BELLAMY & CHILD

EUROPEAN COMMUNITY LAW OF COMPETITION

FIFTH EDITION

APPENDICES

General Editor: P. M. ROTH QC, Barrister

CONTRIBUTORS

DAVID AITMAN
Solicitor

FRANCES BARR
Solicitor

PETER DAVIS
Solicitor

RICHARD FOWLER QC
Barrister

FIONA GASKIN
Solicitor

FRANCES GRAUPNER
Solicitor

DAVID HALL
Solicitor (retired)

REBECCA HAYNES
Barrister

RAYMOND HILL
Barrister

JESSICA JONES
Barrister

STEPHEN MORRIS
Barrister

GEORGE PERETZ
Barrister

VIVIEN ROSE
Barrister

JENNIFER SKILBECK
Barrister

KASSIE SMITH
Barrister

CHRISTOPHER THOMAS
Solicitor

RHODRI THOMPSON
Barrister

CHRISTOPHER VAJDA QC
Barrister

CHARLES WILLIAMS
Barrister

Published in 2001 by
Sweet & Maxwell Limited of
100 Avenue Road, London NW3 3PF
Computerset by Interactive Sciences Ltd, Gloucester
Printed in Great Britain by Clays Ltd, St Ives plc

First edition 1973
Second edition 1978
Third edition 1987
Fourth edition 1993
Fifth edition 2001

BRITISH LIBRARY CATALOGUING IN PUBLICATION DATA
A catalogue record for this book is available from the British Library

No natural forests were destroyed to make this product
only farmed timber was used and re-planted

ISBN 0 421 56440 7

PREFACE

This volume contains the articles of the EC Treaty and the ECSC Treaty that are of particular importance for the application of competition law, followed by all the legislative instruments adopted and the guidelines and notices issued by the Community institutions in the competition field that are of relevance as at 30 April 2001. Three United Kingdom statutory instruments relating to EC competition law are also reproduced. In addition, this volume includes a Table setting out the fines imposed by the European Commission for infringements of the competition rules in the period 1985–2000.

In addition to amending the EU Treaties, the Treaty of Amsterdam provides that the articles of the Treaty on European Union and the EC Treaty should be sequentially re-numbered in accordance with an annexed Table of Equivalences. The Table of Equivalences from the Annex to the Treaty of Amsterdam is in Appendix 1.

Article 12 of the Treaty of Amsterdam provides that the cross-references within the re-numbered Treaties shall be adapted in consequence, and that references in all other instruments or acts shall be understood as references to the articles of those Treaties as re-numbered. For convenience, the references to articles of the EC Treaty in all the Council and Commission regulations, notices and guidelines included in this volume have been amended accordingly to state the articles as re-numbered.[1]

The provisions of the EC Treaty set out in Appendices 3 and 6 incorporate the further amendments made by the Treaty of Nice, which was signed on 26 February 2001 and will enter into force following ratification by all Member States.[2]

Pursuant to Article 2 of Council Regulation 1103/97,[3] every reference in a legal instrument to the ECU was replaced with effect from 1 January 1999 by a reference to the euro at the rate of one euro to one ECU. However, since

---

[1] However, the UK statutory instrument included as Appendix 59 is reproduced in the form in which it was made and should be interpreted in accordance with the Table of Equivalences.
[2] OJ 2001 C80/1. No amendments were made by the Treaty of Nice to the provisions of the EC Treaty in Appendices 2, 4 and 5 or to the provisions of the ECSC Treaty in Appendix 7.
[3] OJ 1997 L162/1.

automatic replacement would complicate the understanding of some pre-1999 instruments, and the main volume contains references to fines imposed in ECUs, references to the ECU have been retained in the materials included in the Appendices.

P.M.R.

Monckton Chambers
Gray's Inn
London
May 2001

CONTENTS

COMMISSION NOTICES: SUBSTANTIVE MATTERS

MERGERS AND CONCENTRATIONS

PROCEDURAL MATTERS

PUBLIC UNDERTAKINGS

TELECOMMUNICATIONS

TRANSPORT

AGRICULTURE

STATE AIDS

TREATY OF AMSTERDAM: TABLES OF EQUIVALENCES

Article 12(1) of the Treaty of Amsterdam provided that the Articles, Titles and Sections of both the Treaty on European Union and the Treaty establishing the European Community, as amended by the Treaty of Amsterdam, should be renumbered in accordance with the following tables of equivalences, which were appended to the Treaty of Amsterdam. This involved removing all the "spent" Articles and renumbering sequentially the Articles that remained, taking account of all the additions.

(*)   Represents a new Article or Title introduced by the Treaty of Amsterdam

Old Number	New Number	Old Number	New Number
A: Treaty on European Union		*Title VI*	*Title VI*
Title I	*Title I*	Article K.1	Article 29
Article A	Article 1	Article K.2	Article 30
Article B	Article 2	Article K.3	Article 31
Article C	Article 3	Article K.4	Article 32
Article D	Article 4	Article K.5	Article 33
Article E	Article 5	Article K.6	Article 34
Article F	Article 6	Article K.7	Article 35
Article F.1 (*)	Article 7	Article K.8	Article 36
Title II	*Title II*	Article K.9	Article 37
Article G	Article 8	Article K.10	Article 38
Title III	*Title III*	Article K.11	Article 39
Article H	Article 9	Article K.12	Article 40
Title IV	*Title IV*	Article K.13	Article 41
Article I	Article 10	Article K.14	Article 42
Title V	*Title V*	*Title VIa (*)*	*Title VII*
Article J.1	Article 11	Article K.15	Article 43
Article J.2	Article 12	Article K.16	Article 44
Article J.3	Article 13	Article K.17	Article 45
Article J.4	Article 14	*Title VII*	*Title VIII*
Article J.5	Article 15	Article L	Article 46
Article J.6	Article 16	Article M	Article 47
Article J.7	Article 17	Article N	Article 48
Article J.8	Article 18	Article O	Article 49
Article J.9	Article 19	Article P	Article 50
Article J.10	Article 20	Article Q	Article 51
Article J.11	Article 21	Article R	Article 52
Article J.12	Article 22	Article S	Article 53
Article J.13	Article 23		
Article J.14	Article 24	*B: Treaty establishing the European*	
Article J.15	Article 25	*Community*	
Article J.16	Article 26	*Part One*	*Part One*
Article J.17	Article 27	Article 1	Article 1
Article J.18	Article 28	Article 2	Article 2

Old Number	New Number	Old Number	New Number
Article 3	Article 3	*Title III*	*Title III*
Article 3a	Article 4	*Chapter 1*	*Chapter 1*
Article 3b	Article 5	Article 48	Article 39
Article 3c (*)	Article 6	Article 49	Article 40
Article 4	Article 7	Article 50	Article 41
Article 4a	Article 8	Article 51	Article 42
Article 4b	Article 9	*Chapter 2*	*Chapter 2*
Article 5	Article 10	Article 52	Article 43
Article 5a (*)	Article 11	Article 53 (repealed)	–
Article 6	Article 12	Article 54	Article 44
Article 6a (*)	Article 13	Article 55	Article 45
Article 7 (repealed)	–	Article 56	Article 46
Article 7a	Article 14	Article 57	Article 47
Article 7b (repealed)	–	Article 58	Article 48
Article 7c	Article 15	*Chapter 3*	*Chapter 3*
Article 7d (*)	Article 16	Article 59	Article 49
Part Two	*Part Two*	Article 60	Article 50
Article 8	Article 17	Article 61	Article 51
Article 8a	Article 18	Article 62 (repealed)	–
Article 8b	Article 19	Article 63	Article 52
Article 8c	Article 20	Article 64	Article 53
Article 8d	Article 21	Article 65	Article 54
Article 8e	Article 22	Article 66	Article 55
Part Three	*Part Three*	*Chapter 4*	*Chapter 4*
Title I	*Title I*	Articles 67–73a	–
Article 9	Article 23	(repealed)	
Article 10	Article 24	Article 73b	Article 56
Article 11 (repealed)	–	Article 73c	Article 57
Chapter I	*Chapter I*	Article 73d	Article 58
Section 1 (deleted)	–	Article 73e (repealed)	–
Article 12	Article 25	Article 73f	Article 59
Articles 13–17 (repealed)	–	Article 73g	Article 60
Section 2 (deleted)	–	Article 73h (repealed)	–
Articles 18–27 (repealed)	–	*Title IIIa (*)*	*Title IV*
Article 28	Article 26	Article 73i (*)	Article 61
Article 29	Article 27	Article 73j (*)	Article 62
Chapter 2	*Chapter 2*	Article 73k (*)	Article 63
Article 30	Article 28	Article 73l (*)	Article 64
Articles 31–33 (repealed)	–	Article 73m (*)	Article 65
Article 34	Article 29	Article 73n (*)	Article 66
Article 35 (repealed)	–	Article 73o (*)	Article 67
Article 36	Article 30	Article 73p (*)	Article 68
Article 37	Article 31	Article 73q (*)	Article 69
Title II	*Title II*	*Title IV*	*Title V*
Article 38	Article 32	Article 74	Article 70
Article 39	Article 33	Article 75	Article 71
Article 40	Article 34	Article 76	Article 72
Article 41	Article 35	Article 77	Article 73
Article 42	Article 36	Article 78	Article 74
Article 43	Article 37	Article 79	Article 75
Articles 44–45 (repealed)	–	Article 80	Article 76
Article 46	Article 38	Article 81	Article 77
Article 47 (repealed)	–	Article 82	Article 78

Old Number	New Number	Old Number	New Number
Article 83	Article 79	Article 109f	Article 117
Article 84	Article 80	Article 109g	Article 118
Title V	*Title VI*	Article 109h	Article 119
Chapter 1	*Chapter 1*	Article 109i	Article 120
Section 1	*Section 1*	Article 109j	Article 121
Article 85	Article 81	Article 109k	Article 122
Article 86	Article 82	Article 109l	Article 123
Article 87	Article 83	Article 109m	Article 124
Article 88	Article 84	*Title VIa (*)*	*Title VIII*
Article 89	Article 85	Article 109n (*)	Article 125
Article 90	Article 86	Article 109o (*)	Article 126
Section 2 (deleted)	–	Article 109p (*)	Article 127
Article 91 (repealed)	–	Article 109q (*)	Article 128
Section 3	*Section 2*	Article 109r (*)	Article 129
Article 92	Article 87	Article 109s (*)	Article 130
Article 93	Article 88	*Title VII*	*Title IX*
Article 94	Article 89	Article 110	Article 131
Chapter 2	*Chapter 2*	Article 111 (repealed)	–
Article 95	Article 90	Article 112	Article 132
Article 96	Article 91	Article 113	Article 133
Article 97 (repealed)	–	Article 114 (repealed)	–
Article 98	Article 92	Article 115	Article 134
Article 99	Article 93	Article 116 (repealed)	–
Chapter 3	*Chapter 3*	*Title VIIa (*)*	*Title X*
Article 100	Article 94	Article 116 (*)	Article 135
Article 100a	Article 95	*Title VIII*	*Title XI*
Articles 100b–100d	–	*Chapter 1*	*Chapter 1*
(repealed)		Article 117	Article 136
Article 101	Article 96	Article 118	Article 137
Article 102	Article 97	Article 118a	Article 138
Title VI	*Title VII*	Article 118b	Article 139
Chapter 1	*Chapter 1*	Article 118c	Article 140
Article 102a	Article 98	Article 119	Article 141
Article 103	Article 99	Article 119a	Article 142
Article 103a	Article 100	Article 120	Article 143
Article 104	Article 101	Article 121	Article 144
Article 104a	Article 102	Article 122	Article 145
Article 104b	Article 103	*Chapter 2*	*Chapter 2*
Article 104c	Article 104	Article 123	Article 146
Chapter 2	*Chapter 2*	Article 124	Article 147
Article 105	Article 105	Article 125	Article 148
Article 105a	Article 106	*Chapter 3*	*Chapter 3*
Article 106	Article 107	Article 126	Article 149
Article 107	Article 108	Article 127	Article 150
Article 108	Article 109	*Title IX*	*Title XII*
Article 108a	Article 110	Article 128	Article 151
Article 109	Article 111	*Title X*	*Title XIII*
Chapter 3	*Chapter 3*	Article 129	Article 152
Article 109a	Article 112	*Title XI*	*Title XIV*
Article 109b	Article 113	Article 129a	Article 153
Article 109c	Article 114	*Title XII*	*Title XV*
Article 109d	Article 115	Article 129b	Article 154
Chapter 4	*Chapter 4*	Article 129c	Article 155
Article 109e	Article 116	Article 129d	Article 156

Old Number	New Number	Old Number	New Number
Title XIII	*Title XVI*	Article 142	Article 199
Article 130	Article 157	Article 143	Article 200
Title XIV	*Title XVII*	Article 144	Article 201
Article 130a	Article 158	*Section 2*	*Section 2*
Article 130b	Article 159	Article 145	Article 202
Article 130c	Article 160	Article 146	Article 203
Article 130d	Article 161	Article 147	Article 204
Article 130e	Article 162	Article 148	Article 205
Title XV	*Title XVIII*	Article 149 (repealed)	–
Article 130f	Article 163	Article 150	Article 206
Article 130g	Article 164	Article 151	Article 207
Article 130h	Article 165	Article 152	Article 208
Article 130i	Article 166	Article 153	Article 209
Article 130j	Article 167	Article 154	Article 210
Article 130k	Article 168	*Section 3*	*Section 3*
Article 130l	Article 169	Article 155	Article 211
Article 130m	Article 170	Article 156	Article 212
Article 130n	Article 171	Article 157	Article 213
Article 130o	Article 172	Article 158	Article 214
Article 130p	Article 173	Article 159	Article 215
Article 130q	–	Article 160	Article 216
(repealed)		Article 161	Article 217
Title XVI	*Title XIX*	Article 162	Article 218
Article 130r	Article 174	Article 163	Article 219
Article 130s	Article 175	*Section 4*	*Section 4*
Article 130t	Article 176	Article 164	Article 220
Title XVII	*Title XX*	Article 165	Article 221
Article 130u	Article 177	Article 166	Article 222
Article 130v	Article 178	Article 167	Article 223
Article 130w	Article 179	Article 168	Article 224
Article 130x	Article 180	Article 168a	Article 225
Article 130y	Article 181	Article 169	Article 226
Part Four	*Part Four*	Article 170	Article 227
Article 131	Article 182	Article 171	Article 228
Article 132	Article 183	Article 172	Article 229
Article 133	Article 184	Article 173	Article 230
Article 134	Article 185	Article 174	Article 231
Article 135	Article 186	Article 175	Article 232
Article 136	Article 187	Article 176	Article 233
Article 136a	Article 188	Article 177	Article 234
Part Five	*Part Five*	Article 178	Article 235
Title I	*Title I*	Article 179	Article 236
Chapter 1	*Chapter 1*	Article 180	Article 237
Section 1	*Section 1*	Article 181	Article 238
Article 137	Article 189	Article 182	Article 239
Article 138	Article 190	Article 183	Article 240
Article 138a	Article 191	Article 184	Article 241
Article 138b	Article 192	Article 185	Article 242
Article 138c	Article 193	Article 186	Article 243
Article 138d	Article 194	Article 187	Article 244
Article 138e	Article 195	Article 188	Article 245
Article 139	Article 196	*Section 5*	*Section 5*
Article 140	Article 197	Article 188a	Article 246
Article 141	Article 198	Article 188b	Article 247

Old Number	New Number	Old Number	New Number
Article 188c	Article 248	*Part Six*	*Part Six*
Chapter 2	*Chapter 2*	Article 210	Article 281
Article 189	Article 249	Article 211	Article 282
Article 189a	Article 250	Article 212 (*)	Article 283
Article 189b	Article 251	Article 213	Article 284
Article 189c	Article 252	Article 213a (*)	Article 285
Article 190	Article 253	Article 213b	Article 286
Article 191	Article 254	Article 214	Article 287
Article 191a (*)	Article 255	Article 215	Article 288
Article 192	Article 256	Article 216	Article 289
Chapter 3	*Chapter 3*	Article 217	Article 290
Article 193	Article 257	Article 218 (*)	Article 291
Article 194	Article 258	Article 219	Article 292
Article 195	Article 259	Article 220	Article 293
Article 196	Article 260	Article 221	Article 294
Article 197	Article 261	Article 222	Article 295
Article 198	Article 262	Article 223	Article 296
Chapter 4	*Chapter 4*	Article 224	Article 297
Article 198a	Article 263	Article 225	Article 298
Article 198b	Article 264	Article 226 (repealed)	–
Article 198c	Article 265	Article 227	Article 299
Chapter 5	*Chapter 5*	Article 228	Article 300
Article 198d	Article 266	Article 228a	Article 301
Article 198e	Article 267	Article 229	Article 302
Title II	*Title II*	Article 230	Article 303
Article 199	Article 268	Article 231	Article 304
Article 200 (repealed)	–	Article 232	Article 305
Article 201	Article 269	Article 233	Article 306
Article 201a	Article 270	Article 234	Article 307
Article 202	Article 271	Article 235	Article 308
Article 203	Article 272	Article 236 (*)	Article 309
Article 204	Article 273	Article 237 (repealed)	–
Article 205	Article 274	Article 238	Article 310
Article 205a	Article 275	Article 239	Article 311
Article 206	Article 276	Article 240	Article 312
Article 206a (repealed)	–	Articles 241–246	–
Article 207	Article 277	(repealed)	
Article 208	Article 278	*Final Provisions*	*Final Provisions*
Article 209	Article 279		
Article 209a	Article 280	Article 247	Article 313
		Article 248	Article 314

EC TREATY: RULES ON COMPETITION

SECTION 1

Rules applying to undertakings

Article 81 [*ex* Article 85]

1. The following shall be prohibited as incompatible with the common market: all agreements between undertakings, decisions by associations of undertakings and concerted practices which may affect trade between Member States and which have as their object or effect the prevention, restriction or distortion of competition within the common market, and in particular those which:

(a) directly or indirectly fix purchase or selling prices or any other trading conditions;
(b) limit or control production, markets, technical development, or investment;
(c) share markets or sources of supply;
(d) apply dissimilar conditions to equivalent transactions with other trading parties, thereby placing them at a competitive disadvantage;
(e) make the conclusion of contracts subject to acceptance by the other parties of supplementary obligations which, by their nature or according to commercial usage, have no connection with the subject of such contracts.

2. Any agreements or decisions prohibited pursuant to this Article shall be automatically void.

3. The provisions of paragraph 1 may, however, be declared inapplicable in the case of:

— any agreement or category of agreements between undertakings;
— any decision or category of decisions by associations of undertakings;
— any concerted practice or category of concerted practices;

which contributes to improving the production or distribution of goods or to promoting technical or economic progress, while allowing consumers a fair share of the resulting benefit, and which does not:

(a) impose on the undertakings concerned restrictions which are not indispensable to the attainment of these objectives;
(b) afford such undertakings the possibility of eliminating competition in respect of a substantial part of the products in question.

6

Article 82 [*ex* Article 86]

Any abuse by one or more undertakings of a dominant position within the common market or in a substantial part of it shall be prohibited as incompatible with the common market insofar as it may affect trade between Member States.

Such abuse may, in particular, consist in:

(a) directly or indirectly imposing unfair purchase or selling prices or other unfair trading conditions;
(b) limiting production, markets or technical development to the prejudice of consumers;
(c) applying dissimilar conditions to equivalent transactions with other trading parties, thereby placing them at a competitive disadvantage;
(d) making the conclusion of contracts subject to acceptance by the other parties of supplementary obligations which, by their nature or according to commercial usage, have no connection with the subject of such contracts.

Article 83 [*ex* Article 87]

1. The appropriate regulations or directives to give effect to the principles set out in Articles 81 and 82 shall be laid down by the Council, acting by a qualified majority on a proposal from the Commission and after consulting the European Parliament.

2. The regulations or directives referred to in paragraph 1 shall be designed in particular:

(a) to ensure compliance with the prohibitions laid down in Article 81(1) and in Article 82 by making provision for fines and periodic penalty payments;
(b) to lay down detailed rules for the application of Article 81(3), taking into account the need to ensure effective supervision on the one hand, and to simplify administration to the greatest possible extent on the other;
(c) to define, if need be, in the various branches of the economy, the scope of the provisions of Articles 81 and 82;
(d) to define the respective functions of the Commission and of the Court of Justice in applying the provisions laid down in this paragraph;
(e) to determine the relationship between national laws and the provisions contained in this Section or adopted pursuant to this Article.

Article 84 [*ex* Article 88]

Until the entry into force of the provisions adopted in pursuance of Article 83, the authorities in Member States shall rule on the admissibility of agreements, decisions and concerted practices and on abuse of a dominant position in the common market in accordance with the law of their country and with the provisions of Article 81, in particular paragraph 3, and of Article 82.

Article 85 [*ex* Article 89]

1. Without prejudice to Article 84, the Commission shall ensure the application of the principles laid down in Articles 81 and 82. On application by a Member State or on its own initiative, and in co-operation with the competent authorities in the Member States, who shall give it their assistance, the Commission shall investigate cases of suspected infringement of these principles. If it finds that there has been an infringement, it shall propose appropriate measures to bring it to an end.

2. If the infringement is not brought to an end, the Commission shall record such infringement of the principles in a reasoned decision. The Commission may publish its decision and authorise Member States to take the measures, the conditions and details of which it shall determine, needed to remedy the situation.

Article 86 [*ex* Article 90]

1. In the case of public undertakings and undertakings to which Member States grant special or exclusive rights, Member States shall neither enact nor maintain in force any measure contrary to the rules contained in this Treaty, in particular to those rules provided for in Article 12 and Articles 81 to 89.

2. Undertakings entrusted with the operation of services of general economic interest or having the character of a revenue-producing monopoly shall be subject to the rules contained in this Treaty, in particular to the rules on competition, insofar as the application of such rules does not obstruct the performance, in law or in fact, of the particular tasks assigned to them. The development of trade must not be affected to such an extent as would be contrary to the interests of the Community.

3. The Commission shall ensure the application of the provisions of this Article and shall, where necessary, address appropriate directives or decisions to Member States.

SECTION 2

Aids granted by states

Article 87 [*ex* Article 92]

1. Save as otherwise provided in this Treaty, any aid granted by a Member State or through State resources in any form whatsoever which distorts or threatens to distort competition by favouring certain undertakings or the production of certain goods shall, insofar as it affects trade between Member States, be incompatible with the common market.

2. The following shall be compatible with the common market:

(a) aid having a social character, granted to individual consumers, provided that such aid is granted without discrimination related to the origin of the products concerned;
(b) aid to make good the damage caused by natural disasters or exceptional occurrences;
(c) aid granted to the economy of certain areas of the Federal Republic of Germany affected by the division of Germany, insofar as such aid is required in order to compensate for the economic disadvantages caused by that division.

3. The following may be considered to be compatible with the common market:

(a) aid to promote the economic development of areas where the standard of living is abnormally low or where there is serious underemployment;
(b) aid to promote the execution of an important project of common European interest or to remedy a serious disturbance in the economy of a Member State;
(c) aid to facilitate the development of certain economic activities or of certain economic areas, where such aid does not adversely affect trading conditions to an extent contrary to the common interest;
(d) aid to promote culture and heritage conservation where such aid does not affect trading conditions and competition in the Community to an extent that is contrary to the common interest;

(e)   such other categories of aid as may be specified by decision of the Council acting by a qualified majority on a proposal from the Commission.

Article 88 [*ex* Article 93)

1. The Commission shall, in co-operation with Member States, keep under constant review all systems of aid existing in those States. It shall propose to the latter any appropriate measures required by the progressive development or by the functioning of the common market.

2. If, after giving notice to the parties concerned to submit their comments, the Commission finds that aid granted by a State or through States resources is not compatible with the common market having regard to Article 87, or that such aid is being misused, it shall decide that the State concerned shall abolish or alter such aid within a period of time to be determined by the Commission.

If the State concerned does not comply with this decision within the prescribed time, the Commission or any other interested State may, in derogation from the provisions of Articles 226 and 227, refer the matter to the Court of Justice direct.

On application by a Member State, the Council may, acting unanimously, decide that aid which that State is granting or intends to grant shall be considered to be compatible with the common market, in derogation from the provisions of Article 87 or from the regulations provided for in Article 89, if such a decision is justified by exceptional circumstances. If, as regards the aid in question, the Commission has already initiated the procedure provided for in the first sub-paragraph of this paragraph, the fact that the State concerned has made its application to the Council shall have the effect of suspending that procedure until the Council has made its attitude known.

If, however, the Council has not made its attitude known within three months of the said application being made, the Commission shall give its decision on the case.

3. The Commission shall be informed, in sufficient time to enable it to submit its comments, of any plans to grant or alter aid. If it considers that any such plan is not compatible with the common market having regard to Article 87, it shall without delay initiate the procedure provided for in paragraph 2. The Member State concerned shall not put its proposed measures into effect until this procedure has resulted in a final decision.

Article 89 [*ex* Article 94]

The Council, acting by a qualified majority on a proposal from the Commission and after consulting the European Parliament, may make any appropriate regulations for the application of Articles 87 and 88 and may in particular determine the conditions in which Article 88(3) shall apply and the categories of aid exempted from this procedure.

EC TREATY: GENERAL PRINCIPLES

Article 1 [ex Article 1]

By this Treaty, the HIGH CONTRACTING PARTIES establish among themselves a EUROPEAN COMMUNITY.

Article 2 [ex Article 2]

The Community shall have as its task, by establishing a common market and an economic and monetary union and by implementing common policies or activities referred to in Articles 3 and 4, to promote throughout the Community a harmonious and balanced and sustainable development of economic activities, a high level of employment and social protection, equality between men and women, sustainable and non-inflationary growth, a high degree of competitiveness and convergence of economic performance, a high level of protection and improvement of the quality of the environment, the raising of the standard of living and quality of life, and economic and social cohesion and solidarity among Member States.

Article 3 [ex Article 3]

1. For the purposes set out in Article 2, the activities of the Community shall include, as provided in this Treaty and in accordance with the timetable set out therein:

(a) the prohibition, as between Member States, of customs duties and quantitative restrictions on the import and export of goods, and of all other measures having equivalent effect;
(b) a common commercial policy;
(c) an internal market characterised by the abolition, as between Member States, of obstacles to the free movement of goods, persons, services and capital;
(d) measures concerning the entry and movement of persons as provided for in Title IV;
(e) a common policy in the sphere of agriculture and fisheries;
(f) a common policy in the sphere of transport;
(g) a system ensuring that competition in the internal market is not distorted;
(h) the approximation of the laws of Member States to the extent required for the functioning of the common market;
(i) the promotion of co-ordination between employment policies of the Member States with a view to enhancing their effectiveness by developing a co-ordinated strategy for employment;
(j) a policy in the social sphere comprising a European Social Fund;
(k) the strengthening of economic and social cohesion;
(l) a policy in the sphere of the environment;
(m) the strengthening of the competitiveness of Community industry;

(n) the promotion of research and technological development;
(o) encouragement for the establishment and development of trans-European networks;
(p) a contribution to the attainment of a high level of health protection;
(q) a contribution to education and training of quality and to the flowering of the cultures of the Member States;
(r) a policy in the sphere of development co-operation;
(s) the association of the overseas countries and territories in order to increase trade and promote jointly economic and social development;
(t) a contribution to the strengthening of consumer protection;
(u) measures in the spheres of energy, civil protection and tourism.

2. In all the activities referred to in this Article, the Community shall aim to eliminate inequalities, and to promote equality, between men and women.

Article 5 [ex Article 3b]

The Community shall act within the limits of the powers conferred upon it by this Treaty and of the objectives assigned to it therein.

In areas which do not fall within its exclusive competence, the Community shall take action in accordance with the principle of subsidiarity, only if and insofar as the objectives of the proposed action cannot be sufficiently achieved by the Member States and can therefore, by reason of the scale or effects of the proposed action, be better achieved by the Community.

Any action by the Community shall not go beyond what is necessary to achieve the objectives of this Treaty.

Article 6 [ex Article 3c]

Environmental protection requirements must be integrated into the definition and implementation of the Community policies and activities referred to in Article 3, in particular with a view to promoting sustainable development.

Article 7 [ex Article 4]

1. The tasks entrusted to the Community shall be carried out by the following institutions:

— a EUROPEAN PARLIAMENT,
— a COUNCIL,
— a COMMISSION,
— a COURT OF JUSTICE,
— a COURT OF AUDITORS.

Each institution shall act within the limits of the powers conferred upon it by this Treaty.

2. The Council and the Commission shall be assisted by an Economic and Social Committee and a Committee of the Regions acting in an advisory capacity.

Article 8 [ex Article 4a]

A European System of Central Banks (hereinafter referred to as "ESCB") and a European Central Bank (hereinafter referred to as "ECB") shall be established in accordance with the procedures laid down in this Treaty; they shall act within the limits of the powers conferred upon them by this Treaty and by the Statute of the ESCB and of the ECB (hereinafter referred to as 'Statute of the ESCB') annexed thereto.

Article 9 [*ex* Article 4b]

A European Investment Bank is hereby established, which shall act within the limits of the powers conferred upon it by this Treaty and the Statute annexed thereto.

Article 10 [*ex* Article 5]

Member States shall take all appropriate measures, whether general or particular, to ensure fulfilment of the obligations arising out of this Treaty or resulting from action taken by the institutions of the Community. They shall facilitate the achievement of the Community's tasks.

They shall abstain from any measure which could jeopardise the attainment of the objectives of this Treaty.

Article 11

[1. Member States which intend to establish enhanced cooperation between themselves in one of the areas referred to in this Treaty shall address a request to the Commission, which may submit a proposal to the Council to that effect. In the event of the Commission not submitting a proposal, it shall inform the Member States concerned of the reasons for not doing so.

2. Authorisation to establish enhanced cooperation as referred to in paragraph 1 shall be granted, in compliance with Articles 43 to 45 of the Treaty on European Union, by the Council, acting by a qualified majority on a proposal from the Commission and after consulting the European Parliament. When enhanced cooperation relates to an area covered by the procedure referred to in Article 251 of this Treaty, the assent of the European Parliament shall be required.

A member of the Council may request that the matter be referred to the European Council. After that matter has been raised before the European Council, the Council may act in accordance with the first subparagraph of this paragraph.

3. The acts and decisions necessary for the implementation of enhanced cooperation activities shall be subject to all the relevant provisions of this Treaty, save as otherwise provided in this Article and in Articles 43 to 45 of the Treaty on European Union.]

[Article 11a

Any Member State which wishes to participate in enhanced cooperation established in accordance with Article 11 shall notify its intention to the Council and to the Commission, which shall give an opinion to the Council within three months of the date of receipt of that notification. Within four months of the date of receipt of that notification, the Commission shall take a decision on it, and on such specific arrangements as it may deem necessary.]

Amendment

Article 11 [*ex* Article 5a] was introduced by the Treaty of Nice and replaces the previous wording.

Article 11a was inserted by the Treaty of Nice.

Article 14 [*ex* Article 7a]

1. The Community shall adopt measures with the aim of progressively establishing the internal market over a period expiring on 31 December 1992, in accordance with the provisions of this Article and of Articles 15, 26, 47(2), 49, 80, 93 and 95 and without prejudice to the other provisions of this Treaty.

2. The internal market shall comprise an area without internal frontiers in which the free movement of goods, persons, services and capital is ensured in accordance with the provisions of this Treaty.

3. The Council, acting by a qualified majority on a proposal from the Commission, shall determine the guidelines and conditions necessary to ensure balanced progress in all the sectors concerned.

(*Formerly paragraph 2 of Article 7b.*)

Article 15 [*ex* Article 7c]

When drawing up its proposals with a view to achieving the objectives set out in Article 14, the Commission shall take into account the extent of the effort that certain economies showing differences in development will have to sustain during the period of establishment of the internal market and it may propose appropriate provisions.

If these provisions take the form of derogations, they must be of a temporary nature and must cause the least possible disturbance to the functioning of the common market.

Article 16 [*ex* Article 7d]

Without prejudice to Articles 73, 86 and 87, and given the place occupied by services of general economic interest in the shared values of the Union as well as their role in promoting social and territorial cohesion, the Community and the Member States, each within their respective powers and within the scope of application of this Treaty, shall take care that such services operate on the basis of principles and conditions which enable them to fulfil their missions.

EC TREATY: FREE MOVEMENT OF GOODS

Article 23 [ex Article 9]

1. The Community shall be based upon a customs union which shall cover all trade in goods and which shall involve the prohibition between Member States of customs duties on imports and exports and of all charges having equivalent effect, and the adoption of a common customs tariff in their relations with third countries.

2. The provisions of Article 25 and of Chapter 2 of this Title shall apply to products originating in Member States and to products coming from third countries which are in free circulation in Member States.

Article 24 [ex Article 10]

Products coming from a third country shall be considered to be in free circulation in a Member State if the import formalities have been complied with and any customs duties or charges having equivalent effect which are payable have been levied in that Member State, and if they have not benefited from a total or partial drawback of such duties or charges. (*Formerly paragraph 1.*)

Article 25 [ex Article 12]

Customs duties on imports and exports and charges having equivalent effect shall be prohibited between Member States. This prohibition shall also apply to customs duties of a fiscal nature.

Article 28 [ex Article 30]

Quantitative restrictions on imports and all measures having equivalent effect shall be prohibited between Member States.

Article 29 [ex Article 34]

Quantitative restrictions on exports, and all measures having equivalent effect, shall be prohibited between Member States. (*Formerly paragraph 1.*)

Article 30 [ex Article 36]

The provisions of Articles 28 and 29 shall not preclude prohibitions or restrictions on imports, exports or goods in transit justified on grounds of public morality, public policy or public security; the protection of health and life of humans, animals or plants; the protection of national treasures possessing artistic, historic or archaeological value; or the protection of industrial and commercial property. Such prohibitions or restrictions shall not, however, constitute a means of arbitrary discrimination or a disguised restriction on trade between Member States.

Article 31 [ex Article 37]

1. Member States shall adjust any State monopolies of a commercial character so as to ensure that no discrimination regarding the conditions under which goods are procured and marketed exists between nationals of Member States.

The provisions of this Article shall apply to any body through which a Member State, in law or in fact, either directly or indirectly, supervises, determines or appreciably influences imports or exports between Member States. These provisions shall likewise apply to monopolies delegated by the State to others.

2. Member States shall refrain from introducing any new measure which is contrary to the principles laid down in paragraph 1 or which restricts the scope of the Articles dealing with the prohibition of customs duties and quantitative restrictions between Member States.

3. If a State monopoly of a commercial character has rules has which are designed to make it easier to dispose of agricultural products or obtain for them the best return, steps should be taken in applying the rules contained in this Article to ensure equivalent safeguards for the employment and standard of living of the producers concerned.

EC TREATY: AGRICULTURE

Article 32 [*ex* Article 38]

1. The common market shall extend to agriculture and trade in agricultural products. "Agricultural products" means the products of the soil, of stock farming and of fisheries and products of first-stage processing directly related to these products.

2. Save as otherwise provided in Articles 33 to 38, the rules laid down for the establishment of the common market shall apply to agricultural products.

3. The products subject to the provisions of Articles 33 to 38 are listed in Annex I to this Treaty.

4. The operation and development of the common market for agricultural products must be accompanied by the establishment of a common agricultural policy.

Article 33 [*ex* Article 39]

1. The objectives of the common agricultural policy shall be:

(a) to increase agricultural productivity by promoting technical progress and by ensuring the rational development of agricultural production and the optimum utilisation of the factors of production, in particular labour;
(b) thus to ensure a fair standard of living for the agricultural community, in particular by increasing the individual earnings of persons engaged in agriculture;
(c) to stabilise markets;
(d) to assure the availability of supplies;
(e) to ensure that supplies reach consumers at reasonable prices.

2. In working out the common agricultural policy and the special methods for its application, account shall be taken of:

(a) the particular nature of agricultural activity, which results from the social structure of agriculture and from structural and natural disparities between the various agricultural regions;
(b) the need to effect the appropriate adjustments by degrees;
(c) the fact that in the Member States agriculture constitutes a sector closely linked with the economy as a whole.

Article 34 [*ex* Article 40]

1. In order to attain the objectives set out in Article 33, a common organisation of agricultural markets shall be established.

This organisation shall take one of the following forms, depending on the product concerned:

(a) common rules on competition;

16

(b) compulsory co-ordination of the various national market organisations;
(c) a European market organisation.

2. The common organisation established in accordance with paragraph 1 may include all measures required to attain the objectives set out in Article 33, in particular regulation of prices, aids for the production and marketing of the various products, storage and carryover arrangements and common machinery for stabilising imports or exports.

The common organisation shall be limited to pursuit of the objectives set out in Article 33 and shall exclude any discrimination between producers or consumers within the Community.

Any common price policy shall be based on common criteria and uniform methods of calculation.

3. In order to enable the common organisation referred to in paragraph 1 to attain its objectives, one or more agricultural guidance and guarantee funds may be set up.

Article 35 [ex Article 41]

To enable the objectives set out in Article 33 to be attained, provision may be made within the framework of the common agricultural policy for measures such as:

(a) an effective co-ordination of efforts in the spheres of vocational training, of research and of the dissemination of agricultural knowledge. This may include joint financing of projects or institutions;
(b) joint measures to promote consumption of certain products.

Article 36 [ex Article 42]

The provisions of the Chapter relating to rules on competition shall apply to production of and trade in agricultural products only to the extent determined by the Council within the framework of Article 37(2) and (3) and in accordance with the procedure laid down therein, account being taking of the objectives set out in Article 33.

The Council may, in particular, authorise the granting of aid:

(a) for the production of enterprises handicapped by structural or natural conditions;
(b) within the framework of economic development programmes.

Article 37 [ex Article 43]

1. In order to evolve the broad lines of a common agricultural policy, the Commission shall, immediately this Treaty enters into force, convene a conference of the Member States with a view to making a comparison of their agricultural policies, in particular by producing a statement of their resources and needs.

2. Having taken into account the work of the conference provided for in paragraph 1, after consulting the Economic and Social Committee and within two years of the entry into force of this Treaty, the Commission shall submit proposals for working out and implementing the common agricultural policy, including the replacement of the national organisations by one of the forms of common organisation provided for in Article 34(1), and for implementing the measures specified in this Title.

These proposals shall take account of the interdependence of the agricultural matters mentioned in this Title. The Council shall, on a proposal from the Commission and after consulting the European Parliament, acting by a qualified majority, make regulations, issue directives, or take decisions, without prejudice to any recommendations it may also make.

3. The Council may, acting by a qualified majority and in accordance with paragraph 2, replace the national market organisations by the common organisation provided for in Article 34(1) if:

(a) the common organisation offers Member States which are opposed to this measure and which have an organisation of their own for the production in question equivalent safeguards for the employment and standard of living of the producers concerned, account being taken of the adjustments that will be possible and the specialisation that will be needed with the passage of time;

(b) such an organisation ensures conditions for trade within the Community similar to those existing in a national market.

4. If a common organisation for certain raw materials is established before a common organisation exists for the corresponding processed products, such raw materials as are used for processed products intended for export to third countries may be imported from outside the Community.

EC TREATY: THE COMMUNITY COURTS

Article 220

[The Court of Justice and the Court of First Instance, each within its jurisdiction, shall ensure that in the interpretation and application of this Treaty the law is observed.

In addition, judicial panels may be attached to the Court of First Instance under the conditions laid down in Article 225a in order to exercise, in certain specific areas, the judicial competence laid down in this Treaty.]

Amendment

This wording was introduced by the Treaty of Nice and replaces the previous Article 220 [*ex* 164].

Article 221

[The Court of Justice shall consist of one judge per Member State.

The Court of Justice shall sit in chambers or in a Grand Chamber, in accordance with the rules laid down for that purpose in the Statute of the Court of Justice.

When provided for in the Statute, the Court of Justice may also sit as a full Court.]

Amendment

This wording was introduced by the Treaty of Nice and replaces the previous Article 221 [*ex* 165].

Article 222

[The Court of Justice shall be assisted by eight Advocates-General. Should the Court of Justice so request, the Council, acting unanimously, may increase the number of Advocates-General.

It shall be the duty of the Advocate-General, acting with complete impartiality and independence, to make, in open court, reasoned submissions on cases which, in accordance with the Statute of the Court of Justice, require his involvement.]

Amendment

This wording was introduced by the Treaty of Nice and replaces the previous Article 222 [*ex* 166].

Article 225

[1. The Court of First Instance shall have jurisdiction to hear and determine at first instance actions or proceedings referred to in Articles 230, 232, 235, 236 and 238, with the exception of those assigned to a judicial panel and those reserved in the Statute for the Court of Justice. The Statute may provide for the Court of First Instance to have jurisdiction for other classes of action or proceeding.

Decisions given by the Court of First Instance under this paragraph may be subject to a right of appeal to the Court of Justice on points of law only, under the conditions and within the limits laid down by the Statute.

2. The Court of First Instance shall have jurisdiction to hear and determine actions or proceedings brought against decisions of the judicial panels set up under Article 225a.

Decisions given by the Court of First Instance under this paragraph may exceptionally be subject to review by the Court of Justice, under the conditions and within the limits laid down by the Statute, where there is a serious risk of the unity or consistency of Community law being affected.

3. The Court of First Instance shall have jurisdiction to hear and determine questions referred for a preliminary ruling under Article 234, in specific areas laid down by the Statute.

Where the Court of First Instance considers that the case requires a decision of principle likely to affect the unity or consistency of Community law, it may refer the case to the Court of Justice for a ruling.

Decisions given by the Court of First Instance on questions referred for a preliminary ruling may exceptionally be subject to review by the Court of Justice, under the conditions and within the limits laid down by the Statute, where there is a serious risk of the unity or consistency of Community law being affected.]

Amendment

This wording was introduced by the Treaty of Nice and replaces the previous Article 225 [*ex* 168a].

[Article 225a

The Council, acting unanimously on a proposal from the Commission and after consulting the European Parliament and the Court of Justice or at the request of the Court of Justice and after consulting the European Parliament and the Commission, may create judicial panels to hear and determine at first instance certain classes of action or proceeding brought in specific areas.

The decision establishing a judicial panel shall lay down the rules on the organisation of the panel and the extent of the jurisdiction conferred upon it.

Decisions given by judicial panels may be subject to a right of appeal on points of law only or, when provided for in the decision establishing the panel, a right of appeal also on matters of fact, before the Court of First Instance.

The members of the judicial panels shall be chosen from persons whose independence is beyond doubt and who possess the ability required for appointment to judicial office. They shall be appointed by the Council, acting unanimously.

The judicial panels shall establish their Rules of Procedure in agreement with the Court of Justice. Those Rules shall require the approval of the Council, acting by a qualified majority.

Unless the decision establishing the judicial panel provides otherwise, the provisions of this Treaty relating to the Court of Justice and the provisions of the Statute of the Court of Justice shall apply to the judicial panels.]

Amendment

This Article was inserted by the Treaty of Nice.

Article 226 [ex Article 169]

If the Commission considers that a Member State has failed to fulfil an obligation under this Treaty, is shall deliver a reasoned opinion on the matter after giving the State concerned the opportunity to submit its observations.

If the State concerned does not comply with the opinion within the period laid down by the Commission, the latter may bring the matter before the Court of Justice.

Article 227 [ex Article 170]

A Member State which considers that another Member State has failed to fulfil an obligation under this Treaty may bring the matter before the Court of Justice.

Before the Member State brings an action against another Member State for an alleged infringement of an obligation under this Treaty, it shall bring the matter before the Commission.

The Commission shall deliver a reasoned opinion after each of the States concerned has been given the opportunity to submit its own case and its observations on the other party's case both orally and in writing.

If the Commission has not delivered an opinion within three months of the date on which the matter was brought before it, the absence of such opinion shall not prevent the matter from being brought before the Court of Justice.

Article 228 [ex Article 171]

1. If the Court of Justice finds that a Member State has failed to fulfil an obligation under this Treaty, the State shall be required to take the necessary measures to comply with the judgment of the Court of Justice.

2. If the Commission considers that the Member State concerned has not taken such measures it shall, after giving that State the opportunity to submit its observations, issue a reasoned opinion specifying the points on which the Member State concerned has not complied with the judgment of the Court of Justice.

If the Member State concerned fails to take the necessary measures to comply with the Court's judgment within the time-limit laid down by the Commission, the latter may bring the case before the Court of Justice. In so doing it shall specify the amount of the lump sum or penalty payment to be paid by the Member State concerned which it considers appropriate in the circumstances.

If the Court of Justice finds that the Member State concerned has not complied with its judgment it may impose a lump sum or penalty payment on it.

This procedure shall be without prejudice to Article 227.

Article 229 [ex Article 172]

Regulations adopted jointly by the European Parliament and the Council, and by the Council, pursuant to the provisions of this Treaty, may give the Court of Justice unlimited jurisdiction with regard to the penalties provided for in such regulations.

[Article 229a

Without prejudice to the other provisions of this Treaty, the Council, acting unanimously on a proposal from the Commission and after consulting the European Parliament, may adopt provisions to confer jurisdiction, to the extent that it shall determine, on the Court of Justice in disputes relating to the application of acts adopted on the basis of this Treaty which create Community industrial property rights. The Council shall recommend those provisions to the Member States for adoption in accordance with their respective constitutional requirements.]

Amendment

Article 229a was inserted by the Treaty of Nice.

Article 230 [*ex* Article 173]

The Court of Justice shall review the legality of acts adopted jointly by the European Parliament and the Council, of acts of the Council, of the Commission and of the ECB, other than recommendations and opinions, and of acts of the European Parliament intended to produce legal effects *vis-à-vis* third parties.

[It shall for this purpose have jurisdiction in actions brought by a Member State, the European Parliament, the Council or the Commission on grounds of lack of competence, infringement of an essential procedural requirement, infringement of this Treaty or of any rule of law relating to its application, or misuse of powers.

The Court of Justice shall have jurisdiction under the same conditions in actions brought by the Court of Auditors and by the ECB for the purpose of protecting their prerogatives.]

Any natural or legal person may, under the same conditions, institute proceedings against a decision addressed to that person or against a decision which, although in the form of a regulation or a decision addressed to another person, is of direct and individual concern to the former.

The proceedings provided for in this Article shall be instituted within two months of the publication of the measure, or of its notification to the plaintiff, or, in the absence thereof, of the day on which it came to the knowledge of the latter, as the case may be.

Amendment

The text in square brackets was inserted by the Treaty of Nice replacing the previous second and third paragraphs of Article 230.

Article 231 [*ex* Article 174]

If the action is well founded, the Court of Justice shall declare the act concerned to be void.

In the case of a regulation, however, the Court of Justice shall, if it considers this necessary, state which of the effects of the regulation which it has declared void shall be considered as definitive.

Article 232 [*ex* Article 175]

Should the European Parliament, the Council or the Commission, in infringement of this Treaty, fail to act, the Member States and the other institutions of the Community may bring an action before the Court of Justice to have the infringement established.

The action shall be admissible only if the institution concerned has been called upon to act. If, within two months of being so called upon, the institution concerned has not defined its position, the action may be brought within a further period of two months.

Any natural or legal person may, under the conditions laid down in the preceding paragraphs, complain to the Court of Justice that an institution of the Community has failed to address to that person any act other than a recommendation or an opinion.

The Court of Justice shall have jurisdiction, under the same conditions, in actions or proceedings brought by the ECB in the areas falling within the latter's field of competence and in actions or proceedings brought against the latter.

Article 233 [*ex* Article 176]

The institution or institutions whose act has been declared void or whose failure to act has been declared contrary to this Treaty shall be required to take the necessary measures to comply with the judgment of the Court of Justice.

This obligation shall not affect any obligation which may result from the application of the second paragraph of Article 288.

This Article shall also apply to the ECB.

Article 234 [*ex* Article 177]

The Court of Justice shall have jurisdiction to give preliminary rulings concerning:

(a) the interpretation of this Treaty;
(b) the validity and interpretation of acts of the institutions of the Community and of the ECB;
(c) the interpretation of the statutes of bodies established by an act of the Council, where those statutes so provide.

Where such a question is raised before any court or tribunal of a Member State, that court or tribunal may, if it considers that a decision on the question is necessary to enable it to give judgment, request the Court of Justice to give a ruling thereon.

Where any such question is raised in a case pending before a court or tribunal of a Member State against whose decisions there is no judicial remedy under national law, that court or tribunal shall bring the matter before the Court of Justice.

Article 242 [*ex* Article 185]

Actions brought before the Court of Justice shall not have suspensory effect. The Court of Justice may, however, if it considers that circumstances so require, order that application of the contested act be suspended.

Article 243 [*ex* Article 186]

The Court of Justice may in any cases before it prescribe any necessary interim measures.

ECSC TREATY (COAL AND STEEL)

Article 4

The following are recognised as incompatible with the common market for coal and steel and shall accordingly be prohibited within the Community, as provided in this Treaty:

(a) import and export duties, or charges having equivalent effect, and quantitative restrictions on the movement of products;
(b) measures or practices which discriminate between producers, between purchasers or between consumers, especially in prices and delivery terms or transport rates and conditions, and measures or practices which interfere with the purchaser's free choice of supplier;
(c) subsidies or aids granted by States, or special charges imposed by States, in any form whatsoever;
(d) restrictive practices which tend towards the sharing or exploiting of markets.

Article 60

1. Pricing practices contrary to Articles 2, 3 and 4 shall be prohibited, in particular:

— unfair competitive practices, especially purely temporary or purely local price reductions tending towards the acquisition of a monopoly position with the common market;
— discriminatory practices involving, within the common market, the application by a seller of dissimilar conditions to comparable transactions, especially on grounds of the nationality of the buyer.

The [Commission] may define the practices covered by this prohibition by decisions taken after consulting the Consultative Committee and the Council.
2. For these purposes:

(a) the price lists and conditions of sale applied by undertakings within the common market must be made public to the extent and in the manner prescribed by the [Commission] after consulting the Consultative Committee. If the [Commission] finds that an undertaking's choice of point on which it bases its price lists is abnormal and in particular makes it possible to evade the provisions of sub-paragraph (b), it shall make appropriate recommendations to that undertaking;
(b) the methods of quotation used must not have the effect that prices charged by an undertaking in the common market, when reduced to their equivalent at the point chosen for its price lists, result in:
— increases over the price shown in the price list in question for a comparable transaction; or
— reductions below that price the amount of which exceeds either:

— the extent enabling the quotation to be aligned on the price list, based on another point which secures the buyer the most advantageous delivered terms; or

— the limits fixed, by the decision of the [Commission] after the Consultative Committee has delivered its opinion, for each category of product, with due regard, where appropriate, for the origin and destination of products.

Such decisions shall be taken when found necessary to avoid disturbances in the whole or any part of the common market or disequilibria resulting from a difference between the methods of quotation used for a product and for materials involved in making it. Such decisions shall not preclude undertakings from aligning their quotations on those of undertakings outside the Community, on condition that the transactions are notified to the [Commission], which may, in the event of abuse, restrict or abrogate the right of the undertakings concerned to take advantage of this exception.

Article 63

1. If the [Commission] finds that discrimination is being systematically practised by purchasers, in particular under provisions governing contracts entered into by bodies dependent on a public authority, it shall make appropriate recommendations to the Governments concerned.

2. Where the [Commission] considers it necessary, it may decide that:

(a) undertakings must frame their conditions of sale in such a way that their customers and commission agents acting on their behalf shall be under an obligation to comply with the rules made by the [Commission] in application of this Chapter;

(b) undertakings shall be held responsible for infringements of this obligation by their direct agents or by commission agents acting on their behalf.

In the event of an infringement of this obligation by a purchaser, the [Commission] may restrict or, should the infringement be repeated, temporarily prohibit dealings with that purchaser by Community undertakings. If this is done, the purchaser shall have the right, without prejudice to Article 33, to bring an action before the court.

3. In addition, the [Commission] is empowered to make to the Member States concerned any appropriate recommendations to ensure that the rules laid down for the application of Article 60(1) are duly observed by all distributive undertakings and agencies in the coal and steel sectors.

Article 64

The [Commission] may impose upon undertakings which infringe the provisions of this Chapter or decisions taken thereunder fines not exceeding twice the value of the sales effected in disregard thereof. If the infringement is repeated, this maximum shall be doubled.

Article 65

1. All agreements between undertakings, decisions by associations of undertakings and concerted practices tending directly or indirectly to prevent, restrict or distort normal competition within the common market shall be prohibited, and in particular those tending:

(a) to fix or determine prices;

(b) to restrict or control production, technical development or investments;

(c) to share markets, products, customers or sources of supply.

2. However, the [Commission] shall authorise specialisation agreements or joint-buying or joint-selling agreements in respect of particular products, if it finds that:

(a) such specialisation or such joint-buying or selling will make for a substantial improvement in the production or distribution of those products;
(b) the agreement in question is essential in order to achieve these results and is not more restrictive than is necessary for that purpose; and
(c) the agreement is not liable to give the undertakings concerned the power to determine the prices, or to control or restrict the production or marketing, of a substantial part of the products in question within the common market, or to shield them against effective competition from other undertakings within the common market.

If the [Commission] finds that certain agreements are strictly analogous in nature and effect to those referred to above, having particular regard to the fact that this paragraph applies to distributive undertakings, it shall authorise them also when satisfied that they meet the same requirements.

Authorisations may be granted subject to specified conditions and for limited periods. In such cases the [Commission] shall renew an authorisation once or several times if it finds that the requirements of sub-paragraphs (a) to (c) are still met at the time of renewal.

The [Commission] shall revoke or amend an authorisation if it finds that as a result of a change in circumstances the agreement no longer meets these requirements, or that the actual results of the agreement or of the application thereof are contrary to the requirements for its authorisation.

Decisions granting, renewing, amending, refusing or revoking an authorisation shall be published together with the reasons therefor; the restrictions imposed by the second paragraph of Article 47 shall not apply thereto.

3. The [Commission] may, as provided in Article 47, obtain any information needed for the application of this Article, either by making a special request to the parties concerned or by means of regulations stating the kinds of agreement, decision or practice which must be communicated to it.

4. Any agreement or decision prohibited by paragraph 1 of this Article shall be automatically void and may not be relied upon before any court or tribunal in the Member States.

The [Commission] shall have sole jurisdiction, subject to the right to bring actions before the Court, to rule whether any such agreement or decision is compatible with this Article.

5. On any undertaking which has entered into an agreement which is automatically void, or has enforced or attempted to enforce, by arbitration, penalty, boycott or any other means, an agreement or decision which is automatically void or an agreement for which authorisation has been refused or revoked, or has obtained an authorisation by means of information which it knew to be false or misleading, or has engaged in practices prohibited by paragraph 1 of this Article, the [Commission] may impose fines or periodic penalty payments not exceeding twice the turnover on the products which were the subject of the agreement, decision or practice, prohibited by this Article; if, however, the purpose of the agreement, decision or practice is to restrict production, technical development or investment, this maximum may be raised to 10 per cent of the annual turnover of the undertakings in question in the case of fines, and 20 per cent of the daily turnover in the case of periodic penalty payments.

Article 66

1. Any transaction shall require the prior authorisation of the [Commission], subject to the provisions of paragraph 3 of this Article, if it has in itself the direct or indirect effect of bringing about within the territories referred to in the first paragraph of Article 79, as a result of action by any person or undertaking or group of persons or undertakings, a

concentration between undertakings at least one of which is covered by Article 80, whether the transaction concerns a single product or a number of different products, and whether it is effected by merger, acquisition of shares or parts of the undertaking or assets, loan, contract or any other means of control. For the purpose of applying these provisions, the [Commission] shall, by regulations made after consulting the Council, define what constitutes control of an undertaking.

2. The [Commission] shall grant the authorisation referred to in the preceding paragraph if it finds that the proposed transaction will not give to the persons or undertakings concerned the power, in respect of the product or products within its jurisdiction:

— to determine prices, to control or restrict production or distribution or to hinder effective competition in a substantial part of the market for those products; or
— to evade the rules of competition instituted under this Treaty, in particular by establishing an artificially privileged position involving a substantial advantage in access to supplies or markets.

In assessing whether this is so, the [Commission] shall, in accordance with the principle of non-discrimination laid down in Article 4(b), take account of the size of like undertakings in the Community, to the extent it considers justified in order to avoid or correct disadvantages resulting from unequal competitive conditions

The [Commission] may make its authorisation subject to any conditions which it considers appropriate for the purposes of this paragraph.

Before ruling on a transaction concerning undertakings at least one of which is not subject to Article 80, the [Commission] shall obtain the comments of the Governments concerned.

3. The [Commission] shall exempt from the requirement of prior authorisation such classes of transactions as it finds should, in view of the size of the assets or undertakings concerned, taken in conjunction with the kind of concentration to be effected, be deemed to meet the requirements of paragraph 2. Regulations made to this effect, with the assent of the Council, shall also lay down the conditions governing such exemption.

4. Without prejudice to the application of Article 47 to undertakings within its jurisdiction, the [Commission] may, either by regulations made after consultation with the Council stating the kind of transaction to be communicated to it or by a special request under these regulations to the parties concerned, obtain from the natural or legal persons who have acquired or regrouped or are intending to acquire or regroup the rights or assets in question any information needed for the application of this Article concerning transactions liable to produce the effect referred to in paragraph 1.

5. If a concentration should occur which the [Commission] finds has been effected contrary to the provision of paragraph 1 but which nevertheless meets the requirements of paragraph 2, the [Commission] shall make its approval of that concentration subject to payment by the persons who have acquired or regrouped the rights or assets in question of the fine provided for in the second sub-paragraph of paragraph 6; the amount of the fine shall not be less than half of the maximum determined in that sub-paragraph should it be clear that authorisation ought to have been applied for. If the fine is not paid, the [Commission] shall take the steps hereinafter provided for in respect of concentrations found to be unlawful.

If a concentration should occur which the [Commission] finds cannot fulfil the general or specific conditions to which an authorisation under paragraph 2 would be subject, the [Commission] shall, by means of a reasoned decision, declare the concentration unlawful and, after giving the parties concerned the opportunity to submit their comments, shall order separation of the undertakings or assets improperly concentrated or cessation of joint control, and any other measures which it considers appropriate to return the undertakings or assets in question to independent operation and restore normal conditions of competition. Any person directly concerned may institute proceedings against such decisions, as provided in Article 33. By way of derogation from Article 33, the Court shall have unlimited jurisdiction to assess whether the transaction effected is a concentration within the meaning of paragraph 1 and of regulations made in application thereof. The institution of proceedings shall have suspensory effect. Proceedings may not be instituted until the measures provided for above have been ordered, unless the [Commission] agrees to the institution of separate proceedings against the decision declaring the transaction unlawful.

The [Commission] may at any time, unless the third paragraph of Article 39 is applied, take or cause to be taken such interim measures of protection as it may consider necessary to safeguard the interests of competing undertakings and of third parties, and to forestall any step which might hinder the implementation of its decisions. Unless the Court decides otherwise, proceedings shall not have suspensory effect in respect of such interim measures.

The [Commission] shall allow the parties concerned a reasonable period in which to comply with its decisions, on expiration of which it may impose daily penalty payments not exceeding one-tenth of 1 per cent of the value of the rights or assets in question.

Article 67

1. Any action by a Member State which is liable to have appreciable repercussions on conditions of competition in the coal or the steel industry shall be brought to the knowledge of the [Commission] by the Government concerned.

2. If the action is liable, by substantially increasing differences in production costs otherwise than through changes in productivity, to provoke a serious disequilibrium, the [Commission], after consulting the Consultative Committee and the Council, may take the following steps:

If the action taken by that State is having harmful effects on the coal or steel undertakings within the jurisdiction of that State, the [Commission] may authorise it to grant aid to these undertakings, the amount, conditions and duration of which shall be determined in agreement with the [Commission]. The same shall apply in the case of any change in wages and working conditions which would have the same effects, even if not resulting from any action by the State.

If the action taken by that State is having harmful effects on the coal or steel undertakings within the jurisdiction of other Member States, the [Commission] shall make a recommendation to that State with a view to remedying these effects by such measures as that State may consider most compatible with its own economic equilibrium.

3. If the action taken by that State reduces differences in production costs by allowing special benefits to or imposing special charges on the coal or steel undertakings within its jurisdiction in comparison with the other industries in the same country, the [Commission] is empowered to make the necessary recommendations to that State after consulting the Consultative Committee and the Council.

Article 80

For the purposes of this Treaty, "undertaking" means any undertaking engaged in production in the coal or the steel industry within the territories referred to in the first paragraph of Article 79 and also, for the purposes of Articles 65 and 66 and of information required for their application and proceedings in connection with them, any undertaking or agency regularly engaged in distribution other than sale to domestic consumers or small craft industries.

APPENDIX 8

REGULATION 19/65[1]

On the Application of Article 81(3) of the Treaty to Certain Categories of Agreements and Concerted Practices

THE COUNCIL OF THE EUROPEAN ECONOMIC COMMUNITY

Having regard to the Treaty establishing the European Economic Community, and in particular Artiolo 83 thereof;

Having regard to the proposal from the Commission;

Having regard to the Opinion of the European Parliament;

Having regard to the Opinion of the Economic and Social Committee;

Whereas Article 81(1) of the Treaty may in accordance with Article 81(3) be declared inapplicable to certain categories of agreements, decisions and concerted practices which fulfil the conditions contained in Article 81(3);

Whereas the provisions for implementation of Article 81(3) must be adopted by way of regulation pursuant to Article 83;

Whereas in view of the large number of notifications submitted in pursuance of Regulation 17 it is desirable that in order to facilitate the task of the Commission it should be enabled to declare by way of regulation that the provisions of Article 81(1) do not apply to certain categories of agreements and concerted practices;

Whereas it should be laid down under what conditions the Commission, in close and constant liaison with the competent authorities of the Member States, may exercise such powers after sufficient experience has been gained in the light of individual decisions and it becomes possible to define categories of agreements and concerted practices in respect of which the conditions of Article 81(3) may be considered as being fulfilled;

Whereas the Commission has indicated by the action it has taken, in particular by Regulation 153, that there can be no easing of the procedures prescribed by Regulation 17 in respect of certain types of agreements and concerted practices that are particularly liable to distort competition in the common market;

Whereas under Article 6 of Regulation 17 the Commission may provide that a decision taken pursuant to Article 81(3) of the Treaty shall apply with retroactive effect; whereas it is desirable that the Commission be also empowered to adopt, by regulation, provisions to the like effect;

Whereas under Article 7 of Regulation 17 agreements, decisions and concerted practices may, by decision of the Commission, be exempted from prohibition in particular if they are modified in such manner that they satisfy the requirements of Article 81(3); whereas it is desirable that the Commission be enabled to grant like exemption by regulation to such agreements and concerted practices if they are modified in such manner as to fall within a category defined in an exempting regulation;

Whereas, since there can be no exemption if the conditions set out in Article 81(3) are not satisfied, the Commission must have power to lay down by decision the conditions that

[1] JO 1965, 533 OJ 1965–6, 35.

must be satisfied by an agreement or concerted practice which owing to special circumstances has certain effects incompatible with Article 81(3).

HAS ADOPTED THIS REGULATION

Article 1

[1. Without prejudice to the application of Regulation No. 17 and in accordance with Article 81(3) of the Treaty the Commission may by regulation declare that Article 81(1) shall not apply to:

(a) categories of agreements which are entered into by two or more undertakings, each operating, for the purposes of the agreement, at a different level of the production or distribution chain, and which relate to the conditions under which the parties may purchase, sell or resell certain goods or services;
(b) categories of agreements to which only two undertakings are party and which include restrictions imposed in relation to the acquisition or use of industrial property rights, in particular of patents, utility models, designs or trade marks, or to the rights arising out of contracts for assignment of, or the right to use, a method of manufacture or knowledge relating to the use or to the application of industrial processes];

2. The regulation shall define the categories of agreements to which it applies and shall specify in particular:

(a) the restrictions or clauses which must not be contained in the agreements;
(b) [...] the other conditions which must be satisfied.

3. Paragraphs (1) and (2) shall apply by analogy to categories of concerted practices [...].

Amendment

Paragraphs 1, 2(b) and 3 were amended by Council Regulation No. 1215/99 OJ 1999 L148/1.

[Article 1a

A regulation pursuant to Article 1 may stipulate the conditions which may lead to the exclusion from its application or certain parallel networks of similar agreements or concerted practices operating on particular markets; when these circumstances are fulfilled the Commission may establish this by means of regulation and fix a period at the expiry of which the Regulation pursuant to Article 1 would no longer be applicable in respect of the relevant agreements or concerted practices on that market; such period must not be shorter than six months.]

Amendment

Article 1a was added by Council Regulation No. 1215/99.

Article 2

1. A regulation pursuant to Article 1 shall be made for a specific period.
2. It may be repealed or amended where circumstances have changed with respect to any factor which was basic to its being made; in such case, a period shall be fixed for

modification of the agreements and concerted practices to which the earlier regulation applies.

Article 3

A regulation pursuant to Article 1 may stipulate that it shall apply with retroactive effect to agreements and concerted practices to which, at the date of entry into force of that regulation, a decision issued with retroactive effect in pursuance of Article 6 of Regulation 17 would have applied.

Article 4

1. A regulation pursuant to Article 1 may stipulate that the prohibition contained in Article 81(1) of the Treaty shall no apply, for such period as shall be fixed by that regulation, to agreements and concerted practices already in existence on March 13, 1962, which do not satisfy the conditions of Article 81(3), [; or]
[A regulation pursuant to Article 1 may stipulate that the prohibition contained in Article 81(1) of the Treaty shall not apply, for such period as shall be fixed by that regulation, to agreements and concerted practices already in existence at the date of accession to which Article 81 applies by virtue of accession and which do not satisfy the conditions of Article 81(3) where:]

— within three months from the entry into force of the regulation, they are so modified as to satisfy the said conditions in accordance with the provisions of the regulation; and
— the modifications are brought to the notice of the Commission within the time limit fixed by the regulation.

[The provisions of the preceding subparagraph shall apply in the same way in the case of the accession of the Hellenic Republic, the Kingdom of Spain and of the Portuguese Republic.]
[The provisions of the preceding subparagraphs shall apply in the same way in the case of the accession of Austria, Finland and Sweden.]
2. Paragraph 1 shall apply to agreements and concerted practices which had to be notified before February 1, 1963, in accordance with Article 5 of Regulation 17, only where they have been so notified before that date.
[Paragraph 1 shall not apply to agreements and concerted practices to which Article 81(1) of the Treaty applies by virtue of accession and which must be notified before July 1, 1973, in accordance with Articles 5 and 25 of Regulation 17, unless they have been so notified before that date.]
[Paragraph 1 shall not apply to agreements and concerted practices to which Article 81(1) of the Treaty applies by virtue of the accession of the Hellenic Republic and which must be notified before July 1, 1981, in accordance with Articles 5 and 25 of Regulation 17, unless they have been so notified before that date.]
[Paragraph 2 shall not apply to agreements and concerted practices to which Article 81(1) of the Treaty applies by virtue of the accession of the Kingdom of Spain and of the Portuguese Republic and which must be notified before July 1, 1986, in accordance with Articles 5 and 25 of Regulation 17, unless they have been so notified before that date.]
[Paragraph 1 shall not apply to agreements and concerted practices to which Article 81(1) of the Treaty applies by virtue of the accession of Austria, Finland and Sweden and which must be notified within six months of accession, in accordance with Articles 5 and 25 of Regulation No 17, unless they have been so notified within that period. The present paragraph shall not apply to agreements and concerted practices which at the date of accession already fall under Article 53(1) of the EEA Agreement.]

3. The benefit of the provisions laid down pursuant to paragraph 1 may not be claimed in actions pending at the date of entry into force of a regulation adopted pursuant to Article 1; neither may it be relied on as grounds for claims for damages against third parties.

Amendments

In paragraph 1 the second sub-paragraph was added by the Act concerning the conditions of Accession and Adjustments to the Treaties, Annex I, v. Competition.

In paragraph 1 the third sub-paragraph was added by the Act of Accession of the Hellenic Republic, Annex I(V)(3). It was subsequently replaced by the Act of Accession of the Kingdom of Spain and the Portuguese Republic, Annex I(IV)(7).

In paragraph 1 the fourth sub-paragraph was added by the Act of Accession of the Republic of Austria, the Republic of Finland and the Kingdom of Sweden, Annex 1(III)(A)(1) as appended by Council Decision 95/1, Article 39.

In paragraph 2 the second sub-paragraph was added by the Act concerning the conditions of Accession and Adjustments to the Treaties, Annex I, v. Competition,

In paragraph 2 the third sub-paragraph was added by the Act of Accession of the Hellenic Republic, Annex I(V)(3);

In paragraph 2 the fourth sub-paragraph was added by the Act of Accession of the Kingdom of Spain and the Portuguese Republic, Annex I(IV)(7).

In paragraph 2, the fifth sub-paragraph was added by the Act of Accession of the Republic of Austria, the Republic of Finland and the Kingdom of Sweden, Annex 1(III)(A)(1), as amended by Council Decision 95/1, Article 39.

Article 5

Before adopting a regulation, the Commission shall publish a draft thereof and invite all persons concerned to submit their comments within such time limit, being not less than one month, as the Commission shall fix.

Article 6

1. The Commission shall consult the Advisory Committee on Restrictive Practices and Monopolies:

[(a) with regard to a regulation pursuant to Article 1 before publishing a draft regulation and before adopting a regulation;
(b) with regard to a regulation pursuant to Article 1a before publishing a draft regulation if requested by a Member State, and before adopting a regulation.]

2. Article 10(5) and (6) of Regulation 17, relating to consultation with the Advisory Committee, shall apply by analogy, it being understood that joint meetings with the Commission shall take place not earlier than one month after dispatch of the notice convening them.

Amendment

Paragraph 1(a) and (b) were amended by Council Regulation No. 1215/99.

Article 7

1. Where the Commission, either on its own initiative or at the request of a Member State or of natural or legal persons claiming a legitimate interest, finds that in any particular case agreements or concerted practices to which a regulation adopted pursuant

to Article 1 of this regulation applies have nevertheless certain effects which are incompatible with the conditions laid down in Article 81(3) of the Treaty, it may withdraw the benefit of application of that regulation and issue a decision in accordance with Articles 6 and 8 of Regulation 17, without any notification under Article 4(1) of Regulation 17 being required.

[2. When in any particular case agreements or concerted practices to which a regulation adopted pursuant to Article 1 applies have certain effects which are incompatible with the conditions laid down in Article 81(3) of the Treaty in the territory of a Member State, or in part thereof, which has all the characteristics of a distinct market, the competent authority in that Member State may on its own initiative or at the request of the Commission or of natural legal persons claiming a legitimate interest withdraw the benefit of application of that regulation.]

Amendment

Paragraph 2 was added by Council Regulation 1215/99.

Article 8

The Commission shall, before 1 January 1970, submit to the Council a proposal for a regulation for such amendment of this regulation as may prove necessary in the light of experience.

Done at Brussels, 2 March 1965.

REGULATION 2821/71[1]

On the Application of Article 81(3) of the Treaty to Categories of Agreements, Decisions and Concerted Practices

THE COUNCIL OF THE EUROPEAN COMMUNITIES

Having regard to the Treaty establishing the European Economic Community, and in particular Article 83 thereof;

Having regard to the proposal from the Commission;

Having regard to the Opinion of the European Parliament;

Having regard to the Opinion of the Economic and Social Committee;

Whereas Article 81(1) of the Treaty may in accordance with Article 81(3) be declared inapplicable to categories of agreements, decisions and concerted practices which fulfil the conditions contained in Article 81(3);

Whereas the provisions for implementation of Article 81(3) must be adopted by way of regulation pursuant to Article 83;

Whereas the creation of a common market requires that undertakings be adapted to the conditions of the enlarged market and whereas co-operation between undertakings can be a suitable means of achieving this;

Whereas agreements, decisions and concerted practices for co-operation between undertakings which enable the undertakings to work more rationally and adapt their productivity and competitiveness to the enlarged market may, in so far as they fall within the prohibition contained in Article 81(1), be exempted therefrom under certain conditions; whereas this measure is necessary in particular as regards agreements, decisions and concerted practices relating to the application of standards and types, research and development of products or processes up to the stage of industrial application, exploitation of the results thereof and specialisation;

Whereas it is desirable that the Commission be enabled to declare by way of regulation that the provisions of Article 81(1) do not apply to those categories of agreements, decisions and concerted practices, in order to make it easier for undertakings to co-operate in ways which are economically desirable and without adverse effect from the point of view of competition policy;

Whereas it should be laid down under what conditions the Commission, in close and constant liaison with the competent authorities of the Member States, may exercise such powers;

Whereas under Article 6 of Regulation 17 the Commission may provide that a decision taken in accordance with Article 81(3) of the Treaty shall apply with retroactive effect; whereas it is desirable that the Commission be empowered to issue regulations whose provisions are to the like effect;

Whereas under Article 7 of Regulation 17 agreements, decisions and concerted practices may by decision of the Commission be exempted from prohibition, in particular if they are modified in such manner that Article 81(3) applies to them; whereas it is desirable

---

[1] JO 1971 L285/46, OJ 1971 1032.

that the Commission be enabled to grant by regulation like exemption to such agreements, decisions and concerted practices if they are modified in such manner as to fall within a category defined in an exempting regulation;

Whereas the possibility cannot be excluded that, in a specific case, the conditions set out in Article 81(3) may not be fulfilled; whereas the Commission must have power to regulate such a case in pursuance of Regulation 17 by way of decision having effect for the future;

HAS ADOPTED THIS REGULATION:

Article 1

1. Without prejudice to the application of Regulation 17 the Commission may, by regulation and in accordance with Article 81(3) of the Treaty, declare that Article 81(1) shall not apply to categories of agreements between undertakings, decisions of associations of undertakings and concerted practices which have as their object:

(a) the application of standards or types;
(b) the research and development of products or processes up to the stage of industrial application, and exploitation of the results, including provisions regarding industrial property rights and confidential technical knowledge;
(c) specialisation, including agreements necessary for achieving it.

2. Such regulation shall define the categories of agreements, decisions and concerted practices to which it applies and shall specify in particular:

(a) the restrictions or clauses which may, or may not, appear in the agreements, decisions and concerted practices;
(b) the clauses which must be contained in the agreements, decisions and concerted practices or the other conditions must be satisfied.

Article 2

1. Any regulation pursuant to Article 1 shall be made for a specified period.
2. It may be repealed or amended where circumstances have changed with respect to any of the facts which were basic to its being made; in such case, a period shall be fixed for modification of the agreements, decisions and concerted practices to which the earlier regulation applies.

Article 3

A regulation pursuant to Article 1 may provide that it shall apply with retroactive effect to agreements, decisions and concerted practices to which, at the date of entry into force of that regulation, a decision issued with retroactive effect in pursuance of Article 6 of Regulation 17 would have applied.

Article 4

1. A regulation pursuant to Article 1 may provide that the prohibition contained in Article 81(1) of the Treaty shall not apply, for such period as shall be fixed by that regulation, to agreements, decisions and concerted practices already in existence on 13 March 1962, which do not satisfy the conditions of Article 81(3), where:

— within six months from the entry into force of the regulation, they are so modified as to satisfy the said conditions in accordance with the provisions of the regulation; and

— the modifications are brought to the notice of the Commission within the time limit fixed by the regulation.

[A regulation adopted pursuant to Article 1 may lay down that the prohibition referred to in Article 81(1) of the Treaty shall not apply, for the period fixed in the same regulation, to agreements and concerted practices which existed at the date of accession and which, by virtue of accession, come within the scope of Article 81 and do not fulfil the conditions set out in Article 81(3).]

[The provisions of the preceding sub-paragraph shall apply in the same way in the case of the accession of the Hellenic Republic, the Kingdom of Spain and of the Portuguese Republic.]

[The provisions of the preceding sub-paragraphs shall apply in the same way in the case of the accession of Austria, Finland and Sweden.]

2. Paragraph 1 shall apply to agreements, decisions and concerted practices which had to be notified before 1 February 1963, in accordance with Article 5 of Regulation 17, only where they have been so notified before that date.

[Paragraph 1 shall be applicable to those agreements and concerted practices which, by virtue of the accession, come within the scope of Article 81(1) of the Treaty and for which notification before 1 July 1973 is mandatory, in accordance with Articles 5 and 25 of Regulation 17, only if notification was given before that date.]

[Paragraph 1 shall not apply to agreements and concerted practices to which Article 81(1) of the Treaty applies by virtue of the accession of the Hellenic Republic and which must be notified before 1 July 1981, in accordance with Articles 5 and 25 of Regulation 17, unless they have been so notified before that date.]

[Paragraph 1 shall not apply to agreements and concerted practices to which Article 81(1) of the Treaty applies by virtue of the accession of the Kingdom of Spain and of the Portuguese Republic and which must be notified before 1 July 1986, in accordance with Articles 5 and 25 of Regulation 17, unless they have been so notified before that date.]

[Paragraph 1 shall not apply to agreements and concerted practices to which Article 81 of the Treaty applies by virtue of the accession of Austria, Finland and Sweden and which must be notified within six months of the accession, in accordance with Articles 5 and 25 of Regulation 17, unless they have been so notified within that period. The present paragraph shall not apply to agreements and concerted practices which at the date of accession already fall under Article 53(1) of the EEA Agreement.]

3. The benefit of the provisions laid down pursuant to paragraph 1 may not be claimed in actions pending at the date of entry into force of a regulation adopted pursuant to Article 1; neither may it be relied on as grounds for claims for damages against third parties.

Amendments

In paragraph 1 the second sub-paragraph was added by Regulation 2743/72, Article 1 (JO 1972, L291/144; OJ 1972 (28–30 Dec.), 60).

In paragraph 1 the third sub-paragraph was added by the Act of Accession of the Hellenic Republic, Annex I(V)(5). It was subsequently replaced by the Act of Accession of the Kingdom of Spain and the Portuguese Republic, Annex I(IV)(9).

In paragraph 1 the fourth sub-paragraph was added by the Act of Accession of the Republic of Austria, the Republic of Finland and the Kingdom of Sweden, Annex 1(III)(A)(2), as amended by Council Decision 95/1, Article 39.

In paragraph 2 the second sub-paragraph was added by Regulation 2743/72, Article 1.

In paragraph 2 the third sub-paragraph was added by the Act of Accession of the Hellenic Republic, Annex I(V)(5).

In paragraph 2 the fourth sub-paragraph was added by the Act of Accession of the Kingdom of Spain and the Portuguese Republic, Annex I(IV)(9).

In paragraph 2 the fifth sub-paragraph was added by the Act of Accession of the Republic of Austria, the Republic of Finland and the Kingdom of Sweden, Annex 1(III)(A)(2), as amended by Council Decision 95/1, Article 39.

Article 5

Before making a regulation, the Commission shall publish a draft thereof to enable all persons and organisations concerned to submit their comments within such time limit, being not less than one month, as the Commission shall fix.

Article 6

1. The Commission shall consult the Advisory Committee on Restrictive Practices and Monopolies:

(a) before publishing a drafting regulation;
(b) before making a regulation.

2. Paragraphs (5) and (6) of Article 10 of Regulation 17, relating to consultation with the Advisory Committee, shall apply by analogy, it being understood that joint meetings with the Commission shall take place not earlier than one month after dispatch of the notice convening them.

Article 7

Where the Commission, either on its own initiative or at the request of a Member State or of natural or legal persons claiming a legitimate interest, finds that in any particular case agreements, decisions or concerted practices to which a regulation made pursuant to Article 1 of this regulation applies have nevertheless certain effects which are incompatible with the conditions laid down in Article 81(3) of the Treaty, it may withdraw the benefit of application of that regulation and take a decision in accordance with Articles 6 and 8 of Regulation 17, without any notification under Article 4(1) of Regulation 17 being required.

Done at Brussels, 20 December 1971.

APPENDIX 10

REGULATION 1534/91[1]

On the Application of Article 81(3) of the Treaty to Certain Categories of Agreements, Decisions and Concerted Practices in the Insurance Sector

THE COUNCIL OF THE EUROPEAN COMMUNITIES

Having regard to the Treaty establishing the European Economic Community, and in particular Article 83 thereof,
Having regard to the proposal from the Commission,[2]
Having regard to the opinion of the European Parliament,[3]
Having regard to the opinion of the Economic and Social Committee,[4]
Whereas Article 81(1) of the Treaty may, in accordance with Article 81(3), be declared inapplicable to categories of agreements, decisions and concerted practices when satisfying the requirements of Article 81(3);
Whereas the detailed rules for the application of Article 81(3) of the Treaty must be adopted by way of a Regulation based on Article 83 of the Treaty;
Whereas co-operation between undertakings in the insurance sector is, to a certain extent, desirable to ensure the proper functioning of this sector and may at the same time promote consumers' interests;
Whereas the application of Council Regulation (EEC) No. 4064/89 of 21 December 1989 on the control of concentrations between undertakings[5] enables the Commission to exercise close supervision on issues arising from concentrations in all sectors, including the insurance sector;
Whereas exemptions granted under Article 81(3) of the Treaty cannot themselves affect Community and national provisions safeguarding consumers' interests in this sector;
Whereas agreements, decisions and concerted practices serving such aims may, in so far as they fall within the prohibition contained in Article 81(1) of the Treaty, be exempted therefrom under certain conditions; whereas this applies in particular to agreements, decisions and concerted practices relating to the establishment of common risk premium tariffs based on collectively ascertained statistics or the number of claims, the establishment of standard policy conditions, common coverage of certain types of risks, the settlement of claims, the testing and acceptance of security devices, and registers of, and information on, aggravated risks;
Whereas in view of the large number of notifications submitted pursuant to Council Regulation No. 17 of 6 February 1962: First Regulation implementing Articles 81 and 82 of the Treaty,[6] as last amended by the Act of Accession of Spain and Portugal, it is desirable that in order to facilitate the Commission's task, it should be enabled to declare,

---

[1] OJ 1991 L143/1.
[2] OJ 1990 C16/13.
[3] OJ 1990 C260/57.
[4] OJ 1990 C182/10.
[5] OJ 1989 L395/1.
[6] OJ 1962, No. 13, 204/62.

by way of Regulation, that the provisions of Article 81(1) of the Treaty are inapplicable to certain categories of agreements, decisions and concerted practices;

Whereas it should be laid down under which conditions the Commission, in close and constant liaison with the competent authorities of the Member States, may exercise such powers;

Whereas, in the exercise of such powers, the Commission will take account not only of the risk of competition being eliminated in a substantial part of the relevant market and of any benefit that might be conferred on policyholders resulting from the agreements, but also of the risk which the proliferation of restrictive clauses and the operation of accommodation companies would entail for policyholders;

Whereas the keeping of registers and the handling of information on aggravated risks should be carried out subject to the proper protection of confidentiality;

Whereas, under Article 6 of Regulation No. 17, the Commission may provide that a decision taken in accordance with Article 81(3) of the Treaty shall apply with retroactive effect; whereas the Commission should also be able to adopt provisions to such effect in a Regulation;

Whereas, under Article 7 of Regulation No. 17, agreements, decisions and concerted practices may, by decision of the Commission, be exempted from prohibition, in particular if they are modified in such manner that they satisfy the requirements of Article 81(3) of the Treaty; whereas it is desirable that the Commission be enabled to grant by Regulation like exemption to such agreements, decisions and concerted practices if they are modified in such manner as to fall within a category defined in an exempting Regulation;

Whereas it cannot be ruled out that, in specific cases, the conditions set out in Article 81(3) of the Treaty may not be fulfilled; whereas the Commission must have the power to regulate such cases pursuant to Regulation No. 17 by way of a Decision having effect for the future,

HAS ADOPTED THIS REGULATION:

Article 1

1. Without prejudice to the application of Regulation No. 17 the Commission may, by means of a Regulation and in accordance with Article 81(3) of the Treaty, declare that Article 81(1) shall not apply to categories of agreements between undertakings, decisions of associations of undertakings and concerted practices in the insurance sector which have as their object co-operation with respect to:

(a) the establishment of common risk premium tariffs based on collectively ascertained statistics or the number of claims;
(b) the establishment of common standard policy conditions;
(c) the common coverage of certain types of risks;
(d) the settlement of claims;
(e) the testing and acceptance of security devices;
(f) registers of, and information on, aggravated risks, provided that the keeping of these registers and the handling of this information is carried out subject to the proper protection of confidentiality.

2. The Commission Regulation referred to in paragraph 1, shall define the categories of agreements, decisions and concerted practices to which it applies and shall specify in particular:

(a) the restrictions or clauses which may, or may not, appear in the agreements, decisions and concerted practices;
(b) the clauses which must be contained in the agreements, decisions and concerted practices or the other conditions which must be satisfied.

Article 2

Any Regulation adopted pursuant to Article 1 shall be of limited duration.

It may be repealed or amended where circumstances have changed with respect to any of the facts which were essential to its being adopted; in such case, a period shall be fixed for modification of the agreements, decisions and concerted practices to which the earlier Regulation applies.

Article 3

A Regulation adopted pursuant to Article 1 may provide that it shall apply with retroactive effect to agreements, decisions and concerted practices to which, at the date of entry into force of the said Regulation, a decision taken with retroactive effect pursuant to Article 6 of Regulation No. 17 would have applied.

Article 4

1. A Regulation adopted pursuant to Article 1 may provide that the prohibition contained in Article 81(1) of the Treaty shall not apply, for such period as shall be fixed in that Regulation, to agreements, decisions and concerted practices already in existence on 13 March 1962 which do not satisfy the conditions of Article 81(3) where:

— within six months from the entry into force of the said Regulation, they are so modified as to satisfy the said conditions in accordance with the provisions of the said Regulation; and
— the modifications are brought to the notice of the Commission within the time limit fixed by the said Regulation.

The provisions of the first sub-paragraph shall apply in the same way to those agreements, decisions and concerted practices existing at the date of accession of new Member States to which Article 81(1) of the Treaty applies by virtue of accession and which do not satisfy the conditions of Article 81(3).

2. Paragraph 1 shall apply to agreements, decisions and concerted practices which had to be notified before 1 February 1963, in accordance with Article 5 of Regulation No. 17, only where they have been so notified before that date.

Paragraph 1 shall not apply to agreements, decisions and concerted practices existing at the date of accession of new Member States to which Article 81(1) of the Treaty applies by virtue of accession and which had to be notified within six months from the date of accession in accordance with Articles 5 and 25 of Regulation No. 17, unless they have been so notified within the said period.

3. The benefit of provisions adopted pursuant to paragraph 1 may not be invoked in actions pending at the date of entry into force of a Regulation adopted pursuant to Article 1; neither may it be invoked as grounds for claims for damages against third parties.

Article 5

Where the Commission proposes to adopt a Regulation, it shall publish a draft thereof to enable all persons and organisations concerned to submit to it their comments within such time limit, being not less than one month, as it shall fix.

Article 6

1. The Commission shall consult the Advisory Committee on Restrictive Practices and Monopolies:

(a) before publishing a draft Regulation;
(b) before adopting a Regulation.

2. Article 10(5) and (6) of Regulation No. 17, relating to consultation of the Advisory Committee, shall apply. However, joint meetings with the Commission shall take place not earlier than one month after dispatch of the notice convening them.

Article 7

Where the Commission, either on its own initiative or at the request of a Member State or of natural or legal persons claiming a legitimate interest, finds that, in any particular case, agreements, decisions and concerted practices, to which a Regulation adopted pursuant to Article 1 applies, have nevertheless certain effects which are incompatible with the conditions laid down in Article 81(3) of the Treaty, it may withdraw the benefit of application of the said Regulation and take a decision in accordance with Articles 6 and 8 of Regulation No. 17, without any notification under Article 4(1) of Regulation No. 17 being required.

Article 8

Not later than six years after the entry into force of the Commission Regulation provided for in Article 1, the Commission shall submit to the European Parliament and the Council a report on the functioning of this Regulation, accompanied by such proposals for amendments to this Regulation as may appear necessary in the light of experience.

This Regulation shall be binding in its entirety and directly applicable in all Member States.

Done at Brussels, 31 May 1991.

APPENDIX 11

REGULATION 2790/99[1]

On the Application of Article 81(3) of the Treaty to Categories of Vertical Agreements and Concerted Practices

(Text with EEA relevance)

THE COMMISSION OF THE EUROPEAN COMMUNITIES

Having regard to the Treaty establishing the European Community,

Having regard to Council Regulation No. 19/65/EEC of 2 March 1965 on the application of Article 81(3) of the Treaty to certain categories of agreements and concerted practices,[2] as last amended by Regulation (EC) No. 1215/1999[3], and in particular Article 1 thereof,

Having published a draft of this Regulation,[4]

Having consulted the Advisory Committee on Restrictive Practices and Dominant Positions,

Whereas:

(1) Regulation No. 19/65/EEC empowers the Commission to apply Article 81(3) of the Treaty (formerly Article 85(3)) by regulation to certain categories of vertical agreements and corresponding concerted practices falling within Article 81(1).

(2) Experience acquired to date makes it possible to define a category of vertical agreements which can be regarded as normally satisfying the conditions laid down in Article 81(3).

(3) This category includes vertical agreements for the purchase or sale of goods or services where these agreements are concluded between non-competing undertakings, between certain competitors or by certain associations of retailers of goods; it also includes vertical agreements containing ancillary provisions on the assignment or use of intellectual property rights; for the purposes of this Regulation, the term "vertical agreements" includes the corresponding concerted practices.

(4) For the application of Article 81(3) by regulation, it is not necessary to define those vertical agreements which are capable of falling within Article 81(1); in the individual assessment of agreements under Article 81(1), account has to be taken of several factors, and in particular the market structure on the supply and purchase side.

(5) The benefit of the block exemption should be limited to vertical agreements for which it can be assumed with sufficient certainty that they satisfy the conditions of Article 81(3).

(6) Vertical agreements of the category defined in this Regulation can improve economic efficiency within a chain of production or distribution by facilitating better

---

[1] OJ 1999 L336/21
[2] OJ 36, 1965, 533/65.
[3] OJ 1999 L148/1.
[4] OJ 1999 C 270/1.

42

co-ordination between the participating undertakings; in particular, they can lead to a reduction in the transaction and distribution costs of the parties and to an optimisation of their sales and investment levels.

(7) The likelihood that such efficiency-enhancing effects will outweigh any anti-competitive effects due to restrictions contained in vertical agreements depends on the degree of market power of the undertakings concerned and, therefore, on the extent to which those undertakings face competition from other suppliers of goods or services regarded by the buyer as interchangeable or substitutable for one another, by reason of the products' characteristics, their prices and their intended use.

(8) It can be presumed that, where the share of the relevant market accounted for by the supplier does not exceed 30%, vertical agreements which do not contain certain types of severely anti-competitive restraints generally lead to an improvement in production or distribution and allow consumers a fair share of the resulting benefits; in the case of vertical agreements containing exclusive supply obligations, it is the market share of the buyer which is relevant in determining the overall effects of such vertical agreements on the market.

(9) Above the market share threshold of 30%, there can be no presumption that vertical agreements falling within the scope of Article 81(1) will usually give rise to objective advantages of such a character and size as to compensate for the disadvantages which they create for competition.

(10) This Regulation should not exempt vertical agreements containing restrictions which are not indispensable to the attainment of the positive effects mentioned above; in particular, vertical agreements containing certain types of severely anti-competitive restraints such as minimum and fixed resale prices, as well as certain types of territorial protection, should be excluded from the benefit of the block exemption established by this Regulation irrespective of the market share of the undertakings concerned.

(11) In order to ensure access to or to prevent collusion on the relevant market, certain conditions are to be attached to the block exemption: to this end, the exemption of non-compete obligations should be limited to obligations which do not exceed a definite duration; for the same reasons, any direct or indirect obligation causing the members of a selective distribution system not to sell the brands of particular competing suppliers should be excluded from the benefit of this Regulation.

(12) The market share limitation, the non-exemption of certain vertical agreements and the conditions provided for in this Regulation normally ensure that the agreements to which the block exemption applies do not enable the participating undertakings to eliminate competition in respect of a substantial part of the products in question.

(13) In particular cases in which the agreements falling under this Regulation nevertheless have effects incompatible with Article 81(3), the Commission may withdraw the benefit of the block exemption; this may occur in particular where the buyer has significant market power in the relevant market in which it resells the goods or provides the services or where parallel networks of vertical agreements have similar effects which significantly restrict access to a relevant market or competition therein; such cumulative effects may for example arise in the case of selective distribution or non-compete obligations.

(14) Regulation No. 19/65/EEC empowers the competent authorities of Member States to withdraw the benefit of the block exemption in respect of vertical agreements having effects incompatible with the conditions laid down in Article 81(3), where such effects are felt in their respective territory, or in a part thereof, and where such territory has the characteristics of a distinct geographic market; Member States should ensure that the exercise of this power of withdrawal does not prejudice the uniform application throughout the common market of the Community competition rules or the full effect of the measures adopted in implementation of those rules.

(15) In order to strengthen supervision of parallel networks of vertical agreements which have similar restrictive effects and which cover more than 50% of a given market, the

Commission may declare this Regulation inapplicable to vertical agreements containing specific restraints relating to the market concerned, thereby restoring the full application of Article 81 to such agreements.

(16) This Regulation is without prejudice to the application of Article 82.

(17) In accordance with the principle of the primacy of Community law, no measure taken pursuant to national laws on competition should prejudice the uniform application throughout the common market of the Community competition rules or the full effect of any measures adopted in implementation of those rules, including this Regulation.

HAS ADOPTED THIS REGULATION:

Article 1

For the purposes of this Regulation:

(a) "competing undertakings" means actual or potential suppliers in the same product market; the product market includes goods or services which are regarded by the buyer as interchangeable with or substitutable for the contract goods or services, by reason of the products' characteristics, their prices and their intended use;

(b) "non-compete obligation" means any direct or indirect obligation causing the buyer not to manufacture, purchase, sell or resell goods or services which compete with the contract goods or services, or any direct or indirect obligation on the buyer to purchase from the supplier or from another undertaking designated by the supplier more than 80% of the buyer's total purchases of the contract goods or services and their substitutes on the relevant market, calculated on the basis of the value of its purchases in the preceding calendar year;

(c) "exclusive supply obligation" means any direct or indirect obligation causing the supplier to sell the goods or services specified in the agreement only to one buyer inside the Community for the purposes of a specific use or for resale;

(d) "selective distribution system" means a distribution system where the supplier undertakes to sell the contract goods or services, either directly or indirectly, only to distributors selected on the basis of specified criteria and where these distributors undertake not to sell such goods or services to unauthorised distributors;

(e) "intellectual property rights" includes industrial property rights, copyright and neighbouring rights;

(f) "know-how" means a package of non-patented practical information, resulting from experience and testing by the supplier, which is secret, substantial and identified: in this context, "secret" means that the know-how, as a body or in the precise configuration and assembly of its components, is not generally known or easily accessible: "substantial" means that the know-how includes information which is indispensable to the buyer for the use, sale or resale of the contract goods or services: "identified" means that the know-how must be described in a sufficiently comprehensive manner so as to make it possible to verify that it fulfils the criteria of secrecy and substantiality;

(g) "buyer" includes an undertaking which, under an agreement falling within Article 81(1) of the Treaty, sells goods or services on behalf of another undertaking.

Article 2

1. Pursuant to Article 81(3) of the Treaty and subject to the provisions of this Regulation, it is hereby declared that Article 81(1) shall not apply to agreements or concerted practices entered into between two or more undertakings each of which operates, for the purposes of the agreement, at a different level of the production or

distribution chain, and relating to the conditions under which the parties may purchase, sell or resell certain goods or services ("vertical agreements").

This exemption shall apply to the extent that such agreements contain restrictions of competition falling within the scope of Article 81(1) ("vertical restraints").

2. The exemption provided for in paragraph 1 shall apply to vertical agreements entered into between an association of undertakings and its members, or between such an association and its suppliers, only if all its members are retailers of goods and if no individual member of the association, together with its connected undertakings, has a total annual turnover exceeding EUR 50 million; vertical agreements entered into by such associations shall be covered by this Regulation without prejudice to the application of Article 81 to horizontal agreements concluded between the members of the association or decisions adopted by the association.

3. The exemption provided for in paragraph 1 shall apply to vertical agreements containing provisions which relate to the assignment to the buyer or use by the buyer of intellectual property rights, provided that those provisions do not constitute the primary object of such agreements and are directly related to the use, sale or resale of goods or services by the buyer or its customers. The exemption applies on condition that, in relation to the contract goods or services, those provisions do not contain restrictions of competition having the same object or effect as vertical restraints which are not exempted under this Regulation.

4. The exemption provided for in paragraph 1 shall not apply to vertical agreements entered into between competing undertakings; however, it shall apply where competing undertakings enter into a non-reciprocal vertical agreement and:

(a) the buyer has a total annual turnover not exceeding EUR 100 million, or
(b) the supplier is a manufacturer and a distributor of goods, while the buyer is a distributor not manufacturing goods competing with the contract goods, or
(c) the supplier is a provider of services at several levels of trade, while the buyer does not provide competing services at the level of trade where it purchases the contract services.

5. This Regulation shall not apply to vertical agreements the subject-matter of which falls within the scope of any other block exemption regulation.

Article 3

1. Subject to paragraph 2 of this Article, the exemption provided for in Article 2 shall apply on condition that the market share held by the supplier does not exceed 30% of the relevant market on which it sells the contract goods or services.

2. In the case of vertical agreements containing exclusive supply obligations, the exemption provided for in Article 2 shall apply on condition that the market share held by the buyer does not exceed 30% of the relevant market on which it purchases the contract goods or services.

Article 4

The exemption provided for in Article 2 shall not apply to vertical agreements which, directly or indirectly, in isolation or in combination with other factors under the control of the parties, have as their object:

(a) the restriction of the buyer's ability to determine its sale price, without prejudice to the possibility of the supplier's imposing a maximum sale price or recommending a sale price, provided that they do not amount to a fixed or minimum sale price as a result of pressure from, or incentives offered by, any of the parties;
(b) the restriction of the territory into which, or of the customers to whom, the buyer may sell the contract goods or services, except;

— the restriction of active sales into the exclusive territory or to an exclusive customer group reserved to the supplier or allocated by the supplier to another buyer, where such a restriction does not limit sales by the customers of the buyer,

— the restriction of sales to end users by a buyer operating at the wholesale level of trade,

— the restriction of sales to unauthorised distributors by the members of a selective distribution system, and

— the restriction of the buyer's ability to sell components, supplied for the purposes of incorporation, to customers who would use them to manufacture the same type of goods as those produced by the supplier,

(c) the restriction of active or passive sales to end users by members of a selective distribution system operating at the retail level of trade, without prejudice to the possibility of prohibiting a member of the system from operating out of an unauthorised place of establishment;

(d) the restriction of cross-supplies between distributors within a selective distribution system, including between distributors operating at different levels of trade;

(e) the restriction agreed between a supplier of components and a buyer who incorporates those components, which limits the supplier to selling the components as spare parts to end-users or to repairers or other service providers not entrusted by the buyer with the repair or servicing of its goods.

Article 5

The exemption provided for in Article 2 shall not apply to any of the following obligations contained in vertical agreements:

(a) any direct or indirect non-compete obligation, the duration of which is indefinite or exceeds five years. A non-compete obligation which is tacitly renewable beyond a period of five years is to be deemed to have been concluded for an indefinite duration. However, the time limitation of five years shall not apply where the contract goods or services are sold by the buyer from premises and land owned by the supplier or leased by the supplier from third parties not connected with the buyer, provided that the duration of the non-compete obligation does not exceed the period of occupancy of the premises and land by the buyer;

(b) any direct or indirect obligation causing the buyer, after termination of the agreement, not to manufacture, purchase, sell or resell goods or services, unless such obligation:

— relates to goods or services which compete with the contract goods or services, and

— is limited to the premises and land from which the buyer has operated during the contract period, and

— is indispensable to protect know-how transferred by the supplier to the buyer,

and provided that the duration of such non-compete obligation is limited to a period of one year after termination of the agreement; this obligation is without prejudice to the possibility of imposing a restriction which is unlimited in time on the use and disclosure of know-how which has not entered the public domain;

(c) any direct or indirect obligation causing the members of a selective distribution system not to sell the brands of particular competing suppliers.

Article 6

The Commission may withdraw the benefit of this Regulation, pursuant to Article 7(1) of Regulation No. 19/65/EEC, where it finds in any particular case that vertical agreements to which this Regulation applies nevertheless have effects which are incompatible with the conditions laid down in Article 81(3) of the Treaty, and in particular where access to the relevant market or competition therein is significantly restricted by the cumulative effect of parallel networks of similar vertical restraints implemented by competing suppliers or buyers.

Article 7

Where in any particular case vertical agreements to which the exemption provided for in Article 2 applies have effects incompatible with the conditions laid down in Article 81(3) of the Treaty in the territory of a Member State, or in a part thereof, which has all the characteristics of a distinct geographic market, the competent authority of that Member State may withdraw the benefit of application of this Regulation in respect of that territory, under the same conditions as provided in Article 6.

Article 8

1. Pursuant to Article 1a of Regulation No. 19/65/EEC, the Commission may by regulation declare that, where parallel networks of similar vertical restraints cover more than 50% of a relevant market, this Regulation shall not apply to vertical agreements containing specific restraints relating to that market.

2. A regulation pursuant to paragraph 1 shall not become applicable earlier than six months following its adoption.

Article 9

1. The market share of 30% provided for in Article 3(1) shall be calculated on the basis of the market sales value of the contract goods or services and other goods or services sold by the supplier, which are regarded as interchangeable or substitutable by the buyer, by reason of the products' characteristics, their prices and their intended use: if market sales value data are not available, estimates based on other reliable market information, including market sales volumes, may be used to establish the market share of the undertaking concerned. For the purposes of Article 3(2), it is either the market purchase value or estimates thereof which shall be used to calculate the market share.

2. For the purposes of applying the market share threshold provided for in Article 3 the following rules shall apply:

(a) the market share shall be calculated on the basis of data relating to the preceding calendar year;
(b) the market share shall include any goods or services supplied to integrated distributors for the purposes of sale;
(c) if the market share is initially not more than 30% but subsequently rises above that level without exceeding 35%, the exemption provided for in Article 2 shall continue to apply for a period of two consecutive calendar years following the year in which the 30% market share threshold was first exceeded;
(d) if the market share is initially not more than 30% but subsequently rises above 35%, the exemption provided for in Article 2 shall continue to apply for one calendar year following the year in which the level of 35% was first exceeded;
(e) the benefit of points (c) and (d) may not be combined so as to exceed a period of two calendar years.

Article 10

1. For the purpose of calculating total annual turnover within the meaning of Article 2(2) and (4), the turnover achieved during the previous financial year by the relevant party to the vertical agreement and the turnover achieved by its connected undertakings in

respect of all goods and services, excluding all taxes and other duties, shall be added together. For this purpose, no account shall be taken of dealings between the party to the vertical agreement and its connected undertakings or between its connected undertakings.

2. The exemption provided for in Article 2 shall remain applicable where, for any period of two consecutive financial years, the total annual turnover threshold is exceeded by no more than 10%.

Article 11

1. For the purposes of this Regulation, the terms "undertaking", "supplier" and "buyer" shall include their respective connected undertakings.

2. "Connected undertakings" are:

(a) undertakings in which a party to the agreement, directly or indirectly;
  — has the power to exercise more than half the voting rights, or
  — has the power to appoint more than half the members of the supervisory board, board of management or bodies legally representing the undertaking, or
  — has the right to manage the undertaking's affairs;
(b) undertakings which directly or indirectly have, over a party to the agreement, the rights or powers listed in (a);
(c) undertakings in which an undertaking referred to in (b) has, directly or indirectly, the rights or powers listed in (a);
(d) undertakings in which a party to the agreement together with one or more of the undertakings referred to in (a), (b) or (c), or in which two or more of the latter undertakings, jointly have the rights or powers listed in (a);
(e) undertakings in which the rights or the powers listed in (a) are jointly held by:
  — parties to the agreement or their respective connected undertakings referred to in (a) to (d), or
  — one or more of the parties to the agreement or one or more of their connected undertakings referred to in (a) to (d) and one or more third parties.

3. For the purposes of Article 3, the market share held by the undertakings referred to in paragraph 2(e) of this Article shall be apportioned equally to each undertaking having the rights or the powers listed in paragraph 2(a).

Article 12

1. The exemptions provided for in Commission Regulations (EEC) No. 1983/83,[5] 1984/83[6] and (EEC) No. 4087/88[7] shall continue to apply until 31 May 2000.

2. The prohibition laid down in Article 81(1) of the EC Treaty shall not apply during the period from 1 June 2000 to 31 December 2001 in respect of agreements already in force on 31 May 2000 which do not satisfy the conditions for exemption provided for in this Regulation but which satisfy the conditions for exemption provided for in Regulations (EEC) No. 1983/83, (EEC) No. 1984/83 or (EEC) No. 4087/88.

---

[5] OJ 1983 L173/1.
[6] OJ 1983 L173/5.
[7] OJ 1988 L359/46.

Article 13

This Regulation shall enter into force on 1 January 2000.

It shall apply from 1 June 2000, except for Article 12(1) which shall apply from 1 January 2000.

This Regulation shall expire on 31 May 2010.

This Regulation shall be binding in its entirety and directly applicable in all Member States.

Done at Brussels, 22 December 1999.

APPENDIX 12

REGULATION 1983/83[1]

On the Application of Article 81(3) of the Treaty to Categories of Exclusive Distribution Agreements

THE COMMISSION OF THE EUROPEAN COMMUNITIES

Having regard to the Treaty establishing the European Economic Community,
Having regard to Council Regulation 19/65 of 2 March 1965 on the application of Article 81(3) of the Treaty to certain categories of agreements and concerted practices, as last amended by the Act of Accession of Greece, and in particular Article 1 thereof,
Having published a draft of this Regulation,
Having consulted the Advisory Committee on Restrictive Practices and Dominant Positions,

(1) Whereas Regulation No. 19/65/EEC empowers the Commission to apply Article 81(3) of the Treaty by regulation to certain categories of bilateral exclusive distribution agreements and analogous concerted practices falling within Article 81(1);
(2) Whereas experience to date makes it possible to define a category of agreements and concerted practices which can be regarded as normally satisfying the conditions laid down in Article 81(3);
(3) Whereas exclusive distribution agreements of the category defined in Article 1 of this Regulation may fall within the prohibition contained in Article 81(1) of the Treaty; whereas this will apply only in exceptional cases to exclusive agreements of this kind to which only undertakings from one Member State are party and which concert the resale of goods within that Member State; whereas however, to the extent that such agreements may affect trade between Member States and also satisfy all the requirements set out in this Regulation there is no reason to withhold from them the benefit of the exemption by category;
(4) Whereas it is not necessary expressly to exclude from the defined category those agreements which do not fulfil the conditions of Article 81(1) of the Treaty;
(5) Whereas exclusive distribution agreements lead in general to an improvement in distribution because the undertaking is able to concentrate its sales activities, does not need to maintain numerous business relations with a larger number of dealers and is able, by dealing with only one dealer, to overcome more easily distribution difficulties in international trade resulting from linguistic, legal and other differences;
(6) Whereas exclusive distribution agreements facilitate the promotion of sales of a product and lead to intensive marketing and to continuity of supplies while at the same time rationalising distribution; whereas they stimulate competition between the products of different manufacturers; whereas the appointment of an exclusive distributor who will take over sales promotion, customer services and carrying of stocks is often the most effective way, and sometimes indeed the only way, for the manufacturer to enter a market and compete with other manufacturers already present;

---

[1] OJ 1983 L173/1. Printed as amended by corrigendum (OJ 1983 L281/24).

whereas this is particularly so in the case of small and medium-sized undertakings; whereas it must be left to the contracting parties to decide whether and to what extent they consider it desirable to incorporate in the agreements terms providing for the promotion of sales;

(7) Whereas, as a rule, such exclusive distribution agreements also allow consumers a fair share of the resulting benefit as they gain directly from the improvement in distribution, and their economic and supply position is improved as they can obtain products manufactured in particular in other countries more quickly and more easily;

(8) Whereas this Regulation must define the obligations restricting competition which may be included in exclusive distribution agreements; whereas the other restrictions on competition allowed under this Regulation in addition to the exclusive supply obligation produce a clear division of functions between the parties and compel the exclusive distributor to concentrate his sales efforts on the contract goods and for the contract territory; whereas they are, where they are agreed only for the duration of the agreement, generally necessary in order to attain the improvement in the distribution of goods sought through exclusive distribution; whereas it may be left to the contracting parties to decide which of these obligations they include in their agreements; whereas further restrictive obligations and in particular those which limit the exclusive distributor's choice of customers or his freedom to determine his prices and conditions of sale cannot be exempted under this Regulation;

(9) Whereas the exemption by category should be reserved for agreements for which it can be assumed with sufficient certainty that they satisfy the conditions of Article 81(3) of the Treaty;

(10) Whereas it is not possible, in the absence of a case-by-case examination, to consider that adequate improvements in distribution occur where a manufacturer entrusts the distribution of his goods to another manufacturer with whom he is in competition; whereas such agreements should, therefore, be excluded from the exemption by category; whereas certain derogations from this rule in favour of small and medium-sized undertakings can be allowed;

(11) Whereas consumers will be assured of a fair share of the benefits resulting from exclusive distribution only if parallel imports remain possible; whereas agreements relating to goods which the user can obtain only from the exclusive distributor should therefore be excluded from the exemption by category; whereas the parties cannot be allowed to abuse industrial property rights or other rights in order to create absolute territorial protection; whereas this does not prejudice the relationship between competition law and industrial property rights, since the sole object here is to determine the conditions for exemption by category;

(12) Whereas, since competition at the distribution stage is ensured by the possibility of parallel imports, the exclusive distribution agreements covered by this Regulation will not normally afford any possibility of eliminating competition in respect of a substantial part of the products in question; whereas this is also true of agreements that allot to the exclusive distributor a contract territory covering the whole of the common market;

(13) Whereas, in particular cases in which agreements or concerted practices satisfying the requirements of this Regulation nevertheless have effects incompatible with Article 81(3) of the Treaty, the Commission may withdraw the benefit of the exemption by category from the undertakings party to them;

(14) Whereas agreements and concerted practices which satisfy the conditions set out in this Regulation need not be notified; whereas an undertaking may nonetheless in a particular case where real doubt exists, request the Commission to declare whether its agreements comply with this Regulation;

(15) Whereas this Regulation does not affect the applicability of Commission Regulation (EEC) No. 3604/82 of 23 December 1982 on the application of Article 81(3) of the Treaty to categories of specialisation agreements, whereas it does not exclude the application of Article 82 of the Treaty.

HAS ADOPTED THIS REGULATION:

Article 1

Pursuant to Article 81(3) of the Treaty and subject to the provisions of this Regulation, it is hereby declared that Article 81(1) of the Treaty shall not apply to agreements to which only two undertakings are party and whereby one party agrees with the other to supply certain goods for resale within the whole or a defined area of the common market only to that other.

Article 2

1. Apart from the obligation referred to in Article 1 no restriction on competition shall be imposed on the supplier other than the obligation not to supply the contract goods to users in the contract territory.

2. No restriction on competition shall be imposed on the exclusive distributor other than:

(a) the obligation not to manufacture or distribute goods which compete with the contract goods;
(b) the obligation to obtain the contract goods for resale only from the other party;
(c) the obligation to refrain, outside the contract territory and in relation to the contract goods, from seeking customers, from establishing any branch, and from maintaining any distribution depot.

3. Article 1 shall apply notwithstanding that the exclusive distributor undertakes all or any of the following obligations:

(a) to purchase complete ranges of goods or minimum quantities;
(b) to sell the contract goods under trademarks, or packed and presented as specified by the other party;
(c) to take measures for promotion of sales, in particular:
— to advertise,
— to maintain a sales network or stock of goods,
— to provide customer and guarantee services,
— to employ staff having specialised or technical training.

Article 3

Article 1 shall not apply where:

(a) manufacturers of identical goods or of goods which are considered by users as equivalent in view of their characteristics, price and intended use enter into reciprocal exclusive distribution agreements between themselves in respect of such goods;
(b) manufacturers of identical goods or of goods which are considered by users as equivalent in view of their characteristics, price and intended use enter into a non-reciprocal exclusive distribution agreement between themselves in respect of such goods unless at least one of them has a total annual turnover of no more than 100 million [ECU];
(c) users can obtain the contract goods in the contract territory only from the exclusive distributor and have no alternative source of supply outside the contract territory;
(d) one or both of the parties makes it difficult for intermediaries or users to obtain the contract goods from other dealers inside the common market or, in so far as no alternative source of supply is available there, from outside the common market, in particular where one or both of them:

1. exercises industrial property rights so as to prevent dealers or users from obtaining outside, or from selling in, the contract territory properly marked or otherwise properly marketed contract goods;
2. exercises other rights to take other measures so as to prevent dealers or users from obtaining outside, or from selling, in the contract territory, contract goods.

Article 4

1. Article 3(a) and (b) shall also apply where the goods there referred to are manufactured by an undertaking connected with a party to the agreement.
2. Connected undertakings are:

(a) undertakings in which a party to the agreement, directly or indirectly:
   — owns more than half the capital or business assets, or
   — has the power to exercise more than half the voting rights, or
   — has the power to appoint more than half the members of the supervisory board, board of directors or bodies legally representing the undertaking, or
   — has the right to manage the affairs;
(b) undertakings which directly or indirectly have in or over a party to the agreement the rights or powers listed in (a);
(c) undertakings in which an undertaking referred to in (b) directly or indirectly has the rights or powers listed in (a).

3. Undertakings in which the parties to the agreement or undertakings connected with them jointly have the rights or powers set out in paragraph 2(a) shall be considered to be connected with each of the parties to the agreement.

Article 5

1. For the purpose of Article 3(b), the ECU is the unit of account used for drawing up the budget of the Community pursuant to Articles 277 and 279 of the Treaty.
2. Article 1 shall remain applicable where during any period of two consecutive financial years the total turnover referred to in Article 3(b) is exceeded by no more than 10 per cent.
3. For the purpose of calculating total turnover within the meaning of Article 3(b), the turnovers achieved during the last financial year by the party to the agreement and connected undertakings in respect of all goods and services, excluding all taxes and other duties, shall be added together. For this purpose, no account shall be taken of dealings between the parties to the agreement or between these undertakings and undertakings connected with them or between the connected undertakings.

Article 6

The Commission may withdraw the benefit of this Regulation, pursuant to Article 7 of Regulation No. 19/65/EEC, when it finds in a particular case that an agreement which is exempted by this Regulation nevertheless has certain effects which are incompatible with the conditions set out in Article 81(3) of the Treaty, and in particular where:

(a) the contract goods are not subject, in the contract territory, to effective competition from identical goods or goods considered by users as equivalent in view of their characteristics, price and intended use;
(b) access by other suppliers to the different stages of distribution within the contract territory is made difficult to a significant extent;

(c) for reasons other than those referred to in Article 3(c) and (d) it is not possible for intermediaries or users to obtain supplies of the contract goods from dealers outside the contract territory on the terms there customary;

(d) the exclusive distributor:
1. without any objectively justified reason refuses to supply in the contract territory categories of purchasers who cannot obtain contract goods elsewhere on suitable terms or applies to them differing prices or conditions of sale;
2. sells the contract goods at excessively high prices.

Article 7

In the period 1 July 1983 to 31 December 1986, the prohibition in Article 81(1) of the Treaty shall not apply to agreements which were in force on 1 July 1983 or entered into force between 1 July and 31 December 1983 and which satisfy the exemption conditions of Regulation No. 67/67/EEC.

[The provisions of the preceding paragraph shall apply in the same way to agreements which were in force on the date of accession of the Kingdom of Spain and of the Portuguese Republic and which, as a result of accession, fall within the scope of Article 81(1) of the Treaty.]

Amendment

The second paragraph was added by the Act of Accession of the Kingdom of Spain and the Republic of Portugal, Annex I(IV)(10).

[Article 7a

The prohibition in Article 81 of the Treaty shall not apply to agreements which were in existence at the date of accession of Austria, Finland and Sweden and which, by reason of this accession, fall within the scope of Article 81(1) if, within six months from the date of accession, they are so amended that they comply with the conditions laid down in this Regulation. However, this Article shall not apply to agreements which at the date of accession already fall under Article 53 of the EEA Agreement.]

Amendment

Article 7a was inserted by the Act of Accession of the Republic of Austria, the Republic of Finland and the Kingdom of Sweden, Annex 1(III)(D)(1), as amended by Council Decision 95/1, Article 39.

Article 8

This Regulation shall not apply to agreements entered into for the resale of drinks in premises used for the sale and consumption of beer or for the resale of petroleum products in service stations.

Article 9

This Regulation shall apply *mutatis mutandis* to concerted practices of the type defined in Article 1.

Article 10

This Regulation shall enter into force on 1 July 1983. It shall expire on 31 December 1999.

Done at Brussels, 22 June 1983.

Amendment

The date of expiry in Article 10 was amended by Article 1 of Regulation 1582/97.[2] But see now Article 12 of Regulation 2790/1999, Appendix 11, *ante*.

---

[2] OJ 1997 L214/27.

APPENDIX 13

REGULATION 1984/83

*On the Application of Article 81(3) of the Treaty to Categories of Exclusive
Purchasing Agreements[1]*

THE COMMISSION OF THE EUROPEAN COMMUNITIES

Having regard to the Treaty establishing the European Economic Community,

Having regard to Council Regulation 19/65 of 2 March 1965 on the application of
Article 81(3) of the Treaty to certain categories of agreements and concerted practices, as
last amended by the Act of Accession of Greece, and in particular Article 1 thereof,

Having published a draft of this Regulation,

Having consulted the Advisory Committee on Restrictive Practices and Dominant
Positions.

(1) Whereas Regulation No. 19/65/EEC empowers the Commission to apply Article
81(3) of the Treaty by regulation to certain categories of bilateral exclusive purchasing agreements entered into for the purpose of the resale of goods and corresponding
concerted practices falling within Article 81;

(2) Whereas experience to date makes it possible to define three categories of agreements
and concerted practices which can be regarded as normally satisfying the conditions
laid down in Article 81(3); whereas the first category comprises exclusive purchasing
agreements of short and medium duration in all sectors of the economy; whereas the
other two categories comprise long-term exclusive purchasing agreements entered
into for the resale of beer in premises used for the sale and consumption (beer supply
agreements) and of petroleum products in filling stations (service-station agreements);

(3) Whereas exclusive purchasing agreements of the categories defined in this Regulation
may fall within the prohibition contained in Article 81(1) of the Treaty; whereas this
will often be the case with agreements concluded between undertakings from different Member States; whereas an exclusive purchasing agreement to which undertakings from only one Member State are party and which concerns the resale of goods
within that Member State may also be caught by the prohibition; whereas this is in
particular the case where it is one of a number of similar agreements which together
may affect trade between Member States;

(4) Whereas it is not necessary expressly to exclude from the defined categories those
agreements which do not fulfil the conditions of Article 81(1) of the Treaty;

(5) Whereas the exclusive purchasing agreements defined in this Regulation lead in
general to an improvement in distribution; whereas they enable the supplier to plan
the sales of his goods with greater precision and for a longer period and ensure that
the reseller's requirements will be met on a regular basis for the duration of the
agreement; whereas this allows the parties to limit the risk to them of variations in
market conditions and to lower distribution costs;

---

[1] OJ 1983 L173/5. Printed as amended by corrigendum (OJ 1983 L281/24).

(6) Whereas such agreements also facilitate the promotion of the sales of a product and lead to intensive marketing because the supplier, in consideration for the exclusive purchasing obligation, is as a rule under an obligation to contribute to the improvement of the structure of the distribution network, the quality of the promotional effort or the sales success; whereas, at the same time they stimulate competition between the products of different manufacturers; whereas the appointment of several resellers, who are bound to purchase exclusively from the manufacturer and who take over sales promotion, customer services and carrying of stock, is often the most effective way, and sometimes the only way, for the manufacturer to penetrate a market and compete with other manufacturers already present; whereas this is particularly so in the case of small and medium-sized undertakings; whereas it must be left to the contracting parties to decide whether and to what extent they consider it desirable to incorporate in their agreements terms concerning the promotion of sales;

(7) Whereas, as a rule, exclusive purchasing agreements between suppliers and resellers also allow consumers a fair share of the resulting benefit as they gain the advantages of regular supply and are able to obtain the contract goods more quickly and more easily;

(8) Whereas this Regulation must define the obligations restricting competition which may be included in an exclusive purchasing agreement; whereas the other restrictions of competition allowed under this Regulation in addition to the exclusive purchasing obligation lead to a clear division of functions between the parties and compel the reseller to concentrate his sales efforts on the contract goods; whereas they are, where they are agreed only for the duration of the agreement, generally necessary in order to attain the improvement in the distribution of goods sought through exclusive purchasing; whereas further restrictive obligations and in particular those which limit the reseller's choice of customers or his freedom to determine his prices and conditions of sale cannot be exempted under this Regulation;

(9) Whereas the exemption by categories should be reserved for agreements for which it can be assumed with sufficient certainty that they satisfy the conditions of Article 81(3) of the Treaty;

(10) Whereas it is not possible, in the absence of a case-by-case examination, to consider that adequate improvements in distribution occur where a manufacturer imposes an exclusive purchasing obligation with respect to his goods on a manufacturer with whom he is in competition; whereas such agreements should, therefore, be excluded from the exemption by categories; whereas certain derogations from this rule in favour of small and medium-sized undertakings can be allowed;

(11) Whereas certain conditions must be attached to the exemption by categories so that access by other undertakings to the different stages of distribution can be ensured; whereas, to this end, limits must be set to the scope and to the duration of the exclusive purchasing obligation; whereas it appears appropriate as a general rule to grant the benefit of a general exemption from the prohibition on restrictive agreements only to exclusive purchasing agreements which are concluded for a specified product or range of products and for not more than five years;

(12) Whereas, in the case of beer supply agreements and service-station agreements, different rules should be laid down which take account of the particularities of the markets in question;

(13) Whereas these agreements are generally distinguished by the fact that, on the one hand, the supplier confers on the reseller special commercial or financial advantages by contributing to his financing, granting him or obtaining for him a loan on favourable terms, equipping him with a site or premises for conducting his business, providing him with equipment or fittings, or undertaking other investments for his benefit and that, on the other hand, the reseller enters into a long-term exclusive purchasing obligation which in most cases is accompanied by a ban on dealing in competing products;

(14) Whereas beer supply and service-station agreements, like the other exclusive purchasing agreements dealt with in this Regulation, normally produce an appreciable

improvement in distribution in which consumers are allowed a fair share of the resulting benefit;

(15) Whereas the commercial and financial advantages conferred by the supplier on the reseller make it significantly easier to establish, modernise, maintain and operate premises used for the sale and consumption of drinks and service stations; whereas the exclusive purchasing obligation and the ban on dealing in competing products imposed on the reseller incite the reseller to devote all the resources at his disposal to the sale of the contract goods; whereas such agreements lead to durable co-operation between the parties allowing them to improve or maintain the quality of the contract goods and of the services to the customer and sales efforts of the reseller; whereas they allow long-term planning of sales and consequently a cost-effective organisation of production and distribution; whereas the pressure of competition between products of different makes obliges the undertakings involved to determine the number and character of premises used for the sale and consumption of drinks and service stations, in accordance with the wishes of customers;

(16) Whereas consumers benefit from the improvements described, in particular because they are ensured supplies of goods of satisfactory quality at fair prices and conditions while being able to choose between the products of different manufacturers;

(17) Whereas the advantages produced by beer supply agreements and service-station agreements cannot otherwise be secured to the same extent and with the same degree of certainty; whereas the exclusive purchasing obligation on the reseller and the non-competition clause imposed on him are essential components of such agreements and thus usually indispensable for the attainment of these advantages; whereas, however, this is true only as long as the reseller's obligation to purchase from the supplier is confined in the case of premises used for the sale and consumption of drinks to beers and other drinks of the types offered by the supplier, and in the case of service stations to petroleum-based fuel for motor vehicles and other petroleum-based fuels; whereas the exclusive purchasing obligation for lubricants and related petroleum-based products can be accepted only on condition that the supplier provides for the reseller or finances the procurement of specific equipment for the carrying out of lubrication work; whereas this obligation should only relate to products intended for use within the service-station;

(18) Whereas, in order to maintain the reseller's commercial freedom and to ensure access to the retail level of distribution on the part of other suppliers, not only the scope but also the duration of the exclusive purchasing obligation must be limited; whereas it appears appropriate to allow drinks suppliers a choice between a medium-term exclusive purchasing agreement covering a range of drinks and a long-term exclusive purchasing agreement for beer; whereas it is necessary to provide special rules for those premises used for the sale and consumption of drinks which the supplier lets to the reseller; whereas, in this case, the reseller must have the right to obtain, under the conditions specified in this Regulation, other drinks, except beer, supplied under the agreement or of the same type but bearing a different trademark; whereas a uniform maximum duration should be provided for service-station agreements, with the exception of tenancy agreements between the supplier and the reseller, which takes account of the long-term character of the relationship between the parties;

(19) Whereas to the extent that Member States provide, by law or administrative measures, for the same upper limit of duration for the exclusive purchasing obligation upon the reseller as in service-station agreements laid down in this Regulation but provide for a permissible duration which varies in proportion to the consideration provided by the supplier or generally provide for a shorter duration than that permitted by this Regulation, such laws or measures are not contrary to the objectives of this Regulation which, in this respect, merely sets an upper limit to the duration of service-station agreements; whereas the application and enforcement of such national laws or measures must therefore be regarded as compatible with the provisions of this Regulation;

(20) Whereas the limitations and conditions provided for in this Regulation are such as to guarantee effective competition on the markets in question; whereas, therefore, the agreements to which the exemption by category applies do not normally enable the participating undertakings to eliminate competition for a substantial part of the products in question;

(21) Whereas, in particular cases in which agreements or concerted practices satisfying the conditions of this Regulation nevertheless have effects incompatible with Article 81(3) of the Treaty, the Commission may withdraw the benefit of the exemption by category from the undertakings party thereto;

(22) Whereas agreements and concerted practices which satisfy the conditions set out in this Regulation need not be notified; whereas an undertaking may nonetheless, in a particular case where real doubt exists, request the Commission to declare whether its agreements comply with this Regulation;

(23) Whereas this Regulation does not affect the applicability of Commission Regulation (EEC) No. 3604/82 of 23 December 1982 on the application of Article 81(3) of the Treaty to categories of specialisation agreements; whereas it does not exclude the application of Article 82 of the Treaty;

HAS ADOPTED THIS REGULATION

TITLE I

GENERAL PROVISIONS

Article 1

Pursuant to Article 81(3) of the Treaty, and subject to the conditions set out in Articles 2 to 5 of this Regulation, it is hereby declared that Article 81(1) of the Treaty shall not apply to agreements to which only two undertakings are party and whereby one party, the reseller, agrees with the other, the supplier, to purchase certain goods specified in the agreement for resale only from the supplier or from a connected undertaking or from another undertaking which the supplier has entrusted with the sale of his goods.

Article 2

1. No other restriction of competition shall be imposed on the supplier than the obligation not to distribute the contract goods or goods which compete with the contract goods in the reseller's principal sales area and at the reseller's level of distribution.

2. Apart from the obligation described in Article 1, no other restriction of competition shall be imposed on the reseller than the obligation not to manufacture or distribute goods which compete with the contract goods.

3. Article 1 shall apply notwithstanding that the reseller undertakes any or all of the following obligations:

(a) to purchase complete ranges of goods;
(b) to purchase minimum quantities of goods which are subject to the exclusive purchasing obligation;
(c) to sell the contract goods under trademarks, or packed and presented as specified by the supplier;
(d) to take measures for the promotion of sales, in particular:
— to advertise,
— to maintain a sales network or stock of goods,
— to provide customer and guarantee services,

— to employ staff having specialised or technical training.

Article 3

Article 1 shall not apply where:

(a) manufacturers of identical goods or of goods which are considered by users as equivalent in view of their characteristics, price and intended use enter into reciprocal exclusive purchasing agreements between themselves in respect of such goods;
(b) manufacturers of identical goods or of goods which are considered by users as equivalent in view of their characteristics, price and intended use enter into a non-reciprocal exclusive purchasing agreement between themselves in respect of such goods, unless at at least one of them has a total annual turnover of no more than 100 million ECU;
(c) the exclusive purchasing obligation is agreed for more than one type of goods where these are neither by their nature nor according to commercial usage connected to each other;
(d) the agreement is concluded for an indefinite duration or for a period of more than five years.

Article 4

1. Article 3(a) and (b) shall also apply where the goods there referred to are manu-factured by an undertaking connected with a party to the agreement.
2. Connected undertakings are:

(a) undertakings in which a party to the agreement, directly or indirectly:
    — owns more than half the capital or business assets, or
    — has the power to exercise more than half the voting rights, or
    — has the power to appoint more than half the members of the supervisory board, board of directors or bodies legally representing the undertakings, or
    — has the right to manage the affairs;
(b) undertakings which directly or indirectly have in or over a party to the agreement the rights or powers listed in (a);
(c) undertakings in which an undertaking referred to in (b) directly or indirectly has the rights or powers listed in (a).

3. Undertakings in which the parties to the agreement or undertakings connected with them jointly have the rights or powers set out in paragraph 2(a) shall be considered to be connected with each of the parties to the agreement.

Article 5

1. For the purpose of Article 3(b), the ECU is the unit of account used for drawing up the budget of the Community pursuant to Articles 277 and 279 of the Treaty.
2. Article 1 shall remain applicable where during any period of two consecutive financial years the total turnover referred to in Article 3(b) is exceeded by no more than 10 per cent.
3. For the purpose of calculating total turnover within the meaning of Article 3(b), the turnovers achieved during the last financial year by the party to the agreement and connected undertakings in respect of all goods and services, excluding all taxes and other duties, shall be added together. For this purpose, no account shall be taken of dealings between the parties to the agreement or between these undertakings and undertakings connected with them or between the connected undertakings.

TITLE II

SPECIAL PROVISIONS FOR BEER SUPPLY AGREEMENTS

Article 6

1. Pursuant to Article 81(3) of the Treaty, and subject to Articles 7 to 9 of this Regulation, it is hereby declared that Article 81(1) of the Treaty shall not apply to agreements to which only two undertakings are party and whereby one party, the reseller, agrees with the other, the supplier, in consideration for according special commercial or financial advantages, to purchase only from the supplier, an undertaking connected with the supplier or another undertaking entrusted by the supplier with the distribution of his goods, certain beers, or certain beers and certain other drinks, specified in the agreement for resale in premises used for the sale and consumption of drinks and designated in the agreement.

2. The declaration in paragraph 1 shall also apply where exclusive purchasing obligations of the kind described in paragraph 1 are imposed on the reseller in favour of the supplier by another undertaking which is itself not a supplier.

Article 7

1. Apart from the obligation referred to in Article 6, no restriction on competition shall be imposed on the reseller other than:

(a) the obligation not to sell beers and other drinks which are supplied by other undertakings and which are of the same type as the beers or other drinks supplied under the agreement in the premises designated in the agreement;

(b) the obligation, in the event that the reseller sells in the premises designated in the agreement beers which are supplied by other undertakings and which are of a different type from the beers supplied under the agreement, to sell such beers only in bottles, cans or other small packages, unless the sale of such beers in draught form is customary or is necessary to satisfy a sufficient demand from consumers;

(c) the obligation to advertise goods supplied by other undertakings within or outside the premises designated in the agreement only in proportion to the share of these goods in the total turnover realised in the premises.

2. Beers or other drinks of the same type are those which are not clearly distinguishable in view of their composition, appearance and taste.

Article 8

1. Article 6 shall not apply where:

(a) the supplier or a connected undertaking imposes on the reseller exclusive purchasing obligations for goods other than drinks or for services;

(b) the supplier restricts the freedom of the reseller to obtain from an undertaking of his choice either services or goods for which neither an exclusive purchasing obligation nor a ban on dealing in competing products may be imposed;

(c) the agreement is concluded for an indefinite duration or for a period of more than five years and the exclusive purchasing obligation relates to specified beers and other drinks;

(d) the agreement is concluded for an indefinite duration or for a period of more than 10 years and the exclusive purchasing obligation relates only to specified beers;

(e) the supplier obliges the reseller to impose the exclusive purchasing obligation on his successor for a longer period than the reseller would himself remain tied to the supplier.

2. Where the agreement relates to premises which the supplier lets to the reseller or allows the reseller to occupy on some other basis in law or in fact, the following provisions shall also apply:

(a) notwithstanding paragraphs (1)(c) and (d), the exclusive purchasing obligations and bans on dealing in competing products specified in this Title may be imposed on the reseller for the whole period for which the reseller in fact operates the premises;

(b) the agreement must provide for the reseller to have the right to obtain:
  — drinks, except beer, supplied under the agreement from other undertakings where these undertakings offer them on more favourable conditions which the supplier does not meet,
  — drinks, except beer, which are of the same type as those supplied under the agreement but which bear different trade marks, from other undertakings where the supplier does not offer them.

Article 9

Articles 2(1) and (3), 3(a) and (b), 4 and 5 shall apply *mutatis mutandis.*

TITLE III

SPECIAL PROVISIONS FOR SERVICE AGREEMENTS

Article 10

Pursuant to Article 81(3) of the Treaty and subject to Articles 11 to 13 of this Regulation, it is hereby declared that Article 81(1) of the Treaty shall not apply to agreements to which only two undertakings are party and whereby one party, the reseller agrees with the other, the supplier, in consideration for the according of special commercial or financial advantages, to purchase only from the supplier, an undertaking connected with the supplier or another undertaking entrusted by the supplier with the distribution of his goods, certain petroleum-based motor-vehicle fuels or certain petroleum-based motor-vehicle and other fuels specified in the agreement for resale in a service station designated in the agreement.

Article 11

Apart from the obligation referred to in Article 10 no restriction on competition shall be imposed on the reseller other than:

(a) the obligation not to sell motor-vehicle fuel and other fuels which are supplied by other undertakings in the service station designated in the agreement;

(b) the obligation not to use lubricants or related petroleum-based products which are supplied by other undertakings within the service station designated in the agreement where the supplier or a connected undertaking has made available to the reseller, or financed, a lubrication bay or other motor-vehicle lubrication equipment;

(c) the obligation to advertise goods supplied by other undertakings within or outside the service station designated in the agreement only in proportion to the share of these goods in the total turnover realised in the service station;

(d) the obligation to have equipment owned by the supplier or a connected undertaking or financed by the supplier or a connected undertaking serviced by the supplier or an undertaking designated by him.

Article 12

1. Article 10 shall not apply where:

(a) the supplier or a connected undertaking imposes on the reseller exclusive purchasing obligations for goods other than motor-vehicle and other fuels or for services, except in the case of the obligations referred to in Article 11(b) and (d);

(b) the supplier restricts the freedom of the reseller to obtain, from an undertaking of his choice, goods or services for which under the provisions of this Title neither an exclusive purchasing obligation nor a ban on dealing in competing products may be imposed;

(c) the agreement is concluded for an indefinite duration or for a period of more than 10 years;

(d) the supplier obliges the reseller to impose the exclusive purchasing obligation on his successor for a longer period than the reseller would himself remain tied to the supplier.

2. Where the agreement relates to a service station which the supplier lets to the reseller, or allows the reseller to occupy on some other basis, in law or in facts, exclusive purchasing obligations or prohibitions of competition indicated in this Title may, notwithstanding paragraph 1(c), be imposed on the reseller for the whole period for which the reseller in fact operates the premises.

Article 13

Articles 2(1) and (3), and 3(a) and (b), 4 and 5 of this Regulation shall apply *mutatis mutandis*.

Title IV

Miscellaneous Provisions

Article 14

The Commission may withdraw the benefit of this Regulation, pursuant to Article 7 of Regulation No. 19/65/EEC, when it finds in a particular case that an agreement which is exempted by this Regulation nevertheless has certain effects which are incompatible with the conditions set out in Article 81(3) of the Treaty, and in particular where:

(a) the contract goods are not subject, in a substantial part of the common market, to effective competition from identical goods or goods considered by users as equivalent in view of their characteristics, price and intended use;

(b) access by of [*sic*] other suppliers to the different stages of distribution in a substantial part of the common market is made difficult to a significant extent;
(c) the supplier without any objectively justified reason:
1.   refuses to supply categories of resellers who cannot obtain the contract goods elsewhere on suitable terms or applies to them differing prices or conditions of sale;
2.   applies less favourable prices or conditions of sale to resellers bound by an exclusive purchasing obligation as compared with other resellers at the same level of distribution.

Article 15

1. In the period 1 July 1983 to 31 December 1986, the prohibition in Article 81(1) of the Treaty shall not apply to agreements of the kind described in Article 1 which either were in force on 1 July 1983 or entered into force between 1 July and 31 December 1983 and which satisfy the exemption conditions under Regulation No. 67/67/EEC.

2. In the period 1 July 1983 to 31 December 1988, the prohibition in Article 81(1) of the Treaty shall not apply to agreements of the kinds described in Articles 6 and 10 which either were in force on 1 July 1983 or entered into force between 1 July and 31 December 1983 and which satisfy the exemption conditions of Regulation No. 67/67/EEC.

3. In the case of agreements of the kinds described in Articles 6 and 10, which were in force on 1 July 1983 and which expire after 31 December 1988, the prohibition in Article 81(1) of the Treaty shall not apply in the period from 1 January 1989 to the expiry of the agreement but at the latest to the expiry of this Regulation to the extent that the supplier releases the reseller, before 1 January 1989, from all obligations which would prevent the application of the exemption under Titles II and III.

[4. The provisions of the preceding paragraphs shall apply in the same way to the agreements referred to respectively in those paragraphs, which were in force on the date of accession of the Kingdom of Spain and of the Portuguese Republic and which, as a result of accession, fall within the scope of Article 81(1) of the Treaty.]

Amendment

Paragraph 4 was added by the Act of Accession of the Kingdom of Spain and the Portuguese Republic, Annex I(IV)(II).

[Article 15a

The prohibition in Article 81(1) of the Treaty shall not apply to agreements which were in existence at the date of accession of Austria, Finland and Sweden and which, by reason of this accession, fall within the scope of Article 81(1) if, within six months from the date of accession they are so amended that they comply with the conditions laid down in this Regulation. However, this Article shall not apply to agreements which at the date of accession already fall under Article 53(1) of the EEA Agreement.]

Amendment

Article 15a was inserted by the Act of Accession of the Republic of Austria, the Republic of Finland and the Kingdom of Sweden, Annex 1(III)(D)(2), as amended by Council Decision 95/1, Article 39.

Article 16

This Regulation shall not apply to agreements by which the supplier undertakes with the reseller to supply only to the reseller certain goods for resale, in the whole or in a defined part of the Community, and the reseller undertakes with the supplier to purchase these goods only from the supplier.

Article 17

This Regulation shall not apply where the parties or connected undertakings, for the purpose of resale in one and the same premises used for the sale and consumption of drinks or service station, enter into agreements both of the kind referred to in Title I and of a kind referred to in Title II or III.

Article 18

This Regulation shall apply *mutatis mutandis* to the categories of concerted practices defined in Articles 1, 6 and 10.

Article 19

This Regulation shall enter into force on 1 July 1983. It shall expire on 31 December 1999.

Done at Brussels, 22 June 1983.

Amendment

The date of expiry in Article 19 was amended by Article 2 of Regulation 1582/97.[2] But see now Article 12 of Regulation 2790/1999, App. 11, *ante*.

---

[2] OJ 1997 L214/27.

COMMISSION NOTICE

On Regulations 1983/83 and 1984/83[1]

I. Introduction

1. Commission Regulation No. 67/67/EEC of March 22, 1967 on the application of Article 81(3) of the Treaty to certain categories of exclusive dealing agreements expired on June 30, 1983 after being in force for over 15 years. With Regulations (EEC) No. 1983/83 and (EEC) No. 1984/83, the Commission has adapted the block exemption of exclusive distribution agreements and exclusive purchasing agreements to the intervening developments in the common market and in Community law. Several of the provisions in the new Regulations are new. A certain amount of interpretative guidance is therefore called for. This will assist undertakings in bringing their agreements into line with the new legal requirements and will also help ensure that the Regulations are applied uniformly in all the Member States.

2. In determining how a given provision is to be applied, one must take into account, in addition to the ordinary meaning of the words used, the intention of the provision as this emerges from the preamble. For further guidance, reference should be made to the principles that have been evolved in the case law of the Court of Justice of the European Communities and in the Commission's decisions on individual cases.

3. This notice sets out the main consideration which will determine the Commission's view of whether or not an exclusive distribution or purchasing agreement is covered by the block exemption. The notice is without prejudice to the jurisdiction of national courts to apply the Regulations, although it may well be of persuasive authority in proceedings before such courts. Nor does the notice necessarily indicate the interpretation which might be given to the provisions by the Court of Justice.

II. Exclusive distribution and exclusive purchasing agreements (Regulations (EEC) No. 1983/83 and (EEC) No. 1984/83)

1. Similarities and differences

4. Regulations (EEC) No. 1983/83 and (EEC) No. 1984/83 are both concerned with exclusive agreements between two undertakings for the purpose of the resale of goods. Each deals with a particular type of such agreements. Regulation (EEC) No. 1983/83 applies to exclusive distribution agreements, Regulation (EEC) No. 1984/83 to exclusive purchasing agreements. The distinguishing feature of exclusive distribution agreements is that one party, the supplier, allots to the other, the reseller, a defined territory (the contract territory) on which the reseller has to concentrate his sales effort, and in return undertakes not to supply any other reseller in that territory. In exclusive purchasing agreements, the reseller agrees to purchase the contract goods only from the other party and not from any

---

[1] OJ 1984 C101/2. Printed as amended by OJ 1992 C121/2.

other supplier. The supplier is entitled to supply other resellers in the same sales area and at the same level of distribution. Unlike an exclusive distributor, the tied reseller is not protected against competition from other resellers who, like himself, receive the contract goods direct from the supplier. On the other hand, he is free of restrictions as to the area over which he may make his sales effort.

5. In keeping with their common starting point, the Regulations have many provisions that are the same or similar in both Regulations. This is true of the basic provision in Article 1, in which the respective subject-matters of the block exemption, the exclusive supply or purchasing obligation, are defined, and of the exhaustive list of restrictions of competition which may be agreed in addition to the exclusive supply or purchasing obligation (Article 2(1) and (2)), the non-exhaustive enumeration of other obligations which do not prejudice the block exemption (Article 2(3)), the inapplicability of the block exemption in principle to exclusive agreements between competing manufacturers (Articles 3(a) and (b), 4 and 5), the withdrawal of the block exemption in individual cases (Article 6 of Regulation (EEC) No. 1983/83 and Article 14 of Regulation (EEC) No. 1984/83), the transitional provisions (Article 7 of Regulation (EEC) No. 1983/83 and Article 15(1) of Regulation (EEC) No. 1984/83), and the inclusion of concerted practices within the scope of the Regulations (Article 9 of Regulation (EEC) No. 1983/83 and Article 18 of Regulation (EEC) No. 1984/83). In so far as their wording permits, these parallel provisions are to be interpreted in the same way.

6. Different rules are laid down in the Regulations wherever they need to take account of matters which are peculiar to the exclusive distribution agreements or exclusive purchasing agreements respectively. This applies in Regulation (EEC) No. 1983/83, to the provisions regarding the obligation on the exclusive distributor not actively to promote sales outside the contract territory (Article 2(2)(c)) and the inapplicability of the block exemption to agreements which give the exclusive distributor absolute territorial protection (Article 3(c) and (d)) and, in Regulation (EEC) No. 1984/83, to the provisions limiting the scope and duration of the block exemption for exclusive purchasing agreements in general (Article 3(c) and (d)) and for beer-supply and service-station agreements in particular (Titles II and III).

7. The scope of the two Regulations has been defined so as to avoid any overlap (Article 16 of Regulation (EEC) No. 1984/83).

2. Basic provision

(Article 1)

8. Both Regulations apply only to agreements entered into for the purpose of the resale of goods to which not more than two undertakings are party.

(a) "For resale"

9. The notion of resale requires that the goods concerned be disposed of by the purchasing party to others in return for consideration. Agreements on the supply or purchase of goods which the purchasing party transforms or processes into other goods or uses or consumes in manufacturing other goods are not agreement for resale. The same applies to the supply of components which are combined with other components into a different product. The criterion is that the goods distributed by the reseller are the same as those the other party has supplied to him for that purpose. The economic identity of the goods is not affected if the reseller merely breaks up and packages the goods in smaller quantities, or repackages them, before resale.

10. Where the reseller performs additional operations to improve the quality, durability, appearance or taste of the goods (such as rust-proofing of metals, sterilisation of food or the addition of colouring matter or flavourings to drugs), the position will mainly depend on how much value the operation adds to the goods. Only a slight addition in value can be taken not to change the economic identity of the goods. In determining the precise

67

dividing line in individual cases, trade usage in particular must be considered. The Commission applies the same principles to agreements under which the reseller is supplied with a concentrated extract for a drink which he has to dilute with water, pure alcohol or another liquid and to bottle before reselling.

(b) "Goods"

11. Exclusive agreements for the supply of services rather than the resale of goods are not covered by the Regulations. The block exemption still applies, however, where the reseller provides customer or after-sales services incidentally to the resale of the goods. Nevertheless, a case where the charge for the service is higher than the price of the goods would fall outside the scope of the Regulations.

12. The hiring out of goods in return for payment comes closer, economically speaking, to a resale of goods than to provision of services. The Commission therefore regards exclusive agreements under which the purchasing party hires out or leases to others the goods supplied to him as covered by the Regulations.

(c) "Only two undertakings party"

13. To be covered by the block exemption, the exclusive distribution or purchasing agreement must be between only one supplier and one reseller in each case. Several undertakings forming one economic unit count as one undertaking.

14. This limitation on the number of undertakings that may be party relates solely to the individual agreement. A supplier does not lose the benefit of the block exemption if he enters into exclusive distribution or purchasing agreements covering the same goods with several resellers.

15. The supplier may delegate the performance of his contractual obligations to a connected or independent undertaking which he has entrusted with the distribution of his goods, so that the reseller has to purchase the contract goods from the latter undertaking. This principle is expressly mentioned only in Regulation (EEC) No. 1984/83 (Articles 1, 6 and 10), because the question of delegation arises mainly in connection with exclusive purchasing agreements. It also applies, however, to exclusive distribution agreements under Regulation (EEC) No. 1983/83.

16. The involvement of undertakings other than the contracting parties must be confined to the execution of deliveries. The parties may accept exclusive supply or purchase obligations only for themselves, and not impose them on third parties, since otherwise more than two undertakings would be party to the agreement. The obligation of the parties to ensure that the obligations they have accepted are respected by connected undertakings is, however, covered by the block exemption.

3. Other restrictions on competition that are exempted

(Article 2(1) and (2))

17. Apart from the exclusive supply obligation (Regulation (EEC) No. 1983/83) or exclusive purchase obligation (Regulation (EEC) No. 1984/83), obligations defined in Article 1 which must be present if the block exemption is to apply, the only other restrictions of competition that may be agreed by the parties are those set out in Article 2(1) and (2). If they agree on further obligations restrictive of competition, the agreement as a whole is no longer covered by the block exemption and requires individual exemption. For example, an agreement will exceed the bounds of the Regulations if the parties relinquish the possibility of independently determining their prices or conditions of business or undertake to refrain from or even prevent, cross-border trade, which the Regulations expressly state must not be impeded. Among other clauses which in general are not permissible under the Regulations are those which impede the reseller in his free choice of customers.

18. The obligations restrictive of competition that are exempted may be agreed only for the duration of the agreement. This also applied to restrictions accepted by the supplier or reseller on competing with the other party.

4. Obligations upon the reseller which do not prejudice the block exemption

(Article 2(3))

19. The obligations cited in this provision are examples of clauses which generally do not restrict competition. Undertakings are therefore free to include one, several or all of these obligations in their agreements. However, the obligations may not be formulated or applied in such a way as to take on the character of restrictions of competition that are not permitted. To forestall this danger, Article 2(3)(b) of Regulation (EEC) No. 1984/83 expressly allows minimum purchase obligations only for goods that are subject to an exclusive purchasing obligation.

20. As part of the obligation to take measures for promotion of sales and in particular to maintain a distribution network (Article 2(3)(c) of Regulation (EEC) No. 1983/83 and Article 2(3)(d) of Regulation (EEC) No. 1984/83), the reseller may be forbidden to supply the contract goods to unsuitable dealers. Such clauses are unobjectionable if admission to the distribution network is based on objective criteria of a qualitative nature relating to the professional qualifications of the owner of the business or his staff or the suitability of his business premises, if the criteria are the same for all potential dealers, and if the criteria are actually applied in a non-discriminatory manner. Distribution systems which do not fulfil these conditions are not covered by the block exemption.

5. Inapplicability of the block exemption to exclusive agreements between competing manufacturers

(Articles 3(a) and (b), 4 and 5)

21. The block exemption does not apply if either the parties themselves or undertakings connected with them are manufacturers, manufacture goods belonging to the same product market, and enter into exclusive distribution or purchasing agreements with one another in respect of those goods. Only identical or equivalent goods are regarded as belonging to the same product market. The goods in question must be interchangeable. Whether or not this is the case must be judged from the vantage point of the user, normally taking the characteristics, price and intended use of the goods together. In certain cases, however, goods can form a separate market on the basis of their characteristics, their price or their intended use alone. This is true especially where consumer preferences have developed. The above provisions are applicable regardless of whether or not the parties of the undertakings connected with them are based in the Community and whether or not they are already actually in competition with one another in the relevant goods inside or outside the Community.

22. In principle both reciprocal and non-reciprocal exclusive agreements between competing manufacturers are not covered by the block exemption and are therefore subject to individual scrutiny of their compatibility with Article 85 of the Treaty, but there is an exemption for non-reciprocal agreements of the abovementioned kind where one or both of the parties are undertakings with a total annual turnover of no more than 100 million ECU (Article 3(b)). Annual turnover is used as a measure of the economic strength of the undertakings involved. Therefore, the aggregate turnover from goods and services of all types and not only from the contract goods, is to be taken. Turnover taxes and other turnover-related levies are not included in turnover. Where a party belongs to a group of connected undertakings, the world-wide turnover of the group, excluding intra-group sales (Article 5(3)), is to be used.

23. The total turnover limit can be exceeded during any period of two successive financial years by up to 10 per cent. without loss of the block exemption. The block

exemption is lost if, at the end of the second financial year, the total turnover over the preceding two years has been over 220 million ECU (Article 5(2)).

6. Withdrawal of the block exemption in individual cases

(Article 6 of Regulation (EEC) No. 1983/83 and Article 14 of Regulation (EEC) No. 1984/83)

24. The situations described are meant as illustrations of the sort of situations in which the Commission can exercise its powers under Article 7 of Council Regulation No. 19/65/EEC to withdraw a block exemption. The benefit of the block exemption can only be withdrawn by a decision in an individual case following proceedings under Regulation No. 17. Such a decision cannot have retroactive effect. It may be coupled with an individual exemption subject to conditions or obligations or, in an extreme case, with the finding of an infringement and an order to bring it to an end.

7. Transitional provisions

(Article 7 of Regulation (EEC) No. 1983/83 and Article 15(1) of Regulation (EEC) No. 1984/83)

25. Exclusive distribution or exclusive purchasing agreements which were concluded and entered into force before January 1, 1984 continue to be exempted under the provisions of Regulation No. 67/67/EEC until December 31, 1986. Should the parties wish to apply such agreements beyond January 1, 1987, they will either have to bring them into line with the provisions of the new Regulations or to notify them to the Commission. Special rules apply in the case of beer-supply and service-station agreements (see paragraphs 64 and 65 below).

8. Concerted practices

(Article 9 of Regulation (EEC) No. 1983/83 and Article 18 of Regulation (EEC) No. 1984/83)

26. These provisions bring within the scope of the Regulations exclusive distribution and purchasing arrangements which are operated by undertakings but are not the subject of a legally-binding agreement.

III. Exclusive distribution agreements (Regulation (EEC) No. 1983/83)

1. Exclusive supply obligation

(Article 1)

27. The exclusive supply obligation does not prevent the supplier from providing the contract goods to other resellers who afterwards sell them in the exclusive distributor's territory. It makes no difference whether the other dealers concerned are established outside or inside the territory. The supplier is not in breach of his obligation to the exclusive distributor provided that he supplies the resellers who wish to sell the contract goods in the territory only at their request and that the goods are handed over outside the territory. It does not matter whether the reseller takes delivery of the goods himself or through an intermediary, such as a freight forwarder. However, supplies of this nature are only permissible if the reseller and not the supplier pays the transport costs of the goods into the contract territory.

28. The goods supplied to the exclusive distributor must be intended for resale in the contract territory. This basic requirement does not, however, mean that the exclusive distributor cannot sell the contract goods to customers outside his contract territory should

he receive orders from them. Under Article 2(2)(c), the supplier can prohibit them only from seeking customers in other areas, but not from supplying them.

29. It would also be incompatible with the Regulation for the exclusive distributor to be restricted to supplying only certain categories of customers (*e.g.* specialist retailers) in his contract territory and prohibited from supplying other categories (*e.g.* department stores), which are supplied by other resellers appointed by the supplier for that purpose.

2. Restrictions on competition by the supplier

(Article 2(1))

30. The restriction on the supplier himself supplying the contract goods to final users in the exclusive distributor's contract territory need not be absolute. Clauses permitting the supplier to supply certain customers in the territory—with or without payment of compensation to the exclusive distributor—are compatible with the block exemption provided the customers in question are not resellers. The supplier remains free to supply the contract goods outside the contract territory to final users based in the territory. In this case the position is the same as for dealers (see paragraph 27 above).

3. Inapplicability of the block exemption in cases of absolute territorial protection

(Articles 3(c) and (d))

31. The block exemption cannot be claimed for agreements that give the exclusive distributor absolute territorial protection. If the situation described in Article 3(c) obtains, the parties must ensure either that the contract goods can be sold in the contract territory by parallel importers or that users have a real possibility of obtaining them from undertakings outside the contract territory, if necessary outside the Community, at the prices and on the terms there prevailing. The supplier can represent an alternative source of supply for the purposes of this provision if he is prepared to supply the contract goods on request to final users located in the contract territory.

32. Article 3(d) is chiefly intended to safeguard the freedom of dealers and users to obtain the contract goods in other Member States. Action to impede imports into the Community from third countries will only lead to loss of the block exemption if there are no alternative sources of supply in the Community. This situation can arise especially where the exclusive distributor's contract territory covers the whole or the major part of the Community.

33. The block exemption ceases to apply as from the moment that either of the parties takes measures to impede parallel imports into the contract territory. Agreements in which the supplier undertakes with the exclusive distributor to prevent his other customers from supplying into the contract territory are ineligible for the block exemption from the outset. This is true even if the parties agree only to prevent imports into the Community from third countries. In this case it is immaterial whether or not there are alternative sources of supply in the Community. The inapplicability of the block exemption follows from the mere fact that the agreement contains restrictions on competition which are not covered by Article 2(1).

IV. Exclusive purchasing agreements (Regulation (EEC) No. 1984/83)

1. Structure of the Regulation

34. Title I of the Regulation contains general provisions for exclusive purchasing agreements and Titles II and III special provisions for beer-supply and service-station agreements. The latter types of agreement are governed exclusively by the special

provisions, some of which (Articles 9 and 13), however, refer to some of the general provisions, Article 17 also excludes the combination of agreements of the kind referred to in Title I with those of the kind referred to in Titles II or III to which the same undertakings or undertakings connected with them are party. To prevent any avoidance of the special provisions for beer-supply and service-station agreements, it is also made clear that the provisions governing the exclusive distribution of goods do not apply to agreements entered into for the resale of drinks on premises used for the sale or consumption of beer or the resale of petroleum products in service stations (Article 8 of Regulation (EEC) No. 1983/83).

2. Exclusive purchasing obligation

(Article 1)

35. The Regulation only covers agreements whereby the reseller agrees to purchase all his requirements for the contract goods from the other party. If the purchasing obligation relates to only part of such requirements, the block exemption does not apply. Clauses which allow the reseller to obtain the contract goods from other suppliers, should these sell them more cheaply or on more favourable terms than the other party are still covered by the block exemption. The same applies to clauses releasing the reseller from his exclusive purchasing obligation should the other party be unable to supply.

36. The contract goods must be specified by brand or denomination in the agreement. Only if this is done will it be possible to determine the precise scope of the reseller's exclusive purchasing obligation (Article 1) and of the ban on dealing in competing products (Article 2(2)).

3. Restriction on competition by the supplier

(Article 2(1))

37. This provision allows the reseller to protect himself against direct competition from the supplier in his principal sales area. The reseller's principal sales area is determined by his normal business activity. It may be more closely defined in the agreement. However, the supplier cannot be forbidden to supply dealers who obtain the contract goods outside this area and afterwards resell them to customers inside it or to appoint other resellers in the area.

4. Limits of the block exemption

(Article 3(c) and (d))

38. Article 3(c) provides that the exclusive purchasing obligation can be agreed for one or more products, but in the latter case the products must be so related as to be thought of as belonging to the same range of goods. The relationship can be founded on technical (e.g. a machine, accessories and spare parts for it) or commercial grounds (e.g. several products used for the same purpose) or on usage in the trade (different goods that are customarily offered for sale together). In the latter case, regard must be had to the usual practice at the reseller's level of distribution on the relevant market, taking into account all relevant dealers and not only particular forms of distribution. Exclusive purchasing agreements covering goods which do not belong together can only be exempted from the competition rules by an individual decision.

39. Under Article 3(d), exclusion purchasing agreements concluded for an indefinite period are not covered by the block exemption. Agreements which specify a fixed term but are automatically renewable unless one of the parties gives notice to terminate are to be considered to have been concluded for an indefinite period.

V. Beer-supply agreements (Title II of Regulation (EEC) No. 1984/83)

[1. Agreements of minor importance

40. It is recalled that the Commission's Notice on agreements of minor importance[2] states that the Commission holds the view that agreements between undertakings do not fall under the prohibition of Article 81(1) of the EEC Treaty if certain conditions as regards market share and turnover are met by the undertakings concerned. Thus, it is evident that when an undertaking, brewery or wholesaler, surpasses the limits as laid down in the above notice, the agreements concluded by it may fall under Article 81(1) of the EEC Treaty. The notice, however, does not apply where in a relevant market competition is restricted by the cumulative effects of parallel networks of similar agreements which would not individually fall under Article 81(1) of the EEC Treaty if the notice was applicable. Since the markets for beer will frequently be characterised by the existence of cumulative effects, it seems appropriate to determine which agreements can nevertheless be considered *de minimis*.

The Commission is of the opinion that an exclusive beer supply agreement concluded by a brewery, in the sense of Article 6, and including Article 8(2) of Regulation (EEC) 1984/83 does not, in general, fall under Article 81(1) of the EEC Treaty if:

— the market share of that brewery is not higher than 1 per cent on the national market for the resale of beer in premises used for the sale and consumption of drinks, and
— if that brewery does not produce more than 200,000 hl of beer per annum.

However, these principles do not apply if the agreement in question is concluded for more than seven and a half years in as far as it covers beer and other drinks, and for 15 years if it covers only beer.

In order to establish the market share of the brewery and its annual production, the provisions of Article 4(2) of Regulation (EEC) 1984/83 apply.

As regards exclusive beer supply agreements in the sense of Article 6, and including Article 8(2) of Regulation (EEC) 1984/83 which are concluded by wholesalers, the above principles apply *mutatis mutandis* by taking account of the position of the brewery whose beer is the main subject of the agreement in question.

The present communication does not preclude that in individual cases even agreements between undertakings which do not fulfil the above criteria, in particular here the number of outlets tied to them is limited as compared to the number of outlets existing on the market, may still have only a negligible effect on trade between Member States or on competition, and would therefore not be caught by Article 81(1) of the EEC Treaty.

Neither does this communication in any way prejudice the application of national law to the agreements covered by it.]

Amendment

Paragraph 40 was added by the Commission Notice concerning Regulations 1983/83 and 1984/83 on the application of Article 81(3) of the EEC Treaty, OJ 1992 C121/2.

2. Exclusive purchasing obligation

(Article 6)
41. The beers and other drinks covered by the exclusive purchasing obligation must be specified by brand or denomination in the agreement. An exclusive purchasing obligation can only be imposed on the reseller for drinks which the supplier carries at the time the

---

[2] OJ 1986 C231/2.

contract takes effect and provided that they are supplied in the quantities required, at sufficiently regular intervals and at prices and on conditions allowing normal sales to the consumer. Any extension of the exclusive purchasing obligation to drinks not specified in the agreement requires an additional agreement, which must likewise satisfy the requirements of Title II of the Regulation. A change in the brand or denomination of a drink which in other respects remains unchanged does not constitute such an extension of the exclusive purchasing obligation.

42. The exclusive purchasing obligation can be agreed in respect of one or more premises used for the sale and consumption of drinks which the reseller runs at the time the contract takes effect. The name and location of the premises must be stated in the agreement. Any extension of the exclusive purchasing obligation to other such premises requires an additional agreement, which must likewise satisfy the provisions of Title II of the Regulation.

43. The concept of "premises used for the sale and consumption of drinks" covers any licensed premises used for this purpose. Private clubs are also included. Exclusive purchasing agreements between the supplier and the operator of an off-licence shop are governed by the provisions of Title I of the Regulation.

44. Special commercial or financial advantages are those going beyond what the reseller could normally expect under an agreement. The explanations given in the 13th recital are illustrations. Whether or not the supplier is affording the reseller special advantages depends on the nature, extent and duration of the obligation undertaken by the parties. In doubtful cases usage in the trade is the decisive element.

45. The reseller can enter into exclusive purchasing obligations both with a brewery in respect of beers of a certain type and with a drinks wholesaler in respect of beers of another type and/or other drinks. The two agreements can be combined into one document. Article 6 also covers cases where the drinks wholesaler performs several functions at once, signing the first agreement on the brewery's and the second on his own behalf and also undertaking delivery of all the drinks. The provisions of Title II do not apply to the contractual relations between the brewery and the drinks wholesaler.

46. Article 6(2) makes the block exemption also applicable to cases in which the supplier affords the owner of premises financial or other help in equipping them as a public house, restaurant, etc., and in return the owner imposes on the buyer or tenant of the premises an exclusive purchasing obligation in favour of the supplier. A similar situation, economically speaking, is the transmission of an exclusive purchasing obligation from the owner of a public house to his successor. Under Article 8(1)(e) this is also, in principle, permissible.

3. Other restrictions of competition that are exempted

(Article 7)

47. The list of permitted obligations given in Article 7 is exhaustive. If any further obligations restricting competition are imposed on the reseller, the exclusive purchasing agreement as a whole is no longer covered by the block exemption.

48. The obligation referred to in paragraph 1(a) applies only so long as the supplier is able to supply the beers or other drinks specified in the agreement and subject to the exclusive purchasing obligation in sufficient quantities to cover the demand the reseller anticipates for the products from his customers.

49. Under paragraph 1(b), the reseller is entitled to sell beer of other types in draught form if the other party has tolerated this in the past. If this is not the case, the reseller must indicate that there is sufficient demand from his customers to warrant the sale of other draught beers. The demand must be deemed sufficient if it can be satisfied without a simultaneous drop in sales of the beers specified in the exclusive purchasing agreement. It is definitely not sufficient if sales of the additional draught beer turn out to be so slow that there is a danger of its quality deteriorating. It is for the reseller to assess the potential demand of his customers for other types of beer; after all, he bears the risk if his forecasts are wrong.

50. The provision in paragraph 1(c) is not only intended to ensure the possibility of advertising products supplied by other undertakings to the minimum extent necessary in any given circumstances. The advertising of such products should also reflect their relative importance *vis–à–vis* the competing products of the supplier who is party to the exclusive purchasing agreement. Advertising for products which the public house has just begun to sell may not be excluded or unduly impeded.

51. The Commission believes that the designations of types customary in inter-State trade and within the individual Member States may afford useful pointers to the interpretation of Article 7(2). Nevertheless the alternative criteria stated in the provision itself are decisive. In doubtful cases, whether or not two beers are clearly distinguishable by their composition, appearance or taste depends on custom at the place where the public house is situated. The parties may, if they wish, jointly appoint an expert to decide the matter.

4. Agreements excluded from the block exemption

(Article 8)

52. The reseller's right to purchase drinks from third parties may be restricted only to the extent allowed by Articles 6 and 7. In his purchases of goods other than drinks and in his procurement of services which are not directly connected with the supply of drinks by the other party, the reseller must remain free to choose his supplier. Under Article 8(1)(a) and (b), any action by the other party or by an undertaking connected with or appointed by him or acting at his instigation or with his agreement to prevent the reseller exercising his rights in this regard will entail the loss of the block exemption. For the purposes of these provisions it makes no difference whether the reseller's freedom is restricted by contract, informal understanding, economic pressures or other practical measures.

53. The installation of amusement machines in tenanted public houses may by agreement be made subject to the owner's permission. The owner may refuse permission on the ground that this would impair the character of the premises or he may restrict the tenant to particular types of machines. However, the practice of some owners of tenanted public houses to allow the tenant to conclude contracts for the installation of such machines only with certain undertakings which the owner recommends is, as a rule, incompatible with this Regulation, unless the undertakings are selected on the basis of objective criteria of a qualitative nature that are the same for all potential providers of such equipment and are applied in a non-discriminatory manner. Such criteria may refer to the reliability of the undertaking and its staff and the quality of the services it provides. The supplier may not prevent a public house tenant from purchasing amusement machines rather than renting them.

54. The limitation of the duration of the agreement in Article 8(1)(c) and (d) does not affect the parties' right to renew their agreement in accordance with the provisions of Title II of the Regulation.

55. Article 8(2)(b) must be interpreted in the light both of the aims of the Community competition rules and of the general legal principle whereby contracting parties must exercise their rights in good faith.

56. Whether or not a third undertaking offers certain drinks covered by the exclusive purchasing obligation on more favourable terms than the other party for the purposes of the first indent of Article 8(2)(b) is to be judged in the first instance on the basis of a comparison of prices. This should take into account the various factors that go to determine the prices. If a more favourable offer is available and the tenant wishes to accept it, he must inform the other party of his intentions without delay so that the other party has an opportunity of matching the terms offered by the third undertaking. If the other party refuses to do so or fails to let the tenant have his decision within a short period, the tenant is entitled to purchase the drinks from the other undertaking. The Commission will ensure that exercise of the brewery's or drinks wholesaler's right to match the prices quoted by another supplier does not make it significantly harder for other suppliers to enter the market.

57. The tenant's right provided for in the second indent of Article 8(2)(b) to purchase drinks of another brand or denomination from third undertakings obtains in cases where the other party does not offer them. Here the tenant is not under a duty to inform the other party of his intentions.

58. The tenant's rights arising from Article 8(2)(b) override any obligation to purchase minimum quantities imposed upon him under Article 9 in conjunction with Article 2(3)(b) to the extent that this is necessary to allow the tenant full exercise of those rights.

VI. Service-station agreements (Title III of Regulation (EEC) No. 1984/83)

1. Exclusive purchasing obligation

(Article 10)

59. The exclusive purchasing obligation can cover either motor vehicle fuels (*e.g.* petrol, diesel fuel, LPG, kerosene) alone or motor vehicle fuels and other fuels (*e.g.* heating oil, bottled gas, paraffin). All the goods concerned must be petroleum-based products.

60. The motor vehicle fuels covered by the exclusive purchasing obligations must be for use in motor-powered land or water vehicles or aircraft. The term "service station" is to be interpreted in a correspondingly wide sense.

61. The Regulation applies to petrol stations adjoining public roads and fuelling installations on private property not open to public traffic.

2. Other restrictions on completion that are exempted

(Article 11)

62. Under Article 11(b) only the use of lubricants and related petroleum-based products supplied by other undertakings can be prohibited. This provision refers to the servicing and maintenance of motor vehicles, *i.e.* to the reseller's activity in the field of provision of services. It does not affect the reseller's freedom to purchase the said products from other undertakings for resale in the service station. The petroleum-based products related to lubricants referred to in paragraph (b) are additives and brake fluids.

63. For the interpretation of Article 11(c), the considerations stated in paragraph 49[3] above apply by analogy.

3. Agreements excluded from the block exemption

(Article 12)

64. These provisions are analogous to those of Article 8(1)(a), (b), (d) and (e) and 8(2)(a). Reference is therefore made to paragraphs 51 and 53[4] above.

VII. Transitional provisions for beer-supply and service-station agreements (Article 15(2) and (3))

65. Under Article 15(2), all beer-supply and service-station agreements which were concluded and entered into force before January 1, 1984 remain covered by the provision of Regulation No. 67/67/EEC until December 31, 1988. From January 12, 1989 they must comply with the provisions of Titles II and III of Regulation (EEC) No. 1984/83. Under Article 15(3), in the case of agreements which were in force on July 1, 1983, the same

---

[3] The paragraph numbers were renumbered by the amendment in OJ 1992 C121/2. Paragraph 49 should therefore read paragraph 50.

[4] Now paragraphs 52 and 54.

principle applies except that the 10–year maximum duration for such agreements laid down in Article 8(1)(d) and Article 12(1)(c) may be exceeded.

66. The sole requirement for the eligible beer-supply and service-station agreements to continue to enjoy the block exemption beyond January 1, 1989 is that they be brought into line with the new provisions. It is left to the undertakings concerned how they do so. One way is for the parties to agree to amend the original agreement, another for the supplier unilaterally to release the reseller from all obligations that would prevent the application of the block exemption after January 1, 1989. The latter method is only mentioned in Article 15(3) in relation to agreements in force on July 1, 1983. However, there is no reason why this possibility should not also be open to parties to agreements entered into between July 1, 1983 and January 1, 1984.

67. Parties lose the benefit of application of the transitional provisions if they extend the scope of their agreement as regards persons, places or subject-matter, or incorporate into it additional obligations restrictive of competition. The agreement then counts as a new agreement. The same applies if the parties substantially change the nature or extent of their obligations to one another. A substantial change in this sense includes a revision of the purchase price of the goods supplied to the reseller or of the rent for a public house or service station which goes beyond mere adjustment to the changing economic environment.

APPENDIX 15

REGULATION 4087/88[1]

*On the Application of Article 81(3) of the Treaty to Categories of Franchise
Agreements*

THE COMMISSION OF THE EUROPEAN COMMUNITIES

Having regard to the Treaty establishing the European Economic Community,

Having regard to Council Regulation No 19/65/EEC of 2 March, 1965, on the application of Article 81(3) of the Treaty to certain categories of agreements and concerted practices,[2] as last amended by the Act of Accession of Spain and Portugal, and in particular Article 1 thereof,

Having published a draft of this Regulation,[3]

Having consulted the Advisory Committee on Restrictive Practices and Dominant Positions,

Whereas:

(1) Regulation No. 19/65/EEC empowers the Commission to apply Article 81(3) of the Treaty by Regulation to certain categories of bilateral exclusive agreements falling within the scope of Article 81(1) which either have as their object the exclusive distribution or exclusive purchase of goods, or include restrictions imposed in relation to the assignment or use of industrial property rights.

(2) Franchise agreements consist essentially of licences of industrial or intellectual property rights relating to trade marks or signs and know-how, which can be combined with restrictions relating to supply or purchase of goods.

(3) Several types of franchise can be distinguished according to their object: industrial franchise concerns the manufacturing of goods, distribution franchise concerns the sale of goods, and service franchise concerns the supply of services.

(4) It is possible on the basis of the experience of the Commission to define categories of franchise agreements which fall under Article 81(1) but can normally be regarded as satisfying the conditions laid down in Article 81(3). This is the case for franchise agreements whereby one of the parties supplies goods or provides services to end users. On the other hand, industrial franchise agreements should not be covered by this Regulation. Such agreements, which usually govern relationships between producers, present different characteristics than the other types of franchise. They consist of manufacturing licences based on patents and/or technical know-how, combined with trade-mark licences. Some of them may benefit from other block exemptions if they fulfil the necessary conditions.

(5) This Regulation covers franchise agreements between two undertakings, the franchisor and the franchisee, for the retailing of goods or the provision of services to end users, or a combination of these activities, such as the processing or adaptation of goods to fit specific needs of their customers. It also covers cases where the relationship between

---

[1] OJ 1988 L359/46.
[2] JO 1965 533.
[3] OJ 1987 C229/3.

franchisor and franchisees is made through a third undertaking, the master franchisee. It does not cover wholesale franchise agreements because of the lack of experience of the Commission in that field.

(6) Franchise agreements as defined in this Regulation can fall under Article 81(1). They may in particular affect intra-Community trade where they are concluded between undertakings from different Member States or where they form the basis of a network which extends beyond the boundaries of a single Member State.

(7) Franchise agreements as defined in this Regulation normally improve the distribution of goods and/or the provision of services as they give franchisors the possibility of establishing a uniform network with limited investments, which may assist the entry of new competitors on the market, particularly in the case of small and medium-sized undertakings, thus increasing interbrand competition. They also allow independent traders to set up outlets more rapidly and with a higher chance of success than if they had to do so without the franchisor's experience and assistance. They have therefore the possibility of competing more efficiently with large distribution undertakings.

(8) As a rule, franchise agreements also allow consumers and other end users a fair share of the resulting benefit, as they combine the advantage of a uniform network with the existence of traders personally interested in the efficient operation of their business. The homogeneity of the network and the constant co-operation between the franchisor and the franchisees ensures a constant quality of the products and services. The favourable effect of franchising on interbrand competition and the fact that consumers are free to deal with any franchisee in the network guarantees that a reasonable part of the resulting benefits will be passed on to the consumers.

(9) This Regulation must define the obligations restrictive of competition which may be included in franchise agreements. This is the case in particular for the granting of an exclusive territory to the franchisees combined with the prohibition on actively seeking customers outside that territory, which allows them to concentrate their efforts on their allotted territory. The same applies to the granting of an exclusive territory to a master franchisee combined with the obligation not to conclude franchise agreements with third parties outside that territory. Where the franchisees sell or use in the process of providing services, goods manufactured by the franchisor or according to its instructions and or bearing its trade mark, an obligation on the franchisees not to sell, or use in the process of the provision of services, competing goods, makes it possible to establish a coherent network which is identified with the franchised goods. However, this obligation should only be accepted with respect to the goods which form the essential subject-matter of the franchise. It should notably not relate to accessories or spare parts for these goods.

(10) The obligations referred to above thus do not impose restrictions which are not necessary for the attainment of the above-mentioned objectives. In particular, the limited territorial protection granted to the franchisees is indispensable to protect their investment.

(11) It is desirable to list in the Regulation a number of obligations that are commonly found in franchise agreements and that are normally not restrictive of competition and to provide that if, because of the particular economic or legal circumstances, they fall under Article 81(1), they are also covered by the exemption. This list, which is not exhaustive, includes in particular clauses which are essential either to preserve the common identity and reputation of the network or to prevent the know-how made available and the assistance given by the franchisor from benefiting competitors.

(12) The Regulation must specify the conditions which must be satisfied for the exemption to apply. To guarantee that competition is not eliminated for a substantial part of the goods which are the subject of the franchise, it is necessary that parallel imports remain possible. Therefore, cross deliveries between franchisees should always be possible. Furthermore, where a franchise network is combined with another distribution system, franchisees should be free to obtain supplies from authorised distributors. To better inform consumers, thereby helping to ensure that they receive a fair share of the resulting benefits, it must be provided that the franchisee shall be obliged to indicate its status as an independent undertaking, by any appropriate means which does not jeopardise

the common identity of the franchised network. Furthermore, where the franchisees have to honour guarantees for the franchisor's goods, this obligation should also apply to goods supplied by the franchisor, other franchisees or other agreed dealers.

(13) The Regulation must also specify restrictions which may not be included in franchise agreements if these are to benefit from the exemption granted by the Regulation, by virtue of the fact that such provisions are restrictions falling under Article 81(1) for which there is no general presumption that they will lead to the positive effects required by Article 81(3). This applies in particular to market sharing between competing manufacturers, to clauses unduly limiting the franchisee's choice of suppliers or customers, and to cases where the franchisee is restricted in determining its prices. However, the franchisor should be free to recommend prices to the franchisees, where it is not prohibited by national laws and to the extent that it does not lead to concerted practices for the effective application of these prices.

(14) Agreements which are not automatically covered by the exemption because they contain provisions that are not expressly exempted by the Regulations and not expressly excluded from exemption may nonetheless generally be presumed to be eligible for application of Article 81(3). It will be possible for the Commission rapidly to establish whether this is the case for a particular agreement. Such agreements should therefore be deemed to be covered by the exemption provided for in this Regulation where they are notified to the Commission and the Commission does not oppose the application of the exemption within a specified period of time.

(15) If individual agreements exempted by this Regulation nevertheless have effects which are incompatible with Article 81(3), in particular as interpreted by the administrative practice of the Commission and the case law of the Court of Justice, the Commission may withdraw the benefit of the block exemption. This applies in particular where competition is significantly restricted because of the structure of the relevant market.

(16) Agreements which are automatically exempted pursuant to this Regulation need not be notified. Undertakings may nevertheless in a particular case request a decision pursuant to Council Regulation No. 17[4] as last amended by the Act of Accession of Spain and Portugal.

(17) Agreements may benefit from the provisions either of this Regulation or of another Regulation, according to their particular nature and provided that they fulfil the necessary conditions of application. They may not benefit from a combination of the provisions of this Regulation with those of another block exemption Regulation.

HAS ADOPTED THIS REGULATION

Article 1

1. Pursuant to Article 81(3) of the Treaty and subject to the provisions of this Regulation, it is hereby declared that Article 81(1) of the Treaty shall not apply to franchise agreements to which two undertakings are party, which include one or more of the restrictions listed in Article 2.

2. The exemption provided for in paragraph 1 shall also apply to master franchise agreements to which two undertakings are party. Where applicable, the provisions of this Regulation concerning the relationship between franchisor and franchisee shall apply *mutatis mutandis* to the relationship between franchisor and master franchisee and between master franchisee and franchisee.

3. For the purposes of this Regulation:

(a) "franchise" means a package of industrial or intellectual property rights relating to trade marks, trade names, shop signs, utility models, designs, copyrights, know-how

---

[4] JO 1962 204.

or patents, to be exploited for the resale of goods or the provision of services to end users;

(b) "franchise agreement" means an agreement whereby one undertaking, the franchisor, grants the other, the franchisee, in exchange for direct or indirect financial consideration, the right to exploit a franchise for the purposes of marketing specified types of goods and/or services; it includes at least obligations relating to:
   — the use of a common name or shop sign and a uniform presentation of contract premises and/or means of transport;
   — the communication by the franchisor to the franchisee of know-how;
   — the continuing provision by the franchisor to the franchisee of commercial or technical assistance during the life of the agreement;

(c) "master franchise agreement" means an agreement whereby one undertaking, the franchisor, grants the other, the master franchisee, in exchange of direct or indirect financial consideration, the right to exploit a franchise for the purposes of concluding franchise agreements with third parties, the franchisees;

(d) "franchisor's goods" means goods produced by the franchisor or according to its instructions, and/or bearing the franchisor's name or trade mark;

(e) "contract premises" means the premises used for the exploitation of the franchise or, when the franchise is exploited outside those premises, the base from which the franchisee operates the means of transport used for the exploitation of the franchise (contract means of transport);

(f) "know-how" means a package of non-patented practical information, resulting from experience and testing by the franchisor, which is secret, substantial and identified;

(g) "secret" means that the know-how, as a body or in the precise configuration and assembly of its components, is not generally known or easily accessible; it is not limited in the narrow sense that each individual component of the know-how should be totally unknown or unobtainable outside the franchisor's business;

(h) "substantial" means that the know-how includes information which is of importance for the sale of goods or the provision of services to end users, and in particular for the presentation of goods for sale, the processing of goods in connection with the provision of services, methods of dealing with customers, and administration and financial management; the know-how must be useful for the franchisee by being capable, at the date of conclusion of the agreement, of improving the competitive position of the franchisee, in particular by improving the franchisee's performance or helping it to enter a new market;

(i) "identified" means that the know-how must be described in sufficiently comprehensive manner so as to make it possible to verify that it fulfils the criteria of secrecy and substantiality; the description of the know-how can either be set out in the franchise agreement or in a separate document or recorded in any other appropriate form.

Article 2

The exemption provided for in Article 1 shall apply to the following restrictions of competition:

(a) an obligation on the franchisor, in a defined area of the common market, the contract territory, not to:
   — grant the right to exploit all or part of the franchise to third parties,
   — itself exploit the franchise, or itself market the goods or services which are the subject-matter of the franchise under a similar formula,
   — itself supply the franchisor's goods to third parties;

(b) an obligation on the master franchisee not to conclude franchise agreement with third parties outside its contract territory;

(c) an obligation on the franchisee to exploit the franchisee only from the contract premises;

(d) an obligation on the franchisee to refrain, outside the contract territory, from seeking customers for the goods or the services which are the subject-matter of the franchise;

(e) an obligation on the franchisee not to manufacture, sell or use in the course of the provision of services, goods competing with the franchisor's goods which are the subject-matter of the franchisee; where the subject-matter of the franchise is the sale or use in the course of the provision of services of both certain types of goods and spare parts or accessories therefor, that obligation may not be imposed in respect of these spare parts or accessories.

Article 3

1. Article 1 shall apply notwithstanding the presence of any of the following obligations on the franchisee, in so far as they are necessary to protect the franchisor's industrial or intellectual property rights or to maintain the common identity and reputation of the franchised network:

(a) to sell, or use in the course of the provision of services, exclusively goods matching minimum objective quality specifications laid down by the franchisor;

(b) to sell, or use in the course of the provision of services, goods which are manufactured only by the franchisor or by third parties [designated]* designed by it, where it is impracticable, owing to the nature of the goods which are the subject-matter of the franchise, to apply objective quality specifications;

(c) not to engage, directly or indirectly, in any similar business in a territory where it would compete with a member of the franchised network, including the franchisor; the franchisee may be held to this obligation after termination of the agreement, for a reasonable period which may not exceed one year, in the territory where it has exploited the franchise;

(d) not to acquire financial interests in the capital of a competing undertaking, which would give the franchisee the power to influence the economic conduct of such undertaking;

(e) to sell the goods which are the subject-matter of the franchise only to end users, to other franchisees and to resellers within other channels of distribution supplied by the manufacturer of these goods or with its consent;

(f) to use its best endeavours to sell the goods or provide the services that are the subject-matter of the franchise; to offer for sale a minimum range of goods, achieve a minimum turnover, plan its orders in advance, keep minimum stocks and provide customer and warranty services;

(g) to pay to the franchisor a specified proportion of its revenue for advertising and itself carry out advertising for the nature of which it shall obtain the franchisor's approval.

2. Article 1 shall apply notwithstanding the presence of any of the following obligations on the franchisee:

(a) not to disclose to third parties the know-how provided by the franchisor; the franchisee may be held to this obligation after termination of the agreement;

(b) to communicate to the franchisor any experience gained in exploiting the franchise and to grant it, and other franchisees, a non-exclusive licence for the know-how resulting from that experience;

(c) to inform the franchisor of infringements of licensed industrial or intellectual property rights, to take legal action against infringers or to assist the franchisor in any legal actions against infringers;

---

* Editor's note: The misprint in the official English text ("designed") has been corrected by reference to the other foreign language texts.

(d) not to use know-how licensed by the franchisor for purposes other than the exploitation of the franchise; the franchisee may be held to this obligation after termination of the agreement;

(e) to attend or have its staff attend training courses arranged by the franchisor;

(f) to apply the commercial methods devised by the franchisor, including any subsequent modification thereof, and use the licensed industrial or intellectual property rights;

(g) to comply with the franchisor's standards for the equipment and presentation of the contract premises and/or means of transport;

(h) to allow the franchisor to carry out checks of the contract premises and/or means of transport, including the goods sold and the services provided, and the inventory and accounts of the franchisee;

(i) not without the franchisor's consent to change the location of the contract premises;

(j) not without the franchisor's consent to assign the rights and obligations under the franchise agreement.

3. In the event that, because of particular circumstances, obligations referred to in paragraph 2 fall within the scope of Article 81(1), they shall also be exempted even if they are not accompanied by any of the obligations exempted by Article 1.

Article 4

The exemption provided for in Article 1 shall apply on condition that:

(a) the franchisee is free to obtain the goods that are the subject-matter of the franchise from other franchisees; where such goods are also distributed through another network of authorised distributors, the franchisee must be free to obtain the goods from the latter;

(b) where the franchisor obliges the franchisee to honour guarantees for the franchisor's goods, that obligation shall apply in respect of such goods supplied by any member of the franchised network or other distributors which give a similar guarantee, in the common market;

(c) the franchisee is obliged to indicate its status as an independent undertaking; this indication shall however not interfere with the common identity of the franchised network resulting in particular from the common name or shop sign and uniform appearance of the contract premises and/or means of transport.

Article 5

The exemption granted by Article 1 shall not apply where:

(a) undertakings producing goods or providing services which are identical or are considered by users as equivalent in view of their characteristics, price and intended use, enter into franchise agreements in respect of such goods or services;

(b) without prejudice to Article 2(e) and Article 3(1)(b), the franchisee is prevented from obtaining supplies of goods of a quality equivalent to those offered by the franchisor;

(c) without prejudice to Article 2(e), the franchisee is obliged to sell, or use in the process of providing services, goods manufactured by the franchisor or third parties designated by the franchisor and the franchisor refuses, for reasons other than protecting the franchisor's industrial or intellectual property rights, or maintaining the common identity and reputation of the franchised network, to designate as authorised manufacturers third parties proposed by the franchisee;

(d) the franchisee is prevented from continuing to use the licensed know-how after termination of the agreement where the know-how has become generally known or easily accessible, other than by breach of an obligation by the franchisee;

(e) the franchisee is restricted by the franchisor, directly or indirectly, in the determination of sale prices for the goods or services which are the subject-matter of the
franchise, without prejudice to the possibility for the franchisor of recommending
sale prices;

(f) the franchisor prohibits the franchisee from challenging the validity of the industrial
or intellectual property rights which form part of the franchise, without prejudice to
the possibility for the franchisor of terminating the agreement in such a case;

(g) franchisees are obliged not to supply within the common market the goods or services
which are the subject-matter of the franchise to end users because of their place of
residence.

Article 6

1. The exemption provided for in Article 1 shall also apply to franchise agreements
which fulfil the conditions laid down in Article 4 and include obligations restrictive of
competition which are not covered by Articles 2 and 3(3) and do not fall within the scope
of Article 5, on condition that the agreements in question are notified to the Commission
in accordance with the provisions of Commission Regulation No. 27,[5] and that the
Commission does not oppose such exemption within a period of six months.

2. The period of six months shall run from the date on which the notification is received
by the Commission. Where, however, the notification is made by registered post, the
period shall run from the date shown on the postmark of the place of posting.

3. Paragraph 1 shall apply only if:

(a) express reference is made to this Article in the notification or in a communication
accompanying it; and

(b) the information furnished with the notification is complete and in accordance with the
facts.

4. The benefit of paragraph 1 can be claimed for agreements notified before the entry
into force of this Regulation by submitting a communication to the Commission referring
expressly to this Article and to the notification. Paragraphs 2 and 3(b) shall apply *mutatis
mutandis*.

5. The Commission may oppose exemption. It shall oppose exemption if it receives a
request to do so from a Member State within three months of the forwarding to the
Member State of the notification referred to in paragraph 1 or the communication referred
to in paragraph 4. This request must be justified on the basis of considerations relating to
the competition rules of the Treaty.

6. The Commission may withdraw its opposition to the exemption at any time.
However, where that opposition was raised at the request of a Member State, it may be
withdrawn only after consultation of the Advisory Committee on Restrictive Practices and
Dominant Positions.

7. If the opposition is withdrawn because the undertakings concerned have shown that
the conditions of Article 81(3) are fulfilled, the exemption shall apply from the date of the
notification.

8. If the opposition is withdrawn because the undertakings concerned have amended
the agreement so that the conditions of Article 81(3) are fulfilled, the exemption shall
apply from the date on which the amendments take effect.

9. If the Commission opposes exemption and its opposition is not withdrawn, the
effects of the notification shall be governed by the provisions of Regulation No. 17.

---

[5] JO 1962 1118, OJ 1985 L240/1.

Article 7

1. Information acquired pursuant to Article 6 shall be used only for the purposes of this Regulation.

2. The Commission and the authorities of the Member States, their officials and other servants shall not disclose information acquired by them pursuant to this Regulation of a kind that is covered by the obligation of professional secrecy.

3. Paragraphs 1 and 2 shall not prevent publication of general information or surveys which do not contain information relating to particular undertakings or associations of undertakings.

Article 8

The Commission may withdraw the benefit of this Regulation, pursuant to Article 7 of Regulation No. 19/65/EEC, where it finds in a particular case that an agreement exempted by this Regulation nevertheless has certain effects which are incompatible with the conditions laid down in Article 81(3) of the Treaty, and in particular where territorial protection is awarded to the franchisee and:

(a) access to the relevant market or competition therein is significantly restricted by the cumulative effect of parallel networks of similar agreements established by competing manufacturers or distributors;

(b) the goods or services which are the subject-matter of the franchise do not face, in a substantial part of the common market, effective competition from goods or services which are identical or considered by users as equivalent in view of their characteristics, price and intended use;

(c) the parties, or one of them, prevent end users, because of their place of residence, from obtaining, directly or through intermediaries, the goods or services which are the subject-matter of the franchise within the common market, or use differences in specifications concerning those goods or services in different Member States, to isolate markets;

(d) franchisees engage in concerted practices relating to the sale prices of the goods or services which are the subject-matter of the franchise;

(e) the franchisor uses its right to check the contract premises and means of transport, or refuses its agreement to requests by the franchisee to move the contract premises or assign its rights and obligations under the franchise agreement, for reasons other than protecting the franchisor's industrial or intellectual property rights, maintaining the common identity and reputation of the franchised network or verifying that the franchisee abides by its obligations under the agreement.

[Article 8a

The prohibition in Article 81(1) of the Treaty shall not apply to the franchise agreements which were in existence at the date of accession of Austria, Finland and Sweden and which, by reason of this accession, fall within the scope of Article 81(1) if, within the six months from the date of accession, they are so amended that they comply with the conditions laid down in this Regulation. However, this Article shall not apply to agreements which at the date of accession already fall under Article 53(1) of the EEA Agreement.]

Amendment

Article 8a was added by the Act of Accession of the Republic of Austria, the Republic of Finland and the Kingdom of Sweden, Annex 1(III)(D)(7), as amended by Council Decision 95/1, Article 39.

Article 9

This Regulation shall enter into force on 1 February, 1989.
It shall remain in force until 31 December, 1999.
This Regulation shall be binding in its entirety and directly applicable in all Member States.

Done at Brussels, 30 November, 1988.

APPENDIX 16

REGULATION 1475/95[1]

*On the Application of Article 81(3) of the Treaty to Certain Categories of
Motor Vehicle Distribution and Servicing Agreements*

THE COMMISSION OF THE EUROPEAN COMMUNITIES

Having regard to the Treaty establishing the European Community.

Having regard to the Council Regulation No. 19/65/EEC of 2 March 1965 on the application of Article 81(3) of the Treaty to certain categories of agreement and concerted practices,[2] as last amended by the Act of Accession of Austria, Finland and Sweden, and in particular Article 1 thereof,

Having published a draft of this Regulation,[3]

Having consulted the Advisory Committee on Restrictive Practices and Dominant Positions,

Whereas:

(1) Under Regulation No. 19/65/EEC the Commission is empowered to declare by means of a Regulation that Article 81(3) of the Treaty applies to certain categories of agreements falling within Article 81(1) to which only two undertakings are party and by which one party agrees with the other to supply only to that other certain goods for resale within a defined area of the common market. The experience gained in dealing with many motor vehicle distribution and servicing agreements allows a category of agreement to be defined which can generally be regarded as satisfying the conditions laid down in Article 81(3). These are agreements for a definite or an indefinite period, by which the supplying party entrusts to the reselling party the task of promoting the distribution and servicing of certain products of the motor vehicle industry in a defined area and by which the supplier undertakes to supply contract goods for resale only to the dealer, or only to a limited number of undertakings within the distribution network besides the dealer, within the contract territory.

A list of definitions for the purpose of this Regulation is set out in Article 10.

(2) Notwithstanding that the obligations listed in Articles 1, 2 and 3 normally have as their object or effect the prevention, restriction or distortion of competition within the common market and are normally liable to affect trade between Member States, the prohibition in Article 81(1) of the Treaty may nevertheless be declared inapplicable to these agreements by virtue of Article 81(3), albeit only under certain restrictive conditions.

(3) The applicability of Article 81(1) of the Treaty to distribution and servicing agreements in the motor vehicle industry stems in particular from the fact that the restrictions on competition and obligations agreed within the framework of a manufacturer's distribution system, and listed in Articles 1 to 4 of this Regulation, are generally imposed in the same or similar form throughout the common market. The motor vehicle

---

[1] OJ 1995 L145/25.
[2] OJ 1965 L36/533.
[3] OJ 1994 C379/16.

manufacturers cover the whole common market or substantial parts of it by means of a cluster of agreements involving similar restrictions on competition and affect in this way not only distribution and servicing within Member States but also trade between them.

(4) The exclusive and selective distribution clauses can be regarded as indispensable measures of rationalisation in the motor vehicle industry, because motor vehicles are consumer durables which at both regular and irregular intervals require expert maintenance and repair, not always in the same place. Motor vehicle manufacturers co-operate with the selected dealers and repairers in order to provide specialised servicing for the product. On grounds of capacity and efficiency alone, such a form of co-operation cannot be extended to an unlimited number of dealers and repairers. The linking of servicing and distribution must be regarded as more efficient than a separation between a distribution organisation for new vehicles on the one hand and a servicing organisation which would also distribute spare parts on the other, particularly as, before a new vehicle is delivered to the final consumer, the undertaking within the distribution system must give it a technical inspection according to the manufacturer's specification.

(5) However, obligatory recourse to the authorised network is not in all respects indispensable for efficient distribution. It should therefore be provided that the supply of contract goods to resellers may not be prohibited where they:

— belong to the same distribution system (Article 3(10)(a)), or
— purchase spare parts for their own use in effecting repairs or maintenance (Article 3(10)(b)).

Measures taken by a manufacturer or by undertakings within the distribution system with the object of protecting the selective distribution system are compatible with the exemption under this Regulation. This applies in particular to a dealer's obligation to sell vehicles to a final consumer using the services of an intermediary only where that consumer has authorised that intermediary to act as his agent (Article 3(11)).

(6) It should be possible to prevent wholesalers not belonging to the distribution system from reselling parts originating from motor vehicle manufacturers. It may be supposed that the system, beneficial to the consumer, whereby spare parts are readily available across the whole contract range, including those parts with a low turnover, could not be maintained without obligatory recourse to the authorised network.

(7) The ban on dealing in competing products may be exempted on condition that it does not inhibit the dealer from distributing vehicles of other makes in a manner which avoids all confusion between makes (Article 3(3)). The obligation to refrain from selling products of other manufacturers other than in separate sales premises, under separate management, linked to the general obligation to avoid confusion between different makes, guarantees exclusivity of distribution of each make in each place of sale. This last obligation has to be implemented in good faith by the dealer so that the promotion, sale and after-sales service cannot, in any manner, cause confusion in the eyes of the consumer or result in unfair practices on the part of the dealer with regard to suppliers of competing makes. In order to maintain the competitiveness of competing products, the separate management of different sales premises has to be carried out by distinct legal entities. Such an obligation provides an incentive for the dealer to develop sales and servicing of contract goods and thus promote competition in the supply of those products and competing products. These provisions do not prevent the dealer from offering and providing maintenance and repair services for competing makes of motor vehicle in the same workshop, subject to the option of obliging the dealer not to allow third parties to benefit unduly from investments made by the supplier (Article 3(4)).

(8) However, bans on dealing in competing products cannot be regarded in all circumstances as indispensable to efficient distribution. Dealers must be free to obtain from third parties supplies of parts which match the quality of those offered by the manufacturer, and to use and sell them. In this regard, it can be presumed that all parts coming from the same source of product are identical in characteristics and origin; it is for spare-part manufacturers offering parts to dealers to confirm, if need be, that such parts correspond to

those supplies to the manufacturer of the vehicle. Moreover, dealers must retain their freedom to choose parts which are usable in motor vehicles within the contract range and which match or exceed the quality standard. Such a limit on the ban on dealing in competing products takes account of both the importance of vehicle safety and the maintenance of effective competition (Article 3(5) and Article 4(1)(6) and (7)).

(9) The restrictions imposed on the dealer's activities outside the allotted area lead to more intensive distribution and servicing efforts in an easily supervised contract territory, to knowledge of the market based on closer contact with consumers, and to more demand-orientated supply (Article 3(8) and (9)). However, demand for contract goods must remain flexible and should not be limited on a regional basis. Dealers must not be confined to satisfying the demand for contract goods within their contract territories, but must also be able to meet demand from persons and undertakings in other areas of the common market. Advertising by dealers in a medium which is directed at customers outside the contract territory should not be prevented, because it does not run counter to the obligation to promote sales within the contact territory. The acceptable means of advertising do not include direct personal contact with the customer, whether by telephone or other form of telecommunication, doorstep canvassing or by individual letter.

(10) So as to give firms greater legal certainty, certain obligations imposed on the dealer that do not stand in the way of exemption should be specified regarding the observation of minimum distribution and servicing standards (Article 4(1)(1)), regularity of orders (Article 4(1)(2)), the achievement of quantitative sales or stock targets agreed by the parties or determined by an expert third party in the event of disagreement (Article 4(1)(3) to (5)) and the arrangements made for after-sales service (Article 4(1)(6) to (9). Such obligations are directly related to the obligations in Articles 1, 2 and 3, and influence their restrictive effect. They may therefore be exempted, for the same reasons as the latter, where they fall in individual cases under the prohibition contained in Article 81(1) of the Treaty (Article 4(2)).

(11) Pursuant to Regulation No. 19/65/EEC, the conditions which must be satisfied if the declaration of inapplicability is to take effect must be specified.

(12) Under Article 5(1)(1)(a) and (b) it is a condition of exemption that the undertaking should honour the guarantee and provide free servicing, vehicle recall work, and repair and maintenance services necessary for the safe and reliable functioning of the vehicle, irrespective of where in the common market the vehicle was purchased. These provisions are intended to prevent limitation of the consumer's freedom to buy anywhere in the common market.

(13) Article 5(1)(2)(a) is intended to allow the manufacturer to build up a co-ordinated distribution system, but without hindering the relationship of confidence between dealers and sub-dealers. Accordingly, if the supplier reserves the right to approve appointments of sub-dealers by the dealer, he must not be allowed to withhold such approval arbitrarily.

(14) Article 5(1)(2)(b) requires the supplier not to impose on a dealer within the distribution system any requirements, as defined in Article 4(1), which are discriminatory or inequitable.

(15) Article 5(1)(12)(c) is intended to counter the concentration of the dealer's demand on the supplier which might follow from cumulation of discounts. The purpose of this provision is to allow spare-parts suppliers which do not offer as wide a range of goods as the manufacturer to compete on equal terms.

(16) Article 5(1)(2)(d) makes the exemption subject to the condition that the dealer must be able to purchase for customers in the common market volume-produced passenger cars with the technical features appropriate to their place of residence or to the place where the vehicle is to be registered, in so far as the corresponding model is also supplied by the manufacturer through undertakings within the distribution system in that place (Article 10(10)). This provision obviates the danger that the manufacturer and undertakings within the distribution network might make use of product differentiation as between parts of the common market to partition the market.

(17) Article 5(2) makes the exemption dependent on other minimum conditions which aim to prevent the dealer, owing to the obligations which are imposed on him, from

becoming economically over-dependent on the supplier and from abandoning the competitive activity which is nominally open to him because to pursue it would be against the interests of the manufacturer or other undertakings within the distribution network.

(18) Under Article 5(2)(1), the dealer may, for objectively justified reasons, oppose the application of excessive obligations covered by Article 3(3).

(19) Article 5(2)(2) and (3) and Article 5(3) lay down minimum requirements for exemption concerning the duration and termination of the distribution and servicing agreement, because the combined effect of the investments the dealer makes in order to improve the distribution the servicing of contract goods and short-term agreement or one terminable at short notice is greatly to increase the dealer's dependence on the supplier. In order to avoid obstructing the development of flexible and efficient distribution structures, however, the suppliers should be entitled to terminate the agreement where there is a need to reorganise all or a substantial part of the network. To allow rapid settlement of any disputes, provision should be made for reference to an expert third party or arbitrator who will decide in the event of disagreement, without prejudice to the parties' right to bring the matter before a competent court in conformity with the relevant provisions of national law.

(20) Pursuant to Regulation No. 19/65/EEC, the restrictions or provisions which must not be contained in the agreements, if the declaration of inapplicability or Article 81(1) of the Treaty under this Regulation is to take effect, are to be specified (Article 6(1), (1) to (5)). Moreover, practices of the parties which lead to automatic loss of the benefit of exemption when committed systematically and repeatedly shall be defined (Article 6(1)(6) to (12)).

(21) Agreements under which one motor vehicle manufacturer entrusts the distribution of his products to another must be excluded from the block exemption, because of their far-reaching impact on competition (Article 6(1)(1)).

(22) In order to ensure that the parties remain within the limits of the Regulation, any agreements whose object goes beyond the products or services referred to in Article 1 or which stipulate restrictions of competition not exempted by this Regulation should also be excluded from the exemption (Article 6(1)(2) and (3)).

(23) The exemption similarly does not apply where the parties agree between themselves obligations concerning goods covered by this Regulation which would be acceptable in the combination of obligations which is exempted by Commission Regulation (EEC) No. 1983/83[4] or (EEC) No. 1984/83,[5] as last amended by the Act of Accession of Austria, Finland and Sweden, regarding the application of Article 81(3) of the Treaty to categories of exclusive distribution agreements and exclusive purchasing agreements respectively, but which go beyond the scope of the obligations exempted by this Regulation (Article 6(1)(4)).

(24) In order to protect dealers' investments and prevent any circumvention by suppliers of the rules governing the termination of agreements, it should be confirmed that the exemption does not apply where the supplier reserves the right to amend unilaterally during the period covered by the contract terms of the exclusive territorial dealership granted to the dealer (Article 6(1)(5)).

(25) In order to maintain effective competition at the distribution stage, it is necessary to provide that the manufacturers or supplier will lose the benefit of exemption where he restricts the dealer's freedom to develop his own policy on resale prices (Article 6(1)(6)).

(26) The principle of a single market required that consumers shall be able to purchase motor vehicles wherever in the Community prices or terms are most favourable and even to resell them, provided that the resale is not effected for commercial purposes. The benefits of this Regulation cannot therefore be accorded to manufacturers or suppliers who impede parallel imports or exports through measures taken in respect of consumers, authorised intermediaries or undertakings within the network (Article 6(1)(7) and (8)).

---

[4] OJ 1983 L173/1.
[5] OJ 1983 L173/5.

(27) So as to ensure, in the interests of consumers, effective competition on the maintenance and repair markets, the exemption must also be withheld from manufacturers or suppliers who impede independent spare-part producers' and distributors' access to the markets or restrict the freedom of resellers or repairers, whether or not they belong to the network, to purchase and use such spare parts where they match the quality of the original spare parts. The dealer's right to procure spare parts with matching quality from external undertakings of his choice and the corresponding right for those undertakings to furnish spare parts to resellers of their choice, as well as their freedom to affix their trade mark or logo, are provided for subject to compliance with the industrial property rights applicable to those spare parts (Article 6(1)(9) to (11)).

(28) In order to give final consumers genuine opportunities of choice as between repairers belonging to the network and independent repairers, it is appropriate to impose upon manufacturers the obligation to give repairers outside the network the technical information necessary for the repair and maintenance of their makes of car, whilst taking into account the legitimate interest of the manufacturers to decide itself the mode of exploitation of its intellectual property rights as well as its identified, substantial, secret know-how when granting licences to third parties. However, these rights must be exercised in a manner which avoids all discrimination or other abuse (Article 6(1)(12)).

(29) For reasons of clarity, the legal effects arising from inapplicability of the exemption in the various situations referred to in the Regulation should be defined (Article 6(2) and (3)).

(30) Distribution and servicing agreements can be exempted, subject to the conditions laid down in Articles 5 and 6, so long as the application of obligations covered by Articles 1 to 4 brings about an improvement in distribution and servicing to the benefit of the consumer and effective competition exists, not only between manufacturers' distribution systems but also to a certain extent within each system within the common market. As regards the categories of products set out in Article 1, the conditions necessary for effective competition, including competition in trade between Member States, may be taken to exist at present, so that European consumers may be considered in general to take an equitable share in the benefit from the operation of such competition.

(31) Since the provisions of Commission Regulation (EEC) No. 123/85 of 12 December 1984 on the application of Article 81(3) of the Treaty to certain categories of motor vehicle distribution and servicing agreements,[6] as last amended by the Act of Accession of Austria, Finland and Sweden, are applicable until 30 June 1995, provision should be made for transitional arrangements in respect of agreements still running on that date which satisfy the exemption conditions laid down by that Regulation (Article 7). The Commission's powers to withdraw the benefit of exemption or to alter its scope in a particular case should be spelled out and several important categories of cases should be listed by way of example (Article 8). Where the Commission makes use of its power of withdrawal as provided for in Article 8(2), it should take into account any price differentials which do not principally result from the imposition of national fiscal measures or currency fluctuations between the Member States (Article 8).

(32) In accordance with Regulation No. 19/65/EEC, the exemption must be defined for a limited period. A period of seven years is appropriate for taking account of the specific characteristics of the motor vehicle sector and the foreseeable changes in competition in that sector. However, the Commission will regularly appraise the application of the Regulation by drawing up a report by 31 December 2000 (Articles 11 and 13).

(33) Agreements which fulfil the conditions set out in this Regulation need not be notified. However, in the case of doubt undertakings are free to notify their agreements to the Commission in accordance with Council Regulation No. 17[7] as last amended by the Act of Accession of Austria, Finland and Sweden.

(34) The sector-specific character of the exemption by category for motor vehicles broadly rules out any regulations containing general exemptions by category as regards

---

[6] OJ 1985 L15/16.
[7] OJ 1962 L13/204.

distribution. Such exclusion should be confirmed in respect of Commission Regulation (EEC) No. 4087/88 of 30 November 1988 concerning the application of Article 81(3) of the Treaty to categories of franchise agreements,[8] as last amended by the Act of Accession of Austria, Finland and Sweden, without prejudice to the right of undertakings to seek an individual exemption under Regulation No. 17. On the other hand, as regards Regulations (EEC) No. 1983/83 and (EEC) No. 1984/83, which make provision for a more narrowly drawn framework of exemptions for undertakings, it is possible to allow them to choose. As for Commission Regulations (EEC) No. 417/85[9] and (EEC) No. 418/85,[10] as last amended by the Act of Accession of Austria, Finland and Sweden, which relate to the application of Article 81(3) of the Treaty for categories of specialisation agreements and to categories of research and development agreements, respectively, but whose emphasis is not on distribution, applicability is not called in question (Article 12).

(35) This Regulation is without prejudice to the application of Article 82 of the Treaty.

HAS ADOPTED THIS REGULATION

Article 1

Pursuant to Article 81(3) of the Treaty it is hereby declared that subject to the conditions laid down in this Regulation Article 81(1) shall not apply to agreements to which only two undertakings are party and in which one contracting party agrees to supply, within a defined territory of the common market

— only to the other party, or
— only to the other party and to a specified number of other undertakings within the distribution system,

for the purpose of resale, certain new motor vehicles intended for use on public roads and having three or more road wheels, together with spare parts therefor.

Article 2

The exemption shall also apply where the obligation referred to in Article 1 is combined with an obligation on the supplier neither to sell contract goods to final consumers nor to provide them with servicing for contract goods in the contract territory.

Article 3

The exemption shall also apply where the obligation referred to in Article 1 is combined with an obligation on the dealer:
1. not, without the supplier's consent, to modify contract goods or corresponding goods, unless such modification has been ordered by a final consumer and concerns a particular motor vehicle within the range covered by the contract, purchased by that final consumer;
2. not to manufacture products which compete with contract goods;
3. not to sell new motor vehicles offered by persons other than the manufacturer *except* on separate sales premises, under separate management, in the form of a distinct legal entity and in a manner which avoids confusion between makes;

---

[8] OJ 1988 L359/46.
[9] OJ 1985 L53/1.
[10] OJ 1985 L53/5.

4. not to permit a third party to benefit unduly, through any after-sales service performed in a common workshop, from investments made by a supplier, notably in equipment or the training of personnel;

5. neither to sell spare parts which compete with contract goods without matching them in quality nor to use them for repair or maintenance of contract goods or corresponding goods;

6. without the supplier's consent, neither to conclude distribution or servicing agreements with undertakings operating in the contract territory for contract goods or corresponding goods not to alter or terminate such agreements;

7. to impose upon undertakings with which the dealer has concluded agreements in accordance with point 6 obligations comparable to those which the dealer has accepted in relation to the supplier and which are covered by Articles 1 to 4 and are in conformity with Articles 5 and 6;

8. outside the contract territory:

(a) not to maintain branches or depots for the distribution of contract goods or corresponding goods,
(b) not to solicit customers for contract goods or corresponding goods, by personalised advertising;

9. not to entrust third parties with the distribution or servicing of contract goods or corresponding goods outside the contract territory;

10. not to supply to a reseller:

(a) contract goods or corresponding goods unless the reseller is an undertaking within the distribution system, or
(b) spare parts within the contract range unless the reseller uses them for the repair or maintenance of a motor vehicle;

11. not to sell motor vehicles within the contract range or corresponding goods to final consumers using the services of an intermediary unless that intermediary has prior written authority from such consumers to purchase a specified motor vehicle or where it is taken away by him, to collect it.

Article 4

1. The exemption shall apply notwithstanding any obligation whereby the dealer undertakes to:

(1) comply, in distribution, sales and after-sales servicing with minimum standards, regarding in particular:

(a) the equipment of the business premises and the technical facilities for servicing;
(b) the specialised, technical training of staff;
(c) advertising;
(d) the collection, storage and delivery of contract goods or corresponding goods and sales and after-sales servicing;
(e) the repair and maintenance of contract goods and corresponding goods, particularly as regards the safe and reliable functioning of motor vehicles;

(2) order contract goods from the supplier only at certain times or within certain periods, provided that the interval between ordering dates does not exceed three months;

(3) endeavour to sell, within the contract territory and during a specified period, a minimum quantity of contract goods, determined by the parties by common agreement or, in the vent of disagreement between the parties as to the minimum number of contractual goods to be sold annually, by an expert third party, account is being taken in particular of

sales previously achieved in the territory and of forecast sales for the territory and at national level;

(4) keep in stock such quantity of contract goods as may be determined in accordance with the procedure in (3);

(5) keep such demonstration vehicles within the contract range, or such number thereof, as may be determined in accordance with the procedure in (3);

(6) perform work under guarantee, free servicing and vehicle-recall work for contract goods and corresponding goods;

(7) use only spare parts within the contract range or corresponding spare parts for work under guarantee, free servicing and vehicle-recall work in respect of contract goods or corresponding goods;

(8) inform customers, in a general manner, of the extent to which spare parts from other sources might be used for the repair or maintenance of contract goods or corresponding goods;

(9) inform customers whenever spare parts from other sources have been used for the repair or maintenance of contract goods or corresponding goods.

2. The exemption shall also apply to the obligations referred to in (1) above where such obligations fall in individual cases under the prohibition contained in Article 81(1).

Article 5

1. In all cases, the exemption shall apply only if:
    (1) the dealer undertakes:

(a) in respect of motor vehicles within the contract range or corresponding thereto which have been supplied in the common market by another undertaking within the distribution network;
    — to honour guarantees and to perform free servicing and vehicle-recall work to an extent which corresponds to the dealer's obligation covered by Article 4(1)(6),
    — to carry out repair and maintenance work in accordance with Article 4(1)(1)(e);
(b) to impose upon the undertakings operating within the contract territory with which the dealer has concluded distribution and servicing agreements as provided for in Article 3(6) an obligation to honour guarantees and to perform free servicing and vehicle-recall work at least to the extent to which the dealer himself is so obliged;

    (2) the supplier:

(a) does not without objectively valid reasons withhold consent to conclude, alter or terminate sub-agreements referred to in Article 3(6);
(b) does not apply, in relation to the dealer's obligations referred to in Article 4(1), minimum requirements or criteria for estimates such that the dealer is subject to discrimination without objective reasons or is treated inequitably;
(c) distinguishes, in any scheme for aggregating quantities or values of goods obtained by the dealer from the supplier and from connected undertakings within a specified period for the purpose of calculating discounts, at least between supplies of
    — motor vehicles within the contract range,
    — spare parts within the contract range, for supplies of which the dealer is dependent on undertakings within the distribution network, and
    — other goods;
(d) supplies to the dealer, for the purpose of performance of a contract of sale concluded between the dealer and a final customer in the common market, any passenger car which corresponds to a model within the contract range and which is marketed by the manufacturer or with the manufacturer's consent in the Member State in which the vehicle is to be registered.

2. Where the dealer has, in accordance with Article 4(1), assumed obligations for the improvement of distribution and servicing structures, the exemption shall apply provided that:

(1) the supplier releases the dealer from the obligations referred to in Article 3(3) where the dealer shows that there are objective reasons for doing so;
(2) the agreement is for a period of at least five years or, if for an indefinite period, the period of notice for regular termination of the agreement is at least two years for both parties; this period is reduced to at least one year where:
— the supplier is obliged by law or by special agreement to pay appropriate compensation on termination of the agreement, or
— the dealer is a new entrant to the distribution system and the period of the agreement, or the period of notice for regular termination of the agreement, is the first agreed by that dealer;
(3) each party undertakes to give the other at least six months' prior notice of intention not to renew an agreement concluded for a definite period.

3. The conditions for exemption laid down in (1) and (2) shall not affect:

— the right of the supplier to terminate the agreement subject to at least one year's notice in a case where it is necessary to reorganise the whole or a substantial part of the network,
— the right of one party to terminate the agreement for cause where the other party fails to perform one of its basic obligations.

In each case, the parties must, in the event of a disagreement, accept a system for the quick resolution of the dispute, such as recourse to an expert third party or an arbitrator, without prejudice to the parties' right to apply to a competent court in conformity with the provisions of national law.

Article 6

1. The exemption shall not apply where:

(1) both parties to the agreement or their connected undertakings are motor vehicle manufacturers; or
(2) the parties link their agreement to stipulations concerning products or services other than those referred to in this Regulation or apply their agreement to such products or services; or
(3) in respect of motor vehicles having three or more road wheel, spare parts or services therefor, the parties agree restrictions of competition that are not expressly exempted by this Regulation; or
(4) in respect of motor vehicles having three or more road wheels or spare parts therefor, the parties make agreements or engage in concerted practices which are exempted from the prohibition in Article 81(1) of the Treaty under Regulations (EEC) No. 1983/83 or (EEC) No. 1984/83 to an extent exceeding the scope of this Regulation; or
(5) the parties agree that the supplier reserves the right to conclude distribution and servicing agreements for contract goods with specified further undertakings operating within the contract territory, or to alter the contract territory; or
(6) the manufacturer, the supplier or another undertaking directly or indirectly restricts the dealer's freedom to determine prices and discounts in reselling contract goods or corresponding goods; or
(7) the manufacturer, the supplier or another undertaking within the network directly or indirectly restricts the freedom of final consumers, authorised intermediaries or dealers to obtain from an undertaking belonging to the network of their choice within

the common market contract goods or corresponding goods or to obtain servicing for such goods, or the freedom of final consumers to resell the contract goods or corresponding goods, when the sale is not effected for commercial purposes; or

(8) the supplier, without any objective reason, grants dealers remunerations calculated on the basis of the place of destination of the motor vehicles resold or the place of residence of the purchaser; or

(9) the supplier directly or indirectly restricts the dealer's freedom under Article 3(5) to obtain from a third undertaking of his choice spare parts which compete with contract goods and which match their quality; or

(10) the manufacturer directly or indirectly restricts the freedom of suppliers of spare parts to supply such products to resellers of their choice, including those which are undertakings within the distribution system, provided that such parts match the quality of contract goods; or

(11) the manufacturer directly or indirectly restricts the freedom of spare part manufacturers to place effectively and in an easily visible manner their trade mark or logo on parts supplied for the initial assembly or for the repair or maintenance of contract goods or corresponding goods; or

(12) the manufacturer refuses to make accessible, where appropriate upon payment, to repairers who are not undertakings within the distribution system, the technical information required for the repair or maintenance of the contractual or corresponding goods or for the implementing of environmental protection measures, provided that the information is not covered by an intellectual property right or does not constitute identified, substantial, secret know-how; in such case, the necessary technical information shall not be withheld improperly.

2. Without prejudice to the consequences for the other provisions of the agreement, in the vases specified in paragraph 1(1) to (5), the inapplicability of the exemption shall apply to *all* the clauses restrictive of competition contained in the agreement concerned; in the cases specified in paragraph 1(6) to (12), it shall apply only to the clauses restrictive of competition agreed respectively on behalf of the manufacturer, the supplier or another undertaking within the network which is engaged in the practice complained of.

3. Without prejudice to the consequences for the other provisions of the agreement, in the cases specified in paragraph 1(6) to (12), the inapplicability of the exemption shall only apply to the clauses restrictive of competition in favour of the other manufacturer, the supplier or another undertaking within the network which appear in the distribution and servicing agreements concluded for a geographic area within the common market in which the objectionable practice distorts competition, and only for the duration of the practice complained of.

Article 7

The prohibition laid down in Article 81(1) of the Treaty shall not apply during the period from 1 October 1995 to 30 September 1996 to agreements already in force on 1 October 1995 which satisfy the conditions for exemption provided for in Commission Regulation (EEC) No. 123/85.

Article 8

The Commission may withdraw the benefit of the application of this Regulation, pursuant to Article 7 of Regulation No. 19/65/EEC, where it finds that in an individual case an agreement which falls within the scope of this Regulation nevertheless has effects which are incompatible with the provisions of Article 81(3) of the Treaty, and in particular:

(1) where, in the common market or a substantial part thereof, contract goods or corresponding goods are not subject to competition from products considered by consumers as similar by reason of their characteristics, price and intended use;

(2) where prices or conditions of supply for contract goods or for corresponding goods are continually being applied which differ substantially as between Member States, such substantial differences being chiefly due to obligations exempted by this Regulation;

(3) where the manufacturer or an undertaking within the distribution system in supplying the distributors with contract goods or corresponding goods apply, unjustifiably, discriminatory prices or sales conditions.

Article 9

This Regulation shall apply *mutatis mutandis* to concerted practices falling within the categories covered by this Regulation.

Article 10

For the purposes of this Regulation the following terms shall have the following meanings:

1. "distribution and servicing agreements" are framework agreements between two undertakings, for a definite or indefinite period, whereby the party supplying goods entrusts to the other the distribution and servicing of those goods;

2. "parties" are the undertakings which are party to an agreement within the meaning of Article 1, "the supplier" being the undertaking which supplies the contract goods, and "the dealer" the undertaking entrusted by the supplier with the distribution and servicing of contract goods;

3. the "contract territory" is the defined territory of the common market to which the obligation of exclusive supply in the meaning of Article 1 applies;

4. "contract goods" are new motor vehicles intended for use on public roads and having three or more road wheels, and spare parts therefor, which are the subject of an agreement within the meaning of Article 1;

5. the "contract range" refers to the totality of the contract goods;

6. "spare parts" are parts which are to be installed in or upon a motor vehicle so as to replace components of that vehicle. They are to be distinguished from other parts and accessories, according to trade usage;

7. the "manufacturer" is the undertaking:
    (a) which manufactures or procures the manufacture of the motor vehicles in the contract range, or
    (b) which is connected with an undertaking described at (a);

8. "connected undertakings" are:
    (a) undertakings one of which directly or indirectly;
    — holds more than half of the capital or business assets of the other, or
    — has the power to exercise more than half the voting rights in the other, or
    — has the power to appoint more than half the members of the supervisory board, board of directors or bodies legally representing the other, or
    — has the right to manage the affairs of the other;
    (b) undertakings in relation to which a third undertaking is able directly or indirectly to exercise such rights or powers as are mentioned in (a) above,

9. "undertakings within the distribution system" are, besides the parties to the agreement, the manufacturer and undertakings which are entrusted by the manufacturers or with the manufacturer's consent with the distribution of servicing of contract goods or corresponding goods;

10. a "passenger car which corresponds to a model within the contract range" is a passenger car:

— manufactured or assembled in volume by the manufacturer and
— identical as to body style, drive-line, chassis, and type of motor with a passenger car within the contract range;

11. "corresponding goods", "corresponding motor vehicles" and "corresponding parts" are those which are similar in kind to those in the contract range, are distributed by the manufacturer or with the manufacturer's consent, and are the subject of a distribution or servicing agreement with an undertaking within the distribution system;

12. "resale" includes all transactions by which a physical or legal person—"the reseller"—disposes of a motor vehicle which is still in a new condition and which he had previously acquired in his own name and on his own behalf, irrespective of the legal description applied under civil law or the format of the transaction which effects such resale. The terms resale shall include all leasing contracts which provide for a transfer of ownership or an option to purchase prior to the expiry of the contract;

13. "distribute" and "sell" include other forms of supply by the dealer such as leasing.

Article 11

1. The Commission will evaluate on a regular basis the application of this Regulation, particularly as regards the impact of the exempted system of distribution on price differentials of contract goods between the different Member States and on the quality of service to final users.

2. The Commission will collate the opinions of associations and experts representing the various interested parties, particularly consumer organisations.

3. The Commission will draw up a report on the evaluation of this Regulation on or before 31 December 2000, particularly taking into account the criteria provided for in paragraph 1.

Article 12

Regulation (EEC) No. 4087/88 is not applicable to agreements concerning the products or services referred to in this Regulation.

Article 13

This Regulation shall enter into force on 1 July 1995.

It shall apply from 1 October 1995 until 30 September 2002.

The provisions of Regulation (EEC) No. 123/85 shall continue to apply until 30 September 1995.

This Regulation shall be binding in its entirety and directly applicable in all Member States.

Done at Brussels, June 28, 1995.

COMMISSION EXPLANATORY BROCHURE ON THE DISTRIBUTION OF MOTOR VEHICLES*

REGARDING REGULATION 1475/95

CONTENTS

Foreword

In the Member States of the European Union, motor vehicle manufacturers distribute their products through selected dealer networks. The distribution agreements making up the networks contain provisions which restrict competition and which may affect trade between Member States. Therefore they fall within the scope of Article 81(1) of the EC Treaty.

The prohibition laid down in Article 81(1) of the EC Treaty may be declared inapplicable if the agreement as a whole brings about overall economic advantages which outweigh the disadvantages for competition. Exemptions may be granted on a case-by-case basis or

---

* Published on the DG Comp website at, http://europa.eu.int/comm/competition/car_sector/ distribution/.

by regulation for certain category of agreements. Commission Regulation (EEC) No. 123/85, which contained such a group exemption, expired on 30 June 1995 and has been replaced by Commission Regulation (EC) No. 1475/95 on the application of Article 81(3) of the Treaty to certain categories of motor vehicle distribution and servicing agreements.[1] The Commission adopted this Regulation on 28 June 1995.

The Regulation contains several adjustments to stimulate competition in the car sector, to improve the functioning of a single market in cars and to re-balance the diverse interests in question. These adjustments aim in particular to:

— give dealers, the great majority of whom are small or medium sized enterprises, greater commercial independence *vis–à–vis* manufacturers;
— give independent spare-part manufacturers and distributors easier access to the various markets, notably the outlets provided by the car manufacturers' networks;
— improve the position of consumers in accordance with the principles underlying the internal market;
— make the dividing line between acceptable and unacceptable agreements and behaviour clearer.

As these changes are important for the distribution and servicing of vehicles, this brochure is intended as a legally non binding guide to the Regulation which is aimed particularly at distributors and consumers. It is not a detailed commentary on each provision of the Regulation. Its objective is to give answers to questions which are likely to arise in practice while applying the new regulatory framework for manufacturers, dealers, spare part producers and independent repairers. Moreover, it is intended to provide consumers with information as to how the Regulation guarantees the freedom to buy a car anywhere in the Community in accordance with the principles of the single market.

I. CLARIFICATION OF THE SCOPE OF EXEMPTION:

1. Scope of the Regulation

[Article 1]

Pursuant to Article 81(3) of the Treaty it is hereby declared that subject to the conditions laid down in this Regulation Article 81(1) shall not apply to agreements to which only two undertakings are party and in which one contracting party agrees to supply, within a defined territory of the common market.

— only to the other party, or
— only to the other party and to a specified number of other undertakings within the distribution system.

for the purpose of resale, certain new motor vehicles intended for use on public roads and having three or more road wheels, together with spare parts therefor.

Question 1:   Does the Regulation apply to the distribution and servicing of all kinds of motor vehicles? Does the Regulation apply to the separate distribution of vehicle spare parts?

The Regulation applies to the distribution of motor vehicles which (1) are new and (2) intended for use on public roads and (3) have three or more road wheels [Article 1].

---

[1] OJ 1996 L145/25. [App. 16]

Used motor vehicles are not subject to the Regulation. The dividing line between new and used motor vehicles has to be drawn in accordance with commercial usage in a manner which prevents any circumvention of the Regulation.

Agricultural vehicles such as tractors are not subject to the Regulation, as their main use is not on public roads.

The Regulation does not apply to the distribution and servicing of motorbikes.

The separate distribution of automotive replacement parts without any connection to the distribution of vehicles is not covered either.

2. "Black List" Clauses and Practices

[Article 6]

1. The exemption shall not apply where:

(1) both parties to the agreement or their connected undertakings are motor vehicle manufacturers; or

(2) the parties link their agreement to stipulations concerning products or services other than those referred to in this Regulation or apply their agreement to such products or services; or

(3) in respect of motor vehicles having three or more road wheels, spare parts or services therefor, the parties agree restrictions of competition that are not expressly exempted by this Regulation; or

(4) in respect of motor vehicles having three or more road wheels or spare parts therefor, the parties make agreements or engage in concerted practices which are exempted from the prohibition in Article 81(1) of the Treaty under Regulations (EEC) No. 1983/83 or (EEC) No. 1984/83 to an extent exceeding the scope of this Regulation; or

(5) the parties agree that the supplier reserves the right to conclude distribution and servicing agreements for contract goods with specified further undertakings operating within the contract territory, or to alter the contract territory; or

(6) the manufacturer, the supplier or another undertaking directly or indirectly restricts the dealer's freedom to determine prices and discounts in reselling contract goods or corresponding goods; or

(7) the manufacturer, the supplier or another undertaking within the network directly or indirectly restricts the freedom of final consumers, authorised intermediaries or dealers to obtain from an undertaking belonging to the network of their choice within the common market contract goods or corresponding goods or to obtain servicing for such goods, or the freedom of final consumers to resell the contract goods or corresponding goods, when the sale is not effected for commercial purposes; or

(8) the supplier, without any objective reason, grants dealers remunerations calculated on the basis of the place of destination of the motor vehicles resold or the place of residence of the purchaser; or

(9) the supplier directly or indirectly restricts the dealer's freedom under Article 3(5) to obtain from a third undertaking of this choice spare parts which compete with contract goods and which match their quality; or

(10) the manufacturer directly or indirectly restricts the freedom of suppliers of spare-parts to supply such products to resellers of their choice, including those which are undertakings within the distribution system, provided that such parts match the quality of contract goods; or

(11) the manufacturer directly or indirectly restricts the freedom of spare-part manufacturers to place effectively and in an easily visible manner their trade mark or logo on parts supplied for the initial assembly or for the repair or maintenance of contract goods or corresponding goods; or

(12) the manufacturer refuses to make accessible, where appropriate upon payment, to repairers who are not undertakings within the distribution system, the technical

information required for the repair or maintenance of the contractual or correspond-ing goods or for the implementing of environmental protection measures, provided that the information is not covered by an intellectual property right or does not constitute identified, substantial, secret know-how; in such case, the necessary techni-cal information shall not be withheld improperly.

2. Without prejudice to the consequences for the other provisions of the agreement, in the cases specified in paragraph 1(1) to (5), the inapplicability of the exemption shall apply to all the clauses restrictive of competition contained in the agreement concerned; in the cases specified in paragraph 1(6) to (12), it shall apply only to the clauses restrictive of competition agreed respectively on behalf of the manufacturer, the supplier or another undertaking within the network which is engaged in the practice complained of.

3. Without prejudice to the consequences for the other provisions of the agreement, in the cases specified in paragraph 1(6) to (12), the inapplicability of the exemption shall only apply to the clauses restrictive of competition agreed in favour of the manufacturer, the supplier or another undertaking within the network which appear in the distribution and servicing agreements concluded for a geographic area within the common market in which the objectionable practice distorts competition, and only for the duration of the practice complained of.

Question 2: Are there any clauses and/or practices which, under this Regulation, may not be included in exclusive and selective distribution agreements?

(a) The Regulation includes in Article 6(1)(1) to (5) a list of *clauses* which should not be used in an agreement for the distribution of cars ("black clauses") and which render the Regulation inapplicable, namely leading to an automatic loss of the benefit of the group exemption, if incorporated into exclusive and selective distribution agreements.

The group exemption does not apply:

— if the two parties to an agreement are both motor vehicle manufacturers[2] [Article 6(1)(1)];
— if the obligations in the agreement are extended to products and services other than motor vehicles and spare parts [Article 6(1)(2)];
— if the agreement contains obligations in favour of the manufacturer or the dealer which are more far-reaching than permitted under the Regulation [Article 6(1)(3)];
— if the parties agree between themselves obligations which would be acceptable under Commission Regulation (EEC) No. 1983/83[3] concerning exclusive distribu-tion agreements or under Commission Regulation (EEC) No. 1984/83[4] concerning exclusive purchasing agreements but which go further than is permitted by this Regulation [Article 6(1)(4)];
— If the manufacturer or supplier is given in the agreement the unilateral right to alter the contract territory during the period of the agreement, or to conclude distribution and service agreements with other companies in the contract territory [Article 6(1)(5)].

(b) Furthermore, the list contains "black practices" which also lead to the automatic loss of the exemption, if committed systematically or repeatedly [Article 6(1)(6) to (12), Recital 20].

"Repeatedly" means that the practice must have been committed several times. An isolated practice is sufficient only where it is part of a plan, in which case it is considered to be committed "systematically".

---

[2] A reference to manufacturer includes, where appropriate, a reference to supplier.
[3] OJ 1983 L173/1.
[4] OJ 1983 L173/5.

"Black practices" are:

— where the manufacturer, the supplier or another undertaking within the network fixes the resale price for vehicles, spare parts or other contract goods and corresponding goods [Article 6(1)(6)];
— where the manufacturer, the supplier or another undertaking within the network directly or indirectly impedes final consumers, their intermediaries or authorised dealers from buying a vehicle where they consider it to be most advantageous [Article 6(1)(7)];
— where the manufacturer or the supplier, without objective reasons, makes the remuneration of a dealer dependent on the destination of sale [Article 6(1)(8)];
— where the manufacturer or the supplier directly or indirectly interferes with its dealer(s) buying spare parts of equal quality from a spare part supplier of his choice [Article 6(1)(9)];
— where the manufacturer or the supplier directly or indirectly interferes with sales by a spare-part supplier although the spare part supplier offers spare-parts of equal quality to those bought by the manufacturer [Article 6(1)(10)];
— where the manufacturer directly or indirectly hinders spare-part manufacturers from affixing their trade mark or logo on spare parts bought by the manufacturer or supplied to the network [Article 6(1)(11)];
— where the manufacturer does not pass on technical information necessary for the maintenance of its vehicles to independent repairers without objectively justified reasons for this refusal [Article 6(1)(12)].

The content of the "Black List" clauses and practices are further explained below in the context of the rights of dealers (Chapter II), spare-part producers and resellers (Chapter III) and consumers (Chapter IV).

Question 3:   What does the automatic loss of the benefit of the exemption mean for the distribution system?

The legal consequences differ depending on whether the inapplicability of the group exemption is due to the incorporation of "black clauses" in the exclusive and selective distribution agreement or whether this is due to a "black practice".

(a) "Black clauses" [Article 6(1)(1) to (5)]:

If the parties agree to include a prohibited clause in their distribution agreement, the group exemption is inapplicable not only with regard to the prohibited clause(s) but with regard to all other restrictions of competition which are included in the agreement concerned. Therefore, the restrictive provisions in the distribution agreement, which would normally be allowed by Articles 1 to 4 of the Regulation, are no longer exempted. It makes no difference whether such restrictions are in favour of the manufacturer or of the dealer.

As the Regulation does not then apply to exempt these restrictive clauses, they are prohibited by EC Competition Law (Article 81(1) of the Treaty) and are null and void from the date of the agreement. In addition, the Commission is entitled to fine the parties to the agreement [Article 15(2)(a) of Council Regulation No 17/62].

The parties may notify an exclusive and selective distribution agreement containing "black clauses" to receive individual exemption. Such individual exemption will only be justifiable in an exceptional situation relating to the specific circumstances of an individual case. A notification provides immunity from fines unless and until the Commission informs the undertakings concerned that after preliminary examination it considers that Article 81(1) of the Treaty applies and that application of Article 81(3) is not justified [Article 15(6) of Council Regulation No. 17/62] and adopts a decision lifting immunity from fines.

The Regulation does not say whether the non-restrictive clauses in the exclusive and selective distribution agreement remain valid in such a situation. This is, in principle, a question of national law, and therefore for the competent national court to decide.

(b) "Black practices" [Article 6(1)(6) to (12)]:

These are mostly actions on the part of a manufacturer, importer or authorised dealer, and have consequences only for the company engaged in the practice [Article 6(2)].

In cases of "black practices", all clauses in an exclusive and selective distribution agreement which are restrictive of competition and which benefit the company responsible are no longer covered by the group exemption. The consequences of the misconduct are limited to the contract territory where the distortion of competition takes place. However, if competition is distorted in a larger area, the exemption is no longer applicable for all the distribution contracts concluded for this area. The benefit of the exemption is only lost for so long as the objectionable conduct lasts.

This means, in practice, that if the manufacturer or importer is responsible, the authorised dealers are released from any obligation which has been imposed on them in favour of the manufacturer/importer under the agreement.

Moreover, even where "black practices" are imposed, *e.g.* by the manufacturer, but accepted by the dealer because he complies with them, such behaviour is considered a concerted practice and prohibited (Article 81(1) of the Treaty). As in the case of the "black clauses" (see above), the Commission can fine the parties to the agreement [Article 15(2)(a) of Council Regulation No 17/62].

(c) National courts in Member States which find "black clauses" and "black practices" which infringe EC competition law (Article 81(1) of the Treaty) can—as well as finding that the agreement or parts of it are prohibited and void—grant injunctions and award damages.

3. Withdrawal of the Benefit of the Exemption

[Article 8]

The Commission may withdraw the benefit of the application of this Regulation, pursuant to Article 7 of Regulation No 19/65/EEC, where it finds that in an individual case an agreement which falls within the scope of this Regulation nevertheless has effects which are incompatible with the provisions of Article 81(3) of the Treaty, and in particular:

(1) where, in the common market or a substantial part thereof, contract goods or corresponding goods are not subject to competition from products considered by consumers as similar by reason of their characteristics, price and intended use;

(2) where prices or conditions of supply for contract goods or for corresponding goods are continually being applied which differ substantially as between Member States, such substantial differences being chiefly due to obligations exempted by this Regulation;

(3) where the manufacturer or an undertaking within the distribution system in supplying the distributors with contract goods or corresponding goods apply, unjustifiably, discriminatory prices or sales conditions.

Question 4: Are there any other circumstances in which an agreement may lose the benefit of the group exemption?

The Regulation lists in Article 8 examples of situations in which the Commission has the power to withdraw the benefit of the group exemption or to alter its scope in a particular case. In contrast to the effects of the Black List, in these cases the benefit of the exemption is not automatically lost but is subject to an official procedure by the Commission. The Commission may begin a procedure for withdrawal either upon complaint or on its own initiative.

Although the Commission may withdraw the benefit of the exemption for other reasons, the circumstances listed are those in which withdrawal is most likely. These are:

— where the contract goods are not subject to effective competition [Article 8(1)];
— where the distribution system leads over a considerable period to differentials in price and sales conditions between Member States [Article 8(2)];
— where the manufacturer or an undertaking within the distribution system applies, unjustifiably, discriminatory prices or sales conditions to its dealers [Article 8(3)].

The Commission has already published in connection with Regulation (EEC) No. 123/85 a Notice[5] which explains what are acceptable and unacceptable price differentials. This Commission Notice remains applicable under the new Regulation as well as the other Commission Notice concerning the clarification of the activities of motor vehicle intermediaries.[6]

4. Duration of the Regulation

[Article 7]

The prohibition laid down in Article 81(1) of the Treaty shall not apply during the period from 1 October 1995 to 30 September 1996 to agreements already in force on 1 October 1995 which satisfy the conditions for exemption provided for in Commission Regulation (EEC) No. 123/85.

[Article 13]

This Regulation shall enter into force on 1 July 1995.
It shall apply from 1 October 1995 until 30 September 2002.
The provisions of Regulation (EEC) No. 123/85 shall continue to apply until 30 September 1995.

Question 5: From what date does Regulation (EC) No. 1475/95 apply and when does it expire?

Regulation (EC) No. 1475/95 entered into force on 1 July 1995. It says that until 30 September 1995, the provisions of Regulation (EEC) No. 123/85 continue to apply [Article 13], in order to give the interested parties sufficient time to adapt their distribution systems to the changes brought about by the new Regulation.

A further transition period of one year is provided for exclusive and selective distribution agreements which are already in force on 1 October 1995 and which satisfy the conditions for exemption set by Regulation (EEC) No. 123/85 [Article 7]. Therefore, from 1 October 1996 onwards, all exclusive and selective distribution agreements which are to benefit from the group exemption have to comply with Regulation (EC) No. 1475/95.

Regulation (EC) No. 1475/95 will be in force for 7 years and expires on 30 September 2002.

II. STRENGTHENING THE COMPETITIVENESS OF DEALERS:

1. Multi-Dealerships

[Article 3]

The exemption shall also apply where the obligation referred to in Article 1 is combined with an obligation on the dealer:

---

[5] OJ 1985 C17/4.
[6] OJ 1991 C329/20.

. . .

3. not to sell new motor vehicles offered by persons other than the manufacturer except on separate sales premises, under separate management, in the form of a distinct legal entity and in a manner which avoids confusion between makes;

4. not to permit a third party to benefit unduly, through any after-sales service performed in a common workshop, from investments made by a supplier, notably in equipment or the training of personnel;

. . .

6. without the supplier's consent, neither to conclude distribution or servicing agreements with undertakings operating in the contract territory for contract goods or corresponding goods nor to alter or terminate such agreements; . . .

[Article 4]

1. The exemption shall apply notwithstanding any obligation whereby the dealer undertakes to:

(1) comply, in distribution, sales and after-sales servicing with minimum standards, regarding in particular;

(a) the equipment of the business premises and the technical facilities for servicing;
(b) the specialised technical training of staff;
(c) advertising;
(d) the collection, storage and delivery of contract goods or corresponding goods and sales and after-sales servicing;
(e) the repair and maintenance of contract goods and corresponding goods, particularly as regards the safe and reliable functioning of motor vehicles;

(2) order contract goods from the supplier only at certain times or within certain periods, provided that the interval between ordering dates does not exceed three months;

(3) endeavour to sell, within the contract territory and during a specified period, a minimum quantity of contract goods, determined by the parties by common agreement or, in the event of disagreement between the parties as to the minimum number of contractual goods to be sold annually, by an expert third party, account being taken in particular of sales previously achieved in the territory and of forecast sales for the territory and at national level;

(4) keep in stock such quantity of contract goods as may be determined in accordance with the procedure in (3);

(5) keep such demonstration vehicles within the contract range, or such number thereof, as may be determined in accordance with the procedure in (3);

(6) perform work under guarantee, free servicing and vehicle-recall work for contract goods and corresponding goods;

(7) use only spare parts within the contract range or corresponding spare parts for work under guarantee, free servicing and vehicle-recall work in respect of contract goods or corresponding goods;

(8) inform customers, in a general manner, of the extent to which spare parts from other sources might be used for the repair or maintenance of contract goods or corresponding goods;

(9) inform customers whenever spare parts from other sources have been used for the repair or maintenance of contract goods or corresponding goods. . . .

[Article 5]

1. In all cases, the exemption shall apply only if:

. . .

(2) the supplier:

(a) does not without objectively valid reasons withhold consent to conclude, alter or terminate sub-agreements referred to in Article 3(6);

. . .

2. Where the dealer has, in accordance with Article 4(1), assumed obligations for the improvement of distribution and servicing structures, the exemption shall apply provided that:

(1) the supplier releases the dealer from the obligations referred to in Article 3(3) where the dealer shows that there are objective reasons for doing so; . . .

[Article 6]

1. The exemption shall not apply where:

. . .

(2) the parties link their agreement to stipulations concerning products or services other than those referred to in this Regulation or apply their agreement to such products or services; or

(3) in respect of motor vehicles having three or more road wheels, spare parts or services therefor, the parties agree restrictions of competition that are not expressly exempted by this Regulation; or . . .

Question 6: Can a dealer sell more than one make of motor vehicle from the same sales premises?

If a manufacturer wishes to benefit from the group exemption, its dealers must be given the right to sell competing makes.

The Regulation, however, allows the manufacturer to oblige the dealer to have (1) separate sales premises (2) under separate management (3) in the form of a distinct legal entity and (4) in a manner which avoids confusion between makes [see Article 3(3), Recital 7].

"Separate sales premises" may be located in the same building.

"Separate management" means in principle keeping separate records, accounts and sales forces.

The third condition, "in the form of a distinct legal entity", makes it clear that for each dealership a company has to be set up. It is the national law of the Member State in question which defines the requirements for the legal structure of such a company.

"In a manner which avoids confusion between makes" means, for example, that promotional literature on one make of vehicle should be kept separate from literature on the other. The attire of sales personnel should also respect this condition since the fixing of several manufacturers trademarks might cause confusion for consumers.

Question 7: Can the manufacturer always impose on the dealer the four obligations designed to maintain the separation of makes?

No, if the manufacturer has obliged the dealer to comply with minimum standards for the improvement of distribution and servicing structures (*e.g.* the collection, storage and delivery of contract goods or corresponding goods and sales and after sales servicing [described in Article 4(1)]), he must release the dealer from obligations relating to the separating of makes (see Question 6), provided that the dealer shows that there are objective reasons for so doing [Article 5(2)(1)].

It will depend on the facts of the case whether the manufacturer must release the dealer from all four obligations or only from those which have a detrimental effect on the dealer's business in that particular case.

An objective reason will be considered to exist if the obligations designed to maintain the separation of makes turn out to be excessive in a particular case [Recital 18]. One example of an objective reason is where the obligation(s) prevent the dealer from operating on an economically viable basis.

Question 8: Can a manufacturer discourage the development of "multi-brand" dealerships?

The Regulation's main objective is to open markets in terms of geography, products and competitors. This is why the Regulation permits multimarketing dealerships in general and leaves it in the sole discretion of the dealer to decide whether he wants to sell a second make. The dealer's freedom to take an autonomous economic decision may not be restricted directly or indirectly by the manufacturer. Measures aimed at stipulating "one brand" dealerships by a manufacturer, *i.e.* by way of rebate systems which accord higher rebates to the dealer if he maintains an exclusive dealership, would be considered as a restriction of competition that is not expressly exempted by the Regulation [Article 6(1)(3)], leading to an automatic loss of the benefit of the exemption.

Question 9: Is a dealer entitled to repair different makes in one workshop?

Yes. The manufacturer may not ask his dealers to instal separate workshops [Article 3(4)].

On the other hand, he may ask his dealers not to permit a third party to benefit unduly from the investments made by him, for example where the manufacturer has borne the costs of purchasing technical equipment used in the dealer's workshop. The manufacturer may require that this equipment may not be used to repair vehicles of another make. However, the financing of the equipment by the manufacturer may not be imposed.

The requirement may be more difficult to fulfil with regard to training of personnel. In this respect "unduly" means that a dealer has to make sure that knowledge obtained from the manufacturer which is not simply useful for repair work but which imparts additional qualifications in the form of specific know-how to the personnel may not be used for other makes. This may lead in practice to the result that a dealer may have to nominate the personnel working for a specific make.

Question 10: Can a dealer participate in the distribution of competing makes through investment in other undertakings?

Dealers are free, even within the contract territory, to own or invest in companies which belong to the networks of competing manufacturers.

Question 11: Can a dealer appoint subagents?

Yes, but subject to the manufacturer's prior consent. The manufacturer can only refuse its consent if it gives objectively valid reasons which should be applied without discrimination, and in an equitable and reasonable manner [Articles 3(6) and 5(1)(2)(a)].

Question 12: Can a manufacturer oblige its dealers to cooperate with specific finance institutions or insurance companies?

The Regulation does not allow such a clause in the agreement. Bank or insurance services are not among the products and services dealt with in the Regulation. Under Article 6(1)(2), the exemption does not apply in such a case.

2. Quantitative Purchasing Targets

[Article 4]

1. The exemption shall apply notwithstanding any obligation whereby the dealer undertakes to:

. . .

(3) endeavour to sell, within the contract territory and during a specified period, a minimum quantity of contract goods, determined by the parties by common agreement or, in the event of disagreement between the parties as to the minimum number of contractual goods to be sold annually, by an expert third party, account being taken in particular of sales previously achieved in the territory and of forecast sales for the territory and at national level;

(4) keep in stock such quantity of contract goods as may be determined in accordance with the procedure in (3);

(5) keep such demonstration vehicles within the contract range, or such number thereof, as may be determined in accordance with the procedure in (3); . . .

[Article 3]

The exemption shall also apply where the obligation referred to in Article 1 is combined with an obligation on the dealer:

. . .

10. not to supply to a reseller:

(a) contract goods or corresponding goods unless the reseller is an undertaking within the distribution system, or . . .

[Article 6]

1. The exemption shall not apply where:

. . .

(3) in respect of motor vehicles having three or more road wheels, spare parts or services therefor, the parties agree restrictions of competition that are not expressly exempted by this Regulation; or . . .

Question 13: Can the dealer have sales targets and stock requirements imposed by the manufacturer?

Sales targets and stock requirements can only be set by agreement between the manufacturer and dealer. Neither party to the agreement is given the final say. In the event of disagreement between the parties on the annual agreement of these quantities, the matter must be referred to an expert third party [Article 4(1) points 3, 4, and 5; Questions 17 to 19] or to a national court.

The Regulation starts with the assumption that the parties normally agree on an annual basis the minimum number of sales, stock and demonstration vehicles. Minimum requirements agreed for a shorter period may only be of an indicative nature. If they are made binding, this may result in an automatic loss of the benefit of the group exemption [Article 6(1)(3)]. This means that the dealer is free from the obligation to endeavour to sell the agreed minimum quantity of contract goods within that shorter period.

Question 14: Is there a general right for a dealer within the distribution network to obtain new motor vehicles in other parts of the Common Market?

An authorised dealer may not be prevented from selling to or purchasing from another authorised dealer within the Community. The Regulation only permits the manufacturer to impose on its dealers the obligation not to sell to a reseller who does not belong to its distribution system [Article 3(10)(a)]. The dealer may not be obliged to purchase only from the manufacturer. If the distribution agreement contains an obligation of the dealer to purchase only from the manufacturer, such obligation would be a "black clause" and the exemption would not apply [Article 6(1)(3)].

3. Duration and Termination of the Agreement

[Article 5]

. . .

2. Where the dealer has, in accordance with Article 4(1), assumed obligations for the improvement of distribution and servicing structures, the exemption shall apply provided that:

. . .

(2) the agreement is for a period of at least five years or, if for an indefinite period, the period of notice for regular termination of the agreement is at least two years for both parties; this period is reduced to at least one year where:

— the supplier is obliged by law or by special agreement to pay appropriate compensation on termination of the agreement, or
— the dealer is a new entrant to the distribution system and the period of the agreement, or the period of notice for regular termination of the agreement, is the first agreed by that dealer;

(3) each party undertakes to give the other at least six months' prior notice of intention not to renew an agreement concluded for a definite period.
3. The conditions for exemption laid down in (1) and (2) shall not affect;

— the right of the supplier to terminate the agreement subject to at least one year's notice in a case where it is necessary to reorganise the whole or a substantial part of the network,
— the right of one party to terminate the agreement for cause where the other party fails to perform one of its basic obligations.

In each case, the parties must, in the event of disagreement, accept a system for the quick resolution of the dispute, such as recourse to an expert third party or an arbitrator, without prejudice to the parties' right to apply to a competent court in conformity with the provisions of national law.

[Article 6]

1. The exemption shall not apply where:
. . .

(5) the parties agree that the supplier reserves the right to conclude distribution and servicing agreements for contract goods with specified further undertakings operating within the contract territory, or to alter the contract territory; or . . .

Question 15: What is the minimum duration of the agreement and the period of notice for termination?

The parties may conclude an agreement for a definite period, or for an indefinite period [Article 5(2)].
If the parties choose the former, then they have to agree on a minimum duration of five years. There must also be a clause that in case one party does not want to renew the

agreement, this party has to inform the other of its intention at least six months before the agreement is due to expire [Article 5(2)(3)]. If the parties conclude the agreement for an indefinite period, then they are deemed to agree on a two year period of notice for termination. Agreements can be terminated on one year's notice if the manufacturer undertakes to pay damages [Article 5(2)(2) first indent] or if the agreement is concluded with a newcomer to the network [Article 5(2)(2) second indent].

Question 16: Are there any possibilities for early termination of the agreement?

The Regulation introduces the possibility of early termination in two cases:

(a) The manufacturer has the right to terminate the agreement early (on one year's notice) where it needs to restructure the whole or a substantial part of the network. Whether it is necessary to reorganise is established between the parties by agreement or at the dealer's request by an expert third party or an arbitrator. Recourse to an expert third party or an arbitrator does not affect the right of either party to apply to a national court under national law [Article 5(3)]. Where the supplier provides for himself in the contract unilateral rights of termination exceeding the limits set by the Regulation, he automatically loses the benefit of the group exemption [Article 6(1)(5); see above I.2.].

This possibility for early termination has been introduced to provide the manu- facturer with an instrument for flexible adaptation to changes in distribution struc- tures [Recital 19]. A need for reorganising may arise due to the behaviour of competitors or due to other economic developments, irrespective of whether these are motivated by internal decisions of a manufacturer or external influences, *e.g.* the closure of a company employing a large workforce in a specific area. In view of the wide variety of situations which may arise, it would be unrealistic to list all the possible reasons.

Whether or not a "substantial part" of the network is affected, must be decided in the light of the specific organisation of a manufacturer's network in each case. "Substantial" implies both an economic and a geographical aspect, which may be limited to the network, or a part of it, in a given Member State. The manufacturer has to reach an agreement—either with or without the intermediation of an expert third party or arbitrator—with the dealer, whose distribution agreement will be terminated, but not with other dealers (who are only indirectly affected by an early termina- tion).

(b) Both parties to the agreement have the right to terminate the agreement at any time without notice, where the other party fails to perform one of its basic obligations. Again, the parties must establish whether the reason for early termination is suffi- cient, by common accord or, in case of disagreement, by recourse to an expert third party or an arbitrator and/or by application to a competent court in conformity with the provisions of national law [Article 5(3)]. One reason for early termination might be where a party infringes contractual obligations allowed under Articles 1 to 4 of the Regulation.

4. Recourse to Expert Third Party or Arbitrator

[Article 4]

1. The exemption shall apply notwithstanding any obligation whereby the dealer undertakes to:
. . .
(3) endeavour to sell, within the contract territory and during a specified period, a minimum quantity of contract goods, determined by the parties by common agreement or, in the event of disagreement between the parties as to the minimum number of contractual

goods to be sold annually, by an expert third party, account being taken in particular of sales previously achieved in the territory and of forecast sales for the territory and at national level;

(4) keep in stock such quantity of contract goods as may be determined in accordance with the procedure in (3);

(5) keep such demonstration vehicles within the contract range, or such number thereof, as may be determined in accordance with the procedure in (3); ...

[Article 5]

3. The conditions for exemption laid down in (1) and (2) shall not affect;

— the right of the supplier to terminate the agreement subject to at least one year's notice in a case where it is necessary to reorganise the whole or a substantial part of the network.
— the right of one party to terminate the agreement for cause where the other party fails to perform one of its basic obligations.

In each case, the parties, in the event of disagreement, accept a system for the quick resolution of the dispute, such as recourse to an expert third party or an arbitrator, without prejudice to the parties' right to apply to a competent court in conformity with the provisions of national law.

Question 17: In what circumstances does the Regulation call upon the manufacturer and dealer, in the event of disagreement between them, to refer to an expert third party or an arbitrator?

The Regulation says that the manufacturer and dealer should refer to an expert third party when they disagree with regard to the annual setting of (1) sales targets [Article 4(1)(3)]; (2) stock requirements [Article 4(1)(4)] and (3) the keeping of demonstration vehicles [Article 4(1)(5)].

Recourse to an expert third party or an arbitrator is provided for in the case of early termination of the agreement. The Regulation leaves the parties free to decide whether they wish to refer to an expert third party or to an arbitrator [Article 5(3)].

However, the parties are not restricted to the use of an expert third party or an arbitrator only in these cases. They can adopt such procedures in other cases of dispute if they both agree so to do.

Question 18: How will the right to apply to a competent court interact with recourse to an expert third party or arbitrator?

The Regulation says that to resolve disputes, to establish a quick and efficient system of settlement, the parties must first go to an expert or an arbitrator. However, this obligation is without prejudice to the parties' right to apply to a competent national court to the extent this is allowed under national law.

Question 19: Who can act as an expert third party or an arbitrator and how should an expert third party or arbitrator be nominated?

Any person, accepted by both parties as being qualified to act in such a capacity, may be appointed as expert third party or arbitrator.

The parties are free to decide, should the situation arise, whom they wish to nominate and whether they prefer to appoint one, two, three or more people to be the expert(s) or arbitrator(s). However, no party is allowed to decide unilaterally who will be the expert or arbitrator. In the event of disagreement the parties shall adopt the nomination procedures which are normally used in such cases, *e.g.* nomination by the president of the court of first instance, by the president of the chambers for commerce and industry. It seems advisable that the contract between the manufacturer and dealer should specify what kind of nomination procedure they wish to use should the situation arise.

5. Direct Sales

[Article 2]

The exemption shall also apply where the obligation referred to in Article 1 is combined with an obligation on the supplier neither to sell contract goods to final consumers nor to provide them with servicing for contract goods in the contract territory.

Question 20: May the manufacturer reserve the right to make direct sales to final consumers?

Article 2 of the Regulation exempts an obligation on the manufacturer neither to sell contract goods to final consumers nor to provide them with servicing for contract goods in the contract territory. It follows from this provision that in the absence of such a contractual obligation, the manufacturer is free to supply final consumers in the contract territory. On the other hand, it is clear that customer restrictions may not be imposed on the dealer and that they lead to the automatic loss of the benefit of the group exemption. Therefore, the manufacturer may not prevent the dealer from supplying those final consumers whom the manufacturer himself wishes to supply.

Moreover, the manufacturer should take care not to affect by such behaviour the economic viability of the dealer's business because, in such a case, the basis of the agreement itself may be destroyed. It is for a national court to solve any dispute.

III. IMPROVED MARKET ACCESS FOR SPARE PART PRODUCERS/DISTRIBUTORS AND FOR INDEPENDENT REPAIRERS:

1. Spare Parts

[Article 3]

The exemption shall also apply where the obligation referred to in Article 1 is combined with an obligation on the dealer:

. . .

5. neither to sell spare parts which compete with contract goods without matching them in quality nor to use them for repair or maintenance of contract goods or corresponding goods;

. . .

10. not to supply to a reseller:

(a) contract goods or corresponding goods unless the reseller is an undertaking within the distribution system, or
(b) spare parts within the contract range unless the reseller uses them for the repair or maintenance of a motor vehicle; . . .

[Article 4]

1. The exemption shall apply notwithstanding any obligation whereby the dealer undertakes to

. . .

(7) use only spare parts within the contract range or corresponding spare parts for work under guarantee, free servicing and vehicle-recall work in respect of contract goods or corresponding goods;

(8) inform customers, in a general manner, of the extent to which spare parts from other sources might be used for the repair or maintenance of contract goods or corresponding goods;

(9) inform customers whenever spare parts from other sources have been used for the repair or maintenance of contract goods or corresponding goods. . . .

[Article 5]

1. In all cases, the exemption shall apply only if:

(c) distinguishes, in any scheme for aggregating quantities or values of goods obtained by the dealer from the supplier and from connected undertakings within a specified period for the purpose of calculating discounts, at least between supplies of
— motor vehicles within the contract range,
— spare parts within the contract range, for supplies of which the dealer is dependent on undertakings within the distribution network, and
— other goods; . . .

[Article 6]

1. The exemption shall not apply where:
. . .

(2) the parties link their agreement to stipulations concerning products or services other than those referred to in this Regulation or apply their agreement to such products or services; or
. . .

(9) the supplier directly or indirectly restricts the dealer's freedom under Article 3(5) to obtain from a third undertaking of his choice spare parts which compete with contract goods and which match their quality; or

(10) the manufacturer directly or indirectly restricts the freedom of suppliers of spare-parts to supply such products to resellers of their choice, including those which are undertakings within the distribution system, provided that such parts match the quality of contract goods; or

(11) the manufacturer directly or indirectly restricts the freedom of spare-part manufacturers to place effectively and in an easily visible manner their trade mark or logo on parts supplied for the initial assembly or for the repair or maintenance of contract goods or corresponding goods; or . . .

[Article 10]

For the purposes of this Regulation the following terms shall have the following meanings:
. . .

4. "contract goods" are new motor vehicles intended for use on public roads and having three or more road wheels, and spare parts therefor, which are the subject of an agreement within the meaning of Article 1;

5. the "contract range" refers to the totality of the contract goods;

6. "spare parts" are parts which are to be installed in or upon a motor vehicle so as to replace components of that vehicle. They are to be distinguished from other parts and accessories, according to trade usage;

. . .

11. "corresponding goods", "corresponding motor vehicles" and "corresponding parts" are those which are similar in kind to those in the contract range, are distributed by the manufacturer or with the manufacturer's consent, and are the subject of a distribution or servicing agreement with an undertaking within the distribution system; . . .

Question 21: Do all vehicle parts and accessories fall under the term "spare parts" as used in the Regulation?

No, only parts which are to be installed in or upon a motor vehicle so as to replace components of that vehicle are spare parts within the meaning of the Regulation. The distinction follows trade usage [Article 10(6)]. For example: oil and other liquids are not considered as "spare parts" under the Regulation. Consequently, dealers are free to get those products wherever they wish and the manufacturer cannot justify restrictions imposed on its dealers with regard to the sourcing of such parts and accessories through reference to the Regulation. Nor is it possible for the parties to include parts and accessories, which fall outside the definition of "spare part", within the scope of the Regulation by agreement. If they do so, they will automatically lose the benefit of the group exemption [Article 6(1)(2)].

Question 22: What control can be exercised by a manufacturer over the sourcing of spare parts for use in the normal repair and maintenance of contract vehicles?

So as to ensure effective competition on the maintenance and repair markets, the Regulation starts from the assumption that dealers must be free to out-source spare parts, as this is in the interest of consumers. Nevertheless, the Regulation enables the manufacturer to verify the quality of spare parts, as this is important with regard to safety and consumer satisfaction.

This is why the manufacturer may impose on its dealers the obligation neither to sell spare parts which compete with contract goods without matching them in quality nor to use parts of lower quality for repair or maintenance of contract goods or corresponding goods [Article 3(5)]. This means that dealers are free to out-source spare parts (1) if the parts do not compete with those promoted by the manufacturer or (2) if the parts compete with contract goods but they match the quality of those products.

However, the manufacturer can require its dealers to inform customers about the use of spare parts from other sources in repair and maintenance work, first in a general manner before repair work has been undertaken [Article 4(1)(8)] and second, after the completion of the repair work where out-sourced spare parts have been used, as to their specific use [Article 4(1)(9)].

Question 23: What is meant by "matching" the quality of the spare parts sourced by the manufacturer? How will the matching quality of spare parts furnished by independent suppliers be controlled?

Recital (8) of the Regulation says that it can be presumed that all parts coming from the same source of production, regardless of whether supplied to the car manufacturer or to a dealer belonging to the network, are identical in characteristics and origin. If the dealer wishes to be certain that the parts offered to him correspond to those supplied to the manufacturer of the vehicle, he should ask the spare parts supplier for confirmation.

Where such parts have not been supplied to the car manufacturer, the question of equivalence in quality must be solved according to the general rules of national law.

Question 24: Do the same rules apply to the use of spare parts in guarantee work?

No, the manufacturer may oblige its dealers to use only its spare parts (*i.e.* those within the contract range or corresponding spare parts) for work under guarantee, free servicing and vehicle-recall work [Article 4(1)(7)].

Spare parts within the contract range or corresponding spare parts are either sourced and distributed by the manufacturer to its dealers [Article 10(4) and (5)] or sold by another undertaking to the authorised dealers with the manufacturer's consent. In the latter case, such spare parts must additionally be the subject of a distribution or servicing agreement between an authorised dealer and the manufacturer or between the manufacturer and a spare-part supplier [Article 10(11)].

Question 25: Why must a manufacturer, in aggregating quantities or values of goods for the purpose of calculating discounts to be granted to a dealer, differentiate between discounts given for motor vehicles within the contract range and for spare parts and for other goods?

The purpose is to avoid dealers having to rely solely on the manufacturer's supply because of special discounts given by him, thus closing the distribution system to independent spare-part suppliers [Article 5(1)(2)(c)].

Therefore, the Regulation imposes the obligation on the manufacturer to differentiate between discounts given to the dealer (1) for the ordering of motor vehicles, (2) for the ordering of spare parts for supplies of which the dealer is dependent on undertakings within the distribution network, *e.g.* bodywork spare-parts and (3) other spare-parts which are used for the normal maintenance of a vehicle and which are equally available outside the distribution network. If these three "baskets" are not kept separate for the accounting of discounts, it could lead to the result that a dealer receives such a high discount from the manufacturer because of the high amount of goods purchased, that no other spare-part manufacturer or supplier could make a competitive price.

Question 26: What are the legal consequences if a manufacturer tries to hinder dealers from purchasing spare parts from competing producers which are of matching quality?

The manufacturer loses the benefit of the exemption, if, directly or indirectly, he restricts the freedom of authorised distributors to purchase from third parties spare parts which match the quality of the contract products [Article 6(1)(9)].

Question 27: What rights are protected by the Regulation on independent suppliers of spare parts and on resellers?

The Regulation opens the market for independent suppliers of spare parts (described above) and resellers. The supply of contract goods [Article 10(4)] to resellers may not be prohibited where they belong to the same distribution system [Article 3(10)(a)], or where the purchase of spare parts is for their own use in effecting repairs or maintenance [Article 3(10)(b)].

These rights of suppliers of spare parts and resellers are safeguarded by the Black List. The manufacturer will automatically lose the benefit of the group exemption, if he directly or indirectly restricts:

— the freedom of spare-part suppliers to supply such products of matching quality to resellers of their choice, including those which are undertakings within the distribution system [Article 6(1)(10)];

— the spare-part manufacturers are hindered from affixing effectively and in an easily visible manner their trade mark or logo on the spare parts bought by the manufacturer or supplied to the network [Article 6(1)(11)].

2. Technical Information

[Article 6]

1. The exemption shall not apply where:
. . .

(12) the manufacturer refuses to make accessible, where appropriate upon payment, to repairers who are not undertakings within the distribution system, the technical information required for the repair or maintenance of the contractual or corresponding goods or for the implementing of environmental protection measures, provided that the information is not covered by an intellectual property right or does not constitute identified, substantial, secret know-how; in such case, the necessary technical information shall not be withheld improperly . . .

Question 28: To what degree is the manufacturer obliged under the Regulation to provide access for independent repairers to technical information required for the repair or maintenance of vehicles produced by the manufacturer?

Independent garage owners are often unable to provide repair services because the manufacturer makes the relevant technical knowledge available only to firms which are network members. The consumer is thus deprived of a considerable part of his freedom of choice for the maintenance and repair of his car.

The Regulation takes account of this problem by imposing the obligation on manufacturers to make accessible to non-network firms the technical information necessary for the repair and maintenance of their makes of motor vehicles, provided this information is not covered by the manufacturer's intellectual property rights or does not constitute identified, substantial and secret know-how. Even in such cases, the necessary technical information may not be withheld in a discriminatory or abusive manner [Article 6(1)(12), Recital 28].

However, the manufacturer may ask from the independent repairer payment for the supply of technical information. In such a case, the amount requested should be reasonable and neither discriminatory nor prohibitive.

The term "intellectual property right" includes rights such as patents, copyrights, registered designs and industrial and commercial property.

The wording "identified, substantial, secret know-how" is interpreted according to the definition given in Article 1(7)(1) to (4) of Regulation (EEC) No. 556/89[7] as amended by Commission Regulation (EEC) No 151/93.[8]

IV. INCREASING CONSUMERS' CHOICE IN ACCORDANCE WITH THE PRINCIPLES OF THE SINGLE MARKET:

1. Parallel Imports

[Article 3]

The exemption shall also apply where the obligation referred to in Article 1 is combined with an obligation on the dealer:

---

[7] OJ 1989 L61/1.
[8] OJ 1993 L21/8.

. . .

10 not to supply to a reseller:

(a) contract goods or corresponding goods unless the reseller is an undertaking within the distribution system, or
(b) spare parts within the contract range unless the reseller uses them for the repair or maintenance of a motor vehicle,

11. not to sell motor vehicles within the contract range or corresponding goods to final consumers using the services of an intermediary unless that intermediary has prior written authority from such consumers to purchase a specified motor vehicle or where it is taken away by him, to collect it.

[Article 5]

1. In all cases, the exemption shall apply only if:
(1) the dealer undertakes:

(a) in respect of motor vehicles within the contract range or corresponding thereto which have been supplied in the common market by another undertaking within the distribution network:
   — to honour guarantees and to perform free servicing and vehicle-recall work to an extent which corresponds to the dealer's obligation covered by Article 4(1)(6).
   — to carry out repair and maintenance work in accordance with Article 4(1)(1)(e);
(b) to impose upon the undertakings operating within the contract territory with which the dealer has concluded distribution and servicing agreements as provided for in Article 3(6) an obligation to honour guarantees and to perform free servicing and vehicle-recall work at least to the extent to which the dealer himself is so obliged: . . .

[Article 6]

1. The exemption shall not apply where:

(6) the manufacturer, the supplier or another undertaking directly or indirectly restricts the dealer's freedom to determine prices and discounts in reselling contract goods or corresponding goods; or
(7) the manufacturer, the supplier or another undertaking within the network directly or indirectly restricts the freedom of final consumers, authorised intermediaries or dealers to obtain from an undertaking belonging to the network of their choice within the common market contract goods or corresponding goods or to obtain servicing for such goods, or the freedom of final consumers to resell the contract goods or corresponding goods, when the sale is not effected for commercial purposes; or
(8) the supplier, without any objective reason, grants dealers remunerations calculated on the basis of the place of destination of the motor vehicles resold or the place of residence of the purchaser; or . . .

[Article 10]

For the purposes of this Regulation the following terms shall have the following meaning.

. . .

12. "resale" includes all transactions by which a physical or legal person—"the reseller"—disposes of a motor vehicle which is still in a new condition and which he had previously acquired in his own name and on his own behalf, irrespective of the legal description applied under civil law or the format of the transaction which effects such resale. The terms resale shall include all leasing contracts which provide for a transfer of ownerships or an option to purchase prior to the expiry of the contract; . . .

Question 29: Is a consumer, who is a resident of an E.U. Member State, free to buy a vehicle wherever he considers it to be most advantageous within the Common Market?

The consumer's freedom to buy anywhere in the Common Market is one of the fundamental achievements of the European Community and the Regulation reinforces this right. The consumer's right is not accompanied by an obligation imposed on dealers to sell since it is normally in a dealer's interest to maximise sales. A dealer within the Common Market may not reject a consumer's offer to buy or ask for a higher price simply because the consumer is a resident of another E.U. Member State.

The Regulation reinforces the right of a consumer resident in one Member State to buy a motor vehicle in another Member State:

— The consumer can be requested to complete only the same documentation and in the usual manner as is normally and lawfully required of a consumer resident in the Member State where the vehicle is bought. Usually such documentation relates to the name and address of the consumer.
— Under the Regulation the producer and all dealers should honour the guarantee and provide free servicing, vehicle recall work, and repair and maintenance services necessary for the safe and reliable functioning of the vehicle, irrespective of where and from whom in the Common Market the vehicle was purchased [Article 5(1)(1)(a) and (b) and Recital 26].
— The manufacturer, the supplier or another undertaking within the network who directly or indirectly restricts the freedom of final consumers, authorised inter-mediaries or authorised dealers to obtain a new motor vehicle from whichever authorised dealer they choose within the Common Market automatically loses the benefit of the exemption [Article 6(1)(7)].

Question 30: What formalities apply if a consumer appoints an intermediary to purchase a motor vehicle in another Member State on the consumer's behalf?

The intermediary must have prior authorisation in writing from the consumer to purchase and/or to collect a specified vehicle [Article 3(11)]. The Commission has already published under Regulation (EEC) No. 123/85 a Commission Notice,[9] which remains applicable.

The written authorisation must enable the dealer to identify the final consumer by name and address. The dealer may require such authorisation to include the name and address of the intermediary. Moreover, the authorisation has to specify the vehicle together with the essential details chosen by the consumer, such as make and model together with the signature of the consumer and the date of signing.

If an intermediary cannot show such authorisation the manufacturer may oblige his dealer(s) not to sell to him [Article 3(10)].

Question 31: Does the use of an intermediary alter the rights accorded to the consumer under the Regulation with regard to purchase or after-sales service?

The right of an authorised intermediary to purchase a motor vehicle on behalf of the final consumer in a Member State other than where the final consumer is resident is given

[9] OJ 1991 C329/20. (App. 19, *post*).

the same protection as the consumer's right to conclude personally such a transaction [see Article 6(1)(7)].

Question 32: Can a manufacturer stipulate the resale price charged by or discounts given by a dealer to a consumer?

Although it is true that a manufacturer may recommend prices, he may neither directly nor indirectly impose on the dealer fixed prices. Neither minimum and maximum resale prices may be fixed by the manufacturer. It is up to the dealer to decide his own policy on resale prices and discounts. If the manufacturer restricts the dealer's freedom with regard to resale prices and discounts, such behaviour will lead to the automatic loss of the exemption for the manufacturer [Article 6(1)(6)].

Question 33: Is the consumer restricted in disposing of the car?

The consumer is free to sell the motor vehicle at any time provided he is not a disguised independent reseller [Article 6(1)(7), Article 10(12)]. The manufacturer, importer or another undertaking within the distribution network may not impose an obligation on the final consumer to sell the vehicle only after a certain period of time and/or after a certain mileage reading.

Question 34: In what way(s) does the Regulation prevent a manufacturer from interfering with parallel imports/exports?

The scope of the rights of consumers, intermediaries and dealers to conduct parallel imports/exports has been discussed above. The manufacturer is, therefore, unable to interfere with these rights without losing the benefit of the exemption.

Additionally, a manufacturer cannot base the payment to a dealer (including rebate systems) on the destination of the vehicle being sold, without having objective reasons [Article 6(1)(8), Recital 26]. "Objective reasons" should be applied without discrimination, and in an equitable and reasonable manner. The manufacturer is, for example, not allowed to give greater remuneration to the dealer for sales to customers resident within the contract territory without objective reason. This prohibition therefore avoids indirect pressure being imposed on the dealer to sell only within the contract territory. An objective reason would be if the legal situation changes in a given Member State, *e.g.* tax which has lead to a change in the calculation basis of list prices.

2. Honouring of Manufacturer's Guarantee

[Article 4]

1. The exemption shall apply notwithstanding any obligation whereby the dealer undertakes to:

(a) comply, in distribution, sales and after-sales servicing with minimum standards, regarding in particular; ...

(e) the repair and maintenance of contract goods and corresponding goods, particularly as regards the safe and reliable functioning of motor vehicles; ...

[Article 5]

1. In all cases, the exemption shall apply only if:
(1) the dealer undertakes:

(a) in respect of motor vehicles within the contract range or corresponding thereto which have been supplied in the common market by another undertaking within the distribution network:
— to honour guarantees and to perform free servicing and vehicle-recall work to an extent which corresponds to the dealer's obligation covered by Article 4(1)(6),
— to carry out repair and maintenance work in accordance with Article 4(1)(1)(e);
. . .

[Article 6]

1. The exemption shall not apply where:
. . .
(7) the manufacturer, the supplier or another undertaking within the network directly or indirectly restricts the freedom of final consumers, authorised intermediaries or dealers to obtain from an undertaking belonging to the network of their choice within the common market contract goods or corresponding goods or to obtain servicing for such goods, or the freedom of final consumers to resell the contract goods or corresponding goods, when the sale is not effected for commercial purposes; or . . .

Question 35: Having purchased the motor vehicle in another Member State, where can the consumer have normal servicing or guarantee work carried out?

The consumer is entitled to seek to have such a vehicle serviced by any undertaking belonging to the network which distributed the vehicle. Hence it is unnecessary for the consumer to return to the dealer in the Member State of purchase [Article 5(1)(1)(a) and Article 4(1)(1)(e)]. The consumer can also turn for servicing to an independent repairer even though there is a risk that in this case the manufacturer can refuse to honour guarantee services thereafter.

Under the Regulation, authorised dealers are expressly obliged to honour the manufacturer's guarantee, to perform free servicing and vehicle recall work on vehicles within their contract or a corresponding range which were supplied in the Common Market by another undertaking within the same distribution network, but only to the extent to which the dealers are obliged under the terms of their distributorship to service vehicles which they themselves have supplied [Article 5(1)(1)(a), Recital 12]. This provision ensures that a final consumer can have the benefit of the manufacturer's guarantee, free servicing and vehicle recall work available from every dealer of the manufacturer's network throughout the Community.

The guarantee period begins at the time when a car leaves the manufacturer's network, *i.e.* the delivery of a car by an authorised dealer. It makes no difference whether the consumer himself or an authorised intermediary collects the vehicle from the authorised dealer. A final consumer who purchases a car from an independent reseller, should be aware that a part of the guarantee period given by the manufacturer could already have expired as the reseller could have bought the car from an authorised dealer of the manufacturer's network some months previously.

Where a manufacturer, importer, dealer or another company within the network impedes the principle of Community-wide guarantee services, it will lose the benefit of the exemption [Article 6(1)(7)].

3. Advertising Outside the Contract Territory

[Article 3]

The exemption shall also apply where the obligation referred to in Article 1 is combined with an obligation on the dealer:

. . .

8. outside the contract territory:

(b) not to solicit customers for contract goods or corresponding goods, by personalised advertising; . . .

Question 36: To what extent is a dealer free to advertise outside the contract territory?

As the Regulation aims at reinforcing flexible demand for contract goods, customers must be in a position to choose the offer which suits them best. The Regulation, therefore, provides that the dealer must be free to seek customers outside his territory by means *e.g.* of media, posters, general brochures or advertisements in newspapers [Article 3(8)(b)]. The manufacturer can only oblige his dealer not to seek customers by personalised advertising, *i.e.* telephone or other form of telecommunication, doorstep canvassing or by direct mail.

[Article 3]

The exemption shall also apply where the obligation referred to in Article 1 is combined with an obligation on the dealer:
. . .

10. not to supply to a reseller:

(a) contract goods or corresponding goods unless the reseller is an undertaking within the distribution system, or
(b) spare parts within the contract range unless the reseller uses them for the repair or maintenance of a motor vehicle; . . .

[Article 10]

For the purposes of this Regulation the following terms shall have the following meanings:
. . .

12. "resale" includes all transactions by which a physical or legal person—"the reseller"—disposes of a motor vehicle which is still in a new condition and which he had previously acquired in his own name and on his own behalf, irrespective of the legal description applied under civil law or the format of the transaction which effects such resale. The terms resale shall include all leasing contracts which provide for a transfer of ownership or an option to purchase prior to the expiry of the contract;

13. "distribute" and "sell" include other forms of supply by the dealer such as leasing.

Question 37: What is the position if a consumer wishes to lease a vehicle from a dealer?

The Regulation makes it clear that a dealer can lease cars as well as selling them [Article 10(13)]. This ensures that any dealer who offers leasing contracts to customers may still benefit from exemption under the Regulation and will still be required to comply with obligations imposed under the Regulation for the protection of consumers, for example as to the servicing of vehicles.

Question 38: Is a dealer entitled to sell to leasing companies?

Yes, the supply to leasing companies is a legitimate part of the activities of dealers as leasing companies are normally considered to be final consumers. However, the supplier may prevent the dealer from supplying contract goods to leasing companies which in fact act as resellers and which do not belong to the distribution network [Article 3(10)]. Article 10(12) makes it clear that leasing contracts which involve a transfer of ownership or a purchase option prior to the expiry of the contract are in reality sales contracts, and that the leasing company in such cases is treated as a reseller.

V. Interaction with Other Provisions of Community Law

[Article 12]

Regulation (EEC) No. 4087/88 is not applicable to agreements concerning the products or services referred to in this Regulation.

[Article 6]

1. The exemption shall not apply where:

. . .

(4) in respect of motor vehicles having three or more road wheels or spare parts therefor, the parties make agreements or engage in concerted practices which are exempted from the prohibition in Article 81(1) of the Treaty under Regulations (EEC) No. 1984/83 or (EEC) No. 198/83 to an extent exceeding the scope of this Regulation, or . . .

Question 39: What effect does the Regulation have on the other group exemption Regulations which relate to the distribution of goods or services?

The Regulation excludes the application of Commission Regulation (EEC) No. 4087/88 concerning franchising agreements[10] on agreements concerning the distribution and servicing of new motor vehicles and the spare parts therefor [Article 12]. The reason is that Regulation 1475/95 has been specifically written for car distribution and is intended to safeguard and balance all the interests involved. Producers can seek an individual exemption if they wish to organise their distribution network as a franchise system.

The other group exemption regulations concerning the distribution of goods, Commission Regulation (EEC) No. 1983/83[11] and (EEC) No 1984/83,[12] remain applicable to cars. This means that producers are free to choose to organise their distribution system according to Regulation 1475/95 or according to these two other group exemptions. It is, however, not possible to combine provisions of those Regulations with provisions of Regulation 1475/85 if the other Regulations allow the introduction of obligations which favour the manufacturer or the dealer and which are more far-reaching than those permitted under Regulation 1475/95 [Article 6(1)(4)].

The group exemption regulations concerning specialisation[13] and research and development agreements[14] are applicable without any restriction since their emphasis does not lay on the distribution of goods.

---

[10] OJ 1988 L359/46.
[11] OJ 1983 L173/1.
[12] OJ 1983 L173/5.
[13] Commission Regulation (EEC) No. 417/85, OJ 1985 L53/1.
[14] Commission Regulation (EEC) No. 418/85, OJ 1985 L53/5.

Question 40: Can Article 82 of the Treaty apply to an exclusive and selective distribution agreement which falls within the scope of Regulation 1475/95?

Yes, the application of Regulation 1475/95—as with any other group exemption regulation—does not preclude the application of Article 82 of the Treaty. The scope of application of Article 82 of the Treaty is different from that of Article 81 since Article 82 requires that the undertaking in question has a dominant position in the relevant market. Article 81 of the Treaty—under which a group exemption is granted—prohibits agreements and concerted practices which restrict competition within the Common Market.

APPENDIX 18

CLARIFICATION OF THE ACTIVITIES OF MOTOR VEHICLE INTERMEDIARIES[1]

This notice is to supplement the notice[2] published with Regulation (EEC) No. 123/85 in order to clarify the scope of the activities of the intermediaries mentioned in that Regulation. The relationship between an intermediary and the person for whom he or it is acting is primarily governed by their contract and by the national law applicable, and does not affect the rights and obligations of third parties to the contract. This notice does not therefore summarize all the obligations of an intermediary.

1. Principles

The following guidelines, which are in line with the balanced objectives pursued by Regulation (EEC) No. 123/85, are based on two principles. The first is that the intermediary referred to in the Regulation is a provider of services acting for the account of a purchaser and final user; he cannot assume risks normally associated with ownership, and is given prior written authority by an identified principal, whose name and address are given, to exercise such activity. The second is the principle of the transparency of the authorization, and in particular the requirement that, under national law, the intermediary pass on to the purchaser all the benefits obtained in the negotiations carried out on his behalf.

In this context, three groups of criteria should be distinguished:

(a) with regard to the validity of the authorization and to the provision of assistance;
(b) with regard to the intermediary's scope for advertising;
(c) with regard to the intermediary's possibilities of supply.

The Commission's experience suggests that the following guidelines and criteria appear appropriate for dealing with the practical requirements. Activities which do not conform to these guidelines and criteria will justify the presumption, in the absence of evidence to the contrary, that an intermediary is acting beyond the limits set by Article 3(11) of Regulation (EEC) No. 123/85, or creating a confusion in the mind of the public on this point by giving the impression that he is a reseller.

2. Practical criteria

(a) The validity of the authorization and the service of assistance

The intermediary is free to organize the structure of his activities. However, operations involving a network of independent undertakings using a common name or other common

---

[1] OJ 1991 C329/20. (App. 19, *post*).
[2] OJ 1985 C17.

distinctive signs could create the misleading impression of an authorized distribution system.

An intermediary may use an outlet in the same building as a supermarket if the outlet is outside the premises where the principal activities of the supermarket are carried on, provided that he complies with the principles set out in the present notice.

Although he cannot assume the risks of ownership, the intermediary must be free to assume the transport and storage risks associated with the vehicle and the credit risks relating to the final purchaser for the financing of the purchase in a foreign country. The services must be provided in total transparency with regard to the various services offered and to payment, and this must be verifiable through the presentation of detailed and exhaustive accounts to the purchaser.

The intermediary must list in detail to the client, in a document which may be separable from the written authorization, the various services offered to him and must give him the possibility to choose those which suit him. In this document, an intermediary not supplying the full range of services associated with the putting into circulation of an imported vehicle should state which services he is not supplying.

(b) Advertising by the intermediary

The intermediary must be able to advertise, though without creating in potential purchasers' minds any confusion between himself and a reseller. Subject to this restriction, he should be able to:

— concentrate his activities, and thus his advertising, on a given brand or on a particular model, provided that he expressly adds an appropriate disclaimer indicating that he is not a reseller, but acts as an intermediary offering his services,
— provide full information on the price which he can obtain, making it clear that the price indicated is his best estimate,
— display cars which have been bought by his clients using his services, or a particular type or model which he can obtain for them, provided that he expressly and visibly makes it clear that he is acting as an intermediary offering his services and not as a reseller, and that types or models which he displays are not for sale,
— use all logos and brand names, in accordance with the applicable rules of law, but without creating any confusion in the mind of the public with regard to the fact that he is an intermediary and not part of the distribution network of the manufacturer or manufacturers concerned.

Where a supermarket carries on a distinct activity as an intermediary, all necessary measures must be taken to avoid confusion in the minds of buyers (final users) with its principal commercial activities conducted under its usual or distinctive sign.

(c) Supply of the intermediaries

In general, the intermediary is free to organize his business relationship with the various dealers in the distribution networks of the different manufacturers; this should not lead the intermediary to establish with such dealers a relationship which is privileged and contrary to contractual obligations accepted in accordance with Regulation (EEC) No. 123/85, especially Articles 3(8)(a) and (b), (9) and (4)(1)(3). In particular the intermediary must obtain supplies on conditions which are normal in the market, and he must not:

— make agreements by which he undertakes obligations to buy,
— receive discounts different from those which are customary on the market of the country in which the car is purchased.

In this context, sales of more than 10% of his annual sales by any one authorized dealer through any one intermediary would create the presumption of a privileged relationship contrary to the Articles cited above.

APPENDIX 19

COMMISSION NOTICE[1]

On Regulation 123/85

In Regulation (EEC) No. 123/85 on the block exemption of motor vehicle distribution agreements the Commission recognises that exclusive and selective distribution in this industry is in principle compatible with Article 81(3) of the Treaty. This assessment is subject to a number of conditions. At the request of some of the commercial sectors involved, this notice sets out some of those conditions and lays down certain administrative principles for the procedures which the Commission might initiate under Article 7 of Council Regulation No. 19/65/EEC in combination with Article 10, points 3 and 4 of the Regulation (EEC) No. 123/85, taking account of the present stage of integration of the European Community.

I

1. Freedom of movement of European consumers and limited availability of vehicle models

The Commission starts from the position that the common market affords advantages to European consumers, and that this is especially so where there is effective competition. Accordingly, Regulation (EEC) No. 123/85 presupposes that in the motor vehicles sector effective competition exists between manufacturers and between their distribution networks. The European consumer must derive a fair share of the benefits which flow from the distribution and servicing agreements. Admittedly, the consumer may benefit from the fact that servicing is carried out by specialists (Article 3, points 3 and 5) and that such service can be obtained throughout the network from dealers and repairers who are obliged to observe minimum requirements (Article 4(1)).

However, the European consumer's basic rights include above all the right to buy a motor vehicle and to have it maintained or repaired wherever prices and quality are most advantageous to him.

(a) This right to buy relates to new vehicles from a manufacturer each of whose dealers offers them in a form and specification mainly required by final consumers in the dealer's contract territory (contract goods).
(b) In the interests of competition at the various stages of distribution in the common market and in those of European consumers, a certain limited availability of other vehicles within the distribution system is also considered indispensable. Any dealer within the distribution system must be able to order from a supplier within the distribution system any volume-produced passenger car which a final consumer has

---

[1] O.J. 1985 C17/4. Although Reg. 123/85 has been superseded by Reg. 1475/95, the Commission's Explanatory Brochure on Reg. 1475/95 (App. 17), states that this Notice remains valid as regards interpretation of the analogous provisions of the later Regulation.

ordered from him and intends to register in another Member State, in the form and specification marketed by the manufacturer or with his consent in that Member State (passenger cars corresponding to those in the contract programme, Article 5(1), point 2(d) and Article 13, point 10 of Regulation (EEC) No. 123/85)[2]:

This provision does not oblige the manufacturer to produce vehicles which he would not otherwise offer within the common market. Nor does it oblige the manufacturer to sell particular vehicle models in any particular part of the common market where he does not, or does not yet, wish to market them. He is only obliged to supply to a dealer within his distribution system a new passenger car required by that dealer to fulfil a contract with a final consumer and intended for another Member State where that dealer's contract programme includes cars of a corresponding kind.

2. Abusive hindrance

The European consumer must not be subject to abusive hindrance either in the exporting country, where he wishes to buy a vehicle, or in the country of destination, where he seeks to register it. The restrictions inherent in an exempted exclusive and selective distribution system do not represent abuses. However, further agreements or concerted practices between undertakings in the distribution system that limit the European consumer's final freedom to purchase do jeopardise the exemption given by the Regulation, as do unilateral measures on the part of a manufacturer or his importers or dealers which have a widespread effect against consumers' interests (Article 10, point 2).[3] Examples are: dealers refuse to perform guarantee work on vehicles which they have not sold and which have been imported from other Member States; manufacturers or their importers withhold their co-operation in the registration of vehicles which European consumers have imported from other Member States; abnormally long delivery periods.

3. Intermediaries

The European consumer must be able to make use of the services of individuals or undertakings to assist in purchasing a new vehicle in another Member State (Article 3, points 10 and 11). However, except as regards contracts between dealers within the distribution system for the sale of contract goods, undertakings within the distribution system can be obliged not to supply new motor vehicles within the contract programme or corresponding vehicles to or through a third party who represents himself as an authorised reseller of new vehicles within the contract programme or corresponding vehicles or carries on an activity equivalent to that of a reseller. It is for the intermediary or the consumer to give the dealer within the distribution system documentary evidence that the intermediary, in buying and accepting delivery of a vehicle, is acting on behalf and for account of the consumer.

II

The Commission may withdraw the benefit of the application of Regulation (EEC) No. 123/85, pursuant to Article 7 of Regulation No. 19/65/EEC where it finds that in an individual case an agreement which falls within the scope of Regulation (EEC) No. 123/85 nevertheless has effects which are incompatible with the provisions of Article 81(3) of the Treaty, and in particular

— where, over a considerable period, prices or conditions of supply for contract goods or for corresponding goods are applied which differ substantially as between Member

---

[2] See now Art. 10, point 10 of Reg. 1475/95.
[3] See now Art. 6(1), point 7 of Reg. 1475/95.

States, and such substantial differences are chiefly due to obligations exempted by Regulation (EEC) No. 123/85 (Article 10, point 3)[4];

— where, in agreements concerning the supply to the dealer of passenger cars which correspond to a model within the contract programme, prices or conditions which are not objectively justifiable are applied, with the object or effect of partitioning the common market (Article 10, point 4).[5]

The Commission may pursue such proceedings in individual cases, upon application (particularly on the basis of complaints from consumers) or on its own initiative, in accordance with the procedural rules laid down in Council Regulation No. 17 and Commission Regulation No. 99/63/EEC under which the parties concerned must be informed of the objections raised and given an opportunity to respond to them before the Commission adopts a decision. Whether the Commission initiates such proceedings depends chiefly on the results of preliminary inquiries, the circumstances of the case and the degree of prejudice to the public interest.

Price differentials for motor vehicles as between Member States are to a certain extent a reflection of the particular play of supply and demand in the areas concerned. Substantial price differences generally give reason to suspect that national measures or private restrictive practices are behind them.

In view of the present stage of integration of the common market, for the time being certain circumstances will not of themselves justify an investigation of whether an agreement exempted by Regulation (EEC) No. 123/85 is incompatible with the conditions of Article 81(3) of the Treaty. For the time being, the Commission does not propose to carry out investigations into private practices under Article 10, point 3[6] or 4[7] of Regulation (EEC) No. 123/85 where the following circumstances obtain (this does not exclude intervention by the Commission in particular cases).

1. Price differentials between Member States (Article 10, point 3[8] in association with Article 13, point 11)[9]

Recommended net prices for resale to final consumers (list prices) of a motor vehicle within the contract programme in one Member State and of the same or a corresponding motor vehicle in another Member State differ, and

(a) the difference expressed in ECU does not exceed 12 per cent. of the lower price, or, over a period of less than one year, exceeds that percentage either
   — by not more than a further 6 per cent. of the list price, or
   — only in respect of an insignificant portion of the motor vehicles within the contract programme, or

(b) the difference is to be attributed, following analysis of the objective datas, to the fact that
   — the purchaser of the vehicle in one of those Member States must pay taxes, charges or fees amounting in total to more than 100 per cent. of the new price, or
   — the freedom to set the price or margin for the resale of the vehicle is directly or indirectly subject in one of those Member States to restriction by national measures lasting longer than one year;
   and that such measures do not represent infringements of the Treaty.

---

[4] See now Art. 8(2) of Reg. 1475/95.
[5] See now Art. 8(3) of Reg. 1475/95.
[6] See now Art. 8(2) of Reg. 1475/95.
[7] See now Art. 8(3) of Reg. 1475/95.
[8] See n. 4 above.
[9] See now Art. 10, point 11 of Reg. 1475/95.

In so far as they are public knowledge, prices net of discounts shall replace recommended net prices. Particular account will be taken, for an appropriate period, of alterations of the parties within the European Monetary System or fluctuations in exchange rates in a Member State.

2. Price differentials between passenger cars within the contract programme and corresponding cars (Article 10, point 4[10] in association with Article 5(1), point 2(d) and Article 13, point 10)[11]

When selling to a dealer a passenger car corresponding to a model within the contract programme, the supplier charges an objectively justifiable supplement on account of special distribution costs and any differences in equipment and specification.

In a Member State where pricing is affected in the manner described at II 1(b) above, the supplier charges a further supplement; however, he does not exceed the price which would be charged in similar cases in that Member State not subject to such effects in which the lowest price net of tax is recommended for the sale to a final consumer of that vehicle within the contract programme (or, as the case may be, of a corresponding vehicle).

3. Where the limits indicated above are exceeded, the Commission may open a procedure on its own initiative under Article 10, points 3[12] and 4[13] of Regulation (EEC) No. 123/85; whether it does so or not will depend mainly on the results of investigations that may be made as to whether the exempted agreement is in fact the principal cause of actual price differences in the meaning of Article 10, point 3[14] or 4[15] or, as the case may be, has led to a partitioning of the common market or is, in the light of experience, liable to do so. Price comparisons made in this connection will take account of differences in equipment and specification and in ancillary items such as the extent of the guarantee, delivery services or registration formalities.

III

1. The rights of Member States, persons and associations of persons to make applications to the Commission under Article 3 of Council Regulation No. 17 (*i.e.* complaints) are unaffected. The Commission will examine such complaints with all due diligence.
2. This notice is without prejudice to any finding of the Court of Justice of the European Communities or of courts of the Member States.
3. Any withdrawal of or amendment to this notice will be effected by publication in the *Official Journal of the European Communities*.

---

[10] See now Art. 8(3) of Reg. 1475/95.
[11] See now Art. 10, point 10 of Reg. 1475/95.
[12] See n. 4 above.
[13] See n. 10 above.
[14] See n. 4 above.
[15] See n. 10 above.

APPENDIX 20

REGULATION 417/85[1]

On the Application of Article 81(3) of the Treaty to Categories of Specialisation Agreements

THE COMMISSION OF THE EUROPEAN COMMUNITIES

Having regard to the Treaty establishing the European Economic Community,

Having regard to Council Regulation 2821/71 of 20 December 1971 on the application of Article 81(3) of the Treaty to categories of agreements, decisions and concerted practices, as last amended by the Act of Accession of Greece, and in particular Article 1 thereof,

Having published a draft of this Regulation,

Having consulted the Advisory Committee on Restrictive Practices and Dominant Positions,

Whereas:

(1) Regulation (EEC) No. 2821/71 empowers the Commission to apply Article 81(3) of the Treaty by Regulation to certain categories of agreements, decisions and concerted practices falling within the scope of Article 81(1) which relate to specialisation, including agreements necessary for achieving it.

(2) Agreements on specialisation in present or future production may fall within the scope of Article 81(1).

(3) Agreements on specialisation in production generally contribute to improving the production or distribution of goods, because undertakings concerned can concentrate on the manufacture of certain products and thus operate more efficiently and supply the products more cheaply. It is likely that, given effective competition, consumers will receive a fair share of the resulting benefit.

(4) Such advantages can arise equally from agreements whereby each participant gives up the manufacture of certain products in favour of another participant and from agreements whereby the participants undertake to manufacture certain products or have them manufactured only jointly.

(5) The Regulation must specify what restrictions of competition may be included in specialisation agreements. The restrictions of competition that are permitted in the Regulation in addition to reciprocal obligations to give up manufacture are normally essential for the making and implementation of such agreements. These restrictions are therefore, in general, indispensable for the attainment of the desired advantages for the participating undertakings and consumers. It may be left to the parties to decide which of these provisions they include in their agreements.

(6) The exemption must be limited to agreements which do not give rise to the possibility of eliminating competition in respect of a substantial part of the products in question.

---

[1] OJ 1985 L53/1. Printed as amended by Commission Reg. (EEC) No. 151/93, OJ 1993 L21/8; and Commission Reg. (EC) No. 2236/97, OJ 1997 L306/12.

The Regulation must therefore apply only as long as the market share and turnover of the participating undertakings do not exceed a certain limit.

(7) It is, however, appropriate to offer undertakings which exceed the turnover limit set in the Regulation a simplified means of obtaining the legal certainty provided by the block exemption. This must allow the Commission to exercise effective supervision as well as simplifying its administration of such agreements.

(8) In order to facilitate the conclusion of long-term specialisation agreements, which can have a bearing on the structure of the participating undertakings, it is appropriate to fix the period of validity of the Regulation at 13 years. If the circumstances on the basis of which the Regulation was adopted should change significantly within this period, the Commission will make the necessary amendments.

(9) Agreements, decisions and concerted practices which are automatically exempted pursuant to this Regulation need not be notified. Undertakings may none the less in an individual case request a decision pursuant to Council Regulation No. 17, as last amended by the Act of Accession of Greece, Spain, Austria, Portugal, Sweden.

HAS ADOPTED THIS REGULATION:

Article 1

Pursuant to Article 81(3) of the Treaty and subject to the provisions of this Regulation, it is hereby declared that Article 81(1) of the Treaty shall not apply to agreements on specialisation whereby, for the duration of the agreement, undertakings accept reciprocal obligations:

(a) not to manufacture certain products or have them manufactured, but to leave it to other parties to manufacture the products or have them manufactured; or

(b) to manufacture certain products or have them manufactured only jointly.

Article 2

1. [Article 1 shall also apply to the following restrictions of competition:]

(a) an obligation not to conclude with third parties specialisation agreements relating to identical products or to products considered by users to be equivalent in view of their characteristics, price and intended use;

(b) an obligation to procure products which are the subject of the specialisation exclusively from another party, a joint undertaking or an undertaking jointly charged with their manufacture, except where they are obtainable on more favourable terms elsewhere and the other party, the joint undertaking or the undertaking charged with manufacture is not prepared to offer the same terms;

[(c) an obligation to grant other parties the exclusive right, within the whole or a defined area of the common market, to distribute products which are the subject of the specialisation, provided that intermediaries and users can also obtain the products from other suppliers and the parties do not render it difficult for intermediaries and users to thus obtain the products;

(d) an obligation to grant one of the parties the exclusive right to distribute products which are the subject of the specialisation provided that that party does not distribute products of a third undertaking which compete with the contract products;

(e) an obligation to grant the exclusive right to distribute products which are the subject of the specialisation to a joint undertaking or to a third undertaking, provided that the joint undertaking or third undertaking does not manufacture or distribute products which compete with the contract products;

(f) an obligation to grant the exclusive right to distribute within the whole or a defined area of the common market the products which are the subject of the specialisation

133

to joint undertakings or third undertakings which do not manufacture or distribute products which compete with the contract products, provided that users and inter- mediaries can also obtain the contract products from other suppliers and that neither the parties nor the joint undertakings or third undertakings entrusted with the exclusive distribution of the contract products render it difficult for users and intermediaries to thus obtain the contract products.]

2. Article 1 shall also apply where the parties undertake obligations of the types referred to in paragraph 1 but with a more limited scope than is permitted by that para- graph.

[2a. Article 1 shall not apply if restrictions of competition other than those set out in paragraphs 1 and 2 are imposed upon the parties by agreement, decision or concerted practice.]

3. Article 1 shall apply notwithstanding that any of the following obligations, in particular, are imposed:

(a) an obligation to supply other parties with products which are the subject of the specialisation and in so doing to observe minimum standards of quality;
(b) an obligation to maintain minimum stocks of products which are the subject of the specialisation and of replacement parts for them;
(c) an obligation to provide customer and guarantee services for products which are the subject of the specialisation.

Amendment

Article 2 was amended by Commission Regulation (EEC) No. 151/93.

Article 3

[1. Article 1 shall apply only if

(a) the products which are the subject of the specialisation together with the participating undertakings' other products which are considered by users to be equivalent in view of their characteristics, price and intended use do not represent more than 20 per cent. of the market for all such products in the common market or a substantial part thereof; and
(b) the aggregate turnover of all the participating undertakings does not exceed ECU 1,000 million.

2. If pursuant to point (d), (e) or (f) of Article 2(1), one of the parties, a joint undertaking, a third undertaking or more than one joint undertaking or third undertaking are entrusted with the distribution of the products which are the subject of the special- isation, Article 1 shall apply only if:

(a) the products which are the subject of the specialisation together with the participating undertakings' other products which are considered by users to be equivalent in view of their characteristics, price and intended use do not represent more than 10 per cent. of the market for all such products in the common market or a substantial part thereof; and
(b) the aggregate annual turnover of all the participating undertakings does not exceed ECU 1,000 million.

3. Article 1 shall continue to apply if the market shares and turnover referred to in paragraphs 1 and 2 are exceeded during any period of two consecutive financial years by not more than one-tenth.

4. Where the limits laid down in paragraph 3 are also exceeded, Article 1 shall continue to apply for a period of six months following the end of the financial year during which they were exceeded.]

Amendment

Article 3 was replaced by Commission Regulation (EEC) No. 151/93.

Article 4

1. The exemption provided for in Article 1 shall also apply to agreements involving participating undertakings whose aggregate turnover exceeds the limits laid down in Article 3(1)(b), (2)[(b) and (3)], on condition that the agreements in question are notified to the Commission in accordance with the provisions of Commission Regulation No. 27, and that the Commission does not oppose such exemption within a period of six months.

2. The period of six months shall run from the date on which the notification is received by the Commission. Where, however, the notification is made by registered post, the period shall run from the date shown on the postmark of the place of posting.

3. Paragraph 1 shall apply only if:

(a) express reference is made to this Article in the notification or in a communication accompanying it; and
(b) the information furnished with the notification is complete and in accordance with the facts.

4. The benefit of paragraph 1 may be claimed for agreements notified before the entry into force of this Regulation by submitting a communication to the Commission referring expressly to this Article and to the notification. Paragraphs 2 and 3(b) shall apply *mutatis mutandis*.

5. The Commission may oppose the exemption. It shall oppose exemption if it receives a request to do so from a Member State within three months of the forwarding to the Member State of the notification referred to in paragraph 1 or of the communication referred to in paragraph 4. This request must be justified on the basis of considerations relating to the competition rules of the Treaty.

6. The Commission may withdraw the opposition to the exemption at any time. However, where the opposition was raised at the request of a Member State and this request is maintained, it may be withdrawn only after consultation of the Advisory Committee on Restrictive Practices and Dominant Positions.

7. If the opposition is withdrawn because the undertakings concerned have shown that the conditions of Article 81(3) are fulfilled, the exemption shall apply from the date of notification.

8. If the opposition is withdrawn because the undertakings concerned have amended the agreement so that the conditions of Article 81(3) are fulfilled, the exemption shall apply from the date on which the amendments take effect.

9. If the Commission opposes exemption and the opposition is not withdrawn, the effects of the notification shall be governed by the provisions of Regulation No. 17.

Article 5

1. Information acquired pursuant to Article 4 shall be used only for the purposes of this Regulation.

2. The Commission and the authorities of the Member States, their officials and other servants shall not disclose information acquired by them pursuant to this Regulation of a kind that is covered by the obligation of professional secrecy.

3. Paragraphs 1 and 2 shall not prevent publication of general information or surveys which do not contain information relating to particular undertakings or associations of undertakings.

Article 6

For the purpose of calculating annual turnover within the meaning of Article 3(1)(*b*) [and (2)(*b*)], the turnovers achieved during the last financial year by the participating undertakings in respect of all goods and services excluding tax shall be added together. For this purpose, no account shall be taken of dealings between the participating undertakings or between these undertakings and a third undertaking jointly charged with manufacture [or sale].

Article 7

1. [For the purposes of Article 3(1) and (2), and Article 6, participating undertakings are:]

(a) undertakings party to the agreement;
(b) undertakings in which a party to the agreement, directly or indirectly:
— owns more than half the capital or business assets,
— has the power to exercise more than half the voting rights,
— has the power to appoint at least half the members of the supervisory board, board of management or bodies legally representing the undertakings, or
— has the right to manage the affairs;
(c) undertakings which directly or indirectly have in or over a party to the agreement the rights or powers listed in (b);
(d) undertakings in or over which an undertaking referred to in (c) directly or indirectly has the rights or powers listed in (b).

2. Undertakings in which the undertakings referred to in paragraph 1(a) to (d) directly or indirectly jointly have the rights or powers set out in paragraph 1(b) shall also be considered to be participating undertakings.

Article 8

The Commission may withdraw the benefit of this Regulation, pursuant to Article 7 of Regulation (EEC) No. 2821/71, where it finds in a particular case that an agreement exempted by this Regulation nevertheless has effects which are incompatible with the conditions set out in Article 81(3) of the Treaty, and in particular where:

(a) the agreement is not yielding significant results in terms of rationalisation or consumers are not receiving a fair share of the resulting benefit; or
(b) the products which are the subject of the specialisation are not subject in the common market or a substantial part thereof to effective competition from identical products or products considered by users to be equivalent in view of their characteristics, price and intended use.

Article 9

This Regulation shall apply *mutatis mutandis* to decisions of associations of undertakings and concerted practices.

[Article 9a

The prohibition in Article 81(1) of the Treaty shall not apply to the specialisation agreements which were in existence at the date of the accession of the Kingdom of Spain and of the Portuguese Republic and which, by reason of this accession, fall within the scope of Article 81(1), if, before 1 July 1986, they are so amended that they comply with the conditions laid down in this Regulation.]

[As regards agreements to which Article 81 of the Treaty applies as a result of the Accession of Austria, Finland and Sweden, the preceding paragraph shall apply *mutatis mutandis* on the understanding that the relevant dates shall be the date of accession of those countries and six months after the date of accession respectively. However, this paragraph shall not apply to agreements which at the date of accession already fall under Article 53(1) of the EEA Agreement.]

Amendments

This Article was inserted by the Act of Accession of the Kingdom of Spain and the Portuguese Republic, Annex I(IV)(14).

The second paragraph was added by the Act of Accession of the Republic of Austria, the Republic of Finland and the Kingdom of Sweden, Annex 1(III)(D)(5), as amended by Council Decision 95/1, Article 39.

Article 10

1. This Regulation shall enter into force on 1 March 1985. It shall apply until 31 December [2000].
2. Commission Regulation (EEC) No. 3604/82 is hereby repealed.

Amendment

Paragraph 1 was amended by Commission Reg. No. 2236/97, OJ 1997 L306/12.

Done at Brussels, 19 December 1984.

REGULATION 2658/2000[1]

On the Application of Article 81(3) of the Treaty to Categories of Specialisation Agreements

(Text with EEA relevance)

THE COMMISSION OF THE EUROPEAN COMMUNITIES,

Having regard to the Treaty establishing the European Community,

Having regard to Council Regulation (EEC) No 2821/71 of 20 December 1971 on the application of Article 81(3) of the Treaty to categories of agreements, decisions and concerted practices,[2] as last amended by the Act of Accession of Austria, Finland and Sweden, and in particular Article 1(1)(c) thereof,

Having published a draft of this Regulation,[3]

Having consulted the Advisory Committee on Restrictive Practices and Dominant Positions,

Whereas:

(1) Regulation (EEC) No 2821/71 empowers the Commission to apply Article 81(3) (formerly Article 85(3)) of the Treaty by regulation to certain categories of agreements, decisions and concerted practices falling within the scope of Article 81(1) which have as their object specialisation, including agreements necessary for achieving it.

(2) Pursuant to Regulation (EEC) No 2821/71, in particular, the Commission has adopted Regulation (EEC) No 417/85 of 19 December 1984 on the application of Article 81(3) of the Treaty to categories of specialisation agreements,[4] as last amended by Regulation (EC) No 2236/97.[5] Regulation (EEC) No 417/85 expires on 31 December 2000.

(3) A new regulation should meet the two requirements of ensuring effective protection of competition and providing adequate legal security for undertakings. The pursuit of these objectives should take account of the need to simplify administrative supervision and the legislative framework to as great extent as possible. Below a certain level of market power it can, for the application of Article 81(3), in general be presumed that the positive effects of specialisation agreements will outweigh any negative effects on competition.

---

[1] OJ 2000 L304/3.
[2] OJ 1971 L285/46.
[3] OJ 2000 C118/3.
[4] OJ 1985 L53/7.
[5] OJ 1997 L306/12.

(4) Regulation (EEC) No 2821/71 requires the exempting regulation of the Commission to define the categories of agreements, decisions and concerted practices to which it applies, to specify the restrictions or clauses which may, or may not, appear in the agreements, decisions and concerted practices, and to specify the clauses which must be contained in the agreements, decisions and concerted practices or the other conditions which must be satisfied.

(5) It is appropriate to move away from the approach of listing exempted clauses and to place greater emphasis on defining the categories of agreements which are exempted up to a certain level of market power and on specifying the restrictions or clauses which are not to be contained in such agreements. This is consistent with an economics-based approach which assesses the impact of agreements on the relevant market.

(6) For the application of Article 81(3) by regulation, it is not necessary to define those agreements which are capable of falling within Article 81(1). In the individual assessment of agreements under Article 81(1), account has to be taken of several factors, and in particular the market structure on the relevant market.

(7) The benefit of the block exemption should be limited to those agreements for which it can be assumed with sufficient certainty that they satisfy the conditions of Article 81(3).

(8) Agreements on specialisation in production generally contribute to improving the production or distribution of goods, because the undertakings concerned can concentrate on the manufacture of certain products and thus operate more efficiently and supply the products more cheaply. Agreements on specialisation in the provision of services can also be said to generally give rise to similar improvements. It is likely that, given effective competition, consumers will receive a fair share of the resulting benefit.

(9) Such advantages can arise equally from agreements whereby one participant gives up the manufacture of certain products or provision of certain services in favour of another participant ("unilateral specialisation"), from agreements whereby each participant gives up the manufacture of certain products or provision of certain services in favour of another participant ("reciprocal specialisation") and from agreements whereby the participants undertake to jointly manufacture certain products or provide certain services ("joint production").

(10) As unilateral specialisation agreements between non-competitors may benefit from the block exemption provided by Commission Regulation (EC) No 2790/1999 of 22 December 1999 on the application of Article 81(3) of the Treaty to categories of vertical agreements and concerted practices,[6] the application of the present Regulation to unilateral specialisation should be limited to agreements between competitors.

(11) All others agreements entered into between undertakings relating to the conditions under which they specialise in the production of goods and/or services should fall within the scope of this Regulation. The block exemption should also apply to provisions contained in specialisation agreements which do not constitute the primary object of such agreements, but are directly related to and necessary for their implementation, to certain related purchasing and marketing arrangements.

(12) To ensure that the benefits of specialisation will materialise without one party leaving the market downstream of production, unilateral and reciprocal specialisation agreements should only be covered by this Regulation where they provide for supply and purchase obligations. These obligations may, but do not have to, be of an exclusive nature.

(13) It can be presumed that, where the participating undertakings' share of the relevant market does not exceed 20%, specialisation agreements as defined in this Regulation will, as a general rule, give rise to economic benefits in the form of economies of

---

[6] OJ 1999 L336/21.

scale or scope or better production technologies, while allowing consumers a fair share of the resulting benefits.

(14) This Regulation should not exempt agreements containing restrictions which are not indispensable to attain the positive effects mentioned above. In principle certain severe anti-competitive restraints relating to the fixing of prices charged to third parties, limitation of output or sales, and allocation of markets or customers should be excluded from the benefit of the block exemption established by this Regulation irrespective of the market share of the undertakings concerned.

(15) The market share limitation, the non-exemption of certain agreements and the conditions provided for in this Regulation normally ensure that the agreements to which the block exemption applies do not enable the participating undertakings to eliminate competition in respect of a substantial part of the products or services in question.

(16) In particular cases in which the agreements falling under this Regulation nevertheless have effects incompatible with Article 81(3) of the Treaty, the Commission may withdraw the benefit of the block exemption.

(17) In order to facilitate the conclusion of specialisation agreements, which can have a bearing on the structure of the participating undertakings, the period of validity of this Regulation should be fixed at 10 years.

(18) This Regulation is without prejudice to the application of Article 82 of the Treaty.

(19) In accordance with the principle of primacy of Community law, no measure taken pursuant to national laws on competition should prejudice the uniform application throughout the common market of the Community competition rules or the full effect of any measures adopted in implementation of those rules, including this Regulation,

HAS ADOPTED THIS REGULATION:

Article 1

Exemption

1. Pursuant to Article 81(3) of the Treaty and subject to the provisions of this Regulation, it is hereby declared that Article 81(1) shall not apply to the following agreements entered into between two or more undertakings (hereinafter referred to as "the parties") which relate to the conditions under which those undertakings specialise in the production of products (hereinafter referred to as "specialisation agreements"):

(a) unilateral specialisation agreements, by virtue of which one party agrees to cease production of certain products or to refrain from producing those products and to purchase them from a competing undertaking, while the competing undertaking agrees to produce and supply these products; or

(b) reciprocal specialisation agreements, by virtue of which two or more parties on a reciprocal basis agree to cease or refrain from producing certain but different products and to purchase these products from the other parties, who agree to supply them; or

(c) joint production agreements, by virtue of which two or more parties agree to produce certain products jointly.

This exemption shall apply to the extent that such specialisation agreements contain restrictions of competition falling within the scope of Article 81(1) of the Treaty.

2. The exemption provided for in paragraph 1 shall also apply to provisions contained in specialisation agreements, which do not constitute the primary object of such agreements, but are directly related to and necessary for their implementation, such as those concerning the assignment or use of intellectual property rights.

The first subparagraph does, however, not apply to provisions which have the same object as the restrictions of competition enumerated in Article 4(1).

Article 2

Definitions

For the purposes of this Regulation:

1. "Agreement" means an agreement, a decision of an association of undertakings or a concerted practice.

2. "Participating undertakings" means undertakings party to the agreement and their respective connected undertakings.

3. "Connected undertakings" means:

(a) undertakings in which a party to the agreement, directly or indirectly:
  (i) has the power to exercise more than half the voting rights, or
  (ii) has the power to appoint more than half the members of the supervisory board, board of management or bodies legally representing the undertaking, or
  (iii) has the right to manage the undertaking's affairs;
(b) undertakings which directly or indirectly have, over a party to the agreement, the rights or powers listed in (a);
(c) undertakings in which an undertaking referred to in (b) has, directly or indirectly, the rights or powers listed in (a);
(d) undertakings in which a party to the agreement together with one or more of the undertakings referred to in (a), (b) or (c), or in which two or more of the latter undertakings, jointly have the rights or powers listed in (a);
(e) undertakings in which the rights or the powers listed in (a) are jointly held by:
  (i) parties to the agreement or their respective connected undertakings referred to in (a) to (d), or
  (ii) one or more of the parties to the agreement or one or more of their connected undertakings referred to in (a) to (d) and one or more third parties.

4. "Product" means a good and/or a service, including both intermediary goods and/or services and final goods and/or services, with the exception of distribution and rental services.

5. "Production" means the manufacture of goods or the provision of services and includes production by way of subcontracting.

6. "Relevant market" means the relevant product and geographic market(s) to which the products, which are the subject matter of a specialisation agreement, belong.

7. "Competing undertaking" means an undertaking that is active on the relevant market (an actual competitor) or an undertaking that would, on realistic grounds, undertake the necessary additional investments or other necessary switching costs so that it could enter the relevant market in response to a small and permanent increase in relative prices (a potential competitor).

8. "Exclusive supply obligation" means an obligation not to supply a competing undertaking other than a party to the agreement with the product to which the specialisation agreement relates.

9. "Exclusive purchase obligation" means an obligation to purchase the product to which the specialisation agreement relates only from the party which agrees to supply it.

Article 3

Purchasing and marketing arrangements

The exemption provided for in Article 1 shall also apply where:

(a) the parties accept an exclusive purchase and/or exclusive supply obligation in the context of a unilateral or reciprocal specialisation agreement or a joint production agreement, or

(b) the parties do not sell the products which are the object of the specialisation agreement independently but provide for joint distribution or agree to appoint a third party distributor on an exclusive or non-exclusive basis in the context of a joint production agreement provided that the third party is not a competing undertaking.

Article 4

Market share threshold

The exemption provided for in Article 1 shall apply on condition that the combined market share of the participating undertakings does not exceed 20% of the relevant market.

Article 5

Agreements not covered by the exemption

1. The exemption provided for in Article 1 shall not apply to agreements which, directly or indirectly, in isolation or in combination with other factors under the control of the parties, have as their object:

(a) the fixing of prices when selling the products to third parties;
(b) the limitation of output or sales; or
(c) the allocation of markets or customers.

2. Paragraph 1 shall not apply to:

(a) provisions on the agreed amount of products in the context of unilateral or reciprocal specialisation agreements or the setting of the capacity and production volume of a production joint venture in the context of a joint production agreement;

(b) the setting of sales targets and the fixing of prices that a production joint venture charges to its immediate customers in the context of point (b) of Article 3.

Article 6

Application of the market share threshold

1. For the purposes of applying the market share threshold provided for in Article 4 the following rules shall apply:

(a) the market share shall be calculated on the basis of the market sales value; if market sales value data are not available, estimates based on other reliable market information, including market sales volumes, may be used to establish the market share of the undertaking concerned;

(b) the market share shall be calculated on the basis of data relating to the preceding calendar year;

(c) the market share held by the undertakings referred to in point (3)(e) shall be apportioned equally to each undertaking having the rights or the powers listed in point (3)(a) of Article 2.

2. If the market share referred to in Article 4 is initially not more than 20% but subsequently rises above this level without exceeding 25%, the exemption provided for in Article 1 shall continue to apply for a period of two consecutive calendar years following the year in which the 20% threshold was first exceeded.

3. If the market share referred to in Article 4 is initially not more than 20% but subsequently rises above 25%, the exemption provided for in Article 1 shall continue to apply for one calendar year following the year in which the level of 25% was first exceeded.

4. The benefit of paragraphs (2) and (3) may not be combined so as to exceed a period of two calendar years.

Article 7

Withdrawal

The Commission may withdraw the benefit of this Regulation, pursuant to Article 7 of Regulation (EEC) No 2821/71, where, either on its own initiative or at the request of a Member State or of a natural or legal person claiming a legitimate interest, it finds in a particular case that an agreement to which the exemption provided for in Article 1 applies nevertheless has effects which are incompatible with the conditions laid down in Article 81(3) of the Treaty, and in particular where:

(a) the agreement is not yielding significant results in terms of rationalisation or consumers are not receiving a fair share of the resulting benefit; or

(b) the products which are the subject of the specialisation are not subject in the common market or a substantial part thereof to effective competition from identical products or products considered by users to be equivalent in view of their characteristics, price and intended use.

Article 8

Transition period

The prohibition laid down in Article 81(1) of the Treaty shall not apply during the period from 1 January 2001 to 30 June 2002 in respect of agreements already in force on 31 December 2000 which do not satisfy the conditions for exemption provided for in this Regulation but which satisfy the conditions for exemption provided for in Regulation (EEC) No 417/85.

Article 9

Period of validity

This Regulation shall enter into force on 1 January 2001.

It shall expire on 31 December 2010.

This Regulation shall be binding in its entirety and directly applicable in all Member States.

Done at Brussels, 29 November 2000.

APPENDIX 22

REGULATION 418/85[1]

On the Application of Article 81(3) of the Treaty to Categories of Research and Development Agreements

THE COMMISSION OF THE EUROPEAN COMMUNITIES

Having regard to the Treaty establishing the European Economic Community,

Having regard to Council Regulation 2821/71 of 20 December 1971 on the application of Article 81(3) of the Treaty to categories of agreements, decisions and concerted practices, as last amended by the Act of Accession of Greece, and in particular Article 1 thereof,

Having published a draft of this Regulation,

Having consulted the Advisory Committee on Restrictive Practices and Dominant Positions,

Whereas:

(1) Regulation (EEC) No. 2821/71 empowers the Commission to apply Article 81(3) of the Treaty by Regulation to certain categories of agreements, decisions and concerted practices falling within the scope of Article 81(1) which have as their object the research and development of products or processes up to the stage of industrial application, and exploitation of the results, including provisions regarding industrial property rights and confidential technical knowledge.

(2) As stated in the Commission's 1968 notice concerning agreements, decisions and concerted practices in the field of cooperation between enterprises, agreements on the joint execution of research work or the joint development of the results of the research, up to but not including the stage of industrial application, generally do not fall within the scope of Article 81(1) of the Treaty. In certain circumstances, however, such as where the parties agree not to carry out other research and development in the same field, thereby forgoing the opportunity of gaining competitive advantages over the other parties, such agreements may fall within Article 81(1) and should therefore not be excluded from this Regulation.

(3) Agreements provided for both joint research and development and joint exploitation of the results may fall within Article 81(1) because the parties jointly determine how the products developed are manufactured or the processes developed are applied or how related intellectual property rights or know-how are exploited.

(4) Cooperation research and development and in the exploitation of the results generally promotes technical and economical progress by increasing the dissemination of technical knowledge between the parties and avoiding duplication of research and development work, by stimulating new advances through the exchange of complementary technical knowledge, and by rationalising the manufacture of the products or application of the processes arising out of the research and development.

---

[1] OJ 1985 L53/5. Printed as amended by Commission Reg. (EEC) No. 151/93, OJ 1993 L21/8.

These aims can be achieved only where the research and development programme and its objectives are clearly defined and each of the parties is given the opportunity of exploiting any of the results of the programme that interest it; where universities or research institutes participate and are not interested in the industrial exploitation of the results, however, it may be agreed that they may use the said results solely for the purpose of further research.

(5) Consumers can generally be expected to benefit from the increased volume and effectiveness of research and development through the introduction of new or improved products or services or the reduction of prices brought about by new or improved processes.

(6) This Regulation must specify the restrictions of competition which may be included in the exempted agreements. The purpose of the permitted restrictions is to concentrate the research activities of the parties in order to improve their chances of success, and to facilitate the introduction of new products and services onto the market. These restrictions are generally necessary to secure the desired benefits for the parties and consumers.

(7) The joint exploitation of results can be considered as the natural consequence of joint research and development. It can take different forms ranging from manufacture to the exploitation of intellectual property rights or know-how that substantially contributes to technical or economic progress. In order to attain the benefits and objectives described above and to justify the restrictions of competition which are exempted, the joint exploitation must relate to products or processes for which the use of the results of the research and development is decisive. Joint exploitation is not therefore justified where it relates to improvements which were not made within the framework of a joint research and development programme but under an agreement having some other principal objective, such as the licensing of intellectual property rights, joint manufacture or specialisation, and merely containing ancillary provisions on joint research and development.

(8) The exemption granted under the Regulation must be limited to agreements which do not afford the undertakings the possibility of eliminating competition in respect of a substantial part of the products in question. In order to guarantee that several independent poles of research can exist in the common market in any economic sector, it is necessary to exclude from the block exemption agreements between competitors whose combined share of the market for products capable of being improved or replaced by the results of the research and development exceeds a certain level at the time the agreement is entered into.

(9) In order to guarantee the maintenance of effective competition during joint exploitation of the results, it is necessary to provide that the block exemption will cease to apply if the parties' combined shares of the market for the products rising out of the joint research and development become too great. However, it should be provided that the exemption will continue to apply, irrespective of the parties' market shares, for a certain period after the commencement of joint exploitation, so as to await stabilisation of their market shares, particularly after the introduction of an entirely new product, and to guarantee a minimum period of return on the generally substantial investments involved.

(10) Agreements between undertakings which do not fulfil the market share conditions laid down in the Regulation may, in appropriate cases, be granted an exemption by individual decision, which will in particular take account of world competition and the particular circumstances prevailing in the manufacture of high technology products.

(11) It is desirable to list in the Regulation a number of obligations that are commonly found in research and development agreements but that are normally not restrictive of competition and to provide that, in the event that, because of the particular economic or legal circumstances, they should fall within Article 81(1), they also would be covered by the exemption. The list is not exhaustive.

(12) The Regulation must specify what provisions may not be included in agreements if these are to benefit from the block exemption by virtue of the fact that such provisions are restrictions falling within Article 81(1) for which there can be no general presumption that they will lead to the positive effects required by Article 81(3).

(13) Agreements which are not automatically covered by the exemption because they include provisions that are not expressly exempted by the Regulation and are not expressly excluded from exemption are none the less capable of benefiting from the general presumption of compatibility with Article 81(3) on which the block exemption is based. It will be possible for the Commission rapidly to establish whether this is the case for a particular agreement. Such an agreement should therefore be deemed to be covered by the exemption provided for in this Regulation where it is notified to the Commission and the Commission does not oppose the application of the exemption within a specific period of time.

(14) Agreements covered by this Regulation may also take advantage of provisions contained in other block exemption Regulations of the Commission, and in particular Regulation (EEC) No. 417/85 on specialisation agreements, Regulation (EEC) No. 1983/83 on exclusive distribution agreements, Regulation (EEC) No. 1984/83, on exclusive purchasing agreements and Regulation (EEC) No. 2349/84 on patent licensing agreements, if they fulfil the conditions set out in these Regulations. The provisions of the aforementioned Regulations are, however not applicable in so far as this Regulation contains specific rules.

(15) If individual agreements exempted by this Regulation nevertheless have effects which are incompatible with Article 81(3), the Commission may withdraw the benefit of the block exemption.

(16) The Regulation should apply with retroactive effect to agreements in existence when the Regulation comes into force where such agreements already fulfil its conditions or are modified to do so. The benefit of these provisions may not be claimed in actions pending at the date of entry into force of this Regulation, nor may it be relied on as grounds for claims for damages against third parties.

(17) Since research and development cooperation agreements are often of a long-term nature, especially where the cooperation extends to the exploitation of the results, it is appropriate to fix the period of validity of the Regulation at 13 years. If the circumstances on the basis of which the Regulation was adopted should change significantly within this period, the Commission will make the necessary amendments.

(18) Agreements which are automatically exempted pursuant to this Regulation need not be notified. Undertakings may nevertheless in a particular case request a decision pursuant to Council Regulation No. 17, as last amended by the Act of Accession of Greece.

HAS ADOPTED THIS REGULATION:

Article 1

1. Pursuant to Article 81(3) of the Treaty and subject to the provisions of this Regulation, it is hereby declared that Article 81(1) of the Treaty shall not apply to agreements entered into between undertakings for the purpose of:

(a) joint research and development of products or processes and joint exploitation of the results of that research and development;

(b) joint exploitation of the results of research and development of products or processes jointly carried out pursuant to a prior agreement between the same undertakings; or

(c) joint research and development of products or processes excluding joint exploitation of the results, in so far as such agreements fall within the scope of Article 81(1).

2. For the purposes of this Regulation:

(a) *research and development of products or processes* means the acquisition of technical knowledge and the carrying out of theoretical analysis, systematic study or experimentation, including experimental production, technical testing of products or processes, the establishment of the necessary facilities and the obtaining of intellectual property rights for the results;
(b) *contract processes* means processes arising out of the research and development;
(c) *contract products* means products or services arising out of the research and development or manufactured or provided applying the contract processes;
(d) *exploitation of the results* means the manufacture of the contract products or the application of the contract processes or the assignment or licensing of intellectual property rights or the communication of know-how required for such manufacture or application;
(e) *technical knowledge* means technical knowledge which is either protected by an intellectual property right or is secret (know-how).

3. Research and development or the exploitation of the results are carried out *jointly* where:

(a) the work involved is:
   — carried out by a joint team, organisation or undertaking,
   — jointly entrusted to a third party, or
   — allocated between the parties by way of specialisation in research, development or production;
(b) the parties collaborate in any way in the assignment or the licensing of intellectual property rights or the communication of know-how, within the meaning of paragraph 2(*d*), to third parties.

Article 2

The exemption provided for in Article 1 shall apply on condition that:

(a) the joint research and development work is carried out within the framework of a programme defining the objectives of the work and the field in which it is to be carried out;
(b) all the parties have access to the results of the work;
(c) where the agreement provides only for joint research and development, each party is free to exploit the results of the joint research and development and any pre-existing technical knowledge necessary therefor independently;
(d) the joint exploitation relates only to results which are protected by intellectual property rights or constitute know-how which substantially contributes to technical or economic progress and that the results are decisive for the manufacture of the contract products or the application of the contract processes;
(f) undertakings charged with manufacture by way of specialisation in production are required to fulfil orders for supplies from all the parties.

Amendment

Article 2(e) was deleted according to Commission Regulation (EEC) No. 151/93.

Article 3

1. Where the parties are not competing manufacturers of products capable of being improved or replaced by the contract products, the exemption provided for in Article 1

shall apply for the duration of the research and development programme and, where the results are jointly exploited, for five years from the time the contract products are first put on the market within the common market.

2. Where two or more of the parties are competing manufacturers within the meaning of paragraph 1, the exemption provided for in Article 1 shall apply for the period specified in paragraph 1 only if, at the time the agreement is entered into, the parties' combined production of the products capable of being improved or replaced by the contract products does not exceed 20 per cent. of the market for such products in the common market or a substantial part thereof.

3. After the end of the period referred to in paragraph 1, the exemption provided for in Article 1 shall continue to apply as long as the production of the contract products together with the parties' combined production of other products which are considered by users to be equivalent in view of their characteristics, price and intended use do not exceed 20 per cent. of the total market for such products in the common market or a substantial part thereof. Where contract products are components used by the parties of the manufacture of other products, reference shall be made to the markets for such of those latter products for which the components represent a significant part.

[3a. Where one of the parties, a joint undertaking, a third undertaking or more than one joint undertaking or third undertaking are entrusted with the distribution of the products which are the subject of the agreement under Article 4(1)(fa), (fb) or (fc), the exemption provided for in Article 1 shall apply only if the parties production of the products referred to in paragraphs 2 and 3 does not exceed 10 per cent. of the market for all such products in the common market or a substantial part thereof.

4. The exemption provided for in Article 1 shall continue to apply where the market shares referred to in paragraphs 3 and 4 are exceeded during any period of two consecutive financial years by not more than one-tenth.

5. Where the limits laid down in paragraph 5 are also exceeded, the exemption provided for in Article 1 shall continue to apply for a period of six months following the end of the financial year during which they were exceeded.]

Amendment

Article 3 was amended by Commission Regulation (EEC) No. 151/93.

Article 4

1. The exemption provided for in Article 1 shall also apply to the following restrictions of competition imposed on the parties:

(a) an obligation not to carry out independently research and development in the field to which the programme relates or in a closely connected field during the execution of the programme;

(b) an obligation not to enter into agreements with third parties on research and development in the field to which the programme relates or in a closely connected field during the execution of the programme;

(c) an obligation to procure the contract products exclusively from parties, joint organisations or undertakings or third parties, jointly charged with their manufacture;

(d) an obligation not to manufacture the contract products or apply the contract processes in territories reserved for other parties;

(e) an obligation to restrict the manufacture of the contract products or application of the contract processes to one or more technical fields of application, except where two or more of the parties are competitors within the meaning of Article 3 at the time the agreement is entered into;

(f) an obligation not to pursue, for a period of five years from the time the contract products are first put on the market within the common market, an active policy of putting the products on the market in territories reserved for other parties, and in particular not to engage in advertising specifically aimed at such territories or to establish any branch or maintain any distribution depot there for the distribution of the products, provided that users and intermediaries can obtain the contract products from other suppliers and the parties do not render it difficult for intermediaries and users to thus obtain the products;

[(fa) an obligation to grant one of the parties the exclusive right to distribute the contract products, provided that that party does not distribute products manufactured by a third producer which compete with the contract products;

(fb) an obligation to grant the exclusive right to distribute the contract products to a joint undertaking or a third undertaking, provided that the joint undertaking or third undertaking does not manufacture or distribute products which compete with the contract products;

(fc) an obligation to grant the exclusive right to distribute the contract products in the whole or a defined area of the common market to joint undertakings or third undertakings which do not manufacture or distribute products which compete with the contract products, provided that users and intermediaries are also able to obtain the contract products from other suppliers and neither the parties nor the joint undertakings or third undertakings entrusted with the exclusive distribution of the contract products render it difficult for users and intermediaries to thus obtain the contract products.]

(g) an obligation on the parties to communicate to each other any experience they may gain in exploiting the results and to grant each other non-exclusive licences for inventions relating to improvements or new applications.

2. The exemption provided for in Article 1 shall also apply where in a particular agreement the parties undertake obligations of the types referred to in paragraph 1 but with a more limited scope than is permitted by that paragraph.

Amendment

Article 4 was amended by Commission Regulation (EEC) No. 151/93.

Article 5

1. Article 1 shall apply notwithstanding that any of the following obligations, in particular, are imposed on the parties during the currency of the agreement.

(a) an obligation to communicate patented or non-patented technical knowledge necessary for the carrying out of the research and development programme for the exploitation of its results;

(b) an obligation not to use any know-how received from another party for purposes other than carrying out the research and development programme and the exploitation of its results;

(c) an obligation to obtain and maintain in force intellectual property rights for the contract products or processes;

(d) an obligation to preserve the confidentiality of any know-how received or jointly developed under the research and development programme; this obligation may be imposed even after the expiry of the agreement;

(e) an obligation:
  (i) to inform other parties of infringements of their intellectual property rights,
  (ii) to take legal action against infringers, and
  (iii) to assist in any such legal action or share with the other parties in the costs thereof;

(f) an obligation to pay royalties or render services to other parties to compensate for unequal contributions to the joint research and development or unequal exploitation of its results;

(g) an obligation to share royalties received from third parties with other parties;

(h) an obligation to supply other parties with minimum quantities of contract products and to observe minimum standards of quality.

2. In the event that, because of particular circumstances, the obligations referred to in paragraph 1 fall within the scope of Article 81(1), they also shall be covered by the exemption. The exemption provided for in this paragraph shall also apply where in a particular agreement the parties undertake obligations of the types referred to in paragraph 1 but with a more limited scope than is permitted by that paragraph.

Article 6

The exemption provided for in Article 1 shall not apply where the parties, by agreement, decision or concerted practice:

(a) are restricted in their freedom to carry out research and development independently or in cooperation with third parties in a field unconnected with that to which the programme relates or, after its completion, in the field to which the programme relates or in a connected field;

(b) are prohibited after completion of the research and development programme from challenging the validity of intellectual property rights which the parties hold in the common market and which are relevant to the programme or, after the expiry of the agreement, from challenging the validity of intellectual property rights which the parties hold in the common market and which protect the results of the research and development;

(c) are restricted as to the quantity of the contract products they may manufacture or sell or as to the number of operations employing the contract process they may carry out;

(d) are restricted in their determination of prices, components of prices or discounts when selling the contract products to third parties;

(e) are restricted as to the customers they may serve, without prejudice to Article 4(1)(e);

(f) are prohibited from putting the contract products on the market or pursuing an active sales policy for them in territories within the common market that are reserved for other parties after the end of the period referred to in Article 4(1)(f);

[(g) are required not to grant licences to third parties to manufacture the contract products or to apply the contract processes even though the exploitation by the parties themselves of the results of the joint research and development is not provided for or does not take place;]

(h) are required:
  — to refuse without any objectively justified reason to meet demand from users or dealers established in their respective territories who would market the contract products in other territories within the common market, or
  — to make it difficult for users or dealers to obtain the contract products from other dealers within the common market, and in particular to exercise intellectual property rights or take measures so as to prevent users or dealers from obtaining, or from putting on the market within the common market, products which have been lawfully put on the market within the common market by another party or with its consent.

Amendment

Article 6(g) was replaced by Commission Regulation (EEC) No. 151/93.

Article 7

1. The exemption provided for in this Regulation shall also apply to agreements of the kind described in Article 1 which fulfil the conditions laid down in Articles 2 and 3 and which contain obligations restrictive of competition which are not covered by Articles 4 and 5 and do not fall within the scope of Article 6, on condition that the agreements in question are notified to the Commission in accordance with the provisions of Commission Regulation No. 27, and that the Commission does not oppose such exemption within a period of six months.

2. The period of six months shall run from the date on which the notification is received by the Commission. Where, however, the notification is made by registered post, the period shall run from the date shown on the postmark of the place of posting.

3. Paragraph 1 shall apply only if:

(a) express reference is made to this Article in the notification or in a communication accompanying it, and
(b) the information furnished with the notification is complete and in accordance with the facts.

4. The benefit of paragraph 1 may be claimed for agreements notified before the entry into force of this Regulation by submitting a communication to the Commission referring expressly to this Article and to the notification. Paragraphs 2 and 3(*b*) shall apply *mutatis mutandis*.

5. The Commission may oppose the exemption. It shall oppose exemption if it receives a request to do so from a Member State within three months of the forwarding to the Member State of the notification referred to in paragraph 1 or of the communication referred to in paragraph 4. This request must be justified on the basis of considerations relating to the competition rules of the Treaty.

6. The Commission may withdraw the opposition to the exemption at any time. However, where the opposition was raised at the request of a Member State and this request is maintained, it may be withdrawn only after consultation of the Advisory Committee on Restrictive Practices and Dominant Positions.

7. If the opposition is withdrawn because the undertakings concerned have shown that the conditions of Article 81(3) are fulfilled, the exemption shall apply from the date of notification.

8. If the opposition is withdrawn because the undertakings concerned have amended the agreement so that the conditions of Article 81(3) are fulfilled, the exemption shall apply from the date on which the amendments take effect.

9. If the Commission opposes exemption and the opposition is not withdrawn, the effects of the notification shall be governed by the provisions of Regulation No. 17.

Article 8

1. Information acquired pursuant to Article 7 shall be used only for the purposes of this Regulation.

2. The Commission and the authorities of the Member States, their officials and other servants shall not disclose information acquired by them pursuant to this Regulation of a kind that is covered by the obligation of professional secrecy.

3. Paragraphs 1 and 2 shall not prevent publication of general information or surveys which do not contain information relating to particular undertakings or associations of undertakings.

Article 9

1. The provisions of this Regulation shall also apply to rights and obligations which the parties create for undertakings connected with them. The market shares held and the

actions and measures taken by connected undertakings shall be treated as those of the parties themselves.

2. Connected undertakings for the purposes of this Regulation are:

(a) undertakings in which a party to the agreement, directly or indirectly:
  — owns more than half the capital or business assets,
  — has the power to exercise more than half the voting rights,
  — has the power to appoint more than half the members of the supervisory board, board of directors or bodies legally representing the undertakings, or
  — has the right to manage the affairs;
(b) undertakings which directly have in or over a party to the agreement the rights or powers listed in (a);
(c) undertakings in or over which an undertaking referred to in (b) directly or indirectly has the rights or powers listed in (a);

3. Undertakings in which the parties to the agreement or undertakings connected with them jointly have, directly or indirectly, the rights or powers set out in paragraph 2(*a*) shall be considered to be connected with each of the parties to the agreement.

Article 10

10. The Commission may withdraw the benefit of this Regulation, pursuant to Article 7 of Regulation (EEC) No. 2821/71, where it finds in a particular case that an agreement exempted by this Regulation nevertheless has certain effects which are incompatible with the conditions laid down in Article 81(3) of the Treaty, and in particular where:

(a) the existence of the agreement substantially restricts the scope of third parties to carry out research and development in the relevant field because of the limited research capacity available elsewhere;
(b) because of the particular structure of supply, the existence of the agreement substantially restricts the access of third parties to the market for the contract products;
(c) without any objectively valid reason, the parties do not exploit the results of the joint research and development;
(d) the contract products are not subject in the whole or a substantial part of the common market to effect competition from identical products or products considered by users as equivalent in view of their characteristics, price and intended use.

Article 11

1. In the case of agreements notified to the Commission before 1 March 1985, the exemption provided for in Article 1 shall have retroactive effect from the time at which the conditions for application of this Regulation were fulfilled or, where the agreement does not fall within Article 4(2)(3)(*b*) of Regulation No. 17, not earlier than the date of notification.

2. In the case of agreements existing on 13 March 1962 and notified to the Commission before 1 February 1963, the exemption shall have retroactive effect from the time at which the conditions for application of this Regulation were fulfilled.

3. Where agreements were in existence on 13 March 1962 and which were notified to the Commission before 1 February 1963, or which are covered by Article 4(2)(3)(*b*) of Regulation No. 17 and were notified to the Commission before 1 January 1967, are amended before 1 September 1985 so as to fulfil the conditions for application of this Regulation, such amendment being communicated to the Commission before 1 October 1985, the prohibition laid down in Article 81(1) of the Treaty shall not apply in respect of the period prior to the amendment. The communication of amendments shall take effect

from the date of their receipt by the Commission. Where the communication is sent by registered post, it shall take effect from the date shown on the postmark of the place of posting.

4. In the case of agreements to which Article 81 of the Treaty applies as a result of the accession of the United Kingdom, Ireland and Denmark, paragraphs 1 to 3 shall apply except where the relevant dates shall be 1 January 1973 instead of 13 March 1962 and 1 July 1973 instead of 1 February 1963 and 1 January 1967.

5. In the case of agreements to which Article 81 of the Treaty applies as a result of the accession of Greece, paragraphs 1 to 3 shall apply except that the relevant dates shall be 1 January 1981 instead of 13 March 1962 and 1 July 1981 instead of 1 February 1963 and 1 January 1967.

[6. As regards agreements to which Article 81 of the Treaty applies as a result of the accession of the Kingdom of Spain and of the Portuguese Republic, paragraphs 1 to 3 shall apply except that the relevant dates should be 1 January 1986 instead of 13 March 1962 and 1 July 1986 instead of 1 February 1963, 1 January 1967, 1 March 1985 and 1 September 1985. The amendments made to the agreements in accordance with the provisions of paragraph 3 need not be notified to the Commission.]

[7. As regards agreements to which Article 81 of the Treaty applies as a result of the Accession of Austria, Finland and Sweden, paragraphs 1 to 3 shall apply *mutatis mutandis* on the understanding that the relevant dates shall be the date of accession instead of 13 March 1962 and six months after the accession instead of 1 February 1963, 1 January 1967, 1 March 1985 and 1 September 1985. The amendment made to those agreements in accordance with the provisions of paragraph 3 need not be notified to the Commission. However this paragraph shall not apply to agreements which at the date of accession already fall under Article 53(1) of the EEA Agreement.]

Amendments

Paragraph 6 was added by the Act of Accession of the Kingdom of Spain and the Republic of Portugal, Annex I(IV)(15).

Paragraph 7 was added by the Act of Accession of the Republic of Austria, the Republic of Finland and the Kingdom of Sweden, Annex 1(III)(D)(6), as amended by Council Decision 95/1, Article 39.

Article 12

This Regulation shall apply *mutatis mutandis* to decisions of associations of undertakings.

Article 13

This Regulation shall enter into force on 1 March 1985. It shall apply until 31 December [2000].

Amendment

Article 13 was amended by Commission Regulation No. 2236/97, OJ 1997 L306/12.

Done at Brussels, 19 December 1984.

APPENDIX 23

REGULATION 2659/2000[1]

*On the Application of Article 81(3) of the Treaty to Categories of Research
and Development Agreements*

(Text with EEA relevance)

THE COMMISSION OF THE EUROPEAN COMMUNITIES

Having regard to the Treaty establishing the European Community,

Having regard to Council Regulation (EEC) No 2821/71 of 20 December 1971 on application of Article 81(3) of the Treaty to categories of agreements, decisions and concerted practices,[2] as last amended by the Act of Accession of Austria, Finland and Sweden, and in particular Article 1(1)(b) thereof,

Having published a draft of this Regulation,[3]

Having consulted the Advisory Committee on Restrictive Practices and Dominant Positions,

Whereas:

(1) Regulation (EEC) No 2821/71 empowers the Commission to apply Article 81(3) (formerly Article 85(3)) of the Treaty by regulation to certain categories of agreements, decisions and concerted practices falling within the scope of Article 81(1) which have as their object the research and development of products or processes up to the stage of industrial application, and exploitation of the results, including provisions regarding intellectual property rights.

(2) Article 163(2) of the Treaty calls upon the Community to encourage undertakings, including small and medium-sized undertakings, in their research and technological development activities of high quality, and to support their efforts to cooperate with one another. Pursuant to Council Decision 1999/65/EC of 22 December 1998 concerning the rules for the participation of undertakings, research centres and universities and for the dissemination of research results for the implementation of the fifth framework programme of the European Community (1998 to 2002)[4] and Commission Regulation (EC) No 996/1999[5] on the implementation of Decision 1999/65/EC, indirect research and technological development (RTD) actions supported under the fifth framework programme of the Community are required to be carried out cooperatively.

(3) Agreements on the joint execution of research work or the joint development of the results of the research, up to but not including the stage of industrial application,

---

[1] OJ 2000 L304/7.
[2] OJ 1971 L285/46.
[3] OJ 2000 C118/3.
[4] OJ 1999 L26/46.
[5] OJ 1999 L122/9.

154

generally do not fall within the scope of Article 81(1) of the Treaty. In certain circumstances, however, such as where the parties agree not to carry out other research and development in the same field, thereby forgoing the opportunity of gaining competitive advantages over the other parties, such agreements may fall within Article 81(1) and should therefore not be included within the scope of this Regulation.

(4) Pursuant to Regulation (EEC) No 2821/71, the Commission has, in particular, adopted Regulation (EEC) No 418/85 of 19 December 1984 on the application of Article 81(3) of the Treaty to categories of research and development agreements,[6] as last amended by Regulation (EC) No 2236/97.[7] Regulation (EEC) No 418/85 expires on 31 December 2000.

(5) A new regulation should meet the two requirements of ensuring effective protection of competition and providing adequate legal security for undertakings. The pursuit of these objectives should take account of the need to simplify administrative supervision and the legislative framework to as great an extent as possible. Below a certain level of market power it can, for the application of Article 81(3), in general be presumed that the positive effects of research and development agreements will outweigh any negative effects on competition.

(6) Regulation (EEC) No 2821/71 requires the exempting regulation of the Commission to define the categories of agreements, decisions and concerted practices to which it applies, to specify the restrictions or clauses which may, or may not, appear in the agreements, decisions and concerted practices, and to specify the clauses which must be contained in the agreements, decisions and concerted practices or the other conditions which must be satisfied.

(7) It is appropriate to move away from the approach of listing exempted clauses and to place greater emphasis on defining the categories of agreements which are exempted up to a certain level of market power and on specifying the restrictions or clauses which are not to be contained in such agreements. This is consistent with an economics based approach which assesses the impact of agreements on the relevant market.

(8) For the application of Article 81(3) by regulation, it is not necessary to define those agreements which are capable of falling within Article 81(1). In the individual assessment of agreements under Article 81(1), account has to be taken of several factors, and in particular the market structure on the relevant market.

(9) The benefit of the block exemption should be limited to those agreements for which it can be assumed with sufficient certainty that they satisfy the conditions of Article 81(3).

(10) Cooperation in research and development and in the exploitation of the results generally promotes technical and economic progress by increasing the dissemination of know-how between the parties and avoiding duplication of research and development work, by stimulating new advances through the exchange of complementary know-how, and by rationalising the manufacture of the products or application of the processes arising out of the research and development.

(11) The joint exploitation of results can be considered as the natural consequence of joint research and development. It can take different forms such as manufacture, the exploitation of intellectual property rights that substantially contribute to technical or economic progress, or the marketing of new products.

(12) Consumers can generally be expected to benefit from the increased volume and effectiveness of research and development through the introduction of new or improved products or services or the reduction of prices brought about by new or improved processes.

(13) In order to attain the benefits and objectives of joint research and development the benefit of this Regulation should also apply to provisions contained in research and

---

[6] OJ 1985 L53/5.
[7] 1997 L306/12.

development agreements which do not constitute the primary object of such agreements, but are directly related to and necessary for their implementation.

(14) In order to justify the exemption, the joint exploitation should relate to products or processes for which the use of the results of the research and development is decisive, and each of the parties is given the opportunity of exploiting any results that interest it. However, where academic bodies, research institutes or undertakings which supply research and development as a commercial service without normally being active in the exploitation of results participate in research and development, they may agree to use the results of research and development solely for the purpose of further research. Similarly, non-competitors may agree to limit their right to exploitation to one or more technical fields of application to facilitate cooperation between parties with complementary skills.

(15) The exemption granted under this Regulation must be limited to research and development agreements which do not afford the undertakings the possibility of eliminating competition in respect of a substantial part of the products or services in question. It is necessary to exclude from the block exemption agreements between competitors whose combined share of the market for products or services capable of being improved or replaced by the results of the research and development exceeds a certain level at the time the agreement is entered into.

(16) In order to guarantee the maintenance of effective competition during joint exploitation of the results, provision should be made for the block exemption to cease to apply if the parties' combined share of the market for the products arising out of the joint research and development becomes too great. The exemption should continue to apply, irrespective of the parties' market shares, for a certain period after the commencement of joint exploitation, so as to await stabilisation of their market shares, particularly after the introduction of an entirely new product, and to guarantee a minimum period of return on the investments involved.

(17) This Regulation should not exempt agreements containing restrictions which are not indispensable to attain the positive effects mentioned above. In principle certain severe anti-competitive restraints such as limitations on the freedom of parties to carry out research and development in a field unconnected to the agreement, the fixing of prices charged to third parties, limitations on output or sales, allocation of markets or customers, and limitations on effecting passive sales for the contract products in territories reserved for other parties should be excluded from the benefit of the block exemption established by this Regulation irrespective of the market share of the undertakings concerned.

(18) The market share limitation, the non-exemption of certain agreements, and the conditions provided for in this Regulation normally ensure that the agreements to which the block exemption applies do not enable the participating undertakings to eliminate competition in respect of a substantial part of the products or services in question.

(19) In particular cases in which the agreements falling under this Regulation nevertheless have effects incompatible with Article 81(3) of the Treaty, the Commission may withdraw the benefit of the block exemption.

(20) Agreements between undertakings which are not competing manufacturers of products capable of being improved or replaced by the results of the research and development will only eliminate effective competition in research and development in exceptional circumstances. It is therefore appropriate to enable such agreements to benefit from the block exemption irrespective of market share and to address such exceptional cases by way of withdrawal of its benefit.

(21) As research and development agreements are often of a long-term nature, especially where the cooperation extends to the exploitation of the results, the period of validity of this Regulation should be fixed at 10 years.

(22) This Regulation is without prejudice to the application of Article 82 of the Treaty.

(23) In accordance with the principle of primacy of Community law, no measure taken pursuant to national laws on competition should prejudice the uniform application

throughout the common market of the Community competition rules or the full effect of any measures adopted in implementation of those rules, including this Regulation,

HAS ADOPTED THIS REGULATION:

Article 1

Exemption

1. Pursuant to Article 81(3) of the Treaty and subject to the provisions of this Regulation, it is hereby declared that Article 81(1) shall not apply to agreements entered into between two or more undertakings (hereinafter referred to as "the parties") which relate to the conditions under which those undertakings pursue:

(a) joint research and development of products or processes and joint exploitation of the results of that research and development;
(b) joint exploitation of the results of research and development of products or processes jointly carried out pursuant to a prior agreement between the same parties; or
(c) joint research and development of products or processes excluding joint exploitation of the results.

This exemption shall apply to the extent that such agreements (hereinafter referred to as "research and development agreements") contain restrictions of competition falling within the scope of Article 81(1).

2. The exemption provided for in paragraph 1 shall also apply to provisions contained in research and development agreements which do not constitute the primary object of such agreements, but are directly related to and necessary for their implementation, such as an obligation not to carry out, independently or together with third parties, research and development in the field to which the agreement relates or in a closely connected field during the execution of the agreement.

The first subparagraph does, however, not apply to provisions which have the same object as the restrictions of competition enumerated in Article 5(1).

Article 2

Definitions

For the purposes of this Regulation:

1. "agreement" means an agreement, a decision of an association of undertakings or a concerted practice;

2. "participating undertakings" means undertakings party to the research and development agreement and their respective connected undertakings;

3. "connected undertakings" means:

(a) undertakings in which a party to the research and development agreement, directly or indirectly:
    (i) has the power to exercise more than half the voting rights,
    (ii) has the power to appoint more than half the members of the supervisory board, board of management or bodies legally representing the undertaking, or
    (iii) has the right to manage the undertaking's affairs;
(b) undertakings which directly or indirectly have, over a party to the research and development agreement, the rights or powers listed in (a);
(c) undertakings in which an undertaking referred to in (b) has, directly or indirectly, the rights or powers listed in (a);

(d) undertakings in which a party to the research and development agreement together with one or more of the undertakings referred to in (a), (b) or (c), or in which two or more of the latter undertakings, jointly have the rights or powers listed in (a);

(e) undertakings in which the rights or the powers listed in (a) are jointly held by:

    (i) parties to the research and development agreement or their respective connected undertakings referred to in (a) to (d), or

    (ii) one or more of the parties to the research and development agreement or one or more of their connected undertakings referred to in (a) to (d) and one or more third parties;

4. "research and development" means the acquisition of know-how relating to products or processes and the carrying out of theoretical analysis, systematic study or experimentation, including experimental production, technical testing of products or processes, the establishment of the necessary facilities and the obtaining of intellectual property rights for the results;

5. "product" means a good and/or a service, including both intermediary goods and/or services and final goods and/or services;

6. "contract process" means a technology or process arising out of the joint research and development;

7. "contract product" means a product arising out of the joint research and development or manufactured or provided applying the contract processes;

8. "exploitation of the results" means the production or distribution of the contract products or the application of the contract processes or the assignment or licensing of intellectual property rights or the communication of know-how required for such manufacture or application;

9. "intellectual property rights" includes industrial property rights, copyright and neighbouring rights;

10. "know-how" means a package of non-patented practical information, resulting from experience and testing, which is secret, substantial and identified: in this context, "secret" means that the know-how is not generally known or easily accessible; "substantial" means that the know-how includes information which is indispensable for the manufacture of the contract products or the application of the contract processes; "identified" means that the know-how is described in a sufficiently comprehensive manner so as to make it possible to verify that it fulfils the criteria of secrecy and substantiality;

11. research and development, or exploitation of the results, are carried out "jointly" where the work involved is:

(a) carried out by a joint team, organisation or undertaking,

(b) jointly entrusted to a third party, or

(c) allocated between the parties by way of specialisation in research, development, production or distribution;

12. "competing undertaking" means an undertaking that is supplying a product capable of being improved or replaced by the contract product (an actual competitor) or an undertaking that would, on realistic grounds, undertake the necessary additional investments or other necessary switching costs so that it could supply such a product in response to a small and permanent increase in relative prices (a potential competitor);

13. "relevant market for the contract products" means the relevant product and geographic market(s) to which the contract products belong.

Article 3

Conditions for exemption

1. The exemption provided for in Article 1 shall apply subject to the conditions set out in paragraphs 2 to 5.

2. All the parties must have access to the results of the joint research and development for the purposes of further research or exploitation. However, research institutes, academic bodies, or undertakings which supply research and development as a commercial service without normally being active in the exploitation of results may agree to confine their use of the results for the purposes of further research.

3. Without prejudice to paragraph 2, where the research and development agreement provides only for joint research and development, each party must be free independently to exploit the results of the joint research and development and any pre-existing know-how necessary for the purposes of such exploitation. Such right to exploitation may be limited to one or more technical fields of application, where the parties are not competing undertakings at the time the research and development agreement is enter into.

4. Any joint exploitation must relate to results which are protected by intellectual property rights or constitute know-how, which substantially contribute to technical or economic progress and the results must be decisive for the manufacture of the contract products or the application of the contract processes.

5. Undertakings charged with manufacture by way of specialisation in production must be required to fulfil orders for supplies from all the parties, except where the research and development agreement also provides for joint distribution.

Article 4

Market share threshold and duration of exemption

1. Where the participating undertakings are not competing undertakings, the exemption provided for in Article 1 shall apply for the duration of the research and development. Where the results are jointly exploited, the exemption shall continue to apply for seven years from the time the contract products are first put on the market within the common market.

2. Where two or more of the participating undertakings are competing undertakings, the exemption provided for in Article 1 shall apply for the period referred to in paragraph 1 only if, at the time the agreement is entered into, the combined market share of the participating undertakings does not exceed 25% of the relevant market for the products capable of being improved or replaced by the contract products.

3. After the end of the period referred to in paragraph 1, the exemption shall continue to apply as long as the combined market share of the participating undertakings does not exceed 25% of the relevant market for the contract products.

Article 5

Agreements not covered by the exemption

1. The exemption provided for in Article 1 shall not apply to research and development agreements which, directly or indirectly, in isolation or in combination with other factors under the control of the parties, have as their object:

(a) the restriction of the freedom of the participating undertakings to carry out research and development independently or in cooperation with third parties in a field uncon-nected with that to which the research and development relates or, after its comple-tion, in the field to which it relates or in a connected field;

(b) the prohibition to challenge after completion of the research and development the validity of intellectual property rights which the parties hold in the common market and which are relevant to the research and development or, after the expiry of the research and development agreement, the validity of intellectual property rights which the parties hold in the common market and which protect the results of the research and development, without prejudice to the possibility to provide for termination of the research and development agreement in the event of one of the parties challenging the validity of such intellectual property rights;

(c) the limitation of output or sales;

(d) the fixing of prices when selling the contract product to third parties;

(e) the restriction of the customers that the participating undertakings may serve, after the end of seven years from the time the contract products are first put on the market within the common market;

(f) the prohibition to make passive sales of the contract products in territories reserved for other parties;

(g) the prohibition to put the contract products on the market or to pursue an active sales policy for them in territories within the common market that are reserved for other parties after the end of seven years from the time the contract products are first put on the market within the common market;

(h) the requirement not to grant licences to third parties to manufacture the contract products or to apply the contract processes where the exploitation by at least one of the parties of the results of the joint research and development is not provided for or does not take place;

(i) the requirement to refuse to meet demand from users or resellers in their respective territories who would market the contract products in other territories within the common market; or

(j) the requirement to make it difficult for users or resellers to obtain the contract products from other resellers within the common market, and in particular to exercise intellectual property rights or take measures so as to prevent users or resellers from obtaining, or from putting on the market within the common market, products which have been lawfully put on the market within the Community by another party or with its consent.

2. Paragraph 1 does not apply to:

(a) the setting of production targets where the exploitation of the results includes the joint production of the contract products;

(b) the setting of sales targets and the fixing of prices charged to immediate customers where the exploitation of the results includes the joint distribution of the contract products.

Article 6

Application of the market share threshold

1. For the purposes of applying the market share threshold provided for in Article 4 the following rules shall apply:

(a) the market share shall be calculated on the basis of the market sales value; if market sales value data are not available, estimates based on other reliable market information, including market sales volumes, may be used to establish the market share of the undertaking concerned;

(b) the market share shall be calculated on the basis of data relating to the preceding calendar year;

(c) the market share held by the undertakings referred to in point 3(e) of Article 2 shall be apportioned equally to each undertaking having the rights or the powers listed in point 3(a) of Article 2.

2. If the market share referred to in Article 4(3) is initially not more than 25% but subsequently rises above this level without exceeding 30%, the exemption provided for in

Article 1 shall continue to apply for a period of two consecutive calendar years following the year in which the 25% threshold was first exceeded.

3. If the market share referred to in Article 4(3) is initially not more than 25% but subsequently rises above 30%, the exemption provided for in Article 1 shall continue to apply for one calendar year following the year in which the level of 30% was first exceeded.

4. The benefit of paragraphs 2 and 3 may not be combined so as to exceed a period of two calendar years.

Article 7

Withdrawal

The Commission may withdraw the benefit of this Regulation, pursuant to Article 7 of Regulation (EEC) No 2821/71, where, either on its own initiative or at the request of a Member State or of a natural or legal person claiming a legitimate interest, it finds in a particular case that a research and development agreement to which the exemption provided for in Article 1 applies nevertheless has certain effects which are incompatible with the conditions laid down in Article 81(3) of the Treaty, and in particular where:

(a) the existence of the research and development agreement substantially restricts the scope for third parties to carry out research and development in the relevant field because of the limited research capacity available elsewhere;

(b) because of the particular structure of supply, the existence of the research and development agreement substantially restricts the access of third parties to the market for the contract products;

(c) without any objectively valid reason, the parties do not exploit the results of the joint research and development;

(d) the contract products are not subject in the whole or a substantial part of the common market to effective competition from identical products or products considered by users as equivalent in view of their characteristics, price and intended use;

(e) the existence of the research and development agreement would eliminate effective competition in research and development on a particular market.

Article 8

Transitional period

The prohibition laid down in Article 81(1) of the Treaty shall not apply during the period from 1 January 2001 to 30 June 2002 in respect of agreements already in force on 31 December 2000 which do not satisfy the conditions for exemption provided for in this Regulation but which satisfy the conditions for exemption provided for in Regulation (EEC) No 418/85.

Article 9

Period of validity

This Regulation shall enter into force on 1 January 2001.

It shall expire on 31 December 2010.

This Regulation shall be binding in its entirety and directly applicable in all Member States.

Done at Brussels, 29 November 2000.

APPENDIX 24

REGULATION 240/96[1]

On the Application of Article 81(3) of the Treaty to Certain Categories of Technology Transfer Agreements[2]

THE COMMISSION OF THE EUROPEAN COMMUNITIES

Having regard to the Treaty establishing the European Community.

Having regard to Council Regulation No. 19/65/EEC of 2 March 1965 on the application of Article 81(3) of the Treaty to certain categories of agreements and concerted practices[3] as last amended by the Act of Accession of Austria, Finland and Sweden, and in particular Article 1 thereof,

Having published a draft of this Regulation,[4]

After consulting the Advisory Committee on Restrictive Practices and Dominant Positions,

Whereas:

(1) Regulation No. 19/65/EEC empowers the Commission to apply Article 81(3) of the Treaty by regulation to certain categories of agreements and concerted practices falling within the scope of Article 81(1) which include restrictions imposed in relation to the acquisition or use of industrial property rights—in particular of patents, utility models, designs or trademarks—or to the rights arising out of contracts for assignment of, or the right to use, a method of manufacture of knowledge relating to use or to the application of industrial processes.

(2) The Commission has made use of this power by adopting Regulation (EEC) No. 2349/84 of 23 July 1984 on the application of Article 81(3) of the Treaty to certain categories of patent licensing agreements,[5] as last amended by Regulation (EC) No. 2131/95,[6] and Regulation (EEC) No. 556/89 of 30 November 1988 on the application of Article 81(3) of the Treaty to certain categories of know-how licensing agreements,[7] as last amended by the Act of Accession of Austria, Finland and Sweden.

(3) These two block exemptions ought to be combined into a single regulation covering technology transfer agreements, and the rules governing patent licensing agreements and agreements for the licensing of know-how ought to be harmonized and simplified as far as possible, in order to encourage the dissemination of technical knowledge in the Community and to promote the manufacture of technically more sophisticated products. In those circumstances Regulation (EEC) No. 556/89 should be repealed.

---

[1] OJ 1996 L31/2.
[2] Text with EEA relevance.
[3] OJ 1965 C36/533.
[4] OJ 1994 C178/3.
[5] OJ 1974 L219/15.
[6] OJ 1995 L214/6.
[7] OJ 1989 L61/1.

162

(4) This Regulation should apply to the licensing of Member States' own patents, Community patents[8] and European patents[9] ("pure" patent licensing agreements). It should also apply to agreements for the licensing of non-patented technical information such as descriptions of manufacturing processes, recipes, formulae, designs or drawings, commonly termed "know-how" ("pure" know-how licensing agreements), and to combined patent and know-how licensing agreements ("mixed" agreements), which are playing an increasingly important role in the transfer of technology. For the purposes of this Regulation, a number of terms are defined in Article 10.

(5) Patent or know-how licensing agreements are agreements whereby one undertaking which holds a patent or know-how ("the licensor") permits another undertaking ("the licensee") to exploit the patent thereby licensed, or communicates the know-how to it, in particular for purposes of manufacture, use or putting on the market. In the light of experience acquired so far, it is possible to define a category of licensing agreements covering all or part of the common market which are capable of falling within the scope of Article 81(1) but which can normally be regarded as satisfying the conditions laid down in Article 81(3), where patents are necessary for the achievement of the objects of the licensed technology by a mixed agreement or where know-how—whether it is ancillary to patents or independent of them—is secret, substantial and identified in any appropriate form. These criteria are intended only to ensure that the licensing of the know-how or the grant of the patent licence justifies a block exemption of obligations restricting competition. This is without prejudice to the right of the parties to include in the contract provisions regarding other obligations, such as the obligation to pay royalties, even if the block exemption no longer applies.

(6) It is appropriate to extend the scope of this Regulation to pure or mixed agreements containing the licensing of intellectual property rights other than patents (in particular, trademarks, design rights and copyright, especially software protection), when such additional licensing contributes to the achievement of the objects of the licensed technology and contains only ancillary provisions.

(7) Where such pure or mixed licensing agreements contain not only obligations relating to territories within the common market but also obligations relating to non-member countries, the presence of the latter does not prevent this Regulation from applying to the obligations relating to territories within the common market. Where licensing agreements for non-member countries or for territories which extend beyond the frontiers of the Community have effects within the common market which may fall within the scope of Article 81(1), such agreements should be covered by this Regulation to the same extent as would agreements for territories within the common market.

(8) The objective being to facilitate the dissemination of technology and the improvement of manufacturing processes, this Regulation should apply only where the licensee himself manufactures the licensed products or has them manufactured for his account, or where the licensed products is a service, provides the service himself or has the service provided for his account, irrespective of whether or not the licensee is also entitled to use confidential information provided by the licensor for the promotion and sale of the licensed product. The scope of this Regulation should therefore exclude agreements solely for the purpose of sale. Also to be excluded from the scope of this Regulation are agreements relating to marketing know-how communicated in the context of franchising arrangements and certain licensing agreements entered into in connection with arrangements such as joint ventures or patent pools and other arrangements in which a licence is granted in exchange for other licences not related to improvements to or new applications of the licensed technology. Such agreements pose different problems which cannot at present be dealt with in a single regulation (Article 5).

(9) Given the similarity between sale and exclusive licensing, and the danger that the requirements of this Regulation might be evaded by presenting as assignments what are

---

[8] Convention for the European patent for the common market (Community Patent Convention) of 15 December 1975, O.J. 1976 L17/1.

[9] Convention on the grant of European patents (European Patent Convention) of 5 October 1973.

in fact exclusive licenses restrictive of competition, this Regulation should apply to agreements concerning the assignment and acquisition of patents or know-how where the risk associated with exploitation remains with the assignor. It should also apply to licensing agreements in which the licensor is not the holder of the patent or know-how but is authorised by the holder to grant the licence (as in the case of sub-licences) and to licensing agreements in which the parties' rights or obligations are assumed by connected undertakings (Article 6).

(10) Exclusive licensing agreements, *i.e.* agreements in which the licensor undertakes not to exploit the licensed technology in the licensed territory himself or to grant further licences there, may not be in themselves incompatible with Article 81(1) where they are concerned with the introduction and protection of a new technology in the licensed territory, by reason of the scale of the research which has been undertaken, of the increase in the level of competition, in particular inter-brand competition, and of the competitiveness of the undertakings concerned resulting from the dissemination of innovation within the Community. In so far as agreements of this kind fall, in other circumstances, within the scope of Article 81(1), it is appropriate to include them in Article 1 in order that they may also benefit from the exemption.

(11) The exemption of export bans on the licensor and on the licensees does not prejudice any developments in the case law of the Court of Justice in relation to such agreements, notably with respect to Articles 28 to 30 and Article 81(1). This is also the case, in particular, regarding the prohibition on the licensee from selling the licensed product in territories granted to other licensees (passive competition).

(12) The obligations listed in Article 1 generally contribute to improving the production of goods and to promoting technical progress. They make the holders of patents or know-how more willing to grant licences and licensees more inclined to undertake the investment required to manufacture, use and put on the market a new product or to use a new process. Such obligations may be permitted under this Regulation in respect of territories where the licensed product is protected by patents as long as these remain in force.

(13) Since the point at which the know-how ceases to be secret can be difficult to determine, it is appropriate, in respect of territories where the licensed technology comprises know-how only, to limit such obligations to a fixed number of years. Moreover, in order to provide sufficient periods of protection, it is appropriate to take as the starting point for such periods the date on which the product is first put on the market in the Community by a licensee.

(14) Exemption under Article 81(3) of longer periods of territorial protection for know-how agreements, in particular in order to protect expensive and risky investment or where the parties were not competitors at the date of the grant of the licence, can be granted only by individual decision. On the other hand, parties are free to extend the term of their agreements in order to exploit any subsequent improvement and to provide for the payment of additional royalties. However, in such cases, further periods of territorial protection may be allowed only starting from the date of licensing of the secret improvements in the Community, and by individual decision. Where the research for improvements results in innovations which are distinct from the licensed technology the parties may conclude a new agreement benefiting from an exemption under this Regulation.

(15) Provision should also be made for exemption of an obligation on the licensee not to put the product on the market in the territories of other licensees, the permitted period for such an obligation (this obligation would ban not just active competition but passive competition too) should, however be limited to a few years from the date on which the licensed product is first put on the market in the Community by a licensee, irrespective of whether the licensed technology comprises know-how, patents or both in the territories concerned.

(16) The exemption of territorial protection should apply for the whole duration of the periods thus permitted, as long as the patents remain in force or the know-how remains secret and substantial. The parties to a mixed patent and know-how licensing agreement

must be able to take advantage in a particular territory of the period of protection conferred by a patent or by the know-how, whichever is the longer.

(17) The obligations listed in Article 1 also generally fulfil the other conditions for the application of Article 81(3). Consumers will, as a rule, be allowed a fair share of the benefit resulting from the improvement in the supply of goods on the market. To safeguard this effect, however, it is right to exclude from the application of Article 1 cases where the parties agree to refuse to meet demand from users or resellers within their respective territories who would resell for export, or to take other steps to impede parallel imports. The obligations referred to above thus only impose restrictions which are indispensable to the attainment of their objectives.

(18) It is desirable to list in this Regulation a number of obligations that are commonly found in licensing agreements but are normally not restrictive of competition, and to provide that in the event that because of the particular economic or legal circumstances they should fall within Article 81(1), they too will be covered by the exemption. This list, in Article 2, is not exhaustive.

(19) This Regulation must also specify what restrictions or provisions may not be included in licensing agreements if these are to benefit from the block exemption. The restrictions listed in Article 3 may fall under the prohibition of Article 81(1), but in their case there can be no general presumption that, although they relate to the transfer of technology, they will lead to the positive effects required by Article 81(3), as would be necessary for the granting of a block exemption. Such restrictions can be declared exempt only by an individual decision, taking account of the market position of the undertakings concerned and the degree of concentration on the relevant market.

(20) The obligations on the licensee to cease using the licensed technology after the termination of the agreement (Article 2(1)(3)) and to make improvements available to the licensor (Article 2(1)(4)) do not generally restrict competition. The post-term use ban may be regarded as a normal feature of licensing, as otherwise the licensor would be forced to transfer his know-how or patents in perpetuity. Undertakings by the licensee to grant back to the licensor a licence for improvements to the licensed know-how and/or patents are generally not restrictive of competition if the licensee is entitled by the contract to share in future experience and inventions made by the licensor. On the other hand, a restrictive effect on competition arises where the agreement obliges the licensee to assign to the licensor rights to improvements of the originally licensed technology that he himself has brought about (Article 3(6)).

(21) The list of clauses which do not prevent exemption also includes an obligation on the licensee to keep paying royalties until the end of the agreement independently of whether or not the licensed know-how has entered into the public domain through the action of third parties or of the licensee himself (Article 2(1)(7)). Moreover, the parties must be free, in order to facilitate payment, to spread the royalty payments for the use of the licensed technology over a period extending beyond the duration of the licensed patents, in particular by setting lower royalty rates. As a rule, parties do not need to be protected against the foreseeable financial consequences of an agreement freely entered into, and they should therefore be free to choose the appropriate means of financing the technology transfer and sharing between them the risks of such use. However, the setting of rates of royalty so as to achieve one of the restrictions listed in Article 3 renders the agreement ineligible for the block exemption.

(22) An obligation on the licensee to restrict his exploitation of the licensed technology to one or more technical fields of application ("fields of use") or to one or more product markets is not caught by Article 81(1) either, since the licensor is entitled to transfer the technology only for a limited purpose (Article 2(1)(8)).

(23) Clauses whereby the parties allocate customers within the same technological field of use or the same product market, either by an actual prohibition on supplying certain classes of customer or through an obligation with an equivalent effect, would also render the agreement ineligible for the block exemption where the parties are competitors for the contract products (Article 3(4)). Such restrictions between undertakings which are not

competitors remain subject to the opposition procedure. Article 3 does not apply to cases where the patent or know-how licence is granted in order to provide a single customer with a second source of supply. In such a case, a prohibition on the second licensee from supplying persons other than the customer concerned is an essential condition for the grant of a second licence, since the purpose of the transaction is not to create an independent supplier in the market. The same applies to limitations on the quantities the licensee may supply to the customer concerned (Article 2(1)(13)).

(24) Besides the clauses already mentioned, the list of restrictions which render the block exemption inapplicable also includes restrictions regarding the selling prices of the licensed product or the quantities to be manufactured or sold, since they seriously limit the extent to which the licensee can exploit the licensed technology and since quantity restrictions particularly may have the same effect as export bans (Article 3(1) and (5)). This does not apply where a licence is granted for use of the technology in specific production facilities and where both a specific technology is communicated for the setting-up, operation and maintenance of these facilities and the licensee is allowed to increase the capacity of the facilities or to set up further facilities for its own use on normal commercial terms. On the other hand, the licensee may lawfully be prevented from using the transferred technology to set up facilities for third parties, since the purpose of the agreement is not to permit the licensee to give other producers access to the licensor's technology while it remains secret or protected by patent (Article 2(1)(12)).

(25) Agreements which are not automatically covered by the exemption because they contain provisions that are not expressly exempted by this Regulation and not expressly excluded from exemption, including those listed in Article 4(2), may, in certain circumstances, nonetheless be presumed to be eligible for application of the block exemption. It will be possible for the Commission rapidly to establish whether this is the case on the basis of the information undertakings are obliged to provide under Commission Regulation (EC) No. 3385/94.[10] The Commission may waive the requirement to supply specific information required in form A/B but which it does not deem necessary. The Commission will generally be content with communication of the text of the agreement and with an estimate, based on directly available data, of the market structure and the licensee's market share. Such agreements should therefore be deemed to be covered by the exemption provided for in this Regulation where they are notified to the Commission and the Commission does not oppose the application of the exemption within a specified period of time.

(26) Where agreements exempted under this Regulation nevertheless have effects incompatible with Article 81(3), the Commission may withdraw the block exemption, in particular where the licensed products are not faced with real competition in the licensed territory (Article 7). This could also be the case where the licensee has a strong position on the market. In assessing the competition the Commission will pay special attention to cases where the licensee has more than 40 per cent of the whole market for the licensed products and of all the products or services which customers consider interchangeable or substitutable on account of their characteristics, prices and intended use.

(27) Agreements which come within the terms of Articles 1 and 2 and which have neither the object nor the effect of restricting competition in any other way need no longer be notified. Nevertheless, undertakings will still have the right to apply in individual cases for negative clearance or for exemption under Article 81(3) in accordance with Council Regulation No. 17,[11] as last amended by the Act of Accession of Austria, Finland and Sweden. They can in particular notify agreements obliging the licensor not to grant other licences in the territory, where the licensee's market share exceeds or is likely to exceed 40 per cent.

---

[10] OJ 1994 L377/31.
[11] OJ 1962 13/204.

Has adopted this regulation:

Article 1

1. Pursuant to Article 81(3) of the Treaty and subject to the conditions set out below, it is hereby declared that Article 81(1) of the Treaty shall not apply to pure patent licensing or know-how licensing agreements and mixed patent and know-how licensing agreements, including those agreements containing ancillary provisions relating to intellectual property rights other than patents to which only two undertakings are party and which include one or more of the following obligations:

(1) an obligation on the licensor not to license other undertakings to exploit the licensed technology in the licensed territory;
(2) an obligation on the licensor not to exploit the licensed technology in the licensed territory himself;
(3) an obligation on the licensee not to exploit the licensed technology in the territory of the licensor within the common market;
(4) an obligation on the licensee not to manufacture or use the licensed product, or use the licensed process in territories within the common market which are licensed to other licensees;
(5) an obligation on the licensee not to pursue an active policy of putting the licensed product on the market in the territories within the common market which are licensed to other licensees, and in particular not to engage in advertising specifically aimed at those territories or to establish any branch or maintain a distribution depot there;
(6) an obligation on the licensee not to put the licensed product on the market in the territories licensed to other licensees within the common market in response to unsolicited orders;
(7) an obligation on the licensee to use only the licensor's trademark or get up to distinguish the licensed product during the term of the agreement, provided that the licensee is not prevented from identifying himself as the manufacturer of the licensed products;
(8) an obligation on the licensee to limit his production of the licensed product to the quantities he requires in manufacturing his own products and to sell the licensed product only as an integral part of or a replacement part for his own products or otherwise in connection with the sale of his own products, provided that such quantities are freely determined by the licensee.

2. Where the agreement is a pure patent licensing agreement, the exemption of the obligations referred to in paragraph 1 is granted only to the extent that and for as long as the licensed product is protected by parallel patents, in the territories respectively of the licensee (points (1), (2), (7) and (8)), the licensor (point (3)) and other licensees (points (4) and (5)). The exemption of the obligation referred to in point (6) of paragraph 1 is granted for a period not exceeding five years from the date when the licensed product is first put on the market within the common market by one of the licensees, to the extent that and for as long as, in these territories, this product is protected by parallel patents.

3. Where the agreement is a pure know-how licensing agreement, the period for which the exemption of the obligations referred to in points (1) to (5) of paragraph 1 is granted may not exceed ten years from the date when the licensed product is first put on the market within the common market by one of the licensees.

The exemption of the obligation referred to in point (6) of paragraph 1 is granted for a period not exceeding five years from the date when the licensed product is first put on the market within the common market by one of the licensees.

The obligations referred to in points (7) and (8) of paragraph 1 are exempted during the lifetime of the agreement for as long as the know-how remains secret and substantial.

However, the exemption in paragraph 1 shall apply only where the parties have identified in any appropriate form the initial know-how and any subsequent improvements to it which become available to one party and are communicated to the other party pursuant to the terms of the agreement and to the purpose thereof, and only for as long as the know-how remains secret and substantial.

Where the agreement is a mixed patent and know-how licensing agreement, the exemption of the obligations referred to in points (1) to (5) of paragraph 1 shall apply in Member States in which the licensed technology is protected by necessary patents for as long as the licensed product is protected in those Member States by such patents if the duration of such protection exceeds the periods specified in paragraph 3.

The duration of the exemption provided in point (6) of paragraph 1 may not exceed the five-year period provided for in paragraphs 2 and 3.

However, such agreements qualify for the exemption referred to in paragraph 1 only for as long as the patents remain in force or to the extent that the know-how is quantified and for as long as it remains secret and substantiated, whichever period is the longer.

5. The exemption provided for in paragraph 1 shall also apply where in a particular agreement the parties undertake obligations of the types referred to in that paragraph but with a more limited scope than is permitted by that paragraph.

Article 2

1. Article 1 shall apply notwithstanding the presence in particular of any of the following clauses, which are generally not restrictive of competition:

(1) an obligation on the licensee not to divulge the know-how communicated by the licensor; the licensee may be held to this obligation after the agreement has expired;

(2) an obligation on the licensee not to grant sublicences or assign the licence;

(3) an obligation on the licensee not to exploit the licensed know-how or patents after termination of the agreement in so far and as long as the know-how is still secret or the patents are still in force;

(4) an obligation on the licensee to grant to the licensor a licence in respect of his own improvements to or his new applications of the licensed technology, provided:
   — that, in the case of severable improvements, such a licence is not exclusive, so that the licensee is free to use his own improvements or to license them to third parties, in so far as that does not involve disclosure of the know-how communicated by the licensor that is still secret,
   — and that the licensor undertakes to grant an exclusive or non-exclusive licence of his own improvements to the licensee;

(5) an obligation on the licensee to observe minimum quality specifications, including technical specifications, for the licensed product or to procure goods or services from the licensor or from an undertaking designated by the licensor, in so far as these quality specifications, products or services are necessary for:
   (a) a technically proper exploitation of the licensed technology; or
   (b) ensuring that the product of the licensee conforms to the minimum quality specifications that are applicable to the licensor and other licensees;
   and to allow the licensor to carry out related checks;

(6) obligations:
   (a) to inform the licensor of misappropriation of the know-how or of infringements of the licensed patents; or
   (b) to take or to assist the licensor in taking legal action against such misappropriation or infringements;

(7) an obligation on the licensee to continue paying the royalties:

(a) until the end of the agreement in the amounts, for the periods and according to the methods freely determined by the parties, in the event of the know-how becoming publicly known other than by action of the licensor, without prejudice to the payment of any additional damages in the event of the know-how becoming publicly known by the action of the licensee in breach of the agreement;

(b) over a period going beyond the duration of the licensed patents, in order to facilitate payment;

(8) an obligation on the licensee to restrict his exploitation of the licensed technology to one or more technical fields of application covered by the licensed technology or to one or more product markets;

(9) an obligation on the licensee to pay a minimum royalty or to produce a minimum quantity of the licensed product or to carry out a minimum number of operations exploiting the licensed technology;

(10) an obligation on the licensor to grant the licensee any more favourable terms that the licensor may grant to another undertaking after the agreement is entered into;

(11) an obligation on the licensee to mark the licensed product with an indication of the licensors name or of the licensed patent;

(12) an obligation on the licensee not to use the licensor's technology to construct facilities for third parties; this is without prejudice to the right of the licensee to increase the capacity of his facilities or to set up additional facilities for his own use on normal commercial terms, including the payment of additional royalties;

(13) an obligation on the licensee to supply only a limited quantity of the licensed product to a particular customer, where the licence was granted so that the customer might have a second source of supply inside the licensed territory; this provision shall also apply where the customer is the licensee, and the licence which was granted in order to provide a second source of supply provides that the customer is himself to manufacture the licensed products or to have them manufactured by a subcontractor;

(14) a reservation by the licensor of the right to exercise the rights conferred by a patent to oppose the exploitation of the technology by the licensee outside the licensed territory;

(15) a reservation by the licensor of the right to terminate the agreement if the licensee contests the secret or substantial nature of the licensed know-how or challenges the validity of licensed patents within the common market belonging to the licensor or undertakings connected with him;

(16) a reservation by the licensor of the right to terminate the licence agreement of a patent if the licensee raises the claim that such a patent is not necessary;

(17) an obligation on the licensee to use his best endeavours to manufacture and market the licensed product;

(18) a reservation by the licensor of the right to terminate the exclusivity granted to the licensee and to stop licensing improvements to him when the licensee enters into competition within the common market with the licensor, with undertakings connected with the licensor or with other undertakings in respect of research and development, production, use or distribution of competing products, and to require the licensee to prove that the licensed know-how is not being used for the production of products and the provision of services other than those licensed.

2. In the event that, because of particular circumstances, the clauses referred to in paragraph 1 fall within the scope of Article 81(1), they shall also be exempted even if they are not accompanied by any of the obligations exempted by Article 1.

3. The exemption in paragraph 2 shall also apply where an agreement contains clauses of the types referred to in paragraph 1 but with a more limited scope than is permitted by that paragraph.

Article 3

Article 1 and Article 2(2) shall not apply where:

(1) one party is restricted in the determination of prices, components of prices or discounts for the licensed products;

(2) one party is restricted from competing within the common market with the other party, with undertakings connected with the other party or with other undertakings in respect of research and development, production, use or distribution of competing products without prejudice to the provisions of Article 2(1)(17) and (18);

(3) one or both of the parties are required without any objectively justified reason:
   (a) to refuse to meet orders from users or resellers in their respective territories who would market products in other territories within the common market:
   (b) to make it difficult for users or resellers to obtain the products from other resellers within the common market, and in particular to exercise intellectual property rights or take measures so as to prevent users or resellers from obtaining outside, or from putting on the market in the licensed territory products which have been lawfully put on the market within the common market by the licensor or with his consent;
   or do so as a result of a concerted practice between them;

(4) the parties were already competing manufacturers before the grant of the licence and one of them is restricted, within the same technical field of use or within the same product market, as to the customers he may serve, in particular by being prohibited from supplying certain classes of user, employing certain forms of distribution or, with the aim of sharing customers, using certain types of packaging for the products, save as provided in Article 1(1)(7) and Article 2(1)(13);

(5) the quantity of the licensed products one party may manufacture or sell or the number of operations exploiting the licensed technology he may carry out or subject to limitations, save as provided in Article (1)(8) and Article 2(1)(13);

(6) the licensee is obliged to assign in whole or in part to the licensor rights to improvements to or new applications of the licensed technology;

(7) the licensor is required, albeit in separate agreements or through automatic prolongation of the initial duration of the agreement by the inclusion of any new improvements, for a period exceeding that referred to in Article 1(2) and (3) not to license other undertakings to exploit the licensed technology in the licensed territory, or a party is required for a period exceeding that referred to in Article 1(2) and (3) or Article 1(4) not to exploit the licensed technology in the territory of the other party or of other licensees.

Article 4

1. The exemption provided for in Articles 1 and 2 shall also apply to agreements containing obligations restrictive of competition which are not covered by those Articles and do not fall within the scope of Article 3, on condition that the agreements in question are notified to the Commission in accordance with the provisions of Articles 1, 2 and 3 of Regulation (EC) No. 3385/94 and that the Commission does not oppose such exemption within a period of four months.

2. Paragraph 1 shall apply, in particular, where:

(a) the licensee is obliged at the time the agreement is entered into to accept quality specifications or further licences or to procure goods or services which are not necessary for a technically satisfactory exploitation of the licensed technology or for ensuring that the production of the licensee conforms to the quality standards that are respected by the licensor and other licensees;

(b) the licensee is prohibited from contesting the secrecy or the substantiality of the licensed know-how or from challenging the validity of patents licensed within the common market belonging to the licensor or undertakings connected with him.

3. The period of four months referred to in paragraph 1 shall run from the date on which the notification takes effect in accordance with Article 4 of Regulation (EC) No. 3385/94.

4. The benefit of paragraphs 1 and 2 may be claimed for agreements notified before the entry into force of this Regulation by submitting a communication to the Commission referring expressly to this Article and to the notification. Paragraph 3 shall apply *mutatis mutandis*.

5. The Commission may oppose the exemption within a period of four months. It shall oppose exemption if it receives a request to do so from a Member State within two months of the transmission to the Member State of the notification referred to in paragraph 1 or of the communication referred to in paragraph 4. This request must be justified on the basis of considerations relating to the competition rules of the Treaty.

6. The Commission may withdraw the opposition to the exemption at any time. However, where the opposition was raised at the request of a Member State and this request is maintained, it may be withdrawn only after consultation of the Advisory Committee on Restrictive Practices and Dominant Positions.

7. If the opposition is withdrawn because the undertakings concerned have shown that the conditions of Article 81(3) are satisfied, the exemption shall apply from the date of notification.

8. If the opposition is withdrawn because the undertakings concerned have amended the agreement so that the conditions of Article 81(3) are satisfied, the exemption shall apply from the date on which the amendments take effect.

9. If the Commission opposes exemption and the opposition is not withdrawn, the effects of the notification shall be governed by the provisions of Regulation No. 17.

Article 5

1. This Regulation shall not apply to:

(1) agreements between members of a patent or know-how pool which relate to the pooled technologies;
(2) licensing agreements between competing undertakings which hold interests in a joint venture, or between one of them and the joint venture, if the licensing agreements relate to the activities of the joint venture;
(3) agreements under which one party grants the other a patent and/or know-how licence and in exchange the other party, albeit in separate agreements or through connected undertakings, grants the first party a patent, trademark or know-how licence or exclusive sales rights, where the parties are competitors in relation to the products covered by those agreements;
(4) licensing agreements containing provisions relating to intellectual property rights other than patents which are not ancillary;
(5) agreements entered into solely for the purpose of sale.

2. This Regulation shall nevertheless apply:

(1) to agreements to which paragraph 1(2) applies, under which a parent undertaking grants the joint venture a patent or know-how licence, provided that the licensed products and the other goods and services of the participating undertakings which are considered by users to be interchangeable or substitutable in view of their characteristics, price and intended use represent:
    — in case of a licence limited to production, not more than 20 per cent, and
    — in case of a licence covering production and distribution, not more than 10 per cent;

171

of the market for the licensed products and all interchangeable or substitutable goods and services;

(2) to agreements to which paragraph 1(1) applies and to reciprocal licences within the meaning of paragraph 1(3), provided the parties are not subject to any territorial restriction within the common market with regard to the manufacture, use or putting on the market of the licensed products or to the use of the licensed or pooled technologies.

3. This Regulation shall continue to apply where, for two consecutive financial years, the market shares in paragraph 2(1) are not exceeded by more than one-tenth; where that limit is exceeded, this Regulation shall continue to apply for a period of six months from the end of the year in which the limit was exceeded.

Article 6

This Regulation shall also apply to:

(1) agreements where the licensor is not the holder of the know-how or the patentee, but is authorised by the holder or the patentee to grant a licence;
(2) assignments of know-how, patents or both where the risk associated with exploitation remains with the assignor, in particular where the sum payable in consideration of the assignment is dependent on the turnover obtained by the assignee in respect of products made using the know-how or the patents, the quantity of such products manufactured or the number of operations carried out employing the know-how or the patents:
(3) licensing agreements in which the rights or obligations of the licensor or the licensee are assumed by undertakings connected with them.

Article 7

The Commission may withdraw the benefit of this Regulation, pursuant to Article 7 of Regulation No. 19/65/EEC, where it finds in a particular case that an agreement exempted by this Regulation nevertheless has certain effects which are incompatible with the conditions laid down in Article 81(3) of the Treaty, and in particular where:

(1) the effect of the agreement is to prevent the licensed products from being exposed to effective competition in the licensed territory from identical goods or services or from goods or services considered by users as interchangeable or substitutable in view of their characteristics, price and intended use, which may in particular occur where the licensee's market share exceeds 40 per cent;
(2) without prejudice to Article 1(1)(6), the licensee refuses, without any objectively justified reason, to meet unsolicited orders from users or resellers in the territory of other licensees;
(3) the parties:
  (a) without any objectively justified reason, refuse to meet orders from users or resellers in their respective territories who would market the products in other territories within the common market; or
  (b) make it difficult for users or resellers to obtain the products from other resellers within the common market, and in particular where they exercise intellectual property rights or take measures so as to prevent resellers or users from obtaining outside, or from putting on the market in the licensed territory products which have been lawfully put on the market within the common market by the licensor or with his consent;
(4) the parties were competing manufacturers at the date of the grant of the licence and obligations on the licensee to produce a minimum quantity or to use his best

endeavours as referred to in Article 2(1), (9) and (17) respectively have the effect of preventing the licensee from using competing technologies.

Article 8

1. For purposes of this Regulation:

(a) patent applications;
(b) utility models;
(c) applications for registration of utility models;
(d) topographies of semiconductor products;
(e) *certificats d'utilité* and *certificats d'addition* under French law;
(f) application for *certificats d'utilité* and *certificats d'addition* under French law;
(g) supplementary protection certificates for medicinal products or other products for which such supplementary protection certificates may be obtained;
(h) plant breeder's certificates,

shall be deemed to be patents.

2. This Regulation shall also apply to agreements relating to the exploitation of an invention if an application within the meaning of paragraph 1 is made in respect of the invention for a licensed territory after the date when the agreements were entered into but within the time limits set by the national law or the international convention to be applied.

3. This Regulation shall furthermore apply to pure patent or know-how licensing agreements or to mixed agreements whose initial duration is automatically prolonged by the inclusion of any new improvements, whether patented or not, communicated by the licensor, provided that the licensee has the right to refuse such improvements or each party has the right to terminate the agreement at the expiry of the initial term of an agreement and at least every three years thereafter.

Article 9

1. Information acquired pursuant to Article 4 shall be used only for the purposes of this Regulation.

2. The Commission and the authorities of the Member States, their officials and other servants shall not disclose information acquired by them pursuant to this Regulation of the kind covered by the obligation of professional secrecy.

3. The provisions of paragraphs 1 and 2 shall not prevent publication of general information or surveys which do not contain information relating to particular undertakings or associations of undertakings.

Article 10

For purposes of this Regulation:

(1) "know-how" means a body of technical information that is secret, substantial and identified in any appropriate form;
(2) "secret" means that the know-how package as a body or in the precise configuration and assembly of its components is not generally known or easily accessible, so that part of its value consists in the lead which the licensee gains when it is communicated to him; it is not limited to the narrow sense that each individual component of the know-how should be totally unknown or unobtainable outside the licensor's business;
(3) "substantial" means that the know-how includes information which must be useful, *i.e.* can reasonably be expected at the date of conclusion of the agreement to be

capable of improving the competitive position of the licensee, for example by helping him to enter a new market or giving him an advantage in competition with other manufacturers or providers of services who do not have access to the licensed secret know-how or other comparable secret know-how;

(4) "identified" means that the know-how is described or recorded in such a manner as to make it possible to verify that it satisfies the criteria of secrecy and substantiality and to ensure that the licensee is not unduly restricted in his exploitation of his own technology, to be identified the know-how can either be set out in the licence agreement or in a separate document or recorded in any other appropriate form at the latest when the know-how is transferred or shortly thereafter, provided that the separate document or other record can be made available if the need arises;

(5) "necessary patents" are patents where a licence under the patent is necessary for the putting into effect of the licensed technology in so far as, in the absence of such a licence, the realisation of the licensed technology would not be possible or would be possible only to a lesser extent or in more difficult or costly conditions. Such patents must therefore be of technical, legal or economic interest to the licensee;

(6) "licensing agreement" means pure patent licensing agreements and pure know-how licensing agreements as well as mixed patent and know-how licensing agreements;

(7) "licensed technology" means the initial manufacturing know-how or the necessary product and process patents, or both, existing at the time the first licensing agreement is concluded, and improvements subsequently made to the know-how or patents, irrespective of whether and to what extent they are exploited by the parties or by other licensees;

(8) "the licensed products" are goods or services the production or provision of which requires the use of the licensed technology;

(9) "the licensee's market share" means the proportion which the licensed products and other goods or services provided by the licensee, which are considered by users to be interchangeable or substitutable for the licensed products in view of their character- istics, price and intended use, represent the entire market for the licensed products and all other interchangeable or substitutable goods and services in the common market or a substantial part of it;

(10) "exploitation" refers to any use of the licensed technology in particular in the production, active or passive sales in a territory even if not coupled with manufacture in that territory, or leasing of the licensed products;

(11) "the licensed territory" is the territory covering all or at least part of the common market where the licensee is entitled to exploit the licensed technology;

(12) "territory of the licensor" means territories in which the licensor has not granted any licences for patents and/or know-how covered by the licensing agreement;

(13) "parallel patents" means patents which, in spite of the divergences which remain in the absence of any unification of national rules concerning industrial property, protect the same invention in various Member States;

(14) "connected undertakings" means:
  (a) undertakings in which a party to the agreement, directly or indirectly:
    — owns more than half the capital or business assets, or
    — has the power to exercise more than half the voting rights, or
    — has the power to appoint more than half the members of the supervisory board, board of directors, or bodies legally representing the undertaking, or
    has the right to manage the affairs of the undertaking;
  (b) undertakings which, directly or indirectly, have in or over a party to the agree- ment the rights or powers listed in (a);
  (c) undertakings in which an undertaking referred to in (b), directly or indirectly, has the rights or powers listed in (a);
  (d) undertakings in which the parties to the agreement or undertakings connected with them jointly have the rights or powers listed in (a): such jointly controlled

undertakings are considered to be connected with each of the parties to the agreement;

(15) "ancillary provisions" are provisions relating to the exploitation of intellectual property rights other than patents, which contain no obligations restrictive of competition other than those also attached to the licensed know-how or patents and exempted under this Regulation;

(16) "obligation" means both contractual obligation and a concerted practice;

(17) "competing manufacturers" or manufacturers of "competing products" means manufacturers who sell products which, in view of their characteristics, price and intended use, are considered by users to be interchangeable or substitutable for the licensed products.

Article 11

1. Regulation (EEC) No. 556/89 is hereby repealed with effect from 1 April 1996.

2. Regulation (EEC) No. 2349/84 shall continue to apply until 31 March 1996.

3. The prohibition in Article 81(1) of the Treaty shall not apply to agreements in force on 31 March 1996 which fulfil the exemption requirements laid down by Regulation (EEC) No. 2349/84 or (EEC) No. 556/89.

Article 12

1. The Commission shall undertake regular assessments of the application of this Regulation, and in particular of the opposition procedure provided for in Article 4.

2. The Commission shall draw up a report on the operation of this Regulation before the end of the fourth year following its entry into force and shall, on that basis assess whether any adaptation of the Regulation is desirable.

Article 13

This Regulation shall enter into force on 1 April 1996.

It shall apply until 31 March 2006.

Article 11(2) of this Regulation shall, however, enter into force on 1 January 1996.

This Regulation shall be binding in its entirety and directly applicable in all Member States.

Done at Brussels, 31 January 1996.

APPENDIX 25

REGULATION 3932/92[1]

On the Application of Article 81(3) of the Treaty to Certain Categories of Agreements, Decisions and Concerted Practices in the Insurance Sector

THE COMMISSION OF THE EUROPEAN COMMUNITIES

Having regard to the Treaty establishing the European Economic Community,

Having regard to Council Regulation (EEC) No. 1534/91 of 31 May 1991 on the application of Article 81(3) of the Treaty to certain categories of agreements, decisions and concerted practices in the insurance sector,[2]

Having published a draft of this Regulation,[3]

Having consulted the Advisory Committee on Restrictive Practices and Dominant Positions,

Whereas:

(1) Regulation (EEC) No. 1534/91 empowers the Commission to apply Article 81(3) of the Treaty by regulation to certain categories of agreements, decisions and concerted practices in the insurance sector which have as their object:

(a) co-operation with respect to the establishment of common risk premium tariffs based on collectively ascertained statistics or the number of claims;
(b) the establishment of common standard policy conditions;
(c) the common coverage of certain types of risks;
(d) the settlement of claims;
(e) the testing and acceptance of security devices;
(f) registers of, and information on, aggravated risks.

(2) The Commission by now has acquired sufficient experience in handling individual cases to make use of such power in respect of the categories of agreements specified in points (a), (b), (c) and (e) of the list.

(3) In many cases, collaboration between insurance companies in the aforementioned fields goes beyond what the Commission has permitted in its notice concerning co-operation between enterprises,[4] and is caught by the prohibition in Article 81(1). It is therefore appropriate to specify the obligations restrictive of competition which may be included in the four categories of agreements covered by it.

---

[1] OJ 1992 L398/7.
[2] OJ 1991 L143/1.
[3] OJ 1992 C207/2.
[4] OJ 1968 C75/3. Corrigendum O.J. 1968 C84/14.

176

(4) It is further necessary to specify for each of the four categories the conditions which must be satisfied before the exemption can apply. These conditions have to ensure that the collaboration between insurance undertakings is and remains compatible with Article 81(3).

(5) It is finally necessary to specify for each of these categories the situations in which the exemption does not apply. For this purpose it has to define the clauses which may not be included in the agreements covered by it because they impose undue restrictions on the parties, as well as other situations falling under Article 81(1) for which there is no general presumption that they will yield the benefits required by Article 81(3).

(6) Collaboration between insurance undertakings or within associations of undertakings in the compilation of statistics on the number of claims, the number of individual risks insured, total amounts paid in respect of claims and the amount of capital insured makes it possible to improve the knowledge of risks and facilitates the rating of risks for individual companies. The same applies to their use to establish indicative pure premiums or, in the case of insurance involving capitalisation, frequency tables. Joint studies on the probable impact of extraneous circumstances that may influence the frequency or scale of claims, or the yield of different types of investments, should also be included. It is, however, necessary to ensure that the restrictions are only exempted to the extent to which they are necessary to attain these objectives. It is therefore appropriate to stipulate that concerted practices on commercial premiums—that is to say, the premiums actually charged to policyholders, comprising a loading to cover administrative, commercial and other costs, plus a loading for contingencies or profit margins—are not exempted, and that even pure premiums can serve only for reference purposes.

(7) Standard policy conditions or standard individual clauses for direct insurance and standard models illustrating the profits of a life insurance policy have the advantage of improving the comparability of cover for the consumer and of allowing risks to be classified more uniformly. However, they must not lead either to the standardisation of products or to the creation of too captive a customer base. Accordingly, the exemption should apply on condition that they are not binding, but serve only as models.

(8) Standard policy conditions may in particular not contain any systematic exclusion of specific types of risk without providing for the express possibility of including that cover by agreement and may not provide for the contractual relationship with the policyholder to be maintained for an excessive period or go beyond the initial object to the policy. This is without prejudice to obligations arising from Community or national law.

(9) In addition, it is necessary to stipulate that the common standard policy conditions must be generally accessible to any interested person, and in particular to the policyholder, so as to ensure that there is real transparency and therefore benefit for consumers.

(10) The establishment of co-insurance or co-reinsurance groups designed to cover an unspecified number of risks must be viewed favourably in so far as it allows a greater number of undertakings to enter the market and, as a result, increases the capacity for covering, in particular, risks that are difficult to cover because of their scale, rarity or novelty.

(11) However, so as to ensure effective competition it is appropriate to exempt such groups subject to the condition that the participants shall not hold a share of the relevant market in excess of a given percentage. The percentage of 15 per cent. appears appropriate in the case of co-reinsurance groups. The percentage should be reduced to 10 per cent. in the case of co-insurance groups. This is because the mechanism of co-insurance requires uniform policy conditions and commercial premiums, with the result that residual competition between members of a co-insurance group is particularly reduced. As regards catastrophe risks or aggravated risks, those figures shall be calculated only with reference to the market share of the group itself.

(12) In the case of co-reinsurance groups, it is necessary to cover the determination of the risk premium including the probable cost of covering the risks. It is further necessary to cover the determination of the operating cost of the co-reinsurance and the remuneration of the participants in their capacity as co-reinsurers.

(13) It should be legitimate in both cases to declare group cover for the risks brought into the group to be subject to (a) the application of common or accepted conditions of cover, (b) the requirement that agreement be obtained prior to the settlement of all (or all large) claims, (c) to joint negotiation of retrocession, and (d) to a ban on retroceding individual shares. The requirement that all risks be brought into the group should however be excluded because that would be an excessive restriction of competition.

(14) The establishment of groups constituted only by reinsurance companies need not be covered by this Regulation due to lack of sufficient experience in this field.

(15) The new approach in the realm of technical harmonisation and standardisation, as defined in the Council resolution of 7 May 1985,[5] and also the global approach to certification and testing, which was presented by the Commission in its communication to the Council of 15 June 1989[6] and which was approved by the Council in its resolution of 21 December 1989,[7] are essential to the functioning of the internal market because they promote competition, being based on standard quality criteria throughout the Community.

(16) It is in the hope of promoting those standard quality criteria that the Commission permits insurance undertakings to collaborate in order to establish technical specifications and rules concerning the evaluation and certification of the compliance of security devices, which as far as possible should be uniform at a European level, thereby ensuring their use in practice.

(17) Co-operation in the evaluation of security devices and of the undertakings installing and maintaining them is useful in so far as it removes the need for repeated individual evaluation. Accordingly, the Regulation should define the conditions under which the formulation of technical specifications and procedures for certifying such security devices and the undertakings installing or maintaining them are authorised. The purpose of such conditions is to ensure that all manufacturers and installation and maintenance undertakings may apply for evaluation, and that the evaluation and certification are guided by objective and well-defined criteria.

(18) Lastly, such agreements must not result in an exhaustive list; each undertaking must remain free to accept devices and installation and maintenance undertakings not approved jointly.

(19) If individual agreements exempted by this Regulation nevertheless have effects which are incompatible with Article 81(3), as interpreted by the administrative practice of the Commission and the case-law of the Court of Justice, the Commission must have the power to withdraw the benefit of the block exemption. This applies for example where studies on the impact of future developments are based on unjustifiable hypotheses; or where recommended standard policy conditions contain clauses which create, to the detriment of the policyholder, a significant imbalance between the rights and obligations arising from the contract; or where groups are used or managed in such a way as to give one or more participating undertakings the means of acquiring or reinforcing a preponderant influence on the relevant market, or if these groups result in market sharing, or if policyholders encounter unusual difficulties in finding cover for aggravated risks outside a group. This last consideration would normally not apply where a group covers less than 25 per cent. of those risks.

(20) Agreements which are exempted pursuant to this Regulation need not be notified. Undertakings may nevertheless in cases of doubt notify their agreements pursuant to Council Regulation No. 17,[8] as last amended by the Act of Accession of Spain and Portugal,

---

[5] OJ 1985 C136/1.
[6] OJ 1989 C267/3.
[7] OJ 1990 C10/1.
[8] OJ 1962, No. 13, p. 204/62.

Has Adopted This Regulation:

TITLE I

GENERAL PROVISIONS

Article 1

Pursuant to Article 81(3) of the Treaty and subject to the provisions of this Regulation, it is hereby declared that Article 81(1) of the Treaty shall not apply to agreements, decisions by associations of undertakings and concerted practices in the insurance sector which seek co-operation with respect to:

(a) the establishment of common risk-premium tariffs based on collectively ascertained statistics or on the number of claims;
(b) the establishment of standard policy conditions;
(c) the common coverage of certain types of risks;
(d) the establishment of common rules on the testing and acceptance of security devices.

TITLE II

CALCULATION OF THE PREMIUM

Article 2

The exemption provided for in Article 1(a) hereof shall apply to agreements, decisions and concerted practices which relate to:

(a) the calculation of the average cost of risk cover (pure premiums) or the establishment and distribution of mortality tables, and tables showing the frequency of illness, accident and invalidity, in connection with insurance involving an element of capitalisation—such tables being based on the assembly of data, spread over a number of risk-years chosen as an observation period, which relate to identical or comparable risks in sufficient number to constitute a base which can be handled statistically and which will yield figures on (*inter alia*):
— the number of claims during the said period,
— the number of individual risks insured in each risk-year of the chosen observation period,
— the total amounts paid or payable in respect of claims arisen during the said period,
— the total amount of capital insured for each risk-year during the chosen observation period,
(b) the carrying-out of studies on the probable impact of general circumstances external to the interested undertakings on the frequency or scale of claims, or the profitability of different types of investment, and the distribution of their results.

179

Article 3

The exemption shall apply on condition that:

(a) the calculations, tables or study results referred to in Article 2, when compiled and distributed, include a statement that they are purely illustrative;

(b) the calculations or tables referred to in Article 2(a) do not include in any way loadings for contingencies, income deriving from reserves, administrative or commercial costs comprising commissions payable to intermediaries, fiscal or para-fiscal contributions or the anticipated profits of the participating undertakings;

(c) the calculations, tables or study results referred to in Article 2 do not identify the insurance undertakings concerned.

Article 4

The exemption shall not benefit undertakings or associations of undertakings which enter into an undertaking or commitment among themselves, or which oblige other undertakings, not to use calculations or tables that differ from those established pursuant to Article 2(a), or not to depart from the results of the studies referred to in Article 2(b).

Title III

Standard Policy Conditions for Direct Insurance

Article 5

1. The exemption provided for in Article 1(b) shall apply to agreements, decisions and concerted practices which have as their object the establishment and distribution of standard policy conditions for direct insurance.

2. The exemption shall also apply to agreements, decisions and concerted practices which have as their object the establishment and distribution of common models illustrating the profits to be realised from an insurance policy involving an element of capitalisation.

Article 6

1. The exemption shall apply on condition that the standard policy conditions referred to in Article 5(1):

(a) are established and distributed with an explicit statement that they are purely illustrative; and

(b) expressly mention the possibility that different conditions may be agreed; and

(c) are accessible to any interested person and provided simply upon request.

2. The exemption shall apply on condition that the illustrative models referred to in Article 5(2) are established and distributed only by way of guidance.

Article 7

1. The exemption shall not apply where the standard policy conditions referred to in Article 5(1) contain clauses which:

(a) exclude from the cover losses normally relating to the class of insurance concerned, without indicating explicitly that each insurer remains free to extend the cover to such events;

(b) make the cover of certain risks subject to specific conditions, without indicating explicity that each insurer remains free to waive them;

(c) impose comprehensive cover including risks to which a significant number of policyholders is not simultaneously exposed, without indicating explicitly that each insurer remains free to propose separate cover;

(d) indicate the amount of the cover or the part which the policyholder must pay himself (the "excess");

(e) allow the insurer to maintain the policy in the event that he cancels part of the cover, increases the premium without the risk or the scope of the cover being changed (without prejudice to indexation clauses), or otherwise alters the policy conditions without the express consent of the policyholder;

(f) allow the insurer to modify the term of the policy without the express consent of the policyholder;

(g) impose on the policyholder in the non-life assurance sector a contract period of more than three years;

(h) impose a renewal period of more than one year where the policy is automatically renewed unless notice is given upon the expiry of a given period;

(i) require the policyholder to agree to the reinstatement of a policy which has been suspended on account of the disappearance of the insured risk, if he is once again exposed to a risk of the same nature;

(j) require the policyholder to obtain cover from the same insurer for different risks;

(k) require the policyholder, in the event of disposal of the object of insurance, to make the acquirer take over the insurance policy.

2. The exemption shall not benefit undertakings or associations of undertakings which concert or undertake among themselves, or oblige other undertakings not to apply conditions other than those referred to in Article 5(1).

Article 8

Without prejudice to the establishment of specific insurance conditions for particular social or occupational categories of the population, the exemption shall not apply to agreements decisions and concerted practices which exclude the coverage of certain risk categories because of the characteristics associated with the policyholder.

Article 9

1. The exemption shall not apply where, without prejudice to legally imposed obligations, the illustrative models referred to in Article 5(2) include only specified interest rates or contain figures indicating administrative costs.

2. The exemption shall not benefit undertakings or associations of undertakings which concert or undertake among themselves, or oblige other undertakings not to apply models illustrating the benefits of an insurance policy other than those referred to in Article 5(2).

Title IV

COMMON COVERAGE OF CERTAIN TYPES OF RISKS

Article 10

1. The exemption under Article 1(c) hereof shall apply to agreements which have as their object the setting-up and operation of groups of insurance undertakings or of insurance undertakings and reinsurance undertakings for the common coverage of a specific category of risks in the form of co-insurance or co-reinsurance.

2. For the purposes of this Regulation:

(a) "co-insurance groups" means groups set up by insurance undertakings which:
— agree to underwrite in the name and for the account of all the participants the insurance of a specified risk category, or
— entrust the underwriting and management of the insurance of a specified risk category in their name and on their behalf to one of the insurance undertakings, to a common broker or to a common body set up for this purpose;
(b) "co-reinsurance groups" means groups set up by insurance undertakings, possibly with the assistance of one or more re-insurance undertakings:
— in order to reinsure mutually all or part of their liabilities in respect of a specified risk category,
— incidentally, to accept in the name and on behalf of all the participants the re-insurance of the same category of risks.

3. The agreements referred to in paragraph 1 may determine:

(a) the nature and characteristics of the risks covered by the co-insurance or co-reinsurance;
(b) the conditions governing admission to the group;
(c) the individual own-account shares of the participants in the risks co-insured or co-reinsured;
(d) the conditions for individual withdrawal of the participants;
(e) the rules governing the operation and management of the group.

4. The agreements alluded to in paragraph 2(b) may further determine:

(a) the shares in the risks covered which the participants to not pass on for co-reinsurance (individual retentions);
(b) the cost of co-reinsurance, which includes both the operating costs of the group and the remuneration of the participants in their capacity as co-reinsurers.

Article 11

1. The exemption shall apply on condition that:

(a) the insurance products underwritten by the participating undertakings or on their behalf do not, in any of the markets concerned, represent:
— in the case of co-insurance groups, more than 10 per cent. of all the insurance products that are identical or regarded as similar from the point of view of the risks covered and of the cover provided,
— in the case of co-reinsurance groups, more than 15 per cent. of all the insurance products that are identical or regarded as similar from the point of view of the risks covered and of the cover provided;

(b) each participating undertaking has the right to withdraw from the group, subject to a period of notice of not more than six months, without incurring any sanctions.

2. By way of derogation from paragraph 1, the respective percentages of 10 and 15 per cent. apply only to the insurance products brought into the group, to the exclusion of identical or similar products underwritten by the participating companies or on their behalf and which are not brought into the group, where this group covers:

— catastrophe risks where the claims are both rare and large,
— aggravated risks which involve a higher probability of claims because of the character-istics of the risk insured.

This derogation is subject to the following conditions:

— that none of the concerned undertakings shall participate in another group that covers risks on the same market, and
— with respect to groups which cover aggravated risks, that the insurance products brought into the group shall not represent more than 15 per cent. of all identical or similar products underwritten by the participating companies or on their behalf on the market concerned.

Article 12

Apart from the obligations referred to in Article 10, no restriction on competition shall be imposed on the undertakings participating in a co-insurance group other than:

(a) the obligation, in order to qualify for the co-insurance cover within the group, to
  — take preventive measures into account,
  — use the general or specific insurance conditions accepted by the group,
  — use the commercial premiums set by the group;
(b) the obligation to submit to the group or approval any settlement of a claim relating to a co-insured risk;
(c) the obligation to entrust to the group the negotiation of reinsurance agreements on behalf of all concerned;
(d) a ban on reinsuring the individual share of the co-insured risk.

Article 13

Apart from the obligations referred to in Article 10, no restriction on competition shall be imposed on the undertakings participating in a co-reinsurance group other than:

(a) the obligation, in order to qualify for the co-reinsurance cover, to
  — take preventive measures into account,
  — use the general or specific insurance conditions accepted by the group,
  — use a common risk-premium tariff for direct insurance calculated by the group, regard being had to the probable cost of risk cover or, where there is not sufficient experience to establish such a tariff, a risk premium accepted by the group,
  — participate in the cost of the co-reinsurance;
(b) the obligation to submit to the group for approval the settlement of claims relating to the co-reinsured risks and exceeding a specified amount, or to pass such claims on to it for settlement;
(c) the obligation to entrust to the group the negotiation of retrocession agreements on behalf of all concerned;
(d) a ban on reinsuring the individual retention or retroceding the individual share.

Title V

Security Devices

Article 14

The exemption provided for in Article 1(d) shall apply to agreements, decisions and concerted practices which have as their object the establishment, recognition and distribution of:

— technical specifications, in particular technical specifications intended as future European norms, and also procedures for assessing and certifying the compliance with such specifications of security devices and their installation and maintenance,
— rules for evaluation and approval of installation undertakings or maintenance undertakings.

Article 15

The exemption shall apply on condition that:

(a) the technical specifications and compliancy assessment procedures are precise, technically justified and in proportion to the performance to be attained by the security device concerned;
(b) the rules for the evaluation of installation undertakings and maintenance undertakings are objective, relate to their technical competence and are applied in a non-discriminatory manner;
(c) such specifications and rules are established and distributed with the statement that insurance undertakings are free to accept other security devices or approve other installation and maintenance undertakings which do not comply with these technical specifications or rules;
(d) such specifications and rules are provided simply upon request to any interested person;
(e) such specifications include a classification based on the level of performance obtained;
(f) a request for an assessment may be submitted at any time by any applicant;
(g) the evaluation of conformity does not impose on the applicant any expenses that are disproportionate to the costs of the approval procedure;
(h) the devices and installation undertakings and maintenance undertakings that meet the assessment criteria are certified to this effect in a non-discriminatory manner within a period of six months of the date of application, except where technical considerations justify a reasonable additional period;
(i) the fact of compliance or approval is certified in writing;
(j) the grounds for a refusal to issue the certificate of compliance are given in writing by attaching a duplicate copy of the records of the tests and controls that have been carried out;
(k) the grounds for a refusal to take into account a request for assessment are provided in writing;
(l) the specifications and rules are applied by bodies observing the appropriate provisions of norms in the series EN 45 000.

TITLE VI

MISCELLANEOUS PROVISIONS

Article 16

1. The provisions of this Regulation shall also apply where the participating undertakings lay down rights and obligations for the undertakings connected with them. The market shares, legal acts or conduct of the connected undertakings shall be considered to be those of the participating undertakings.

2. "Connected undertakings" for the purposes of this Regulation means:

(a) undertakings in which a participating undertaking, directly or indirectly:
   — owns more than half the capital or business assets, or
   — has the power to exercise more than half the voting rights, or
   — has the power to appoint more than half the members of the supervisory board, board of directors or bodies legally representing the undertaking, or
   — has right to manage the affairs of the undertaking;
(b) undertakings which directly or indirectly have in or over a participating undertaking the rights or powers listed in (a);
(c) undertakings in which an undertaking referred to in (b) directly or indirectly has the rights or powers listed in (a).

3. Undertakings in which the participating undertakings or undertakings connected with them have directly or indirectly the rights or powers set out in paragraph 2(a) shall be considered to be connected with each of the participating undertakings.

Article 17

The Commission may withdraw the benefit of this Regulation, pursuant to Article 7 of 1534/91, where it finds in a particular case that an agreement, decision or concerted practice exempted under this Regulation nevertheless has certain effects which are incompatible with the conditions laid down in Article 81(3) of the EEC Treaty, and in particular where,

— in the cases referred to in Title II, the studies are based on unjustifiable hypotheses,
— in the cases referred to in Title III, the standard policy conditions contain clauses other than those listed in Article 7(1) which create, to the detriment of the policyholder, a significant imbalance between the rights and obligations arising from the contract,
— in the cases referred to in Title IV:
   (a) the undertakings participating in a group would not, having regard to the nature, characteristics and scale of the risks concerned, encounter any significant difficulties in operating individually on the relevant market without organising themselves in a group;
   (b) one or more participating undertakings exercise a determining influence on the commercial policy of more than one group on the same market;
   (c) the setting-up or operation of a group may, through the conditions governing admission, the definition of the risks to be covered, the agreements on retrocession or by any other means, result in the sharing of the markets for the insurance products concerned or from neighbouring products;
   (d) an insurance group which benefits from the provisions of Article 11(2) has such a position with respect to aggravated risks that the policyholders encounter considerable difficulties in finding cover outside this group.

Article 18

1. As regards agreements existing on 13 March 1962 and notified before 1 February 1963 and agreements, whether notified or not, to which Article 4(2)(1) of Regulation No. 17 applies, the declaration of inapplicability of Article 81(1) of the Treaty contained in this Regulation shall have retroactive effect from the time at which the conditions for application of this Regulation were fulfilled.

2. As regards all other agreements notified before this Regulation entered into force, the declaration of inapplicability of Article 81(1) of the Treaty contained in this Regulation shall have retroactive effect from the time at which the conditions for application of this Regulation were fulfilled, or from the date of notification, whichever is later.

Article 19

If agreements existing on 13 March 1962 and notified before 1 February 1963, or agreements covered by Article 4(2)(1) of Regulation No. 17 and notified before 1 January 1967, are amended before 31 December 1993 so as to fulfil the conditions for application of this Regulation, and if the amendment is communicated to the Commission before 1 April 1994, the prohibition in Article 81(1) of the Treaty shall not apply in respect of the period prior to the amendment. The communication shall take effect from the time of its receipt by the Commission. Where the communication is sent by registered post, it shall take effect from the date shown on the postmark of the place of posting.

Article 20

1. As regards agreements covered by Article 81 of the Treaty as a result of the accession of the United Kingdom, Ireland and Denmark, Articles 18 and 19 shall apply, on the understanding that the relevant dates shall be 1 January 1973 instead of 13 March 1962 and 1 July 1973 instead of 1 February 1963 and 1 January 1967.

2. As regards agreements covered by Article 81 of the Treaty as a result of the accession of Greece, Articles 18 and 19 shall apply, on the understanding that the relevant dates shall be 1 January 1981 instead of 13 March 1962 and 1 July 1981 instead of 1 February 1963 and 1 January 1967.

3. As regards agreements covered by Article 81 of the Treaty as a result of the accession of Spain and Portugal, Articles 18 and 19 shall apply, on the understanding that the relevant dates shall be 1 January 1986 instead of 13 March 1962 and 1 July 1986 instead of 1 February 1963 and 1 January 1967.

[4. As regards agreements covered by Article 81 of the Treaty as a result of the accession of Austria, Finland and Sweden, Articles 18 and 19 shall apply *mutatis mutandis* on the understanding that the relevant dates shall be the date of accession instead of 13 March 1962 and six months after the date of accession instead of 1 February 1963, 1 January 1967, 31 December 1993 and 1 April 1994. The amendments made to the agreements in accordance with Article 19 need not be notified to the Commission. However, the present paragraph shall not apply to agreements which at the date of accession already fall under Article 53(1) of the EEA Agreement.]

Amendment

Para. 4 was added by the Act of Accession of the Republic of Austria, the Republic of Finland and the Kingdom of Sweden, Annex 1(III)(D)(9), as amended by Council Decision 95/1, Article 39.

Article 21

This Regulation shall enter into force on 1 April 1993.
　It shall apply until 31 March 2003.
　This Regulation shall be binding in its entirety and directly applicable in all Member States.

Done at Brussels, 21 December 1992.

APPENDIX 26

COMMISSION NOTICE[1]

On the Definition of Relevant Market for the Purposes of Community Competition Law

(Text with EEA relevance)

I. Introduction

1. The purpose of this notice is to provide guidance as to how the Commission applies the concept of relevant product and geographic market in its ongoing enforcement of Community competition law, in particular the application of Council Regulation No 17 and (EEC) No 4064/89, their equivalents in other sectoral applications such as transport, coal and steel, and agriculture, and the relevant provisions of the EEA Agreement.[2] Throughout this notice, references to Articles 81 and 82 of the Treaty and to merger control are to be understood as referring to the equivalent provisions in the EEA Agreement and the ECSC Treaty.

2. Market definition is a tool to identify and define the boundaries of competition between firms. It serves to establish the framework within which competition policy is applied by the Commission. The main purpose of market definition is to identify in a systematic way the competitive constraints that the undertakings involved[3] face. The objective of defining a market in both its product and geographic dimension is to identify those actual competitors of the undertakings involved that are capable of constraining those undertakings' behaviour and of preventing them from behaving independently of effective competitive pressure. It is from this perspective that the market definition makes it possible *inter alia* to calculate market shares that would convey meaningful information regarding market power for the purposes of assessing dominance or for the purposes of applying Article 81.

3. It follows from point 2 that the concept of "relevant market" is different from other definitions of market often used in other contexts. For instance, companies often use the term "market" to refer to the area where it sells its products or to refer broadly to the industry or sector where it belongs.

4. The definition of the relevant market in both its product and its geographic dimensions often has a decisive influence on the assessment of a competition case. By rendering public the procedures which the Commission follows when considering market definition

---

[1] OJ 1997 C372/5.

[2] The focus of assessment in State aid cases is the aid recipient and the industry/sector concerned rather than identification of competitive constraints faced by the aid recipient. When consideration of market power and therefore of the relevant market are raised in any particular case, elements of the approach outlined here might serve as a basis for the assessment of State aid cases.

[3] For the purposes of this notice, the undertakings involved will be, in the case of a concentration, the parties to the concentration; in investigations within the meaning of Article 82 of the Treaty, the undertaking being investigated or the complainants; for investigations within the meaning of Article 81, the parties to the Agreement.

and by indicating the criteria and evidence on which it relies to reach a decision, the Commission expects to increase the transparency of its policy and decision-making in the area of competition policy.

5. Increased transparency will also result in companies and their advisers being able to better anticipate the possibility that the Commission may raise competition concerns in an individual case. Companies could, therefore, take such a possibility into account in their own internal decision-making when contemplating, for instance, acquisitions, the creation of joint ventures, or the establishment of certain agreements. It is also intended that companies should be in a better position to understand what sort of information the Commission considers relevant for the purposes of market definition.

6. The Commission's interpretation of "relevant market" is without prejudice to the interpretation which may be given by the Court of Justice or the Court of First Instance of the European Communities.

II. Definition of relevant market

Definition of relevant product market and relevant geographic market

7. The Regulations based on Article 81 and 82 of the Treaty, in particular in section 6 of Form A/B with respect to Regulation No 17, as well as in section 6 of Form CO with respect to Regulation (EEC) No 4064/89 on the control of concentrations having a Community dimension have laid down the following definitions, "Relevant product markets" are defined as follows:

"A relevant product market comprises all those products and/or services which are regarded as interchangeable or substitutable by the consumer, by reason of the products' characteristics, their prices and their intended use".

8. "Relevant geographic markets" are defined as follows:

"The relevant geographic market comprises the area in which the undertakings concerned are involved in the supply and demand of products or services, in which the conditions of competition are sufficiently homogeneous and which can be distinguished from neighbouring areas because the conditions of competition are appreciably different in those area".

9. The relevant market within which to assess a given competition issue is therefore established by the combination of the product and geographic markets. The Commission interprets the definitions in paragraphs 7 and 8 (which reflect the case-law of the Court of Justice and the Court of First Instance as well as its own decision-making practice) according to the orientations defined in this notice.

Concept or relevant market and objectives of Community competition policy

10. The concept of relevant market is closely related to the objectives pursued under Community competition policy. For example, under the Community's merger control, the objective in controlling structural changes in the supply of a product/service is to prevent the creation or reinforcement of a dominant position as a result of which effective competition would be significantly impeded in a substantial part of the common market. Under the Community's competition rules, a dominant position is such that a firm or group of firms would be in a position to behave to an appreciable extent independently of its competitors, customers and ultimately of its consumers.[4] Such a position would usually

---

[4] Definition given by the Court of Justice in its judgment of 13 February 1979 in Case 85/76, *Hoffmann-La Roche* [1979] ECR 461, and confirmed in subsequent judgments.

arise when a firm or group of firms accounted for a large share of the supply in any given market, provided that other factors analysed in the assessment (such as entry barriers, customers' capacity to react, etc.) point in the same direction.

11. The same approach is followed by the Commission in its application of Article 82 of the Treaty to firms that enjoy a single or collective dominant position. Within the meaning of Regulation No 17, the Commission has the power to investigate and bring to an end abuses of such a dominant position, which must also be defined by reference to the relevant market. Markets may also need to be defined in the application of Article 81 of the Treaty, in particular, in determining whether an appreciable restriction of competition exists or in establishing if the condition pursuant to Article 81(3)(b) for an exemption from the application of Article 81(1) is met.

12. The criteria for defining the relevant market are applied generally for the analysis of certain types of behaviour in the market and for the analysis of structural changes in the supply of products. This methodology, though, might lead to different results depending on the nature of the competition issue being examined. For instance, the scope of the geographic market might be different when analysing a concentration, where the analysis is essentially prospective, from an analysis of past behaviour. The different time horizon considered in each case might lead to the result that different geographic markets are defined for the same products depending on whether the Commission is examining a change in the structure of supply, such as a concentration or a cooperative joint venture, or examining issues relating to certain past behaviour.

Basic principles for market definition

Competitive constraints

13. Firms are subject to three main sources or competitive constraints: demand substitutability, supply substitutability and potential competition. From an economic point of view, for the definition of the relevant market, demand substitution constitutes the most immediate and effective disciplinary force on the suppliers of a given product, in particular in relation to their pricing decisions. A firm or a group of firms cannot have a significant impact on the prevailing conditions of sale, such as prices, if its customers are in a position to switch easily to available substitute products or to suppliers located elsewhere. Basically, the exercise of market definition consists in identifying the effective alternative sources of supply for the customers of the undertakings involved, in terms both of products/services and of geographic location of suppliers.

14. The competitive constraints arising from supply side substitutability other than those described in paragraphs 20 to 23 and from potential competition are in general less immediate and in any case require an analysis of additional factors. As a result such constraints are taken into account at the assessment stage of competition analysis.

Demand substitution

15. The assessment of demand substitution entails a determination of the range of products which are viewed as substitutes by the consumer. One way of making this determination can be viewed as a speculative experiment, postulating a hypothetical small, lasting change in relative prices and evaluating the likely reactions of customers to that increase. The exercise of market definition focuses on prices for operational and practical purposes, and more precisely on demand substitution arising from small, permanent changes in relative prices. This concept can provide clear indications as to the evidence that is relevant in defining markets.

16. Conceptually, this approach means that, starting from the type of products that the undertakings involved sell and the area in which they sell them, additional products and areas will be included in, or excluded from, the market definition depending on whether

competition from these other products and areas affect or restrain sufficiently the pricing of the parties' products in the short term.

17. The question to be answered is whether the parties' customers would switch to readily available substitutes or to suppliers located elsewhere in response to a hypothetical small (in the range 5% to 10%) but permanent relative price increase in the products and areas being considered. If substitution were enough to make the price increase unprofitable because of the resulting loss of sales, additional substitutes and areas are included in the relevant market. This would be done until the set of products and geographical areas is such that small, permanent increases in relative prices would be profitable. The equivalent analysis is applicable in cases concerning the concentration of buying power, where the starting point would then be the supplier and the price test serves to identify the alternative distribution channels or outlets for the supplier's products. In the application of these principles, careful account should be taken of certain particular situations as described within paragraphs 56 and 58.

18. A practical example of this test can be provided by its application to a merger of, for instance, soft-drink bottlers. An issue to examine in such a case would be to decide whether different flavours of soft drinks belong to the same market. In practice, the question to address would be whether consumers of flavour A would switch to other flavours when confronted with a permanent price increase of 5% to 10% for flavour A. If a sufficient number of consumers would switch to, say, flavour B, to such an extent that the price increase for flavour A would not be profitable owing to the resulting loss of sales, then the market would comprise at least flavours A and B. The process would have to be extended in addition to other available flavours until a set of products is identified for which a price rise would not induce a sufficient substitution in demand.

19. Generally, and in particular for the analysis of merger cases, the price to take into account will be the prevailing market price. This may not be the case where the prevailing price has been determined in the absence of sufficient competition. In particular for the investigation of abuses of dominant positions, the fact that the prevailing price might already have been substantially increased will be taken into account.

Supply substitution

20. Supply-side substitutability may also be taken into account when defining markets in those situations in which its effects are equivalent to those of demand substitution in terms of effectiveness and immediacy. This means that suppliers are able to switch production to the relevant products and market them in the short term[5] without incurring significant additional costs or risks in response to small and permanent changes in relative prices. When these conditions are met, the additional production that is put on the market will have a disciplinary effect on the competitive behaviour of the companies involved. Such an impact in terms of effectiveness and immediacy is equivalent to the demand substitution effect.

21. These situations typically arise when companies market a wide range of qualities or grades of one product; even if, for a given final customer or group of consumers, the different qualities are not substitutable, the different qualities will be grouped into one product market, provided that most of the suppliers are able to offer and sell the various qualities immediately and without the significant increases in costs described above. In such cases, the relevant product market will encompass all products that are substitutable in demand and supply, and the current sales of those products will be aggregated so as to give the total value or volume of the market. The same reasoning may lead to group different geographic areas.

22. A practical example of the approach to supply-side substitutability when defining product markets is to be found in the case of paper. Paper is usually supplied in a range of different qualities, from standard writing paper to high quality papers to be used, for

---

[5] That is such a period that does not entail a significant adjustment of existing tangible and intangible assets (see paragraph 23).

instance, to publish art books. From a demand point of view, different qualities of paper cannot be used for any given use, i.e. an art book or a high quality publication cannot be based on lower quality papers. However, paper plants are prepared to manufacture the different qualities, and production can be adjusted with negligible costs and in a short time-frame. In the absence of particular difficulties in distribution, paper manufacturers are able therefore, to compete for orders of the various qualities, in particular if orders are placed with sufficient lead time to allow for modification of production plans. Under such circumstances, the Commission would not define a separate market for each quality of paper and its respective use. The various qualities of paper are included in the relevant market, and their sales added up to estimate total market value and volume.

23. When supply-side substitutability would entail the need to adjust significantly existing tangible and intangible assets, additional investments, strategic decisions or time delays, it will not be considered at the stage of market definition. Examples where supply-side substitution did not induce the Commission to enlarge the market are offered in the area of consumer products, in particular for branded beverages. Although bottling plants may in principle bottle different beverages, there are costs and lead times involved (in terms of advertising, product testing and distribution) before the products can actually be sold. In these cases, the effects of supply-side substitutability and other forms of potential competition would then be examined at a later stage.

Potential competition

24. The third source of competitive constraint, potential competition, is not taken into account when defining markets, since the conditions under which potential competition will actually represent an effective competitive constraint depend on the analysis of specific factors and circumstances related to the conditions of entry. If required, this analysis is only carried out at a subsequent stage, in general once the position of the companies involved in the relevant market has already been ascertained, and when such position gives rise to concerns from a competition point of view.

III. Evidence relied on to define relevant markets

The process of defining the relevant market in practice

Product dimension

25. There is a range of evidence permitting an assessment of the extent to which substitution would take place. In individual cases, certain types of evidence will be determinant, depending very much on the characteristics and specificity of the industry and products or services that are being examined. The same type of evidence may be of no importance in other cases. In most cases, a decision will have to be based on the consideration of a number of criteria and different items of evidence. The Commission follows an open approach to empirical evidence, aimed at making an effective use of all available information which may be relevant in individual cases. The Commission does not follow a rigid hierarchy of different sources of information or types of evidence.

26. The process of defining relevant markets may be summarized as follows: on the basis of the preliminary information available or information submitted by the undertakings involved, the Commission will usually be in a position to broadly establish the possible relevant markets within which, for instance, a concentration or a restriction of competition has to be assessed. In general, and for all practical purposes when handling individual cases, the question will usually be to decide on a few alternative possible relevant markets. For instance, with respect to the product market, the issue will often be to establish whether product A and product B belong or do not belong to the same product market, it is often the case that the inclusion of product B would be enough to remove any competition concerns.

27. In such situations it is not necessary to consider whether the market includes additional products, or to reach a definitive conclusion on the precise product market. If under the conceivable alternative market definitions the operation in question does not raise competition concerns, the question of market definition will be left open, reducing thereby the burden on companies to supply information.

Geographic dimension

28. The Commission's approach to geographic market definition might be summarized as follows: it will take a preliminary view of the scope of the geographic market on the basis of broad indications as to the distribution of market shares between the parties and their competitors, as well as a preliminary analysis of pricing and price differences at national and Community or EEA level. This initial view is used basically as a working hypothesis to focus the Commission's enquiries for the purposes of arriving at a precise geographic market definition.

29. The reasons behind any particular configuration of prices and market shares need to be explored. Companies might enjoy high market shares in their domestic markets just because of the weight of the past, and conversely, a homogeneous presence of companies throughout the EEA might be consistent with national or regional geographic markets. The initial working hypothesis will therefore be checked against an analysis of demand characteristics (importance of national or local preferences, current patterns of purchases of customers, product differentiation/brands, other) in order to establish whether companies in different areas do indeed constitute a real alternative source of supply for consumers. The theoretical experiment is again based on substitution arising from changes in relative prices, and the question to answer is again whether the customers of the parties would switch their orders to companies located elsewhere in the short term and at a negligible cost.

30. If necessary, a further check on supply factors will be carried out to ensure that those companies located in differing areas do not face impediments in developing their sales on competitive terms throughout the whole geographic market. This analysis will include an examination of requirements for a local presence in order to sell in that area the conditions of access to distribution channels, costs associated with setting up a distribution network, and the presence or absence of regulatory barriers arising from public procurement, price regulations, quotas and tariffs limiting trade or production, technical standards, monopolies, freedom of establishment, requirements for administrative authorizations, packaging regulations, etc. In short, the Commission will identify possible obstacles and barriers isolating companies located in a given area from the competitive pressure of companies located outside that area, so as to determine the precise degree of market interpenetration at national, European or global level.

31. The actual pattern and evolution of trade flows offers useful supplementary indications as to the economic importance of each demand or supply factor mentioned above, and the extent to which they may or may not constitute actual barriers creating different geographic markets. The analysis of trade flows will generally address the question of transport costs and the extent to which these may hinder trade between different areas, having regard to plant location, costs of production and relative price levels.

Market integration in the Community

32. Finally, the Commission also takes into account the continuing process of market integration, in particular in the Community, when defining geographic markets, especially in the area of concentrations and structural joint ventures. The measures adopted and implemented in the internal market programme to remove barriers to trade and further integrate the Community markets cannot be ignored when assessing the effects on

competition of a concentration or a structural joint venture. A situation where national markets have been artificially isolated from each other because of the existence of legislative barriers that have now been removed will generally lead to a cautious assessment of past evidence regarding prices, market shares or trade patterns. A process of market integration that would, in the short term, lead to wider geographic markets may therefore be taken into consideration when defining the geographic market for the purposes of assessing concentrations and joint ventures.

The process of gathering evidence

33. When a precise market definition is deemed necessary, the Commission will often contact the main customers and the main companies in the industry to enquire into their views about the boundaries of product and geographic markets and to obtain the necessary factual evidence to reach a conclusion. The Commission might also contact the relevant professional associations, and companies active in upstream markets, so as to be able to define, in so far as necessary, separate product and geographic markets, for different levels of production or distribution of the products/services in question. It might also request additional information to the undertakings involved.

34. Where appropriate, the Commission will address written requests for information to the market players mentioned above. These requests will usually include questions relating to the perceptions of companies about reactions to hypothetical price increases and their views of the boundaries of the relevant market. They will also ask for provision of the factual information the Commission deems necessary to reach a conclusion on the extent of the relevant market. The Commission might also discuss with marketing directors or other officers of those companies to gain a better understanding on how negotiations between suppliers and customers take place and better understand issues relating to the definition of the relevant market. Where appropriate, they might also carry out visits or inspections to the premises of the parties, their customers and/or their competitors, in order to better understand how products are manufactured and sold.

35. The type of evidence relevant to reach a conclusion as to the product market can be categorized as follows:

Evidence to define markets—product dimension

36. An analysis of the product characteristics and its intended use allows the Commission, as a first step, to limit the field of investigation of possible substitutes. However, product characteristics and intended use are insufficient to show whether two products are demand substitutes. Functional interchangeability or similarity in characteristics may not, in themselves, provide sufficient criteria, because the responsiveness of customers to relative price changes may be determined by other considerations as well. For example, there may be different competitive contraints in the original equipment market for car components and in spare parts, thereby leading to a separate delineation of two relevant markets. Conversely, differences in product characteristics are not in themselves sufficient to exclude demand substitutability, since this will depend to a large extent on how customers value different characteristics.

37. The type of evidence the Commission considers relevant to assess whether two products are demand substitutes can be categorized as follows:

38. *Evidence of substitution in the recent past.* In certain cases, it is possible to analyse evidence relating to recent past events or shocks in the market that offer actual examples of substitution between two products. When available, this sort of information will normally be fundamental for market definition. If there have been changes in relative prices in the past (all else being equal), the reactions in terms of quantities demanded will be determinant in establishing substitutability. Launches of new products in the past can

194

also offer useful information, when it is possible to precisely analyse which products have lost sales to the new product.

39. There are a number of *quantitative tests* that have specifically been designed for the purpose of delineating markets. These tests consist of various econometric and statistical approaches estimates of elasticities and cross-price elasticities[6] for the demand of a product, tests based on similarity of price movements over time, the analysis of causality between price series and similarity of price levels and/or their convergence. The Commission takes into account the available quantitative evidence capable of withstanding rigorous scrutiny for the purposes of establishing patterns of substitution in the past.

40. *Views of customers and competitors.* The Commission often contacts the main customers and competitors of the companies involved in its enquiries, to gather their views on the boundaries of the product market as well as most of the factual information it requires to reach a conclusion on the scope of the market. Reasoned answers of customers and competitors as to what would happen if relative prices for the candidate products were to increase in the candidate geographic area by a small amount (for instance of 5% to 10%) are taken into account when they are sufficiently backed by factual evidence.

41. *Consumer preferences.* In the case of consumer goods, it may be difficult for the Commission to gather the direct views of end consumers about substitute products. *Marketing studies* that companies have commissioned in the past and that are used by companies in their own decision-making as to pricing of their products and/or marketing actions may provide useful information for the Commission's delineation of the relevant market. Consumer surveys on usage patterns and attitudes, data from consumer's purchasing patterns, the views expressed by retailers and more generally, market research studies submitted by the parties and their competitors are taken into account to establish whether an economically significant proportion of consumers consider two products as substitutable, also taking into account the importance of brands for the products in question. The methodology followed in consumer surveys carried out *ad hoc* by the undertakings involved or their competitors for the purposes of a merger procedure or a procedure pursuant to Regulation No. 17 will usually be scrutinized with utmost care. Unlike pre-existing studies, they have not been prepared in the normal course of business for the adoption of business decisions.

42. *Barriers and costs associated with switching demand to potential substitutes.* There are a number of barriers and costs that might prevent the Commission from considering two *prima facie* demand substitutes as belonging to one single product market. It is not possible to provide an exhaustive list of all the possible barriers to substitution and of switching costs. These barriers or obstacles might have a wide range of origins, and in its decisions, the Commission has been confronted with regulatory barriers or other forms of State intervention, constraints arising in downstream markets, need to incur specific capital investment or loss in current output in order to switch to alternative inputs, the location of customers, specific investment in production process, learning and human capital investment, retooling costs or other investments, uncertainty about quality and reputation of unknown suppliers, and others.

43. *Different categories of customers and price discrimination.* The extent of the product market might be narrowed in the presence of distinct groups of customers. A distinct group of customers for the relevant product may constitute a narrower, distinct market when such a group could be subject to price discrimination. This will usually be the case when two conditions are met: (a) it is possible to identify clearly which group an individual customer belongs to at the moment of selling the relevant products to him, and (b) trade among customers or arbitrage by third parties should not be feasible.

---

[6] Own-price elasticity of demand for product X is a measure of the responsiveness of demand for X to percentage change in its own price. Cross-price elasticity between products X and Y is the responsiveness of demand for product X to percentage change in the price of product Y.

Evidence for defining markets—geographic dimension

44. The type of evidence the Commission considers relevant to reach a conclusion as to the geographic market can be categorized as follows:

45. *Past evidence of diversion of orders to other areas.* In certain cases, evidence on changes in prices between different areas and consequent reactions by customers might be available. Generally, the same quantitative tests used for product market definition might as well be used in geographic market definition, bearing in mind that international comparisons of prices might be more complex due to a number of factors such as exchange rate movements, taxation and product differentiation.

46. *Basic demand characteristics.* The nature of demand for the relevant product may in itself determine the scope of the geographical market. Factors such as national preferences or preferences for national brands, language, culture and life style, and the need for a local presence have a strong potential to limit the geographic scope of competition.

47. *Views of customers and competitors.* Where appropriate, the Commission will contact the main customers and competitors of the parties in its enquiries, to gather their views on the boundaries of the geographic market as well as most of the factual information it requires to reach a conclusion on the scope of the market when they are sufficiently backed by factual evidence.

48. *Current geographic pattern of purchases.* An examination of the customers' current geographic pattern of purchases provides useful evidence as to the possible scope of the geographic market. When customers purchase from companies located anywhere in the Community or the EEA on similar terms, or they procure their supplies through effective tendering procedures in which companies from anywhere in the Community or the EEA submit bids, usually the geographic market will be considered to be Community-wide.

49. *Trade flows/pattern of shipments.* When the number of customers is so large that it is not possible to obtain through them a clear picture of geographic purchasing patterns, information on trade flows might be used alternatively, provided that the trade statistics are available with a sufficient degree of detail for the relevant products. Trade flows, and above all, the rationale behind trade flows provide useful insights and information for the purpose of establishing the scope of the geographic market but are not in themselves conclusive.

50. *Barriers and switching costs associated to divert orders to companies located in other areas.* The absence of trans-border purchases or trade flows, for instance, does not necessarily mean that the market is at most national in scope. Still, barriers isolating the national market have to be identified before it is concluded that the relevant geographic market in such a case is national. Perhaps the clearest obstacle for a customer to divert its orders to other areas is the impact of transport costs and transport restrictions arising from legislation or from the nature of the relevant products. The impact of transport costs will usually limit the scope of the geographic market for bulky, low-value products, bearing in mind that a transport disadvantage might also be compensated by a comparative advantage in other costs (labour costs or raw materials). Access to distribution in a given area, regulatory barriers still existing in certain sectors, quotas and custom tariffs might also constitute barriers isolating a geographic area from the competitive pressure of companies located outside that area. Significant switching costs in procuring supplies from companies located in other countries constitute additional sources of such barriers.

51. On the basis of the evidence gathered, the Commission will then define a geographic market that could range from a local dimension to a global one, and there are examples of both local and global markets in past decisions of the Commission.

52. The paragraphs above describe the different factors which might be relevant to define markets. This does not imply that in each individual case it will be necessary to obtain evidence and assess each of these factors. Often in practice the evidence provided by a subset of these factors will be sufficient to reach a conclusion, as shown in the past decisional practice of the Commission.

IV. Calculation of market share

53. The definition of the relevant market in both its product and geographic dimensions allows the identification the suppliers and the customers/consumers active on that market. On that basis, a total market size and market shares for each supplier can be calculated on the basis of their sales of the relevant products in the relevant area. In practice, the total market size and market shares are often available from market sources, i.e. companies' estimates, studies commissioned from industry consultants and/or trade associations. When this is not the case, or when available estimates are not reliable, the Commission will usually ask each supplier in the relevant market to provide its own sales in order to calculate total market size and market shares.

54. If sales are usually the reference to calculate market shares, there are nevertheless other indications that, depending on the specific products or industry in question, can offer useful information such as, in particular, capacity, the number of players in bidding markets, units of fleet as in aerospace, or the reserves held in the case of sectors such as mining.

55. As a rule of thumb, both volume sales and value sales provide useful information. In cases of differentiated products, sales in value and their associated market share will usually be considered to better reflect the relative position and strength of each supplier.

V. Additional considerations

56. There are certain areas where the application of the principles above has to be undertaken with care. This is the case when considering primary and secondary markets, in particular, when the behaviour of undertakings at a point in time has to be analysed pursuant to Article 82. The method of defining markets in these cases is the same, i.e. assessing the responses of customers based on their purchasing decisions to relative price changes, but taking into account as well, constraints on substitution imposed by conditions in the connected markets. A narrow definition of market for secondary products, for instance, spare parts, may result when compatibility with the primary product is important. Problems of finding compatible secondary products together with the existence of high prices and a long lifetime of the primary products may render relative price increases of secondary products profitable. A different market definition may result if significant substitution between secondary products is possible or if the characteristics of the primary products make quick and direct consumer responses to relative price increases of the secondary products feasible.

57. In certain cases, the existence of chains of substitution might lead to the definition of a relevant market where products or areas at the extreme of the market are not directly substitutable. An example might be provided by the geographic dimension of a product with significant transport costs. In such cases, deliveries from a given plant are limited to a certain area around each plant by the impact of transport costs. In principle, such an area could constitute the relevant geographic market. However, if the distribution of plants is such that there are considerable overlaps between the areas around different plants, it is possible that the pricing of those products will be constrained by a chain substitution effect, and lead to the definition of a broader geographic market. The same reasoning may apply if product B is a demand substitute for products A and C. Even if products A and C are not direct demand substitutes, they might be found to be in the same relevant product market since their respective pricing might be constrained by substitution to B.

58. From a practical perspective, the concept of chains of substitution has to be corroborated by actual evidence, for instance related to price interdependence at the extremes of the chains of substitution, in order to lead to an extension of the relevant market in an individual case. Price levels at the extremes of the chains would have to be of the same magnitude as well.

APPENDIX 27

COMMISSION NOTICE

Concerning the Assessment of Cooperative Joint Ventures Pursuant to Article 81 of the EC Treaty[1]

I. Introduction

1. Joint Ventures (JVs), as referred to in this Notice, embody a special, institutionally fixed form of cooperation between undertakings. They are versatile instruments at the disposal of the parents, with the help of which different goals can be pursued and attained.

2. JVs can form the basis and the framework for cooperation in all fields of business activity. Their potential area of application includes, *inter alia*, the procuring and processing of data, the organization of working systems and procedures, taxation and business consultancy, the planning and financing of investment, the implementation of research and development plans, the acquisition and granting of licences for the use of intellectual property rights, the supply of raw materials or semi-finished products, the manufacture of goods, the provision of services, advertising, distribution and customer service.

3. JVs can fulfil one or more of the aforementioned tasks. Their activity can be limited in time or be of an unlimited duration. The broader the concrete and temporal framework of the cooperation, the stronger it will influence the business policy of the parents in relation to each other and to third parties. If the JV concerns market-orientated matters such as purchasing, manufacturing, sales or the provision of services, it will normally lead to coordination, if not even to a uniformity of the competitive behaviour of the parents at that particular economic level. This is all the more true where a JV fulfils all the functions of a normal undertaking and consequently behaves on the market as an independent supplier or purchaser. The creation of a JV which combines wholly or in part the existing activities of the parents in a particular economic area or takes over new activities for the parents, brings, over and above that, a change in the structure of the participating enterprises.

4. The assessment of cooperative joint ventures pursuant to Article 81(1) and (3) does not depend on the legal form which the parents choose for their cooperation. The applicability of the prohibition of restrictive practices depends, on the contrary, on whether the creation or the activities of the JV may affect trade between Member States and have as their object or effect the prevention, restriction or distortion of competition within the common market. The question whether an exemption can be granted to a JV will depend on the one hand on its overall economic benefits and on the other hand on the nature and scope of the restrictions of competition it entails.

5. In view of the variety of situations which come into consideration it is impossible to make general comments on the compliance of JVs with competition law. For a large proportion of JVs, whether or not they fall within the scope of application of Article 81 depends on their particular activity.[2] For other JVs, prohibition will occur only if particular

---

[1] OJ 1993 C43/2.
[2] See below III.1, point 15.

198

legal and factual circumstances coincide, the existence of which must be determined on a case-by-case basis.[3] Exemptions from the prohibition are based on the analysis of the overall economic balance, the results of which can turn out differently.[4] Cooperative joint ventures can however be divided into different categories, which are each open to the same competition law analysis.

6. In the Commission Notice of 1968 concerning agreements, decisions and concerted practices in the field of cooperation between enterprises,[5] the Commission listed a series of types of cooperation which *by their nature* are not prohibited because they do not have as their object or effect the restriction of competition within the meaning of Article 81(1). The 1986 Notice on agreements of minor importance[6] sets out quantitative criteria for those arrangements which are not prohibited because they have no *appreciable* impact on competition or inter-State trade. Both Notices apply to JVs. Commission Regulations (EEC) No. 417/85, (EEC) No. 418/85, (EEC) No. 2349/84 and (EEC) No. 556/89 on the application of Article 81(3) of the Treaty to specialization agreements,[7] research and development agreements,[8] patent licensing agreements[9] and know-how licensing agreements,[10] as amended by Regulation (EEC) No. ... /93,[11] include JVs amongst the beneficiaries of these group exemptions.[12] Further general indications on the assessment of cooperative JVs for competition purposes can be found in the numerous decisions and notices of the Commission in individual cases.[13]

7. The Commission will hereinafter summarize its administrative practice to date. In this way undertakings will be informed about both the legal and economic criteria which will guide the Commission in the future application of Article 81(1) and (3) to cooperative joint ventures. This Notice applies to all JVs which do not fall within the scope of application of Article 3 of Council Regulation (EEC) No. 4064/89 of 21 December 1989 on the control of concentrations between undertakings.[14] It forms the counterpart of the Notice regarding concentrative and cooperative operations[15] and the Notice on restrictions ancillary to concentrations[16] which clarify the abovementioned Regulation. Links between undertakings other than JVs will not be dealt with in this Notice, even though they often have similar effects on competition in the common market and on trade between Member States. Having regard to the experience of the Commission, however, no generally applicable conclusions can yet be drawn.

8. This notice is without prejudice to the power of national courts in the Member States to apply Article 81(1) and group exemptions under Article 81(3) on the basis of their own jurisdiction. Nevertheless it constitutes a factor which the national courts can take into account when deciding a dispute before them. It is also without prejudice to any interpretation which may be given by the Court of Justice of the European Communities.

II. The concept of cooperative joint ventures

9. The concept of cooperative joint ventures can be derived from Regulation (EEC) No. 4064/89. According to Article 3(1), a JV is an undertaking under the joint control of several other undertakings, the parents. Control, according to Article 3(3), consists of the

---

[3] See below III.2 and 3, points 17 *et seq.* and 32 *et seq.*
[4] See below IV.1 and 2, points 43 *et seq.* and 52 *et seq.*
[5] OJ 1968 C75/3; corrected by OJ 1968 C84/14.
[6] OJ 1986 C231/2.
[7] OJ 1985 L53/1.
[8] OJ 1985 L53/5.
[9] OJ 1984 L219/15; corrected by OJ 1985 L280/32.
[10] OJ 1989 L61/1.
[11] OJ 1993 L ... /... [Since published as Reg. 151/93 OJ 1993 L21/8].
[12] See below IV.1, points 43 *et seq.*
[13] For references and summaries see the Commission Competition Policy Reports.
[14] OJ 1989 L395/1; corrected by OJ 1990 L257/13.
[15] OJ 1990 C203/10.
[16] OJ 1990 C203/5.

possibility of exercising a decisive influence on the activities of the undertaking. Whether joint control, the prerequisite of every JV, exists, is determined by the legal and factual circumstances of the individual case. For details refer to the Notice regarding concentrative and cooperative operations.[17]

10. According to Article 3(2) of Regulation (EEC) No. 4064/89, any JV which does not fulfil the criteria of a concentration, is cooperative in nature. Under the second subparagraph, this applies to:

— all JVs, the activities of which are not to be performed on a lasting basis, especially those limited in advance by the parents to a short time period,
— JVs which do not perform all the functions of an autonomous economic entity, especially those charged by their parents simply with the operation of particular functions of an undertaking (partial-function JVs),
— JVs which perform all the functions of an autonomous economic entity (full-function JVs) where they give rise to coordination of competitive behaviour by the parents in relation to each other or to the JV.

The delimitation of cooperative and concentrative operations can be difficult in individual cases. The abovementioned Commission Notice[18] contains detailed instructions for the solution of this problem. Additional indications can also be gained from the practice of the Commission under Regulation (EEC) No. 4064/89.[19]

11. Cooperative JVs are outside the scope of the provisions on merger control. The determination of the cooperative character of a JV has however no substantive legal effects. It simply means that the JV is subject to the procedures set out in Regulation No. 17[20] or Regulations (EEC) No. 1017/68,[21] (EEC) No. 4056/86[22] or (EEC) No. 3975/87[23] in the determination of its compliance with Article 81(1) and (3).

III. Assessment pursuant to Article 81

1. General comments

12. JVs can be caught by the prohibition of cartels only where they fulfil all the requisite elements pursuant to Article 81(1).

13. The creation of a JV is usually based on an agreement between undertakings and sometimes on a decision of an association of undertakings. The exercise of control as well as the management of the business is likewise usually governed by contract. Where there is no agreement, which is the case for instance in the acquisition of a joint controlling interest in an existing company by the purchase of shares on the stock exchange, the continued existence of the JV depends on the parent companies, coordinating their policy towards the JV and their manner of controlling it.

---

[17] See points 6 to 14.
[18] See points 15 and 16.
[19] See on the one hand Decisions (pursuant to Article 6(1)(a) of Regulation (EEC) No. 4064/89); *Renault/Volvo*; *Baxter/Nestlé/Salvia*; *Apollinaris/Schweppes*; *Elf/Enterprise*; *Sunrise*; *BSN/Nestlé/ Cokoladovny*; *Flachglas/Vegla*; *Eureko, Herbal/IRR*; *Koipe-Tabacalera/Elosua*; on the other hand Decisions (pursuant to Article 6(1)(b) of Regulation (EEC) No. 4064/89); *Sanofi/Sterling Drugs*; *Elf/BC/Cepsa*; *Dräger/IBM/HMP*; *Thomson/Pilkington*; *UAP/Transatlantic/Sun Life*; *TNT/ GD/Net*; *Lucas/Eaton*; *Courtaulds/SNIA*; *Volvo/Atlas*; *Ericsson/Kolbe*; *Spar/Dansk Supermarked*; *Generali/BCHA*; *Mondi/Frantschach*; *Eucom/Digital*; *Ericsson/Ascom*; *Thomas Cook/LTU/West LB*; *Elf-Atochem/Rohm & Haas*; *Rhône-Poulenc/SNIA*; *Northern Telecom/Matra Telecommunications*; *Avesta/British Steel, NCC/AGA/Axel Johnson*; (References and summaries in the Commission Competition Policy Reports).
[20] OJ 1962 No. 13 204/62.
[21] OJ 1968 L175/10.
[22] OJ 1986 L378/4.
[23] OJ 1987 L374/1.

14. Whether the aforementioned agreements, decisions or concerted practices are likely to affect trade between Member States, can be decided only on a case-by-case basis. Where the JV's actual or foreseeable effects on competition are limited to the territory of one Member State or to territories outside the Community, Article 81(1) will not apply.

15. Article 81(1) does not therefore apply to certain categories of JV because they do not have as their object or effect the prevention, restriction or distortion of competition. This is particularly true for:

— JVs formed by parents which all belong to the same group and which are not in a position freely to determine their market behaviour: in such a case its creation is merely a matter of internal organization and allocation of tasks within the group,
— JVs of minor economic importance within the meaning of the 1986 Notice[24]; there is no *appreciable* restriction of competition where the combined turnover of the participating undertakings does not exceed ECU 200 million and their market share is not more than 5%,
— JVs with activities neutral to competition within the meaning of the 1968 Notice on cooperation between enterprises[25]: the types of cooperation referred to therein do not restrict competition because:
— they have as their sole object the procurement of non-confidential information and therefore serve in the preparation of autonomous decisions of the participating enterprises,[26]
— they have as their sole object management cooperation,[27]
— they have as their sole object cooperation in fields removed from the market,[28]
— they are concerned solely with technical and organizational arrangements,[29]
— they concern solely arrangements between non-competitors,[30]
— even though they concern arrangements between competitors, they neither limit the parties' competitive behaviour nor affect the market position of third parties.[31]

The aforementioned characteristics for distinguishing between conduct restrictive of competition and conduct which is neutral from a competition point of view are not fixed, but form part of the general development of Community law. They must therefore be construed and applied in the light of the case-law of the Court of Justice as well as of the Commission's decisions. In addition, general Commission notices are modified from time to time in order to adapt them to the evolution of the law.

16. JVs which do not fall into any of the abovementioned categories must be individually examined to see whether they have the object or effect of restricting competition. The basic principles of the Notice on cooperation can be useful in such examination. The Commission will explain below on what criteria it assesses the restrictive character of a JV.

2. Criteria for the establishment of restrictions of competition

17. The appraisal of a cooperative JV in the light of the competition rules will focus on the relationship between the enterprises concerned and on the effects of their cooperation on third parties. In this respect the first task is to check whether the creation or operation of the JV is likely to prevent, restrict or distort competition between the parents. Secondly, it is necessary to examine whether the operation in question is likely to affect appreciably

---

[24] OJ 1986 C231/2.
[25] OJ 1968 C75/3; corrected by OJ 1968 C93/14.
[26] See II, point 1.
[27] See II, point 2.
[28] See II, point 3.
[29] See II, point 4.
[30] See II, points 5 and 6.
[31] See II, points 7 and 8.

the competitive position of third parties, especially with regard to supply and sales possibilities. The relationship of the parents to the JV requires a separate legal assessment only if the JV is a full-function undertaking. However, even here the assessment must always take into account the relationship of the parents to each other and to third parties. Prevention, restriction or distortion of competition will be brought about by a JV only if its creation or activity affects the conditions of competition on the relevant market. The evaluation of a JV pursuant to Article 81(1) therefore always implies defining the relevant geographic and product market. The criteria to apply in that process are to be drawn from the *de minimis* Notice and the Commission's previous decisions. Special attention must be paid to networks of JVs which are set up by the same parents, by one parent with different partners or by different parents in parallel. They form an important element of the market structure and may therefore be of decisive influence in determining whether the creation of a JV leads to restrictions of competition.

(a) Competition between parent companies

18. Competition between parent companies can be prevented, restricted or distorted through cooperation in a JV only to the extent that companies are already actual or potential competitors. The assumption of potential competitive circumstances presupposes that each parent alone is in a position to fulfil the tasks assigned to the JV and that it does not forfeit its capabilities to do so by the creation of the JV. An economically realistic approach is necessary in the assessment of any particular case.

19. The Commission has developed a set of questions, which aim to clarify the theoretical and practical existing possibilities for the parents to perform the tasks individually instead of together.[32] Although these questions are designed to apply in particular to the case of manufacturing of goods, they are also relevant to the provisions of services. They are as follows:

— *Contribution to the JV*
  Does each parent company have sufficient financial resources to carry out the planned investment? Does each parent company have sufficient managerial qualifications to run the JV? Does each parent company have access to the necessary input products?
— *Production of the JV*
  Does each parent know the production technique? Does each parent make the upstream or downstream products himself and does it have access to the necessary production facilities?
— *Sales by the JV*
  Is actual or potential demand such as to enable each parent company to manufacture the product on its own? Does each parent company have access to the distribution channels needed to sell the product manufactured by the JV?
— *Risk factors*
  Can each parent company on its own bear the technical and financial risks associated with the production operations of the JV?
— *Access to the relevant market*
  What is the relevant geographic and product market? What are the barriers to entry into that market? Is each parent company capable of entering that market on its own? Can each parent overcome existing barriers within a reasonable time and without undue effort or cost?

20. The parents of a JV are potential competitors, in so far as in the light of the above factors, which may be given different weight from case to case, they could reasonably be expected to act autonomously. In that connection, analysis must focus on the various stages of the activity of an undertaking. The economic pressure towards cooperation at the

---

[32] See Thirteenth Competition Policy Report (1983), point 55.

R&D stage does not normally eliminate the possibility of competition between the participating undertakings at the production and distribution stages. The pooling of the production capacity of several undertakings, when it is economically unavoidable and thus objectionable as regards competition law, does not necessarily imply that these undertakings should also cooperate in the distribution of the products concerned.

(b) Competition between the parent companies and the JV

21. The relationship between the parents and the JV takes a specific significance when the JV is a full-function JV and is in competition with, or is a supplier or a customer of, at least one of the parents. The applicability of the prohibition on cartels depends on the circumstances of the individual case. As anti-competitive behaviour between the parents will as a rule also influence business relationships between the parents and the JV and conversely, anti-competitive behaviour by the JV and one of the parents will always affect relationships between the parents, a global analysis of all the different relationships is necessary. The Commission's decisions offer plenty of examples of this.

22. The restriction of competition, within the meaning of Article 81(1), between parents and JVs typically manifests itself in the division of geographical markets, product markets (especially through specialization) or customers. In such cases the participating undertakings reduce their activity to the role of potential competitors. If they remain active competitors, they will usually be tempted to reduce the intensity of competition by coordinating their business policy, especially as to prices and volume of production or sales or by voluntarily restraining their efforts.

(c) Effects of the JV on the position of third parties

23. The restrictive effect on third parties depends on the JV's activities in relation to those of its parents and on the combined market power of the undertakings concerned.

24. Where the parent companies leave it to the JV to handle their purchases or sales, the choice available to suppliers or customers may be appreciably restricted. The same is true when the parents arrange for the JV to manufacture primary or intermediate products or to process products which they themselves have produced. The creation of a JV may even exclude from the market the parents' traditional suppliers and customers. That risk increases in step with the degree of oligopolisation of the market and the existence of exclusive or preferential links between the JV and its parents.

25. The existence of a JV in which economically significant undertakings pool their respective market power may even be a barrier to market entry by potential competitors and/or impede the growth of the parents' competitors.

(d) Assessment of the appreciable effect of restrictions of competition

26. The scale of a JV's effects on competition depends on a number of factors, the most important of which are:

— the market shares of the parent companies and the JV, the structure of the relevant market and the degree of concentration in the sector concerned,
— the economic and financial strength of the parent companies, and any commercial or technical edge which they may have in comparison to their competitors,
— the market proximity of the activities carried out by the JV,
— whether the fields of activity of the parent companies and the JV are identical or interdependent,
— the scale and significance of the JV's activities in relation to those of its parents,
— the extent to which the arrangements between the firms concerned are restrictive,
— the extent to which market access by third parties is restricted.

(e) JV networks

27. JV networks can particularly restrict competition because they increase the influence of the individual JV on the business policy of the parents and on the market position of third parties. The assessment under competition law must take into account the different ways of arranging JV networks just as much as the cumulative effects of parallel existing networks.

28. Often competing parent companies set up several JVs which are active in the same product market but in different geographical markets. On the top of the restrictions of competition which can already be attributed to each JV, there will then be those which arise in the relationships between the individual JVs. The ties between the parents are strengthened by the creation of every further JV so that any competition which still exists between them will be further reduced.

29. The same is true in the case where competing parents set up several JVs for complementary products which they themselves intend to process or for non-complementary products which they themselves distribute. The extent and intensity of the restrictive effects on competition are also increased in such cases. Competition is most severely restricted where undertakings competing within the same oligopolistic economic sector set up a multitude of JVs for related products or for a great variety of intermediate products. These considerations are also valid for the service sector.

30. Even where a JV is created by non-competing undertakings and does not, on its own, cause any restriction of competition, it can be anti-competitive if it belongs to a network of JVs set up by one of the parents for the same product market with different partners, because competition between the JVs may then be prevented, restricted or distorted.[33] If the different partners are actual or potential competitors, there will additionally be restrictive effects in the relationships between them.

31. Parallel networks of JVs, involving different parent companies, simply reveal the degree of personal and financial connection between the undertakings of an economic sector or between several economic sectors. They form, in so far as they are comparable to the degree of concentration on the relevant market, an important aspect of the economic environment which has to be taken into account in the assessment from a competition point of view of both the individual networks and the participating JVs.

3. Assessment of the most important types of JV

(a) Joint ventures between non-competitors

32. This group rarely causes problems for competition, whether the JV fulfils merely partial or the full functions of an undertaking. In the first case one must simply examine whether market access of third parties is significantly affected by the cooperation between the parents.[34] In the second case the emphasis of the examination is on the same question and the problem of competition restrictions between one of the parents and the JV[35] is usually only of secondary significance.

33. JVs between non-competitors created for research and development, for production or for distribution of goods including customer service do not in principle fall within Article 81(1). The non-application of the prohibition is justified by the combination of complementary knowledge, products and services in the JV. That is, however, subject to the reservation that there remains room for a sufficient number of R&D centres, production units and sales channels in the respective area of economic activity of the JV.[36] The

---

· [33] See Decision *Optical Fibres*, OJ 1986 L236/30.

[34] See above III.2 (c) points 23, 24 and 25.

[35] See above III.2 (b) points 21 and 22.

[36] See Section II of the Notice on cooperation, points 3 and 6, and Regulation (EEC) No. 418/85 on the application of Article 81(3) of the Treaty to categories of research and development agreements, OJ 1985 L53/5.

same reasoning also applies to the assessment of purchasing JVs for customers from different business sectors. Such JVs are unobjectionable from a competition point of view as long as they leave suppliers with sufficient possibilities of customer choice.

34. JVs which manufacture exclusively for their parents primary or intermediate products or undertake processing for one or more of their parents do not, as a rule, restrict competition. A significant restriction of the supply and sales possibilities of third parties, a prerequisite for the application of the prohibition, can occur only if the parents have a strong market position in the supply or demand of the relevant products.

35. In the assessment of a full-function JV it is essential whether the activities the JV pursues are closely linked to those of the parents. In addition, the relationship of the activities of the parents to each other is of importance. If the JV trades in a product market which is upstream or downstream of the market of a parent, restrictions of competition can occur in relation to third parties, if the participants are undertakings with market power.[37] If the market of the JV is upstream of the market of one of the parents and at the same time downstream of the market of another parent, the JV functions as a connection between the two parents and also possibly as a vertical multi-level integration instrument. In such a situation the exclusive effects with regard to third parties are reinforced. Whether it fulfils the requisite minimum degree for the application of Article 81(1) can be decided only on an individual basis. If the JV and one of the parents trade in the same product market, then coordination of their market behaviour is probable if not inevitable.[38]

(b) Joint ventures by competitors

36. In this situation the effects of the JV on competition between the parents and on the market position of third parties must be analysed. The relationship between the activities of the JV and those of the parents is of decisive importance. In the absence of any interplay, Article 81(1) will usually not be applicable. The competition law assessment of the different types of JV leads to the following results.

37. A research and development JV may, in exceptional cases, restrict competition if it excludes individual activity in this area by the parents or if competition by the parents on the market for the resulting products will be restricted. This will normally be the case where the JV also assumes the exploitation of the newly developed or improved products or processes.[39] Whether the restriction of competition between the parents and the ensuing possible secondary effects on third parties are appreciable can be decided only on a case-by-case basis.

38. Sales JVs, selling the products of competing manufacturers, restrict competition between the parents on the supply side and limit the choice of purchasers. They belong to the category of traditional horizontal cartels which are subject to the prohibition of Article 81(1),[40] when they have an appreciable effect on the market.

39. Purchasing JVs set up by competitors can give the participants an advantageous position on the demand side and reduce the choice of suppliers. Depending on the importance of the jointly-sold products to the production and sales activities of the parents, the cooperation can also lead to a considerable weakening of price competition between the participating undertakings. This applies even more so when the purchase

---

[37] No negative effect was found by the Commission in Decision 86/405/EEC (*Optical Fibres*), OJ 1986 L236/30, and in Decision 90/410/EEC (*Elopak/Metal Box-Odin*), OJ 1990 L209/15.

[38] See above III.2 (b) point 22, and Decision 87/100/EEC (*Mitchell Cotts/Sofiltra*), OJ 1987 L41/31.

[39] See Notice in cooperation, II, point 3 and Regulation (EEC) No. 418/85 (cited in footnote 8).

[40] See the following decisions: *NCH*, OJ 1972 L22/16; *Cementregeling voor Nederland*, OJ 1972 L303/7; *Cimbel*, OJ 1972 L303/24; *CSV*, OJ 1978 L242/15; *UIP*, OJ 1989 L226/25 and *Astra*, OJ L . . . [since published at OJ 1993 L20/23].

price makes up a significant part of the total cost of the products distributed by the parents. The application of Article 81(1) depends on the circumstances of the individual case.[41]

40. JVs which manufacture primary or intermediate products for competing parent companies, which are further processed by them into the final product, must be assessed on the same principles. On the other hand, if the JV undertakes the processing of basic materials supplied by the parents, or the processing of half-finished into fully-finished products, with the aim of resupplying the parents, then competition between the participating undertakings, taking into consideration the market proximity of their cooperation and the inherent tendency to align prices, will usually exist only in a weaker form.[42] This is particularly so when the entire production activities of the parents are concentrated in the JV and the parents withdraw to the role of pure distributors. This leads to the standardization of manufacturing costs and the quality of the products so that essentially the only competition between the parents is on trade margins. This is a considerable restriction of competition which cannot be remedied by the parents marketing the products under different brand names.[43]

41. Different situations must be distinguished when assessing full-function JVs between competing undertakings.[44]

— Where the JV operates on the same market as its parents, the normal consequence is that competition between all participating undertakings will be restricted.
— Where the JV operates on a market upstream or downstream of that of the parents with which it has supply or delivery links, the effects on competition will be the same as in the case of a production JV.
— Where the JV operates on a market adjacent to that of its parents, competition can only be restricted when there is a high degree of interdependence between the two markets. This is especially the case when the JV manufactures products which are complementary to those of its parents.

Combinations of various types of JV are often found in economic life so that an overall assessment of the resultant restrictions of competition between participating undertakings and the consequences of the cooperation on third parties must be carried out. In addition the economic circumstances must be taken into account, especially the association of a JV to a network with other JVs and the existence of several parallel JV networks within the same economic sector.[45]

42. Even JVs between competitors, which are usually caught by the prohibition in Article 81(1), must be examined to see whether in the actual circumstances of the individual case they have as their object or effect the restriction, prevention or distortion of competition. This will not be the case where cooperation in the form of a JV can objectively be seen as the only possibility for the parents to enter a new market or to

---

[41] See the following decisions: *Socemas*, OJ 1968 L201/4; *Intergroup*, OJ 1975 L212/23; *National Sulphuric Acid Association I*, OJ 1980 L260/24 and *(II)*, OJ 1989 L190/25; *Filmeinkauf Deutscher Fernsehanstalten*, OJ 1989 L284/36; and *IJsselcentrale*, OJ 1991 L28/32.

[42] See Notice in *Exxon/Shell*, OJ L . . . / . . . [since published at OJ 1993 C92/2].

[43] See Decision 91/38/EEC (*KSB/Goulds/Lowara/ITT*), OJ 1991 L19/25, the anti-competitive character of joint economic production is acknowledged in principle in Regulation (EEC) No. 417/85 on the application of Article 81(3) of the EEC Treaty to categories of specialization agreements, OJ 1985 L53/1.

[44] See in particular the following decisions: *Bayer/Gist-Brocades*, OJ 1976 L30/13; *United Reprocessors* and *KEWA*, OJ 1976 L51/7, 15; *Vacuum Interrupters I*, OJ 1977 L48/32, and *II*, OJ 1980 L383/1; *De Laval/Stork I*, OJ 1977 L215/11, and *II*, OJ 1988 L59/32; *GEC/Weir*, OJ 1977 L327/26; *WANO/Schwarzpulver*, OJ 1978 L322/26; *Langenscheidt/Hachette*, OJ 1982 L39/25; *Amersham/Buchler*, OJ 1982 L314/34; *Rockwell/Iveco*, OJ 1983 L224/19; *Carbon Gas Technologie*, OJ 1983 L376/17; *Enichem/ICI*, OJ 1988 L50/18; *Bayer/BP Chemicals*, OJ 1988 L150/35; *Iveco/Ford*, OJ 1988 L230/39; *Alcatel Espace/ANT*, OJ 1990 L32/19; *Konsortium ECR 900*, OJ 1990 L228/31; *Screensport/EBU-Eurosport*, OJ 1991 L63/32; *Eirpage*, OJ 1991 L306/22; *Procter and Gamble/Finaf*, OJ 1992 C3/2 and *Infonet*, OJ 1992 C7/3.

[45] See above III.2 (e), points 27 to 31.

remain in their existing market, provided that their presence will strengthen competition or prevent it from being weakened. Under these conditions the JV will neither reduce existing competition nor prevent potential competition from being realized. The prohibition in Article 81(1) will therefore not apply.[46]

IV. Assessment pursuant to Article 81(3)

1. Group exemptions

43. JVs falling within the scope of Article 81(1) are exempted from the prohibition if they fulfil the conditions of a group exemption. Two Commission regulations legalize cooperation between undertakings in the form of JVs. Two other Commission regulations authorize certain restrictive agreements on the transfer of technology to a JV by its parents. The field of application of these group exemption regulations will be considerably expanded, notably for JVs, by Regulation (EEC) No. ... /93.[47]

(a) Specialization Regulation

44. Regulation (EEC) No. 417/85 on the application of Article 81(3) to categories of specialization agreements[48] includes, *inter alia*, agreements whereby several undertakings leave the manufacture of certain products to a JV set up by them. This transfer can be for existing or future production. The creation and use of production JVs are exempted only if the aggregate market share of the participating undertakings does not exceed 20% and the cumulated turnover does not exceed ECU 1 000 million. Agreements between more sizeable undertakings, the turnover of which exceeds ECU 1 000 million, also benefit from the group exemption if they are properly notified and the Commission does not object to the agreement within six months. This procedure is not applicable when the market share threshold is exceeded.

45. The abovementioned rules apply exclusively to cooperation at the production level. The JV must supply all its production—which can include primary, intermediate or finished products—to its parents. The latter are not permitted to be active as manufacturers in the JV's area of production, but they may manufacture other products belonging to that product market. Products made by the JV are then sold by the parents, each of which can deal as exclusive distributor for a given territory.

46. Agreements in which the parents entrust JVs with the distribution of the contract products are also covered by the group exemption, though only under more rigorous conditions. The aggregate market share of the participating undertakings must not exceed 10%. In this case also, there is a turnover threshold of ECU 1 000 million, the effect of which undertakings can avoid by resorting to the opposition procedure. Regulation (EEC) No. 417/85 leaves the undertakings concerned free to organize their cooperation at the production and distribution stages. It allows for separate production followed by joint distribution of the contract products through a sales JV, as well as for the merging of production and distribution in a full-function JV, or the separation of both functions through the creation of a production JV and a sales JV. The production and/or distribution of the contract products can be entrusted to several JVs instead of one, which may, as the

---

[46] See the following decisions: *Alliance des constructeurs français de machines-outils*, OJ 1968 L201/1; *SAFCO*, OJ 1972 L13/44; *Metaleurop*, OJ 1990 L179/41; *Elopak/Metal Box-Odin*, OJ 1990 L209/15; *Konsortium ECR 900*, OJ 1990 L228/31.
[47] OJ No. L..., ... [since published as Reg. 151/93, OJ 1993 L21/8].
[48] OJ 1985 L53/1.

case may be, fulfil their function on the basis of exclusive contracts in various territories.

(b) Research and development Regulation

47. Regulation (EEC) No. 418/85 on the application of Article 81(3) to categories of research and development agreements[49] provides for the exemption of JVs whose activities can range from R&D to the joint exploitation of results. The term exploitation covers the manufacture of new or improved products as well as the use of new or improved production processes, the marketing of products derived from R&D activities and the granting of manufacturing, use or distribution licences to third parties. The exemption is subject to the requirement that the joint R&D contributes substantially to technical or economic progress and is essential to the manufacture of new or improved products.

48. Regulation (EEC) No. 418/85 also links exemption from the prohibition to quantitative conditions in the form of a two-fold market share limit. Cooperation in the form of a JV dealing with R&D, production and licensing policy will be permitted for parents who have an aggregate market share of up to 20%. In the area of R&D as well as manufacture, the Regulation allows all forms of coordination of behaviour because it does not require specialization. The parents can themselves remain or become active within the field of activity of the JV. They are also allowed to determine in what way they wish to use the possibilities of production by themselves or the licensing of third parties. By the allocation of contract territories the parents can protect themselves for the duration of the contract from the manufacture and use of the contract products by other partners in the reserved territories; furthermore, they can prevent other partners from pursuing an active marketing policy in those territories for five years after the introduction of the new or improved product into the common market. If, on the contrary, the partners entrust one or more JVs with the distribution of the contract products, a market share threshold of 10% is applicable to the whole of their cooperation. As Regulation (EEC) No. 418/85 does not provide for a turnover threshold, all undertakings regardless of their size can benefit from the group exemption.

(c) Patent-licensing and know-how licensing Regulations

49. Regulation (EEC) No. 2349/84 on the application of Article 81(3) of the Treaty to categories of patent licensing agreements[50] applies also to such agreements between any one of the parents and the JV affecting the activities of the JV. If the parents are competitors on the market of the contract products, the group exemption applies only up to a certain market share limit. This is 20% if the JV simply carries on manufacturing or 10% if it carries on the manufacture and marketing of the licensed products.

50. Regulation (EEC) No. 2349/84 also permits the granting of exclusive territorial manufacture and distribution licences to the JV, the protection of the licence territories of the JV and of the parents against active and passive competition by other participants for the duration of the contract and the protection of the licence territory of the JV against other licensees. The parents can protect the JV from an active distribution policy by other licensees for the full duration of the contract. During an initial five-year period from the introduction of a product into the common market, it is possible to forbid direct imports of contract products by other licensees into the JV's licensed territory.

51. Regulation (EEC) No. 556/89 on the application of Article 81(3) of the Treaty to certain categories of know-how licensing agreements[51] contains similar provisions, except that the territorial protection between the JV and the parents is limited to 10 years, beginning from the signature of the first know-how agreement concluded for a territory

---

[49] OJ 1985 L53/5.
[50] OJ 1984 L219/15.
[51] OJ 1989 L61/1.

inside the Community. This point in time also marks the beginning of the period for which the JV can be protected against active competition (10 years) and passive competition (five years) by other licensees.

2. Individual exemptions

(a) General comments

52. JVs which fall within Article 81(1) without fulfilling the conditions for the application of a group exemption regulation are not inevitably unlawful. They can be exempted by an individual decision of the Commission in so far as they fulfil the four conditions of Article 81(3). According to Articles 4, 5 and 15 of Regulation No. 17 an individual exemption can be issued only if the participating undertakings have notified the agreement, decision or concerted practice on which cooperation is based, to the Commission. Certain arrangements which are less harmful to the development of the common market are dispensed from the requirement to notify by Article 4(2) of Regulation No. 17. They can therefore be exempted without prior notification. The same applies to transport cartels within the meaning of Regulations (EEC) No. 1017/68, (EEC) No. 4056/86 and (EEC) No. 3975/87.

53. The Commission must, pursuant to Article 81(3), examine:

— whether the JV contributes to improving the production or distribution of goods or to promoting technical or economic progress,
— whether consumers are allowed a fair share of the resulting benefit,
— whether the parents or the JV are subject to restrictions which are not indispensable for the attainment of these objectives, and
— whether the cooperation in the JV affords the undertakings concerned the possibility of eliminating competition in respect of a substantial part of the products or services in question.

An exemption from the prohibition in Article 81(1) can be issued only if the answer to the first two questions is in the affirmative and the answer to the second two questions is negative.

(b) Principles of assessment

54. In order to fulfil the first two conditions of Article 81(3) the JV must bring appreciable objective advantages for third parties, especially consumers, which at least equal the consequent detriment to competition.

55. Advantages in the abovementioned sense, which can be pursued and attained with the aid of a JV, include, in the Commission's opinion, in particular, the development of new or improved products and processes which are marketed by the originator or by third parties under licence. In addition, measures opening up new markets, leading to the sales expansion of the undertaking in new territories or the enlargement of its supply range by new products, will in principle be assessed favourably. In all these cases the undertakings in question contribute to dynamic competition, consolidating the internal market and strengthening the competitiveness of the relevant economic sector. Production and sales increases can also be a pro-competitive stimulant. On the other hand, the rationalization of production activities and distribution networks are rather a means of adapting supply to a shrinking or stagnant demand. It leads, however, to cost savings which, under effective competition, are usually passed on to customers as lower prices. Plans for the reduction of production capacity however lead mostly to price rises. Agreements of this latter type will be judged favourably only if they serve to overcome a structural crisis, to accelerate the removal of unprofitable production capacity from the market and thereby to reestablish competition in the medium term.

56. The commission will give a negative assessment to agreements which have as their main purpose the coordination of actual or potential competition between the participating undertakings. This is especially so for joint price-fixing, the reduction of production and sales by establishing quotas, the division of markets and contractual prohibitions or restrictions on investment. JVs which are created or operated essentially to achieve such aims are nothing but classic cartels the anti-competitive effects of which are well known.

57. The pros and cons of a JV will be weighed against each other on an overall economic balance, by means of which the type and the extent of the respective advantages and risks can be assessed. If the parents are economically and financially powerful and have, over and above that a high market-share, their exemption applications will need a rigorous examination. The same applies to JVs which reinforce an existing narrow oligopoly or belong to a network of JVs.

58. The acceptance pursuant to Article 81(3)(a) of restrictions on the parents or the JV depends above all on the type and aims of the cooperation. In this context, the decisive factor is usually whether the contractual restriction on the parties' economic freedom is directly connected with the creation of the JV and can be considered indispensable for its existence.[52] It is only for the restriction of global competition that Article 81(3)(b) sets an absolute limit. Competition must be fully functioning at all times. Agreements which endanger its effectiveness cannot benefit from individual exemption. This category includes JVs which, through the combination of activities of the parents, achieve, consolidate or strengthen a dominant position.

(c) Assessment of the most important types of JV

59. Pure research and development JVs which do not fulfil the conditions for group exemption under Regulation (EEC) No. 418/85 can still in general be viewed positively. This type of cooperation normally offers important economic benefits without adversely affecting competition. That is also the case where the parents entrust the JV with the further task of granting licences to third parties. If the JV also takes on the manufacture of the jointly researched and developed product, the assessment for the purpose of exemption must include the principles which apply to production JVs.[53] JVs which are responsible for R&D, licensing, production and distribution are full-function JVs and must be analysed accordingly.[54]

60. Sales JVs belong to the category of classic horizontal cartels. They have as a rule the object and effect of coordinating the sales policy of competing manufacturers. In this way they not only close off price competition between the parents but also restrict the volume of goods to be delivered by the participants within the framework of the system for allocating orders. The Commission will therefore in principle assess sales JVs negatively.[55] The Commission takes a positive view however of those cases where joint distribution of the contract products is part of a global cooperation project which merits favourable treatment pursuant to Article 81(3) and for the success of which it is indispensable. The most important examples are sales JVs between manufacturers who have concluded a reciprocal specialization agreement, but wish to continue to offer the whole range of products concerned, or sales JVs set up for the joint exploitation of the results of joint R&D, even at the distribution stage. In other cases, an exemption can be envisaged only in certain specific circumstances.[56]

61. Purchasing JVs contribute to the rationalization of ordering and to the better use of transport and store facilities but are at the same time an instrument for the setting of

---

[52] See below V.2, points 70 et seq.
[53] See below points 62 and 63.
[54] See below point 64.
[55] See the *NCH, Cementregeling voor Nederland, Cimbel* and *CSV* decisions (all cited in footnote 40) and Astra, OJ 1993 L . . . , . . . [since published at OJ 1993 L20/23].
[56] See Decision 89/467/EEC (*UIP*) (cited in footnote 40).

uniform purchase prices and conditions and often of purchase quotas. By combining their demand power in a JV, the parents can obtain a position of excessive influence *vis–à–vis* the other side of the market and distort competition between suppliers. Consequently, the disadvantages often outweigh the possible benefits which can accompany purchasing JVs, particularly those between competing producers. The Commission is correspondingly prepared to grant exemptions only in exceptional cases and then only if the parents retain the possibility of purchasing individually.[57] No decision has, however, concerned the most important of the purchasing JVs so far.

62. Production JVs can serve different economic purposes. They will often be set up to create new capacity for the manufacture of particular products which are also manufactured by the parents.[58] In other cases the JV will be entrusted with the manufacture of a new product in the place of the parents.[59] Finally, the JV can be entrusted with the combination of the production capacities of the parents and their expansion or reduction as necessary.

63. In view of the various tasks of production JVs their assessment for exemption purposes will be carried out according to different yardsticks. JVs, for the expansion of production capacity or product range, can contribute not only to the prevention of parallel investment—which results in costs savings—but also to the stimulation of competition. The combination or reduction of existing production capacity is primarily a reationalization measure and is usually of a defensive nature. It is not always obvious that measures of this kind benefit third parties, especially consumers and they must therefore be justified individually. Generally applicable quantitative thresholds, for instance in the form of market share limits, cannot be fixed for production JVs. The more the competition between the parents is restricted, the more emphasis must be put on the maintenance of competition with third parties. The market share limit of 20% in the group exemption regulations can serve as a starting point for the assessment of production JVs in individual cases.

64. Full-function JVs, in so far as they are not price-fixing, quota-fixing or market-sharing cartels or vehicles for a coordination of the investment policies conducted by the parents which goes beyond the individual case, often form elements of dynamic competition and then deserve a favourable assessment.[60] As cooperation also includes distribution, the Commission has to take special care in assessing individual cases that no position of market power will be created or strengthened by entrusting the JV with all the functions of an undertaking, combined with the placing at its disposal of all the existing resources of the parents. To assess whether a full-function JV raises problems of compatibility with the competition rules or not, an important point of reference is the aggregate market share limit of 10% contained in the group exemption regulations. Below this threshold it can be assumed that the effect of exclusion from the market of third parties and the danger of creating or reinforcing barriers to market entry will be kept within justifiable limits. A prerequisite is however that the market structure will continue to guarantee effective competition. If the said threshold is exceeded, an exemption will be considered only after a careful examination of each individual case.

---

[57] See the *National Sulphuric Acid Association, Filmeinkauf deutscher Fernsehanstalten, IJsselcentrale* decisions (all cited in footnote 41).

[58] See *Exxon/Shell* (footnote 42).

[59] See the *KSB/Goulds/Lowara/ITT* decision (cited in footnote 43).

[60] See the following decisions: *Amersham/Buchler*, OJ 1982 L314/34; *Rockwell/Iveco*, OJ 1983 L224/19; *Carbon Gas Technologie*, OJ 1983 L376/17; *Enichem/ICI*, OJ 1988 L50/18; *Bayer/BP Chemicals*, OJ 1988 L150/35; *Iveco/Ford*, OJ 1988 L230/39; *Alcatel Espace/ANT*, OJ 1990 L32/19; *Eirpage*, OJ 1991 L306/22; *Bayer/Gist-Brocades*, OJ 1976 L30/13; *United Reprocessors and KEWA*, OJ 1976 L51/7; *Vacuum Interrupters I*, OJ 1977 L48/32 and *II*, OJ 1980 L383/1; *De Laval/Stork I*, OJ 1977 L215/11 and *II*, OJ 1988 L59/32; *GEC/Weir*, OJ 1977 L327/26; *Langenscheidt/Hachette*, OJ 1982 L39/25; *Procter and Gamble/Finaf*, OJ 1992 C3/2; and *INFONET*, OJ 1992 C7/3.

V. Ancillary restrictions

1. Principles of assessment

65. A distinction must be made between restrictions of competition which arise from the creation and operation of a JV, and additional agreements which would, on their own, also constitute restrictions of competition by limiting the freedom of action in the market of the participating undertakings. Such additional agreements are either directly related to and necessary for the establishment and operation of the JV in so far as they cannot be dissociated from it without jeopardizing its existence, or are simply concluded at the same time as the JV's creation without having those features.

66. Additional agreements which are directly related to the JV and necessary for its existence must be assessed together with the JV. They are treated under the rules of competition as ancillary restrictions if they remain subordinate in importance to the main object of the JV. In particular, in determining the "necessity" of the restriction, it is proper not only to take account of its nature, but equally to ensure that its duration, subject matter and geographical field of application do not exceed what the creation and operation of the JV normally requires.

67. If a JV does not fall within the scope of Article 81(1), then neither do any additional agreements which, while restricting competition on their own, are ancillary to the JV in the manner described above. Conversely, if a JV falls within the scope of Article 81(1), then so will any ancillary restrictions. The exemption from prohibition is based for both on the same principles. Ancillary restrictions require no special justification under Article 81(3). They will generally be exempted for the same period as the JV.

68. Additional agreements which are not ancillary to the JV normally fall within the scope of Article 81(1), even though the JV itself may not. For them to be granted an exemption under Article 81(3), a specific assessment of their benefits and disadvantages must be made. This assessment must be carried out separately from that of the JV.

69. In view of the diversity of JVs and of the additional restrictions that may be linked to them, only a few examples can be given of the application of existing principles. They are drawn from previous Commission practice.

2. Assessment of certain additional restrictions

70. Assessment of whether additional restrictions constitute an ancillary agreement must distinguish between those which affect the JV and those which affect the parents.

(a) Restrictions on the JV

71. Of the restrictions which affect the JV, those which give concrete expression to its object, such as contract clauses which specify the product range or the location of production, may be regarded as ancillary. Additional restrictions which go beyond the definition of the venture's object and which relate to quantities, prices or customers may not. The same can be said for export bans.

72. When the setting-up of the JV involves the creation of new production capacity or the transfer of technology from the parent, the obligation imposed on the JV not to manufacture or market products competing with the licensed products may usually be regarded as ancillary. The JV must seek to ensure the success of the new production unit, without depriving the parent companies of the necessary control over exploitation and dissemination of their technology.[61]

73. In certain circumstances, other restrictions on the JV can be classified as ancillary such as contract clauses which limit the cooperation to a certain area or to a specific

---

[61] *Mitchell Cotts/Sofiltra* (footnote 38).

technical application of the transferred technology. Such restrictions must be seen as the inevitable consequences of the parent's wish to limit the cooperation to a specific field of activity without jeopardizing the object and existence of the JV.[62]

74. Lastly, where the parent companies assign to the JV certain stages of production or the manufacture of certain products, obligations on the JV to purchase from or supply its parents may also be regarded as ancillary, at least during the JV's starting-up period.

(b) Restrictions on the parent companies

75. Restrictions which prohibit the parent companies from competing with the JV or from actively competing with it in its area of activity, may be regarded as ancillary at least during the JV's starting-up period. Additional restrictions relating to quantities, prices or customers, and export bans obviously go beyond what is required for the setting-up and operation of the JV.

76. The Commission has in one case regarded as ancillary, a territorial restriction imposed on a parent company where the JV was granted an exclusive manufacturing licence in respect of fields of technical application and product markets in which both the JV and the parent were to be active.[63] This decision was limited, however, to the starting-up period of the JV and appeared necessary for the parents to become established in a new geographical market with the help of the JV. In another case, the grant to the JV of an exclusive exploitation licence without time-limit was regarded as indispensable for its creation and operation. In this case the parent company granting the licence was not active in the same field of application or on the same product market as that for which the licence was granted.[64] This will generally be the case with JVs undertaking new activities in respect of which the parent companies are neither actual nor potential competitors.

---

[62] *Elopak/Metal Box-Odin* (footnote 37).
[63] *Mitchell Cotts/Sofiltra* (footnote 38).
[64] *Elopak/Metal Box-Odin* (footnote 37).

COMMISSION NOTICE

Guidelines on the applicability of Article 81 of the EC Treaty to horizontal cooperation agreements[1]

(Text with EEA relevance)

1. INTRODUCTION

1.1. Purpose

1. These guidelines set out the principles for the assessment of horizontal cooperation agreements under Article 81 of the Treaty. A cooperation is of a "horizontal nature" if an agreement or concerted practice is entered into between companies operating at the same level(s) in the market. In most instances, horizontal cooperation amounts to cooperation between competitors. It covers for example areas such as research and development (R & D), production, purchasing or commercialisation.

2. Horizontal cooperation may lead to competition problems. This is for example the case if the parties to a cooperation agree to fix prices or output, to share markets, or if the cooperation enables the parties to maintain, gain or increase market power and thereby causes negative market effects with respect to prices, output, innovation or the variety and quality of products.

3. On the other hand, horizontal cooperation can lead to substantial economic benefits. Companies need to respond to increasing competitive pressure and a changing market place driven by globalisation, the speed of technological progress and the generally more dynamic nature of markets. Cooperation can be a means to share risk, save costs, pool know-how and launch innovation faster. In particular for small and medium-sized enterprises cooperation is an important means to adapt to the changing market place.

4. The Commission, while recognising the economic benefits that can be generated by cooperation, has to ensure that effective competition is maintained. Article 81 provides the legal framework for a balanced assessment taking into account both anti-competitive effects as well as economic benefits.

5. In the past, two Commission notices and two block exemption regulations provided guidance for the assessment of horizontal cooperation under Article 81. Commission Regulation (EEC) No 417/85,[2] as last amended by Regulation (EC) No 2236/97[3] and Commission Regulation (EEC) No 418/85,[4] as last amended by Regulation (EC) No 2236/97, provided for the exemption of certain forms of specialisation agreement and research and development agreement (R & D) respectively. Those two Regulations have

---

[1] OJ 2001 C3/2.
[2] OJ 1985 L53/1.
[3] OJ 1997 L306/12.
[4] OJ 1985 L53/5.

now been replaced by the Commission Regulation (EC) No 2658/2000 of 29 November 2000 on the application of Article 81(3) of the Treaty to categories of specialisation agreements[5] ("the Specialisation block exemption Regulation") and Commission Regulation (EC) No 2659/2000 of 29 November 2000 on the application of Article 81(3) of the Treaty to categories of research and development agreements[6] ("the R & D block exemption Regulation"). The two notices provided guidance in respect of certain types of cooperation agreement falling outside Article 81[7] and the assessment of co-operative joint ventures.[8]

6. Changing markets have generated an increasing variety and use of horizontal cooperation. More complete and updated guidance is needed to improve clarity and transparency regarding the applicability of Article 81 in this area. Within the assessment greater emphasis has to be put on economic criteria to better reflect recent developments in enforcement practice and the case law of the Court of Justice and Court of First Instance of the European Communities.

7. The purpose of these guidelines is to provide an analytical framework for the most common types of horizontal cooperation. This framework is primarily based on criteria that help to analyse the economic context of a cooperation agreement. Economic criteria such as the market power of the parties and other factors relating to the market structure, form a key element of the assessment of the market impact likely to be caused by a cooperation and therefore for the assessment under Article 81. Given the enormous variety in types and combinations of horizontal cooperation and market circumstances in which they operate, it is impossible to provide specific answers for every possible scenario. The present analytical framework based on economic criteria will nevertheless assist businesses in assessing the compatibility of an individual cooperation agreement with Article 81.

8. The guidelines not only replace the Notices referred to in paragraph 5, but also cover a wider range of the most common types of horizontal agreements. They complement the R & D block exemption Regulation and the Specialisation block exemption Regulation.

1.2. Scope of the guidelines

9. These guidelines cover agreements or concerted practices (hereinafter referred to as "agreements") entered into between to or more companies operating at the same level(s) in the market, e.g. at the same level of production or distribution. Within this context the focus is on cooperation between competitors. The term "competitors" as used in these guidelines includes both actual[9] and potential.[10]

---

[5] OJ 2000 L304/3.

[6] OJ 2000 L304/7.

[7] OJ 1968 C75/3.

[8] OJ 1993 C43/2.

[9] A firm is treated as an actual competitor if it is either active on the same relevant market or if, in the absence of the agreement, it is able to switch production to the relevant products and market them in the short term without incurring significant additional costs or risks in response to a small and permanent increase in relative prices (immediate supply-side substitutability). The same reasoning may lead to the grouping of diferent geographic areas. However, when supply-side substitutability would entail the need to adjust significantly existing tangible and intangible assets, to make additional investments, to take strategic decisions or to incur time delays, a company will not be treated as a competitor but as a potential competitor (see below). See Commission Notice on the definition of the relevant market for the purposes of Community competition law (OJ 1997 C372/5, paragraphs 20–23).

[10] A firm is treated as a potential competitor if there is evidence that, absent the agreement, this firm could and would be likely to undertake the necessary additional investments or other changes necessary switching costs so that it could enter the relevant market in response to a small and permanent increase in relative prices. This assessment has to be based on realistic grounds, the mere theoretical possibility to enter a market is not sufficient (see Commission Notice on the definition of the relevant market for the purposes of Community competition law (paragraph 24);

10. The present guidelines do not, however, address all possible horizontal agreements. They are only concerned with those types of cooperation which potentially generate efficiency gains, namely agreements on R & D production, purchasing, commercialisation, standardisation, and environmental agreements. Other types of horizontal agreements between competitors, for example on the exchange of information or on minority shareholdings, are to be addressed separately.

11. Agreements that are entered into between companies operating at a different level of the production or distribution chain, that is to say vertical agreements, are in principle excluded from these guidelines and dealt with in Commission Regulation (EC) No. 2790/1999[11] (the "Block Exemption Regulation on Vertical Restraints") and the Guide lines on vertical restraints.[12] However, to the extent that vertical agreements, e.g. distribution agreements, are concluded between competitors, the effects of the agreement on the market and the possible competition problems can be similar to horizontal agreements. Therefore, these agreements have to be assessed according to the principles described in the present guidelines. This does not exclude the additional application of the Guidelines on Vertical Restraints to these agreements to asses the vertical restraints included in such agreements.[13]

12. Agreements may combine different stages of cooperation, for example R & D and the production of its results. Unless they fall under Council Regulation (EEC) No 4064/89 of 21 December 1989 on the control of concentrations between undertakings,[14] as last amended by Regulation (EC) No 1310/97[15] ("the Merger Regulation"), these agreements are covered by the guidelines. The centre of gravity of the cooperation determines which section of the present guidelines applies to the agreement in question. In the determination of the centre of gravity, account is taken in particular of two factors: firstly, the starting point of the cooperation, and, secondly, the degree of integration of the different functions which are being combined. A cooperation involving both joint R & D and joint production of the results would thus normally be covered in the section on "Agreements on Research and Development", as the joint production will only take place if the joint R & D is successful. This implies that the results of the joint R & D are decisive for production. The R & D agreement can thus be regarded as the starting point of the cooperation. This assessment would change if the agreement foresaw a full integration in the area of production and only a partial integration of some R & D activities. In this case, the possible anti-competitive effects and economic benefits of the cooperation would largely relate to the joint production, and the agreement would therefore be examined according to the principles set out in the section on "Production Agreements". More complex arrangements such as strategic alliances that combine a number of different areas and instruments of cooperation in varying ways are not covered by the guidelines. The assessment of each individual area of cooperation within an alliance may be carried out with the help of the corresponding chapter in the guidelines. However, complex arrangements must also be analysed in their totality. Due to the variety of areas an alliance may combine, it is impossible to give general guidance for such an overall assessment.

---

see also the Commission's Thirteenth Report on Competition Policy, point 55 and Commission Decision 90/410/EEC in case *Elopak/Metal Box-Odin* (OJ 1990 L209/15). Market entry needs to take place sufficiently fast so that the threat of potential entry is a constraint on the market participants' behaviour. Normally, this means that entry has to occur within a short period. The Guidelines on Vertical Restraints (OJ 2000 C291/1), paragraph 26, consider a period of maximum 1 year for the purposes of application of the Block Exemption Regulation on Vertical Restraints (see footnote 11). However, in individual cases longer time periods can be taken into account. The time period needed by companies already active on the market to adjust their capacities can be used as a yardstick to determine this period.

[11] OJ 1999 L336/21.

[12] OJ 2000 C291/1.

[13] The delineation between horizontal and vertical agreements will be further developed in the chapters on joint purchasing (Chapter 4) and joint commercialisation (Chapter 5). See also the Guidelines on Vertical Restraints, paragraphs 26 and 29.

[14] OJ 1989 L395/1. Corrected version OJ 1990 L257/13.

[15] OJ 1997 L180/1.

Alliances or other forms of cooperation that primarily declare intentions are impossible to assess under the competition rules as long as they lack a precise scope.

13. The criteria set out in these guidelines apply to cooperation concerning both goods and services, collectively referred to as "products". However, the guidelines do not apply to the extent that sector-specific rules apply, as is the case for agriculture, transport or insurance.[16] Operations that come under the Merger Regulation are also not the subject of the present guidelines.

14. Article 81 only applies to those horizontal cooperation agreements which may affect trade between Member States. These guidelines are not concerned with the analysis of the capability of a given agreement to affect trade. The following principles on the applicability of Article 81 are therefore based on the assumption that trade between Member States is affected. In practice, however, this issue needs to be examined on a case-by-case basis.

15. Article 81 does not apply to agreements which are of minor importance because they are not capable of appreciably restricting competition by object or effect. These guidelines are without prejudice to the application of the present or any future "de minimis" notice.[17]

16. The assessment under Article 81 as described in these guidelines is without prejudice to the possible parallel application of Article 82 of the Treaty to horizontal cooperation agreements. Furthermore, these guidelines are without prejudice to the interpretation that may be given by the Court of First Instance and the Court of Justice of the European Communities in relation to the application of Article 81 to horizontal cooperation agreements.

1.3. Basic principles for the assessment under Article 81

1.3.1. Article 81(1)

17. Article 81(1) applies to horizontal cooperation agreements which have as their object or effect the prevention, restriction or distortion of competition (hereinafter referred to as "restrictions of competition").

18. In some cases the nature of a cooperation indicates from the outset the applicability of Article 81(1). This is the case for agreements that have as their object a restriction of competition by means of price fixing, output limitation or sharing of markets or customers. These agreements are presumed to have negative market effects. It is therefore not necessary to examine their actual effects on competition and the market in order to establish that they fall within Article 81(1).

19. Many horizontal cooperation agreements, however, do not have as their object a restriction of competition. Therefore, an analysis of the effects of the agreement is necessary. For this analysis it is not sufficient that the agreement limits competition

---

[16] Council Regulation 26/62 (OJ 1962/30, 993) (agriculture).
Council Regulation (EEC) No 1017/68 (OJ 1968 L175/1) (transport by rail road and inland waterway);
Council Regulation (EEC) No 4056/86 (OJ 1986, L378/4) (maritime transport);
Council Regulation (EEC) No 3975/87 (OJ 1987 L374/1) (air transport);
Council Regulation (EEC) No 3976/87 (OJ 1987 L374/9) (air transport);
Commission Regulation (EEC) No 1617/93 (OJ 1993 L155/18) (Block exemption concerning joint planning and coordination of schedules, joint operations, consultation on passenger and cargo tariffs on scheduled air services and slot allocation at airports);
Council Regulation (EEC) No 479/92 (OJ 1992 L55/3) (Liner shipping companies);
Commission Regulation (EC) No 870/95 (OJ 1995 L89/7) (Block exemption covering certain agreements between liner shipping companies);
Council Regulation (EEC) No 1534/91 (OJ 1991 L143/1) (insurance sector);
Commission Regulation (EEC) No 3932/92 (OJ 1992 L398/7) (Block exemption covering certain agreements in the insurance sector).
[17] See Notice on agreements of minor importance (OJ 1997 C372/13).

between the parties. It must also be likely to affect competition in the market to such an extent that negative market effects as to prices, output, innovation or the variety or quality of goods and services can be expected.

20. Whether the agreement is able to cause such negative market effects depends on the economic context taking into account both the nature of the agreement and the parties' combined market power which determines—together with other structural factors—the capability of the cooperation to affect overall competition to such a significant extent.

Nature of the agreement

21. The nature of an agreement relates to factors such as the area and objective of the cooperation, the competitive relationship between the parties and the extent to which they combine their activities. These factors indicate the likelihood of the parties coordinating their behaviour in the market.

22. Certain types of agreement, for instance most R & D agreements or cooperation to set standards or improve environmental conditions, are less likely to include restrictions with respect to prices and output. If these types of agreements have negative effects at all these are likely to be on innovation or the variety of products. They may also give rise to foreclosure problems.

23. Other types of cooperation such as agreements on production or purchasing typically cause a certain degree of commonality in (total) costs. If this degree is significant, the parties may more easily coordinate market prices and output. A significant degree of commonality in costs can only be achieved under certain conditions: First, the area of cooperation, e.g. production and purchasing, has to account for a high proportion of the total costs in a given market. Secondly, the parties need to combine their activities in the area of cooperation to a significant extent. This is, for instance, the case, where they jointly manufacture or purchase an important intermediate product or a high proportion of their total output of a final product.

Agreements that do not fall under Article 81(1)

24. Some categories of agreements do not fall under Article 81(1) because of their very nature. This is normally true for cooperation that does not imply a coordination of the parties' competitive behaviour in the market such as:

— cooperation between non-competitors,
— cooperation between competing companies that cannot independently carry out the project or activity covered by the cooperation,
— cooperation concerning an activity which does not influence the relevant parameters of competition.

These categories of cooperation could only come under Article 81(1) if they involve firms with significant market power[18] and are likely to cause foreclosure problems *vi-à-vis* third parties.

Agreements that almost always fall under Article 81(1)

25. Another category of agreements can be assessed from the outset as normally falling under Article 81(1). This concerns cooperation agreements that have the object to restrict competition by means of price fixing, output limitation or sharing of markets or customers. These restrictions are considered to be the most harmful, because they directly interfere

---

[18] Companies may have significant market power below the level of market dominance, which is the threshold for the application of Article 82.

with the outcome of the competitive process. Price fixing and output limitation directly lead to customers paying higher prices or not receiving the desired quantities. The sharing of markets or customers reduces the choice available to customers and therefore also leads to higher prices or reduced output. It can therefore be presumed that these restrictions have negative market effects. They are therefore almost always prohibited.[19]

Agreements that may fall under Article 81(1)

26. Agreements that do not belong to the above-mentioned categories need further analysis in order to decide whether they fall under Article 81(1). The analysis has to include market-related criteria such as the market position of the parties and other structural factors.

Market power and market structure

27. The starting point for the analysis is the position of the parties in the markets affected by the cooperation. This determines whether or not they are likely to maintain, gain or increase market power through the cooperation, i.e. have the ability to cause negative market effects as to prices, output, innovation or the variety or quality of goods and services. To carry out this analysis the relevant market(s) have to be defined by using the methodology of the Commission's market definition notice.[20] Where specific types of markets are concerned such as purchasing or technology markets, these guidelines will provide additional guidance.

28. If the parties together have a low combined market share,[21] a restrictive effect of the cooperation is unlikely and no further analysis normally is required. If one of just two parties has only an insignificant market share and if it does not possess important resources, even a high combined market share normally cannot be seen as indicating a restrictive effect on competition in the market.[22] Given the variety of cooperation types and the different effects they may cause in different market situations, it is impossible to give a general market share threshold above which sufficient market power for causing restrictive effects can be assumed.

29. In addition to the market position of the parties and the addition of market shares, the market concentration, i.e. the position and number of competitors, may have to be taken into account as an additional factor to assess the impact of the cooperation on market competition. As an indicator the Herfindahl-Hirshman Index ("HHI"), which sums up the squares of the individual market shares of all competitors,[23] can be used: With an HHI

---

[19] This does, however, exceptionally not apply to a production joint venture. It is inherent to the functioning of such a joint venture that decisions on output are taken jointly by the parties. If the joint venture also markets the jointly manufactured goods, then decisions on prices need to be taken jointly by the parties to such an agreement. In this case, the inclusion of provisions on prices or output does not automatically cause the agreement to fall under Article 81(1). The provisions on prices or output will have to be assessed together with the other effects of the joint venture on the market to determine the applicability of Article 81(1) (see paragraph 90).

[20] Sce Commission Notice on the definition of the relevant market for the purposes of Community competition law (OJ 1997 C372/5).

[21] Market shares should normally be calculated on the basis of the market sales value (see Article 6 of the R & D Block Exemption Regulation and Article 6 of the Specialisation Block Exemption Regulation). In determining the market share of a party in a given market, account must be taken of the undertakings which are connected to the parties (see point 2 of Article 2 of the Block Exemption Regulation and point 2 of Article 2 of the Specialisation Block Exemption Regulation).

[22] If there are more than two parties, then the collective share of all cooperating competitors has to be significantly greater than the share of the largest single participating competitor.

[23] A market consisting of four firms with shares of 30%, 25%, 25% and 20%, has a HHI of 2550 (900+625+625+400) pre-cooperation. If the first two market leaders would cooperate, the HHI would change to 4050 (3025+625+400) post-cooperation. The HHI post-cooperation is relevant for the assessment of the possible market effects of a cooperation.

below 1 000 the market concentration can be characterised as low, between 1 000 and 1 800 as moderate and above 1 800 as high. Another possible indicator would be the leading firm concentration ratio, which sums up the individual market shares of the leading competitors.[24]

30. Depending on the market position of the parties and the concentration in the market, other factors such as the stability of market shares over time, entry barriers and the likelihood of market entry, the countervailing power of buyers/suppliers or the nature of the products (e.g. homogeneity, maturity) have to be considered as well. Where an impact on competition in innovation is likely and can not be assessed adequately on the basis of existing markets, specific factors to analyse these impacts may have to be taken into account (see Chapter 2, R & D agreements).

1.3.2. Article 81(3)

31. Agreements that come under Article 81(1) may be exempted provided the conditions of Article 81(3) are fulfilled. This is the case if the agreement

— contributes to improving the production or distribution of products or to promoting technical or economic progress
— allows consumers a fair share of the resulting benefit

and does not

— impose restrictions which are not indispensible to the attainment of the above listed objectives
— afford the possibility of eliminating competition in respect of a substantial part of the products in question.

Economic benefits

32. The first condition requires that the agreement contributes to improving the production or distribution of products or to promoting technical or economic progress. As these benefits relate to static or dynamic efficiencies, they can be referred to as "economic benefits". Economic benefits may outweigh restrictive effects on competition. For instance, a cooperation may enable firms to offer goods or services at lower prices, better quality or to launch innovation more quickly. Most efficiencies stem from the combination and integration of different skills or resources. The parties must demonstrate that the efficiencies are likely to be caused by the cooperation and cannot be achieved by less restrictive means (see also below). Efficiency claims must be substantiated. Speculations or general statements on cost savings are not sufficient.

33. The Commission does not take into account cost savings that arise from output reduction, market sharing, or from the mere exercise of market power.

Fair share for the consumers

34. Economic benefits have to favour not only the parties to the agreement, but also the consumers. Generally, the transmission of the benefits to the consumers will depend on the intensity of competition within the relevant market. Competitive pressures will normally ensure that cost-savings are passed on by way of lower prices or that companies have an incentive to bring new products to the market as quickly as possible. Therefore, if

---

[24] E.g. the three-firm concentration ratio CR3 is the sum of the market shares of the leading three competitors in a market.

sufficient competition which effectively constrains the parties to the agreement is maintained on the market, the competitive process will normally ensure that the consumers receive a fair share of the economic benefits.

Indispensability

35. The restriction of competition must be necessary to achieve the economic benefits. If there are less restrictive means to achieve similar benefits, the claimed efficiencies cannot be used to justify the restrictions of competition. Whether or not individual restrictions are necessary depends on market circumstances and on the duration of the agreement. For instance, exclusivity agreements may prevent a participating party from free riding and may therefore be acceptable. Under certain circumstances they may, however, not be necessary and worsen a restrictive effect.

No elimination of competition

36. The last criterion of elimination of competition for a substantial part of the products in question is related to the question of dominance. Where an undertaking is dominant or becoming dominant as a consequence of a horizontal agreement, an agreement which produces anti-competitive effects within the meaning of Article 81 can in principle not be exempted.

Block Exemption Regulations for R & D and Specialisation

37. Under certain conditions the criteria of Article 81(3) can be assumed to be fulfilled for specified categories of agreements. This is in particular the case for R & D and production agreements where the combination of complementary skills or assets can be the source of substantial efficiencies. These guidelines should be seen as a complement to the R & D and Specialisation block exemption Regulations. Those block exemption Regulations exempt most common forms of agreements in the fields of production/specialisation up to a market share threshold of 20% and in the field of R & D up to a market share threshold of 25% provided that the agreements fulfil the conditions for application of the block exemption and do not contain "hard core" restrictions ("black clauses") that render the block exemption inapplicable. The block exemption Regulations do not provide severability for hardcore restrictions. If there are one or more hardcore restrictions, the benefit of the block exemption Regulation is lost for the entire agreement.

1.4. Structure of the following chapters on types of cooperation

38. The guidelines are divided into chapters relating to certain types of agreements. Each chapter is structured according to the analytical framework described above under point 1.3. Where necessary, specific guidance on the definition of relevant markets is given (e.g. in the field of R & D or with respect to purchasing markets).

2. AGREEMENTS ON RESEARCH AND DEVELOPMENT

2.1. Definition

39. R & D agreements may vary in form and scope. They range from outsourcing certain R & D activities to the joint improvement of existing technologies or to a cooperation concerning the research, development and marketing of completely new products. They may take the form of a cooperation agreement or of a jointly controlled company. This chapter applies to all forms of R & D agreements including related agreements concerning

the production or commercialisation of the R & D results provided that the cooperation's centre of gravity lies in R & D, with the exception of mergers and joint ventures falling under the Merger Regulation.

40. Cooperation in R & D may reduce duplicative, unnecessary costs, lead to significant cross fertilisation of ideas and experience and thus result in products and technologies being developed more rapidly than would otherwise be the case. As a general rule, R & D cooperation tends to increase overall R & D activities.

41. Small and medium-sized enterprises (SMEs) form a dynamic and heterogeneous community which is confronted by many challenges, including the growing demands of larger companies for which they often work as sub-contractors. In R & D intensive sectors, fast growing SMEs, more often called "start-up companies", also aim at becoming a leader in fast-developing market segments. To meet those challenges and to remain competitive, SMEs need constantly to innovate. Through R & D cooperation there is a likelihood that overall R & D by SMEs will increase and that they will be able to compete more vigorously with stronger market players.

42. Under certain circumstances, however, R & D agreements may cause competition problems such as restrictive effects on prices, output, innovation, or variety or quality of products.

2.2. Relevant markets

43. The key to defining the relevant market when assessing the effects of an R & D agreement is to identify those products, technologies or R & D efforts, that will act as a competitive constraint on the parties. At one end of the spectrum of possible situations, the innovation may result in a product (or technology) which competes in an existing product (or technology) market. This is the case with R & D directed towards slight improvements or variations, such as new models of certain products. Here, possible effects concern the market for existing products. At the other end, innovation may result in an entirely new product which creates its own new market (e.g. of the spectrum of a new vaccine for a previously incurable disease). In such a case, existing markets are only relevant if they are somehow related to the innovation in question. Consequently, and if possible, the effects of the cooperation on innovation have to be assessed. However, most of the cases probably concern situations in between these two extremes, i.e. situations in which innovation efforts may create products (or technology) which, over time, replace existing ones (e.g. CDs which have replaced records). A careful analysis of those situations may have to cover both existing markets and the impact of the agreement on innovation.

Existing markets

(a) Product markets

44. When the cooperation concerns R & D for the improvement of existing products, these existing products including its close substitutes form the relevant market concerned by the cooperation.[25]

45. If the R & D efforts aim at a significant change of an existing product or even at a new product replacing existing ones, substitution with the existing products may be imperfect or long-term. Consequently, the old and the potentially emerging new products are not likely to belong to the same relevant market. The market for existing products may nevertheless be concerned, if the pooling of R & D efforts is likely to result in the co-ordination of the parties' behaviour as suppliers of existing products. An exploitation of power in the existing market, however, is only possible if the parties together have a strong position with respect to both the existing product market and R & D efforts.

---

[25] For market definition see the Commission Notice on the definition of the relevant market.

46. If the R & D concerns an important component of a final product, not only the market for this component may be relevant for the assessment, but the existing market for the final product as well. For instance, if car manufacturers cooperate in R & D related to a new type of engine, the car market may be affected by this R & D cooperation. The market for final products, however, is only relevant for the assessment, if the component at which the R & D is aimed, is technically or economically a key element of these final products and if the parties to the R & D agreement are important competitors with respect to the final products.

(b) Technology markets

47. R & D cooperation may not only concern products but also technology. When rights to intellectual property are marketed separately from the products concerned to which they relate, the relevant technology market has to be defined as well. Technology markets consist of the intellectual property that is licensed and its close substitutes, i.e. other technologies which customers could use as a substitute.

48. The methodology for defining technology markets follows the same principles as product market definition.[26] Starting from the technology which is marketed by the parties, one needs to identify those other technologies to which customers could switch in response to a small but permanent increase in relative prices. Once these technologies are identified, one can calculate market shares by dividing the licensing income generated by the parties with the total licensing income of all sellers of substitutable technologies.

49. The parties' position in the market for existing technology is a relevant assessment criterion where the R & D cooperation concerns the significant improvement of existing technology or a new technology that is likely to replace the existing technology. The parties' market share can however only be taken as a starting point for this analysis. In technology markets, particular emphasis must be put on potential competition. If companies, who do not currently license their technology, are potential entrants on the technology market they could constrain the ability of the parties to raise the price for their technology (see Example 3 below).

Competition in innovation (R & D efforts)

50. R & D cooperation may not—or not only—affect competition in existing markets, but competition in innovation. This is the case where cooperation concerns the development of new products/technology which either may—if emerging—one day replace existing ones or which are being developed for a new intended use and will therefore not replace existing products but create a completely new demand. The effects on competition in innovation are important in these situations, but can in some cases not be sufficiently assessed by analysing actual or potential competition in existing product/technology markets. In this respect, two scenarios can be distinguished, depending on the nature of the innovative process in a given industry.

51. In the first scenario, which is for instance present in the pharmaceutical industry, the process of innovation is structured in such a way that it is possible at an early stage to identify R & D poles. R & D poles are R & D efforts directed towards a certain new product or technology, and the substitutes for that R & D, i.e. R & D aimed at developing substitutable products or technology for those developed by the cooperation and having comparable access to resources as well as a similar timing. In this case, it can be analysed if after the agreement there will be a sufficient number of R & D poles left. The starting point of the analysis is the R & D of the parties. Then credible competing R & D poles have to be identified. In order to assess the credibility of competing poles, the following

---

[26] See Commission Notice on the definition of the relevant market; see also, for example, Commission Decision 94/811/EC of 8 June 1994 in Case No IV/M269—*Shell/Montecatini* (OJ 1994 L332/48).

aspects have to be taken into account: the nature, scope and size of possible other R & D efforts, their access to financial and human resources, know-how/patents, or other specialised assets as well as their timing and their capability to exploit possible results. An R & D pole is not a credible competitor if it can not be regarded as a close substitute for the parties' R & D effort from the viewpoint of, for instance, access to resources or timing.

52. In the second scenario, the innovative efforts in an industry are not clearly structured so as to allow the identification of R & D poles. In this situation, the Commission would, absent exceptional circumstances, not try to assess the impact of a given R & D cooperation on innovation, but would limit its assessment to product and/or technology markets which are related to the R & D cooperation in question.

Calculation of market shares

53. The calculation of market shares, both for the purposes of the R & D block exemption Regulation and of these guidelines, has to reflect the distinction between existing markets and competition in innovation. At the beginning of a cooperation the reference point is the market for products capable of being improved or replaced by the products under development. If the R & D agreement only aims at improving or refining existing products, this market includes the products directly concerned by the R & D. Market shares can thus be calculated on the basis of the sales value of the existing products. If the R & D aims at replacing an existing product, the new product will, if successful, become a substitute to the existing products. To assess the competitive position of the parties, it is again possible to calculate market shares on the basis of the sales value of the existing products. Consequently, the R & D block exemption Regulation bases its exemption of these situations on the market share in "the relevant market for the products capable of being improved or replaced by the contract products". For an automatic exemption, this market share may not exceed 25%.[27]

54. If the R & D aims at developing a product which will create a complete new demand, market shares based on sales cannot be calculated. Only an analysis of the effects of the agreement on competition in innovation is possible. Consequently, the R & D block exemption Regulation exempts these agreements irrespective of market share for a period of seven years after the product is first put on the market.[28] However, the benefit of the block exemption may be withdrawn if the agreement would eliminate effective competition in innovation.[29] After the seven year period, market shares based on sales value can be calculated, and the market share threshold of 25% applies.[30]

2.3. Assessment under Article 81(1)

2.3.1. Nature of the agreement

2.3.1.1. Agreements that do not fall under Article 81(1)

55. Most R & D agreements do not fall under Article 81(1). First, this can be said for agreements relating to cooperation in R & D at a rather theoretical stage, far removed from the exploitation of possible results.

56. Moreover, R & D cooperation between non-competitors does generally not restrict competition.[31] The competitive relationship between the parties has to be analysed in the

---

[27] Article 4(2) of the R & D Block Exemption Regulation.
[28] Article 4(1) of the R & D Block Exemption Regulation.
[29] Article 7(e) of the R & D Block Exemption Regulation.
[30] Article 4(3) of the R & D Block Exemption Regulation.
[31] An R & D cooperation between non-competitors can however produce foreclosure effects under Article 81(1) if it relates to an exclusive exploitation of results and if it is concluded between firms, one of which has significant market power with respect to key technology.

context of affected existing markets and/or innovation. If the parties are not able to carry out the necessary R & D independently, there is no competition to be restricted. This can apply, for example, to firms bringing together complementary skills, technologies and other resources. The issue of potential competition has to be assessed on a realistic basis. For instance, parties cannot be defined as potential competitors simply because the cooperation enables them to carry out the R & D activities. The decisive question is whether each party independently has the necessary means as to assets, know-how and other resources.

57. R & D cooperation by means of outsourcing of previously captive R & D is often carried out by specialised companies, research institutes or academic bodies which are not active in the exploitation of the results. Typically such agreements are combined with a transfer of know-how and/or an exclusive supply clause concerning possible results. Due to the complementary nature of the co-operating parties in these scenarios, Article 81(1) does not apply.

58. R & D cooperation which does not include the joint exploitation of possible results by means of licensing, production and/or marketing rarely falls under Article 81(1). Those "pure" R & D agreements can only cause a competition problem, if effective competition with respect to innovation is significantly reduced.

2.3.1.2. Agreements that almost always fall under Article 81(1)

59. If the true object of an agreement is not R & D but the creation of a disguised cartel, i.e. otherwise prohibited price fixing, output limitation or market allocation, it falls under Article 81(1). However, an R & D agreement which includes the joint exploitation of possible future results is not necessarily restrictive of competition.

2.3.1.3. Agreements that may fall under Article 81(1)

60. R & D agreements that cannot be assessed from the outset as clearly non-restrictive may fall under Article 81(1)[32] and have to be analysed in their economic context. This applies to R & D cooperation which is set up at a stage rather close to the market launch and which is agreed between companies that are competitors on either existing product/technology markets or on innovation markets.

2.3.2 Market power and market structures

61. R & D cooperation can cause negative market effects in three respects: First, it may restrict innovation, secondly it may cause the coordination of the parties' behaviour in existing markets and thirdly, foreclosure problems may occur at the level of the exploitation of possible results. These types of negative market effects, however, are only likely to emerge when the parties to the cooperation have significant power on the existing markets and/or competition with respect to innovation is significantly reduced. Without market power there is no incentive to co-ordinate behaviour on existing markets or to reduce or slow down innovation. A foreclosure problem may only arise in the context of cooperation involving at least one player with significant market power for a key technology and the exclusive exploitation of results.

62. There is no absolute market share threshold which indicates that an R & D agreement creates some degree of market power and thus falls under Article 81(1). However, R & D agreements are exempted provided that they are concluded between parties with a combined market share not exceeding 25% and that the other conditions for

---

[32] Pursuant to Article 4 (2)(3) of Regulation No. 17, agreements which have as their sole object joint research and development need not to, but may, be notified to the Commission.

the application of the R & D Block Exemption Regulation are fulfilled. Therefore, for most R & D agreements, restrictive effects only have to be analysed if the parties' combined market share exceeds 25%.

63. Agreements falling outside the R & D Block Exemption Regulation due to a stronger market position of the parties do not necessarily restrict competition. However, the stronger the combined position of the parties on existing markets and/or the more competition in innovation is restricted, the more likely is the application of Article 81(1) and the assessment requires a more detailed analysis.

64. If the R & D is directed at the improvement or refinement of existing products/ technology possible effects concern the relevant market(s) for these existing products/ technology. Effects on prices, output and/or innovation in existing markets are, however, only likely if the parties together have a strong position, entry is difficult and few other innovation activities are identifiable. Furthermore, if the R & D only concerns a relatively minor input of a final product, effects as to competition in these final products are, if invariably, very limited. In general, a distinction has to be made between pure R & D agreements and more comprehensive cooperation involving different stages of the exploitation of results (i.e. licensing, production, marketing). As said above, pure R & D agreements rarely come under Article 81(1). This is in particular true for R & D directed towards a limited improvement of existing products/technology. If, in such a scenario, the R & D cooperation includes joint exploitation only by means of licensing, restrictive effects such as foreclosure problems are unlikely. If, however, joint production and/or marketing of the slightly improved products/technology are included, the cooperation has to be examined more closely. First, negative effects as to prices and output in existing markets are more likely if strong competitors are involved in such a situation . Secondly, the cooperation may come closer to a production agreement because the R & D activities may de facto not form the centre of gravity of such a collaboration.

65. If the R & D is directed at an entirely new product (or technology) which creates its own new market, price and output effects on existing markets are rather unlikely. The analysis has to focus on possible restrictions of innovation concerning, for instance, the quality and variety of possible future products/technology or the speed of innovation. Those restrictive effects can arise where two or more of the few firms engaged in the development of such a new product, start to cooperate at a stage where they are each independently rather near to the launch of the product. In such a case, innovation may be restricted even by a pure R & D agreement. In general, however, R & D cooperation concerning entirely new products is pro-competitive. This principle does not change significantly if the joint exploitation of the results, even joint marketing, is involved. Indeed, the issue of joint exploitation in these situations is only relevant where foreclosure from key technologies plays a role. Those problems would, however, not arise where the parties grant licences to third parties.

66. Most R & D agreements will lie somewhere in between the two situations described above. They may therefore have effects on innovation as well as repercussions on existing markets. Consequently, both the existing market and the effect on innovation may be of relevance for the assessment with respect to the parties' combined positions, concentration ratios, number of players/innovators and entry conditions. In some cases there can be restrictive price/output effects on existing markets and a negative impact on innovation by means of slowing down the speed of development. For instance, if significant competitors on an existing technology market cooperate to develop a new technology which may one day replace existing products, this cooperation is likely to have restrictive effects if the parties have significant market power on the existing market (which would give an incentive to exploit it), and if they also have a strong position with respect to R & D. A similar effect can occur, if the major player in an existing market cooperates with a much smaller or even potential competitor who is just about to emerge with a new product/ technology which may endanger the incumbent's position.

67. Agreements may also fall outside the block exemption irrespective of the market power of the parties. This applies for instance to agreements which restrict access of a

party to the results of the work because they do not, as a general rule, promote technical and economic progress by increasing the dissemination of technical knowledge between the parties.[33] The Block exemption provides for a specific exception to this general rule in the case of academic bodies, research Regulation institutes or specialised companies which provide R & D as a service and which are not active in the industrial exploitation of the results of research and development.[34] Nevertheless, it should be noted that agreements containing exclusive access rights may, where they fall under Article 81(1), meet the criteria for exemption under Article 81(3), particularly where exclusive access rights are economically indispensible in view of the market, risks and scale of the investment required to exploit the results of the research and development.

2.4. Assessment under Article 81(3)

2.4.1. Economic benefits

68. Most R & D agreements—with or without joint exploitation of possible results—bring about economic benefits by means of cost savings and cross fertilisation of ideas and experience, thus resulting in improved or new products and technologies being developed more rapidly than would otherwise be the case. Under these conditions it appears reasonable to provide for the exemption of such agreements which result in a restriction of competition up to a market share threshold below which it can, for the application of Article 81(3), in general, be presumed that the positive effects of research and development agreements will outweigh any negative effects on competition. Therefore, the R & D Block Exemption Regulation exempts those R & D agreements which fulfill certain conditions (see Article 3) and which do not include hard core restrictions (see Article 5), provided that the combined market share of the parties in the affected existing market(s) does not exceed 25%.

69. If considerable market power is created or increased by the cooperation, the parties have to demonstrate significant benefits in carrying out R & D, a quicker launch of new products/technology or other efficiencies.

2.4.2. Indispensability

70. An R & D agreement cannot be exempted if it imposes restrictions that are not indispensable to the attainment of the above-mentioned benefits. The individual clauses listed in Article 5 of the R & D block exemption Regulation will in most cases render an exemption impossible following an individual assessment too, and can therefore be regarded as a good indication of restrictions that are not indispensable to the cooperation.

2.4.3. No elimination of competition

71. No exemption will be possible, if the parties are afforded the possibility of eliminating competition in respect of a substantial part of the products (or technologies) in question. Where as a consequence of an R & D agreement an undertaking is dominant or becoming dominant either on an existing market or with respect to innovation, such an agreement

---

[33] See Article 3(2) of the R & D Block Exemption Regulation.
[34] See Article 3(2) of the R & D Block Exemption Regulation.

which produces anti-competitive effects in the meaning of Article 81 can in principle not be exempted. For innovation this is the case, for example, if the agreement combines the only two existing poles of research.

Time of the assessment and duration of the exemption

72. R & D agreements extending to the joint production and marketing of new products/technology require particular attention as to the time of the assessment.

73. At the beginning of an R & D cooperation, its success and factors such as the parties' future market position as well as the development of future product or technology markets are often not known. Consequently, the assessment at the point in time when the cooperation is formed is limited to the (then) existing product or technology markets and/or innovation markets as described in this chapter. If, on the basis of this analysis, competition is not likely to be eliminated, the R & D agreement can benefit from an exemption. This will normally cover the duration of the R & D phase plus, in as far as the joint production and marketing of the possible results is concerned, an additional phase for a possible launch and market introduction. The reason for this additional exemption phase is that the first companies to reach the market with a new product/technology will often enjoy very high initial market shares and successful R & D is also often rewarded by intellectual property protection. A strong market position due to this "first mover advantage" cannot normally be interpreted as elimination of competition. Therefore, the block exemption covers R & D agreements for an additional period of seven years (i.e. beyond the R & D phase) irrespective of whether or not the parties obtain with their new products/technology a high share within this period. This also applies to the individual assessment of cases falling outside the block exemption provided that the criteria of Article 81(3) as to the other aspects of the agreement are fulfilled. This does not exclude the possibility that a period of more than 7 years also meets the criteria of Article 81(3) if it can be shown to be the minimum period of time necessary to guarantee an adequate return on the investment involved.

74. If a new assessment of an R & D cooperation is made after that period—for instance, following a complaint—the analysis has to be based on the (then) existing market situation. The block exemption still continues to apply if the parties' share on the (then) relevant market does not exceed 25%. Similarly, Article 81(3) continues to apply to R & D agreements falling outside the block exemption provided that the criteria for an exemption are fulfilled.

2.5. Examples

75. Example 1

Situation: There are two major companies on the European market for the manufacture of existing electronic components: A (30%) and B (30%). They have each made significant investment in the R & D necessary to develop miniaturised electronic components and have developed early prototypes. They now agree to pool these R & D efforts by setting up a JV to complete the R & D and produce the components, which will be sold back to the parents, who will commercialise them separately. The remainder of the market consists of small firms without sufficient resources to undertake the necessary investments.

Analysis: Miniaturised electronic components, while likely to compete with the existing components in some areas, are essentially a new technology and an analysis must be made of the poles of research destined towards this future market. If the JV goes ahead then only one route to the necessary manufacturing technology will exist, whereas it would appear likely that A and B could reach the market individually with separate products. While the agreement could have advantages in bringing a new technology

228

forward quicker, it also reduces variety and creates a commonality of costs between the parties. Furthermore, the possibility for the parties to exploit their strong position on the existing market must be taken into account. Since they would face no competition at the R & D level, their incentives to pursue the new technology at a high pace could be severely reduced. Although some of these concerns could be remedied by requiring the parties to license key know-how for manufacturing miniature components to third parties on reasonable terms, it may not be possible to remedy all concerns and fulfil the conditions for an exemption.

76. Example 2

Situation: A small research company A which does not have its own marketing organisation has discovered and patented a pharmaceutical substance based on new technology that will revolutionise the treatment of a certain disease. Company A enters into an R & D agreement with a large pharmaceutical producer B of products that have so far been used for treating the disease. Company B lacks any similar R & D programme. For the existing products company B has a market share of around 75% in all Member States, but patents are expiring over the next five-year period. There exist two other poles of research at approximately the same stage of development using the same basic new technology. Company B will provide considerable funding and know-how for product development, as well as future access to the market. Company B is granted a license for the exclusive production and distribution of the resulting product for the duration of the patent. It is expected that the parties could jointly bring the product to market in five to seven years.

Analysis: The product is likely to belong to a new relevant market. The parties bring complementary resources and skills to the cooperation, and the probability of the product coming to market increases substantially. Although Company B is likely to have considerable market power on the existing market, this power will be decreasing shortly and the existence of other poles of research are likely to eliminate any incentive to reduce R & D efforts. The exploitation rights during the remaining patent period are likely to be necessary for Company B to make the considerable investments needed and Company A has no own marketing resources. The agreement is therefore unlikely to restrict competition.

77. Example 3

Situation: Two engineering companies that produce vehicle components, agree to set up a JV to combine their R & D efforts to improve the production and performance of an existing component. They also pool their existing technology licensing businesses in this area, but will continue to manufacture separately. The two companies have market shares in Europe of 15% and 20% on the OEM product market. There are two other major competitors together with several in-house research programmes by large vehicle manufacturers. On the world-wide market for the licensing of technology for these products they have shares of 20% and 25% measured in terms of revenue generated, and there are two other major technologies. The product life cycle for the component is typically two to three years. In each of the last five years one of the major firms has introduced a new version or upgrade.

Analysis: Since neither company's R & D effort is aimed at a completely new product, the markets to consider are for the existing components and for the licensing of relevant technology. Although their existing R & D programmes broadly overlap, the reduced duplication through the cooperation could allow them to spend more on R & D than individually. Several other technologies exist and the parties' combined market share on the OEM market does not bring them into a dominant position. Although their market share on the technology market, at 45%, is very high, there are competing technologies. In addition, the vehicle manufactures, who do not currently licence their technology, are also potential entrants on this market thus constraining the ability of the parties to raise prices. As described, the JV is likely to benefit from an exemption.

3. PRODUCTION AGREEMENTS (INCLUDING SPECIALISATION AGREEMENTS)

3.1 Definition

78. Production agreements may vary in form and scope. They may take the form of joint production through a joint venture,[35] i.e. a jointly controlled company that runs one or several production facilities, or can be carried out by means of specialisation or subcontracting agreements whereby one party agrees to carry out the production of a certain product.

79. Generally, one can distinguish three categories of production agreements: Joint production agreements, whereby the parties agree to produce certain products jointly, (unilateral or reciprocal) specialisation agreements, whereby the parties agree unilaterally or reciprocally to cease production of a product and to purchase it from the other party, and subcontracting agreements whereby one party (the "contractor") entrusts to another party (the "subcontractor") the production of a product.

80. Subcontracting agreements are vertical agreements. They are therefore, to the extent that they contain restrictions of competition, covered by the Block Exemption Regulation and the Guidelines on Vertical Restraints. There are however two exceptions to this rule: Subcontracting agreements between competitors,[36] and subcontracting agreements between non-competitors involving the transfer of know-how to the subcontractor.[37]

81. Subcontracting agreements between competitors are covered by these guidelines.[38] Guidance for the assessment of subcontracting agreements between non-competitors involving the transfer of know-how to the subcontractor is given in a separate Notice.[39]

3.2. Relevant markets

82. In order to assess the competitive relationship between the co-operating parties, the relevant product and geographic market(s) directly concerned by the cooperation (i.e. the market(s) to which products subject to the agreement belong) must first be defined. Secondly, a production agreement in one market may also affect the competitive behaviour of the parties in a market which is downstream or upstream or a neighbouring market closely related to the market directly concerned by the cooperation[40] (so-called "spill-over markets"). However, spill-over effects only occur if the cooperation in one market necessarily results in the co-ordination of competitive behaviour in another market, i.e. if

---

[35] As indicated above, joint ventures which fall under the Merger Regulation are not the subject of these guidelines. Full-function joint ventures below Community dimension are normally dealt with by the competition authorities of the Member States. The application of Regulation No. 17 could be relevant only where such a full-function joint venture would lead to a restriction of competition resulting from the coordination of the parent companies outside the joint venture ("spill-over effect"). In this respect, the Commission has declared that it will leave the assessment of such operations to the Member States as far as possible (see Statement for the Council Minutes on Regulation (EC) No 1310/97, pt. 4).

[36] Article 2(4) of the Block Exemption Regulation on Vertical Restraints.

[37] Article 2(3) of the Block Exemption Regulation on Vertical Restraints. See also Guidelines on Vertical Restraints, paragraph 33, which notes that subcontracting arrangements between non-competitors under which the buyer provides only specifications to the supplier which describe the goods or services to be supplied are covered by the Block Exemption Regulation on Vertical Restraints.

[38] If a subcontracting agreement between competitors stipulates that the contractor will cease production of the product to which the agreement relates, the agreement constitutes a unilateral specialisation agreement which is covered, subject to certain conditions, by the Specialisation Block Exemption Regulation.

[39] Notice concerning the assessment of certain subcontracting agreements in relation to Article 81(1) of the EEC Treaty, OJ 1979 C1/2).

[40] As also referred to in Article 2(4) of the Merger Regulation.

the markets are linked by interdependencies, and if the parties are in a strong position on the spill-over market.

3.3. Assessment under Article 81(1)

3.3.1. Nature of the agreement

83. The main source of competition problems that may arise from production agreements is the co-ordination of the parties' competitive behaviour as suppliers. This type of competition problem arises where the co-operating parties are actual or potential competitors on at least one of these relevant market(s), i.e. on the markets directly concerned by the cooperation and/or on possible spill-over markets.

84. The fact that the parties are competitors does not automatically cause the coordination of their behaviour. In addition, the parties normally need to cooperate with regard to a significant part of their activities in order to achieve a substantial degree of commonality of costs. The higher the degree of commonality of costs, the greater the potential for a limitation of price competition, especially in the case of homogeneous products.

85. In addition to co-ordination concerns, production agreements may also create foreclosure problems and other negative effects towards third parties. They are not caused by a competitive relationship between the parties, but by a strong market position of at least one of the parties (e.g. on an upstream market for a key component, which enables the parties to raise the costs of their rivals in a downstream market) in the context of a more vertical or complementary relationship between the co-operating parties. Therefore, the possibility of foreclosure mainly needs to be examined in the case of joint production of an important component and of subcontracting agreements (see below).

3.3.1.1. Agreements that do not fall under Article 81(1)

86. Unless foreclosure problems arise, production agreements between non-competitors are not normally caught by Article 81(1). This is also true for agreements whereby inputs or components which have so far been manufactured for own consumption (captive production) are purchased from a third party by way of subcontracting or unilateral specialisation, unless there are indications that the company which so far has only produced for own consumption could have entered the merchant market for sales to third parties without incurring significant additional costs or risks in response to small, permanent changes in relative market prices.

87. Even production agreements between competitors do not necessarily come under Article 81(1). First, cooperation between firms which compete on markets closely related to the market directly concerned by the cooperation, cannot be defined as restricting competition, if the cooperation is the only commercially justifiable possible way to enter a new market, to launch a new product or service or to carry out a specific project.

88. Secondly, an effect on the parties' competitive behaviour as market suppliers is highly unlikely if the parties have a small proportion of their total costs in common. For instance, a low degree of commonality in total costs can be assumed where two or more companies agree on specialisation/joint production of an intermediate product which only accounts for a small proportion of the production costs of the final product and, consequently, the total costs. The same applies to a subcontracting agreement between competitors where the input which one competitor purchases from another only accounts for a small proportion of the production costs of the final product. A low degree of commonality of total costs can also be assumed where the parties jointly manufacture a final product, but only a small proportion as compared to their total output of the final product. Even if a significant proportion is jointly manufactured, the degree of commonality of total costs may nevertheless be low or moderate, if the cooperation concerns heterogeneous products which require costly marketing.

231

89. Thirdly, subcontracting agreements between competitors do not fall under Article 81(1) if they are limited to individual sales and purchases on the merchant market without any further obligations and without forming part of a wider commercial relationship between the parties.[41]

3.3.1.2. Agreements that almost always fall under Article 81(1)

90. Agreements which fix the prices for market supplies of the parties, limit output or share markets or customer groups have the object of restricting competition and almost always fall under Article 81(1). This does, however, not apply to cases

— where the parties agree on the output directly concerned by the production agreement (e.g. the capacity and production volume of a joint venture or the agreed amount of outsourced products), or:
— where a production joint venture that also carries out the distribution of the manufactured products sets the sales prices for these products, provided that the price fixing by the joint venture is the effect of integrating the various functions.[42]

In both scenarios the agreement on output or prices will not be assessed separately, but in light of the overall effects of the joint venture on the market in order to determine the applicability of Article 81(1).

3.3.1.3. Agreements that may fall under Article 81(1)

91. Production agreements that cannot be characterised as clearly restrictive or non-restrictive on the basis of the above factors may fall under Article 81(1)[43] and have to be analysed in their economic context. This applies to cooperation agreements between competitors which create a significant degree of commonality of costs, but do not involve hard core restrictions as described above.

3.3.2. Market power and market structures

92. The starting point for the analysis is the position of the parties in the market(s) concerned. This is due to the fact that without market power the parties to a production agreement do not have an incentive to coordinate their competitive behaviour as suppliers. Secondly, there is no effect on competition in the market without market power of the parties, even if the parties would coordinate their behaviour.

93. There is no absolute market share threshold which indicates that a production agreement creates some degree of market power and thus falls under Article 81(1). However, agreements concerning unilateral or reciprocal specialisation as well as joint production are block exempted provided that they are concluded between parties with a combined market share not exceeding 20% in the relevant market(s) and that the other conditions for the application of the Specialisation block exemption Regulation are fulfilled. Therefore, for agreements covered by the block exemption, restrictive effects only have to be analysed if the parties' combined market share exceeds 20%.

---

[41] As any subcontracting agreement such an agreement can however fall under Article 81(1) if it contains vertical restraints, such as restrictions on passive sales, resale price maintenance, etc.

[42] A production joint venture which also carries out joint distribution is, however, in most of the cases a full-function joint venture.

[43] Pursuant to Article 4(2)(3) of Council Regulation No 17, agreements which have as their sole object specialisation in the manufacture of products need, under certain conditions, not to be notified to the Commission. They may, however, be notified.

94. Agreements which are not covered by the block exemption Regulation require a more detailed analysis. The starting point is the market position of the parties. This will normally be followed by the concentration ratio and the number of players as well as by other factors as described in Chapter 1.

95. Usually the analysis will only involve the relevant market(s) with which the cooperation is directly concerned. Under certain circumstances, e.g. if the parties have a very strong combined position on up- or downstream markets or on markets otherwise closely related to the markets with which the cooperation is directly concerned, these spill-over markets may however have to be analysed as well. This applies in particular to cooperation in upstream markets by firms which also enjoy a strong combined market position further downstream. Similarly, problems of foreclosure may need to be examined if the parties individually have a strong position as either suppliers or buyers of an input.

Market position of the parties, concentration ratio, number of players and other structural factors

96. If the parties' combined market share is larger than 20%, the likely impact of the production agreement on the market must be assessed. In this respect market concentration as well as market shares will be a significant factor. The higher the combined market share of the parties, the higher the concentration in the market concerned. However, a moderately higher market share than allowed for in the block exemption does not necessarily imply a high concentration ratio. For instance, a combined market share of the parties of slightly more than 20% may occur in a market with a moderate concentration (HHI below 1800). In such a scenario a restrictive effect is unlikely. In a more concentrated market, however, a market share of more than 20% may, alongside other elements, lead to a restriction of competition (see also example 1 below). The picture may nevertheless change, if the market is very dynamic with new participants entering the market and market positions changing frequently.

97. For joint production, network effects, i.e. links between a significant number of competitors, can also play an important role. In a concentrated market the creation of an additional link may tip the balance and make collusion in this market likely, even if the parties have a significant, but still moderate, combined market share (see example 2 below).

98. Under specific circumstances a cooperation between potential competitors may also raise competition concerns. This is, however, limited to cases where a strong player in one market cooperates with a realistic potential entrant, for instance, with a strong supplier of the same product or service in a neighbouring geographic market. The reduction of potential competition creates particular problems if actual competition is already weak and threat of entry is a major source of competition.

Cooperation in upstream markets

99. Joint production of an important component or other input to the parties' final product can cause negative market effects under certain circumstances:

— Foreclosure problems (see example 3 below) provided that the parties have a strong position on the relevant input market (non-captive use) and that switching between captive and non-captive use would not occur in the presence of a small but permanent relative price increase for the product in question.
— Spill-over effects (see example 4 below) provided that the input is an important component of costs and that the parties have a strong position in the downstream market for the final product.

Subcontracting agreements between competitors

100. Similar problems can arise if a competitor subcontracts an important component or other input to its final product from a competitor. This can also lead to:

— Foreclosure problems provided that the parties have a strong position as either suppliers or buyers on the relevant input market (non-captive use). Subcontracting could then either lead to other competitors not being able to obtain this input at a competitive price or to other suppliers not being able to supply the input competitively if they will be losing a large part of their demand.
— Spill-over effects provided that the input is an important component of costs and that the parties have a strong position in the downstream market for the final product.

Specialisation agreements

101. Reciprocal specialisation agreements with market shares beyond the threshold of the block exemption will almost always fall under Article 81(1) and have to be examined carefully because of the risk of market partitioning (see example 5 below).

3.4. Assessment under Article 81(3)

3.4.1. Economic benefits

102. Most common types of production agreements can be assumed to cause some economic benefits in the form of economies of scale or scope or better production technologies unless they are an instrument for price fixing, output restriction or market and customer allocation. Under these conditions it appears reasonable to provide for the exemption of such agreements which result in a restriction of competition up to a market share threshold below which it can, for the application of Article 81(3), in general, be presumed that the positive effects of production agreements will outweigh any negative effects on competition. Therefore, agreements concerning unilateral or reciprocal special- isation as well as joint production are block exempted (Specialisation block exemption Regulation) provided that they do not contain hard core restrictions (see Article 5) and that they are concluded between parties with a combined market share not exceeding 20% in the relevant market(s).

103. For those agreements not covered by the block exemption the parties have to demonstrate improvements of production or other efficiencies. Efficiencies that only benefit the parties or cost savings that are caused by output reduction or market allocation cannot be taken into account.

3.4.2. Indispensability

104. Restrictions that go beyond what is necessary to achieve the economic benefits described above will not be accepted. For instance, parties should not be restricted in their competitive behaviour on output outside the cooperation.

3.4.3. No elimination of competition

105. No exemption will be possible, if the parties are afforded the possibility of eliminat- ing competition in respect of a substantial part of the products in question. Where as a consequence of a production agreement an undertaking is dominant or becoming domi- nant, such an agreement which produces anti-competitive effects in the meaning of Article 81 can in principle not be exempted. This has to be analysed on the relevant market to

which the products subject to the cooperation belong and on possible spill-over markets.

3.5. Examples

Joint production

106. The following two examples concern hypothetical cases causing competition problems on the relevant market to which the jointly manufactured products belong.

107. Example 1
Situation: Two suppliers, A and B, of the basic chemical product X decide to build a new production plant controlled by a joint venture. This plant will produce roughly 50% of their final output. X is a homogeneous product and is not substitutable with other products, i.e. forms a relevant market on its own. The market is rather stagnant. The parties will not significantly increase total output, but close down two old factories and shift capacity to the new plant. A and B each have a market share of 20%. There are three other significant suppliers each with 10–15% market share and several smaller players.
Analysis: It is likely that this joint venture would have an effect on the competitive behaviour of the parties because co-ordination would give them considerable market power, if not even a dominant position. Severe restrictive effects in the market are probable. High efficiency gains which may outweigh these effects are unlikely in such a scenario where a significant increase in output cannot be expected.

108. Example 2
Situation: Two suppliers, A and B, form a production joint venture on the same relevant market as in example 1. The joint venture also produces 50% of the parties' total output. A and B each have 15% market share. There are 3 other players: C with a market share of 30%, D with 25% and E with 15%. B already has a joint production plant with E.
Analysis: Here the market is characterised by very few players and rather symmetric structures. The joint venture creates an additional link between the players. Co-ordination between A and B would de facto further increase concentration and also link E to A and B. This cooperation is likely to cause a severe restrictive effect, and—as in example 1—high efficiency gains cannot be expected.
109. Example 3 also concerns the relevant market to which the jointly manufactured products belong, but demonstrates the importance of criteria other than market share (here: switching between captive and non-captive production).

110. Example 3
Situation: A and B set up a production joint venture for an intermediate product X through restructuring current plants. The joint venture sells X exclusively to A and B. It produces 40% of A's total output of X and 50% of B's total output. A and B are captive users of X and are also suppliers of the non-captive market. A's share of total industry output of X is 10%, B's share amounts to 20% and the share of the joint venture to 14%. On the non-captive market, however, A and B have respectively 25% and 35% market share.
Analysis: Despite the parties' strong position on the non-captive market the cooperation may not eliminate effective competition in the market for X, if switching costs between captive and non-captive use are small. However, only very rapid switching would counteract the high market share of 60%. Otherwise this production venture raises serious competition concerns which cannot be outweighed even by significant economic benefits.
111. Example 4 concerns cooperation regarding an important intermediate product with spill-over effects on a down-stream market.

112. Example 4

Situation: A and B set up a production joint venture for an intermediate product X. They will close their own factories, which have been manufacturing X, and will cover their needs of X exclusively from the joint venture. The intermediate product accounts for 50% of the total costs of the final product Y. A and B each have a share of 20% in the market for Y. There are two other significant suppliers of Y each with 15% market share and several smaller competitors.

Analysis: Here the commonality of costs is high; furthermore, the parties would gain market power through co-ordination of their behaviour on the market Y. The case raises competition problems and the assessment is almost identical to example 1 although here the cooperation is taking place in an upstream market.

Reciprocal specialisation

113. Example 5

Situation: A and B each manufacture and supply the homogeneous products X and Y, which belong to different markets. A's market share of X is 28% and of Y it is 10%. B's share of X is 10% and of Y it is 30%. Because of scale economies they conclude a reciprocal specialisation agreement according to which A will in future only produce X and B will produce only Y. Both agree on cross-supplies so that they will both remain in the markets as suppliers. Due to the homogeneous nature of the products, distribution costs are minor. There are two other manufacturing suppliers of X and Y with market shares of roughly 15% each, the remaining suppliers have 5–10% shares.

Analysis: The degree of commonality of costs is extremely high, only the relatively minor distribution costs remain separate. Consequently, there is very little room for competition left. The parties would gain market power through co-ordination of their behaviour on the markets for X and Y. Furthermore, it is likely that the market supplies of Y from A and X from B will diminish over time. The case raises competition problems which the economies of scale are unlikely to outweigh.

The scenario may change if X and Y were heterogeneous products with a very high proportion of marketing and distribution costs (e.g. 65–70% of total costs). Furthermore, if the offer of a complete range of the differentiated products was a condition for competing successfully, the withdrawal of one or more parties as suppliers of X and/or Y would be unlikely. In such a scenario the criteria for exemption may be fulfilled (provided that the economies are significant), despite the high market shares.

Subcontracting between competitors

114. Example 6

Situation: A and B are competitors in the market for the final product X. A has a market share of 15%, B of 20%. Both also produce the intermediate product Y, which is an input into the production of X, but is also used to produce other products. It accounts for 10% of the cost of X. A only produces Y for internal consumption, while B is also selling Y to third party customers. Its market share for Y is 10%. A and B agree on a subcontracting agreement, whereby A will purchase 60% of its requirements of Y from B. It will continue to produce 40% of its requirements internally to not lose the know-how related to the production of Y.

Analysis: As A has only produced Y for internal consumption, it first needs to be analysed if A is a realistic potential entrant into the merchant market for sales of Y to third parties. If this is not the case, then the agreement does not restrict competition with respect to Y. Spill-over effects into the market for X are also unlikely in view of the low degree of commonality of costs created by the agreement.

If A were to be regarded a realistic potential entrant into the merchant market for sales of Y to third parties, the market position of B in the market for Y would need to be taken into account. As B's market share is rather low, the result of the analysis would not change.

236

4. PURCHASING AGREEMENTS

4.1. Definition

115. This chapter focuses on agreements concerning the joint buying of products. Joint buying can be carried out by a jointly controlled company, by a company in which many firms hold a small stake, by a contractual arrangement or even looser form of cooperation.

116. Purchasing agreements are often concluded by small and medium-sized enterprises to achieve volumes and discounts similar to their bigger competitors. These agreements between small and medium-sized enterprises are therefore normally pro-competitive. Even if a moderate degree of market power is created, this may be outweighed by economies of scale provided the parties actually bundle volume.

117. Joint purchasing may involve both horizontal and vertical agreements. In these cases a two-step analysis is necessary. First, the horizontal agreements have to be assessed according to the principles described in the present guidelines. If this assessment leads to the conclusion that a cooperation between competitors in the area of purchasing is acceptable, a further assessment will be necessary to examine the vertical agreements concluded with suppliers or individual sellers. The latter assessment will follow the rules of the Block Exemption Regulation and the Guidelines on Vertical Restraints.[44]

118. An example would be an association formed by a group of retailers for the joint purchasing of products. Horizontal agreements concluded between the members of the association or decisions adopted by the association have to be assessed first as a horizontal agreement according to the present guidelines. Only if this assessment is positive does it become relevant to assess the resulting vertical agreements between the association and an individual members or between the association and suppliers. These agreements are covered—up to a certain limit—by the block exemption for vertical restraints.[45] Those agreements falling outside the vertical block exemption will not be presumed to be illegal but may need individual examination.

4.2. Relevant markets

119. There are two markets which may be affected by joint buying: First, the market(s) with which the cooperation is directly concerned, i.e. the relevant purchasing market(s). Secondly, the selling market(s), i.e. the market(s) downstream where the participants of the joint purchasing arrangement are active as sellers.

120. The definition of relevant purchasing markets follows the principles described in the Commission Notice on the definition of the relevant market and is based on the concept of substitutability to identify competitive constraints. The only difference to the definition of "selling markets" is that substitutability has to be defined from the viewpoint of supply and not from the viewpoint of demand. In other words: the suppliers' alternatives are decisive in identifying the competitive constraints on purchasers. These could be analysed for instance by examining the suppliers' reaction to a small but lasting price *decrease*. If the market is defined, the market share can be calculated as the percentage for which the purchases by the parties concerned account out of the total sales of the purchased product or service in the relevant market.

121. Example 1

A group of car manufacturers agree to buy product X jointly. Their combined purchases of X account for 15 units. All the sales of X to car manufacturers account for 50 units. However, X is also sold to manufacturers of products other than cars. All sales of X account for 100 units. Thus, the (purchasing) market share of the group is 15%.

---

[44] See Guidelines on Vertical Restraints, paragraph 29.
[45] Article 2(2) of Block Exemption Regulation on Vertical Restraints.

122. If the parties are in addition competitors on one or more selling markets, these markets are also relevant for the assessment. Restrictions of competition on these markets are more likely if the parties will achieve market power by coordinating their behaviour and if the parties have a significant proportion of their total costs in common. This is, for instance, the case if retailers which are active in the same relevant retail market(s) jointly purchase a significant amount of the products they offer for resale. It may also be the case if competing manufacturers and sellers of a final product jointly purchase a high proportion of their input together. The selling markets have to be defined by applying the methodology described in the Commission Notice on the definition of the relevant market.

4.3. Assessment under Article 81(1)

4.3.1. Nature of the agreement

4.3.1.1. Agreements that do not fall under Article 81(1)

123. By their very nature joint buying agreements will be concluded between companies that are at least competitors on the purchasing markets. If, however, competing purchasers cooperate who are not active on the same relevant market further downstream (e.g. retailers which are active in different geographic markets and cannot be regarded as realistic potential competitors), Article 81(1) will rarely apply unless the parties have a very strong position in the buying markets, which could be used to harm the competitive position of other players in their respective selling markets.

4.3.1.2. Agreements that almost always fall under Article 81(1)

124. Purchasing agreements only come under Article 81(1) by their nature if the cooperation does not truly concern joint buying, but serves as a tool to engage in a disguised cartel, i.e. otherwise prohibited price fixing, output limitation or market allocation.

4.3.1.3. Agreements that may fall under Article 81(1)

125. Most purchasing agreements have to be analysed in their legal and economic context. The analysis has to cover both the purchasing and the selling markets.

4.3.2. Market power and market structures

126. The starting point for the analysis is the examination of the parties' buying power. Buying power can be assumed if a purchasing agreement accounts for a sufficiently large proportion of the total volume of a purchasing market so that prices can be driven down below the competitive level or access to the market can be foreclosed to competing buyers. A high degree of buying power over the suppliers of a market may bring about inefficiencies such as quality reductions, lessening of innovation efforts, or ultimately suboptimal supply. However, the primary concerns in the context of buying power are that lower prices may not be passed on to customers further downstream and that it may cause cost increases for the purchasers' competitors on the selling markets because either suppliers will try to recover price reductions for one group of customers by increasing prices for other customers or competitors have less access to efficient suppliers. Consequently, purchasing markets and selling markets are characterised by interdependencies as set out below.

Interdependencies between purchasing and selling market(s)

127. The cooperation of competing purchasers can appreciably restrict competition by means of creating buying power. Whilst the creation of buying power can lead to lower prices for customers, buying power is not always pro-competitive and may even, under certain circumstances, cause severe negative effects on competition.

128. First, lower purchasing costs resulting from the exercise of buying power cannot be seen as pro-competitive, if the purchasers together have power on the selling markets. In this case, the cost savings are probably not passed on to consumers. The more combined power the parties have on their selling markets, the higher is the incentive for the parties to coordinate their behaviour as sellers. This may be facilitated if the parties achieve a high degree of commonality of costs through joint purchasing. For instance, if a group of large retailers buys a high proportion of their products together, they will have a high proportion of their total cost in common. The negative effects of joint buying can therefore be rather similar to joint production.

129. Secondly, power on the selling markets may be created or increased through buying power which is used to foreclose competitors or to raise rivals' costs. Significant buying power by one group of customers may lead to foreclosure of competing buyers by limiting their access to efficient suppliers. It can also cause cost increases for its competitors because suppliers will try to recover price reductions for one group of customers by increasing prices for other customers (e.g. rebate discrimination by suppliers of retailers). This is only possible if the suppliers of the purchasing markets also have a certain degree of market power. In both cases, competition in the selling markets can be further restricted by buying power.

130. There is no absolute threshold which indicates that a buying cooperation creates some degree of market power and thus falls under Article 81(1). However, in most cases, it is unlikely that market power exists if the parties to the agreement have a combined market share of below 15% on the purchasing market(s) as well as a combined market share of below 15% on the selling market(s). In any event, at that level of market share it is likely that the conditions of Article 81(3) explained below are fulfilled by the agreement in question.

131. A market share above this threshold does not automatically indicate that a negative market effect is caused by the cooperation but requires a more detailed assessment of the impact of a joint buying agreement on the market, involving factors such as the market concentration and possible countervailing power of strong suppliers. Joint buying that involves parties with a combined market share significantly above 15% in a concentrated market is likely to come under Article 81(1), and efficiencies that may outweigh the restrictive effect have to be shown by the parties.

4.4. Assessment under Article 81(3)

4.4.1. Economic benefits

132. Purchasing agreements can bring about economic benefits such as economies of scale in ordering or transportation which may outweigh restrictive effects. If the parties together have significant buying or selling power, the issue of efficiencies has to be examined carefully. Cost savings that are caused by the mere exercise of power and which do not benefit consumers cannot be taken into account.

4.4.2. Indispensability

133. Purchasing agreements cannot be exempted if they impose restrictions that are not indispensable to the attainment of the above mentioned benefits. An obligation to buy exclusively through the cooperation can in certain cases be indispensable to achieve the

necessary volume for the realisation of economies of scale. However, such an obligation has to be assessed in the context of the individual case.

4.4.3. No elimination of competition

134. No exemption will be possible, if the parties are afforded the possibility of eliminating competition in respect of a substantial part of the products in question. This assessment has to cover buying and selling markets. The combined market shares of the parties can be regarded as a starting point. It then needs to be evaluated whether these market shares are indicative of a dominant position, and whether there are any mitigating factors, such as countervailing power of suppliers on the purchasing markets or potential for market entry in the selling markets. Where as a consequence of a purchasing agreement an undertaking is dominant or becoming dominant on either the buying or selling market, such an agreement which produces anti-competitive effects in the meaning of Article 81 can in principle not be exempted.

4.5. Examples

135. Example 2
Situation: Two manufacturers, A and B, decide to jointly buy component X. They are competitors on their selling market. Together their purchases represent 35% of the total sales of X in the EEA, which is assumed to be the relevant geographic market. There are 6 other manufacturers (competitors of A and B on their selling market) accounting for the remaining 65% of the purchasing market; one having 25%, the others accounting for significantly less. The supply side is rather concentrated with 6 suppliers of component X, two with 30% market share each, and the rest with between 10 and 15% (HHI of 2300–2500). On their selling market, A and B achieve a combined market share of 35%.

Analysis: Due to the parties' market power in their selling market, the benefits of possible cost savings may not be passed on to final consumers. Furthermore, the joint buying is likely to increase the costs of the parties' smaller competitors because the two powerful suppliers probably recover price reductions for the group by licensing smaller customers' prices. Increasing concentration in the downstream market may be the result. In addition, the cooperation may lead to further concentration among suppliers because smaller ones, which may already work near or below minimum optimal scale, may be driven out of business if they cannot reduce prices further. Such a case probably causes a significant restriction of competition which may not be outweighed by possible efficiency gains from bundling volume.

136. Example 3
Situation: 150 small retailers conclude an agreement to form a joint buying organisation. They are obliged to buy a minimum volume through the organisation which accounts for roughly 50% of each retailer's total costs. The retailers can buy more than the minimum volume through the organisation, and they may also buy outside the cooperation. They have a combined market share of 20% on each of the purchasing and the selling market(s). A and B are their two large competitors, A has a 25% share on each of the markets concerned, B 35%. The remaining smaller competitors have also formed a buying group. The 150 retailers achieve economies by combining a significant amount of volume and buying tasks.

Analysis: The retailers may achieve a high degree of commonality of costs if they ultimately buy more than the agreed minimum volume together. However, together they only have a moderate market position on the buying and the selling market. Furthermore, the cooperation brings about some economies of scale. This cooperation is likely to be exempted.

137. Example 4

Situation: Two supermarket chains conclude an agreement to jointly buy products which account for roughly 50% of their total costs. On the relevant buying markets for the different categories of products the parties have shares between 25% and 40%, on the relevant selling market (assuming there is only one geographic market concerned) they achieve 40%. There are five other significant retailers each with 10–15% market share. Market entry is not likely.

Analysis: It is likely that this joint buying arrangement would have an effect on the competitive behaviour of the parties because coordination would give them significant market power. This is particularly the case if entry is weak. The incentive to coordinate behaviour is higher if the costs are similar. Similar margins of the parties would add an incentive to have the same prices. Even if efficiencies are caused by the cooperation, it is not likely to be exempted due to the high degree of market power.

138. Example 5

Situation: Small cooperatives conclude an agreement to form a joint buying organisation. They are obliged to buy a minimum volume through the organisation. The parties can buy more than the minimum volume through the organisation, but they may also buy outside the cooperation. Each of the parties has a total market share of 5% on each of the purchasing and selling markets, giving a combined market share of 25%. There are two other significant retailers each with 20–25% market share and a number of smaller retailers with market shares below 5%.

Analysis: The setting up of the joint buying organisation is likely to give the parties a market position on both the purchasing and selling markets of a degree which enables them to compete with the two largest retailers. Moreover, the presence of these two other players with similar levels of market position is likely to result in the efficiencies of the agreement being passed on to consumers. In such a scenario the agreement is likely to be exempted.

5. COMMERCIALISATION AGREEMENTS

5.1. Definition

139. The agreements covered in this section involve cooperation between competitors in the selling, distribution or promotion of their products. These agreements can have a widely varying scope, depending on the marketing functions which are being covered by the cooperation. At one end of the spectrum, there is joint selling that leads to a joint determination of all commercial aspects related to the sale of the product including price. At the other end, there are more limited agreements that only address one specific marketing function, such as distribution, service, or advertising.

140. The most important of these more limited agreements would seem to be distribution agreements. These agreements are generally covered by the Block Exemption Regulation and Guidelines on Vertical Restraints unless the parties are actual or potential competitors. In this case, the Block Exemption Regulation only covers non-reciprocal vertical agreements between competitors, if (a) the buyer, together with its connected undertakings, has an annual turnover not exceeding EUR 100 million, or (b) the supplier is a manufacturer and a distributor or products and the buyer is a distributor who is not also a manufacturer of products competing with the contract products or (c) the supplier is a provider of services at several levels of trade, while the buyer does not provide competing services at the level of trade where it purchases the contract services.[46] If competitors agree to distribute their products on a reciprocal basis there is a possibility in certain cases that the agreements have as their object or effect the partitioning of markets between the parties or that they lead to collusion. The same is true for non-reciprocal

---

[46] Article 2(4) of Block Exemption Regulation on Vertical Restraints.

agreements between competitors exceeding a certain size. These agreements have thus first to be assessed according to the principles set out below. If this assessment leads to the conclusion that a cooperation between competitors in the area of distribution would in principle be acceptable, a further assessment will be necessary to examine the vertical restraints included in such agreements. This assessment should be based on the principles set out in the Guidelines on Vertical Restraints.

141. A further distinction should be drawn between agreements where the parties agree only on joint commercialisation and agreements where the commercialisation is related to another cooperation. This can be for instance the case as regards joint production or joint purchasing. These agreements will be dealt with as in the assessment of those types of cooperation.

5.2. Relevant markets

142. To assess the competitive relationship between the co-operating parties, first the relevant product and geographic market(s) directly concerned by the cooperation (i.e. the market(s) to which products subject to the agreement belong) have to be defined. Secondly, a commercialisation agreement in one market may also affect the competitive behaviour of the parties in a neighbouring market closely related to the market directly concerned by the cooperation.

5.3. Assessment under Article 81(1)

5.3.1. Nature of the agreement

5.3.1.1. Agreements that do not fall under Article 81(1)

143. The commercialisation agreements covered by this section only fall under the competition rules if the parties to the agreements are competitors. If the parties clearly do not compete with regard to the products or services covered by the agreement, the agreement cannot create competition problems of a horizontal nature. However, the agreement can fall under Article 81(1) if it contains vertical restraints, such as restrictions on passive sales, resale price maintenance, etc. This also applies if a cooperation in commercialisation is objectively necessary to allow one party to enter a market it could not have entered individually, for example because of the costs involved. A specific application of this principle would be consortia arrangements that allow the companies involved to mount a credible tender for projects that they would not be able to fulfil, or would not have bid for, individually. As they are therefore not potential competitors for the tender, there is no restriction of competition.

5.3.1.2. Agreements that almost always fall under Article 81(1)

144. The principle competition concern about a commercialisation agreement between competitors is price fixing. Agreements limited to joint selling have as a rule the object and effect of co-ordinating the pricing policy of competing manufacturers. In this case they not only eliminate price competition between the parties but also restrict the volume of products to be delivered by the participants within the framework of the system for allocating orders. They therefore restrict competition between the parties on the supply side and limit the choice of purchasers and fall under Article 81(1).

145. This appreciation does not change if the agreement is non-exclusive. Article 81(1) continues to apply even where the parties are free to sell outside the agreement, as long as it can be presumed that the agreement will lead to an overall coordination of the prices charged by the parties.

242

5.3.1.3. Agreements that may fall under Article 81(1)

146. For commercialisation arrangements that fall short of joint selling there will be two major concerns. The first is that the joint commercialisation provides a clear opportunity for exchanges of sensitive commercial information particularly on marketing strategy and pricing. The second is that, depending on the cost structure of the commercialisation, a significant input to the parties' final costs may be common. As a result the actual scope for price competition at the final sales level may be limited. Joint commercialisation agreements therefore can fall under Article 81(1) if they either allow the exchange of sensitive commercial information, or if they influence a significant part of the parties' final cost.

147. A specific concern related to distribution arrangements between competitors which are active in different geographic markets is that they can lead to or be an instrument of market partitioning. In the case of reciprocal agreements to distribute each other's products, the parties to the agreement allocate markets or customers and eliminate competition between themselves. The key question in assessing an agreement of this type is if the agreement in question is objectively necessary for the parties to enter each other's market. If it is, the agreement does not create competition problems of a horizontal nature. However, the distribution agreement can fall under Article 81(1) if it contains vertical restraints, such as restrictions on passive sales, resale price maintenance, etc. If the agreement is not objectively necessary for the parties to enter each other's market, it falls under Article 81(1). If the agreement is not reciprocal, the risk of market partitioning is less pronounced. It needs however to be assessed if the non-reciprocal agreement constitutes the basis for a mutual understanding to not enter each other's market or is a means to control access to or competition on the "importing" market.

5.3.2. Market power and market structure

148. As indicated above, agreements that involve price fixing will always fall under Article 81(1) irrespective of the market power of the parties. They may, however, be exemptable under Article 81(3) under the conditions described below.

149. Commercialisation agreements between competitors which do not involve price fixing are only subject to Article 81(1) if the parties to the agreement have some degree of market power. In most cases, it is unlikely that market power exists if the parties to the agreement have a combined market share of below 15%. In any event, at that level of market share it is likely that the conditions of Article 81(3) explained below are fulfilled by the agreement in question.

150. If the parties' combined market share is greater than 15%, the likely impact of the joint commercialisation agreement on the market must be assessed. In this respect market concentration, as well as market shares will be a significant factor. The more concentrated the market the more useful information about prices or marketing strategy to reduce uncertainty and the greater the incentive for the parties to exchange such information.[47]

5.4. Assessment under Article 81(3)

5.4.1. Economic benefits

151. The efficiencies to be taken into account when assessing whether a joint commercialisation agreement can be exempted will depend upon the nature of the activity. Price fixing

---

[47] The exchange of sensitive and detailed information which takes place in an oligopolistic market might as such be caught by Article 81(1). The judgments of 28 May 1998 in the "Tractor" cases (C–8/958 P: *New Holland Ford* and C–7/95 P: *John Deere*) and of 11 March 1999 in the "*Steel Beams*" cases (T–134/94, T–136/94, T–137/94, T–138/94, T–141/94, T–145/94, T–147/94, T–148/94, T–151/94, T–156/94 and T–157/94) provide useful clarification in this respect.

can generally not be justified, unless it is indispensable for the integration of other marketing functions, and this integration will generate substantial efficiencies. The size of the efficiencies generated depends *inter alia* on the importance of the joint marketing activities for the overall cost structure of the product in question. Joint distribution is thus more likely to generate significant efficiencies for producers of widely distributed con sumer products than for producers of industrial products which are only bought by a limited number of users.

152. In addition, the claimed efficiencies should not be savings which result only from the elimination of costs that are inherently part of competition, but must result from the integration of economic activities. A reduction of transport costs which is only a result of customer allocation without any integration of the logistical system can therefore not be regarded as an efficiency that would make an agreement exemptable.

153. Claimed efficiency benefits must be demonstrated. An important element in this respect would be the contribution by both parties of significant capital, technology, or other assets. Cost savings through reduced duplication of resources and facilities can also be accepted. If, on the other hand, the joint commercialisation represents no more than a sales agency with no investment, it is likely to be a disguised cartel and as such cannot fulfil the conditions of Article 81(3).

5.4.2. Indispensability

154. A commercialisation agreement cannot be exempted if it imposes restrictions that are not indispensable to the attainment of the abovementioned benefits. As discussed above, the question of indispensability is especially important for those agreements involving price fixing or the allocation of markets.

5.4.3. No elimination of competition

155. No exemption will be possible, if the parties are afforded the possibility of eliminating competition in respect of a substantial part of the products in question. In making this assessment, the combined market shares of the parties can be regarded as a starting point. One then needs to evaluate whether these market shares are indicative of a dominant position, and whether there are any mitigating factors, such as the potential for market entry. Where as a consequence of a commercialisation agreement an undertaking is dominant or becoming dominant, such an agreement which produces anti-competitive effects in the meaning of Article 81 can in principle not be exempted.

5.5. Examples

156. Example 1
Situation: 5 small food producers, each with 2% market share of the overall food market, agree to: combine their distribution facilities; market under a common brand name; and sell their products at a common price. This involves significant investment in warehousing, transport, advertising, marketing and a sales force. It significantly reduces their cost base, representing typically 50% of the price at which they sell, and allows them to offer a quicker, more efficient distribution system. The customers of the food producers are large retail chains.

Three large multinational food groups dominate the market, each with 20% market share. The rest of the market is made up of small independent producers. The product ranges of the parties to this agreement overlap in some significant areas, but in no product market does their combined market share exceed 15%.

Analysis: The agreement involves price fixing and thus falls under Article 81(1), even though the parties to the agreement cannot be considered as having market power. However, the integration of the marketing and distribution appears to provide significant efficiencies which are of benefit to customers both in terms of improved service, and lower costs. The question is therefore whether the agreement is exemptable under Article 81(3). To answer this question it must be established whether the price fixing is indispensable for the integration of the other marketing functions and the attainment of the economic benefits. In this case, the price fixing can be regarded as indispensable, as the clients— large retail chains—do not want to deal with a multitude of prices. It is also indispensable as the aim—a common brand—can only be credibly achieved if all aspects of marketing, including price, are standardised. As the parties do not have market power and the agreement creates significant efficiencies it is compatible with Article 81.

157. Example 2
   Situation: 2 producers of ball bearings, each having a market share of 5%, create a sales joint venture which will market the products, determine the prices and allocate orders to the parent companies. They retain the right to sell outside this structure. Deliveries to customers continue to be made directly from the parents' factories. They claim that this will create efficiencies as the joint sales force can demonstrate the parties' products at the same time to the same client thus eliminating a wasteful duplication of sales efforts. In addition, the joint venture would, wherever possible, allocate orders to the closest factory possible, thus reducing transport costs.
   Analysis: The agreement involves price fixing and thus falls under Article 81(1), even though the parties to the agreement cannot be considered as having market power. It is not exemptable under Article 81(3), as the claimed efficiencies are only cost reductions derived from the elimination of competition between the parties.

158. Example 3
   Situation: 2 producers of soft drinks are active in 2 different, neighbouring Member States. Both have a market share of 20% in their home market. They agree to reciprocally distribute each other's product in their respective geographic market.
   Both markets are dominated by a large multi-national soft drink producer, having a market share of 50% in each market.
   Analysis: The agreement falls under Article 81(1) if the parties can be presumed to be potential competitors. Answering this question would thus require an analysis of the barriers to entry into the respective geographic markets. If the parties could have entered each other's market independently, then their agreement eliminates competition between them. However, even though the market shares of the parties indicate that they could have some market power, an analysis of the market structure indicates that this is not the case. In addition, the reciprocal distribution agreement benefits customers as it increases the available choice in each geographic market. The agreement would thus be exemptable even if it were considered to be restrictive of competition.

6. AGREEMENT ON STANDARDS

6.1. Definition

159. Standardisation agreements have as their primary objective the definition of technical or quality requirements with which current or future products, production processes or methods may comply.[48] Standardisation agreements can cover various issues, such as standardisation of different grades or sizes of a particular product or technical specifications in markets where compatibility and interoperability with other products or systems is essential. The terms of access to a particular quality mark or for approval by a regulatory body can also be regarded as a standard.

---

[48] Standardisation can take different forms, ranging from the adoption of national consensus based standards by the recognised European or national standards bodies, through consortia and fora, to agreements between single companies. Although Community law defines standards in a narrow way, these guidelines qualify as standards for all agreements as defined in this paragraph.

160. Standards related to the provision of professional services, such as rules of admission to a liberal profession, are not covered by these guidelines.

6.2. Relevant markets

161. Standardisation agreements produce their effects on three possible markets, which will be defined according to the Commission notice on market definition. First, the product market(s) to which the standard(s) relates. Standards on entirely new products may raise issues similar to those raised for R & D agreements, as far as market definition is concerned (see Point 2.2). Second, the service market for standard setting, if different standard setting bodies or agreements exist. Third, where relevant, the distinct market for testing and certification.

6.3. Assessment under Article 81(1)

162. Agreements to set standards[49] may be either concluded between private undertakings or set under the aegis of public bodies or bodies entrusted with the operation of services of general economic interest, such as the standards bodies recognised under Directive 98/34/EC.[50] The involvement of such bodies is subject to the obligations of Member States regarding the preservation of non-distorted competition in the Community.

6.3.1. Nature of the agreement

6.3.1.1. Agreements that do not fall under Article 81(1)

163. Where participation in standard setting is unrestricted and transparent, standardisation agreements as defined above, which set no obligation to comply with the standard or which are parts of a wider agreement to ensure compatibility of products, do not restrict competition. This normally applies to standards adopted by the recognised standards bodies which are based on non-discriminatory, open and transparent procedures.

164. No appreciable restriction exists for those standards that have a negligible coverage of the relevant market, as long as it remains so. No appreciable restriction is found either in agreements which pool together SMEs to standardise access forms or conditions to collective tenders or those that standardise aspects such as minor product characteristics, forms and reports, which have an insignificant effect on the main factors affecting competition in the relevant markets.

6.3.1.2. Agreements that almost always fall under Article 81(1)

165. Agreements that use a standard as a means amongst other parts of a broader restrictive agreement aimed at excluding actual or potential competitors will almost always be caught by Article 81(1). For instance, an agreement whereby a national association of manufacturers set a standard and put pressure on third parties not to market products that did not comply with the standard would be in this category.

---

[49] Pursuant to Article 4(2)(3) of Regulation No. 17, agreements which have as their sole object the development or the uniform application of standards and types need not, but may, be notified to the Commission.

[50] Directive 98/34/EC of the European Parliament and of the Council on 22 June 1998 laying down a procedure for the provision of information in the field of technical standards and regulations (OJ 1998 L204/37).

6.3.1.3. *Agreements that may fall under Article 81(1)*

166. Standardisation agreements may be caught by Article 81(1) insofar as they grant the parties joint control over production and/or innovation, thereby restricting their ability to compete on product characteristics, while affecting third parties like suppliers or purchasers of the standardised products. The assessment of each agreement must take into account the nature of the standard and its likely effect on the markets concerned, on the one hand, and the scope of possible restrictions that go beyond the primary objective of standardisation, as defined above, on the other.

167. The existence of a restriction of competition in standardisation agreements depends upon the extent to which the parties remain free to develop alternative standards or products that do not comply with the agreed standard. Standardisation agreements may restrict competition where they prevent the parties from either developing alternative standards or commercialising products that do not comply with the standard. Agreements that entrust certain bodies with the exclusive right to test compliance with the standard go beyond the primary objective of defining the standard and may also restrict competition. Agreements that impose restrictions on marking of conformity with standards, unless imposed by regulatory provisions, may also restrict competition.

6.3.2. *Market power and market structures*

168. High market shares held by the parties in the market(s) affected will not necessarily be a concern for standardisation agreements. Their effectiveness is often proportional to the share of the industry involved in setting and/or applying the standard. On the other hand, standards that are not accessible to third parties may discriminate or foreclose third parties or segment markets according to their geographic scope of application. Thus, the assessment whether the agreement restricts competition will focus, necessarily on an individual basis, on the extent to which such barriers to entry are likely to be overcome.

6.4. Assessment under Article 81(3)

6.4.1. *Economic benefits*

169. The Commission generally takes a positive approach towards agreements that promote economic interpenetration in the common market or encourage the development of new markets and improved supply conditions. To materialise those economic benefits, the necessary information to apply the standard must be available to those wishing to enter the market and an appreciable proportion of the industry must be involved in the setting of the standard in a transparent manner. It will be for the parties to demonstrate that any restrictions on the setting, use or access to the standard provide economic benefits.

170. In order to reap technical or economic benefits, standards should not limit innovation. This will depend primarily on the lifetime of the associated products, in connection with the market development stage (fast growing, growing, stagnant . . .). The effects on innovation must be analysed on a case-by-case basis. The parties may also have to provide evidence that collective standardisation is efficiency-enhancing for the consumer when a new standard may trigger unduly rapid obsolescence of existing products, without objective additional benefits.

6.4.2. *Indispensability*

171. By their nature, standards will not include all possible specifications or technologies. In some cases, it would be necessary for the benefit of the consumers or the economy at large to have only one technological solution. However, this standard must be set on a

non-discriminatory basis. Ideally, standards should be technology neutral. In any event, it must be justifiable why one standard is chosen over another.

172. All competitors in the market(s) affected by the standard should have the possibility of being involved in discussions. Therefore, participation in standard setting should be open to all, unless the parties demonstrate important inefficiencies in such participation or unless recognised procedures are foreseen for the collective representation of interests, as in formal standards bodies.

173. As a general rule there should be a clear distinction between the setting of a standard and, where necessary, the related R & D, and the commercial exploitation of that standard. Agreements on standards should cover no more than what is necessary to ensure their aims, whether this is technical compatibility or a certain level of quality. For instance, it should be very clearly demonstrated why it is indispensable to the emergence of the economic benefits that an agreement to disseminate a standard in an industry where only one competitor offers an alternative should oblige the parties to the agreement to boycott the alternative.

6.4.3. No elimination of competition

174. There will clearly be a point at which the specification of a private standard by a group of firms that are jointly dominant is likely to lead to the creation of a de facto industry standard. The main concern will then be to ensure that these standards are as open as possible and applied in a clear non-discriminatory manner. To avoid elimination of competition in the relevant market(s), access to the standard must be possible for third parties on fair, reasonable and non-discriminatory terms.

175. To the extent that private organisations or groups of companies set a standard or their proprietary technology becomes a de facto standard, then competition will be eliminated if third parties are foreclosed from access to this standard.

6.5 Examples

176. Example 1
Situation: EN 60603–7:1993 defines the requirements to connect television receivers to video-generating accessories such as video recorders and video games. Although the standard is not legally binding, in practice manufacturers both of television receivers and of video games use the standard, as the market requires.

Analysis: Article 81(1) is not infringed. The standard has been adopted by recognised standards bodies, at national, European and international level, through open and transparent procedures, and is based on national consensus reflecting the position of manufacturers and consumers. All manufacturers are allowed to use the standard.

177. Example 2
Situation: A number of video cassette manufacturers agree to develop a quality mark or standard to denote the fact that the videocassette meets certain minimum technical specifications. The manufacturers are free to produce videocassettes which do not conform to the standard and the standard is freely available to other developers.

Analysis: Provided that the agreement does not otherwise restrict competition, Article 81(1) is not infringed, as participation in standard setting is unrestricted and transparent, and the standardisation agreement does not set an obligation to comply with the standard. If the parties agreed only to produce videocassettes which conform to the new standard, the agreement would limit technical development and prevent the parties from selling different products, which would infringe Article 81(1).

178. Example 3
Situation: A group of competitors active in various markets which are interdependent with products that must be compatible, and with over 80% of the relevant markets, agree to jointly develop a new standard that will be introduced in competition with other

standards already present in the market, widely applied by their competitors. The various products complying with the new standard will not be compatible with existing standards. Because of the significant investment needed to shift and to maintain production under the new standard, the parties agree to commit a certain volume of sales to products complying with the new standard so as to create a "critical mass" in the market. They also agree to limit their individual production volume of products not complying with the standard to the level attained last year.

Analysis: This agreement, owing to the parties' market power and the restrictions on production, falls under Article 81(1) while not being likely to fulfil the conditions of paragraph 3, unless access to technical information were provided on a non-discriminatory basis and reasonable terms to other suppliers wishing to compete.

7. ENVIRONMENTAL AGREEMENTS

7.1. Definition

179. Environmental agreements[51] are those by which the parties undertake to achieve pollution abatement, as defined in environmental law, or environmental objectives, in particular, those set out in Article 174 of the Treaty. Therefore, the target or the measures agreed need to be directly linked to the reduction of a pollutant or a type of waste identified as such in relevant regulations.[52] This excludes agreements that trigger pollution abatement as a by-product of other measures.

180. Environmental agreements may set out standards on the environmental performance of products (inputs or outputs) or production processes.[53] Other possible categories may include agreements at the same level of trade, whereby the parties provide for the common attainment of an environmental target such as recycling of certain materials, emission reductions, or the improvement of energy-efficiency.

181. Comprehensive, industry-wide schemes are set up in many Member States for complying with environmental obligations on take-back or recycling. Such schemes usually comprise a complex set of arrangements, some of which are horizontal, while others are vertical in character. To the extent that these arrangements contain vertical restraints they are not subject to these guidelines.

7.2. Relevant markets

182. The effects are to be assessed on the markets to which the agreement relates, which will be defined according to the Notice on the definition of the relevant market for the purposes of Community competition law. When the pollutant is not itself a product, the relevant market encompasses that of the product into which the pollutant is incorporated. As for collection/recycling agreements, in addition to their effects on the market(s) on which the parties are active as producers or distributors, the effects on the market of collection services potentially covering the good in question must be assessed as well.

---

[51] The term "agreement" is used in the sense defined by the Court of Justice and the Court of First Instance in the case law on Article 81. It does not necessarily correspond to the definition of an "agreement" in Commission documents dealing with environmental issues such as the Communication on environmental agreements COM(96) 561 final of 27.11.1996.

[52] For instance, a national agreement phasing out a pollutant or waste identified as such in relevant Community directives may not be assimilated to a collective boycott on a product which circulates freely in the Community.

[53] To the extent that some environmental agreements could be assimilated to standardisation, the same assessment principles for standardisation apply to them.

7.3. Assessment under Article 81(1)

183. Some environmental agreements may be encouraged or made necessary by State authorities in the exercise of their public prerogatives. The present guidelines do not deal with the question of whether such State intervention is in conformity with the Member State's obligations under the Treaty. They only address the assessment that must be made as to the compatibility of the agreement with Article 81.

7.3.1. Nature of the agreement

7.3.1.1. Agreements that do not fall under Article 81(1)

184. Some environmental agreements are not likely to fall within the scope of the prohibition of Article 81(1), irrespective of the aggregate market share of the parties.

185. This may arise if no precise individual obligation is placed upon the parties or if they are loosely committed to contributing to the attainment of a sector-wide environmental target. In this latter case, the assessment will focus on the discretion left to the parties as to the means that are technically and economically available in order to attain the environmental objective agreed upon. The more varied such means, the less appreciable the potential restrictive effects.

186. Similarly, agreements setting the environmental performance of products or processes that do not appreciably affect product and production diversity in the relevant market or whose importance is marginal for influencing purchase decisions do not fall under Article 81(1). Where some categories of a product are banned or phased out from the market, restrictions cannot be deemed appreciable in so far as their share is minor in the relevant geographic market or, in the case of Community-wide markets, in all Member States.

187. Finally, agreements which give rise to genuine market creation, for instance recycling agreements, will not generally restrict competition, provided that and for as long as, the parties would not be capable of conducting the activities in isolation, whilst other alternatives and/or competitors do not exist.

7.3.1.2. Agreements that almost always come under Article 81(1)

188. Environmental agreements come under Article 81(1) by their nature if the cooperation does not truly concern environmental objectives, but serves as a tool to engage in a disguised cartel, i.e. otherwise prohibited price fixing, output limitation or market allocation, or if the cooperation is used as a means amongst other parts of a broader restrictive agreement which aims at excluding actual or potential competitors.

7.3.1.3. Agreements that may fall under Article 81(1)

189. Environmental agreements covering a major share of an industry at national or EC level are likely to be caught by Article 81(1) where they appreciably restrict the parties' ability to devise the characteristics of their products or the way in which they produce them, thereby granting them influence over each other's production or sales. In addition to restrictions between the parties, an environmental agreement may also reduce or substantially affect the output of third parties, either as suppliers or as purchasers.

190. For instance, environmental agreements, which may phase out or significantly affect an important proportion of the parties' sales as regards their products or production processes, may fall under Article 81(1) when the parties hold a significant proportion of the market. The same applies to agreements whereby the parties allocate individual pollution quotas.

191. Similarly, agreements whereby parties holding significant market shares in a substantial part of the common market appoint an undertaking as exclusive provider of collection and/or recycling services for their products, may also appreciably restrict competition, provided other actual or realistic potential providers exist.

7.4. Assessment under Article 81(3)

7.4.1. Economic benefits

192. The Commission takes a positive stance on the use of environmental agreements as a policy instrument to achieve the goals enshrined in Article 2 and Article 174 of the Treaty as well as in Community environmental action plans,[54] provided such agreements are compatible with competition rules.[55]

193. Environmental agreements caught by Article 81(1) may attain economic benefits which, either at individual or aggregate consumer level, outweigh their negative effects on competition. To fulfil this condition, there must be net benefits in terms of reduced environmental pressure resulting from the agreement, as compared to a baseline where no action is taken. In other words, the expected economic benefits must outweigh the costs.[56]

194. Such costs include the effects of lessened competition along with compliance costs for economic operators and/or effects on third parties. The benefits might be assessed in two stages. Where consumers individually have a positive rate of return from the agreement under reasonable payback periods, there is no need for the aggregate environmental benefits to be objectively established. Otherwise, a cost-benefit analysis may be necessary to assess whether net benefits for consumers in general are likely under reasonable assumptions.

7.4.2. Indispensability

195. The more objectively the economic efficiency of an environmental agreement is demonstrated, the more clearly each provision might be deemed indispensable to the attainment of the environmental goal within its economic context.

196. An objective evaluation of provisions which might "prima facie" be deemed not to be indispensable must be supported with a cost-effectiveness analysis showing that alternative means of attaining the expected environmental benefits, would be more economically or financially costly, under reasonable assumptions. For instance, it should be very clearly demonstrated that a uniform fee, charged irrespective of individual costs for waste collection, is indispensable for the functioning of an industry-wide collection system.

7.4.3. No elimination of competition

197. Whatever the environmental and economic gains and the necessity of the intended provisions, the agreement must not eliminate competition in terms of product or process differentiation, technological innovation or market entry in the short or, where relevant,

---

[54] Vth Environmental Action Programme (OJ 1993 C138/1); European Parliament and Council Decision No. 2179/98/EC of 24 September 1998 (OJ 1998 L275/1).

[55] Communication on environmental agreements COM(96) 561 final of 27.11.1996, paragraphs 27–29 and Article 3(1)(f) of EP and Council Decision *ut supra*. The communication includes a "Checklist for Environmental Agreements" identifying the elements that should generally be included in such an agreement.

[56] This is consistent with the requirement to take account of the potential benefits and costs of action or lack of action set forth in Article 231(3) of the Treaty and Article 7(d) of European Parliament and Council Decision *ut supra*.

medium term. For instance, in the case of exclusive collection rights granted to a collection/recycling operator who has potential competitors, the duration of such rights should take into account the possible emergence of an alternative to the operator.

7.5. Examples

198. Example

Situation: Almost all Community producers and importers of a given domestic appliance (e.g. washing machines) agree, with the encouragement of a public body, to no longer manufacture and import into the Community products which do not comply with certain environmental criteria (e.g. energy efficiency). Together, the parties hold 90% of the Community market. The products which will be thus phased out of the market account for a significant proportion of total sales. They will be replaced with more environmentally friendly, but also more expensive products. Furthermore, the agreement indirectly reduces the output of third parties (e.g. electric utilities, suppliers of components incorporated in the products phased out).

Analysis: The agreement grants the parties control of individual production and imports and concerns an appreciable proportion of their sales and total output, whilst also reducing third parties' output. Consumer choice, which is partly focused on the environmental characteristics of the product, is reduced and prices will probably rise. Therefore, the agreement is caught by Article 81(1). The involvement of the public authority is irrelevant for this assessment.

However, newer products are more technically advanced and by reducing the environmental problem indirectly aimed at (emissions from electricity generation), they will not inevitably create or increase another environmental problem (e.g. water consumption, detergent use). The net contribution to the improvement of the environmental situation overall outweighs increased costs. Furthermore, individual purchasers of more expensive products will also rapidly recoup the cost increase as the more environmentally friendly products have lower running costs. Other alternatives to the agreement are shown to be less certain and less cost-effective in delivering the same net benefits. Varied technical means are economically available to the parties in order to manufacture products which do comply with the environmental characteristics agreed upon and competition will still take place for other product characteristics. Therefore, the conditions for an exemption under Article 81(3) are fulfilled.

APPENDIX 29

COMMISSION NOTICE

Guidelines on vertical restraints[1]

(Text with EEA relevance)

CONTENTS

---

[1] OJ 2000 C291/1.

I Introduction

1 Purpose of the Guidelines

(1) These Guidelines set out the principles for the assessment of vertical agreements under Article 81 of the EC Treaty. What are considered vertical agreements is defined in Article 2(1) of Commission Regulation (EC) No. 2790/1999 of 22 December 1999 on the application of Article 81(3) of the Treaty to categories of vertical agreements and concerted practices[2] (Block Exemption Regulation) (see paragraphs 23 to 45). These Guidelines are without prejudice to the possible parallel application of Article 82 of the Treaty to vertical agreements. The Guidelines are structured in the following way:

— Section II (paragraphs 8 to 20) describes vertical agreements which generally fall outside Article 81(1);
— Section III (paragraphs 21 to 70) comments on the application of the Block Exemption Regulation;
— Section IV (paragraphs 71 to 87) describes the principles concerning the withdrawal of the block exemption and the disapplication of the Block Exemption Regulation;
— Section V (paragraphs 88 to 99) addresses market definition and market share calculation issues;
— Section VI (paragraphs 100 to 229) describes the general framework of analysis and the enforcement policy of the Commission in individual cases concerning vertical agreements.

(2) Throughout these Guidelines the analysis applies to both goods and services, although certain vertical restraints are mainly used in the distribution of goods. Similarly, vertical agreements can be concluded for intermediate and final goods and services. Unless otherwise stated, the analysis and arguments in the text apply to all types of goods

---

[2] OJ 1999 L336/21.

and services and to all levels of trade. The term "products" includes both goods and services. The term "supplier" and "buyer" are used for all levels of trade.

(3) By issuing these Guidelines the Commission aims to help companies to make their own assessment of vertical agreements under the EC competition rules. The standards set forth in these Guidelines must be applied in circumstances specific to each case. This rules out a mechanical application. Each case must be evaluated in the light of its own facts. The Commission will apply the Guidelines reasonably and flexibly.

(4) These Guidelines are without prejudice to the interpretation that may be given by the Court of First Instance and the Court of Justice of the European Communities in relation to the application of Article 81 to vertical agreements.

2 Applicability of Article 81 to vertical agreements

(5) Article 81 of the EC Treaty applies to vertical agreements that may affect trade between Member States and that prevent, restrict or distort competition (hereinafter referred to as "vertical restraints").[3] For vertical restraints, Article 81 provides an appropriate legal framework for assessment, recognising the distinction between anti-competitive and pro-competitive effects: Article 81(1) prohibits those agreements which appreciably restrict or distort competition, while Article 81(3) allows for exemption of those agreements which confer sufficient benefits to outweigh the anti-competitive effects.

(6) For most vertical restraints, competition concerns can only arise if there is insufficient inter-brand competition, i.e. if there is some degree of market power at the level of the supplier or the buyer or at both levels. If there is insufficient inter-brand competition, the protection of inter- and intra-brand competition becomes important.

(7) The protection of competition is the primary objective of EC competition policy, as this enhances consumer welfare and creates an efficient allocation of resources. In applying the EC competition rules, the Commission will adopt an economic approach which is based on the effects on the market; vertical agreements have to be analysed in their legal and economic context. However, in the case of restrictions by object as listed in Article 4 of the Block Exemption Regulation, the Commission is not required to assess the actual effects on the market. Market integration is an additional goal of EC competition policy. Market integration enhances competition in the Community. Companies should not be allowed to recreate private barriers between Member States where State barriers have been successfully abolished.

II Vertical agreements which generally fall outside Article 81(1)

1 Agreements of minor importance and SMEs

(8) Agreements which are not capable of appreciably affecting trade between Member States or capable of appreciably restricting competition by object or effect are not caught by Article 81(1). The Block Exemption Regulation applies only to agreements falling within the scope of application of Article 81(1). These Guidelines are without prejudice to the application of the present or any future "de minimis" notice.[4]

(9) Subject to the conditions set out in points 11, 18 and 20 of the "de minimis" notice concerning hardcore restrictions and cumulative effect issues, vertical agreements entered into by undertakings whose market share on the relevant market does not exceed 10% are generally considered to fall outside the scope of Article 81(1). There is no presumption

---

[3] See inter alia judgment of the Court of Justice of the European Communities in Joined Cases 56/64 and 58/64 Grundig-Consten v. Commission [1966] ECR 299; Case 56/65 Technique Minière v. Machinenbau Ulm [1966] ECR 235; and of the Court of First Instance of the European Communities in Case T–77/92 Parker Pen v. Commission [1994] ECR II–549.

[4] See Notice on agreements of minor importance of 9 December 1997, OJ 1997 C372/13.

that vertical agreements concluded by undertakings having more than 10% market share automatically infringe Article 81(1). Agreements between undertakings whose market share exceeds the 10% threshold may still not have an appreciable effect on trade between Member States or may not constitute an appreciable restriction of competition.[5] Such agreements need to be assessed in their legal and economic context. The criteria for the assessment of individual agreements are set out in paragraphs 100 to 229.

(10) As regards hardcore restrictions defined in the "*de minimis*" notice, Article 81(1) may apply below the 10% threshold, provided that there is an appreciable effect on trade between Member States and on competition. The applicable case law of the Court of Justice and the Court of First Instance is relevant in this respect.[6] Reference is also made to the particular situation of launching a new product or entering a new market which is dealt with in these Guidelines (paragraph 119, point 10).

(11) In addition, the Commission considers that, subject to cumulative effect and hardcore restrictions, agreements between small and medium-sized undertakings as defined in the Annex to Commission Recommendation 96/280/EC[7] are rarely capable of appreciably affecting trade between Member States or of appreciably restricting competition within the meaning of Article 81(1), and therefore generally fall outside the scope of Article 81(1). In cases where such agreements nonetheless meet the conditions for the application of Article 81(1), the Commission will normally refrain from opening proceedings for lack of sufficient Community interest unless those undertakings collectively or individually hold a dominant position in a substantial part of the common market.

2 Agency agreements

(12) Paragraphs 12 to 20 replace the Notice on exclusive dealing contracts with commercial agents of 1962.[8] They must be read in conjunction with Council Directive 86/653/EC.[9]

Agency agreements cover the situation in which a legal or physical person (the agent) is vested with the power to negotiate and/or conclude contracts on behalf of another person (the principal), either in the agent's own name or in the name of the principal, for the:

— purchase of goods or services by the principal, or
— sale of goods or services supplied by the principal.

(13) In the case of genuine agency agreements, the obligations imposed on the agent as to the contracts negotiated and/or concluded on behalf of the principal do not fall within the scope of application of Article 81(1). The determining factor in assessing whether Article 81(1) is applicable is the financial or commercial risk borne by the agent in relation to the activities for which he has been appointed as an agent by the principal. In this respect it is not material for the assessment whether the agent acts for one or several principals. Non-genuine agency agreements may be caught by Article 81(1), in which case the Block Exemption Regulation and the other sections of these Guidelines will apply.

(14) There are two types of financial or commercial risk that are material to the assessment of the genuine nature of an agency agreement under Article 81(1). First there are the risks which are directly related to the contracts concluded and/or negotiated by the agent on behalf of the principal, such as financing of stocks. Secondly, there are the risks

---

[5] See judgment of the Court of First Instance in Case T–7/93 *Langnese-Iglo v. Commission* [1995] ECR II–1533, paragraph 98.
[6] See judgment of the Court of Justice in Case 5/69, *Völk v. Vervaecke* [1969] ECR 295; Case 1/71 *Cadillon v. Höss* [1971] ECR 351; and Case C–306/96 *Javico v. Yves Saint Laurent* [1998] ECR I–1983, paragraphs 16 and 17.
[7] OJ 1996 L107/4.
[8] OJ 1962 139, 2921/62.
[9] OJ 1986 L382/17.

related to market-specific investments. These are investments specifically required for the type of activity for which the agent has been appointed b the principal, i.e. which are required to enable the agent to conclude and/or negotiate this type of contract. Such investments are usually sunk, if upon leaving that particular field of activity the investment cannot be used for other activities or sold other than at a significant loss.

(15) The agency agreement is considered a genuine agency agreement and consequently falls outside Article 81(1) if the agent does not bear any, or bears only insignificant, risks in relation to the contracts concluded and/or negotiated on behalf of the principal and in relation to market-specific investments for that field of activity. In such a situation, the selling or purchasing function forms part of the principal's activities, despite the fact that the agent is a separate undertaking. The principal thus bears the related financial and commercial risks and the agent does not exercise an independent economic activity in relation to the activities for which he has been appointed as an agent by the principal. In the opposite situation the agency agreement is considered a non-genuine agency agreement and may fall under Article 81(1). In that case the agent does bear such risks and will be treated as an independent dealer who must remain free in determining his marketing strategy in order to be able to recover his contract- or market-specific investments. Risks that are related to the activity of providing agency services in general, such as the risk of the agent's income being dependent upon his success as an agent or general investments in for instance premises or personnel, are not material to this assessment.

(16) The question of risk must be assessed on a case-by-case basis, and with regard to the economic reality of the situation rather than the legal form. Nonetheless, the Commission considers that Article 81(1) will generally not be applicable to the obligations imposed on the agent as to the contracts negotiated and/or concluded on behalf of the principal where property in the contract goods bought or sold does not vest in the agent, or the agent does not himself supply the contract services and where the agent:

— does not contribute to the costs relating to the supply/purchase of the contract goods or services, including the costs of transporting the goods. This does not preclude the agent from carrying out the transport service, provided that the costs are covered by the principal;
— is not, directly or indirectly, obliged to invest in sales promotion, such as contributions to the advertising budgets of the principal;
— does not maintain at his own cost or risk stocks of the contract goods, including the costs of financing the stocks and the costs of loss of stocks and can return unsold goods to the principal without charge, unless the agent is liable for fault (for example, by failing to comply with reasonable security measures to avoid loss of stocks);
— does not create and/or operate an after-sales service, repair service or a warranty service unless it is fully reimbursed by the principal;
— does not make market-specific investments in equipment, premises or training of personnel, such as for example the petrol storage tank in the case of petrol retailing or specific software to sell insurance policies in case of insurance agents;
— does not undertake responsibility towards third parties for damage caused by the product sold (product liability), unless, as agent, he is liable for fault in this respect;
— does not take responsibility for customers' non-performance of the contract, with the exception of the loss of the agent's commission, unless the agent is liable for fault (for example, by failing to comply with reasonable security or anti-theft measures or failing to comply with reasonable measures to report theft to the principal or police or to communicate to the principal all necessary information available to him on the customer's financial reliability).

(17) This list is not exhaustive. However, where the agent incurs one or more of the above risks or costs, then Article 81(1) may apply as with any other vertical agreement.

(18) If an agency agreement does not fall within the scope of application of Article 81(1), then all obligations imposed on the agent in relation to the contracts concluded and/ or negotiated on behalf of the principal fall outside Article 81(1). The following obligations on the agent's part will generally be considered to form an inherent part of an agency agreement, as each of them relates to the ability of the principal to fix the scope of activity of the agent in relation to the contract goods or services, which is essential if the principal is to take the risks and therefore to be in a position to determine the commercial strategy:

— limitations on the territory in which the agent may sell these goods or services;
— limitations on the customers to whom the agent may sell these goods or services;
— the prices and conditions at which the agent must sell or purchase these goods or services.

(19) In addition to governing the conditions of sale or purchase of the contract goods or services by the agent on behalf of the principal, agency agreements often contain provisions which concern the relationship between the agent and the principal. In particular, they may contain a provision preventing the principal from appointing other agents in respect of a given type of transaction, customer or territory (exclusive agency provisions) and/or a provision preventing the agent from acting as an agent or distributor of undertakings which compete with the principal (non-compete provisions). Exclusive agency provisions concern only intra-brand competition and will in general not lead to anti-competitive effects. Non-compete provisions, including post-term non-compete provisions, concern inter-brand competition and may infringe Article 81(1) if they lead to foreclosure on the relevant market where the contract goods or services are sold or purchased (see Section VI.2.1).

(20) An agency agreement may also fall within the scope of Article 81(1), even if the principal bears all the relevant financial and commercial risks, where it facilitates collusion. This could for instance be the case when a number of principals use the same agents while collectively excluding others from using these agents, or when they use the agents to collude on marketing strategy or to exchange sensitive market information between the principals.

III Application of the Block Exemption Regulation

1 Safe harbour created by the Block Exemption Regulation

(21) The Block Exemption Regulation creates a presumption of legality for vertical agreements depending on the market share of the supplier or the buyer. Pursuant to Article 3 of the Block Exemption Regulation, it is in general the market share of the supplier on the market where it sells the contract goods or services which determines the applicability of the block exemption. This market share may not exceed the threshold of 30% in order for the block exemption to apply. Only where the agreement contains an exclusive supply obligation, as defined in Article 1(c) of the Block Exemption Regulation, is it the buyer's market share on the market where it purchases the contract goods or services which may not exceed the threshold of 30% in order for the block exemption to apply. For market share issues see Section V (paragraphs 88 to 99).

(22) From an economic point of view, a vertical agreement may have effects not only on the market between supplier and buyer but also on markets downstream of the buyer. The simplified approach of the Block Exemption Regulation, which only takes into account the market share of the supplier or the buyer (as the case may be) on the market between these two parties, is justified by the fact that below the threshold of 30% the effects on downstream markets will in general be limited. In addition, only having to consider the market between supplier and buyer makes the application of the Block

Exemption Regulation easier and enhances the level of legal certainty, while the instrument of withdrawal (see paragraphs 71 to 87) remains available to remedy possible problems on other related markets.

2 Scope of the Block Exemption Regulation

(i) Definition of vertical agreements

(23) Vertical agreements are defined in Article 2(1) of the Block Exemption Regulation as "agreements or concerted practices entered into between two or more undertakings each of which operates, for the purposes of the agreement, at a different level of the production or distribution chain, and relating to the condition under which the parties may purchase, sell or resell certain goods or services".

(24) There are three main elements in this definition:

— the agreement or concerted practice is between two or more undertakings. Vertical agreements with final consumers not operating as an undertaking are not covered. More generally, agreements with final consumers do not fall under Article 81(1), as that Article applies only to agreements between undertakings, decisions by associations of undertakings and concerted practices. This is without prejudice to the possible application of Article 82 of the Treaty;

— the agreement or concerted practice is between undertakings each operating, for the purposes of the agreement, at a different level of the production or distribution chain. This means for instance that one undertaking produces a raw material which the other undertaking uses as an input, or that the first is a manufacturer, the second a wholesaler and the third a retailer. This does not preclude an undertaking from being active at more than one level of the production or distribution chain;

— the agreements or concerted practices relate to the conditions under which the parties to the agreement, the supplier and the buyer, "may purchase, sell or resell certain goods or services". This reflects the purpose of the Block Exemption Regulation to cover purchase and distribution agreements. These are agreements which concern the conditions for the purchase, sale or resale of the goods or services supplied by the supplier and/or which concern the conditions for the sale by the buyer of the goods or services which incorporate these goods or services. For the application of the Block Exemption Regulation both the goods or services supplied by the supplier and the resulting goods or services are considered to be contract goods or services. Vertical agreements relating to all final and intermediate goods and services are covered. The only exception is the automobile sector, as long as this sector remains covered by a specific block exemption such as that granted by Commission Regulation (EC) No. 1475/95.[10] The goods or services provided by the supplier may be resold by the buyer or may be used as an input by the buyer to produce his own goods or services.

(25) The Block Exemption Regulation also applies to goods sold and purchased for renting to third parties. However, rent and lease agreements as such are not covered, as no good or service is being sold by the supplier to the buyer. More generally, the Block Exemption Regulation does not cover restrictions or obligations to that do not relate to the conditions of purchase, sale and resale, such as an obligation preventing parties from carrying out independent research and development which the parties may have included in an otherwise vertical agreement. In addition, Articles 2(2) to (5) directly or indirectly

---

[10] OJ 1995 L145/25.

exclude certain vertical agreements from the application of the Block Exemption Regulation.

(ii) Vertical agreements between competitors

(26) Article 2(4) of the Block Exemption Regulation explicitly excludes from its application "vertical agreements entered into between competing undertakings". Vertical agreements between competitors will be dealt with, as regards possible collusion effects, in the forthcoming Guidelines on the applicability of Article 81 to horizontal co-operation.[11] However, the vertical aspects of such agreements need to be assessed under these Guidelines. Article 1(a) of the Block Exemption Regulation defines competing undertakings as "actual or potential suppliers in the same product market", irrespective of whether or not they are competitors on the same geographic market. Competing undertakings are undertakings that are actual or potential suppliers of the contract goods or services or goods or services that are substitutes for the contract goods or services. A potential supplier is an undertaking that does not actually produce a competing product but could and would be likely to do so in the absence of the agreement in response to a small and permanent increase in relative prices. This means that the undertaking would be able and likely to undertake the necessary additional investments and supply the market within one year. This assessment has to be based on realistic grounds; the mere theoretical possibility of entering a market is not sufficient.[12]

(27) There are three exceptions to the general exclusion of vertical agreements between competitors, all three being set out in Article 2(4) and relating to non-reciprocal agreements. Non-reciprocal means, for instance, that while one manufacturer becomes the distributor of the products of another manufacturer, the latter does not become the distributor of the products of the first manufacturer. Non-reciprocal agreements between competitors are covered by the Block Exemption Regulation where (1) the buyer has a turnover not exceeding EUR 100 million, or (2) the supplier is a manufacturer and distributor of goods, while the buyer is only a distributor and not also a manufacturer of competing goods, or (3) the supplier is a provider of services operating at several levels of trade, while the buyer does not provide competing services at the level of trade where it purchases the contract services. The second exception covers situations of dual distribution, i.e. the manufacturer of particular goods also acts as a distributor of the goods in competition with independent distributors of his goods. A distributor who provides specifications to a manufacturer to produce particular goods under the distributor's brand name is not to be considered a manufacturer of such own-brand goods. The third exception covers similar situations of dual distribution, but in this case for services, when the supplier is also a provider of services at the level of the buyer.

(iii) Associations of retailers

(28) Article 2(2) of the Block Exemption Regulation includes in its application vertical agreements entered into by an association of undertakings which fulfils certain conditions and thereby excludes from the Block Exemption Regulation vertical agreements entered into by all other associations. Vertical agreements entered into between an association and its members, or between an association and its suppliers, are covered by the Block Exemption Regulation only if all the members are retailers of goods (not services) and if each individual member of the association has a turnover not exceeding EUR 50 million. Retailers are distributors reselling goods to final consumers. Where only a limited number

---

[11] Draft text published in OJ 2000 C118/14.

[12] See Commission Notice on the definition of the relevant market for the purposes of Community competition law, OJ 1997 C372/5, at paras. 20–24, the Commission's Thirteenth Report on Competition Policy, point 55, and Commission Decision 90/410 in Case No. IV/32.009—Elopak/Metal Box-Odin, OJ 1990 L209/15.

of the members of the association have a turnover not significantly exceeding the EUR 50 million threshold, this will normally not change the assessment under Article 81.

(29) An association of undertakings may involve both horizontal and vertical agreements. The horizontal agreements have to be assessed according to the principles set out in the forthcoming Guidelines on the applicability of Article 81 to horizontal cooperation. If this assessment leads to the conclusion that a cooperation between undertakings in the area of purchasing or selling is acceptable, a further assessment will be necessary to examine the vertical agreements concluded by the association with its suppliers or its individual members. The latter assessment will follow the rules of the Block Exemption Regulation and these Guidelines. For instance, horizontal agreements concluded between the members of the association or decisions adopted by the association, such as the decision to require the members to purchase from the association or the decision to allocate exclusive territories to the members have to be assessed first as a horizontal agreement. Only if this assessment is positive does it become relevant to assess the vertical agreements between the association and individual members or between the association and suppliers.

(iv) Vertical agreements containing provisions on intellectual property rights (IPRs)

(30) Article 2(3) of the Block Exemption Regulation includes in its application vertical agreements containing certain provisions relating to the assignment of IPRs to or use of IPRs by the buyer and thereby excludes from the Block Exemption Regulation all other vertical agreements containing IPR provisions. The Block Exemption Regulation applies to vertical agreements containing IPR provisions when five conditions are fulfilled:

— the IPR provisions must be part of a vertical agreement, i.e. an agreement with conditions under which the parties may purchase, sell or resell certain goods or services;
— the IPRs must be assigned to, or for use by, the buyer;
— the IPR provisions must not constitute the primary object of the agreement;
— the IPR provisions must be directly related to the use, sale or resale of goods or services by the buyer or his customers. In the case of franchising where marketing forms the object of the exploitation of the IPRs, the goods or services are distributed by the master franchisee or the franchisees;
— the IPR provisions, in relation to the contract goods or services, must not contain restrictions of competition having the same object or effect as vertical restraints which are not exempted under the Block Exemption Regulation.

(31) These conditions ensure that the Block Exemption Regulation applies to vertical agreements where the use, sale or resale of goods or services can be performed more effectively because IPRs are assigned to or transferred for use by the buyer. In other words, restrictions concerning the assignment or use of IPRs can be covered when the main object of the agreement is the purchase or distribution of goods or services.

(32) The first condition makes clear that the context in which the IPRs are provided is an agreement to purchase or distribute goods or an agreement to purchase or provide services and not an agreement concerning the assignment or licensing of IPRs for the manufacture of goods, nor a pure licensing agreement. The Block Exemption Regulation does not cover for instance:

— agreements where a party provides another party with a recipe and licenses the other party to produce a drink with this recipe;
— agreements under which one party provides another party with a mould or master copy and licenses the other party to produce and distribute copies;
— the pure licence of a trade mark or sign for the purposes of merchandising;

— sponsorship contracts concerning the right to advertise oneself as being an official sponsor of an event;

— copyright licensing such as broadcasting contracts concerning the right to record and/ or the right to broadcast an event.

(33) The second condition makes clear that the Block Exemption Regulation does not apply when the IPRs are provided by the buyer to the supplier, no matter whether the IPRs concern the manner of manufacture or of distribution. An agreement relating to the transfer of IPRs to the supplier and containing possible restrictions on the sales made by the supplier is not covered by the Block Exemption Regulation. This means in particular that sub-contracting involving the transfer of know-how to a sub-contractor[13] does not fall within the scope of application of the Block Exemption Regulation. However, vertical agreements under which the buyer provides only specifications to the supplier which describe the goods or services to be supplied are covered by the Block Exemption Regulation.

(34) The third condition makes clear that in order to be covered by the Block Exemption Regulation the primary object of the agreement must not be the assignment or licensing of IPRs. The primary object must be the purchase or distribution of goods or services and the IPR provisions must serve the implementation of the vertical agreement.

(35) The fourth condition requires that the IPR provisions facilitate the use, sale or resale of goods or services by the buyer or his customers. The goods or services for use or resale are usually supplied by the licensor but may also be purchased by the licensee from a third supplier. The IPR provisions will normally concern the marketing of goods or services. This is for instance the case in a franchise agreement where the franchisor sells to the franchisee goods for resale and in addition licenses the franchisee to use his trade mark and know-how to market the goods. Also covered is the case where the supplier of a concentrated extract licenses the buyer to dilute and bottle the extract before selling it as a drink.

(36) The fifth condition signifies in particular that the IPR provisions should not have the same object or effect as any of the hardcore restrictions listed in Article 4 of the Block Exemption Regulation or any of the restrictions excluded from the coverage of the Block Exemption Regulation by Article 5 (see paragraphs 46 to 61).

(37) Intellectual property rights which may be considered to serve the implementation of vertical agreements within the meaning of Article 2(3) of the Block Exemption Regulation generally concern three main areas: trade marks, copyright and know-how.

Trade mark

(38) A trade mark licence to a distributor may be related to the distribution of the licensor's products in a particular territory. If it is an exclusive licence, the agreement amounts to exclusive distribution.

Copyright

(39) Resellers of goods covered by copyright (books, software, etc.) may be obliged by the copyright holder only to resell under the condition that the buyer, whether another reseller or the end user, shall not infringe the copyright. Such obligations on the reseller, to the extent that they fall under Article 81(1) at all, are covered by the Block Exemption Regulation.

(40) Agreements under which hard copies of software are supplied for resale and where the reseller does not acquire a licence to any rights over the software but only has the right

---

[13] See Notice on sub-contracting, OJ 1979 C1/2.

262

to resell the hard copies, are to be regarded as agreements for the supply of goods for resale for the purpose of the Block Exemption Regulation. Under this form of distribution the licence of the software only takes place between the copyright owner and the user of the software. This may take the form of a "shrink wrap" licence, i.e. a set of conditions included in the package of the hard copy which the end user is deemed to accept by opening the package.

(41) Buyers of hardware incorporating software protected by copyright may be obliged by the copyright holder not to infringe the copyright, for example not to make copies and resell the software or not to make copies and use the software in combination with other hardware. Such use-restrictions, to the extent that they fall within Article 81(1) at all, are covered by the Block Exemption Regulation.

Know-how

(42) Franchise agreements, with the exception of industrial franchise agreements, are the most obvious example where know-how for marketing purposes is communicated to the buyer. Franchise agreements contain licences of intellectual property rights relating to trade marks or signs and know-how for the use and distribution of goods or the provision of services. In addition to the licence of IPR, the franchisor usually provides the franchisee during the life of the agreement with commercial or technical assistance, such as procurement services, training, advice on real estate, financial planning, etc. The licence and the assistance are integral components of the business method being franchised.

(43) Licensing contained in franchise agreements is covered by the Block Exemption Regulation if all five conditions listed in point 30 are fulfilled. This is usually the case as under most franchise agreements, including master franchise agreements, the franchisor provides goods and/or services, in particular commercial or technical assistance services, to the franchisee. The IPRs help the franchisee to resell the products supplied by the franchisor or by a supplier designated by the franchisor or to use those products and sell the resulting goods or services. Where the franchise agreement only or primarily concerns licensing of IPRs, such an agreement is not covered by the Block Exemption Regulation, but it will be treated in a way similar to those franchise agreements which are covered by the Block Exemption Regulation.

(44) The following IPR-related obligations are generally considered to be necessary to protect the franchisor's intellectual property rights and are, if these obligations fall under Article 81(1), also covered by the Block Exemption Regulation:

(a) an obligation on the franchisee not to engage, directly or indirectly, in any similar business;

(b) an obligation on the franchisee not to acquire financial interests in the capital of a competing undertaking such as would give the franchisee the power to influence the economic conduct of such undertaking;

(c) an obligation on the franchisee not to disclose to third parties the know-how provided by the franchisor as long as this know-how is not in the public domain;

(d) an obligation on the franchisee to communicate to the franchisor any experience gained in exploiting the franchise and to grant it, and other franchisees, a non-exclusive licence for the know-how resulting from that experience;

(e) an obligation on the franchisee to inform the franchisor of infringements of licensed intellectual property rights, to take legal action against infringers or to assist the franchisor in any legal actions against infringers;

(f) an obligation on the franchisee not to use know-how licensed by the franchisor for purposes other than the exploitation of the franchise;

(g) an obligation on the franchisee not to assign the rights and obligations under the franchise agreement without the franchisor's consent.

(v) Relationship to other block exemption regulations

(45) Article 2(5) states that the Block Exemption Regulation does "not apply to vertical agreements the subject matter of which falls within the scope of any other block exemption regulation". This means that the Block Exemption Regulation does not apply to vertical agreements covered by Commission Regulation (EC) No. 240/96[14] on technology transfer, Commission Regulation (EC) No. 1475/1995[15] for car distribution or Regulations (EC) No. 417/85[16] and (EC) No. 418/85[17] exempting vertical agreements concluded in connection with horizontal agreements, as last amended by Regulation (EC) No. 2236/97[18] or any future regulations of that kind.

3 Hardcore restrictions under the Block Exemption Regulation

(46) The Block Exemption Regulation contains in Article 4 a list of hardcore restrictions which lead to the exclusion of the whole vertical agreement from the scope of application of the Block Exemption Regulation. This list of hardcore restrictions applies to vertical agreements concerning trade within the Community. In so far as vertical agreements concern exports outside the Community or imports/reimports from outside the Community, see the judgment in *Javico v. Yves Saint Laurent*. Individual exemption of vertical agreements containing such hardcore restrictions is also unlikely.

(47) The hardcore restriction set out in Article 4(a) of the Block Exemption Regulation concerns resale price maintenance (RPM), that is agreements or concerted practices having as their direct or indirect object the establishment of a fixed or minimum resale price or a fixed or minimum price level to be observed by the buyer. In the case of contractual provisions or concerted practices that directly establish the resale price, the restriction is clear cut. However, RPM can also be achieved through indirect means. Examples of the latter are an agreement fixing the distribution margin, fixing the maximum level of discount the distributor can grant from a prescribed price level, making the grant of rebates or reimbursement of promotional costs by the supplier subject to the observance of a given price level, linking the prescribed resale prices to the resale prices of competitors, threats, intimidation, warnings, penalties, delay or suspension of deliveries or contract terminations in relation to observance of a given price level. Direct or indirect means of achieving price fixing can be made more effective when combined with measures to identify price-cutting distributors, such as the implementation of a price monitoring system, or the obligation on retailers to report other members of the distribution network who deviate from the standard price level. Similarly, direct or indirect price fixing can be made more effective when combined with measures which may reduce the buyer's incentive to lower the resale price, such as the supplier printing a recommended resale price on the product or the supplier obliging the buyer to apply a most-favoured-customer clause. The same indirect means and the same "supportive" measures can be used to make maximum or recommended prices work as RPM. However, the provision of a list of recommended prices or maximum prices by the supplier to the buyer is not considered in itself as leading to RPM.

(48) In the case of agency agreements, the principal normally establishes the sales price, as the agent does not become the owner of the goods. However, where an agency agreement falls within Article 81(1) (see paragraphs 12 to 20), an obligation preventing or restricting the agent from sharing his commission, fixed or variable, with the customer would be a hardcore restriction under Article 4(a) of the Block Exemption Regulation.

---

[14] OJ 1996 L31/2.
[15] OJ 1995 L145/25.
[16] OJ 1985 L53/1.
[17] OJ 1985 L53/5.
[18] OJ 1997 L306/12.

The agent should thus be left free to lower the effective price paid by the customer without reducing the income for the principal.[19]

(49) The hardcore restriction set out in Article 4(b) of the Block Exemption Regulation concerns agreements or concerted practices that have as their direct or indirect object the restriction of sales by the buyer, in as far as those restrictions relate to the territory into which or the customers to whom the buyer may sell the contract goods or services. That hardcore restriction relates to market partitioning by territory or by customer. That may be the result of direct obligations, such as the obligation not to sell to certain customers or to customers in certain territories or the obligation to refer orders from these customers to other distributors. It may also result from indirect measures aimed at inducing the distributor not to sell to such customers, such as refusal or reduction of bonuses or discounts, refusal to supply, reduction of supplied volumes or limitation of supplied volumes to the demand within the allocated territory or customer group, threat of contract termination or profit pass-over obligations. It may further result from the supplier not providing a Community-wide guarantee service, whereby all distributors are obliged to provide the guarantee service and are reimbursed for this service by the supplier, even in relation to products sold by other distributors into their territory. These practices are even more likely to be viewed as a restriction of the buyer's sales when used in conjunction with the implementation by the supplier of a monitoring system aimed at verifying the effective destination of the supplied goods, e.g. the use of differentiated labels or serial numbers. However, a prohibition imposed on all distributors to sell to certain end users is not classified as a hardcore restriction if there is an objective justification related to the product, such as a general ban on selling dangerous substances to certain customers for reasons of safety or health. It implies that also the supplier himself does not sell to these customers. Nor are obligations on the reseller relating to the display of the supplier's brand name classified as hardcore.

(50) There are four exceptions to the hardcore restriction in Article 4(b) of the Block Exemption Regulation. The first exception allows a supplier to restrict active sales by his direct buyers to a territory or a customer group which has been allocated exclusively to another buyer or which the supplier has reserved to itself. A territory or customer group is exclusively allocated when the supplier agrees to sell his product only to one distributor for distribution in a particular territory or to a particular customer group and the exclusive distributor is protected against active selling into his territory or to his customer group by the supplier and all the other buyers of the supplier inside the Community. The supplier is allowed to combine the allocation of an exclusive territory and an exclusive customer group by for instance appointing an exclusive distributor for a particular customer group in a certain territory. This protection of exclusively allocated territories or customer groups must, however, permit passive sales to such territories or customer groups. For the application of Article 4(b) of the Block Exemption Regulation, the Commission interprets "active" and "passive" sales as follows:

— "Active" sales mean actively approaching individual customers inside another distributor's exclusive territory or exclusive customer group by for instance direct mail or visits; or actively approaching a specific customer group or customers in a specific territory allocated exclusively to another distributor through advertisement in media or other promotions specifically targeted at that customer group or targeted at customers in that territory; or establishing a warehouse or distribution outlet in another distributor's exclusive territory.
— "Passive" sales mean responding to unsolicited requests from individual customers including delivery of goods or services to such customers. General advertising or promotion in media or on the Internet that reaches customers in other distributors' exclusive territories or customer groups but which is a reasonable way to reach

---

[19] See, for instance, Commission Decision 91/562/EEC in Case No. IV/32.737—Eirpage, OJ 1991 L306/22, in particular point (6).

customers outside those territories or customer groups, for instance to reach customers in non-exclusive territories or in one's own territory, are passive sales.

(51) Every distributor must be free to use the Internet to advertise or to sell products. A restriction on the use of the Internet by distributors could only be compatible with the Block Exemption Regulation to the extent that promotion on the Internet or sales over the Internet would lead to active selling into other distributors' exclusive territories or customer groups. In general, the use of the Internet is not considered a form of active sales into such territories or customer groups, since it is a reasonable way to reach every customer. The fact that it may have effects outside one's own territory or customer group results from the technology, i.e. the easy access from everywhere. If a customer visits the website of a distributor and contacts the distributor and if such contact leads to a sale, including delivery, then that is considered passive selling. The language used on the website or in the communication plays normally no role in that respect. In so far as a website is not specifically targeted at customers primarily inside the territory or customer group exclusively allocated to another distributor, for instance with the use of banners or links in pages of providers specifically available to these exclusively allocated customers, the website is not considered a form of active selling. However, unsolicited emails sent to individual customers or specific customer groups are considered active selling. The same considerations apply to selling by catalogue. Notwithstanding what has been said before, the supplier may require quality standards for the use of the Internet site to resell his goods, just as the supplier may require quality standards for a shop or for advertising and promotion in general. The latter may be relevant in particular for selective distribution. An outright ban on Internet or catalogue selling is only possible if there is an objective justification. In any case, the supplier cannot reserve to itself sales and/or advertising over the Internet.

(52) There are three other exceptions to the second hardcore restriction set out in Article 4(b) of the Block Exemption Regulation. All three exceptions allow for the restriction of both active and passive sales. Thus, it is permissible to restrict a wholesaler from selling to end users, to restrict an appointed distributor in a selective distribution system from selling, at any level of trade, to unauthorised distributors in markets where such a system is operated, and to restrict a buyer of components supplied for incorporation from reselling them to competitors of the supplier. The term "component" includes any intermediate goods and the term "incorporation" refers to the use of any input to produce goods.

(53) The hardcore restriction set out in Article 4(c) of the Block Exemption Regulation concerns the restriction of active or passive sales to end users, whether professional end users or final consumers, by members of a selective distribution network. This means that dealers in a selective distribution system, as defined in Article 1(d) of the Block Exemption Regulation, cannot be restricted in the users or purchasing agents acting on behalf of these users to whom they may sell. For instance, also in a selective distribution system the dealer should be free to advertise and sell with the help of the Internet. Selective distribution may be combined with exclusive distribution provided that active and passive selling is not restricted anywhere. The supplier may therefore commit itself to supplying only one dealer or a limited number of dealers in a given territory.

(54) In addition, in the case of selective distribution, restrictions can be imposed on the dealer's ability to determine the location of his business premises. Selected dealers may be prevented from running their business from different premises or from opening a new outlet in a different location. If the dealer's outlet is mobile ("shop on wheels"), an area may be defined outside which the mobile outlet cannot be operated.

(55) The hardcore restriction set out in Article 4(d) of the Block Exemption Regulation concerns the restriction of cross-supplies between appointed distributors within a selective distribution system. This means that an agreement or concerted practice may not have as its direct or indirect object to prevent or restrict the active or passive selling of the contract products between the selected distributors. Selected distributors must remain free to purchase the contract products from other appointed distributors within the network,

operating either at the same or at a different level of trade. This means that selective distribution cannot be combined with vertical restraints aimed at forcing distributors to purchase the contract products exclusively from a given source, for instance exclusive purchasing. It also means that within a selective distribution network no restrictions can be imposed on appointed wholesalers as regards their sales of the product to appointed retailers.

(56) The hardcore restriction set out in Article 4(e) of the Block Exemption Regulation concerns agreements that prevent or restrict end users, independent repairers and service providers from obtaining spare parts directly from the manufacturer of these spare parts. An agreement between a manufacturer of spare parts and a buyer who incorporates these parts into his own products (an original equipment manufacturer, or OEM) may not, either directly or indirectly, prevent or restrict sales by the manufacturer of these spare parts to end users, independent repairers or service providers. Indirect restrictions may arise in particular when the supplier of the spare parts is restricted in supplying technical information and special equipment which are necessary for the use of spare parts by users, independent repairers or service providers. However, the agreement may place restrictions on the supply of the spare parts to the repairers or service providers entrusted by the original equipment manufacturer with the repair or servicing of his own goods. In other words, the OEM may require his own repair and service network to buy the spare parts from it.

4 Conditions under the Block Exemption Regulation

(57) Article 5 of the Block Exemption Regulation excludes certain obligations from the coverage of the Block Exemption Regulation even though the market share threshold is not exceeded. However, the Block Exemption Regulation continues to apply to the remaining part of the vertical agreement if that part is severable from the non-exempted obligations.

(58) The first exclusion is provided in Article 5(a) of the Block Exemption Regulation and concerns non-compete obligations. Non-compete obligations are obligations that require the buyer to purchase from the supplier or from another undertaking designated by the supplier more than 80% of the buyer's total purchases during the previous year of the contract goods and services and their substitutes (see the definition in Article 1(b) of the Block Exemption Regulation), thereby preventing the buyer from purchasing competing goods or services or limiting such purchases to less than 20% of total purchases. Where for the year preceding the conclusion of the contract no relevant purchasing data for the buyer are available, the buyer's best estimate of his annual total requirements may be used. Such non-compete obligations are not covered by the Block Exemption Regulation when their duration is indefinite or exceeds five years. Non-compete obligations that are tacitly renewable beyond a period of five years are also not covered by the Block Exemption Regulation. However, non-compete obligations are covered when their duration is limited to five years or less, or when renewal beyond five years requires explicit consent of both parties and no obstacles exist that hinder the buyer from effectively terminating the non-compete obligation at the end of the five-year period. If for instance the agreement provides for a five-year non-compete obligation and the supplier provides a loan to the buyer, the repayment of that loan should not hinder the buyer from effectively terminating the non-compete obligation at the end of the five-year period; the repayment needs to be structured in equal or decreasing instalments and should not increase over time. This is without prejudice to the possibility, in the case for instance of a new distribution outlet, to delay repayment for the first one or two years until sales have reached a certain level. The buyer must have the possibility to repay the remaining debt where there is still an outstanding debt at the end of the non-compete obligation. Similarly, when the supplier provides the buyer with equipment which is not relationship-specific, the buyer should have the possibility to take over the equipment at its market asset value at the end of the non-compete obligation.

(59) The five-year duration limit does not apply when the goods or services are resold by the buyer "from premises and land owned by the supplier or leased by the supplier from third parties not connected with the buyer". In such cases the non-compete obligation may be of the same duration as the period of occupancy of the point of sale by the buyer (Article 5(a) of the Block Exemption Regulation). The reason for this exception is that it is normally unreasonable to expect a supplier to allow competing products to be sold from premises and land owned by the supplier without his permission. Artificial ownership constructions intended to avoid the five-year limit cannot benefit from this exception.

(60) The second exclusion from the block exemption is provided for in Article 5(b) of the Block Exemption Regulation and concerns post term non-compete obligations. Such obligations are normally not covered by the Block Exemption Regulation, unless the obligation is indispensable to protect know-how transferred by the supplier to the buyer, is limited to the point of sale from which the buyer has operated during the contract period, and is limited to a maximum period of one year. According to the definition in Article 1(f) of the Block Exemption Regulation the know-how needs to be "substantial", meaning "that the know-how includes information which is indispensable to the buyer for the use, sale or resale of the contract goods or services".

(61) The third exclusion from the block exemption is provided for in Article 5(c) of the Block Exemption Regulation and concerns the sale of competing goods in a selective distribution system. The Block Exemption Regulation covers the combination of selective distribution with a non-compete obligation, obliging the dealers not to resell competing brands in general. However, if the supplier prevents his appointed dealers, either directly or indirectly, from buying products for resale from specific competing suppliers, such an obligation cannot enjoy the benefit of the Block Exemption Regulation. The objective of the exclusion of this obligation is to avoid a situation whereby a number of suppliers using the same selective distribution outlets prevent one specific competitor or certain specific competitors from using these outlets to distribute their products (foreclosure of a competing supplier which would be a form of collective boycott).[20]

5 No presumption of illegality outside the Block Exemption Regulation

(62) Vertical agreements falling outside the Block Exemption Regulation will not be presumed to be illegal but may need individual examination. Companies are encouraged to do their own assessment without notification. In the case of an individual examination by the Commission, the latter will bear the burden of proof that the agreement in question infringes Article 81(1). When appreciable anti-competitive effects are demonstrated, undertakings may substantiate efficiency claims and explain why a certain distribution system is likely to bring about benefits which are relevant to the conditions for exemption under Article 81(3).

6 No need for precautionary notification

(63) Pursuant to Article 4(2) of Council Regulation No. 17 of 6 February 1962, First Regulation implementing Articles 81 and 82 of the Treaty,[21] as last amended by Regulation (EC) No. 1216/1999,[22] vertical agreements can benefit from an exemption under Article 81(3) from their date of entry into force, even if notification occurs after that date. This means in practice that no precautionary notification needs to be made. If a dispute arises, an undertaking can still notify, in which case the Commission can exempt the vertical agreement with retroactive effect from the date of entry into force of the

---

[20] An example of indirect measures having such exclusionary effects can be found in Commission Decision 92/428 in Case No. IV/33.542—*Parfum Givenchy* (OJ 1992 L236/11).

[21] OJ 1962 13, 204/62.

[22] OJ 1999 L148/5.

agreement if all four conditions of Article 81(3) are fulfilled. A notifying party does not have to explain why the agreement was not notified earlier and will not be denied retroactive exemption simply because it did not notify earlier. Any notification will be reviewed on its merits. This amendment to Article 4(2) of Regulation No. 17 should eliminate artificial litigation before national courts and thus strengthen the civil enforceability of contracts. It also takes account of the situation where undertakings have not notified because they assumed the agreement was covered by the Block Exemption Regulation.

(64) Since the date of notification no longer limits the possibility of exemption by the Commission, national courts have to assess the likelihood that Article 81(3) will apply in respect of vertical agreements falling within Article 81(1). If such likelihood exists, they should suspend proceedings pending adoption of a position by the Commission. However, national courts may adopt interim measures pending the assessment by the Commission of the applicability of Article 81(3), in the same way as they do when they refer a preliminary question to the Court of Justice under Article 234 of the EC Treaty. No suspension is necessary in respect of injunction proceedings, where national courts themselves are empowered to assess the likelihood of application of Article 81(3).[23]

(65) Unless there is litigation in national courts or complaints, notifications of vertical agreements will not be given priority in the Commission's enforcement policy. Notifications as such do not provide provisional validity for the execution of agreements. Where undertakings have not notified an agreement because they assumed in good faith that the market share threshold under the Block Exemption Regulation was not exceeded, the Commission will not impose fines.

7 Severability

(66) The Block Exemption Regulation exempts vertical agreements on condition that no hardcore restriction, as set out in Article 4, is contained in or practised with the vertical agreement. If there are one or more hardcore restrictions, the benefit of the Block Exemption Regulation is lost for the entire vertical agreement. There is no severability for hardcore restrictions.

(67) The rule of severability does apply, however, to the conditions set out in Article 5 of the Block Exemption Regulation. Therefore, the benefit of the block exemption is only lost in relation to that part of the vertical agreement which does not comply with the conditions set out in Article 5.

8 Portfolio of products distributed through the same distribution system

(68) Where a supplier uses the same distribution agreement to distribute several goods/services some of these may, in view of the market share threshold, be covered by the Block Exemption Regulation while others may not. In that case, the Block Exemption Regulation applies to those goods and services for which the conditions of application are fulfilled.

(69) In respect of the goods or services which are not covered by the Block Exemption Regulation, the ordinary rules of competition apply, which means:

— there is no block exemption but also no presumption of illegality;
— if there is an infringement of Article 81(1) which is not exemptable, consideration may be given to whether there are appropriate remedies to solve the competition problem within the existing distribution system;
— if there are no such appropriate remedies, the supplier concerned will have to make other distribution arrangements.

This situation can also arise where Article 82 applies in respect of some products but not in respect of others.

---

[23] Case C–234/89, *Delimitis v. Henninger Bräu* [1991] ECR I–935 at paragraph 52.

9 Transitional period

(70) The Block Exemption Regulation applies from 1 June 2000. Article 12 of the Block Exemption Regulation provides for a transitional period for vertical agreements already in force before 1 June 2000 which do not satisfy the conditions for exemption provided in the Block Exemption Regulation, but which do satisfy the conditions for exemption under the Block Exemption Regulations which expired on 31 May 2000 (Commission Regulations (EEC) No. 1983/83, (EEC) No. 1984/83 and (EEC) No. 4087/88). The Commission Notice concerning Regulations (EEC) Nos. 1983/83 and 1984/83 also ceases to apply on 31 May 2000. The latter agreements may continue to benefit from these outgoing Regulations until 31 December 2001. Agreements of suppliers with a market share not exceeding 30% who signed with their buyers non-compete agreements with a duration exceeding five years are covered by the Block Exemption Regulation if on 1 January 2002 the non-compete agreements have no more than five years to run.

IV Withdrawal of the Block Exemption and disapplication of the Block Exemption Regulation

1 Withdrawal procedure

(71) The presumption of legality conferred by the Block Exemption Regulation may be withdrawn if a vertical agreement, considered either in isolation or in conjunction with similar agreements enforced by competing suppliers or buyers, comes within the scope of Article 81(1) and does not fulfil all the conditions of Article 81(3). This may occur when a supplier, or a buyer in the case of exclusive supply agreements, holding a market share not exceeding 30%, enters into a vertical agreement which does not give rise to objective advantages such as to compensate for the damage which it causes to competition. This may particularly be the case with respect to the distribution of goods to final consumers, who are often in a much weaker position than professional buyers of intermediate goods. In the case of sales to final consumers, the disadvantages caused by a vertical agreement may have a stronger impact than in a case concerning the sale and purchase of inter-mediate goods. When the conditions of Article 81(3) are not fulfilled, the Commission may withdraw the benefit of the Block Exemption Regulation under Article 6 and establish an infringement of Article 81(1).

(72) Where the withdrawal procedure is applied, the Commission bears the burden of proof that the agreement falls within the scope of Article 81(1) and that the agreement does not fulfil all four conditions of Article 81(3).

(73) The conditions for an exemption under Article 81(3) may in particular not be fulfilled when access to the relevant market or competition therein is significantly restricted by the cumulative effect of parallel networks of similar vertical agreements practised by competing suppliers or buyers. Parallel networks of vertical agreements are to be regarded as similar if they contain restraints producing similar effects on the market. Similar effects will normally occur when vertical restraints practised by competing suppliers or buyers come within one of the four groups listed in paragraphs 104 to 114. Such a situation may arise for example when, on a given market, certain suppliers practise purely qualitative selective distribution while other suppliers practise quantitative selective distribution. In such circumstances, the assessment must take account of the anti-competitive effects attributable to each individual network of agreements. Where appropriate, withdrawal may concern only the quantitative limitations imposed on the number of authorised distributors. Other cases in which a withdrawal decision may be taken include situations where the buyer, for example in the context of exclusive supply or exclusive distribution, has significant market power in the relevant downstream market where he resells the goods or provides the services.

(74) Responsibility for an anti-competitive cumulative effect can only be attributed to those undertakings which make an appreciable contribution to it. Agreements entered into

by undertakings whose contribution to the cumulative effect is insignificant do not fall under the prohibition provided for in Article 81(1)[24] and are therefore not subject to the withdrawal mechanism. The assessment of such a contribution will be made in accordance with the criteria set out in paragraphs 137 to 229.

(75) A withdrawal decision can only have *ex nunc* effect, which means that the exempted status of the agreements concerned will not be affected until the date at which the withdrawal becomes effective.

(76) Under Article 7 of the Block Exemption Regulation, the competent authority of a Member State may withdraw the benefit of the Block Exemption Regulation in respect of vertical agreements whose anti-competitive effects are felt in the territory of the Member State concerned or a part thereof, which has all the characteristics of a distinct geographic market. Where a Member State has not enacted legislation enabling the national competition authority to apply Community competition law or at least to withdraw the benefit of the Block Exemption Regulation, the Member State may ask the Commission to initiate proceedings to this effect.

(77) The Commission has the exclusive power to withdraw the benefit of the Block Exemption Regulation in respect of vertical agreements restricting competition on a relevant geographic market which is wider than the territory of a single Member State. When the territory of a single Member State, or a part thereof, constitutes the relevant geographic market, the Commission and the Member State concerned have concurrent competence for withdrawal. Often, such cases lend themselves to decentralised enforcement by national competition authorities. However, the Commission reserves the right to take on certain cases displaying a particular Community interest, such as cases raising a new point of law.

(78) National decisions of withdrawal must be taken in accordance with the procedures laid down under national law and will only have effect within the territory of the Member State concerned. Such national decisions must not prejudice the uniform application of the Community competition rules and the full effect of the measures adopted in implementation of those rules.[25] Compliance with this principle implies that national competition authorities must carry out their assessment under Article 81 in the light of the relevant criteria developed by the Court of Justice and the Court of First Instance and in the light of notices and previous decisions adopted by the Commission.

(79) The Commission considers that the consultation mechanisms provided for in the Notice on co-operation between national competition authorities and the Commission[26] should be used to avert the risk of conflicting decisions and duplication of procedures.

2 Disapplication of the Block Exemption Regulation

(80) Article 8 of the Block Exemption Regulation enables the Commission to exclude from the scope of the Block Exemption Regulation, by means of regulation, parallel networks of similar vertical restraints where these more than 50% of a relevant market. Such a measure is not addressed to individual undertakings but concerns all undertakings whose agreements are defined in the regulation disapplying the Block Exemption Regulation.

(81) Whereas the withdrawal of the benefit of the Block Exemption Regulation under Article 6 implies the adoption of a decision establishing an infringement of Article 81 by an individual company, the effect of a regulation under Article 8 is merely to remove, in respect of the restraints and the markets concerned, the benefit of the application of the Block Exemption Regulation and to restore the full application of Article 81(1) and (3). Following the adoption of a regulation declaring the Block Exemption inapplicable in respect of certain vertical restraints on a particular market, the criteria developed by the

---

[24] Judgment in the *Delimitis* case.

[25] Judgment of the Court of Justice in Case 14/68, *Walt Wilhelm v. Bundeskartellamt* [1969] ECR 1, paragraph 4, and judgment in *Delimitis*.

[26] OJ 1997 C313/3, points 49 to 53.

relevant case law of the Court of Justice and the Court of First Instance and by notices and previous decisions adopted by the Commission will guide the application of Article 81 to individual agreements. Where appropriate, the Commission will take a decision in an individual case, which can provide guidance to all the undertakings operating on the market concerned.

(82) For the purpose of calculating the 50% market coverage ratio, account must be taken of each individual network of vertical agreements containing restraints, or combinations of restraints, producing similar effects on the market. Similar effects normally result when the restraints come within one of the four groups listed in paragraphs 104 to 114.

(83) Article 8 does not entail an obligation on the part of the Commission to act where the 50% market-coverage ratio is exceeded. In general, disapplication is appropriate when it is likely that access to the relevant market or competition therein is appreciably restricted. This may occur in particular when parallel networks of selective distribution covering more than 50% of a market make use of selection criteria which are not required by the nature of the relevant goods or discriminate against certain forms of distribution capable of selling such goods.

(84) In assessing the need to apply Article 8, the Commission will consider whether individual withdrawal would be a more appropriate remedy. This may depend, in particular, on the number of competing undertakings contributing to a cumulative effect on a market or the number of affected geographic markets within the Community.

(85) Any regulation adopted under Article 8 must clearly set out its scope. This means, first, that the Commission must define the relevant product and geographic market(s) and, secondly, that it must identify the type of vertical restraint in respect of which the Block Exemption Regulation will no longer apply. As regards the latter aspect, the Commission may modulate the scope of its regulation according to the competition concern which it intends to address. For instance, while all parallel networks of single branding-type arrangements shall be taken into account in view of establishing the 50% market coverage ratio, the Commission may nevertheless restrict the scope of the disapplication regulation only to non-compete obligations exceeding a certain duration. Thus, agreements of a shorter duration or of a less restrictive nature might be left unaffected, in consideration of the lesser degree of foreclosure attributable to such restraints. Similarly, when on a particular market selective distribution is practised in combination with additional restraints such as non-compete or quantity-forcing on the buyer, the disapplication regulation may concern only such additional restraints. Where appropriate, the Commission may also provide guidance by specifying the market share level which, in the specific market context, may be regarded as insufficient to bring about a significant contribution by an individual undertaking to the cumulative effect.

(86) The transitional period of not less than six months that the Commission will have to set under Article 8(2) should allow the undertakings concerned to adapt their agreements to take account of the regulation disapplying the Block Exemption Regulation.

(87) A regulation disapplying the Block Exemption Regulation will not affect the exempted status of the agreements concerned for the period preceding its entry into force.

V Market definition and market share calculation issues

1 Commission Notice on definition of the relevant market

(88) The Commission Notice on definition of the relevant market for the purposes of Community competition law[27] provides guidance on the rules, criteria and evidence which the Commission uses when considering market definition issues. That Notice will not be further explained in these Guidelines and should serve as the basis for market definition

---

[27] OJ 1997 C372/5.

issues. These Guidelines will only deal with specific issues that arise in the context of vertical restraints and that are not dealt with in the general notice on market definition.

2 The relevant market for calculating the 30% market share threshold under the Block Exemption Regulation

(89) Under Article 3 of the Block Exemption Regulation, it is in general the market share of the supplier that is decisive for the application of the block exemption. In the case of vertical agreements concluded between an association of retailers and individual members, the association is the supplier and needs to take into account its market share as a supplier. Only in the case of executive supply as defined in Article 1(c) of the Block Exemption Regulation is it the market share of the buyer, and only that market share, which is decisive of the application of the Block Exemption Regulation.

(90) In order to calculate the market share, it is necessary to determine the relevant market. For this, the relevant product market and the relevant geographic market must be defined. The relevant product market comprises any goods or services which are regarded by the buyer as interchangeable, by reason of their characteristics, prices and intended use. The relevant geographic market comprises the area in which the undertakings concerned are involved in the supply and demand of relevant goods or services, in which the conditions of competition are sufficiently homogeneous, and which can be distinguished from neighbouring geographic areas because, in particular, conditions of competition are appreciably different in those areas.

(91) For the application of the Block Exemption Regulation, the market share of the supplier is his share on the relevant product and geographic market on which he sells to his buyers.[28] In the example given in paragraph 92, this is market A. The product market depends in the first place on substitutability from the buyers' perspective. When the supplied product is used as an input to produce other products and is generally not recognisable in the final product, the product market is normally defined by the direct buyers' preferences. The customers of the buyers will normally not have a strong preference concerning the inputs used by the buyers. Usually the vertical restraints agreed between the supplier and buyer of the input only relate to the sale and purchase of the intermediate product and not to the sale of the resulting product. In the case of distribution of final goods, what are substitutes for the direct buyers will normally be influenced or determined by the preferences of the final consumers. A distributor, as reseller, cannot ignore the preferences of final consumers when he purchases final goods. In addition, at the distribution level the vertical restraints usually concern not only the sale of products between supplier and buyer, but also their resale. As different distribution formats usually compete, markets are in general not defined by the form of distribution that is applied. Where suppliers generally sell a portfolio of products, the entire portfolio may determine the product market when the portfolios and not the individual products are regarded as substitutes by the buyers. As the buyers on market A are professional buyers, the geographic market is usually wider than the market where the product is resold to final consumers. Often, this will lead to the definition of national markets or wider geographic markets.

(92) In the case of exclusive supply, the buyer's market share is his share of all purchases on the relevant purchase market.[29] In the example below, this is also market A.

---

[28] For example, the Dutch market for new replacement truck and bus tyres in the *Michelin* case (Case 322/81 *Nederlandsche Banden-Industrie Michelin v. Commission* [1983] ECR 3461), the various meat markets in the Danish slaughterhouse case: Commission Decision 2000/42/EC in Case No. IV/M.1313—*Danish Crown/Vestjyske Slagterier*, OJ 2000 L20/1.

[29] For an example of purchase markets, see Commission Decision 1999/674/EC in Case No. IV/M.1221—*Rewe/Meinl*, OJ 1999 L274/1.

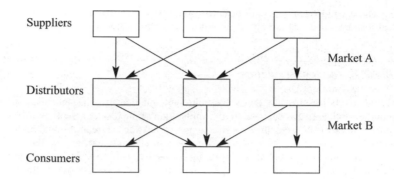

Suppliers

Market A

Distributors

Market B

Consumers

(93) Where a vertical agreement involves three parties, each operating at a different level of trade, their market shares will have to be below the market share threshold of 30% at both levels in order to benefit from the block exemption. If for instance, in an agreement between a manufacturer, a wholesaler (or association of retailers) and a retailer, a non-compete obligation is agreed, then the market share of both the manufacturer and the wholesaler (or association of retailers) must not exceed 30% in order to benefit from the block exemption.

(94) Where a supplier produces both original equipment and the repair or replacement parts for this equipment, the supplier will often be the only or the major supplier on the after-market for the repair and replacement parts. This may also arise where the supplier (OEM supplier) sub-contracts the manufacturing of the repair or replacement parts. The relevant market for application of the Block Exemption Regulation may be the original equipment market including the spare parts or a separate original equipment market and after-market depending on the circumstances of the case, such as the effects of the restrictions involved, the lifetime of the equipment and importance of the repair or replacement costs.[30]

(95) Where the vertical agreement, in addition to the supply of the contract goods, also contains IPR provisions—such as a provision concerning the use of the supplier's trade mark—which help the buyer to market the contract goods, the supplier's market share on the market where he sells the contract goods is decisive for the application of the Block Exemption Regulation. Where a franchisor does not supply goods to be resold but provides a bundle of services combined with IPR provisions which together form the business method being franchised, the franchisor needs to take account of his market share as a provider of a business method. For that purpose, the franchisor needs to calculate his market share on the market where the business method is exploited, which is the market where the franchisees exploit the business method to provide goods or services to end users. The franchisor must base his market share on the value of the goods or services supplied by his franchisees on this market. On such a market the competitors may be providers of other franchised business methods but also suppliers of substitutable goods or services not applying franchising. For instance, without prejudice to the definition of such market, if there was a market for fast-food services, a franchisor operating on such a market would need to calculate his market share on the basis of the relevant sales figures of his franchisees on this market. If the franchisor, in addition to the business method, also supplies certain inputs, such as meat and spices, then the franchisor also needs to calculate his market share on the market where these goods are sold.

---

[30] See for example *Pelikan/Kyocera* in XXV Report on Competition Policy, point 87, and Commission Decision 91/595/EEC in Case No. IV/M.12—*Varta/Bosch*, OJ 1991 L320/26, Commission Decision in Case No. IV/M.1094—*Caterpillar/Perkins Engines*, OJ 1998 C94/28, and Commission Decision in Case No. IV/M.768—*Lucas/Varity*, OJ 1996 C266/6. See also *Eastman Kodak Co v. Image Technical Services Inc.*, Supreme Court of the United States, No. 90 1029. See also point 56 of the Commission Notice on the definition of relevant market for the purposes of Community competition law.

3 The relevant market for individual assessment

(96) For individual assessment of vertical agreements not covered by the Block Exemption Regulation, additional markets may need to be investigated besides the relevant market defined for the application of the Block Exemption Regulation. A vertical agreement may not only have effects on the market between supplier and buyer but may also have effects on downstream markets. For an individual assessment of a vertical agreement the relevant markets at each level of trade affected by restraints contained in the agreement will be examined:

(i) For "intermediate goods or services" that are incorporated by the buyer into his own goods or services, vertical restraints generally have effects only on the market between supplier and buyer. A non-compete obligation imposed on the buyer for instance may foreclose other suppliers but will not lead to reduced in-store competition downstream. However, in cases of exclusive supply the position of the buyer on his downstream market is also relevant because the buyer's foreclosing behaviour may only have appreciable negative effects if he has market power on the downstream market.

(ii) For "final products" an analysis limited to the market between supplier and buyer is less likely to be sufficient since vertical restraints may have negative effects of reduced inter-brand and/or intra-brand competition on the resale market, that is on the market downstream of the buyer. For instance, exclusive distribution may not only lead to foreclosure effects on the market between the supplier and the buyer, but may above all lead to less intra-brand competition in the resale territories of the distributors. The resale market is in particular important if the buyer is a retailer selling to final consumers. A non-compete obligation agreed between a manufacturer and a wholesaler may foreclose this wholesaler to other manufacturers but a loss of in-store competition is not very likely at the wholesale level. The same agreement concluded with a retailer may however cause this added loss of in-store inter-brand competition on the resale market.

(iii) In cases of individual assessment of an "after-market", the relevant market may be the original equipment market or the after-market depending on the circumstances of the case. In any event, the situation on a separate after-market will be evaluated taking account of the situation on the original equipment market. A less significant position on the original equipment market will normally reduce possible anti-competitive effects on the after-market.

4 Calculation of the market share under the Block Exemption Regulation

(97) The calculation of the market share needs to be based in principle on value figures. Where value figures are not available substantiated estimates can be made. Such estimates may be based on other reliable market information such as volume figures (see Article 9(1) of the Block Exemption Regulation).

(98) In-house production, that is production of an intermediate product for own use, may be very important in a competition analysis as one of the competitive constraints or to accentuate the market position of a company. However, for the purpose of market definition and the calculation of market share for intermediate goods and services, in-house production will not be taken into account.

(99) However, in the case of dual distribution of final goods, i.e. where a producer of final goods also acts as a distributor on the market, the market definition and market share calculation need to include the goods sold by the producer and competing producers through their integrated distributors and agents (see Article 9(2)(b) of the Block Exemption Regulation). "Integrated distributors" are connected undertakings within the meaning of Article 11 of the Block Exemption Regulation.

VI Enforcement policy in individual cases

(100) Vertical restraints are generally less harmful than horizontal restraints. The main reason for treating a vertical restraint more leniently than a horizontal restraint lies in the fact that the latter may concern an agreement between competitors producing identical or substitutable goods or services. In such horizontal relationships the exercise of market power by one company (higher price of its product) may benefit its competitors. This may provide an incentive to competitors to induce each other to behave anti-competitively. In vertical relationships the product of the one is the input for the other. This means that the exercise of market power by either the upstream or downstream company would normally hurt the demand for the product of the other. The companies involved in the agreement therefore usually have an incentive to prevent the exercise of market power by the other.

(101) However, this self-restraining character should not be over-estimated. When a company has no market power it can only try to increase its profits by optimising its manufacturing and distribution process, with or without the help of vertical restraints. However, when it does have market power it can also try to increase its profits at the expense of its direct competitors by raising their costs and at the expense of its buyers and ultimately consumers by trying to appropriate some of their surplus. This can happen when the upstream and downstream company share the extra profits or when one of the two uses vertical restraints to appropriate all the extra profits.

(102) In the assessment of individual cases, the Commission will adopt an economic approach in the application of Article 81 to vertical restraints. This will limit the scope of application of Article 81 to undertakings holding a certain degree of market power where inter-brand competition may be insufficient. In those cases, the protection of inter-brand and intra-brand competition is important to ensure efficiencies and benefits for consumers.

1 The framework of analysis

1.1 Negative effects of vertical restraints

(103) The negative effects on the market that may result from vertical restraints which EC competition law aims at preventing are the following:

(i) foreclosure of other suppliers or other buyers by raising barriers to entry;
(ii) reduction of inter-brand competition between the companies operating on a market, including facilitation of collusion amongst suppliers or buyers; by collusion is meant both explicit collusion and tacit collusion (conscious parallel behaviour);
(iii) reduction of intra-brand competition between distributors of the same brand;
(iv) the creation of obstacles to market integration including, above all, limitations on the freedom of consumers to purchase goods or services in any Member State they may choose.

(104) Such negative effects may result from various vertical restraints. Agreements which are different in form may have the same substantive impact on competition. To analyse these possible negative effects, it is appropriate to divide vertical restraints into four groups: a single branding group, a limited distribution group, a resale price maintenance group and a market partitioning group. The vertical restraints within each group have largely similar negative effects on competition.

(105) The classification into four groups is based upon what can be described as the basic components of vertical restraints. In paragraphs 103 to 136, the four different groups are analysed. In 137 to 229, vertical agreements are analysed as they are used in practice because many vertical agreements make use of more than one of these components.

Single branding group

(106) Under the heading of "single branding" come those agreements which have as their main element that the buyer is induced to concentrate his orders for a particular type of product with one supplier. This component can be found amongst others in non-compete and quantity-forcing on the buyer, where an obligation or incentive scheme agreed between the supplier and the buyer makes the latter purchase his requirements for a particular product and its substitutes only, or mainly, from one supplier. The same component can be found in tying, where the obligation or incentive scheme relates to a product that the buyer is required to purchase as a condition of purchasing another distinct product. The first product is referred to as the "tied" product and the second is referred to as the "tying" product.

(107) There are four main negative effects on competition: (1) other suppliers in that market cannot sell to the particular buyers and this may lead to foreclosure of the market or, in the case of tying, to foreclosure of the market for the tied product; (2) it makes market shares more rigid and this may help collusion when applied by several suppliers; (3) as far as the distribution of final goods is concerned, the particular retailers will only sell one brand and there will therefore be no inter-brand competition in their shops (no in-store competition); and (4) in the case of tying, the buyer may pay a higher price for the tied product than he would otherwise do. All these effects may lead to a reduction in inter-brand competition.

(108) The reduction in inter-brand competition may be mitigated by strong initial competition between suppliers to obtain the single branding contracts, but the longer the duration of the non-compete obligation, the more likely it will be that this effect will not be strong enough to compensate for the reduction in inter-brand competition.

Limited distribution group

(109) Under the heading of "limited distribution" come those agreements which have as their main element that the manufacturer sells to only one or a limited number of buyers. This may be to restrict the number of buyers for a particular territory or group of customers, or to select a particular kind of buyer. This component can be found amongst others in:

— exclusive distribution and exclusive customer allocation, where the supplier limits his sales to only one buyer for a certain territory or class of customers;
— exclusive supply and quantity-forcing on the supplier, where an obligation or incentive scheme agreed between the supplier and the buyer makes the former sell only or mainly to one buyer;
— selective distribution, where the conditions imposed on or agreed with the selected dealers usually limit their number;
— after-market sales restrictions which limit the component supplier's sales possibilities.

(110) There are three main negative effects on competition: (1) certain buyers within that market can no longer buy from that particular supplier, and this may lead in particular in the case of exclusive supply to foreclosure of the purchase market, (2) when most or all of the competing suppliers limit the number of retailers, this may facilitate collusion, either at the distributor's level or at the supplier's level, and (3) since fewer distributors will offer the product it will also lead to a reduction of intra-brand competition. In the case of wide exclusive territories or exclusive customer allocation the result may be total elimination of intra-brand competition. This reduction of intra-brand competition can in turn lead to a weakening of inter-brand competition.

Resale price maintenance group

(111) Under the heading "resale price maintenance" (RPM) come those agreements whose main element is that the buyer is obliged or induced to resell not below a certain price, at a certain price or not above a certain price. This group comprises minimum, fixed, maximum and recommended resale prices. Maximum and recommended resale prices, which are not hardcore restrictions, may still lead to a restriction of competition by effect.

(112) There are two main negative effects of RPM on competition: (1) a reduction in intra-brand price competition, and (2) increased transparency on prices. In the case of fixed or minimum RPM, distributors can no longer compete on price for that brand, leading to a total elimination of intra-brand price competition. A maximum or recommended price may work as a focal point for resellers, leading to a more or less uniform application of that price level. Increased transparency on price and responsibility for price changes makes horizontal collusion between manufacturers or distributors easier, at least in concentrated markets. The reduction in intra-brand competition may, as it leads to less downward pressure on the price for the particular goods, have as an indirect effect a reduction of inter-brand competition.

Market partitioning group

(113) Under the heading of "market partitioning" come agreements whose main element is that the buyer is restricted in where he either sources or resells a particular product. This component can be found in exclusive purchasing, where an obligation or incentive scheme agreed between the supplier and the buyer makes the latter purchase his requirements for a particular product, for instance beer of brand X, exclusively from the designated supplier, but leaving the buyer free to buy and sell competing products, for instance competing brands of beer. It also includes territorial resale restrictions, the allocation of an area of primary responsibility, restrictions on the location of a distributor and customer resale restrictions.

(114) The main negative effect on competition is a reduction of intra-brand competition that may help the supplier to partition the market and thus hinder market integration. This may facilitate price discrimination. When most or all of the competing suppliers limit the sourcing or resale possibilities of their buyers this may facilitate collusion, either at the distributors' level or at the suppliers' level.

1.2 Positive effects of vertical restraints

(115) It is important to recognise that vertical restraints often have positive effects by, in particular, promoting non-price competition and improved quality of services. When a company has no market power, it can only try to increase its profits by optimising its manufacturing or distribution processes. In a number of situations vertical restraints may be helpful in this respect since the usual arm's length dealings between supplier and buyer, determining only price and quantity of a certain transaction, can lead to a sub-optimal level of investments and sales.

(116) While trying to give a fair overview of the various justifications for vertical restraints, these Guidelines do not claim to be complete or exhaustive. The following reasons may justify the application of certain vertical restraints:

(1) To "solve a 'free-rider' problem". One distributor may free-ride on the promotion efforts of another distributor. This type of problem is most common at the wholesale and retail level. Exclusive distribution or similar restrictions may be helpful in avoiding such free-riding. Free-riding can also occur between suppliers, for instance where one invests in promotion at the buyer's premises, in general at the retail level,

278

that may also attract customers for its competitors. Non-compete type restraints can help overcome this situation of free-riding.

For there to be a problem, there needs to be a real free-rider issue. Free-riding between buyers can only occur on pre-sales services and not on after-sales services. The product will usually need to be relatively new or technically complex as the customer may otherwise very well know what he or she wants, based on past purchases. And the product must be of a reasonably high value as it is otherwise not attractive for a customer to go to one shop for information and to another to buy. Lastly, it must not be practical for the supplier to impose on all buyers, by contract, effective service requirements concerning pre-sales services.

Free-riding between suppliers is also restricted to specific situations, namely in cases where the promotion takes place at the buyer's premises and is generic, not brand specific.

(2) To "open up or enter new markets". Where a manufacturer wants to enter a new geographic market, for instance by exporting to another country for the first time, this may involve special "first time investments" by the distributor to establish the brand in the market. In order to persuade a local distributor to make these investments it may be necessary to provide territorial protection to the distributor so that he can recoup these investments by temporarily charging a higher price. Distributors based in other markets should then be restrained for a limited period from selling in the new market. This is a special case of the free-rider problem described under point (1).

(3) The "certification free-rider issue". In some sectors, certain retailers have a reputation for stocking only "quality" products. In such a case, selling through these retailers may be vital for the introduction of a new product. If the manufacturer cannot initially limit his sales to the premium stores, he runs the risk of being de-listed and the product introduction may fail. This means that there may be a reason for allowing for a limited duration a restriction such as exclusive distribution or selective distribution. It must be enough to guarantee introduction of the new product but not so long as to hinder large-scale dissemination. Such benefits are more likely with "experience" goods or complex goods that represent a relatively large purchase for the final consumer.

(4) The so-called "hold-up problem". Sometimes there are client-specific investments to be made by either the supplier or the buyer, such as in special equipment or training. For instance, a component manufacturer that has to build new machines and tools in order to satisfy a particular requirement of one of his customers. The investor may not commit the necessary investments before particular supply arrangements are fixed.

However, as in the other free-riding examples, there are a number of conditions that have to be met before the risk of under-investment is real or significant. Firstly, the investment must be relationship-specific. An investment made by the supplier is considered to be relationship-specific when, after termination of the contract, it cannot be used by the supplier to supply other customers and can only be sold at a significant loss. An investment made by the buyer is considered to be relationship-specific when, after termination of the contract, it cannot be used by the buyer to purchase and/or use products supplied by other suppliers and can only be sold at a significant loss. An investment is thus relationship-specific because for instance it can only be used to produce a brand-specific component or to store a particular brand and thus cannot be used profitably to produce or resell alternatives. Secondly, it must be a long-term investment that is not recouped in the short run. And thirdly, the investment must be asymmetric, i.e. one party to the contract invests more than the other party. When these conditions are met, there is usually a good reason to have a vertical restraint for the duration it takes to depreciate the investment. The appropriate vertical restraint will be of the non-compete type or quantity-forcing type when the investment is made by the supplier and of the exclusive distribution, exclusive customer-allocation or exclusive supply type when the investment is made by the buyer.

279

(5) The "specific hold-up problem that may arise in the case of transfer of substantial know-how". The know-how, once provided, cannot be taken back and the provider of the know-how may not want it to be used for or by his competitors. In as far as the know-how was not readily available to the buyer, is substantial and indispensable for the operation of the agreement, such a transfer may justify a non-compete type of restriction. This would normally fall outside Article 81(1).

(6) "Economies of scale in distribution". In order to have scale economies exploited and thereby see a lower retail price for his product, the manufacturer may want to concentrate the resale of his products on a limited number of distributors. For this he could use exclusive distribution, quantity forcing in the form of a minimum purchasing requirement, selective distribution containing such a requirement or exclusive purchasing.

(7) "Capital market imperfections". The usual providers of capital (banks, equity markets) may provide capital sub-optimally when they have imperfect information on the quality of the borrower or there is an inadequate basis to secure the loan. The buyer or supplier may have better information and be able, through an exclusive relationship, to obtain extra security for his investment. Where the supplier provides the loan to the buyer this may lead to non-compete or quantity forcing on the buyer. Where the buyer provides the loan to the supplier this may be the reason for having exclusive supply or quantity forcing on the supplier.

(8) "Uniformity and quality standardisation". A vertical restraint may help to increase sales by creating a brand image and thereby increasing the attractiveness of a product to the final consumer by imposing a certain measure of uniformity and quality standardisation on the distributors. This can for instance be found in selective distribution and franchising.

(117) The eight situations mentioned in paragraph 116 make clear that under certain conditions vertical agreements are likely to help realise efficiencies and the development of new markets and that this may offset possible negative effects. The case is in general strongest for vertical restraints of a limited duration which help the introduction of new complex products or protect relationship-specific investments. A vertical restraint is sometimes necessary for as long as the supplier sells his product to the buyer (see in particular the situations described in paragraph 116, points (1), (5), (6) and (8)).

(118) There is a large measure of substitutability between the different vertical restraints. This means that the same inefficiency problem can be solved by different vertical restraints. For instance, economies of scale in distribution may possibly be achieved by using exclusive distribution, selective distribution, quantity forcing or exclusive purchasing. This is important as the negative effects on competition may differ between the various vertical restraints. This plays a role when indispensability is discussed under Article 81(3).

1.3 General rules for the evaluation of vertical restraints

(119) In evaluating vertical restraints from a competition policy perspective, some general rules can be formulated:

(1) For most vertical restrains competition concerns can only arise if there is insufficient inter-brand competition, i.e. if there exists a certain degree of market power at the level of the supplier or the buyer or both. Conceptually, market power is the power to raise price above the competitive level and, at least in the short term, to obtain supra-normal profits. Companies may have market power below the level of market dominance, which is the threshold for the application of Article 82. Where there are many firms competing in an unconcentrated market, it can be assumed that non-hardcore vertical restraints will not have appreciable negative effects. A market is deemed unconcentrated when the HHI index, i.e. the sum of the squares of the individual market shares of all companies in the relevant market, is below 1,000.

(2) Vertical restraints which reduce inter-brand competition are generally more harmful than vertical restraints that reduce intra-brand competition. For instance, non-compete obligations are likely to have more net negative effects than exclusive distribution. The former, by possibly foreclosing the market to other brands, may prevent those brands from reaching the market. The latter, while limiting intra-brand competition, does not prevent goods from reaching the final consumer.

(3) Vertical restraints from the limited distribution group, in the absence of sufficient inter-brand competition, may significantly restrict the choices available to consumers. They are particularly harmful when more efficient distributors or distributors with a different distribution format are foreclosed. This can reduce innovation in distribution and denies consumers the particular service or price-service combination of these distributors.

(4) Exclusive dealing arrangements are generally worse for competition than non-exclusive arrangements. Exclusive dealing makes, by the express language of the contract or its practical effects, one party fulfil all or practically all its requirements from another party. For instance, under a non-compete obligation the buyer purchases only one brand. Quantity forcing, on the other hand, leaves the buyer some scope to purchase competing goods. The degree of foreclosure may therefore be less with quantity forcing.

(5) Vertical restraints agreed for non-branded goods and services are in general less harmful than restraints affecting the distribution of branded goods and services. Branding tends to increase product differentiation and reduce substitutability of the product, leading to a reduced elasticity of demand and an increased possibility to raise price. The distinction between branded and non-branded goods or services will often coincide with the distinction between intermediate goods and services and final goods or services.

Intermediate goods and services are sold to undertakings for use as an input to produce other goods or services and are generally not recognisable in the final goods or services. The buyers of intermediate products are usually well-informed customers, able to assess quality and therefore less reliant on brand and image. Final goods are, directly or indirectly, sold to final consumers who often rely more on brand and image. As distributors (retailers, wholesalers) have to respond to the demand of final consumers, competition may suffer more when distributors are foreclosed from selling one or a number of brands than when buyers of intermediate products are prevented from buying competing products from certain sources of supply.

The undertakings buying intermediate goods or services normally have specialist departments or advisers who monitor developments in the supply market. Because they effect sizeable transactions, search costs are in general not prohibitive. A loss of intra-brand competition is therefore less important at the intermediate level.

(6) In general, a combination of vertical restraints aggravates their negative effects. However, certain combinations of vertical restraints are better for competition than their use in isolation from each other. For instance, in an exclusive distribution system, the distributor may be tempted to increase the price of the products as intra-brand competition has been reduced. The use of quantity forcing or the setting of a maximum resale price may limit such price increases.

(7) Possible negative effects of vertical restraints are reinforced when several suppliers and their buyers organise their trade in a similar way. These so-called cumulative effects may be a problem in a number of sectors.

(8) The more the vertical restraint is linked to the transfer of know-how, the more reason there may be to expect efficiencies to arise and the more a vertical restraint may be necessary to protect the know-how transferred or the investment costs incurred.

(9) The more the vertical restraint is linked to investments which are relationship-specific, the more justification there is for certain vertical restraints. The justified duration will depend on the time necessary to depreciate the investment.

(10) In the case of a new product, or where an existing product is sold for the first time on a different geographic market, it may be difficult for the company to define the

market or its market share may be very high. However, this should not be considered a major problem, as vertical restraints linked to opening up new product or geographic markets in general do not restrict competition. This rule holds, irrespective of the market share of the company, for two years after the first putting on the market of the product. It applies to all non-hardcore vertical restraints and, in the case of a new geographic market, to restrictions on active and passive sales imposed on the direct buyers of the supplier located in other markets to intermediaries in the new market. In the case of genuine testing of a new product in a limited territory or with a limited customer group, the distributors appointed to sell the new product on the test market can be restricted in their active selling outside the test market for a maximum period of 1 year without being caught by Article 81(1).

1.4 Methodology of analysis

(120) The assessment of a vertical restraint involves in general the following four steps:

(1) First, the undertakings involved need to define the relevant market in order to establish the market share of the supplier or the buyer, depending on the vertical restraint involved (see paragraphs 88 to 99, in particular 89 to 95).
(2) If the relevant market share does not exceed the 30% threshold, the vertical agreement is covered by the Block Exemption Regulation, subject to the hardcore restrictions and conditions set out in that regulation.
(3) If the relevant market share is above the 30% threshold, it is necessary to assess whether the vertical agreement falls within Article 81(1).
(4) If the vertical agreement falls within Article 81(1), it is necessary to examine whether it fulfils the conditions for exemption under Article 81(3).

1.4.1 Relevant factors for the assessment under Article 81(1)

(121) In assessing cases above the market share threshold of 30%, the Commission will make a full competition analysis. The following factors are the most important to establish whether a vertical agreement brings about an appreciable restriction of competition under Article 81(1):

(a) market position of the supplier;
(b) market position of competitors;
(c) market position of the buyer;
(d) entry barriers;
(e) maturity of the market;
(f) level of trade;
(g) nature of the product;
(h) other factors.

(122) The importance of individual factors may vary from case to case and depends on all other factors. For instance, a high market share of the supplier is usually a good indicator of market power, but in the case of low entry barriers it may not indicate market power. It is therefore not possible to provide strict rules on the importance of the individual factors. However the following can be said:

Market position of the supplier

(123) The market position of the supplier is established first and foremost by his market share on the relevant product and geographic market. The higher his market share, the greater his market power is likely to be. The market position of the supplier is further

strengthened if he has certain cost advantages over his competitors. These competitive advantages may result from a first mover advantage (having the best site, etc.), holding essential patents, having superior technology, being the brand leader or having a superior portfolio.

Market position of competitors

(124) The same indicators, that is market share and possible competitive advantages, are used to describe the market position of competitors. The stronger the established competitors are and the greater their number, the less risk there is that the supplier or buyer in question will be able to foreclose the market individually and the less there is a risk of a reduction of inter-brand competition. However, if the number of competitors becomes rather small and their market position (size, costs, R & D potential, etc.) is rather similar, this market structure may increase the risk of collusion. Fluctuating or rapidly changing market shares are in general an indication of intense competition.

Market position of the buyer

(125) Buying power derives from the market position of the buyer. The first indicator of buying power is the market share of the buyer on the purchase market. This share reflects the importance of his demand for his possible suppliers. Other indicators focus on the market position of the buyer on his resale market including characteristics such as a wide geographic spread of his outlets, own brands of the buyer/distributor and his image amongst final consumers. The effect of buying power on the likelihood of anti-competitive effects is not the same for the different vertical restraints. Buying power may in particular increase the negative effects in case of restraints from the limited distribution and market partitioning groups such as exclusive supply, exclusive distribution and quantitative selective distribution.

Entry barriers

(126) Entry barriers are measured by the extent to which incumbent companies can increase their price above the competitive level, usually above minimum average total cost, and make supra-normal profits without attracting entry. Without any entry barriers, easy and quick entry would eliminate such profits. In as far as effective entry, which would prevent or erode the supra-normal profits, is likely to occur within one or two years, entry barriers can be said to be low.

(127) Entry barriers may result from a wide variety of factors such as economies of scale and scope, government regulations, especially where they establish exclusive rights, state aid, import tariffs, intellectual property rights, ownership of resources where the supply is limited, due to for instance natural limitations,[31] essential facilities, a first mover advantage and brand loyalty of consumers created by strong advertising. Vertical restraints and vertical integration may also work as an entry barrier by making access more difficult and foreclosing (potential) competitors. Entry barriers may be present at only the supplier or buyer level or at both levels.

(128) The question whether certain of these factors should be described as entry barriers depends on whether they are related to sunk costs. Sunk costs are those costs that have to be incurred to enter or be active on a market but that are lost when the market is exited. Advertising costs to build consumer loyalty are normally sunk costs, unless an exiting firm could either sell its brand name or use it somewhere else without a loss. The more costs are sunk, the more potential entrants have to weigh the risks of entering the

---

[31] See Commission Decision 97/26/EC (Case No. IV/M.619—*Gencor/Lonrho*), OJ 1997 L11/30.

market and the more credibly incumbents can threaten that they will match new competition, as sunk costs make it costly for incumbents to leave the market. If, for instance, distributors are tied to a manufacturer via a non-compete obligation, the foreclosing effect will be more significant if setting up its own distributors will impose sunk costs on the potential entrant.

(129) In general, entry requires sunk costs, sometimes minor and sometimes major. Therefore, actual competition is in general more effective and will weigh more in the assessment of a case than potential competition.

Maturity of the market

(130) A mature market is a market that has existed for some time, where the technology used is well known and widespread and not changing very much, where there are no major brand innovations and in which demand is relatively stable or declining. In such a market negative effects are more likely than in more dynamic markets.

Level of trade

(131) The level of trade is linked to the distinction between intermediate and final goods and services. As indicated earlier, negative effects are in general less likely at the level of intermediate goods and services.

Nature of the product

(132) The nature of the product plays a role in particular for final products in assessing both the likely negative and the likely positive effects. When assessing the likely negative effects, it is important whether the products on the market are more homogeneous or heterogeneous, whether the product is expensive, taking up a large part of the consumer's budget, or is inexpensive and whether the product is a one-off purchase or repeatedly purchased. In general, when the product is more heterogeneous, less expensive and resembles more a one-off purchase, vertical restraints are more likely to have negative effects.

Other factors

(133) In the assessment of particular restraints other factors may have to be taken into account. Among these factors can be the cumulative effect, i.e. the coverage of the market by similar agreements, the duration of the agreements, whether the agreement is "imposed" (mainly one party is subject to the restrictions or obligations) or "agreed" (both parties accept restrictions or obligations), the regulatory environment and behaviour that may indicate or facilitate collusion like price leadership, pre-announced price changes and discussions on the "right" price, price rigidity in response to excess capacity, price discrimination and past collusive behaviour.

1.4.2 Relevant factors for the assessment under Article 81(3)

(134) There are four cumulative conditions for the application of Article 81(3):

— the vertical agreement must contribute to improving production or distribution or to promoting technical or economic progress;
— the vertical agreement must allow consumers a fair share of these benefits;
— the vertical agreement must not impose on the undertakings concerned vertical restraints which are not indispensable to the attainment of these benefits;

— the vertical agreement must not afford such undertakings the possibility of eliminating competition in respect of a substantial part of the products in question.

(135) The last criterion of elimination of competition for a substantial part of the products in question is related to the question of dominance. Where an undertaking is dominant or becoming dominant as a consequence of the vertical agreement, a vertical restraint that has appreciable anti-competitive effects can in principle not be exempted. The vertical agreement may however fall outside Article 81(1) if there is an objective justification, for instance if it is necessary for the protection of relationship-specific investments or for the transfer of substantial know-how without which the supply or purchase of certain goods or services would not take place.

(136) Where the supplier and the buyer are not dominant, the other three criteria become important. The first, concerning the improvement of production or distribution and the promotion of technical or economic progress, refers to the type of efficiencies described in paragraphs 115 to 118. These efficiencies have to be substantiated and must produce a net positive effect. Speculative claims on avoidance of free-riding or general statements on cost savings will not be accepted. Cost savings that arise from the mere exercise of market power or from anti-competitive conduct cannot be accepted. Secondly, economic benefits have to favour not only the parties to the agreement, but also the consumer. Generally the transmission of the benefits to consumers will depend on the intensity of competition on the relevant market. Competitive pressures will normally ensure that cost savings are passed on by way of lower prices or that companies have an incentive to bring new products to the market as quickly as possible. Therefore, if sufficient competition which effectively constrains the parties to the agreement is maintained on the market, the competitive process will normally ensure that consumers receive a fair share of the economic benefits. The third criterion will play a role in ensuring that the least anti-competitive restraint is chosen to obtain certain positive effects.

2 Analysis of specific vertical restraints

(137) Vertical agreements may contain a combination of two or more of the components of vertical restraints described in paragraphs 103 to 114. The most common vertical restraints and combinations of vertical restrains are analysed below following the methodology of analysis developed in paragraphs 120 to 136.

2.1 Single branding

(138) A non-compete arrangement is based on an obligation or incentive scheme which makes the buyer purchase practically all his requirements on a particular market from only one supplier. It does not mean that the buyer can only buy directly from the supplier, but that the buyer will not buy and resell or incorporate competing goods or services. The possible competition risks are foreclosure of the market to competing suppliers and potential suppliers, facilitation of collusion between suppliers in case of cumulative use and, where the buyer is a retailer selling to final consumers, a loss of in-store inter-brand competition. All three restrictive effects have a direct impact on inter-brand competition.

(139) Single branding is exempted by the Block Exemption Regulation when the supplier's market share does not exceed 30% and subject to a limitation in time of five years for the non-compete obligation. Above the market share threshold or beyond the time limit of five years, the following guidance is provided for the assessment of individual cases.

(140) The "market position of the supplier" is of main importance to assess possible anti-competitive effects of non-compete obligations. In general, this type of obligation is imposed by the supplier and the supplier has similar agreements with other buyers.

(141) It is not only the market position of the supplier that is of importance but also the extent to and the duration for which he applies a non-compete obligation. The higher his

tied market share, i.e. the part of his market share sold under a single branding obligation, the more significant foreclosure is likely to be. Similarly, the longer the duration of the non-compete obligations, the more significant foreclosure is likely to be. Non-compete obligations shorter than one year entered into by non-dominant companies are in general not considered to give rise to appreciable anti-competitive effects or net negative effects. Non-compete obligations between one and five years entered into by non-dominant companies usually require a proper balancing of pro- and anti-competitive effects, while non-compete obligations exceeding five years are for most types of investment not considered necessary to achieve the claimed efficiencies or the efficiencies are not sufficient to outweigh their foreclosure effect. Dominant companies may not impose non-compete obligations on their buyers unless they can objectively justify such commercial practice within the context of Article 82.

(142) In assessing the supplier's market power, the "market position of his competitors" is important. As long as the competitors are sufficiently numerous and strong, no appreciable anti-competitive effects can be expected. It is only likely that competing suppliers will be foreclosed if they are significantly smaller than the supplier applying the non-compete obligation. Foreclosure of competitors is not very likely where they have similar market positions and can offer similarly attractive products. In such a case foreclosure may however occur for potential entrants when a number of major suppliers enter into non-compete contracts with a significant number of buyers on the relevant market (cumulative effect situation). This is also a situation where non-compete agreements may facilitate collusion between competing suppliers. If individually these suppliers are covered by the Block Exemption Regulation, a withdrawal of the block exemption may be necessary to deal with such a negative cumulative effect. A tied market share of less than 5% is not considered in general to contribute significantly to a cumulative foreclosure effect.

(143) In cases where the market share of the largest supplier is below 30% and the market share of the five largest suppliers (concentration rate (CR) 5) is below 50%, there is unlikely to be a single or a cumulative anti-competitive effect situation. If a potential entrant cannot penetrate the market profitably, this is likely to be due to factors other than non-compete obligations, such as consumer preferences. A competition problem is unlikely to arise when, for instance, 50 companies, of which none has an important market share, compete fiercely on a particular market.

(144) "Entry barriers" are important to establish whether there is real foreclosure. Wherever it is relatively easy for competing suppliers to create new buyers or find alternative buyers for the product, foreclosure is unlikely to be a real problem. However, there are often entry barriers, both at the manufacturing and at the distribution level.

(145) "Countervailing power" is relevant, as powerful buyers will not easily allow themselves to be cut off from the supply of competing goods or services. Foreclosure which is not based on efficiency and which has harmful effects on ultimate consumers is therefore mainly a risk in the case of dispersed buyers. However, where non-compete agreements are concluded with major buyers this may have a strong foreclosure effect.

(146) Lastly, "the level of trade" is relevant for foreclosure. Foreclosure is less likely in case of an intermediate product. When the supplier of an intermediate product is not dominant, the competing suppliers still have a substantial part of demand that is "free". Below the level of dominance a serious foreclosure effect may however arise for actual or potential competitors where there is a cumulative effect. A serious cumulative effect is unlikely to arise as long as less than 50% of the market is tied. When the supplier is dominant, any obligation to buy the products only or mainly from the dominant supplier may easily lead to significant foreclosure effects on the market. The stronger his dominance, the higher the risk of foreclosure of other competitors.

(147) Where the agreement concerns supply of a final product at the wholesale level, the question whether a competition problem is likely to arise below the level of dominance depends in large part on the type of wholesaling and the entry barriers at the wholesale level. There is no real risk of foreclosure if competing manufacturers can easily establish their own wholesaling operation. Whether entry barriers are low depend in part on the type

of wholesaling, i.e. whether or not wholesalers can operate efficiently with only the product concerned by the agreement (for example ice cream) or whether it is more efficient to trade in a whole range of products (for example frozen foodstuffs). In the latter case, it is not efficient for a manufacturer selling only one product to set up his own wholesaling operation. In that case anti-competitive effects may arise below the level of dominance. In addition, cumulative effect problems may arise if several suppliers tie most of the available wholesalers.

(148) For final products, foreclosure is in general more likely to occur at the retail level, given the significant entry barriers for most manufacturers to start retail outlets just for their own products. In addition, it is at the retail level that non-compete agreements may lead to reduced in-store inter-brand competition. It is for these reasons that for final products at the retail level, significant anti-competitive effects may start to arise, taking into account all other relevant factors, if a non-dominant supplier ties 30% or more of the relevant market. For a dominant company, even a modest tied market share may already lead to significant anti-competitive effects. The stronger its dominance, the higher the risk of foreclosure of other competitors.

(149) At the retail level a cumulative foreclosure effect may also arise. When all companies have market shares below 30% a cumulative foreclosure effect is unlikely if the total tied market share is less than 40% and withdrawal of the block exemption is therefore unlikely. This figure may be higher when other factors like the number of competitors, entry barriers, etc. are taken into account. When not all companies have market shares below the threshold of the Block Exemption Regulation but none is dominant, a cumulative foreclosure effect is unlikely if the total tied market share is below 30%.

(150) Where the buyer operates from premises and land owned by the supplier or leased by the supplier from a third party not connected with the buyer, the possibility of imposing effective remedies for a possible foreclosure effect will be limited. In that case intervention by the Commission below the level of dominance is unlikely.

(151) In certain sectors the selling of more than one brand from a single site may be difficult, in which case a foreclosure problem can better be remedied by limiting the effective duration of contracts.

(152) A so-called "English clause", requiring the buyer to report any better offer and allowing him only to accept such an offer when the supplier does not match it, can be expected to have the same effect as a non-compete obligation, especially when the buyer has to reveal who makes the better offer. In addition, by increasing the transparency of the market it may facilitate collusion between the suppliers. An English clause may also work as quantity-forcing. Quantity-forcing on the buyer is a weaker form of non-compete, where incentives or obligations agreed between the supplier and the buyer make the latter concentrate his purchases to a large extent with one supplier. Quantity-forcing may for example take the form of minimum purchase requirements or non-linear pricing, such as quantity rebate schemes, loyalty rebate schemes or a two-part tariff (fixed fee plus a price per unit). Quantity-forcing on the buyer will have similar but weaker foreclosure effects than a non-compete obligation. The assessment of all these different forms will depend on their effect on the market. In addition, Article 82 specifically prevents dominant companies from applying English clauses or fidelity rebate schemes.

(153) Where appreciable anti-competitive effects are established, the question of a possible exemption under Article 81(3) arises as long as the supplier is not dominant. For non-compete obligations, the efficiencies described in paragraph 116, points 1 (free riding between suppliers), 4, 5 (hold-up problems) and 7 (capital market imperfections) may be particularly relevant.

(154) In the case of an efficiency as described in paragraph 116, points 1, 4 and 7, quantity forcing on the buyer could possibly be a less restrictive alternative. A non-compete obligation may be the only viable way to achieve an efficiency as described in paragraph 116, point 5 (hold-up problem related to the transfer of know-how).

(155) In the case of a relationship-specific investment made by the supplier (see efficiency 4 in paragraph 116), a non-compete or quantity forcing agreement for the period

of depreciation of the investment will in general fulfil the conditions of Article 81(3). In the case of high relationship-specific investments, a non-compete obligation exceeding five years may be justified. A relationship-specific investment could, for instance, be the installation or adaptation of equipment by the supplier when this equipment can be used afterwards only to produce components for a particular buyer. General or market-specific investments in (extra) capacity are normally not relationship-specific investments. However, where a supplier creates new capacity specifically linked to the operations of a particular buyer, for instance a company producing metal cans which creates new capacity to produce cans on the premises of or next to the canning facility of a food producer, this new capacity may only be economically viable when producing for this particular customer, in which case the investment would be considered to be relationship-specific.

(156) Where the supplier provides the buyer with a loan or provides the buyer with equipment which is not relationship-specific, this in itself is normally not sufficient to justify the exemption of a foreclosure effect on the market. The instance of capital market imperfection, whereby it is more efficient for the supplier of a product than for a bank to provide a loan, will be limited (see efficiency 7 in paragraph 116). Even if the supplier of the product were to be the more efficient provider of capital, a loan could only justify a non-compete obligation if the buyer is not prevented from terminating the non-compete obligation and repaying the outstanding part of the loan at any point in time and without payment of any penalty. This means that the repayment of the loan should be structured in equal or decreasing instalments and should not increase over time and that the buyer should have the possibility to take over the equipment provided by the supplier at its market asset value. This is without prejudice to the possibility, in case for example of a new point of distribution, to delay repayment for the first one or two years until sales have reached a certain level.

(157) The transfer of substantial know-how (efficiency 5 in paragraph 116) usually justifies a non-compete obligation for the whole duration of the supply agreement, as for example in the context of franchising.

(158) Below the level of dominance the combination of non-compete with exclusive distribution may also justify the non-compete obligation lasting the full length of the agreement. In the latter case, the non-compete obligation is likely to improve the distribution efforts of the exclusive distributor in his territory (see paragraphs 161 to 177).

(159) Example of non-compete

The market leader in a national market for an impulse consumer product, with a market share of 40%, sells most of its products (90%) through tied retailers (tied market share 36%). The agreements oblige the retailers to purchase only from the market leader for at least four years. The market leader is especially strongly represented in the more densely populated areas like the capital. Its competitors, 10 in number, of which some are only locally available, all have much smaller market shares, the biggest having 12%. These 10 competitors together supply another 10% of the market via tied outlets. There is strong brand and product differentiation in the market. The market leader has the strongest brands. It is the only one with regular national advertising campaigns. It provides its tied retailers with special stocking cabinets for its product.

The result on the market is that in total 46% (36% + 10%) of the market is foreclosed to potential entrants and to incumbents not having tied outlets. Potential entrants find entry even more difficult in the densely populated areas where foreclosure is even higher, although it is there that they would prefer to enter the market. In addition, owing to the strong band and product differentiation and the high search costs relative to the price of the product, the absence of in-store inter-brand competition leads to an extra welfare loss for consumers. The possible efficiencies of the outlet exclusivity, which the market leader claims result from reduced transport costs and a possible hold-up problem concerning the stocking cabinets, are limited and do not outweigh the negative effects on competition. The efficiencies are limited, as the transport costs are linked to quantity and not exclusivity and the stocking cabinets do not contain special know-how and are not brand specific. Accordingly, it is unlikely that the conditions for exemption are fulfilled.

(160) Example of quantity forcing

A product X with a 40% market share sells 80% of its products through contracts which specify that the reseller is required to purchase at least 75% of its requirements for that type of product from X. In return X is offering financing and equipment at favourable rates. The contracts have a duration of five years in which repayment of the loan is foreseen in equal instalments. However, after the first two years buyers have the possibility to terminate the contract with a six-month notice period if they repay the outstanding loan and take over the equipment at its market asset value. At the end of the five-year period the equipment becomes the property of the buyer. Most of the competing producers are small, twelve in total, with the biggest having a market share of 20%, and engage in similar contracts with different durations. The producers with market shares below 10% often have contracts with longer durations and with less generous termination clauses. The contracts of producer X leave 25% of requirements free to be supplied by competitors. In the last three years, two new producers have entered the market and gained a combined market share of around 8%, partly by taking over the loans of a number of resellers in return for contracts with these resellers.

Producer X's tied market share is 24% ($0.75 \times 0.80 \times 40\%$). The other producer's tied market share is around 25%. Therefore, in total around 49% of the market is foreclosed to potential entrants and to incumbents not having tied outlets for at least the first two years of the supply contracts. The market shows that the resellers often have difficulty in obtaining loans from banks and are too small in general to obtain capital through other means like the issuing of shares. In addition, producer X is able to demonstrate that concentrating his sales on a limited number of resellers allows him to plan his sales better and to save transport costs. In the light of the 25% non-tied part in the contracts of producer X, the real possibility for early termination of the contract, the recent entry of new producers and the fact that around half the resellers are not tied, the quantity forcing of 75% applied by producer X is likely to fulfil the conditions for exemption.

2.2 Exclusive distribution

(161) In an exclusive distribution agreement the supplier agrees to sell his products only to one distributor for resale in a particular territory. At the same time the distributor is usually limited in his active selling into other exclusively allocated territories. The possible competition risks are mainly reduced intra-brand competition and market partitioning, which may in particular facilitate price discrimination. When most or all of the suppliers apply exclusive distribution this may facilitate collusion, both at the suppliers' and distributors' level.

(162) Exclusive distribution is exempted by the Block Exemption Regulation when the supplier's market share does not exceed 30%, even if combined with other non-hardcore vertical restraints, such as a non-compete obligation limited to five years, quantity forcing or exclusive purchasing. A combination of exclusive distribution and selective distribution is only exempted by the Block Exemption Regulation if active selling in other territories is not restricted. Above the 30% market share threshold, the following guidance is provided for the assessment of exclusive distribution in individual cases.

(163) The market position of the supplier and his competitors is of major importance, as the loss of intra-brand competition can only be problematic if inter-brand competition is limited. The stronger the "position of the supplier", the more serious is the loss of intra-brand competition. Above the 30% market share threshold there may be a risk of a significant reduction of intra-brand competition. In order to be exemptable, the loss of intra-brand competition needs to be balanced with real efficiencies.

(164) The "position of the competitors" can have a dual significance. Strong competitors will generally mean that the reduction in intra-brand competition is out-weighed by sufficient inter-brand competition. However, if the number of competitors becomes rather small and their market position is rather similar in terms of market share, capacity and distribution network, there is a risk of collusion. The loss of intra-brand competition can increase this risk, especially when several suppliers operate similar distribution systems. Multiple exclusive dealerships, i.e. when different suppliers appoint the same

exclusive distributor in a given territory, may further increase the risk of collusion. If a dealer is granted the exclusive right to distribute two or more important competing products in the same territory, inter-brand competition is likely to be substantially restricted for those brands. The higher the cumulative market share of the brands distributed by the multiple dealer, the higher the risk of collusion and the more inter-brand competition will be reduced. Such cumulative effect situations may be a reason to withdraw the benefit of the Block Exemption Regulation when the market shares of the suppliers are below the threshold of the Block Exemption Regulation.

(165) "Entry barriers" that may hinder suppliers from creating new distributors of finding alternative distributors are less important in assessing the possible anti-competitive effects of exclusive distribution. Foreclosure of other suppliers does not arise as long as exclusive distribution is not combined with single branding.

(166) Foreclosure of other distributors is not a problem if the supplier which operates the exclusive distribution system appoints a high number of exclusive distributors in the same market and these exclusive distributors are not restricted in selling to other non-appointed distributors. Foreclosure of other distributors may however become a problem where there is "buying power" and market power downstream, in particular in the case of very large territories where the exclusive distributor becomes the exclusive buyer for a whole market. An example would be a supermarket chain which becomes the only distributor of a leading brand on a national food retail market. The foreclosure of other distributors may be aggravated in the case of multiple exclusive dealership. Such a case, covered by the Block Exemption Regulation when the market share of each supplier is below 30%, may give reason for withdrawal of the block exemption.

(167) "Buying power" may also increase the risk of collusion on the buyers' side when the exclusive distribution arrangements are imposed by important buyers, possibly located in different territories, on one or several suppliers.

(168) "Maturity of the market" is important, as loss of intra-brand competition and price discrimination may be a serious problem in a mature market but may be less relevant in a market with growing demand, changing technologies and changing market positions.

(169) "The level of trade" is important as the possible negative effects may differ between the wholesale and retail level. Exclusive distribution is mainly applied in the distribution of final goods and services. A loss of intra-brand competition is especially likely at the retail level if coupled with large territories, since final consumers may be confronted with little possibility of choosing between a high price/high service and a low price/low service distributor for an important brand.

(170) A manufacturer which chooses a wholesaler to be his exclusive distributor will normally do so for a larger territory, such as a whole Member State. As long as the wholesaler can sell the products without limitation to downstream retailers there are not likely to be appreciable anti-competitive effects if the manufacturer is not dominant. A possible loss of intra-brand competition at the wholesale level may be easily outweighed by efficiencies obtained in logistics, promotion, etc., especially when the manufacturer is based in a different country. Foreclosure of other wholesalers within that territory is not likely as a supplier with a market share above 30% usually has enough bargaining power not to choose a less efficient wholesaler. The possible risks for inter-brand competition of multiple exclusive dealerships are however higher at the wholesale than at the retail level.

(171) The combination of exclusive distribution with single branding may add the problem of foreclosure of the market to other suppliers, especially in case of a dense network of exclusive distributors with small territories or in case of a cumulative effect. This may necessitate application of the principles set out above on single branding. However, when the combination does not lead to significant foreclosure, the combination of exclusive distribution and single branding may be pro-competitive by increasing the incentive for the exclusive distributor to focus his efforts on the particular brand. Therefore, in the absence of such a foreclosure effect, the combination of exclusive distribution

with non-compete is exemptable for the whole duration of the agreement, particularly at the wholesale level.

(172) The combination of exclusive distribution with exclusive purchasing increases the possible competition risks of reduced intra-brand competition and market partitioning which may in particular facilitate price discrimination. Exclusive distribution already limits arbitrage by customers, as it limits the number of distributors and usually also restricts the distributors in their freedom of active selling. Exclusive purchasing, requiring the exclusive distributors to buy their supplies for the particular brand directly from the manufacturer, eliminates in addition possible arbitrage by the exclusive distributors, who are prevented from buying from other distributors in the system. This enhances the possibilities for the supplier to limit intra-brand competition while applying dissimilar conditions of sale. The combination of exclusive distribution and exclusive purchasing is therefore unlikely to be exempted for suppliers with a market share above 30% unless there are very clear and substantial efficiencies leading to lower prices to all final consumers. Lack of such efficiencies may also lead to withdrawal of the block exemption where the market share of the supplier is below 30%.

(173) The "nature of the product" is not very relevant to assessing the possible anti-competitive effects of exclusive distribution. It is however, relevant when the issue of possible efficiencies is discussed; that is, after an appreciable anti-competitive effect is established.

(174) Exclusive distribution may lead to efficiencies, especially where investments by the distributors are required to protect or build up the brand image. In general, the case for efficiencies is strongest for new products, for complex products, for products whose qualities are difficult to judge before consumption (so-called experience products) or of which the qualities are difficult to judge even after consumption (so-called credence products). In addition, exclusive distribution may lead to savings in logistic costs due to economies of scale in transport and distribution.

(175) Example of exclusive distribution at the wholesale level:

In the market for a consumer durable, A is the market leader. A sells its product through exclusive wholesalers. Territories for the wholesalers correspond to the entire Member State for small Member States, and to a region for larger Member States. These exclusive distributors take care of sales to all the retailers in their territories. They do not sell to final consumers. The wholesalers are in charge of promotion in their markets. This includes sponsoring of local events, but also explaining and promoting the new products to the retailers in their territories. Technology and product innovation are evolving fairly quickly on this market, and pre-sale service to retailers and to final consumers plays an important role. The wholesalers are not required to purchase all their requirements of the brand of supplier A from the producer himself, and arbitrage by wholesalers or retailers is practicable because the transport costs are relatively low compared to the value of the product. The wholesalers are not under a non-compete obligation. Retailers also sell a number of brands of competing suppliers, and there are no exclusive or selective distribution agreements at the retail level. On the European market of sales to wholesalers A has around 50% market share. Its market share on the various national retail markets varies between 40% and 60%. A has between 6 and 10 competitors on every national market: B, C and D are its biggest competitors and are also present on each national market, with market shares varying between 20% and 5%. The remaining producers are national producers, with smaller market shares. B, C and D have similar distribution networks, whereas the local producers tend to sell their products directly to retailers.

On the wholesale market described above, the risk of reduced intra-brand competition and price discrimination is low. Arbitrage is not hindered, and the absence of intra-brand competition is not very relevant at the wholesale level. At the retail level neither intra- nor inter-brand competition are hindered. Moreover, inter-brand competition is largely unaffected by the exclusive arrangements at the wholesale level. This makes it likely, if anti-competitive effects exist, that the conditions for exemption are fulfilled.

(176) Example of multiple exclusive dealerships in an oligopolistic market:

In a national market for a final product, there are four market leaders, who each have a market share of around 20%. These four market leaders sell their product through exclusive distributors at the retail level. Retailers are given an exclusive territory which corresponds to the town in which they are located or a district of the town for large towns. In most territories, the four market leaders happen to appoint the same exclusive retailer ("multiple dealership"), often centrally located and rather specialised in the product. The remaining 20% of the national market is composed of small local producers, the largest of these producers having a market share of 5% on the national market. These local producers sell their products in general through other retailers, in particular because the exclusive distributors of the four largest suppliers show in general little interest in selling less well-known and cheaper brands. There is strong brand and product differentiation on the market. The four market leaders have large national advertising campaigns and strong brand images, whereas the fringe producers do not advertise their products at the national level. The market is rather mature, with stable demand and no major product and technological innovation. The product is relatively simple.

In such an oligopolistic market, there is a risk of collusion between the four market leaders. This risk is increased through multiple dealerships. Intra-brand competition is limited by the territorial exclusivity. Competition between the four leading brands is reduced at the retail level, since one retailer fixes the price of all four brands in each territory. The multiple dealership implies that, if one producer cuts the price for its brand, the retailer will not be eager to transmit this price cut to the final consumer as it would reduce its sales and profits made with the other brands. Hence, producers have a reduced interest in entering into price competition with one another. Inter-brand price competition exists mainly with the low brand image goods of the fringe producers. The possible efficiency arguments for (joint) exclusive distributors are limited, as the product is relatively simple, the resale does not require any specific investments or training and advertising is mainly carried out at the level of the producers.

Even though each of the market leaders has a market share below the threshold, exemption under Article 81(3) may not be justified and withdrawal of the block exemption may be necessary.

(177) Example of exclusive distribution combined with exclusive purchasing

Manufacturer A is the European market leader for a bulky consumer durable, with a market share of between 40% and 60% in most national retail markets. In every Member State, it has about seven competitors with much smaller market shares, the largest of these competitors having a market share of 10%. These competitors are present on only one or two national markets. A sells its product through its national subsidiaries to exclusive distributors at the retail level, which are not allowed to sell actively into each other's territories. In addition, the retailers are obliged to purchase manufacturer A's products exclusively from the national subsidiary of manufacturer A in their own country. The retailers selling the brand of manufacturer A are the main resellers of that type of product in their territory. They handle competing brands, but with varying degrees of success and enthusiasm. A applies price differences of 10% to 15% between markets and smaller differences within markets. This is translated into smaller price differences at the retail level. The market is relatively stable on the demand and the supply side, and there are no significant technological changes.

In these markets, the loss of intra-brand competition results not only from the territorial exclusivity at the retail level but is aggravated by the exclusive purchasing obligation imposed on the retailers. The exclusive purchase obligation helps to keep markets and territories separate by making arbitrage between the exclusive retailers impossible. The exclusive retailers also cannot sell actively into each other's territory and in practice tend to avoid delivering outside their own territory. This renders price discrimination possible. Arbitrage by consumers or independent traders is limited due to the bulkiness of the product.

The possible efficiency arguments of this system, linked to economies of scale in transport and promotion efforts at the retailers' level, are unlikely to outweigh the negative effect of price discrimination and reduced intra-brand competition. Consequently, it is unlikely that the conditions for exemption are fulfilled.

2.3 Exclusive customer allocation

(178) In an exclusive customer allocation agreement, the supplier agrees to sell its products only to one distributor for resale to a particular class of customers. At the same time, the distributor is usually limited in his active selling to other exclusively allocated classes of customers. The possible competition risks are mainly reduced intra-brand competition and market partitioning, which may in particular facilitate price discrimination. When most or all of the suppliers apply exclusive customer allocation, this may facilitate collusion, both at the suppliers' and distributors' level.

(179) Exclusive customer allocation is exempted by the Block Exemption Regulation when the supplier's market share does not exceed the 30% market share threshold, even if combined with other non-hardcore vertical restraints such as non-compete, quantity-forcing or exclusive purchasing. A combination of exclusive customer allocation and selective distribution is normally hardcore, as active selling to end-users by the appointed distributors is usually not left free. Above the 30% market share threshold, the guidance provided in paragraphs 161 to 177 applies *mutatis mutandis* to the assessment of exclusive customer allocation, subject to the following specific remarks.

(180) The allocation of customers normally makes arbitrage by the customers more difficult. In addition, as each appointed distributor has his own class of customers, non-appointed distributors not falling within such a class may find it difficult to obtain the product. This will reduce possible arbitrage by non-appointed distributors. Therefore, above the 30% market share threshold of the Block Exemption Regulation exclusive customer allocation is unlikely to be exemptable unless there are clear and substantial efficiency effects.

(181) Exclusive customer allocation is mainly applied to intermediate products and at the wholesale level when it concerns final products, where customer groups with different specific requirements concerning the product can be distinguished.

(182) Exclusive customer allocation may lead to efficiencies, especially when the distributors are required to make investments in for instance specific equipment, skills or know-how to adapt to the requirements of their class of customers. The depreciation period of these investments indicates the justified duration of an exclusive customer allocation system. In general the case is strongest for new or complex products and for products requiring adaptation to the needs of the individual customer. Identifiable differentiated needs are more likely for intermediate products, that is products sold to different types of professional buyers. Allocation of final consumers is unlikely to lead to any efficiencies and is therefore unlikely to be exempted.

(183) Example of exclusive customer allocation

A company has developed a sophisticated sprinkler installation. The company has currently a market share of 40% on the market for sprinkler installations. When it started selling the sophisticated sprinkler it had a market share of 20% with an older product. The installation of the new type of sprinkler depends on the type of building that it is installed in and on the use of the building (office, chemical plant, hospital, etc.). The company has appointed a number of distributors to sell and install the sprinkler installation. Each distributor needed to train its employees for the general and specific requirements of installing the sprinkler installation for a particular class of customers. To ensure that distributors would specialise, the company assigned to each distributor an exclusive class of customers and prohibited active sales to each others' exclusive customer classes. After five years, all the exclusive distributors will be allowed to sell actively to all classes of customers, thereby ending the system of exclusive customer allocation. The supplier may then also start selling to new distributors. The market is quite dynamic, with two recent entries and a number of technological developments. Competitors, with market shares between 25% and 5%, are also upgrading their products.

As the exclusivity is of limited duration and helps to ensure that the distributors may recoup their investments and concentrate their sales efforts first on a certain class of customers in order to learn the trade, and as the possible anti-competitive effects seem limited in a dynamic market, the conditions for exemption are likely to be fulfilled.

2.4 Selective distribution

(184) Selective distribution agreements, like exclusive distribution agreements, restrict on the one hand the number of authorised distributors and on the other the possibilities of resale. The difference with exclusive distribution is that the restriction of the number of dealers does not depend on the number of territories but on selection criteria linked in the first place to the nature of the product. Another difference with exclusive distribution is that the restriction on resale is not a restriction on active selling to a territory but a restriction on any sales to non-authorised distributors, leaving only appointed dealers and final customers as possible buyers. Selective distribution is almost always used to distribute branded final products.

(185) The possible competition risks are a reduction in intra-brand competition and, especially in case of cumulative effect, foreclosure of certain type(s) of distributors and facilitation of collusion between suppliers or buyers. To assess the possible anti-competitive effects of selective distribution under Article 81(1), a distinction needs to be made between purely qualitative selective distribution and quantitative selective distribution. Purely qualitative selective distribution selects dealers only on the basis of objective criteria required by the nature of the product such as training of sales personnel, the service provided at the point of sale, a certain range of the products being sold, etc.[32] The application of such criteria does not put a direct limit on the number of dealers. Purely qualitative selective distribution is in general considered to fall outside Article 81(1) for lack of anti-competitive effects, provided that three conditions are satisfied. First, the nature of the product in question must necessitate a selective distribution system, in the sense that such a system must constitute a legitimate requirement, having regard to the nature of the product concerned, to preserve its quality and ensure its proper use. Secondly, resellers must be chosen on the basis of objective criteria of a qualitative nature which are laid down uniformly for all potential resellers and are not applied in a discriminatory manner. Thirdly, the criteria laid down must not go beyond what is necessary.[33] Quantitative selective distribution adds further criteria for selection that more directly limit the potential number of dealers by, for instance, requiring minimum or maximum sales, by fixing the number of dealers, etc.

(186) Qualitative and quantitative selective distribution is exempted by the Block Exemption Regulation up to 30% market share, even if combined with other non-hardcore vertical restraints, such as non-compete or exclusive distribution, provided active selling by the authorised distributors to each other and to end users is not restricted. The Block Exemption Regulation exempts selective distribution regardless of the nature of the product concerned. However, where the nature of the product does not require selective distribution, such a distribution system does not generally bring about sufficient efficiency enhancing effects to counterbalance a significant reduction in intra-brand competition. If appreciable anti-competitive effects occur, the benefit of the Block Exemption Regulation is likely to be withdrawn. In addition, the following guidance is provided for the assessment of selective distribution in individual cases which are not covered by the Block Exemption Regulation or in the case of cumulative effects resulting from parallel networks of selective distribution.

---

[32] See for example judgment of the Court of First Instance in Case T–88/92, *Groupement d'achat Édouard Leclerc v. Commission* [1996] ECR II–1961.

[33] See judgments of the Court of Justice in Case 31/80, *L'Oréal v. PVBA* [1980] ECR 3775, paragraphs 15 and 16; Case 26/76, *Metro I* [1977] ECR 1875, paragraphs 20 and 21; Case 107/82, *AEG* [1983] ECR 3151, paragraph 35; and of the Court of First Instance in Case T–19/91, *Vichy v. Commission* [1992] ECR II–415, paragraph 65.

(187) The market position of the supplier and his competitors is of central importance in assessing possible anti-competitive effects, as the loss of intra-brand competition can only be problematic if inter-brand competition is limited. The stronger the position of the supplier, the more problematic is the loss of intra-brand competition. Another important factor is the number of selective distribution networks present in the same market. Where selective distribution is applied by only one supplier in the market which is not a dominant undertaking, quantitative selective distribution does not normally create net negative effects provided that the contract goods, having regard to their nature, require the use of a selective distribution system and on condition that the selection criteria applied are necessary to ensure efficient distribution of the goods in question. The reality, however, seems to be that selective distribution is often applied by a number of the suppliers in a given market.

(188) The position of competitors can have a dual significance and plays in particular a role in case of a cumulative effect. Strong competitors will mean in general that the reduction in intra-brand competition is easily outweighed by sufficient inter-brand competition. However, when a majority of the main suppliers apply selective distribution there will be a significant loss of intra-brand competition and possible foreclosure of certain types of distributors as well as an increased risk of collusion between those major suppliers. The risk of foreclosure of more efficient distributors has always been greater with selective distribution than with exclusive distribution, given the restriction on sales to non-authorised dealers in selective distribution. This is designed to give selective distribution systems a closed character, making it impossible for non-authorised dealers to obtain supplies. This makes selective distribution particularly well suited to avoid pressure by price discounters on the margins of the manufacturer, as well as on the margins of the authorised dealers.

(189) Where the Block Exemption Regulation applies to individual networks of selective distribution, withdrawal of the block exemption or disapplication of the Block Exemption Regulation may be considered in case of cumulative effects. However, a cumulative effect problem is unlikely to arise when the share of the market covered by selective distribution is below 50%. Also, no problem is likely to arise where the market coverage ratio exceeds 50%, but the aggregate market share of the five largest suppliers (CR5) is below 50%. Where both the CR5 and the share of the market covered by selective distribution exceed 50%, the assessment may vary depending on whether or not all five largest suppliers apply selective distribution. The stronger the position of the competitors not applying selective distribution, the less likely the foreclosure of other distributors. If all five largest suppliers apply selective distribution, competition concerns may in particular arise with respect to those agreements that apply quantitative selection criteria by directly limiting the number of authorised dealers. The conditions of Article 81(3) are in general unlikely to be fulfilled if the selective distribution systems at issue prevent access to the market by new distributors capable of adequately selling the products in question, especially price discounters, thereby limiting distribution to the advantage of certain existing channels and to the detriment of final consumers. More indirect forms of quantitative selective distribution, resulting for instance from the combination of purely qualitative selection criteria with the requirement imposed on the dealers to achieve a minimum amount of annual purchases, are less likely to produce net negative effects, if such an amount does not represent a significant proportion of the dealer's total turnover achieved with the type of products in question and it does not go beyond what is necessary for the supplier to recoup his relationship-specific investment and/or realise economies of scale in distribution. As regards individual contributions, a supplier with a market share of less than 5% is in general not considered to contribute significantly to a cumulative effect.

(190) "Entry barriers" are mainly of interest in the case of foreclosure of the market to non-authorised dealers. In general entry barriers will be considerable as selective distribution is usually applied by manufacturers of branded products. It will in general take time and considerable investment for excluded retailers to launch their own brands or obtain competitive supplies elsewhere.

(191) "Buying power" may increase the risk of collusion between dealers and thus appreciably change the analysis of possible anti-competitive effects of selective distribution. Foreclosure of the market to more efficient retailers may especially result where a strong dealer organisation imposes selection criteria on the supplier aimed at limiting distribution to the advantage of its members.

(192) Article 5(c) of the Block Exemption Regulation provides that the supplier may not impose an obligation causing the authorised dealers, either directly or indirectly, not to sell the brands of particular competing suppliers. This condition aims specifically at avoiding horizontal collusion to exclude particular brands through the creation of a selective club of brands by the leading suppliers. This kind of obligation is unlikely to be exemptable when the CR5 is equal to or above 50%, unless none of the suppliers imposing such an obligation belongs to the five largest suppliers in the market.

(193) Foreclosure of other suppliers is normally not a problem as long as other suppliers can use the same distributors, i.e. as long as the selective distribution system is not combined with single branding. In the case of a dense network of authorised distributors or in the case of a cumulative effect, the combination of selective distribution and a non-compete obligation may pose a risk of foreclosure to other suppliers. In that case the principles set out above on single branding apply. Where selective distribution is not combined with a non-compete obligation, foreclosure of the market to competing suppliers may still be a problem when the leading suppliers apply not only purely qualitative selection criteria, but impose on their dealers certain additional obligations such as the obligation to reserve a minimum shelf-space for their products or to ensure that the sales of their products by the dealer achieve a minimum percentage of the dealer's total turnover. Such a problem is unlikely to arise if the share of the market covered by selective distribution is below 50% or, where this coverage ratio is exceeded, if the market share of the five largest suppliers is below 50%.

(194) Maturity of the market is important, as loss of intra-brand competition and possible foreclosure of suppliers or dealers may be a serious problem in a mature market but is less relevant in a market with growing demand, changing technologies and changing market positions.

(195) Selective distribution may be efficient when it leads to savings in logistical costs due to economies of scale in transport and this may happen irrespective of the nature of the product (efficiency 6 in paragraph 116). However, this is usually only a marginal efficiency in selective distribution systems. To help solve a free rider problem between the distributors (efficiency 1 in paragraph 116) or to help create a brand image (efficiency 8 in paragraph 116), the nature of the product is very relevant. In general the case is strongest for new products, for complex products, for products of which the qualities are difficult to judge before consumption (so-called experience products) or of which the qualities are difficult to judge even after consumption (so-called credence products). The combination of selective and exclusive distribution is likely to infringe Article 81 if it is applied by a supplier whose market share exceeds 30% or in case of cumulative effects, even though active sales between the territories remain free. Such a combination may exceptionally fulfil the conditions of Article 81(3) if it is indispensable to protect substantial and relationship-specific investments made by the authorised dealers (efficiency 4 in paragraph 116).

(196) To ensure that the least anti-competitive restraint is chosen, it is relevant to see whether the same efficiencies can be obtained at a comparable cost by for instance service requirements alone.

(197) Example of quantitative selective distribution:

In a market for consumer durables, the market leader (brand A), with a market share of 35%, sells its product to final consumers through a selective distribution network. There are several criteria for admission to the network: the shop must employ trained staff and provide pre-sales services, there must be a specialised area in the shop devoted to the sales of the product and similar hi-tech products, and the shop is required to sell a wide range of models of the supplier and to display them in an attractive manner. Moreover, the number of admissible retailers in the network is directly limited through the establishment of a maximum number of retailers per number of inhabitants in each province or urban area. Manufacturer A has 6 competitors in this market. Its largest competitors, B, C and D, have market shares of respectively 25, 15 and 10%, whilst the other producers have smaller market shares. A is the only manufacturer to use selective distribution. The selective distributors of brand A always handle a few competing brands. However, competing brands are also widely sold in shops which are not members of A's selective distribution network. Channels of distribution are various: for instance, brands B and C are sold in most of A's selected shops, but also in other shops providing a high quality service and in hypermarkets. Brand D is mainly sold in high service shops. Technology is evolving quite rapidly in this market, and the main suppliers maintain a strong quality image for their products through advertising.

In this market, the coverage ratio of selective distribution is 35%. Inter-brand competition is not directly affected by the selective distribution system of A. Intra-brand competition for brand A may be reduced, but consumers have access to low service/low price retailers for brands B and C, which have a comparable quality image to brand A. Moreover, access to high service retailers for other brands is not foreclosed, since there is no limitation on the capacity of selected distributors to sell competing brands, and the quantitative limitation on the number of retailers for brand A leaves other high service retailers free to distribute competing brands. In this case, in view of the service requirements and the efficiencies these are likely to provide and the limited effect on intra-brand competition the conditions for exempting A's selective distribution network are likely to be fulfilled.

(198) Example of selective distribution with cumulative effect:

On a market for a particular sports article, there are seven manufacturers, whose respective market shares are: 25%, 20%, 15%, 15%, 10%, 8% and 7%. The five largest manufacturers distribute their products through quantitative selective distribution, whilst the two smallest use different types of distribution systems, which results in a coverage ratio of selective distribution of 85%. The criteria for access to the selective distribution networks are remarkably uniform amongst manufacturers: shops are required to have trained personnel and to provide pre-sale services, there must be a specialised area in the shop devoted to the sales of the article and a minimum size for this area is specified. The shop is required to sell a wide range of the brand in question and to display the article in an attractive manner, the shop must be located in a commercial street, and this type of article must represent at least 30% of the total turnover of the shop. In general, the same dealer is appointed selective distributor for all five brands. The two brands which do not use selective distribution usually sell through less specialised retailers with lower service levels. The market is stable, both on the supply and on the demand side, and there is strong brand image and product differentiation. The five market leaders have strong brand images, acquired through advertising and sponsoring, whereas the two smaller manufacturers have a strategy of cheaper products, with no strong brand image.

In this market, access by general price discounters to the five leading brands is denied. Indeed, the requirement that this type of article represents at least 30% of the activity of the dealers and the criteria on presentation and pre-sales services rule out most price discounters from the network of authorised dealers. As a consequence, consumers have no choice but to buy the five leading brands in high service/ high price shops. This leads to reduced inter-brand competition between the five leading brands. The fact that the two smallest brands can be bought in low service/ low price shops does not compensate for this, because the brand image of the five market leaders is much better. Inter-brand competition is also limited through multiple dealership. Even though there exists some degree of intra-brand competition and the number of retailers is not directly limited, the criteria for admission are strict enough to lead to a small number of retailers for the five leading brands in each territory.

The efficiencies associated with these quantitative selective distribution systems are low: the product is not very complex and does not justify a particularly high service. Unless the manufacturers can prove that there are clear efficiencies linked to their network of selective distribution, it is probable that the block exemption will have to be withdrawn because of its cumulative effects resulting in less choice and higher prices for consumers.

2.5 Franchising

(199) Franchise agreements contain licences of intellectual property rights relating in particular to trade marks or signs and know-how for the use and distribution of goods or services. In addition to the licence of IPRs, the franchisor usually provides the franchisee during the life of the agreement with commercial or technical assistance. The licence and the assistance are integral components of the business method being franchised. The franchisor is in general paid a franchise fee by the franchisee for the use of the particular business method. Franchising may enable the franchisor to establish, with limited investments, a uniform network for the distribution of his products. In addition to the provision of the business method, franchise agreements usually contain a combination of different vertical restraints concerning the products being distributed, in particular selective distribution and/or non-compete and/or exclusive distribution or weaker forms thereof.

(200) The coverage by the Block Exemption Regulation of the licensing of IPRs contained in franchise agreements is dealt with in paragraphs 23 to 45. As for the vertical restraints on the purchase, sale and resale of goods and services within a franchising arrangement, such as selective distribution, non-compete or exclusive distribution, the Block Exemption Regulation applies up to the 30% market share threshold for the franchisor or the supplier designated by the franchisor.[34] The guidance provided earlier in respect of these types of restraints applies also to franchising, subject to the following specific remarks:

(1) In line with general rule 8 (see paragraph 119), the more important the transfer of know-how, the more easily the vertical restraints fulfil the conditions for exemption.
(2) A non-compete obligation on the goods or services purchased by the franchisee falls outside Article 81(1) when the obligation is necessary to maintain the common identity and reputation of the franchised network. In such cases, the duration of the non-compete obligation is also irrelevant under Article 81(1), as long as it does not exceed the duration of the franchise agreement itself.

(201) Example of franchising:
A manufacturer has developed a new format for selling sweets in so-called fun shops where the sweets can be coloured specially on demand from the consumer. The manufacturer of the sweets has also developed the machines to colour the sweets. The manufacturer also produces the colouring liquids. The quality and freshness of the liquid is of vital importance to producing good sweets. The manufacturer made a success of its sweets through a number of own retail outlets all operating under the same trade name and with the uniform fun image (style of lay-out of the shops, common advertising etc.). In order to expand sales the manufacturer started a franchising system. The franchisees are obliged to buy the sweets, liquid and colouring machine from the manufacturer, to have the same image and operate under the trade name, pay a franchise fee, contribute to common advertising and ensure the confidentiality of the operating manual prepared by the franchisor. In addition, the franchisees are only allowed to sell from the agreed premises, are only allowed to sell to end users or other franchisees and are not allowed to sell other sweets. The franchisor is obliged not to appoint another franchisee nor operate a retail outlet himself in a given contract territory. The franchisor is also under the obligation to update and further develop its products, the business outlook and the

---

[34] See also paragraphs *AEG* [1983] ECR 3151, paragraph 35; and of the Court of First Instance in Case T–19/91, *Vichy v. Commission* [1992] ECR II–415, paragraph 65. See also paragraphs 89 to 95, in particular paragraph 95.

operating manual and make these improvements available to all retail franchisees. The franchise agreements are concluded for a duration of 10 years.

Sweet retailers buy their sweets on a national market from either national producers that cater for national tastes or from wholesalers which import sweets from foreign producers in addition to selling products from national producers. On this market the franchisor's products compete with other brands of sweets. The franchisor has a market share of 30% on the market for sweets sold to retailers. Competition comes from a number of national and international brands, sometimes produced by large diversified food companies. There are many potential points of sale of sweets in the form of tobacconists, general food retailers, cafeterias and specialised sweet shops. On the market for machines for colouring food the franchisor's market share is below 10%.

Most of the obligations contained in the franchise agreements can be assessed as being necessary to protect the intellectual property rights or maintain the common identity and reputation of the franchised network and fall outside Article 81(1). The restrictions on selling (contract territory and selective distribution) provide an incentive to the franchisees to invest in the colouring machine and the franchise concept and, if not necessary for, at least help to maintain the common identity, thereby offsetting the loss of intra-brand competition. The non-compete clause excluding other brands of sweets from the shops for the full duration of the agreements does allow the franchisor to keep the outlets uniform and prevent competitors from benefiting from its trade name. It does not lead to any serious foreclosure in view of the great number of potential outlets available to other sweet producers. The franchise agreements of this franchisor are likely to fulfil the conditions for exemption under Article 81(3) in as far as the obligations contained therein fall under Article 81(1).

2.6 Exclusive supply

(202) Exclusive supply as defined in Article 1(c) of the Block Exemption Regulation is the extreme form of limited distribution in as far as the limit on the number of buyers is concerned: in the agreement it is specified that there is only one buyer inside the Community to which the supplier may sell a particular final product. For intermediate goods or services, exclusive supply means that there is only one buyer inside the Community or that there is only one buyer inside the Community for the purposes of a specific use. For intermediate goods or services, exclusive supply is often referred to as industrial supply.

(203) Exclusive supply as defined in Article 1(c) of the Block Exemption Regulation is exempted by Article 2(1) read in conjuction with Article 3(2) of the Block Exemption Regulation up to 30% market share of the buyer, even if combined with other non-hardcore vertical restraints such as non-compete. Above the market share threshold the following guidance is provided for the assessment of exclusive supply in individual cases.

(204) The main competition risk of exclusive supply is foreclosure of other buyers. The market share of the buyer on the upstream purchase market is obviously important for assessing the ability of the buyer to "impose" exclusive supply which forecloses other buyers from access to supplies. The importance of the buyer on the downstream market is however the factor which determines whether a competition problem may arise. If the buyer has no market power downstream, then no appreciable negative effects for consumers can be expected. Negative effects can however be expected when the market share of the buyer on the downstream supply market as well as the upstream purchase market exceeds 30%. Where the market share of the buyer on the upstream market does not exceed 30%, significant foreclosure effects may still result, especially when the market share of the buyer on his downstream market exceeds 30%. In such cases withdrawal of the block exemption may be required. Where a company is dominant on the downstream market, any obligation to supply the products only or mainly to the dominant buyer may easily have significant anti-competitive effects.

(205) It is not only the market position of the buyer on the upstream and downstream market that is important but also the extent to and the duration for which he applies an exclusive supply obligation. The higher the tied supply share, and the longer the duration of the exclusive supply, the more significant the foreclosure is likely to be. Exclusive supply agreements shorter than five years entered into by non-dominant companies usually require a balancing of pro- and anti-competitive effects, while agreements lasting longer than five years are for most types of investments not considered necessary to achieve the claimed efficiencies or the efficiencies are not sufficient to outweigh the foreclosure effect of such long-term exclusive supply agreements.

(206) The market position of the competing buyers on the upstream market is important as it is only likely that competing buyers will be foreclosed for anti-competitive reasons, *i.e.* to increase their costs, if they are significantly smaller than the foreclosing buyer. Foreclosure of competing buyers is not very likely where these competitors have similar buying power and can offer the suppliers similar sales possibilities. In such a case foreclosure could only occur for potential entrants, who may not be able to secure supplies when a number of major buyers all enter into exclusive supply contracts with the majority of suppliers on the market. Such a cumulative effect may lead to withdrawal of the benefit of the Block Exemption Regulation.

(207) Entry barriers at the supplier level are relevant to establishing whether there is real foreclosure. In as far as it is efficient for competing buyers to provide the goods or services themselves via upstream vertical integration, foreclosure is unlikely to be a real problem. However, often there are significant entry barriers.

(208) Countervailing power of suppliers is relevant, as important suppliers will not easily allow themselves to be cut off from alternative buyers. Foreclosure is therefore mainly a risk in the case of weak suppliers and strong buyers. In the case of strong suppliers the exclusive supply may be found in combination with non-compete. The combination with non-compete brings in the rules developed for single branding. Where there are relationship-specific investments involved on both sides (hold-up problem) the combination of exclusive supply and non-compete, *i.e.* reciprocal exclusivity in industrial supply agreements is usually justified up to the level of dominance.

(209) Lastly, the level of trade and the nature of the product are relevant for foreclosure. Foreclosure is less likely in the case of an intermediate product or where the product is homogeneous. Firstly, a foreclosed manufacturer that uses a certain input usually has more flexibility to respond to the demand of his customers than the wholesaler/retailer has in responding to the demand of the final consumer for whom brands may play an important role. Secondly, the loss of a possible source of supply matters less for the foreclosed buyers in the case of homogeneous products than in the case of a heterogeneous product with different grades and qualities.

(210) For homogeneous intermediate products, anti-competitive effects are likely to be exemptable below the level of dominance. For final branded products or differentiated intermediate products where there are entry barriers, exclusive supply may have appreciable anti-competitive effects where the competing buyers are relatively small compared to the foreclosing buyer, even if the latter is not dominant on the downstream market.

(211) Where appreciable anti-competitive effects are established, an exemption under Article 81(3) is possible as long as the company is not dominant. Efficiencies can be expected in the case of a hold-up problem (paragraph 116, points 4 and 5), and this is more likely for intermediate products than for final products. Other efficiencies are less likely. Possible economies of scale in distribution (paragraph 116, point 6) do not seem likely to justify exclusive supply.

(212) In the case of a hold-up problem and even more so in the case of scale economies in distribution, quantity forcing on the supplier, such as minimum supply requirements, could well be a less restrictive alternative.

(213) Example of exclusive supply:

On a market for a certain type of components (intermediate product market) supplier A agrees with buyer B to develop, with its own know-how and considerable investment in new machines and with the help of specifications supplied by buyer B, a different version of the component. B will have to make considerable investments to incorporate the new component. It is agreed that A will supply the new product only to buyer B for a period of five years from the date of first entry on the market. B is obliged to buy the new product only from A for the same period of five years. Both A and B can continue to sell and buy respectively other versions of the component elsewhere. The market share of buyer B on the upstream component market and on the downstream final goods market is 40%. The market share of the component supplier is 35%. There are two other component suppliers with around 20–25% market share and a number of small suppliers.

Given the considerable investments, the agreement is likely to fulfil the conditions for exemption in view of the efficiencies and the limited foreclosure effect. Other buyers are foreclosed from a particular version of a product of a supplier with 35% market share and there are other component suppliers that could develop similar new products. The foreclosure of part of buyer B's demand to other suppliers is limited to a maximum of 40% of the market.

(214) Exclusive supply is based on a direct or indirect obligation causing the supplier only to sell to one buyer. Quantity forcing on the supplier is based on incentives agreed between the supplier and the buyer that make the former concentrate his sales mainly with one buyer. Quantity forcing on the supplier may have similar but more mitigated effects than exclusive supply. The assessment of quantity forcing will depend on the degree of foreclosure of other buyers on the upstream market.

2.7 Tying

(215) Tying exists when the supplier makes the sale of one product conditional upon the purchase of another distinct product from the supplier or someone designated by the latter. The first product is referred to as the tying product and the second is referred to as the tied product. If the tying is not objectively justified by the nature of the products or commercial usage, such practice may constitute an abuse within the meaning of Article 82.[35] Article 81 may apply to horizontal agreements or concerted practices between competing suppliers which make the sale of one product conditional upon the purchase of another distinct product. Tying may also constitute a vertical restraint falling under Article 81 where it results in a single branding type of obligation (see paragraphs 138 to 160) for the tied product. Only the latter situation is dealt with in these Guidelines.

(216) What is to be considered as a distinct product is determined first of all by the demand of the buyers. Two products are distinct if, in the absence of tying, from the buyers' perspective, the products are purchased by them on two different markets. For instance, as customers want to buy shoes with laces, it has become commercial usage for shoe manufacturers to supply shoes with laces. Therefore, the sale of shoes with laces is not a tying practice. Often combinations have become accepted practice because the nature of the product makes it technically difficult to supply one product without the supply of another product.

(217) The main negative effect of tying on competition is possible foreclosure on the market of the tied product. Tying means that there is at least a form of quantity-forcing on the buyer in respect of the tied product. Where in addition a non-compete obligation is agreed in respect of the tied product, this increases the possible foreclosure effect on the market of the tied product. Tying may also lead to supra-competitive prices, especially in three situations. Firstly, when the tying and tied product are partly substitutable for the buyer. Secondly, when the tying allows price discrimination according to the use the customer makes of the tying product, for example the tying of ink cartridges to the sale of photocopying machines (metering). Thirdly, when in the case of long-term contracts or in the case of after-markets with original equipment with a long replacement time, it becomes difficult for the customers to calculate the consequences of the tying. Lastly,

---

[35] Judgment of the Court of Justice in Case C–333/94 P, *Tetrapak v. Commission* [1996] ECR I–5987, paragraph 37.

tying may also lead to higher entry barriers both on the market of the tying and on the market of the tied product.

(218) Tying is exempted by Article 2(1) read in conjunction with Article 3 of the Block Exemption Regulation when the market share of the supplier on both the market of the tied product and the market of the tying product does not exceed 30%. It may be combined with other non-hardcore vertical restraints such as non-compete or quantity forcing in respect of the tying product, or exclusive purchasing. Above the market share threshold the following guidance is provided for the assessment of tying in individual cases.

(219) The market position of the supplier on the market of the tying product is obviously of main importance to assess possible anti-competitive effects. In general this type of agreement is imposed by the supplier. The importance of the supplier on the market of the tying product is the main reason why a buyer may find it difficult to refuse a tying obligation.

(220) To assess the supplier's market power, the market position of his competitors on the market of the tying product is important. As long as his competitors are sufficiently numerous and strong, no anti-competitive effects can be expected, as buyers have sufficient alternatives to purchase the tying product without the tied product, unless other suppliers are applying similar tying. In addition, entry barriers on the market of the tying product are relevant to establish the market position of the supplier. When tying is combined with a non-compete obligation in respect of the tying product, this considerably strengthens the position of the supplier.

(221) Buying power is relevant, as important buyers will not easily be forced to accept tying without obtaining at least part of the possible efficiencies. Tying not based on efficiency is therefore mainly a risk where buyers do not have significant buying power.

(222) Where appreciable anti-competitive effects are established, the question of a possible exemption under Article 81(3) arises as long as the company is not dominant. Tying obligations may help to produce efficiencies arising from joint production or joint distribution. Where the tied product is not produced by the supplier, an efficiency may also arise from the supplier buying large quantities of the tied product. For tying to be exemptable it must, however, be shown that at least part of these cost reductions are passed on to the consumer. Tying is therefore normally not exemptable when the retailer is able to obtain, on a regular basis, supplies of the same or equivalent products on the same or better conditions than those offered by the supplier which applies the tying practice. Another efficiency may exist where tying helps to ensure a certain uniformity and quality standardisation (see efficiency 8 in paragraph 116). However, it needs to be demonstrated that the positive effects cannot be realised equally efficiently by requiring the buyer to use or resell products satisfying minimum quality standards, without requiring the buyer to purchase these from the supplier or someone designated by the latter. The requirements concerning minimum quality standards would not normally fall within Article 81(1). Where the supplier of the tying product imposes on the buyer the suppliers from which the buyer must purchase the tied product, for instance because the formulation of minimum quality standards is not possible, this may also fall outside Article 81(1), especially where the supplier of the tying product does not derive a direct (financial) benefit from designating the suppliers of the tied product.

(223) The effect of supra-competitive prices is considered anti-competitive in itself. The effect of foreclosure depends on the tied percentage of total sales on the market of the tied product. On the question of what can be considered appreciable foreclosure under Article 81(1), the analysis for single branding can be applied. Above the 30% market share threshold exemption of tying is unlikely, unless there are clear efficiencies that are transmitted, at least in part, to consumers. Exemption is even less likely when tying is combined with non-compete, either in respect of the tied or in respect of the tying product.

(224) Withdrawal of the block exemption is likely where no efficiencies result from tying or where such efficiencies are not passed on to the consumer (see paragraph 222). Withdrawal is also likely in the case of a cumulative effect where a majority of the

suppliers apply similar tying arrangements without the possible efficiencies being transmitted at least in part to consumers.

2.8 Recommended and maximum resale prices

(225) The practice of recommending a resale price to a reseller or requiring the reseller to respect a maximum resale price is—subject to the comments in paragraphs 46 to 56 concerning RPM—covered by the Block Exemption Regulation when the market share of the supplier does not exceed the 30% threshold. For cases above the market share threshold and for cases of withdrawal of the block exemption the following guidance is provided.

(226) The possible competition risk of maximum and recommended prices is firstly that the maximum or recommended price will work as a focal point for the resellers and might be followed by most or all of them. A second competition risk is that maximum or recommended prices may facilitate collusion between suppliers.

(227) The most important factor for assessing possible anti-competitive effects of maximum or recommended resale prices is the market position of the supplier. The stronger the market position of the supplier, the higher the risk that a maximum resale price or a recommended resale price leads to a more or less uniform application of that price level by the resellers, because they may use it as a focal point. They may find it difficult to deviate from what they perceive to be the preferred resale price proposed by such an important supplier on the market. Under such circumstances the practice of imposing a maximum resale price or recommending a resale price may infringe Article 81(1) if it leads to a uniform price level.

(228) The second most important factor for assessing possible anti-competitive effects of the practice of maximum and recommended prices is the market position of competitors. Especially in a narrow oligopoly, the practice of using or publishing maximum or recommended prices may facilitate collusion between the suppliers by exchanging information on the preferred price level and by reducing the likelihood of lower resale prices. The practice of imposing a maximum resale price or recommending resale prices leading to such effects may also infringe Article 81(1).

2.9 Other vertical restraints

(229) The vertical restraints and combinations described above are only a selection. There are other restraints and combinations for which no direct guidance is provided here. They will however be treated according to the same principles, with the help of the same general rules and with the same emphasis on the effect on the market.

APPENDIX 30

COMMISSION NOTICE[1]

On Subcontracting Agreements

1. In this Notice the Commission of the European Communities gives its view as to subcontracting agreements in relation to Article 81(1) of the Treaty establishing the European Economic Community. This class of agreement is at the present time a form of work distribution which concerns firms of all sizes, but which offers opportunities for development in particular to small and medium-sized firms.

The Commission considers that agreements under which one firm, called "the contractor," whether or not in consequence of a prior order from a third party, entrusts to another, called "the subcontractor", the manufacture of goods, the supply of services or the performance of work under the contract's instructions, to be provided to the contractor or performed on his behalf, are not of themselves caught by the prohibition in Article 81(1).

To carry out certain subcontracting agreements in accordance with the contractor's instructions, the subcontractor may have to make use of particular technology or equipment which the contractor will have to provide. In order to protect the economic value of such technology or equipment, the contractor may wish to restrict their use by the subcontractor to whatever is necessary for the purpose of the agreement. The question arises whether such restrictions are caught by Article 81(1). They are assessed in this Notice with due regard to the purpose of such agreements, which distinguishes them from ordinary patent and know-how licensing agreements.

2. In the Commission's view, Article 81(1) does not apply to clauses whereby:

— technology or equipment provided by the contractor may not be used except for the purposes of the subcontracting agreement,
— technology or equipment provided by the contractor may not be made available to third parties,
— the goods, services or work resulting from the use of such technology or equipment may be supplied only to the contractor or performed on his behalf,

provided that and in so far as this technology or equipment is necessary to enable the subcontractor under reasonable conditions to manufacture the goods, to supply the services or to carry out the work in accordance with the contractor's instructions. To that extent the subcontractor is providing goods, services or work in respect of which he is not an independent supplier in the market.

The above proviso is satisfied where performance of the subcontracting agreement makes necessary the use of the subcontractor of:

— industrial property rights of the contractor or at his disposal, in the form of patents, utility models, designs protected by copyright, registered designs or other rights, or

---

[1] OJ 1979 C1/2.

304

— secret knowledge or manufacturing processes (know-how) of the contractor or at his disposal, or of

— studies, plans or documents accompanying the information given which have been prepared by or for the contractor, or

— dies, patterns or tools, and accessory equipment that are distinctively the contractor's,

which, even though not covered by industrial property rights nor containing any element of secrecy, permit the manufacture of goods which differ in form, function or composition from other goods manufactured or supplied on the market.

However, the restrictions mentioned above are not justifiable where the subcontractor has at his disposal or could under reasonable conditions obtain access to the technology and equipment needed to produce the goods, provide the services or carry out the work. Generally, this is the case when the contractor provides no more than general information which merely describes the work to be done. In such circumstances the restrictions could deprive the subcontractor of the possibility of developing his own business in the fields covered by the agreement.

3. The following restrictions in connection with the provision of technology by the contractor may in the Commission's view also be imposed by subcontracting agreements without giving ground for objection under Article 81(1):

— an undertaking by either of the parties not to reveal manufacturing processes or other know-how of a secret character, or confidential information given by the other party during the negotiation and performance of the agreement, as long as the know-how or information in question has not become public knowledge,

— an undertaking by the subcontractor not to make use, even after expiry of the agreement, of manufacturing processes or other know-how of a secret character received by him during the currency of the agreement, as long as they have not become public knowledge,

— an undertaking by the subcontractor to pass on to the contractor on a non-exclusive basis any technical improvements which he has made during the currency of the agreement, or, where a patentable invention has been discovered by the subcontractor, to grant non-exclusive licences in respect of inventions relating to improvements and new applications of the original invention to the contractor for the term of the patent held by the latter.

This undertaking by the subcontractor may be exclusive in favour of the contractor in so far as improvements and inventions made by the subcontractor during the currency of the agreement are incapable of being used independently of the contractor's secret know-how or patent, since this does not constitute an appreciable restriction of competition.

However, any undertaking by the subcontractor regarding the right to dispose of the results of his own reserch and development work may restrain competition, where such results are capable of being used independently. In such circumstances, the subcontracting relationship is not sufficient to displace the ordinary competition rules on the disposal of industrial property rights or secret know-how.

4. Where the subcontractor is authorised by a subcontracting agreement to use a specified trade mark, trade name or get up, the contractor may at the same time forbid such use by the subcontractor in the case of goods, services or work which are not to be supplied to the contractor.

5. Although this Notice should in general obviate the need for firms to obtain a ruling on the legal position by an individual Commission Decision, it does not affect the right of the firms concerned to apply for negative clearance as defined by Article 2 of Regulation No. 17 or to notify the agreement to the Commission under Article 4(1) of that Regulation.

The 1968 Notice on cooperation between enterprises, which lists a number of agreements that by their nature are not to be regarded as anti-competitive, is thus supplemented in the subcontracting field.[2] The Commission also reminds firms that, in order to promote cooperation between small and medium-sized businesses, it has published a notice concerning agreements of minor importance which do not fall under Article 81(1) of the Treaty establishing the European Economic Community.

This Notice is without prejudice to the view that may be taken of subcontracting agreements by the Court of Justice of the European Communities.

---

[2] [Editor's Note: the 1968 Notice has been replaced by the Guidelines on the applicability of Article 81 to horizontal cooperation agreements, App. 28 *post*. See those Guidelines at §§6, 81.]

COMMISSION NOTICE[1]

On Agreements of Minor Importance which do not fall within the meaning of Article 81(1) of the Treaty Establishing the European Community

(Text with EEA relevance)

I.

1. The Commission considers it important to facilitate cooperation between undertakings where such cooperation is economically desirable without presenting difficulties from the point of view of competition policy. To this end, it published the notice concerning agreements, decisions and concerted practices in the field of cooperation between enterprises[2] listing a number of agreements that by their nature cannot be regarded as being in restraint of competition. Furthermore, in the notice concerning its assessment of certain subcontracting agreements[3] the Commission considered that that type of contract, which offers all undertakings opportunities for development, does not automatically fall within the scope of Article 81(1). The notice concerning the assessment of cooperative joint ventures pursuant to Article 81 of the EC Treaty[4] describes in detail the conditions under which the agreements in question do not fall under the prohibition of restrictive agreements. By issuing this notice which replaces the Commission notice of 3 September 1986,[5] the Commission is taking a further step towards defining the scope of Article 81(1), in order to facilitate cooperation between undertakings.

2. Article 81(1) prohibits agreements which may affect trade between Member States and which have as their object or effect the prevention, restriction or distortion of competition within the common market. The Court of Justice of the European Communities has clarified that this provision is not applicable where the impact of the agreement on intra-Community trade or on competition is not appreciable. Agreements which are not capable of significantly affecting trade between Member States are not caught by Article 81. They should therefore be examined on the basis, and within the framework, of national legislation alone. This is also the case for agreements whose actual or potential effect remains limited to the territory of only one Member State or of one or more third countries. Likewise, agreements which do not have as their object or their effect an appreciable restriction of competition are not caught by the prohibition contained in Article 81(1).

3. In this notice the Commission, by setting quantitative criteria and by explaining their application, has given a sufficiently concrete meaning to the term "appreciable" for

---

[1] OJ 1997 C372/13.
[2] OJ 1968 C75/3, as corrected in OJ 1968 C84/14.
[3] OJ 1979 C1/2.
[4] OJ 1993 C43/2.
[5] OJ 1986 C231/2.

undertakings to be able to judge for themselves whether their agreements do not fall within the prohibition pursuant to Article 81(1) by virtue of their minor importance. The quantitiative definition of appreciability, however, serves only as a guideline: in individual cases even agreements between undertakings which exceed the threshold set out below may still have only a negligible effect on trade between Member States or on competition within the common market and are therefore not caught by Article 81(1). This notices does not contain an exhaustive description of restictions which fall outside Article 81(1). It is generally recognized that even agreements which are not of minor importance can escape the prohibition on agreements on account of their exclusively favourable impact on competition.

4. The benchmarks provided by the Commission in this notice should eliminate the need to have the legal status of agreements covered by it established through individual Commission decisions; notification for this purpose will no longer be necessary for such agreements. However, if it is doubtful whether, in an individual case, an agreement is likely to affect trade between Member States or to restrict competition to any significant extent, undertakings are free to apply for negative clearance or to notify the agreement pursuant to Council Regulations No 17[6], (EEC) No 1017/69[7], (EEC) No 4056/86[8] and (EEC) No. 3975/87[9].

5. In cases covered by this notice, and subject to points 11 and 20, the Commission will not institute any proceedings either on application or on its own initiative. Where undertakings have failed to notify an agreement falling within the scope of Article 81(1) because they assumed in good faith that the agreement was covered by this notice, the Commission will not consider imposing fines.

6. This notice is likewise applicable to decisions by associations of undertakings and to concerted practices.

7. This notice is without prejudice to the competence of national courts to apply Article 81. However, it constitutes a factor which those courts may take into account when deciding a pending case. It is also without prejudice to any interpretation of Article 81 which may be given by the Court of Justice or the Court of First Instance of the European Communities.

8. This notice is without prejudice to the application of national competition laws.

II.

9. The Commission holds the view that agreements between undertakings engaged in the production or distribution of goods or in the provision of services do not fall under the prohibition in Article 81(1) if the aggregate market shares held by all of the participating undertakings do not exceed, on any of the relevant markets:

(a) the 5% threshold, where the agreement is made between undertakings operating at the same level of production or of marketing ("horizontal" agreement);
(b) the 10% threshold, where the agreement is made between undertakings operating at different economic levels ("vertical" agreement).

In the case of a mixed horizontal/vertical agreement or where it is difficult to classify the agreement as either horizontal or vertical, the 5% threshold is applicable.

10. The Commission also holds the view that the said agreements do not fall under the prohibition of Article 81(1) if the market shares given at point 9 are exceeded by no more than one 10th during two successive financial years.

---

[6] OJ 13, 21.2.1962, p. 204/62.
[7] OJ L 175, 23.7.1968, p. 1.
[8] OJ L 378, 31.12.1986, p. 4.
[9] OJ L 374, 31.12.1987, p. 1.

11. With regard to:

(a) horizontal agreements which have as their object
  — to fix prices or to limit production or sales, or
  — to share markets or sources of supply,
(b) vertical agreements which have as their object
  — to fix resale prices, or
  — to confer territorial protection on the participating undertakings or third under-
    takings,

the applicability of Article 81(1) cannot be ruled out even where the aggregate market shares held by all of the participating undertakings remain below the thresholds mentioned in points 9 and 10.

The Commission considers, however, that in the first instance it is for the authorities and courts of the Member States to take action on any agreements envisaged above in (a) and (b). Accordingly, it will only intervene in such cases when it considers that the interest of the Community so demands, and in particular if the agreements impair the proper functioning of the internal market.

12. For the purposes of this notice, "participating undertakings" are:

(a) undertakings being parties to the agreement;
(b) undertakings in which a party to the agreement, directly or indirectly,
  — owns more than half of the capital or business assets, or
  — has the power to exercise more than half of the voting rights, or
  — has the power to appoint more than half of the members of the supervisory board,
    board of management or bodies legally representing the undertakings, or
  — has to the right to manage the undertaking's business;
(c) undertakings which directly or indirectly have over a party to the agreement the rights
    or powers listed in (b);
(d) undertakings over which an undertaking referred to in (c) has, directly or indirectly,
    the rights or powers listed in (b).

Undertakings over which several undertakings as referred to in (a) to (d) jointly have, directly or indirectly, the rights or powers set out in (b) shall also be considered to be participating undertakings.

13. In order to calculate the market share, it is necessary to determine the relevant market; for this, the relevant product market and the relevant geographic market must be defined.

14. The relevant product market comprises any products or services which are regarded as interchangeable or substitutable by the consumer, by reason of their characteristics, prices and intended use.

15. The relevant geographic market comprises the area in which the participating undertakings are involved in the supply of relevant products or services, in which the conditions of competition are sufficiently homogeneous, and which can be distinguished from neighbouring geographic areas because, in particular, conditions of competition are appreciably different in those areas.

16. When applying points 14 and 15, reference should be had to the notice on the definition of the relevant market under Community competition law[10].

17. In the case of doubt about the delimitation of the relevant geographic market, undertakings may take the view that their agreement has no appreciable effect on intra-Community trade or on competition when the market share thresholds indicated in points 9 and 10 are not exceeded in any Member State. This view, however, does not preclude the application of national competition law to the agreements in question.

---

[10] OJ C372, 9.12.1997, p. 5.

18. Chapter II of this notice shall not apply where in a relevant market competition is restricted by the cumulative effects of parallel networks of similar agreements established by several manufacturers or dealers.

III.

19. Agreements between small and medium-sized undertakings, as defined in the Annex to Commission Recommendation 96/280/EC[11] are rarely capable of significantly affecting trade between Member States and competition within the common market. Consequently, as a general rule, they are not caught by the prohibition in Article 81(1). In cases where such agreements exceptionally meet the conditions for the application of that provision, they will not be of sufficient Community interest to justify any intervention. This is why the Commission will not institute any proceedings, either on request or on its own initiative, to apply the provisions of Article 81(1) to such agreements, even if the thresholds set out in points 9 and 10 above are exceeded.

20. The Commission nevertheless reserves the right to intervene in such agreements:

(a) where they significantly impede competition in a substantial part of the relevant market,

(b) where, in the relevant market, competition is restricted by the cumulative effect of parallel networks of similar agreements made between several producers or dealers.

---

[11] OJ L 107, 30.4.1996, p. 4.

APPENDIX 32

ANNEX TO COMMISSION RECOMMENDATION 96/280[1]

Definition of small and medium-sized enterprises adopted by the Commission

Article 1

1. Small and medium-sized enterprises, hereinafter referred to as "SMEs", are defined as enterprises which:

— have fewer than 250 employees, and
— have either,
    an annual turnover not exceeding ECU 40 million, or
    an annual balance-sheet total not exceeding ECU 27 million,
— conform to the criterion of independence as defined in paragraph 3.

2. Where it is necessary to distinguish between small and medium-sized enterprises, the "small enterprise" is defined as an enterprise which:

— has fewer than 50 employees and
— has either,
    an annual turnover not exceeding ECU 7 million, or
    an annual balance-sheet total not exceeding ECU 5 million,
— conforms to the criterion of independence as defined in paragraph 3.

3. Independent enterprises are those which are not owned as to 25% or more of the capital or the voting rights by one enterprise, or jointly by several enterprises, falling outside the definition of an SME or a small enterprise, whichever may apply. This threshold may be exceeded in the following two cases:

— if the enterprise is held by public investment corporations, venture capital companies or institutional investors, provided no control is exercised either individually or jointly,
— if the capital is spread in such a way that it is not possible to determine by whom it is held and if the enterprise declares that it can legitimately presume that it is not owned as to 25% or more by one enterprise, or jointly by several enterprises, falling outside the definitions of an SME or a small enterprise, whichever may apply.

4. In calculating the thresholds referred to in paragraphs 1 and 2, it is therefore necessary to cumulate the relevant figures for the beneficiary enterprise and for all the enterprises which it directly or indirectly controls through possession of 25% or more of the capital or of the voting rights.

5. Where it is necessary to distinguish micro-enterprises from other SMEs, these are defined as enterprises having fewer than 10 employees.

---

[1] OJ 1996 L107/4, 8.

311

6. Where, at the final balance sheet date, an enterprise exceeds or falls below the employee thresholds or financial ceilings, this is to result in its acquiring or losing the status of "SME", "medium-sized enterprise", "small enterprise" or "micro-enterprise" only if the phenomenon is repeated over two consecutive financial years.

7. The number of persons employed corresponds to the number of annual working units (AWU), that is to say, the number of full-time workers employed during one year with part-time and seasonal workers being fractions of AWU. The reference year to be considered is that of the last approved accounting period.

8. The turnover and balance sheet total thresholds are those of the last approved 12-month accounting period. In the case of newly-established enterprises whose accounts have not yet been approved, the thresholds to apply shall be derived from a reliable estimate made in the course of the financial year.

Article 2

The Commission will amend the ceilings chosen for the turnover and balance-sheet total as the need arises and normally every four years from the adoption of this Recommendation, to take account of changing economic circumstances in the Community.

Article 3

1. The Commission undertakes to adopt the appropriate measures to ensure that the definition of SMEs, as set out in Article 1, applies to all programmes managed by it in which the terms "SME", "medium-sized enterprise", "small enterprise" or "micro-enterprise" are mentioned.

2. The Commission undertakes to adopt the appropriate measures to adapt the statistics that it produces in line with the following size-classes:

— 0 employees,
— 1 to 9 employees,
— 10 to 49 employees,
— 50 to 249 employees,
— 250 to 499 employees,
— 500 employees plus.

3. Current Community programmes defining SMEs with criteria other than those mentioned in Article 1 will continue, during a transitional period, to be implemented to the benefit of the enterprises which were considered SMEs when these programmes were adopted. Any modification of the SME definition within these programmes can be made only by adopting the definition contained herein and by replacing the divergent definition with a reference to this Recommendation. This transitional period should in principle end at the latest on 31 December 1997. However, legally binding commitments entered into by the Commission on the basis of these programmes will remain unaffected.

4. When the Fourth Council Directive 78/660/EEC is amended, the Commission will propose that the existing criteria for defining SMEs be replaced by a reference to the definition contained in this Recommendation.

5. Any provisions adopted by the Commission which mention the terms "SME", "medium-sized enterprise", "small enterprise" or "micro-enterprise", or any other such term, will refer to the definition contained in this Recommendation.

REGULATION 4064/89[1]

On the Control of Concentrations Between Undertakings

THE COUNCIL OF THE EUROPEAN COMMUNITIES

Having regard to the Treaty establishing the European Economic Community, and in particular Articles 83 and 308 thereof,

Having regard to the proposal from the Commission,[2]

Having regard to the opinion of the European Parliament,[3]

Having regard to the opinion of the Economic and Social Committee,[4]

Whereas—

[1] For the achievement of the aims of the Treaty establishing the European Economic Community, Article 3(1)(g) gives the Community the objective of instituting a system ensuring that competition in the Common Market is not distorted;

[2] This system is essential for the achievement of the internal market by 1992 and its further development;

[3] The dismantling of internal frontiers is resulting and will continue to result in major corporate reorganisations in the Community, particularly in the form of concentrations;

[4] Such a development must be welcomed as being in line with the requirements of dynamic competition and capable of increasing the competitiveness of European industry, improving the conditions of growth and raising the standard of living in the Community;

[5] However, it must be ensured that the process of reorganisation does not result in lasting damage to competition; whereas Community law must therefore include provisions governing those concentrations which may significantly impede effective competition in the Common Market or in a substantial part of it;

[6] Articles 81 and 82, while applicable, according to the case law of the Court of Justice, to certain concentrations, are not, however, sufficient to control all operations which may prove to be incompatible with the system of undistorted competition envisaged in the Treaty;

[7] A new legal instrument should therefore be created in the form of a Regulation to permit effective control of all concentrations from the point of view of their effect on the

---

[1] Corrected text at OJ 1990 L257/13, as amended by Reg. 1310/97, OJ 1997 L180/1, corr. by OJ 1998 L40/17. The consolidated text of the substantive Regulation follows the unofficial version published by the European Commission. The consolidation of the Recitals follows the version published at [1997] 5 CMLR 387 (prep. by Celia Hampton).

[2] OJ 1988 C130/4, [1988] 4 CMLR 472, OJ 1996 C350/8 & 10.

[3] OJ 1988 C309/55; OJ 1996 C362/130.

[4] OJ 1988 C208/11 OJ 1997 C56/71.

structure of competition in the Community and to be the only instrument applicable to such concentrations;

[8] This Regulation should therefore be based not only on Article 83 but, principally, on Article 308 of the Treaty, under which the Community may give itself the additional powers of action necessary for the attainment of its objectives, including with regard to concentrations on the markets for agricultural products listed in Annex II to the Treaty;

[9] The provisions to be adopted in this Regulation should apply to significant structural changes the impact of which on the market goes beyond the national borders of any one Member State;

[10] The scope of application of this Regulation should therefore be defined according to the geographical area of activity of the undertakings concerned and be limited by quantitative thresholds in order to cover those concentrations which have a Community dimension; [at the end of an initial phase of the application of this Regulation, these thresholds should be reviewed in the light of the experience gained–*now redundant*]

[10A—Reg. 1310/97 Recital 4] At the end of the initial phase of application of ... [5] Regulation [1310/97] the Commission should report to the Council on the implementation of all applicable thresholds and criteria, so that the Council is in a position, acting in accordance with Article 202 of the Treaty, to change the criteria or adjust the thresholds laid down in this Regulation;

[11] A concentration with a Community dimension exists where the combined aggregate turnover of the undertakings concerned exceeds given levels world-wide and within the Community and where at least two of the undertakings concerned have their sole or main fields of activities in different Member States or where, although the undertakings in question act mainly in one and the same Member State, at least one of them has substantial operations in at least one other Member State; whereas that is also the case where the concentrations are effected by undertakings which do not have their principal fields of activities in the Community but which have substantial operations there;

[11A—Reg. 1310/97 Recital 1] Concentrations with a significant impact in several Member States that fall below the thresholds referred to in [Article 1(2)] *Regulation 4064/89 of 21 December 1989 on the control of concentrations between undertakings* may qualify for examination under a number of national merger control systems; whereas multiple notification of the same transaction increases legal uncertainty, effort and cost for companies and may lead to conflicting assessments;

[11B—Reg. 1310/97 Recital 2] Extending the scope of Community merger control to concentrations with a significant impact in several Member States will ensure that a "one-stop shop" system applies and will allow, in compliance with the subsidiarity principle, for an appreciation of the competition impact of such concentrations in the Community as a whole;

[11C—Reg. 1310/97 Recital 3] Additional criteria should be established for the application of Community merger control in order to meet the above-mentioned objectives; whereas those criteria should consist of new thresholds established in terms of the total turnover of the undertakings concerned achieved world-wide, at Community level and in at least three Member States;

[12] Whereas the arrangements to be introduced for the control of concentrations should, without prejudice to Article 86(2) of the Treaty, respect the principle of non-discrimination between the public and the private sectors; whereas, in the public sector, calculation of the turnover of an undertaking concerned in a concentration needs, therefore, to take account of undertakings making up an economic unit with an independent power of decision, irrespective of the way in which their capital is held or of the rules of administrative supervision applicable to them;

[12A—Reg. 1310/97 Recital 6] For the purposes of calculating the turnover of credit and financial institutions, banking income is a better criterion than a proportion of assets, because it reflects more accurately the economic reality of the whole banking sector;

---

[5] The word "this" has been omitted.

[13] It is necessary to establish whether concentrations with a Community dimension are compatible or not with the Common Market from the point of view of the need to maintain and develop effective competition in the Common Market; in so doing, the Commission must place its appraisal within the general framework of the achievement of the fundamental objectives referred to in Article 2 of the Treaty, including that of strengthening the Community's economic and social cohesion, referred to in Article 158;

[14] This Regulation should establish the principle that a concentration with a Community dimension which creates or strengthens a position as a result of which effective competition in the Common Market or in a substantial part of it is significantly impeded is to be declared incompatible with the Common Market;

[15] Concentrations which, by reason of the limited market share of the undertakings concerned, are not liable to impede effective competition may be presumed to be compatible with the Common Market; whereas, without prejudice to Articles 81 and 82 of the Treaty, an indication to this effect exists, in particular, where the market share of the undertakings concerned does not exceed 25 per cent either in the Common Market or in a substantial part of it,

[16] The Commission should have the task of taking all the decisions necessary to establish whether or not concentrations with a Community dimension are compatible with the Common Market, as well as decisions designed to restore effective competition;

[17] To ensure effective control undertakings should be obliged to give prior notification of concentrations with a Community dimension and provision should be made for the suspension of concentrations for a limited period, and for the possibility of extending or waiving a suspension where necessary; whereas in the interests of legal certainty the validity of transactions must nevertheless be protected as much as necessary;

[17A—Reg. 1310/97 Recital 9] To ensure effective control, concentrations should be suspended until a final decision has been taken; whereas, on the other hand, it should be possible to waive a suspension, where appropriate; whereas, in deciding whether or not to grant a waiver, the Commission should take account of all pertinent factors, such as the nature and gravity of damage to the undertakings concerned by a concentration or to third parties, and the threat to competition posed by the concentration;

[18] A period within which the Commission must initiate proceedings in respect of a notified concentration and periods within which it must give a final decision on the compatibility or incompatibility with the Common Market of a notified concentration should be laid down;

[18A—Reg. 1310/97 Recital 12] It should be possible to suspend exceptionally the period within which the Commission must take a decision within the first phase of the procedure;

[19] The undertakings concerned must be afforded the right to be heard by the Commission when proceedings have been initiated; whereas the members of the management and supervisory bodies and the recognised representatives of the employees of the undertakings concerned, and third parties showing a legitimate interest, must also be given the opportunity to be heard;

[20] The Commission should act in close and constant liaison with the competent authorities of the Member States from which it obtains comments and information;

[21] For the purposes of this Regulation, and in accordance with the case law of the Court of Justice, the Commission must be afforded the assistance of the Member States and must also be empowered to require information to be given and to carry out the necessary investigations in order to appraise concentrations;

[22] Compliance with this Regulation must be enforceable by means of fines and periodic penalty payments; whereas the Court of Justice should be given unlimited jurisdiction in that regard pursuant to Article 229 of the Treaty;

[23—Reg. 1310/97 Recital 5] It is appropriate to define the concept of concentration in such a manner as to cover operations bringing about a lasting change in the structure of the undertakings concerned; whereas in the specific case of joint ventures it is appropriate to include within the scope and procedure of [this] Regulation *(4064/89)* all full-function joint ventures; whereas, in addition to the dominance test set out in Article 2 *of that Regulation*, it should be provided that the Commission apply the criteria of Article 81(1) and (3) of the Treaty to such joint ventures, to the extent that their creation has as its direct consequence an appreciable restriction of competition between undertakings that remain independent; whereas, if the effects of such joint ventures on the market are primarily structural, Article 81(1) does not as a general rule apply; whereas Article 81(1) may apply if two or more parent companies remain active in the market of the joint venture, or, possibly, if the creation of the joint venture has as its object or effect the prevention, restriction or distortion of competition between the parent companies in upstream, downstream or neighbouring markets; whereas, in this context, the appraisal of all competition aspects of the creation of the joint venture must be made within the same procedure;

Recital 23 has been superseded by the above recital in Reg. 1310/97: It is appropriate to define the concept of concentration in such a manner as to cover only operations bringing about a lasting change in the structure of the undertakings concerned; whereas it is therefore necessary to exclude from the scope of this Regulation those operations which have as their object or effect the co-ordination of the competitive behaviour of undertakings which remain independent, since such operations fall to be examined under the appropriate provisions of the Regulations implementing Article 81 and 82 of the Treaty; whereas it is appropriate to make this distinction specifically in the case of the creation of joint ventures;]

[24] There is no co-ordination of competitive behaviour within the meaning of this Regulation where two or more undertakings agree to acquire jointly control of one or more other undertakings with the object and effect of sharing amongst themselves such undertakings or their assets;

[25] This Regulation should still apply where the undertakings concerned accept restrictions directly related and necessary to the implementation of the concentration;

[25A—Reg. 1310/97 Recital 7] It should be expressly provided that decisions taken at the end of the first phase of the procedure cover restrictions directly related and necessary for the implementation of a concentration;

[25B—Reg. 1310/97 Recital 8] The Commission may declare a concentration compatible with the Common Market in the second phase of the procedure, following commitments by the parties that are proportional to and would entirely eliminate the competition problem; whereas it is also appropriate to accept commitments in the first phase of the procedure where the competition problem is readily identifiable and can easily be remedied; whereas it should be expressly provided that in these cases the Commission may attach to its decision conditions and obligations; whereas transparency and effective consultation of Member States and interested third parties should be ensured in both phases of the procedure;

[26] The Commission should be given exclusive competence to apply this Regulation subject to review by the Court of Justice;

[27] The Member States may not apply their national legislation on competition to concentrations with a Community dimension, unless this Regulation makes provision therefor; whereas the relevant powers of national authorities should be limited to cases where, failing intervention by the Commission, effective competition is likely to be significantly impeded within the territory of a Member State and where the competition interests of that Member State cannot be sufficiently protected otherwise by this Regulation; whereas the Member States concerned must act promptly in such cases; whereas this Regulation cannot, because of the diversity of national law, fix a single deadline for the adoption of remedies;

[28] Furthermore, the exclusive application of this Regulation to concentrations with a Community dimension is without prejudice to Article 296 of the Treaty, and does not prevent the Member States from taking appropriate measures to protect legitimate interests other than those pursued by this Regulation, provided that such measures are compatible with the general principles and other provisions of Community law;

[28A—Reg. 1310/97 Recital 10] The rules governing the referral of concentrations between the Commission and Member States should be reviewed at the same time as the additional criteria for implementation of Community merger control are established; whereas these rules protect the competition interests of the Member States in an adequate manner and take due account of legal security and the "one-stop shop" principle; whereas, however, certain aspects of the referral procedures should be improved or clarified;

[28B—Reg. 1310/97 Recital 11] In particular, the Commission can declare a concentration incompatible with the Common Market only if it impedes effective competition in a substantial part thereof; whereas the application of national competition law is, therefore, particularly appropriate where a concentration affects competition on a distinct market within a Member State that does not constitute a substantial part of the Common Market; whereas in this case it should not be necessary to demonstrate, in the request for referral, that the concentration threatens to create or to strengthen a dominant position on this distinct market;

[29] Concentrations not covered by this Regulation come, in principle, within the jurisdiction of the Member States; whereas, however, the Commission should have the power to act, at the request of a Member State concerned, in cases where effective competition could be significantly impeded within that Member State's territory;

[29A—Reg. 1310/97 Recital 13] It should be expressly provided that two or more Member States may make a joint request pursuant to Article 22 *of Regulation 4064/89; whereas to ensure effective control, provision should be made for the suspension of concentrations referred to the Commission by one or more Member States (Article 22(4))*;

[30] The conditions in which concentrations involving Community undertakings are carried out in non-Member countries should be observed, and provision should be made for the possibility of the Council giving the Commission an appropriate mandate for negotiation with a view to obtaining non-discriminatory treatment for Community undertakings;

[30A—Reg. 1310/97 Recital 14] The Commission should be given the power to adopt implementing provisions where necessary,

[31] This Regulation in no way detracts from the collective rights of employees as recognised in the undertakings concerned.
HAS ADOPTED THIS REGULATION:

Article 1

Scope

1. Without prejudice to Article 22, this Regulation shall apply to all concentrations with a Community dimension as defined in paragraphs 2 and 3.

2. For the purposes of this Regulation, a concentration has a Community dimension where:

(a) the combined aggregate world-wide turnover of all the undertakings concerned is more than 5,000 million ECUs; and
(b) the aggregate Community-wide turnover of each of at least two of the undertakings concerned is more than 250 million ECUs,

unless each of the undertakings concerned achieves more than two-thirds of its aggregate Community-wide turnover within one and the same Member State.

3. For the purposes of this Regulation, a concentration that does not meet the thresholds laid down in paragraph 2 has a Community dimension where:

(a) the combined aggregate world-wide turnover of all the undertakings concerned is more than 2,500 million ECUs;
(b) in each of at least three Member States, the combined aggregate turnover of all the undertakings concerned is more than 100 million ECUs;

(c) in each of at least three Member States included for the purpose of point (b), the aggregate turnover of each of at least two of the undertakings concerned is more than 25 million ECUs; and
(d) the aggregate Community-wide turnover of each of at least two of the undertakings concerned is more than 100 million ECUs;

unless each of the undertakings concerned achieves more than two-thirds of its aggregate Community-wide turnover within one and the same Member State.

4. Before 1 July 2000 the Commission shall report to the Council on the operation of the thresholds and criteria set out in paragraphs 2 and 3.

5. Following the report referred to in paragraph 4 and on a proposal from the Commission, the Council, acting by a qualified majority, may revise the thresholds and criteria mentioned in paragraph 3.

Article 2

Appraisal of concentrations

1. Concentrations within the scope of this Regulation shall be appraised in accordance with the following provisions with a view to establishing whether or not they are compatible with the Common Market.

In making this appraisal, the Commission shall take into account:

(a) the need to maintain and develop effective competition within the Common Market in view of, among other things, the structure of all the markets concerned and the actual or potential competition from undertakings located either within or outwith the Community;
(b) the market position of the undertakings concerned and their economic and financial power, the alternatives available to suppliers and users, their access to suppliers or markets, any legal or other barriers to entry, supply and demand trends for the relevant goods and services, the interests of the intermediate and ultimate consumers, and the development of technical and economic progress provided that it is to consumers' advantage and does not form an obstacle to competition.

2. A concentration which does not create or strengthen a dominant position as a result of which effective competition would be significantly impeded in the Common Market or in a substantial part of it shall be declared compatible with the Common Market (*see also Recital 15*).

3. A concentration which creates or strengthens a dominant position as a result of which effective competition would be significantly impeded in the Common Market or in a substantial part of it shall be declared incompatible with the Common Market.

4. To the extent that the creation of a joint venture constituting a concentration pursuant to Article 3 has as its object or effect the co-ordination of the competitive behaviour of undertakings that remain independent, such co-ordination shall be appraised in accordance with the criteria of Article 81(1) and (3) of the Treaty, with a view to establishing whether or not the operation is compatible with the Common Market.

In making this appraisal, the Commission shall take into account in particular:

— whether two or more parent companies retain to a significant extent activities in the same market as the joint venture or in a market which is downstream or upstream from that of the joint venture or in a neighbouring market closely related to this market,
— whether the co-ordination which is the direct consequence of the creation of the joint venture affords the undertakings concerned the possibility of eliminating competition in respect of a substantial part of the products or services in question.

318

Article 3

Definition of concentration

1. A concentration shall be deemed to arise where:

(a) two or more previously independent undertakings merge, or
(b) — one or more persons already controlling at least one undertaking, or
— one or more undertakings

acquire, whether by purchase of securities or assets, by contract or by any other means, direct or indirect control of the whole or parts of one or more other undertakings.

2. The creation of a joint venture performing on a lasting basis all the functions of an autonomous economic entity shall constitute a concentration within the meaning of paragraph 1(b).

3. For the purposes of this Regulation, control shall be constituted by rights, contracts or any other means which, either separately or in combination and having regard to the considerations of fact or law involved, confer the possibility of exercising decisive influence on an undertaking, in particular by:

(a) ownership or the right to use all or part of the assets of an undertaking;
(b) rights or contracts which confer decisive influence on the composition, voting or decisions of the organs of an undertaking.

4. Control is acquired by persons or undertakings which:

(a) are holders of the rights or entitled to rights under the contracts concerned; or
(b) while not being holders of such rights or entitled to rights under such contracts, have the power to exercise the rights deriving therefrom.

5. A concentration shall not be deemed to arise where:

(a) credit institutions or other financial institutions or insurance companies, the normal activities of which include transactions and dealing in securities for their own account or for the account of others, hold on a temporary basis securities which they have acquired in an undertaking with a view to reselling them, provided that they do not exercise voting rights in respect of those securities with a view to determining the competitive behaviour of that undertaking or provided that they exercise such voting rights only with a view to preparing the disposal of all or part of that undertaking or of its assets or the disposal of those securities and that any such disposal takes place within one year of the date of acquisition; that period may be extended by the Commission on request where such institutions or companies can show that the disposal was not reasonably possible within the period set;
(b) control is acquired by an officeholder according to the law of a Member State relating to liquidation, winding up, insolvency, cessation of payments, compositions or analogous proceedings;
(c) the operations referred to in paragraph 1(b) are carried out by the financial holding companies referred to in Article 5(3) of the Fourth Council Directive 78/660 on the annual accounts of certain types of companies,[6] as last amended by Directive 84/569,[7] provided however that the voting rights in respect of the holding are exercised, in particular in relation to the appointment of members of the management and supervisory bodies of the undertakings in which they have holdings, only to

---

[6] OJ 1978 L222/11.
[7] OJ 1984 L314/28.

maintain the full value of those investments and not to determine directly or indirectly the competitive conduct of those undertakings.

Article 4

Prior notification of concentrations

1. Concentrations with a Community dimension defined in this Regulation shall be notified to the Commission not more than one week after the conclusion of the agreement, or the announcement of the public bid, or the acquisition of a controlling interest. That week shall begin when the first of those events occurs.

2. A concentration which consists of a merger within the meaning of Article 3(1)(a) or in the acquisition of joint control within the meaning of Article 3(1)(b) shall be notified jointly by the parties to the merger or by those acquiring joint control as the case may be. In all other cases, the notification shall be effected by the person or undertaking acquiring control of the whole or parts of one or more undertakings.

3. Where the Commission finds that a notified concentration falls within the scope of this Regulation, it shall publish the fact of the notification, at the same time indicating the names of the parties, the nature of the concentration and the economic sectors involved. The Commission shall take account of the legitimate interest of undertakings in the protection of their business secrets.

Article 5

Calculation of turnover

1. Aggregate turnover within the meaning of Article 1(2) shall comprise the amounts derived by the undertakings concerned in the preceding financial year from the sale of products and the provision of services falling within the undertakings; ordinary activities after deduction of sales rebates and of value added tax and other taxes directly related to turnover. The aggregate turnover of an undertaking concerned shall not include the sale of products or the provision of services between any of the undertakings referred to in paragraph 4.

Turnover, in the Community or in a Member State, shall comprise products sold and services provided to undertakings or consumers, in the Community or in that Member State as the case may be.

2. By way of derogation from paragraph 1, where the concentration consists in the acquisition of parts, whether or not constituted as legal entities, of one or more undertakings, only the turnover relating to the parts which are the subject of the transaction shall be taken into account with regard to the seller or sellers.

However, two or more transactions within the meaning of the first subparagraph which take place within a two-year period between the same persons or undertakings shall be treated as one and the same concentration arising on the date of the last transaction.

3. In place of turnover the following shall be used:

(a) for credit institutions and other financial institutions, as regards Article 1(2) and (3), the sum of the following income items as defined in Council Directive 86/635 on the annual accounts and consolidated accounts of banks and other financial institutions,[8] after deduction of value added tax and other taxes directly related to those items, where appropriate:
   (i) interest income and similar income;
   (ii) income from securities;
       — income from shares and other variable yield securities,

---

[8] OJ 1986 L372/1.

— income from participating interests,
— income from shares in affiliated undertakings;
(iii) commissions receivable;
(iv) net profit on financial operations;
(v) other operating income.

The turnover of a credit or financial institution in the Community or in a Member State shall comprise the income items, as defined above, which are received by the branch or division of that institution established in the Community or in the Member State in question, as the case may be;

(b) for insurance undertakings, the value of gross premiums written which shall comprise all amounts received and receivable in respect of insurance contracts issued by or on behalf of the insurance undertakings, including also outgoing reinsurance premiums, and after deduction of taxes and parafiscal contributions or levies charged by reference to the amounts of individual premiums or the total volume of premiums; as regards Article 1(2)(b) and (3)(b), (c) and (d) and the final part of Article 1(2) and (3), gross premiums received from Community residents and from residents of one Member State respectively shall be taken into account.

4. Without prejudice to paragraph 2, the aggregate turnover of an undertaking concerned within the meaning of Article 1(2) and (3) shall be calculated by adding together the respective turnovers of the following:

(a) the undertaking concerned;
(b) those undertakings in which the undertaking concerned, directly or indirectly:
— owns more than half the capital or business assets, or
— has the power to appoint more than half the members of the supervisory board, the administrative board or bodies legally representing the undertakings, or
— has the right to manage the undertakings' affairs;
(c) those undertakings which have in the undertaking concerned the rights or powers listed in (b);
(d) those undertakings in which an undertaking as referred to in (c) has the rights or powers listed in (b);
(e) those undertakings in which two or more undertakings as referred to in (a) to (d) jointly have the rights or powers listed in (b).

5. Where undertakings concerned by the concentration jointly have the rights or powers listed in paragraph 4(b), in calculating the aggregate turnover of the undertakings concerned for the purposes of Article 1(2) and (3):

(a) no account shall be taken of the turnover resulting from the sale of products or the provision of services between the joint undertaking and each of the undertakings concerned or any other undertaking connected with any one of them, as set out in paragraph 4(b) to (e);
(b) account shall be taken of the turnover resulting from the sale of products and the provision of services between the joint undertaking and any third undertakings. This turnover shall be apportioned equally amongst the undertakings concerned.

Article 6

Examination of the notification and initiation of proceedings

1. The Commission shall examine the notification as soon as it is received.

(a) Where it concludes that the concentration notified does not fall within the scope of this Regulation, it shall record that finding by means of a decision.

(b) Where it finds that the concentration notified, although falling within the scope of this Regulation, does not raise serious doubts as to its compatibility with the Common Market, it shall decide not to oppose it and shall declare that it is compatible with the Common Market.

The decision declaring the concentration compatible shall also cover restrictions directly related and necessary to the implementation of the concentration.

(c) Without prejudice to paragraph 2, where the Commission finds that the concentration notified falls within the scope of this Regulation and raises serious doubts as to its compatibility with the Common Market, it shall decide to initiate proceedings.

2. Where the Commission finds that, following modification by the undertakings concerned, a notified concentration no longer raises serious doubts within the meaning of paragraph 1(c), it may decide to declare the concentration compatible with the Common Market pursuant to paragraph 1(b).

The Commission may attach to its decision under paragraph 1(b) conditions and obligations intended to ensure that the undertakings concerned comply with the commitments they have entered into *vis–à–vis* the Commission with a view to rendering the concentration compatible with the Common Market.

3. The Commission may revoke the decision it has taken pursuant to paragraph 1(a) or (b) where:

(a) the decision is based on incorrect information for which one of the undertakings is responsible or where it has been obtained by deceit; or
(b) the undertakings concerned commit a breach of an obligation attached to the decision.

4. In the cases referred to in paragraph 1(b), the Commission may take a decision under paragraph 1, without being bound by the deadlines referred to in Article 10(1).

5. The Commission shall notify its decision to the undertakings concerned and the competent authorities of the Member States without delay.

Article 7

Suspension of concentrations

1. A concentration as defined in Article 1 shall not be put into effect either before its notification or until it has been declared compatible with the Common Market pursuant to a decision under Article 6(1)(b) or Article 8(2) or on the basis of a presumption according to Article 10(6).

2. [Deleted]

3. Paragraph 1 shall not prevent the implementation of a public bid which has been notified to the Commission in accordance with Article 4(1), provided that the acquirer does not exercise the voting rights attached to the securities in question or does so only to maintain the full value of those investments and on the basis of a derogation granted by the Commission under paragraph 4.

4. The Commission may, on request, grant a derogation from the obligations imposed in paragraph 1 or 3. The request to grant a derogation must be reasoned. In deciding on the request, the Commission shall take into account *inter alia* the effects of the suspension on one or more undertakings concerned by a concentration or on a third party and the threat to competition posed by the concentration. That derogation may be made subject to conditions and obligations in order to ensure conditions of effective competition. A derogation may be applied for and granted at any time, even before notification or after the transaction.

5. The validity of any transaction carried out in contravention of paragraph 1 shall be dependent on a decision pursuant to Article 6(1)(b) or Article 8(2) or (3) or on a presumption pursuant to Article 10(6).

This Article shall, however, have no effect on the validity of transactions in securities including those convertible into other securities admitted to trading on a market which is regulated and supervised by authorities recognised by public bodies, operates regularly and is accessible directly or indirectly to the public, unless the buyer and seller knew or ought to have known that the transaction was carried out in contravention of paragraph 1.

Article 8

Powers of decision of the Commission

1. Without prejudice to Article 9, all proceedings initiated pursuant to Article 6(1)(c) shall be closed by means of a decision as provided for in paragraphs 2 to 5.

2. Where the Commission finds that, following modification by the undertakings concerned if necessary, a notified concentration fulfils the criterion laid down in Article 2(2) and, in the cases referred to in Article 2(4), the criteria laid down in Article 81(3) of the Treaty, it shall issue a decision declaring the concentration compatible with the Common Market.

It may attach to its decision conditions and obligations intended to ensure that the undertakings concerned comply with the commitments they have entered into *vis-à-vis* the Commission with a view to rendering the concentration compatible with the Common Market. The decision declaring the concentration compatible with the Common Market shall also cover restrictions directly related and necessary to the implementation of the concentration.

3. Where the Commission finds that a concentration fulfils the criterion defined in Article 2(3) or, in the cases referred to in Article 2(4), does not fulfil the criteria laid down in Article 81(3) of the Treaty, it shall issue a decision declaring that the concentration is incompatible with the Common Market.

4. Where a concentration has already been implemented, the Commission may, in a decision pursuant to paragraph 3 or by separate decision, require the undertakings or assets brought together to be separated or the cessation of joint control or any other action that may be appropriate in order to restore conditions of effective competition.

5. The Commission may revoke the decision it has taken pursuant to paragraph 2 where:

(a) the declaration of compatibility is based on incorrect information for which one of the undertakings is responsible or where it has been obtained by deceit; or
(b) the undertakings concerned commit a breach of an obligation attached to the decision.

6. In the cases referred to in paragraph 5, the Commission may take a decision under paragraph 3, without being bound by the deadline referred to in Article 10(3).

Article 9

Referral to the competent authorities of the Member States

1. The Commission may, by means of a decision notified without delay to the undertakings concerned and the competent authorities of the Member States, refer a notified concentration to the competent authorities of a Member State concerned in the following circumstances.

2. Within three weeks of the date of receipt of the copy of the notification a Member State may inform the Commission, which shall inform the undertakings concerned, that:

(a) a concentration threatens to create or to strengthen a dominant position as a result of which effective competition will be significantly impeded on a market within that Member State, which presents all the characteristics of a distinct market, or
(b) a concentration affects competition on a market within that Member State, which presents all the characteristics of a distinct market and which does not constitute a substantial part of the Common Market.

3. If the Commission considers that, having regard to the market for the products or services in question and the geographical reference market within the meaning of paragraph 7, there is such a distinct market and that such a threat exists, either:

(a) it shall itself deal with the case in order to maintain or restore effective competition on the market concerned; or
(b) it shall refer the whole or part of the case to the competent authorities of the Member State concerned with a view to the application of that State's national competition law.

In cases where a Member State informs the Commission that a concentration affects competition in a distinct market within its territory that does not form a substantial part of the Common Market, the Commission shall refer the whole or part of the case relating to the distinct market concerned, if it considers that such a distinct market is affected.

4. A decision to refer or not to refer pursuant to paragraph 3 shall be taken:

(a) as a general rule within the six-week period provided for in Article 10(1), second subparagraph, where the Commission, pursuant to Article 6(1)(b), has not initiated proceedings; or
(b) within three months at most of the notification of the concentration concerned where the Commission has initiated proceedings under Article 6(1)(c), without taking the preparatory steps in order to adopt the necessary measures under Article 8(2), second subparagraph, (3) or (4) to maintain or restore effective competition on the market concerned.

5. If within the three months referred to in paragraph 4(b) the Commission, despite a reminder from the Member State concerned, has not taken a decision on referral in accordance with paragraph 3 nor has it taken the preparatory steps referred to in paragraph 4(b), it shall be deemed to have taken a decision to refer the case to the Member State concerned in accordance with paragraph 3(b).

6. The publication of any report or the announcement of the findings of the examination of the concentration by the competent authority of the Member State concerned shall be effected not more than four months after the Commission's referral.

7. The geographical reference market shall consist of the area in which the undertakings concerned are involved in the supply and demand of products or services, in which the conditions of competition are sufficiently homogeneous and which can be distinguished from neighbouring areas because, in particular, conditions of competition are appreciably different in those areas. This assessment should take account in particular of the nature and characteristics of the products or services concerned, of the existence of entry barriers, of consumer preferences, of appreciable differences of the undertakings' market shares between the area concerned and neighbouring areas or of substantial price differences.

8. In applying the provisions of this Article, the Member State concerned may take only the measures strictly necessary to safeguard or restore effective competition on the market concerned.

9. In accordance with the relevant provisions of the Treaty, any Member State may appeal to the Court of Justice, and in particular request the application of Article 243, for the purpose of applying its national competition law.

10. This Article may be re-examined at the same time as the thresholds referred to in Article 1.

Article 10

Time limits for initiating proceedings and for decisions

1. The decisions referred to in Article 6(1) must be taken within one month at most. That period shall begin on the day following that of the receipt of a notification or, if the information to be supplied with the notification is incomplete, on the day following that of the receipt of the complete information.

That period shall be increased to six weeks if the Commission receives a request from a Member State in accordance with Article 9(2) or where, after notification of a concentration, the undertakings concerned submit commitments pursuant to Article 6(2), which are intended by the parties to form the basis for a decision pursuant to Article 6(1)(b).

2. Decisions taken pursuant to Article 8(2) concerning notified concentrations must be taken as soon as it appears that the serious doubts referred to in Article 6(1)(c) have been removed, particularly as a result of modifications made by the undertakings concerned, and at the latest by the deadline laid down in paragraph 3.

3. Without prejudice to Article 8(6), decisions taken pursuant to Article 8(3) concerning notified concentrations must be taken within not more than four months of the date on which proceedings are initiated.

4. The periods set by paragraphs 1 and 3 shall exceptionally be suspended where, owing to circumstances for which one of the undertakings involved in the concentration is responsible, the Commission has had to request information by decision pursuant to Article 11 or to order an investigation by decision pursuant to Article 13.

5. Where the Court of Justice gives a judgment which annuls the whole or part of a Commission decision taken under this Regulation, the periods laid down in this Regulation shall start again from the date of the judgment.

6. Where the Commission has not taken a decision in accordance with Article 6(1)(b) or (c) or Article 8(2) or (3) within the deadlines set in paragraphs 1 and 3 respectively, the concentration shall be deemed to have been declared compatible with the Common Market, without prejudice to Article 9.

Article 11

Requests for information

1. In carrying out the duties assigned to it by this Regulation, the Commission may obtain all necessary information from the governments and competent authorities of the Member States, from the persons referred to in Article 3(1)(b), and from undertakings and associations of undertakings.

2. When sending a request for information to a person, an undertaking or an association of undertakings, the Commission shall at the same time send a copy of the request to the competent authority of the Member State within the territory of which the residence of the person or the seat of the undertaking or association of undertakings is situated.

3. In its request the Commission shall state the legal basis and the purpose of the request and also the penalties provided for in Article 14(1)(c) for supplying incorrect information.

4. The information requested shall be provided, in the case of undertakings, by their owners or their representatives and, in the case of legal persons, companies or firms, or of

associations having no legal personality, by the persons authorised to represent them by law or by their statutes.

5. Where a person, an undertaking or an association of undertakings does not provide the information requested within the period fixed by the Commission or provides incomplete information, the Commission shall by decision require the information to be provided. The decision shall specify what information is required, fix an appropriate period within which it is to be supplied and state the penalties provided for in Articles 14(1)(c) and 15(1)(a) and the right to have the decision reviewed by the Court of Justice.

6. The Commission shall at the same time send a copy of its decision to the competent authority of the Member State within the territory of which the residence of the person or the seat of the undertaking or association of undertakings is situated.

Article 12

Investigations by the authorities of the Member States

1. At the request of the Commission, the competent authorities of the Member States shall undertake the investigations which the Commission considers to be necessary under Article 13(1), or which it has ordered by decision pursuant to Article 13(3). The officials of the competent authorities of the Member States responsible for conducting those investigations shall exercise their powers upon production of an authorisation in writing issued by the competent authority of the Member State within the territory of which the investigation is to be carried out. Such authorisation shall specify the subject matter and purpose of the investigation.

2. If so requested by the Commission or by the competent authority of the Member State within the territory of which the investigation is to be carried out, officials of the Commission may assist the officials of that authority in carrying out their duties.

Article 13

Investigative powers of the Commission

1. In carrying out the duties assigned to it by this Regulation, the Commission may undertake all necessary investigations into undertakings and associations of undertakings.

To that end the officials authorised by the Commission shall be empowered:

(a) to examine the books and other business records;
(b) to take or demand copies of or extracts from the books and business records;
(c) to ask for oral explanations on the spot;
(d) to enter any premises, land and means of transport of undertakings.

2. The officials of the Commission authorised to carry out the investigations shall exercise their powers on production of an authorisation in writing specifying the subject matter and purpose of the investigation and the penalties provided for in Article 14(1)(d) in cases where production of the required books or other business records is incomplete. In good time before the investigation, the Commission shall inform, in writing, the competent authority of the Member State within the territory of which the investigation is to be carried out of the investigation and of the identities of the authorised officials.

3. Undertakings and associations of undertakings shall submit to investigations ordered by decision of the Commission. The decision shall specify the subject matter and purpose of the investigation, appoint the date on which it shall begin and state the penalties provided for in Articles 14(1)(d) and 15(1)(b) and the right to have the decision reviewed by the Court of Justice.

4. The Commission shall in good time and in writing inform the competent authority of the Member State within the territory of which the investigation is to be carried out of its intention of taking a decision pursuant to paragraph 3. It shall hear the competent authority before taking its decision.

5. Officials of the competent authority of the Member State within the territory of which the investigation is to be carried out may, at the request of that authority or of the Commission, assist the officials of the Commission in carrying out their duties.

6. Where an undertaking or association of undertakings opposes an investigation ordered pursuant to this Article, the Member State concerned shall afford the necessary assistance to the officials authorised by the Commission to enable them to carry out their investigation. To this end the Member States shall, after consulting the Commission, take the necessary measures within one year of the entry into force of this Regulation.

Article 14

Fines

1. The Commission may by decision impose on the persons referred to in Article 3(1)(b), undertakings or associations of undertakings fines of from 1,000 to 50,000 ECUs where intentionally or negligently:

(a) they fail to notify a concentration in accordance with Article 4;
(b) they supply incorrect or misleading information in a notification pursuant to Article 4;
(c) they supply incorrect information in response to a request made pursuant to Article 11 or fail to supply information within the period fixed by a decision taken pursuant to Article 11;
(d) they produce the required books or other business records in incomplete form during investigations under Article 12 or 13, or refuse to submit to an investigation ordered by decision taken pursuant to Article 13.

2. The Commission may by decision impose fines not exceeding 10 per cent of the aggregate turnover of the undertakings concerned within the meaning of Article 5 on the persons or undertakings concerned where, either intentionally or negligently, they:

(a) fail to comply with an obligation imposed by decision pursuant to Article 7(4) or 8(2), second subparagraph;
(b) put into effect a concentration in breach of Article 7(1) or disregard a decision taken pursuant to Article 7(2);
(c) put into effect a concentration declared incompatible with the Common Market by decision pursuant to Article 8(3) or do not take the measures ordered by decision pursuant to Article 8(4).

3. In setting the amount of a fine, regard shall be had to the nature and gravity of the infringement.

4. Decisions taken pursuant to paragraphs 1 and 2 shall not be of criminal law nature.

Article 15

Periodic penalty payments

1. The Commission may by decision impose on the persons referred to in Article 3(1)(b), undertakings or associations of undertakings concerned periodic penalty payments of up

to 25,000 ECUs for each day of delay calculated from the date set in the decision, in order to compel them:

(a) to supply complete and correct information which it has requested by decision pursuant to Article 11;
(b) to submit to an investigation which it has ordered by decision pursuant to Article 13.

2. The Commission may by decision impose on the persons referred to in Article 3(1)(b) or on undertakings periodic penalty payments of up to 100,000 ECUs for each day of delay calculated from the date set in the decision, in order to compel them:

(a) to comply with an obligation imposed by decision pursuant to Article 7(4) or Article 8(2), second subparagraph; or
(b) to apply the measures ordered by decision pursuant to Article 8(4).

3. Where the persons referred to in Article 3(1)(b), undertakings or associations of undertakings have satisfied the obligation which it was the purpose of the periodic penalty payment to enforce, the Commission may set the total amount of the periodic penalty payments at a lower figure than that which would arise under the original decision.

Article 16

Review by the Court of Justice

The Court of Justice shall have unlimited jurisdiction within the meaning of Article 229 of the Treaty to review decisions whereby the Commission has fixed a fine or periodic penalty payments; it may cancel, reduce or increase the fine or periodic penalty payments imposed.

Article 17

Professional secrecy

1. Information acquired as a result of the application of Articles 11, 12, 13 and 18 shall be used only for the purposes of the relevant request, investigation or hearing.
2. Without prejudice to Articles 4(3), 18 and 20, the Commission and the competent authorities of the Member States, their officials and other servants shall not disclose information they have acquired through the application of this Regulation of the kind covered by the obligation of professional secrecy.
3. Paragraphs 1 and 2 shall not prevent publication of general information or of surveys which do not contain information relating to particular undertakings or associations of undertakings.

Article 18

Hearing of the parties and of third persons

1. Before taking any decision provided for in Article 7(4), Article 8(2) second subparagraph, and (3) to (5) and Articles 14 and 15, the Commission shall give the persons, undertakings and associations of undertakings concerned the opportunity, at every stage of the procedure up to the consultation of the Advisory Committee, of making known their views on the objections against them.

2. By way of derogation from paragraph 1, a decision to grant a derogation from suspension as referred to in Article 7(4) may be taken provisionally, without the persons, undertakings or associations of undertakings concerned being given the opportunity to make known their views beforehand, provided that the Commission gives them that opportunity as soon as possible after having taken its decision.

3. The Commission shall base its decision only on objections on which the parties have been able to submit their observations. The rights of the defence shall be fully respected in the proceedings. Access to the file shall be open at least to the parties directly involved, subject to the legitimate interest of undertakings in the protection of their business secrets.

4. In so far as the Commission or the competent authorities of the Member States deem it necessary, they may also hear other natural or legal persons. Natural or legal persons showing a sufficient interest and especially members of the administrative or management bodies of the undertakings concerned or the recognised representatives of their employees shall be entitled, upon application, to be heard.

Article 19

Liaison with the authorities of the Member States

1. The Commission shall transmit to the competent authorities of the Member States copies of notifications within three working days and, as soon as possible, copies of the most important documents lodged with or issued by the Commission pursuant to this Regulation.

Such documents shall include commitments which are intended by the parties to form the basis for a decision pursuant to Articles 6(1)(b) or 8(2).

2. The Commission shall carry out the procedures set out in this Regulation in close and constant liaison with the competent authorities of the Member States, which may express their views upon those procedures. For the purposes of Article 9 it shall obtain information from the competent authority of the Member State as referred to in paragraph 2 of that Article and give it the opportunity to make known its views at every stage of the procedure up to the adoption of a decision pursuant to paragraph 3 of that Article; to that end it shall give it access to the file.

3. An Advisory Committee on concentrations shall be consulted before any decision is taken pursuant to Article 8(2) to (5), 14 or 15, or any provisions are adopted pursuant to Article 23.

4. The Advisory Committee shall consist of representatives of the authorities of the Member States. Each Member State shall appoint one or two representatives; if unable to attend, they may be replaced by other representatives. At least one of the representatives of a Member State shall be competent in matters of restrictive practices and dominant positions.

5. Consultation shall take place at a joint meeting convened at the invitation of and chaired by the Commission. A summary of the case, together with an indication of the most important documents and a preliminary draft of the decision to be taken for each case considered, shall be sent with the invitation. The meeting shall take place not less than 14 days after the invitation has been sent. The Commission may in exceptional cases shorten that period as appropriate in order to avoid serious harm to one or more of the undertakings concerned by a concentration.

6. The Advisory Committee shall deliver an opinion on the Commission's draft decision, if necessary by taking a vote. The Advisory Committee may deliver an opinion even if some members are absent and unrepresented. The opinion shall be delivered in writing and appended to the draft decision. The Commission shall take the utmost account of the opinion delivered by the Committee. It shall inform the Committee of the manner in which its opinion has been taken into account.

7. The Advisory Committee may recommend publication of the opinion. The Commission may carry out such publication. The decision to publish shall take due account of the

legitimate interest of undertakings in the protection of their business secrets and of the interest of the undertakings concerned in such publications taking place.

Article 20

Publication of decisions

1. The Commission shall publish the decisions which it takes pursuant to Article 8(2) to (5) in the *Official Journal of the European Communities*.
2. The publication shall state the names of the parties and the main content of the decision; it shall have regard to the legitimate interest of undertakings in the protection of their business secrets.

Article 21

Jurisdiction

1. Subject to review by the Court of Justice, the Commission shall have sole jurisdiction to take the decisions provided for in this Regulation.
2. No Member State shall apply its national legislation on competition to any consideration that has a Community dimension.

The first subparagraph shall be without prejudice to any Member State's power to carry out any enquiries necessary for the application to Article 9(2) or after referral, pursuant to Article 9(3), first subparagraph, indent (b), or (5), to take the measures strictly necessary for the application of Article 9(8).

3. Notwithstanding paragraphs 1 and 2, Member States may take appropriate measures to protect legitimate interests other than those taken into consideration by this Regulation and compatible with the general principles and other provisions of Community law.

Public security, plurality of the media and prudential rules shall be regarded as legitimate interests within the meaning of the first subparagraph.

Any other public interest must be communicated to the Commission by the Member State concerned and shall be recognised by the Commission after an assessment of its compatibility with the general principles and other provisions of Community law before the measures referred to above may be taken. The Commission shall inform the Member State concerned of its decision within one month of that communication.

Article 22

Application of the Regulation

1. This Regulation alone shall apply to concentrations as defined in Article 3, and Regulations 17, 1017/68, 4086/86 and 3975/87 shall not apply, except in relation to joint ventures that do not have a Community dimension and which have [as] their object or effect the co-ordination of the competitive behaviour of undertakings that remain independent.

3. If the Commission finds, at the request of a Member State or at the joint request of two or more Member States, that a concentration as defined in Article 3 that has no Community dimension within the meaning of Article 1 creates or strengthens a dominant position as a result of which effective competition would be significantly impeded within the territory of the Member State or States making the joint request, it may, in so far as that concentration affects trade between Member States, adopt the decisions provided for in Article 8(2), second subparagraph, (3) and (4).

4. Articles 2(1)(a) and (b), 5, 6, 8 and 10 to 20 shall apply to a request made pursuant to paragraph 3. Article 7 shall apply to the extent that the concentration has not been put

into effect on the date on which the Commission informs the parties that a request has been made.

The period within which proceedings may be initiated pursuant to Article 10(1) shall begin on the day following that of the receipt of the request from the Member State or States concerned. The request must be made within one month at most of the date on which the concentration was made known to the Member State or to all Member States making a joint request or affected. This period shall begin on the date of the first of those events.

5. Pursuant to paragraph 3 the Commission shall take only the measures strictly necessary to maintain or store effective competition within the territory of the Member State or States at the request of which it intervenes.

Article 23

Implementing provisions

The Commission shall have the power to adopt implementing provisions concerning the form, content and other details of notifications pursuant to Article 4, time-limits pursuant to Articles 7, 9, 10 and 22, and hearings pursuant to Article 18.

The Commission shall have the power to lay down the procedure and time limits for the submission of commitments pursuant to Articles 6(2) and 8(2).

Article 24

Relations with non-Member countries

1. The Member States shall inform the Commission of any general difficulties encountered by their undertakings with concentrations as defined in Article 3 in a non-Member country.

2. Initially not more than one year after the entry into force of this Regulation and thereafter periodically the Commission shall draw up a report examining the treatment accorded to Community undertakings, in the terms referred to in paragraphs 3 and 4, as regards concentrations in non-Member countries. The Commission shall submit those reports to the Council, together with any recommendations.

3. Whenever it appears to the Commission, either on the basis of the reports referred to in paragraph 2 or on the basis of other information, that a non-Member country does not grant Community undertakings treatment comparable to that granted by the Community to undertakings from that non-Member country, the Commission may submit proposals to the Council for an appropriate mandate for negotiation with a view to obtaining comparable treatment for Community undertakings.

4. Measures taken under this Article shall comply with the obligations of the Community or of the Member States, without prejudice to Article 307 of the Treaty, under international agreements, whether bilateral or multilateral.

Article 25

Entry into force

1. This Regulation shall enter into force on 21 September 1990.

2. This Regulation shall not apply to any concentration which was the subject of an agreement or announcement or where control was acquired within the meaning of Article 4(1) before the date of this Regulation's entry into force and it shall not in any circumstances apply to any concentration in respect of which proceedings were initiated before that date by a Member State's authority with responsibility for competition.

[3. As regards concentrations to which this Regulation applies by virtue of accession, the date of accession shall be substituted for the date of entry into force of this Regulation. The provision of paragraph 2, second alternative, applies in the same way to proceedings initiated by a competition authority of the new Member States or by the EFTA Surveillance Authority.]

This Regulation shall be binding in its entirety and directly applicable in all Member States.

Amendment

Para. 3 was added by the Act of Accession of the Republic of Austria, the Republic of Finland and the Kingdom of Sweden, Annex 1 (III)(B)(4), as amended by Council Decision 95/1, Article 39.

Entry into force of amendments made by Regulation 1310/97

... Regulation [1310/97] shall not apply to any concentration which was the subject of an agreement or announcement or where control was acquired within the meaning of Article 4(1) of Regulation 4064/89, before 1 March 1998 and it shall not in any circumstances apply to any concentration in respect of which proceedings were initiated before 1 March 1998 by a Member State's authority with responsibility for competition.

... Regulation [1310/97] shall enter into force on 1 March 1998.

... Regulation [1310/97] shall be binding in its entirety and directly applicable in all Member States.

NOTES ON COUNCIL REGULATION (EEC) 4064/89

For all appropriate purposes and in particular with a view to clarifying the scope of certain articles of the regulation, the following texts are drawn to the notice of interested parties:

re Article 1

- The Commission considers that the threshold for world turnover as set in Article 1(2)(a) of this regulation for the initial stage of implementation must be lowered to ECU 2,000 million at the end of that period. The *de minimis* threshold as set out in (b) should also be revised in the light of experience and the trend of the main threshold. It therefore undertakes to submit a proposal to that effect to the Council in due course.
- The Council and the Commission state their readiness to consider taking other factors into account in addition to turnover when the thresholds are revised.
- The Council and the Commission consider that the review of the thresholds as provided for in Article 1(3) will have to be combined with a special re-examination of the method of calculation of the turnover of joint undertakings as referred to in Article 5(5).

re Article 2

- The Commission states that among the factors to be taken into consideration for the purpose of establishing the compatibility or incompatibility of a concentration—factors as referred to in Article 2(1) and explained in Recital 13—account should be taken in particular of the competitiveness of undertakings located in regions which are greatly in need of restructuring owing *inter alia* to slow development.
- Under the first subparagraph of Article 2(1), the Commission has to establish in respect of each concentration covered by the regulation whether that concentration is compatible or incompatible with the common market.

The appraisal necessary for this purpose will have to be made on the basis of the same factors as defined in Article 2(1)(a) and (b) and within the context of a single appraisal procedure.

If, at the end of the first stage of appraisal (within one month of notification), the Commission reaches the conclusion that the concentration is not likely to create or reinforce a dominant position within the meaning of Article 2(3), it will decide against initiating proceedings. Such a decision will then establish the concentration's compatibility with the common market. It will be presented in the form of a letter and will be notified to the undertakings concerned and to the competent authorities of the Member States.

If the Commission has decided to initiate proceedings because it concludes that there is prima facie a real risk of creating or reinforcing a dominant position, and if further investigation (within a maximum period of four months of the initiation of proceedings) confirms this suspicion it will declare the concentration incompatible with the common market. If, on the contrary, the initial assumption is proved to be unfounded in the light of the further investigation, possibly in view of the changes made by the undertakings concerned to their initial project, the Commission will adopt a final decision noting that the operation is compatible with operation of the common market.

The decision on compatibility is therefore only the counterpart to a decision on incompatibility or prohibition.

- The Commission considers that the concept of "the structure of all the markets concerned" refers both to markets within the Community and to those outside it.
- The Commission considers that the concept of technical and economic progress must be understood in the light of the principles enshrined in Article 85(3) of the Treaty, as interpreted by the case law of the Court of Justice.

re Article 3(2), first indent

The Commission considers that this rule also applies to consortia in the liner trades sector.

re Article 5(3)(a)

The Council and the Commission consider that the criterion defined as a proportion of assets should be replaced by a concept of banking income as referred to in Directive 86/635 on the annual accounts and consolidated accounts of banks and other financial institutions, either at the actual time of entry into force of the relevant provisions of that directive or at the time of the review of thresholds referred to in Article 1 of this regulation and in the light of experience acquired.

re Article 9

- The Council and the Commission consider that, when a specific market represents a substantial part of the common market, the referral procedure provided for in Article 9 should only be applied in exceptional cases. There are indeed grounds for taking as a basis the principle that a concentration which creates or reinforces a dominant position in a substantial part of the common market must be declared incompatible with the common market. The Council and the Commission consider that such an application of Article 9 should be confined to cases in which the interests in respect of competition of the Member State concerned could not be adequately protected in any other way.

    They consider that the review of Article 9 referred to in paragraph 10 thereof should be carried out in the light of the experience gained in its application (which it is envisaged will be exceptional), having regard to the importance of the principle of exclusivity and the need to provide clarity and certainty for firms, with a view to considering whether it remains appropriate to include it in the regulation.

- The Commission states that the preparatory steps within the meaning of Article 9(4)(b) which must be taken during the period of three months are preliminary measures which should lead to a final decision within the remaining period of two-and-a-half months and normally take the form of the notification of objections within the meaning of Article 18(1).

re Articles 9(5) and 10(5)

The Commission states that it intends, in all cases of concentrations which are duly notified, to take the decisions provided for in Article 6(1), Article 8(2) and (3) and Article 9(3). Any Member State or undertaking concerned may ask the Commission to give written confirmation of its position with regard to the concentration.

re Articles 12 and 13

The Commission states that, pursuant to the principle of proportionality, it will carry out investigations within the meaning of Articles 12 and 13 only where particular circumstances so require.

re Article 19

The Council and the Commission agree that the arrangements for publication referred to in Article 19(7) will be reviewed after four years in the light of the experience acquired.

re Article 21(3)

1. Application of the general clause on "legitimate interests" must be subject to the following principles:

- It shall create no new rights for Member States and shall be restricted to sanctioning the recognition in Community law of their present reserved powers to intervene in certain aspects of concentrations affecting the territory coming within their jurisdiction on grounds other than those covered by this regulation. The application of this clause therefore reaffirms Member States' ability on those grounds either to prohibit a concentration or to make it subject to additional conditions and requirements. It does not imply the attribution to them of any power to authorise concentrations which the Commission may have prohibited under this regulation.
- Nor, by invoking the protection of the legitimate interests referred to, may a Member State justify itself on the basis of considerations which the Commission must take into account in assessing concentrations on a European scale. While mindful of the need to conserve and develop effective competition in the common market as required by the Treaty, the Commission must—in line with consistent decisions of the Court of Justice concerning the application of the rules of competition contained in the Treaty—place its assessment of the compatibility of a concentration in the overall context of the achievement of the fundamental objectives of the Treaty mentioned in Article 2, as well as that of strengthening the Community's economic and social cohesion referred to in Article 158.
- In order that the Commission may recognise the compatibility of the public interest claimed by a Member State with the general principles and other provisions of Community law, it is essential that prohibitions or restrictions placed on the forming of concentrations should constitute neither a form of arbitrary discrimination nor a disguised restriction in trade between Member States.
- In application of the principle of necessity or efficacity and of the rule of proportionality, measures which may be taken by Member States must satisfy the criterion of appropriateness for the objective and must be limited to the minimum of action necessary to ensure protection of the legitimate interest in question. The Member States must therefore choose, where alternatives exist, the measure which is objectively the least restrictive to achieve the end pursued.

2. The Commission considers that the three specific categories of legitimate interests which any Member State may freely cite under this provision are to be interpreted as follows:

- The reference to "public security" is made without prejudice to the provisions of Article 296 on national defence, which allow a Member State to intervene in respect of a concentration which would be contrary to the essential interests of its security and is connected with the production of or trade in arms, munitions and war material. The restriction set by that article concerning products not intended for specifically military purposes should be complied with.

There may be wider considerations of public security, both in the sense of Article 297 and in that of Article 30, in addition to defence interests in the strict sense. Thus the requirement for public security, as interpreted by the Court of Justice, could cover security of supplies to the country in question of a product or service considered of vital or essential interest for the protection of the population's health.

- The Member States' right to plead the "plurality of the media" recognises the legitimate concern to maintain diversified sources of information for the sake of plurality of opinion and multiplicity of views.
- Legitimate invocation may also be made of the prudential rules in Member States, which relate in particular to financial services: the application of these rules is normally confined to national bodies for the surveillance of banks, stockbroking firms and insurance companies. They concern, for example, the good repute of individuals, the honesty of transactions and the rules of solvency. These specific prudential criteria are also the subject of efforts aimed at a minimum degree of harmonisation being made in order to ensure uniform "rules of play" in the Community as a whole.

re Article 22

- The Commission states that it does not normally intend to apply Articles 81 and 82 of the Treaty establishing the European Economic Community to concentrations as defined in Article 3 other than by means of this regulation.

However, it reserves the right to take action in accordance with the procedures laid down in Article 85 of the Treaty, for concentrations as defined in Article 3, but which do not have a Community dimension within the meaning of Article 1, in cases not provided for by Article 22.

In any event, it does not intend to take action in respect of concentrations with a world-wide turnover of less than ECU 2,000 million or below a minimum Community turnover level of ECU 100 million or which are not covered by the threshold of two-thirds provided for in the last part of the sentence in Article 1(2), on the grounds that below such levels a concentration would not normally significantly affect trade between Member States.

- The Council and the Commission note that the Treaty establishing the European Economic Community contains no provisions making specific reference to the prior control of concentrations.

Acting on a proposal from the Commission, the Council has therefore decided, in accordance with Article 308 of the Treaty, to set up a new mechanism for the control of concentrations.

The Council and the Commission consider, for pressing reasons of legal security, that this new regulation will apply solely and exclusively to concentrations as defined in Article 3.

- The Council and the Commission state that the provisions of Article 22(3) to (5) in no way prejudice the power of Member States other than that at whose request the

Commission intervenes to apply their national laws within their respective territories.

STATEMENTS FOR THE COUNCIL MINUTES ON

The Adoption of Regulation 1310/97 Amending Regulation 4064/39*

1. Re Article 1

(a) *"The Commission* states that the operation of the thresholds laid down in Article 1 will be considered in each of its annual reports on competition policy."

(b) *"The Commission* states that it will request Member States to inform it, if possible, of cases notified under national legislation on the control of concentrations solely because the two-thirds rule applies, thus enabling it to report on the effects of that rule as requested by the European Parliament and the Economic and Social Committee."

(c) *Re paragraph 4*

"The Council agrees that the drafting of the report provided for in Article 1(4) will necessitate in particular the collection by the Commission from Member States, to the extent permitted by their national legislation, of information relating to concentrations notified in several States. In this context it will be particularly helpful if every six months Member States send the Commission a list of concentrations notified in accordance with their national law. It would also be advisable for them to include in their national notification forms the obligation for notifying parties to indicate the other Member States in which the concentration must also be notified in order to be able to give this information to the Commission.

The Commission states that it considers the close and regular collaboration of Member States, to the extent permitted by their national legislation and in the manner indicated by the Council above, to be fundamental to the preparation of a useful report. It will supplement this information by approaching undertakings directly, relying where appropriate on Article 11 of the Regulation."

2. Re Article 2(4)

"The Commission states that it does not normally intend to use its powers to revoke an exemption given pursuant to Article 81(3) of the Treaty under this Regulation.

It will do so only in exceptional cases where, in particular, the coordination of the competitive behaviour of the parent companies affords them the possibility of eliminating competition in respect of a substantial part of the products or services in question. In exercising its power to revoke an exemption, the Commission shall, in line with the principle of proportionality, take into account the time lapsed since the exemption was granted, the effect of a revocation on the investment made by the parties and the nature of the joint venture as an on-going concern.

The Commission will also take into account any modifications proposed by the parties that would eliminate the competition problem at hand.

The Commission emphasizes that in all circumstances the powers available to it under Article 82 of the Treaty remain fully applicable should an abuse be detected following an exemption granted in the context of Article 81(3) of the Treaty."

3. Re Article 3(2)

— *"The Commission* states that this Regulation does not apply to consortia in the liner trades sector."

---

* Published in Merger control law in the European Union (DG IV, 1998).

— *"The United Kingdom delegation* states that its agreement to the extension of the scope of this Regulation to cover cooperative joint ventures does not prejudice its position on any future proposals to extend Regulations implementing Articles 81 and 82 of the Treaty to aviation services outside the Community."

4. Re Article 22(1)

(1) *"The Commission* states that it will continue its efforts to decentralize the application of Articles 81 and 82 of the Treaty and to improve the worksharing between the Commission and the Member States in this field.

(2) With respect to full-function joint ventures below the thresholds of the Merger Regulation, the Commission underlines that it is normally for the competition authorities of the Member States to deal with such joint ventures since they are defined in Article 3(2) of the Merger Regulation as concentrations without a Community dimension. The residual power to apply Regulation No 17 or other implementing regulations to joint ventures below the thresholds is limited to those joint ventures which may have an appreciable effect on trade between Member States. Where a national authority intends to prohibit a case on the grounds of the creation of a dominant position by the joint venture itself, whether on the basis of the national rules on merger control or on restrictive practices, there is no scope for an exemption to be granted by the Commission under Article 81(3). The application of Regulation No 17 could be relevant only where a projected prohibition decision would be based on a restriction of competition resulting from the coordination of the parent companies outside the joint venture ("spill-over effect"). In this respect, the Commission states that it will leave the assessment of such operations to the Member States as far as possible. In this context, reference is made to the notice on cooperation between national competition authorities and the Commission.

(3) The Commission states that it will continue with determination the efforts which it has already undertaken, in terms of procedure and internal organization, to ensure that full-function joint ventures which do not fall under the present Regulation are examined within deadlines and by methods which are as close as possible to those provided for in the present Regulation. It will not, however, be possible to achieve identical treatment, in particular as a result of the procedural rules in force and the limited resources available to the Commission in this area. The Commission will every year send the competent authorities of the Member States a report on the duration of and the methods used for the examination of full-function joint ventures which do not fall within the scope of the present Regulation, whilst endeavouring to make clear the progress made in the area of convergence during the preceding year."

5. Re Article 23, second subparagraph

"The Commission states that the time limit for the submission of commitments intended to form the basis for a decision based on Article 6(1)(b) will be no more than three weeks from the date of receipt of the notification."

REGULATION 447/98[1]

*On the Notifications, Time Limits and Hearings Provided for in Council
Regulation (EEC) No 4064/89 on the Control of Concentrations Between
Undertakings*

(Text with EEA relevance)

THE COMMISSION OF THE EUROPEAN COMMUNITIES,

Having regard to the Treaty establishing the European Community,
  Having regard to the Agreement on the European Economic Area,
  Having regard to Council Regulation (EEC) No 4064/89 of 21 December 1989 on the
control of concentrations between undertakings,[2] as last amended by Regulation (EC) No
1310/97,[3] and in particular Article 23 thereof,
  Having regard to Council Regulation No 17 of 6 February 1962, First Regulation
implementing Articles 81 and 82 of the Treaty,[4] as last amended by the Act of Accession
of Austria, Finland and Sweden, and in particular Article 24 thereof,
  Having regard to Council Regulation (EEC) No 1017/68 of 19 July 1968 applying rules
of competition to transport by rail, road and inland waterway,[5] as last amended by the Act
of Accession of Austria, Finland and Sweden, and in particular Article 29 thereof,
  Having regard to Council Regulation (EEC) No 4056/86 of 22 December 1986 laying
down detailed rules for the application of Articles 81 and 82 of the Treaty to maritime
transport,[6] as amended by the Act of Accession of Austria, Finland and Sweden, and in
particular Article 26 thereof,
  Having regard to Council Regulation (EEC) No 3975/87 of 14 December 1987 laying
down the procedure for the application of the rules on competition to undertakings in the
air transport sector,[7] as last amended by Regulation (EEC) No 2410/92,[8] and in particular
Article 19 thereof,
  Having consulted the Advisory Committee on Concentrations,
  (1) Whereas Regulation (EEC) No 4064/89 and in particular Article 23 thereof has
been amended by Regulation (EC) No 1310/97;
  (2) Whereas Commission Regulation (EC) No 3384/94,[9] implementing Regulation
(EEC) No 4064/89, must be modified in order to take account of those amendments;
whereas experience in the application of Regulation (EC) No 3384/94 has revealed the

---

[1] OJ 1998 L61/1, of 1–3–98
[2] OJ 1989 L395/1; corrected version, OJ 1990 L257/13.
[3] OJ 1997 L180/1.
[4] OJ 1962 15/204.
[5] OJ 1968 L175/1.
[6] OJ 1986 L378/4.
[7] OJ 1987 L374/1.
[8] OJ 1992 L240/18.
[9] OJ 1994 L377/1.

need to improve certain procedural aspects thereof; whereas for the sake of clarity it should therefore be replaced by a new regulation;

(3) Whereas the Commission has adopted Decision 94/810/ECSC, EC of 12 December 1994 on the terms of reference of hearing officers in competition procedures before the Commission[10];

(4) Whereas Regulation (EEC) No 4064/89 is based on the principle of compulsory notification of concentrations before they are put into effect; whereas, on the one hand, a notification has important legal consequences which are favourable to the parties to the concentration plan, while, on the other hand, failure to comply with the obligation to notify renders the parties liable to a fine and may also entail civil law disadvantages for them; whereas it is therefore necessary in the interests of legal certainty to define precisely the subject matter and content of the information to be provided in the notification;

(5) Whereas it is for the notifying parties to make full and honest disclosure to the Commission of the facts and circumstances which are relevant for taking a decision on the notified concentration;

(6) Whereas in order to simplify and expedite examination of the notification, it is desirable to prescribe that a form be used;

(7) Whereas since notification sets in motion legal time limits pursuant to Regulation (EEC) No 4064/89, the conditions governing such time-limits and the time when they become effective must also be determined;

(8) Whereas rules must be laid down in the interests of legal certainty for calculating the time limits provided for in Regulation (EEC) No 4064/89; whereas in particular, the beginning and end of the period and the circumstances suspending the running of the period must be determined, with due regard to the requirements resulting from the exceptionally short legal time-limits referred to above; whereas in the absence of specific provisions the determination of rules applicable to periods, dates and time-limits should be based on the principles of Council Regulation (EEC, Euratom) No 1182/71[11];

(9) Whereas the provisions relating to the Commission's procedure must be framed in such a way as to safeguard fully the right to be heard and the rights of defence; whereas for these purposes the Commission should distinguish between the parties who notify the concentration, other parties involved in the concentration plan, third parties and parties regarding whom the Commission intends to take a decision imposing a fine or periodic penalty payments;

(10) Whereas the Commission should give the notifying parties and other parties involved, if they so request, an opportunity before notification to discuss the intended concentration informally and in strict confidence; whereas in addition it should, after notification, maintain close contact with those parties to the extent necessary to discuss with them any practical or legal problems which it discovers on a first examination of the case and if possible to remove such problems by mutual agreement;

(11) Whereas in accordance with the principle of the rights of defence, the notifying parties must be given the opportunity to submit their comments on all the objections which the Commission proposes to take into account in its decisions; whereas the other parties involved should also be informed of the Commission's objections and granted the opportunity to express their views;

(12) Whereas third parties having sufficient interest must also be given the opportunity of expressing their views where they make a written application;

(13) Whereas the various persons entitled to submit comments should do so in writing, both in their own interest and in the interest of good administration, without prejudice to their right to request a formal oral hearing where appropriate to supplement the written procedure; whereas in urgent cases, however, the Commission must be able to proceed immediately to formal oral hearings of the notifying parties, other parties involved or third parties;

---

[10] OJ 1994 L330/67.
[11] OJ 1971 L124/1.

(14) Whereas it is necessary to define the rights of persons who are to be heard, to what extent they should be granted access to the Commission's file and on what conditions they may be represented or assisted;

(15) Whereas the Commission must respect the legitimate interest of undertakings in the protection of their business secrets and other confidential information;

(16) Whereas, in order to enable the Commission to carry out a proper assessment of commitments that have the purpose of rendering the concentration compatible with the common market, and to ensure due consultation with other parties involved, third parties and the authorities of the Member States as provided for in Regulation (EEC) No 4064/89, in particular Article 18(1) and (4) thereof, the procedure and time-limits for submitting such commitments as provided for in Article 6(2) and Article 8(2) of Regulation (EEC) No 4064/89 must be laid down;

(17) Whereas it is also necessary to define the rules for fixing and calculating the time limits for reply fixed by the Commission;

(18) Whereas the Advisory Committee on Concentrations must deliver its opinion on the basis of a preliminary draft decision; whereas it must therefore be consulted on a case after the inquiry into that case has been completed; whereas such consultation does not, however, prevent the Commission from reopening an inquiry if need be,

HAS ADOPTED THIS REGULATION:

CHAPTER I

NOTIFICATIONS

Article 1

Persons entitled to submit notifications

1. Notifications shall be submitted by the persons or undertakings referred to in Article 4(2) of Regulation (EEC) No 4064/89.

2. Where notifications are signed by representatives of persons or of undertakings, such representatives shall produce written proof that they are authorised to act.

3. Joint notifications should be submitted by a joint representative who is authorised to transmit and to receive documents on behalf of all notifying parties.

Article 2

Submission of notifications

1. Notifications shall be submitted in the manner prescribed by form CO as shown in the Annex. Joint notifications shall be submitted on a single form.

2. One original and 23 copies of the form CO and the supporting documents shall be submitted to the Commission at the address indicated in form CO.

3. The supporting documents shall be either originals or copies of the originals; in the latter case the notifying parties shall confirm that they are true and complete.

4. Notifications shall be in one of the official languages of the Community. This language shall also be the language of the proceeding for the notifying parties. Supporting documents shall be submitted in their original language. Where the original language is not one of the official languages of the Community, a translation into the language of the proceeding shall be attached.

5. Where notifications are made pursuant to Article 57 of the EEA Agreement, they may also be in one of the official languages of the EFTA States or the working language

of the EFTA Surveillance Authority. If the language chosen for the notifications is not an official language of the Community, the notifying parties shall simultaneously supplement all documentation with a translation into an official language of the Community. The language which is chosen for the translation shall determine the language used by the Commission as the language of the proceedings for the notifying parties.

Article 3

Information and documents to be provided

1. Notifications shall contain the information, including documents, requested by form CO. The information must be correct and complete.

2. The Commission may dispense with the obligation to provide any particular information, including documents, requested by form CO where the Commission considers that such information is not necessary for the examination of the case.

3. The Commission shall without delay acknowledge in writing to the notifying parties or their representatives receipt of the notification and of any reply to a letter sent by the Commission pursuant to Article 4(2) and (4).

Article 4

Effective date of notification

1. Subject to paragraphs 2, 3 and 4, notifications shall become effective on the date on which they are received by the Commission.

2. Where the information, including documents, contained in the notification is incomplete in a material respect, the Commission shall inform the notifying parties or their representatives in writing without delay and shall set an appropriate time-limit for the completion of the information. In such cases, the notification shall become effective on the date on which the complete information is received by the Commission.

3. Material changes in the facts contained in the notification which the notifying parties know or ought to have known must be communicated to the Commission without delay. In such cases, when these material changes could have a significant effect on the appraisal of the concentration, the notification may be considered by the Commission as becoming effective on the date on which the information on the material changes is received by the Commission; the Commission shall inform the notifying parties or their representatives of this in writing and without delay.

4. Incorrect or misleading information shall be considered to be incomplete information.

5. When the Commission publishes the fact of the notification pursuant to Article 4(3) of Regulation (EEC) No 4064/89, it shall specify the date upon which the notification has been received. Where, further to the application of paragraphs 2, 3 and 4, the effective date of notification is later than the date specified in this publication, the Commission shall issue a further publication in which it will state the later date.

Article 5

Conversion of notifications

1. Where the Commission finds that the operation notified does not constitute a concentration within the meaning of Article 3 of Regulation (EEC) No 4064/89, it shall inform the notifying parties or their representatives in writing. In such a case, the Commission shall, if requested by the notifying parties, as appropriate and subject to paragraph 2 of this Article, treat the notification as an application within the meaning of Article 2 or a

notification within the meaning of Article 4 of Regulation No 17, as an application within the meaning of Article 12 or a notification within the meaning of Article 14 of Regulation (EEC) No 1017/68, as an application within the meaning of Article 12 of Regulation (EEC) No 4056/86 or as an application within the meaning of Article 3(2) or of Article 5 of Regulation (EEC) No 3975/87.

2. In cases referred to in paragraph 1, second sentence, the Commission may require that the information given in the notification be supplemented within an appropriate time-limit fixed by it in so far as this is necessary for assessing the operation on the basis of the Regulations referred to in that sentence. The application or notification shall be deemed to fulfil the requirements of such Regulations from the date of the original notification where the additional information is received by the Commission within the time-limit fixed.

CHAPTER II

TIME-LIMITS

Article 6

Beginning of periods

1. The period referred to in Article 9(2) of Regulation (EEC) No 4064/89 shall start at the beginning of the working day following the date of the receipt of the copy of the notification by the Member State.

2. The period referred to in Article 9(4)(b) of Regulation (EEC) No 4064/89 shall start at the beginning of the working day following the effective date of the notification, within the meaning of Article 4 of this Regulation.

3. The period referred to in Article 9(6) of Regulation (EEC) No 4064/89 shall start at the beginning of the working day following the date of the Commission's referral.

4. The periods referred to in Article 10(1) of Regulation (EEC) No 4064/89 shall start at the beginning of the working day following the effective date of the notification, within the meaning of Article 4 of this Regulation.

5. The period referred to in Article 10(3) of Regulation (EEC) No 4064/89 shall start at the beginning of the working day following the day on which proceedings were initiated.

6. The period referred to in Article 22(4), second subparagraph, second sentence, of Regulation (EEC) No 4064/89 shall start at the beginning of the working day following the date of the first of the events referred to.

Article 7

End of periods

1. The period referred to in Article 9(2) of Regulation (EEC) No 4064/89 shall end with the expiry of the day which in the third week following that in which the period began is the same day of the week as the day from which the period runs.

2. The period referred to in Article 9(4)(b) of Regulation (EEC) No 4064/89 shall end with the expiry of the day which in the third month following that in which the period began falls on the same date as the day from which the period runs. Where such a day does not occur in that month, the period shall end with the expiry of the last day of that month.

3. The period referred to in Article 9(6) of Regulation (EEC) No 4064/89 shall end with the expiry of the day which in the fourth month following that in which the period began falls on the same date as the day from which the period runs. Where such a day does not occur in that month, the period shall end with the expiry of the last day of that month.

4. The period referred to in Article 10(1), first subparagraph, of Regulation (EEC) No 4064/89 shall end with the expiry of the day which in the month following that in which the period began falls on the same date as the day from which the period runs. Where such a day does not occur in that month, the period shall end with the expiry of the last day of that month.

5. The period referred to in Article 10(1), second subparagraph, of Regulation (EEC) No 4064/89 shall end with the expiry of the day which in the sixth week following that in which the period began is the same day of the week as the day from which the period runs.

6. The period referred to in Article 10(3) of Regulation (EEC) No 4064/89 shall end with the expiry of the day which in the fourth month following that in which the period began falls on the same date as the day from which the period runs. Where such a day does not occur in that month, the period shall end with the expiry of the last day of that month.

7. The period referred to in Article 22(4), second subparagraph, second sentence, of Regulation (EEC) No 4064/89 shall end with the expiry of the day which in the month following that in which the period began falls on the same date as the day from which the period runs. Where such a day does not occur in that month, the period shall end with the expiry of the last day of that month.

8. Where the last day of the period is not a working day, the period shall end with the expiry of the following working day.

Article 8

Recovery of holidays

Once the end of the period has been determined in accordance with Article 7, if public holidays or other holidays of the Commission referred to in Article 23 fall within the periods referred to in Articles 9, 10 and 22 of Regulation (EEC) No 4064/89, a corresponding number of working days shall be added to those periods.

Article 9

Suspension of time limit

1. The periods referred to in Article 10(1) and (3) of Regulation (EEC) No 4064/89 shall be suspended where the Commission, pursuant to Article 11(5) and Article 13(3) of that Regulation, has to take a decision because:

(a) information which the Commission has requested pursuant to Article 11(1) of Regulation (EEC) No 4064/89 from one of the notifying parties or another involved party, as defined in Article 11 of this Regulation, is not provided or not provided in full within the time limit fixed by the Commission;

(b) information which the Commission has requested pursuant to Article 11(1) of Regulation (EEC) No 4064/89 from a third party, as defined in Article 11 of this Regulation, is not provided or not provided in full within the time limit fixed by the Commission owing to circumstances for which one of the notifying parties or another involved party, as defined in Article 11 of this Regulation, is responsible;

(c) one of the notifying parties or another involved party, as defined in Article 11 of this Regulation, has refused to submit to an investigation deemed necessary by the

Commission on the basis of Article 13(1) of Regulation (EEC) No 4064/89 or to cooperate in the carrying out of such an investigation in accordance with that pro-vision;

(d) the notifying parties have failed to inform the Commission of material changes in the facts contained in the notification.

2. The periods referred to in Article 10(1) and (3) of Regulation (EEC) No 4064/89 shall be suspended:

(a) in the cases referred to in paragraph 1(a) and (b), for the period between the end of the time limit fixed in the request for information and the receipt of the complete and correct information required by decision;

(b) in the cases referred to in paragraph 1(c), for the period between the unsuccessful attempt to carry out the investigation and the completion of the investigation ordered by decision;

(c) in the cases referred to in paragraph 1(d), for the period between the occurrence of the change in the facts referred to therein and the receipt of the complete and correct information requested by decision or the completion of the investigation ordered by decision.

3. The suspension of the time limit shall begin on the day following that on which the event causing the suspension occurred. It shall end with the expiry of the day on which the reason for suspension is removed. Where such a day is not a working day, the suspension of the time-limit shall end with the expiry of the following working day.

Article 10

Compliance with the time-limits

1. The time limits referred to in Article 9(4) and (5), and Article 10(1) and (3) of Regulation (EEC) No 4064/89 shall be met where the Commission has taken the relevant decision before the end of the period.
2. The time limit referred to in Article 9(2) of Regulation (EEC) No 4064/89 shall be met where a Member State informs the Commission before the end of the period in writing.
3. The time limit referred to in Article 9(6) of Regulation (EEC) No 4064/89 shall be met where the competent authority of the Member State concerned publishes any report or announces the findings of the examination of the concentration before the end of the period.
4. The time limit referred to in Article 22(4), second subparagraph, second sentence, of Regulation (EEC) No 4064/89 shall be met where the request made by the Member State or the Member States is received by the Commission before the end of the period.

CHAPTER III

HEARING OF THE PARTIES AND OF THIRD PARTIES

Article 11

Parties to be heard

For the purposes of the rights to be heard pursuant to Article 18 of Regulation (EEC) No 4064/89, the following parties are distinguished:

(a) notifying parties, that is, persons or undertakings submitting a notification pursuant to Article 4(2) of Regulation (EEC) No 4064/89;
(b) other involved parties, that is, parties to the concentration plan other than the notifying parties, such as the seller and the undertaking which is the target of the concentration;
(c) third parties, that is, natural or legal persons showing a sufficient interest, including customers, suppliers and competitors, and especially members of the administration or management organs of the undertakings concerned or recognised workers' representatives of those undertakings;
(d) parties regarding whom the Commission intends to take a decision pursuant to Article 14 or 15 of Regulation (EEC) No 4064/89.

Article 12

Decisions on the suspension of concentrations

1. Where the Commission intends to take a decision pursuant to Article 7(4) of Regulation (EEC) No 4064/89 which adversely affects one or more of the parties, it shall, pursuant to Article 18(1) of that Regulation, inform the notifying parties and other involved parties in writing of its objections and shall fix a time limit within which they may make known their views.

2. Where the Commission, pursuant to Article 18(2) of Regulation (EEC) No 4064/89, has taken a decision referred to in paragraph 1 of this Article provisionally without having given the notifying parties and other involved parties the opportunity to make known their views, it shall without delay send them the text of the provisional decision and shall fix a time limit within which they may make known their views.

Once the notifying parties and other involved parties have made known their views, the Commission shall take a final decision annulling, amending or confirming the provisional decision. Where they have not made known their views within the time limit fixed, the Commission's provisional decision shall become final with the expiry of that period.

3. The notifying parties and other involved parties shall make known their views in writing or orally within the time limit fixed. They may confirm their oral statements in writing.

Article 13

Decisions on the substance of the case

1. Where the Commission intends to take a decision pursuant to Article 8(2), second subparagraph, or Article 8(3), (4) or (5) of Regulation (EEC) No 4064/89, it shall, before consulting the Advisory Committee on Concentrations, hear the parties pursuant to Article 18(1) and (3) of that Regulation.

2. The Commission shall address its objections in writing to the notifying parties.

The Commission shall, when giving notice of objections, set a time limit within which the notifying parties may inform the Commission of their views in writing.

The Commission shall inform other involved parties in writing of these objections.

The Commission shall also set a time limit within which those other involved parties may inform the Commission of their views in writing.

3. After having addressed its objections to the notifying parties, the Commission shall, upon request, give them access to the file for the purpose of enabling them to exercise their rights of defence.

The Commission shall, upon request, also give the other involved parties who have been informed of the objections access to the file in so far as this is necessary for the purposes of preparing their observations.

4. The parties to whom the Commission's objections have been addressed or who have been informed of those objections shall, within the time limit fixed, make known in writing their views on the objections. In their written comments, they may set out all matters relevant to the case and may attach any relevant documents in proof of the facts set out. They may also propose that the Commission hear persons who may corroborate those facts. They shall submit one original and 29 copies of their response to the Commission at the address indicated in form CO.

5. Where the Commission intends to take a decision pursuant to Article 14 or 15 of Regulation (EEC) No 4064/89 it shall, before consulting the Advisory Committee on Concentrations, hear pursuant to Article 18(1) and (3) of that Regulation the parties regarding whom the Commission intends to take such a decision.

The procedure provided for in paragraph 2, first and second subparagraphs, paragraph 3, first subparagraph, and paragraph 4 is applicable, *mutatis mutandis*.

Article 14

Oral hearings

1. The Commission shall afford the notifying parties who have so requested in their written comments the opportunity to put forward their arguments orally in a formal hearing if such parties show a sufficient interest. It may also in other cases afford such parties the opportunity of expressing their views orally.

2. The Commission shall afford other involved parties who have so requested in their written comments the opportunity to express their views orally in a formal hearing if they show a sufficient interest. It may also in other cases afford such parties the opportunity of expressing their views orally.

3. The Commission shall afford parties on whom it proposes to impose a fine or periodic penalty payment who have so requested in their written comments the opportunity to put forward their arguments orally in a formal hearing. It may also in other cases afford such parties the opportunity of expressing their views orally.

4. The Commission shall invite the persons to be heard to attend on such date as it shall appoint.

5. The Commission shall invite the competent authorities of the Member States, to take part in the hearing.

Article 15

Conduct of formal oral hearings

1. Hearings shall be conducted by the Hearing Officer.

2. Persons invited to attend shall either appear in person or be represented by legal representatives or by representatives authorised by their constitution as appropriate. Undertakings and associations of undertakings may be represented by a duly authorised agent appointed from among their permanent staff.

3. Persons heard by the Commission may be assisted by their legal adviser or other qualified persons admitted by the Hearing Officer.

4. Hearings shall not be public. Each person shall be heard separately or in the presence of other persons invited to attend. In the latter case, regard shall be had to the legitimate interest of the undertakings in the protection of their business secrets and other confidential information.

5. The statements made by each person heard shall be recorded.

347

Article 16

Hearing of third parties

1. If third parties apply in writing to be heard pursuant to Article 18(4), second sentence, of Regulation (EEC) No 4064/89, the Commission shall inform them in writing of the nature and subject matter of the procedure and shall fix a time limit within which they may make known their views.

2. The third parties referred to in paragraph 1 shall make known their views in writing within the time limit fixed. The Commission may, where appropriate, afford the parties who have so requested in their written comments the opportunity to participate in a formal hearing. It may also in other cases afford such parties the opportunity of expressing their views orally.

3. The Commission may likewise afford to any other third parties the opportunity of expressing their views.

Article 17

Confidential information

1. Information, including documents, shall not be communicated or made accessible in so far as it contains business secrets of any person or undertaking, including the notifying parties, other involved parties or of third parties, or other confidential information the disclosure of which is not considered necessary by the Commission for the purpose of the procedure, or where internal documents of the authorities are concerned.

2. Any party which makes known its views under the provisions of this Chapter shall clearly identify any material which it considers to be confidential, giving reasons, and provide a separate non-confidential version within the time limit fixed by the Commission.

CHAPTER IV

COMMITMENTS RENDERING THE CONCENTRATION COMPATIBLE

Article 18

Time limits for commitments

1. Commitments proposed to the Commission by the undertakings concerned pursuant to Article 6(2) of Regulation (EEC) No 4064/89 which are intended by the parties to form the basis for a decision pursuant to Article 6(1)(b) of that Regulation shall be submitted to the Commission within not more than three weeks from the date of receipt of the notification.

2. Commitments proposed to the Commission by the undertakings concerned pursuant to Article 8(2) of Regulation (EEC) No 4064/89 which are intended by the parties to form the basis for a decision pursuant to that Article shall be submitted to the Commission within not more than three months from the date on which proceedings were initiated. The Commission may in exceptional circumstances extend this period.

3. Articles 6 to 9 shall apply *mutatis mutandis* to paragraphs 1 and 2 of this Article.

Article 19

Procedure for commitments

1. One original and 29 copies of commitments proposed to the Commission by the undertakings concerned pursuant to Article 6(2) or Article 8(2) of Regulation (EEC) No 4064/89 shall be submitted to the Commission at the address indicated in form CO.

2. Any party proposing commitments to the Commission pursuant to Articles 6(2) or Article 8(2) of Regulation (EEC) No 4064/89 shall clearly identify any material which it considers to be confidential, giving reasons, and provide a separate non-confidential version within the time limit fixed by the Commission.

CHAPTER V

MISCELLANEOUS PROVISIONS

Article 20

Transmission of documents

1. Transmission of documents and invitations from the Commission to the addressees may be effected in any of the following ways:

(a) delivery by hand against receipt;
(b) registered letter with acknowledgement of receipt;
(c) fax with a request for acknowledgement of receipt;
(d) telex;
(e) electronic mail with a request for acknowledgement of receipt.

2. Unless otherwise provided in this Regulation, paragraph 1 also applies to the transmission of documents from the notifying parties, from other involved parties or from third parties to the Commission.

3. Where a document is sent by telex, by fax or by electronic mail, it shall be presumed that it has been received by the addressee on the day on which it was sent.

Article 21

Setting of time limits

In fixing the time limits provided for pursuant to Article 4(2), Article 5(2), Article 12(1) and (2), Article 13(2) and Article 16(1), the Commission shall have regard to the time required for preparation of statements and to the urgency of the case. It shall also take account of working days as well as public holidays in the country of receipt of the Commission's communication.

These time limits shall be set in terms of a precise calendar date.

Article 22

Receipt of documents by the Commission

1. In accordance with the provisions of Article 4(1) of this Regulation, notifications must be delivered to the Commission at the address indicated in form CO or have been

dispatched by registered letter to the address indicated in form CO before the expiry of the period referred to in Article 4(1) of Regulation (EEC) No 4064/89.

Additional information requested to complete notifications pursuant to Article 4(2) and (4) or to supplement notifications pursuant to Article 5(2) must reach the Commission at the aforesaid address or have been dispatched by registered letter before the expiry of the time limit fixed in each case.

Written comments on Commission communications pursuant to Article 12(1) and (2), Article 13(2) and Article 16(1) must have reached the Commission at the aforesaid address before the expiry of the time limit fixed in each case.

2. Time limits referred to in subparagraphs two and three of paragraph 1 shall be determined in accordance with Article 21.

3. Should the last day of a time limit fall on a day which is not a working day or which is a public holiday in the country of dispatch, the time limit shall expire on the following working day.

Article 23

Definition of working days

The expression "working days" in this Regulation means all days other than Saturdays, Sundays, public holidays and other holidays as determined by the Commission and published in the *Official Journal of the European Communities* before the beginning of each year.

Article 24

Repeal

Regulation (EEC) No 3384/94 is repealed.

Article 25

Entry into force

This Regulation shall enter into force on 21 March 1998.

This Regulation shall be binding in its entirety and directly applicable in all Member States.

Done at Brussels, 1 March 1998.

FORM CO RELATING TO THE NOTIFICATION OF A CONCENTRATION PURSUANT TO REGULATION (EEC) NO 4064/89

INTRODUCTION

A. The purpose of this form

This form specifies the information that must be provided by an undertaking or undertakings when notifying the Commission of a concentration with a Community dimension. A "concentration" is defined in Article 3 of Regulation (EEC) No 4064/89 (hereinafter referred to as "the Merger Regulation") and "Community dimension" in Article 1 thereof.

Your attention is drawn to the Merger Regulation and to Regulation (EC) No 447/98 (hereinafter referred to as "the Implementing Regulation") and to the corresponding provisions of the Agreement on the European Economic Area.[12]

Experience has shown that prenotification meetings are extremely valuable to both the notifying parties and the Commission in determining the precise amount of information required in a notification and, in the large majority of cases, will result in a significant reduction of the information required. Accordingly, notifying parties are encouraged to consult the Commission regarding the possibility of dispensing with the obligation to provide certain information (see Section B(g) on the possibility of dispensation).

B. The need for a correct and complete notification

All information required by this form must be correct and complete. The information required must be supplied in the appropriate section of this form. Annexes to this form shall only be used to supplement the information supplied in the form itself.

In particular you should note that:

(a) In accordance with Article 10(1) of the Merger Regulation and Article 4(2) and (4) of the Implementing Regulation, the time limits of the Merger Regulation linked to the notification will not begin to run until all the information that has to be supplied with the notification has been received by the Commission. This requirement is to ensure that the Commission is able to assess the notified concentration within the strict time-limits provided by the Merger Regulation.

(b) The notifying parties should check carefully, in the course of preparing their notification, that contact names and numbers, and in particular fax numbers, provided to the Commission are accurate, relevant and up-to-date.

---

[12] Hereinafter referred to as "the EEA Agreement"; see in particular Article 57 of the EEA Agreement (point 1 of Annex XIV to the EEA Agreement and Protocol 4 to the Agreement between the EFTA States on the establishment of a Surveillance Authority and a Court of Justice), as well as Protocols 21 and 24 to the EEA Agreement and Article 1, and the Agreed Minutes of the Protocol adjusting the EEA Agreement. In particular, any reference to EFTA States shall be understood to mean those EFTA States which are Contracting Parties to the EEA Agreement.

(c) Incorrect or misleading information in the notification will be considered to be incomplete information (Article 4(4) of the Implementing Regulation).

(d) If a notification is incomplete, the Commission will inform the notifying parties or their representatives of this in writing and without delay. The notification will only become effective on the date on which the complete and accurate information is received by the Commission (Article 10(1) of the Merger Regulation, Article 4(2) and (4) of the Implementing Regulation).

(e) Article 14(1)(b) of the Merger Regulation provides that incorrect or misleading information, where supplied intentionally or negligently, can make the notifying party or parties liable to fines of up to ECU 50 000. In addition, pursuant to Article 6(3)(a) and Article 8(5)(a) of the Merger Regulation the Commission may also revoke its decision on the compatibility of a notified concentration where it is based on incorrect information for which one of the undertakings is responsible.

(f) You may request that the Commission accept that the notification is complete notwithstanding the failure to provide information required by this form, if such information is not reasonably available to you in part or in whole (for example, because of the unavailability of information on a target company during a contested bid).

The Commission will consider such a request, provided that you give reasons for the unavailability of that information, and provide your best estimates for missing data together with the sources for the estimates. Where possible, indications as to where any of the requested information that is unavailable to you could be obtained by the Commission should also be provided.

(g) You may request that the Commission accept that the notification is complete notwithstanding the failure to provide information required by this form, if you consider that any particular information requested by this form, in the full or short form version, may not be necessary for the Commission's examination of the case.

The Commission will consider such a request, provided that you give reasons why that information is not relevant and necessary to its inquiry into the notified operation. You may explain this during your pre-notification contacts with the Commission and/ or in your notification and ask the Commission to dispense with the obligation to provide that information, pursuant to Article 3(2) of the Implementing Regulation.

C. Notification in short form

(a) In cases where a joint venture has no, or *de minimis*, actual or foreseen activities within the EEA territory, the Commission intends to allow notification of the operation by means of short form. Such cases occur where joint control is acquired by two or more undertakings, and where:

(i) the turnover[13] of the joint venture and/or the turnover of the contributed activities,[14] is less than ECU 100 million in the EEA territory; and

---

[13] The turnover of the joint venture should be determined according to the most recent audited accounts of the parent companies, or the joint venture itself, depending upon the availability of separate accounts for the resources combined in the joint venture.

[14] The expression "and/or" refers to the variety of situations covered by the short form; for example:

— in the case of the joint acquisition of a target company, the turnover to be taken into account is the turnover of this target (the joint venture),

— in the case of the creation of a joint venture to which the parent companies contribute their activities, the turnover to be taken into account is that of the contributed activities,

— in the case of entry of a new controlling party into an existing joint venture, the turnover of the joint venture and the turnover of the activities contributed by the new parent company (if any) must be taken into account.

(ii) the total value of assets[15] transferred to the joint venture is less than ECU 100 million in the EEA territory.[16]

(b) If you consider that the operation to be notified meets these qualifications, you may explain this in your notification and ask the Commission to dispense with the obligation to provide the full-form notification, pursuant to Article 3(2) of the Implementing Regulation, and to allow you to notify by means of short form.

(c) Short-form notification allows the notifying parties to limit the information provided in the notification to the following sections and questions:
— Section 1,
— Section 2, except questions 2.1 (a, b and d), 2.3.4, and 2.3.5,
— Section 3, only questions 3.1 and 3.2 (a),
— Section 5, only questions 5.1 and 5.3,
— Section 6,
— Section 10,
— Section 11 (optional for the convenience of the parties), and
— Section 12,
— the five largest independent customers, the five largest independent suppliers, and the five largest competitors in the markets in which the joint venture will be active. Provide the name, address, telephone number, fax number and appropriate contact person of each such customer, supplier and competitor.

(d) In addition, with respect to the affected markets of the joint venture as defined in Section 6, indicate for the EEA territory, for the Community as a whole, for each Member State and EFTA State, and where different, in the opinion of the notifying parties, for the relevant geographic market, the sales in value and volume, as well as the market shares, for the year preceding the operation.

(e) The Commission may require full, or where appropriate partial, notification under the form CO where:
— the notified operation does not meet the short-form thresholds, or
— this appears to be necessary for an adequate investigation with respect to possible competition problems.

In such cases, the notification may be considered incomplete in a material respect pursuant to Article 4(2) of the Implementing Regulation. The Commission will inform the notifying parties or their representatives of this in writing and without delay and will fix a deadline for the submission of a full or, where appropriate, partial notification. The notification will only become effective on the date on which all information required is received.

D. Who must notify

In the case of a merger within the meaning of Article 3(1)(a) of the Merger Regulation or the acquisition of joint control in an undertaking within the meaning of Article 3(1)(b) of the Merger Regulation, the notification shall be completed jointly by the parties to the merger or by those acquiring joint control as the case may be.

In case of the acquisition of a controlling interest in one undertaking by another, the acquirer must complete the notification.

In the case of a public bid to acquire an undertaking, the bidder must complete the notification.

---

[15] The total value of assets of the joint venture should be determined according to the last regularly prepared and approved balance sheet of each parent company. The term "assets" includes: (1) all tangible and intangible assets that will be transferred to the joint venture (examples of tangible assets include production plants, wholesale or retail outlets, and inventory of goods), and (2) any amount of credit or any obligations of the joint venture which any parent company of the joint venture has agreed to extend or guarantee.

[16] Where the assets transferred generate turnover, then neither the value of the assets nor that of the turnover may exceed ECU 100 million.

Each party completing the notification is responsible for the accuracy of the information which it provides.

E. How to notify

The notification must be completed in one of the official languages of the European Community. This language will thereafter be the language of the proceedings for all notifying parties. Where notifications are made in accordance with Article 12 of Protocol 24 to the EEA Agreement in an official language of an EFTA State which is not an official language of the Community, the notification must simultaneously be supplemented with a translation into an official language of the Community.

The information requested by this form is to be set out using the sections and paragraph numbers of the form, signing a declaration as provided in Section 12, and annexing supporting documentation.

Supporting documents are to be submitted in their original language; where this is not an official language of the Community, they must be translated into the language of the proceeding (Article 2(4) of the Implementing Regulation).

Supporting documents may be originals or copies of the originals. In the latter case, the notifying party must confirm that they are true and complete.

One original and 23 copies of the form CO and all supporting documents must be provided.

The notification must be delivered to the Commission on working days as defined by Article 23 of the Implementing Regulation. In order to enable it to be registered on the same day, it must be delivered before 17.00 on Mondays to Thursdays and before 16.00 on Fridays, at the following address:

Commission of the European Communities
Directorate-General for Competition (DG IV)
Merger Task Force
150 avenue de Cortenberg/Kortenberglaan 150
B–1049 Brussels.

F. Confidentiality

Article 287 of the Treaty and Article 17(2) of the Merger Regulation as well as the corresponding provisions of the EEA Agreement[17] require the Commission, the Member States, the EFTA Surveillance Authority and the EFTA States, their officials and other servants not to disclose information they have acquired through the application of the Regulation of the kind covered by the obligation of professional secrecy. The same principle must also apply to protect confidentiality between notifying parties.

If you believe that your interests would be harmed if any of the information you are asked to supply were to be published or otherwise divulged to other parties, submit this information separately with each page clearly marked "Business Secrets". You should also give reasons why this information should not be divulged or published.

In the case of mergers or joint acquisitions, or in other cases where the notification is completed by more than one of the parties, business secrets may be submitted under separate cover, and referred to in the notification as an annex. All such annexes must be included in the submission in order for a notification to be considered complete.

---

[17] See, in particular, Article 122 of the EEA Agreement, Article 9 of Protocol 24 to the EEA Agreement and Article 17(2) of Chapter XIII of Protocol 4 to the Agreement between the EFTA States on the establishment of a Surveillance Authority and a Court of Justice (ESA Agreement).

G. Definitions and instructions for purposes of this form

Notifying party or parties: in cases where a notification is submitted by only one of the undertakings party to an operation, "notifying parties" is used to refer only to the undertaking actually submitting the notification.

Party(parties) to the concentration: these terms relate to both the acquiring and acquired parties, or to the merging parties, including all undertakings in which a controlling interest is being acquired or which is the subject of a public bid.

Except where otherwise specified, the terms "notifying party(parties)" and "party(parties) to the concentration" include all the undertakings which belong to the same groups as those "parties".

Affected markets: Section 6 of this form requires the notifying parties to define the relevant product markets, and further to identify which of those relevant markets are likely to be affected by the notified operation. This definition of affected market is used as the basis for requiring information for a number of other questions contained in this form. The definitions thus submitted by the notifying parties are referred to in this form as the affected market(s). This term can refer to a relevant market made up either of products or of services.

Year: all references to the word "year" in this form should be read as meaning calendar year, unless otherwise stated. All information requested in this form must, unless otherwise specified, relate to the year preceding that of the notification.

The financial data requested in Sections 2.3 to 2.5 must be provided in ecus at the average conversion rates prevailing for the years or other periods in question.

All references contained in this form are to the relevant Articles and paragraphs of Council Regulation (EEC) No 4064/89, unless otherwise stated.

SECTION 1

Background information

1.1. Information on notifying party (or parties)

Give details of:

1.1.1. name and address of undertaking;
1.1.2. nature of the undertaking's business;
1.1.3. name, address, telephone number, fax number and/or telex of, and position held by, the appropriate contact person.

1.2. Information on other parties[18] to the concentration

For each party to the concentration (except the notifying party or parties) give details of:

---

[18] This includes the target company in the case of a contested bid, in which case the details should be completed as far as is possible.

1.2.1. name and address of undertaking;

1.2.2. nature of undertaking's business;

1.2.3. name, address, telephone number, fax number and/or telex of, and position held by the appropriate contact person.

1.3. Address for service

Give an address (in Brussels if available) to which all communications may be made and documents delivered.

1.4. Appointment of representatives

Where notifications are signed by representatives of undertakings, such representatives must produce written proof that they are authorised to act.

If a joint notification is being submitted, has a joint representative been appointed?

If yes, please give the details requested in Sections 1.4.1 to 1.4.4.

If no, please give details of information of any representatives who have been authorised to act for each of the parties to the concentration, indicating whom they represent:

1.4.1. name of representative;

1.4.2. address of representative;

1.4.3. name of person to be contacted (and address, if different from 1.4.2);

1.4.4. telephone number, fax number and/or telex.

Section 2

Details of the concentration

2.1. Describe the nature of the concentration being notified. In doing so state:

(a) whether the proposed concentration is a full legal merger, an acquisition of sole or joint control, a full-function joint venture within the meaning of Article 3(2) of the Merger Regulation or a contract or other means of conferring direct or indirect control within the meaning of Article 3(3) of the Merger Regulation;

(b) whether the whole or parts of parties are subject to the concentration;

(c) a brief explanation of the economic and financial structure of the concentration;

(d) whether any public offer for the securities of one party by another party has the support of the former's supervisory boards of management or other bodies legally representing that party;

(e) the proposed or expected date of any major events designed to bring about the completion of the concentration;

(f) the proposed structure of ownership and control after the completion of the concentration;

(g) any financial or other support received from whatever source (including public authorities) by any of the parties and the nature and amount of this support.

2.2. List the economic sectors involved in the concentration

2.3. For each of the undertakings concerned by the concentration[19] provide the following data[20] for the last financial year:

2.3.1. worldwide turnover;
2.3.2. Community-wide turnover;
2.3.3. EFTA-wide turnover;
2.3.4. turnover in each Member State;
2.3.5. turnover in each EFTA State;
2.3.6. the Member State, if any, in which more than two thirds of Community-wide turnover is achieved[21];
2.3.7. the EFTA State, if any, in which more than two thirds of EFTA-wide turnover is achieved.

2.4. For the purposes of Article 1(3) of the Merger Regulation, if the operation does not meet the thresholds set out in Article 1(2), provide the following data for the last financial year:

2.4.1. the Member States, if any, in which the combined aggregate turnover of all the undertakings concerned is more than ECU 100 million;
2.4.2. the Member States, if any, in which the aggregate turnover of each of at least two of the undertakings concerned is more than ECU 25 million.

2.5. Provide the following information with respect to the last financial year:

2.5.1. does the combined turnover of the undertakings concerned in the territory of the EFTA States equal 25% or more of their total turnover in the EEA territory?
2.5.2. does each of at least two undertakings concerned have a turnover exceeding ECU 250 million in the territory of thc EFTA States?

SECTION 3

Ownership and control[22]

For each of the parties to the concentration provide a list of all undertakings belonging to the same group.
This list must include:

3.1. all undertakings or persons controlling these parties, directly or indirectly;

---

[19] See Commission notice on the concept of undertakings concerned.
[20] See, generally, the Commission notice on calculation of turnover. Turnover of the acquiring party or parties to the concentration should include the aggregated turnover of all undertakings within the meaning of Article 5(4). Turnover of the acquired party or parties should include the turnover relating to the parts subject to the transaction within the meaning of Article 5(2). Special provisions are contained in Article 5(3), (4) and 5(5) for credit, insurance, other financial institutions and joint undertakings.
[21] See Guidance Note III for the calculation of turnover in one Member State with respect to Community-wide turnover.
[22] See Article 3(3), (4) and (5) and Article 5(4).

3.2.   all undertakings active on any affected market[23] that are controlled, directly or indirectly:
(a) by these parties;
(b) by any other undertaking identified in 3.1.

For each entry listed above, the nature and means of control should be specified.

The information sought in this section may be illustrated by the use of organisation charts or diagrams to show the structure of ownership and control of the undertakings.

SECTION 4

Personal and financial links and previous acquisitions

With respect to the parties to the concentration and each undertaking or person identified in response to Section 3, provide:

4.1.   a list of all other undertakings which are active on affected markets (affected markets are defined in Section 6 in which the undertakings, or persons, of the group hold individually or collectively 10% or more of the voting rights, issued share capital or other securities;
in each case identify the holder and state the percentage held;

4.2.   a list for each undertaking of the members of their boards of management who are also members of the boards of management or of the supervisory boards of any other undertaking which is active on affected markets; and (where applicable) for each undertaking a list of the members of their supervisory boards who are also members of the boards of management of any other undertaking which is active on affected markets;
in each case identify the name of the other undertaking and the positions held;

4.3.   details of acquisitions made during the last three years by the groups identified above (Section 3) of undertakings active in affected markets as defined in Section 6.
Information provided here may be illustrated by the use of organisation charts or diagrams to give a better understanding.

SECTION 5

Supporting documentation

Notifying parties must provide the following:

5.1.   copies of the final or most recent versions of all documents bringing about the concentration, whether by agreement between the parties to the concentration, acquisition of a controlling interest or a public bid;

5.2.   in a public bid, a copy of the offer document; if it is unavailable at the time of notification, it should be submitted as soon as possible and not later than when it is posted to shareholders;

---

[23] See Section 6 for the definition of affected markets.

5.3.   copies of the most recent annual reports and accounts of all the parties to the concentration;

5.4.   where at least one affected market is identified:
copies of analyses, reports, studies and surveys submitted to or prepared for any member(s) of the board of directors, the supervisory board, or the shareholders' meeting, for the purpose of assessing or analysing the concentration with respect to competitive conditions, competitors (actual and potential), and market conditions.

SECTION 6

Market definitions

The relevant product and geographic markets determine the scope within which the market power of the new entity resulting from the concentration must be assessed.[24]

The notifying party or parties must provide the data requested having regard to the following definitions:

I. Relevant product markets

A relevant product market comprises all those products and/or services which are regarded as interchangeable or substitutable by the consumer, by reason of the products' characteristics, their prices and their intended use. A relevant product market may in some cases be composed of a number of individual products and/or services which present largely identical physical or technical characteristics and are interchangeable.

Factors relevant to the assessment of the relevant product market include the analysis of why the products or services in these markets are included and why others are excluded by using the above definition, and having regard to, for example, substitutability, conditions of competition, prices, cross-price elasticity of demand or other factors relevant for the definition of the product markets.

II. Relevant geographic markets

The relevant geographic market comprises the area in which the undertakings concerned are involved in the supply and demand of relevant products or services, in which the conditions of competition are sufficiently homogeneous and which can be distinguished from neighbouring geographic areas because, in particular, conditions of competition are appreciably different in those areas.

Factors relevant to the assessment of the relevant geographic market include the nature and characteristics of the products or services concerned, the existence of entry barriers, consumer preferences, appreciable differences in the undertakings' market shares between neighbouring geographic areas or substantial price differences.

III. Affected markets

For purposes of information required in this form, affected markets consist of relevant product markets where, in the EEA territory, in the Community, in the territory of the EFTA States, in any Member State or in any EFTA State:

---

[24] See Commission notice on the definition of the relevant market for the purposes of Community competition law.

(a) two or more of the parties to the concentration are engaged in business activities in the same product market and where the concentration will lead to a combined market share of 15% or more. These are horizontal relationships;

(b) one or more of the parties to the concentration are engaged in business activities in a product market, which is upstream or downstream of a product market in which any other party to the concentration is engaged, and any of their individual or combined market shares is 25% or more, regardless of whether there is or is not any existing supplier/customer relationship between the parties to the concentration. These are vertical relationships.

On the basis of the above definitions and market share thresholds, provide the following information:

6.1. Identify each affected market within the meaning of Section III, at:

(a) the EEA, Community or EFTA level;
(b) the individual Member States or EFTA States level.

IV. Markets related to affected markets within the meaning of Section III

6.2. Describe the relevant product and geographic markets concerned by the notified operation, which are closely related to the affected market(s) (in upstream, downstream and horizontal neighbouring markets), where any of the parties to the concentration are active and which are not themselves affected markets within the meaning of Section III.

V. Non-affected markets

6.3. In case there are no affected markets in the meaning of Section 6.1, describe the product and geographic scope of the markets on which the notified operation would have an impact.

SECTION 7

Information on affected markets

For each affected relevant product market, for each of the last three financial years[25]:

(a) for the EEA territory,
(b) for the Community as a whole,
(c) for the territory of the EFTA States as a whole,
(d) individually for each Member State and EFTA State where the parties to the concentration do business,
(e) and, where in the opinion of the notifying parties, the relevant geographic market is different,

provide the following:

---

[25] Without prejudice to Article 3(2) of the Implementing Regulation, the information required under 7.1 and 7.2 below must be provided with regard to all the territories under (a), (b), (c), (d) and (e).

7.1.   an estimate of the total size of the market in terms of sales value (in ecus) and volume (units).[26] Indicate the basis and sources for the calculations and provide documents where available to confirm these calculations;

7.2.   the sales in value and volume, as well as an estimate of the market shares, of each of the parties to the concentration;

7.3.   an estimate of the market share in value (and where appropriate volume) of all competitors (including importers) having at least 10% of the geographic market under consideration. Provide documents where available to confirm the calculation of these market shares and provide the name, address, telephone number, fax number and appropriate contact person, of these competitors;

7.4.   an estimate of the total value and volume and source of imports from outside the EEA territory and identify:

(a)   the proportion of such imports that are derived from the groups to which the parties to the concentration belong,

(b)   an estimate of the extent to which any quotas, tariffs or non-tariff barriers to trade, affect these imports, and

(c)   an estimate of the extent to which transportation and other costs affect these imports,

7.5.   the extent to which trade among States within the EEA territory is affected by:

(a)   transportation and other costs, and

(b)   other non-tariff barriers to trade;

7.6.   the manner in which the parties to the concentration produce and sell the products and/or services; for example, whether they manufacture locally, or sell through local distribution facilities;

7.7.   a comparison of price levels in each Member State and EFTA State by each party to the concentration and a similar comparison of price levels between the Community, the EFTA States and other areas where these products are produced (e.g. eastern Europe, the United States of America, Japan, or other relevant areas);

7.8.   the nature and extent of vertical integration of each of the parties to the concentration compared with their largest competitors.

SECTION 8

General conditions in affected markets

8.1. Identify the five largest independent[27] suppliers to the parties and their individual shares of purchases from each of these suppliers (of raw materials or goods used for purposes of producing the relevant products). Provide the name, address, telephone number, fax number and appropriate contact person, of these suppliers.

---

[26] The value and volume of a market should reflect output less exports plus imports for the geographic areas under consideration.

[27] That is suppliers which are not subsidiaries, agents or undertakings forming part of the group of the party in question. In addition to those five independent suppliers the notifying parties can, if they consider it necessary for a proper assessment of the case, identify the intra-group suppliers. The same will apply in 8.5 in relation with customers.

Structure of supply in affected markets

8.2. Explain the distribution channels and service networks that exist on the affected markets. In so doing, take account of the following where appropriate:

(a) the distribution systems prevailing on the market and their importance. To what extent is distribution performed by third parties and/or undertakings belonging to the same group as the parties identified in Section 3?
(b) the service networks (for example, maintenance and repair) prevailing and their importance in these markets. To what extent are such services performed by third parties and/or undertakings belonging to the same group as the parties identified in Section 3?

8.3. Where appropriate, provide an estimate of the total Community-wide and EFTA-wide capacity for the last three years. Over this period what proportion of this capacity is accounted for by each of the parties to the concentration, and what have been their respective rates of capacity utilisation.

8.4. If you consider any other supply-side considerations to be relevant, they should be specified.

Structure of demand in affected markets

8.5. Identify the five largest independent customers of the parties in each affected market and their individual share of total sales for such products accounted for by each of those customers. Provide the name, address, telephone number, fax number and appropriate contact person, of each of these customers.

8.6. Explain the structure of demand in terms of:

(a) the phases of the markets in terms of, for example, take-off, expansion, maturity and decline, and a forecast of the growth rate of demand;
(b) the importance of customer preferences, in terms of brand loyalty, product differentiation and the provision of a full range of products;
(c) the degree of concentration or dispersion of customers;
(d) segmentation of customers into different groups with a description of the "typical customer" of each group;
(e) the importance of exclusive distribution contracts and other types of long-term contracts;
(f) the extent to which public authorities, government agencies, State enterprises or similar bodies are important participants as a source of demand.

Market entry

8.7. Over the last five years, has there been any significant entry into any affected markets? If the answer is "yes", where possible provide their name, address, telephone number, fax number and appropriate contact person, and an estimate of their current market shares.

8.8. In the opinion of the notifying parties are there undertakings (including those at present operating only in extra-Community or extra-EEA markets) that are likely to enter the market? If the answer is "yes", please explain why and identify such entrants by name, address, telephone number, fax number and appropriate contact person, and an estimate of the time within which such entry is likely to occur.

8.9. Describe the various factors influencing entry into affected markets that exist in the present case, examining entry from both a geographical and product viewpoint. In so doing, take account of the following where appropriate:

(a) the total costs of entry (R & D, establishing distribution systems, promotion, advertising, servicing, etc.) on a scale equivalent to a significant viable competitor, indicating the market share of such a competitor;

(b) any legal or regulatory barriers to entry, such as government authorisation or standard setting in any form;

(c) any restrictions created by the existence of patents, know-how and other intellectual property rights in these markets and any restrictions created by licensing such rights;

(d) the extent to which each of the parties to the concentration are licensees or licensors of patents, know-how and other rights in the relevant markets;

(e) the importance of economies of scale for the production of products in the affected markets;

(f) access to sources of supply, such as availability of raw materials.

Research and development

8.10. Give an account of the importance of research and development in the ability of a firm operating on the relevant market(s) to compete in the long term. Explain the nature of the research and development in affected markets carried out by the parties to the concentration.

In so doing, take account of the following, where appropriate:

(a) trends and intensities of research and development[28] in these markets and for the parties to the concentration;

(b) the course of technological development for these markets over an appropriate time period (including developments in products and/or services, production processes, distribution systems, etc.);

(c) the major innovations that have been made in these markets and the undertakings responsible for these innovations;

(d) the cycle of innovation in these markets and where the parties are in this cycle of innovation.

Cooperative agreements

8.11. To what extent do cooperative agreements (horizontal or vertical) exist in the affected markets?

8.12. Give details of the most important cooperative agreements engaged in by the parties to the concentration in the affected markets, such as research and development, licensing, joint production, specialisation, distribution, long term supply and exchange of information agreements.

Trade associations

8.13. With respect to the trade associations in the affected markets:

(a) identify those in which the parties to the concentration are members;

---

[28] Research and development intensity is defined as research development expenditure as a proportion of turnover.

(b) identify the most important trade associations to which the customers and suppliers of the parties to the concentration belong.

Provide the name, address, telephone number, fax number and appropriate contact person of all trade associations listed above.

Section 9

General market information

Market data on conglomerate aspects

Where any of the parties to the concentration hold individually a market share of 25% or more for any product market in which there is no horizontal or vertical relationship as described above, provide the following information:

9.1. a description of each product market and explain why the products and/or services in these markets are included (and why others are excluded) by reason of their characteristics, prices and their intended use;

9.2. an estimate of the value of the market and the market shares of each of the groups to which the parties belong for each product market identified in 9.1 for the last financial year:

(a) for the EEA territory as a whole;
(b) for the Community as a whole;
(c) for the territory of the EFTA States as a whole;
(d) individually for each Member State and EFTA State where the groups to which the parties belong do business;
(e) and, where different, for the relevant geographic market.

Overview of the markets

9.3. Describe the worldwide context of the proposed concentration, indicating the position of each of the parties to the concentration outside of the EEA territory in terms of size and competitive strength.

9.4. Describe how the proposed concentration is likely to affect the interests of intermediate and ultimate consumers and the development of technical and economic progress.

Section 10

Cooperative effects of a joint venture

10. For the purpose of Article 2(4) of the Merger Regulation please answer the following questions:

(a) Do two or more parents retain to a significant extent activities in the same market as the joint venture or in a market which is downstream or upstream from that of the joint venture or in a neighbouring market closely related to this market?[29]

If the answer is affirmative, please indicate for each of the markets referred to here:

— the turnover of each parent company in the preceding financial year,
— the economic significance of the activities of the joint venture in relation to this turnover,
— the market share of each parent.

If the answer is negative, please justify your answer.

(b) If the answer to (a) is affirmative and in your view the creation of the joint venture does not lead to coordination between independent undertakings that restricts competition within the meaning of Article 81(1) of the EC Treaty, give your reasons.

(c) Without prejudice to the answers to (a) and (b) and in order to ensure that a complete assessment of the case can be made by the Commission, please explain how the criteria of Article 81(3) apply.

Under Article 81(3), the provisions of Article 81(1) may be declared inapplicable if the operation:

(i) contributes to improving the production or distribution of goods, or to promoting technical or economic progress;

(ii) allows consumers a fair share of the resulting benefit;

(iii) does not impose on the undertakings concerned restrictions which are not indispensable to the attainment of these objectives; and

(iv) does not afford such undertakings the possibility of eliminating competition in respect of a substantial part of the products in question.

For guidance, please refer to form A/B, and in particular Sections 16 and 17 thereof, annexed to Commission Regulation (EC) No 3385/94.[30]

SECTION 11

General matters

Ancillary restraints

11.1. If the parties to the concentration, and/or other involved parties (including the seller and minority shareholders), enter into ancillary restrictions directly related and necessary to the implementation of the concentration, these restrictions may be assessed in conjunction with the concentration itself (see Article 6(1)(b) and Article 8(2) of the Merger Regulation, recital 25 to the Merger Regulation, recital 7 to Regulation (EC) No 1310/97 and the Commission notice on restrictions ancillary to concentrations).[31]

(a) identify each ancillary restriction in the agreements provided with the notification for which you request an assessment in conjunction with the concentration; and

---

[29] For market definitions refer to Section 6.
[30] OJ L377, 31.12.1994, p. 28.
[31] OJ L180, 9.7.1997, p. 1.

(b) explain why these are directly related and necessary to the implementation of the concentration.

Conversion of notification

11.2. In the event that the Commission finds that the operation notified does not constitute a concentration within the meaning of Article 3 of the Merger Regulation, do you request that it be treated as an application for negative clearance from, or a notification to obtain an exemption from Article 81 of the EC Treaty?

SECTION 12

Declaration

Article 1(2) of the Implementing Regulation states that where notifications are signed by representatives of undertakings, such representatives must produce written proof that they are authorised to act. Such written authorisation must accompany the notification.

The notification must conclude with the following declaration which is to be signed by or on behalf of all the notifying parties:

The undersigned declare that, to the best of their knowledge and belief, the information given in this notification is true, correct, and complete, that complete copies of documents required by form CO, have been supplied, and that all estimates are identified as such and are their best estimates of the underlying facts and that all the opinions expressed are sincere.

They are aware of the provisions of Article 14(1)(b) of the Merger Regulation.

Place and date:

Signatures:

Name/s:

On behalf of:

GUIDANCE NOTE I

CALCULATION OF TURNOVER FOR INSURANCE UNDERTAKINGS

(Article 5(3)(A))

For the calculation of turnover for insurance undertakings, we give the following example (proposed concentration between insurance A and B):

I. Consolidated profit and loss account

(million ECU)

Income	Insurance A		Insurance B	
Gross premiums written	5 000		300	
gross premiums received from Community residents		(4 500)		(300)
gross premiums received from residents of one (and the same) Member State X		(3 600)		(270)
Other income	500		50	
Total income	5 500		350	

II. Calculation of turnover

1. Aggregate worldwide turnover is replaced by the value of gross premiums written worldwide, the sum of which is ECU 5 300 million.
2. Community-wide turnover is replaced, for each insurance undertakings, by the value of gross premiums written with Community residents. For each of the insurance undertakings, this amount is more than ECU 250 million.
3. Turnover within one (and the same) Member State X is replaced, for insurance undertakings, by the value of gross premiums written with residents of one (and the same) Member State X. For insurance A, it achieves 80% of its gross premiums written with Community residents within Member State X, whereas for insurance B, it achieves 90% of its gross premiums written with Community residents in that Member State X.

III. Conclusion

Since

(a) the aggregate worldwide turnover of insurances A and B, as replaced by the value of gross premiums written worldwide, is more than ECU 5 000 million;
(b) for each of the insurance undertakings, the value of gross premiums written with Community residents is more than ECU 250 million; but
(c) each of the insurance undertakings achieves more than two thirds of its gross premiums written with Community residents in one (and the same) Member State X,

the proposed concentration would not fall under the scope of the Regulation.

GUIDANCE NOTE II

CALCULATION OF TURNOVER FOR JOINT UNDERTAKINGS

A. Creation of a joint undertaking (Article 3(2))

In a case where two (or more) undertakings create a joint undertaking that constitutes a concentration, turnover is calculated for the undertakings concerned.

367

B. Existence of a joint undertaking (Article 5(5))

For the calculation of turnover in case of the existence of a joint undertaking C between two undertakings A and B concerned in a concentration, we give the following example:

I. Profit and loss accounts

(million ECU)

Turnover	Undertaking A	Undertaking B
Sales revenues worldwide	10 000	2 000
— Community	(8 000)	(1 500)
— Member State Y	(4 000)	(900)

(million ECU)

Turnover	Joint undertaking C	
Sales revenues worldwide	100	
— with undertaking A		(20)
— with undertaking B		(10)
Turnover with third undertakings	700	
— Community-wide		(60)
— in Member State Y		(50)

II. Consideration of the joint undertaking

(a) The undertaking C is jointly controlled (in the meaning of Article 3(3) and (4)) by the undertakings A and B concerned by the concentration, irrespective of any third undertaking participating in that undertaking C.
(b) The undertaking C is not consolidated A and B in their profit and loss accounts.
(c) The turnover of C resulting from operations with A and B shall not be taken into account.
(d) The turnover of C resulting from operations with any third undertaking shall be apportioned equally amongst the undertakings A and B, irrespective of their individual shareholdings in C.

III. Calculation of turnover

(a) Undertaking A's aggregate worldwide turnover shall be calculated as follows: ECU 10 000 million and 50% of C's worldwide turnover with third undertakings (i.e. ECU 35 million), the sum of which is ECU 10 035 million.

Undertaking B's aggregate worldwide turnover shall be calculated as follows: ECU 2 000 million and 50% of C's world-wide turnover with third undertakings (i.e. ECU 35 million), the sum of which is ECU 2 035 million.
(b) The aggregate worldwide turnover of the undertakings concerned is ECU 12 070 million.

(c) Undertaking A achieves ECU 4 025 million within Member State Y (50% of C's turnover in this Member State taken into account), and a Community-wide turnover of ECU 8 030 million (including 50% of C's Community-wide turnover).

Undertaking B achieves ECU 925 million within Member State Y (50% of C's turnover in this Member State taken into account), and a Community-wide turnover of ECU 1 530 million (including 50% of C's Community-wide turnover).

IV. Conclusion

Since

(a) the aggregate worldwide turnover of undertakings A and B is more than ECU 5 000 million;
(b) each of the undertakings concerned by the concentration achieves more than ECU 250 million within the Community;
(c) each of the undertakings concerned (undertaking A 50,1% and undertaking B 60,5%) achieves less than two thirds of its Community-wide turnover in one (and the same) Member State Y;

the proposed concentration would fall under the scope of the Regulation.

GUIDANCE NOTE III

APPLICATION OF THE TWO-THIRDS RULE

(Article 1)

For the application of the two thirds rule for undertakings, we give the following examples (proposed concentration between undertakings A and B):

I. Consolidated profit and loss accounts

Example 1   *(million ECU)*

Turnover	Undertaking A	Undertaking B
Sales revenues worldwide	10 000	500
— within the Community	(8 000)	(400)
— in Member State X	(6 000)	(200)

Example 2(a)   *(million ECU)*

Turnover	Undertaking A	Undertaking B
Sales revenues worldwide	4 800	500
— within the Community	(2 400)	(400)
— in Member State X	(2 100)	(300)

Example 2(b)
Same figures as in example 2(a) but undertaking B achieves ECU 300 million in Member State Y.

II. *Application of the two-thirds rule*

Example 1

1. Community-wide turnover is, for undertaking A, ECU 8 000 million and for under-taking B ECU 400 million.

2. Turnover in one (and the same) Member State X is, for undertaking A (ECU 6 000 million), 75% of its Community-wide turnover and is, for undertaking B (ECU 200 million), 50% of its Community-wide turnover.

3. Conclusion: In this case, although undertaking A achieves more than two thirds of its Community-wide turnover in Member State X, the proposed concentration would fall under the scope of the Regulation due to the fact that undertaking B achieves less than two thirds of its Community-wide turnover in Member State X.

Example 2(a)

1. Community-wide turnover of undertaking A is ECU 2 400 million and of undertaking B, ECU 400 million.

2. Turnover in one (and the same) Member State X is, for undertaking A, ECU 2 100 million (i.e. 87,5% of its Community-wide turnover); and, for undertaking B, ECU 300 million (i.e. 75% of its Community-wide turnover).

3. Conclusion: In this case, each of the undertakings concerned achieves more than two thirds of its Community-wide turnover in one (and the same) Member State X; the proposed concentration would not fall under the scope of the Regulation.

Example 2(b)

Conclusion: In this case, the two thirds rule would not apply due to the fact that undertakings A and B achieve more than two thirds of their Community-wide turnover in different Member States X and Y. Therefore, the proposed concentration would fall under the scope of the Regulation.

APPENDIX 35

COMMISSION NOTICE[1]

On the Concept of Concentration under Council Regulation (EEC) No 4064/89 on the Control of Concentrations Between Undertakings

(Text with EEA relevance)

I. Introduction

1. The purpose of this Notice is to provide guidance as to how the Commission interprets the term "concentration" used in Article 3 of Council Regulation (EEC) No 4064/89[2] as last amended by Regulation (EC) No 1310/97[3] (hereinafter referred to as "the Merger Regulation"). This formal guidance on the interpretation of Article 3 should enable firms to establish more quickly, in advance of any contact with the Commission, whether and to what extent their operations may be covered by Community merger control.

This Notice replaces the Notice on the notion of a concentration.[4]

---

[1] OJ 1998 C66/5.
[2] OJ 1989 L395/1; corrected version OJ 1990 L257/13.
[3] OJ 1997 L180/1.
[4] OJ 1994 C385/5.

This Notice deals with paragraphs (1), (3), (4) and (5) of Article 3. The interpretation of Article 3 in relation to joint ventures, dealt with in particular under Article 3(2), is set out in the Commission's Notice on the concept of full-function joint ventures.

2. The guidance set out in this Notice reflects the Commission's experience in applying the Merger Regulation since it entered into force on 21 December 1990. The principles contained here will be applied and further developed by the Commission in individual cases.

3. According to recital 23 to Regulation (EEC) No 4064/89, the concept of concentration is defined as covering only operations which bring about a lasting change in the structure of the undertakings concerned. Article 3(1) provides that such a structural change is brought about either by a merger between two previously independent undertakings or by the acquisition of control over the whole or part of another undertaking.

4. The determination of the existence of a concentration under the Merger Regulation is based upon qualitative rather than quantitative criteria, focusing on the concept of control. These criteria include considerations of both law and fact. It follows, therefore, that a concentration may occur on a legal or a *de facto* basis.

5. Article 3(1) of the Merger Regulation defines two categories of concentration:

— those arising from a merger between previously independent undertakings (point (a));
— those arising from an acquisition of control (point (b)).

These are treated respectively in Sections II and III below.

II. MERGERS BETWEEN PREVIOUSLY INDEPENDENT UNDERTAKINGS

6. A merger within the meaning of Article 3(1)(a) of the Merger Regulation occurs when two or more independent undertakings amalgamate into a new undertaking and cease to exist as separate legal entities. A merger may also occur when an undertaking is absorbed by another, the latter retaining its legal identity while the former ceases to exist as a legal entity.

7. A merger within the meaning of Article 3(1)(a) may also occur where, in the absence of a legal merger, the combining of the activities of previously independent undertakings results in the creation of a single economic unit.[5] This may arise in particular where two or more undertakings, while retaining their individual legal personalities, establish contractually a common economic management.[6] If this leads to a *de facto* amalgamation of the undertakings concerned into a genuine common economic unit, the operation is considered to be a merger. A prerequisite for the determination of a common economic unit is the existence of a permanent, single economic management. Other relevant factors may include internal profit and loss compensation as between the various undertakings within the group, and their joint liability externally. The *de facto* amalgamation may be reinforced by cross-shareholdings between the undertakings forming the economic unit.

---

[5] In determining the previous independence of undertakings, the issue of control may be relevant. Control is considered generally in paragraphs 12 *et seq.* below. For this specific issue, minority shareholders are deemed to have control if they have previously obtained a majority of votes on major decisions at shareholders meetings. The reference period in this context is normally three years.

[6] This could apply for example, in the case of a "Gleichordnungskonzern" in German law, certain "Groupements d'Intérêt Economique" in French law, and certain partnerships.

III. ACQUISITION OF CONTROL

8. Article 3(1)(b) provides that a concentration occurs in the case of an acquisition of control. Such control may be acquired by one undertaking acting alone or by two or more undertakings acting jointly.

Control may also be acquired by a person in circumstances where that person already controls (whether solely or jointly) at least one other undertaking or, alternatively, by a combination of persons (which controls another undertaking) and/or undertakings. The term "person" in this context extends to public bodies[7] and private entities, as well as individuals.

As defined, a concentration within the meaning of the Merger Regulation is limited to changes in control. Internal restructuring within a group of companies, therefore, cannot constitute a concentration.

An exceptional situation exists where both the acquiring and acquired undertakings are public companies owned by the same State (or by the same public body). In this case, whether the operation is to be regarded as an internal restructuring depends in turn on the question whether both undertakings were formerly part of the same economic unit within the meaning of recital 12 to Regulation (EEC) No 4064/89. Where the undertakings were formerly part of different economic units having an independent power of decision, the operation will be deemed to constitute a concentration and not an internal restructuring.[8] Such independent power of decision does not normally exist, however, where the undertakings are within the same holding company.[9]

9. Whether an operation gives rise to an acquisition of control depends on a number of legal and/or factual elements. The acquisition of property rights and shareholders' agreements are important, but are not the only elements involved: purely economic relationships may also play a decisive role. Therefore, in exceptional circumstances, a situation of economic dependence may lead to control on a *de facto* basis where, for example, very important long-term supply agreements or credits provided by suppliers or customers, coupled with structural links, confer decisive influence.[10]

There may also be acquisition of control even if it is not the declared intention of the parties.[11] Moreover, the Merger Regulation clearly defines control as having "the possibility of exercising decisive influence" rather than the actual exercise of such influence.

10. Control is nevertheless normally acquired by persons or undertakings which are the holders of the rights or are entitled to rights conferring control (Article 3(4)(a)). There may be exceptional situations where the formal holder of a controlling interest differs from the person or undertaking having in fact the real power to exercise the rights resulting from this interest. This may be the case, for example, where an undertaking uses another person or undertaking for the acquisition of a controlling interest and exercises the rights through this person or undertaking, even though the latter is formally the holder of the rights. In such a situation, control is acquired by the undertaking which in reality is behind the operation and in fact enjoys the power to control the target undertaking (Article 3(4)(b)). The evidence needed to establish this type of indirect control may include factors such as the source of financing or family links.

---

[7] Including the State itself, e.g. Case IV/M.157—*Air France/Sabena*, of 5 October 1992 in relation to the Belgian State, or other public bodies such as the Treuhand in Case IV/M.308—*Kali und Salz/MDK/Treuhand*, of 14 December 1993.

[8] Case IV/M.097—*Péchiney/Usinor*, of 24 June 1991; Case IV/M.216—*CEA Industrie/France Telecom/SGS-Thomson*, of 22 February 1993.

[9] See paragraph 55 of the Notice on the concept of undertakings concerned.

[10] For example, in the *Usinor/Bamesa* decision adopted by the Commission under the ECSC Treaty. See also Case IV/M.258—*CCIE/GTE*, of 25 September 1992, and Case IV/M.697—*Lockheed Martin Corporation/Loral Corporation*, of 27 March 1996.

[11] Case IV/M.157—*Air France/Sabena*, of 5 October 1992.

11. The object of control can be one or more undertakings which constitute legal entities, or the assets of such entities, or only some of these assets.[12] The assets in question, which could be brands or licences, must constitute a business to which a market turnover can be clearly attributed.

12. The acquisition of control may be in the form of sole or joint control. In both cases, control is defined as the possibility of exercising decisive influence on an undertaking on the basis of rights, contracts or any other means (Article 3(3)).

1. Sole control

13. Sole control is normally acquired on a legal basis where an undertaking acquires a majority of the voting rights of a company. It is not in itself significant that the acquired shareholding is 50% of the share capital plus one share[13] or that it is 100% of the share capital.[14] In the absence of other elements, an acquisition which does not include a majority of the voting rights does not normally confer control even if it involves the acquisition of a majority of the share capital.

14. Sole control may also be acquired in the case of a "qualified minority". This can be established on a legal and/or de facto basis.

On a legal basis it can occur where specific rights are attached to the minority shareholding. These may be preferential shares leading to a majority of the voting rights or other rights enabling the minority shareholder to determine the strategic commercial behaviour of the target company, such as the power to appoint more than half of the members of the supervisory board or the administrative board.

A minority shareholder may also be deemed to have sole control on a de facto basis. This is the case, for example, where the shareholder is highly likely to achieve a majority at the shareholders' meeting, given that the remaining shares are widely dispersed.[15] In such a situation it is unlikely that all the smaller shareholders will be present or represented at the shareholders' meeting. The determination of whether or not sole control exists in a particular case is based on the evidence resulting from the presence of shareholders in previous years. Where, on the basis of the number of shareholders attending the shareholders' meeting, a minority shareholder has a stable majority of the votes at this meeting, then the large minority shareholder is taken to have sole control.[16]

Sole control can also be exercised by a minority shareholder who has the right to manage the activities of the company and to determine its business policy.

15. An option to purchase or convert shares cannot in itself confer sole control unless the option will be exercised in the near future according to legally binding agreements.[17] However, the likely exercise of such an option can be taken into account as an additional element which, together with other elements, may lead to the conclusion that there is sole control.

16. A change from joint to sole control of an undertaking is deemed to be a concentration within the meaning of the Merger Regulation because decisive influence exercised alone is substantially different from decisive influence exercised jointly.[18] For the same reason, an operation involving the acquisition of joint control of one part of an undertaking and sole control of another part is in principle regarded as two separate concentrations under the Merger Regulation.[19]

---

[12] Case IV/M.286—*Zürich/MMIr, of 2 April 1993.*
[13] Case IV/M.296—*Crédit Lyonnais/BFG Bank,* of 11 January 1993.
[14] Case IV/M.299—*Sara Lee/BP Food Division,* of 8 February 1993.
[15] Case IV/M.025—*Arjomari/Wiggins Teape,* of 10 February 1990.
[16] Case IV/M.343—*Société Générale de Belgique/Générale de Banque,* of 3 August 1993.
[17] Judgment in Case T 2/93, *Air France v. Commission* [1994] ECR II–323.
[18] This issue is dealt with in paragraphs 30, 31 and 32 of the Notice on the concept of undertakings concerned.
[19] Case IV/M.409—*ABB/Renault Automation,* of 9 March 1994.

17. The concept of control under the Merger Regulation may be different from that applied in specific areas of legislation concerning, for example, prudential rules, taxation, air transport or the media. In addition, national legislation within a Member State may provide specific rules on the structure of bodies representing the organisation of decision-making within an undertaking, in particular, in relation to the rights of representatives of employees. While such legislation may confer some power of control upon persons other than the shareholders, the concept of control under the Merger Regulation is related only to the means of influence normally enjoyed by the owners of an undertaking. Finally, the prerogatives exercised by a State acting as a public authority rather than as a shareholder, in so far as they are limited to the protection of the public interest, do not constitute control within the meaning of the Merger Regulation to the extent that they have neither the aim nor the effect of enabling the State to exercise a decisive influence over the activity of the undertaking.[20]

2. Joint control

18. As in the case of sole control, the acquisition of joint control (which includes changes from sole control to joint control) can also be established on a legal or *de facto* basis. There is joint control if the shareholders (the parent companies) must reach agreement on major decisions concerning the controlled undertaking (the joint venture).

19. Joint control exists where two or more undertakings or persons have the possibility of exercising decisive influence over another undertaking. Decisive influence in this sense normally means the power to block actions which determine the strategic commercial behaviour of an undertaking. Unlike sole control, which confers the power upon a specific shareholder to determine the strategic decisions in an undertaking, joint control is characterized by the possibility of a deadlock situation resulting from the power of two or more parent companies to reject proposed strategic decisions. It follows, therefore, that these shareholders must reach a common understanding in determining the commercial policy of the joint venture.

2.1. Equality in voting rights or appointment to decision-making bodies

20. The clearest form of joint control exists where there are only two parent companies which share equally the voting rights in the joint venture. In this case, it is not necessary for a formal agreement to exist between them. However, where there is a formal agreement, it must be consistent with the principle of equality between the parent companies, by laying down, for example, that each is entitled to the same number of representatives in the management bodies and that none of the members has a casting vote.[21] Equality may also be achieved where both parent companies have the right to appoint an equal number of members to the decision-making bodies of the joint venture.

2.2. Veto rights

21. Joint control may exist even where there is no equality between the two parent companies in votes or in representation in decision-making bodies or where there are more than two parent companies. This is the case where minority shareholders have additional rights which allow them to veto decisions which are essential for the strategic commercial behaviour of the joint venture.[22] These veto rights may be set out in the statute of the joint venture or conferred by agreement between its parent companies. The veto rights themselves may operate by means of a specific quorum required for decisions taken at the

---

[20] Case IV/M.493—*Tractebel/Distrigaz II*, of 1 September 1994.

[21] Case IV/M.272—*Matra/CAP Gemini Sogeti*, of 17 March 1993.

[22] Case T 2/93—*Air France v. Commission* (*ibid*). Case IV/M.010—Conagra/Idea, of 3 May 1991.

shareholders' meeting or by the board of directors to the extent that the parent companies are represented on this board. It is also possible that strategic decisions are subject to approval by a body, e.g. supervisory board, where the minority shareholders are represented and form part of the quorum needed for such decisions.

22. These veto rights must be related to strategic decisions on the business policy of the joint venture. They must go beyond the veto rights normally accorded to minority shareholders in order to protect their financial interests as investors in the joint venture. This normal protection of the rights of minority shareholders is related to decisions on the essence of the joint venture, such as changes in the statute, an increase or decrease in the capital or liquidation. A veto right, for example, which prevents the sale or winding-up of the joint venture does not confer joint control on the minority shareholder concerned.[23]

23. In contrast, veto rights which confer joint control typically include decisions and issues such as the budget, the business plan, major investments or the appointment of senior management. The acquisition of joint control, however, does not require that the acquirer has the power to exercise decisive influence on the day-to-day running of an undertaking. The crucial element is that the veto rights are sufficient to enable the parent companies to exercise such influence in relation to the strategic business behaviour of the joint venture. Moreover, it is not necessary to establish that an acquirer of joint control of the joint venture will actually make use of its decisive influence. The possibility of exercising such influence and, hence, the mere existence of the veto rights, is sufficient.

24. In order to acquire joint control, it is not necessary for a minority shareholder to have all the veto rights mentioned above. It may be sufficient that only some, or even one such right, exists. Whether or not this is the case depends upon the precise content of the veto right itself and also the importance of this right in the context of the specific business of the joint venture.

Appointment of management and determination of budget

25. Normally the most important veto rights are those concerning decisions on the appointment of the management and the budget. The power to co-determine the structure of the management confers upon the holder the power to exercise decisive influence on the commercial policy of an undertaking. The same is true with respect to decisions on the budget since the budget determines the precise framework of the activities of the joint venture and, in particular, the investments it may make.

Business plan

26. The business plan normally provides details of the aims of a company together with the measures to be taken in order to achieve those aims. A veto right over this type of business plan may be sufficient to confer joint control even in the absence of any other veto right. In contrast, where the business plan contains merely general declarations concerning the business aims of the joint venture, the existence of a veto right will be only one element in the general assessment of joint control but will not, on its own, be sufficient to confer joint control.

Investments

27. In the case of a veto right on investments, the importance of this right depends, first, on the level of investments which are subject to the approval of the parent companies and, secondly, on the extent to which investments constitute an essential feature of the market in which the joint venture is active. In relation to the first criterion, where the level of

---

[23] Case IV/M.062—*Eridania/ISI*, of 30 July 1991.

investments necessitating approval of the parent companies is extremely high, this veto right may be closer to the normal protection of the interests of a minority shareholder than to a right conferring a power of co-determination over the commercial policy of the joint venture. With regard to the second, the investment policy of an undertaking is normally an important element in assessing whether or not there is joint control. However, there may be some markets where investment does not play a significant role in the market behaviour of an undertaking.

Market-specific rights

28. Apart from the typical veto rights mentioned above, there exist a number of other veto rights related to specific decisions which are important in the context of the particular market of the joint venture. One example is the decision on the technology to be used by the joint venture where technology is a key feature of the joint venture's activities. Another example relates to markets characterised by product differentiation and a significant degree of innovation. In such markets, a veto right over decisions relating to new product lines to be developed by the joint venture may also be an important element in establishing the existence of joint control.

Overall context

29. In assessing the relative importance of veto rights, where there are a number of them, these rights should not be evaluated in isolation. On the contrary, the determination of whether or not joint control exists is based upon an assessment of these rights as a whole. However, a veto right which does not relate either to commercial policy and strategy or to the budget or business plan cannot be regarded as giving joint control to its owner.[24]

2.3. Joint exercise of voting rights

30. Even in the absence of specific veto rights, two or more undertakings acquiring minority shareholdings in another undertaking may obtain joint control. This may be the case where the minority shareholdings together provide the means for controlling the target undertaking. This means that the minority shareholders, together, will have a majority of the voting rights; and they will act together in exercising these voting rights. This can result from a legally binding agreement to this effect, or it may be established on a *de facto* basis.
    31. The legal means to ensure the joint exercise of voting rights can be in the form of a holding company to which the minority shareholders transfer their rights, or an agreement by which they undertake to act in the same way (pooling agreement).
    32. Very exceptionally, collective action can occur on a *de facto* basis where strong common interests exist between the minority shareholders to the effect that they would not act against each other in exercising their rights in relation to the joint venture.
    33. In the case of acquisitions of minority shareholdings, the prior existence of links between the minority shareholders or the acquisition of the shareholdings by means of concerted action will be factors indicating such a common interest.
    34. In the case where a new joint venture is established, as opposed to the acquisition of minority shareholdings in a pre-existing company, there is a higher probability that the parent companies are carrying out a deliberate common policy. This is true, in particular, where each parent company provides a contribution to the joint venture which is vital for its operation (e.g. specific technologies, local know-how or supply agreements). In these circumstances, the parent companies may be able to operate the joint venture with full cooperation only with each other's agreement on the most important strategic decisions

---

[24] Case IV/M.295—*SITA-RPC/SCORI*, of 19 March 1993.

even if there is no express provision for any veto rights. The greater the number of parent companies involved in such a joint venture, however, the more remote is the likelihood of this situation occurring.

35. In the absence of strong common interests such as those outlined above, the possibility of changing coalitions between minority shareholders will normally exclude the assumption of joint control. Where there is no stable majority in the decision-making procedure and the majority can on each occasion be any of the various combinations possible amongst the minority shareholders, it cannot be assumed that the minority shareholders will jointly control the undertaking. In this context, it is not sufficient that there are agreements between two or more parties having an equal shareholding in the capital of an undertaking which establish identical rights and powers between the parties. For example, in the case of an undertaking where three shareholders each own one-third of the share capital and each elect one-third of the members of the Board of Directors, the shareholders do not have joint control since decisions are required to be taken on the basis of a simple majority. The same considerations also apply in more complex structures, for example, where the capital of an undertaking is equally divided between three share-holders and where the Board of Directors is composed of twelve members, each of the shareholders A, B and C electing two, another two being elected by A, B and C jointly, whilst the remaining four are chosen by the other eight members jointly. In this case also there is no joint control, and hence no control at all within the meaning of the Merger Regulation.

2.4. Other considerations related to joint control

36. Joint control is not incompatible with the fact that one of the parent companies enjoys specific knowledge of and experience in the business of the joint venture. In such a case, the other parent company can play a modest or even non-existent role in the daily management of the joint venture where its presence is motivated by considerations of a financial, long-term-strategy, brand image or general policy nature. Nevertheless, it must always retain the real possibility of contesting the decisions taken by the other parent company, without which there would be sole control.

37. For joint control to exist, there should not be a casting vote for one parent company only. However, there can be joint control when this casting vote can be exercised only after a series of stages of arbitration and attempts at reconciliation or in a very limited field.[25]

2.5. Joint control for a limited period

38. Where an operation leads to joint control for a starting-up period[26] but, according to legally binding agreements, this joint control will be converted to sole control by one of the shareholders, the whole operation will normally be considered to be an acquisition of sole control.

3. Control by a single shareholder on the basis of veto rights

39. An exceptional situation exists where only one shareholder is able to veto strategic decisions in an undertaking, but this shareholder does not have the power, on his own, to impose such decisions. This situation occurs either where one shareholder holds 50% in an undertaking whilst the remaining 50% is held by two or more minority shareholders, or where there is a quorum required for strategic decisions which in fact confers a veto

---

[25] Case IV/M.425—*British Telecom/Banco Santander*, of 28 March 1994.
[26] This starting-up period must not exceed three years. Case IV/M.425—*British Telecom/Banco Santander, ibid.*

right upon only one minority shareholder.[27] In these circumstances, a single shareholder possesses the same level of influence as that normally enjoyed by several jointly-controlling shareholders, i.e. the power to block the adoption of strategic decisions. However, this shareholder does not enjoy the powers which are normally conferred on an undertaking with sole control, i.e. the power to impose strategic decisions. Since this shareholder can produce a deadlock situation comparable to that in normal cases of joint control, he acquires decisive influence and therefore control within the meaning of the Merger Regulation.[28]

4. Changes in the structure of control

40. A concentration may also occur where an operation leads to a change in the structure of control. This includes the change from joint control to sole control as well as an increase in the number of shareholders exercising joint control. The principles for determining the existence of a concentration in these circumstances are set out in detail in the Notice on the concept of undertakings concerned.[29]

IV. EXCEPTIONS

41. Article 3(5) sets out three exceptional situations where the acquisition of a controlling interest does not constitute a concentration under the Merger Regulation.

42. First, the acquisition of securities by companies whose normal activities include transactions and dealing in securities for their own account or for the account of others is not deemed to constitute a concentration if such an acquisition is made in the framework of these businesses and if the securities are held on only a temporary basis (Article 3(5)(a)). In order to fall within this exception, the following requirements must be fulfilled:

— the acquiring undertaking must be a credit or other financial institution or insurance company the normal activities of which are described above,
— the securities must be acquired with a view to their resale,
— the acquiring undertaking must not exercise the voting rights with a view to determining the strategic commercial behaviour of the target company or must exercise these rights only with a view to preparing the total or partial disposal of the undertaking, its assets or securities,
— the acquiring undertaking must dispose of its controlling interest within one year of the date of the acquisition, that is, it must reduce its shareholding within this one-year period at least to a level which no longer confers control. This period, however, may be extended by the Commission where the acquiring undertaking can show that the disposal was not reasonably possible within the one-year period.

43. Secondly, there is no change of control, and hence no concentration within the meaning of the Merger Regulation, where control is acquired by an office-holder according to the law of a Member State relating to liquidation, winding-up, insolvency, cessation of payments, compositions or analogous proceedings (Article 3(5)(b));

---

[27] Case IV/M.258—*CCIE/GTE*, of 25 September 1992, where the veto rights of only one shareholder were exercisable through a member of the board appointed by this shareholder.
[28] Since this shareholder is the only undertaking acquiring a controlling influence, only this shareholder is obliged to submit a notification under the Merger Regulation.
[29] Paragraphs 30 to 48.

44. Thirdly, a concentration does not arise where a financial holding company within the meaning of the Fourth Council Directive 78/660/EEC[30] acquires control, provided that this company exercises its voting rights only to maintain the full value of its investment and does not otherwise determine directly or indirectly the strategic commercial conduct of the controlled undertaking.

45. In the context of the exceptions under Article 3(5), the question may arise whether a rescue operation constitutes a concentration under the Merger Regulation. A rescue operation typically involves the conversion of existing debt into a new company, through which a syndicate of banks may acquire joint control of the company concerned. Where such an operation meets the criteria for joint control, as outlined above, it will normally be considered to be a concentration.[31] Although the primary intention of the banks is to restructure the financing of the undertaking concerned for its subsequent resale, the exception set out in Article 3(5)(a) is normally not applicable to such an operation. This is because the restructuring programme normally requires the controlling banks to determine the strategic commercial behaviour of the rescued undertaking. Furthermore, it is not normally a realistic proposition to transform a rescued company into a commercially viable entity and to resell it within the permitted one-year period. Moreover, the length of time needed to achieve this aim may be so uncertain that it would be difficult to grant an extension of the disposal period.

V. Final

46. The Commission's interpretation of Article 3 as set out in this Notice is without prejudice to the interpretation which may be given by the Court of Justice or the Court of First Instance of the European Communities.

---

[30] OJ 1978 L222/11, as last amended by the Act of Accession of Austria, Finland and Sweden. Article 5(3) of this Directive defines financial holding companies as "those companies the sole objective of which is to acquire holdings in other undertakings, and to manage such holdings and turn them to profit, without involving themselves directly or indirectly in the management of those undertakings, the foregoing without prejudice to their rights as shareholders".

[31] Case IV/M.116—*Kelt/American Express*, of 20 August 1991.

APPENDIX 36

COMMISSION NOTICE[1]

On the Concept of Full-function Joint Ventures under Council Regulation (EEC) No 4064/89 On the Control of Concentrations Between Undertakings

(Text with EEA relevance)

I. INTRODUCTION

II. JOINT VENTURES UNDER ARTICLE 3 OF THE MERGER REGULATION

 1. Joint control
 2. Structural change of the undertakings

III. FINAL

I. Introduction

1. The purpose of this notice is to provide guidance as to how the Commission interprets Article 3 of Council Regulation (EEC) No 4064/89[2] as last amended by Regulation (EC) No 1310/97[3] (hereinafter referred to as the Merger Regulation) in relation to joint ventures.[4]

2. This Notice replaces the Notice on the distinction between concentrative and cooperative joint ventures. Changes made in this Notice reflect the amendments made to the Merger Regulation as well as the experience gained by the Commission in applying the Merger Regulation since its entry into force on 21 September 1990. The principles set out in this Notice will be followed and further developed by the Commission's practice in individual cases.

3. Under the Community competition rules, joint ventures are undertakings which are jointly controlled by two or more other undertakings.[5] In practice joint ventures encompass a broad range of operations, from merger-like operations to cooperation for particular functions such as R & D, production or distribution.

---

[1] OJ 1998 C66/1.
[2] OJ 1989 L395/1, corrected version 1990 L257/13.
[3] OJ 1997 L180/1.
[4] The Commission intends, in due course, to provide guidance on the application of Article 2(4) of the Merger Regulation. Pending the adoption of such guidance, interested parties are referred to the principles set out in paragraphs 17 to 20 of Commission Notice on the distinction between concentrative and cooperative joint ventures, OJ 1994 C385/1.
[5] The concept of joint control is set out in the Notice on the concept of concentration.

4. Joint ventures fall within the scope of the Merger Regulation if they meet the requirements of a concentration set out in Article 3 thereof.

5. According to recital 23 to Council Regulation (EEC) No 4064/89 it is appropriate to define the concept of concentration in such a manner as to cover only operations bringing about a lasting change in the structure of the undertakings concerned.

6. The structural changes brought about by concentrations frequently reflect a dynamic process of restructuring in the markets concerned. They are permitted under the Merger Regulation unless they result in serious damage to the structure of competition by creating or strengthening a dominant position.

7. The Merger Regulation deals with the concept of full-function joint ventures in Article 3(2) as follows:

"The creation of a joint venture performing on a lasting basis all the functions of an autonomous economic entity shall constitute a concentration within the meaning of paragraph 1(b)."

II. JOINT VENTURES UNDER ARTICLE 3 OF THE MERGER REGULATION

8. In order to be a concentration within the meaning of Article 3 of the Merger Regulation, an operation must fulfil the following requirements:

1. Joint control

9. A joint venture may fall within the scope of the Merger Regulation where there is an acquisition of joint control by two or more undertakings, that is, its parent companies (Article 3(1)(b)). The concept of control is set out in Article 3(3). This provides that control is based on the possibility of exercising decisive influence over an undertaking, which is determined by both legal and factual considerations.

10. The principles for determining joint control are set out in detail in the Commission's Notice on the concept of concentration.[6]

2. Structural change of the undertakings

11. Article 3(2) provides that the joint venture must perform, on a lasting basis, all the functions of an autonomous economic entity. Joint ventures which satisfy this requirement bring about a lasting change in the structure of the undertakings concerned. They are referred to in this Notice as "full-function" joint ventures.

12. Essentially this means that a joint venture must operate on a market, performing the functions normally carried out by undertakings operating on the same market. In order to do so the joint venture must have a management dedicated to its day-to-day operations and access to sufficient resources including finance, staff, and assets (tangible and intangible) in order to conduct on a lasting basis its business activities within the area provided for in the joint-venture agreement.[7]

---

[6] Paragraphs 18 to 39.

[7] Case IV/M.527—*Thomson CSF/Deutsche Aerospace*, of 2 December 1994 (paragraph 10)—intellectual rights, Case IV/M.560 *EDS/Lufthansa* of 11 May 1995 (paragraph 11)—outsourcing, Case IV/M.585—*Voest Alpine Industrieanlagenbau GmbH/Davy International Ltd*, of 7 September 1995 (paragraph 8)—joint venture's right to demand additional expertise and staff from its parent companies, Case IV/M.686—*Nokia/Autoliv*, of 5 February 1996 (paragraph 7), joint venture able to terminate "service agreements" with parent company and to move from site retained by parent company, Case IV/M.791—*British Gas Trading Ltd/Group 4 Utility Services Ltd*, of 7 October 1996 (paragraph 9), joint venture's intended assets will be transferred to leasing company and leased by joint venture.

13. A joint venture is not full-function if it only takes over one specific function within the parent companies' business activities without access to the market. This is the case, for example, for joint ventures limited to R & D or production. Such joint ventures are auxiliary to their parent companies' business activities. This is also the case where a joint venture is essentially limited to the distribution or sales of its parent companies' products and, therefore, acts principally as a sales agency. However, the fact that a joint venture makes use of the distribution network or outlet of one or more of its parent companies normally will not disqualify it as "full-function" as long as the parent companies are acting only as agents of the joint venture.[8]

14. The strong presence of the parent companies in upstream or downstream markets is a factor to be taken into consideration in assessing the full-function character of a joint venture where this presence leads to substantial sales or purchases between the parent companies and the joint venture. The fact that the joint venture relies almost entirely on sales to its parent companies or purchases from them only for an initial start-up period does not normally affect the full-function character of the joint venture. Such a start-up period may be necessary in order to establish the joint venture on a market. It will normally not exceed a period of three years, depending on the specific conditions of the market in question.[9]

Where sales from the joint venture to the parent companies are intended to be made on a lasting basis, the essential question is whether, regardless of these sales, the joint venture is geared to play an active role on the market. In this respect the relative proportion of these sales compared with the total production of the joint venture is an important factor. Another factor is whether sales to the parent companies are made on the basis of normal commercial conditions.[10]

In relation to purchases made by the joint venture from its parent companies, the full-function character of the joint venture is questionable in particular where little value is added to the products or services concerned at the level of the joint venture itself. In such a situation, the joint venture may be closer to a joint sales agency. However, in contrast to this situation where a joint venture is active in a trade market and performs the normal functions of a trading company in such a market, it normally will not be an auxiliary sales agency but a full-function joint venture. A trade market is characterised by the existence of companies which specialise in the selling and distribution of products without being vertically integrated in addition to those which are integrated, and where different sources of supply are available for the products in question. In addition, many trade markets may require operators to invest in specific facilities such as outlets, stockholding, warehouses, depots, transport fleets and sales personnel. In order to constitute a full-function joint venture in a trade market, an undertaking must have the necessary facilities and be likely to obtain a substantial proportion of its supplies not only from its parent companies but also from other competing sources.[11]

15. Furthermore, the joint venture must be intended to operate on a lasting basis. The fact that the parent companies commit to the joint venture the resources described above normally demonstrates that this is the case. In addition, agreements setting up a joint venture often provide for certain contingencies, for example, the failure of the joint

---

[8] Case IV/M.102—*TNT/Canada Post* etc. of 2 December 1991 (paragraph 14).

[9] Case IV/M.560—*EDS/Lufthansa* of 11 May 1995 (paragraph 11); Case IV/M.686 *Nokia/Autoliv* of 5 February 1996 (paragraph 6); to be contrasted with Case IV/M.904—*RSB/Tenex/Fuel Logistics* of 2 April 1997 (paragraph 15–17) and Case IV/M.979—*Preussag/Voest-Alpine* of 1 October 1997 (paragraph 9–12). A special case exists where sales by the joint venture to its parent are caused by a legal monopoly downstream of the joint venture (Case IV/M.468—*Siemens/Italtel* of 17 February 1995 (paragraph 12), or where the sales to a parent company consist of by-products, which are of minor importance to the joint venture (Case IV/M.550—*Union Carbide/Enichem* of 13 March 1995 (paragraph 14).

[10] Case IV/M.556—*Zeneca/Vanderhave* of 9 April 1996 (paragraph 8); Case IV/M.751—*Bayer/Hüls* of 3 July 1996 (paragraph 10).

[11] Case IV/M.788—*AgrEVO/Marubeni* of 3 September 1996 (paragraphs 9 and 10).

venture or fundamental disagreement as between the parent companies.[12] This may be achieved by the incorporation of provisions for the eventual dissolution of the joint venture itself or the possibility for one or more parent companies to withdraw from the joint venture. This kind of provision does not prevent the joint venture from being considered as operating on a lasting basis. The same is normally true where the agreement specifies a period for the duration of the joint venture where this period is sufficiently long in order to bring about a lasting change in the structure of the undertakings concerned,[13] or where the agreement provides for the possible continuation of the joint venture beyond this period. By contrast, the joint venture will not be considered to operate on a lasting basis where it is established for a short finite duration. This would be the case, for example, where a joint venture is established in order to construct a specific project such as a power plant, but it will not be involved in the operation of the plant once its construction has been completed.

III. FINAL

16. The creation of a full-function joint venture constitutes a concentration within the meaning of Article 3 of the Merger Regulation. Restrictions accepted by the parent companies of the joint venture that are directly related and necessary for the implementation of the concentration ("ancillary restrictions"), will be assessed together with the concentration itself.[14]

Further, the creation of a full-function joint venture may as a direct consequence lead to the coordination of the competitive behaviour of undertakings that remain independent. In such cases Article 2(4) of the Merger Regulation provides that those cooperative effects will be assessed within the same procedure as the concentration. This assessment will be made in accordance with the criteria of Article 81(1) and (3) of the Treaty with a view to establishing whether or not the operation is compatible with the common market.

The applicability of Article 81 of the Treaty to other restrictions of competition, that are neither ancillary to the concentration, nor a direct consequence of the creation of the joint venture, will normally have to be examined by means of Regulation No 17.

17. The Commission's interpretation of Article 3 of the Merger Regulation with respect to joint ventures is without prejudice to the interpretation which may be given by the Court of Justice or the Court of First Instance of the European Communities.

---

[12] Case IV/M.891—*Deutsche Bank/Commerzbank/J.M. Voith* of 23 April 1997 (paragraph 7).

[13] Case IV/M.791—*British Gas Trading Ltd/Group 4 Utility Services Ltd* of 7 October 1996, (paragraph 10); to be contrasted with Case IV/M.722—*Teneo/Merill Lynch/Bankers Trust* of 15 April 1996 (paragraph 15).

[14] See Commission Notice regarding restrictions ancillary to concentrations, OJ 1990 C203/5.

COMMISSION NOTICE[1]

On the Distinction between Concentrative and Co-operative Joint Ventures

Under Council Regulation (EEC) No. 4064/89 of 21 December 1989 on the control of concentrations between undertakings

I. INTRODUCTION

1. The purpose of this notice is to provide guidance as to how the Commission interprets Article 3 of Regulation (EEC) No. 4064/89[2] (hereinafter referred to as "the Merger Regulation") in relation to joint ventures.

2. This notice replaces the notice on the same subject adopted by the Commission on 25 July 1990.[3] Changes made in the current notice reflect the experience gained by the Commission in applying the Merger Regulation since its entry into force on 21 September 1990. The principles set out in this notice will be followed and further developed by the Commission's practice in individual cases.

3. Under the Community competition rules joint ventures are undertakings which are jointly controlled by two or more other undertakings.[4] In practice joint ventures encompass a broad range of operations, from merger-like operations to co-operation for particular functions such as R&D, production or distribution.

4. Joint ventures fall within the scope of the Merger Regulation if they meet the requirements of a concentration set out in Article 3 thereof.

5. According to recital 23 of the Merger Regulation "it is appropriate to define the concept of concentration in such a manner as to cover only operations bringing about a lasting change in the structure of the undertakings concerned . . . it is therefore necessary to exclude from the scope of this Merger Regulation those operations which have as their object or effect the co-ordination of competitive behaviour of undertakings which remain independent . . . "

6. The structural changes brought about by concentrations frequently reflect a dynamic process of restructuring in the markets concerned. They are permitted under the Merger Regulation unless they result in serious damage to the structure of competition by creating or strengthening a dominant position.

In this respect concentrations are to be contrasted with arrangements between independent undertakings whereby they co-ordinate their competitive behaviour. The latter do not, in principle, involve a lasting change in structure of undertakings. It is therefore appropriate to submit such arrangements to the prohibition laid down in Article 81(1) of the

---

[1] OJ 1994 C385/1.
[2] OJ 1989 C395/1, corrected version OJ 1990 L257/13.
[3] OJ 1990 C203/10.
[4] The concept of joint control is set out in the notice on the notion of a concentration.

EEC Treaty where they affect trade between Member States and have as their object or effect the prevention, restriction or distortion of competition within the common market, and they can be exempted from this prohibition only where they fulfil the requirements of Article 81(3). For this reason, co-operative arrangements are dealt with under Regulation (EEC) No. 17,[5] (EEC) No. 1017/68,[6] (EEC) No. 4056/86,[7] or (EEC) No. 3975/87[8] implementing Articles 81 and 82.[9]

7. The Merger Regulation deals with the distinction between concentrative and co-operative operations in Article 3(2)[10] as follows:

"An operation, including the creation of a joint venture, which has as its object or effect the co-ordination of the competitive behaviour of undertakings which remain independent shall not constitute a concentration within the meaning of paragraph 1(b).

The creation of a joint venture performing on a lasting basis all the functions of an autonomous economic entity, which does not give rise to co-ordination of the competitive behaviour of the parties amongst themselves or between them and the joint venture, shall constitute a concentration within the meaning of paragraph 1(b)."

8. Although Article 3(2), second subparagraph, refers to co-ordination between parent companies and the joint venture, this has to be interpreted in the light of recital 23 and Article 3(2), first subparagraph, the purpose of which is to exclude from the scope of the Merger Regulation operations which lead to the co-ordination of behaviour between "undertakings which remain independent". For the purposes of the distinction between co-operative and concentrative joint ventures therefore, the co-ordination between the parent companies and the joint venture referred to in the second subparagraph is relevant only in so far as it is an instrument for producing or reinforcing the co-ordination between the parent companies.

II. Joint Ventures Under Article 3 of the Merger Regulation

9. In order to be a concentration within the meaning of Article 3 of the Merger Regulation an operation must fulfil the following requirements:

1. Joint control

10. A joint venture may fall within the scope of the Merger Regulation where there is an acquisition of joint control by two or more undertakings, that is, its parent companies (Article 3(1)(b)). The concept of control is set out in Article 3(3). This provides that control is based on the possibility of exercising decisive influence on an undertaking, which is determined by both legal and factual considerations.

11. The principles for determining joint control are set out in detail in the Commission's notice on the notion of concentration.[11]

2. Structural change of the undertakings

12. Article 3(2), second subparagraphs stipulates that the joint venture must perform, on a lasting basis, all the functions of an autonomous economic entity.

---

[5] OJ 1962 13/204.
[6] OJ 1968 L175/1.
[7] OJ 1986 L378/4.
[8] OJ 1987 L374/1.
[9] See Commission Notice concerning the assessment of co-operative joint ventures pursuant to Article 81 of the EEC Treaty, OJ 1993 C43/2.
[10] Whilst Article 3(2) first subparagraph, is not confined to joint ventures, its application to operations other than joint ventures is not dealt with in the context of the present notice.
[11] Paragraphs 18 to 39.

13. Essentially this means that the joint venture must operate on a market, performing the functions normally carried out by other undertakings operating on the same market. In order to do so the joint venture must have sufficient financial and other resources including finance, staff, and assets (tangible and intangible) in order to operate a business activity on a lasting basis. In respect of intellectual property rights it is sufficient that these rights are licensed to the joint venture for its duration.[12] Joint ventures which satisfy this requirement are commonly described as "full-function" joint ventures.

14. A joint venture is not full-function venture if it only takes over one specific function within the parent companies' business activities without access to the market. This is the case, for example, for joint ventures limited to R&D or production. Such joint ventures are auxiliary to their parent companies' business activities. This is also the case where a joint venture is essentially limited to the distribution or sales of its parent companies' products and, therefore, acts principally as a sales agency. However, the fact that a joint venture makes use of the distribution network or outlet of one or more of its parent companies, normally will not disqualify it as "full-function" as long as the parent companies are acting only as agents of the joint venture.[13]

15. The strong presence of the parent companies in upstream or downstream markets is a factor to be taken into consideration in assessing the full-function character of a joint venture where this presence leads to substantial sales or purchases between the parent companies and the joint venture. The fact that the joint venture relies almost entirely on sales to its parent companies or purchases from them only for an initial start-up period does not normally affect the full-function character of the joint venture. Such a start-up period may be necessary in order to establish the joint venture on a market. It will normally not exceed a time period of three years, depending on the specific conditions of the market in question.[14]

Where sales from the joint venture to the parent companies are intended to be made on a lasting basis the essential question is whether regardless of these sales the joint venture is geared to play an active role on the market. In this respect the relative proportion of these sales compared with the total production of the joint venture is an important factor. Another factor is that sales to the parent companies are made on the basis of normal commercial conditions.[15]

In relation to purchases made by the joint venture from its parent companies, the full-function character of the joint venture is questionable in particular where little value is added to the products or services concerned at the level of the joint venture itself. In such a situation, the joint venture may be closer to a joint sales agency. However, in contrast to this situation where a joint venture is active in a trade market and performs the normal functions of a trading company in such a market, it normally will not be an auxiliary sales agency but a full-function joint venture. A trade market is characterised by the existence of companies which specialise in the selling and distribution of products without being vertically integrated in addition to those which may be integrated, and where different sources of supply are available for the products in question. In addition, many trade markets may require operators to invest in specific facilities such as outlets, stockholding, warehouses, depots, transport fleets and sales personnel. In order to constitute a full-function joint venture in a trading market, it must have the necessary facilities and be likely to obtain a substantial proportion of its supplies not only from its parent companies but also from other competing sources.[16]

16. Furthermore, the joint venture must be intended to operate on a lasting basis. The fact that the parent companies commit to the joint venture the resources described above

---

[12] Case IV/M.236, *Ericsson/Ascom* of 8 July 1992 (paragraph 11).

[13] Case IV/M.102, *TNT/Canada Post* etc. of 2 December 1991; Case IV/M.149, *Lucas/Eaton* of 9 December 1991.

[14] Case IV/M.394, *Mannesmann/RWE/Deutsche Bank* of 22 December 1983 (paragraph 9).

[15] Case IV/M.266, *Rhône-Poulenc Chimie/SITA* of 26 November 1992 (paragraph 15), to be contrasted with Case IV/M.168, *Flachglas/VEGLA* of 13 April 1992.

[16] Case IV/M.179, *Spar/Dansk Supermarked* of 3 February 1992 (food retail); Case IV/M.326, *Toyota Motor Corp./Walter Frey Holding/Toyota France* 1 July 1993 (car distribution).

normally demonstrates that this is the case. In addition, agreements setting up a joint venture often provide for certain contingencies, for example, the failure of the joint venture or fundamental disagreement as between the parent companies.[17] This may be achieved by the incorporation of provisions for the eventual dissolution of the joint venture itself or the possibility for one or more parent companies to withdraw from the joint venture. This kind of provision does not prevent the joint venture from being considered as operating on a lasting basis. The same is normally true where the agreement specifies a period for the duration of the joint venture where this period is sufficiently long in order to bring about a lasting change in the structure of the undertaking concerned,[18] or where the agreement provides for the possible continuation of the joint venture beyond this period. By contrast, the joint venture will not be considered to operate on a lasting basis where it is established for a short finite duration. This would be the case, for example, where a joint venture is established in order to construct a specific project such as a power plant, but it will not be involved in the operation of the plant once its construction has been completed.

3. Co-operative aspects

17. The creation of a full-function joint venture normally constitutes a concentration within the meaning of Article 3 of the Merger Regulation unless its object or effect is co-ordination of the competitive behaviour of independent undertakings which is likely to result in a restriction of competition within the meaning of Article 81(1). In order to assess whether a joint venture is co-operative in nature it is necessary to determine whether there is co-ordination between the parent companies in relation to prices, markets, output or innovation. The co-ordination between the parent companies and the joint venture referred to in the second subparagraph of Article 3(2) is relevant only in so far as it is an instrument for producing or reinforcing the co-ordination between the parent companies. Where there is a restriction of competition of this kind the Commission will have to examine the applicability of Article 81 to the whole operation by means of Regulation No. 17. Where the factors leading to this restriction of competition can be separated from the creation of the joint venture itself, the former will be assessed under Regulation No. 17, the latter under the rules on merger control.[19]

3.1. Product market

18. The following typical situations illustrate where co-ordination of the competitive behaviour of the parent companies resulting in an appreciable restriction of competition may or may not occur:

— there is no possibility of co-ordination of the competitive behaviour of independent undertakings where the parent companies transfer their entire business activities to the joint venture or their total activities in a given industrial sector,

— co-ordination can normally be excluded where the parent companies are not active in the market of the joint venture or transfer to the joint venture all their activities in this market or where only one parent company remains active in the joint venture's market. The same is true where the parent companies retain only minor activities in the market of the joint venture,

— by contrast to the above, there is normally a high probability of co-ordination where two or more parent companies retain to a significant extent activities in the same

---

[17] Case IV/M.408, *RWE/Mannesmann* of 28 February 1994 (paragraph 6).

[18] Case IV/M.259, *British Airways/TAT* of 27 October 1992 (paragraph 10).

[19] Case IV/M.179, *Spar/Dansk Supermarked* of 3 February 1992 (paragraph 8). Case IV/M.263, *Ahold/Jeronimo Martins* of 29 September 1992 (paragraph 8).

product market as the joint venture itself in so far as these activities are in the same geographic market,[20]

— there is also a probability of co-ordination where the, parent companies or the joint venture specialise in specific segments of an overall product market, unless these segments are of minor importance in view of the main activities of the parent companies or the joint venture respectively or there are objective reasons for the parent companies to retain their activities outside the joint venture, *e.g.* technology related to other activities of the parent companies. In the latter case each of the parent companies retains a genuine interest in their specific segments. The existence of the joint venture therefore does not normally of itself justify the assumption that they would co-ordinate their behaviour with regard to these activities,

— where a network of co-operative links already exists between the parent companies in the joint venture's market the main object or effect of the joint venture may be to add a further link and thereby strengthen already existing co-ordination of competitive behaviour,[21]

— where the parent companies are active in a market which is downstream from the joint venture's market co-ordination of their competitive behaviour may occur where the joint venture is their main supplier and relatively little further value is added at the level of the parent companies; equally, where the parent companies are active in a market which is upstream from the joint venture's market co-ordination of their competitive behaviour may occur where their main customer is the joint venture either in general or in a particular geographic market,

— where two or more parent companies have a significant activity in a neighbouring market and this neighbouring market is of significant economic importance compared with that of the joint venture, the collaboration within the joint venture may lead to the co-ordination of the parent companies' competitive behaviour on this neighbouring market.[22] In this context a neighbouring market is a separate but closely related market to the market of the joint venture, both markets having common characteristics including technology, customers or competitors.

3.2. Geographic market

19. The parent companies and the joint venture may be active in the same product market but in different geographic markets. In this context two situations may be particularly relevant: the parent companies and the joint venture are each in different geographic markets, or the parent companies are in the same geographic market which is nevertheless different from that of the joint venture. In these situations co-ordination may or may not occur as follows:

— where the parent companies and the joint venture are all in different geographic markets, the Commission will examine closely the likelihood of co-ordination between the parent companies. In doing so the Commission will consider interaction between markets, and foreseeable developments in the emergence of wider geographic markets particularly in the light of the market integration process in the Community.[23] The same applies where one parent company and the joint venture are in the same

---

[20] Case IV/M.088, *Elf Enterprise* of 24 July 1991 (paragraph 6); Case IV/M.117 *Koipe—Tabacalera/Elosua* of 28 July 1992 (paragraphs 10 to 14). In principle, the same would apply where, following the creation of the joint venture, the parent companies, while no longer active in the joint venture's market, nevertheless remain potential competitors in this market. However, this can normally be excluded since it is unlikely that the parents would re-enter the market on their own, in particular, where they have transferred their respective activities to the joint venture, or where they commit significant investment to the joint venture.

[21] Case IV/M.176, *Sunrise* of 13 January 1992 (paragraph 34).

[22] Case IV/M.293, *Philips/Thomson/SAGEM* of 18 January 1993 (paragraph 19).

[23] See Case IV/M.207, *Eureko* of 27 April 1992 (paragraph 16(b)) which can be contrasted with Case IV/M.319, *BHF/CCF/Charterhouse* of 30 August 1993 (paragraph 6).

geographic market while the other parent companies are all in different geographic markets,
— where the parent companies are in the same geographic market, which is different from that of the joint venture, there is scope for co-ordination of the competitive behaviour of the parent companies where the joint venture's activities have a substantial economic importance when compared with the parent companies' activities on their home market and where there is interaction between the parent companies' and joint venture's markets or such interaction is likely to evolve in the near future. By contrast, where the joint venture's activities account for only a small proportion of the overall activities of the parent companies in the products concerned, the conclusion that collaboration in the joint venture would lead to co-ordination on the parent companies' market would be justified only in exceptional cases,
— in any event, where the co-ordination of competitive behaviour of the parent companies takes place on geographic markets outside the Community or the EEA and has no appreciable effect on competition within the Community/EEA the joint venture is considered to be concentrative despite this co-ordination;

20. In relation to the abovementioned paragraphs, the fact that a joint venture leads to co-ordination of the competitive behaviour of the parent companies does not prevent the assumption of a concentration where these co-operative elements are only of minor economic importance relative to the operation as a whole (*de minimis*).

However a high accumulation of minor elements of co-ordination may lead to a situation where the operation as a whole has to be considered as co-operative.

III. FINAL

21. The Commission's interpretation of Article 3 with respect to joint ventures is without prejudice to the interpretation which may be given by the Court of Justice or the Court of First Instance of the European Communities.

APPENDIX 38

COMMISSION NOTICE[1]

*On the Concept of Undertakings Concerned Under Council Regulation (EEC)
No 4064/89 on the Control of Concentrations Between Undertakings*

(Text with EEC relevance)

I. INTRODUCTION

II. THE CONCEPT OF UNDERTAKING CONCERNED

III. IDENTIFYING THE UNDERTAKINGS CONCERNED IN DIFFERENT
TYPES OF OPERATIONS

---

[1] OJ 1998 C66/14.

I. Introduction

1. The purpose of this notice is to clarify the Commission's interpretation of the term "undertakings concerned" used in Articles 1 and 5 of Council Regulation (EEC) No 4064/89[2] as last amended by Regulation (EC) No 1310/97[3] (hereinafter referred to as "the Merger Regulation") and to help identify the undertakings concerned in the most typical situations which have arisen in cases dealt with by the Commission to date. The principles set out in this notice will be followed and further developed by the Commission's practice in individual cases.

This Notice replaces the Notice on the notion of undertakings concerned.[4]

2. According to Article 1 of the Merger Regulation, the Regulation only applies to operations that satisfy two conditions. First, several undertakings must merge, or one or more undertakings must acquire control of the whole or part of other undertakings through the proposed operation, which must qualify as a concentration within the meaning of Article 3 of the Regulation. Secondly, those undertakings must meet the turnover thresholds set out in Article 1.

3. From the point of view of determining jurisdiction, the undertakings concerned are, broadly speaking, the actors in the transaction in so far as they are the merging, or acquiring and acquired parties; in addition, their total aggregate economic size in terms of turnover will be decisive in determining whether the thresholds are met.

4. The Commission's interpretation of Articles 1 and 5 with respect to the concept of undertakings concerned is without prejudice to the interpretation which may be given by the Court of Justice or by the Court of First Instance of the European Communities.

II. The Concept of Undertaking Concerned

5. Undertakings concerned are the direct participants in a merger or acquisition of control. In this respect, Article 3(1) of the Merger Regulation provides that:

"A concentration shall be deemed to arise where:
(a) two or more previously independent undertakings merge, or
(b) — one or more persons already controlling at least one undertaking, or
— one or more undertakings
acquire, whether by purchase of securities or assets, by contract or by any other means, direct or indirect control of the whole or parts of one or more other undertakings"

6. In the case of a merger, the undertakings concerned will be the undertakings that are merging.

7. In the remaining cases, it is the concept of "acquiring control" that will determine which are the undertakings concerned. On the acquiring side, there can be one or more companies acquiring sole or joint control. On the acquired side, there can be one or more companies as a whole or parts thereof, when only one of their subsidiaries or some of their assets are the subject of the transaction. As a general rule, each of these companies will be an undertaking concerned within the meaning of the Merger Regulation. However, the particular features of specific transactions require some refinement of this principle, as will be seen below when analysing different possible scenarios.

8. In concentrations other than mergers or the setting-up of new joint ventures, i.e. in cases of sole or joint acquisition of pre-existing companies or parts of them, there is an

---

[2] OJ 1989 L395/1; corrected version 1990 L257/13.
[3] OJ 1997 L180/1.
[4] OJ 1994 C385/12.

important party to the agreement that gives rise to the operation who is to be ignored when identifying the undertakings concerned: the seller. Although it is clear that the operation cannot proceed without his consent, his role ends when the transaction is completed since, by definition, from the moment the seller has relinquished all control over the company, his links with it disappear. Where the seller retains joint control with the acquiring company (or companies), it will be considered to be one of the undertakings concerned.

9. Once the undertakings concerned have been identified in a given transaction, their turnover for the purposes of determining jurisdiction should be calculated according to the rules set out in Article 5 of the Merger Regulation.[5] One of the main provisions of Article 5 is that where the undertaking concerned belongs to a group, the turnover of the whole group should be included in the calculation. All references to the turnover of the undertakings concerned in Article 1 should therefore be understood as the turnover of their entire respective groups.

10. The same can be said with respect to the substantive appraisal of the impact of a concentration in the market place. When Article 2 of the Merger Regulation provides that the Commission is to take into account "the market position of the undertakings concerned and their economic and financial power", that includes the groups to which they belong.

11. It is important, when referring to the various undertakings which may be involved in a procedure, not to confuse the concept of "undertakings concerned" under Articles 1 and 5 with the terminology used in the Merger Regulation and in Commission Regulation (EC) No 447/98 of 1 March 1998 on the notifications, time-limits and hearings provided for in Council Regulation (EEC) No 4064/89 (hereinafter referred to as the "Implementing Regulation")[6] referring to the various undertakings which may be involved in a procedure. This terminology refers to the notifying parties, other involved parties, third parties and parties who may be subject to fines or periodic penalty payments, and they are defined in Chapter III of the Implementing Regulation, along with their respective rights and duties.

III. IDENTIFYING THE UNDERTAKINGS CONCERNED IN DIFFERENT TYPES OF OPERATIONS

1. Mergers

12. In a merger, several previously independent companies come together to create a new company or, while remaining separate legal entities, to create a single economic unit. As mentioned earlier, the undertakings concerned are each of the merging entities.

2. Acquisition of sole control

2.1. Acquisition of sole control of the whole company

13. Acquisition of sole control of the whole company is the most straightforward case of acquisition of control; the undertakings concerned will be the acquiring company and the acquired or target company.

---

[5] The rules for calculating turnover in accordance with Article 5 are detailed in the Commission Notice on calculation of turnover.

[6] OJ 1998 L61/1.

2.2. Acquisition of sole control of part of a company

14. The first subparagraph of Article 5(2) of the Merger Regulation provides that when the operation concerns the acquisition of parts of one or more undertakings, only those parts which are the subject of the transaction shall be taken into account with regard to the seller. The concept of "parts" is to be understood as one or more separate legal entities (such as subsidiaries), internal subdivisions within the seller (such as a division or unit), or specific assets which in themselves could constitute a business (e.g. in certain cases brands or licences) to which a market turnover can be clearly attributed. In this case, the undertakings concerned will be the acquirer and the acquired part(s) of the target company.

15. The second subparagraph of Article 5(2) includes a special provision on staggered operations or follow-up deals, whereby if several acquisitions of parts by the same purchaser from the same seller occur within a two-year period, these transactions are to be treated as one and the same operation arising on the date of the last transaction. In this case, the undertakings concerned are the acquirer and the different acquired part(s) of the target company taken as a whole.

2.3. Acquisition of sole control after reduction or enlargement of the target company

16. The undertakings concerned are the acquiring company and the target company or companies, in their configuration at the date of the operation.

17. The Commission bases itself on the configuration of the undertakings concerned at the date of the event triggering the obligation to notify under Article 4(1) of the Merger Regulation, namely the conclusion of the agreement, the announcement of the public bid or the acquisition of a controlling interest. If the target company has divested an entity or closed a business prior to the date of the event triggering notification or where such a divestment or closure is a pre-condition for the operation,[7] then sales of the divested entity or closed business are not to be included when calculating turnover. Conversely, if the target company has acquired an entity prior to the date of the event triggering notification, the sales of the latter are to be added.[8]

2.4. Acquisition of sole control through a subsidiary of a group

18. Where the target company is acquired by a group through one of its subsidiaries, the undertakings concerned for the purpose of calculating turnover are the target company and the acquiring subsidiary. However, regarding the actual notification, this can be made by the subsidiary concerned or by its parent company.

19. All the companies within a group (parent companies, subsidiaries, etc.) constitute a single economic entity, and therefore there can only be one undertaking concerned within the one group—i.e. the subsidiary and the parent company cannot each be considered as separate undertakings concerned, either for the purposes of ensuring that the threshold requirements are fulfilled (for example, if the target company does not meet the ECU 250 million Community-turnover threshold), or that they are not (for example, if a group was split into two companies each with a Community turnover below ECU 250 million).

20. However, even though there can only be one undertaking concerned within a group, Article 5(4) of the Merger Regulation provides that it is the turnover of the whole group

---

[7] See judgment of the Court of First Instance of 24 March 1994 in Case T–3/93—*Air France v. Commission* [1994] ECR II–21.

[8] The calculation of turnover in the case of acquisitions or divestments subsequent to the date of the last audited accounts is dealt with in the Commission Notice on calculation of turnover, paragraph 27.

to which the undertaking concerned belongs that shall be included in the threshold calculations.[9]

3. Acquisition of joint control

3.1. Acquisition of joint control of a newly-created company

21. In the case of acquisition of joint control of a newly-created company, the undertakings concerned are each of the companies acquiring control of the newly set-up joint venture (which, as it does not yet exist, cannot be considered to be an undertaking concerned and moreover, as yet, has no turnover of its own).

3.2. Acquisition of joint control of a pre-existing company

22. In the case of acquisition of joint control of a pre-existing company or business,[10] the undertakings concerned are each of the companies acquiring joint control on the one hand, and the pre-existing acquired company or business on the other.
   23. However, where the pre-existing company was under the sole control of one company and one or several new shareholders acquire joint control while the initial parent company remains, the undertakings concerned are each of the jointly-controlling companies (including this initial shareholder). The target company in this case is not an undertaking concerned, and its turnover is part of the turnover of the initial parent company.

3.3. Acquisition of joint control with a view to immediate partition of assets

24. Where several undertakings come together solely for the purpose of acquiring another company and agree to divide up the acquired assets according to a pre-existing plan immediately upon completion of the transaction, there is no effective concentration of economic power between the acquirers and the target company since the assets acquired are jointly held and controlled for only a "legal instant". This type of acquisition with a view to immediate partition of assets will in fact be considered to be several operations, whereby each of the acquiring companies acquires its relevant part of the target company. For each of these operations, the undertakings concerned will therefore be the acquiring company and that part of the target which it is acquiring (just as if there was an acquisition of sole control of part of a company).
   25. This scenario is referred to in recital 24 of Regulation (EEC) No 4064/89, which states that the Regulation applies to agreements whose sole object is to divide up the assets acquired immediately after the acquisition.

4. Acquisition of control by a joint venture

26. In transactions where a joint venture acquires control of another company, the question arises whether or not, from the point of view of the acquiring party, the joint venture should be regarded as a single undertaking concerned (the turnover of which would include the turnover of its parent companies), or whether each of its parent companies should individually be regarded as undertakings concerned. In other words, the

---

[9] The calculation of turnover in the case of company groups is dealt with in the Commission Notice on calculation of turnover, paragraphs 36 to 42.
[10] i.e. two or more companies (companies A, B, etc.) acquire a pre-existing company (company X). For changes in the shareholding in cases of joint control of an existing joint venture, see Section III.6.

issue is whether or not to "lift the corporate veil" of the intermediate undertaking (the vehicle). In principle, the undertaking concerned is the direct participant in the acquisition of control. However, there may be circumstances where companies set up "shell" companies, which have little or no turnover of their own, or use an existing joint venture which is operating on a different market from that of the target company in order to carry out acquisitions on behalf of the parent companies. Where the acquired or target company has a Community turnover of less than ECU 250 million, the question of determining the undertakings concerned may be decisive for jurisdictional purposes.[11] In this type of situation, the Commission will look at the economic reality of the operation to determine which are the undertakings concerned.

27. Where the acquisition is carried out by a full-function joint venture, i.e. a joint venture which has sufficient financial and other resources to operate a business activity on a lasting basis[12] and is already operating on a market, the Commission will normally consider the joint venture itself and the target company to be the undertakings concerned (and not the joint venture's parent companies).

28. Conversely, where the joint venture can be regarded as a vehicle for an acquisition by the parent companies, the Commission will consider each of the parent companies themselves to be the undertakings concerned, rather than the joint venture, together with the target company. This is the case in particular where the joint venture is set up especially for the purpose of acquiring the target company, where the joint venture has not yet started to operate, where an existing joint venture has no legal personality or full-function character as referred to above or where the joint venture is an association of undertakings. The same applies where there are elements which demonstrate that the parent companies are in fact the real players behind the operation. These elements may include a significant involvement by the parent companies themselves in the initiation, organisation and financing of the operation. Moreover, where the acquisition leads to a substantial diversification in the nature of the joint venture's activities, this may also indicate that the parent companies are the real players in the operation. This will normally be the case when the joint venture acquires a target company operating on a different product market. In those cases, the parent companies are regarded as undertakings concerned.

29. In the *TNT* case,[13] joint control over a joint venture (JVC) was to be acquired by a joint venture (GD NET BV) between five postal administrations and another acquiring company (TNT Ltd). In this case, the Commission considered that the joint venture GD NET BV was simply a vehicle set up to enable the parent companies (the five postal administrations) to participate in the resulting JVC joint venture in order to facilitate decision-making amongst themselves and to ensure that the parent companies spoke and acted as one; this configuration would ensure that the parent companies could exercise a decisive influence with the other acquiring company, TNT, over the resulting joint venture JVC and would avoid the situation where that other acquirer could exercise sole control

---

[11] The target company hypothetically has an aggregate Community turnover of less than ECU 250 million, and the acquiring parties are two (or more) undertakings, each with a Community turnover exceeding ECU 250 million. If the target is acquired by a "shell" company set up between the acquiring undertakings, there would only be one company (the "shell" company) with a Community turnover exceeding ECU 250 million, and thus one of the cumulative threshold conditions for Community jurisdiction would not be fulfilled (namely, the existence of at least two undertakings with a Community turnover exceeding ECU 250 million). Conversely, if instead of acting through a "shell" company, the acquiring undertakings acquire the target company themselves, then the turnover threshold would be met and the Merger Regulation would apply to this transaction. The same considerations apply to the national turnover thresholds referred to in Article 1(3).

[12] The criteria determining the full-function nature of a joint venture are contained in the Commission Notice on the concept of full-function joint ventures.

[13] Case IV/M.102—*TNT/Canada Post, DBP Postdienst, La Poste, PTT Post and Sweden Post*, of 2 December 1991.

because of the postal administrations' inability to reach a unified position on any decision.

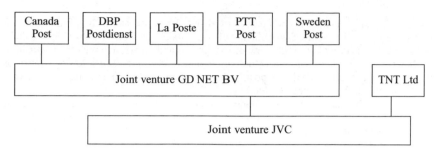

5. Change from joint control to sole control

30. In the case of a change from joint control to sole control, one shareholder acquires the stake previously held by the other shareholder(s). In the case of two shareholders, each of them has joint control over the entire joint venture, and not sole control over 50% of it; hence the sale of all of his shares by one shareholder to the other does not lead the sole remaining shareholder to move from sole control over 50% to sole control over 100% of the joint venture, but rather to move from joint control to sole control of the entire company (which, subsequent to the operation, ceases to be a "joint" venture).

31. In this situation, the undertakings concerned are the remaining (acquiring) shareholder and the joint venture. As is the case for any other seller, the "exiting" shareholder is not an undertaking concerned.

32. The *ICI/Tioxide* case[14] involved such a change from joint (50/50) control to sole control. The Commission considered that " . . . decisive influence exercised solely is substantially different to decisive influence exercised jointly, since the latter has to take into account the potentially different interests of the other party or parties concerned . . . By changing the quality of decisive influence exercised by ICI on Tioxide, the transaction will bring about a durable change of the structure of the concerned parties . . . ". In this case, the undertakings concerned were held to be ICI (as acquirer) and Tioxide as a whole (as acquiree), but not the seller Cookson.

6. Change in the shareholding in cases of joint control of an existing joint venture

33. The decisive element in assessing changes in the shareholding of a company is whether the operation leads to a change in the quality of control. The Commission assesses each operation on a case-by-case basis, but under certain hypotheses, there will be a presumption that the given operation leads, or does not lead, to such a change in the quality of control, and thus constitutes, or does not constitute, a notifiable concentration.

34. A distinction must be made according to the circumstances of the change in the shareholding; firstly, one or more existing shareholders can exit; secondly, one or more new additional shareholders can enter; and thirdly, one or more existing shareholders can be replaced by one or more new shareholders.

---

[14] Case IV/M.023—*ICI/Tioxide*, of 28 November 1990.

6.1. Reduction in the number of shareholders leading to a change from joint to sole control

35. It is not the reduction in the number of shareholders *per se* which is important, but rather the fact that if some shareholders sell their stakes in a given joint venture, these stakes are then acquired by other (new or existing) shareholders, and thus the acquisition of these stakes or additional contractual rights may lead to the acquisition of control or may strengthen an already existing position of control (e.g. additional voting rights or veto rights, additional board members, etc.).

36. Where the number of shareholders is reduced, there may be a change from joint control to sole control (see also Section III.5.), in which case the remaining shareholder acquires sole control of the company. The undertakings concerned will be the remaining (acquiring) shareholder and the acquired company (previously the joint venture).

37. In addition to the shareholder with sole control of the company, there may be other shareholders, for example with minority stakes, but who do not have a controlling interest in the company; these shareholders are not undertakings concerned as they do not exercise control.

6.2. Reduction in the number of shareholders not leading to a change from joint to sole control

38. Where the operation involves a reduction in the number of shareholders having joint control, without leading to a change from joint to sole control and without any new entry or substitution of shareholders acquiring control (see Section III.6.3.), the proposed transaction will normally be presumed not to lead to a change in the quality of control and will therefore not be a notifiable concentration. This would be the case where, for example, five shareholders initially have equal stakes of 20% each and where, after the operation, one shareholder exits and the remaining four shareholders each have equal stakes of 25%.

39. However, this situation would be different where there is a significant change in the quality of control, notably where the reduction in the number of shareholders gives the remaining shareholders additional veto rights or additional board members, resulting in a new acquisition of control by at least one of the shareholders, through the application of either the existing or a new shareholders' agreement. In this case, the undertakings concerned will be each of the remaining shareholders which exercise joint control and the joint venture. In *Avesta II*,[15] the fact that the number of major shareholders decreased from four to three led to one of the remaining shareholders acquiring negative veto rights (which it had not previously enjoyed) because of the provisions of the shareholders' agreement which remained in force.[16] This acquisition of full veto rights was considered by the Commission to represent a change in the quality of control.

6.3. Any other changes in the composition of the shareholding

40. Finally, in the case where, following changes in the shareholding, one or more shareholders acquire control, the operation will constitute a notifiable operation as there is a presumption that it will normally lead to a change in the quality of control.

41. Irrespective of whether the number of shareholders decreases, increases or remains the same subsequent to the operation, this acquisition of control can take any of the following forms:

---

[15] Case IV/M.452—*Avesta II*, of 9 June 1994.

[16] In this case, a shareholder who was a party to the shareholders' agreement sold its stake of approximately 7%. As the exiting shareholder had shared veto rights with another shareholder who remained, and as the shareholders' agreement remained unchanged, the remaining shareholder now acquired full veto rights.

— entry of one or more new shareholders (change from sole to joint control, or situation of joint control both before and after the operation),

— acquisition of a controlling interest by one or more minority shareholders (change from sole to joint control, or situation of joint control both before and after the operation),

— substitution of one or more shareholders (situation of joint control both before and after the operation).

42. The question is whether the undertakings concerned are the joint venture and the new shareholder(s) who would together acquire control of a pre-existing company, or whether all of the shareholders (existing and new) are to be regarded as undertakings concerned acquiring control of a new joint venture. This question is particularly relevant when there is no express agreement between one (or more) of the existing shareholders and the new shareholder(s), who might only have had an agreement with the "exiting" shareholder(s), i.e. the seller(s).

43. A change in the shareholding through the entry or substitution of shareholders is considered to lead to a change in the quality of control. This is because the entry of a new parent company, or the substitution of one parent company for another, is not comparable to the simple acquisition of part of a business as it implies a change in the nature and quality of control of the whole joint venture, even when, both before and after the operation, joint control is exercised by a given number of shareholders.

44. The Commission therefore considers that the undertakings concerned in cases where there are changes in the shareholding are the shareholders (both existing and new) who exercise joint control and the joint venture itself. As mentioned earlier, non-controlling shareholders are not undertakings concerned.

45. An example of such a change in the shareholding is the *Synthomer/Yule Catto* case,[17] in which one of two parent companies with joint control over the pre-existing joint venture was replaced by a new parent company. Both parent companies with joint control (the existing one and the new one) and the joint venture were considered to be undertakings concerned.

7. "Demergers" and the break-up of companies

46. When two undertakings merge or set up a joint venture, then subsequently demerge or break up their joint venture, and in particular the assets[18] are split between the "demerging" parties, particularly in a configuration different from the original, there will normally be more than one acquisition of control (see the Annex).

47. For example, undertakings A and B merge and then subsequently demerge with a new asset configuration. There will be the acquisition by undertaking A of various assets (assets which may previously have been owned by itself or by undertaking B and assets jointly acquired by the entity resulting from the merger), with similar acquisitions by undertaking B. Similarly, a break-up of a joint venture can be deemed to involve a change from joint control over the joint venture's entire assets to sole control over the divided assets.[19]

48. A break-up of a company in this way is "asymmetrical". For such a demerger, the undertakings concerned (for each break-up operation) will be, on the one hand, the original parties to the merger and, on the other, the assets that each original party is acquiring. For the break-up of a joint venture, the undertakings concerned (for each break-up operation) will be, on the one hand, the original parties to the joint venture, each as

---

[17] Case IV/M.376—*Synthomer/Yule Catto*, of 22 October 1993.

[18] The term "assets" as used here means specific assets which in themselves could constitute a business (e.g. a subsidiary, a division of a company or, in some cases, brands or licences) to which a market turnover can be clearly attributed.

[19] Case IV/M.197—*Solvay-Laporte/Interox*, of 30 April 1992.

acquirer, and, on the other, that part of the joint venture that each original party is acquiring.

8. Exchange of assets

49. In those transactions where two (or more) companies exchange assets, regardless of whether these constitute legal entities or not, each acquisition of control constitutes an independent concentration. Although it is true that both transfers of assets in a swap are usually considered by the parties to be interdependent, that they are often agreed in a single document and that they may even take place simultaneously, the purpose of the Merger Regulation is to assess the impact of the operation resulting from the acquisition of control by each of the companies. The legal or even economic link between those operations is not sufficient for them to qualify as a single concentration.

50. Hence the undertakings concerned will be, for each property transfer, the acquiring companies and the acquired companies or assets.

9. Acquisitions of control by individual persons

51. Article 3(1) of the Merger Regulation specifically provides that a concentration is deemed to arise, *inter alia*, where "one or more persons already controlling at least one undertaking" acquire control of the whole or parts of one or more undertakings. This provision indicates that acquisitions of control by individuals will bring about a lasting change in the structure of the companies concerned only if those individuals carry out economic activities of their own. The Commission considers that the undertakings concerned are the target company and the individual acquirer (with the turnover of the undertaking(s) controlled by that individual being included in the calculation of the individual's turnover).

52. This was the view taken in the Commission decision in the *Asko/Jacobs/Adia* case,[20] where Asko, a German holding company with substantial retailing assets, and Mr Jacobs, a private Swiss investor, acquired joint control of Adia, a Swiss company active mainly in personnel services. Mr Jacobs was considered to be an undertaking concerned because of the economic interests he held in the chocolate, confectionery and coffee sectors.

10. Management buy-outs

53. An acquisition of control of a company by its own managers is also an acquisition by individuals, and what has been said above is therefore also applicable here. However, the management of the company may pool its interests through a "vehicle company", so that it acts with a single voice and also to facilitate decision-making. Such a vehicle company may be, but is not necessarily, an undertaking concerned. The general rule on acquisitions of control by a joint venture applies here (see Section III.4.).

54. With or without a vehicle company, the management may also look for investors in order to finance the operation. Very often, the rights granted to these investors according to their shareholding may be such that control within the meaning of Article 3 of the Merger Regulation will be conferred on them and not on the management itself, which may simply enjoy minority rights. In the *CWB/Goldman Sachs/Tarkett* decision,[21] the two companies managing the investment funds taking part in the transaction were those acquiring joint control, and not the managers.

---

[20] Case IV/M.082—*Asko/Jacobs/Adia*, of 16 May 1991.
[21] Case IV/M.395—*CWB/Goldman Sachs/Tarkett*, of 21 February 1994.

11. Acquisition of control by a state-owned company

55. In those situations where a State-owned company merges with or acquires control of another company controlled by the same State,[22] the question arises as to whether these transactions really constitute concentrations within the meaning of Article 3 of the Merger Regulation or rather internal restructuring operations of the "public sector group of companies".[23] In this respect, recital 12 of Regulation (EEC) No 4064/89 sets out the principle of non-discrimination between public and private sectors and declares that "in the public sector, calculation of the turnover of an undertaking concerned in a concentration needs, therefore, to take account of undertakings making up an economic unit with an independent power of decision, irrespective of the way in which their capital is held or of the rules of administrative supervision applicable to them".

56. A merger or acquisition of control arising between two companies owned by the same State may constitute a concentration and, if so, both of them will qualify as undertakings concerned, since the mere fact that two companies are both owned by the same State does not necessarily mean that they belong to the same "group". Indeed, the decisive issue will be whether or not these companies are both part of the same industrial holding and are subject to a coordinated strategy. This was the approach taken in the SGS/Thomson decision.[24]

---

[22] The term "State" as used here means any legal public entity, i.e. not only Member States, but also regional or local public entities such as provinces, departments, Länder, etc.

[23] See also Commission Notice on the concept of concentration, paragraph 8.

[24] Case IV/M.216—*CEA Industrie/France Telecom/Finmeccanica/SGS-Thomson*, of 22 February 1993.

Annex

"DEMERGERS" AND BREAK-UP OF COMPANIES[25]

Merger Scenario

Before merger

Company A	Company B

After merger

Merged company
Combined assets

After breaking up the merger

Company A:	Company B:
Divided assets of merged company:	Divided assets of merged company:
— some (initial) assets of A	— some (initial) assets of A
— some (initial) assets of B	— some (initial) assets of B
— some (subsequent) assets of the merged company	— some (subsequent) assets of the merged company

---

[25] The term "assets" as used here means specific assets which in themselves could constitute a business (e.g. a subsidiary, a division of a company or, in some cases, brands or licences) to which a market turnover can be clearly attributed.

Joint venture scenario (JV)

Before JV

Company A	Assets of A for the JV		Assets of B for the JV	Company B

After JV

Company A	——	Joint venture	——	Company B
		Combined assets		

After breaking up the JV

Company A	Divided assets of joint venture
	— some (initial) assets of A
	— some (initial) assets of B
	— some (subsequent) assets
	  of the JV
		Divided assets of joint venture
		— some (initial) assets of A
		— some (initial) assets of B
		— some (subsequent) assets
		  of the JV
			Company B

APPENDIX 39

COMMISSION NOTICE[1]

On Calculation of Turnover under Council Regulation (EEC) No 4064/89 on the Control of Concentrations Between Undertakings

(Text with EEA relevance)

I. "ACCOUNTING" DETERMINATION OF TURNOVER

    1. Turnover as a reflection of business activity
        1.1.   The concept of turnover
        1.2.   Ordinary activities
    2. "Net" turnover
        2.1.   The deduction of rebates and taxes
        2.2.   The deduction of "internal" turnover
    3. Adjustment of turnover calculation rules for the different types of operations
        3.1.   The general rule
        3.2.   Acquisition of parts of companies
        3.3.   Staggered operations
        3.4.   Turnover of groups
        3.5.   Turnover of State-owned companies

II. GEOGRAPHICAL ALLOCATION OF TURNOVER

    1. General rule
    2. Conversion of turnover into ecu

III. CREDIT AND OTHER FINANCIAL INSTITUTIONS AND INSURANCE UNDERTAKINGS

    1. Definitions
    2. Calculation of turnover

1. The purpose of this Notice is to expand upon the text of Articles 1 and 5 of Council Regulation (EEC) No 4064/89[2] as last amended by Council Regulation (EC) No 1310/97[3] (hereinafter referred to as "the Merger Regulation") and in so doing to elucidate certain procedural and practical questions which have caused doubt or difficulty.

2. This Notice is based on the experience gained by the Commission in applying the Merger Regulation to date. The principles it sets out will be followed and further developed by the Commission's practice in individual cases.

---

[1] OJ 1998 C66/25.
[2] OJ 1989 L395/1; corrected version OJ 1990 L257/13.
[3] OJ 1997 L180/1.

This Notice replaces the Notice on calculation of turnover.[4]

3. The Merger Regulation has a two fold test for Commission jurisdiction. One test is that the transaction must be a concentration within the meaning of Article 3.[5] The second comprises the turnover thresholds contained in Article 1 and designed to identify those transactions which have an impact upon the Community and can be deemed to be of "Community interest". Turnover is used as a proxy for the economic resources being combined in a concentration, and is allocated geographically in order to reflect the geographic distribution of those resources.

Two sets of thresholds are set out in Article 1, in paragraph 2 and paragraph 3 respectively. Article 1(2) sets out the thresholds which must first be checked in order to establish whether the transaction has a Community dimension. In this respect, the worldwide turnover threshold is intended to measure the overall dimension of the undertakings concerned; the Community turnover threshold seek to determine whether the concentration involves a minimum level of activities in the Community; and the two-thirds rule aims to exclude purely domestic transactions from Community jurisdiction.

Article 1(3) must only be applied in the event that the thresholds set out in Article 1(2) are not met. This second set of thresholds is designed to tackle those transactions which fall short of achieving Community dimension under Article 1(2), but would need to be notified under national competition rules in at least three Member States (so called "multiple notifications"). For this purpose, Article 1(3) provides for lower turnover thresholds, both worldwide and Community-wide, to be achieved by the undertakings concerned. A concentration has a Community dimension if these lower thresholds are fulfilled and the undertakings concerned achieve jointly and individually a minimum level of activities in at least three Member States. Article 1(3) also contains a two-thirds rule similar to that of Article 1(2), which aims to identify purely domestic transactions.

4. The thresholds as such are designed to establish jurisdiction and not to assess the market position of the parties to the concentration nor the impact of the operation. In so doing they include turnover derived from, and thus the resources devoted to, all areas of activity of the parties, and not just those directly involved in the concentration. Article 1 of the Merger Regulation sets out the thresholds to be used to determine a concentration with a "Community dimension" while Article 5 explains how turnover should be calculated.

5. The fact that the thresholds of Article 1 of the Merger Regulation are purely quantitative, since they are only based on turnover calculation instead of market share or other criteria, shows that their aim is to provide a simple and objective mechanism that can be easily handled by the companies involved in a merger in order to determine if their transaction has a Community dimension and is therefore notifiable.

6. The decisive issue for Article 1 of the Merger Regulation is to measure the economic strength of the undertakings concerned as reflected in their respective turnover figures, regardless of the sector where such turnover was achieved and of whether those sectors will be at all affected by the transaction in question. The Merger Regulation has thereby given priority to the determination of the overall economic and financial resources that are being combined through the merger in order to decide whether the latter is of Community interest.

7. In this context, it is clear that turnover should reflect as accurately as possible the economic strength of the undertakings involved in a transaction. This is the purpose of the set of rules contained in Article 5 of the Merger Regulation which are designed to ensure that the resulting figures are a true representation of economic reality.

8. The Commission's interpretation of Articles 1 and 5 with respect to calculation of turnover is without prejudice to the interpretation which may be given by the Court of Justice or the Court of First Instance of the European Communities.

---

[4] OJ 1994 C385/21.
[5] See the Notice on the concept of concentration.

I. "Accounting" Calculation of Turnover

1. Turnover as a reflection of activity

1.1. The concept of turnover

9. The concept of turnover as used in Article 5 of the Merger Regulation refers explicitly to "the amounts derived from the sale of products and the provision of services". Sale, as a reflection of the undertaking's activity, is thus the essential criterion for calculating turnover, whether for products or the provision of services. "Amounts derived from sale" generally appear in company accounts under the heading "sales".

10. In the case of products, turnover can be determined without difficulty, namely by identifying each commercial act involving a transfer of ownership.

11. In the case of services, the factors to be taken into account in calculating turnover are much more complex, since the commercial act involves a transfer of "value".

12. Generally speaking, the method of calculating turnover in the case of services does not differ from that used in the case of products: the Commission takes into consideration the total amount of sales. Where the service provided is sold directly by the provider to the customer, the turnover of the undertaking concerned consists of the total amount of sales for the provision of services in the last financial year.

13. Because of the complexity of the service sector, this general principle may have to be adapted to the specific conditions of the service provided. Thus, in certain sectors of activity (such as tourism and advertising), the service may be sold through the intermediary of other suppliers. Because of the diversity of such sectors, many different situations may arise. For example, the turnover of a service undertaking which acts as an intermediary may consist solely of the amount of commissions which it receives.

14. Similarly, in a number of areas such as credit, financial services and insurance, technical problems in calculating turnover arise which will be dealt with in Section III.

1.2. Ordinary activities

15. Article 5(1) states that the amounts to be included in the calculation of turnover must correspond to the "ordinary activities" of the undertakings concerned.

16. With regard to aid granted to undertakings by public bodies, any aid relating to one of the ordinary activities of an undertaking concerned is liable to be included in the calculation of turnover if the undertaking is itself the recipient of the aid and if the aid is directly linked to the sale of products and the provision of services by the undertaking and is therefore reflected in the price.[6] For example, aid towards the consumption of a product allows the manufacturer to sell at a higher price than that actually paid by consumers.

17. With regard to services, the Commission looks at the undertaking's ordinary activities involved in establishing the resources required for providing the service. In its Decision in the Accor/Wagons-Lits case,[7] the Commission decided to take into account the item "other operating proceeds" included in Wagons-Lits's profit and loss account. The Commission considered that the components of this item which included certain income from its car-hire activities were derived from the sale of products and the provision of services by Wagons-Lits and were part of its ordinary activities.

---

[6] See Case IV/M.156—*Cereol/Continentale Italiana* of 27 November 1991. In this case, the Commission excluded Community aid from the calculation of turnover because the aid was not intended to support the sale of products manufactured by one of the undertakings involved in the merger, but the producers of the raw materials (grain) used by the undertaking, which specialized in the crushing of grain.

[7] Case IV/M.126—*Accor/Wagons-Lits*, of 28 April 1992.

2. "Net" turnover

18. The turnover to be taken into account is "net" turnover, after deduction of a number of components specified in the Regulation. The Commission's aim is to adjust turnover in such a way as to enable it to decide on the real economic weight of the undertaking.

2.1. The deduction of rebates and taxes

19. Article 5(1) provides for the "deduction of sales rebates and of value added tax and other taxes directly related to turnover". The deductions thus relate to business components (sales rebates) and tax components (value added tax and other taxes directly related to turnover).
   20. "Sales rebates" should be taken to mean all rebates or discounts which are granted by the undertakings during their business negotiations with their customers and which have a direct influence on the amounts of sales.
   21. As regards the deduction of taxes, the Merger Regulation refers to VAT and "other taxes directly related to turnover". As far as VAT is concerned, its deduction does not in general pose any problem. The concept of "taxes directly related to turnover" is a clear reference to indirect taxation since it is directly linked to turnover, such as, for example, taxes on alcoholic beverages.

2.2. The deduction of "internal" turnover

22. The first subparagraph of Article 5(1) states that "the aggregate turnover of an undertaking concerned shall not include the sale of products or the provision of services between any of the undertakings referred to in paragraph 4", i.e. those which have links with the undertaking concerned (essentially parent companies or subsidiaries).
   23. The aim is to exclude the proceeds of business dealings within a group so as to take account of the real economic weight of each entity. Thus, the "amounts" taken into account by the Merger Regulation reflect only the transactions which take place between the group of undertakings on the one hand and third parties on the other.

3. Adjustment of turnover calculation rules for the different types of operations

3.1. The general rule

24. According to Article 5(1) of the Merger Regulation, aggregate turnover comprises the amounts derived by the undertakings concerned in the preceding financial year from the sale of products and the provision of services. The basic principle is thus that for each undertaking concerned the turnover to be taken into account is the turnover of the closest financial year to the date of the transaction.
   25. This provision shows that since there are usually no audited accounts of the year ending the day before the transaction, the closest representation of a whole year of activity of the company in question is the one given by the turnover figures of the most recent financial year.
   26. The Commission seeks to base itself upon the most accurate and reliable figures available. As a general rule therefore, the Commission will refer to audited or other definitive accounts. However, in cases where major differences between the Community's accounting standards and those of a non-member country are observed, the Commission may consider it necessary to restate these accounts in accordance with Community standards in respect of turnover. The Commission is, in any case, reluctant to rely on management or any other form of provisional accounts in any but exceptional circumstances (see the next paragraph). Where a concentration takes place within the first months

of the year and audited accounts are not yet available for the most recent financial year, the figures to be taken into account are those relating to the previous year. Where there is a major divergence between the two sets of accounts, and in particular, when the final draft figures for the most recent years are available, the Commission may decide to take those draft figures into account.

27. Notwithstanding paragraph 26, an adjustment must always be made to account for acquisitions or divestments subsequent to the date of the audited accounts. This is necessary if the true resources being concentrated are to be identified. Thus if a company disposes of part of its business at any time before the signature of the final agreement or the announcement of the public bid or the acquisition of a controlling interest bringing about a concentration, or where such a divestment or closure is a pre-condition for the operation[8] the part of the turnover to be attributed to that part of the business must be subtracted from the turnover of the notifying party as shown in its last audited accounts. Conversely, the turnover to be attributed to assets of which control has been acquired subsequent to the preparation of the most recent audited accounts must be added to a company's turnover for notification purposes.

28. Other factors that may affect turnover on a temporary basis such as a decrease in orders for the product or a slow-down in the production process within the period prior to the transaction will be ignored for the purposes of calculating turnover. No adjustment to the definitive accounts will be made to incorporate them.

29. Regarding the geographical allocation of turnover, since audited accounts often do not provide a geographical breakdown of the sort required by the Merger Regulation, the Commission will rely on the best figures available provided by the companies in accordance with the rule laid down in Article 5(1) of the Merger Regulation (see Section II.1).

3.2. Acquisitions of parts of companies

30. Article 5(2) of the Merger Regulation provides that "where the concentration consists in the acquisition of parts, whether or not constituted as legal entities, of one or more undertakings, only the turnover relating to the parts which are the subject of the transaction shall be taken into account with regard to the seller or sellers".

31. This provision states that when the acquirer does not purchase an entire group, but only one, or part, of its businesses, whether or not constituted as a subsidiary, only the turnover of the part acquired should be included in the turnover calculation. In fact, although in legal terms the seller as a whole (with all its subsidiaries) is an essential party to the transaction, since the sale-purchase agreement cannot be concluded without him, he plays no role once the agreement has been implemented. The possible impact of the transaction on the market will depend only on the combination of the economic and financial resources that are the subject of a property transfer with those of the acquirer and not on the remaining business of the seller who remains independent.

3.3. Staggered operations

32. Sometimes certain successive transactions are only individual steps within a wider strategy between the same parties. Considering each transaction alone, even if only for determining jurisdiction, would imply ignoring economic reality. At the same time, whereas some of these staggered operations may be designed in this fashion because they will better meet the needs of the parties, others could be structured like this in order to circumvent the application of the Merger Regulation.

33. The Merger Regulation has foreseen these scenarios in Article 5(2), second subparagraph, which provides that "two or more transactions within the meaning of the first

---

[8] See Judgment of the Court of First Instance in Case T–3/93, *Air France v. Commission*, [1994] ECR II–21.

subparagraph which take place within a two-year period between the same persons or undertakings shall be treated as one and the same concentration arising on the date of the last transaction".

34. In practical terms, this provision means that if company A buys a subsidiary of company B that represents 50% of the overall activity of B and one year later it acquires the other subsidiary (the remaining 50% of B), both transactions will be taken as one. Assuming that each of the subsidiaries attained a turnover in the Community of only ECU 200 million, the first transaction would not be notifiable unless the operation fulfilled the conditions set out in Article 1(3). However, since the second transaction takes place within the two-year period, both have to be notified as a single transaction when the second occurs.

35. The importance of the provision is that previous transactions (within two years) become notifiable with the most recent transaction once the thresholds are cumulatively met.

3.4. Turnover of groups

36. When an undertaking concerned in a concentration within the meaning of Article 1 of the Merger Regulation[9] belongs to a group, the turnover of the group as a whole is to be taken into account in order to determine whether the thresholds are met. The aim is again to capture the total volume of the economic resources that are being combined through the operation.

37. The Merger Regulation does not define the concept of group in abstract terms but focuses on whether the companies have the right to manage the undertaking's affairs as the yardstick to determine which of the companies that have some direct or indirect links with an undertaking concerned should be regarded as part of its group.

38. Article 5(4) of the Merger Regulation provides the following:

"Without prejudice to paragraph 2 [acquisitions of parts], the aggregate turnover of an undertaking concerned within the meaning of Article 1(2) and (3) shall be calculated by adding together the respective turnovers of the following:
(a) the undertaking concerned;
(b) those undertakings in which the undertaking concerned directly or indirectly:
— owns more than half the capital or business assets, or
— has the power to exercise more than half the voting rights, or
— has the power to appoint more than half the members of the supervisory board, the administrative board or bodies legally representing the undertakings, or
— has the right to manage the undertaking's affairs;
(c) those undertakings which have in an undertaking concerned the rights or powers listed in (b);
(d) those undertakings in which an undertaking as referred to in (c) has the rights or powers listed in (b);
(e) those undertakings in which two or more undertakings as referred to in (a) to (d) jointly have the rights or powers listed in (b)."

This means that the turnover of the company directly involved in the transaction (point (a)) should include its subsidiaries (point (b)), its parent companies (point (c)), the other subsidiaries of its parent companies (point (d)) and any other undertaking jointly controlled by two or more of the companies belonging to the group (point (e)). A graphic example is as follows:
The undertaking concerned and its group:

---

[9] See the Commission Notice on the concept of undertakings concerned.

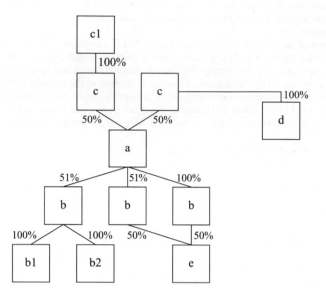

a: The undertaking concerned
b: Its subsidiaries and their own subsidiaries (b1 and b2)
c: Its parent companies and their own parent companies (c1)
d: Other subsidiaries of the parent companies of the undertaking concerned
e: Companies jointly controlled by two (or more) companies of the group

Note: these letters correspond to the relevant points of Article 5(4).
   Several remarks can be made from this chart:

1. As long as the test of control of point (b) is fulfilled, the whole turnover of the subsidiary in question will be taken into account regardless of the actual shareholding of the controlling company. In the example, the whole turnover of the three subsidiaries (called b) of the undertaking concerned (a) will be included.
2. When any of the companies identified as belonging to the group also controls others, these should also be incorporated into the calculation. In the example, one of the subsidiaries of a (called b) has in turn its own subsidiaries b1 and b2.
3. When two or more companies jointly control the undertaking concerned (a) in the sense that the agreement of each and all of them is needed in order to manage the undertaking affairs, the turnover of all of them should be included.[10] In the example, the two parent companies (c) of the undertaking concerned (a) would be taken into account as well as their own parent companies (c1 in the example). Although the Merger Regulation does not explicitly mention this rule for those cases where the undertaking concerned is in fact a joint venture, it is inferred from the text of Article 5(4)(c), which uses the plural when referring to the parent companies. This interpretation has been consistently applied by the Commission.
4. Any intra-group sale should be subtracted from the turnover of the group (see paragraph 22).

---

[10] See Commission Notice on the concept of undertakings concerned (paragraphs 26–29).

39. The Merger Regulation also deals with the specific scenario that arises when two or more undertakings concerned in a transaction exercise joint control of another company. Pursuant to point (a) of Article 5(5), the turnover resulting from the sale of products or the provision of services between the joint venture and each of the undertakings concerned or any other company connected with any one of them in the sense of Article 5(4) should be excluded. The purpose of such a rule is to avoid double counting. With regard to the turnover of the joint venture generated from activities with third parties, point (b) of Article 5(5) provides that it should be apportioned equally amongst the undertakings concerned, to reflect the joint control.[11]

40. Following the principle of point (b) of Article 5(5) by analogy, in the case of joint ventures between undertakings concerned and third parties, the Commission's practice has been to allocate to each of the undertakings concerned the turnover shared equally by all the controlling companies in the joint venture. In all these cases, however, joint control has to be demonstrated.

The practice shows that it is impossible to cover in the present Notice the whole range of scenarios which could arise in respect of turnover calculation of joint venture companies or joint control cases. Whenever ambiguities arise, an assessment should always give priority to the general principles of avoiding double counting and of reflecting as accurately as possible the economic strength of the undertakings involved in the transaction.[12]

41. It should be noted that Article 5(4) refers only to the groups that already exist at the time of the transaction, i.e. the group of each of the undertakings concerned in an operation, and not to the new structures created as a result of the concentration. For example, if companies A and B, together with their respective subsidiaries, are going to merge, it is A and B, and not the new entity, that qualify as undertakings concerned, which implies that the turnover of each of the two groups should be calculated independently.

42. Since the aim of this provision is simply to identify the companies belonging to the existing groups for the purposes of turnover calculation, the test of having the right to manage the undertaking's affairs in Article 5(4)[13] is somewhat different from the test of control set out in Article 3(3), which refers to the acquisition of control carried out by means of the transaction subject to examination. Whereas the former is simpler and easier to prove on the basis of factual evidence, the latter is more demanding because in the absence of an acquisition of control no concentration arises.

3.5. Turnover of State-owned companies

43. While Article 5(4) sets out the method for determining the economic grouping to which an undertaking concerned belongs for the purpose of calculating turnover, it should be read in conjunction with recital 12 to Regulation (EEC) No 4064/89 in respect of State-owned enterprises. This recital states that in order to avoid discrimination between the public and private sector, account should be taken "of undertakings making up an economic unit with an independent power of decision, irrespective of the way in which their capital is held or of the rules of administrative supervision applicable to them". Thus the mere fact that two companies are both State-owned should not automatically lead to the conclusion that they are part of a group for the purposes of Article 5. Rather, it should be considered whether there are grounds to consider that each company constitutes an independent economic unit.

---

[11] For example, company A and company B set up a joint venture C. These two parent companies exercise at the same time joint control of company D, although A has 60% and B 40% of the capital. When calculating the turnover of A and B at the time they set up the new joint venture C, the turnover of D with third parties is attributed in equal parts to A and B.

[12] See for example Case IV/M.806—*BA/TAT*, of 26 August 1996.

[13] See for example Case IV/M.126—*Accor/Wagons-Lits*, of 28 April 1992, and Case IV/M.940—*UBS/Mister Minit*, of 9 July 1997.

44. Thus where a State-owned company is not part of an overall industrial holding company and is not subject to any coordination with other State-controlled holdings, it should be treated as an independent group for the purposes of Article 5, and the turnover of other companies owned by that State should not be taken into account. Where, however, a Member State's interests are grouped together in holding companies, or are managed together, or where for other reasons it is clear that State-owned companies form part of an "economic unit with an independent power of decision", then the turnover of those businesses should be considered part of the group of the undertaking concerned's for the purposes of Article 5.

II. GEOGRAPHICAL ALLOCATION OF TURNOVER

1. General rule

45. The thresholds other than those set by Article 1(2)(a) and Article 1(3)(a) select cases which have sufficient turnover within the Community in order to be of Community interest and which are primarily cross-border in nature. They require turnover to be allocated geographically to achieve this. The second subparagraph of Article 5(1) provides that the location of turnover is determined by the location of the customer at the time of the transaction:

> "Turnover, in the Community or in a Member State, shall comprise products sold and services provided to undertakings or consumers, in the Community or in that Member State as the case may be."

46. The reference to "products sold" and "services provided" is not intended to discriminate between goods and services by focusing on where the sale takes place in the case of goods but the place where a service is provided (which might be different from where the service was sold) in the case of services. In both cases, turnover should be attributed to the place where the customer is located because that is, in most circumstances, where a deal was made, where the turnover for the supplier in question was generated and where competition with alternative suppliers took place.[14] The second subparagraph of Article 5(1) does not focus on where a good or service is enjoyed or the benefit of the good or service derived. In the case of a mobile good, a motor car may well be driven across Europe by its purchaser but it was purchased at only one place—Paris, Berlin or Madrid say. This is also true in the case of those services where it is possible to separate the purchase of a service from its delivery. Thus in the case of package holidays, competition for the sale of holidays through travel agents takes place locally, as with retail shopping, even though the service may be provided in a number of distant locations. This turnover is, however, earned locally and not at the site of an eventual holiday.

47. This applies even where a multinational corporation has a Community buying strategy and sources all its requirements for a good or service from one location. The fact that the components are subsequently used in ten different plants in a variety of Member States does not alter the fact that the transaction with a company outside the group occurred in only one country. The subsequent distribution to other sites is purely an internal question for the company concerned.

48. Certain sectors do, however, pose very particular problems with regard to the geographical allocation of turnover (see Section III).

---

[14] If the place where the customer was located when purchasing the goods or service and the place where the billing was subsequently made are different, turnover should be allocated to the former.

2. Conversion of turnover into ECU

49. When converting turnover figures into ecu great care should be taken with the exchange rate used. The annual turnover of a company should be converted at the average rate for the twelve months concerned. This average can be obtained from the Commission. The audited annual turnover figures should not be broken down into component quarterly, monthly, or weekly sales figures which are converted individually at the corresponding average quarterly, monthly or weekly rates, with the ecu figures then added to give a total for the year.

50. When a company has sales in a range of currencies, the procedure is no different. The total turnover given in the consolidated audited accounts and in that company's reporting currency is converted into ecu at the average rate for the twelve months. Local currency sales should not be converted directly into ecu since these figures are not from the consolidated audited accounts of the company.

III. CREDIT AND OTHER FINANCIAL INSTITUTIONS AND INSURANCE UNDERTAKINGS

1. Definitions

51. The specific nature of banking and insurance activities is formally recognized by the Merger Regulation which includes specific provisions dealing with the calculation of turnover for these sectors.[15] Although the Merger Regulation does not provide a definition of the terms, "credit institutions and other financial institutions" within the meaning of point (a) of Article 5(3), the Commission in its practice has consistently adopted the definitions provided in the First and Second Banking Directives:

— "Credit institution means an undertaking whose business is to receive deposits or other repayable funds from the public and to grant credits for its own account".[16]
— "Financial institution shall mean an undertaking other than a credit institution, the principal activity of which is to acquire holdings or to carry one or more of the activities listed in points 2 to 12 in the Annex".[17]

52. From the definition of "financial institution" given above, it is clear that on the one hand holding companies must be regarded as financial institutions and, on the other hand, that undertakings which perform on a regular basis as a principal activity one or more activities expressly mentioned in points 2 to 12 of the abovementioned Annex must also be regarded as financial institutions within the meaning of point (a) of Article 5(3) of the Merger Regulation. These activities include:

— lending (*inter alia*, consumer credit, mortgage credit, factoring, . . .),
— financial leasing,
— money transmission services,
— issuing and managing instruments of payment (credit cards, travellers' cheques and bankers' drafts),

---

[15] See Article 5(3) of the Merger Regulation.
[16] Article 1 of First Council Directive 77/780/EEC of 12 December 1977 on the coordination of laws, regulations and administrative provisions relating to the taking up and pursuit of the business of credit institutions (OJ L 322, 17.12.1977, p. 30).
[17] Article 1(6) of Second Council Directive 89/646/EEC of 15 December 1989 on the coordination of laws, regulations and administrative provisions relating to the taking up and pursuit of the business of credit institutions (OJ L 386, 30.12.1989, p. 1).

— guarantees and commitments,
— trading on own account or on account of customers in money market instruments, foreign exchange, financial futures and options, exchange and interest rate instruments, and transferable securities,
— participation in share issues and the provision of services related to such issues,
— advice to undertakings on capital structure, industrial strategy and related questions and advice and services relating to mergers and the purchase of undertakings,
— money broking,
— portfolio management and advice,
— safekeeping and administration of securities.

2. Calculation of turnover

53. The methods of calculation of turnover for credit and other financial institutions and for insurance undertakings are described in Article 5(3) of the Merger Regulation. The purpose of this Section is to provide an answer to supplementary questions related to turnover calculation for the abovementioned types of undertakings which were raised during the first years of the application of the Merger Regulation.

2.1. Credit and financial institutions (other than financial holding companies)

2.1.1. General

54. There are normally no particular difficulties in applying the banking income criterion for the definition of the worldwide turnover to credit institutions and other kinds of financial institutions. Difficulties may arise for determining turnover within the Community and also within individual Member States. For this purpose, the appropriate criterion is that of the residence of the branch or division, as provided by Article 5(3)(a)(v), second subparagraph, of the Merger Regulation.

2.1.2. Turnover of leasing companies

55. There is a fundamental distinction to be made between financial leases and operating leases. Basically, financial leases are made for longer periods than operating leases and ownership is generally transferred to the lessee at the end of the lease term by means of a purchase option included in the lease contract. Under an operating lease, on the contrary, ownership is not transferred to the lessee at the end of the lease term and the costs of maintenance, repair and insurance of the leased equipment are included in the lease payments. A financial lease therefore functions as a loan by the lessor to enable the lessee to purchase a given asset. A financial leasing company is thus a financial institution within the meaning of point (a) of Article 5(3) and its turnover has to be calculated by applying the specific rules related to the calculation of turnover for credit and other financial institutions. Given that operational leasing activities do not have this lending function, they are not considered as carried out by financial institutions, at least as primary activities, and therefore the general turnover calculation rules of Article 5(1) should apply.[18]

2.2. Insurance undertakings

2.2.1. Gross premiums written

56. The application of the concept of gross premiums written as a measure of turnover for insurance undertakings has raised supplementary questions notwithstanding the definition

---

[18] See Case IV/M.234—*GECC/Avis Lease*, 15 July 1992.

provided in point (b) of Article 5(3) of the Merger Regulation. The following clarifications are appropriate:

— "gross" premiums written are the sum of received premiums (which may include received reinsurance premiums if the undertaking concerned has activities in the field of reinsurance). Outgoing or outward reinsurance premiums, i.e. all amounts paid and payable by the undertaking concerned to get reinsurance cover, are already included in the gross premiums written within the meaning of the Merger Regulation,

— wherever the word "premiums" is used (gross premiums, net (earned) premiums, outgoing reinsurance premiums, etc.), these premiums are related not only to new insurance contracts made during the accounting year being considered but also to all premiums related to contracts made in previous years which remain in force during the period taken into consideration.

2.2.2. *Investments of insurance undertakings*

57. In order to constitute appropriate reserves allowing for the payment of claims, insurance undertakings, which are also considered as institutional investors, usually hold a huge portfolio of investments in shares, interest-bearing securities, land and property and other assets which provide an annual revenue which is not considered as turnover for insurance undertakings.

58. With regard to the application of the Merger Regulation, a major distinction should be made between pure financial investments, in which the insurance undertaking is not involved in the management of the undertakings where the investments have been made, and those investments leading to the acquisition of an interest giving control in a given undertaking thus allowing the insurance undertaking to exert a decisive influence on the business conduct of the subsidiary or affiliated company concerned. In such cases Article 5(4) of the Merger Regulation would apply, and the turnover of the subsidiary or affiliated company should be added to the turnover of the insurance undertaking for the determination of the thresholds laid down in the Merger Regulation.[19]

2.3. *Financial holding companies*[20]

59. A financial holding company is a financial institution and therefore the calculation of its turnover should follow the criteria established in point (a) of Article 5(3) for the calculation of turnover for credit and other financial institutions. However, since the main purpose of a financial holding is to acquire and manage participation in other undertakings, Article 5(4) also applies, (as for insurance undertakings), with regard to those participations allowing the financial holding company to exercise a decisive influence on the business conduct of the undertakings in question. Thus, the turnover of a financial holding is basically to be calculated according to Article 5(3), but it may be necessary to add turnover of undertakings falling within the categories set out in Article 5(4) ("Article 5(4) companies").

In practice, the turnover of the financial holding company (non-consolidated) must first be taken into account. Then the turnover of the Article 5(4) companies must be added, whilst taking care to deduct dividends and other income distributed by those companies to the financial holdings. The following provides an example for this kind of calculation:

---

[19] See Case IV/M.018—*AG/AMEV*, of 21 November 1990.
[20] The principles set out in this paragraph for financial holdings may to a certain extent be applied to fund management companies.

ECU million

1. Turnover related to financial activities (from non-consolidated P&L)   3 000
2. Turnover related to insurance Article 5(4) companies (gross premiums written)   300
3. Turnover of industrial Article 5(4) companies   2 000
4. Deduct dividends and other income derived from Article 5(4) companies 2 and 3   (200)
5. Total turnover financial holding and its group   5 100

60. In such calculations different accounting rules, in particular those related to the preparation of consolidated accounts, which are to some extent harmonised but not identical within the Community, may need to be taken into consideration. Whilst this consideration applies to any type of undertaking concerned by the Merger Regulation, it is particularly important in the case of financial holding companies[21] where the number and the diversity of enterprises controlled and the degree of control the holding holds on its subsidiaries, affiliated companies and other companies in which it has shareholding requires careful examination.

61. Turnover calculation for financial holding companies as described above may in practice prove onerous. Therefore a strict and detailed application of this method will be necessary only in cases where it seems that the turnover of a financial holding company is likely to be close to the Merger Regulation thresholds; in other cases it may well be obvious that the turnover is far from the thresholds of the Merger Regulation, and therefore the published accounts are adequate for the establishment of jurisdiction.

---

[21] See for example Case IV/M.166—*Torras/Sarrió*, of 24 February 1992, Case IV/M.213—*Hong Kong and Shanghai Bank/Midland*, of 21 May 1992, IV/M.192—*Banesto/Totta*, of 14 April 1992.

APPENDIX 40

COMMISSION NOTICE[1]

Regarding Restrictions Ancillary to Concentrations

I. Introduction

1. Council Regulation (EEC) No. 4064/89 of 21 December 1989 on the control of concentrations between undertakings ("the Regulation")[2] states in its 25th recital that its application is not excluded where the undertakings concerned accept restrictions which are directly related and necessary to the implementation of the concentration, hereinafter referred to as "ancillary restrictions". In the scheme of the Regulation, such restrictions are to be assessed together with the concentration itself. It follows, as confirmed by Article 8(2), second subparagraph, last sentence of the Regulation, that a decision declaring the concentration compatible also covers these restrictions. In this situation, under the provisions of Article 22, paragraphs 1 and 2, the Regulation is solely applicable, to the exclusion of Regulation No. 17[3] as well as Regulations (EEC) No. 1017/18,[4] (EEC) No. 4056/86[5] and (EEC) No. 3975/87.[6] This avoids parallel Commission proceedings, one concerned with the assessment of the concentration under the Regulation, and the other aimed at the application of Articles 81 and 82 to the restrictions which are ancillary to the concentration.

2. In this notice, the Commission sets out to indicate the interpretation it gives to the notion of "restrictions directly related and necessary to the implementation of the concentration". Under the Regulation such restrictions must be assessed in relation to the concentration, whatever their treatment might be under Articles 81 and 82 if they were to be considered in isolation or in a different economic context. The Commission endeavours, within the limits set by the Regulation, to take the greatest account of business practice and of the conditions necessary for the implementation of concentrations.

This notice is without prejudice to the interpretation which may be given by the Court of Justice of the European Communities.

II. Principles of evaluation

3. The "restrictions" meant are those agreed on between the parties to the concentration which limit their own freedom of action in the market. They do not include restrictions to the detriment of third parties. If such restrictions are the inevitable consequence of the concentration itself, they must be assessed together with it under the provisions of Article 2 of the Regulation. If on the contrary, such restrictive effects on third parties are separable

---

[1] OJ 1990 C203/5.
[2] OJ 1989 L395/1.
[3] OJ 1962 13/204–62.
[4] OJ 1968 L175/1.
[5] OJ 1986 L378/4.
[6] OJ 1987 L374/1.

from the concentration they may, if appropriate, be the subject of an assessment of compatibility with Articles 81 and 82 of the EEC Treaty.

4. For restrictions to be considered "directly related" they must be ancillary to the implementation of the concentration, that is to say subordinate in importance to the main object of the concentration. They cannot be substantial restrictions wholly different in nature from those which result from the concentration itself. Neither are they contractual arrangements which are among the elements constituting the concentration, such as those establishing economic unity between previously independent parties, or organising joint control by two undertakings of another undertaking. As integral parts of the concentration, the latter arrangements constitute the very subject matter of the evaluation to be carried out under the Regulation.

Also excluded, for concentrations which are carried out in stages, are the contractual arrangements relating to the stages before the establishment of control within the meaning of Article 3, paragraphs 1 and 3 of the Regulation. For these, Articles 81 and 82 remain applicable as long as the conditions set out in Article 3 are not fulfilled.

The notion of directly related restrictions likewise excludes from the application of the Regulation additional restrictions agreed at the same time which have no direct link with the concentration. It is not enough that the additional restrictions exist in the same context as the concentration.

5. The restrictions must likewise be "necessary to the implementation of the concentration," which means that in their absence the concentration could not be implemented or could only be implemented under more uncertain conditions, at substantially higher cost, over an appreciably longer period or with considerably less probability of success. This must be judged on an objective basis.

6. The question of whether a restriction meets these conditions cannot be answered in general terms. In particular as concerns the necessity of the restriction, it is proper not only to take account of its nature, but equally to ensure, in applying the rule of proportionality, that its duration and subject-matter, and geographic field of application, do not exceed what the implementation of the concentration reasonably requires. If alternatives are available for the attainment of the legitimate aim pursued, the undertakings must choose the one which is objectively the least restrictive of competition.

These principles will be followed and further developed by the Commission's practice in individual cases. However, it is already possible, on the basis of past experience, to indicate the attitude the Commission will take to those restrictions most commonly encountered in relation to the transfer of undertakings or parts of undertakings, the division of undertakings or of their assets following a joint acquisition of control, or the creation of a concentrative joint ventures.

III. Evaluation of common ancillary restrictions in cases of the transfer of an undertaking

A. Non-competition clauses

1. Among the ancillary restrictions which meet the criteria set out in the Regulation are contractual prohibitions on competition which are imposed on the vendor in the context of a concentration achieved by the transfer of an undertaking or part of an undertaking. Such prohibitions guarantee the transfer to the acquirer of the full value of the assets transferred, which in general include both physical assets and intangible assets such as the goodwill which the vendor has accumulated or the know-how he has developed. These are not only directly related to the concentration, but are also necessary for its implementation because, in their absence, there would be reasonable grounds to expect that the sale of the undertaking or part of an undertaking could not be accomplished satisfactorily. In order to take over fully the value of the assets transferred, the acquirer must be able to benefit from some protection against competitive acts of the vendor in order to gain the loyalty of

customers and to assimilate and exploit the know-how. Such protection cannot generally be considered necessary when *de facto* the transfer is limited to physical assets (such as land, buildings or machinery) or to exclusive industrial and commercial property rights (the holders of which could immediately take action against infringements by the transferor of such rights).

However, such a prohibition on competition is justified by the legitimate objective sought of implementing the concentration only when its duration, its geographical field of application, its subject matter and the persons subject to it do not exceed what is reasonably necessary to that end.

2. With regard to the acceptable duration of a prohibition on competition, a period of five years has been recognised as appropriate when the transfer of the undertaking includes the goodwill and know-how, and a period of two years when it includes only the goodwill. However, these are not absolute rules; they do not preclude a prohibition of longer duration in particular circumstances, where for example the parties can demonstrate that customer loyalty will persist for a period longer than two years or that the economic life-cycle of the products concerned is longer than five years and should be taken into account.

3. The geographic scope of the non-competition clause must be limited to the area where the vendor had established the products or services before the transfer. It does not appear objectively necessary that the acquirer be protected from competition by the vendor in territories which the vendor had not previously penetrated.

4. In the same manner, the non-competition clause must be limited to products and services which form the economic activity of the undertaking transferred. In particular, in the case of a partial transfer of assets, it does not appear that the acquirer needs to be protected from the competition of the vendor in the products or services which constitute the activities which the vendor retains after the transfer.

5. The vendor may bind himself, his subsidiaries and commercial agents. However, an obligation to impose similar restrictions on others would not qualify as an ancillary restriction. This applies in particular to clauses which would restrict the scope for resellers or users to import or export.

6. Any protection of the vendor is not normally an ancillary restriction and is therefore to be examined under Articles 81 and 82 of the EEC Treaty.

B. *Licences of industrial and commercial property rights and of know-how*

1. The implementation of a transfer of an undertaking or part of an undertaking generally includes the transfer to the acquirer, with a view to the full exploitation of the assets transferred, of rights to industrial or commercial property or know-how. However, the vendor may remain the owner of the rights in order to exploit them for activities other than those transferred. In these cases, the usual means for ensuring that the acquirer will have the full use of the assets transferred is to conclude licensing agreements in his favour.

2. Simple or exclusive licences of patents, similar rights or existing know-how can be accepted as necessary for the completion of the transaction, and likewise agreements to grant such licences. They may be limited to certain fields of use, to the extent that they correspond to the activities of the undertaking transferred. Normally it will not be necessary for such licences to include territorial limitations on manufacture which reflect the territory of the activity transferred. Licences may be granted for the whole duration of the patent or similar rights or the duration of the normal economic life of the know-how. As such licences are economically equivalent to a partial transfer of rights, they need not be limited in time.

3. Restrictions in licence agreements, going beyond what is provided above, fall outside the scope of the Regulation. They must be assessed on their merits according to Article 81(1) and (3). Accordingly, where they fulfil the conditions required, they may

benefit from the block exemptions provided for by Regulation (EEC) No. 2349/84 on patent licences[7] or Regulation (EEC) No. 559/89 on know-how licences.[8]

4. The same principles are to be applied by analogy in the case of licences of trademarks, business names or similar rights. There may be situations where the vendor wishes to remain the owner of such rights in relation to activities retained, but the acquirer needs the rights to use them to market the products constituting the object of the activity of the undertaking or part of an undertaking transferred.

In such circumstances, the conclusion of agreements for the purpose of avoiding confusion between trade marks may be necessary.

C. Purchase and supply agreements

1. In many cases, the transfer of an undertaking or part of an undertaking can entail the disruption of traditional lines of internal procurement and supply resulting from the previous integration of activities within the economic entity of the vendor. To make possible the break up of the economic unity of the vendor and the partial transfer of the assets to the acquirer under reasonable conditions, it is often necessary to maintain, at least for a transitional period, similar links between the vendor and the acquirer. This objective is normally attained by the conclusion of purchase and supply agreements between the vendor and the acquirer of the undertaking or part of an undertaking. Taking account of the particular situation resulting from the break up of the economic unity of the vendor such obligations, which may lead to restrictions of competition, can be recognised as ancillary. They may be in favour of the vendor as well as the acquirer.

2. The legitimate aim of such obligations may be to ensure the continuity of supply to one or other of the parties of products necessary to the activities retained (for the vendor) or taken over (for the acquirer). Thus, there are grounds for recognising, for a transitional period, the need for supply obligations aimed at guaranteeing the quantities previously supplied within the vendor's integrated business or enabling their adjustment in accordance with the development of the market.

Their aim may also be to provide continuity of outlets for one or the other of the parties, as they were previously assured within the single economic entity. For the same reason, obligations providing for fixed quantities, possibly with a variation clause, may be recognised as necessary.

3. However, there does not appear to be a general justification for exclusive purchase or supply obligations. Save in exceptional circumstances, for example resulting from the absence of a market or the specificity of products, such exclusivity is not objectively necessary to permit the implementation of a concentration in the form of a transfer of an undertaking or part of an undertaking.

In any event, in accordance with the principle of proportionality, the undertakings concerned are bound to consider whether there are no alternative means to the ends pursued, such as agreements for fixed quantities, which are less restrictive than exclusivity.

4. As for the duration of procurement and supply obligations, this must be limited to a period necessary for the replacement of the relationship of dependency by autonomy in the market. The duration of such a period must be objectively justified.

IV. Evaluation of ancillary restrictions in the case of a joint acquisition

1. As set out in the 24th recital, the Regulation is applicable when two or more undertakings agree to acquire jointly the control of one or more other undertakings, in particular by means of a public tender offer, where the object or effect is the division among themselves of the undertakings or their assets. This is a concentration implemented

---

[7] OJ 1984 L219/15.
[8] OJ 1989 L61/1.

in two successive stages; the common strategy is limited to the acquisition of control. For the transaction to be concentrative, the joint acquisition must be followed by a clear separation of the undertakings or assets concerned.

2. For this purpose, an agreement by the joint acquirers of an undertaking to abstain from making separate competing offers for the same undertaking, or otherwise acquiring control, may be considered an ancillary restriction.

3. Restrictions limited to putting the division into effect are to be considered directly related and necessary to the implementation of the concentration. This will apply to arrangements made between the parties for the joint acquisition of control in order to divide among themselves the production facilities or the distribution networks together with the existing trademarks of the undertaking acquired in common. The implementation of this division may not in any circumstances lead to the coordination of the future behaviour of the acquiring undertakings.

4. To the extent that such a division involves the break up of a pre-existing economic entity, arrangements that make the break up possible under reasonable conditions must be considered ancillary. In this regard, the principles explained above in relation to purchase and supply arrangements over a transitional period in cases of transfer of undertakings should be applied by analogy.

V. Evaluation of ancillary restrictions in cases of concentrative joint ventures within the meaning of Article 3(2) subparagraph 2 of the Regulation

This evaluation must take account of the characteristics peculiar to concentrative joint ventures, the constituent elements of which are the creation of an autonomous economic entity exercising on a long-term basis all the functions of an undertaking, and the absence of coordination of competitive behaviour between the parent undertakings and between them and the joint venture. This condition implies in principle to the withdrawal of the parent undertakings from the market assigned to the joint venture and, therefore, their disappearance as actual or potential competitors of the new entity.

A. Non-competition obligations

To the extent that a prohibition on the parent undertakings competing with the joint venture aims at expressing the reality of the lasting withdrawal of the parents from the market assigned to the joint venture, it will be recognised as an integral part of the concentration.

B. Licences for industrial and commercial property rights and know-how

The creation of a new autonomous economic entity usually involves the transfer of the technology necessary for carrying on the activities assigned to it, in the form of a transfer of rights and related know-how. Where the parent undertakings intend nonetheless to retain the property rights, particularly with the aim of exploitation in other fields of use, the transfer of technology to the joint venture may be accomplished by means of licences. Such licences may be exclusive, without having to be limited in duration or territory, for they serve only as a substitute for the transfer of property rights. They must therefore be considered necessary to the implementation of the concentration.

C. Purchase and supply obligations

If the parent undertakings remain present in a market upstream or downstream of that of the joint venture, any purchase and supply agreements are to be examined in accordance with the principles applicable in the case of the transfer of an undertaking.

DRAFT COMMISSION NOTICE

On Restrictions Directly Related and Necessary to Concentrations

I. Introduction

1. Council Regulation (EEC) No 4064/89 of 21 December 1989,[1] as amended by Council Regulation (EC) No 1310/97 of 30 June 1997,[2] on the control of concentrations between undertakings ("the Regulation") states in its 25th recital[3] that its application is not excluded where the undertakings concerned accept restrictions which are directly related and necessary to the implementation of the concentration. Pursuant to Article 6(1)(b), second subparagraph and Article 8(2), second subparagraph, last sentence, of the Regulation, a decision declaring the concentration compatible also covers these restrictions. In this situation, under the provisions of Article 22, paragraph 1, the Regulation is solely applicable, to the exclusion of Regulation No 17[4] as well as Regulations (EEC) No 1017/68,[5] (EEC) No 4056/86[6] and (EEC) No 3975/87.[7] The Commission assesses such restrictions together with the concentration itself. This avoids parallel Commission proceedings, one concerned with the assessment of the concentration under the Regulation, and the other aimed at the application of Article 81[8] to restrictions which are directly related and necessary to the implementation of the concentration.

    2. In this notice, the Commission sets out to indicate the interpretation it gives to the notion of "restrictions directly related and necessary to the implementation of the concentration". Under the Regulation, such restrictions must be assessed in relation to the concentration, whatever their treatment might be under Articles 81 and 82 if they were to be considered in isolation or in a different economic context. The guidance given in the following sections reflects past Commission experience and practice in this field.

3. This notice is without prejudice to the interpretation which may be given by the Community courts.

II. Principles of evaluation

4. Contractual arrangements which are among the elements constituting the concentration and agreements establishing control within the meaning of Article 3, paragraph 3, including all agreements which relate to assets necessary to carry out the main object of

---

[1] OJ No L 395, 30.12.1989, p. 1, corrected version OJ L 257, 21.9.1990, p. 13.
[2] OJ No L 180, 9.7.1997, p. 1, corrigendum OJ L 40, 13.2.1998, p. 17.
[3] Also see 7th recital of Council Regulation (EC) No 1310/97, OJ reference as in footnote (2) above.
[4] OJ No 13, 21.2.1962, p. 204/62.
[5] OJ No L 175, 23.7.1968, p. 1.
[6] OJ No L 378, 31.12.1986, p. 4.
[7] OJ No L 374, 31.12.1987, p. 1.
[8] Previously Article 85 of the EEC Treaty (numbering revised by the Treaty of Amsterdam).

the concentration, are integral parts of the concentration. The latter arrangements constitute the very subject matter of the evaluation to be carried out under the Regulation.

5. In addition to these agreements, the parties to the concentration may enter into other agreements which do not form part of the concentration, and which limit the parties' freedom of action in the market. If such agreements contain restrictions that are directly related and necessary to the concentration itself, they must be assessed together with it under the provisions of Article 2 of the Regulation. If not, their restrictive effects may, if appropriate, be examined separately by the Commission in order to assess their compatibility with Articles 81 and 82 of the EEC Treaty. For reasons of legal certainty, only binding agreements will be assessed as directly related and necessary to the implementation of a concentration.

6. The agreements must be "necessary to the implementation of the concentration", which means that in their absence the concentration could not be implemented or could only be implemented under more uncertain conditions, at substantially higher cost, over an appreciably longer period or with considerably higher difficulty. Agreements which aim at protecting the value transferred, maintaining the continuity of supply after the break-up of a former economic entity, or which enable the start-up of a new entity, usually meet these criteria. This must be judged on an objective basis.

7. In determining whether or not a restriction is necessary, it is proper not only to take account of its nature, but equally to ensure that its duration, subject matter and geographical field of application, do not exceed what the implementation of the concentration reasonably requires. Where there is more than one method of achieving the desired result, the undertakings must choose the one which is least restrictive.

8. For concentrations which are carried out in stages, the contractual arrangements relating to the stages before the establishment of control within the meaning of Article 3, paragraphs 1 and 3 of the Regulation cannot be considered as directly related and necessary to the concentration. For these agreements, Articles 81 and 82 remain applicable for as long as the conditions set out in Article 3 are not fulfilled. The notion of directly related restrictions likewise excludes from the application of the Regulation those agreements which have no direct link with the concentration. It is thus not sufficient that the additional restrictions exist in the same context as the concentration.

9. The Commission will not take a definitive view on the appreciability of the restrictive character of an agreement it finds directly related and necessary to the implementation of the concentration.[9]

III. Evaluation of common clauses in cases of the acquisition of an undertaking

10. Restrictions agreed between the parties in the context of a transfer of an undertaking may be to the benefit of the buyer or of the vendor. In general terms, the need for the buyer to benefit from certain protection is more compelling than the corresponding need for the vendor. It is the buyer who needs to be assured that he will be able to run the acquired business so as to recoup the investment made in the acquired business. Thus, restrictions which benefit the vendor either are not directly related and necessary for the concentration or, when they are, they are unlikely to need to go as far, in scope and/or duration, as those which benefit the acquirer.

A. Non-competition clauses

11. Restrictions which meet the criteria set out in the Regulation include contractual prohibitions on competition which are imposed on the vendor in the context of a

---

[9] See for example cases No IV/M.527—*UAP/Provincial*, 7.11.1994; No IV/M.612—*RWE-DEA/Enichem Augusta*, 27.7.1995; No IV/M.651—*AT&T-Philips*, 3.2.1996; No IV/M.861—*Textron/Kautex*, 16.12.1996.

concentration achieved by the transfer of an undertaking or part of an undertaking. Such prohibitions guarantee the transfer to the acquirer of the full value of the assets transferred, which in general include both physical assets and intangible assets such as the goodwill which the vendor has accumulated or the know-how he has developed. These are not only directly related to the concentration, but are also necessary for its implementation because, in their absence, there would be reasonable grounds to expect that the sale of the undertaking or part of an undertaking could not be accomplished.

12. In order to obtain the full value of the assets transferred, the acquirer must be able to benefit from some protection against competition from the vendor in order to gain the loyalty of customers and to assimilate and exploit the know-how. However, such a prohibition is justified by the legitimate objective of implementing the concentration only when its duration, its geographical field of application, its subject matter and the persons subject to it do not exceed what is reasonably necessary to achieve that end. Such protection cannot generally be considered necessary when, *de facto*, the transfer is limited to physical assets (such as land, buildings or machinery) or to exclusive industrial and commercial property rights (the holders of which could immediately take action against infringements by the transferor of such rights).

13. Prohibitions for periods of up to three years are generally justified when the transfer of the undertaking includes elements of goodwill and know-how, and for periods of up to two years when it includes only goodwill. Prohibitions of longer duration can only be justified in a limited range of circumstances, for example where the parties can demonstrate that customer loyalty will persist for more than two years or where there is a transfer of know-how that equally justifies an additional period of protection.

14. The geographical scope of a non-competition clause must be limited to the area where the vendor offered the relevant products or services before the transfer. The presumption is that the acquirer does not need to be protected from competition from the vendor in territories not previously penetrated by the vendor, unless such protection can be justified by the notifying parties.

15. In the same manner, non-competition clauses must be limited to products and services which form the economic activity of the undertaking transferred. Here again, in the absence of a full justification from the notifying parties, the presumption is that the acquirer does not need to be protected from competition from the vendor in those products or services markets in which the transferred undertaking was not active before the transfer.

16. The vendor may bind himself, his subsidiaries and commercial agents. However, an obligation to impose similar restrictions on others would not be regarded as directly related and necessary to the implementation of the concentration. This applies in particular to clauses which would restrict the scope for resellers or users to import or export.

17. Non-solicitation and confidentiality clauses are evaluated in the same way as non-compete clauses, to the extent that their restrictive effect does not exceed that of a non-compete clause. However, since the scope of these clauses may be narrower than that of non-compete clauses, they are likely to be found directly related and necessary to the concentration in a larger number of circumstances.

B. Licence agreements

18. The implementation of a transfer of an undertaking or part of an undertaking generally includes the transfer to the acquirer, with a view to the full exploitation of the assets transferred, of rights to industrial or commercial property or know-how. However, the vendor may remain the owner of the rights in order to exploit them for activities other than those transferred. In these cases, the usual means for ensuring that the acquirer will have the full use of the assets transferred is to conclude licensing agreements in his favour. Likewise, where the vendor has transferred intellectual property rights with the business he may want to continue using some or all of these rights for activities other than those transferred. In such a case the acquirer will grant a licence to the vendor.

19. Licences of patents,[10] similar rights or know-how, can be considered necessary for the implementation of the concentration. They may equally be considered as an integral part to the concentration. These licences may be limited to certain fields of use, to the extent that they correspond to the activities of the undertaking transferred. It is not normally necessary to include territorial limitations on manufacture, where these reflect the territory of the transferred activity. Nor do such licences need to be time-limited. Restrictions in licence agreements, which go beyond the above provisions, such as those which protect the licensor rather than the licensee, are not usually necessary for the implementation of the concentration. Instead, they will be assessed in accordance with Article 81 of the EEC Treaty. Where they fulfil the conditions required, such agreements may fall under Regulation (EC) No 240/96.[11] In the case of a licence granted from the seller of a business to the buyer, the seller can be made subject to a territorial restriction in the licence agreement under the same conditions as laid down for non-competition clauses in the context of the sale of a business.

20. Similarly, in the case of licences of trademarks, business names, design rights, copyright or similar rights, there may be situations where the vendor wishes to remain the owner of such rights in relation to activities retained, but the acquirer needs the rights to use them in order to market the goods or services produced by the undertaking or part of an undertaking transferred. Here, the same considerations as above apply.

21. Agreements relating to the use of business names/trademarks will normally be analysed in the context of the corresponding licence of the relevant intellectual property right.

C. Purchase and supply obligations

22. In many cases, the transfer of an undertaking or part of an undertaking can entail the disruption of traditional lines of purchase and supply which existed as a result of the previous integration of activities within the economic unity of the vendor. To enable the break-up of the economic unity of the vendor and the partial transfer of the assets to the acquirer under reasonable conditions, it is often necessary to maintain, at least for a transitional period, the existing or similar links between the vendor and the acquirer. This objective is normally attained by purchase and supply obligations for the vendor and/or the acquirer of the undertaking or part of an undertaking. Taking into account the particular situation resulting from the break-up of the economic unity of the vendor, such obligations, which may lead to restrictions of competition, can be recognised as directly related and necessary to implementation of the concentration. They may be in favour of the vendor as well as the acquirer, depending on the particular circumstances.

23. The aim of such obligations may be, quite legitimately, to ensure the continuity of supply to one or other of the parties of products necessary for carrying out the activities retained (for the vendor) or taken over (for the acquirer). Thus, there are grounds for recognising, for a transitional period, the need for supply obligations aimed at guaranteeing the quantities previously supplied within the vendor's integrated business or providing for their adjustment to the foreseeable demand forecasts.

24. Their aim may also be to provide continuity of purchases for the vendor or the acquirer, as they were previously assured within the single economic entity.

25. Supply obligations, which the notifying parties consider directly related and necessary to the concentration and which benefit the vendor, will require particularly careful justification by the parties.

---

[10] Including patent applications, utility models, topographies of semiconductor products, certificats d'utilité and certificats d'addition under French law and applications for these, supplementary protection certificates for medicinal products or other products for which supplementary protection certificates may be obtained and plant breeder's certificates (as referred to in Article 8 of Commission Regulation (EC) 240/96 of 31.1.1996, OJ No L 31, 9.2.1996, p. 2).

[11] OJ No L 31, 9.2.1996, p. 2.

26. Both supply and purchase obligations, providing for fixed quantities, possibly with a variation clause, and may be recognised as directly related and necessary.

27. However, the presumption is that obligations which provide for excessive or unlimited quantities, or which confer preferred supplier or purchaser status, are not normally necessary. Any such obligations would need to be justified by the parties. Likewise, there is no general justification for exclusive purchase or supply obligations. Save in exceptional circumstances, for example resulting from the absence of a market or the specificity of the products in question, such exclusivity is not necessary to permit the implementation of a concentration in the form of a transfer of an undertaking or part of an undertaking.

28. In any event, the undertakings concerned are bound to consider whether any alternative, less restrictive means of providing the necessary continuity exist, such as agreements for fixed quantities.

29. The duration of purchase and supply obligations must be limited to a period necessary for the replacement of the relationship of dependency by autonomy in the market. Given the variety of potential supply arrangements (eg commodities, consumer goods, services) it is impossible to have a general presumption which would apply across the whole range of options. The presumption for goods such as complex industrial products is that this type of obligation is not normally justified for longer than a transitional period of three years. The Commission will use this starting presumption in determining what constitutes a necessary duration in relation to the particular goods or services in question. In any event, the duration of such a period must be justified by the notifying parties.

30. Service agreements are, occasionally, equivalent in their effect to supply arrangements. In this case the same considerations as above apply.

31. As for distribution arrangements, they may also be considered as ancillary restraints. In any event, the relevant Block Exemption Regulation shall apply.[12]

IV. Evaluation of common clauses in the case of a joint acquisition

32. As set out in the 24th recital, the Regulation is applicable when two or more undertakings agree to acquire jointly the control of one or more other undertakings, in particular by means of a public tender offer, where the object or effect is the division among themselves of the undertakings or their assets. This is a concentration implemented in two successive stages. The common strategy is limited to the acquisition of control. For the transaction to fall under the Merger Regulation, the joint acquisition must be followed by a clear separation of the undertakings or assets concerned.

33. For this purpose, in the context of a joint bid, an agreement by the joint acquirers of an undertaking to abstain from making separate competing offers for the same undertaking, or otherwise acquiring control, may be considered directly related and necessary to the implementation of the concentration.

34. Restrictions limited to putting the division into effect are to be considered directly related and necessary to the implementation of the concentration. This will apply to arrangements made between the parties for the joint acquisition of control in order to divide among themselves the production facilities or distribution networks, together with the existing trademarks of the undertaking acquired jointly. The implementation of this division may not in any circumstances lead to the coordination of the future behaviour of the acquiring undertakings.

35. To the extent that such a division involves the break-up of a pre-existing economic entity, arrangements that make the break-up possible under reasonable conditions must be considered directly related and necessary to the implementation of the concentration. In

---

[12] Commission Regulation No 1983/83 of 22.6.1983; Commission Regulation No 1984/83 of 22.6.1983.

this regard, the principles explained above in relation to purchase and supply arrangements over a transitional period in cases of transfer of undertakings should also be applied here.

V. Evaluation of common clauses in cases of joint ventures within the meaning of Article 3(2) subparagraph 2 of the Regulation

36. This evaluation must take account of the characteristics peculiar to joint ventures, the constituent elements of which are the creation of an autonomous economic entity performing on a long-term basis all the functions of an undertaking.

A. Non-competition obligations

37. Prohibitions on competition between parent undertakings and a joint venture may be considered as directly related and necessary to the implementation of the concentration.
38. Non-competition clauses may reflect, *inter alia*, the need to ensure good faith during negotiations, the need to utilise fully the joint venture's assets or to enable the joint venture to assimilate know-how and goodwill provided by the parents, or the need to protect the parents' interests in the joint venture from competitive acts facilitated, inter alia, by privileged access to know-how and goodwill transferred or developed by the joint venture.
39. The duration of a non-competition clause must be duly justified by the parties. For periods of up to two or three years they can be justified on similar grounds and conditions as in the case of non-compete clauses in the context of a transfer of an undertaking.
40. Prohibitions on competition between parent undertakings and a joint venture which extend beyond the life of the joint venture may never be regarded as directly related and necessary to the implementation of the concentration.
41. The geographical scope of a non-competition clause should be limited to the area where the parents offered the relevant products or services prior to establishing the joint venture. In the same manner, non-competition clauses must be limited to products and services which form the economic activity of the joint venture. If the joint venture is set up to enter a new market, reference will be made to the products, services and territories in which it is called to operate under the joint venture agreement or by-laws. The presumption is that a parent's interest in the joint venture does not need to be protected from competition from the other parent in markets other than those in which the joint venture will be active at its outset. Any departure from this principle must be justified by the notifying parties.
42. Additionally, the presumption is that prohibitions on competition between non-controlling parents and a joint venture are not normally directly related and necessary to the implementation of a concentration. Again, any departure from this principle must be justified by the notifying parties.
43. Non-solicitation and confidentiality clauses are evaluated in the same way as non-compete clauses, to the extent that their restrictive effect does not exceed that of a non-compete clause. However, since the scope of confidentiality clauses in particular may be narrower than non-compete clauses, they may be found directly related and necessary to the concentration in a larger number of circumstances.

B. Licence agreements

44. A licence granted by the parents to the joint venture may be considered necessary for the implementation of the concentration. They may equally be considered as an integral part of the concentration. This applies regardless of whether or not the licence is an exclusive one, or whether or not it is time-limited. The licence may be restricted to a particular field of use, which corresponds to the activities of the joint venture. It may also be limited to the contractual territory of activity of the joint venture.

45. Licence agreements between parents, however, are not considered directly related and necessary to the implementation of a joint venture.

46. Likewise, licence agreements granted by the joint venture to one of the parents, or cross-licence agreements, are neither integral nor necessary for the creation of the joint venture. However, if intellectual property rights have been transferred by a parent to the JV, a licence from the JV to this parent can be regarded as directly related and necessary under the same conditions as in the case of the sale of a business.

47. Licence agreements which are not considered as directly related and necessary may nevertheless fall under Regulation (EC) No 240/96.

C. Purchase and supply obligations

48. If the parent undertakings remain present in a market upstream or downstream of that of the joint venture, any purchase and supply agreements, including distribution agreements, are to be examined in accordance with the principles applicable in the case of the transfer of an undertaking.

VI. Procedure

49. Where the notifying parties request that agreements be considered directly related and necessary to the implementation of the concentration, the agreements should be individually identified and the parties should explain the rationale behind the request in Form CO. Requests which fail to comply with these requirements, or which concern restrictions which are not binding on the parties to a concentration, will not be dealt with by the Commission in any decision clearing the concentration in question.

TREATMENT OF ANCILLARY RESTRAINTS UNDER THE MERGER REGULATION

Introduction

1. This paper explains the changes proposed by the Commission to its Notice on restrictions directly related and necessary to concentrations.

2. The wording of the text in the Notice has been streamlined and descriptions of the economic justifications for a restriction to be regarded as necessary have been added, namely the protection of the value transferred from free riding, the maintenance of the continuity of supply relations after the break up of a former economic entity and the enabling of the start-up of a new entity.

Principles of evaluation

3. The term "ancillary" has a specific meaning in competition law but it is not used in the Merger Regulation. Consequently, the Commission takes the view that in future it would be preferable to refer to the actual wording of the Merger Regulation. The new Notice therefore contains the phrase "restrictions directly related and necessary to the implementation of the concentration", as employed in Article 6(1)(b) paragraph 2 and in Article 8(2) of the Merger Regulation. This means that for a clause to be examined together with the concentration it must be "directly related" (ie "subordinate in importance to the main object of the concentration") and "necessary" (ie in the absence of such restrictions, the concentration would not be implemented) for the concentration to take place.

4. The paper does not tackle the question whether the clauses concerned have any appreciable restrictive effect within the meaning of Article 81(1) (ex–85(1)) of the EEC Treaty. Such an evaluation is outside the scope of the assessment of ancillary restrictions under the Merger Regulation.

Non-compete clauses

5. Non-compete covenants are amongst the most common clauses agreed upon by the parties to a concentration that may be considered as directly related to, and necessary for, its implementation within the meaning of Articles 6(1)(b) and (2) and 8(2) of the Merger Regulation. Other provisions similar in scope include non-solicitation clauses and confidentiality provisions. These clauses may, for this purpose, be treated as non-compete clauses to the extent that they are designed to prevent competition between the parties to the concentration.

6. Non-compete clauses may be justified on several grounds and serve several purposes. The parties must always provide an explanation of the rationale underlying non-compete restrictions and fully justify their request for them to be viewed as directly related and necessary to the concentration.

7. In case of a **transfer of an undertaking**, a general presumption can be made that non-compete restrictions on the vendor are necessary and directly related to the sale for two or three years respectively if either goodwill alone or goodwill and know-how (that must remain available to the vendor) are involved. On the question of product and geographical scope, the starting presumption is that the restriction should be limited to those products and services and the geographical area where the vendor had established the products or services before the transfer. The parties may seek coverage for a longer duration or for a wider product or geographical area but it is for them to demonstrate the need for any such extension.

8. The same presumption applies to **joint ventures**, in particular where the joint venture needs to assimilate know-how and goodwill provided by the parents. However, the parties to the joint venture agreement may agree a non-compete clause for a longer

duration, up to the whole life of the joint venture. In such a case they should justify that the agreements at issue are necessary and directly related on grounds which may include, inter alia, the expression of the parents' lasting withdrawal from the market, the need to protect the JV's start-up or ensure that it utilises fully its assets, or to protect the JV from free-riding by the parents. The acceptable duration will depend on the aim of the restriction in question, and may be limited in time or extend up to the life of the JV. The duration may not extend beyond the termination of the JV, as in such cases the restriction is unrelated to the concentration in question and moreover not proportionate to its aim. The principles applicable to transfers of undertakings in relation to product and geographic scope of non-compete restrictions also apply to JVs.

9. Non-compete restrictions on **non-controlling shareholders** give rise to specific considerations. Here the starting presumption is that they are not, in principle, regarded as directly related and necessary to the concentration. Here again, the parties bear the burden of reversing this negative presumption, by proving that the restrictions are necessary.

10. **Non-solicitation and confidentiality clauses** will be evaluated in the same way as non-compete clauses, to the extent that their restrictive effect does not exceed that of a non-compete clause. Otherwise, when the restrictions implied go beyond a non-compete restriction, further justification must be provided. However, since the scope of confidentiality clauses in particular may be narrower than non-compete clauses, they may be found directly related and necessary to the concentration in a larger number of circumstances.

Licences of technical and commercial property rights and of know-how

11. The following licence agreements will be covered by the Notice: all patent and know-how licensing agreements within the meaning of the block exemption regulation on technology transfer (Regulation 240/96) as well as agreements on trademarks, related rights (design rights, copyright) and business names. Agreements on all these rights will need to be assessed using similar criteria.

12. In the case of a **transfer of a business**, the wording of the old Notice has been redrafted without making any material changes. It is proposed to add a phrase which allows territorial restrictions in cases where a licence is given by the buyer to the seller.

13. The creation of a **joint venture** usually involves the transfer of the technology necessary for carrying on the activities assigned to it. If the parents want to remain the owners of the property rights in order to exploit them for other activities, they will license the technology to the JV. Such licences may serve as a substitute for the transfer of property rights. Consequently, the licence may be considered to be an integral part of the operation, in particular if the duration is unlimited. Indeed, there is no difference between this and a scenario in which a parent does not transfer the property title for a piece of land but instead grants a lease.

14. This argument applies regardless of whether the licence is a simple (simple licences do not normally involve any restriction of competition whatsoever) or an exclusive licence, limited or unlimited in time. The licence may be limited to a certain field of use which corresponds to the activities of the JV. The licence may also be limited to the territory of the JV.

15. If the scope of the licence is wider than the scope of activities of the JV, the provisions or elements of the licence agreement (field of use, geographic scope, possibility of sublicenses) may not necessarily be anti-competitive but it cannot be said that they are an integral part of the operation. It is also difficult to argue that these licence agreements are necessary for the implementation of the JV. Therefore, unless the notifying parties are able to demonstrate otherwise, such agreements are not ancillary. Regulation 240/96 provides guidance on the extent to which certain clauses can be considered to be restrictive.

16. Licence agreements between the parents or licences granted from the joint venture to the parent are not generally necessary for the creation of the joint venture. Instead, they need to be dealt with under Article 81 (ex–85) of the Treaty.

Purchase and supply agreements

17. The present Notice provides that purchase and supply agreements between the vendor and the acquirer, or between a parent and its joint venture, may be considered directly related and necessary to the implementation of the concentration for a transitional period. The aim of such agreements may be to prevent any disruption in procurement resulting from the break-up of previously integrated activities and, thereby, to ensure the continuity of supplies while establishing links with new suppliers. They may also aim to guarantee the continuity of outlets for one or more parties. Such obligations, which may lead to restrictions of competition, can thus be recognised as directly related and necessary to take concentration for a given period.

18. For the sake of clarity, in the following paragraphs of this section the terms "vendor", "buyer", "parents" and "JV" are intended to refer to the parties to the concentration, whereas the terms "supplier" and "customer" are intended to refer to the parties to the supply contract.

19. Different types of purchase and supply clauses governing the relationship between the vendor and the buyer (or the parents and the joint venture) can be identified. The vendor (parents) and the buyer (JV) may take within these agreements both the roles of supplier or customer. The most common clauses are:

(i) obligations to purchase/supply a given quantity;
(ii) obligations to purchase/supply without limitation;
(iii) preferred supplier/preferred customer status; and
(iv) exclusive purchase/supply arrangements.

20. For the purpose of the present analysis, other arrangements such as outsourcing, service and distribution may be considered to be similar to purchase and supply arrangements and can therefore be subsumed within this category when assessing whether they are necessary and directly related to the implementation of a concentration. However, for the purpose of this paper, these clauses are dealt with under the heading "other" clauses.

21. The type of obligation (ie the scope of the restriction involved) and its duration are the key considerations when assessing whether a supply agreement is directly related and necessary to a concentration. The parties must always provide an explanation of the rationale underlying supply agreements and justify their request in terms of these two factors.

22. Supply agreements which the notifying parties consider directly related and necessary to the concentration and which benefit the vendor or the supplier, will require particularly careful justification by the parties.

23. As regards the **type of obligation**, the Commission will favour agreements providing obligations to supply/purchase given quantities (provided such quantities are not too large compared to the total capacity of the supplier or to the total sourcing of the customer or as large as to imply de facto exclusivity) over obligations where there are no quantitative limitations or which provide for exclusivity arrangements. Indeed, there should be a negative presumption against any such form of "non-limitation" and against exclusivity. This presumption may be rebutted by the parties.

24. In terms of **duration**, the large number of case-specific and sector-specific considerations do provide a basis for the Commission to give precise guidance. Comparable commercial practice in the sector can provide an important reference in determining an acceptable duration. However for complex intermediate products three years are normally viewed as an acceptable duration. In the case of specific market conditions such as limited sources of supply, this duration can be extended up to a maximum of five years. A longer period would be acceptable only under exceptional circumstances (in the past this has occurred primarily in the chemical industry, either because other supply facilities were unavailable or difficult to access or where the supply arrangements prior to the transaction were highly integrated and economically interdependent within one group).

25. Beyond this general approach, the duration accepted will diminish in proportion to any increase in the restrictive effect of the obligation. Thus, obligations for very substantial quantities (relative to total supply/sourcing) or without limitations will only be acceptable for a strictly limited duration, and should possibly be accompanied by a variation clause providing, for example, for a decrease in the quantities concerned.

"Other" clauses

26. The Commission has also considered certain categories of agreements which do not easily lend themselves to categorisation within the existing categories of the Notice (namely non-competition clauses, licences of industrial and commercial property rights and of know-how, purchase and supply agreements). The Commission has nevertheless concluded that such clauses might, on the basis of their purpose and rationale, be subsumed within one of the existing categories.

27. Agreements relating to the **use of names/trademarks** (in particular obligations not to use a certain name/trademark) can be dealt together with agreements relating to the transfer or licence of such names/trademarks, to the extent that they simply constitute an additional guarantee for the acquirer.

28. The treatment of **Outsourcing agreements**, as ancillary restraints will be subsumed within the purchase/supply agreements category, given that the rationale for both types of agreement is basically the same. Equally, **distribution agreements** will be treated as supply agreements.

29. **Agreements relating to the lease of premises or utilities** and **agreements relating to assets which are not transferred** but which nevertheless relate to the core business of the activity being transferred, are to be considered as part of the notified concentration and, therefore, technically do not constitute ancillary restraints.

Procedural issues

30. Form CO requires notifying parties to identify each ancillary restriction in the agreements provided with the notification and to explain why these are directly related and necessary to the implementation of the concentration. **The parties' requests must be sufficiently reasoned**, referring to precise clauses and not simply to complete agreements, identified in general terms. The Commission will not consider non-binding agreements or simple declarations of intentions as eligible for scrutiny as ancillary retraints.

31. Where notifying parties' requests are not sufficiently reasoned, the normal practice will be for the Commission to inform the parties that their request under section 11.1 is not admissible as such and that they will not be covered in its final decision.

32. From a strictly legal point of view, the Commission should establish the anti-competitive nature of the notified clause and examine the question whether these clauses appear to be necessary and directly related to the concentration. The question whether an appreciable restriction of competition exists is, however, very difficult to answer in the majority of cases, within the very short time available. Nevertheless, if the clauses identified by the notifying parties are directly related and necessary to the concentration, they are automatically covered by the decision adopted under the Merger Regulation. If, on the other hand, these provisions are not considered directly related and necessary to the concentration, then the decision adopted under the Merger Regulation will not prejudge their legal status. The assessment of these clauses will then normally be carried out by DG IV Directorates in charge of the application of Articles 81 and 82 (ex–85 and 86).

APPENDIX 42

COMMISSION NOTICE[1]

Concerning Alignment of Procedures for Processing Mergers under the ECSC and EC Treaties

(Text with EEA relevance)

I. INTRODUCTION

1. The following provisions relate to mergers governed by the ECSC Treaty. They are designed to increase transparency and improve compliance with the rights of the defence in connection with the examination of such mergers and to expedite decision making. To this end, they are based on an alignment of certain rules with those governing mergers covered by Council Regulation (EEC) No 4064/89 of 21 December 1989 on the control of concentrations between undertakings.[2]

2. The Commission hopes, in this context, to meet the expectations of undertakings, in particular as regards merger operations which are covered by the ECSC and EC Treaties at the same time. This notice should also be seen as an attempt at simplification, albeit within the limits imposed by having two separate treaties. The rules thus introduced should make it possible for ECSC undertakings to familiarise themselves with the procedures of law against the background of the forthcoming expiry of the ECSC Treaty.

II. MAIN PROCEDURAL CHANGES ENVISAGED WITH REGARD TO MERGER CONTROL PURSUANT TO THE ECSC TREATY

Publication of the fact of notification

3. The Commission will from now on publish in the *Official Journal of the European Communities* the fact of notification in the case of mergers covered by the ECSC Treaty. It will state in particular the names of the interested parties, the nature of the merger operation and the economic sectors concerned. Publication will take account of the legitimate interest of undertakings in not having their business secrets divulged.

---

[1] OJ 1998 L66/36.
[2] OJ 1989 L395/1; corrected version: OJ 1990 L257/14.

Statement of objections where the commission plans to subject the authorisation of a merger to conditions or even to prohibit an operation

4. The sending of a statement of objections prior to the conditional authorisation or prohibition of a merger does not appear explicitly in Article 66 of the ECSC Treaty. It is provided for only in the event of a pecuniary sanction (Article 36 of the ECSC Treaty) or of a decision requiring a demerger or other measures designed to restore effective competition where a merger has already been carried out (second paragraph of Article 66(5) of the ECSC Treaty). The Commission believes, however, that it can commit itself to sending such a statement in pursuance of the general principle of the protection of the rights of the defence, which is recognised by the Court as a general principle of Community law. It will therefore base its decisions only on those objections on which the interested parties have been able to express their views.

Of course, this does not prevent the Commission from allowing undertakings to alter their merger proposals on their own initiative, thus making it unnecessary to send a statement of objections, in particular where the competition problem perceived is easily identifiable, limited in scope and easy to resolve, as currently happens in the Community field.

Access to the file and possibility of making oral observations (hearing)

5. The possibility of access to the Commission file and making oral observations (at a hearing) when a statement of objections has been sent is the logical consequence of such a statement.

Accordingly, the Commission confirms that it will give such an opportunity to interested natural or legal persons. It will apply in this context, and by analogy, the rules in Articles 14 to 16 of Commission Regulation (EC) No 3384/94 of 21 December 1994 on the notification, time-limits and hearings provided for in Council Regulation (EEC) No 4064/89 on the control of concentrations between undertakings,[3] which is an implementing regulation, and in accordance with Commission Decision 94/810/ECSC, EC of 12 December 1994 on the terms of reference of hearing officers in competition procedures before the Commission[4] and the Commission notice on the internal rules of procedure for processing requests for access to the file in cases pursuant to Articles 81 and 82 of the EC Treaty, Articles 65 and 66 of the ECSC Treaty and Council Regulation (EEC) No 4064/89.[5]

Publication in the *Official Journal of the European Communities* of the final decisions adopted after communication of the objections, and the public nature of all authorisation decisions

6. Final decisions adopted after the objections have been communicated will be systematically published in the *Official Journal of the European Communities*. Similarly, all authorisation decisions will be made public. Publication will respect business secrecy in accordance with Article 47 of the ECSC Treaty.

Time-limits

7. A statement of objections will be sent at the latest within ten weeks of notification of the merger operation. The final decision, where a statement of objections has been sent, will be taken at the latest within five months of notification. These time-limits presuppose

---

[3] OJ 1994 L377/1.
[4] OJ 1994 L330/67.
[5] OJ 1997 C23/3.

that undertakings use form CO annexed to Regulation (EC) No 3384/94 and supply the Commission with five copies of the notification. Where the Commission considers it unnecessary to send a statement of objections, it will endeavour to adopt its decision within one month of notification.

8. As regards the effective date of notification, the Commission will apply by analogy the provisions of Article 4 of the abovementioned Regulation (EC) No 3384/94. As far as the application of paragraph 5 of that Article is concerned, the terms "pursuant to Article 4(3) of Regulation (EEC) No 4064/89" are to be read as "pursuant to point 3 of this notice". As regards the time-limits of ten weeks and five months mentioned at point 7 above, these will start to run on the working day following that on which the notification becomes effective. The time-limit of ten weeks will end on the same weekday as that on which it commenced. The time-limit of five months will end on the same numerical date as that of its commencement: where no such date occurs in that month, the time-limit will end with the expiry of the last day of the month. Where the last day is not a working day, the time-limit will end with the expiry of the first working day which follows. Working days are taken into account in the time-limits, in accordance with the rules laid down in Article 8 of the abovementioned Regulation (EC) No 3384/94 and are defined in the same way as in Article 22 of that Regulation.

9. The Commission will give favourable consideration to requests for dispensation from supplying certain information required in the form CO where those requests are submitted to it in a prenotification, limiting the information required to that which is strictly necessary for examining the cases.

III. IMPLEMENTATION

10. The Commission will apply the above rules, where they are not already in force, to notified mergers from 1 March 1998.

APPENDIX 43

MERGER: BEST PRACTICE GUIDELINES[1]

One of the fundamental principles underlying the EC Merger Regulation is that in all cases that do not involve "serious doubts", a clearance decision is taken by the Commission within one month from notification. The confidence of European industry and of legal practitioners in the Commission's regulation of mergers is dependent on the Commission being able to process the majority of cases that do not raise competition issues within the one month period.

Declarations of incompleteness under Article 4(2) of the Implementing Regulation have only been made in a few cases (17 cases out of a total of 172 notifications in 1997 and 17 cases out of a total of 196 notifications until 13.11.1998).

However there has been a certain increase in declarations of incompleteness in recent years. Members of the ECLF Committee have had an open discussion with the Merger Task Force with a view to coming to a better understanding of the reasons for these declarations.

We have been informed that declarations according to Article 4(2) are still only made in exceptional circumstances. The Merger Task Force has explained that notifications have been declared incomplete for principally the following reasons:

- In some cases it was not technically possible to accept a notification. These cases include for example notifications made by two parties while they should have been made by three or more parties, or notifications made before there were sufficiently clear legally binding agreements.
- A number of notifications have been poor in terms of the drafting and adequacy of the information provided.
- In some cases the Merger Task Force has identified late during the one month period potential affected markets that should have been identified by the notifying parties in good faith during the pre-notification stage and in the notification itself.

As a more general point, it was explained that in a number of cases in which the notification has been declared incomplete the notification was not preceded by a pre-notification contact, or such contact has been very limited. The consequence of this is that in the absence of any pre-notification discussions there is a higher risk of a declaration of incompleteness.

It is in the interests of the Commission, European business and the legal community to ensure that declarations of incompleteness are kept to the minimum. With this in mind, we have developed the following best practice guidelines in consultation with the Merger Task Force. We recognise that it will not be possible for notifying parties to follow these guidelines in all circumstances.

---

[1] Published on the DG Competition website at http://europa.eu.int/comm/dg04/merger/en/best_practice_gl.htm

Guidelines

- — It is always appropriate even in straightforward cases to have pre-notification contacts with the Merger Task Force case team. Notifying parties should submit a briefing memorandum at least three working days before a first meeting. This first meeting should take place preferably at least one or two weeks before the expected date of notification. In more difficult cases, a more protracted pre-notification period may well be appropriate.
  — Following this first meeting, the parties should provide before notification the Merger Task Force with a substantially complete draft Form CO. The Merger Task Force should be given in general one week to review the draft before a further meeting or being asked to comment on the phone on the adequacy of the draft.
- At pre-notification meetings, a discussion should take place on what should and what should not be included in the notification. Indeed, it may not be necessary to provide all information specified in *Form CO*. However all requests to omit any part of the information specified should be discussed in detail and agreed with the Merger Task Force beforehand.
- Potentially affected markets should be openly discussed with the case team in good faith, even if the notifying parties take a different view on market definition. Furthermore, wherever there may be uncertainty or differences of view over market definitions, it will be more prudent to produce market shares on one or more alternative basis— e.g. by national markets as well as by an EU-wide one.
- Notifying parties and their advisers should take care to ensure that the information contained in Form CO has been carefully prepared and verified. Contact details for customers and competitors should be carefully checked to ensure that the Merger Task Force's investigations are not delayed.
- At meetings in general (both at the pre-notification stage and during notification), it is preferable that cases are discussed with both legal advisers and business representatives who have a good understanding of the relevant markets.

Provided these guidelines are complied with, the Merger Task Force case team will in principle be prepared to confirm informally the adequacy of a draft notification at the pre-notification stage or, if appropriate to identify in what specific respects it is incomplete.

Despite these guidelines, we recognise that it will not be possible for the Merger Task Force to exclude the fact that it may have to declare a notification incomplete in appropriate cases.

COMMISSION NOTICE[1]

On a Simplified Procedure for Treatment of Certain Concentrations under Council Regulation (EEC) No 4064/89

(Text with EEA relevance)

1. This notice sets out a simplified procedure under which the Commission intends to treat certain concentrations that do not raise competition concerns. The notice is based on experience gained by the Commission in applying Council Regulation (EEC) No 4064/89 of 21 December 1989 on the control of concentrations between undertakings,[2] as last amended by Regulation (EC) No 1310/97[3] (the "Merger Regulation") to date, which has shown that certain categories of notified concentrations are normally cleared without having raised any substantive doubts, provided that there were no special circumstances.

2. By following the procedure outlined in the following sections, the Commission aims to make Community merger control more focused and effective.

I. Overview of the simplified procedure

3. This notice sets out the conditions under which the simplified procedure will be applied, together with the procedure itself. Pre-notification contact between the notifying parties and the Commission in such cases is encouraged. When all necessary conditions are met, and provided there are no special circumstances, the Commission will adopt a short-form clearance decision within one month from the date of notification, pursuant to Article 6(1)(b) of the Merger Regulation. Where it considers it appropriate in any particular case, the Commission may, naturally, launch an investigation and/or adopt a full decision within the time-limits laid down in Article 10(1) of the Merger Regulation.

II. Categories of concentrations suitable for treatment under the simplified procedure

Eligible concentrations

4. The simplified procedure will apply to the following categories of concentrations:

(a) two or more undertakings acquire joint control of a joint venture, provided that the joint venture has no, or negligible, actual or foreseen activities within the territory of the European Economic Area (EEA). Such cases occur where:

---

[1] OJ 2000 C217/32.
[2] OJ 1984 L395/1; Corrigendum: OJ 1990 L257/13.
[3] OJ 1997 L180/1; Corrigendum: OJ 1998 L40/1.

(i) the turnover[4] of the joint venture and/or the turnover of the contributed activities[5] is less than EUR 100 million in the EEA territory; and

(ii) the total value of assets[6] transferred to the joint venture is less than EUR 100 million in the territory[7];

(b) two or more undertakings merge, or one or more undertakings acquire sole or joint control of another undertaking, provided that none of the parties to the concentration are engaged in business activities in the same product and geographical market, or in a product market which is upstream or downstream of a product market in which any other party to the concentration is engaged[8];

(c) two or more undertakings merge, or one or more undertakings acquire sole or joint control of another undertaking:

(i) and two or more of the parties to the concentration are engaged in business activities in the same product and geographical market (horizontal relationships); or

(ii) one or more of the parties to the concentration are engaged in business activities in a product market which is upstream or downstream of a product market in which any other party to the concentration is engaged (vertical relationships),[9] provided that their combined market share is not 15% or more for horizontal and 25% or more for vertical relationships.[10]

5. The Commission's experience in applying the Merger Regulation to date has shown that, except in exceptional circumstances, concentrations falling into the above categories do not combine market positions in a way that would give rise to competition concerns.

Safeguards and exclusions

6. In assessing whether a concentration falls into one of the above categories, the Commission will ensure that all relevant circumstances are established with sufficient clarity. Given that market definitions may be a key element in this assessment, the parties are invited to provide information on possible alternative market definitions during the pre-notification phase (see point 10). Notifying parties are responsible for describing all

---

[4] The turnover of the joint venture should be determined according to the most recent audited accounts of the parent companies, or the joint venture itself, depending upon the availability of separate accounts for the resources combined in the joint venture.

[5] The expression "and/or" refers to the variety of situations covered; for example:
— in the case of a joint acquisition of a target company, the turnover to be taken into account is the turnover of this target (the joint venture),
— in the case of the creation of a joint venture to which the parent companies contribute their activities, the turnover to be taken into account is that of the contributed activities,
— in the case of entry of a new controlling party into an existing joint venture, the turnover of the joint venture and the turnover of the activities contributed by the new parent company (if any) must be taken into account.

[6] The total value of assets of the joint venture should be determined according to the last regularly prepared and approved balance sheet of each parent company. The term "assets" includes: (1) all tangible and intangible assets that will be transferred to the joint venture (examples of tangible assets include production plants, wholesale or retail outlets, and inventory of goods; examples of intangible assets include intellectual property, goodwill, etc.), and (2) any amount of credit or any obligations of the joint venture which any parent company of the joint venture has agreed to extend or guarantee.

[7] Where the assets transferred generate turnover, then neither the value of the assets nor that of the turnover may exceed EUR 100 million.

[8] See Commission notice on the definition of relevant market for the purposes of Community competition law (OJ 1997 C372/5).

[9] See footnote 7.

[10] This means that only concentrations, which do not lead to affected markets, as defined in Section 6 III of Form CO, fall into this category. The thresholds for horizontal and vertical relationships apply to market shares both at national and at EEA levels and to any alternative product market

alternative relevant product and geographic markets on which the notified concentration could have an impact and for providing data and information relating to the definition of such markets.[11] The Commission retains the discretion to take the ultimate decision on market definition, basing its decision on an analysis of the facts of the case. Where it is difficult to define the relevant markets or to determine the parties' market shares, the Commission will not apply the simplified procedure.

7. While it can normally be assumed that concentrations falling into the above categories will not raise serious doubts as to their compatibility with the common market, there may nonetheless be certain situations, which exceptionally require a closer investigation and/or full decision. In such cases, the Commission may refrain from applying the simplified procedure.

8. The following are indicative examples of types of cases which may be excluded from the simplified procedure. Certain types of concentrations may increase the parties' market power, for instance by combining technological, financial or other resources, even if the parties to the concentration do not operate in the same market. Concentrations involving conglomerate aspects may also be unsuitable for the simplified procedure, in particular, where one or more of the parties to the concentration holds individually a market share of 25% or more in any product market in which there is no horizontal or vertical relationship between the parties. In other cases, it may not be possible to determine the parties' precise market shares. This is often the case when the parties operate in new or little developed markets. Concentrations in markets with high entry barriers, with a high degree of concentration or other known competition problems may also be unsuitable. Finally, the Commission may not apply the simplified procedure where an issue of coordination as referred to in Article 2(4) of the Merger Regulation arises.

9. If a Member State expresses substantiated concerns about the notified concentration within three weeks of receipt of the copy of the notification, or if a third party expresses substantiated concerns within the time-limit laid down for such comments, the Commission will adopt a full decision. The time-limits set out in Article 10(1) of the Merger Regulation apply. The simplified procedure will not be applied if a Member State requests the referral of a notified concentration pursuant to Article 9 of the Merger Regulation.

III. Procedural provisions

Pre-notification contacts

10. Experience has shown that the business community has found pre-notification contacts between notifying parties and the Commission beneficial.[12] In particular, such contacts allow the Commission and the notifying parties to determine the precise amount of information to be provided in a notification. Notifying parties are therefore advised to engage in pre-notification contacts, particularly where they request the Commission to waive full-form notification in accordance with Article 3(2) of Commission Regulation (EC) No 447/98[13] on the grounds that the operation to be notified will not raise competition concerns.

---

definition that may have to be considered in a given case. It is important that the underlying market definitions set out in the notification are precise enough to justify the assessment that these thresholds are not met, and that all possible alternative market definitions are mentioned (including geographic markets narrower than national).

[11] As with all other notifications, the Commission may revoke the short-form decision if it is based on incorrect information for which one of the undertakings concerned is responsible (Article 6(3)(a) of the Merger Regulation).

[12] See the ECLF Committee's best practice guidelines, reproduced on the Commission's website at: http://europa.eu.int/comm/competition/mergers/others/best_practice_gl.html

[13] OJ 1998 C61/1.

Publication of the fact of notification

11. The information to be published in the *Official Journal of the European Communities* upon receipt of a notification[14] will include: the names of the parties to the concentration, the nature of the concentration and the economic sectors involved, as well as an indication that, on the basis of the information provided by the notifying party, the concentration may qualify for a simplified procedure. Interested parties will then have the opportunity to submit observations, in particular on circumstances which might require an investigation.

Short-form decision

12. If the Commission is satisfied that the concentration qualifies for the simplified procedure, it will normally issue a short-form decision. The concentration will thus be declared compatible with the common market, within one month from the date of notification, pursuant to Article 10(1) and (6) of the Merger Regulation. However, in the period leading up to the one-month deadline, the option of reverting to a normal first phase merger procedure and thus launching investigations and/or adopting a full decision remains open to the Commission, should it judge such action appropriate in the case in question.

Publication of the short-form decision

13. The Commission will publish a notice of the fact of the decision in the *Official Journal of the European Communities* as it does for full clearance decisions. The public version of the decision will be made available on the Internet for a limited period. The short-form decision will contain the information about the notified concentration published in the Official Journal at the time of notification (names of the parties, nature of the concentration and economic sectors concerned) and a statement in the decision that the concentration is declared compatible with the common market because it falls within one or more of the categories described in the notice on simplified procedure, with the applicable category(ies) being explicitly identified.

IV. Restrictions directly related to and necessary for the implementation of the concentration

14. Unless otherwise decided by the Commission, the simplified procedure for the approval of concentrations will also apply to restrictions directly related and necessary to the implementation of the concentration. The approval of a concentration by a short-form decision will cover, pursuant to Article 6(1)(b), second subparagraph, of the Merger Regulation, restrictions which are specified by the notifying parties and which are directly related and necessary to the implementation of the concentration. It should be noted in this regard that the criteria of direct relation and necessity are objective in nature[15]; restrictions are not ancillary simply because the parties regard them as such.

---

[14] Article 4, paragraph 3, of the Merger Regulation.
[15] See Commission notice on restrictions directly related and necessary to concentrations (OJ 1990 C203/5 p. 5). This notice sets out those categories of restrictions that, on the basis of the Commission's experience of applying the Merger Regulation to date, can be considered directly related and necessary to the implementation of a concentration.

EXPLANATORY NOTE*

Commission Notice on a Simplified Procedure for Treatment of Certain Concentrations under Council Regulation (EEC) No 4064/89

On 28 June 2000, in parallel to launching the merger review, the Commission adopted the principle of a Notice, which renders merger procedures more efficient already within the present legislative framework. The text of the Notice will be adopted and published in the Official Journal in due course. The Notice will also be put on the COMP Web Site in all language versions immediately after adoption. The simplified procedure will be applied after the publication of the Notice in the Official Journal.

The Notice is based on the experience gained in the application of Merger Regulation, which has shown that certain categories of concentrations do not normally raise competition concerns and are therefore cleared.

The Commission Notice on a simplified procedure for treatment of certain concentrations under Council Regulation (EEC) No 4064/89 identifies three categories of cases, which would qualify for a short-form decision adopted by the Commission at the end of the usual one-month-review. The Notice applies to concentrations where:

- two or more undertakings acquire joint control over a joint venture, provided that the joint venture has no, or negligible, actual or foreseen activities within the EEA territory (turnover of less than 100 million euros and assets less than 100 million euros in the European Economic Area, 15 EU states plus Norway, Iceland and Liechtenstein);
- none of the parties are engaged in business activities in the same product and geographical market (horizontal relationships), or in a product market which is upstream or downstream of a product market in which any other party to the concentration is engaged (vertical relationships); and
- two or more of the parties are engaged in business activities in the same product and geographical market or upstream or downstream market, provided that their combined market share is not 15% or more for horizontal and 25% or more for vertical relationships.

The short-form decision will contain information about the parties, nature of the concentration and economic sectors concerned as well as a statement that the concentration is declared compatible with the common market because it falls within one or more of the categories contained in the Notice, with the applicable category(ies) being explicitly identified. Like in all full clearance decisions, the Commission will publish the fact of the adoption of the decision in the *Official Journal of the European Communities* and for a limited period, the decision will be made available on the COMP Web Site on the Internet.

The simplified procedure can reduce the administrative burden on notifying parties. It will still give the Member States and third parties the same possibilities to comment or intervene as under the ordinary procedure. The Commission may also, if necessary, at any time revert to the ordinary investigative procedures.*

---

* Published on the DG Competition website.

---

[1] OJ 2001 C68/3.

I. Introduction

1. Council Regulation (EEC) No 4064/89 of 21 December 1989 on the control of concentrations between undertakings,[2] as last amended by Regulation (EC) No 1310/97[3] (hereinafter referred to as "the Merger Regulation") expressly provides that the Commission may decide to declare a concentration compatible with the common market following modification by the parties.[4] Recital 8 of Council Regulation (EC) No 1310/97 states that "the Commission may declare a concentration compatible with the common market in the second phase[5] of the procedure, following commitments by the parties that are proportional to and would entirely eliminate the competition problem . . . ". Recital 8 also provides for "commitments in the first phase[6] of the procedure where the competition problem is readily identifiable and can easily be remedied. . . . Transparency and effective consultation of Member States and interested third parties should be ensured in both phases of the procedure."

2. The purpose of this notice is to provide guidance on modifications to concentrations, including, in particular, commitments to modify a concentration. Such modifications are more commonly described as "remedies" since their object is to reduce the merging parties' market power and to restore conditions for effective competition which would be distorted as a result of the merger creating or strengthening a dominant position. The guidance set out in this notice reflects the Commission's evolving experience with the assessment, acceptance and implementation of remedies under the Merger Regulation since its entry into force on 21 September 1990. The principles contained here will be applied and further developed and refined by the Commission in individual cases. The guidance provided on commitments is without prejudice to the interpretation which may be given by the Court of Justice or by the Court of First Instance of the European Communities.

3. This notice sets out the general principles applicable to remedies acceptable to the Commission, the main types of commitments that have been accepted by the Commission in cases under the Merger Regulation, the specific requirements which proposals of commitments need to fulfil in both phases of the procedure, and the main requirements for the implementation of commitments.

II. General Principles

4. Under the Merger Regulation, the Commission assesses the compatibility of a notified concentration with the common market on the basis of its effect on the structure of competition in the Community.[7] The test for compatibility under Article 2(2) and (3) of the Merger Regulation is whether or not a concentration would create or strengthen a dominant position as a result of which effective competition would be significantly

---

[2] OJ 1989 L395/1, corrected version OJ 1990 L257/13.
[3] OJ 1997 L180/1.
[4] The references to "parties" and "merging parties" also cover situations with one notifying party.
[5] Referred to hereinafter as "phase II".
[6] Referred to hereinafter as "phase I".
[7] Recital 7 of the Merger Regulation.

impeded in the common market or a substantial part of it.[8] A concentration that creates or strengthens a dominant position as described above is incompatible with the common market and the Commission is required to prohibit it.

5. Where a concentration raises competition concerns in that it could lead to the creation or strengthening of a dominant position, the parties may seek to modify the concentration in order to resolve the competition concerns raised by the Commission and thereby gain clearance of their merger. Such modifications may be offered and implemented in advance of a clearance decision. However, it is more common that the parties submit commitments with a view to rendering the concentration compatible with the common market within a specific period following clearance.

6. It is the responsibility of the Commission to show that a concentration creates or strengthens market structures which are liable to impede significantly effective competition in the common market. It is the responsibility of the parties to show that the proposed remedies, once implemented, eliminate the creation or strengthening of such a dominant position identified by the Commission. To this end, the parties are required to show clearly, to the Commission's satisfaction in accordance with its obligations under the Merger Regulation, that the remedy restores conditions of effective competition in the common market on a permanent basis.

7. In assessing whether or not a remedy will restore effective competition the Commission will consider all relevant factors relating to the remedy itself, including *inter alia* the type, scale and scope of the remedy proposed, together with the likelihood of its successful, full and timely implementation by the parties. Moreover, these factors have to be judged by reference to the structure and particular characteristics of the market in which the competition concerns arise, including of course the position of the parties and other players on the market. It follows that it is incumbent on the parties from the outset to remove any uncertainties as to any of these factors which might cause the Commission to reject the remedy proposed.

8. More generally, the Commission will take into account the fact that any remedy, so long as it remains a commitment which is not yet fulfilled, carries with it certain uncertainties as to its eventual outcome. This general factor must also be taken into consideration by the parties when presenting a remedy to the Commission.

9. In the *Gencor* case,[9] the Court of First Instance established the principle that the basic aim of commitments is to ensure competitive market structures. Accordingly, commitments that would amount merely to a promise to behave in a certain way, for example a commitment not to abuse a dominant position created or strengthened by the proposed concentration, are as such not considered suitable to render the concentration compatible with the common market. According to the Court,[10] commitments which are structural in nature, such as the commitment to sell a subsidiary, are, as a rule, preferable from the point of view of the Regulation's objective, inasmuch as such a commitment prevents the creation or strengthening of a dominant position previously identified by the Commission and does not, moreover, require medium or long-term monitoring measures. Nevertheless, the possibility cannot automatically be ruled out that other types of commitments may themselves also be capable of preventing the emergence or strengthening of a

---

[8] In the case of the creation of a joint venture, the Commission will also examine the concentration under Article 2(4) of the Merger Regulation. In this respect, the Commission examines whether or not the creation of the joint venture has as its object or effect the coordination of the competitive behaviour of undertakings that remain independent. Such coordination will be appraised in accordance with the criteria of Article 81(1) and (3) of the Treaty, with view to establishing whether or not the operation is compatible with the common market. The principles set out in this notice would normally also apply to cases dealt with under Article 2(4).

[9] Judgment of Court of First Instance of 25 March 1999 in Case T–102/96 *Gencor v. Commission* [1999] ECR II–753, at paragaph 316.

[10] Op. cit., at paragraph 319.

dominant position. However, whether such commitments can be accepted has to be determined on a case-by-case basis.

10. Once the concentration has been implemented, despite the possibility of some interim safeguards, the desired conditions of competition on the market cannot actually be restored until the commitments have been fulfilled. Therefore, commitments must be capable of being implemented effectively and within a short period. Commitments should not require additional monitoring once they have been implemented.[11]

11. The Commission may accept commitments in either phase of the procedure. However, given the fact that an in-depth market investigation is only carried out in phase II, commitments submitted to the Commission in phase I must be sufficient to clearly rule out "serious doubts" within the meaning of Article 6(1)(c) of the Merger Regulation.[12] Pursuant to Article 10(2) of the Merger Regulation, the Commission has to take a clearance decision as soon as the serious doubts established in the decision pursuant to Article 6(1)(c) of the Merger Regulation are removed as a result of commitments submitted by the parties. This rule applies in particular to commitments proposed at an early stage of phase-II proceedings.[13] After an in-depth investigation and where the Commission in a Statement of Objections has reached the preliminary view that the merger leads to the creation or strengthening of a dominant position within the meaning of Article 2(3) of the Merger Regulation, the commitments have to eliminate the creation or strengthening of such a dominant position.

12. Whilst commitments have to be offered by the parties, the Commission may ensure the enforceability of commitments by making its authorisation subject to compliance with them.[14] A distinction must be made between conditions and obligations. The requirement for achievement of each measure that gives rise to the structural change of the market is a condition—for example, that a business is to be divested. The implementing steps which are necessary to achieve this result are generally obligations on the parties, e.g. such as the appointment of a trustee with an irrevocable mandate to sell the business. Where the undertakings concerned commit a breach of an obligation, the Commission may revoke clearance decisions issued either under Article 6(2) or Article 8(2) of the Merger Regulation, acting pursuant to Article 6(3) or Article 8(5)(b), respectively. The parties may also be subject to fines and periodic penalty payments as provided in Articles 14(2)(a) and 15(2)(a) respectively of the Merger Regulation. Where, however, the situation rendering the concentration compatible with the common market does not materialise,[15] that is, where the condition is not fulfilled, the compatibility decision no longer stands. In such circumstances, the Commission may, pursuant to Article 8(4) of the Merger Regulation, order any appropriate action necessary to restore conditions of effective competition.[16] In addition, the parties may also be subject to fines as provided in Article 14(2)(c).

---

[11] Only in exceptional circumstances will the Commission consider commitments which require further monitoring: Commission Decision 97/816/EC (IV/M.877—*Boeing/McDonnell Douglas*; OJ 1997 L336/16).

[12] Commitments in phase I can only be accepted in certain types of situation. The competition problem needs to be so straightforward and the remedies so clear-cut that it is not necessary to enter into an in-depth investigation.

[13] Commission Decision of 30 March 1999 (IV/JV.15—*BT/AT&T*); Commission Decision 2000/45/EC (IV/M.1532—*BP Amoco/Arco*; OJ 2001 L18/1).

[14] If the Commission's final assessment of a case shows that there are no competition concerns or that the resolution of the concerns does not depend on a particular element of the submitted commitments, the parties, being informed, may withdraw them. If the parties do not withdraw them, the Commission may either take note of their proposals in the decision or ignore them. Where the Commission takes note of them, it will explain in its decision that they do not constitute a condition for clearance.

[15] The same principle applies where the situation that originally rendered the concentration compatible is subsequently reversed; see the last sentence of paragraph 49.

[16] These measures may also lead to periodic penalty payments as provided in Article 15(2)(b).

III. Types of Remedy Acceptable to the Commission[17]

1. Divestiture

13. Where a proposed merger threatens to create or strengthen a dominant position which would impede effective competition, the most effective way to restore effective competition, apart from prohibition, is to create the conditions for the emergence of a new competitive entity or for the strengthening of existing competitors via divestiture.

Viable business

14. The divested activities must consist of a **viable business** that, if operated by a suitable purchaser, can compete effectively with the merged entity on a lasting basis. Normally a viable business is an **existing** one that can operate on a **stand-alone-basis**, which means independently of the merging parties as regards the supply of input materials or other forms of cooperation other than during a transitory period.

15. In proposing a viable business for divestiture, the parties must take into account the uncertainties and risks related to the transfer of a business to a new owner. These risks may limit the competitive impact of the divested business, and, therefore, may lead to a market situation where the competition concerns of the Commission will not necessarily be eliminated.

Object of the divestiture

16. Where the competition problem results from horizontal overlap, the most appropriate business has to be divested.[18] This might be the business of the acquiring company in cases of a hostile bid where the notifying party's knowledge of the business to be acquired is more limited. A commitment to divest activities of the target company might, in such circumstances, increase the risk that this business might not result in a viable competitor which could effectively compete in the market on a lasting basis.

17. In determining which overlapping business should be divested, the ability of the business to be operated on a stand-alone-basis is an important consideration.[19] In order to assure a viable business, it might be necessary to include in a divestiture those activities which are related to markets where the Commission did not raise competition concerns because this would be the only possible way to create an effective competitor in the affected markets.[20]

18. Although it has been accepted in certain specific circumstances,[21] a divestiture consisting of a combination of certain assets from both the purchaser and the target may create additional risks as to the viability and efficiency of the resulting business. It will, therefore, be assessed with great care. In exceptional cases, a divestiture package including only brands and supporting production assets may be sufficient to create the conditions

---

[17] The following overview is non-exhaustive.

[18] Where the competition problem arises in vertical integration cases, divestiture may also resolve the competition concern.

[19] Commission Decision of 29 September 1999 (IV/M.1383—*Exxon/Mobil*, at paragraph 860); Commission Decision of 9 February 2000 (COMP/M.1641—*Linde/AGA*, at paragraph 94).

[20] Commission Decision 1999/229/EC (IV/M.913—*Siemens/Elektrowatt*; OJ 1999 L880, 1, at paragraph 134); Commission Decision 2000/718/EC (COMP/M.1578—*Sanitec/Sphinx*; OJ 2000 L294/1, at paragraph 255); Commission Decision of 8 March 2000 (COMP/M.1802—*Unilever/Amora Maille*); Commission Decision of 28 September 2000 (COMP/M.1990—*Unilever/Bestfoods*; OJ 2000 C311/6).

[21] Commission Decision 96/222/EC (IV/M.603—*Crown Cork & Seal/Carnaud/Metalbox*; OJ 1996 L75/38).

for effective competition.[22] In such circumstances, the Commission would have to be convinced that the buyer could integrate these assets effectively and immediately.

Suitable purchaser

19. The condition for a clearance decision by the Commission is that the viable business will have been transferred to a suitable purchaser[23] within a specific deadline. The two elements of the viable business and the suitable purchaser are thus inter-linked. The potential of a business to attract a suitable purchaser is, therefore, an important element of the Commission's assessment of the appropriateness of the proposed commitment.[24]

20. There are cases where the viability of the divestiture package depends, in view of the assets being part of the business, to a large extent on the identity of the purchaser. In such circumstances, the Commission will not clear the merger unless the parties undertake not to complete the notified operation before having entered into a binding agreement with a purchaser for the divested business (known as the "upfront buyer"), approved by the Commission.[25]

21. Once a divestiture of a business is made a condition of the clearance decision, it is a matter for the parties to find a suitable purchaser for this business. The parties may therefore add, on their own initiative, other assets to make the package more attractive to buyers.[26]

Alternative divestiture commitments

22. In certain cases, the implementation of the parties' preferred divestiture option (of a viable business solving the competition concerns) might be uncertain or difficult in view of, for instance, third parties' pre-emption rights or uncertainty as to the transferability of key contracts, intellectual property rights or employees, as the case may be. Nevertheless, the parties may consider that they would be able to divest this business within the appropriate short time period.

23. In such circumstances, the Commission cannot take the risk that, in the end, effective competition will not be restored. Accordingly, it is up to the parties to set out in the commitment an alternative proposal, which has to be at least equal if not better suited to restore effective competition, as well as a clear timetable as to how and when the other alternative will be implemented.[27]

Removal of structural links

24. Divestiture commitments may not be limited to overcoming competition problems created by horizontal overlaps. The divestiture of an existing shareholding in a joint venture may be necessary in order to sever a structural link with a major competitor.[28]

25. In other cases, a possible remedy could be the divestiture of minority shareholdings or the elimination of interlocking directorates in order to increase the incentives for competing on the market.[29]

---

[22] Commission Decision 96/435/EC (IV/M.623—*Kimberly-Clark/Scott Paper*; OJ 1996 L183/1).

[23] See para. 49 for the purchaser standards.

[24] IV/M.913—*Siemens/Elektrowatt*: cited above.

[25] Commission Decision of 13 December 2000 (COMP/M.2060—*Bosch/Rexroth*).

[26] IV/M.1532—*BP Amoco/Arco* (cited above) where the commitment was to divest the interests in certain gas pipelines and processing facilities in the North Sea, also the interests in the related gas fields were divested.

[27] Commission Decision of 8 April 1999 (COMP/M.1453—*AXA/GRE*; OJ 2000 C30/6).

[28] Commission Decision 98/455/EC (IV/M.942—*VEBA/Degussa*; OJ 1998 L201/102).

[29] Commission Decision of 9 February 2000 (COMP/M.1628—*TotalFina/Elf*); Commission Decision of 13 June 2000 (COMP/M.1673—*VEBA/VIAG*); Commission Decision of 1 September 2000 (COMP/M.1980—*Volvo/Renault*; OJ 2000 C301/23).

2. Other remedies

26. Whilst being the preferred remedy, divestiture is not the only remedy acceptable to the Commission. First, there may be situations where a divestiture of a business is impossible.[30] Secondly, competition problems can also result from specific features, such as the existence of exclusive agreements, the combination of networks ("network effects") or the combination of key patents. In such circumstances, the Commission has to determine whether or not other types of remedy may have a sufficient effect on the market to restore effective competition.

27. The change in the market structure resulting from a proposed concentration can cause existing contractual arrangements to be inimical to effective competition. This is in particular true for exclusive long-term supply and distribution agreements if such agreements limit the market potential available for competitors. Where the merged entity will have a considerable market share, the foreclosure effects resulting from **existing exclusive agreements** may contribute to the creation of a dominant position.[31] In such circumstances, the termination of existing exclusive agreements[32] may be considered appropriate to eliminate the competitive concerns if there is clearly no evidence that *de facto* exclusivity is being maintained.

28. The change in the market structure resulting from a proposed concentration can lead to major barriers or impediments to entry into the relevant market. Such barriers may arise from control over infrastructure, in particular networks, or key technology including patents, know-how or other intellectual property rights. In such circumstances, remedies may aim at facilitating market entry by ensuring that competitors will have **access to the necessary infrastructure**[33] or **key technology**.

29. Where the competition problem is created by control over key technology, a divestiture of such technology[34] is the preferable remedy as it eliminates a lasting relationship between the merged entity and its competitors. However, the Commission may accept licensing arrangements (preferably exclusive licences without any field-of-use restrictions on the licensee) as an alternative to divestiture where, for instance, a divestiture would have impeded efficient, on-going research. The Commission has pursued this approach in mergers involving for example, the pharmaceutical industry.[35]

30. Owing to the specifics of the competition problems raised by a given concentration in several markets, the parties may have to offer **remedy packages** which comprise a combination of divestiture remedies and other remedies that facilitate market entry by granting network access or access to specific content.[36] Such packages may be appropriate to remedy specific foreclosure problems arising, for instance, in concentrations in the

---

[30] IV/M.877—*Boeing/McDonnell Douglas* (cited above). The Commission's investigations revealed that no existing aircraft manufacturer was interested in acquiring Douglas Aircraft Company (DAC, the commercial aircraft division of McDonnell Douglas) from Boeing, nor was it possible to find a potential entrant to the commercial jet aircraft market who might achieve entry through the acquisition of DAC.

[31] Commission Decision 98/475/EC (IV/M.986—*AGFA Gevaert/DuPont*; OJ 1998 L211/22).

[32] Commission Decision of 28 October 1999 (IV/M.1571—*New Holland/Case*: OJ 2000 C130/11); Commission Decision of 19 April 1999 (IV/M.1467 *Rohm and Haas/Morton*; OJ 1999 C157/7).

[33] Commission Decision of 5 October 1992 (IV/M.157—*Air France/SABENA*: OJ 1992 C272/1); Commission Decision of 27 November 1992 (IV/M.259—*British Airways/TAT*; OJ 1992 C326/1); Commission Decision of 20 July 1995 (IV/M.616—*Swissair/SABENA*; OJ 1995 C200/10); Commission Decision of 13 October 1999 (IV/M.1439—*Telia/Telenor*); Commission Decision of 12 April 2000 (COMP/M.1795—*Vodafone/Mannesmann*).

[34] Commission Decision of 9 August 1999 (IV/M.1378—*Hoechst/Rhône-Poulenc*; OJ 1994 C254/5); Commission Decision of 1 December 1999 (COMP/M.1601—*Allied Signal/Honeywell*); Commission Decision of 3 May 2000 (COMP/M.1671—*Dow/UCC*).

[35] Commission Decision of 28 February 1995 (IV/M.555—*Glaxo/Wellcome*; OJ 1995 C65/3).

[36] COMP/M.1439—*Telia/Telenor*; COMP/M.1795—*Vodafone Airtouch/Mannesmann* (cited above); Commission Decision of 13 October 2000 (COMP/M.2050—*Vivendi/Canal+/Seagram*; OJ 2000 C311/3).

telecommunication and media sectors. In addition, there may be transactions affecting mainly one product market where, however, only a package including a variety of other commitments will be able to remedy the competitive concerns raised by the specific concentration on an overall basis.[37]

IV. Situations Where Remedies are Difficult, if not Impossible

31. The Commission is willing to explore solutions to the competition problems raised by a concentration, provided that these solutions are convincing and effective. There are, however, concentrations where remedies adequate to eliminate competition concerns within the common market cannot be found.[38] In such circumstances, the only possibility is prohibition.

32. Where the parties submit proposed remedies that are so extensive and complex that it is not possible for the Commission to determine with the required degree of certainty that effective competition will be restored in the market, an authorisation decision cannot be granted.[39]

V. Specific Requirements for Submission of Commitments

1. Phase I

33. Pursuant to Article 6(2) of the Merger Regulation the Commission may declare a concentration compatible with the common market, where it is confident that following modification a notified concentration no longer raises serious doubts within the meaning of paragraph 1(c). Parties can submit proposals for commitments to the Commission on an informal basis, even before notification. Where the parties submit proposals for commitments together with the notification or within three weeks from the date of receipt of the notification,[40] the deadline for the Commission's decision pursuant to Article 6(1) of the Merger Regulation is extended from one month to six weeks.

34. In order to form the basis for a decision pursuant to Article 6(2), proposals for commitments must meet the following requirements:

 (a) they shall be submitted in due time, at the latest on the last day of the three-week period;
 (b) they shall specify the commitments entered into by the parties in a sufficient degree of detail to enable a full assessment to be carried out;

---

[37] Commission Decision 97/816/EC (IV/M.877—*Boeing/McDonnell Douglas*; OJ 1997 L336/16); COMP/M.1673—*VEBA/VIAG*.

[38] Commission Decision 94/922/EC (*MSG Media Service*, OJ 1994 L364/1); Commission Decision 96/177/EC (*Nordic Satellite Distribution*, OJ 1996 L53/20); Commission Decision 96/342/EC (*RTL/Veronica/Endemol*, OJ 1996 L134/32); Commission Decision 1999/153/EC (*Bertelsmann/Kirch/Premiere*; OJ 1999 L53/1); Commission Decision 1999/154/EC (*Deutsche Telekom Beta-Research*; OJ 1999 L53/31); Commission Decision 97/610/EC (*St. Gobain/Wacker Chemie/NOM*; OJ 1997 L247/1); Commission Decision 91/619/EEC (*Aerospatiale/Alenia/De Havilland*, OJ 1991 L334/42); Commission Decision 97/26/EC (*Gencor/Lonrho*, OJ 1997 L11/30); Commission Decision 2000/276/EC (M.1524—*Airtours/First Choice*; OJ 2000 L93/1).

[39] Commission Decision of 15 March 2000 (COMP/M.1672—*Volvo/Scania*); Commission Decision of 28 June 2000 (COMP/M.1741—*WorldCom/Sprint*).

[40] Article 18(1) of Commission Regulation (EC) No 447/98 (Implementing Regulation), OJ 1998 L61/1.

(c) they shall explain how the commitments offered solve the competition concerns identified by the Commission.

At the same time as submitting the commitments, the parties need to supply a non-confidential version of the commitments, for purposes of market testing.[41]

35. Proposals submitted by the parties in accordance with these requirements will be assessed by the Commission. The Commission will consult the authorities of the Member States on the proposed commitments and, when considered appropriate, also third parties in the form of a market test. In addition, in cases involving a geographic market that is wider than the European Economic Area ("EEA") or where, for reasons related to the viability of the business, the scope of the business to be divested is wider than the EEA territory, the proposed remedies may also be discussed with non-EEA competition author-ities in the framework of the Community's bilateral cooperation agreements with these countries.

36. Where the assessment confirms that the proposed commitments remove the grounds for serious doubts, the Commission clears the merger in phase I.

37. Where the assessment shows that the commitments offered are not sufficient to remove the competitive concerns raised by the merger, the parties will be informed accordingly. Given that phase I remedies are designed to provide a straightforward answer to a readily identifiable competition concern,[42] only limited modifications can be accepted to the proposed commitments. Such modifications, presented as an immediate response to the result of the consultations, include clarifications, refinements and/or other improve-ments which ensure that the commitments are workable and effective.

38 If the parties have not removed the serious doubts, the Commission will issue an Article 6(1)(c) decision and open proceedings.

2. Phase II

39. Pursuant to Article 8(2) of the Merger Regulation, the Commission must declare a concentration compatible with the common market, where following modification a notified concentration no longer creates or strengthens a dominant position within the meaning of Article 2(3) of the Merger Regulation. Commitments proposed to the Com-mission pursuant to Article 8(2) must be submitted to the Commission within not more than three months from the day on which proceedings were initiated. An extension of this period shall only be taken into consideration on request by the parties setting forth the exceptional circumstances which, according to them, justify it. The request for extension must be received within the three-month period. An extension is only possible in case of exceptional circumstances and where in the particular case there is sufficient time to make a proper assessment of the proposal by the Commission and to allow adequate consulta-tion with Member States and third parties.[43]

40. The Commission is available to discuss suitable commitments prior to the end of the three-month period. The parties are encouraged to submit draft proposals dealing with both substantive and procedural aspects which are necessary to ensure that the commit-ments are fully workable.

41. Proposals for commitments submitted in order to form the basis for a decision pursuant to Article 8(2) must meet the following requirements:

(a) they shall be submitted in due time, at the latest on the last day of the three-month period;

---

[41] By way of a market test, customers, competitors, suppliers and other companies which might be affected or have specific expertise are requested to indicate to the Commission their reasoned opinion as to the effectiveness of the commitment.

[42] See recital 8 of Council Regulation (EC) No 1310/97 referred to in paragraph 1.

[43] M.1439—*Telia/Telenor*; and in Commission Decision 98/335/EC (M.754—*Anglo American/ Lonrho*; OJ 1998 L149/21).

(b) they shall address all competition problems raised in the Statement of Objections and not subsequently abandoned. In this respect, they must specify the substantive and implementing terms entered into by the parties in sufficient detail to enable a full assessment to be carried out;

(c) they shall explain how the commitments offered solve the competition concerns.

At the same time as submitting the commitments, the parties shall supply a non-confidential version of the commitments, for purposes of market testing.

42. Proposals submitted by the parties in accordance with these requirements will be assessed by the Commission. If the assessment confirms that the proposed commitments remove the competition concerns, following consultation with the authorities of the Member States, discussions with non-Member States authorities[44] and, when considered appropriate, with third parties in the form of a market test, a clearance decision will be submitted for Commission approval.

43. Conversely, where the assessment leads to the conclusion that the proposed commitments appear not to be sufficient to resolve the competition concerns raised by the concentration, the parties will be informed accordingly. Where the parties subsequently modify the proposed commitments, the Commission may only accept these modified commitments[45] where it can clearly determine—on the basis of its assessment of information already received in the course of the investigation, including the results of prior market testing, and without the need for any other market test—that such commitments, once implemented, resolve the competition problems identified and allow sufficient time for proper consultation of Member States.

VI. REQUIREMENTS FOR IMPLEMENTATION OF COMMITMENTS

44. Commitments are offered as a means of securing a clearance, with the implementation normally taking place after the decision. These commitments require safeguards to ensure their successful and timely implementation. These implementing provisions will form part of the commitments entered into by the parties *vis-à-vis* the Commission. They have to be considered on a case-by-case basis. This is in particular true for the fixed time periods laid down for the implementation, which should in general be as short as is feasible. Consequently, it is not possible to standardise these requirements totally.

45. The following guidance is intended to assist the parties in framing commitment proposals. The principles are based on the framework of a divestiture commitment, which, as was seen above, is the most typical commitment. However, many of the principles discussed below are equally applicable to other types of commitments.

1. Essential features of divestment commitments

46. In a typical divestment commitment, the business to be divested normally consists of a combination of tangible and intangible assets, which could take the form of a pre-existing company or group of companies, or of a business activity which was not previously incorporated in its own right. Thus the parties,[46] when submitting a divestiture commitment, have to give a precise and exhaustive definition of the intended subject of divestment (hereafter referred to as "the description of the business" or "the description"). The description has to contain all the elements of the business that are necessary for the business to act as a viable competitor in the market: tangible (such as R&D, production, distribution, sales and marketing activities) and intangible (such as intellectual

---

[44] See para. 35.
[45] COMP/M.1628—*TotalFina/Elf*, LPG, cited above, at paragraph 345.
[46] Commitments must be signed by a person duly authorised to do so.

property rights, goodwill) assets, personnel, supply and sales agreements (with appropriate guarantees about the transferability of these), customer lists, third party service agreements, technical assistance (scope, duration, cost, quality) and so forth. In order to avoid any misunderstanding about the business to be divested, assets that are used within the business but that should not, according to the parties, be divested, have to be identified separately.

47. The description has to provide for a mechanism whereby the acquirer of the business can retain and select the appropriate personnel. Such a mechanism is required both for the personnel that are currently working in the business unit as it is operated and for the personnel that provide essential functions for the business such as, for instance, group R&D and information technology staff even where such personnel are currently employed by another business unit of the parties. This mechanism is without prejudice to the application of the Council Directives on collective redundancies[47]; on safeguarding employees rights in the event of transfers of undertakings[48]; and on informing and consulting employees[49] as well as national provisions implementing those Directives.

48. The divestment has to be completed within a fixed time period agreed between the parties and the Commission, which takes account of all relevant circumstances. The package will specify what kind of agreement—binding letter of intent, final agreement, transfer of legal title—is required by what date. The deadline for the divestment should start on the day of the adoption of the Commission decision.

49. In order to ensure the effectiveness of the commitment, the sale to a proposed purchaser is subject to prior approval by the Commission. The purchaser is normally required to be a viable existing or potential competitor, independent of and unconnected to the parties, possessing the financial resources,[50] proven expertise and having the incentive to maintain and develop the divested business as an active competitive force in competition with the parties. In addition, the acquisition of the business by a particular proposed purchaser must neither be likely to create new competition problems nor give rise to a risk that the implementation of the commitment will be delayed. These conditions are hereinafter referred to as "the purchaser standards". In order to maintain the structural effect of a remedy, the merged entity cannot, even in the absence of an explicit clause in the commitments, subsequently acquire influence over the whole or parts of the divested business unless the Commission has previously found that the structure of the market has changed to such an extent that the absence of influence over the divested business is no longer necessary to render the concentration compatible with common market.

2. Interim preservation of the business to be divested—the hold-separate trustee

50. It is the parties' responsibility to reduce to the minimum any possible risk of loss of competitive potential of the business to be divested resulting from the uncertainties inherent to the transfer of a business. Pending divestment, the Commission will require the parties to offer commitments to maintain the independence, economic viability, marketability and competitiveness of the business.

---

[47] Council Directive 98/59/EC of 20 July 1998 on the approximation of the laws of the Member States relating to collective redundancies (OJ 1998 L225/16).

[48] Council Directive 77/187/EEC of 14 February 1977 on the approximation of the laws of the Member States relating to the safeguarding of employees' rights in the event of transfers of undertakings, businesses or parts of a business (OJ 1977 L61/26) as amended by Council Directive 98/50/EC (OJ 1998 L201/88).

[49] Council Directive 94/45/EC of 22 September 1994 on the establishment of a European Works Council or a procedure in Community-scale undertakings and Community-scale groups of undertakings for the purposes of informing and consulting employees (OJ 1994 L254/64), as amended by Directive 97/74/EC (OJ 1998 L10/22).

[50] The Commission does not accept seller-financed divestitures because of the impact this has on the divested company's independence.

51. These commitments will be designed to keep the business separate from the business retained by the parties, and to ensure that it is managed as a distinct and saleable business. The parties will be required to ensure that all relevant tangible and intangible assets of the divestiture package are maintained, pursuant to good business practice and in the ordinary course of business. This relates in particular to the maintenance of fixed assets, know-how or commercial information of a confidential or proprietary nature, the customer base and the technical and commercial competence of the employees. Furthermore, the parties must maintain the same conditions of competition as regards the divestiture package as those applied before the merger, so as to continue the business as it is currently conducted. This includes providing relevant administrative and management functions, sufficient capital, and a line of credit, and it may include other conditions specific to maintaining competition in an industry.

52. As the Commission cannot, on a daily basis, be directly involved in overseeing compliance with these interim preservation measures, it therefore approves the appointment of a trustee to oversee the parties' compliance with such preservation measures (a so-called "hold-separate trustee"). The hold-separate trustee will act in the best interests of the business to be divested. The commitment will set out the specific details of the trustee's mandate. The trustee's mandate, to be approved by the Commission, together with the trustee appointment, will include for example, responsibilities for supervision, which include the right to propose, and, if deemed necessary, impose, all measures which the trustee considers necessary to ensure compliance with any of the commitments, and periodic compliance reports.

3. Implementation of the commitments—the divestiture trustee

53. The commitment will also set out the specific details and procedures relating to the Commission's oversight of the implementation of the divestiture: for example, criteria for approval of the purchaser, periodic reporting requirements, and approval of the prospectus or advertising material. Here, too, it is noted that the Commission cannot, on a daily basis, be directly involved in managing the divestment. Consequently, in most cases, the Commission considers it appropriate to approve the appointment of a trustee with responsibilities for overseeing the implementation of the commitments (the "divestiture trustee").

54. The divestiture trustee's role will vary on a case-by-case basis, but will generally include supervision which includes the right to propose, and if deemed necessary, impose all measures which the trustee requires to ensure compliance with any of the commitments, and reporting at regular intervals. Where appropriate, the trustee's role will span two phases: in the first phase, he or she will be responsible for overseeing the parties' efforts to find a potential purchaser. If the parties do not succeed in finding an acceptable purchaser within the time frame set out in their commitments, then in the second phase, the trustee will be given an irrevocable mandate to dispose of the business within a specific deadline at any price, subject to the prior approval of the Commission.

4. Approval of the trustee and the trustee mandate

55. Depending on the types of commitments involved and the facts of the case, the divestiture trustee may or may not be the same person or institution as the hold-separate trustee. The trustee will normally be an investment bank, management consulting or accounting company or similar institution. The parties shall suggest the trustee (or a number of trustees) to the Commission. The trustee shall be independent of the parties, possess the necessary qualifications to carry out the job and shall not be, or become, exposed to a conflict of interests. It is the parties' responsibility to supply the Commission with adequate information for it to verify that the trustee fulfils these requirements. The Commission will review and approve the terms of the trustee's appointment, which should be irrevocable unless "good cause" is shown to the Commission for the appointment of a new trustee.

56. The parties are responsible for remuneration of each trustee for all services rendered in the execution of their responsibilities, and the remuneration structure must be such as to not impede the trustee's independence and effectiveness in fulfilling his mandate. The trustee will assume specified duties designed to ensure compliance in good faith with the commitments on behalf of the Commission, and these duties will be defined in the trustee's mandate. The mandate must include all provisions necessary to enable the trustee to fulfil its duties under the commitments accepted by the Commission. It is subject to the Commission's approval.

57. When the specific commitments with which the trustee has been entrusted have been implemented—that is to say, when legal title for the divestiture package to be divested has passed or at the end of some specific obligations which continue post-divestiture—the mandate will provide for the trustee to request the Commission for a discharge from further responsibilities. Even after the discharge has been given, the Commission has the discretion to require the reappointment of the trustee, if subsequently it appears to the Commission that the relevant commitments might not have been fully and properly implemented.

5. Approval of the purchaser and the purchase agreement

58. The parties or the trustee can only proceed with the sale if the Commission approves a proposed purchaser and the purchase agreement on the basis of the arrangements set out in the commitment. The parties or the trustee will be required to demonstrate satisfactorily to the Commission that the proposed buyer meets the requirements of the commitments, which means the purchaser's standards, and that the business is sold in a manner consistent with the commitment. The Commission will formally communicate its view to the parties. Before doing so, the Commission officials may have discussed with the proposed purchaser its incentives for competing with the merged entity on the basis of its business plans. Where different purchasers are being proposed for different parts of the package, the Commission will assess whether each individual proposed purchaser is acceptable and that the total package solves the competition problem.

59. Where the Commission determines that the acquisition of the divestiture package by the proposed purchaser, in the light of the information available to the Commission, threatens to create *prima facie* competition problems[51] or other difficulties, which may delay the timely implementation of the commitment or indicate the lack of appropriate incentives for the purchaser to compete with the merged entity, the proposed purchaser will not be considered acceptable. In this case, the Commission will formally communicate its view that the buyer does not satisfy the purchaser's standards.[52]

60. Where the purchase result in a concentration that has a Community dimension, this new operation will have to be notified under the Merger Regulation and cleared under normal procedures.[53] Where this is not the case, the Commission's approval of a purchaser is without prejudice to the jurisdiction of merger control of national authorities.

---

[51] This is most likely to arise where the market structure is already highly concentrated and where the remedy would transfer the market share to another market player.

[52] COMP/M.1628—*TotalFina/Elf*—motorway service stations.

[53] Commission Decision of 29 September 1999 (Case M.1383—*Exxon/Mobil*) and the Commission Decisions of 2 February 2000 in the follow-up cases M.1820—*BP/JV Dissolution* (not published) and M.1822—*Mobil/JV Dissolution* (OJ 2000 C112/6).

APPENDIX 46

THE EEC MERGER CONTROL (CONSEQUENTIAL PROVISIONS) REGULATIONS 1990

(S.I. 1990 No. 1563)

Made ... 27th July 1990
Coming into force ... 21st September 1990

Whereas a draft of these Regulations has been approved by resolution of each House of Parliament:

Now, therefore, the Secretary of State, being designated (S.I. 1990/1304) for the purposes of section 2(2) of the European Communities Act 1972 (1972 c. 68) in relation to measures relating to the control of concentrations between undertakings, in exercise of the powers conferred on him by the said section 2(2) and by section 75F(1) and (2) of the Fair Trading Act 1973 (1973 c. 41; sections 75A to 75F of that Act were inserted by section 146 of the Companies Act 1989 (c. 40)) hereby makes the following Regulations:

1.—(1) These Regulations may be cited as the EEC Merger Control (Consequential Provisions) Regulations 1990 and shall come into force on 21st September 1990.

(2) In these Regulations, "the Merger Control Regulation" means Council Regulation (EEC) No. 4064/89 on the control of concentrations between undertakings (O.J. 1989 No. L395/1), and expressions used in that Regulation shall bear the same meaning in these Regulations.

2. For the purpose of determining the effect of giving a merger notice and the steps which may be or are to be taken by any persons in connection with such a notice in a case in which the arrangements in question are or would result in a concentration with a Community dimension, section 75B of the Fair Trading Act 1973 is amended by omitting the word "or" at the end of paragraph (b) of subsection (7) and adding the following at the end of that subsection:

"or,
(d) it appears to him that the notified arrangements are, of if carried into effect would result in, a concentration with a Community dimension within the meaning of Council Regulation (EEC) No. 4064/89 of 21st December 1989 on the control of concentrations between undertakings."

3. A merger reference may be made under section 64 of the Fair Trading Act 1973 in a case in which the relevant enterprises ceased to be distinct enterprises at a time and in circumstances not falling within subsection (4) of that section if by reason of the Merger Control Regulation or anything done under or in accordance with it the reference could not have been made earlier than six months before the date on which it is to be made.

Explanatory Note

(This note is not part of the Regulations)

These Regulations make provision consequential upon Council Regulation (EEC) No. 4064/89 on the control of concentrations between undertakings ("the Merger Control Regulation").

Regulation 2 amends the provision of the Fair Trading Act 1973 about restriction on the power to make a merger reference where prior notice has been given (inserted by the Companies Act 1989) by providing that the Director General of Fair Trading may reject a merger notice where it appears to him that the merger is also a "concentration with a Community dimension" within the Merger Control Regulation.

Regulation 3 enables a merger reference to be made later than the time limit in section 64(4) of the Fair Trading Act 1973 if it is made within six months of the removal of any restriction on the making of the reference created by the Merger Control Regulation.

THE EEC MERGER CONTROL (DISTINCT MARKET INVESTIGATIONS) REGULATIONS 1990

(S.I. 1990 No. 1715)

Made ... 20th August 1990
Laid before Parliament ... 22nd August 1990
Coming into force ... 21st September 1990

The Secretary of State being designated (S.I. 1990/1304) for the purposes of section 2(2) of the European Communities Act 1972 (1972 c. 68) in relation to measures relating to the control of concentrations between undertakings, in exercise of the powers conferred on him by the said section 2(2) hereby makes the following Regulations:

1.—(1) These Regulations may be cited as the EEC Merger Control (Distinct Market Investigations) Regulations 1990 and shall come into force on 21st September 1990.

(2) In these Regulations, "the Merger Control Regulation" means Council Regulation (EEC) No. 4064/89 on the control of concentrations between undertakings (O.J. 1990 No. L395/1, and expressions used in that Regulation shall bear the same meaning in these Regulations.

2. At any time after the Commission has transmitted to the competent authorities of the United Kingdom a copy of the notification to the Commission of a concentration with a Community dimension, the Director General of Fair Trading ("the Director") may, for the purpose of furnishing information to the Commission under the second sentence of Article 19(2) of the Merger Control Regulation, and by notice in writing signed by him—

(a) require any person to produce, at a time and place specified in the notice, to the Director or to any person appointed by him for the purpose, any documents which are specified or described in the notice and which are documents in his custody or under his control and relating to any matter relevant to the furnishing of information as aforesaid, or

(b) require any person carrying on any business to furnish to the Director such estimates, returns or other information as may be specified or described in the notice, and specify the time, the manner and the form in which such estimates, returns or information are to be furnished;

but no person shall be compelled by virtue of this regulation to produce any documents which he could not be compelled to produce in civil proceedings before the High Court or, in Scotland, the Court of Session or, in complying with any requirement for the furnishing of information, to give any information which he could not be compelled to give in evidence in such proceedings.

3.—(1) Subsections (6) to (8) of section 85 of the Fair Trading Act 1973 (1973 c. 41) shall, subject to paragraph (2) below, apply in relation to a notice under Regulation 2 above as they apply in relation to a notice under subsection (1) of that section, but as if—

(a) the reference in subsection (6) of that section to a fine not exceeding the prescribed sum were a reference to a fine not exceeding an amount equal to level 5 on the standard scale, and

(b) in subsection (7) of that section, for the words from "any one" to "the Commission" there were substituted "the Director".

(2) In punishing a defaulter under subsection (7A) of the said section 85, the court shall not impose any penalty which could not be imposed on summary conviction for an offence created in exercise of the powers conferred by section 2(2) of the European Communities Act 1972.

4. Sections 93B (furnishing false or misleading information to the Director) and 133 (restrictions on disclosure of information) of the Fair Trading Act 1973 shall apply as if these Regulations were contained in Part V of that Act and the references in—

(a) subsection (3)(a) of the said section 93B to a fine not exceeding the statutory maximum, and

(b) subsection (5)(a) of the said section 133 to a fine not exceeding the prescribed sum were references to a fine not exceeding an amount equal to level 5 on the standard scale.

EXPLANATORY NOTE

(This note is not part of the Regulations)

These Regulations confer investigative powers (based on section 3(7) of the Competition Act 1980) upon the Director General of Fair Trading for the purpose of furnishing information to the European Commission under Council Regulation (EEC) No. 4064/89 (on the control of concentrations between undertakings) when a concentration with a Community dimension (as defined in that Regulation) may impede competition in a distinct market within the United Kingdom. The enforcement provisions of section 81(6) to (8) of the Fair Trading Act 1973 apply. Sections 93B and 133 of that Act also apply.

REGULATION 17[1]

The Council of the European Economic Community

Having regard to the Treaty establishing the European Economic Community, and in particular Article 83 thereof;

Having regard to the proposal from the Commission;

Having regard to the Opinion of the Economic and Social Committee;

Having regard to the Opinion of the European Parliament;

Whereas, in order to establish a system ensuring that competition shall not be distorted in the common market, it is necessary to provide for balanced application of Articles 81 and 82 in a uniform manner in the Member States;

Whereas in establishing the rules for applying Article 81(3) account must be taken of the need to ensure effective supervision and to simplify administration to the greatest possible extent;

Whereas it is accordingly necessary to make it obligatory, as a general principle, for undertakings which seek application of Article 81(3) to notify to the Commission their agreements, decisions and concerted practices;

Whereas, on the one hand, such agreements, decisions and concerted practices are probably very numerous and cannot therefore all be examined at the same time and, on the other hand, some of them have special features which may make them less prejudicial to the development of the common market;

Whereas there is consequently a need to make more flexible arrangements for the time being in respect of certain categories of agreement, decision and concerted practice without prejudicing their validity under Article 81;

Whereas it may be in the interest of undertakings to know whether any agreements, decisions or practices to which they are party, or propose to become party, may lead to action on the part of the Commission pursuant to Article 81(1) or Article 82;

Whereas, in order to secure uniform application of Articles 81 and 82 in the common market, rules must be made under which the Commission, acting in close and constant liaison with the competent authorities of the Member States, may take the requisite measures for applying those Articles;

Whereas for this purpose the Commission must have the co-operation of the competent authorities of the Member States and be empowered, throughout the common market, to require such information to be supplied and to undertake such investigations as are necessary to bring to light any agreement, decision or concerted practice prohibited by Article 81(1) or any abuse of a dominant position prohibited by Article 82;

Whereas, in order to carry out its duty of ensuring that the provisions of the Treaty are applied, the Commission must be empowered to address to undertakings or associations

---

[1] JO 1962, 13/204 OJ 1959–62, 87, as am. by Reg. 1216/1999, OJ 1999 L/148/5.

of undertakings recommendations and decisions for the purpose of bringing to an end infringements of Articles 81 and 82;

Whereas compliance with Articles 81 and 82 and the fulfilment of obligations imposed on undertakings and associations of undertakings under this Regulation must be enforceable by means of fines and periodic penalty payments;

Whereas undertakings concerned must be accorded the right to be heard by the Commission, third parties whose interests may be affected by a decision must be given the opportunity of submitting their comments beforehand, and it must be ensured that wide publicity is given to decisions taken;

Whereas all decisions taken by the Commission under this Regulation are subject to review by the Court of Justice under the conditions specified in the Treaty; whereas it is moreover desirable to confer upon the Court of Justice, pursuant to Article 229, unlimited jurisdiction in respect of decisions under which the Commission imposes fines or periodic penalty payments;

Whereas this Regulation may enter into force without prejudice to any other provisions that may hereafter be adopted pursuant to Article 83;

HAS ADOPTED THIS REGULATION:

Article 1

Basic provision

Without prejudice to Articles 6, 7 and 23 of this Regulation, agreements, decisions and concerted practices of the kind described in Article 81(1) of the Treaty and the abuse of a dominant position in the market, within the meaning of Article 82 of the Treaty, shall be prohibited, no prior decision to that effect being required.

Article 2

Negative clearance

Upon application by the undertakings or associations of undertakings concerned, the Commission may certify that, on the basis of the facts in its possession, there are no grounds under Article 81(1) or Article 82 of the Treaty for action on its part in respect of an agreement, decision or practice.[2]

---

[2] The Commission has published the following *Notice on procedures concerning applications for negative clearance pursuant to Article 2 of Regulation 17*, OJ 1982 C343/4:

"In publishing this notice below, it is the intention of the Commission to open the way for a more flexible administrative practice in assessing applications for negative clearance under Article 2 of Regulation No. 17/62, which empowers the Commission to certify that Article 81(1) of the EEC Treaty does not apply to an agreement. Experience has, indeed, shown that in certain cases a 'comfort letter' closing the procedure sent by the Commission's Directorate-General for Competition was an appropriate response to an application for negative clearance. However, in order to enhance the declaratory value of such a letter, and without prejudice to the possibility of terminating the procedure by a formal decision, the Commission is now publishing the essential content of such agreements pursuant to Article 19(3) of Regulation No. 17/62, so as to give interested third parties an opportunity to make known their views. In appropriate cases, it would be possible to send a comfort letter closing the procedure after publication, so as to simplify and shorten the procedure.

Cases closed by a comfort letter following publication will be brought to the attention of interested third parties by the subsequent publication of a notice in the *Official Journal of the European Communities*."

Article 3

Termination of infringements

1. Where the Commission, upon application or upon its own initiative, finds that there is infringement of Article 81 or Article 82 of the Treaty, it may by decision require the undertakings or associations of undertakings concerned to bring such infringement to an end.

2. Those entitled to make application are:

(a) Member States;

(b) natural or legal persons who claim a legitimate interest.

Without prejudice to the other provisions of this Regulation, the Commission may, before taking a decision under paragraph 1, address to the undertakings or associations of undertakings concerned recommendations for termination of the infringement.

Article 4

Notification of new agreements, decisions and practices

1. Agreements, decisions and concerted practices of the kind described in Article 81(1) of the Treaty which come into existence after the entry into force of this Regulation and in respect of which the parties seek application of Article 81(3) must be notified to the Commission. Until they have been notified, no decision in application of Article 81(3) may be taken.

2. Paragraph 1 shall not apply to agreements, decisions or concerted practices where:

(1) the only parties thereto are undertakings from one Member State and the agreements, decisions or practices do not relate either to imports or to exports between Member States;

[(2) (a) the agreements or concerted practices are entered into by two or more under-takings, each operating for the purposes of the agreement, at a different level of the production or distribution chain, and relate to the conditions under which the parties may purchase, sell or resell certain goods or services;

(b) not more than two undertakings are party thereto, and the agreements only impose restrictions on the exercise of the rights of the assignee or user of industrial property rights, in particular patents, utility models, designs or trade marks, or of the person entitled under a contract to the assignment, or grant, of the right to use a method of manufacture or knowledge relating to the use and to the application of industrial processes.]

(3) they have as their sole object:

(a) the development or uniform application of standards or types; or

(b) joint research and development;

(c) specialisation in the manufacture of products, including agreements necessary for achieving this,

— where the products which are the subject of specialisation do not, in a substantial part of the common market, represent more than 15 per cent. of the volume of business done in identical products or those considered by consumers to be similar by reason of their characteristics, price and use, and

— where the total annual turnover of the participating undertakings does not exceed 200 million units of account.

These agreements, decisions and practices may be notified to the Commission.[3]

Amendment

The revised text of para. 2(2) was inserted by Regulation 1216/1999.

Article 5

Notification of existing agreements, decisions and practices

1. Agreements, decisions and concerted practices of the kind described in Article 81(1) of the Treaty which are in existence at the date of entry into force of this Regulation and in respect of which the parties seek application of Article 81(3) shall be notified to the Commission before 1 November 1962. However, notwithstanding the foregoing provisions, any agreements, decisions and concerted practices to which not more than two undertakings are party shall be notified before 1 February 1963.

2. Paragraph 1 shall not apply to agreements, decisions or concerted practices falling within Article 4(2); these may be notified to the Commission.

Article 6

Decisions pursuant to Article 81(3)

1. Whenever the Commission takes a decision pursuant to Article 81(3) of the Treaty, it shall specify therein the date from which the decision shall take effect. Such date shall not be earlier than the date of notification.

2. The second sentence of paragraph 1 shall not apply to agreements, decisions or concerted practices falling within Article 4(2) and Article 5(2), nor to those falling within Article 5(1) which have been notified within the time limit specified in Article 5(1).

---

[3] The Commission has published the following *Notice on procedures concerning notifications pursuant to Article 4 of Regulation 17*, OJ 1983 C295/6:

"In publishing this notice, it is the intention of the Commission to open the way for a more flexible administrative practice in assessing notifications under Article 4 of Regulation 17/62 in the light of its past experience in this area. This has shown that in certain cases a provisional letter sent by the Commission's Directorate-General for Competition would be an appropriate response to a notification made for the purposes of obtaining an Article 81(3) Decision. However, in order to enhance the declaratory value of such a letter, and without prejudice to the possibility of terminating the procedure by a formal Decision, the Commission will now publish the essential content of such agreements pursuant to Article 19(3) of Regulation No. 17/62, so as to give interested third parties an opportunity to make known their views. In the light of the comments received after publication, it would then be possible, in appropriate cases, to send a provisional letter, so as to simplify and shorten the procedure. Such letters will not have the status of Decisions and will therefore not be capable of obtaining an appeal to the Court of Justice. They will state that the Directorate-General for Competition, in agreement with the undertakings concerned, does not consider it necessary to pursue the formal procedure through to the adoption of a Decision under Article 81(3) in accordance with Article 6 of Regulation No. 17/62.

A list of the cases dealt with by dispatch of provisional letters following publication will be appended to the Report on Competition Policy."

Article 7

Special provisions for existing agreements, decisions and practices

1. Where agreements, decisions and concerted practices in existence at the date of entry into force of this Regulation and notified within the time limits specified in Article 5(1) do not satisfy the requirements of Article 81(3) of the Treaty and the undertakings or associations of undertakings concerned cease to give effect to them or modify them in such manner that they no longer fall within the prohibition contained in Article 81(1) or that they satisfy the requirements of Article 81(3), the prohibition contained in Article 81(1) shall apply only for a period fixed by the Commission. A decision by the Commission pursuant to the foregoing sentence shall not apply as against undertakings and associations of undertakings which did not expressly consent to the notification.

2. Paragraph 1 shall apply to agreements, decisions and concerted practices falling within Article 4(2) which are in existence at the date of entry into force of this Regulation if they are notified before 1 January 1967.

Article 8

Duration and revocation of decisions under Article 81(3)

1. A decision in application of Article 81(3) of the Treaty shall be issued for a specified period and conditions and obligations may be attached thereto.

2. A decision may on application be renewed if the requirements of Article 81(3) of the Treaty continue to be satisfied.

3. The Commission may revoke or amend its decision or prohibit specified acts by the parties:

(a) where there has been a change in any of the facts which were basic to the making of the decision;
(b) where the parties commit a breach of any obligation attached to the decision;
(c) where the decision is based on incorrect information or was induced by deceit;
(d) where the parties abuse the exemption from the provisions of Article 81(1) of the Treaty granted to them by the decision.

In cases to which sub-paragraphs (*b*), (*c*) or (*d*) apply, the decision may be revoked with retroactive effect.

Article 9

Powers

1. Subject to review of its decision by the Court of Justice, the Commission shall have sole power to declare Article 81(1) inapplicable pursuant to Article 81(3) of the Treaty.

2. The Commission shall have power to apply Article 81(1) and Article 82 of the Treaty; this power may be exercised notwithstanding that the time limits specified in Article 5(1) and in Article 7(2) relating to notification have not expired.

3. As long as the Commission has not initiated any procedure under Articles 2, 3 or 6, the authorities of the Member States shall remain competent to apply Article 81(1) and Article 82 in accordance with Article 84 of the Treaty; they shall remain competent in this respect notwithstanding that the time limits specified in Article 5(1) and in Article 7(2) relating to notification have not expired.

Article 10

Liaison with the authorities of the Member States

1. The Commission shall forthwith transmit to the competent authorities of the Member States a copy of the application and notifications together with copies of the most important documents lodged with the Commission for the purpose of establishing the existence of infringements of Articles 81 or 82 of the Treaty or of obtaining negative clearance or a decision in application of Article 81(3).

2. The Commission shall carry out the procedure set out in paragraph 1 in close and constant liaison with the competent authorities of the Member States; such authorities shall have the right to express their views upon that procedure.

3. An Advisory Committee on Restrictive Practices and Monopolies shall be consulted prior to the taking of any decision following upon a procedure under paragraph 1, and of any decision concerning the renewal, amendment or revocation of a decision pursuant to Article 81(3) of the Treaty.

4. The Advisory Committee shall be composed of officials competent in the matter of restrictive practices and monopolies. Each Member State shall appoint an official to represent it who, if prevented from attending, may be replaced by another official.

5. The consultation shall take place at a joint meeting convened by the Commission; such meeting shall be held not earlier than 14 days after dispatch of the notice convening it. The notice shall, in respect of each case to be examined, be accompanied by a summary of the case together with an indication of the most important documents, and a preliminary draft decision.

6. The Advisory Committee may deliver an opinion notwithstanding that some of its members or their alternates are not present. A report of the outcome of the consultative proceedings shall be annexed to the draft decision. It shall not be made public.

Article 11

Request for information

1. In carrying out the duties assigned to it by Article 85 and by provisions adopted under Article 83 of the Treaty, the Commission may obtain all necessary information from the Governments and competent authorities of the Member States and from undertakings and associations of undertakings.

2. When sending a request for information to an undertaking or association of undertakings, the Commission shall at the same time forward a copy of the request to the competent authority of the Member State in whose territory the seat of the undertaking or association of undertakings is situated.

3. In its request the Commission shall state the legal basis and the purpose of the request and also the penalties provided for in Article 15(1)(*b*) for supplying incorrect information.

4. The owners of the undertakings or their representatives and, in the case of legal persons, companies or firms, or of associations having no legal personality, the persons authorised to represent them by law or by their constitution shall supply the information requested.

5. Where an undertaking or association of undertakings does not supply the information requested within the time limit fixed by the Commission, or supplies incomplete information, the Commission shall by decision require the information to be supplied. The decision shall specify what information is required, fix an appropriate time limit within which it is to be supplied and indicate the penalties provided for in Article 15(1)(*b*) and Article 16(1)(*c*) and the right to have the decision reviewed by the Court of Justice.

6. The Commission shall at the same time forward a copy of its decision to the competent authority of the Member State in whose territory the seat of the undertaking or association of undertakings is situated.

Article 12

Inquiry into sectors of the economy

1. If in any sector of the economy the trend of trade between Member States, price movements, inflexibility of prices or other circumstances suggest that in the economic sector concerned competition is being restricted or distorted within the common market, the Commission may decide to conduct a general inquiry into that economic sector and in the course thereof may request undertakings in the sector concerned to supply the information necessary for giving effect to the principles formulated in Articles 81 and 82 of the Treaty and for carrying out the duties entrusted to the Commission.

2. The Commission may in particular request every undertaking or association of undertakings in the economic sector concerned to communicate to it all agreements, decisions and concerted practices which are exempt from notification by virtue of Article 4(2) and Article 5(2).

3. When making inquiries pursuant to paragraph 2, the Commission shall also request undertakings or groups of undertakings whose size suggests that they occupy a dominant position within the common market or a substantial part thereof to supply to the Commission such particulars of the structure of the undertakings and of their behaviour as are requisite to an appraisal of their position in the light of Article 82 of the Treaty.

4. Article 10(3) to (6) and Articles 11, 13 and 14 shall apply correspondingly.

Article 13

Investigations by the authorities of the Member States

1. At the request of the Commission, the competent authorities of the Member States shall undertake the investigations which the Commission considers to be necessary under Article 14(1), or which it has ordered by decision pursuant to Article 14(3). The officials of the competent authorities of the Member States responsible for conducting these investigations shall exercise their powers upon production of an authorisation in writing issued by the competent authority of the Member State in whose territory the investigation is to be made. Such authorisation shall specify the subject matter and purpose of the investigation.

2. If so requested by the Commission or by the competent authority of the Member State in whose territory the investigation is to be made, the officials of the Commission may assist the officials of such authorities in carrying out their duties.

Article 14

Investigating powers of the Commission

1. In carrying out the duties assigned to it by Article 85 and by provisions adopted under Article 83 of the Treaty, the Commission may undertake all necessary investigations into undertakings and associations of undertakings. To this end the officials authorised by the Commission are empowered:

(a) to examine the books and other business records;
(b) to take copies of or extracts from the books and business records;
(c) to ask for oral explanations on the spot;

(d) to enter any premises land and means of transport of undertakings,

2. The officials of the Commission authorised for the purpose of these investigations shall exercise their powers upon production of an authorisation in writing specifying the subject matter and purpose of the investigation and the penalties provided for in Article 15(1)(c) in cases where production of the required books or other business records is incomplete. In good time before the investigation, the Commission shall inform the competent authority of the Member State in whose territory the same is to be made of the investigation and of the identity of the authorised officials.[4]

3. Undertakings and associations of undertakings shall submit to investigations ordered by decision of the Commission. The decision shall specify the subject matter and purpose

---

[4] *Explanatory note to authorization to investigate under Article 14(2) of Regulation No. 17/62* (Thirteenth Report on Competition Policy pp. 270–272).

"This note is for information only and is without prejudice to any formal interpretation of the Commission's powers of enquiry.

1. The officials of the Commission authorised for the purpose of carrying out an investigation under Article 14(2) of Regulation No. 17 exercise their powers upon production of an authorisation in writing. They prove their identity by means of their staff card.

2. Before starting the investigation the Commission officials shall, at the undertaking's request, provide explanations on the subject matter and purpose of the proposed investigation and also on procedural matters, particularly confidentiality. These explanations cannot modify the authorisation and may not compromise the purpose of, nor unduly delay, the investigation.

3. The authorisation, not being in execution of a Commission decision under Article 14(3), does not oblige the undertaking to submit to the investigation. The undertaking may accordingly refuse the investigation. The Commission officials shall minute this refusal, no particular form being required. The undertaking shall receive a copy of the minute if it so wishes.

4. Where the undertaking is prepared to submit to the investigation, the Commission officials are empowered, pursuant to Article 14(1) of Regulation No. 17:

(a) to examine the books and other business records;
(b) to take copies of or extracts from the books and business records;
(c) to ask for oral explanations on the spot;
(d) to enter any premises, land and means of transport of undertakings.

5. Officials of the competent authority of the Member State in whose territory the investigation is made are entitled to be present at the investigation to assist the officials of the Commission in carrying out their duties. They shall prove their identity in accordance with the relevant national rules.

6. The undertaking may consult a legal adviser during the investigation. However, the presence of a lawyer is not a legal condition for the validity of the investigation, nor must it unduly delay or impede it. Any delay pending a lawyer's arrival must be kept to the strict minimum, and shall be allowed only where the management of the undertaking simultaneously undertakes to ensure that the business records will remain in the place and state they were in when the Commission officials arrived. The officials' acceptance of delay is also conditional upon their not being hindered from entering into and remaining in occupation of offices of their choice. If the undertaking has an in-house legal service, Commission officials are instructed not to delay the investigation by awaiting the arrival of an external legal adviser.

7. Where the undertaking gives oral explanations on the spot on the subject matter of the investigation at the request of the Commission officials, the explanations may be minuted at the request of the undertaking or of the Commission officials. The undertaking shall receive a copy of the minute if it so wishes.

8. The Commission officials are entitled to take copies of or extracts from books and business records. The undertaking may request a signed inventory of the copies and extracts taken by the Commission officials during the investigation. Where the undertaking makes available photocopies of documents at the request of the Commission officials, the Commission shall, at the request of the undertaking, reimburse the cost of the photocopies.

9. In addition to the documents requested by the Commission officials, the undertaking is entitled to draw attention to other documents or information where it considers this necessary for the purpose of protecting its legitimate interest in a complete and objective clarification of the matters raised provided that the investigation is not thereby unduly delayed."

of the investigation, appoint the date on which it is to begin and indicate the penalties provided for in Article 15(1)(c) and Article 16(1)(d) and the right to have the decision reviewed by the Court of Justice.[5]

4. The Commission shall take decisions referred to in paragraph 3 after consultation with the competent authority of the Member State in whose territory the investigation is to be made.

5. Officials of the competent authority of the Member State in whose territory the investigation is to be made may, at the request of such authority or of the Commission, assist the officials of the Commission in carrying out their duties.

6. Where an undertaking opposes an investigation ordered pursuant to this Article, the Member State concerned shall afford the necessary assistance to the officials authorised by the Commission to enable them to make their investigation. Member States shall, after

---

[5] *Explanatory note to authorisation to investigate in execution of a Commission decision under Article 14(3) of Regulation No. 17/62* (Thirteenth Report on Competition Policy pp. 270–272).

"This note is for information only and is without prejudice to any formal interpretation of the Commission's powers of enquiry.

1. Enterprises are legally obliged to submit to an investigation ordered by decision of the Commission under Article 14(3) of Regulation No. 17. Written authorisations serve to name the officials charged with the execution of the decision. They prove their identity by means of their staff card.

2. Officials cannot be required to enlarge upon the subject matter as set out in the decision or to justify in any way the taking of the decision. They may however explain procedural matters, particularly confidentiality, and the possible consequences of a refusal to submit.

3. A certified copy of the decision is to be handed to the undertaking. The minute of notification of service serves only to certify delivery and its signature by the receipient does not imply submission.

4. The Commission officials are empowered, pursuant to Article 14(1) of Regulation No. 17:

(a) to examine the books and other business records;
(b) to take copies of or extracts from the books and business records;
(c) to ask for oral explanations on the spot;
(d) to enter any premises, land and means of transport of undertakings.

5. Officials of the competent authority of the Member State in whose territory the investigation is made are entitled to be present at the investigation to assist the officials of the Commission in carrying out their duties. They shall prove their identity in accordance with the relevant national rules.

6. The undertaking may consult a legal adviser during the investigation. However, the presence of a lawyer is not a legal condition for the validity of the investigation, nor must it unduly delay or impede it. Any delay pending a lawyer's arrival must be kept to the strict minimum, and shall be allowed only where the management of the undertaking simultaneously undertakes to ensure that the business records will remain in the place and state they were in when the Commission officials arrived. The officials' acceptance of delay is also conditional upon their not being hindered from entering into and remaining in occupation of offices of their choice. If the undertaking has an in-house legal service, Commission officials are instructed not to delay the investigation by awaiting the arrival of an external legal adviser.

7. Where the undertaking gives oral explanations on the spot on the subject matter of the investigation at the request of the Commission officials, the explanations may be minuted at the request of the undertaking or of the Commission officials. The undertaking shall receive a copy of the minute if it so wishes.

8. The Commission officials are entitled to take copies of or extracts from books and business records. The undertaking may request a signed inventory of the copies and extracts taken by the Commission officials during the investigation. Where the undertaking makes available photocopies of documents at the request of the Commission officials, the Commission shall, at the request of the undertaking, reimburse the cost of the photocopies.

9. In addition to the documents requested by the Commission officials, the undertaking is entitled to draw attention to other documents or information where it considers this necessary for the purpose of protecting its legitimate interest in a complete and objective clarification of the matters raised provided that the investigation is not thereby unduly delayed."

consultation with the Commission, take the necessary measures to this end before 1 October 1962.

Article 15

Fines

1. The Commission may by decision impose on undertakings or associations of undertakings fines of from 100 to 5,000 units of account where, intentionally or negligently:

(a) they supply incorrect or misleading information in an application pursuant to Article 2 or in a notification pursuant to Articles 4 or 5; or
(b) they supply incorrect information in response to a request made pursuant to Article 11(3) or (5) or to Article 12, or do not supply information within the time limit fixed by a decision taken under Article 11(5); or
(c) they produce the required books or other business records in incomplete form during investigations under Articles 13 or 14, or refuse to submit to an investigation ordered by decision issued in implementation of Article 14(3).

2. The Commission may by decision impose on undertakings or associations of undertakings fines from 1,000 to 1,000,000 units of account, or a sum in excess thereof but not exceeding 10 per cent. of the turnover in the preceding business year of each of the undertakings participating in the infringement where, either intentionally or negligently:

(a) they infringe Article 81(1) or Article 82 of the Treaty; or
(b) they commit a breach of any obligation imposed pursuant to Article 8(1).

In fixing the amount of the fine, regard shall be had both to the gravity and to the duration of the infringement.

3. Article 10(3) to (6) shall apply.

4. Decisions taken pursuant to paragraphs 1 and 2 shall not be of a criminal law nature.

5. The fines provided for in paragraph 2(*a*) shall not be imposed in respect of acts taking place:

(a) after notification to the Commission and before its decision in application of Article 81(3) of the Treaty, provided they fall within the limits of the activity described in the notification;
(b) before notification and in the course of agreements, decisions or concerted practices in existence at the date of entry into force of this Regulation, provided that notification was effected within the time limits specified in Article 5(1) and Article 7(2).

6. Paragraph 5 shall not have effect where the Commission has informed the undertakings concerned that after preliminary examination it is of opinion that Article 81(1) of the Treaty applies and that application of Article 81(3) is not justified.

Article 16

Periodic penalty payments

1. The Commission may by decision impose on undertakings or associations of undertakings periodic penalty payments of from 50 to 1,000 units of account per day, calculated from the date appointed by the decision, in order to compel them:

(a) to put an end to an infringement of Articles 81 or 82 of the Treaty, in accordance with a decision taken pursuant to Article 3 of this Regulation;
(b) to refrain from any act prohibited under Article 8(3);
(c) to supply complete and correct information which it has requested by decision taken pursuant to Article 11(5);
(d) to submit to an investigation which it has ordered by decision taken pursuant to Article 14(3).

2. Where the undertakings or associations or undertakings have satisfied the obligation which it was the purpose of the periodic penalty payment to enforce, the Commission may fix the total amount of the periodic penalty payment at a lower figure than that which would arise under the original decision.

3. Article 10(3) to (6) shall apply.

Article 17

Review by the Court of Justice

The Court of Justice shall have unlimited jurisdiction within the meaning of Article 229 of the Treaty to review decisions whereby the Commission has fixed a fine or periodic penalty payment; it may cancel, reduce or increase the fine or periodic penalty payment imposed.

Article 18

Unit of account

For the purposes of applying Articles 15 to 17 the unit of account shall be that adopted in drawing up the budget of the Community in accordance with Articles 277 and 279 of the Treaty.

Article 19

Hearing of the parties and of third persons

1. Before taking decisions as provided for in Articles 2, 3, 6, 7, 8, 15 and 16, the Commission shall give the undertaking or associations of undertakings concerned the opportunity of being heard on the matters to which the Commission has taken objection.

2. If the Commission or the competent authorities of the Member States consider it necessary, they may also hear other natural or legal persons. Applications to be heard on the part of such persons shall, where they show a sufficient interest, be granted.

3. Where the Commission intends to give negative clearance pursuant to Article 2 or take a decision in application of Article 81(3) of the Treaty, it shall publish a summary of the relevant application or notification and invite all interested third parties to submit their observations within a time limit which it shall fix being not less than one month. Publication shall have regard to the legitimate interest of undertakings in the protection of their business secrets.

Article 20

Professional secrecy

1. Information acquired as a result of the application of Articles 11, 12, 13 and 14 shall be used only for the purpose of the relevant request or investigation.

2. Without prejudice to the provisions of Articles 19 and 21, the Commission and the competent authorities of the Member States, their officials and other servants shall not disclose information acquired by them as a result of the application of this Regulation and of the kind covered by the obligation of professional secrecy.

3. The provisions of paragraphs 1 and 2 shall not prevent publication of general information or surveys which do not contain information relating to particular undertakings or associations of undertakings.

Article 21

Publication of decisions

1. The Commission shall publish the decisions which it takes pursuant to Articles 2, 3, 6, 7 and 8.

2. The publication shall state the names of the parties and the main content of the decision; it shall have regard to the legitimate interest of undertakings in the protection of their business secrets.

Article 22

Special provisions

1. The Commission shall submit to the Council proposals for making certain categories of agreement, decision and concerted practice falling within Article 4(2) or Article 5(2) compulsorily notifiable under Article 4 or 5.

2. Within one year from the date of entry into force of this Regulation, the Council shall examine, on a proposal from the Commission, what special provisions might be made for exempting from the provisions of this Regulation agreements, decisions and concerted practices falling within Article 4(2) or Article 5(2).

Article 23

Transitional provisions applicable to decisions of authorities of the Member States

1. Agreements, decisions and concerted practices of the kind described in Article 81(1) of the Treaty to which, before the entry into force of this Regulation, the competent authority of a Member State has declared Article 81(1) to be inapplicable pursuant to Article 81(3) shall not be subject to compulsory notification under Article 5. The decision of the competent authority of the Member State shall be deemed to be a decision within the meaning of Article 6; it shall cease to be valid upon expiration of the period fixed by such authority but in any event not more than three years after the entry into force of this Regulation. Article 8(3) shall apply.

2. Application for renewal of decisions of the kind described in paragraph 1 shall be decided upon by the Commission in accordance with Article 8(2).

Article 24

Implementing provisions

The Commission shall have power to adopt implementing provisions concerning the form, content and other details of applications pursuant to Article 2 and 3 and of notifications pursuant to Articles 4 and 5, and concerning hearings pursuant to Article 19(1) and (2).

[Article 25

1. As regards agreements, decisions and concerted practices to which Article 81 of the Treaty applies by virtue of accession, the date of accession shall be substituted for the date of entry into force of this Regulation in every place where reference is made in this Regulation to this latter date.

2. Agreements, decisions and concerted practices existing at the date of accession to which Article 81 of the Treaty applies by virtue of accession shall be notified pursuant to Article 8(1) or Article 7(1) and (2) within six months from the date of accession.

3. Fines under Article 15(2)(*a*) shall not be imposed in respect of any act prior to notification of the agreements, decisions and practices to which paragraph 2 applies and which have been notified within the period therein specified.

4. New Member States shall take the measures referred to in Article 14(6) within six months from the date of accession after consulting the Commission.

[5. The provisions of paragraphs 1 to 4 above shall apply in the same way in the case of the accession of the Hellenic Republic, the Kingdom of Spain and of the Portuguese Republic.]]

[6. The provisions of paragraphs 1 to 4 shall apply in the same way in the case of the accession of Austria. Finland and Sweden. However, they do not apply to agreements, decisions and concerted practices which at the date of the accession already fall under Article 53 of the EEA Agreement.]

This regulation shall be binding in its entirety and directly applicable in all Member States.

Done at Brussels, 6 February 1962.

Amendments

Article 25 was added by the Act of 1972 concerning the conditions of Accession and the Adjustments to the Treaty, Annex I.

Para. 5 was added by the 1979 Act of the Hellenic Republic, Annex I(V)(1) and subsequently replaced by the 1985 Act of Accession of the Kingdom of Spain and the Portuguese Republic, Annex I(IV)(5).

Para. 6 was added by the 1994 Act of Accession of the Republic of Austria, the Republic of Finland and the Kingdom of Sweden, as amended by Council Decision 95/1, Article 39.

Note: In the publication of the amendments in the *Official Journal* (English edition), the word "still" appears in the first line of paragraphs (5) and (6). That appears to be a mistranscription that does not correspond to the foreign language versions; in the text above the word "shall" has accordingly been substituted.

APPENDIX 49

REGULATION 3385/94[1]

On the Form, Content and Other Details of Applications and Notifications Provided for in Council Regulation No. 17

THE COMMISSION OF THE EUROPEAN COMMUNITIES,

Having regard to the Treaty establishing the European Community,

Having regard to the Agreement on the European Economic Area,

Having regard to Council Regulation No. 17 of 6 February 1962, First Regulation implementing Articles 81 and 82 of the Treaty,[2] as last amended by the Act of Accession of Spain and Portugal, and in particular Article 24 thereof,

Whereas Commission Regulation No. 27 of 3 May 1962, First Regulation implementing Council Regulation No. 17,[3] as last amended by Regulation (EC) No. 3666/93,[4] no longer meets the requirements of efficient administrative procedure; whereas it should therefore be replaced by a new regulation;

Whereas, on the one hand, applications for negative clearance under Article 2 and notifications under Articles 4, 5 and 25 of Regulation No. 17 have important legal consequences, which are favourable to the parties to an agreement, a decision or a practice, while, on the other hand, incorrect or misleading information in such applications or notifications may lead to the imposition of fines and may also entail civil law disadvantages for the parties; whereas it is therefore necessary in the interests of legal certainty to define precisely the persons entitled to submit applications and notifications, the subject matter and content of the information which such applications and notifications must contain, and the time when they become effective;

Whereas each of the parties should have the right to submit the application or the notification to the Commission; whereas, furthermore, a party exercising the right should inform the other parties in order to enable them to protect their interests; whereas applications and notifications relating to agreements, decisions or practices of associations of undertakings should be submitted only by such association;

Whereas it is for the applicants and the notifying parties to make full and honest disclosure to the Commission of the facts and circumstances which are relevant for coming to a decision on the agreements, decisions or practices concerned;

Whereas, in order to simplify and expedite their examination, it is desirable to prescribe that a form be used for applications for negative clearance relating to Article 81(1) and for notifications relating to Article 81(3); whereas the use of this form should also be possible in the case of applications for negative clearance relating to Article 82;

Whereas the Commission, in appropriate cases, will give the parties, if they so request, an opportunity before the application or the notification to discuss the intended agreement, decision or practice informally and in strict confidence; whereas, in addition, it will, after

---

[1] OJ 1994 L377/1.
[2] OJ No. 13, 21.2.1962, p. 204/62.
[3] OJ No. 35, 10.5.1962, p. 1118/62.
[4] OJ No. L336, 31.12.1993, p. 1.

the application or notification, maintain close contact with the parties to the extent necessary to discuss with them any practical or legal problems which it discovers on a first examination of the case and if possible to remove such problems by mutual agreement;

Whereas the provisions of this Regulation must also cover cases in which applications for negative clearance relating to Article 53(1) or Article 54 of the EEA Agreement, or notifications, relating to Article 53(3) of the EEA Agreement are submitted to the Commission,

HAS ADOPTED THIS REGULATION:

Article 1

Persons entitled to submit applications and notifications

1. The following may submit an application under Article 2 of Regulation No. 17 relating to Article 81(1) of the Treaty or a notification under Articles 4, 5 and 25 of Regulation No. 17:

(a) any undertaking and any association of undertakings being a party to agreements or to concerted practices; and
(b) any association of undertakings adopting decisions or engaging in practices;

which may fall within the scope of Article 81(1).

Where the application or notification is submitted by some, but not all, of the parties, referred to in point (a) of the first subparagraph, they shall give notice to the other parties.

2. Any undertaking which may hold, alone or with other undertakings, a dominant position within the common market or in a substantial part of it, may submit an application under Article 2 of Regulation No. 17 relating to Article 82 of the Treaty.

3. Where the application or notification is signed by representatives of persons, undertakings or associations of undertakings, such representatives shall produce written proof that they are authorized to act.

4. Where a joint application or notification is made, a joint representative should be appointed who is authorized to transmit and receive documents on behalf of all the applicants or notifying parties.

Article 2

Submission of applications and notifications

1. Applications under Article 2 of Regulation No. 17 relating to Article 81(1) of the Treaty and notifications under Articles 4, 5 and 25 of Regulation No. 17 shall be submitted in the manner prescribed by form A/B as shown in the Annex to this Regulation. Form A/B may also be used for applications under Article 2 of Regulation No. 17 relating to Article 82 of the Treaty. Joint applications and joint notifications shall be submitted on a single form.

2. Seventeen copies of each application and notification and three copies of the Annexes thereto shall be submitted to the Commission at the address indicated in Form A/B.

3. The documents annexed to the application or notification shall be either originals or copies of the originals; in the latter case the applicant or notifying party shall confirm that they are true copies of the originals and complete.

4. Applications and notifications shall be in one of the official languages of the Community. This language shall also be the language of the proceeding for the applicant

or notifying party. Documents shall be submitted in their original language. Where the original language is not one of the official languages, a translation into the language of the proceeding shall be attached.

5. Where applications for negative clearance relating to Article 53(1) or Article 54 of the EEA Agreement or notifications relating to Article 53(3) of the EEA Agreement are submitted, they may also be in one of the official languages of the EFTA States or the working language of the EFTA Surveillance Authority. If the language chosen for the application or notification is not an official language of the Community, the applicant or notifying party shall supplement all documentation with a translation into an official language of the Community. The language which is chosen for the translation shall be the language of the proceeding for the applicant or notifying party.

Article 3

Content of applications and notifications

1. Applications and notifications shall contain the information, including documents, required by Form A/B. The information must be correct and complete.

2. Applications under Article 2 of Regulation No. 17 relating to Article 82 of the Treaty shall contain a full statement of the facts, specifying, in particular, the practice concerned and the position of the undertaking or undertakings within the common market or a substantial part thereof in regard to the products or services to which the practice relates.

3. The Community may dispense with the obligation to provide any particular information, including documents, required by Form A/B where the Commission considers that such information is not necessary for the examination of the case.

4. The Commission shall, without delay, acknowledge in writing to the applicant or notifying party receipt of the application or notification, and of any reply to a letter sent by the Commission pursuant to Article 4(2).

Article 4

Effective date of submission of applications and notifications

1. Without prejudice to paragraphs 2 to 5, applications and notifications shall become effective on the date on which they are received by the Commission. Where, however, the application or notification is sent by registered post, it shall become effective on the date shown on the postmark of the place of posting.

2. Where the Commission finds that the information, including documents, contained in the application or notification is incomplete in a material respect, it shall, without delay, inform the applicant or notifying party in writing of this fact and shall fix an appropriate time limit for the completion of the information. In such cases, the application or notification shall become effective on the date on which the complete information is received by the Commission.

3. Material changes in the facts contained in the application or notification which the applicant or notifying party knows or ought to know must be communicated to the Commission voluntarily and without delay.

4. Incorrect or misleading information shall be considered to be incomplete information.

5. Where, at the expiry of a period of one month following the date on which the application or notification has been received, the Commission has not provided the applicant or notifying party with the information referred to in paragraph 2, the application or notification shall be deemed to have become effective on the date of its receipt by the Commission.

Article 5

Repeal

Regulation No. 27 is repealed.

Article 6

Entry into force

This Regulation shall enter into force on 1 March 1995.

This Regulation shall be binding in its entirety and directly applicable in all Member States.

Done at Brussels, 21 December 1994.

FORM A/B

INTRODUCTION

Form A/B, as its Annex, is an integral part of the Commission Regulation (EC) No. 3385/94 of 21 December 1994 on the form, content and other details of applications and notifications provided for in Council Regulation No. 17 (hereinafter referred to as "the Regulation"). It allows undertakings and associations of undertakings to apply to the Commission for negative clearance agreements or practices which may fall within the prohibitions of Article 81(1) and Article 82 of the EC Treaty, or within Articles 53(1) and 54 of the EEA Agreement or to notify such agreement and apply to have it exempted from the prohibition set out in Article 81(1) by virtue of the provisions of Article 81(3) of the EC Treaty or from the prohibition of Article 53(1) by virtue of the provisions of Article 53(3) of the EEA Agreement.

To facilitate the use of the Form A/B the following pages set out:

— in which situations it is necessary to make an application or a notification (Point A),
— to which authority (the Commission or the EFTA Surveillance Authority) the application or notification should be made (Point B),
— for which purposes the application or notification can be used (Point C),
— what information must be given in the application or notification (Points D, E and F),
— who can make an application or notification (Point G),
— how to make an application or notification (Point H),
— how the business secrets of the undertakings can be protected (Point I),
— how certain technical terms used in the operational part of the Form A/B should be interpreted (Point J), and
— the subsequent procedure after the application or notification has been made (Point K).

A. In which situations is it necessary to make an application or a notification?

I. Purpose of the competition rules of the EC Treaty and the EEA Agreement

1. Purpose of the EC Competition Rules

The purpose of the competition rules is to prevent the distortion of competition in the common market by restrictive practices or the abuse of dominant positions. They apply to any enterprise trading directly or indirectly in the common market, wherever established.

Article 81(1) of the EC Treaty (the text of Articles 81 and 82 is reproduced in Annex I to this form) prohibits restrictive agreements, decisions or concerted practices (arrangements) which may affect trade between Member States, and Article 81(2) declares agreements and decisions containing such restrictions void (although the Court of Justice has held that if restrictive terms of agreements are severable, only those terms are void); Article 81(3), however, provides for exemption of arrangements with beneficial effects, if its conditions are met. Article 82 prohibits the abuse of a dominant position which may affect trade between Member States. The original procedures for implementing these Articles, which provide for "negative clearance" and exemption pursuant to Article 81(3), were laid down in Regulation No. 17.

2. Purpose of the EEA competition rules

The competition rules of the Agreement on the European Economic Area (concluded between the Community, the Member States and the EFTA States[5]) are based on the same principles as those contained in the Community competition rules and have the same purpose, i.e. to prevent the distortion of competition in the EEA territory by cartels or the abuse of dominant position. They apply to any enterprise trading directly or indirectly in the EEA territory, wherever established.

Article 53(1) of the EEA Agreement (the text of Articles 53, 54 and 56 of the EEA Agreement is reproduced in Annex I) prohibits restrictive agreements, decisions or concerted practices (arrangements) which may affect trade between the Community and one or more EFTA States (or between EFTA States), and Article 53(2) declares agreements or decisions containing such restrictions void; Article 53(3), however, provides for exemption of arrangements with beneficial effects, if its conditions are met. Article 54 prohibits the abuse of a dominant position which may affect trade between the Community and one or more EFTA States (or between EFTA States). The procedures for implementing these Articles, which provide for "negative clearance" and exemption pursuant to Article 53(3), are laid down in Regulation No. 17, supplemented for EEA purposes, by Protocols 21, 22 and 23 to the EEA Agreement.[6]

II. The scope of the competition rules of the EC Treaty and the EEA Agreement

The applicability of Articles 81 and 82 of the EC Treaty and Articles 53 and 54 of the EEA Agreement depends on the circumstances of each individual case. It presupposes that the arrangement or behaviour satisfies all the conditions set out in the relevant provisions. This question must consequently be examined before any application for negative clearance or any notification is made.

1. Negative clearance

The negative clearance procedure allows undertakings to ascertain whether the Commission considers that their arrangement or their behaviour is or is not prohibited by Article 81(1), or Article 82 of the EC Treaty or by Article 53(1) or Article 54 of the EEA Agreement. This procedure is governed by Article 2 of Regulation No. 17. The negative clearance takes the form of a decision by which the Commission certifies that, on the basis of the facts in its possession, there are no grounds pursuant to Article 81(1) or Article 82

---

[5] See list of Member States and EFTA States in Annex III.
[6] Reproduced in Annex I.

of the EC Treaty or under Article 53(1) or Article 54 of the EEA Agreement for action on its part in respect of the arrangement or behaviour.

There is, however, no point in making an application when the arrangements or the behaviour are manifestly not prohibited by the abovementioned provisions. Nor is the Commission obliged to give negative clearance. Article 2 of Regulation No. 17 states that " . . . the Commission may certify . . . ". The Commission issues negative clearance decisions only where an important problem of interpretation has to be solved. In the other cases it reacts to the application by sending a comfort letter.

The Commission has published several notices relating the interpretation of Article 81(1) of the EC Treaty. They define certain categories of agreements which, by their nature or because of their minor importance, are not caught by the prohibition.[7]

2. Exemption

The procedure for exemption pursuant to Article 81(3) of the EC Treaty and Article 53(3) of the EEA Agreement allows companies to enter into arrangements which, in fact, offer economic advantages but which, without exemption, would be prohibited by Article 81(1) of the EC Treaty or by Article 53(1) of the EEA Agreement. This procedure is governed by Articles 4, 6 and 8 and, for the new Member States, also by Articles 5, 7 and 25 of Regulation No. 17. The exemption takes the form of a decision by the Commission declaring Article 81(1) of the EC Treaty or Article 53(1) of the EEA Agreement to be inapplicable to the arrangements described in the decision. Article 8 requires the Commissioner to specify the period of validity of any such decision, allows the Commission to attach conditions and obligations and provides for decisions to be amended or revoked or specified acts by the parties to be prohibited in certain circumstances, notably if the decisions were based on incorrect information or if there is any material change in the facts.

The Commission has adopted a number of regulations granting exemptions to categories of agreements.[8] Some of these regulations provide that some agreements may benefit from exemption only if they are notified to the Commission pursuant to Article 4 or 5 of Regulation No. 17 with a view to obtaining exemption, and the benefit of the opposition procedure is claimed in the notification.

A decision granting exemption may have retroactive effect, but, with certain exceptions, cannot be made effective earlier than the date of notification (Article 6 of Regulation No. 17). Should the Commission find that notified arrangements are indeed prohibited and cannot be exempted and, therefore, take a decision condemning them, the participants are nevertheless protected, between the date of the notification and the date of the decision, against fines for any infringement described in the notification (Article 3 and Article 15(5) and (6) of Regulation No. 17).

Normally the Commission issues exemption decisions only in cases of particular legal, economic or political importance. In the other cases it terminates the procedure by sending a comfort letter.

B. To which authority should application or notification be made?

The applications and notifications must be made to the authority which has competence for the matter. The Commission is responsible for the application of the competition rules of the EC Treaty. However there is shared competence in relation to the application of the competition rules of the EEA Agreement.

The competence of the Commission and of the EFTA Surveillance Authority to apply the EEA competition rules follows from Article 56 of the EEA Agreement. Applications and notifications relating to agreements, decisions or concerted practices liable to affect

---

[7] See Annex II.
[8] See Annex II.

trade between Member States should be addressed to the Commission unless their effects on trade between Member States or on competition within the Community are not appreciable within the meaning of the Commission notice of 1986 on agreements of minor importance.[9] Furthermore, all restrictive agreements, decisions or concerted practices affecting trade between one Member State and one or more EFTA States fall within the competence of the Commission, provided that the undertakings concerned achieve more than 67 per cent of their combined EEA-wide turnover within the Community.[10] However, if the effects of such agreements, decisions or concerted practices on trade between Member States or on competition within the Community are not appreciable, the notification should, where necessary, be addressed to the EFTA Surveillance Authority. All other agreements, decisions and concerted practices falling under Article 53 of the EEA Agreement should be notified to the EFTA Surveillance Authority (the address of which is given in Annex III).

Applications for negative clearance regarding Article 54 of the EEA Agreement should be lodged with the Commission if the dominant position exists only in the Community, or with the EFTA Surveillance Authority, if the dominant position exists only in the whole of the territory of the EFTA States, or a substantial part of it. Only where the dominant position exists within both territories should the rules outlined above with respect to Article 53 be applied.

The Commission will apply, as a basis for appraisal, the competition rules of the EC Treaty. Where the case falls under the EEA Agreement and is attributed to the Commission pursuant to Article 56 of that Agreement, it will simultaneously apply the EEA rules.

C. The purpose of this form

Form A/B lists the questions that must be answered and the information and documents that must be provided when applying for the following:

— a negative clearance with regard to Article 81(1) of the EC Treaty and/or Article 53(1) of the EEA Agreement, pursuant to Article 2 of Regulation No. 17, with respect to agreements between undertakings, decisions by associations of undertakings and concerted practices,
— an exemption pursuant to Article 81(3) of the EC Treaty and/or Article 53(3) of the EEA Agreement with respect to agreements between undertakings, decisions by associations of undertakings and concerted practices,
— the benefit of the opposition procedure contained in certain Commission regulations granting exemption by category.

This form allows undertakings applying for negative clearance to notify, at the same time, in order to obtain an exemption in the event that the Commission reaches the conclusion that no negative clearance can be granted.

Applications for negative clearance and notifications relating to Article 81 of the EC Treaty shall be submitted in the manner prescribed by form A/B (see Article 2(1), first sentence of the Regulation).

This form can also be used by undertakings that wish to apply for a negative clearance from Article 82 of the EC Treaty or Article 53 of the EEA Agreement, pursuant to Article 2 of Regulation No. 17. Applicants requesting negative clearance from Article 82 are not required to use form A/B. They are nonetheless strongly recommended to give all the information requested below to ensure that their application gives a full statement of the facts (see Article 2(1), second sentence of the Regulation).

---

[9] OJ No. C231, 12.9.1986, p. 2.
[10] For a definition of "turnover" in this context, see Articles 2, 3 and 4 of Protocol 22 to the EEA Agreement reproduced in Annex I.

The applications or notifications made on the form A/B issued by the EFTA side are equally valid. However, if the agreements, decisions or practices concerned fall solely within Articles 81 or 82 of the EC Treaty, i.e. have no EEA relevance whatsoever, it is advisable to use the present form established by the Commission.

D. Which chapters of the form should be completed?

The operational part of this form is sub-divided into four chapters. Undertakings wishing to make an application for a negative clearance or a notification must complete Chapters I, II and IV. An exception to this rule is provided for in the case where the application or notification concerns an agreement concerning the creation of a cooperative joint venture of a structural character if the parties wish to benefit from an accelerated procedure. In this situation Chapters I, III and IV should be completed.

In 1992, the Commission announced that it had adopted new internal administrative rules that provided that certain applications and notifications—those of cooperative joint ventures which are structural in nature—would be dealt with within fixed deadlines. In such cases the services of the Commission will, within two months of receipt of the complete notification of the agreement, inform the parties in writing of the results of the initial analysis of the case and, as appropriate, the nature and probable length of the administrative procedure they intend to engage.

The contents of this letter may vary according to the characteristics of the case under investigation:

— in cases not posing any problems, the Commission will send a comfort letter confirming the compatibility of the agreement with Article 81(1) or (3),
— if a comfort letter cannot be sent because of the need to settle the case by formal decision, the Commission will inform the undertakings concerned of its intention to adopt a decision either granting or rejecting exemption,
— if the Commission has serious doubts as to the compatibility of the agreement with the competition rules, it will send a letter to the parties giving notice of an in-depth examination which may, depending on the case, result in a decision neither prohibiting, exempting subject to conditions and obligations, or simply exempting the agreement in question.

This new accelerated procedure, applicable since 1 January 1993, is based entirely on the principle of self-discipline. The deadline of two months from the complete notification—intended for the initial examination of the case—does not constitute a statutory term and is therefore in no way legally binding. However, the Commission will do its best to abide by it. The Commission reserves the right, moreover, to extend this accelerated procedure to other forms of cooperation between undertakings.

A cooperative joint venture of a structural nature is one that involves an important change in the structure and organization of the business assets of the parties to the agreement. This may occur because the joint venture takes over or extends existing activities of the parent companies or because it undertakes new activities on their behalf. Such operations are characterized by the commitment of significant financial, material and/or non-tangible assets such as intellectual property rights and know-how. Structural joint ventures are therefore normally intended to operate on a medium- or long-term basis.

This concept includes certain "partial function" joint ventures which take over one or several specific functions within the parents' business activity without access to the market, in particular research and development and/or production. It also covers those "full function" joint ventures which give rise to coordination of the competitive behaviour of independent undertakings, in particular between the parties to the joint ventures or between them and the joint venture.

In order to respect the internal deadline, it is important that the Commission has available on notification all the relevant information reasonably available to the notifying parties that is necessary for it to assess the impact of the operation in question on competition. Form A/B therefore contains a special section (Chapter III) that must be completed only by persons notifying cooperative joint ventures of a structural character that wish to benefit from the accelerated procedure.

Persons notifying joint ventures of a structural character that wish to claim the benefit of the aforementioned accelerated procedure should therefore complete Chapters I, III and IV of this form. Chapter III contains a series of detailed questions necessary for the Commission to assess the relevant market(s) and the position of the parties to the joint venture on that (those) market(s).

Where the parties do not wish to claim the benefit of an accelerated procedure for their joint ventures of a structural character they should complete Chapters I, II and IV of this form. Chapter II contains a far more limited range of questions on the relevant market(s) and the position of the parties to the operation in question on that (those) market(s), but sufficient to enable the Commission to commence its examination and investigation.

E. The need for complete information

The receipt of a valid notification by the Commission has two main consequences. First, it affords immunity from fines from the date that the valid notification is received by the Commission with respect to applications made in order to obtain exemption (see Article 15(5) of Regulation No. 17). Second, until a valid notification is received, the Commission cannot grant an exemption pursuant to Article 81(3) of the EC Treaty and/or Article 53(3) of the EEA Agreement, and any exemption that is granted can be effective only from the date of receipt of a valid notification.[11] Thus, whilst there is no legal obligation to notify as such, unless and until an arrangement that falls within the scope of Article 81(1) and/or Article 53(1) has not been notified and is, therefore, not capable of being exempted, it may be declared void by a national court pursuant to Article 81(2) and/or Article 53(2).[12]

Where an undertaking is claiming the benefit of a group exemption by recourse to an opposition procedure, the period within which the Commission must oppose the exemption by category only applies from the date that a valid notification is received. This is also true of the two months' period imposed on the Commission services for an initial analysis of applications for negative clearance and notifications relating to cooperative joint ventures of a structural character which benefit from the accelerated procedure.

A valid application or notification for this purpose means one that is not incomplete (see Article 3(1) of the Regulation). This is subject to two qualifications. First, if the information or documents required by this form are not reasonably available to you in part or in whole, the Commission will accept that a notification is complete and thus valid notwithstanding the failure to provide such information, providing that you give reasons for the unavailability of the information, and provide your best estimates for missing data together with the sources for the estimates. Indications as to where any of the requested information or documents that are unavailable to you could be obtained by the Commission must also be provided. Second, the Commission only requires the submission of information relevant and necessary to its inquiry into the notified operation. In some cases not all the information required by this form will be necessary for this purpose. The Commission may therefore dispense with the obligation to provide certain information required by this form (see Article 3(3) of the Regulation. This provision enables, where appropriate, each application or notification to be tailored to each case so that only the information strictly necessary for the Commission's examination is provided. This avoids unnecessary administrative burdens being imposed on undertakings, in particular on small and medium-sized ones. Where the information or documents required by this form are not provided for this reason, the application or notification should indicate the reasons

---

[11] Subject to the qualification provided for in Article 4(2) of Regulation No. 17.
[12] For further details of the consequences of non-notification see the Commission notice on co-operation between national Courts and the Commission (OJ No. C39, 13.2.1993, p. 6).

why the information is considered to be unnecessary to the Commission's investigation.

Where the Commission finds that the information contained in the application or notification is incomplete in a material respect, it will, within one month from receipt, inform the applicant or the notifying party in writing of this fact and the nature of the missing information. In such cases, the application or notification shall become effective on the date on which the complete information is received by the Commission. If the Commission has not informed the applicant or the notifying party within the one month period that the application or notification is incomplete in a material respect, the application or notification will be deemed to be complete and valid (see Article 4 of the Regulation).

It is also important that undertakings inform the Commission of important changes in the factual situation including those of which they become aware after the application or notification has been submitted. The Commission must, therefore, be informed immediately of any changes to an agreement, decision or practice which is the subject of an application or notification (see Article 4(3) of the Regulation). Failure to inform the Commission of such relevant changes could result in any negative clearance decision being without effect or in the withdrawal of any exemption decision[13] adopted by the Commission on the basis of the notification.

F. The need for accurate information

In addition to the requirement that the application or notification be complete, it is important that you ensure that the information provided is accurate (see Article 3(1) of the Regulation). Article 15(1)(a) of Regulation No. 17 states that the Commission may, by decision, impose on undertakings or associations of undertakings fines of up to ECU 5000 where, intentionally or negligently, they supply incorrect or misleading information in an application for negative clearance or notification. Such information is, moreover, considered to be incomplete (see Article 4(4) of the Regulation), so that the parties cannot benefit from the advantages of the opposition procedure or accelerated procedure (see above, Point E).

G. Who can lodge an application or a notification?

Any of the undertakings party to an agreement, decision or practice of the kind described in Articles 81 or 82 of the EC Treaty and Articles 53 or 54 of the EEA Agreement may submit an application for negative clearance, in relation to Article 81 and Article 53, or a notification requesting an exemption. An association of undertakings may submit an application or a notification in relation to decisions taken or practices pursued into in the operation of the association.

In relation to agreements and concerted practices between undertakings it is common practice for all the parties involved to submit a joint application or notification. Although the Commission strongly recommends this approach, because it is helpful to have the views of all the parties directly concerned at the same time, it is not obligatory. Any of the parties to an agreement may submit an application or notification in their individual capacities, but in such circumstances the notifying party should inform all the other parties to the agreement, decision or practice of that fact (see Article 1(3) of the Regulation). They may also provide them with a copy of the completed form, where relevant once confidential information and business secrets have been deleted (see below, operational part, question 1.2).

Where a joint application or notification is submitted, it has also become common practice to appoint a joint representative to act on behalf of all the undertakings involved,

---

[13] See point (a) of Article 8(3) of Regulation No. 17.

both in making the application or notification, and in dealing with any subsequent contacts with the Commission (see Article 1(4) of the Regulation). Again, whilst this is helpful, it is not obligatory, and all the undertakings jointly submitting an application or a notification may sign it in their individual capacities.

H. How to submit an application or notification

Applications and notifications may be submitted in any of the official languages of the European Community or of an EFTA State (see Article 2(4) and (5) of the Regulation). In order to ensure rapid proceedings, it is, however, recommended to use, in case of an application or notification to the EFTA Surveillance Authority one of the official languages of an EFTA State or the working language of the EFTA Surveillance Authority, which is English, or, in case of an application or notification to the Commission, one of the official languages of the Community or the working language of the EFTA Surveillance Authority. This language will thereafter be the language of the proceeding for the applicant or notifying party.

Form A/B is not a form to be filled in. Undertakings should simply provide the information requested by this form, using its sections and paragraph numbers, signing a declaration as stated in Section 19 below, and annexing the required supporting documentation.

Supporting documents shall be submitted in their original language; where this is not an official language of the Community they must be translated into the language of the proceeding. The supporting documents may be originals or copies of the originals (see Article 2(4) of the Regulation).

All information requested in this form shall, unless otherwise stated, relate to the calendar year preceding that of the application or notification. Where information is not reasonably available on this basis (for example if accounting periods are used that are not based on the calendar year, or the previous year's figures are not yet available) the most recently available information should be provided and reasons given why figures on the basis of the calendar year preceding that of the application or notification cannot be provided.

Financial data may be provided in the currency in which the official audited accounts of the undertaking(s) concerned are prepared or in Ecus. In the latter case the exchange rate used for the conversion must be stated.

Seventeen copies of each application or notification, but only three copies of all supporting documents must be provided (see Article 2(2) of the Regulation).

The application or notification is to be sent to:

Commission of the European Communities,
Directorate-General for Competition (DG IV),
The Registrar,
200, Rue de la Loi,
B–1049 Brussels.

or be delivered by hand during Commission working days and official working hours at the following address:

Commission of the European Communities,
Directorate-General for Competition (DG IV),
The Registrar,
158, Avenue de Cortenberg,
B–1040 Brussels.

483

I. Confidentiality

Article 287 of the EC Treaty, Article 20 of Regulation No. 17, Article 9 of Protocol 23 to the EEA Agreement, Article 122 of the EEA Agreement and Articles 20 and 21 of Chapter II of Protocol 4 to the Agreement between the EFTA States on the establishment of a Surveillance Authority and of a Court of Justice require the Commission, the Member States, the EEA Surveillance Authority and EFTA States not to disclose information of the kind covered by the obligation of professional secrecy. On the other hand, Regulation No. 17 requires the Commission to publish a summary of the application or notification, should it intend to take a favourable decision. In this publication, the Commission ". . . shall have regard to the legitimate interest of undertakings in the protection of their business secrets" (Article 19(3) of Regulation No. 17; see also Article 21(2) in relation to the publication of decisions). In this connection, if an undertaking believes that its interests would be harmed if any of the information it is asked to supply were to be published or otherwise divulged to other undertakings, it should put all such information in a separate annex with each page clearly marked "Business Secrets". It should also give reasons why any information identified as confidential or secret should not be divulged or published. (See below, Section 5 of the operational part that requests a non-confidential summary of the notification.)

J. Subsequent procedure

The application or notification is registered in the Registry of the Directorate-General for Competition (DG IV). The date of receipt by the Commission (or the date of posting if sent by registered post) is the effective date of the submission (see Article 4(1) of the Regulation). However, special rules apply to incomplete applications and notifications (see above under Point E).

The Commission will acknowledge receipt of all applications and notifications in writing, indicating the case number attributed to the file. This number must be used in all future correspondence regarding the notification. The receipt of acknowledgement does not prejudge the question whether the application or notification is valid.

Further information may be sought from the parties or from third parties (Articles 11 to 14 of Regulation No. 17) and suggestions might be made as to amendments to the arrangements that might make them acceptable. Equally, a short preliminary notice may be published in the C series of the *Official Journal of the European Communities*, stating the names of the interested undertakings, the groups to which they belong, the economic sectors involved and the nature of the arrangements, and inviting third party comments (see below, operational part, Section 5).

Where a notification is made together for the purpose of the application of the opposition procedure, the Commission may oppose the grant of the benefit of the group exemption with respect to the notified agreement. If the Commission opposes the claim, and unless it subsequently withdraws its opposition, that notification will then be treated as an application for an individual exemption.

If, after examination, the Commission intends to grant the application for negative clearance or exemption, it is obliged (by Article 19(3) of Regulation No. 17) to publish a summary and invite comments from third parties. Subsequently, a preliminary draft decision has to be submitted to and discussed with the Advisory Committee on Restrictive Practices and Dominant Positions composed of officials of the competent authorities of the Member States in the matter of restrictive practices and monopolies (Article 10 of Regulation No. 17) and attended, where the case falls within the EEA Agreement, by representatives of the EFTA Surveillance Authority and the EFTA States which will already have received a copy of the application or notification. Only then, and providing nothing has happened to change the Commission's intention, can it adopt the envisaged decision.

Files are often closed without any formal decision being taken, for example, because it is found that the arrangements are already covered by a block exemption, or because they do not call for any action by the Commission, at least in circumstances at that time. In such cases comfort letters are sent. Although not a Commission decision, a comfort letter indicates how the Commission's departments view the case on the facts currently in their possession which means that the Commission could where necessary—for example, if it were to be asserted that a contract was void under Article 81(2) of the EC Treaty and/or Article 53(2) of the EEA Agreement—take an appropriate decision to clarify the legal situation.

K. Definitions used in the operational part of this form

Agreement: The word "agreement" is used to refer to all categories of arrangements, i.e. agreements between undertakings, decisions by associations of undertakings and concerted practices.

Year: All references to the word "year" in this form shall be read as meaning calendar year, unless otherwise stated.

Group: A group relationship exists for the purpose of this form where one undertaking:

— owns more than half the capital or business assets of another undertaking, or
— has the power to exercise more than half the voting rights in another undertaking, or
— has the power to appoint more than half the members of the supervisory board, board of directors or bodies legally representing the undertaking, or
— has the right to manage the affairs of another undertaking.

An undertaking which is jointly controlled by several other undertakings (joint venture) forms part of the group of each of these undertakings.

Relevant product market: Questions 6.1 and 11.1 of this form require the undertaking or individual submitting the notification to define the relevant product and/or service market(s) that arc likely to be affected by the agreement in question. That definition(s) is then used as the basis for a number of other questions contained in this form. The definition(s) thus submitted by the notifying parties are referred to in this form as the relevant product market(s). These words can refer to a market made up either of products or of services.

Relevant geographic market: Questions 6.2 and 11.2 of this form require the undertaking or individual submitting the notification to define the relevant geographic market(s) that are likely to be affected by the agreement in question. That definition(s) is then used as the basis for a number of other questions contained in this form. The definition(s) thus submitted by the notifying parties are referred to in this form as the relevant geographic market(s).

Relevant product and geographic market: By virtue of the combination of their replies to questions 6 and 11 the parties provide their definition of the relevant market(s) affected by the notified agreement(s). That (those) definition(s) is (are) then used as the basis for a number of other questions contained in this form. The definition(s) thus submitted by the notifying parties is referred to in this form as the relevant geographic and product market(s).

Notification: This form can be used to make an application for negative clearance and/ or a notification requesting an exemption. The word "notification" is used to refer to either an application or a notification.

Parties and notifying party: The word "party" is used to refer to all the undertakings which are party to the agreement being notified. As a notification may be submitted by only one of the undertakings which are party to an agreement, "notifying party" is used to refer only to the undertakings actually submitting the notification.

OPERATIONAL PART

PLEASE MAKE SURE THAT THE FIRST PAGE OF YOUR APPLICATION OR NOTIFICATION CONTAINS THE WORDS "APPLICATION FOR NEGATIVE CLEARANCE/NOTIFICATION IN ACCORDANCE WITH FORM A/B"

CHAPTER I

Sections concerning the parties, their groups and the agreement (to be completed for all notifications)

Section I

Identity of the undertakings or persons submitting the notification

1.1. Please list the undertakings on behalf of which the notification is being submitted and indicate their legal denomination or commercial name, shortened or commonly used as appropriate (if it differs from the legal denomination).

1.2. If the notification is being submitted on behalf of only one or some of the undertakings party to the agreement being notified, please confirm that the remaining undertakings have been informed of that fact and indicate whether they have received a copy of the notification, with relevant confidential information and business secrets deleted.[14] (In such circumstances a copy of the edited copy of the notification which has been provided to such other undertakings should be annexed to this notification.)

1.3. If a joint notification is being submitted, has a joint representative[15] been appointed[16]?

If yes, please give the details requested in 1.3.1 to 1.3.3 below.

If no, please give details of any representatives who have been authorized to act for each or either of the parties to the agreement indicating who they represent.

1.3.1. Name of representative.
1.3.2. Address of representative.
1.3.3. Telephone and fax number of representative.

1.4. In cases where one or more representatives have been appointed, an authority to act on behalf of the undertaking(s) submitting the notification must accompany the notification.

---

[14] The Commission is aware that in exceptional cases it may not be practicable to inform non-notifying parties to the notified agreement of the fact that it has been notified, or to provide them a copy of the notification. This may be the case, for example, where a standard agreement is being notified that is concluded with a large number of undertakings. Where this is the case you should state the reasons why it has not been practicable to follow the standard procedure set out in this question.

[15] *Note:* For the purposes of this question a representative means an individual or undertaking formally apointed to make the notification or application on behalf of the party or parties submitting the notification. This should be distingushed from the situation where the notification is signed by an officer of the company or companies in question. In the latter situation no representative is appointed.

[16] *Note:* It is not mandatory to appoint representatives for the purpose of completing and/or submitting this notification. This question only requires the identification of representatives where the notifying parties have chosen to appoint them.

Section 2

Information on the parties to the agreement and the groups to which they belong

2.1. State the name and address of the parties to the agreement being notified, and the country of their incorporation.

2.2. State the nature of the business of each of the parties to the agreement being notified.

2.3. For each of the parties to the agreement, give the name of a person that can be contacted, together with his or her name, address, telephone number, fax number and position held in the undertaking.

2.4. Identify the corporate groups to which the parties to the agreement being notified belong. State the sectors in which these groups are active, and the world-wide turnover of each group.[17]

Section 3

Procedural matters

3.1. Please state whether you have made any formal submission to any other competition authorities in relation to the agreement in question. If yes, state which authorities, the individual or department in question, and the nature of the contact. In addition to this, mention any earlier proceedings or informal contacts, of which you are aware, with the Commission and/or the EFTA Surveillance Authority and any earlier proceedings with any national authorities or courts in the Community or in EFTA concerning these or any related agreements.

3.2. Please summarize any reasons for any claim that the case involves an issue of exceptional urgency.

3.3. The Commission has stated that where notifications do not have particular political, economic or legal significance for the Community they will normally be dealt with by means of comfort letter.[18] Would you be satisfied with a comfort letter? If you consider that it would be inappropriate to deal with the notified agreement in this manner, please explain the reasons for this view.

3.4. State whether you intend to produce further supporting facts or arguments not yet available and, if so, on which points.[19]

Section 4

Full details of the arrangements

4.1. Please summarize the nature, content and objectives pursued by the agreement being notified.

4.2. Detail any provisions contained in the agreements which may restrict the parties in their freedom to take independent commercial decisions, for example regarding:

---

[17] For the calculation of turnover in the banking and insurance sectors see Article 3 of Protocol 22 to the EEA Agreement.

[18] See paragraph 14 of the notice on cooperation between national courts and the Commission in applying Articles 81 and 82 of the EC Treaty (OJ No. C39, 13.2.1993, p. 6).

[19] *Note:* In so far as the notifying parties provide the information required by this form that was reasonably available to them at the time of notification, the fact that the parties intend to provide further supporting facts of documentation in due course does not prevent the notification being valid at the time of notification and, in the case of structural joint ventures where the accelerated procedure is being claimed, the two month deadline commencing.

— buying or selling prices, discounts or other trading conditions,
— the quantities of goods to be manufactured or distributed or services to be offered,
— technical development or investment,
— the choice of markets or sources of supply,
— purchases from or sales to third parties,
— whether to apply similar terms for the supply of equivalent goods or services,
— whether to offer different services separately or together.

If you are claiming the benefit of the opposition procedure, identify in this list the restrictions that exceed those automatically exempted by the relevant regulation.

4.3. State between which Member States of the Community and/or EFTA States[20] trade may be affected by the arrangements. Please give reasons for your reply to this question, giving data on trade flows where relevant. Furthermore please state whether trade between the Community or the EEA territory and any third countries is affected, again giving reasons for your reply.

Section 5

Non-confidential Summary

Shortly following receipt of a notification, the Commission may publish a short notice inviting third party comments on the agreement in question.[21] As the objective pursued by the Commission in publishing an informal preliminary notice is to receive third party comments as soon as possible after the notification has been received, such a notice is usually published without first providing it to the notifying parties for their comments. This section requests the information to be used in an informal preliminary notice in the event that the Commission decides to issue one. It is important, therefore, that your replies to these questions do not contain any business secrets or other confidential information.

1. State the names of the parties to the agreement notified and the groups of undertakings to which they belong.

2. Give a short summary of the nature and objectives of the agreement. As a guideline this summary should not exceed 100 words.

3. Identify the product sectors affected by the agreement in question.

CHAPTER II

Section concerning the relevant market (to be completed for all notifications except those relating to structural joint ventures for which accelerated treatment is claimed)

Section 6

The relevant market

A relevant product market comprises all those products and/or services which are regarded as interchangeable or substitutable by the consumer, by reason of the products' characteristics, their prices and their intended use.

---

[20] See list in Annex II.

[21] An example of such a notice figures in Annex I to this Form. Such a notice should be distinguished from a formal notice published pursuant to Article 19(3) of Regulation No. 17. An Article 19(3) notice is relatively detailed, and gives an indication of the Commission's current approach in the case in question. Section 5 seeks only information that will be used in a short preliminary notice, and not a notice published pursuant to Article 19(3).

The following factors are normally considered to be relevant to the determination of the relevant product market and should be taken into account in this analysis[22]:

— the degree of physical similarity between the products/services in question,
— any differences in the end use to which the goods are put,
— differences in price between two products,
— the cost of switching between two potentially competing products,
— established or entrenched consumer preferences for one type or category of product over another,
— industry-wide product classifications (e.g. classifications maintained by trade associations).

The relevant geographic market comprises the area in which the undertakings concerned are involved in the supply of products or services, in which the conditions of competition are sufficiently homogeneous and which can be distinguished from neighbouring areas because, in particular, conditions of competition are appreciably different in those areas.

Factors relevant to the assessment of the relevant geographic market include[23] the nature and characteristics of the products or services concerned, the existence of entry barriers or consumer preferences, appreciable differences of the undertakings' market share or substantial price differences between neighbouring areas, and transport costs.

6.1 In the light of the above please explain the definition of the relevant product market or markets that in your opinion should form the basis of the Commission's analysis of the notification.

In your answer, please give reasons for assumptions or findings, and explain how the factors outlined above have been taken into account. In particular, please state the specific products or services directly or indirectly affected by the agreement being notified and identify the categories of goods viewed as substitutable in your market definition. In the questions figuring below, this (or these) definition(s) will be referred to as "the relevant product market(s)".

6.2. Please explain the definition of the relevant geographic market or markets that in your opinion should form the basis of the Commission's analysis of the notification. In your answer, please give reasons for assumptions or findings, and explain how the factors outlined above have been taken into account. In particular, please identify the countries in which the parties are active in the relevant product market(s), and in the event that you consider the relevant geographic market to be wider than the individual Member States of the community or EFTA on which the parties to the agreement are active, give reasons for this.

In the questions below, this (or these) definition(s) will be referred to as "the relevant geographic market(s)".

Section 7

Group members operating on the same markets as the parties

7.1. For each of the parties to the agreement being notified, provide a list of all undertakings belonging to the same group which are:

7.1.1. active in the relevant product market(s);

---

[22] This list is not, however, exhaustive, and notifying parties may refer to other factors.
[23] This list is not, however, exhaustive, and notifying parties may refer to other factors.

7.1.2. active in markets neighbouring the *relevant market(s)* (i.e. active in products and/ or services that represent imperfect and partial substitutes for those included in your definition of the relevant product market(s)).

Such undertakings must be identified even if they sell the product or service in question in other geographic areas than those in which the parties to the notified agreement operate. Please list the name, place of incorporation, exact product manufactured and the geographic scope of operation of each group member.

Section 8

The position of the parties on the affected relevant product markets

Information requested in this section must be provided for the groups of the parties as a whole. It is not sufficient to provide such information only in relation to the individual undertakings directly concerned by the agreement.

8.1 In relation to each relevant product market(s) identified in your reply to question 6.1 please provide the following information:

8.1.1. the market shares of the parties on the *relevant geographic market* during the previous three years;

8.1.2. where different, the market shares of the parties in (a) the EEA territory as a whole, (b) the Community, (c) the territory of the EFTA States and (d) each EC Member State and EFTA State during the previous three years.[24] For this section, where market shares are less than 20 per cent, please state simply which of the following bands are relevant: 0 to 5 per cent, 5 to 10 per cent, 10 to 15 per cent, 15 to 20 per cent.

For the purpose of answering these questions, market share may be calculated either on the basis of value or volume. Justification for the figures provided must be given. Thus, for each answer, total market value/volume must be stated, together with the sales/ turnover of each of the parties in question. The source or sources of the information should also be given (e.g. official statistics, estimates, etc.), and where possible, copies should be provided of documents from which information has been taken.

Section 9

The position of competitors and customers on the relevant product market(s)

Information requested in this section must be provided for the group of the parties as a whole and not in relation to the individual companies directly concerned by the agreement notified.

For the (all) relevant product and geographic market(s) in which the parties have a combined market share exceeding 15 per cent, the following questions must be answered.

---

[24] *i.e.* Where the relevant geographic market has been defined as world wide, these figures must be given regarding the EEA, the Community, the territory of the EFTA States, and each EC Member State. Where the relevant geographic market has been defined as the Community, these figures must be given for the EEA, the territory of the EFTA States, and each EC Member State. Where the relevant geographic market has been defined as national, these figures must be given for the EEA, the Community and the territory of the EFTA States.

9.1. Please identify the five main competitors of the parties. Please identify the company and give your best estimate as to their market share in the relevant geographic market(s). Please also provide address, telephone number and fax number, and, where possible, the name of a contact person at each company identified.

9.2. Please identify the five main customers of each of the parties. State company name, address, telephone and fax numbers, together with the name of a contact person.

Section 10

Market entry and potential competition in product and geographic terms

For the (all) relevant product and geographic market(s) in which the parties have a combined market share exceeding 15 per cent, the following questions must be answered.

10.1. Describe the various factors influencing entry in product terms into the *relevant product market(s)* that exist in the present case (i.e. what barriers exist to prevent undertakings that do not presently manufacture goods within the relevant product market(s) entering this market(s)). In so doing take account of the following where appropriate:

— to what extent is entry to the markets influenced by the requirement of government authorization or standard setting in any form? Are there any legal or regulatory controls on entry to these markets?
— to what extent is entry to the markets influenced by the availability of raw materials?
— to what extent is entry to the markets influenced by the length of contracts between an undertaking and its suppliers and/or customers?
— describe the importance of research and development and in particular the importance of licensing patents, know-how and other rights in these markets.

10.2. Describe the various factors influencing entry in geographic terms into the relevant geographic market(s) that exist in the present case (i.e. what barriers exist to prevent undertakings already producing and/or marketing products within the relevant product market(s) but in areas outside the relevant geographic market(s) extending the scope of their sales into the relevant geographic market(s)?). Please give reasons for your answers, explaining where relevant, the importance of the following factors:

— trade barriers imposed by law, such as tariffs, quotas etc.,
— local specification or technical requirements,
— procurement policies,
— the existence of adequate and available local distribution and retailing facilities,
— transport costs,
— entrenched consumer preferences for local brands or products,
— language.

10.3. Have any new undertakings entered the relevant product market(s) in geographic areas where the parties sell during the last three years? Please provide this information with respect to both new entrants in product terms and new entrants in geographic terms. If such entry has occurred, please identify the undertaking(s) concerned (name, address, telephone and fax numbers, and, where possible, contact person), and provide your best estimate of their market share in the relevant product and geographic market(s).

Chapter III

Section concerning the relevant market only for structural joint ventures for which accelerated treatment is claimed

Section 11

The relevant market

A relevant product market comprises all those products and/or services which are regarded as interchangeable or substitutable by the consumer, by reason of the products' characteristics, their prices and their intended use.

The following factors are normally considered to be relevant[25] to the determination of the relevant product market and should be taken into account in this analysis:

— the degree of physical similarity between the products/services in question,
— any differences in the end use to which the goods are put,
— differences in price between two products,
— the cost of switching between two potentially competing products,
— established or entrenched consumer preferences for one type or category of product over another,
— different or similar industry-wide product classifications (e.g. classifications maintained by trade associations).

The relevant geographic market comprises the area in which the undertakings concerned are involved in the supply of products or services, in which the conditions of competition are sufficiently homogeneous and which can be distinguished from neighbouring areas because, in particular, conditions of competition are appreciably different in those areas.

Factors relevant to the assessment of the relevant geographic market include[26] the nature and characteristics of the products or services concerned, the existence of entry barriers or consumer preferences, appreciable differences of the undertakings' market share or substantial price differences between neighbouring areas, and transport costs.

Part 11.1

The notifying parties' analysis of the relevant market

11.1.1. In the light of the above, please explain the definition of the relevant product market or markets that in the opinion of the parties should form the basis of the Commission's analysis of the notification.

In your answer, please give reasons for assumptions or findings, and explain how the factors outlined above have been taken into account.

In the questions figuring below, this (or these) definition(s) will be referred to as "the relevant product market(s)".

11.1.2. Please explain the definition of the relevant geographic market or markets that in the opinion of the parties should form the basis of the Commission's analysis of the notification.

---

[25] This list is not, however, exhaustive, and notifying parties may refer to other factors.
[26] This list is not, however, exhaustive, and notifying parties may refer to other factors.

In your answer, please give reasons for assumptions or findings, and explain how the factors outlined above have been taken into account.

Part 11.2

Questions on the relevant product and geographic market(s)

Answers to the following questions will enable the Commission to verify whether the product and geographic market definitions put forward by you in Section 11.1 are compatible with definitions figuring above.

Product market definition

11.2.1. List the specific products or services directly or indirectly affected by the agreement being notified.

11.2.2. List the categories of products and/or services that are, in the opinion of the notifying parties, close economic substitutes for those identified in the reply to question 11.2.1. Where more than one product or service has been identified in the reply to question 11.2.1, a list for each product must be provided for this question.

The products identified in this list should be ordered in their degree of substitutability, first listing the most perfect substitute for the products of the parties, finishing with the least perfect substitute.[27]

---

[27] Close economic substitute; most perfect substitute; least perfect substitute: these definitions are only relevant to those filling out Chapter III of the form, i.e. those notifying structural joint ventures requesting the accelerated procedure).

For any given product (for the purposes of this definition "product" is used to refer to products or services) a chain of substitutes exists. This chain is made up of all conceivable substitutes for the product in question, i.e. all those products that will, to a greater or lesser extent, fulfil the needs of the consumer in question. The substitutes will range from very close (or perfect) ones (products to which consumers would turn immediately in the event of, for example, even a very small price increase for the product in question) to very distant (or imperfect) substitutes (products to which customers would only turn to in the event of a very large price rise for the product in question). When defining the relevant market, and calculating market shares, the Commission only takes into account close economic substitutes of the products in question. Close economic substitutes are ones to which customers would turn to in response to a small but significant price increase for the product in question (say 5 per cent). This enables the Commission to assess the market power of the notifying companies in the context of a relevant market made up of all those products that consumers of the products in question could readily and easily turn to.

However, this does not mean that the Commission fails to take into account the constraints on the competitive behaviour of the parties in question resulting from the existence of imperfect substitutes (those to which a consumer could not turn to in response to a small but significant price increase (say 5 per cent) for the products in question). These effects are taken into account once the market has been defined, and the market shares determined.

It is therefore important for the Commission to have information regarding both close economic substitutes for the products in question, as well as less perfect substitutes.

For example, assume two companies active in the luxury watch sector conclude a research and development agreement. They both manufacture watches costing ECU 1800 to 2000. Close economic substitutes are likely to be watches of other manufacturers in the same or similar price category, and these will be taken into account when defining the relevant product market. Cheaper watches, and in particular disposable plastic watches, will be imperfect substitutes, because it is unlikely that a potential purchaser of a ECU 2000 watch will turn to one costing ECU 20 if the expensive one increased its price by 5 per cent.

Please explain how the factors relevant to the definition of the relevant product market have been taken into account in drawing up this list and in placing the products/services in their correct order.

Geographic market definition

11.2.3. List all the countries in which the parties are active in the relevant product market(s). Where they are active in all countries within any given groups of countries or trading area (e.g. the whole Community or EFTA, the EEA countries, world-wide) it is sufficient to indicate the area in question.

11.2.4. Explain the manner in which the parties produce and sell the goods and/or services in each of these various countries or areas. For example, do they manufacture locally, do they sell through local distribution facilities, or do they distribute through exclusive, or non-exclusive, importers and distributors?

11.2.5. Are there significant trade flows in the goods/services that make up the relevant product market(s) (i) between the EC Member States (please specify which and estimate the percentage of total sales made up by imports in each Member State in which the parties are active), (ii) between all or part of the EC Member States and all or part of the EFTA States (again, please specify and estimate the percentage of total sales made up by imports), (iii) between the EFTA States (please specify which and estimate the percentage of total sales made up by imports in each such State in which the parties are active), and (iv) between all or part of the EEA territory and other countries? (again, please specify and estimate the percentage of total sales made up by imports.)

11.2.6. Which producer undertakings based outside the Community or the EEA territory sell within the EEA territory in countries in which the parties are active in the affected products? How do these undertakings market their products? Does this differ between different EC Member States and/or EFTA States?

Section 12

Group members operating on the same markets as the parties to the notified agreement

12.1. For each of the parties to the agreement being notified, provide a list of all undertakings belonging to the same group which are:

12.1.1. active in the relevant product market(s);

12.1.2. active in markets neighbouring the relevant product market(s) (i.e. active in products/services that represent imperfect and partial substitutes[28] for those included in your definition of the relevant product market(s);

12.1.3. active in markets upstream and/or downstream from those included in the relevant product market(s).

Such undertakings must be identified even if they sell the product or service in question in other geographic areas than those in which the parties to the notified agreement operate. Please list the name, place of incorporation, exact product manufactured and the geographic scope of operation of each group member.

---

[28] The following are considered to be partial substitutes: products and services which may replace each other solely in certain geographic areas, solely during part of the year or solely for certain uses.

Section 13

The position of the parties on the relevant product market(s)

Information requested in this section must be provided for the group of the parties as a whole and not in relation to the individual companies directly concerned by the agreement notified.

13.1 In relation to each relevant product market(s), as defined in your reply to question 11.1.2, please provide the following information:

13.1.1. the market shares of the parties on the relevant geographic market during the previous three years;

13.1.2. where different, the market shares of the parties in (a) the EEA territory as a whole, (b) the Community, (c) the territory of the EFTA States and (d) each EC Member State and EFTA State during the previous three years.[29] For this section, where market shares are less than 20 per cent, please state simply which of the following bands are relevant: 0 to 5 per cent, 5 to 10 per cent, 10 to 15 per cent, 15 to 20 per cent in terms of value or volume.

For the purpose of answering these questions, market share may be calculated either on the basis of value or volume. Justification for the figures provided must be given. Thus, for each answer, total market value/volume must be stated, together with the sales/turnover of each the parties in question. The source of sources of the information should also be given, and where possible, copies should be provided of documents from which information has been taken.

13.2. If the market shares in question 13.1 were to be calculated on a basis other than that used by the parties, would the resultant market shares differ by more than 5 per cent in any market (i.e. if the parties have calculated market shares on the basis of volume, what would be the relevant figure if it was calculated on the basis of value?) If the figure were to differ by more than 5 per cent please provide the information requested in question 13.1 on the basis of both value and volume.

13.3. Give your best estimate of the current rate of capacity utilization of the parties and in the industry in general in the relevant product and geographic market(s).

Section 14

The position of competitors on the relevant product market(s)

Information requested in this section must be provided for the group of the parties as a whole and not in relation to the individual companies directly concerned by the agreement notified.

For the (all) relevant product market(s) in which the parties have a combined market share exceeding 10 per cent in the EEA as a whole, the Community, the EFTA territory or in any EC Member State or EFTA Member State, the following questions must be answered.

14.1. Please identify the competitors of the parties on the relevant product market(s) that have a market share exceeding 10 per cent in any EC Member State, EFTA State, in the territory of the EFTA States, in the EEA, or world-wide. Please identify the company and give your best estimate as to their market share in these geographic areas. Please also

---

[29] i.e. Where the relevant geographic market has been defined as world wide, these figures must be given regarding the EEA, the Community, the territory of the EFTA States, and each E.C. Member State and EFTA State. Where the relevant geographic market has been defined as the Community, these figures must be given for the EEA, the territory of the EFTA States, and each E.C. Member State and EFTA State. Where the market has been defined as national, these figures must be given for the EEA, the Community and the territory of the EFTA States.

provide the address, telephone and fax numbers, and, where possible, the name of a contact person at each company identified.

14.2. Please describe the nature of demand on the relevant product market(s). For example, are there few or many purchasers, are there different categories of purchasers, are government agencies or departments important purchasers?

14.3. Please identify the five largest customers of each of the parties for each *relevant product market(s)*. State company name, address, telephone and fax numbers, together with the name of a contact person.

Section 15

Market entry and potential competition

For the (all) relevant product market(s) in which the parties have a combined market share exceeding 10 per cent in the EEA as a whole, the Community, the EFTA territory or in any EC Member State or EFTA State, the following questions must be answered.

15.1. Describe the various factors influencing entry into the relevant product market(s) that exist in the present case. In so doing take account of the following where appropriate:

— to what extent is entry to the markets influenced by the requirement of government authorization or standard setting in any form? Are there any legal or regulatory controls on entry to these markets?
— to what extent is entry to the markets influenced by the availability of raw materials?
— to what extent is entry to the markets influenced by the length of contracts between an undertaking and its suppliers and/or customers?
— what is the importance of research and development and in particular the importance of licensing patents, know-how and other rights in these markets.

15.2. Have any new undertakings entered the relevant product market(s) in geographic areas where the parties sell during the last three years? If so, please identify the undertaking(s) concerned (name, address, telephone and fax numbers, and, where possible, contact person), and provide your best estimate of their market share in each EC Member State and EFTA State that they are active and in the Community, the territory of the EFTA States and the EEA territory as a whole.

15.3. Give your best estimate of the minimum viable scale for the entry into the relevant product market(s) in terms of appropriate market share necessary to operate profitably.

15.4. Are there significant barriers to entry preventing companies active on the relevant product market(s):

15.4.1. in one EC Member State or EFTA State selling in other areas of the EEA territory;

15.4.2. outside the EEA territory selling into all or parts of the EEA territory. Please give reasons for your answers, explaining, where relevant, the importance of the following factors:

— trade barriers imposed by law, such as tariffs, quotas etc.,
— local specification or technical requirements,
— procurement policies,
— the existence of adequate and available local distribution and retailing facilities,
— transport costs,
— entrenched consumer preferences for local brands or products,
— language.

CHAPTER IV

Final sections to be completed for all notifications

Section 16

Reasons for the application for negative clearance

If you are applying for negative clearance state:

16.1. why, i.e. state which provision or effects of the agreement or behaviour might, in your view, raise questions of compatibility with the Community's and/or the EEA rules of competition. The object of this subheading is to give the Commission the clearest possible idea of the doubts you have about your agreement or behaviour that you wish to have resolved by a negative clearance.

Then, under the following three references, give a statement of the relevant facts and reasons as to why you consider Article 81(1) or 82 of the EC Treaty and/or Article 53(1) or 54 of the EEA Agreement to be inapplicable, i.e.:

16.2. why the agreements or behaviour do not have the object or effect of preventing, restricting or distorting competition within the common market or within the territory of the EFTA State to any appreciable extent, or why your undertaking does not have or its behaviour does not abuse a dominant position; and/or

16.3. why the agreements or behaviour do not have the object or effect of preventing, restricting or distorting competition within the EEA territory to any appreciable extent, or why your undertaking does not have or its behaviour does not abuse a dominant position; and/or

16.4. why the agreements or behaviour are not such as may affect trade between Member States or between the Community and one or more EFTA States, or between EFTA States to any appreciable extent.

Section 17

Reasons for the application for exemption

If you are notifying the agreement, even if only as a precaution, in order to obtain an exemption under Article 81(3) of the E.C. Treaty and/or Article 53(3) of the EEA Agreement, explain how:

17.1. the agreement contributes to improving production or distribution, and/or promoting technical or economic progress. In particular, please explain the reasons why these benefits are expected to result from the collaboration; for example, do the parties to the agreement possess complementary technologies or distribution systems that will produce important synergies? (if, so, please state which). Also please state whether any documents or studies were drawn up by the notifying parties when assessing the feasibility of the operation and the benefits likely to result therefrom, and whether any such documents or studies provided estimates of the savings or efficiencies likely to result. Please provide copies of any such documents or studies;

17.2. a proper share of the benefits arising from such improvement or progress accrues to consumers;

17.3. all restrictive provisions of the agreement are indispensable to the attainment of the aims set out under 17.1 (if you are claiming the benefit of the opposition procedure, it is particularly important that you should identify and justify restrictions that exceed those automatically exempted by the relevant Regulations). In this respect please explain how the benefits resulting from the agreement identified in your reply to question 17.1 could not be achieved, or could not be achieved so quickly or efficiently or only at higher cost or with less certainty of success (i) without the conclusion of the agreement as a whole and (ii) without those particular clauses and provisions of the agreement identified in your reply to question 4.2;

17.4 the agreement does not eliminate competition in respect of a substantial part of the goods or services concerned.

Section 18

Supporting documentation

The completed notification must be drawn up and submitted in one original. It shall contain the last versions of all agreements which are the subject of the notification and be accompanied by the following:

(a) sixteen copies of the notification itself;
(b) three copies of the annual reports and accounts of all the parties to the notified agreement, decision or practice for the last three years;
(c) three copies of the most recent in-house or external long-term market studies or planning documents for the purpose of assessing or analysing the affected markets) with respect to competitive conditions, competitors (actual and potential), and market conditions. Each document should indicate the name and position of the author;
(d) three copies of reports and analyses which have been prepared by or for any officer(s) or director(s) for the purposes of evaluating or analysing the notified agreement.

Section 19

Declaration

The notification must conclude with the following declaration which is to be signed by or on behalf of all the applicants or notifying parties.[30]

"The undersigned declare that the information given in this notification is correct to the best of their knowledge and belief, that complete copies of all documents requested by form A/B have been supplied to the extent that they are in the possession of the group of undertakings to which the applicant(s) or notifying party(ies) belong(s) and are accessible to the latter, that all estimates are identified as such and are their best estimates of the underlying facts and that all the opinions expressed are sincere.

They are aware of the provisions of Article 15(1)(a) of Regulation No. 17.

Place and date:

Signatures:"

Please add the name(s) of the person(s) signing the application or notification and their function(s).

---

[30] Applications and notifications which have not been signed are invalid.

Annex I

Text of Articles 81 and 82 of the EC Treaty, Articles 53, 54 and 56 of the EEA Agreement, and of Articles 2, 3 and 4 of Protocol 22 to that Agreement

Article 81 of the Treaty

1. The following shall be prohibited as incompatible with the common market: all agreements between undertakings, decisions by associations or undertakings and concerted practices which may affect trade between Member States and which have as their object or effect the prevention, restriction or distortion of competition within the common market, and in particular those which:

(a) directly or indirectly fix purchase or selling prices or any other trading conditions;
(b) limit or control production, markets, technical development, or investment;
(c) share markets or sources of supply;
(d) apply dissimilar conditions to equivalent transactions with other trading parties, thereby placing them at a competitive disadvantage;
(e) make the conclusion of contracts subject to acceptance by the other parties of supplementary obligations which, by their nature or according to commercial usage, have no connection with the subject of such contracts.

2. Any agreements or decisions prohibited pursuant to this Article shall be automatically void.

3. The provisions of paragraph 1 may, however, be declared in applicable in the case of:

— any agreement or category of agreements between undertakings,
— any decision or category of decisions by associations or undertakings,
— any concerted practice or category of concerted practices,

which contributes to improving the production or distribution of goods or to promoting technical or economic progress, while allowing consumers a fair share of the resulting benefit, and which does not:

(a) impose on the undertakings concerned restrictions which are not indispensable to the attainment of these objectives;
(b) afford such undertakings the possibility of eliminating competition in respect of a substantial part of the products in question.

Article 82 of the EC Treaty

Any abuse by one or more undertakings of a dominant position within the common market or in a substantial part of it shall be prohibited as incompatible with the common market in so far as it may affect trade between Member States.

Such abuse may, in particular, consist in:

(a) directly or indirectly imposing unfair purchase or selling prices or other unfair trading conditions;

499

(b) limiting production, markets or technical development to the prejudice of consumers;
(c) applying dissimilar conditions to equivalent transactions with other trading parties, thereby placing them at a competitive disadvantage;
(d) making the conclusion of contracts subject to acceptance by the other parties of supplementary obligations which, by their nature or according to commercial usage, have no connection with the subject of such contracts.

ARTICLE 53 OF THE EEA AGREEMENT

1. The following shall be prohibited as incompatible with the functioning of this Agreement: all agreements between undertakings, decisions by associations of undertakings and concerted practices which may affect trade between Contracting Parties and which have as their object or effect the prevention, restriction or distortion of competition within the territory covered by this Agreement, and in particular those which:

(a) directly or indirectly fix purchase or selling prices or any other trading conditions;
(b) limit or control production, markets, technical development, or investment;
(c) share markets or sources of supply;
(d) apply dissimilar conditions to equivalent transactions with other trading parties, thereby placing them at a competitive disadvantage;
(e) make the conclusion of contracts subject to acceptance by the other parties of supplementary obligations which, by their nature or according to commercial usage, have no connection with the subject of such contracts.

2. Any agreement or decisions prohibited pursuant to this Article shall be automatically void.
3. The provisions of paragraph 1 may, however, be declared inapplicable in the case of:

— any agreement or category of agreements between undertakings,
— any decision or category of decisions by associations of undertakings,
— any concerted practice or category of concerted practices,

which contributes to improving the production or distribution of goods or to promoting technical or economic progress, while allowing consumers a fair share of the resulting benefit, and which does not:

(a) impose on the undertakings concerned restrictions which are not indispensable to the attainment of these objectives;
(b) afford such undertakings the possibility of eliminating competition in respect of a substantial part of the products in question.

ARTICLE 54 OF THE EEA AGREEMENT

Any abuse by one or more undertakings of a dominant position within the territory covered by this agreement or in a substantial part of it shall be prohibited as incompatible with the functioning of this Agreement in so far as it may affect trade between Contracting Parties.
Such abuse may, in particular, consist in:

(a) directly or indirectly imposing unfair purchase or selling prices or other unfair trading conditions;

(b) limiting production, markets or technical development to the prejudice of consumers;

(c) applying dissimilar conditions to equivalent transactions with other trading parties, thereby placing them at a competitive disadvantage;

(d) making the conclusion of contracts subject to acceptance by the other parties of supplementary obligations which, by their nature or according to commercial usage, have no connection with the subject of such contracts.

ARTICLE 56 OF THE EEA AGREEMENT

1. Individual cases falling under Article 53 shall be decided upon by the surveillance authorities in accordance with the following provisions:

(a) individual cases where only trade between EFTA States is affected shall be decided upon by the EFTA Surveillance Authority;

(b) without prejudice to subparagraph (c), the EFTA Surveillance Authority decides, as provided for in the provisions set out in Article 58, Protocol 21 and the rules adopted for its implementation, Protocol 23 and Annex XIV, on cases where the turnover of the undertakings concerned in the territory of the EFTA States equals 33 per cent or more of their turnover in the territory covered by this Agreement;

(c) the EC Commission decides on the other cases as well as on cases under (b) where trade between EC Member States is affected, taking into account the provisions set out in Article 58, Protocol 21, Protocol 23 and Annex XIV.

2. Individual cases falling under Article 54 shall be decided upon by the surveillance authority in the territory of which a dominant position is found to exist. The rules set out in paragraph 1(b) and (c) shall apply only if dominance exists within the territories of both surveillance authorities.

3. Individual cases falling under paragraph 1(c), whose effects on trade between EC Member States or on competition within the Community are not appreciable, shall be decided upon by the EFTA Surveillance Authority.

4. The terms "undertaking" and "turnover" are, for the purpose of this Article, defined in Protocol 22.

ARTICLES 2, 3, AND 4 OF PROTOCOL 22 TO THE EEA AGREEMENT

Article 2

"Turnover" within the meaning of Article 56 of the Agreement shall comprise the amounts derived by the undertaking concerned, in the territory covered by this Agreement, in the preceding financial year from the sale of products and the provision of services falling within the undertaking's ordinary scope of activities after deduction of sales rebates and of value-added tax and other taxes directly related to turnover.

Article 3

In place of turnover the following shall be used:

(a) for credit institutions and other financial institutions, their total assets multiplied by the ratio between loans and advances to credit institutions and customers in transactions with residents in the territory covered by this Agreement and the total sum of those loans and advances;

(b) for insurance undertakings, the value of gross premiums received from residents in the territory covered by this Agreement, which shall comprise all amounts received and receivable in respect of insurance contracts issued by or on behalf of the insurance undertakings, including also outgoing reinsurance premiums, and after deduction of taxes and parafiscal contributions or levies charged by reference to the amounts of individual premiums or the total value of premiums.

Article 4

1. In derogation of the definition of the turnover relevant for the application of Article 56 of the Agreement, as contained in Article 2 of this Protocol, the relevant turnover shall be constituted:

(a) as regards agreements, decisions of associations of undertakings and concerted practices related to distribution and supply arrangements between non-competing undertakings, of the amounts derived from the sale of goods or the provision of services which are the subject matter of the agreements, decisions or concerted practices, and from the other goods or services which are considered by users to be equivalent in view of their characteristics, price and intended use;

(b) as regards agreements, decisions of associations of undertakings and concerted practices related to arrangements on transfer of technology between non-competing undertakings, of the amounts derived from the sale of goods or the provision of services which result from the technology which is the subject matter of the agreements, decisions or concerted practices, and of the amounts derived from the sale of those goods or the provision of those services which that technology is designed to improve or replace.

2. However, where at the time of the coming to existence of arrangements as described in paragraph 1(a) and (b) turnover as regards the sale of products or the provision of services is not in evidence, the general provision as contained in Article 2 shall apply.

ANNEX II

LIST OF RELEVANT ACTS

(as of 1 March 1995)

(If you think it possible that your arrangements do not need to be notified by virtue of any of these regulations or notices it may be worth your while to obtain a copy.)

Implementing Regulations[31]

Council Regulation No. of 6 February 1992: First Regulation implementing Articles 81 and 82 of the Treaty (OJ No. 13, 21.2.1962, p. 204/62, English Special Edition 1959–1962, November 1972, p. 87) as amended (OJ No. 58, 10.7.1962, p. 1655/62; OJ No. 162, 7.11.1963, p. 2696/63; OJ No. L285, 29.12.1971, p. 49; OJ No. L73, 27.3.1972, p. 92; OJ No. L291, 19.11.1979, p. 94 and OJ No. L302, 15.11.1985, p. 165).

Commission Regulation (EC) No. 3385/94 of 21 December 1994 on the form, content and other details of applications and notifications provided for in Council Regulation No. 17.

Regulations Granting Block Exemption in Respect of a Wide Range of Agreements

Commission Regulation (EC) No. 1983/83 of 22 June 1983 on the application of Article 81(3) of the Treaty to categories of exclusive distribution agreements (OJ No. L173, 30.6.1983, p. 1, as corrected in OJ No. L281, 13.10.1983, p. 24), as well as this Regulation as adapted for EEA purposes (see point 2 of Annex XIV to the EEA Agreement).

Commission Regulation (EEC) No. 1984/83 of 22 June 1983 on the application of Article 81(3) of the Treaty to categories of exclusive purchasing agreements (OJ No. L173, 30.6.1983, p. 5, as corrected in OJ No. L281, 13.10.1983, p. 24), as well as this Regulation as adapted for EEA purposes (see point 3 of Annex XIV to the EEA Agreement).

See also the Commission notices concerning Regulations (EEC) No. 1983/93 and (EEC) No. 1984/83 (OJ No. C101, 13.4.1984, p. 2 and OJ No. C121, 13.5.1992, p. 2).

Commission Regulation (EEC) No. 2349/84 of 23 July 1984 on the application of Article 81(3) of the Treaty to certain categories of patent licensing agreements (OJ No. L219, 16.8.1984, p. 15, as corrected in OJ No. L113, 26.4.1985, p. 34), as amended (OJ No. L12, 18.1.1995, p. 13), as well as this Regulation as adapted for EEA purposes (see point 5 of Annex XIV to the EEA Agreement). Article 4 of this Regulation provides for an opposition procedure.

Commission Regulation (EEC) No. 123/85 of 12 December 1984 on the application of Article 81(3) of the Treaty to certain categories of motor vehicle distributing and servicing agreements (OJ No. L15, 18.1.1985, p. 16); as well as this Regulation as adapted for EEA purposes (see point 4 of Annex XIV to the EEA Agreement). See also the Commission notices concerning this Regulation (OJ No. C17, 18.1.1985, p. 4 and OJ No. C329, 18.12.1991, p. 20).

Commission Regulation (EEC) No. 417/85 of 19 December 1984 on the application of Article 81(3) of the Treaty to categories of specialization agreements (OJ No. L53, 22.2.1985, p. 1), as amended (OJ No. L21, 29.1.1993, p. 8), as well as this Regulation as adapted for EEA purposes (see point 6 of Annex XIV to the EEA Agreement). Article 4 of this Regulation provides for an opposition procedure.

Commission Regulation (EEC) No. 418/85 of 19 December 1984 on the application of Article 81(3) of the Treaty to categories of research and development cooperation agreements (OJ No. L53, 22.2.1985, p. 5), as amended (OJ No. L21, 29.1.1993, p. 8), as well as this Regulation as adapted for EEA purposes (see point 7 of Annex XIV to the EEA Agreement). Article 7 of this Regulation provides for an opposition procedure.

---

[31] As regards procedural rules applied by the EFTA Surveillance Authority, see Article 3 of Protocol 21 to the EEA Agreement and the relevant provisions in Protocol 4 to the Agreement between the EFTA States on the establishment of a Surveillance Authority and a Court of Justice.

Commission Regulation (EEC) No. 4087/88 of 30 November 1988 on the application of Article 81(3) of the Treaty to categories of franchise agreements (OJ No. L359, 28.12.1988, p. 46), as well as this Regulation as adapted for EEA purposes (see point 8 of Annex XIV to the EEA Agreement). Article 6 of this Regulation provides for an opposition procedure.

Commission Regulation (EEC) No. 556/89 of 30 November 1988 on the application of Article 81(3) of the Treaty to certain categories of know-how licensing agreements (OJ No. L61, 4.3.1989, p. 1), as amended (OJ No. L21, 29.1.1993, p. 8), as well as this Regulation as adapted for EEA purposes (see point 9 of Annex XIV to the EEA Agreement). Article 4 of this Regulation provides for an opposition procedure.

Commission Regulation (EEC) No. 3932/92 of 21 December 1992 on the application of Article 81(3) of the Treaty to certain categories of agreements, decisions and concerted practices in the insurance sector (OJ No. L398, 31.12.1992, p. 7). This Regulation will be adapted for EEA purposes.

NOTICES OF A GENERAL NATURE[32]

Commission notice on exclusive dealing contracts with commercial agents (OJ No. 139, 24.12.1962, p. 2921/62). This states that the Commission does not consider most such agreements to fall under the prohibition of Article 81(1).

Commission notice concerning agreements, decisions and concerted practices in the field of cooperation between enterprises (OJ No. C75, 29.7.1968, p. 3, as corrected in OJ No. C84, 28.8.1968, p. 14). This defines the sorts of cooperation on market studies, accounting, R & D, joint use of production, storage of transport, ad hoc consortia, selling or after-sales service, advertising or quality labelling that the Commission considers not to fall under the prohibition of Article 81(1).

Commission notice concerning its assessment of certain subcontracting agreements in relation to Article 81(1) of the Treaty (OJ No. C1, 3.1.1979, p. 2).

Commission notice on agreements, decisions and concerted practices of minor importance which do not fall under Article 81(1) of the Treaty (OJ No. C231, 12.9.1986, p. 2) as amended by Commission notice (OJ No. C368, 23.12.1994, p. 20)—in the main, those where the parties have less than 5 per cent of the market between them, and a combined annual turnover of less than ECU 300 million.

Commission guidelines on the application of EEC competition rules in the telecommunications sector (OJ No. C233, 6.9.1991, p. 2). These guidelines aim at clarifying the application of Community competition rules to the market participants in the telecommunications sector.

Commission notice on cooperation between national courts and the Commission in applying Articles 81 and 82 (OJ No. C39, 13.2.1993, p. 6). This notice sets out the principles on the basis of which such cooperation takes place.

Commission notice concerning the assessment of cooperative joint ventures pursuant to Article 81 of the EC Treaty (OJ No. C43, 16.2.1993, p. 2). This notice sets out the principles on the assessment of joint ventures.

A collection of these texts (as at 31 December 1989) was published by the Office for Official Publications of the European Communities (references Vol. 1: ISBN 92–826–1307–0, catalogue No. CV-42-90-001-EN-C). An updated collection is in preparation.

Pursuant to the Agreement, these texts will also cover the European Economic Area.

---

[32] See also the corresponding notices published by the EFTA Surveillance Authority.

ANNEX III

LIST OF MEMBER STATES AND EFTA STATES, ADDRESS OF THE COMMISSION
AND OF THE EFTA SURVEILLANCE AUTHORITY, LIST OF COMMISSION
INFORMATION OFFICES WITHIN THE COMMUNITY AND IN EFTA STATES AND
ADDRESSES OF COMPETENT AUTHORITIES IN EFTA STATES

The Member States as at the date of this Annex are: Austria, Belgium, Denmark, Finland, France, Germany, Greece, Ireland, Italy, Luxembourg, the Netherlands, Portugal, Spain, Sweden and the United Kingdom.

The EFTA States which will be Contracting Parties of the EEA Agreement, as at the date of this Annex, are: Iceland, Liechtenstein and Norway.

The address of the Commission's Directorate-General for Competition is:

Commission of the European Communities
Directorate-General for Competition
200 rue de la Loi
B-1049 Brussels
Tel. (322) 299 11 11

The address of the EFTA Surveillance Authority's Competition Directorate is:

EFTA Surveillance Authority
Competition Directorate
1–3 rue Marie-Thérèse
B-1040 Brussels
Tel. (322) 286 17 11

The addresses of the Commission's Information Offices in the Community are:

BELGIUM
73 rue Archimède
B-1040 Bruxelles
Tel. (322) 299 11 11

DENMARK
Højbrohus
Østergade 61
Postboks 144
DK-1004 København K
Tel. (4533) 14 41 40

FEDERAL REPUBLIC OF
GERMANY
Zitelmannstraße 22
D-53113 Bonn
Tel. (49228) 53 00 90

Kurfürstendamm 102
D-10711 Berlin 31
Tel. (4930) 896 09 30
Erhardtstraße 27
D-80331 München
Tel. (4989) 202 10 11

GREECE
2 Vassilissis Sofias
Case Postale 11002
GR-Athina 10674
Tel. (301) 724 39 82/83/84

SPAIN
Calle de Serrano 41
5a Planta
E-28001 Madrid
Tel. (341) 435 17 00

Av. Diagonal, 407 bis
18 Planta
E-08008 Barcelona
Tel. (343) 415 81 77

FRANCE
288, boulevard Saint-Germain
F-75007 Paris
Tel. (331) 40 63 38 00

CMCI
2, rue Henri Barbusse
F-13241 Marseille, Cedex 01
Tel. (3391) 91 46 00

IRELAND
39 Molesworth Street
IRL-Dublin 2
Tel. (3531) 71 22 44

ITALY
Via Poli 29
I-00187
Roma
Tel. (396) 699 11 60

Corso Magenta 61
I-20123 Milano
Tel. (392) 480 15 05

LUXEMBURG
Bâtiment Jean-Monnet
rue Alcide de Gasperi
L-2920 Luxembourg
Tel. (352) 430 11

NETHERLANDS
Postbus 30465 NL-2500 GL Den Haag
Tel. (3170) 346 93 26

AUSTRIA
Hoyosgasse 5
A-1040 Wien
Tel. (431) 505 33 79

PORTUGAL
Centro Europeu Jean Monnet
Largo Jean Monnet, 1-10°
P-1200 Lisboa
Tel. (3511) 54 11 44

FINLAND
31 Pohjoisesplanadi
00100 Helsinki
Tel. (3580) 65 64 20

SWEDEN
PO Box 16396
Hamngatan 6
11147 Stockholm
Tel. (468) 611 11 72

UNITED KINGDOM
8 Storey's Gate
UK-London SW1P 3AT
Tel. (4471) 973 19 92

Windsor House
9/15 Bedford Street
UK-Belfast BT2 7EG
Tel. (44232) 24 07 08

4 Cathedral Road
UK-Cardiff CF1 9SG
Tel. (44222) 37 16 31

9 Alva Street
UK-Edinburgh EH2 4PH
Tel. (4431) 225 20 58

The addresses of the Commission's Information Offices in the EFTA States are:

NORWAY
Postboks 1643 Vika 0119 Oslo 1
Haakon's VII Gate No. 6
0161 Oslo 1
Tel. (472) 83 35 83

Forms for notification and applications, as well as more detailed information on the EEA competition rules, can also be obtained from the following offices:

AUSTRIA
Federal Ministry for Economic
Affairs
Tel. (431) 71 100

LIECHTENSTEIN
Office of National Economy
Division of Economy and Statistics
Tel. (4175) 61 11

FINLAND
Office of Free Competition
Tel. (3580) 73 141

NORWAY
Price Directorate
Tel. (4722) 40 09 00

ICELAND
Directorate of Competition and Fair
Trade
Tel. (3541) 27 422

SWEDEN
Competition Authority
Tel. (468) 700 16 00

APPENDIX 50

REGULATION 2842/98[1]

On the Hearing of Parties in Certain Proceedings under Articles 81 and 82 of the EC Treaty

(Text with EEA relevance)

THE COMMISSION OF THE EUROPEAN COMMUNITIES,

Having regard to the Treaty establishing the European Community,

Having regard to the Agreement on the European Economic Area,

Having regard to Council Regulation No 17 of 6 February 1962, First Regulation implementing Articles 81 and 82 of the Treaty,[2] as last amended by the Act of Accession of Austria, Finland and Sweden, and in particular Article 24 thereof,

Having regard to Council Regulation (EEC) No 1017/68 of 19 July 1968 applying rules of competition to transport by rail, road and inland waterway,[3] as last amended by the Act of Accession of Austria, Finland and Sweden, and in particular Article 29 thereof,

Having regard to Council Regulation (EEC) No 4056/86 of 22 December 1986 laying down detailed rules for the application of Articles 81 and 82 of the Treaty to maritime transport,[4] as last amended by the Act of Accession of Austria, Finland and Sweden, and in particular Article 26 thereof,

Having regard to Council Regulation (EEC) No 3975/87 of 14 December 1987 laying down the procedure for the application of the rules on competition to undertakings in the air transport sector,[5] as last amended by Regulation (EEC) No 2410/92,[6] and in particular Article 19 thereof,

Having consulted the appropriate Advisory Committees on Restrictive Practices and Dominant Positions,

(1) Whereas a great deal of experience has been acquired in the application of Commission Regulation No 99/63/EEC of 25 July 1963 on the hearings provided for in Article 19(1) and (2) of Regulation No 17,[7] Commission Regulation (EEC) No 1630/69 of 8 August 1969 on the hearings provided for in Article 26(1) and (2) of Council Regulation (EEC) No 1017/68 of 19 July 1968,[8] Section II of Commission Regulation (EEC) No 4260/88 of 16 December 1988 on the communications, complaints and applications and the hearings provided for in Council Regulation (EEC) No 4056/86

---

[1] OJ 1998 L354/18, of 22–12–98.
[2] OJ 1962 13/204.
[3] OJ 1968 L175/1.
[4] OJ 1986 L378/4.
[5] OJ 1987 L374/1.
[6] OJ 1992 L240/18.
[7] OJ 1963 127/2268.
[8] OJ 1969 209/11.

laying down detailed rules for the application of Articles 81 and 82 of the Treaty to maritime transport,[9] as last amended by the Act of Accession of Austria, Finland and Sweden, and Section II of Commission Regulation (EEC) No 4261/88 of 16 December 1988 on the complaints, applications and hearings provided for in Council Regulation (EEC) No 3975/87 laying down the procedure for the application of the rules on competition to undertakings in the air transport sector[10];

(2) Whereas that experience has revealed the need to improve certain procedural aspects of those Regulations; whereas it is appropriate for the sake of clarity to adopt a single Regulation on the various hearing procedures laid down by Regulation No 17, Regulation (EEC) No 1017/68, Regulation (EEC) No 4056/86 and Regulation (EEC) No 3975/87; whereas, accordingly, Regulations No 99/63/EEC and (EEC) No 1630/69 should be replaced, and Sections II of Regulations (EEC) No 4260/88 and (EEC) No 4261/88 should be deleted and replaced;

(3) Whereas the provisions relating to the Commission's procedure under Decision 94/810/ECSC, EC of 12 December 1994 on the terms of reference of hearing officers in competition procedures before the Commission[11] should be framed in such a way as to safeguard fully the right to be heard and the rights of defence; whereas for these purposes, the Commission should distinguish between the respective rights to be heard of the parties to which the Commission has addressed objections, of the applicants and complainants, and of other third parties;

(4) Whereas in accordance with the principle of the rights of defence, the parties to which the Commission has addressed objections should be given the opportunity to submit their comments on all the objections which the Commission proposes to take into account in its decisions;

(5) Whereas the applicants and complainants should be granted the opportunity of expressing their views, if the Commission considers that there are insufficient grounds for granting the application or acting on the complaint; whereas the applicant or complainant should be provided with a copy of the non-confidential version of the objections and should be permitted to make known its views in writing where the Commission raises objections;

(6) Whereas other third parties having sufficient interest should also be given the opportunity of expressing their views in writing where they make a written application to do so;

(7) Whereas the various parties entitled to submit comments should do so in writing, both in their own interest and in the interests of sound administration, without prejudice to the possibility of an oral hearing where appropriate to supplement the written procedure;

(8) Whereas it is necessary to define the rights of persons who are to be heard and on what conditions they may be represented or assisted;

(9) Whereas the Commission should continue to respect the legitimate interest of undertakings in the protection of their business secrets and other confidential information;

(10) Whereas compatibility should be ensured between the Commission's current administrative practices and the case-law of the Court of Justice and the Court of First Instance of the European Communities in accordance with the Commission notice on the internal rules of procedure for processing requests for access to the file in cases pursuant to Articles 81 and 82 of the Treaty, Articles 65 and 66 of the ECSC Treaty and Council Regulation (EEC) No 4064/89[12];

---

[9] OJ 1988 L376/1.
[10] OJ 1988 L376/10.
[11] OJ 1994 L330/67.
[12] OJ 1997 C23/3.

(11) Whereas to facilitate the proper conduct of the hearing it is appropriate to allow statements made by each person at a hearing to be recorded;

(12) Whereas in the interest of legal certainty, it is appropriate to set the time limit for the submissions by the various persons pursuant to this Regulation by defining the date by which the submission must reach the Commission;

(13) Whereas the appropriate Advisory Committee under Article 10(3) of Regulation No 17, Article 16(3) of Regulation (EEC) No 1017/68, Article 15(3) of Regulation (EEC) No 4056/86 or Article 8(3) of Regulation (EEC) No 3975/87 must deliver its opinion on the basis of a preliminary draft decision; whereas it should therefore be consulted on a case after the inquiry in that case has been completed; whereas such consultation should not prevent the Commission from reopening an inquiry if need be,

HAS ADOPTED THIS REGULATION:

CHAPTER I

Scope

Article 1

This Regulation shall apply to the hearing of parties under Article 19(1) and (2) of Regulation No 17, Article 26(1) and (2) of Regulation (EEC) No 1017/68, Article 23(1) and (2) of Regulation (EEC) No 4056/86 and Article 16(1) and (2) of Regulation (EEC) No 3975/87.

CHAPTER II

Hearing of parties to which the Commission has addressed objections

Article 2

1. The Commission shall hear the parties to which it has addressed objections before consulting the appropriate Advisory Committee under Article 10(3) of Regulation No 17, Article 16(3) of Regulation (EEC) No 1017/68, Article 15(3) of Regulation (EEC) No 4056/86 or Article 8(3) of Regulation (EEC) No 3975/87.

2. The Commission shall in its decisions deal only with objections in respect of which the parties have been afforded the opportunity of making their views known.

Article 3

1. The Commission shall inform the parties in writing of the objections raised against them. The objections shall be notified to each of them or to a duly appointed agent.

2. The Commission may inform the parties by giving notice in the *Official Journal of the European Communities*, if from the circumstances of the case this appears appropriate,

in particular where notice is to be given to a number of undertakings but no joint agent has been appointed. The notice shall have regard to the legitimate interests of the undertakings in the protection of their business secrets and other confidential information.

3. A fine or a periodic penalty payment may be imposed on a party only if the objections have been notified in the manner provided for in paragraph 1.

4. The Commission shall, when giving notice of objections, set a date by which the parties may inform it in writing of their views.

5. The Commission shall set a date by which the parties may indicate any parts of the objections which in their view contain business secrets or other confidential material. If they do not do so by that date, the Commission may assume that the objections do not contain such information.

Article 4

1. Parties which wish to make known their views on the objections raised against them shall do so in writing and by the date referred to in Article 3(4). The Commission shall not be obliged to take into account written comments received after that date.

2. The parties may in their written comments set out all matters relevant to their defence. They may attach any relevant documents as proof of the facts set out and may also propose that the Commission hear persons who may corroborate those facts.

Article 5

The Commission shall afford to parties against which objections have been raised the opportunity to develop their arguments at an oral hearing, if they so request in their written comments.

CHAPTER III

Hearing of applicants and complainants

Article 6

Where the Commission, having received an application made under Article 3(2) of Regulation No 17 or a complaint made under Article 10 of Regulation (EEC) No 1017/68, Article 10 of Regulation (EEC) No 4056/86 or Article 3(1) of Regulation (EEC) No 3975/87, considers that on the basis of the information in its possession there are insufficient grounds for granting the application or acting on the complaint, it shall inform the applicant or complainant of its reasons and set a date by which the applicant or complainant may make known its views in writing.

Article 7

Where the Commission raises objections relating to an issue in respect of which it has received an application or a complaint as referred to in Article 6, it shall provide an applicant or complainant with a copy of the non-confidential version of the objections and

511

set a date by which the applicant or complainant may make known its views in writing.

Article 8

The Commission may, where appropriate, afford to applicants and complainants the opportunity of orally expressing their views, if they so request in their written comments.

CHAPTER IV

Hearing of other third parties

Article 9

1. If parties other than those referred to in Chapters II and III apply to be heard and show a sufficient interest, the Commission shall inform them in writing of the nature and subject matter of the procedure and shall set a date by which they may make known their views in writing.

2. The Commission may, where appropriate, invite parties referred to in paragraph 1 to develop their arguments at the oral hearing of the parties against which objections have been raised, if they so request in their written comments.

3. The Commission may afford to any other third parties the opportunity of orally expressing their views.

CHAPTER V

General provisions

Article 10

Hearings shall be conducted by the Hearing Officer.

Article 11

1. The Commission shall invite the persons to be heard to attend the oral hearing on such date as it shall appoint.

2. The Commission shall invite the competent authorities of the Member States to take part in the oral hearing.

Article 12

1. Persons invited to attend shall either appear in person or be represented by legal representatives or by representatives authorised by their constitution as appropriate. Undertakings and associations of undertakings may be represented by a duly authorised agent appointed from among their permanent staff.

2. Persons heard by the Commission may be assisted by their legal advisers or other qualified persons admitted by the Hearing Officer.

3. Oral hearings shall not be public. Each person shall be heard separately or in the presence of other persons invited to attend. In the latter case, regard shall be had to the legitimate interest of the undertakings in the protection of their business secrets and other confidential information.

4. The statements made by each person heard shall be recorded on tape. The recording shall be made available to such persons on request, by means of a copy from which business secrets and other confidential information shall be deleted.

Article 13

1. Information, including documents, shall not be communicated or made accessible in so far as it contains business secrets of any party, including the parties to which the Commission has addressed objections, applicants and complainants and other third parties, or other confidential information or where internal documents of the authorities are concerned. The Commission shall make appropriate arrangements for allowing access to the file, taking due account of the need to protect business secrets, internal Commission documents and other confidential information.

2. Any party which makes known its views under the provisions of this Regulation shall clearly identify any material which it considers to be confidential, giving reasons, and provide a separate non-confidential version by the date set by the Commission. If it does not do so by the set date, the Commission may assume that the submission does not contain such material.

Article 14

In setting the dates provided for in Articles 3(4), 6, 7 and 9(1), the Commission shall have regard both to the time required for preparation of the submission and to the urgency of the case. The time allowed in each case shall be at least two weeks; it may be extended.

CHAPTER VI

Final provisions

Article 15

1. Regulations No 99/63/EEC and (EEC) No 1630/69 are repealed.
2. Sections II of Regulations (EEC) No 4260/88 and (EEC) No 4261/88 are deleted.

Article 16

This Regulation shall enter into force on 1 February 1999.

This Regulation shall be binding in its entirety and directly applicable in all Member States.

Done at Brussels, 22 December 1998.

APPENDIX 51

REGULATION 2988/74[1]

Concerning Limitation Periods in Proceedings and the Enforcement of Sanctions under the Rules of the European Economic Community relating to Transport and Competition

THE COUNCIL OF THE EUROPEAN COMMUNITIES

Having regard to the Treaty establishing the European Economic Community, and in particular Articles 71, 75 and 83 thereof;

Having regard to the proposal from the Commission;

Having regard to the Opinion of the European Parliament;

Having regard to the Opinion of the Economic and Social Committee;

Whereas under the rules of the European Economic Community relating to transport and competition the Commission has the power to impose fines, penalties and periodic penalty payments on undertakings or associations of undertakings which infringe Community law relating to information or investigation, or to the prohibition on discrimination, restrictive practices and abuse of dominant position; whereas those rules make no provision for any limitation period;

Whereas it is necessary in the interest of legal certainty that the principle of limitation be introduced and that implementing rules be laid down; whereas, for the matter to be covered fully, it is necessary that provision for limitation be made not only as regards the power to impose fines or penalties, but also as regards the power to enforce decisions, imposing fines, penalties or periodic penalty payments; whereas such provisions should specify the length of limitation periods, the date on which time starts to run and the events which have the effect of interrupting or suspending the limitation period; whereas in this respect the interests of undertakings and associations of undertakings on the one hand, and the requirements imposed by administrative practice, on the other hand, should be taken into account;

Whereas this Regulation must apply to the relevant provisions of Regulation 11 concerning the abolition of discrimination in transport rates and conditions, in implementation of Article 75(3) of the Treaty establishing the European Economic Community, of Regulation 17: first Regulation implementing Articles 81 and 82 of the Treaty, and of Council Regulation 1017/68 of 19 July 1968, applying rules of competition to transport by rail, road and inland waterway; whereas it must also apply to the relevant provisions of future regulations in the fields of European Economic Community law relating to transport and competition.

---

[1] OJ 1974 L319/1.

Has Adopted This Regulation:

Article 1

Limitation periods in proceedings

1. The power of the Commission to impose fines or penalties for infringements of the rules of the European Community relating to transport or competition shall be subject to the following limitation periods;

(a) three years in the case of infringements of provisions concerning applications or notifications of undertakings or associations of undertakings, requests for information, or the carrying out of investigations;
(b) five years in the case of all other infringements.

2. Time shall begin to run upon the day on which the infringement is committed. However, in the case of continuing or repeated infringements, time shall begin to run on the day on which the infringement ceases..

Article 2

Interruption of the limitation period in proceedings

1. Any action taken by the Commission, or by any Member State, acting at the request of the Commission, for the purpose of the preliminary investigation or proceedings in respect of an infringement shall interrupt the limitation period in proceedings. The limitation period shall be interrupted with effect from the date on which the action is notified to at least one undertaking or association of undertakings which have participated in the infringement.
Actions which interrupt the running of the period shall include in particular the following:

(a) written requests for information by the Commission, or by the competent authority of a Member State acting at the request of the Commission; or a Commission decision requiring the requested information;
(b) written authorisations issued to their officials by the Commission or by the competent authority of any Member State at the request of the Commission; or a Commission decision ordering an investigation;
(c) the commencement of proceedings by the Commission;
(d) notification of the Commission's statement of objections.

2. The interruption of the limitation period shall apply for all the undertakings or associations of undertakings which have participated in the infringement.
3. Each interruption shall start time running afresh. However, the limitation period shall expire at the latest on the day on which a period equal to twice the limitation period has elapsed without the Commission having imposed a fine or a penalty; that period shall be extended by the time during which limitation is suspended pursuant to Article 3.

Article 3

Suspension of the limitation period in proceedings

The limitation period in proceedings shall be suspended for as long as the decision of the Commission is the subject of proceedings pending before the Court of Justice of the European Communities.

Article 4

Limitation period for the enforcement of sanctions

1. The power of the Commission to enforce decisions imposing fines, penalties or periodic payments for infringements of the rules of the European Economic Community relating to transport or competition shall be subject to a limitation period of five years.
2. Time shall begin to run on the day on which the decision becomes final.

Article 5

Interruption of the limitation period for the enforcement of sanctions

1. The limitation period for the enforcement of sanctions shall be interrupted:

(a) by notification of a decision varying the original amount of the fine, penalty or periodic penalty payments or refusing an application for variation;
(b) by any action of the Commission, or of a Member State at the request of the Commission, for the purpose of enforcing payments of a fine, penalty or periodic penalty payment.

2. Each interruption shall start time running afresh.

Article 6

Suspension of the limitation period for the enforcement of sanctions

The limitation period for the enforcement of sanctions shall be suspended for so long as:

(a) time to pay is allowed; or
(b) enforcement of payment is suspended pursuant to a decision of the Court of Justice of the European Communities.

Article 7

Application to transitional cases

This Regulation shall also apply in respect of infringements committed before it enters into force.

Article 8

Entry into force

This Regulation shall enter into force on 1 January 1975.
This Regulation shall be binding on its entirety and directly applicable in all Member States.

Done at Brussels, 26 November 1974.

APPENDIX 52

COMMISSION NOTICE[1]

On the Internal Rules of Procedure for Processing Requests for Access to the File in Cases Pursuant to Articles 81 and 82 of the EC Treaty, Articles 65 and 66 of the ECSC Treaty and Council Regulation (EEC) No 4064/89

(Text with EEA relevance)

INTRODUCTION

Access to the file is an important procedural stage in all contentious competition cases (prohibitions with or without a fine, prohibitions of mergers, rejection of complaints, etc.). The Commission's task in this area is to reconcile two opposing obligations, namely that of safeguarding the rights of the defence and that of protecting confidential information concerning firms.

The purpose of this notice is to ensure compatibility between current administrative practice regarding access to the file and the case-law of the Court of Justice of the European Communities and the Court of First Instance, in particular the "Soda-ash" cases.[2] The line of conduct thus laid down concerns cases dealt with on the basis of the competition rules applicable to enterprises: Articles 81 and 82 of the EC Treaty, Regulation (EEC) No 4064/89[3] (hereinafter "the Merger Regulation"), and Articles 65 and 66 of the ECSC Treaty.

Access to the file, which is one of the procedural safeguards designed to ensure effective exercise of the right to be heard[4] provided for in Article 19(1) and (2) of Council Regulation No 17[5] and Article 2 of Commission Regulation No 99/63/EEC,[6] as well as in the corresponding provisions of the Regulations governing the application of Articles 81 and 82 in the field of transport, must be arranged in all cases involving decisions on infringements, decisions rejecting complaints, decisions imposing interim measures and decisions adopted on the basis of Article 15(6) of Regulation No 17.

The guidelines set out below, however, essentially relate to the rights of the undertakings which are the subject of investigations into alleged infringements; they do not relate to the rights of third parties, and complainants in particular.

In merger cases, access to the file by parties directly concerned is expressly provided for in Article 18(3) of the Merger Regulation and in Article 13(3)(a) of Regulation (EC) No 3384/94[7] ("the Implementing Regulation").

---

[1] OJ 1997 C23/3

[2] Court of First Instance judgments in Cases T–30/91, *Solvay v. Commission*, T–36/91, *ICI v. Commission*, and T–37/91, *ICI v. Commission* [1995] ECR II–1775, II–1847 and II–1901.

[3] OJ 1989 L395/1, as corrected in OJ No 1990 L257/13.

[4] Judgment of the Court of First Instance in Joined Cases T–10, 11, 12 and 15/92, *CBR and Others* [1992] ECR II–2667, at paragraph 38.

[5] OJ 1962 13/204.

[6] OJ 1963 127/2268.

[7] OJ 1994 L377/1.

517

I. Scope and limits of access to the file

As the purpose of providing access to the file is to enable the addressees of a statement of objections to express their views on the conclusions reached by the Commission, the firms in question must have access to all the documents making up the "file" of the Commission (DG IV), apart from the categories of documents identified in the *Hercules* judgment,[8] namely the business secrets of other undertakings, internal Commission documents[9] and other confidential information.

Thus not all the documents collected in the course of an investigation are communicable and a distinction must be made between non-communicable and communicable documents.

A. Non-communicable documents

1. Business secrets

Business secrets mean information (documents or parts of documents) for which an undertaking has claimed protection as "business secrets", and which are recognized as such by the Commission.

The non-communicability of such information is intended to protect the legitimate interest of firms in preventing third parties from obtaining strategic information on their essential interests and on the operation or development of their business.[10]

The criteria for determining what constitutes a business secret have not as yet been defined in full. Reference may be made, however, to the case-law, especially the *Akzo* and the *BAT and Reynolds* judgments,[11] to the criteria used in anti-dumping procedures,[12] and to decisions on the subject by the Hearing Officer. The term "business secret" must be construed in its broader sense: according to *Akzo*, Regulation No 17 requires the Commission to have regard to the legitimate interest of firms in the protection of their business secrets.

Business secrets need no longer be protected when they are known outside the firm (or group or association of firms) to which they relate. Nor can facts remain business secrets if, owing to the passage of time or for any other reason, they are no longer commercially important.

Where business secrets provide evidence of an infringement or tend to exonerate a firm, the Commission must reconcile the interest in the protection of sensitive information, the public interest in having the infringement of the competition rules terminated, and the rights of the defence. This calls for an assessment of:

(i) the relevance of the information to determining whether or not an infringement has been committed;
(ii) its probative value;

---

[8] Court of First Instance judgment in Case T–7/89, *Hercules Chemicals v. Commission* [1991] ECR II–1711, paragraph 54.

[9] Internal Commission documents do not form part of the investigation file and are placed in the file of internal documents relating to the case under examination (see points I.A.3 and II.A.2 below).

[10] For example methods of assessing manufacturing and distribution costs, production secrets and processes, supply sources, quantities produced and sold, market shares, customer and distributor lists, marketing plants, cost price structure, sales policy, and information on the internal organization of the firm.

[11] Case 53/85, *Akzo* [1986] ECR 1965, paragraphs 24 to 28, and paragraph 28 in particular on pp. 1991–1992. Cases 142 and 156/84, *BAT and Reynolds v. Commission* [1987] ECR 4487, paragraph 21.

[12] Order of the Court of 30.3.1982 in Case 236/81, *Celanese v. Commission and Council* [1982] ECR 1183.

(iii) whether it is indispensable;
(iv) the degree of sensitivity involved (to what extent would disclosure of the information harm the interests of the firm?);
(v) the seriousness of the infringement.

Each document must be assessed individually to determine whether the need to disclose it is greater than the harm which might result from disclosure.

2. Confidential documents

It is also necessary to protect information for which confidentiality has been requested.

This category includes information making it possible to identify the suppliers of the information who wish to remain anonymous to the other parties, and certain types of information communicated to the Commission on condition that confidentiality is observed, such as documents obtained during an investigation which form part of a firm's property and are the subject of a non-disclosure request (such as a market study commissioned by the firm and forming part of its property). As in the preceding case (business secrets), the Commission must reconcile the legitimate interest of the firm in protecting its assets, the public interest in having breaches of the competition rules terminated, and the rights of the defence. Military secrets also belong in the category of "other confidential information".

As a rule, the confidential nature of documents is not a bar to their disclosure[13] if the information in question is necessary in order to prove an alleged infringement ("inculpatory documents") or if the papers invalidate or rebut the reasoning of the Commission set out in its statement of objections ("exculpatory documents").

3. Internal documents

Internal documents are, by their nature, not the sort of evidence on which the Commission can rely in its assessment of a case. For the most part they consist of drafts, opinions or memos from the departments concerned and relating to ongoing procedures.

The Commission departments must be able to express themselves freely within their institution concerning ongoing cases. The disclosure of such documents could also jeopardize the secrecy of the Commission's deliberations.

It should, moreover, be noted that the secrecy of proceedings is also protected by the code of conduct on public access to Commission and Council documents as set out in Commission Decision 94/90/ECSC, EC, Euratom,[14] as amended by Decision 96/567/ECSC, EC, Euratom[15] as are internal documents relating to inspections and investigations and those whose disclosure could jeopardize the protection of individual privacy, business and industrial secrets or the confidentiality requested by a legal or natural person.

These considerations justify the non-disclosure of this category of documents, which will, in future, be placed in the file of internal documents relating to cases under investigation, which is, as a matter of principle, inaccessible (see point II.A.2).

B. Communicable documents

All documents not regarded as "non-communicable" under the abovementioned criteria are accessible to the parties concerned.

---

[13] Here the procedure described in point II.A.1.3 should be followed.
[14] OJ 1994 L46/58.
[15] OJ 1996 L247/45.

Thus, access to the file is not limited to documents which the Commission regards as "relevant" to an undertaking's rights of defence.

The Commission does not select accessible documents in order to remove those which may be relevant to the defence of an undertaking. This concept, already outlined in the Court of First Instance judgments in *Hercules* and *Cimenteries CBR*,[16] was confirmed and developed in the *Soda-ash* case, where the Court held that "in the defended proceedings for which Regulation No 17 provides it cannot be for the Commission alone to decide which documents are of use for the defence. . . . The Commission must give the advisers of the undertaking concerned the opportunity to examine documents which may be relevant so that their probative value for the defence can be assessed." (Case T–30/91, paragraph 81).

Special note concerning studies:

It should be stressed that studies commissioned in connection with proceedings or for a specific file, whether used directly or indirectly in the proceedings, must be made accessible irrespective of their intrinsic value. Access must be given not only to the results of a study (reports, statistics, etc.), but also to the Commission's correspondence with the contractor, the tender specifications and the methodology of the study.[17]

However, correspondence relating to the financial aspects of a study and the references concerning the contractor remain confidential in the interests of the latter.

II. Procedures for implementing access to the file

A. Preparatory procedure—cases investigated pursuant to Articles 81 and 82

1. Investigation file

1.1. Return of certain documents after inspection visits

In the course of its investigations pursuant to Article 14(2) and (3) of Regulation No 17, the Commission obtains a considerable number of documents, some of which may, following a detailed examination, prove to be irrelevant to the case in question. Such documents are normally returned to the firm as rapidly as possible.

1.2. Request for a non-confidential version of a document

In order to facilitate access to the file at a later stage in proceedings, the undertakings concerned will be asked systematically to:

— detail the information (documents or parts of documents) which they regard as business secrets and the confidential documents whose disclosure would injure them,
— substantiate their claim for confidentiality in writing,

---

[16] In paragraph 54 of *Hercules*, referred to in paragraph 41 of the *Cimenteries* judgment, the Court of First Instance held that the Commission has an obligation to make available to the undertakings all documents, whether in their favour or otherwise, which it has obtained during the course of the investigation, save where the business secrets of other undertakings, the internal documents of the Commission or other confidential information are involved.

[17] As a result of this provision, it is necessary, when drawing up a study contract, to include a specific clause stipulating that the study and the relevant documents (methodology, correspondence with the Commission) may be disclosed by the Commission to third parties.

— give the Commission a non-confidential version of their confidential documents (where confidential passages are deleted).

As regards documents taken during an inspection (Article 14(2) and (3)), requests are made only after the inspectors have returned from their mission.

When an undertaking, in response to a request from the Commission, claims that the information supplied is confidential, the following procedure will be adopted:

(a) at that stage of the proceedings, claims of confidentiality which at first sight seem justified will be accepted provisionally. The Commission reserves the right, however, to reconsider the matter at a later stage of the proceedings;

(b) where it is apparent that the claim of confidentiality is clearly unjustified, for example where it relates to a document already published or distributed extensively, or is excessive where it covers all, or virtually all the documents obtained or sent without any plausible justification, the firm concerned will be informed that the Commission does not agree with the scope of the confidentiality that is claimed. The matter will be dealt with when the final assessment is made of the accessibility of the documents (see below).

1.3. Final assessment of the accessibility of documents

It may prove necessary to grant other undertakings involved access to a document even where the undertaking that has issued it objects, if the document serves as a basis for the decision[18] or is clearly an exculpatory document.

If an undertaking states that a document is confidential but does not submit a non-confidential version, the following procedure applies:

— the undertaking claiming confidentiality will be contacted again and asked for a reasonably coherent non-confidential version of the document.
— if the undertaking continues to object to the disclosure of the information, the competent department applies to the Hearing Officer, who will if necessary implement the procedure leading to a decision pursuant to Article 5(4) of Commission Decision 94/810/ECSC, EC of 12 December 1994 on the terms of reference of hearing officers in competition procedures before the Commission.[19] The undertaking will be informed by letter that the Hearing Officer is examining the question.

1.4. Enumerative list of documents

An enumerative list of documents should be drawn up according to the following principles:

(a) the list should include uninterrupted numbering of all the pages in the investigation file and an indication (using a classification code) of the degree of accessibility of the document and the parties with authorized access;

(b) an access code is given to each document on the list:

— accessible document
— partially accessible document

---

[18] For example, documents which help to define the scope, duration and nature of the infringement, the identity of participants, the harm to competition, the economic context, etc.
[19] OJ 1994 L330/67.

— non-accessible document;

(c) the category of completely non-accessible documents essentially consists of documents containing "business secrets" and other confidential documents. In view of the "*Soda-ash*" case-law, the list will include a summary enabling the content and subject of the documents to be identified, so that any firm having requested access to the file is able to determine in full knowledge of the facts whether the documents are likely to be relevant to its defence and to decide whether to request access despite that classification;

(d) accessible and partially accessible documents do not call for a description of their content in the list as they can be "physically" consulted by all firms, either in their full version or in their non-confidential version. In the latter event, only the sensitive passages are deleted in such a way that the firm with access is able to determine the nature of the information deleted (e.g. turnover).

2. File of internal documents relating to ongoing cases

In order to simplify administration and increase efficiency, internal documents will, in future, be placed in the file of internal documents relating to cases under investigation (non-accessible) containing all internal documents in chronological order. Classification in this category is subject to the control of the Hearing Officer, who will if necessary certify that the papers contained therein are "internal documents".

The following, for example, will be deemed to be internal documents:

(a) requests for instructions made to, and instructions received from, hierarchical superiors on the treatment of cases;

(b) consultations with other Commission departments on a case;

(c) correspondence with other public authorities concerning a case[20];

(d) drafts and other working documents;

(e) individual technical assistance contracts (languages, computing, etc.) relating to a specific aspect of a case.

---

[20] It is necessary to protect the confidentiality of documents obtained from public authorities; this rule applies not only to documents from competition authorities, but also to those from other public authorities, Member States or non-member countries.

Any exception to the principle of non-disclosure of these documents must be firmly justified on the grounds of safeguarding the rights of the defence (e.g. complaint lodged by a Member State pursuant to Article 3 of Regulation No 17). Letters simply expressing interest, whether from a public authority of a Member State or of a third country, are non-communicable in principle.

A distinction must be made, however, between the opinions or comments expressed by other public authorities, which are afforded absolute protection, and any specific documents they may have furnished, which are not always covered by the exception. In the latter case, it is advisable in any event to proceed with circumspection, especially if the documents are from a non-member country, as it is considered of prime importance for the development of international cooperation in the application of the competition rules, to safeguard the relationship of trust between the Commission and non-member countries.

There are two possibilities in this context:

a) There may already be an agreement governing the confidentiality of the information exchanged.

Article VIII(2) of the Agreement between the European Communities and the Government of the United States of America regarding the application of their competition laws (OJ 1995 L95/45) stipulates that exchanges of information and information received under the Agreement must be protected "to the fullest extent possible". The article lays down a point of international law which must be complied with.

b) If there is no such agreement, the same principle of guaranteed confidentiality should be observed.

B. Preparatory procedure—cases examined within the meaning of the Merger Regulation

1. Measures common to the preparatory procedure in cases investigated pursuant to Articles 81 and 82

(a) Return of certain documents after an inspection

On-the-spot inspections are specifically provided for in Article 13 of the Merger Regulation: in such cases, the procedure provided for in point II.A.1.1 for cases examined on the basis of Articles 81 and 82 is applicable.

(b) Enumerative list of documents

The enumerative list of the documents in the Commission file with the access codes will be drawn up in accordance with the criteria set out in point II.A.1.4.

(c) Request for a non-confidential version of a document

In order to facilitate access to the file, firms being investigated will be asked to:

— detail the information (documents or parts of documents) they regard as business secrets and the confidential documents whose disclosure would injure them,
— substantiate their request for confidentiality in writing,
— give the Commission a reasonably coherent non-confidential version of their confidential documents (where confidential passages are deleted).

This procedure will be followed in stage II cases (where the Commission initiates proceedings in respect of the notifying parties) and in stage I cases (giving rise to a Commission decision without initiation of proceedings).

2. Measures specific to preparatory procedures in merger cases

(a) Subsequent procedure in stage II cases

In stage II cases the subsequent procedure is as follows.

Where a firm states that all or part of the documents it has provided are business secrets, the following steps should be taken:

— if the claim appears to be justified, the documents or parts of documents concerned will be regarded as non-accessible to third parties,
— if the claim does not appear to be justified, the competent Commission department will ask the firm, in the course of the investigation and no later than the time at which the statement of objections is sent, to review its position. The firm must either state in writing which documents or parts of documents must be regarded as confidential, or send a non-confidential version of the documents.
  If disagreement regarding the extent of the confidentiality persists, the competent department refers the matter to the Hearing Officer, who may if necessary take the decision provided for in Article 5(4) of Decision 94/810/ECSC, EC.

(b) Specific cases

Article 9(1) of the Merger Regulation provides that "the Commission may, by means of a decision notified without delay to the undertakings concerned . . . refer a notified concentration to the competent authorities of the Member State concerned". In the context of access to the file, the parties concerned should, as a general rule be able to see the request for referral from a national authority, with the exception of any business secrets or other confidential information it may contain.

Article 22(3) of the Merger Regulation provides that "If the Commission finds, at the request of a Member State, that a concentration (. . .) that has no Community dimension (. . .) creates or strengthens a dominant position (. . .) it may (. . .) adopt the decisions provided for in the second subparagraph of Article 8(2), (3) and (4)". Such requests have the effect of empowering the Commission to deal with mergers which would normally fall outside its powers of review. Accordingly, the parties concerned should be granted right of access to the letter from the Member State requesting referral, after deletion of any business secrets or other confidential information.

C. Practical arrangements for access to the file

1. General rule: access by way of consultation on the Commission's premises

Firms are invited to examine the relevant files on the Commission's premises.

If the firm considers, on the basis of the list of documents it has received, that it requires certain non-accessible documents for its defence, it may make a reasoned request to that end to the Hearing Officer.[21]

2. If the file is not too bulky, however, the firm has the choice of being sent all the accessible documents, apart from those already sent with the statement of objections or the letter rejecting the complaint, or of consulting the file on the Commission's premises.

As regards Articles 81 and 82 cases, contrary to a common previous practice, the statement of objections or letter of rejection will in future be accompanied only by the evidence adduced and documents cited on which the objections/rejection letter is based.

Any request for access made prior to submission of the statement of objections will in principle be inadmissible.

D. Particular questions which may arise in connection with complaints and procedures relating to abuse of a dominant position (Articles 81 and 82)

1. Complaints

While complainants may properly be involved in proceedings, they do not have the same rights and guarantees as the alleged infringers. A complainant's right to consult the files does not share the same basis as the rights of defence of the addressees of a statement of objections, and there are no grounds for treating the rights of the complainant as equivalent to those of the firms objected to.

Nevertheless, a complainant who has been informed of the intention to reject his complaint may request access to the documents on which the Commission based its position. Complainants may not, however, have access to any confidential information or other business secrets belonging to the firms complained of, or to third-party firms, which the Commission has obtained in the course of its investigations (Articles 11 and 14 of Regulation No 17).

Clearly, it is even more necessary here to respect the principle of confidentiality as there is no presumption of infringement. In accordance with the judgment in *Fedetab*,[22] Article

---

[21] Special procedure provided for in Decision 94/810/ECSC, EC.

[22] Cases 209–215 and 218/78, *Fedetab* [1980] ECR 3125, paragraph 46.

19(2) of Regulation No 17 gives complainants a right to be heard and not a right to receive confidential information.

2. *Procedures in cases of abuse of a dominant position*

The question of procedures in cases of abuse of a dominant position was referred to by the Court of First instance and the Court of Justice in the *BPB Industries and British Gypsum v. Commission* case.[23]

By definition, firms in a dominant position on a market are able to place very considerable economic or commercial pressure on their competitors or on their trading partners, customers or suppliers.

The Court of First Instance and the Court of Justice thus acknowledged the legitimacy of the reluctance displayed by the Commission in revealing certain letters received from customers of the firm being investigated.

Although it is of value to the Commission for giving a better understanding of the market concerned, the information does not in any way constitute inculpatory evidence, and its disclosure to the firm concerned might easily expose the authors to the risk of retaliatory measures.

---

[23] Judgment of the Court of First Instance in Case T–65/89, *BPB Industries and British Gypsum* [1993] ECR II–389, and judgment of the Court of Justice in Case C–310/93 P in *BPB Industries and British Gypsum* [1995] ECR I–865.

APPENDIX 53

COMMISSION DECISION[1]

On the Terms of Reference of Hearing Officers in Competition Procedures Before the Commission

THE COMMISSION OF THE EUROPEAN COMMUNITIES,

Having regard to the Treaty establishing the European Coal and Steel Community,
Having regard to the Treaty establishing the European Community,
Whereas the treaties establishing the Communities and the rules implementing those treaties in relation to competition matters provide for the right of the parties concerned and of third parties to be heard before a final decision affecting their interests is taken;
Whereas the Commission must ensure that that right is guaranteed in its competition proceedings;
Whereas it is appropriate to entrust the organisation and conduct of the administrative procedures designed to protect the right to be heard to an independent person experienced in competition matters, in the interest of contributing to the objectivity, transparency and efficiency of Commission's competition proceedings;
Whereas the Commission created the post of Hearing Officer for these purposes in 1982 and laid down his terms of reference;
Whereas it is necessary to adapt and consolidate those terms of reference in the light of subsequent developments in Community law,

HAS DECIDED AS FOLLOWS:

Article 1

1. The hearings provided for in the provisions implementing Articles 65 and 66 of the ECSC Treaty, Articles 81 and 82 of the EC Treaty and Council Regulation (EEC) No. 4064/89[2] shall be organised and conducted by the Hearing Officer in accordance with Articles 2 to 10 of this Decision.
2. The implementing provisions referred to in paragraph 1 are:

(a) Article 36(1) of the ECSC Treaty;
(b) Regulation No. 99/63/EEC of the Commission of 25 July 1963 on the hearings provided for in Article 19(1) and (2) of Council Regulation No. 17[3];
(c) Regulation (EEC) No. 1630/69 of the Commission of 8 August 1969 on the hearings provided for in Article 26(1) and (2) of Council Regulation (EEC) No. 1017/68 of 19 July 1968[4];

---

[1] OJ 1994 L330/67.
[2] OJ L395, 30.12.1989, p. 1 (corrected version OJ 1 257, 21.9.1990, p. 13).
[3] OJ 1963 127/2268/63.
[4] OJ 1969 L209/11.

(d) Commission Regulation (EEC) No. 4260/88 of 16 December 1988 on the communications, complaints and applications and the hearings provided for in Council Regulation (EEC) No. 4056/86 laying down detailed rules for the application of Articles 48 and 82 of the treaty to maritime transport[5];

(e) Commission Regulation (EEC) No. 4261/88 of 16 December 1988 on the complaints, applications and hearings provided for in Council Regulation (EEC) No. 3975/87 laying down the procedure for the application of the rules on competition to undertakings in the air transport sector[6];

(f) Commission Regulation (EEC) No. 2367/90 of 25 July 1990, on the notifications, time limits and hearings provided for in Council Regulation (EEC) No. 4064/89 on the control of concentrations between undertakings.[7]

3. Administratively the Hearing Officer shall belong to the Directorate-General for Competition. To ensure the independence of the Hearing Officer in the performance of his duties, he has the right of direct access, as defined in Article 9, to the Member of the Commission with special responsibility for competition.

4. Where the Hearing Officer is unable to act, the Director-General, where appropriate after consultation of the Hearing Officer, shall designate another official, who is least in the grade A3 and is not involved in the case in question, to carry out the duties described herein.

Article 2

1. The Hearing Officer shall ensure that the hearing is properly conducted and thus contribute to the objectivity of the hearing itself and of any decision taken subsequently. The Hearing Officer shall seek to ensure in particular that in the preparation of draft Commission decisions in competition cases due account is taken of all the relevant facts, whether favourable or unfavourable to the parties concerned.

2. In performing his duties the Hearing Officer shall see to it that the rights of the defence are respected, while taking account of the need for effective application of the competition rules in accordance with the regulations in force and the principles laid down by the Court of First Instance and the Court of Justice.

Article 3

1. Decisions as to whether third parties, be they natural or legal persons, are to be heard shall be taken after consulting the Director responsible for investigating the case which is the subject of the procedure.

2. Applications to be heard on the part of third parties shall be submitted in writing, together with a written statement explaining the applicant's interest in the outcome of the procedure.

3. Where it is found that an applicant has not shown a sufficient interest to be heard, he shall be informed in writing of the reasons for such finding. A time limit shall be fixed within which he may submit any further written comments.

Article 4

1. Decisions whether persons are to be heard orally shall be taken after consulting the Director responsible for investigating the case which is the subject of the procedure.

---

[5] OJ 1988 L376/1.
[6] OJ 1988 L376/10.
[7] OJ 1990 L219/5.

2. Applications to be heard orally shall be made in the applicant's written comments on letters which the Commission has addressed to him and shall contain a reasoned statement of the applicant's interest in an oral hearing.

3. The letters referred to in paragraph 2 are those:

— communicating a statement of objections,
— inviting the written comments of a natural or legal person having shown sufficient interest to be heard as a third party,
— informing a complainant that in the Commission's view there are insufficient grounds for finding an infringement and inviting him to submit any further written comments,
— informing a natural or legal person that in the Commission's view that person has not shown sufficient interest to be heard as a third party.

4. Where it is found that the applicant has not shown a sufficient interest to be heard orally, he shall be informed in writing of the reasons for such finding. A time limit shall be fixed within which he may submit any further written comments.

Article 5

1. Where a person, an undertaking or an association of persons or undertakings who or which has received one or more of the letters listed in Article 4(3) has reason to believe that the Commission has in its possession documents which have not been disclosed to it and that those documents are necessary for the proper exercise of the right to be heard, he or it may draw attention to the matter by a reasoned request.

2. The reasoned decision on any such request shall be communicated to the person, undertaking or association that made the request and to any other person, undertaking or association concerned by the procedure.

3. Where it is intended to disclose information which may constitute a business secret of an undertaking, it shall be informed in writing of this intention and the reasons for it. A time limit shall be fixed within which the undertaking concerned may submit any written comments.

4. Where the undertaking concerned objects to the disclosure of the information but it is found that the information is not protected and may therefore be disclosed, that finding shall be stated in a reasoned decision which shall be notified to the undertaking concerned. The decision shall specify the date after which the information will be disclosed. This date shall not be less than one week from the date of notification.

5. Where an undertaking or association of undertakings considers that the time limit imposed for its reply to a letter referred to in Article 4(3) is too short, it may, within the original time limit, draw attention to the matter by a reasoned request. The applicant shall be informed in writing whether the request has been granted.

Article 6

1. Where appropriate in view of the need to ensure that the hearing is properly prepared and particularly that questions of fact are clarified as far as possible, the Hearing Officer may, after consulting the Director responsible for investigating the case, supply in advance to the firms concerned a list of the questions on which he or she wishes them to explain their point of view.

2. For this purpose, after consulting the Director responsible for investigating the case which is the subject of the hearing, the Hearing Officer may hold a meeting with the parties concerned and, where appropriate, the Commission staff, in order to prepare for the hearing itself.

3. For the same purpose the Hearing Officer may ask for prior written notification of the essential contents of the intended statement of persons whom the undertakings concerned have proposed for hearing.

Article 7

1. After consulting the Director responsible for investigating the case, the Hearing Officer shall determine the date, the duration and the place of the hearing, and, where a postponement is requested, the Hearing Officer shall decide whether or not to allow it.

2. The Hearing Officer shall be fully responsible for the conduct of the hearing.

3. In this regard, the Hearing Officer shall decide whether fresh documents should be admitted during the hearing, what persons should be heard on behalf of a party and whether the persons concerned should be heard separately or in the presence of other persons attending the hearing.

4. The Hearing Officer shall ensure that the essential content of the statement made by each person heard shall be recorded in minutes which, where appropriate, shall be read and approved by that person.

Article 8

The Hearing Officer shall report to the Director-General for Competition on the hearing and the conclusions he draws from it. The Hearing Officer may make observations on the further progress of the proceedings. Such observations may relate among other things to the need for further information, the withdrawal of certain objections, or the formulation of further objections.

Article 9

In performing the duties defined in Article 2, the Hearing Officer may, if he deems it appropriate, refer his observations direct to the Member of the Commission with special responsibility for competition.

Article 10

Where appropriate, the Member of the Commission with special responsibility for competition may decide, at the Hearing Officer's request, to attach the Hearing Officer's final report to the draft decision submitted to the Commission, in order to ensure that when it reaches a decision on an individual case it is fully apprised of all relevant information.

Article 11

This Decision revokes and replaces the Commission Decisions of 8 September 1982 and 23 November 1990 on the implementation of hearings in connection with procedures for the application of Articles 65 and 66 of the ECSC Treaty and Articles 81 and 82 of the EC Treaty.

Article 12

This Decision shall enter into force on the day following its publication in the *Official Journal of the European Communities*.

Done at Brussels, 12 December 1994.

COMMISSION NOTICE[1]

On the Non-Imposition or Deduction of Fines in Cartel Cases

A. Introduction

1. Secret cartels between enterprises aimed at fixing prices, production or sales quotas, sharing markets or banning imports or exports are among the most serious restrictions of competition encountered by the Commission.

Such practices ultimately result in increased prices and reduced choice for the consumer. Furthermore, they not only prejudice the interests of Community consumers, but they also harm European industry. By artificially limiting the competition that would normally prevail between them, Community enterprises avoid exactly those pressures that lead them to innovate, both in terms of product development and with regard to the introduction of more efficient production processes. Such practices also lead to more expensive raw materials and components for the Community enterprises that buy from such producers. In the long term, they lead to a loss of competitiveness and, in an increasingly global market-place, reduced employment opportunities.

For all those reasons, the Commission considers that combating cartels is an important aspect of its endeavours to achieve the objectives set out in its 1993 White Paper on Growth, Competitiveness and Employment. This explains why it has increased its efforts to detect cartels in recent years.

2. The Commission is aware that certain enterprises participating in such agreements might wish to terminate their involvement and inform the Commission of the existence of the cartel, but are deterred from doing so by the risk of incurring large fines.

3. In order to take account of this fact, the Commission has decided to adopt the present notice, which sets out the conditions under which enterprises co-operating with the Commission during its investigation into a cartel may be exempted from fines, or may be granted reductions in the fine which would otherwise have been imposed upon them. The Commission will examine whether it is necessary to modify this notice as soon as it has acquired sufficient experience in applying it.

4. The Commission considers that it is in the Community interest in granting favourable treatment to enterprises which co-operate with it in the circumstances set out below. The interests of consumers and citizens in ensuring that such practices are detected and prohibited outweigh the interest in fining those enterprises which co-operate with the Commission, thereby enabling or helping it to detect and prohibit a cartel.

5. Co-operation by an enterprise is only one of several factors which the Commission takes into account when fixing the amount of a fine. This notice does not prejudice the Commission's right to reduce a fine for other reasons.

---

[1] OJ 1996 C207/4.

B. Non-imposition of a fine or a very substantial reduction in its amount

An enterprise which:

(a) informs the Commission about a secret cartel before the Commission has undertaken an investigation, ordered by decision, of the enterprises involved, provided that it does not already have sufficient information to establish the existence of the alleged cartel;
(b) is the first to adduce decisive evidence of the cartel's existence;
(c) puts an end to its involvement in the illegal activity no later than the time at which it discloses the cartel;
(d) provides the Commission with all the relevant information and all the documents and evidence available to it regarding the cartel and maintains continuous and complete co-operation throughout the investigation;
(e) has not compelled another enterprise to take part in the cartel and has not acted as an instigator or played a determining role in the illegal activity,

will benefit from a reduction of at least 75% of the fine or even from total exemption from the fine that would have been imposed if they had not co-operated.

C. Substantial reduction in a fine

Enterprises which both satisfy the conditions set out in Section B, points (b) to (e) and disclose the secret cartel after the Commission has undertaken an investigation ordered by decision on the premises of the parties to the cartel which has failed to provide sufficient grounds for initiating the procedure leading to a decision, will benefit from a reduction of 50% to 75% of the fine.

D. Significant reduction in a fine

1. Where an enterprise co-operates without having met all the conditions set out in Sections B or C, it will benefit from a reduction of 10% to 50% of the fine that would have been imposed it it had not co-operated.
2. Such cases may include the following:

— before a statement of objections is sent, an enterprise provides the Commission with information, documents or other evidence which materially contribute to establishing the existence of the infringement;
— after receiving a statement of objections, an enterprise informs the Commission that it does not substantially contest the facts on which the Commission bases its allegations.

E. Procedure

1. Where an enterprise wishes to take advantage of the favourable treatment set out in this notice, it should contact the Commission's Directorate-General for Competition. Only persons empowered to represent the enterprise for that purpose may take such a step. This notice does not therefore cover requests from individual employees of enterprises.
2. Only on its adoption of a decision will the Commission determine whether or not the conditions set out in Sections B, C and D are met, and thus whether or not to grant any reduction in the fine, or even waive its imposition altogether. It would not be appropriate to grant such a reduction or waiver before the end of the administrative procedure, as those conditions apply throughout such period.

3. Nonetheless, provided that all the conditions are met, non-imposition or reductions will be granted. The Commission is aware that this notice will create legitimate expectations on which enterprises may rely when disclosing the existence of a cartel to the Commission. Failure to meet any of the conditions set out in Section B or C at any stage of the administrative procedure will, however, result in the loss of the favourable treatment set out therein. In such circumstances an enterprise may, however, still enjoy a reduction in the fine, as set out in Section D above.

4. The fact that leniency in respect of fines is granted cannot, however, protect an enterprise from the civil law consequences of its participation in an illegal agreement. In this respect, if the information provided by the enterprise leads the Commission to take a decision pursuant to Article 81(1) of the EC Treaty, the enterprise benefiting from the leniency in respect of the fine will also be named in that decision as having infringed the Treaty and will have the part it played described in full therein. The fact that the enterprise co-operated with the Commission will also be indicated in the decision, so as to explain the reason for the non-imposition or reduction of the fine.

Should an enterprise which has benefited from a reduction in a fine for not substantially contesting the facts then contest them for the first time in proceedings for annulment before the Court of First Instance, the Commission will normally ask that court to increase the fine imposed on that enterprise.

APPENDIX 55

COMMISSION NOTICE[1]

*Guidelines on the Method of Setting Fines Imposed pursuant to Article 15(2)
of Regulation No 17 and Article 65(5) of the ECSC Treaty*

(Text with EEA relevance)

The principles outlined here should ensure the transparency and impartiality of the Commission's decisions, in the eyes of the undertakings and of the Court of Justice alike, while upholding the discretion which the Commission is granted under the relevant legislation to set fines within the limit of 10% of overall turnover. This discretion must, however, follow a coherent and non-discriminatory policy which is consistent with the objectives pursued in penalizing infringements of the competition rules.

The new method of determining the amount of a fine will adhere to the following rules, which start from a basic amount that will be increased to take account of aggravating circumstances or reduced to take account of attenuating circumstances.

1. Basic amount

The basic amount will be determined according to the gravity and duration of the infringement, which are the only criteria referred to in Article 15(2) of Regulation No 17.

A. Gravity

In assessing the gravity of the infringement, account must be taken of its nature, its actual impact on the market, where this can be measured, and the size of the relevant geographic market.

Infringements will thus be put into one of three categories: minor infringements, serious infringements and very serious infringements.

— *minor infringements*:
These might be trade restrictions, usually of a vertical nature, but with a limited market impact and affecting only a substantial but relatively limited part of the Community market.
Likely fines: ECU 1000 to ECU 1 million.
— *serious infringements*:
These will more often than not be horizontal or vertical restrictions of the same type as above, but more rigorously applied, with a wider market impact, and with effects in extensive areas of the common market. There might also be abuse of a dominant position (refusals to supply, discrimination, exclusion, loyalty discounts made by dominant firms in order to shut competitors out of the market, etc.).
Likely fines: ECU 1 million to ECU 20 million.

---

[1] OJ 1998 C 9/3.

— *very serious infringements*:
These will generally be horizontal restrictions such as price cartels and market-sharing quotas, or other practices which jeopardize the proper functioning of the single market, such as the partitioning of national markets and clear-cut abuse of a dominant position by undertakings holding a virtual monopoly (see Decisions 91/297/EEC, 91/298/EEC, 91/299/EEC, 91/300/EEC and 91/301/EEC[2]—*Soda Ash*, 94/815/EC[3]—*Cement*, 94/601/EC[4]—*Cartonboard*, 92/163/EC[5]—*Tetra Pak*, and 94/215/ECSC[6]—*Steel beams*).
Likely fines: above ECU 20 million.

Within each of these categories, and in particular as far as serious and very serious infringements are concerned, the proposed scale of fines will make it possible to apply differential treatment to undertakings according to the nature of the infringement committed.

It will also be necessary to take account of the effective economic capacity of offenders to cause significant damage to other operators, in particular consumers, and to set the fine at a level which ensures that it has a sufficiently deterrent effect.

Generally speaking, account may also be taken of the fact that large undertakings usually have legal and economic knowledge and infrastructures which enable them more easily to recognize that their conduct constitutes an infringement and be aware of the consequences stemming from it under competition law.

Where an infringement involves several undertakings (e.g. cartels), it might be necessary in some cases to apply weightings to the amounts determined within each of the three categories in order to take account of the specific weight and, therefore, the real impact of the offending conduct of each undertaking on competition, particularly where there is considerable disparity between the sizes of the undertakings committing infringements of the same type.

Thus, the principle of equal punishment for the same conduct may, if the circumstances so warrant, lead to different fines being imposed on the undertakings concerned without this differentiation being governed by arithmetic calculation.

B. Duration

A distinction should be made between the following:

— infringements of short duration (in general, less than one year): no increase in amount,
— infringements of medium duration (in general, one to five years): increase of up to 50% in the amount determined for gravity,
— infringements of long duration (in general, more than five years): increase of up to 10% per year in the amount determined for gravity.

This approach will therefore point to a possible increase in the amount of the fine.

Generally speaking, the increase in the fine for long-term infringements represents a considerable strengthening of the previous practice with a view to imposing effective sanctions on restrictions which have had a harmful impact on consumers over a long period. Moreover, this new approach is consistent with the expected effect of the notice of 18 July 1996 on the non-imposition or reduction of fines in cartel cases.[7] The risk of

---

[2] OJ 1991 L152/54.
[3] OJ 1994 L343/1.
[4] OJ 1994 L243/1.
[5] OJ 1992 L72/1.
[6] OJ 1994 L116/1.
[7] OJ 1996 C207/4.

having to pay a much larger fine, proportionate to the duration of the infringement, will necessarily increase the incentive to denounce it or to cooperate with the Commission.

The basic amount will result from the addition of the two amounts established in accordance with the above:

$$x \text{ gravity} + y \text{ duration} = \text{basic amount}$$

2. Aggravating circumstances

The basic amount will be increased where there are aggravating circumstances such as:

— repeated infringement of the same type by the same undertaking(s),
— refusal to cooperate with or attempts to obstruct the Commission in carrying out its investigations,
— role of leader in, or instigator of the infringement,
— retaliatory measures against other undertakings with a view to enforcing practices which constitute an infringement,
— need to increase the penalty in order to exceed the amount of gains improperly made as a result of the infringement when it is objectively possible to estimate that amount,
— other.

3. Attenuating circumstances

The basic amount will be reduced where there are attenuating circumstances such as:

— an exclusively passive or "follow-my-leader" role in the infringement,
— non-implementation in practice of the offending agreements or practices,
— termination of the infringement as soon as the Commission intervenes (in particular when it carries out checks),
— existence of reasonable doubt on the part of the undertaking as to whether the restrictive conduct does indeed constitute an infringement,
— infringements committed as a result of negligence or unintentionally,
— effective cooperation by the undertaking in the proceedings, outside the scope of the Notice of 18 July 1996 on the non-imposition or reduction of fines in cartel cases,
— other.

4. Application of the Notice of 18 July 1996 on the non-imposition or reduction of fines[8]

---

[8] See footnote 7.

APPENDIX 56

FINES IMPOSED

Case	Year	Offence	Fine imposed in ECU	Result on Appeal
Peroxygen Products[1]	1985	Market sharing	500,000 to 3 million	–
John Deere[2]	1985	Export ban	2 million	–
Wood Pulp[3]	1985	Price-fixing	Highest fine 500,000 Total 4.125 million	Most fines annulled
ECS/AKZO[4]	1985	Article [82] Predatory pricing	10 million	Appeal dismissed but fine reduced to 7.5 million
Sperry New-Holland[5]	1985	Export ban	750,000	–
Siemens Fanuc[6]	1985	Mutual exclusive dealing	1 million on each party	
Polypropylene[7]	1986	Price-fixing	Total 57.85 million as follows:	
			Rhone-Poulenc: 500,000;	Appeal dismissed[8]
			Petrofina: 600,000;	Fine reduced to 300,000[9]
			Atochem: 1.75 million;	Appeal dismissed[10]
			BASF: 2.5 million;	Fine reduced to 2,125,000[11]
			Enichem Anic: 750,000.	Fine reduced to 450,000 – Appeal dismissed by ECJ[12]

---

[1] OJ 1985 L35/1, [1985] 1 CMLR 481.
[2] OJ 1985 L35/58, [1985] 2 CMLR 554.
[3] OJ 1985 L85/1, [1985] 3 CMLR 474; on appeal Cases C–89/85, etc., [1993] ECR I–1307, [1993] 4 CMLR 407.
[4] OJ 1985 L374/1, [1986] 3 CMLR 273; on appeal Case C–62/86, [1991] ECR I–3359.
[5] OJ 1985 L376/12, [1988] 4 CMLR 306.
[6] OJ 1985 L376/29, [1988] 4 CMLR 945.
[7] OJ 1986 L230/1, [1988] 4 CMLR 347.
[8] Case T–1/89, [1991] ECR II–867.
[9] Case T–2/89, [1991] ECR II–1087.
[10] Case T–3/89, [1991] ECR II–1177.
[11] Case T–4/89, [1991] ECR II–1523.
[12] Case T–6/89, [1991] ECR II–1623; Case C–49/92P, [1999] ECR I–4125, [2001] 4 CMLR 602.

Case	Year	Offence	Fine imposed in ECU	Result on Appeal
			Hercules: 2.75 million;	Appeals dismissed by CFI and ECJ[13]
			DSM: 2.75 million;	Appeal dismissed by CFI[14]
			Hüls: 2.75 million;	Fine reduced to 2,337,500 – Appeal dismissed by ECJ[15]
			Hoechst: 9 million;	Appeals dismissed by CFI and ECJ[16]
			Shell: 9 million;	Fine reduced to 8,100,000 – Appeal dismissed by ECJ[17]
			Solvay: 2.5 million;	Appeal dismissed[18]
			ICI: 10 million;	Fine reduced to 9 million – Appeal dismissed by ECJ[19]
			Montedipe: 11 million;	Appeals dismissed by CFI and ECJ[20]
			Linz: 1 million.	Appeals dismissed by CFI and ECJ[21]
Roofing Felt[22]	1986	Price fixing	15,000 to 420,000	Appeal dismissed
MELDOC[23]	1986	Price fixing	425,000 to 3.15 million	–
Fatty Acids[24]	1986	Information exchange	150,000	–
Sandoz[25]	1987	Export ban	800,000	Fine reduced to 500,000
Tipp-Ex[26]	1987	Export ban	400,000	Appeal dismissed
Konica[27]	1987	Prevention of parallel imports	150,000	–

[13] Case T–7/89, [1991] ECR II–1711; Case C–51/92P, [1999] ECR I–4235, [1999] 5 CMLR 976.
[14] Case T–8/89, [1991] ECR II–833. See also Case C–5/93P, [1999] ECR I–4695, dismissing application for revision.
[15] Case T–9/89, [1992] ECR II–499; Case C–199/92P, [1999] ECR I–4287, [1999] 5 CMLR 1016.
[16] Case T–10/89, [1992] ECR II–629; Case C–227/92P, [1999] ECR I–4443.
[17] Case T–11/89, [1992] ECR II–757; Case C–234/92P, [1999] ECR I–4501, [1999] 5 CMLR 1142.
[18] Case T–12/89, [1992] ECR II–907.
[19] Case T–13/89, [1992] ECR II–1021; Case C–200/92P, [1999] ECR I–4399, [1999] 5 CMLR 1110.
[20] Case T–14/89, [1992] ECR II–1155, [1993] 4 CMLR 110; Case C–235/92P, [1999] ECR I–4539, [2001] 4 CMLR 691.
[21] Case T–15/89, [1992] ECR II–1275; Case C–245/92P, [1999] ECR I–4643.
[22] OJ 1986 L232/15, [1991] 4 CMLR 130; on appeal Case 246/86 [1989] ECR 2117, [1991] 4 CMLR 96.
[23] OJ 1986 L384/50, [1989] 4 CMLR 853.
[24] OJ 1987 L3/17, [1989] 4 CMLR 445.
[25] OJ 1987 L222/28, [1989] 4 CMLR 628; on appeal Case C–277/87, [1990] ECR I–45.
[26] OJ 1987 L222/1, [1989] 4 CMLR 425; on appeal Case C–279/87, [1990] ECR I–261.
[27] OJ 1988 L78/34, [1988] 4 CMLR 848.

Case	Year	Offence	Fine imposed in ECU	Result on Appeal
Quaker Oats UK[28]	1987	Impending parallel trading	300,000	–
Hilti[29]	1987	Abuse of dominant position	6 million	Appeals dismissed by CFI and ECJ.
British Dental Trade Association[30]	1988	Exclusion of non-United Kingdom supplies	100,000	–
British Sugar[31]	1988	Article [82] predation	300,000	–
Hudson's Bay[32]	1988	Restrictions on members selling through auction rooms of their choice	500,000	Fine reduced to 300,000
Sabena[33]	1988	Article [82]; exclusion of competitors	100,000	–
BPB Industries/ British Gypsum[34]	1988	Article [82]; exclusion of competitors	3 million and 150,000	Appeals dismissed by the CFI and ECJ.
Italian Flat Glass[35]	1988	Price and quota fixing; abuse of dominant position	7 million; 4.7 million and 1.7 million	Fines annulled or reduced to 1 million and 671,428
LdPE[36]	1988	Price and quota fixing	Total 37 million ranging from 500,000 to 5.5 million	Annulled
PVC (No. 1)[37]	1988	Price and quota fixing	Total 23.5 million ranging from 400,000 to 3.5 million	Decision annulled for procedural breaches
Welded Steel Mesh Producers[38]	1989	Price or quota fixing; market sharing	Total of 9.501 million imposed on 14 companies as follows: Tréfilunion: 1,375,000;	Fine reduced to 1,235,000[39]

[28] OJ 1988 L49/19, [1989] 4 CMLR 553.
[29] OJ 1988 L65/19, [1989] 4 CMLR 677; on appeal Case T–30/89, [1991] ECR II–1439; on further appeal Case C–53/92P, [1994] ECR I–667, [1994] 4 CMLR 614.
[30] OJ 1988 L233/15, [1990] 4 CMLR 1021.
[31] OJ 1988 L284/41, [1990] 4 CMLR 196.
[32] OJ 1988 L316/43, [1989] 4 CMLR 340; on appeal Case T–61/89 [1992] ECR II–1931.
[33] OJ 1988 L317/47, [1989] 4 CMLR 662.
[34] OJ 1989 L10/50, [1990] 4 CMLR 464; on appeal Case T–65/89, [1993] ECR II–389, on further appeal Case C–310/93P, [1995] ECR I–865, [1997] 4 CMLR 238.
[35] OJ 1989 L33/44, [1990] 4 CMLR 535; on appeal Cases T–68/89, etc., [1992] ECR II–1403.
[36] OJ 1989 L74/21, [1990] 4 CMLR 382; on appeal Cases T–80/89, etc., [1995] ECR II–729.
[37] OJ 1989 L74/1, [1990] 4 CMLR 345; on appeal Cases T–79/89, etc., [1992] ECR II–315, [1992] 4 CMLR 357; on further appeal Case C–137/92P, [1994] ECR I–2555.
[38] OJ 1989 L260/1, [1991] 4 CMLR 13.
[39] Case T–148/89, [1995] ECR II–1063.

Case	Year	Offence	Fine imposed in ECU	Result on Appeal
			SMN: 50,000;	–
			STPS: 150,000;	Appeal dismissed[40]
			Sotralentz: 228,000;	fine reduced to 57,000[41]
			Tréfilarbed: 1,143,000;	Appeal dismissed[42]
			Cockerill Sambre: 315,000;	fine reduced to 252,000[43]
			Boël: 550,000;	fine reduced to 440,000[44]
			Thibo Bouwstaal: 420,000;	–
			Van Meerksteijn: 375,000;	–
			ZND Bouwstaal: 42,000;	–
			Baustahlgewebe: 4.5 million;	fine reduced by CFI to 3 million; (further reduced by ECJ by 50,000 on account of delay)[45]
			ILRO: 13,000;	Appeal dismissed[46]
			Ferrière Nord (Pittini): 320,000;	Appeals dismissed by CFI and ECJ[47]
			G.B. Martinelli: 20,000.	Appeal dismissed[48]
Bayo-n-ox[49]	1989	Exclusive purchase agreement; prohibition on resale	500,000	–
Soda Ash[50]	1990	Market sharing; abuse of dominant position	4 decisions. Total fines: Solvay, 30 million; ICI 17 million; CFK, 1 million.	Decisions against Solvay and ICI annulled for procedural irregularities. (3 decisions re-adopted in 2000).
Gosme/Martell-DMP[51]	1991	Restrictions on parallel exports	350,000	–

[40] Case T–151/89, [1995] ECR II–1191.
[41] Case T–149/89, [1995] ECR II–1127.
[42] Case T–141/89, [1995] ECR II–791.
[43] Case T–144/89, [1995] ECR II–947.
[44] Case T–142/89, [1995] ECR II–867.
[45] Case T–145/89, [1995] ECR II–987; Case C–185/95P, [1998] ECR I–8417, [1999] 4 CMLR 1203.
[46] Case T–152/89, [1995] ECR II–1197.
[47] Case T–143/89, [1995] ECR II–917; on appeal Case C–219/95 P, [1997] ECR I–4411.
[48] Case T–150/89, [1995] ECR II–1167.
[49] OJ 1990 L21/71, [1990] 4 CMLR 930.
[50] OJ 1991 L152/1, 16, 21, 40, [1994] 4 CMLR 454, 645; on appeal Cases T–30/91, etc., [1995] ECR II–1775, 1821, 1825, 1847, 1901, [1996] 5 CMLR 57 (T–30/91) and 91 (T–32/91) and [1995] All ER(EC) 600 (T–30 & 32/91); on further appeal, Cases C–286 to 288/95P, [2000] ECR I–2341, 2391, [2000] 5 CMLR 413, 454, [2000] All ER(EC) 439.
[51] OJ 1991 L185/23, [1992] 5 CMLR 585.

Case	Year	Offence	Fine imposed in ECU	Result on Appeal
Viho/Toshiba[52]	1991	Export ban	2 million	–
Tetra Pak II[53]	1991	Abuse of dominant position	75 million	Appeal dismissed
Building and construction industry in the Netherlands[54]	1992	Price-fixing; information exchange; market sharing	Total of 22.5 million imposed on 28 companies	Appeals dismissed by the CFI and the ECJ
Aer Lingus[55]	1992	Abuse of dominant position; breach of block exemption requirements	750,000	–
Newitt/Dunlop[56]	1992	Export ban	Dunlop 5 million. All Weather Sports 150,000	Fine reduced from 5 million to 3 million. All Weather Sports annulled.[57]
Eurocheque Helsinki Agreement[58]	1992	Price-fixing	5 million	Fine reduced to 2 million
French W. African Shipowners' committees[59]	1992	Market sharing	Total 15.3 million	–
Viho/Parker Pen[60]	1992	Export ban	Parker; 700,000 Herlitz; 40,000	Parker Pen's fine reduced to 400,000 Herlitz's appeal dismissed
Distribution of railway tickets by travel agents[61]	1992	Price-fixing	1 million	Decision declared void for error of law
CEWAL[62]	1992	Abuse of collective dominance	CMB 9.6 million Dafra Line 200,000	Annulled by ECJ on procedural grounds

[52] OJ 1991 L287/39, [1992] 5 CMLR 180.
[53] OJ 1992 L72/1, [1992] 4 CMLR 551; on appeal Case T–83/91, [1994] ECR II–755; on further appeal Case C–333/94P, [1996] ECR I–5951, [1997] 4 CMLR 662.
[54] OJ 1992 L92/1, [1993] 5 CMLR 135; on appeal Case T–29/92, [1995] ECR II–289; on further appeal Case C–137/95P, [1996] ECR I–1611.
[55] OJ 1992 L96/34.
[56] OJ 1992 L131/32, [1993] 5 CMLR 352; on appeal Case T–43/92, [1994] ECR II–441.
[57] Case T–38/92, [1994] ECR II–211.
[58] OJ 1992 L95/50, [1993] 5 CMLR 323; on appeal Cases T–39 & 40/92, [1994] ECR II–49.
[59] OJ 1992 L134/1, [1993] 5 CMLR 446.
[60] OJ 1992 L233/27, [1993] 5 CMLR 382; on appeal Case T–77/92, [1994] ECR II–549, [1995] 5 CMLR 435; Case T–66/92, [1994] ECR II–531, [1995] 5 CMLR 458.
[61] OJ 1992 L366/47, on appeal Case T–14/93, [1995] ECR II–1503, [1996] 5 CMLR 40.
[62] OJ 1993 L34/20, [1995] 5 CMLR 198; on appeal Cases T–24/93, etc., [1996] ECR II–1019, [1997] 4 CMLR 273; on further appeal Cases C–395 & 396/96P, [2000] ECR I–1365, [2000] 4 CMLR 1076, [2000] All ER (EC) 385.

Case	Year	Offence	Fine imposed in ECU	Result on Appeal
			Nedlloyd 100,000	Fine reduced by CFI to 90,000
			Deutsche Afrika 200,000	Fine reduced by CFI to 180,000
PVC (No. 2)[63]	1994	Price and quota fixing	Total of 18.25 million imposed on 12 companies as follows:	3 fines reduced on appeal
			BASF: 1.5 million;	Appeal dismissed
			DSM: 600,000;	Appeal dismissed
			Elf Atochem: 3.2 million;	Fine reduced to 2,600,000
			Enichem: 2.5 million;	Appeal dismissed
			Hoechst: 1.5 million;	Appeal dismissed
			Hüls: 2.2 million;	Appeal dismissed
			ICI: 2.5 million;	Fine reduced to 1.55 million
			Limburgse Vynil: 750,000;	Appeal dismissed
			Montedison: 1.75 million;	Appeal dismissed
			Société Artesienne de Vynil: 400,000;	Fine reduced to 135,000
			Shell: 850,000;	Appeal dismissed
			Wacker Chemie: 1.5 million.	Appeal dismissed
				Further appeals pending before ECJ for 8 companies
Cartonboard[64]	1994	Price fixing; market sharing	Total of 141.55 million imposed on 19 companies as follows:	Fines reduced by CFI/ECJ as follows:
			Buchmann: 2.2 million;	Fine reduced by CFI to 2.15 million[65]
			Cascades: 16.2 million;	Appeal allowed partly by ECJ: case referred back to CFI[66]
			Enso Española: 1.75 million;	Fine reduced by CFI to 1.2 million.[67] Further appeal to ECJ dismissed

---

[63] OJ 1994 L239/4; on appeal Cases T–305/94, etc., [1999] ECR II–931, [1999] 5 CMLR 303; on further appeal, Cases C–238/99P, etc.
[64] OJ 1994 L243/1, [1994] 5 CMLR 547.
[65] Case T–295/94, [1998] ECR II–813.
[66] Case T–308/94, [1998] ECR II–925; on appeal Case C–279/98P, [2000] ECR I–9693.
[67] Case T–348/94, [1998] ECR II–1875; on appeal Case C–282/98P, [2000] ECR I–9817.

Case	Year	Offence	Fine imposed in ECU	Result on Appeal
			Europa Carton: 2 million;	Appeal dismissed[68]
			Fiskeby Board: 1 million;	Appeal dismissed[69]
			Finnish Board Mills Association: 20 million;	Appeals dismissed by CFI and ECJ[70]
			Gruber & Weber: 1 million;	Fine reduced by CFI to 730,000[71]
			BPB de Eendracht: 1.75 million;	Fine reduced by CFI to 750,000[72]
			NV Koninklijke KNP: 3 million;	Fine reduced by ECJ to €2.6 million[73]
			Laakmann Karton: 2.2 million;	–
			Mo Och Domsjö: 22.75 million;	Appeals dismissed by CFI and ECJ[74]
			Mayr-Melnhof: 21 million;	Fine reduced by CFI to 17 million[75]
			Papeteries de Lancey: 1.5 million;	–
			Rena Kartonfabrik: 200,000;	–
			Sarrió: 15.5 million;	Fine reduced by ECJ to €13.75 million[76]
			SCA Holding: 2.2 million;	Appeal dismissed[77]
			Stora Kopparbergs: 11.25 million;	Appeal allowed in part by ECJ: case referred back to CFI[78]
			Enso-Gutzeit: 3.25 million;	Annulment of Commission decision[79]

---

[68] Case T–304/94, [1998] ECR II–869.

[69] Case T–319/94, [1998] ECR II–1331.

[70] Case T–338/94, [1998] ECR II–1617; on appeal Case C–298/98P, judgment of 16 November 2000.

[71] Case T–310/94, [1998] ECR II–1043.

[72] Case T–311/94, [1998] ECR II–1129.

[73] Case T–309/94, [1998] ECR II–1007; on appeal Case C–248/98P, [2000] ECR I–9641.

[74] Case T–352/94, [1998] ECR II–1989; on appeal Case C–283/98P, [2000] ECR I–9855, [2001] 4 CMLR 322.

[75] Case T–347/94, [1998] ECR II–1749.

[76] Case T–334/94, [1998] ECR II–1439, [1998] 5 CMLR 195; on appeal Case C–291/98P, [2000] ECR I–9991.

[77] Case T–327/94, [1998] ECR II–1373, [1998] 5 CMLR 195; on appeal Case C–297/98P, [2001] 4 CMLR 413.

[78] Case T–354/94, [1998] ECR II–2111; on appeal Case C–286/98P, [2000] ECR I–9925, [2001] 4 CMLR 370.

[79] Case T–337/94, [1998] ECR II–1571.

Case	Year	Offence	Fine imposed in ECU	Result on Appeal
			Moritz J. Weig: 3 million.	Fine reduced by ECJ to €1.9 million[80]
Steel beams cartel[81]	1994	Price fixing; market sharing; information exchange	Total of 104,364,350 imposed on 14 companies as follows:	Fines reduced by CFI as follows:
			NMH Stahlwerkel: 150,000;	Fine reduced to 110,000[82]
			ARBED: 11.2 million;	Fine reduced to 10 million[83]
			Saarstahl: 4.6 million;	–
			Ferdofin: 9.5 million;	–
			Cockerill-Sambre: 4 million;	Fine reduced to 3,580,000[84]
			Thyssen Stahl: 6.5 million;	Fine reduced to 4.4 million[85]
			Unimétal: 12.3 million;	Fine reduced to 8.3 million[86]
			Krupp-Hoesch Stahl: 13,000;	Fine reduced to 9,000[87]
			Preussag: 9.5 million;	Fine reduced to 8,600,000[88]
			British Steel: 32 million;	Fine reduced to 20 million[89]
			Siderurgica Aristrain Madrid: 10.6 million;	Fine reduced to 7.1 million[90]
			Empresa Nacional Siderurgica: 4 million;	Fine reduced to 3.35 million[91]
			Norsk Jernverk: 750;	–
			Inexa Profil: 600.	–
				Appeals pending before ECJ for 7 companies

[80] Case T–317/94, [1998] ECR II–1235; on appeal Case C–280/98P, [2000] ECR I–9757.
[81] OJ 1994 L116/1, [1994] 5 CMLR 353.
[82] Case T–134/94, [1999] ECR II–239.
[83] Case T–137/94, [1999] ECR II–303; on appeal Case C–176/99P.
[84] Case T–138/94, [1999] ECR II–333.
[85] Case T–141/94, [1999] ECR II–347, [1999] 4 CMLR 810; on appeal Case C–194/99P.
[86] Case T–145/94, [1999] ECR II–585.
[87] Case T–147/94, [1999] ECR II–603; on appeal Case C–195/99P.
[88] Case T–148/94, [1999] ECR II–613; on appeal Case C–182/99P.
[89] Case T–151/94, [1999] ECR II–629; on appeal Case C–199/99P.
[90] Case T–156/94, [1999] ECR II–645; on appeal Case C–196/99P.
[91] Case T–157/94, [1999] ECR II–707; on appeal Case C–198/99P.

Case	Year	Offence	Fine imposed in ECU	Result on Appeal
Cement[92]	1994	Price fixing; market sharing	Total of 248 million imposed on 42 companies	Fines on 16 companies annulled; fines on remainder reduced by CFI to €116.67 million. Further appeals to ECJ pending.
Tretorn and others[93]	1994	Export bans	600,000 on manufacturer and 10,000 on distributors.	Fine upheld
Far Eastern Freight Conference[94]	1994	Price-fixing; liner conference.	10,000 imposed on 13 companies	–
HOV SVZ/ MCN[95]	1994	Price discrimination	11 million	Appeals dismissed by CFI and ECJ
BASF Lacke+ Farben/ Accinauto[96]	1995	Export bans	2.7 million on manufacturer and 10,000 on distributor	Appeals dismissed
SCK and FNK[97]	1995	Price-fixing by trade association; ban on hiring from non-affiliated suppliers	11.5 million on FNK for price fixing 300,000; on SCK for other infringements	Appeal by FNK dismissed; Fine on SCK reduced to 100,000
ADALAT[98]	1996	Export bans	3 million	Annulled. Appeal by Commission to ECJ pending.
Fenex[99]	1996	Price-fixing by trade association	1,000	–
Ferry Services[1]	1997	Concerted practice; currency surcharge	450,000 on P&O 245,000 on four others	–
Irish Sugar[2]	1997	Dominant position	8.8 million	Fine reduced by CFI to 7,883,326. Further appeal to ECJ pending
Novalliance/ Systemform[3]	1997	Export ban; restrictions on resale prices	100,000	–

[92] OJ 1994 L343/1, [1995] 4 CMLR 327; on appeal Cases T–25/95, etc., [2000] ECR II–491; on further appeal Cases C–204/00P, etc.
[93] OJ 1994 L378/45; on appeal Case T–49/95, [1996] ECR II–1799, [1997] 4 CMLR 843.
[94] OJ 1994 L378/17.
[95] OJ 1994 L104/34; on appeal Case T–229/94, [1997] ECR II–1689; on further appeal Case C–436/97P, [1999] ECR I–2387, [1999] 5 CMLR 776.
[96] OJ 1995 L272/16, [1996] 4 CMLR 811; on appeal Cases T–175 & 176/95, [1999] ECR II–1581, 1635, [2000] 4 CMLR 33, 67.
[97] OJ 1995 L312/79, [1995] 4 CMLR 565; on appeal Cases T–213/95 & T–18/96, [1997] ECR II–1739, [1998] 4 CMLR 259.
[98] OJ 1996 L201/1, [1996] 5 CMLR 416; on appeal Case T–41/96, [2001] 4 CMLR 126; [2001] All ER(EC) 1; on further appeal, Case C–338/00P.
[99] OJ 1996 L181/28, [1996] 5 CMLR 332.
[1] OJ 1997 L26/23, [1997] 4 CMLR 798.
[2] OJ 1997 L258/1, [1997] 5 CMLR 666; on appeal Case T–228/97, [1999] ECR II–2969, [1999] 5 CMLR 1300, [2000] All ER (EC) 198; on further appeal Case C–497/99P.
[3] OJ 1997 L47/11, [1997] 4 CMLR 876.

Case	Year	Offence	Fine imposed in ECU	Result on Appeal
AAMS[4]	1998	Dominant position	6 million	Appeal pending
British Sugar[5]	1998	Concerted practice	Total of 50.2 million as follows: British Sugar: 39.06 million; Tate & Lyle: 7 million; Napier Brown: 1.08 million; James Budgett Sugars: 1.08 million.	Appeals pending
Volkswagen[6]	1998	Export bans	102 million	Fine reduced by CFI to 90 million. Further appeal to ECJ pending.
Alloy Surcharge[7]	1998	ECSC; concerted practices; price-fixing; information exchange	Acerinox: 3.53 million ALZ: 4.54 million Acciai: 4.54 million Avesta: 2.81 million Krupp Thyssen: 8.1 million Usinor: 3.86 million	
Greek Ferries[8]	1998	Price fixing	Total 9.12 million imposed on six Greek and one Italian ferry operators	Appeals pending
Transatlantic Conference Agreement (TACA)[9]	1998	Concerted practice; price fixing.	Total of 272.98 million imposed on 15 companies as follows: AP Møller-Maersk Line: 27.5 million; Atlantic Container Line: 6.88 million; Hapag Lloyd Container Line: 20.63 million; P&O Nedlloyd Container Line: 41.26 million;	Appeals pending

---

[4] OJ 1998 L252/47, [1998] 5 CMLR 786; on appeal Case T–139/98.
[5] OJ 1999 L76/1, [1999] 4 CMLR 1316; on appeal Cases T–202 & 204/98.
[6] OJ 1998 L124/60, [1998] 5 CMLR 33; on appeal Case T–62/98, [2000] ECR II–2707, [2000] 5 CMLR 853; on further appeal Case C–338/00P.
[7] OJ 1998 L100/55, [1998] 4 CMLR 973; on appeal Cases T–45 & 48/98.
[8] OJ 1999 L109/24, [1999] 5 CMLR 47; on appeal Cases T–56/99, etc.
[9] OJ 1999 L95/1, [1999] 4 CMLR 1415; on appeal Cases T–191/98, etc.

Case	Year	Offence	Fine imposed in ECU	Result on Appeal
			Sea-Land Service: 27.5 million;	
			Mediterranean Shipping: 13.75 million;	
			Orient Overseas Container Line: 20.63 million;	
			Polish Ocean Lines: 6.88 million;	
			DSR/Senator Lines: 13.75 million;	
			Cho Yang Shipping Co: 13.75 million;	
			Neptune Orient Lines: 13.75 million;	
			Nippon Ysen Kausha: 20.63 million;	
			Transportacion Maritima: 6.88 million;	
			Hanjin Shipping Co: 20.63 million;	
			Hyundai Merchant Marine Co: 18.56 million.	
Pre-insulated pipe cartel[10]	1998	Concerted practice; price fixing; market sharing; and information exchange	Total of 92.61 million imposed on 10 companies as follows: ABB Asea Brown Boveri: 70 million; Brugg Rohrsysteme: 925,000; Dansk Rørindustri: 1,475,000; De Henss/Isoplus: 4,950,000; Ke-Kelit Kunststoffwerk: 360,000;	Appeals pending

[10] OJ 1999 L24/1, [1999] 4 CMLR 402; on appeal Cases T–28/99, etc.

Case	Year	Offence	Fine imposed in ECU	Result on Appeal
			Oy KWH Tech: 700,000;	
			Løgstør Ror A/S: 8.9 million;	
			Pan-Isovit: 1.5 million;	
			Sigma Tecnologie Di Rivestimento: 400,000;	
			Tarco Energi A/S: 3 million.	

Case	Year	Offence	Fine imposed in €	Result on Appeal
Football World Cup[11]	1999	Article 82; Discriminatory sales	1,000	–
Lufthansa[12]	1999	Infringement of Code of Conduct for computer reservation systems	10,000	–
British Airways[13]	1999	Article 82	6.8 million	Appeal pending
FEG and TU[14]	1999	Concerted practice; price fixing; collective exclusive dealing	FEG 4.4 million TU 2.15 million	Appeals pending
Seamless Steel Tubes[15]	1999	Market sharing	Total of 99 million on 8 companies as follows: Mannesmannröhren-Werke; Sumitomo Metal Industries; Nippon Steel; Kawasaki Steel; NKK: 13.5 million each; British Steel: 12.6 million; Dalmine: 10.8 million; Vallorec: 8.1 million.	Appeals pending

---

[11] OJ 2000 L5/55, [2000] 4 CMLR 963.
[12] OJ 1999 L244/56.
[13] OJ 2000 L30/1, [2000] 4 CMLR 999; on appeal Case T–219/99.
[14] OJ 2000 L39/1, [2000] 4 CMLR 1208; on appeal Cases T–5 & 6/00.
[15] IP/99/957 of 8 December 1999; on appeal Cases T–44/00, etc.

Case	Year	Offence	Fine imposed in €	Result on Appeal
FETTCSA[16]	2000	Price-fixing	Total of 6.932 million on 15 companies as follows: CMA CGM: 134,000; Hapag-Lloyd Container Line: 368,000; Kawasaki Kisen Kaisha: 620,000; A.P. Møller Maersk Sealand: 836,000; Malaysian International Shipping Corp: 134,000; Mitsui O.S.K. Lines: 620,000; Neptune Orient Lines: 368,000; Nippon Yusen Kaisha: 620,000; Oriental Overseas Container Line: 134,000; P&O Nedlloyd Container Line: 1.24 million; Cho Yang Shipping Co: 134,000; DSR-Senator Lines: 368,000; Evergreen Marine Corp. (Taiwan): 368,000; Hanjin Shipping Co: 620,000; Yangming Marine Transport Corp: 368,000.	Appeals pending
Lysine cartel[17]	2000	Price-fixing; and sales quotas	Total of 110 million on 5 companies as follows: Archer Daniels Midland: 47.3 million; Ajinomoto: 28.3 million;	Appeals pending

---

[16] OJ 2000 L268/1, [2000] 5 CMLR 1011; on appeal Cases T–213/00, etc.
[17] IP/OO/589 of 7 June 2000; on appeal cases T–220/00, etc.

Case	Year	Offence	Fine imposed in €	Result on Appeal
			Cheil: 12.2 million	
			Kyowa: 13.2 million;	
			Senson: 8.9 million.	
Nathan-Bricolux[18]	2000	Export ban; and RPM	Nathan: 60,000 Bricolux: 1,000	
Opel[19]	2000	Export bans	Opel Nederland (General Motors) 43 million	Appeal pending
Soda Ash[20]	2000	Re-adoption of 1990 decisions	Solvay: 23 million; ICI: 10 million	
JCB[21]	2000	Export ban	39.6 million	

---

[18] OJ 2001 L54/1, [2001] 4 CMLR 1122.
[19] OJ 2001 L59/1; on appeal Case T–363/00.
[20] IP/00/1449 of 13 December 2000; see p. 539, n. 50, supra.
[21] IP/00/1526 of 21 December 2000.

COMMISSION NOTICE[1]

On Cooperation between National Courts and the Commission in Applying Articles 81 and 82 of the EC Treaty

I. Introduction

1. The abolition of internal frontiers enables firms in the Community to embark on new activities and Community consumers to benefit from increased competition. The Commission considers that these advantages must not be jeopardized by restrictive or abusive practices of undertakings and that the completion of the internal market thus reaffirms the importance of the Community's competition policy and competition law.

2. A number of national and Community institutions have contributed to the formulation of Community competition law and are responsible for its day-to-day application. For this purpose, the national competition authorities, national and Community courts and the Commission each assume their own tasks and responsibilities, in line with the principles developed by the case-law of the Court of Justice of the European Communities.

3. If the competition process is to work well in the internal market, effective cooperation between these institutions must be ensured. The purpose of this Notice is to achieve this in relations between national courts and the Commission. It spells out how the Commission intends to assist national courts by closer cooperation in the application of Articles 81 and 82 of the EEC Treaty in individual cases.

II. Powers

4. The Commission is the administrative authority responsible for the implementation and for the thrust of competition policy in the Community and for this purpose has to act in the public interest. National courts, on the other hand, have the task of safeguarding the subjective rights of private individuals in their relations with one another.[2]

5. In performing these different tasks, national courts and the Commission possess concurrent powers for the application of Article [81(1)] and Article [82] of the Treaty. In the case of the Commission, the power is conferred by Article 85 and by the provisions adopted pursuant to Article 83. In the case of the national courts, the power derives from the direct effect of the relevant Community rules. In *BRT* v. *Sabam*, the Court of Justice considered that "as the prohibitions of Articles [81(1)] and [82] tend by their very nature to produce direct effects in relations between individuals, these Articles create direct rights in respect of the individuals concerned which the national courts must safeguard".[3]

---

[1] OJ 1993 C39/6.

[2] Case C–234/89, *Delimitis* v. *Henninger Bräu*, [1991] ECR I–935, paragraph 44; Case T–24/90, *Automec* v. *Commission*, [1992] ECR II–2223, paragraphs 73 and 85.

[3] Case 127/73, *BRT* v. *Sabam*, [1974] ECR 51, paragraph 16.

Notice on Cooperation between national courts & Commission

6. In this way, national courts are able to ensure, at the request of the litigants or on their own initiative, that the competition rules will be respected for the benefit of private individuals. In addition, Article 81(2) enables them to determine, in accordance with the national procedural law applicable, the civil law effects of the prohibition set out in Article 81.[4]

7. However, the Commission, pursuant to Article 9 of Regulation No. 17,[5] has sole power to exempt certain types of agreements, decisions and concerted practices from this prohibition. The Commission may exercise this power in two ways. It may take a decision exempting a specific agreement in an individual case. It may also adopt regulations granting block exemptions for certain categories of agreements, decisions or concerted practices, where it is authorized to do so by the Council, in accordance with Article 83.

8. Although national courts are not competent to apply Article 81(3), they may nevertheless apply the decisions and regulations adopted by the Commission pursuant to that provision. The Court has on several occasions confirmed that the provisions of a regulation are directly applicable.[6] The Commission considers that the same is true for the substantive provisions of an individual exemption decision.

9. The powers of the Commission and those of national courts differ not only in their objective and content, but also in the ways in which they are exercised. The Commission exercises its powers according to the procedural rules laid down by regulation No. 17, whereas national courts exercise theirs in the context of national procedural law.

10. In this connection, the Court of Justice has laid down the principles which govern procedures and remedies for invoking directly applicable Community law.

"Although the Treaty has made it possible in a number of instances for private persons to bring a direct action, where appropriate, before the Court of Justice, it was not intended to create new remedies in the national courts to ensure the observance of Community law other than those already laid down by national law. On the other hand ... it must be possible for every type of action provided for by national law to be available for the purpose of ensuring observance of Community provisions having direct effect, on the same conditions concerning the admissibility and procedure as would apply were it a question of ensuring observance of national law".[7]

11. The Commission considers that these principles apply in the event of breach of the Community competition rules; individuals and companies have access to all procedural remedies provided for by national law on the same conditions as would apply if a comparable breach of national law were involved. This equality of treatment concerns not only the definitive finding of a breach of competition rules, but embraces all the legal means capable of contributing to effective legal protection. Consequently, it is the right of parties subject to Community law that national courts should take provisional measures, that an effective end should be brought, by injunction, to the infringement of Community competition rules of which they are victims, and that compensation should be awarded for the damage suffered as a result of infringements, where such remedies are available in proceedings relating to similar national law.

---

[4] Case 56/65, *LTM* v. *MBU*, [1966] ECR 337; Case 48/72, *Brasserie De Haecht* v. *Wilkin-Janssen*, [1973] ECR 77; Case 319/82, *Ciments et Bétons* v. *Kerpen & Kerpen*, [1983] ECR 4173.

[5] Council Regulation No. 17 of 6 February 1962: First Regulation implementing Articles 81 and 82 of the Treaty (OJ 1962 13, 204/62; Special Edition 1959–62, p. 87).

[6] Case 63/75, *Fonderies Roubaix* v. *Fonderies Roux*, [1976] ECR 111; Case C–234/89, *Delimitis* v. *Henninger Bräu*, [1991] ECR I–935.

[7] Case 158/80, *Rewe* v. *Hauptzollamt Kiel*, [1981] ECR 1805, paragraph 44; see also Case 33/76, *Rewe* v. *Landwirtschaftskammer Saarland*, [1976] ECR 1989; Case 79/83, *Harz* v. *Deutsche Tradax*, [1984] ECR 1921; Case 199/82, *Amministrazione delle Finanze dello Stato* v. *San Giorgio*, [1983] ECR 3595.

12. Here the Commission would like to make it clear that the simultaneous application of national competition law is compatible with the application of Community law, provided that it does not impair the effectiveness and uniformity of Community competition rules and the measures taken to enforce them. Any conflicts which may arise when national and Community competition law are applied simultaneously must be resolved in accordance with the principle of the precedence of Community law.[8] The purpose of this principle is to rule out any national measure which could jeopardize the full effectiveness of the provisions of Community law.

III. The exercise of powers by the Commission

13. As the administrative authority responsible for the Community's competition policy, the Commission must serve the Community's general interest. The administrative resources at the Commission's disposal to perform its task are necessarily limited and cannot be used to deal with all the cases brought to its attention. The Commission is therefore obliged, in general, to take all organizational measures necessary for the performance of its task and, in particular, to establish priorities.[9]

14. The Commission intends, in implementing its decision-making powers, to concentrate on notifications, complaints and own-initiative proceedings having particular political, economic or legal significance for the Community. Where these features are absent in a particular case, notifications will normally be dealt with by means of comfort letter and complaints should, as a rule, be handled by national courts or authorities.

15. The Commission considers that there is not normally a sufficient Community interest in examining a case when the plaintiff is able to secure adequate protection of his rights before the national courts.[10] In these circumstances the complaint will normally be filed.

16. In this respect the Commission would like to make it clear that the application of Community competition law by the national courts has considerable advantages for individuals and companies:

— the Commission cannot award compensation for loss suffered as a result of an infringement of Article 81 or Article 82. Such claims may be brought only before the national courts. Companies are more likely to avoid infringements of the Community competition rules if they risk having to pay damages or interest in such an event,
— national courts can usually adopt interim measures and order the ending of infringements more quickly than the Commission is able to do,
— before national courts, it is possible to combine a claim under Community law with a claim under national law. This is not possible in a procedure before the Commission,
— in some Member States, the courts have the power to award legal costs to the successful applicant. This is never possible in the administrative procedure before the Commission.

IV. Application of Articles 81 and 82 by national courts

17. The national court may have to reach a decision on the application of Articles 81 and 82 in several procedural situations. In the case of civil law proceedings, two types of action are particularly frequent: actions relating to contracts and actions for damages. Under the former, the defendant usually relies on Article 81(2) to dispute the contractual obligations invoked by the plaintiff. Under the latter, the prohibitions contained in Article

---

[8] Case 14/68, *Walt Wilhelm and Others* v. *Bundeskartellamt*, [1969] ECR 1; Joined Cases 253/78 and 1 to 3/79, *Procureur de la République* v. *Giry and Guerlain*, [1980] ECR 2327.
[9] Case T–24/90, *Automec* v. *Commission*, [1992] ECR II–2223, paragraph 77.
[10] Case T–24/90, cited above, paragraphs 91 to 94.

81 and 82 are generally relevant in determining whether the conduct which has given rise to the alleged injury is illegal.

18. In such situations, the direct effect of Article 81(1) and Article 82 gives national courts sufficient powers to comply with their obligation to hand down judgment. Nevertheless, when exercising these powers, they must take account of the Commission's powers in order to avoid decisions which could conflict with those taken or envisaged by the Commission in applying Article 81(1) and Article 82, and also Article 81(3).[11]

19. In its case-law the Court of Justice has developed a number of principles which make it possible for such contradictory decisions to be avoided.[12] The Commission feels that national courts could take account of these principles in the following manner.

1. Application of Article 81(1) and (2) and Article 82

20. The first question which national courts have to answer is whether the agreement, decision or concerted practice at issue infringes the prohibitions laid down in Article 81(1) or Article 82. Before answering this question, national courts should ascertain whether the agreement, decision or concerted practice has already been the subject of a decision, opinion or other official statement issued by an administrative authority and in particular by the Commission. Such statements provide national courts with significant information for reaching a judgment, even if they are not formally bound by them. It should be noted in this respect that not all procedures before the Commission lead to an official decision, but that cases can also be closed by comfort letters. Whilst it is true that the Court of Justice has ruled that this type of letter does not bind national courts, it has nevertheless stated that the opinion expressed by the Commission constitutes a factor which the national courts may take into account in examining whether the agreements or conduct in question are in accordance with the provisions of Article 81.[13]

21. If the Commission has not ruled on the same agreement, decision or concerted practice, the national courts can always be guided, in interpreting the Community law in question, by the case-law of the Court of Justice and the existing decisions of the Commission. It is with this in view that the Commission has, in a number of general notices,[14] specified categories of agreements that are not caught by the ban laid down in Article 81(1).

22. On these bases, national courts should generally be able to decide whether the conduct at issue is compatible with Article 81(1) and Article 82. Nevertheless, if the Commission has initiated a procedure in a case relating to the same conduct, they may, if they consider it necessary for reasons of legal certainty, stay the proceedings while awaiting the outcome of the Commission's action.[15] A stay of proceedings may also be envisaged where national courts wish to seek the Commission's views in accordance with the arrangements referred to in this Notice.[16] Finally, where national courts have persistent

---

[11] Case C–234/89, *Delimitis* v. *Henninger Bräu*, [1991] ECR I–935, paragraph 47.

[12] Casc 48/72, *Brasserie de Haecht* v. *Wilkin-Janssen*, [1973] ECR 77; Case 127/73, *BRT* v. *Sabam*, [1974] ECR 51; Case C–234/89, *Delimitis* v. *Henninger Bräu*, [1991] ECR I–935.

[13] Case 99/79, *Lancôme* v. *Etos*, [1980] ECR 2511, paragraph 11.

[14] See the notices on:
— exclusive dealing contracts with commercial agents (OJ 1962 No. 139 2921/62),
— agreements, decisions and concerted practices in the field of cooperation between enterprises (OJ 1968 C75/3, as corrected in OJ 1968 C84/14),
— assessment of certain subcontracting agreements (OJ 1979 C1/2),
— agreements of minor importance (OJ 1986 C231/2).

[15] Case 127/73, *BRT* v. *Sabam*, [1974] ECR 51, paragraph 21. The procedure before the Commission is initiated by an authoritative act. A simple acknowledgement of receipt cannot be considered an authoritative act as such; Case 48/72, *Brasserie de Haecht* v. *Wilkin-Janssen*, [1973] ECR 77, paragraphs 16 and 17.

[16] Case C–234/89, *Delimitis* v. *Henninger Bräu*, [1991] ECR I–935, paragraph 53, Part V of this Notice.

doubts on questions of compatibility, they may stay proceedings in order to bring the matter before the Court of Justice, in accordance with Article 234 of the Treaty.

23. However, where national courts decide to give judgment and find that the conditions for applying Article 81(1) or Article 82 are not met, they should pursue their proceedings on the basis of such a finding, even if the agreement, decision or concerted practice at issue has been notified to the Commission. Where the assessment of the facts shows that the conditions for applying the said Articles are met, national courts must rule that the conduct at issue infringes Community competition law and take the appropriate measures, including those relating to the consequences that attach to infringement of a statutory prohibition under the civil law applicable.

2. Application of Article 81(3)

24. If the national court concludes that an agreement, decision or concerted practice is prohibited by Article 81(1), it must check whether it is or will be the subject of an exemption by the Commission under Article 81(3). Here several situations may arise.

25. (a) The national court is required to respect the exemption decisions taken by the Commission. Consequently, it must treat the agreement, decision or concerted practice at issue as compatible with Community law and fully recognize its civil law effects. In this respect mention should be made of comfort letters in which the Commission services state that the conditions for applying Article 81(3) have been met. The Commission considers that national courts may take account of these letters as factual elements.

26. (b) Agreements, decisions and concerted practices which fall within the scope of application of a block exemption regulation are automatically exempted from the prohibition laid down in Article 81(1) without the need for a Commission decision or comfort letter.[17]

27. (c) Agreements, decisions and concerted practices which are not covered by a block exemption regulation and which have not been the subject of an individual exemption decision or a comfort letter must, in the Commission's view, be examined in the following manner.

28. The national court must first examine whether the procedural conditions necessary for securing exemption are fulfilled, notably whether the agreement, decision or concerted practice has been duly notified in accordance with Article 4(1) of Regulation No. 17. Where no such notification has been made, and subject to Article 4(2) of Regulation No. 17, exemption under Article 81(3) is ruled out, so that the national court may decide, pursuant to Article 81(2), that the agreement, decision or concerted practice is void.

29. Where the agreement, decision or concerted practice has been duly notified to the Commission, the national court will assess the likelihood of an exemption being granted in the case in question in the light of the relevant criteria developed by the case law of the Court of Justice and the Court of First Instance and by previous regulations and decisions of the Commission.

30. Where the national court has in this way ascertained that the agreement, decision or concerted practice at issue cannot be the subject of an individual exemption, it will take the measures necessary to comply with the requirements of Article 81(1) and (2). On the other hand, if it takes the view that individual exemption is possible, the national court should suspend the proceedings while awaiting the Commission's decision. If the national court does suspend the proceedings, it nevertheless remains free, according to the rules of the applicable national law, to adopt any interim measures it deems necessary.

31. In this connection, it should be made clear that these principles do not apply to agreements, decisions and concerted practices which existed before Regulation No. 17 entered into force or before that Regulation became applicable as a result of the accession of a new Member State and which were duly notified to the Commission. The national courts must consider such agreements, decisions and concerted practices to be valid so

---

[17] A list of the relevant regulations and of the official explanatory comments relating to them is given in the Annex to this Notice.

long as the Commission or the authorities of the Member States have not taken a prohibition decision or sent a comfort letter to the parties informing them that the file has been closed.[18]

32. The Commission realizes that the principles set out above for the application of Articles 81 and 82 by national courts are complex and sometimes insufficient to enable those courts to perform their judicial function properly. This is particularly so where the practical application of Article 81(1) and Article 82 gives rise to legal or economic difficulties, where the Commission has initiated a procedure in the same case or where the agreement, decision or concerted practice concerned may become the subject of an individual exemption within the meaning of Article 81(3). National courts may bring such cases before the Court of Justice for a preliminary ruling, in accordance with Article 234. They may also avail themselves of the Commission's assistance according to the procedures set out below.

V. Cooperation between national courts and the Commission

33. Article 10 of the EEC Treaty establishes the principle of constant and sincere cooperation between the Community and the Member States with view to attaining the objectives of the Treaty, including implementation of Article 3(1)(g), which refers to the establishment of a system ensuring that competition in the common market is not distorted. This principle involves obligations and duties of mutual assistance, both for the Member States and for the Community institutions. The Court has thus ruled that, under Article 10 of the EEC Treaty, the Commission has a duty of sincere cooperation vis-à-vis judicial authorities of the Member States, who are responsible for ensuring that Community law is applied and respected in the national legal system.[19]

34. The Commission considers that such cooperation is essential in order to guarantee the strict, effective and consistent application of Community competition law. In addition, more effective participation by the national courts in the day-to-day application of competition law gives the Commission more time to perform its administrative task, namely to steer competition policy in the Community.

35. In the light of these considerations, the Commission intends to work towards closer cooperation with national courts in the following manner.

36. The Commission conducts its policy so as to give the parties concerned useful pointers to the application of competition rules. To this end, it will continue its policy in relation to block exemption regulations and general notices. These general texts, the case-law of the Court of Justice and the Court of First Instance, the decisions previously taken by the Commission and the annual reports on competition policy are all elements of secondary legislation or explanations which may assist national courts in examining individual cases.

37. If these general pointers are insufficient, national courts may, within the limits of their national procedural law, ask the Commission and in particular its Directorate-General for Competition for the following information.

First, they may ask for information of a procedural nature to enable them to discover whether a certain case is pending before the Commission, whether a case has been the subject of a notification, whether the Commission has officially initiated a procedure or whether it has already taken a position through an official decision or through a comfort letter sent by its services. If necessary, national courts may also ask the Commission to give an opinion as to how much time is likely to be required for granting or refusing individual exemption for notified agreements or practices, so as to be able to determine the

---

[18] Case 48/72, *Brasserie de Haecht* v. *Wilkin-Janssen*, [1973] ECR 77; Case 59/77, *De Bloss* v. *Bouyer* [1977] ECR 2359; Case 99/79, *Lancôme* v. *Etos*, [1980] ECR 2511.

[19] Case C–2/88 Imm., *Zwartveld*, [1990] ECR I–3365, paragraph 18; Case C–234/89, *Delimitis* v. *Henninger Bräu*, [1991] ECR I–935, paragraph 53.

conditions for any decision to suspend proceedings or whether interim measures need to be adopted.[20] The Commission, for its part, will endeavour to give priority to cases which are the subject of national proceedings suspended in this way, in particular when the outcome of a civil dispute depends on them.

38. Next, national courts may consult the Commission on points of law. Where the application of Article 81(1) and Article 82 causes them particular difficulties, national courts may consult the Commission on its customary practice in relation to the Community law at issue. As far as Articles 81 and 82 are concerned, these difficulties relate in particular to the conditions for applying these Articles as regards the effect on trade between Member States and as regards the extent to which the restriction of competition resulting from the practices specified in these provisions is appreciable. In its replies, the Commission does not consider the merits of the case. In addition, where they have doubts as to whether a contested agreement, decision or concerted practice is eligible for an individual exemption, they may ask the Commission to provide them with an interim opinion. If the Commission says that the case in question is unlikely to qualify for an exemption, national courts will be able to waive a stay of proceedings and rule on the validity of the agreement, decision or concerted practice.

39. The answers given by the Commission are not binding on the courts which have requested them. In its replies the Commission makes it clear that its view is not definitive and that the right for the national court to refer to the Court of Justice, pursuant to Article 234, is not affected. Nevertheless, the Commission considers that it gives them useful guidance for resolving disputes.

40. Lastly, national courts can obtain information from the Commission regarding factual data: statistics, market studies and economic analyses. The Commission will endeavour to communicate these data, within the limits laid down in the following paragraph, or will indicate the source from which they can be obtained.

41. It is in the interests of the proper administration of justice that the Commission should answer requests for legal and factual information in the shortest possible time. Nevertheless, the Commission cannot accede to such requests unless several conditions are met. First, the requisite data must actually be at its disposal. Secondly, the Commission may communicate this data only in so far as permitted by the general principle of sound administrative practice.

42. For example, Article 287 of the Treaty, as spelt out in Article 20 of Regulation No. 17 for the purposes of the competition rules, requires the Commission not to disclose information of a confidential nature. In addition, the duty of sincere cooperation deriving from Article 10 is one applying to the relationship between national courts and the Commission and cannot concern the position of the parties to the dispute pending before those courts. As *amicus curiae*, the Commission is obliged to respect legal neutrality and objectivity. Consequently, it will not accede to requests for information unless they come from a national court, either directly, or indirectly through parties which have been ordered by the court concerned to provide certain information. In the latter case, the Commission will ensure that its answer reaches all the parties to the proceedings.

43. Over and above such exchange of information, required in specific cases, the Commission is anxious to develop as far as possible a more general information policy. To this end, the Commission intends to publish an explanatory booklet regarding the application of the competition rules at national level.

44. Lastly, the Commission also wishes to reinforce the effect of national competition judgments. To this end, it will study the possibility of extending the scope of the Convention on jurisdiction and the enforcement of judgments in civil and commercial matters to competition cases assigned to administrative courts.[21] It should be noted that,

---

[20] See paragraphs 22 and 30 of this Notice.
[21] Convention of 27 September 1968 (OJ 1978 L304/77).

in the Commission's view, competition judgments are already governed by this Convention where they are handed down in cases of a civil and commercial nature.

VI. Final remarks

45. This Notice does not relate to the competition rules governing the transport sector.[22] Nor does it relate to the competition rules laid down in the Treaty establishing the European Coal and Steel Community.

46. This Notice is issued for guidance and does not in any way restrict the rights conferred on individuals or companies by Community law.

47. This Notice is without prejudice to any interpretation of the Community competition rules which may be given by the Court of Justice of the European Communities.

48. A summary of the answers given by the Commission pursuant to this Notice will be published annually in the Competition Report.

ANNEX

BLOCK EXEMPTIONS

A. ENABLING COUNCIL REGULATIONS

I. Vertical agreements (see under B.I and B.II)
    Council Regulation No. 19/65/EEC of 2 March 1965 on the application of Article 81(3) of the Treaty to certain categories of agreements and concerted practices (OJ 1965–66 Spec. Ed. 35).

II. Horizontal agreements (see under B.III)
    Council Regulation (EEC) No. 2821/71 of 20 December 1971 on the application of Article 81(3) of the Treaty to categories of agreements, decisions and concerted practices (OJ 1971–III Spec. Ed. 1032), modified by Regulation (EEC) No. 2743/72 of 19 December 1972 (OJ 1972 Spec. Ed. 60).

B. COMMISSION BLOCK EXEMPTION REGULATIONS AND EXPLANATORY NOTICES

I. Distribution agreements
    1. Commission Regulation (EEC) No. 1983/83 of 22 June 1983 concerning exclusive distribution agreements (OJ 1983 L173/1).
    2. Commission Regulation (EEC) No. 1984/83 of 22 June 1983 concerning exclusive purchasing agreements (OJ 1983 L173/5).
    3. Commission Notice concerning Commission Regulations (EEC) No. 1983/83 and (EEC) No. 1984/83 (OJ 1984 C101/2).

---

[22] Regulation No. 141/62 of the Council of 26 November 1962 exempting transport from the application of Council Regulation No. 17 (OJ 124 1962 2751/62), as amended by Regulations Nos. 165/65/EEC (OJ 210 1965 3141/65) and 1002/67/EEC (J.O. 306, 1967 1); Regulation (EEC) No. 1017/68 of the Council of 19 July 1968 applying rules of competition to transport by rail, road and inland waterway (OJ 1968 L175/1); Council Regulation (EEC) No. 4056/86 of 22 December 1986 laying down detailed rules for the application of Articles 81 and 82 of the Treaty to maritime transport (OJ 1986 L378/4); Council Regulation (EEC) No. 3975/87 of 14 December 1987 laying down the procedure for the application of the rules on competition to undertakings in the air transport sector (OJ 1987 L374/1).

4. Commission Regulation (EEC) No. 123/85 of 12 December 1984 concerning motor vehicle distribution and servicing agreements (OJ 1985 L15/16).

5. Commission Notice concerning regulation (EEC) No. 123/85 (OJ 1985 C17/4).

6. Commission Notice on the clarification of the activities of motor vehicle intermediaries (OJ 1991 C329/20).

II. Licensing and franchising agreements

1. Commission Regulation (EEC) No. 2349/84 of 23 July 1984 concerning patent licensing agreements (OJ 1984 L219/15; corrigendum OJ 1985 L280/32).

2. Commission Regulation (EEC) No. 4087/88 of 30 November 1988 concerning franchising agreements (OJ 1988 L359/46).

3. Commission Regulation (EEC) No. 556/89 of 30 November 1988 concerning know-how licensing agreements (OJ 1989 L61/1).

III. Cooperative agreements

1. Commission Regulation (EEC) No. 417/85 of 19 December 1984 concerning specialization agreements (OJ 1985 L53/1).

2. Commission Regulation (EEC) No. 418/85 of 19 December 1984 concerning research and development agreements (OJ 1985 L53/5).

COMMISSION NOTICE[1]

On Cooperation Between National Competition Authorities and the Commission in Handling Cases Falling Within the Scope of Articles 81 or 82 of the EC Treaty

(Text with EEA relevance)

I. ROLE OF THE MEMBER STATES AND OF THE COMMUNITY

1. In competition policy the Community and the Member States perform different functions. Whereas the Community is responsible only for implementing the Community rules, Member States not only apply their domestic law but also have a hand in implementing Articles 81 and 82 of the EC Treaty.

2. This involvement of the Member States in Community competition policy means that decision can be taken as closely as possible to the citizen (Article 1 of the Treaty on European Union). The decentralized application of Community competition rules also leads to a better allocation of tasks. If, by reason of its scale or effects, the proposed action can best be taken at Community level, it is for the Commission to act. Otherwise, it is for the competition authority of the Member State concerned to act.

3. Community law is implemented by the Commission and national competition authorities, on the one hand, and national courts, on the other, in accordance with the principles developed by the Community legislature and by the Court of Justice and the Court of First Instance of the European Communities.

It is the task of national courts to safeguard the rights of private persons in their relations with one another.[2] Those rights derive from the fact that the prohibitions in Articles 81(1) and 82[3] and the exemptions granted by regulation[4] have been recognized by the Court of Justice as being directly applicable. Relations between national courts and the Commission in applying Articles 81 and 82 were spelt out in a Notice published by the Commission in 1993.[5] This Notice is the counterpart, for relations with national authorities, to that of 1993 on relations with national courts.

4. As administrative authorities, both the Commission and national competition authorities act in the public interest in performing their general task of monitoring and enforcing the competition rules.[6] Relations between them are determined primarily by this common role of protecting the general interest. Although similar to the Notice on cooperation with national courts, this Notice accordingly reflects this special feature.

---

[1] OJ 1997 C313/3.

[2] Case T–24/90 *Automec v. Commission ("Automec II")* [1992] ECR II–2223, paragraph 85.

[3] Case 127/73 *BRT v. SABAM* [1974] ECR 51, paragraph 16.

[4] Case 63/75 *Fonderies Roubaix-Wattrelos v. Fonderies A. Roux* [1976] ECR 111.

[5] Notice on cooperation between national courts and the Commission in applying Articles 81 and 82 of the EEC Treaty (OJ 1993 C39/3).

[6] *Automec II*, see footnote 1; paragraph 85.

5. The specific nature of the role of the Commission and of national competition authorities is characterized by the powers conferred on those bodies by the Council regulations adopted under Article 83 of the Treaty. Article 9(1) of Regulation No 17[7] thus provides: "Subject to review of its decision by the Court of Justice,[8] the Commission shall have sole power to declare Article 81(1) inapplicable pursuant to Article 81(3) of the Treaty". And Article 9(3) of the same Regulation provides: "As long as the Commission has not initiated any procedure under Article 2,[9] 3[10] or 6,[11] the authorities of the Member States shall remain competent to apply Article 81(1) and Article 82 in accordance with Article 84 of the Treaty."

It follows that, provided their national law has conferred the necessary powers on them, national competition authorities are empowered to apply the prohibitions in Articles 81(1) and 82. On the other hand, for the purposes of applying Article 81(3), they do not have any powers to grant exemptions in individual cases; they must abide by the decisions and regulations adopted by the Commission under that provision. They may also take account of other measures adopted by the Commission in such cases, in particular comfort letters, treating them as factual evidence.

6. The Commission is convinced that enhancing the role of national competition authorities will boost the effectiveness of Articles 81 and 82 of the Treaty and, generally speaking, will bolster the application of Community competition rules throughout the Community. In the interests of safeguarding and developing the single market, the Commission considers that those provisions should be used as widely as possible. Being closer to the activities and businesses that require monitoring, national authorities are often in a better position than the Commission to protect competition.

7. Cooperation must therefore be organized between national authorities and the Commission. If this cooperation is to be fruitful, they will have to keep in close and constant touch.

8. The Commission proposes to set out in this Notice the principles it will apply in future when dealing with the cases described herein. The Notice also seeks to induce firms to approach national competition authorities more often.

9. This Notice describes the practical cooperation which is desirable between the Commission and national authorities. It does not affect the extent of the powers conferred by Community law on either the Commission or national authorities for the purpose of dealing with individual cases.

10. For cases falling within the scope of Community law, to avoid duplication of checks on compliance with the competition rules which are applicable to them, which is costly for the firms concerned, checks should wherever possible be carried out by a single authority (either a Member State's competition authority or the Commission). Control by a single authority offers advantages for businesses.

Parallel proceedings before the Commission, on the one hand, and a national competition authority, on the other, are costly for businesses whose activities fall within the scope both of Community law and of Member States' competition laws. They can lead to the repetition of checks on the same activity, by the Commission, on the one hand, and by the competition authorities of the Member States concerned, on the other.

Businesses in the Community may therefore in certain circumstances find it to their advantage if some cases falling within the scope of Community competition law were dealt with solely by national authorities. In order that this advantage may be enjoyed to the full, the Commission thinks it is desirable that national authorities should themselves apply Community law directly or, failing that, obtain, by applying their domestic law, a result similar to that which would have been obtained had Community law been applied.

---

[7] Council Regulation No 17 of 6 February 1962: First Regulation implementing Articles 81 and 82 of the Treaty; OJ 1962 13/204 (English Special Edition 1959–62, p. 87).

[8] Now by the Court of First Instance and, on appeal, by the Court of Justice.

[9] Negative clearance.

[10] Termination of infringements—prohibition decisions.

[11] Decisions pursuant to Article 81(3).

11. What is more, in addition to the resulting benefits accruing to competition authorities in terms of mobilization of their resources, cooperation between authorities reduces the risk of divergent decisions and hence the opportunities for those who might be tempted to do so to seek out whichever authority seemed to them to be the most favourable to their interests.

12. Member States' competition authorities often have a more detailed and precise knowledge than the Commission of the relevant markets (particularly those with highly specific national features) and the businesses concerned. Above all, they may be in a better position than the Commission to detect restrictive practices that have not been notified or abuses of a dominant position whose effects are essentially confined to their territory.

13. Many cases handled by national authorities involve arguments based on national law and arguments drawn from Community competition law. In the interests of keeping proceedings as short as possible, the Commission considers it preferable that national authorities should directly apply Community law themselves, instead of making firms refer to the Community-law aspects of their cases to the Commission.

14. An increasing number of major issues in the field of Community competition law have been clarified over the last thirty years through the case-law of the Court of Justice and the Court of First Instance and through decisions taken on questions of principle and the exemption regulations adopted by the Commission. The application of that law by national authorities is thereby simplified.

15. The Commission intends to encourage the competition authorities of all Member States to engage in this cooperation. However, the national legislation of several Member States does not currently provide competition authorities with the procedural means of applying Articles 81(1) and 82. In such Member States conduct caught by the Community provisions can be effectively dealt with by national authorities only under national law.

In the Commission's view, it is desirable that national authorities should apply Articles 81 or 82 of the Treaty, if appropriate in conjunction with their domestic competition rules, when handling cases that fall within the scope of those provisions.

16. Where authorities are not in a position to do this and hence can apply only their national law to such cases, the application of that law should "not prejudice the uniform application throughout the common market of the Community rules on cartels and of the full effect of the measures adopted in implementation of those rules".[12] At the very least, the solution they find to a case falling within the scope of Community law must be compatible with that law, Member States being forbidden, given the primacy of Community law over national competition law[13] and the obligation to cooperate in good faith laid down in Article 10 of the Treaty,[14] to take measures capable of defeating the practical effectiveness of Articles 81 and 82.

17. Divergent decisions are more likely to be reached where a national authority applies its national law rather than Community law. Where a Member State's competition authority applies Community law, it is required to comply with any decisions taken previously by the Commission in the same proceedings. Where the case has merely been the subject of a comfort letter, then, according to the Court of Justice, although this type of letter does not bind national courts, the opinion expressed by the Commission constitutes a factor which the national courts may take into account in examining whether the agreements on conduct in question are in accordance with the provisions of Article 81.[15] In the Commission's view, the same holds true for national authorities.

18. Where an infringement of Articles 81 or 82 is established by Commission decision, that decision precludes the application of a domestic legal provision authorizing what the Commission has prohibited. The objective of the prohibitions in Articles 81(1) and 82 is

---

[12] Case 14/68 *Walt Wilhelm and Others v. Bundeskartellamt* [1969] ECR 1, paragraph 4.

[13] *Walt Wilhelm*, see footnote 11; paragraph 6; Case 66/86 *Ahmed Saeed Flugreisen and Others v. Zentrale Zur Bekämpfung Unlauteren Wettbewerbs* [1989] ECR 803, paragraph 48.

[14] Case C–165/91 *Van Munster v. Rijksdienst voor Pensioenen* [1994] ECR I–4661, paragraph 32.

[15] Case 99/79 *Lancôme v. Etos* [1980] ECR 2511, paragraph 11, cited in the abovementioned notice on cooperation between national courts and the Commission in applying Articles 81 and 82.

to guarantee the unity of the common market and the preservation of undistorted competition in that market. They must be strictly complied with if the functioning of the Community regime is not to be endangered.[16]

19. The legal position is less clear as to whether national authorities are allowed to apply their more stringent national competition law where the situation they are assessing has previously been the subject of an individual exemption decision of the Commission or is covered by a block exemption Regulation. In *Walt Wilhelm*, the Court stated that the Treaty "permits the Community authorities to carry out certain positive, though indirect, actions with a view to promoting a harmonious development of economic activities within the whole Community" (paragraph 5 of the judgment). In *Bundeskartellamt v. Volkswagen and VAG Leasing*,[17] the Commission contended that national authorities may not prohibit exempted agreements. The uniform application of Community law would be frustrated every time an exemption granted under Community law was made to depend on the relevant national rules. Otherwise, not only would a given agreement be treated differently depending on the law of each Member State, thus detracting from the uniform application of Community law, but the full effectiveness of an act giving effect to the Treaty—which an exemption under Article 81(3) undoubtedly is—would also be disregarded. In the case in point, however, the Court did not have to settle the question.

20. If the Commission's Directorate-General for Competition sends a comfort letter in which it expresses the opinion that an agreement or a practice is incompatible with Article 81 of the Treaty but states that, for reasons to do with its internal priorities, it will not propose to the Commission that it take a decision thereon in accordance with the formal procedures laid down in Regulation No 17, it goes without saying that the national authorities in whose territory the effects of the agreement or practice are felt may take action in respect of that agreement or practice.

21. In the case of a comfort letter in which the Directorate-General for Competition expresses the opinion that an agreement does restrict competition within the meaning of Article 81(1) but qualifies for exemption under Article 81(3), the Commission will call upon national authorities to consult it before they decide whether to adopt a different decision under Community or national law.

22. As regards comfort letters in which the Commission expresses the opinion that, on the basis of the information in its possession, there is no need for it to take any action under Article 81(1) or Article 82 of the Treaty, "that fact cannot by itself have the result of preventing the national authorities from applying to those agreements" or practices "provisions of national competition law which may be more rigorous than Community law in this respect. The fact that a practice has been held by the Commission not to fall within the ambit of the prohibition contained in Article 81(1) and (2)" or Article 82, "the scope of which is limited to agreements" or dominant positions "capable of affecting trade between Member States, in no way prevents that practice from being considered by the national authorities from the point of view of the restrictive effects which it may produce nationally". (Judgment of the Court of Justice in *Procureur de la République v. Giry and Guerlain*).[18]

II. GUIDELINES ON CASE ALLOCATION

23. Cooperation between the Commission and national competition authorities has to comply with the current legal framework. First, if it is to be caught by Community law and not merely by national competition law, the conduct in question must be liable to have an appreciable effect on trade between Member States. Secondly, the Commission has sole power to declare Article 81(1) of the Treaty inapplicable under Article 81(3).

---

[16] Fourth Report on Competition Policy 1974, point 45.
[17] Case C–266/93 [1995] ECR I–3477; see also the Opinion of Advocate-General Tesauro in the same case, paragraph 51.
[18] Joined Cases 253/78 and 1 to 3/79 *Procureur de la République v. Giry and Guerlain* [1980] ECR 2327, paragraph 18.

24. In practice, decisions taken by a national authority can apply effectively only to restrictions of competition whose impact is felt essentially within its territory. This is the case in particular with the restrictions referred to in Article 4(2)(1) of Regulation No 17, namely agreements, decisions or concerted practices the only parties to which are undertakings from one Member State and which, though they do not relate either to imports or to exports between Member States, may affect intra-Community trade.[19] It is extremely difficult from a legal standpoint for such an authority to conduct investigations outside its home country, such as when on-the-spot inspections need to be carried out on businesses, and to ensure that its decisions are enforced beyond its national borders. The upshot is that the Commission usually has to handle cases involving businesses whose relevant activities are carried on in more than one Member State.

25. A national authority having sufficient resources in terms of manpower and equipment and having had the requisite powers conferred on it, also needs to be able to deal effectively with any cases covered by the Community rules which it proposes to take on. The effectiveness of a national authority's action is dependent on its powers of investigation, the legal means it has at its disposal for settling a case—including the power to order interim measures in an emergency—and the penalties it is empowered to impose on businesses found guilty of infringing the competition rules. Differences between the rules of procedure applicable in the various Member States should not, in the Commission's view, lead to outcomes which differ in their effectiveness when similar cases are being dealt with.

26. In deciding which cases to handle itself, the Commission will take into account the effects of the restrictive practice or abuse of a dominant position and the nature of the infringement.

In principle, national authorities will handle cases the effects of which are felt mainly in their territory and which appear upon preliminary examination unlikely to qualify for exemption under Article 81(3). However, the Commission reserves the right to take on certain cases displaying a particular Community interest.

Mainly national effects

27. First of all, it should be pointed out that the only cases at issue here are those which fall within the scope of Articles 81 and 82.

That being so, the existing and foreseeable effects of a restrictive practice or abuse of a dominant position may be deemed to be closely linked to the territory in which the agreement or practice is applied and to the geographic market for the goods or services in question.

28. Where the relevant geographic market is limited to the territory of a single Member State and the agreement or practice is applied only in that State, the effects of the agreement or practice must be deemed to occur mainly within that State even if, theoretically, the agreement or practice is capable of affecting trade between Member States.

Nature of the infringement: cases that cannot be exempted

29. The following considerations apply to cases brought before the Commission, to cases brought before a national competition authority and to cases which both may have to deal with.

A distinction should be drawn between infringements of Article 81 of the Treaty and infringements of Article 82.

---

[19] It is possible that an agreement, "although it does not relate either to imports or to exports between Member States" within the meaning of Article 4 of Regulation No 17, "may affect trade between Member States" within the meaning of Article 81(1) of the Treaty (judgment of the Court of Justice in Case 43/69 *Bilger v. Jehle* [1970] ECR 127, paragraph 5).

30. The Commission has exclusive powers under Article 81 (3) of the Treaty to declare the provisions of Article 81 (1) inapplicable. Any notified restrictive practice that *prima facie* qualifies for exemption must therefore be examined by the Commission, which will take account of the criteria developed in this area by the Court of Justice and the Court of First Instance and also by the relevant regulations and its own previous decisions.

31. The Commission also has exclusive responsibility for investigation complaints against decisions it has taken under its exclusive powers, such as a decision to withdraw an exemption previously granted by it under Article 81 (3).[20]

32. No such limitation exists, however, on implementation of Article 82 of the Treaty. The Commission and the Member States have concurrent competence to investigate complaints and to prohibit abuses of dominant positions.

Cases of particular significance to the Community

33. Some cases considered by the Commission to be of particular Community interest will more often be dealt with by the Commission even if, inasmuch as they satisfy the requirements set out above (points 27–28 and 29–32), they can be dealt with by a national authority.

34. This category includes cases which raise a new point of law, that is to say, those which have not yet been the subject of a Commission decision or a judgment of the Court of Justice or Court of First Instance.

35. The economic magnitude of a case is not in itself sufficient reason for its being dealt with by the Commission. The position might be different where access to the relevant market by firms from other Member States is significantly impeded.

36. Cases involving alleged anti-competitive behaviour by a public undertaking, an undertaking to which a Member State has granted special or exclusive rights with the meaning of Article 82 (1) of the Treaty, or an undertaking entrusted with the operation of services of general economic interest or having the character of a revenue-producing monopoly within the meaning of Article 82 (2) of the Treaty may also be of particular Community interest.

III. COOPERATION IN CASES WHICH THE COMMISSION DEALS WITH FIRST

37. Cases dealt with by the Commission have three possible origins: own-initiative proceedings, notifications and complaints. By their very nature, own-initiative proceedings do not lend themselves to decentralized processing by national competition authorities.

38. The exclusivity of the Commission's powers to apply Article 81 (3) of the Treaty in individual cases means that cases notified to the Commission under Article 4 (1) of Regulation No 17 by parties seeking exemption under Article 81 (3) cannot be dealt with by a national competition authority on the Commission's initiative. According to the case-law of the Court of First Instance, these exclusive powers confer on the applicant the right to obtain from the Commission a decision on the substance of his request for exemption.[21]

39. National competition authorities may deal, at the Commission's request, with complaints that do not involve the application of Article 81 (3), namely those relating to restrictive practices which must be notified under Articles 4 (1), 5 (1) and 25 of Regulation No 17 but have not been notified to the Commission and those based on alleged infringement of Article 82 of the Treaty. On the other hand, complaints concerning matters falling within the scope of the Commission's exclusive powers, such as withdrawal of exemption, cannot be usefully handled by a national competition authority.[22]

---

[20] *Automec II*, see footnote 1; paragraph 75.
[21] Case T–23/90 *Peugeot v. Commission* [1991] ECR II–653, paragraph 47.
[22] *Automec II*, see footnote 1; paragraph 75.

40. The criteria set out at points 23 to 36 above in relation to the handling of a case by the Commission or a national authority, in particular as regards the territorial extent of the effects of a restrictive practice or dominant position (points 27–28), should be taken into account.

Commission's right to reject a complaint

41. It follows from the case-law of the Court of First Instance that the Commission is entitled under certain conditions to reject a complaint which does not display sufficient Community interest to justify further investigation.[23]

42. The Commission's resultant right to reject a complaint stems from the concurrent competence of the Commission, national courts and—where they have the power— national competition authorities to apply Articles 81 (1) and 82 and from the consequent protection available to complainants before the courts and administrative authorities. With regard to that concurrent competence, it has been consistently held by the Court of Justice and the Court of First Instance that Article 3 of Regulation No 17 (the legal basis for the right to lodge a complaint with the Commission for alleged infringement of Article 81 or Article 82) does not entitle an applicant under that Article to obtain from the Commission a decision within the meaning of Article 249 of the Treaty as to whether or not the alleged infringement has occurred.[24]

Conditions for rejecting a complaint

43. The investigation of a complaint by a national authority presupposes that the following specific conditions, derived from the case-law of the Court of First Instance, are met.

44. The first of these conditions is that, in order to assess whether or not there is a Community interest in having a case investigated further, the Commission must first undertake a careful examination of the questions of fact and law set out in the complaint.[25] In accordance with the obligation imposed on it by Article 253 of the Treaty to state the reasons for its decisions, the Commission has to inform the complainant of the legal and factual considerations which have induced it to conclude that the complaint does not display a sufficient Community interest to justify further investigation. The Commission cannot therefore confine itself to an abstract reference to the Community interest.[26]

45. In assessing whether it is entitled to reject a complaint for lack of any Community interest, the Commission must balance the significance of the alleged infringement as regards the functioning of the common market, the probability of its being able to establish the existence of the infringement, and the extent of the investigative measures required for it to perform, under the best possible conditions, its task of making sure that Articles 81 and 82 are complied with.[27] In particular, as the Court of First Instance held in *BEMIM*,[28] where the effects of the infringements alleged in a complaint are essentially confined to the territory of one Member State and where proceedings have been brought before the courts and competent administrative authorities of that Member State by the complainant against the body against which the complaint was made, the Commission is entitled to reject the complaint for lack of any sufficient Community interest in further investigation of the case, provided however that the rights of the complainant can be

---

[23] *Automec II*, se footnote 1; paragraph 85; cited in Case T–114/92 *BEMIM v. Commission* [1995] ECR II–147, paragraph 80, and in Case T–77/95 *SFEI and Others v. Commission* [1997] ECR II–1, paragraphs 29 and 55.

[24] See in particular Case 125/78, *GEMA v. Commission* [1979] ECR 3173, paragraph 17, and Case T–16/91, *Rendo and Others v. Commission* [1992] ECR II–2417, paragraph 98.

[25] *Automec II*, see footnote 1; paragraph 82.

[26] *Automec II*, see footnote 1; paragraph 85.

[27] *Automec II*, see footnote 1; paragraph 86, cited in *BEMIM*, paragraph 80.

[28] See footnote 22; paragraph 86.

adequately safeguarded. As to whether the effects of the restrictive practice are localized, such is the case in particular with practices to which the only parties are undertakings from one Member State and which, although they do not relate either to imports or to exports between Member States, within the meaning of point 1 of Article 4 (2) of Regulation No 17,[29] are capable of affecting intra-Community trade. As regards the safeguarding of the complainant's rights, the Commission considers that the referral of the matter to the national authority concerned needs must protect them quite adequately. On this latter point, the Commission takes the view that the effectiveness of the national authority's action depends notably on whether that authority is able to take interim measures if it deems it necessary, without prejudice to the possibility, found in the law of certain Member States, that such measures may be taken with the requisite degree of effectiveness by a court.

Procedure

46. Where the Commission considers these conditions to have been met, it will ask the competition authority of the Member State in which most of the effects of the contested agreement or practice are felt if it would agree to investigate and decide on the complaint. Where the competition authority agrees to do so, the Commission will reject the complaint pending before it on the ground that it does not display sufficient Community interest and will refer the matter to the national competition authority, either automatically or at the complainant's request. The Commission will place the relevant documents in its possession at the national authority's disposal.[30]

47. With regard to investigation of the complaint, it should be stressed that, in accordance with the ruling given by the Court of Justice in Case C–67/91[31] (the "*Spanish banks*" case), national competition authorities are not entitled to use as evidence, for the purposes of applying either national rules or the Community competition rules, unpublished information contained in replies to requests for information sent to firms under Article 11 of Regulation No 17 or information obtained as a result of any inspections carried out under Article 14 of that Regulation. This information can nevertheless be taken into account, where appropriate, to justify instituting national proceedings.[32]

IV. COOPERATION IN CASES WHICH A NATIONAL AUTHORITY DEALS WITH FIRST

Introduction

48. At issue here are cases falling within the scope of Community competition law which a national competition authority handles on its own initiative, applying Articles 81 (1) or 82, either alone or in conjunction with its national competition rules, or, where it cannot do so, its national rules alone. This covers all cases within this field which a national authority investigates before the Commission—where appropriate—does so, irrespective of their procedural origin (own-initiative proceedings, notification, complaint,

---

[29] See footnote 18.

[30] However, in the case of information accompanied by a request for confidentiality with a view to protecting the informant's anonymity, an institution which accepts such information is bound, under Article 214 of the Treaty, to comply with such a condition (Case 145/83 *Adams v. Commission* [1985] ECR 3539). The Commission will thus not divulge to national authorities the name of an informant who wishes to remain anonymous unless the person concerned withdraws, at the Commission's request, his request for anonymity *vis-à-vis* the national authority which may be dealing with his complaint.

[31] Case C–67/91 *Dirección General de Defensa de la Competencia v. Asociación Española de Banca Privada (AEB) and Others* [1992] ECR I–4785, operative part.

[32] See footnote 30; paragraphs 39 and 43.

etc.). These cases are therefore those which fulfil the conditions set out in Part II (Guidelines on case allocation) of this Notice.

49. As regards cases which they deal with under Community law, it is desirable that national authorities should systematically inform the Commission of any proceedings they initiate. The Commission will pass on this information to the authorities in the other Member States.

50. This cooperation is especially necessary in regard to cases of particular significance to the Community within the meaning of points 33–36. This category includes (a) all cases raising a new point of law, the aim being to avoid decisions, whether based on national law or on Community law, which are incompatible with the latter; (b) among cases of the utmost importance from an economic point of view, only those in which access by firms from other Member States to the relevant national market is significantly impeded; and (c) certain cases in which a public undertaking or an undertaking treated as equivalent to a public undertaking (within the meaning of Article 86(1) and (2) of the Treaty) is suspected of having engaged in an anti-competitive practice. Each national authority must determine, if necessary after consulting the Commission, whether a given case fits into one of these sub-categories.

51. Such cases will be investigated by national competition authorities in accordance with the procedures laid down by their national law, whether they are acting with a view to applying the Community competition rules or applying their national competition rules.[33]

52. The Commission also takes the view that, like national courts to which competition cases involving Articles 81 or 82 have been referred, national competition authorities applying those provisions are always at liberty, within the limits of their national procedural rules and subject to Article 287 of the Treaty, to seek information from the Commission on the state of any proceedings which the Commission may have set in motion and as to the likelihood of its giving an official ruling, pursuant to Regulation No 17, on cases which they are investigating on their own initiative. Under the same circumstances, national competition authorities may contact the Commission where the concrete application of Article 81(1) or of Article 82 raises particular difficulties, in order to obtain the economic and legal information which the Commission is in a position to supply to them.[34]

53. The Commission is convinced that close cooperation with national authorities will forestall any contradictory decisions. But if, "during national proceedings, it appears possible that the decision to be taken by the Commission at the culmination of a procedure still in progress concerning the same agreement may conflict with the effects of the decision of the national authorities, it is for the latter to take the appropriate measures" (*Walt Wilhelm*) to ensure that measures implementing Community competition law are fully effective. The Commission takes the view that these measures should generally consist in national authorities staying their proceedings pending the outcome of the proceedings being conducted by the Commission. Where a national authority applies its national law, such a stay of proceedings would be based on the principles of the primacy of Community law (*Walt Wilhelm*)[35] and legal certainty, and where it applies Community law, on the principle of legal certainty alone. For its part, the Commission will endeavour to deal as a matter of priority with cases subject to national proceedings thus stayed. A second possibility may, however, be envisaged, whereby the Commission is consulted before adopting the national decision. The consultations would consist, due regard being had to the judgment in the *Spanish banks* case, in exchanging any documents preparatory to the decisions envisaged, so that Member States' authorities might be able to take account of the Commission's position in their own decision without the latter having to be deferred until such time as the Commission's decision has been taken.

---

[33] See footnote 30; paragraph 32.
[34] Case C–234/89 *Delimitis v. Henninger Bräu* [1991] ECR I–935, paragraph 53.
[35] See footnote 11; paragraphs 8, 9 and 5 respectively.

Procedure

In respect of complaints

54. Since complainants cannot force the Commission to take a decision as to whether the infringement they allege has actually occurred, and since the Commission is entitled to reject a complaint which lacks a sufficient Community interest, national competition authorities should not have any special difficulty in handling complaints submitted initially to them involving matters that fall within the scope of the Community competition rules.

In respect of notifications

55. Although they form a very small percentage of all notifications to the Commission, special consideration needs to be given to notifications to the Commission of restrictive practices undergoing investigation by a national authority made for dilatory purposes. A dilatory notification is one where a firm, threatened with a decision banning a restrictive practice which a national authority is poised to take following an investigation under Article 81(1) or under national law, notifies the disputed agreement to the Commission and asks for it to be exempted under Article 81(3) of the Treaty. Such a notification is made in order to induce the Commission to initiate a proceeding under Articles 2, 3 or 6 of Regulation No 17 and hence, by virtue of Article 9(3) of that Regulation, to remove from Member States' authorities the power to apply the provisions of Article 81(1). The Commission will not consider a notification to be dilatory until after it has contacted the national authority concerned and checked that the latter agrees with its assessment. The Commission calls upon national authorities, moreover, to inform it of their own accord of any notifications they receive which, in their view, are dilatory in nature.

56. A similar situation arises where an agreement is notified to the Commission with a view to preventing the imminent initiation of national proceedings which might result in the prohibition of that agreement.[36]

57. The Commission recognizes, of course, that a firm requesting exemption is entitled to obtain from it a decision on the substance of its request (see point 38). However, if the Commission takes the view that such notification is chiefly aimed at suspending the national proceedings, given its exclusive powers to grant exemptions it considers itself justified in not examining it as a matter of priority.

58. The national authority which is investigating the matter and has therefore initiated proceedings should normally ask the Commission for its provisional opinion on the likelihood of its exempting the agreement now notified to it. Such a request will be superfluous where, "in the light of the relevant criteria developed by the case-law of the Court of Justice and the Court of First Instance and by previous regulations and decisions of the Commission, the national authority has ascertained that the agreement, decision or concerted practice at issue cannot be the subject of an individual exemption".[37]

59. The Commission will deliver its provisional opinion on the likelihood of an exemption being granted, in the light of a preliminary examination of the questions of fact and law involved, as quickly as possible once the complete notification is received. Examination of the notification having revealed that the agreement in question is unlikely to qualify for exemption under Article 81 (3) and that its effects are mainly confined to one Member State, the opinion will state that further investigation of the matter is not a Commission priority.

---

[36] With respect to agreements not subject to notification pursuant to point 1 of Article 4 (2) of Regulation No 17, points 56 and 57 of this Notice also apply *mutatis mutandis* to express requests for exemption.

[37] Points 29 and 30 of the Notice on cooperation between national courts and the Commission.

60. The Commission will transmit this opinion in writing to the national authority investigating the case and to the notifying parties. It will state in its letter that it will be highly unlikely to take a decision on the matter before the national authority to which it was referred has taken its final decision and that the notifying parties retain their immunity from any fines the Commission might impose.

61. In its reply, the national authority, after taking note of the Commission's opinion, should undertake to contact the Commission forthwith if its investigation leads it to a conclusion which differs from that opinion. This will be the case if, following its investigation, the national authority concludes that the agreement in question should not be banned under Article 81(1) of the Treaty or, if that provisions cannot be applied, under the relevant national law. The national authority should also undertake to forward a copy of its final decision on the matter to the Commission. Copies of the correspondence will be sent to the competition authorities of the other Member States for information.

62. The Commission will not itself initiate proceedings in the same case before the proceedings pending before the national authority have been completed; in accordance with Article 9 (3) of Regulation No 17, such action would have the effect of taking the matter out of the hands of the national authority. The Commission will do this only in quite exceptional circumstances—in a situation where, against all expectations, the national authority is liable to find that there has been no infringement of Articles 81 or 82 or of its national competition law, or where the national proceedings are unduly long drawn-out.

63. Before initiating proceedings the Commission will consult the national authority to discover the factual or legal grounds for that authority's proposed favourable decision or the reasons for the delay in the proceedings.

V. Concluding Remarks

64. This Notice is without prejudice to any interpretation by the Court of First Instance and the Court of Justice.

65. In the interests of effective, consistent application of Community law throughout the Union, and legal simplicity and certainty for the benefit of undertakings, the Commission calls upon those Member States which have not already done so to adopt legislation enabling their competition authority to implement Articles 81(1) and 82 of the Treaty effectively.

66. In applying this Notice, the Commission and the competent authorities of the Member States and their officials and other staff will observe the principle of professional secrecy in accordance with Article 20 of Regulation No 17.

67. This Notice does not apply to competition rules in the transport sector, owing to the highly specific way in which cases arising in that sector are handled from a procedural point of view.[38]

---

[38] Council Regulation No 141/62 of 26 November 1962 exempting transport from the application of Council Regulation No 17 (OJ 1962 124/2753; English Special Edition 1959–62, p. 291), as amended by Regulations Nos 165/65/EEC (OJ 1965 210/314) and 1002/67/EEC (OJ 1967 306/1; Council Regulation (EEC) No 1017/68 of 19 July 1968 applying rules of competition to transport by rail, road and inland waterway (OJ 1968 L175/1; English Special Edition 1968 I, p. 302); Council Regulation (EEC) No 4056/86 of 22 December 1986 laying down detailed rules for the application of Articles 81 and 82 of the Treaty to maritime transport (OJ 1986 L378/4); Council Regulation (EEC) No 3975/87 of 14 December 1987 laying down the procedure for the application of the rules on competition to undertakings in the air transport sector (OJ 1987 L374/1); and Commission Regulation (EC) No 870/95 of 20 April 1995 on the application of Article 81(3) of the Treaty to certain categories of agreements, decisions and concerted practices between liner shipping companies (consortia) pursuant to Council Regulation (EEC) No 479/92 (OJ 1995 L89/7).

68. The actual application of this Notice, especially in terms of the measures considered desirable to facilitate its implementation, will be the subject of an annual review carried out jointly by the authorities of the Member States and the Commission.

69. This Notice will be reviewed no later than at the end of the fourth year after its adoption.

APPENDIX 59

THE EC COMPETITION LAW (ARTICLES 88 AND 89) ENFORCEMENT REGULATIONS 1996*

(S.I. 1996 No. 2199)

Made	*23rd August 1996*
Laid before Parliament	*27th August 1996*
Coming into force	*28th August 1996*

The Secretary of State, being the Minister designated[1] for the purposes of section 2(2) of the European Communities Act 1972[2] in relation to measures relating to the procedure for, nature of and enforcement of decisions concerning competition between undertakings, in exercise of the powers conferred by that section hereby makes the following Regulations:

Title, commencement and extent

1. (1) These Regulations may be cited as the EC Competition law (Articles 88 and 89) Enforcement Regulations 1996 and shall come into force on the day after the day on which they are laid before Parliament.

(2) These Regulations extend to Northern Ireland.

Interpretation

2. (1) In these Regulations—
"the 1973 Act" means the Fair Trading Act 1973[3];
"Commission" means the Commission of the European Communities;
"the Director" means the Director General of Fair Trading;
"the MMC" means the Monopolies and Mergers Commission;
"practice" means any form of conduct or any other matter which may constitute an abuse of a dominant position;
"qualifying undertaking" means an undertaking which is—

(a) in the case of an individual, a citizen of the United Kingdom and Colonies, or
(b) a body corporate incorporated under the law of the United Kingdom, or of a part of the United Kingdom, or
(c) a person carrying on business in the United Kingdom, either alone or in partnership with one or more other persons.

---

* Ed. Note: The EC Treaty numbers have not been changed in these Regulations and accordingly do not reflect the Amsterdam re-numbering. See the Table of Equivalences in App. 1, *supra.*
[1] S.I. 1996/1912.
[2] 1972 c.68.
[3] 1973 c.41.

(2) References in these Regulations to Articles are (except where the contrary intention appears) references to Articles of the treaty establishing the European Community.

(3) Except in the case of the word "undertaking" in regulations 14, 20, 22 and 24, expressions used in these Regulations and in Article 85, 86, 88 or 89 shall have the meaning they bear in the treaty establishing the European Community.

(4) Any provision of these Regulations which is expressed to apply to, or in relation to, an agreement is to be read as applying equally to, or in relation to, a decision by an association of undertakings or a concerted practice (but with any necessary modifications).

Preliminary investigation by the Director

3. (1) If it appears to the Secretary of State that the United Kingdom might have a duty under Article 88 to rule on the question—

(a) whether or not there is or has been in existence an agreement prohibited by Article 85 to which a qualifying undertaking is a party, or

(b) whether or not the carrying on of a practice by a qualifying undertaking constitutes an infringement of Article 86,

he may ask the Director to carry out an investigation (a "preliminary investigation") and to advise the Secretary of State of the outcome.

(2) In carrying out a preliminary investigation, the Director shall take into account all representations made to him by persons appearing to him to have a substantial interest in the subject matter of the investigation.

Action by the Secretary of State on an agreement

4. (1) This paragraph applies where, following a preliminary investigation by the Director of an agreement, it appears to the Secretary of State—

(a) that there is or has been in existence an agreement, to which at least one of the parties is or was a qualifying undertaking, and

(b) that the United Kingdom has a duty under Article 88 to rule on the question whether or not the agreement is prohibited by Article 85.

(2) Where paragraph (1) applies, the Secretary of State may, if it appears to him that the agreement does not or did not fall within Article 85(1), decide to certify that, on the basis of the facts in his possession, there are no grounds for action on his part in respect of the agreement.

(3) Where paragraph (1) applies, the Secretary of State may, if it appears to him that the agreement falls within Article 85(1) or did so fall, but that the conditions for application of Article 85(3) are met in respect of the agreement, declare the provisions of Article 85(1) inapplicable to the agreement.

(4) Where paragraph (1) applies and the Secretary of State has not made a decision under paragraph (2) or a declaration under paragraph (3), he may refer the agreement to the MMC for investigation and report.

(5) Where, following a preliminary investigation by the Director, it appears to the Secretary of State that there may be, or may have been, in existence an agreement to which at least one of the parties is or was a qualifying undertaking, and that, if so, the United Kingdom would have a duty to rule on the agreement under Article 88, the Secretary of State may refer the suspected agreement to the MMC for investigation and report.

Action by the Secretary of State on a practice

5. (1) This paragraph applies where, following a preliminary investigation by the Director of a practice, it appears to the Secretary of State that—

(a) a practice is being, or has been, carried on by a qualifying undertaking, and
(b) the United Kingdom has a duty under Article 88 to rule on the question whether or not the practice infringes Article 86.

(2) Where paragraph (1) applies, the Secretary of State may, if it appears to him that the practice does not infringe Article 86, decide to certify that, on the basis of the facts in his possession, there are no grounds for action on his part in respect of the practice.

(3) Where paragraph (1) applies and it appears to the Secretary of State that the practice may infringe Article 86, the Secretary of State may refer the practice to the MMC for investigation and report.

(4) Where, following a preliminary investigation by the Director, it appears to the Secretary of State that a practice may be being or may have been carried on by a qualifying undertaking, and that, if so, the United Kingdom would have a duty to rule on the practice under Article 88, the Secretary of State may refer the suspected practice to the MMC for investigation and report.

Publication of decisions by Secretary of State

6. (1) Subject to paragraphs (3) and (4) below, the Secretary of State shall publish any decision to certify taken by him under regulation 4(2) or 5(2) and any declaration made by him under regulation 4(3) together with such an account of his reasons for making the decision or declaration as in his opinion is expedient for facilitating an understanding of his decision or of his declaration.

(2) Any publication of a decision or declaration under paragraph (1) shall be in such manner as appears to the Secretary of State to be appropriate.

(3) If it appears to the Secretary of State that it would be against the public interest to publish a particular matter which he would otherwise include in an account of his reasons required to be published under paragraph (1), the Secretary of State shall exclude that matter from the account before publishing it.

(4) Without prejudice to paragraph (3), if the Secretary of State considers that it would not be in the public interest to disclose any matter which he would otherwise include in an account of his reasons required to be published under paragraph (1),

(a) relating to the private affairs of an individual whose interest would, in the opinion of the Secretary of State, be seriously and prejudicially affected by the publication of that matter, or
(b) relating specifically to the affairs of a particular person whose interests would, in the opinion of the Secretary of State, be seriously and prejudicially affected by the publication of that matter,

the Secretary of State shall exclude that matter from the account before publishing it.

Variation of reference

7. The Secretary of State may at any time vary a reference made by him under these Regulations.

Publication of references

8. On making a reference under these Regulations or a variation of such a reference the Secretary of State shall arrange for the reference or variation to be published in such manner as he thinks most suitable for the purpose of bringing it to the attention of persons who, in his opinion, would be affected by it.

Time limit for report on a reference

9. (1) Every reference under regulation 4, 5 or 20 shall specify a period (not being longer than six months beginning with the date of the reference) within which a report on the reference is to be made.

(2) The Secretary of State may give directions to the MMC allowing such further period for the purpose of reporting on a reference under these Regulations as may be specified in the directions, or, if the period has already been extended once or more than once by directions under this paragraph, allowing to the MMC such further extended period for that purpose as may be so specified.

Functions of the MMC on a reference of an agreement

10. (1) On a reference under regulation 4 the MMC shall investigate and report on the questions—

(a) whether such an agreement which is the subject of the reference exists or has existed;
(b) whether any qualifying undertaking is or was a party to it;
(c) whether the agreement falls within Article 85(1);
(d) whether the agreement affects or has affected competition within the United Kingdom, and, if so, what are those effects.

(2) Where, during an investigation on a reference under regulation 4, it appears to the MMC—

(a) that there may have existed or be in existence an agreement (other than that which is the subject of the reference) to which some or all of the parties to the agreement which is the subject of the reference are party;
(b) that the parties to that other agreement include a qualifying undertaking; and
(c) that the United Kingdom may have a duty to rule on that agreement under Article 88;

the MMC may investigate and report on that agreement as if it had been the subject of the reference.

(3) Where a report of the MMC on a reference under regulation 4 includes the conclusions that—

(a) the agreement which is the subject of the reference (or is treated as the subject by virtue of the preceding paragraph) exists or has existed;
(b) a qualifying undertaking is or was a party to it; and
(c) the agreement falls within Article 85(1);

the MMC shall also investigate and report on the question whether in their opinion the conditions for application of Article 85(3) are met.

Functions of the MMC on reference of a practice

11. (1) On a reference under regulation 5 the MMC shall investigate and report on the questions—

(a) whether the practice which is the subject of the reference is being carried on or has been carried on;

574

(b) whether that practice infringes or has infringed Article 86;
(c) whether any qualifying undertaking is carrying on or has carried on the practice;
(d) whether the infringement of Article 86 has had an effect on competition in the United Kingdom and, if so, what are those effects.

(2) Where, during an investigation on a reference under regulation 5, it appears to the MMC that a practice similar in form and effect to the practice which is the subject of the reference may be being carried on or may have been carried on by a qualifying undertaking and that the United Kingdom may have a duty to rule on that practice under Article 88, the MMC may investigate and report on that practice as if it had been the subject of the reference.

Report of the MMC

12. Any report of the MMC shall include definite conclusions on the questions on which the MMC is required to report under regulation 10, 11 or 20 together with such an account of their reasons for those conclusions as in their opinion is expedient for facilitating a proper understanding of their conclusions.

Recommendations of MMC

13. Where a report of the MMC—

(a) on a reference under regulation 4 includes the conclusions specified in regulation 10(3); or
(b) on a reference under regulation 5 includes the conclusions that a qualifying undertaking has infringed Article 86;

the MMC shall, as part of their investigations, consider what action (if any) should be taken in respect of those conclusions by the Secretary of State or any Minister or public authority and may, if they think fit, include in their report recommendations as to such action.

Undertakings as an alternative to a reference

14. (1) Where the Secretary of State has power to make a reference to the MMC under regulation 4, regulation 5 or regulation 20 he may, instead of making a reference, accept from such of the parties concerned as he considers appropriate undertakings to take such specified action as the Secretary of State considers appropriate—

(a) to terminate or prevent the recurrence of the infringement of Article 85(1) or Article 86 which it appears to the Secretary of State has occurred or may have occurred, or
(b) to enable him to make a declaration under paragraph (2).

(2) Where the Secretary of State has accepted undertakings under this regulation in respect of an agreement, and it appears to him that, if the undertakings are fulfilled, the conditions for application of Article 85(3) will be met in respect of the agreement, he may declare the provisions of Article 85(1) inapplicable to the agreement.

(3) The Secretary of State shall arrange to publish in such manner as appears to him to be appropriate—

(a) any undertakings accepted by him under paragraph (1);
(b) any declaration made by him under paragraph (2);

(c) such an account of his reasons for his decision to accept undertakings, and, if it be the case, for making a declaration as in his opinion is expedient for facilitating an understanding of his decision or his declaration;

(d) any variation or release of such an undertaking.

(4) Regulation 6(3) and (4) shall apply to the account referred to in paragraph (3)(c) as they apply to an account of the Secretary of State's reasons published under regulation 6(1).

(5) Where an undertaking has been accepted under paragraph (1), it shall be the duty of the Director—

(a) to keep under review the carrying out of that undertaking, and from time to time to consider whether, by reason of any change of circumstances, the undertaking is no longer appropriate and either—
   (i) one or more of the parties to it can be released from it, or
   (ii) it needs to be varied or to be superseded by a new undertaking, and

(b) if it appears to him that the undertaking has not been or is not being fulfilled, that any person can be so released or that the undertaking needs to be varied or superseded, to give such advice to the Secretary of State as he may think proper in the circumstances.

(6) Where it appears to the Secretary of State that an undertaking accepted by him under paragraph (1) or which has superseded such an undertaking has not been, is not being, or will not be fulfilled, the Secretary of State may by order made by statutory instrument exercise such one or more of the powers specified in regulation 21 as he may consider it requisite to exercise for the purpose of terminating or preventing the recurrence of the infringement of Article 85 or Article 86 which it appears to the Secretary of State has occurred; and those powers may be so exercised to such extent and in such manner as the Secretary of State considers requisite for that purpose.

(7) In determining whether, or to what extent or in what manner, to exercise any of those powers, the Secretary of State shall take into account any advice given by the Director under paragraph (5).

(8) The provisions contained in an order under paragraph (6) may be different from those contained in the undertaking.

(9) On the making of an order under paragraph (6), the undertaking accepted under paragraph (1) or which has superseded such an undertaking shall be released by virtue of this regulation.

Duty of Director to assist MMC

15. It shall be the duty of the Director, for the purpose of assisting the MMC in carrying out an investigation on a reference made to them under these Regulations, to give to the MMC—

(a) any information which is in his possession and which relates to matters falling within the scope of the investigation and which is either requested by the MMC for that purpose or is information which in his opinion it would be appropriate for that purpose to give to the MMC without any such request, and

(b) any other assistance which the MMC may require and which it is within his power to give in relation to such matters;

and the MMC shall take account of any information given to them for that purpose under this regulation.

Procedures of MMC and General Provisions as to Reports

16. The following provisions of the 1973 Act, namely sections 81 (procedures in carrying out investigations), 82 (general provisions as to reports), 83[4] (laying before Parliament and publication of reports), 85[5] (attendance of witnesses and production of documents), and Part II of Schedule 3[6] (performance of functions of the MMC) shall apply in relation to references under these Regulations and reports of the MMC on such references as if—

(a) a reference under these Regulations was a reference under the 1973 Act;
(b) functions of the MMC under these Regulations were functions in relation to an investigation under the 1973 Act;
(c) a report of the MMC under these Regulations were a report under the 1973 Act;
(d) in section 83 references to the Minister or Ministers were references to the Secretary of State;
(e) in section 85(6) the references to a fine on summary conviction were to a fine not exceeding the statutory maximum;
(f) in paragraph 11 of Schedule 3 the reference to a monopoly reference were to a reference under these Regulations and the reference to section 52 were a reference to regulation 7;
(g) paragraph 16(2) of Schedule 3 were omitted.

Laying aside of references

17. (1) If, at any time during an investigation by the MMC on a reference under these Regulations, it appears to the Secretary of State that the United Kingdom is not under a duty under Article 88 to rule on the agreement or practice which is the subject of the reference, the Secretary of State may direct the MMC to lay the reference aside.

(2) The MMC shall comply with any direction under paragraph (1) but shall furnish to the Secretary of State such information as he may require as to the results until then of their investigations.

Director to receive copies of reports

18. The MMC shall send a copy of every report on a reference under these Regulations to the Director and the Secretary of State shall take account of any advice given to him by the Director with respect to such a report.

Exemptions under Article 85(3)

19. (1) Where—

(a) the report of the MMC on a reference under regulation 4 includes the conclusions specified in regulation 10(3); and

---

[4] Section 83(1) was amended and subsection (1A) inserted by the Competition Act 1980 (c.21), section 22; subsection (3A) was inserted by the Companies Act 1989 (c.40), Schedule 20, paragraph 12.
[5] Section 85(6) was amended by the Magistrates' Courts Act 1980 (c.43), section 32(2); section 85(5) and words in section 85(6) were repealed by the Companies Act 1989, Schedule 24; and section 85(7) was substituted by and subsection (7A) inserted by the Companies Act 1989, Schedule 20, paragraph 13.
[6] Paragraph 10 of Schedule 3 was amended by S.I. 1989/122, article 2.

(b) it appears to the Secretary of State that the United Kingdom is under a duty under Article 88 to rule on the question whether or not the agreement concerned is prohibited by Article 85;

the Secretary of State may, if it appears to him that the conditions for application of Article 85(3) are met in respect of the agreement, declare the provisions of Article 85(1) inapplicable to the agreement.

(2) Before deciding whether to make such a declaration the Secretary of State shall have regard to the recommendations of the MMC and to their opinion as to whether the conditions for application of Article 85(3) are met.

(3) The Secretary of State shall publish any declaration under paragraph (1) in such manner as appears to him to be appropriate.

General provisions about exemptions

20. (1) This regulation applies to any declaration made by the Secretary of State—

(a) under regulation 4(3);
(b) under regulation 14(2);
(c) under regulation 19(1);

and to any renewal of such a declaration under paragraph (3) below.

(2) A declaration to which this regulation applies—

(a) shall have effect from such date as may be stated in the declaration being a date not earlier than the date on which the agreement or these Regulations came into force whichever is the later, and
(b) shall have effect for the period stipulated in the declaration.

(3) The Secretary of State may renew a declaration to which this regulation applies for a further period if it appears to him that the conditions for application of Article 85(3) continue to be met in respect of the agreement at the expiry of the original declaration.

(4) A declaration to which this regulation applies may be made unconditionally or subject to such conditions as the Secretary of State thinks fit.

(5) It shall be the duty of the Director to keep under review the operation of any agreement in respect of which the Secretary of State has made a declaration to which this regulation applies and to advise the Secretary of State if at any time, he considers that the conditions for the application of Article 85(3) cease to be satisfied in respect of the agreement.

(6) If it appears to the Secretary of State in respect of a declaration to which this regulation applies:—

(a) that there has been a material change of circumstances since the declaration was made; or
(b) that any information given in respect of the agreement concerned to the Director, to the MMC or to the Secretary of State is or was in any material respect false or misleading; or
(c) that any person who gave an undertaking under regulation 14 or 22 to the Secretary of State as a result of which the Secretary of State was able to make the declaration has not complied with it;

the Secretary of State may revoke or vary the declaration as he thinks fit.

(7) Before deciding whether to renew, revoke or vary a declaration to which this regulation applies, the Secretary of State may refer the matter to the MMC for investigation and report.

(8) On a reference under paragraph (7) above, the MMC shall investigate and report on the question whether in their opinion the conditions for application of Article 85(3) are met in respect of the agreement which is the subject of the reference.

(9) The MMC shall, as part of their investigations on a reference under paragraph (7) above, consider what action (if any) should be taken in respect of their conclusions by the Secretary of State or any Minister or public authority and may, if they think fit, include in their report recommendations as to such action.

Powers of Secretary of State to make Orders

21. (1) Where—

(a) paragraph (2) applies, or
(b) pursuant to Article 89(2), the Commission has taken a reasoned decision relating to an infringement of Article 85 and has authorised the United Kingdom to take measures needed to remedy the situation;

the Secretary of State may by order made by statutory instrument exercise such one or more of the powers specified in Parts I and II of Schedule 8[7] to the 1973 Act as he considers it requisite to exercise for the purpose of terminating or preventing the recurrence of the infringement of Article 85 concerned or for the purpose of enabling him to make a declaration under regulation 19 or a renewal of such a declaration; and those powers may be so exercised to such extent and in such manner as the Secretary of State considers requisite for that purpose.

(2) This paragraph applies where—

(a) it appears to the Secretary of State that the United Kingdom has a duty under Article 88 to rule on whether or not an agreement which is the subject of a report of the MMC on a reference under regulation 4 is prohibited under Article 85(1), and
(b) the report includes the conclusions specified in regulation 10(3) and the Secretary of State has not declared Article 85(1) inapplicable to the agreement.

(3) Where—

(a) the Secretary of State has received a report of the MMC on a reference under regulation 5(3) which concludes that there is or has been an infringement of Article 86 by one or more undertakings at least one of which is a qualifying undertaking and it appears to the Secretary of State that the United Kingdom has a duty under Article 88 to rule on whether or not that infringement has occurred; or
(b) pursuant to Article 89(2), the Commission has taken a reasoned decision under Article 89(2) relating to an infringement of Article 86 and has authorised the United Kingdom to take measures needed to remedy the situation;

the Secretary of State may by order made by statutory instrument exercise any one or more of the powers specified in paragraph (4) for the purpose of terminating or preventing the recurrence of the infringement of Article 86 concerned.

(4) The powers which may be exercised under paragraph (3) are—

(a) the power to prohibit a person named in the order from carrying on the practice constituting the infringement of Article 86 specified in the report of the MMC or decision of the Commission or from carrying on any other practice which is similar in form and effect to that practice; and

---

[7] Paragraphs 9A, 12A–12C of Part I of Schedule 8 were inserted by the Companies Act, (c.40), Schedule 20, paragraph 19.

(b)   such one or more of the powers specified in Part I or II of Schedule 8 to the 1973 Act as the Secretary of State considers it requisite to exercise for the purpose mentioned in paragraph (3);

and those powers may be so exercised to such extent and in such manner as the Secretary of State considers requisite for the purpose mentioned in paragraph (3).

(5) In determining whether, or to what extent or in what manner, to exercise any of the powers under this regulation the Secretary of State shall have regard to any recommendations included in the report of the MMC.

(6) For the purpose of this regulation and of regulation 14(6), Schedule 8 to the 1973 Act shall be construed as if—

(a)   an order under section 56 were an order under these Regulations;
(b)   paragraph 3 were omitted,
(c)   references to the appropriate Minister were references to the Secretary of State.

(7) It shall be the duty of the Director to keep under review the action (if any) taken in compliance with an order made under regulation 14(6) or under this regulation, and from time to time to consider whether, by reason of any change of circumstances, the order should be varied or revoked or should be superseded by a new order, and—

(a)   if it appears to him that the order has in any respect not been complied with, to consider whether any action (by way of proceedings in accordance with section 93 of the 1973 Act as applied by regulation 24 or otherwise) should be taken for the purpose of securing compliance with the order, and (where in his opinion it is appropriate to do so) to take such action himself or give advice to the Secretary of State or other person by whom such action might be taken; or
(b)   if it appears to him that the order needs to be varied or revoked, or to be superseded by a new order, to give such advice to the Secretary of State as he may think proper in the circumstances.

Undertakings following a report

22. (1) In any circumstances where the Secretary of State has power to make an order under regulation 21 it shall be the duty of the Director to comply with any request of the Secretary of State to consult with any persons mentioned in the request ("the relevant parties") with a view to obtaining from them undertakings to take action indicated in the request made to the Director as being action requisite in the opinion of the Secretary of State, for the purpose of terminating or preventing the recurrence of the infringement of Article 85 or 86 concerned, or of enabling the Secretary of State to make a declaration under regulation 19.

(2) Subsections (2) to (5) of section 88 of the 1973 Act shall apply in relation to consultation under paragraph (1), undertakings given in pursuance of them and orders made under regulation 21, as if—

(a)   references to the appropriate Minister were references to the Secretary of State;
(b)   references to powers under section 56 were to powers under regulation 21;
(c)   references to the "relevant parties" were construed in accordance with paragraph (1) above.

Procedure relating to orders made under these Regulations

23. (1) No order made under these Regulations which exercises any of the powers specified in Part II of Schedule 8 to the 1973 Act and no order varying or revoking any such order shall be made unless a draft of the order has been laid before Parliament and approved by a resolution of each House of Parliament; and the provisions of Schedule 9[8] to the 1973 Act shall apply with respect to the procedure to be followed before laying before Parliament a draft of any such order as they apply to an order such as is mentioned in section 9(1) of the 1973 Act.

(2) Any statutory instrument whereby any order is made under any provision of these Regulations, other than an instrument whereby an order is made to which the preceding paragraph applies, shall be subject to annulment in pursuance of a resolution of either House of Parliament.

(3) Section 91(2) of the 1973 Act shall apply to an order made under these Regulations (other than an order to which paragraph (1) applies) as it applies to an order made under section 56 of the 1973 Act other than an order such as is mentioned in section 91(1) of the 1973 Act.

Provisions as to orders and enforcement

24. Sections 90 (general provisions to orders), 92[9] (investigation of company), 93 (enforcement of orders), and 93A[10] (enforcement of undertakings) of the 1973 Act shall apply in relation to orders made under these Regulations as if—

(a) references to orders made under section 56 of the 1973 Act were references to orders made under these Regulations;
(b) the words "either for all persons or" in subsection (2) of section 90 were omitted;
(c) subsections (5) and (6) of section 90 were omitted;
(d) references to the Minister were references to the Secretary of State;
(e) references to an order to which section 90 of the 1973 Act applies were references to an order made under these Regulations; and
(f) references to undertakings accepted by the Secretary of State under section 75G, of the 1973 Act were to undertakings accepted by the Secretary of State under regulation 14 or regulation 22.

False or misleading information

25. Section 93B (false or misleading information) of the 1973 Act[11] shall apply in relation to information furnished by any person to the Secretary of State, the Director or the MMC in connection with any of their functions under these Regulations as it applies to information furnished to the Secretary of State in connection with any of his functions under Parts IV, V or VI of the 1973 Act.

26. Section 129 of the 1973 Act[12] (time limit for prosecutions) shall apply in relation to offences under these Regulations as it applies to offences under the 1973 Act.

27. Section 132 of the 1973 Act[13] (offences by bodies corporate) shall apply in relation to offences under these Regulations as if—

---

[8] Paragraph 4 of Schedule 9 was amended by the Companies Act 1989 (c.40) Schedule 20, paragraph 20 and Schedule 24.

[9] Subsections (2) and (3) of section 92 were substituted by the Companies Consolidation (Consequential Provisions) Act 1995 (c.9) Schedule 2.

[10] Section 93A was inserted by the Companies Act 1989, section 148.

[11] Section 93B was inserted by the Companies Act 1989, section 151.

[12] Section 129(2) and (4) were amended by the Magistrates' Courts Act 1980 (c.43) Schedule 7, paragraph 118. Subsection (4) has also been amended by S.I. 1981/1675 (N.I. 26), Schedule 6, Pt I, and by S.I. 1980/704 (N.I.6), Schedule 1, Pt II. Section 129(3) was amended by the Criminal Procedure (Scotland) Act 1975 (c.21), section 460(7) and 461, Schedule 10, and by the Criminal Procedure (Consequential Provisions) (Scotland) Act 1995 (c.40), Schedule 4, paragraph 9.

[13] Section 132 was amended by the Companies Act 1989 (c.40) Schedule 20, paragraph 17.

(a) the reference to section 85(6) were a reference to that subsection as it applied by regulation 16, and

(b) the reference to section 93(B) were a reference to that section as it is applied by regulation 25.

Restrictions on disclosure of information

28. (1) Subject to paragraphs (2) to (4), no information with respect to any particular business which has been obtained under or by virtue of the provisions of these Regulations shall, so long as that business continues to be carried on, be disclosed without the consent of the person for the time being carrying on that business.

(2) Paragraph (1) does not apply to any disclosure of information which is made—

(a) for the purpose of facilitating the performance of any functions of the Director, the Civil Aviation Authority, the MMC, or the Secretary of State under these Regulations, or the Fair Trading Act 1973,[14] or the Restrictive Trade Practices Act 1976,[15] or the Resale Prices Act 1976,[16] or the Competition Act 1980,[17] or the Civil Aviation Act 1982,[18] or the Airports Act 1986[19]; or the Licensing of Air Carriers Regulations 1992,[20] or Part IV of the Airports (Northern Ireland) Order 1994,[21] or

(b) for facilitating the performance by the Commission of its functions under Article 89, or

(c) in pursuance of a Community obligation within the meaning of the European Communities Act 1972.

(3) Paragraph (1) does not apply to any disclosure of information which is made for the purpose of any proceedings before the Restrictive Practices Court or of any other legal proceedings, whether civil or criminal under these Regulations, the 1973 Act or the Restrictive Trade Practices Act 1976.

(4) Nothing in paragraph (1) shall be construed—

(a) as limiting the matters which may be included in, or made public as part of, a report of the MMC; or

(b) as applying to any information which has been made public as part of such a report or of a decision or declaration made by the Secretary of State under these Regulations or as part of an account published with such a decision or declaration.

(5) Any person who discloses any information in contravention of this regulation shall be guilty of an offence and shall be liable—

(a) on summary conviction, to a fine not exceeding the statutory maximum;

(b) on conviction on indictment, to imprisonment for a term not exceeding two years or to a fine or to both.

Amendments to other enactments

29. (1) In paragraph (a) of section 133(2) of the 1973 Act (exceptions from the general restriction on the disclosure of information obtained under or by virtue of certain provisions of that Act), after "or the Coal Industry Act 1994" there shall be inserted the words "or the EC Competition Law (Articles 88 and 89) Enforcement Regulations 1996".

[14] 1973 c.41.
[15] 1976 c.34.
[16] 1976 c.53.
[17] 1980 c.21.
[18] 1982 c.16.
[19] 1986 c.31.
[20] S.I. 1992/2992.
[21] S.I. 1994/426 (N.I.1).

(2) In paragraph (a) of section 41(1) of the Restrictive Trade Practices Act 1976 (exceptions from the general restriction on the disclosure of information obtained under or by virtue of that Act), after "or the Coal Industry Act 1994" there shall be inserted the words "or the EC Competition Law (Articles 88 and 89) Enforcement Regulations 1996".

(3) In section 19(3) of the Competition Act 1980, (exceptions from the general restriction on the disclosure of information obtained under or by virtue of that Act) there shall be inserted at the end the following sub-paragraph—

"(q) the EC Competition Law (Articles 88 and 89) Enforcement Regulations 1996;".

(4) In section 74(3) of the Airports Act 1986[22] (exceptions from the general restriction on the disclosure of information obtained under or by virtue of that Act) there shall be inserted at the end the following sub-paragraph—

"(o) the EC Competition Law (Articles 88 and 89) Enforcement Regulations 1996.".

(5) In article 49(3) of the Airports (Northern Ireland) Order 1994[23] (exceptions from the general restriction on the disclosure of information obtained under or by virtue of that Order) there shall be inserted at the end the following sub-paragraph—

"(r) the EC Competition Law (Articles 88 and 89) Enforcement Regulations 1996.".

Past agreements and infringements

30. Nothing in these Regulations shall enable or require the Director or the MMC to investigate or report on an agreement which was determined, or on a practice which has ceased, before these regulations came into force.

John M. Taylor
Parliamentary Under Secretary
23 August 1996   for Corporate and Consumer Affairs
Department of Trade and Industry

EXPLANATORY NOTE

(This note is not part of the Regulations)

These Regulations make provision for the investigation of, and the making and enforcement of decisions in respect of, agreements or practices on which it appears to the Secretary of State the United Kingdom has a duty to rule under Article 88 of the EC Treaty.

Article 88 applies to cases where the Council of Ministers of the European Community has not made regulations under Article 87 giving effect to Articles 85 and 86 of the EC Treaty. Subject to the possibility of exemption under Article 85(3), Article 85 prohibits agreements between undertakings which have as their object or effect the prevention, restriction or distortion of competition within the common market and which may affect trade between Member States. Article 86 prohibits the abuse by one or more undertakings of a dominant position in the common market or in a substantial part of it in so far as it may affect trade between Member States.

---

[22] 1986 c.31.
[23] S.I. 1994/426(N.I.1).

No implementing regulation has been made under Article 87 in respect of air transport services between Member States of the European Community and countries outside the European Community or in respect of international maritime tramp vessel services.

Regulation 3 empowers the Secretary of State to request the Director General of Fair Trading to carry out a preliminary investigation where it appears to the Secretary of State that the United Kingdom might have a duty to rule on whether an agreement or practice is prohibited by Article 85 or 86.

Regulations 4 and 5 provide that the Secretary of State may, following such a preliminary investigation, decide to take no further action in respect of the agreement or practice, or in the case of an agreement, declare that the exemption provided for in Article 85(3) applies. Alternatively, the Secretary of State may decide to refer the matter to the Monopolies and Mergers Commission for investigation and report. Regulation 14 provides that the Secretary of State may accept enforceable undertakings from the persons concerned instead of making a reference to the MMC.

The Regulations make provisions for the publication of decisions to take no further action or exemption declarations made by the Secretary of State following a preliminary investigation (regulation 6) and for the procedures to be followed with regard to the MMC's investigation and report (regulations 7 to 13, and 15 to 18).

Following a report by the MMC which concludes that an agreement exists which falls within Article 85(1), the Secretary of State may declare an exemption or make an order for the purpose of terminating the infringement (regulations 19 and 21(1) and (2)). Where the MMC concludes that an infringement of Article 86 has occurred, the Secretary of State may make an order for the purpose of terminating the infringement (regulation 21(3) and (4)).

As an alternative to making an order, the Secretary of State may accept enforceable undertakings from the persons concerned (regulation 22).

The regulations also enable the Secretary of State to make orders where the Commission of the European Communities authorises the United Kingdom to take measures under Article 89 of the E.C. Treaty (regulations 21(1) and 21(3)).

The regulations contain provisions for the enforcement of orders (regulation 24) and provide for an offence of providing false or misleading information (regulation 25), and for restricting the disclosure of information with respect to a particular business obtained under the Regulations except for permitted purposes (regulation 28).

Regulation 30 provides that the regulations may not be used to investigate agreements or practices which have ended before the regulations come into force.

The Regulations come into force on the day after they are laid before Parliament.

DIRECTIVE 80/723[1]

On the Transparency of Financial Relations Between Member States and Public Undertakings [as well as on Financial Transparency within Certain Undertakings][2]

THE COMMISSION OF THE EUROPEAN COMMUNITIES

Having regard to the Treaty establishing the European Economic Community, and in particular Article 86(3) thereof;

(1) Whereas public undertakings play a substantial role in the national economy of the Member States;

(2) Whereas the Treaty in no way prejudices the rules governing the system of property ownership in Member States and equal treatment of private and public undertakings must therefore be ensured;

(3) Whereas the Treaty requires the Commission to ensure that Member States do not grant undertakings, public or private, aids incompatible with the common market;

(4) Whereas, however, the complexity of the financial relations between national public authorities and public undertakings tends to hinder the performance of this duty;

(5) Whereas a fair and effective application of the aid rules in the Treaty to both public and private undertakings will be possible only if these financial relations are made transparent;

(6) Whereas such transparency applied to public undertakings should enable a clear distinction to be made between the role of the State as public authority and its role as proprietor;

(7) Whereas Article 86(1) confers certain obligations and on the Member States in respect of public undertakings; whereas Article 86(3) requires the Commission to ensure that these obligations are respected, and provides it with the requisite means to this end; whereas this entails defining the conditions for achieving transparency;

(8) Whereas it should be made clear what is to be understood by the terms "public authorities" and "public undertakings";

(9) Whereas public authorities may exercise a dominant influence on the behaviour of public undertakings not only where they are the proprietor or have a majority participation but also by virtue of powers they hold in management or supervisory bodies as a result either of the rules governing the undertaking or of the manner in which the shareholdings are distributed;

(10) Whereas the provision of public funds to public undertakings may take place either directly or indirectly; whereas transparency must be achieved irrespective of the manner in which such provision of public funds is made; whereas it may also be necessary to ensure that adequate information is made available as regards the reasons for such provision of public funds and their actual use;

---

[1] OJ 1980 L195/35, as amended by Dir. 93/84, OJ 1993 L254/16, and Dir. 2000/52, OJ 2000 L 193/75.

[2] Amended by Dir. 2000/52.

(11) Whereas Member States may through their public undertakings seek ends other than commercial ones; whereas in some cases public undertakings are compensated by the State for financial burdens assumed by them as a result;

(12) Whereas transparency should also be ensured in the case of such compensation;

(13) Whereas certain undertakings should be excluded from the application of this Directive by virtue either of the nature of their activities or of the size of their turnover; whereas this applies to certain activities which stand outside the sphere of competition or which are already covered by specific Community measures which ensure adequate transparency, to public undertakings belonging to sectors of activity for which distinct provision should be made, and to those whose business is not conducted on such a scale as to justify the administration burden of ensuring transparency;

(14) Whereas it is predominantly in the manufacturing sector that the Commission has established that a considerable amount of aid has been granted to undertakings but not notified pursuant to Article 88(3) of the Treaty; whereas the first,[3] second,[4] and third[5] State aid surveys confirm that large amounts of State aid continue to be granted illegally;

(15) Whereas a reporting system based on *ex post facto* checks of the financial flows between public authorities and public undertakings will enable the Commission to fulfil its obligations; whereas that system of control must cover specific financial information; whereas such information is not always publicly available and, as it is found in the public arena, is insufficiently detailed to allow a proper evaluation of the financial flows between the State and public undertakings;

(16) Whereas all of the information requested can be regarded as being proportional to the objective pursued, taking account of the fact that such information is already subject to the disclosure obligations under the Fourth Council Directive 78/660/EEC[6] concerning the annual accounts of companies, as last amended by Directive 90/605/EEC.[7]

(17) Whereas, in order to limit the administrative burden on Member States, the reporting system should make use of both publicly available data and information available to majority shareholders; whereas the presentation of consolidated reports is to be permitted; whereas incompatible aid to major undertakings operating in the manufacturing sector will have the greatest distortive effect on competition in the common market; whereas, therefore, such a reporting system may at present be limited to undertakings with a yearly turnover of more that ECU 250 million;

(18) Whereas, although the Commission, when notifying the Directive in 1980, took the view that movements of funds within a public undertakings or group of public undertakings were not subject to the requirements of Directive 80/723/EEC, the inclusion of such information is called for by the new requirements of economic life, which is often influenced by State intervention via public undertakings; whereas, as has been underlined in the case-law of the Court of Justice since 1980,[8] infringements of the provisions of Article 88(3) by Member States have increased appreciably, thereby making the Commission's monitoring tasks in the field of competition more and more difficult; whereas the Commission's powers of vigilance must therefore be increased,

Note

Recitals [14]–[18] are inserted from Dir. 93/84

(19) Whereas various sectors of the economy which were characterised in the past by the existence of national, regional or local monopolies have been or are being opened

---

[3] ISBN 92–825–9535.
[4] ISBN 9–826–0386.
[5] ISBN 92–826–4637.
[6] OJ 1978 L222/11.
[7] OJ 1990 L317/60.
[8] See, for example, the Judgments in Case 290/83 *Commission v. France* [1985] ECR 439 (agriculture credit fund), Joined Cases 67, 68 and 70/85 *Van der Kooy v. Commission* [1988] ECR p. 219, Case 303/88 *Italy v. Commission* [1991] ECR I–1433 (*ENI-Lanerossi*), and Case C–305/89 *Italy v. Commission* [1991] ECR I–1603 (*IRI, Finmeccanica and Alfa Romeo*).

partly or fully to competition in application of the Treaty or by rules adopted by the Member States and the Community. This process has highlighted the importance of ensuring that the rules on competition contained in the Treaty are fairly and effectively applied in these sectors, in particular that there is no abuse of a dominant position within the meaning of Article 82 of the Treaty, and no State aid within the meaning of Article 87 of the Treaty unless it is compatible with the common market, without prejudice to the possible application of Article 86(2) of the Treaty.

(20) Whereas in such sectors Member States often grant special or exclusive rights to particular undertakings, or make payments or give some other kind of compensation to particular undertakings entrusted with the operation of services of general economic interest. These undertakings are often also in competition with other undertakings.

(21) Whereas according to Article 86(2) and (3) of the Treaty it is, in principle, for the Member States to entrust certain undertakings with the operation of services of general economic interest that they define, the Commission being responsible for ensuring the proper application of the provisions of that Article.

(22) Whereas Article 86(1) of the Treaty requires that, in the case of public undertakings and undertakings to which Member States grant special or exclusive rights, Member States must neither enact nor maintain in force any measure contrary to the rules contained in the Treaty. Article 86(2) of the Treaty applies to undertakings entrusted with the operation of services of general economic interest. Article 86(3) of the Treaty requires the Commission to ensure the application of the provisions of Article 86 and to address appropriate directives or decisions to Member States. The interpretative provisions annexed to the Treaty by the Protocol on the system of public broadcasting in the Member States state that the provisions of the Treaty establishing the European Community shall be without prejudice to the competence of the Member States to provide for the funding of public service broadcasting in so far as such funding is granted to broadcasting organisations for the fulfilment of the public service remit conferred, defined and organised by each Member State, and in so far as such funding does not affect trading conditions and competition in the Community to an extent which would be contrary to the common interest, while the realisation of the remit of that public service shall be taken into account. In order to ensure the application of the provisions of Article 86 of the Treaty the Commission must have the necessary information. This entails defining the conditions for achieving transparency.

(23) Whereas complex situations linked to the diverse forms of public and private undertakings granted special or exclusive rights or entrusted with the operation of services of general economic interest as well as the range of activities that might be carried on by a single undertaking and the different degrees of market liberalisation in the various Member States could complicate application of the competition rules, and particularly Article 86 of the Treaty. It is therefore necessary for Member States and the Commission to have detailed data about the internal financial and organisational structure of such undertakings, in particular separate and reliable accounts relating to different activities carried on by the same undertaking. Such information is not always available or is not always sufficiently detailed or reliable.

(24) Whereas such accounts should show the distinction between different activities, the costs and revenues associated with each activity and the methods of cost and revenue assignment and allocation. Such separate accounts should be available in relation to, on the one hand, products or services in respect of which the Member State has granted a special or exclusive right or entrusted the undertaking with the operation of a service of general economic interest, as well as, on the other hand, for each other product or service in respect of which the undertaking is active. The obligation of separation of accounts should not apply to undertakings whose activities are limited to the provision of services of general economic interest and which do not operate activities outside the scope of these services of general economic interest. It does not seem necessary to require separation of accounts within the area of services of general economic interest or within the area of the special or exclusive rights, as far as this is not necessary for the cost and revenue

allocation between these services and products and those outside of the services of general economic interest or the special or exclusive rights.

(25) Whereas requiring Member States to ensure that the relevant undertakings maintain such separate accounts is the most efficient means by which fair and effective application of the rules on competition to such undertakings can be assured. The Commission has adopted a Communication on services of general interest in Europe[9] in which it emphasises their importance. It is necessary to take account of the importance of the sectors concerned, which may involve services of general interest, the strong market position that the relevant undertakings may have and the vulnerability of emerging competition in the sectors being liberalised. In accordance with the principle of proportionality it is necessary and appropriate for the achievement of the basic objective of transparency to lay down rules on such separate accounts. This Directive confines itself to what is necessary in order to achieve the objectives pursued in accordance with the third paragraph of Article 5 of the Treaty.

(26) Whereas in certain sectors provisions adopted by the Community require Member States and certain undertakings to maintain separate accounts. It is necessary to ensure an equal treatment for all economic activities throughout the Community and to extend the requirement to maintain separate accounts to all comparable situations. This Directive should not amend specific rules established for the same purpose in other Community provisions and should not apply to activities of undertakings covered by those provisions.

(27) Whereas in view of the limited potential impact on competition and in order to avoid imposing an excessive administrative burden it is not necessary, at this time, to require enterprises with a total annual net turnover of less than EUR 40 million to maintain separate accounts. In view of the limited potential for an effect on trade between Member States, it is not necessary, at this time, to require separate accounts in relation to the supply of certain categories of services. This Directive should apply without prejudice to any other rules concerning the provision of information by Member States to the Commission.

(28) Whereas in cases where the compensation for the fulfilment of services of general economic interest has been fixed for an appropriate period following an open, transparent and non-discriminatory procedure it does not seem necessary at this time to require such undertakings to maintain separate accounts.

(29) Whereas Article 295 of the Treaty provides that the Treaty is in no way to prejudice the rules in Member States governing the system of property ownership. There should be no unjustified discrimination between public and private undertakings in the application of the rules on competition. This Directive should apply to both public and private undertakings.

(30) Whereas the Member States have differing administrative territorial structures. This Directive should cover public authorities at all levels in each Member State.

Note:

Recitals [19] to [30] are inserted from Dir. 2000/52

(31) Whereas this Directive is without prejudice to other provisions of the Treaty, notably Articles 86(2), 88 and 296;

(32) Whereas, the undertakings in question being in competition with other undertakings, information acquired should be covered by the obligation of professional secrecy;

(33) Whereas this Directive must be applied in close cooperation with the Member States, and where necessary be revised in the light of experience.

---

[9] OJ C 281, 26.9.1996, p. 3.

HAS ADOPTED THIS DIRECTIVE:

Article 1

1. The Member States shall ensure that financial relations between public authorities and public undertakings are transparent as provided in this Directive, so that the following emerge clearly:

(a) public funds made available directly by public authorities to the public undertakings concerned;
(b) public funds made available by public authorities through the intermediary of public undertakings or financial institutions;
(c) the use to which these public funds are actually put.

2. Without prejudice to specific provisions laid down by the Community the Member States shall ensure that the financial and organisational structure of any undertaking required to maintain separate accounts is correctly reflected in the separate accounts, so that the following emerge clearly:

(a) the costs and revenues associated with different activities;
(b) full details of the methods by which costs and revenues are assigned or allocated to different activities.

Amendment:

Article 1 was replaced by Dir. 2000/52. Art. 1(2) applies with effect from 1 January 2002: Art. 2 of Dir. 2000/52.

Article 2

1. For the purpose of this Directive:

(a) "public authorities" means all public authorities, including the State and regional, local and all other territorial authorities;
(b) "public undertakings" means any undertaking over which the public authorities may exercise directly or indirectly a dominant influence by virtue of their ownership of it, their financial participation therein, or the rules which govern it;
(c) "public undertakings operating in the manufacturing sector" means all undertakings whose principal area of activity, defined as being at least 50% of total annual turnover, is in manufacturing. These undertakings are those whose operations fall to be included in Section D—Manufacturing (being subsection DA up to and including subsection DN) of the NACE (Rev. 1) classification;[10]
(d) "undertaking required to maintain separate accounts" means any undertaking that enjoys a special or exclusive right granted by a Member State pursuant to Article 86(1) of the Treaty, or that is entrusted with the operation of a service of general economic interest pursuant to Article 86(2) of the Treaty and receives State aid in any form whatsoever, including any grant, support or compensation, in relation to such service and which carries on other activities;
(e) "different activities" means, on the one hand, all products or services in respect of which a special or exclusive right is granted to an undertaking or all services of general economic interest with which an undertaking is entrusted and, on the other

---

[10] OJ 1993 L83/1.

hand, each other separate product or service in respect of which the undertaking is active;

(f) "exclusive rights" means rights that are granted by a Member State to one undertaking through any legislative, regulatory or administrative instrument, reserving it the right to provide a service or undertake an activity within a given geographical area;

(g) "special rights" means rights that are granted by a Member State to a limited number of undertakings, through any legislative, regulatory or administrative instrument, which, within a given geographical area:

— limits to two or more the number of such undertakings, authorised to provide a service or undertake an activity, otherwise than according to objective, proportional and non-discriminatory criteria, or

— designates, otherwise than according to such criteria, several competing undertakings, as being authorised to provide a service or undertake an activity, or

— confers on any undertaking or undertakings, otherwise than according to such criteria, any legal or regulatory advantages which substantially affect the ability of any other undertaking to provide the same

service or to operate the same activity in the same geographical area under substantially equivalent conditions.

2. A dominant influence on the part of the public authorities shall be presumed when these authorities, directly or indirectly in relation to an undertaking:

(a) hold the major part of the undertaking's subscribed capital; or

(b) control the majority of the votes attaching to shares issued by the undertakings; or

(c) can appoint more than half of the members of the undertaking's administrative, managerial or supervisory body.]

Amendment

Article 2 was replaced by Dir. 2000/52.

Article 3

The transparency referred to in [Article 1(1)][11] shall apply in particular to the following aspects of financial relations between public authorities and public undertakings:

(a) the setting-off of operating losses;

(b) the provision of capital;

(c) non-refundable grants, or loans on privileged terms;

(d) the granting of financial advantages by forgoing profits or the recovery of sums due;

(e) the forgoing of a normal return on public funds used;

(f) compensation for financial burdens imposed by the public authorities.

Article 3A

1. To ensure the transparency referred to in Article 1(2), the Member States shall take the measures necessary to ensure that for any undertaking required to maintain separate accounts:

(a) the internal accounts corresponding to different activities are separate;

---

[11] See n. 2 *supra*.

(b) all costs and revenues are correctly assigned or allocated on the basis of consistently applied and objectively justifiable cost accounting principles;
(c) the cost accounting principles according to which separate accounts are maintained are clearly established.

2. Paragraph 1 shall only apply to activities which are not covered by specific provisions laid down by the Community and shall not affect any obligations of Member States or undertakings arising from the Treaty or from such specific provisions.

Article 4

1. As far as the transparency referred to in Article 1(1) is concerned, this Directive shall not apply to financial relations between the public authorities and

(a) public undertakings, as regards services the supply of which is not liable to affect trade between Member States to an appreciable extent;
(b) central banks;
(c) public credit institutions, as regards deposits of public funds placed with them by public authorities on normal commercial terms;
(d) public undertakings whose total annual net turnover over the period of the two financial years preceding that in which the funds referred to in Article 1(1) are made available or used has been less than EUR 40 million. However, for public credit institutions the corresponding threshold shall be a balance sheet total of EUR 800 million.

2. As far as the transparency referred to in Article 1(2) is concerned, this Directive shall not apply

(a) to undertakings, as regards services the supply of which is not liable to affect trade between Member States to an appreciable extent;
(b) to undertakings whose total annual net turnover over the period of the two financial years preceding any given year in which it enjoys a special or exclusive right granted by a Member State pursuant to Article 86(1) of the Treaty, or in which it is entrusted with the operation of a service of general economic interest pursuant to Article 86(2) of the Treaty is less than EUR 40 million; however, for public credit institutions the corresponding threshold shall be a balance sheet total of EUR 800 million;
(c) to undertakings which have been entrusted with the operation of services of general economic interest pursuant to Article 86(2) of the Treaty if the State aid in any form whatsoever, including any grant, support or compensation they receive was fixed for an appropriate period following an open, transparent and non-discriminating procedure.

Article 5

1. Member States shall ensure that information concerning the financial relations referred to in Article 1(1) be kept at the disposal of the Commission for five years from the end of the financial year in which the public funds were made available to the public undertakings concerned. However, where the same funds are used during a later financial year, the five-year time limit shall run from the end of that financial year.
2. Member States shall ensure that information concerning the financial and organisational structure of undertakings referred to in Article 1(2) be kept at the disposal of the Commission for five years from the end of the financial year to which the information refers.
3. Member States shall, where the Commission considers it necessary so to request, supply to it the information referred to in paragraphs 1 and 2, together with any necessary background information, notably the objectives pursued.

591

Amendment

Article 3A was inserted and Articles 4 to 5 were replaced by Dir. 2000/52.

Article 5A

1. Member States whose public undertakings operate in the manufacturing sector shall supply the financial information as set out in paragraph 2 to the Commission on an annual basis within the timetable contained in paragraph 4.

2. The financial information required for each public undertaking operating in the manufacturing sector and in accordance with paragraph 3 shall be as follows:

(i) The annual report and annual accounts, in accordance with the definition of Council Directive 78/660/EEC.[12] The annual accounts and annual report include the balance sheet and profit/loss account, explanatory notes, together with accounting policies, statements by directors, segmental and activity reports. Moreover, notices of share-holders' meetings and any other pertinent information shall be provided.

The following details, in so far as not disclosed in the annual report and annual accounts of each public undertaking, shall also be provided:

(ii) the provision of any share capital or quasi-capital funds similar in nature to equity, specifying the terms of its or their provision (whether ordinary, preference, deferred or convertible shares and interest rates; the dividend or conversion rights attaching thereto);

(iii) non-refundable grants, or grants which are only refundable in certain circum-stances;

(iv) the award to the enterprise of any loans, including overdrafts and advances on capital injections, with a specification of interest rates and the terms of the loan and its security, if any, given to the lender by the enterprise receiving the loan:

(v) guarantees given to the enterprise by public authorities in respect of loan finance (specifying terms and any charges paid by enterprises for these guarantees);

(vi) dividends paid out and profits retained;

(vii) any other forms of State intervention, in particular, the forgiving of sums due to the State by a public undertaking, including, *inter alia*, the repayment of loans, grants, payment of corporate or social taxes or any similar charges.

3. The information required by paragraph 2 shall be provided for all public under-takings whose turnover for the most recent financial year was more than [EUR][13] 250 million.

The information required above shall be supplied separately for each public undertaking including those located in the Member States, and shall include, where appropriate, details of all intra- and inter-group transactions between different public undertakings, as well as transactions conducted direct between public undertaking and the State. The share capital referred to in paragraph 2(ii) shall include share capital contributed by the State direct and any share capital received contributed by a public holding company or other public undertaking (including financial institutions), whether inside or outside the same group, to a given public undertaking. The relationship between the provider of the finance and the recipient shall always be specified. Similarly, the reports required in paragraph 2 shall be provided for each individual public undertaking separately, as well as for the (sub)-

---

[12] OJ 1978 L222/11.
[13] See n. 2 *supra*.

holding company which consolidates several public undertakings in so far as the consoli-dated sales of the (sub)-holding company lead to its being classified as "manufactur-ing".

Certain public enterprises split their activities into several legally distinct undertakings. For such enterprises the Commission is willing to accept one consolidated report. The consolidation should reflect the economic reality of a group of enterprises operating in the same or closely related sectors. Consolidated reports from diverse, and purely financial, holdings shall not be sufficient.

4. The information required under paragraph 2 shall be supplied to the Commission on an annual basis. The information in respect of the financial year 1992 shall be forwarded to the Commission within two months of publication of this Directive.

For 1993 and subsequent years, the information shall be provided within 15 working days of the date of publication of the annual report of the public undertaking concerned. In any case, and specifically for undertakings which do not publish an annual report the required information shall be submitted not later than nine months following the end of the undertaking's financial year.

In order to assess the number of companies covered by this reporting system, Member States shall supply to the Commission a list of the companies covered by this Article and their turnover, within two months of publication of this Directive. The list is to be updated by 31 March of each year.

5. This Article is applicable to companies owned or controlled by the Treuhandanstalt only from the expiry date of the special reporting system set up for Treuhandanstalt investments.

6. Member States will furnish the Commission with any additional information that it deems necessary in order to complete a thorough appraisal of the data submitted.

Amendment

Article 5A was inserted by Directive 93/84.

Article 6

1. The Commission shall not disclose such information supplied to it pursuant to Article [5(3)] as is of a kind covered by the obligation of professional secrecy.

2. Paragraph 1 shall not prevent publication of general information or surveys which do not contain information relating to particular public undertakings to which this Directive applies.

Article 7

The Commission shall regularly inform the Member States of the results of the operation of this Directive.

Article 8

Member States shall take the measures necessary to comply with the Directive by 31 December 1981. They shall inform the Commission thereof.

Note

Directive 93/824 required that Member States shall adopt the provision necessary for compliance by 1 November 1993. Directive 2000/52 requires that Member States shall adopt the provisions necessary for compliance by 31 July 2001. Both Directives require

Member States to make a reference to the relevant Directive in the adopting provision or at the time of its publication.

Article 9

This Directive is addressed to the Member States.

Done at Brussels, 25 June 1980.

APPENDIX 61

COMMISSION NOTICE[1]

*Guidelines on the Application of EEC Competition Rules in the
Telecommunications Sector*

PREFACE

These guidelines aim at clarifying the application of Community competition rules to the market participants in the telecommunications sector. They must be viewed in the context of the special conditions of the telecommunications sector, and the overall Community telecommunications policy will be taken into account in their application. In particular, account will have to be taken of the actions the Commission will be in a position to propose for the telecommunications industry as a whole, actions deriving from the assessment of the state of play and issues at stake for this industry, as has already been the case for the European electronics and information technology industry in the communication of the Commission of 3 April 1991.[2]

A major political aim, as emphasized by the Commission, the Council, and the European Parliament, must be the development of efficient Europe-wide networks and services, at the lowest cost and of the highest quality, to provide the European user in the single market of 1992 with a basic infrastructure for efficient operation.

The Commission has made it clear in the past that in this context it is considered that liberalization and harmonization in the sector must go hand in hand.

Given the competition context in the telecommunications sector, the telecommunications operators should be allowed, and encouraged, to establish the necessary cooperation mechanisms, in order to create—or ensure—Community-wide full interconnectivity between public networks, and where required between services to enable European users to benefit from a wider range of better and cheaper telecommunications services.

This can and has to be done in compliance with, and respect of, EEC competition rules in order to avoid the diseconomies which otherwise could result. For the same reasons, operators and other firms that may be in a dominant market position should be made aware of the prohibition of abuse of such positions.

The guidelines should be read in the light of this objective. They set out to clarify, *inter alia*, which forms of cooperation amount to undesirable collusion, and in this sense they list what is *not* acceptable. They should therefore be seen as one aspect of an overall Community policy towards telecommunications, and notably of policies and actions to encourage and stimulate those forms of cooperation which promote the development and availability of advanced communications for Europe.

The full application of competition rules forms a major part of the Community's overall approach to telecommunications. These guidelines should help market participants to shape their strategies and arrangements for Europe-wide networks and services from the outset in a manner which allows them to be fully in line with these rules. In the event of significant changes in the conditions which prevailed when the guidelines were drawn up,

---

[1] OJ 1991 C233/2.

[2] The European electronics and information technology industry: state of play, issues at stake and proposals for action, SEC(91) 565, 3 April 1991.

the Commission may find it appropriate to adapt the guidelines to the evolution of the situation in the telecommunications sector.

I. SUMMARY

1. The Commission of the European Communities in its Green Paper on the development of the common market for telecommunications services and equipment (COM(87)290) dated 30 June 1987 proposed a number of Community positions. Amongst these, positions (H) and (I) are as follows:

"(H) strict continuous review of operational (commercial) activities of telecommunications administrations according to Articles 81, 82 and 86 of the EEC Treaty. This applies in particular to practices of cross-subsidization of activities in the competitive services sector and of activities in manufacturing;
(J) strict continuous review of all private providers in the newly opened sectors according to Articles 81 and 82, in order to avoid the abuse of dominant positions;".

2. These positions were restated in the Commission's document of 9 February 1988 "Implementing the Green Paper on the development of the common market for telecommunications services and equipment/state of discussions and proposals by the Commission" (COM(88)48). Among the areas where the development of concrete policy actions is now possible, the Commission indicated the following:

"Ensuring fair conditions of competition:
Ensuring an open competitive market makes continuous review of the telecommunications sector necessary.
The Commission intends to issue guidelines regarding the application of competition rules to the telecommunications sector and on the way that the review should be carried out."

This is the objective of this communication.

The telecommunications sector in many cases requires cooperation agreements, *inter alia*, between telecommunications organizations (TOs) in order to ensure network and services interconnectivity, one-stop shopping and one-stop billing which are necessary to provide for Europe-wide services and to offer optimum service to users. These objectives can be achieved, *inter alia*, by TOs cooperating—for example, in those areas where exclusive or special rights for provision may continue in accordance with Community law, including competition law, as well as in areas where optimum service will require certain features of cooperation. On the other hand the overriding objective to develop the conditions for the market to provide European users with a greater variety of telecommunications services, of better quality and at lower cost requires the introduction and safeguarding of a strong competitive structure. Competition plays a central role for the Community, especially in view of the completion of the single market for 1992. This role has already been emphasized in the Green Paper.

The single market will represent a new dimension for telecoms operators and users. Competition will give them the opportunity to make full use of technological development and to accelerate it, and encouraging them to restructure and reach the necessary economies of scale to become competitive not only on the Community market, but worldwide.

With this in mind, these guidelines recall the main principles which the Commission, according to its mandate under the Treaty's competition rules, has applied and will apply in the sector without prejudging the outcome of any specific case which will have to be considered on the facts.

The objective is, *inter alia*, to contribute to more certainty of conditions for investment in the sector and the development of Europe-wide services.

The mechanisms for creating certainty for individual cases (apart from complaints and ex-officio investigations) are provided for by the notification and negative clearance procedures provided under Regulation No 17, which give a formal procedure for clearing cooperation agreements in this area whenever a formal clearance is requested. This is set out in further detail in this communication.

II. INTRODUCTION

3. The fundamental technological development worldwide in the telecommunications sector[3] has caused considerable changes in the competition conditions. The traditional monopolistic administrations cannot alone take up the challenge of the technological revolution. New economic forces have appeared on the telecoms scene which are capable of offering users the numerous enhanced services generated by the new technologies. This has given rise to and stimulated a wide deregulation process propagated in the Community with various degrees of intensity.

This move is progressively changing the face of the European market structure. New private suppliers have penetrated the market with more and more transnational value-added services and equipment. The telecommunications administrations, although keeping a central role as public services providers, have acquired a business-like way of thinking. They have started competing dynamically with private operators in services and equipment. Wide restructuring, through mergers and joint ventures, is taking place in order to compete more effectively on the deregulated market through economies of scale and rationalization. All these events have a multiplier effect on technological progress.

4. In the light of this, the central role of competition for the Community appears clear, especially in view of the completion of the single market for 1992. This role has already been emphasized in the Green Paper.

5. In the application of competition rules the Commission endeavours to avoid the adopting of State measures or undertakings erecting or maintaining artificial barriers incompatible with the single market. But it also favours all forms of cooperation which foster innovation and economic progress, as contemplated by competition law. Pursuing effective competition in telecoms is not a matter of political choice. The choice of a free market and a competition-oriented economy was already envisaged in the EEC Treaty, and the competition rules of the Treaty are directly applicable within the Community. The abovementioned fundamental changes make necessary the full application of competition law.

6. There is a need for more certainty as to the application of competition rules. The telecommunication administrations together with keeping their duties of public interest, are now confronted with the application of these rules practically without transition from a long tradition of legal protection. Their scope and actual implications are often not easily perceivable. As the technology is fast-moving and huge investments are necessary, in order to benefit from the new possibilities on the market-place, all the operators, public or private, have to take quick decisions, taking into account the competition regulatory framework.

7. This need for more certainty regarding the application of competition rules is already met by assessments made in several individual cases. However, assessments of individual cases so far have enabled a response to only some of the numerous competition questions

---

[3] Telecommunications embraces any transmission, emission or reception of signs, signals, writing, images and sounds or intelligence of any nature by wire, radio, optical and other electromagnetic systems (Article 2 of WATTC Regulation of 9 December 1988).

which arise in telecommunications. Future cases will further develop the Commission's practice in this sector.

Purpose of these guidelines

8. These guidelines are intended to advise public telecommunications operators, other telecommunications service and equipment suppliers and users, the legal profession and the interested members of the public about the general legal and economic principles which have been and are being followed by the Commission in the application of competition rules to undertakings in the telecommunications sector, based on experience gained in individual cases in compliance with the rulings of the Court of Justice of the European Communities.

9. The Commission will apply these principles also to future individual cases in a flexible way, and taking the particular context of each case into account. These guidelines do not cover all the general principles governing the application of competition rules, but only those which are of specific relevance to telecommunication issues. The general principles of competition rules not specifically connected with telecommunications but entirely applicable to these can be found, *inter alia*, in the regulatory acts, the Court judgments and the Commission decisions dealing with the individual cases, the Commission's yearly reports on competition policy, press releases and other public information originating from the Commission.

10. These guidelines do not create enforceable rights. Moreover, they do not prejudice the application of EEC competition rules by the Court of Justice of the European Communities and by national authorities (as these rules may be directly applied in each Member State, by the national authorities, administrative or judicial).

11. A change in the economic and legal situation will not automatically bring about a simultaneous amendment to the guidelines. The Commission, however, reserves the possibility to make such an amendment when it considers that these guidelines no longer satisfy their purpose, because of fundamental and/or repeated changes in legal precedents, methods of applying competition rules, and the regulatory, economic and technical context.

12. These guidelines essentially concern the direct application of competition rules to undertakings, i.e. Articles 81 and 82 of the EEC Treaty. They do not concern those applicable to the Member States, in particular Articles 5 and 86(1) and (3). Principles ruling the application of Article 86 in telecommunications are expressed in Commission Directives adopted under Article 86(3) for the implementation of the Green Paper.[4]

Relationship between competition rules applicable to undertakings and those applicable to Member States

13. The Court of Justice of the European Communities[5] has ruled that while it is true that Articles 81 and 82 of the Treaty concern the conduct of undertakings and not the laws or regulations of the Member States, by virtue of Article 5(2) of the EEC Treaty, Member States must not adopt or maintain in force any measure which could deprive those provisions of their effectiveness. The Court has stated that such would be the case, in

---

[4] Commission Directive 88/301/EEC of 16 May 1988 on competition in the markets in telecommunications terminal equipment (OJ No L 131, 27.5.1988, p. 73).
Commission Directive 90/388/EEC of 28 June 1990 on competition in the markets for telecommunications services (OJ No L 192, 24.7.1990, p. 10).

[5] Judgment of 10.1.1985 in Case 229/83, *Leclerc/gasoline* [1985] ECR 17; Judgment of 11.7.1985 in Case 299/83, *Leclerc/books* [1985] ECR 2517; Judgment of 30.4.1986 in Cases from 209 to 213/84, *Ministère public v. Asjes* [1986] ECR 1425; Judgment of 1.10.1987 in Case 311/85, *Vereniging van Vlaamse Reisbureaus v. Sociale Dienst van de Plaatselijke en Gewestelijke Overheidsdiensten* [1987] ECR 3801.

particular, if a Member State were to require or favour prohibited cartels or reinforce the effects thereof or to encourage abuses by dominant undertakings.

If those measures are adopted or maintained in force *vis-à-vis* public undertakings or undertakings to which a Member State grants special or exclusive rights, Article 86 might also apply.

14. When the conduct of a public undertaking or an undertaking to which a Member State grants special or exclusive rights arises entirely as a result of the exercise of the undertaking's autonomous behaviour, it can only be caught by Articles 81 and 82.

When this behaviour is imposed by a mandatory State measure (regulative or administrative), leaving no discretionary choice to the undertakings concerned, Article 86 may apply to the State involved in association with Articles 81 and 82. In this case Articles 81 and 82 apply to the undertakings' behaviour taking into account the constraints to which the undertakings are submitted by the mandatory State measure.

Ultimately, when the behaviour arises from the free choice of the undertakings involved, but the State has taken a measure which encourages the behaviour or strengthens its effects, Articles 81 and/or 82 apply to the undertakings' behaviour and Article 86 may apply to the State measure. This could be the case, *inter alia*, when the State has approved and/or legally endorsed the result of the undertakings' behaviour (for instance tariffs).

These guidelines and the Article 86 Directives complement each other to a certain extent in that they cover the principles governing the application of the competition rules: Articles 81 and 82 on the one hand, Article 86 on the other.

Application of competition rules and other Community law, including open network provision (ONP) rules

15. Articles 81 and 82 and Regulations implementing those Articles in application of Article 83 of the EEC Treaty constitute law in force and enforceable throughout the Community. Conflicts should not arise with other Community rules because Community law forms a coherent regulatory framework. Other Community rules, and in particular those specifically governing the telecommunications sector, cannot be considered as provisions implementing Articles 81 and 82 in this sector. However it is obvious that Community acts adopted in the telecommunications sector are to be interpreted in a way consistent with competition rules, so to ensure the best possible implementation of all aspects of the Community telecommunications policy.

16. This applies, *inter alia*, to the relationship between competition rules applicable to undertakings and the ONP rules. According to the Council Resolution of 30 June 1988 on the development of the common market for telecommunications services and equipment up to 1992,[6] ONP comprises the "rapid definition, by Council Directives, of technical conditions, usage conditions, and tariff principles for open network provision, starting with harmonized conditions for the use of leased lines". The details of the ONP procedures have been fixed by Directive 90/387/EEC[7] on the establishment of the internal market for telecommunications services through the implementation of open network provision, adopted by Council on 28 June 1990 under Article 95 of the EEC Treaty.

17. ONP has a fundamental role in providing European-wide access to Community-wide interconnected public networks. When ONP harmonization is implemented, a network user will be offered harmonized access conditions throughout the EEC, whichever country they address. Harmonized access will be ensured in compliance with the competition rules as mentioned above, as the ONP rules specifically provide.

ONP rules cannot be considered as competition rules which apply to States and/or to undertakings' behaviour. ONP and competition rules therefore constitute two different but coherent sets of rules. Hence, the competition rules have full application, even when all ONP rules have been adopted.

---

[6] OJ 1988 C257/1.
[7] OJ 1990 L192/1.

18. Competition rules are and will be applied in a coherent manner with Community trade rules in force. However, competition rules apply in a non-discriminatory manner to EEC undertakings and to non-EEC ones which have access to the EEC market.

III. COMMON PRINCIPLES OF APPLICATION OF ARTICLES 81 AND 82

Equal application of Articles 81 and 82

19. Articles 81 and 82 apply directly and throughout the Community to all undertakings, whether public or private, on equal terms and to the same extent, apart from the exception provided in Article 86(2).[8]

The Commission and national administrative and judicial authorities are competent to apply these rules under the conditions set out in Council Regulation No 17.[9]

20. Therefore, Articles 81 and 82 apply both to private enterprises and public telecommunications operators embracing telecommunications administrations and recognized private operating agencies, hereinafter called "telecommunications organizations" (TOs).

TOs are undertakings within the meaning of Articles 81 and 82 to the extent that they exert an economic activity, for the manufacturing and/or sale of telecommunications equipment and/or for the provision of telecommunications services, regardless of other facts such as, for example, whether their nature is economic or not and whether they are legally distinct entities or form part of the State organization.[10] Associations of TOs are associations of undertakings within the meaning of Article 81, even though TOs participate as undertakings in organizations in which governmental authorities are also represented.

Articles 81 and 82 apply also to undertakings located outside the EEC when restrictive agreements are implemented or intended to be implemented or abuses are committed by those undertakings within the common market to the extent that trade between Member States is affected.[11]

Competition restrictions justified under Article 86(2) or by essential requirements

21. The exception provided in Article 86(2) may apply both to State measures and to practices by undertakings. The Services Directive 90/388/EEC, in particular in Article 3, makes provision for a Member State to impose specified restrictions in the licences which it can grant for the provision of certain telecommunications services. These restrictions may be imposed under Article 86(2) or in order to ensure the compliance with State essential requirements specified in the Directive.

22. As far as Article 86(2) is concerned, the benefit of the exception provided by this provision may still be invoked for a TO's behaviour when it brings about competition

---

[8] Article 86(2) states: "Undertakings entrusted with the operation of services of general economic interest or having the character of a revenue-producing monopoly shall be subject to the rules contained in this Treaty, in particular to the rules on competition, in so far as the application of such rules does not obstruct the performance, in law or in fact, of the particular tasks assigned to them. The development of trade must not be affected to such an extent as would be contrary to the interests of the Community".

[9] OJ 1962 73/204 (Special Edition 1959–62, p. 87).

[10] See Judgment of the Court 16.6.1987 in Case 118/85, *Commission v. Italy—Transparency of Financial Relations between Member States and Public Undertakings* [1987] ECR 2599.

[11] See Judgment of the Court of 27.9.1988 in Joined Cases 89, 104, 114, 116, 117, 125, 126, 127, 129/85, *Ålström & others v. Commission* (*"Woodpulp"*), [1988] ECR 5193.

restrictions which its Member State did not impose in application of the Services Directive. However, the fact should be taken into account that in this case the State whose function is to protect the public and the general economic interest, did not deem it necessary to impose the said restrictions. This makes particularly hard the burden of proving that the Article 86(2) exception still applies to an undertakings's behaviour involving these restrictions.

23. The Commission infers from the case law of the Court of Justice[12] that it has exclusive competence, under the control of the Court, to decide that the exception of Article 86(2) applies. The national authorities including judicial authorities can assess that this exception does not apply, when they find that the competition rules clearly do not obstruct the performance of the task of general economic interest assigned to undertakings. When those authorities cannot make a clear assessment in this sense they should suspend their decision in order to enable the Commission to find that the conditions for the application of that provision are fulfilled.

24. As to measures aiming at the compliance with "essential requirements" within the meaning of the Services Directive, under Article 1 of the latter,[13] they can only be taken by Member States and not by undertakings.

The relevant market

25. In order to assess the effects of an agreement on competition for the purposes of Article 81 and whether there is a dominant position on the market for the purposes of Article 82, it is necessary to define the relevant market(s), product or service market(s) and geographic market(s), within the domain of telecommunications. In a context of fast-moving technology the relevant market definition is dynamic and variable.

(a) The product market

26. A product market comprises the totality of the products which, with respect to their characteristics, are particularly suitable for satisfying constant needs and are only to a limited extent interchangeable with other products in terms of price, usage and consumer preference. An examination limited to the objective characteristics only of the relevant products cannot be sufficient: the competitive conditions and the structure of supply and demand on the market must also be taken into consideration.[14]

The Commission can precisely define these markets only within the framework of individual cases.

27. For the guidelines' purpose it can only be indicated that distinct service markets could exist at least for terrestrial network provision, voice communication, data communication and satellites. With regard to the equipment market, the following areas could all be taken into account for the purposes of market definition: public switches, private switches, transmission systems and more particularly, in the field of terminals, telephone sets, modems, telex terminals, data transmission terminals and mobile telephones. The above indications are without prejudice to the definition of further narrower distinct markets. As to other services—such as value-added ones—as well as terminal and network equipment, it cannot be specified here whether there is a market for each of them or for an aggregate of them, or for both, depending upon the interchangeability existing in different geographic markets. This is mainly determined by the supply and the requirements in those markets.

28. Since the various national public networks compete for the installation of the telecommunication hubs of large users, market definition may accordingly vary. Indeed,

---

[12] Case 10/71, *Mueller-Hein* [1971] ECR 723; Judgment of 11.4.1989 in Case 66/86, *Ahmed Saeed* [1989] ECR 803.

[13] " . . . the non-economic reasons in the general interest which may cause a Member State to restrict access to the public telecommunications network or public telecommunications services."

[14] Case 322/81, *Michelin v. Commission*, 9 November 1983, [1983] ECR 3529, Ground 37.

large telecommunications users, whether or not they are service providers, locate their premises depending, *inter alia*, upon the features of the telecommunications services supplied by each TO. Therefore, they compare national public networks and other services provided by the TOs in terms of characteristics and prices.

29. As to satellite provision, the question is whether or not it is substantially interchangeable with terrestrial network provision:

(a) communication by satellite can be of various kinds: fixed service (point to point communication), multipoint (point to multipoint and multipoint to multipoint), one-way or two-way;

(b) satellites' main characteristics are: coverage of a wide geographic area not limited by national borders, insensitivity of costs to distance, flexibility and ease of networks deployment, in particular in the very small aperture terminals (VSAT) systems;

(c) satellites' uses can be broken down into the following categories: public switched voice and data transmission, business value-added services and broadcasting;

(d) a satellite provision presents a broad interchangeability with the terrestrial transmission link for the basic voice and data transmission on long distance. Conversely, because of its characteristics it is not substantially interchangeable but rather complementary to terrestrial transmission links for several specific voice and data transmission uses. These uses are: services to peripheral or less-developed regions, links between non-contiguous countries, reconfiguration of capacity and provision of routing for traffic restoration. Moreover, satellites are not currently substantially interchangeable for direct broadcasting and multipoint private networks for value-added business services. Therefore, for all those uses satellites should constitute distinct product markets. Within satellites, there may be distinct markets.

30. In mobile communications distinct services seem to exist such as cellular telephone, paging, telepoint, cordless voice and cordless data communication. Technical development permits providing each of these systems with more and more enhanced features. A consequence of this is that the differences between all these systems are progressively blurring and their interchangeability increasing. Therefore, it cannot be excluded that in future for certain uses several of those systems be embraced by a single product market. By the same token, it is likely that, for certain uses, mobile systems will be comprised in a single market with certain services offered on the public switched network.

(b) The geographic market

31. A geographic market is an area:

— where undertakings enter into competition with each other, and
— where the objective conditions of competition applying to the product or service in question are similar for all traders.[15]

32. Without prejudice to the definition of the geographic market in individual cases, each national territory within the EEC seems still to be a distinct geographic market as regards those relevant services or products, where:

— the customer's needs cannot be satisfied by using a non-domestic service,
— there are different regulatory conditions of access to services, in particular special or exclusive rights which are apt to isolate national territories,

---

[15] Judgment of 14.2.1978 in Case 27/76, *United Brands v. Commission* [1978] ECR 207, Ground 44. In the telecommunications sector: Judgment of 5.10.1988 in Case 247/86, *Alsatel-Novasam* [1988] ECR 5987.

— as to equipment and network, there are no Community-common standards, whether mandatory or voluntary, whose absence could also isolate the national markets. The absence of voluntary Community-wide standards shows different national customers' requirements.

However, it is expected that the geographic market will progressively extend to the EEC territory at the pace of the progressive realization of a single EEC market.

33. It has also to be ascertained whether each national market or a part thereof is a substantial part of the common market. This is the case where the services of the product involved represent a substantial percentage of volume within the EEC. This applies to all services and products involved.

34. As to satellite uplinks, for cross-border communication by satellite the uplink could be provided from any of several countries. In this case, the geographic market is wider than the national territory and may cover the whole EEC.

As to space segment capacity, the extension of the geographic market will depend on the power of the satellite and its ability to compete with other satellites for transmission to a given area, in other words on its range. This can be assessed only case by case.

35. As to services in general as well as terminal and network equipment, the Commission assesses the market power of the undertakings concerned and the result for EEC competition of the undertakings' conduct, taking into account their interrelated activities and interaction between the EEC and world markets. This is even more necessary to the extent that the EEC market is progressively being opened. This could have a considerable effect on the structure of the markets in the EEC, on the overall competitivity of the undertakings operating in those markets, and in the long run, on their capacity to remain independent operators.

IV. APPLICATION OF ARTICLE 81

36. The Commission recalls that a major policy target of the Council Resolution of 30 June 1988 on the development of the common market for telecommunications services and equipment up to 1992 was that of:

" . . . stimulating European cooperation at all levels, as far as compatible with Community competition rules, and particularly in the field of research and development, in order to secure a strong European presence on the telecommunications markets and to ensure the full participation of all Member States".

In many cases Europe-wide services can be achieved by TOs' cooperation—for example, by ensuring interconnectivity and interoperability

(i) in those areas where exclusive or special rights for provision may continue in accordance with Community law and in particular with the Services Directive 90/388/EEC; and

(ii) in areas where optimum service will require certain features of cooperation, such as so-called "one-stop shopping" arrangements, i.e. the possibility of acquiring Europe-wide services at a single sales point.

The Council is giving guidance, by Directives, Decisions, recommendations and resolutions on those areas where Europe-wide services are most urgently needed: such as by recommendation 86/659/EEC on the coordinated introduction of the integrated services digital network (ISDN) in the European Community[16] and by recommendation

---

[16] OJ 1986 L382/36.

87/371/EEC on the coordinated introduction of public pan-European cellular digital land-based mobile communications in the Community.[17]

The Commission welcomes and fully supports the necessity of cooperation particularly in order to promote the development of trans-European services and strengthen the competitivity of the EEC industry throughout the Community and in the world markets. However, this cooperation can only attain that objective if it complies with Community competition rules. Regulation No 17 provides well-defined clearing procedures for such cooperation agreements. The procedures foreseen by Regulation No 17 are:

(i) the application for negative clearance, by which the Commission certifies that the agreements are not caught by Article 81, because they do not restrict competition and/or do not affect trade between Member States; and

(ii) the notification of agreements caught by Article 81 in order to obtain an exemption under Article 81(3). Although if a particular agreement is caught by Article 81, an exemption can be granted by the Commission under Article 81(3), this is only so when the agreement brings about economic benefits—assessed on the basis of the criteria in the said paragraph 3—which outweigh its restrictions on competition. In any event competition may not be eliminated for a substantial part of the products in question. Notification is not an obligation; but if, for reasons of legal certainty, the parties decide to request an exemption pursuant to Article 4 of Regulation No 17 the agreements may not be exempted until they have been notified to the Commission.

37. Cooperation agreements may be covered by one of the Commission block exemption Regulations or Notices.[18] In the first case the agreement is automatically exempted under Article 81(3). In the latter case, in the Commission's view, the agreement does not appreciably restrict competition and trade between Member States and therefore does not justify a Commission action. In either case, the agreement does not need to be notified; but it may be notified in case of doubt. If the Commission receives a multitude of notifications of similar cooperation agreements in the telecommunications sector, it may consider whether a specific block exemption regulation for such agreements would be appropriate.

38. The categories of agreements[19] which seem to be typical in telecommunications and may be caught by Article 81 are listed below. This list provides examples only and is, therefore, not exhaustive. The Commission is thereby indicating possible competition restrictions which could be caught by Article 81 and cases where there may be the possibility of an exemption.

39. These agreements may affect trade between Member States for the following reasons:

(i) services other than services reserved to TOs, equipment and spatial segment facilities are traded throughout the EEC; agreements on these services and equipment are therefore likely to affect trade. Although at present cross-frontier trade is limited, there is potentially no reason to suppose that suppliers of such facilities will in future confine themselves to their national market;

(ii) as to reserved network services, one can consider that they also are traded throughout the Community. These services could be provided by an operator located in one Member State to customers located in other Member States, which decide to move their telecommunications hub into the first one because it is economically or qualitatively advantageous. Moreover, agreements on these matters are likely to

---

[17] OJ 1987 L196/81.

[18] Reported in "Competition Law in the European Communities" Volume I (situation at 31.12.1989) published by the Commission.

[19] For simplification's sake this term stands also for "decisions by associations" and "concerted practices" within the meaning of Article 81.

affect EEC trade at least to the extent they influence the conditions under which the other services and equipment are supplied throughout the EEC.

40. Finally, to the extent that the TOs hold dominant positions in facilities, services and equipment markets, their behaviour leading to—and including the conclusion of—the agreements in question could also give rise to a violation of Article 82, if agreements have or are likely to have as their effect hindering the maintenance of the degree of competition still existing in the market or the growth of that competition, or causing the TOs to reap trading benefits which they would not have reaped if there had been normal and sufficiently effective competition.

A. Horizontal agreements concerning the provision of terrestrial facilities and reserved services

41. Agreements concerning terrestrial facilities (public switched network or leased circuits) or services (e.g. voice telephony for the general public) can currently only be concluded between TOs because of this legal regime providing for exclusive or special rights. The fact that the Services Directive recognizes the possibility for a Member State to reserve this provision to certain operators does not exempt those operators from complying with the competition rules in providing these facilities or services. These agreements may restrict competition within a Member State only where such exclusive rights are granted to more than one provider.

42. These agreements may restrict the competition between TOs for retaining or attracting large telecommunications users for their telecommunications centres. Such "hub competition" is substantially based upon favourable rates and other conditions, as well as the quality of the services. Member States are not allowed to prevent such competition since the Directive allows only the granting of exclusive and special rights by each Member State in its own territory.

43. Finally, these agreements may restrict competition in non-reserved services from third party undertakings, which are supported by the facilities in question, for example if they impose discriminatory or inequitable trading conditions on certain users.

44.(aa) *Price agreements:* all TOs' agreements on prices, discounting or collection charges for international services, are apt to restrict the hub competition to an appreciable extent. Coordination on or prohibition of discounting could cause particularly serious restrictions. In situations of public knowledge such as exists in respect of the tariff level, discounting could remain the only possibility of effective price competition.

45. In several cases the Court of Justice and the Commission have considered price agreements among the most serious infringements of Article 81.[20]

While harmonization of tariff structures may be a major element for the provision of Community-wide services, this goal should be pursued as far as compatible with Community competition rules and should include definition of efficient pricing principles throughout the Community. Price competition is a crucial, if not the principal, element of customer choice and is apt to stimulate technical progress. Without prejudice to any application for individual exemption that may be made, the justification of any price agreement in terms of Article 81(3) would be the subject of very rigorous examination by the Commission.

46. Conversely, where the agreements concern only the setting up of common tariff structures or principles, the Commission may consider whether this would not constitute one of the economic benefits under Article 81(3) which outweigh the competition restriction. Indeed, this could provide the necessary transparency on tariff calculations and facilitate users' decisions about traffic flow or the location of headquarters or premises.

---

[20] *PVC*, Commission Decision 89/190/EEC, OJ 1989 L74/1; Case 123/85, *BNIC v. Clair* [1985] ECR 391; Case 8/72, *Cementhandelaren v. Commission* [1972] ECR 977; *Polypropylene*, Commission Decision 86/398/EEC (OJ 1986 L230/1) on appeal Case 179/86.

Such agreements could also contribute to achieving one of the Green Paper's economic objectives—more cost-orientated tariffs.

In this connection, following the intervention of the Commission, the CEPT has decided to abolish recommendation PGT/10 on the general principles for the lease of international telecommunications circuits and the establishment of private international networks. This recommendation recommended, *inter alia*, the imposition of a 30% surcharge or an access charge where third-party traffic was carried on an international telecommunications leased circuit, or if such a circuit was interconnected to the public telecommunications network. It also recommended the application of uniform tariff coefficients in order to determine the relative price level of international telecommunications leased circuits. Thanks to the CEPT's cooperation with the Commission leading to the abolition of the recommendation, competition between telecoms operators for the supply of international leased circuits is re-established, to the benefit of users, especially suppliers of non-reserved services. The Commission had found that the recommendation amounted to a price agreement between undertakings under Article 81 of the Treaty which substantially restricted competition within the European Community.[21]

47.(ab) *Agreements on other conditions for the provision of facilities*

These agreements may limit hub competition between the partners. Moreover, they may limit the access of users to the network, and thus restrict third undertakings' competition as to non-reserved services. This applies especially to the use of leased circuits. The abolished CEPT recommendation PGT/10 on tariffs had also recommended restrictions on conditions of sale which the Commission objected to. These restrictions were mainly:

— making the use of leased circuits between the customer and third parties subject to the condition that the communication concern exclusively the activity for which the circuit has been granted,
— a ban on subleasing,
— authorization of private networks only for customers tied to each other by economic links and which carry out the same activity,
— prior consultation between the TOs for any approval of a private network and of any modification of the use of the network, and for any interconnection of private networks.

For the purpose of an exemption under Article 81(3), the granting of special conditions for a particular facility in order to promote its development could be taken into account among other elements. This could foster technologies which reduce the costs of services and contribute to increasing competitiveness of European industry structures. Naturally, the other Article 81(3) requirements should also be met.

48. (ac) *Agreements on the choice of telecommunication routes.*

These may have the following restrictive effects:

(i) to the extent that they coordinate the TOs' choice of the routes to be set up in international services, they may limit competition between TOs as suppliers to users' communications hubs, in terms of investments and production, with a possible effect on tariffs. It should be determined whether this restriction of their business autonomy is sufficiently appreciable to be caught by Article 81. In any event, an argument for an exemption under Article 81(3) could be more easily sustained if common routes designation were necessary to enable interconnections and, therefore, the use of a Europe-wide network;
(ii) to the extent that they reserve the choice of routes already set up to the TOs, and this choice concerns one determined facility, they could limit the use of other facilities

---

[21] See Commission press release IP(90) 188 of 6 March 1990.

and thus services provision possibly to the detriment of technological progress. By contrast, the choice of routes does not seem restrictive in principle to the extent that it constitutes a technical requirement.

49. (ad) *Agreements on the imposition of technical and quality standards on the services provided on the public network*

Standardization brings substantial economic benefits which can be relevant under Article 81(3). It facilitates *inter alia* the provision of pan-European telecommunications services. As set out in the framework of the Community's approach to standardization, products and services complying with standards may be used Community-wide. In the context of this approach, European standards institutions have developed in this field (ETSI and CEN-Cenelec). National markets in the EC would be opened up and form a Community market. Service and equipment markets would be enlarged, hence favouring economies of scale. Cheaper products and services are thus available to users. Standardization may also offer an alternative to specifications controlled by undertakings dominant in the network architecture and in non-reserved services. Standardization agreements may, therefore, lessen the risk of abuses by these undertakings which could block the access to the markets for non-reserved services and for equipment. However, certain standardization agreements can have restrictive effects on competition: hindering innovation, freezing a particular stage of technical development, blocking the network access of some users/service providers. This restriction could be appreciable, for example when deciding to what extent intelligence will in future be located in the network or continue to be permitted in customers' equipment. The imposition of specifications other than those provided for by Community law could have restrictive effects on competition. Agreements having these effects are, therefore, caught by Article 81.

The balance between economic benefits and competition restrictions is complex. In principle, an exemption could be granted if an agreement brings more openness and facilitates access to the market, and these benefits outweigh the restrictions caused by it.

50. Standards jointly developed and/or published in accordance with the ONP procedures carry with them the presumption that the cooperating TOs which comply with those standards fulfil the requirement of open and efficient access (see the ONP Directive mentioned in paragraph 16). This presumption can be rebutted, *inter alia*, if the agreement contains restrictions which are not foreseen by Community law and are not indispensable for the standardization sought.

51. One important Article 81(3) requirement is that users must also be allowed a fair share of the resulting benefit. This is more likely to happen when users are directly involved in the standardization process in order to contribute to deciding what products or services will meet their needs. Also, the involvement of manufacturers or service providers other than TOs seems a positive element for Article 81(3) purposes. However, this involvement must be open and widely representative in order to avoid competition restrictions to the detriment of excluded manufacturers or service providers. Licensing other manufacturers may be deemed necessary, for the purpose of granting an exemption to these agreements under Article 81(3).

52. (ae) *Agreements foreseeing special treatment for TOs' terminal equipment or other companies' equipment for the interconnection or interoperation of terminal equipment with reserved services and facilities*

53. (af) *Agreements on the exchange of information*

A general exchange of information could indeed be necessary for the good functioning of international telecommunications services, and for cooperation aimed at ensuring interconnectivity or one-stop shopping and billing. It should not be extended to competition-sensitive information, such as certain tariff information which constitutes business secrets, discounting, customers and commercial strategy, including that concerning new products. The exchange of this information would affect the autonomy of each TO's commercial policy and it is not necessary to attain the said objectives.

B. Agreements concerning the provision of non-reserved services and terminal equipment

54. Unlike facilities markets, where only the TOs are the providers, in the services markets the actual or potential competitors are numerous and include, besides the TOs, international private companies, computer companies, publishers and others. Agreements on services and terminal equipment could therefore be concluded between TOs, between TOs and private companies, and between private companies.

55. The liberalizing process has led mostly to strategic agreements between (i) TOs, and (ii) TOs and other companies. These agreements usually take the form of joint ventures.

56. (ba) *Agreements between TOs*

The scope of these agreements, in general, is the provision by each partner of a value-added service including the management of the service. Those agreements are mostly based on the "one-stop shopping" principle, i.e. each partner offers to the customer the entire package of services which he needs. These managed services are called managed data network services (MDNS). An MDNS essentially consists of a broad package of services including facilities, value-added services and management. The agreements may also concern such basic services as satellite uplink.

57. *These agreements could restrict competition in the MDNS market and also in the markets for a service or a group of services included in the MDNS*:

(i) between the participating TOs themselves; and
(ii) *vis-à-vis* other actual or potential third-party providers.

58. (i) *Restrictions of competition between TOs*

Cooperation between TOs could limit the number of potential individual MDNS offered by each participating TO.

The agreements may affect competition at least in certain aspects which are contemplated as specific examples of prohibited practices under Article 81(1)(a) to (c), in the event that:

— they fix or recommend, or at least lead (through the exchange of price information) to coordination of prices charged by each participant to customers,
— they provide for joint specification of MDNS products, quotas, joint delivery, specification of customers' systems; all this would amount to controlling production, markets, technical development and investments,
— they contemplate joint purchase of MDNS hardware and/or software, which would amount to sharing markets or sources of supply.

59. (ii) *Restrictive effects on third party undertakings*

Third parties' market entry could be precluded or hampered if the participating TOs:

— refuse to provide facilities to third party suppliers of services,
— apply usage restrictions only to third parties and not to themselves (e.g. a private provider is precluded from placing multiple customers on a leased line facility to obtain lower unit costs),
— favour their MDNS offerings over those of private suppliers with respect to access, availability, quality and price of leased circuits, maintenance and other services,
— apply especially low rates to their MDNS offerings, cross-subsidizing them with higher rates for monopoly services.

Examples of this could be the restrictions imposed by the TOs on private network operators as to the qualifications of the users, the nature of the messages to be exchanged over the network or the use of international private leased circuits.

60. Finally, as the participating TOs hold, individually or collectively, a dominant position for the creation and the exploitation of the network in each national market, any

restrictive behaviour described in paragraph 59 could amount to an abuse of a dominant position under Article 82 (see V below).

61. On the other hand, agreements between TOs may bring economic benefits which could be taken into account for the possible granting of an exemption under Article 81(3). *Inter alia*, the possible benefits could be as follows:

— a European-wide service and "one-stop shopping" could favour business in Europe. Large multinational undertakings are provided with a European communication service using only a single point of contact,
— the cooperation could lead to a certain amount of European-wide standardization even before further EEC legislation on this matter is adopted,
— the cooperation could bring a cost reduction and consequently cheaper offerings to the advantage of consumers,
— a general improvement of public infrastructure could arise from a joint service provision.

62. Only by notification of the cases in question, in accordance with the appropriate procedures under Regulation No 17, will the Commission be able, where requested, to ascertain, on the merits, whether these benefits outweigh the competition restrictions. But in any event, restrictions on access for third parties seem likely to be considered as not indispensable and to lead to the elimination of competition for a substantial part of the products and services concerned within the meaning of Article 81(3), thus excluding the possibility of an exemption. Moreover, if an MDNS agreement strengthens appreciably a dominant position which a participating TO holds in the market for a service included in the MDNS, this is also likely to lead to a rejection of the exemption.

63. The Commission has outlined the conditions for exempting such forms of cooperation in a case concerning a proposed joint venture between 22 TOs for the provision of a Europe-wide MDNS, later abandoned for commercial reasons,[22] The Commission considered that the MDNS project presented the risks of restriction of competition between the operators themselves and private service suppliers but it accepted that the project also offered economic benefits to telecommunications users such as access to Europe-wide services through a single operator. Such cooperation could also have accelerated European standardization, reduced costs and increased the quality of the services. The Commission had informed the participants that approval of the project would have to be subject to guarantees designed to prevent undue restriction of competition in the telecommunications services markets, such as discrimination against private services suppliers and cross-subsidization. Such guarantees would be essential conditions for the granting of an exemption under the competition rules to cooperation agreements involving TOs. The requirement for an appropriate guarantee of non-discrimination and non-cross-subsidization will be specified in individual cases according to the examples of discrimination indicated in Section V below concerning the application of Article 82.

64. (bb) *Agreements between TOs and other service providers*
Cooperation between TOs and other operators is increasing in telecommunications services. It frequently takes the form of a joint venture. The Commission recognizes that it may have beneficial effects. However, this cooperation may also adversely affect competition and the opening up of services markets. Beneficial and harmful effects must therefore be carefully weighed.

65. Such agreements may restrict competition for the provision of telecommunications services:

(i) between the partners; and
(ii) from third parties.

66. (i) Competition between the partners may be restricted when these are actual or potential competitors for the relevant telecommunications service. This is generally the

---

[22] Commission press release IP(89) 948 of 14.12.1989.

case, even when only the other partners and not the TOs are already providing the service. Indeed, TOs may have the required financial capacity, technical and commercial skills to enter the market for non-reserved services and could reasonably bear the technical and financial risk of doing it. This is also generally the case as far as private operators are concerned, when they do not yet provide the service in the geographical market covered by the cooperation, but do provide this service elsewhere. They may therefore be potential competitors in this geographic market.

67. (ii) The cooperation may restrict competition from third parties because:

— there is an appreciable risk that the participant TO, i.e. the dominant network provider, will give more favourable network access to its cooperation partners than to other service providers in competition with the partners,

— potential competitors may refrain from entering the market because of this objective risk or, in any event, because of the presence on the market-place of a cooperation involving the monopolist for the network provision. This is especially the case when market entry barriers are high: the market structure allows only few suppliers and the size and the market power of the partners are considerable.

68. On the other hand, the cooperation may bring economic benefits which outweigh its harmful effect and therefore justify the granting of an exemption under Article 81(3). The economic benefits can consist, *inter alia*, of the rationalization of the production and distribution of telecommunication services, in improvements in existing services or development of new services, or transfer of technology which improves the efficiency and the competitiveness of the European industrial structures.

69. In the absence of such economic benefits a complementarity between partners, i.e. between the provision of a reserved activity and that of a service under competition, is not a benefit as such. Considering it as a benefit would be equal to justifying an involvement through restrictive agreements of TOs in any non-reserved service provision. This would be to hinder a competitive structure in this market.

In certain cases, the cooperation could consolidate or extend the dominant position of the TOs concerned to a non-reserved services market, in violation of Article 82.

70. The imposition or the proposal of cooperation with the service provider as a condition for the provision of the network may be deemed abusive (see paragraph 98(vi)).

71. (bc) *Agreements between service providers other than TOs*

The Commission will apply the same principles indicated in (ba) and (bb) above also to agreements between private service providers, *inter alia*, agreements providing quotas, price fixing, market and/or customer allocation. In principle, they are unlikely to qualify for an exemption. The Commission will be particularly vigilant in order to avoid cooperation on services leading to a strengthening of dominant positions of the partners or restricting competition from third parties. There is a danger of this occurring for example when an undertaking is dominant with regard to the network architecture and its proprietary standard is adopted to support the service contemplated by the cooperation. This architecture enabling interconnection between computer systems of the partners could attract some partners to the dominant partner. The dominant position for the network architecture will be strengthened and Article 82 may apply.

72. In any exemption of agreements between TOs and other services and/or equipment providers, or between these providers, the Commission will require from the partners appropriate guarantees of non-cross-subsidization and non-discrimination. The risk of cross-subsidization and discrimination is higher when the TOs or the other partners provide both services and equipment, whether within or outside the Community.

C. Agreements on research and development (R&D)

73. As in other high technology based sectors, R&D in telecommunications is essential for keeping pace with technological progress and being competitive on the market-place

to the benefit of users. R&D requires more and more important financial, technical and human resources which only few undertakings can generate individually. Cooperation is therefore crucial for attaining the above objectives.

74. The Commission has adopted a Regulation for the block exemption under Article 81(3) of R&D agreements in all sectors, including telecommunications.[23]

75. Agreements which are not covered by this Regulation (or the other Commission block exemption Regulations) could still obtain an individual exemption from the Commission if Article 81(3) requirements are met individually. However, not in all cases do the economic benefits of an R&D agreement outweigh its competition restrictions. In telecommunications, one major asset, enabling access to new markets, is the launch of new products or services. Competition is based not only on price, but also on technology. R&D agreements could constitute the means for powerful undertakings with high market shares to avoid or limit competition from more innovative rivals. The risk of excessive restrictions of competition increases when the cooperation is extended from R&D to manufacturing and even more to distribution.

76. The importance which the Commission attaches to R&D and innovation is demonstrated by the fact that it has launched several programmes for this purpose. The joint companies' activities which may result from these programmes are not automatically cleared or exempted as such in all aspects from the application of the competition rules. However, most of those joint activities may be covered by the Commission's block exemption Regulations. If not, the joint activities in question may be exempted, where required, in accordance with the appropriate criteria and procedures.

77. In the Commission's experience joint distribution linked to joint R&D which is not covered by the Regulation on R&D does not play the crucial role in the exploitation of the results of R&D. Nevertheless, in individual cases, provided that a competitive environment is maintained, the Commission is prepared to consider full-range cooperation even between large firms. This should lead to improving the structure of European industry and thus enable it to meet strong competition in the world market place.

V. APPLICATION OF ARTICLE 82

78. Article 82 applies when:

(i) the undertaking concerned holds an individual or a joint dominant position;
(ii) it commits an abuse of that dominant position; and
(iii) the abuse may affect trade between Member States.

Dominant position

79. In each national market the TOs hold individually or collectively a dominant position for the creation and the exploitation of the network, since they are protected by exclusive or special rights granted by the State. Moreover, the TOs hold a dominant position for some telecommunications services, in so far as they hold exclusive or special rights with respect to those services.[24]

---

[23] Regulation (EEC) No 418/85, OJ 1985 L53/5.
[24] Commission Decision 82/861/EEC in the *"British Telecommunications"* case, point 26, OJ 1982 L360/36, confirmed in the Judgment of 20.3.1985 in Case 41/83, *Italian Republic v. Commission* [1985] ECR 873, generally known as *"British Telecom"*.

80. The TOs may also hold dominant positions on the markets for certain equipment or services, even though they no longer hold any exclusive rights on those markets. After the elimination of these rights, they may have kept very important market shares in this sector. When the market share in itself does not suffice to give the TOs a dominant position, it could do it in combination with the other factors such as the monopoly for the network or other related services and a powerful and wide distribution network. As to the equipment, for example terminal equipment, even if the TOs are not involved in the equipment manufacturing or in the services provision, they may hold a dominant position in the market as distributors.

81. Also, firms other than TOs may hold individual or collective dominant positions in markets where there are no exclusive rights. This may be the case especially for certain non-reserved services because of either the market shares alone of those undertakings, or because of a combination of several factors. Among these factors, in addition to the market shares, two of particular importance are the technological advance and the holding of the information concerning access protocols or interfaces necessary to ensure inter-operability of software and hardware. When this information is covered by intellectual property rights this is a further factor of dominance.

82. Finally, the TOs hold, individually or collectively, dominant positions in the demand for some telecommunication equipment, works or software services. Being dominant for the network and other services provisions they may account for a purchaser's share high enough to give them dominance as to the demand, i.e. making suppliers dependent on them. Dependence could exist when the supplier cannot sell to other customers a substantial part of its production or change a production. In certain national markets, for example in large switching equipment, big purchasers such as the TOs face big suppliers. In this situation, it should be weighed up case by case whether the supplier or the customer position will prevail on the other to such an extent as to be considered dominant under Article 82.

With the liberalization of services and the expansion of new forces on the services markets, dominant positions of undertakings other than the TOs may arise for the purchasing of equipment.

Abuse

83. The Commission's activity may concern mainly the following broad areas of abuses:

A. *TOs' abuses:* in particular, they may take advantage of their monopoly or at least dominant position to acquire a foothold or to extend their power in non-reserved neighbouring markets, to the detriment of competitors and customers.

B. *Abuses by undertaking other than TOs:* these may take advantage of the fundamental information they hold, whether or not covered by intellectual property rights, with the object and/or effect of restricting competition.

C. *Abuses of a dominant purchasing position:* for the time being this concerns mainly the TOs, especially to the extent that they hold a dominant position for reserved activities in the national market. However, it may also increasingly concern other undertakings which have entered the market.

A. *TOs' Abuses*

84. The Commission has recognized in the Green Paper the central role of the TOs, which justifies the maintenance of certain monopolies to enable them to perform their public task. This public task consists in the provision and exploitation of a universal network or, where appropriate, universal service, i.e. one having general coverage and available to all users (including service providers and the TOs themselves) upon request on reasonable and non-discriminatory conditions.

This fundamental obligation could justify the benefit of the exception provided in Article 86(2) under certain circumstances, as laid down in the Services Directive.

85. In most cases, however, the competition rules, far from obstructing the fulfilment of this obligation, contribute to ensuring it. In particular, Article 82 can apply to behaviour of dominant undertakings resulting in a refusal to supply, discrimination, restrictive tying clauses, unfair prices or other inequitable conditions.

If one of these types of behaviour occurs in the provision of one of the monopoly services, the fundamental obligation indicated above is not performed. This could be the case when a TO tries to take advantage of its monopoly for certain services (for instance: network provision) in order to limit the competition they have to face in respect of non-reserved services, which in turn are supported by those monopoly services.

It is not necessary for the purpose of the application of Article 82 that competition be restricted as to a service which is supported by the monopoly provision in question. It would suffice that the behaviour results in an appreciable restriction of competition in whatever way. This means that an abuse may occur when the company affected by the behaviour is not a service provider but an end user who could himself be disadvantaged in competition in the course of his own business.

86. The Court of Justice has set out this fundamental principle of competition in telecommunications in one of its judgments.[25] An abuse within the meaning of Article 82 is committed where, without any objective necessity, an undertaking holding a dominant position on a particular market reserves to itself or to an undertaking belonging to the same group an ancillary activity which might be carried out by another undertaking as part of its activities on a neighbouring but separate market, with the possibility of eliminating all competition from such undertaking.

The Commission believes that this principle applies, not only when a dominant undertaking monopolizes other markets, but also when by anti-competitive means it extends its activity to other markets.

Hampering the provision of non-reserved services could limit production, markets and above all the technical progress which is a key factor of telecommunications. The Commission has already shown these adverse effects of usage restrictions on monopoly provision in its decision in the "*British Telecom*" case.[26] In this Decision it was found that the restrictions imposed by British Telecom on telex and telephone networks usage, namely on the transmission of international messages on behalf of third parties:

(i) limited the activity of economic operators to the detriment of technological progress;
(ii) discriminated against these operators, thereby placing them at a competitive disadvantage *vis-à-vis* TOs not bound by these restrictions; and
(iii) made the conclusion of the contracts for the supply of telex circuits subject to acceptance by the other parties of supplementary obligations which had no connection with such contracts. These were considered abuses of a dominant position identified respectively in Article 82(b), (c) and (d).

This could be done:

(a) as above, by refusing or restricting the usage of the service provided under monopoly so as to limit the provision of non-reserved services by third parties; or
(b) by predatory behaviour, as a result of cross-subsidization.

---

[25] Case 311/84, *Centre belge d'études de marché Télémarketing (CBEM) SA v. Compagnie luxembourgeoise de télédiffusion SA and Information Publicité Benelux SA*, 3 October 1985 [1985] ECR 3261, Grounds 26 and 27.
[26] See note 24.

87. The separation of the TOs' regulatory power from their business activity is a crucial matter in the context of the application of Article 82. This separation is provided in the Article 86 Directives on terminals and on services mentioned in Note 2 above.

(a) Usage restrictions

88. Usage restrictions on provisions of reserved services are likely to correspond to the specific examples of abuses indicated in Article 82. In particular:

— they may limit the provision of telecommunications services in free competition, the investments and the technical progress, to the prejudice of telecommunications consumers (Article 82(b)),
— to the extent that these usage restrictions are not applied to all users, including the TOs themselves as users, they may result in discrimination against certain users, placing them at a competitive disadvantage (Article 82(c)),
— they may make the usage of the reserved services subject to the acceptance of obligations which have no connection with this usage (Article 82(d)).

89. The usage restrictions in question mainly concern public networks (public switched telephone network (PSTN) or public switched data networks (PSDN)) and especially leased circuits. They may also concern other provisions such as satellite uplink, and mobile communication networks. The most frequent types of behaviour are as follows:

(i) *Prohibition imposed by TOs on third parties:*

(*a*) *to connect private leased circuits by means of concentrator, multiplexer or other equipment to the public switched network; and/or*
(*b*) *to use private leased circuits for providing services, to the extent that these services are not reserved, but under competition.*

90. To the extent that the user is granted a licence by State regulatory authorities under national law in compliance with EEC law, these prohibitions limit the user's freedom of access to the leased circuits, the provision of which is a public service. Moreover, it discriminates between users, depending upon the usage (Article 82(c)). This is one of the most serious restrictions and could substantially hinder the development of international telecommunications services (Article 82(b)).

91. When the usage restriction limits the provision of non-reserved service in competition with that provided by the TO itself the abuse is even more serious and the principles of the abovementioned *"Télémarketing"* judgment (Note 23 *supra*) apply.

92. In individual cases, the Commission will assess whether the service provided on the leased circuit is reserved or not, on the basis of the Community regulatory acts interpreted in the technical and economic context of each case. Even though a service could be considered reserved according to the law, the fact that a TO actually prohibits the usage of the leased circuit only to some users and not to others could constitute a discrimination under Article 82(c).

93. The Commission has taken action in respect of the Belgian Régie des télégraphes et téléphones after receiving a complaint concerning an alleged abuse of dominant position from a private supplier of value-added telecommunications services relating to the conditions under which telecommunications circuits were being leased. Following discussions with the Commission, the RTT authorized the private supplier concerned to use the leased telecommunications circuits subject to no restrictions other than that they should not be used for the simple transport of data.

Moreover, pending the possible adoption of new rules in Belgium, and without prejudice to any such rules, the RTT undertook that all its existing and potential clients for leased telecommunications circuits to which third parties may have access shall be governed by the same conditions as those which were agreed with the private sector supplier mentioned above.[27]

(ii) Refusal by TOs to provide reserved services (in particular the network and leased circuits) to third parties

94. Refusal to supply has been considered an abuse by the Commission and the Court of Justice.[28] This behaviour would make it impossible or at least appreciably difficult for third parties to provide non-reserved services. This, in turn, would lead to a limitation of services and of technical development (Article 82(b)) and, if applied only to some users, result in discrimination (Article 82(c)).

(iii) Imposition of extra charges or other special conditions for certain usages of reserved services

95. An example would be the imposition of access charges to leased circuits when they are connected to the public switched network or other special prices and charges for service provision to third parties. Such access charges may discriminate between users of the same service (leased circuits provision) depending upon the usage and result in imposing unfair trading conditions. This will limit the usage of leased circuits and finally non-reserved service provision. Conversely, it does not constitute an abuse provided that it is shown, in each specific case, that the access charges correspond to costs which are entailed directly for the TOs for the access in question. In this case, access charges can be imposed only on an equal basis to all users, including TOs themselves.

96. Apart from these possible additional costs which should be covered by an extra charge, the interconnection of a leased circuit to the public switched network is already remunerated by the price related to the use of this network. Certainly, a leased circuit can represent a subjective value for a user depending on the profitability of the enhanced service to be provided on that leased circuit. However, this cannot be a criterion on which a dominant undertaking, and above all a public service provider, can base the price of this public service.

97. The Commission appreciates that the substantial difference between leased circuits and the public switched network causes a problem of obtaining the necessary revenues to cover the costs of the switched network. However, the remedy chosen must not be contrary to law, i.e. the EEC Treaty, as discriminatory pricing between customers would be.

(iv) Discriminatory price or quality of the service provided

98. This behaviour may relate, *inter alia*, to tariffs or to restrictions or delays in connection to the public switched network or leased circuits provision, in installation, maintenance and repair, in effecting interconnection of systems or in providing information concerning network planning, signalling protocols, technical standards and all other information necessary for an appropriate interconnection and interoperation with the reserved service and which may affect the interworking of competitive services or terminal equipment offerings.

---

[27] Commission Press release IP(90) 67 of 29.1.1990.
[28] Cases 6 and 7/73 *Commercial Solvents v. Commission* [1974] ECR 223; *United Brands v. Commission* (Note 15, above).

(v) Tying the provision of the reserved service to the supply by the TOs or others of terminal equipment to be interconnected or interoperated, in particular through imposition, pressure, offer of special prices or other trading conditions for the reserved service linked to the equipment

(vi) Tying the provision of the reserved service to the agreement of the user to enter into cooperation with the reserved service provider himself as to the non-reserved service to be carried on the network

(vii) Reserving to itself for the purpose of non-reserved service provision or to other service providers information obtained in the exercise of a reserved service in particular information concerning users of a reserved services providers more favourable conditions for the supply of this information

This latter information could be important for the provision of services under competition to the extent that it permits the targeting of customers of those services and the definition of business strategy. The behaviour indicated above could result in a discrimination against undertakings to which the use of this information is denied in violation of Article 82(c). The information in question can only be disclosed with the agreement of the users concerned and in accordance with relevant data protection legislation (see the proposal for a Council Directive concerning the protection of personal data and privacy in the context of public digital telecommunications networks, in particular the integrated services digital network (ISDN) and public digital mobile networks).[29]

(viii) Imposition of unneeded reserved services by supplying reserved and/or non-reserved services when the former reserved services are reasonably separable from the others

99. The practices under (v) (vi) (vii) and (viii) result in applying conditions which have no connection with the reserved service, contravening Article 82(d).

100. Most of these practices were in fact identified in the Services Directive as restrictions on the provision of services within the meaning of Article 49 and Article 82 of the Treaty brought about by State measures. They are therefore covered by the broader concept of "restrictions" which under Article 6 of the Directive have to be removed by Member States.

101. The Commission believes that the Directives on terminals and on services also clarify some principles of application of Articles 81 and 82 in the sector.

The Services Directive does not apply to important sectors such as mobile communications and satellites; however, competition rules apply fully to these sectors. Moreover, as to the services covered by the Directive it will depend very much on the degree of precision of the licences given by the regulatory body whether the TOs still have a discretionary margin for imposing conditions which should be scrutinized under competition rules. Not all the conditions can be regulated in licences: consequently, there could be room for discretionary action. The application of competition rules to companies will therefore depend very much on a case-by-case examination of the licences. Nothing more than a class licence can be required for terminals.

(b) Cross-subsidization

102. Cross-subsidization means that an undertaking allocates all or part of the costs of its activity in one product or geographic market to its activity in another product or

---

[29] Commission document COM(90) 314 of 13.9.1990.

geographic market. Under certain circumstances, cross-subsidization in telecommunications could distort competition, i.e. lead to beating other competitors with offers which are made possible not by efficiency and performance but by artificial means such as subsidies. Avoiding cross-subsidization leading to unfair competition is crucial for the development of service provision and equipment supply.

103. Cross-subsidization does not lead to predatory pricing and does not restrict competition when it is the costs of reserved activities which are subsidized by the revenue generated by other reserved activities since there is no competition possible as to these activities. This form of subsidization is even necessary, as it enables the TOs holders of exclusive rights to perform their obligation to provide a public service universally and on the same conditions to everybody. For instance, telephone provision in unprofitable rural areas is subsidized through revenues from telephone provision in profitable urban areas or long-distance calls. The same could be said of subsidizing the provision of reserved services through revenues generated by activities under competition. The application of the general principle of cost-orientation should be the ultimate goal, in order, *inter alia*, to ensure that prices are not inequitable as between users.

104. Subsidizing activities under competition, whether concerning services or equipment, by allocating their costs to monopoly activities, however, is likely to distort competition in violation of Article 82. It could amount to an abuse by an undertaking holding a dominant position within the Community. Moreover, users of activities under monopoly have to bear unrelated costs for the provision of these activities. Cross-subsidization can also exist between monopoly provision and equipment manufacturing and sale. Cross-subsidization can be carried out through:

— funding the operation of the activities in question with capital remunerated substantially below the market rate;
— providing for those activities premises, equipment, experts and/or services with a remuneration substantially lower than the market price.

105. As to funding through monopoly revenues or making available monopoly material and intellectual means for the starting up of new activities under competition, this constitutes an investment whose costs should be allocated to the new activity. Offering the new product or service should normally include a reasonable remuneration of such investment in the long run. If it does not, the Commission will assess the case on the basis of the remuneration plans of the undertaking concerned and of the economic context.

106. Transparency in the TOs' accounting should enable the Commission to ascertain whether there is cross-subsidization in the cases in which this question arises. The ONP Directive provides in this respect for the definition of harmonized tariff principles which should lessen the number of these cases.

This transparency can be provided by an accounting system which ensures the fully proportionate distribution of all costs between reserved and non-reserved activities. Proper allocation of costs is more easily ensured in cases of structural separation, i.e. creating distinct entities for running each of these two categories of activities.

An appropriate accounting system approach should permit the identification and allocation of all costs between the activities which they support. In this system all products and services should bear proportionally all the relevant costs, including costs of research and development, facilities and overheads. It should enable the production of recorded figures which can be verified by accountants.

107. As indicated above (paragraph 59), in cases of cooperation agreements involving TOs a guarantee of no cross-subsidization is one of the conditions required by the Commission for exemption under Article 81(3). In order to monitor properly compliance with that guarantee, the Commission now envisages requesting the parties to ensure an appropriate accounting system as described above, the accounts being regularly submitted to the Commission. Where the accounting method is chosen, the Commission will reserve the possibility of submitting the accounts to independent audit, especially if any doubt arises as to the capability of the system to ensure the necessary transparency or to detect

any cross-subsidization. If the guarantee cannot be properly monitored, the Commission may withdraw the exemption.

108. In all other cases, the Commission does not envisage requiring such transparency of the TOs. However, if in a specific case there are substantial elements converging in indicating the existence of an abusive cross-subsidization and/or predatory pricing, the Commission could establish a presumption of such cross-subsidization and predatory pricing. An appropriate separate accounting system could be important in order to counter this presumption.

109. Cross-subsidization of a reserved activity by a non-reserved one does not in principle restrict competition. However, the application of the exception provided in Article 86(2) to this non-reserved activity could not as a rule be justified by the fact that the financial viability of the TO in question rests on the non-reserved activity. Its financial viability and the performance of its task of general economic interest can only be ensured by the State where appropriate by the granting of an exclusive or special right and by imposing restrictions on activities competing with the reserved ones.

110. Also cross-subsidization by a public or private operator outside the EEC may be deemed abusive in terms of Article 82 if that operator holds a dominant position for equipment or non-reserved services within the EEC. The existence of this dominant position, which allows the holder to behave to an appreciable extent independently of its competitors and customers and ultimately of consumers, will be assessed in the light of all elements in the EEC and outside.

B. *Abuses by undertakings other than the TOs*

111. Further to the liberalization of services, undertakings other than the TOs may increasingly extend their power to acquire dominant positions in non-reserved markets. They may already hold such a position in some services markets which had not been reserved. When they take advantage of their dominant position to restrict competition and to extend their power, Article 82 may also apply to them. The abuses in which they might indulge are broadly similar to most of those previously described in relation to the TOs.

112. Infringements of Article 82 may be committed by the abusive exercise of industrial property rights in relation with standards, which are of crucial importance for telecommunications. Standards may be either the results of international standardization, or *de facto* standards and the property of undertakings.

113. Producers of equipment or suppliers of services are dependent on proprietary standards to ensure the interconnectivity of their computer resources. An undertaking which owns a dominant network architecture may abuse its dominant position by refusing to provide the necessary information for the interconnection of other architecture resources to its architecture products. Other possible abuses—similar to those indicated as to the TOs—are, *inter alia*, delays in providing the information, discrimination in the quality of the information, discriminatory pricing or other trading conditions, and making the information provision subject to the acceptance by the producer, supplier or user of unfair trading conditions.

114. On 1 August 1984, the Commission accepted a unilateral undertaking from IBM to provide other manufacturers with the technical interface information needed to permit competitive products to be used with IBM's then most powerful range of computers, the System/370. The Commission thereupon suspended the proceedings under Article 82 which it had initiated against IBM in December 1980. The IBM Undertaking[30] also contains a commitment relating to SNA formats and protocols.

115. The question how to reconcile copyrights on standards with the competition requirements is particularly difficult. In any event, copyright cannot be used unduly to restrict competition.

---

[30] Reproduced in full in EC Bulletin 10–1984 (point 3.4.1). As to its continued application, see Commission press release No IP(88) 814 of 15 December 1988.

C. *Abuses of dominant purchasing position*

116. Article 82 also applies to behaviour of undertakings holding a dominant purchasing position. The examples of abuses indicated in that Article may therefore also concern that behaviour.

117. The Council Directive 90/531/EEC[31] based on Articles 54(2), 55, 95 and 133 of the EEC Treaty on the procurement procedures of entities operating in *inter alia* the telecommunications sector regulates essentially:

(i) procurement procedures in order to ensure on a reciprocal basis non-discrimination on the basis of nationality; and
(ii) for products or services for use in reserved markets, not in competitive markets. That Directive, which is addressed to States, does not exclude the application of Article 82 to the purchasing of products within the scope of the Directive. The Commission will decide case by case how to ensure that these different sets of rules are applied in a coherent manner.

118. Furthermore, both in reserved and competitive markets, practices other than those covered by the Directive may be established in violation of Article 82. One example is taking advantage of a dominant purchasing position for imposing excessively favourable prices or other trading conditions, in comparison with other purchasers and suppliers (Article 82(a)). This could result in discrimination under Article 82(c). Also obtaining, whether or not through imposition, an exclusive distributorship for the purchased product by the dominant purchaser may constitute an abusive extension of its economic power to other markets (see *"Télémarketing"* Court judgment (Note 23 *supra*)).

119. Another abusive practice could be that of making the purchase subject to licensing by the supplier of standards for the product to be purchased or for other products, to the purchaser itself, or to other suppliers (Article 82(d)).

120. Moreover, even in competitive markets, discriminatory procedures on the basis of nationality may exist, because national pressures and traditional links of a non-economic nature do not always disappear quickly after the liberalization of the markets. In this case, a systematic exclusion or considerably unfavourable treatment of a supplier, without economic necessity, could be examined under Article 82, especially (b) (limitation of outlets) and (c) (discrimination). In assessing the case, the Commission will substantially examine whether the same criteria for awarding the contract have been followed by the dominant undertaking for all suppliers. The Commission will normally take into account criteria similar to those indicated in Article 27(1) of the Directive.[32] The purchases in question being outside the scope of the Directive, the Commission will not require that transparent purchasing procedures be pursued.

D. *Effect on trade between Member States*

121. The same principle outlined regarding Article 81 applies here. Moreover, in certain circumstances, such as the case of the elimination of a competitor by an undertaking holding a dominant position, although trade between Member States is not directly affected, for the purposes of Article 82 it is sufficient to show that there will be repercussions on the competitive structure of the common market.

---

[31] OJ 1990 L297/1.

[32] (See Note 26) Article 27(1)(a) and (b). The criteria on which the contracting entities shall base the award of the contracts shall be: (a) the most economically advantageous tender involving various criteria such as delivery date, period for completion, running costs, cost-effectiveness, quality, aesthetic and functional characteristics, technical merit, after-sales services and technical assistance, commitments with regard to spare parts, security of supplies and price; or (b) the lowest price only.

VI. Application of Articles 81 and 82 in the Field of Satellites

122. The development of this sector is addressed globally by the Commission in the "Green Paper on a common approach in the field of satellite communications in the European Community" of 20 November 1990 (Doc. COM(90) 490 final). Due to the increasing importance of satellites and the particular uncertainty among undertakings as to the application of competition rules to individual cases in this sector, it is appropriate to address the sector in a distinct section in these guidelines.

123. State regulations on satellites are not covered by the Commission Directives under Article 86 of the EEC Treaty respectively on terminals and services mentioned above except in the Directive on terminals which contemplates receive-only satellite stations not connected to a public network. The Commission's position on the regulatory framework compatible with the Treaty competition rules is stated in the Commission Green Paper on satellites mentioned above.

124. In any event the Treaty competition rules fully apply to the satellites domain, *inter alia*, Articles 81 and 82 to undertakings. Below is indicated how the principles set out above, in particular in Sections IV and V, apply to satellites.

125. Agreements between European TOs in particular within international conventions may play an important role in providing European satellites systems and a harmonious development of satellite services throughout the Community. These benefits are taken into consideration under competition rules, provided that the agreements do not contain restrictions which are not indispensable for the attainment of these objectives.

126. Agreements between TOs concerning the operation of satellite systems in the broadest sense may be caught by Article 81. As to space segment capacity, the TOs are each other's competitors, whether actual or potential. In pooling together totally or partially their supplies of space segment capacity they may restrict competition between themselves. Moreover, they are likely to restrict competition *vis-à-vis* third parties to the extent that their agreements contain provisions with this object or effect: for instance provisions limiting their supplies in quality and/or quantity, or restricting their business autonomy by imposing directly or indirectly a coordination between these third parties and the parties to the agreements. It should be examined whether such agreements could qualify for an exemption under Article 81(3) provided that they are notified. However, restrictions on third parties' ability to compete are likely to preclude such an exemption. It should also be examined whether such agreements strengthen any individual or collective dominant position of the parties, which also would exclude the granting of an exemption. This could be the case in particular if the agreement provides that the parties are exclusive distributors of the space segment capacity provided by the agreement.

127. Such agreements between TOs could also restrict competition as to the uplink with respect to which TOs are competitors. In certain cases the customer for satellite communication has the choice between providers in several countries, and his choice will be substantially determined by the quality, price and other sales conditions of each provider. This choice will be even ampler since uplink is being progressively liberalized and to the extent that the application of EEC rules to State legislations will open up the uplink markets. Community-wide agreements providing directly or indirectly for coordination as to the parties' uplink provision are therefore caught by Article 81.

128. Agreements between TOs and private operators on space segment capacity may be also caught by Article 81, as that provision applies, *inter alia*, to cooperation, and in particular joint venture agreements. These agreements could be exempted if they bring specific benefits such as technology transfer, improvement of the quality of the service or enabling better marketing, especially for a new capacity, outweighing the restrictions. In any event, imposing on customers the bundled uplink and space segment capacity provision is likely to exclude an exemption since it limits competition in uplink provision to the detriment of the customer's choice, and in the current market situation will almost certainly strengthen the TOs' dominant position in violation of Article 82. An exemption is unlikely to be granted also when the agreement has the effect of reducing substantially

the supply in an oligopolistic market, and even more clearly when an effect of the agreement is to prevent the only potential competitor of a dominant provider in a given market from offering its services independently. This could amount to a violation of Article 82. Direct or indirect imposition of any kind of agreement by a TO, for instance by making the uplink subject to the conclusion of an agreement with a third party, would constitute an infringement of Article 82.

VII. RESTRUCTURING IN TELECOMMUNICATIONS

129. Deregulation, the objective of a single market for 1992 and the fundamental changes in the telecommunications technology have caused wide strategic restructuring in Europe and throughout the world as well. They have mostly taken the form of mergers and joint ventures.

(a) Mergers

130. In assessing telecom mergers in the framework of Council Regulation (EEC) No 4064/89 on the control of concentrations between undertakings[33] the Commission will take into account, *inter alia*, the following elements.

131. Restructuring moves are in general beneficial to the European telecommunications industry. They may enable the companies to rationalize and to reach the critical mass necessary to obtain the economies of scale needed to make the important investments in research and development. These are necessary to develop new technologies and to remain competitive in the world market.

However, in certain cases they may also lead to the anti-competitive creation or strengthening of dominant positions.

132. The economic benefits resulting from critical mass must be demonstrated. The concentration operation could result in a mere aggregation of market shares, unaccompanied by restructuring measures or plans. This operation may create or strengthen Community or national dominant positions in a way which impedes competition.

133. When concentration operations have this sole effect, they can hardly be justified by the objective of increasing the competitivity of Community industry in the world market. This objective, strongly pursued by the Commission, rather requires competition in EEC domestic markets in order that the EEC undertakings acquire the competitive structure and attitude needed to operate in the world market.

134. In assessing concentration cases in telecommunications, the Commission will be particularly vigilant to avoid the strengthening of dominant positions through integration. If dominant service providers are allowed to integrate into the equipment market by way of mergers, access to this market by other equipment suppliers may be seriously hindered. A dominant service provider is likely to give preferential treatment to its own equipment subsidiary.

Moreover, the possibility of disclosure by the service provider to its subsidiary of sensitive information obtained from competing equipment manufacturers can put the latter at a competitive disadvantage.

The Commission will examine case by case whether vertical integration has such effects or rather is likely to reinforce the competitive structure in the Community.

135. The Commission has enforced principles on restructuring in a case concerning the GEC and Siemens joint bid for Plessey.[34]

---

[33] OJ 1989 L395/1; Corrigendum OJ No 1990 L257/13.
[34] Commission Decision rejecting Plessey's complaint against the GEC-Siemens bid (Case IV/33.018 *GEC-Siemens/Plessey*), OJ 1990 C239/2.

136. Article 81(1) applies to the acquisition by an undertaking of a minority share-holding in a competitor where, *inter alia*, the arrangements involve the creation of a structure of cooperation between the investor and the other undertakings, which will influence these undertakings' competitive conduct.[35]

(b) Joint ventures

137. A joint venture can be of a cooperative or a concentrative nature. It is of a cooperative nature when it has as its object or effect the coordination of the competitive behaviour of undertakings which remain independent. The principles governing cooperative joint ventures are to be set out in Commission guidelines to that effect. Concentrative joint ventures fall under Regulation (EEC) No 4064/89.[36]

138. In some of the latest joint venture cases the Commission granted an exemption under Article 81(3) on grounds which are particularly relevant to telecommunications. Precisely in a decision concerning telecommunications, the *"Optical Fibres"* case,[37] the Commission considered that the joint venture enabled European companies to produce a high technology product, promoted technical progress, and facilitated technology transfer. Therefore, the joint venture permits European companies to withstand competition from non-Community producers, especially in the USA and Japan, in an area of fast-moving technology characterized by international markets. The Commission confirmed this approach in the *"Canon-Olivetti"* case.[38]

VIII. Impact of the International Conventions on the Application of EEC Competition Rules to Telecommunications

139. International conventions (such as the Convention of International Telecommunication Union (ITU) or Conventions on Satellites) play a fundamental role in ensuring worldwide cooperation for the provision of international services. However, application of such international conventions on telecommunications by EEC Member States must not affect compliance with the EEC law, in particular with competition rules.

140. Article 307 of the EEC Treaty regulates this matter.[39] The relevant obligations provided in the various conventions or related Acts do not pre-date the entry into force of the Treaty. As to the ITU and World Administrative Telegraph and Telephone Conference (WATTC), whenever a revision or a new adoption of the ITU Convention or of the WATTC Regulations occurs, the ITU or WATTC members recover their freedom of action. The Satellites Conventions were adopted much later.

Moreover, as to all conventions, the application of EEC rules does not seem to affect the fulfilment of obligations of Member States *vis-à-vis* third countries. Article 307 does not protect obligations between EEC Member States entered into in international treaties. The purpose of Article 307 is to protect the right of third countries only and it is not intended to crystallize the acquired international treaty rights of Member States to the detriment of the EEC Treaty's objectives or of the Community interest. Finally, even if

---

[35] *British American Tobacco Company Ltd and RJ Reynolds Industries Inc. v. Commission* (Joined Cases 142 and 156/84) of 17.11.1987 [1987] ECR 4487.

[36] OJ 1990 C203/10.

[37] Decision 86/405/EEC, OJ 1986 L236/30.

[38] Decision 88/88/EEC, OJ 1988 L52/51.

[39] "The rights and obligations arising from agreements concluded before the entry into force of this Treaty between one or more Member States on the one hand and one or more third countries on the other, shall not be affected by the provisions of this Treaty. To the extent that such agreements are not compatible with this Treaty, the Member State or States concerned shall take all appropriate steps to eliminate the incompatibilities established. Member States shall, where necessary, assist each other to this end and shall, where appropriate, adopt a common attitude ... "

Article 307(1) did apply, the Member States concerned would nevertheless be obliged to take all appropriate steps to eliminate incompatibility between their obligations *vis-à-vis* third countries and the EEC rules. This applies in particular where Member States acting collectively have the statutory possibility to modify the international convention in question as required, e.g. in the case of the Eutelsat Convention.

141. As to the WATTC Regulations, the relevant provisions of the Regulations in force from 9 December 1988 are flexible enough to give the parties the choice whether or not to implement them or how to implement them.

In any event, EEC Member States, by signing the Regulations, have made a joint declaration that they will apply them in accordance with their obligations under the EEC Treaty.

142. As to the International Telegraph and Telephone Consultative Committee (CCITT) recommendations, competition rules apply to them.

143. Members of the CCITT are, pursuant to Article 11(2) of the International Tele-communications Convention, "administrations" of the Members of the ITU and recognized private operating agencies ("RPOAs") which so request with the approval of the ITU members which have recognized them. Unlike the members of the ITU or the Administrative Conferences which are States, the members of the CCITT are tele-communications administrations and RPOAs. Telecommunications administrations are defined in Annex 2 to the International Telecommunications Conventions as "tout service ou département gouvernemental responsable des mesures à prendre pour exécuter les obligations de la Convention Internationale des télécommunications et des règlements" [any government service or department responsible for the measures to be taken to fulfil the obligations laid down in the International Convention on Telecommunications and Regulations]. The CCITT meetings are in fact attended by TOs. Article 11(2) of the International Telecommunications Convention clearly provides that telecommunications administrations and RPOAs are members of the CCITT by themselves. The fact that, because of the ongoing process of separation of the regulatory functions from the business activity, some national authorities participate in the CCITT is not in contradiction with the nature of undertakings of other members. Moreover, even if the CCITT membership became governmental as a result of the separation of regulatory and operational activities of the telecommunications administrations, Article 86 in association with Article 81 could still apply either against the State measures implementing the CCITT recommendations and the recommendations themselves on the basis of Article 86(1), or if there is no such national implementing measure, directly against the telecommunications organizations which followed the recommendation.[40]

144. In the Commission's view, the CCITT recommendations are adopted, *inter alia*, by undertakings. Such CCITT recommendations, although they are not legally binding, are agreements between undertakings or decisions by an association of undertakings. In any event, according to the case law of the Commission and the European Court of Justice[41] a statutory body entrusted with certain public functions and including some members appointed by the government of a Member State may be an "association of undertakings" if it represents the trading interests of other members and takes decisions or makes agreements in pursuance of those interests.

The Commission draws attention to the fact that the application of certain provisions in the context of international conventions could result in infringements of the EEC competition rules:

— As to the WATTC Regulations, this is the case for the respective provisions for mutual agreement between TOs on the supply of international telecommunications services (Article 1(5)), reserving the choice of telecommunications routes to the TOs (Article 3(3)(3)), recommending practices equivalent to price agreements (Articles 6(6)(1)(2)),

---

[40] See Commission Decision 87/3/EEC *ENI/Montedison*, OJ No L 5, 7.1.1987, p. 13.
[41] See *Pabst & Richarz/BNIA*, OJ 1976 L231/24, *AROW/BNIC*, OJ 1982 L379/1, and Case 123/83 *BNIC v. Clair* [1985] ECR 391.

and limiting the possibility of special arrangements to activities meeting needs within and/or between the territories of the Members concerned (Article 9) and only where existing arrangements cannot satisfactorily meet the relevant telecommunications needs (Opinion PL A).

— CCITT recommendations D1 and D2 as they stand at the date of the adoption of these guidelines could amount to a collective horizontal agreement on prices and other supply conditions of international leased lines to the extent that they lead to a coordination of sales policies between TOs and therefore limit competition between them. This was indicated by the Commission in a CCITT meeting on 23 May 1990. The Commission reserves the right to examine the compatibility of other recommendations with Article 81.

— The agreements between TOs concluded in the context of the Conventions on Satellites are likely to limit competition contrary to Article 81 and/or 82 on the grounds set out in paragraphs 126 to 128 above.

COMMISSION NOTICE[1]

On the application of the competition rules to access agreements in the telecommunications sector framework, relevant markets and principles

(Text with EEA relevance)

PREFACE

In the telecommunications industry, access agreements are central in allowing market participants the benefits of liberalisation.

The purpose of this notice is threefold:

— to set out access principles stemming from Community competition law as shown in a large number of Commission decisions in order to create greater market certainty and more stable conditions for investment and commercial initiative in the telecoms and multimedia sectors;
— to define and clarify the relationship between competition law and sector specific legislation under the Article 95 framework (in particular this relates to the relationship between competition rules and open network provision legislation);
— to explain how competition rules will be applied in a consistent way across the sectors involved in the provision of new services, and in particular to access issues and gateways in this context.

INTRODUCTION

1. The timetable for full liberalisation in the telecommunications sector has now been established, and most Member States had to remove the last barriers to the provision of telecommunications networks and services in a competitive environment to consumers by 1 January 1998.[2] As a result of this liberalisation a second set of related products or

---

[1] OJ 1998 C 265/2.
[2] According to Commission Directives 96/19/EC and 96/2/EC (cited in footnote 4), certain Member States may request a derogation from full liberalisation for certain limited periods. This notice is without prejudice to such derogations, and the Commission will take account of the existence of any such derogation when applying the competition rules to access agreements, as described in this notice.
See:
Commission Decision 97/114/EC of 27 November 1996 concerning the additional implementation periods requested by Ireland for the implementation of Commission Directives 90/388/EEC and 96/2/EC as regards full competition in the telecommunications markets (OJ 1997 L41/8);
Commission Decision 97/310/EC of 12 February 1997 concerning the granting of additional implementation periods to the Portuguese Republic for the implementation of Commission Directives 90/388/EEC and 96/2/EC as regards full competition in the telecommunications markets (OJ 1997 L133/19);

services will emerge as well as the need for access to facilities necessary to provide these services. In this sector, interconnection to the public switched telecommunications network is a typical, but not the only, example of such access. The Commission has stated that it will define the treatment of access agreements in the telecommunications sector under the competition rules.[3] This notice, therefore, addresses the issue of how competition rules and procedures apply to access agreements in the context of harmonised EC and national regulation in the telecommunications sector.

2. The regulatory framework for the liberalisation of telecommunications consists of the liberalisation directives issued under Article 86 of the Treaty and the harmonisation Directives under Article 95, including in particular the open network provision (ONP) framework. The ONP framework provides harmonised rules for access and interconnection to the telecommunications networks and the voice telephony services. The legal framework provided by the liberalisation and harmonisation legislation is the background to any action taken by the Commission in its application of the competition rules. Both the liberalisation legislation (the Article 86 Directives)[4] and the harmonisation legislation (the ONP Directives)[5] are aimed at ensuring the attainment of the objectives of the Community

---

Commission Decision 97/568/EC of 14 May 1997 on the granting of additional implementation periods to Luxembourg for the implementation of Directive 90/388/EEC as regards full competition in the telecommunications markets (OJ 1997 L234/7);
Commission Decision 97/603/EC of 10 June 1997 concerning the granting of additional implementation periods to Spain for the implementation of Commission Directive 90/388/EEC as regards full competition in the telecommunications markets (OJ 1997 L243/48);
Commission Decision 97/607/EC of 18 June 1997 concerning the granting of additional implementation periods to Greece for the implementation of Directive 90/388/EEC as regards full competition in the telecommunications markets (OJ 1997 L245/6).
[3] Communication by the Commission of 3 May 1995 to the European Parliament and the Council, Consultation on the Green Paper on the liberalisation of telecommunications infrastructure and cable television networks, COM(95) 158 final.
[4] Commission Directive 88/301/EEC of 16 May 1988, on competition in the markets in telecommunications terminal equipment (OJ 1988 L131/73);
Commission Directive 90/388/EEC of 28 June 1990 on competition in the markets for telecommunications services (OJ 1990 L192/10) (the "Services Directive");
Commission Directive 94/46/EC of 13 October 1994, amending Directive 88/301/EEC and Directive 90/388/EEC in particular with regard to satellite communications (OJ 1994 L268/15);
Commission Directive 95/51/EC of 18 October 1995 amending Directive 90/388/EEC with regard to the abolition of the restrictions on the use of cable television networks for the provision of already liberalised telecommunications services (OJ 1995 L256/49);
Commission Directive 96/2/EC of 16 January 1996 amending Directive 90/388/EEC with regard to mobile and personal communications (OJ 1996 L20159);
Commission Directive 96/19/EC of 13 March 1996 amending Directive 90/388/EEC with regard to the implementation of full competition in the telecommunications markets (OJ 1996 L75/15) (the "Full Competition Directive").
[5] Interconnection agreements are the most significant form of access agreement in the telecommunications sector. A basic framework for interconnection agreements is set up by the rules on open network provision (ONP), and the application of competition rules must be seen against this background:
Directive 97/13/EC of the European Parliament and of the Council of 10 April 1997 on a common framework for authorisations and individual licences in the field of telecommunications services (OJ 1997 L117/15) (the "Licensing Directive");
Directive 97/33/EC of the European Parliament and of the Council of 30 June 1997 on interconnection in Telecommunications with regard to ensuring universal service and interoperability through application of the principles of open network provision (ONP) (OJ 1997 L199/32) (the "Interconnection Directive");
Council Directive 90/387/EEC of 28 June 1990 on the establishment of the internal market for telecommunications services through the implementation of open network provision (OJ 1990 L192/1) (the "Framework Directive");
Council Directive 92/44/EEC of 5 June 1992 on the application of open network provision to leased lines (OJ 1992 L165/27) (the "Leased Lines Directive");
Directive 95/62/EEC of the European Parliament and of the Council of 13 December 1995 on the

as laid out in Article 3 of the Treaty, and specifically, the establishment of "a system ensuring that competition in the internal market is not distorted" and "an internal market characterised by the abolition, as between Member States, of obstacles to the free movement of goods, persons, services and capital".

3. The Commission has published Guidelines on the application of EEC competition rules in the telecommunications sector.[6] The present notice is intended to build on those Guidelines, which do not deal explicitly with access issues.

4. In the telecommunications sector, liberalisation and harmonisation legislation permit and simplify the task of Community firms in embarking on new activities in new markets and consequently allow users to benefit from increased competition. These advantages must not be jeopardised by restrictive or abusive practices of undertakings: the Community's competition rules are therefore essential to ensure the completion of this development. New entrants must in the initial stages be guaranteed the right to have access to the networks of incumbent telecommunications operators (TOs). Several authorities, at the regional, national and Community levels, have a role in regulating this sector. If the competition process is to work well in the internal market, effective coordination between these institutions must be ensured.

5. Part I of the notice sets out the legal framework and details how the Commission intends to avoid unnecessary duplication of procedures while safe-guarding the rights of undertakings and users under the competition rules. In this context, the Commission's efforts to encourage decentralised application of the competition rules by national courts and national authorities aim at achieving remedies at a national level, unless a significant Community interest is involved in a particular case. In the telecommunications sector, specific procedures in the ONP framework likewise aim at resolving access problems in the first place at a decentralised, national level, with a further possibility for conciliation at Community level in certain circumstances. Part II defines the Commission's approach to market definition in this sector. Part III details the principles that the Commission will follow in the application of the competition rules: it aims to help telecommunications market participants shape their access agreements by explaining the competition law requirements. The principles set out in this Notice apply not only to traditional fixed line telecommunications, but also to all telecommunications, including areas such as satellite communications and mobile communications.

6. The notice is based on the Commission's experience in several cases,[7] and certain studies into this area carried out on behalf of the Commission.[8] As this notice is based on the generally applicable competition rules, the principles set out in this Notice will, to extent that comparable problems arise, be equally applicable in other areas, such as access issues in digital communications sectors generally. Similarly, several of the principles

---

application of open network provision to voice telephony (OJ 1995 L321/6) replaced by Directive 98/10/EC of the European Parliament and of the Council of 26 February 1998 on the application of open network provision (ONP) to voice telephony and on universal service for telecommunications in a competitive environment (OJ 1998 L101/24) (the "Voice Telephony Directive");

Directive 97/66/EC of the European Parliament and of the Council of 15 December 1997 concerning the processing of personal data and the protection of privacy in the telecommunications sector (OJ 1998 L24/1) (the "Data Protection Directive").

[6] OJ 1991 C233/2

[7] In the telecommunications area, notably:

Commission Decision 91/562/EEC of 18 October 1991, *Eirpage* (OJ 1991 L306/22);

Commission Decisions 96/546/EC and 96/547/EC of 17 July 1996, *Atlas and Phoenix* (OJ 996 L239/23 and 57); and

Commission Decision 97/780/EC of 29 October 1997, *Unisource* (OJ 1997 L318/1).

There are also a number of pending cases involving access issues.

[8] Competition aspects of interconnection agreements in the telecommunications sector, June 1995;

Competition aspects of access by service providers to the resources of telecommunications operators, December 1995. See also

Competition Aspects of Access Pricing, December 1995.

contained in the Treaty will be of relevance to any company occupying a dominant position including those in fields other than telecommunications.

7. The present notice is based on issues which have arisen during the initial stages of transition from monopolies to competitive markets. Given the convergence of the tele-communications, broadcasting and information technology sectors,[9] and the increased competition on these markets, other issues will emerge. This may make it necessary to adapt the scope and principles set out in this notice to these new sectors.

8. The principles set out in this document will apply to practices outside the Community to the extent that such practices have an effect on competition within the Community and affect trade between Member States. In applying the competition rules, the Commission is obliged to comply with the Community's obligations under the WTO tele-communications agreement.[10] The Commission also notes that there are continuing discussions with regard to the international accounting rates system in the context of the ITU. The present notice is without prejudice to the Commission's position in these discussions.

9. This notice does not in any way restrict the rights conferred on individuals or undertakings by Community law, and is without prejudice to any interpretation of the Community competition rules that may be given by the Court of Justice or the Court of First Instance of the European Communities. This notice does not purport to be a comprehensive analysis of all possible competition problems in this sector: other problems already exist and more are likely to arise in the future.

10. The Commission will consider whether the present notice should be amended or added to in the light of experience gained during the first period of a liberalised telecommunications environment.

PART I—FRAMEWORK

1. Competition rules and sector specific regulation

11. Access problems in the broadest sense of the word can be dealt with at different levels and on the basis of a range of legislative provisions, of both national and Community origin. A service provider faced with an access problem such as a TO's unjustified refusal to supply (or on reasonable terms) a leased line needed by the applicant to provide services to its customers could therefore contemplate a number of routes to seek a remedy. Generally speaking, aggrieved parties will experience a number of benefits, at least in an initial stage, in seeking redress at a national level. At a national level, the applicant has two main choices, namely (1) specific national regulatory procedures now established in accordance with Community law and harmonised under Open Network Provision (see footnote 4), and (2) an action under national and/or Community law before a national court or national competition authority.[11]

---

[9] See the Commission's Green Paper of 3 December 1997 on the Convergence of the Tele-communications, Media and Information Technology sectors and the implications for Regulation—Towards an information society approach (COM(97) 623).

[10] See Council Decision 97/838/EC of 28 November 1997 concerning the conclusion on behalf of the European Community, as regards matters within its competence, of the results of the WTO negotiations on basic telecommunications services (OJ 1997 L347/45).

[11] In the case of the ONP Leased Lines Directive, a first stage is foreseen which allows the aggrieved user to appeal to the National Regulatory Authority. This can offer a number of advantages. In the telecommunications areas where experience has shown that companies are often hesitant to be seen as complainants against the TO on which they heavily depend not only with respect to the specific point of conflict but also much broader and far-reaching sense, the procedures foreseen under ONP are an attractive option. ONP procedures furthermore can cover a broader range of access problems than could be approached on the basis of the competition rules. Finally, these procedures can offer

12. Complaints made to the Commission under the competition rules in the place of or in addition to national courts, national competition authorities and/or to national regulatory authorities under ONP procedures will be dealt with according to the priority which they deserve in view of the urgency, novelty and transnational nature of the problem involved and taking into account the need to avoid duplicate proceedings (see points 23 *et seq.*).

13. The Commission recognises that national regulatory authorities (NRAs)[12] have different tasks, and operate in a different legal framework from the Commission when the latter is applying the competition rules. First, the NRAs operate under national law, albeit often implementing European law. Secondly, that law, based as it is on considerations of telecommunications policy, may have objectives different to, but consistent with, the objectives of Community competition policy. The Commission cooperates as far as possible with the NRAs, and NRAs also have to cooperate between themselves in particular when dealing with cross-border issues.[13] Under Community law, national authorities, including regulatory authorities and competition authorities, have a duty not to approve any practice or agreement contrary to Community competition law.

14. Community competition rules are not sufficient to remedy all of the various problems in the telecommunications sector. NRAs therefore have a significantly wider ambit and a significant and far-reaching role in the regulation of the sector. It should also be noted that as a matter of Community law, the NRAs must be independent.[14]

15. It is also important to note that the ONP Directives impose on TOs having significant market power certain obligations of transparency and non-discrimination that go beyond those that would normally be imposed under Article 82 of the Treaty. ONP Directives lay down obligations relating to transparency, obligations to supply and pricing practices. These obligations are enforced by the NRAs, which also have jurisdiction to take steps to ensure effective competition.[15]

16. In relation to Article 82, this notice is written, for convenience, in most respects as if there was one telecommunications operator occupying a dominant position. This will not necessarily be the case in all Member States: for example new telecommunications networks offering increasingly wide coverage will develop progressively. These alternative telecommunications networks may, or may ultimately, be large and extensive enough to be partly or even wholly substitutable for the existing national networks, and this should be kept in mind. The existence and the position on the market of competing operators will be relevant in determining whether sole or joint dominant positions exist: references to the existence of a dominant position in this notice should be read with this in mind.

17. Given the Commission's responsibility for the Community's competition policy, the Commission must serve the Community's general interest. The administrative resources at the Commission's disposal to perform its task are necessarily limited and

---

users the advantage of proximity and familiarity with national administrative procedures; language is also a factor to be taken into account.

Under the ONP Leased Lines Directive, if a solution cannot be found at the national level, a second stage is organised at the European level (conciliation procedure). An agreement between the parties involved must then be reached within two months, with a possible extension of one month if the parties agree.

[12] An NRA is a national telecommunications regulatory body created by a Member State in the context of the services directive as amended, and the ONP framework. The list of NRAs is published regularly in the *Official Journal of the European Communities*, and a copy of the latest list can be found at http://www.ispo.cec.be.

[13] Articles 9 and 17 of the Interconnection Directive.

[14] Article 7 of the Services Directive (see footnote 4), and Article 5a of the ONP Framework Directive (see footnote 5). See also Communication by the Commission to the European Parliament and the Council on the status and implementation of Directive 90/388/EEC on competition in the markets for telecommunications services (OJ 1995 C275/2).

See also the judgment of the Court of Justice of the European Communities in Case C–91/94, *Thierry Tranchant and Telephones Stores* [1995] ECR I–3911.

[15] The Interconnection Directive cited in footnote 5, Article 9(3).

cannot be used to deal with all the cases brought to its attention. The Commission is therefore obliged, in general, to take all organisational measures necessary for the performance of its task and, in particular, to establish priorities.[16]

18. The Commission has therefore indicated that it intends, in using its decision-making powers, to concentrate on notifications, complaints and own-initiative proceedings having particular political, economic or legal significance for the Community.[17] Where these features are absent in a particular case, notifications will not normally be dealt with by means of a formal decision, but rather a comfort letter (subject to the consent of the parties), and complaints should, as a rule, be handled by national courts or other relevant authorities. In this context, it should be noted that the competition rules are directly effective[18] so that Community competition law is enforceable in the national courts. Even where other Community legislation has been respected, this does not remove the need to comply with the Community competition rules.[19]

19. Other national authorities, in particular NRAs acting within the ONP framework, have jurisdiction over certain access agreements (which must be notified to them). However, notification of an agreement to an NRA does not make notification of an agreement to the Commission unnecessary. The NRAs must ensure that actions taken by them are consistent with Community competition law.[20] This duty requires them to refrain from action that would undermine the effective protection of Community law rights under the competition rules.[21] Therefore, they may not approve arrangements which are contrary to the competition rules.[22] If the national authorities act so as to undermine those rights, the Member State may itself be liable for damages to those harmed by this action.[23] In addition, NRAs have jurisdiction under the ONP directives to take steps to ensure effective competition.[24]

20. Access agreements in principle regulate the provision of certain services between independent undertakings and do not result in the creation of an autonomous entity which

---

[16] Judgments of the Court of First Instance of the European Communities: Case T–24/90, *Automec v. Commission* [1992] ECR II–2223, at paragraph 77 and Case T–114/92 *BEMIM* [1995] ECR II–147.

[17] Notice on cooperation between national courts and the Commission in applying Articles 81 and 82 of the EC Treaty (OJ C39, 13.2.1993, p. 6, at paragraph 14).
Notice on cooperation between national competition authorities and the Commission (OJ 1997 C313/3).

[18] Case 127/73, *BRT v. SABAM* [1974] ECR 51.

[19] Case 66/86, *Ahmed Saeed* [1989] ECR 838.

[20] They must not, for example, encourage or reinforce or approve the results of anti-competitive behaviour:
— *Ahmed Saeed*, see footnote 19;
— Case 153/93, *Federal Republic of Germany v. Delta Schiffahrtsges.* [1994] ECR I–2517,
— Case 267/86, *Van Eycke* [1988] ECR 4769.

[21] Case 13/77, *GB-Inno-BM/ATAB* [1977] ECR 2115, at paragraph 33:
— "while it is true that Article [82] is directed at undertakings, nonetheless it is also true that the Treaty imposes a duty on Member States not to adopt or maintain in force any measure which could deprive the provision of its effectiveness."

[22] For further duties of national authorities see:
Case 103/88, *Fratelli Costanzo* [1989] ECR 1839.
See *Ahmed Saeed*, cited in footnote 18:
— "Articles 10 and 86 of the EEC Treaty must be interpreted as (i) prohibiting the national authorities from encouraging the conclusion of agreements on tariffs contrary to Article [81(1)] or Article [82] of the Treaty, as the case may be; (ii) precluding the approval by those authorities of tariffs resulting from such agreements".

[23] Joined Cases C–6/90, and C–9/90 *Francovich* [1991] ECR I–5357;
Joined Cases C–46/93, *Brasserie de Pêcheur v. Germany* and Case C–48/93, *R v. Secretary of State for Transport ex parte Factortame and others* [1996] ECR I–1029.

[24] For example, recital 18 of the Leased Lines Directive and Article 9(3) of the Interconnection Directive, see footnote 5.

would be distinct from the parties to the agreements. Access agreements are thus generally outside the scope of the Merger Regulation.[25]

21. Under Regulation No 17,[26] the Commission could be seised of an issue relating to access agreements by way of a notification of an access agreement by one or more of the parties involved,[27] by way of a complaint against a restrictive access agreement or against the behaviour of a dominant company in granting or refusing access,[28] by way of a Commission own-initiative procedure into such a grant or refusal, or by way of a sector inquiry.[29] In addition, a complainant may request that the Commission take interim measures in circumstances where there is an urgent risk of serious and irreparable harm to the complainant or to the public interest.[30] It should however, be noted in cases of great urgency that procedures before national courts can usually result more quickly in an order to end the infringements than procedures before the Commission.[31]

22. There are a number of areas where agreements will be subject to both the competition rules and national or European sector specific measures, most notably Internal Market measures. In the telecommunications sector, the ONP Directives aim at establishing a regulatory regime for access agreements. Given the detailed nature of ONP rules and the fact that they may go beyond the requirements of Article 82, undertakings operating in the telecommunications sector should be aware that compliance with the Community competition rules does not absolve them of their duty to abide by obligations imposed in the ONP context, and *vice versa*.

2. Commission action in relation to access agreements[32]

23. Access agreements taken as a whole are of great significance, and it is therefore appropriate for the Commission to spell out as clearly as possible the Community legal framework within which these agreements should be concluded. Access agreements having restrictive clauses will involve issues under Article 81. Agreements which involve dominant, or monopolist, undertakings involve Article 82 issues: concerns arising from the dominance of one or more of the parties will generally be of greater significance in the context of a particular agreement than those under Article 81.

Notifications

24. In applying the competition rules, the Commission will build on the ONP Directives which set a framework for action at the national level by the NRAs. Where agreements fall within Article 81(1), they must be notified to the Commission if they are to benefit from an exemption under Article 81(3). Where agreements are notified, the Commission intends to deal with some notifications by way of formal decisions, following appropriate publicity in the *Official Journal of the European Communities*, and in accordance with the principles set out below. Once the legal principles have been clearly established, the Commission then proposes to deal by way of comfort letter with other notifications raising the same issues.

---

[25] Council Regulation (EEC) No. 4064/89 of 21 December 1989 on the control of concentrations between undertakings (OJ L395, 30.12.1989, p. 1); corrected version (OJ L257, 21.9.1990, p. 13).

[26] Council Regulation No. 17 of 6 February 1962, First Regulation implementing Articles 85 and 86 of the Treaty (OJ 13, 21.2.1962, p. 204).

[27] Articles 2 and 4(1) of Regulation No. 17.

[28] Article 3 of Regulation No. 17.

[29] Articles 3 and 12 of Regulation No. 17.

[30] Case 792/79R, *Camera Care v. Commission* [1980] ECR 119.
See also Case T–44/90, *La Cinq v. Commission* [1992] ECR II–1.

[31] See point 16 of the Notice cited in footnote 17.

[32] Article 2 or Article 4(1) of Regulation No. 17.

3. Complaints

25. Natural or legal persons with a legitimate interest may, under certain circumstances, submit a complaint to the Commission, requesting that the Commission by decision require that an infringement of Article 81 or Article 82 of the Treaty be brought to an end. A complainant may additionally request that the Commission take interim measures where there is an urgent risk of serious and irreparable harm.[33] A prospective complainant has other equally or even more effective options, such as an action before a national court. In this context, it should be noted that procedures before the national courts can offer considerable advantages for individuals and companies, such as in particular[34]:

— national courts can deal with and award a claim for damages resulting from an infringement of the competition rules,
— national courts can usually adopt interim measures and order the termination of an infringement more quickly than the Commission is able to do,
— before national courts, it is possible to combine a claim under Community law with a claim under national law,
— legal costs can be awarded to the successful applicant before a national court.

Furthermore, the specific national regulatory principles as harmonised under ONP Directives can offer recourse both at the national level and, if necessary, at the Community level.

3.1. Use of national and ONP procedures

26. As referred to above[35] the Commission will take into account the Community interest of each case brought to its attention. In evaluating the Community interest, the Commission examines " ... the significance of the alleged infringement as regards the functioning of the common market, the probability of establishing the existence of the infringement and the scope of the investigation required in order to fulfil, under the best possible conditions, its task of ensuring that Articles [81] and [82] are complied with ... ".[36]

Another essential element in this evaluation is the extent to which a national judge is in a position to provide an effective remedy for an infringement of Article 81 or 82. This may prove difficult, for example, in cases involving extra-territorial elements.

27. Article 81(1) and Article 82 of the Treaty produce direct effects in relations between individuals which must be safeguarded by national courts.[37] As regards actions before the NRA, the Interconnection Directive provides that such an authority has power to intervene and order changes in relation to both the existence and content of access agreements. NRAs must take into account "the need to stimulate a competitive market" and may impose conditions on one or more parties, *inter alia*, "to ensure effective competition".[38]

28. The Commission may itself be seised of a dispute either pursuant to the competition rules, or pursuant to an ONP conciliation procedure. Multiple proceedings might lead to unnecessary duplication of investigative efforts by the Commission and the national authorities. Where complaints are lodged with the Commission under Article 3 of Regulation No 17 while there are related actions before a relevant national or European authority or court, the Directorate-General for Competition will generally not initially

---

[33] *Camera Care and La Cinq*, referred to at footnote 30.
[34] See point 16 of the Notice cited in footnote 17.
[35] See point 18.
[36] See *Automec*, cited in footnote 16, at paragraph 86.
[37] *BRT v. SABAM*, cited in footnote 18.
[38] Article 9(1) and (3) of the ONP Interconnection Directive.

pursue any investigation as to the existence of an infringement under Article 81 or 82 of the Treaty. This is subject, however, to the following points.

3.2. Safeguarding complainant's rights

29. Undertakings are entitled to effective protection of their Community law rights.[39] Those rights would be undermined if national proceedings were allowed to lead to an excessive delay of the Commission's action, without a satisfactory resolution of the matter at a national level. In the telecommunications sector, innovation cycles are relatively short, and any substantial delay in resolving an access dispute might in practice be equivalent to a refusal of access, thus prejudging the proper determination of the case.

30. The Commission therefore takes the view that an access dispute before an NRA should be resolved within a reasonable period of time, normally speaking not extending beyond six months of the matter first being drawn to the attention of that authority. This resolution could take the form of either a final determination of the action or another form of relief which would safeguard the rights of the complainant. If the matter has not reached such a resolution then, *prima facie*, the rights of the parties are not being effectively protected, and the Commission would in principle, upon request by the complainant, begin its investigations into the case in accordance with its normal procedures, after consultation and in cooperation with the national authority in question. In general, the Commission will not begin such investigations where there is already an ongoing action under ONP conciliation procedures.

31. In addition, the Commission must always look at each case on its merits: it will take action if it feels that in a particular case, there is a substantial Community interest affecting, or likely to affect, competition in a number of Member States.

3.3. Interim measures

32. As regards any request for interim measures, the existence or possibility of national proceedings is relevant to the question of whether there is a risk of serious and irreparable harm. Such proceedings should, *prima facie*, remove the risk of such harm and it would therefore not be appropriate for the Commission to grant interim measures in the absence of evidence that the risk would nevertheless remain.

33. The availability of and criteria for interim injunctive relief is an important factor which the Commission must take into account in reaching this *prima facie* conclusion. If interim injunctive relief were not available, or if such relief was not likely adequately to protect the complainant's rights under Community law, the Commission would consider that the national proceedings did not remove the risk of harm, and could therefore commence its examination of the case.

4. Own-initiative investigation and sector inquiries

34. If it appears necessary, the Commission will open an own-initiative investigation. It can also launch a sector inquiry, subject to consultation of the Advisory Committee of Member State competition authorities.

5. Fines

35. The Commission may impose fines of up to 10% of the annual worldwide turnover of undertakings which intentionally or negligently breach Article 81(1) or Article 82.[40] Where agreements have been notified pursuant to Regulation No 17 for an exemption

---

[39] Case 14/83, *Von Colson* [1984] ECR 1891.
[40] Article 15(2) of Regulation No. 17.

under Article 81(3), no fine may be levied by the Commission in respect of activities described in the notification[41] for the period following notification. However, the Commission may withdraw the immunity from fines by informing the undertakings concerned that, after preliminary examination, it is of the opinion that Article 81(1) of the Treaty applies and that application of Article 81(3) is not justified.[42]

36. The ONP Interconnection Directive has two particular provisions which are relevant to fines under the competition rules. First, it provides that interconnection agreements must be communicated to the relevant NRAs and made available to interested third parties, with the exception of those parts which deal with the commercial strategy of the parties.[43] Secondly, it provides that the NRA must have a number of powers which it can use to influence or amend the interconnection agreements.[44] These provisions ensure that appropriate publicity is given to the agreements, and provide the NRA with the opportunity to take steps, where appropriate, to ensure effective competition on the market.

37. Where an agreement has been notified to an NRA, but has not been notified to the Commission, the Commission does not consider it would be generally appropriate as a matter of policy to impose a fine in respect of the agreement, even if the agreement ultimately proves to contain conditions in breach of Article 81. A fine would, however, be appropriate in some cases, for example where:

(a) the agreement proves to contain provisions in breach of Article 82; and/or
(b) the breach of Article 81 is particularly serious.

The Commission has recently published Guidelines on how fines will be calculated.[45]

38. Notification to the NRA is not a substitute for a notification to the Commission and does not limit the possibility for interested parties to submit a complaint to the Commission, or for the Commission to begin an own-initiative investigation into access agreements. Nor does such notification limit the rights of a party to seek damages before a national court for harm caused by anti-competitive agreements.[46]

Part II—Relevant Markets

39. In the course of investigating cases within the framework set out in Part I above, the Commission will base itself on the approach to the definition of relevant markets set out in the Commission's Notice on the definition of the relevant market for the purposes of Community competition law.[47]

40. Firms are subject to three main sources of competitive constraints; demand substitutability, supply substitutability and potential competition, with the first constituting the most immediate and effective disciplinary force on the suppliers of a given product or service. Demand substitutability is therefore the main tool used to define the relevant product market on which restrictions of competition for the purposes of Article 81(1) and Article 82 can be identified.

41. Supply substitutability may in appropriate circumstances be used as a complementary element to define relevant markets. In practice it cannot be clearly distinguished from potential competition. Supply side substitutability and potential competition are used for the purpose of determining whether the undertaking has a dominant position or whether

---

[41] Article 15(5) of Regulation No. 17.
[42] Article 15(6) of Regulation No. 17.
[43] Article 6(c) of the Interconnection Directive.
[44] *Inter alia*, at Article 9 of the Interconnection Directive.
[45] Guidelines on the method of setting fines imposed pursuant to Article 15(2) of Regulation No. 17 and Article 65(5) of the ECSC Treaty (OJ C9, 14.1.1998, p. 3).
[46] See footnote 23.
[47] OJ C372, 9.12.1997, p. 5.

the restriction of competition is significant within the meaning of Article 81, or whether there is elimination of competition.

42. In assessing relevant markets it is necessary to look at developments in the market in the short term.

The following sections set out some basic principles of particular relevance to the telecommunications sector.

1. Relevant product market

43. Section 6 of Form A/B defines the relevant product market as follows:

"A relevant product market comprises all those products and/or services which are regarded as interchangeable or substitutable by the consumer, by reason of the products' characteristics, their prices and their intended use".

44. Liberalisation of the telecommunications sector will lead to the emergence of a second type of market, that of access to facilities which are currently necessary to provide these liberalised services. Interconnection to the public switched telecommunications network would be a typical example of such access. Without interconnection, it will not be commercially possible for third parties to provide, for example, comprehensive voice telephony services.

45. It is clear, therefore, that in the telecommunications sector there are at least two types of relevant markets to consider—that of a service to be provided to end users and that of access to those facilities necessary to provide that service to end-users (information, physical network, etc.). In the context of any particular case, it will be necessary to define the relevant access and services markets, such as interconnection to the public telecommunications network, and provision of public voice telephony services, respectively.

46. When appropriate, the Commission will use the test of a relevant market which is made by asking whether, if all the suppliers of the services in question raised their prices by 5 to 10%, their collective profits would rise. According to this test, if their profits would rise, the market considered is a separate relevant market.

47. The Commission considers that the principles under competition law governing these markets remain the same regardless of the particular market in question. Given the pace of technological change in this sector, any attempt to define particular product markets in this notice would run the risk of rapidly becoming inaccurate or irrelevant. The definition of particular product markets—for example, the determination of whether call origination and call termination facilities are part of the same facilities market—is best done in the light of a detailed examination of an individual case.

1.1. Services market

48. This can be broadly defined as the provision of any telecommunications service to users. Different telecommunications services will be considered substitutable if they show a sufficient degree of interchangeability for the end-user, which would mean that effective competition can take place between the different providers of these services.

1.2. Access to facilities

49. For a service provider to provide services to end-users it will often require access to one or more (upstream or downstream) facilities. For example, to deliver physically the service to end-users, it needs access to the termination points of the telecommunications network to which these end-users are connected. This access can be achieved at the physical level through dedicated or shared local infrastructure, either self provided or leased from a local infrastructure provider. It can also be achieved either through a service

provider who already has these end-users as subscribers, or through an interconnection provider who has access directly or indirectly to the relevant termination points.

50. In addition to physical access, a service provider may need access to other facilities to enable it to market its service to end-users: for example, a service provider must be able to make end-users aware of its services. Where one organisation has a dominant position in the supply of services such as directory information, similar concerns arise as with physical access issues.

51. In many cases, the Commission will be concerned with physical access issues, where what is necessary is access to the network facilities of the dominant TO.[48]

52. Some incumbent TOs may be tempted to resist providing access to third party service providers or other network operators, particularly in areas where the proposed service will be in competition with a service provided by the TO itself. This resistance will often manifest itself as unjustified delay in giving access, a reluctance to allow access or a willingness to allow it only under disadvantageous conditions. It is the role of the competition rules to ensure that these prospective access markets are allowed to develop, and that incumbent TOs are not permitted to use their control over access to stifle developments on the services markets.

53. It should be stressed that in the telecommunications sector, liberalisation can be expected to lead to the development of new, alternative networks which will ultimately have an impact on access market definition involving the incumbent telecommunications operator.

2. Relevant geographic market

54. Relevant geographic markets are defined in Form A/B as follows:

"The relevant geographic market comprises the area in which the undertakings concerned are involved in the supply and demand of products or services, in which the conditions of competition are sufficiently homogeneous and which can be distinguished from neighbouring areas because the conditions of competition are appreciably different in those areas."

55. As regards the provision of telecommunication services and access markets, the relevant geographic market will be the area in which the objective conditions of competition applying to service providers are similar, and competitors are able to offer their services. It will therefore be necessary to examine the possibility for these service providers to access an end-user in any part of this area, under similar and economically viable conditions. Regulatory conditions such as the terms of licences, and any exclusive or special rights owned by competing local access providers are particularly relevant.[49]

---

[48] Interconnection is defined in the Full Competition Directive as " . . . the physical and logical linking of the telecommunications facilities of organisations providing telecommunications networks and/or telecommunications services, in order to allow the users of one organisation to communicate with the users of the same or another organisation or to access services provided by third organisations."
In the Full Competition Directive and ONP Directives, telecommunications services are defined as "services, whose provision consists wholly or partly in the transmission and/or routing of signals on a telecommunications network."
It therefore includes the transmission of broadcasting signals and CATV networks.
A telecommunications network is itself defined as " . . . the transmission equipment and, where applicable, switching equipment and other resources which permit the conveyance of signals between defined termination points by wire, by radio, by optical or by other electromagnetic means".

[49] Commission Decision 94/894/EC of 13 December 1994, *Eurotunnel* (OJ 1994 L354/66).

PART III—PRINCIPLES

56. The Commission will apply the following principles in cases before it.

57. The Commission has recognised that "Articles 85 and 86 ... constitute law in force and enforceable throughout the Community. Conflicts should not arise with other Community rules because Community law forms a coherent regulatory framework ... it is obvious that Community acts adopted in the telecommunications sector are to be interpreted in a way consistent with competition rules, so as to ensure the best possible implementation of all aspects of the Community telecommunications policy ... This applies, *inter alia*, to the relationship between competition rules applicable to undertakings and the ONP rules".[50]

58. Thus, competition rules continue to apply in circumstances where other Treaty provisions or secondary legislation are applicable. In the context of access agreements, the internal market and competition provisions of Community law are both important and mutually reinforcing for the proper functioning of the sector. Therefore in making an assessment under the competition rules, the Commission will seek to build as far as possible on the principles established in the harmonisation legislation. It should also be borne in mind that a number of the competition law principles set out below are also covered by specific rules in the context of the ONP framework. Proper application of these rules should often avoid the need for the application of the competition rules.

59. As regards the telecommunications sector, attention should be paid to the cost of universal service obligations. Article 86(2) of the Treaty may justify exceptions to the principles of Articles 81 and 82. The details of universal service obligations are a regulatory matter. The field of application of Article 86(2) has been specified in the Article 86 Directives in the telecommunications sector, and the Commission will apply the competition rules in this context.

60. Articles 81 and 82 of the Treaty apply in the normal manner to agreements or practices which have been approved or authorised by a national authority,[51] or where the national authority has required the inclusion of terms in an agreement at the request of one or more of the parties involved.

61. However, if a NRA were to require terms which were contrary to the competition rules, the undertakings involved would in practice not be fined, although the Member State itself would be in breach of Article 3(h) and Article 10 of the Treaty[52] and therefore subject to challenge by the Commission under Article 226. Additionally, if an undertaking having special or exclusive rights within the meaning of Article 86, or a State-owned undertaking, were required or authorised by a national regulator to engage in behaviour constituting an abuse of its dominant position, the Member State would also be in breach of Article 86(1) and the Commission could adopt a decision requiring termination of the infringement.[53]

62. NRAs may require strict standards of transparency, obligations to supply and pricing practices on the market, particularly where this is necessary in the early stages of liberalisation. When appropriate, legislation such as the ONP framework will be used as an aid in the interpretation of the competition rules.[54] Given the duty resting on NRAs to ensure that effective competition is possible, application of the competition rules is likewise required for an appropriate interpretation of the ONP principles. It should also be noted that many of the issues set out below are also covered by rules under the Full Competition Directive and the ONP Licensing and Data Protection Directives: effective

---

[50] See Guidelines cited in footnote 6, at paragraphs 15 and 16.

[51] Commission Decision 82/896/EEC of 15 December 1982, *AROW/BNIC* (OJ 1982 L379/19).

[52] See footnote 20.

[53] Joined Cases C–48 and 66/90 *Netherlands and others v. Commission*, [1992] ECR I–565.

[54] See *Ahmed Saeed*, cited in footnote 19, where internal market legislation relating to pricing was used as an aid in determining what level of prices should be regarded as unfair for the purposes of Article 82.

enforcement of this regulatory framework should prevent many of the competition issues set out below from arising.

1. Dominance (Article 82)

63. In order for an undertaking to provide services in the telecommunications services market, it may need to obtain access to various facilities. For the provision of tele-communications services, for example, interconnection to the public switched telecommunications network will usually be necessary. Access to this network will almost always be in the hands of a dominant TO. As regards access agreements, dominance stemming from control of facilities will be the most relevant to the Commission's appraisal.

64. Whether or not a company is dominant does not depend only on the legal rights granted to that company. The mere ending of legal monopolies does not put an end to dominance. Indeed, notwithstanding the liberalisation Directives, the development of effective competition from alternative network providers with adequate capacity and geographic reach will take time.

65. The judgment of the Court of Justice in *Tetra Pak*[55] is also likely to prove important in the telecommunications sector. The Court held that given the extremely close links between the dominated and non-dominated market, and given the extremely high market share on the dominated market, Tetra Pak was "in a situation comparable to that of holding a dominant position on the markets in question as a whole".

The *Tetra Pak* case concerned closely related horizontal markets: the analysis is equally applicable, however, to closely related vertical markets which will be common in the telecommunications sector. In the telecommunications sector, it is often the case that a particular operator has an extremely strong position on infrastructure markets, and on markets downstream of that infrastructure. Infrastructure costs also typically constitute the single largest cost of the downstream operations. Further, operators will often face the same competitors on both the infrastructure and downstream markets.

66. It is therefore possible to envisage a number of situations where there will be closely related markets, together with an operator having a very high degree of market power on at least one of those markets.

67. It these circumstances are present, it may be appropriate for the Commission to find that the particular operator was in a situation comparable to that of holding a dominant position on the markets in question as a whole.

68. In the telecommunications sector, the concept of "essential facilities" will in many cases be of relevance in determining the duties of dominant TOs. The expression essential facility is used to describe a facility or infrastructure which is essential for reaching customers and/or enabling competitors to carry on their business, and which cannot be replicated by any reasonable means.[56]

69. A company controlling the access to an essential facility enjoys a dominant position within the meaning of Article 82. Conversely, a company may enjoy a dominant position pursuant to Article 82 without controlling an essential facility.

1.1. Services market

70. One of the factors used to measure the market power of an undertaking is the sales attributable to that undertaking, expressed as a percentage of total sales in the market for

---

[55] On each market, Tetra Pak was faced with the same potential customers and actual competitors. Case C–333/94 P, *Tetra Pak International SA v. Commission* [1996] ECR I–5951.

[56] See also the definition included in the "Additional commitment on regulatory principles by the European Communities and their Member States" used by the Group on basic telecommunications in the context of the World Trade Organisation (WTO) negotiations:

"Essential facilities mean facilities of a public telecommunications transport network and service that:

(a) are exclusively or predominantly provided by a single or limited number of suppliers; and

(b) cannot feasibly be economically or technically substituted in order to provide a service."

substitutable services in the relevant geographic area. As regards the services market, the Commission will assess, *inter alia*, the turnover generated by the sale of substitutable services, excluding the sale or internal usage of interconnection services and the sale or internal usage of local infrastructure,[57] taking into consideration the competitive conditions and the structure of supply and demand on the market.

1.2. Access to facilities

71. The concept of "access" as referred to in point 45 can relate to a range of situations, including the availability of leased lines enabling a service provider to build up its own network, and interconnection in the strict sense, that is interconnecting two telecommunication networks, for example mobile and fixed. In relation to access it is probable that the incumbent operator will remain dominant for some time after the legal liberalisation has taken place. The incumbent operator, which controls the facilities, is often also the largest service provider, and it has in the past not needed to distinguish between the conveyance of telecommunications services and the provision of these services to end-users. Traditionally, an operator who is also a service provider has not required its downstream operating arm to pay for access, and therefore it has not been easy to calculate the revenue to be allocated to the facility. In a case where an operator is providing both access and services it is necessary to separate so far as possible the revenues as the basis for the calculation of the company's share of whichever market is involved. Article 8(2) of the Interconnection Directive addresses this issue by introducing a requirement for separate accounting for "activities related to interconnection—covering both interconnection services provided internally and interconnection services provided to others—and other activities". The proposed Commission Recommendation on Accounting Separation in the context of Interconnection will also be helpful in this regard.

72. The economic significance of obtaining access also depends on the coverage of the network with which interconnection is sought. Therefore, in addition to using turnover figures, the Commission will, where possible, also take into account the number of customers who have subscribed to services offered by the dominant company comparable with those which the service provider requesting access intends to provide. Accordingly, market power for a given undertaking will be measured partly by the number of subscribers who are connected to termination points of the telecommunications network of that undertaking expressed as a percentage of the total number of subscribers connected to termination points in the relevant geographic area.

Supply-side substitutability

73. As stated in point 41, supply-side substitutability is also relevant to the question of dominance. A market share of over 50%[58] is usually sufficient to demonstrate dominance although other factors will be examined. For example, the Commission will examine the existence of other network providers, if any, in the relevant geographic area to determine

---

[57] Case 6/72 *Continental Can* [1973] ECR 215.

[58] It should be noted in this context that under the ONP framework an organisation may be notified as having significant market power. The determination of whether an organisation does or does not have significant market power depends on a number of factors, but the starting presumption is that an organisation with a market share of more than 25% will normally be considered to have significant market power. The Commission will take account of whether an undertaking has been notified as having significant market power under the ONP rules in its appraisal under the competition rules. It is clear, however, that the notion of significant market power generally describes a position of economic power on a market less than that of dominance: the fact that an undertaking has significant market power under the ONP rules will generally therefore not lead to a presumption of dominance, although in a particular situation, this may prove to be the case. One important factor to be taken into consideration, however, will be whether the market definition used in the ONP procedures is appropriate for use in applying the competition rules.

whether such alternative infrastructures are sufficiently dense to provide competition to the incumbent's network and the extent to which it would be possible for new access providers to enter the market.

Other relevant factors

74. In addition to market share data, and supply-side substitutability, in determining whether an operator is dominant the Commission will also examine whether the operator has privileged access to facilities which cannot reasonably be duplicated within an appropriate time frame, either for legal reasons or because it would cost too much.

75. As competing access providers appear and challenge the dominance of the incumbent, the scope of the rights they receive from Member States' authorities, and notably their territorial reach, will play an important part in the determination of market power. The Commission will closely follow market evolution in relation to these issues and will take account of any altered market conditions in its assessment of access issues under the competition rules.

1.3. Joint dominance

76. The wording of Article 82 makes it clear that the Article also applies when more than one company shares a dominant position. The circumstances in which a joint dominant position exists, and in which it is abused, have not yet been fully clarified by the case law of the Community judicature or the practice of the Commission, and the law is still developing.

77. The words of Article 82 ("abuse by one or more undertakings") describe something different from the prohibition of anti-competitive agreements or concerted practices in Article 81. To hold otherwise would be contrary to the usual principles of interpretation of the Treaty, and would render the words pointless and without practical effect. This does not, however, exclude the parallel application of Articles 81 and 82 to the same agreement or practice, which has been upheld by the Commission and the Court in a number of cases,[59] nor is there anything to prevent the Commission from taking action only under one of the provisions, when both apply.

78. Two companies, each dominant in a separate national market, are not the same as two jointly dominant companies. For two or more companies to be in a joint dominant position, they must together have substantially the same position *vis-à-vis* their customers and competitors as a single company has if it is in a dominant position. With specific reference to the telecommunications sector, joint dominance could be attained by two telecommunications infrastructure operators covering the same geographic market.

79. In addition, for two or more companies to be jointly dominant it is necessary, though not sufficient, for there to be no effective competition between the companies on the relevant market. This lack of competition may in practice be due to the fact that the companies have links such as agreements for cooperation, or interconnection agreements. The Commission does not, however, consider that either economic theory or Community law implies that such links are legally necessary for a joint dominant position to exist.[60] It is a sufficient economic link if there is the kind of interdependence which often comes about in oligopolistic situations. There does not seem to be any reason in law or in economic theory to require any other economic link between jointly dominant companies. This having been said, in practice such links will often exist in the telecommunications sector where national TOs nearly inevitably have links of various kinds with one another.

---

[59] Case 85/76 *Hoffmann-La Roche* [1979] ECR 461.
Commission Decision 89/113/EEC of 21 December 1988, *Decca Navigator System* (OJ 1989 L43/27).
[60] Commission Decision 92/553/EEC of 22 July 1992, *Nestlé/Perrier* (OJ 1992 L356/1).

80. To take as an example access to the local loop, in some Member States this could well be controlled in the near future by two operators—the incumbent TO and a cable operator. In order to provide particular services to consumers, access to the local loop of either the TO or the cable television operator is necessary. Depending on the circumstances of the case and in particular on the relationship between them, it is possible that neither operator holds a dominant position: together, however, they may hold a joint monopoly of access to these facilities. In the longer term, technological developments may lead to other local loop access mechanisms being viable, such as energy networks: the existence of such mechanisms will be taken into account in determining whether dominant positions or joint dominant positions exist.

2. Abuse of dominance

81. Application of Article 82 presupposes the existence of a dominant position and some link between the dominant position and the alleged abusive conduct. It will often be necessary in the telecommunications sector to examine a number of associated markets, one or more of which may be dominated by a particular operator. In these circumstances, there are a number of possible situations where abuses could arise:

— conduct on the dominated market having effects on the dominated market,[61]
— conduct on the dominated market having effects on markets other than the dominated market,[62]
— conduct on a market other than the dominated market and having effects on the dominated market,[63]
— conduct on a market other than the dominated market and having effects on a market other than the dominated market.[64]

82. Although the factual and economic circumstances of the telecommunications sector are often novel, in many cases it is possible to apply established competition law principles. When looking at competition problems in this sector, it is important to bear in mind existing case law and Commission decisional practice on, for example, leveraging market power, discrimination and bundling.

2.1. Refusal to grant access to facilities and application of unfavourable terms

83. A refusal to give access may be prohibited under Article 82 if the refusal is made by a company which is dominant because of its control of facilities, as incumbent TOs will usually be for the foreseeable future. A refusal may have "the effect of hindering the maintenance of the degree of competition still existing in the market or the growth of that competition".[65]

A refusal will only be abusive if it has exploitative or anti-competitive effects. Service markets in the telecommunications sector will initially have few competitive players and refusals will therefore generally affect competition on those markets. In all cases of refusal, any justification will be closely examined to determine whether it is objective.

84. Broadly there are three relevant scenarios:

---

[61] The most common situation.
[62] Joined Cases 6/73 and 7/73 *Commercial Solvents v. Commission* [1974] ECR 223 and Case 311/84 *CBEM v. CLT and IPB* [1985] ECR 3261.
[63] Case C–62/86, *AKZO v. Commission* [1991] ECR I–3359 and Case T–65/89 *BPB Industries and British Gypsum v. Commission* [1993] ECR II–389.
[64] Case C–333/94 P, *Tetra Pak International v. Commission* [1996] ECR I–5951. In this fourth case, application of Article 82 can only be justified by special circumstances (*Tetra Pak*, at paragraphs 29 and 30).
[65] Case 85/76, *Hoffmann-La Roche* [1979] ECR 461.

(a) a refusal to grant access for the purposes of a service where another operator has been given access by the access provider to operate on that services market;

(b) a refusal to grant access for the purposes of a service where no other operator has been given access by the access provider to operate on that services market;

(c) a withdrawal of access from an existing customer.

Discrimination

85. As to the first of the above scenarios, it is clear that a refusal to supply a new customer in circumstances where a dominant facilities owner is already supplying one or more customers operating in the same downstream market would constitute discriminatory treatment which, if it would restrict competition on that downstream market, would be an abuse. Where network operators offer the same, or similar, retail services as the party requesting access, they may have both the incentive and the opportunity to restrict competition and abuse their dominant position in this way. There may, of course, be justifications for such refusal—for example, *vis-à-vis* applicants which represent a potential credit risk. In the absence of any objective justifications, a refusal would usually be an abuse of the dominant position on the access market.

86. In general terms, the dominant company's duty is to provide access in such a way that the goods and services offered to downstream companies are available on terms no less favourable than those given to other parties, including its own corresponding downstream operations.

Essential facilities

87. As to the second of the above situations, the question arises as to whether the access provider should be obliged to contract with the service provider in order to allow the service provider to operate on a new service market. Where capacity constraints are not an issue and where the company refusing to provide access to its facility has not provided access to that facility, either to its downstream arm or to any other company operating on that services market, then it is not clear what other objective justification there could be.

88. In the transport field,[66] the Commission has ruled that a firm controlling an essential facility must give access in certain circumstances.[67] The same principles apply to the telecommunications sector. If there were no commercially feasible alternatives to

---

[66] Commission Decision 94/19/EC of 21 December 1993, *Sea Containers v. Stena Sealink*—Interim measure (OJ L15, 18.1.1994, p. 8).
Commission Decision 94/119/EEC of 21 December 1993, *Port of Rødby (Denmark)* (OJ 1994 L55/52).

[67] See also (among others):
Judgments of the Court of Justice and the Court of First Instance:
Cases 6 and 7/73 *Commercial Solvents v. Commission* [1974] ECR 223;
Case 311/84, *Télémarketing* [1985] ECR 3261;
Case C–18/88 *RTT v. GB-Inno* [1991] ECR I–5941;
Case C–260/89, *Elliniki Radiophonia Teleorassi* [1991] ECR I–2925;
Cases T–69, T–70 and T–76/89, *RTE, BBC and ITP v. Commission* [1991] ECR II–485, 535, 575;
Case C–271/90, *Spain v. Commission* [1992] ECR I–5833;
Cases C–241 and 242/91 *P, RTE and ITP Ltd v. Commission (Magill)*, [1995] ECR I–743.
Commission Decisions:
Commission Decision 76/185/ECSC of 29 October 1975, *National Carbonising Company* (OJ 1976 L35/6).
Commission Decision 88/589/EEC of 4 November 1988, *London European/Sabena* (OJ 1988 L317/47).
Commission Decision 92/213/EEC of 26 February 1992, *British Midland v. Aer Lingus* (OJ 1992 L96/34); *B&I v. Sealink* (1992) 5 CMLR 255; EC Bulletin, No. 6—1992, point 1.3.30.

the access being requested, then unless access is granted, the party requesting access would not be able to operate on the service market. Refusal in this case would therefore limit the development of new markets, or new products on those markets, contrary to Article 82(b), or impede the development of competition on existing markets. A refusal having these effects is likely to have abusive effects.

89. The principle obliging dominant companies to contract in certain circumstances will often be relevant in the telecommunications sector. Currently, there are monopolies or virtual monopolies in the provision of network infrastructure for most telecom services in the Community. Even where restrictions have already been, or will soon be, lifted, competition in downstream markets will continue to depend upon the pricing and conditions of access to upstream network services that will only gradually reflect competitive market forces. Given the pace of technological change in the telecommunications sector, it is possible to envisage situations where companies would seek to offer new products or services which are not in competition with products or services already offered by the dominant access operator, but for which this operator is reluctant to provide access.

90. The Commission must ensure that the control over facilities enjoyed by incumbent operators is not used to hamper the development of a competitive telecommunications environment. A company which is dominant on a market for services and which commits an abuse contrary to Article 82 on that market may be required, in order to put an end to the abuse, to supply access to its facility to one or more competitors on that market. In particular, a company may abuse its dominant position if by its actions it prevents the emergence of a new product or service.

91. The starting point for the Commission's analysis will be the identification of an existing or potential market for which access is being requested. In order to determine whether access should be ordered under the competition rules, account will be taken of a breach by the dominant company of its duty not to discriminate (see below) or of the following elements, taken cumulatively:

(a) access to the facility in question is generally essential in order for companies to compete on that related market.[68]

The key issue here is therefore what is essential. It will not be sufficient that the position of the company requesting access would be more advantageous if access were granted—but refusal of access must lead to the proposed activities being made either impossible or seriously and unavoidably uneconomic.

Although, for example, alternative infrastructure may as from 1 July 1996 be used for liberalised services, it will be some time before this is in many cases a satisfactory alternative to the facilities of the incumbent operator. Such alternative infrastructure does not at present offer the same dense geographic coverage as that of the incumbent TO's network;

(b) there is sufficient capacity available to provide access;

(c) the facility owner fails to satisfy demand on an existing service or product market, blocks the emergence of a potential new service or product, or impedes competition on an existing or potential service or product market;

(d) the company seeking access is prepared to pay the reasonable and non-discriminatory price and will otherwise in all respects accept non-discriminatory access terms and conditions;

(e) there is no objective justification for refusing to provide access.

Relevant justifications in this context could include an overriding difficulty of providing access to the requesting company, or the need for a facility owner which has undertaken investment aimed at the introduction of a new product or service to have sufficient time and opportunity to use the facility in order to place that new product or service on the market. However, although any justification will have to be

---

[68] It would be insufficient to demonstrate that one competitor needed access to a facility in order to compete in the downstream market. It would be necessary to demonstrate that access is necessary for all except exceptional competitors in order for access to be made compulsory.

examined carefully on a case-by-case basis, it is particularly important in the tele-communications sector that the benefits to end-users which will arise from a competitive environment are not undermined by the actions of the former State monopolists in preventing competition from emerging and developing.

92. In determining whether an infringement of Article 82 has been committed, account will be taken both of the factual situation in that and other geographic areas, and, where relevant, the relationship between the access requested and the technical configuration of the facility.

93. The question of objective justification will require particularly close analysis in this area. In addition to determining whether difficulties cited in any particular case are serious enough to justify the refusal to grant access, the relevant authorities must also decide whether these difficulties are sufficient to outweigh the damage done to competition if access is refused or made more difficult and the downstream service markets are thus limited.

94. Three important elements relating to access which could be manipulated by the access provider in order, in effect, to refuse to provide access are timing, technical configuration and price.

95. Dominant TOs have a duty to deal with requests for access efficiently: undue and inexplicable or unjustified delays in responding to a request for access may constitute an abuse. In particular, however, the Commission will seek to compare the response to a request for access with:

(a) the usual time frame and conditions applicable when the responding party grants access to its facilities to its own subsidiary or operating branch;
(b) responses to requests for access to similar facilities in other Member States;
(c) the explanations given for any delay in dealing with requests for access.

96. Issues of technical configuration will similarly be closely examined in order to determine whether they are genuine. In principle, competition rules require that the party requesting access must be granted access at the most suitable point for the requesting party, provided that this point is technically feasible for the access provider. Questions of technical feasibility may be objective justifications for refusing to supply—for example, the traffic for which access is sought must satisfy the relevant technical standards for the infrastructure—or there may be questions of capacity restraints, where questions of rationing may arise.[69]

97. Excessive pricing for access, as well as being abusive in itself,[70] may also amount to an effective refusal to grant access.

98. There are a number of elements of these tests which require careful assessment. Pricing questions in the telecommunications sector will be facilitated by the obligations under ONP Directives to have transparent cost-accounting systems.

Withdrawal of supply

99. As to the third of the situations referred to in point 84, some previous Commission decisions and the case law of the Court have been concerned with the withdrawal of supply from downstream competitors. In *Commercial Solvents*, the Court held that "an undertaking which has a dominant position on the market in raw materials and which, with the object of reserving such raw material for manufacturing its own derivatives, refuses to supply a customer, which is itself a manufacturer of these derivatives, and therefore risks

---

[69] As noted in point 91.
[70] See point 105.

eliminating all competition on the part of this customer, is abusing its dominant position within the meaning of Article 82."[71]

100. Although this case dealt with the withdrawal of a product, there is no difference in principle between this case and the withdrawal of access. The unilateral termination of access agreements raises substantially similar issues to those examined in relation to refusals. Withdrawal of access from an existing customer will usually be abusive. Again, objective reasons may be provided to justify the termination. Any such reasons must be proportionate to the effects on competition of the withdrawal.

2.2. Other forms of abuse

101. Refusals to provide access are only one form of possible abuse in this area. Abuses may also arise in the context of access having been granted. An abuse may occur *inter alia* where the operator is behaving in a discriminatory manner or the operator's actions otherwise limit markets or technical development. The following are non-exhaustive examples of abuse which can take place.

Network configuration

102. Network configuration by a dominant network operator which makes access objectively more difficult for service providers[72] could constitute an abuse unless it were objectively justifiable. One objective justification would be where the network configuration improves the efficiency of the network generally.

Tying

103. This is of particular concern where it involves the tying of services for which the TO is dominant with those for which it is not.[73] Where the vertically integrated dominant network operator obliges the party requesting access to purchase one or more services[74] without adequate justification, this may exclude rivals of the dominant access provider from offering those elements of the package independently. This requirement could thus constitute an abuse under Article 82.

The Court has further held that " ... even where tied sales of two products are in accordance with commercial usage or there is a natural link between the two products in question, such sales may still constitute abuse within the meaning of Article 82 unless they are objectively justified ... ".[75]

Pricing

104. In determining whether there is a pricing problem under the competition rules, it will be necessary to demonstrate that costs and revenues are allocated in an appropriate way. Improper allocation of costs and interference with transfer pricing could be used as mechanisms for disguising excessive pricing, predatory pricing or a price squeeze.

---

[71] Cases 6 and 7/73, *Commercial Solvents* [1974] ECR 223.

[72] That is to say, to use the network to reach their own customers.

[73] This is also dealt with under the ONP framework: see Article 7(4) of the Interconnection Directive, Article 12(4) of the Voice Telephony Directive and Annex II to the ONP Framework Directive.

[74] Including those which are superfluous to the party requesting access, or indeed those which may constitute services which that party itself would like to provide for its customers.

[75] *Tetra Pak International*, cited in footnote 64.

Excessive Pricing

105. Pricing problems in connection with access for service providers to a dominant operator's facilities will often revolve around excessively high prices[76]: In the absence of another viable alternative to the facility to which access is being sought by service providers, the dominant or monopolistic operator may be inclined to charge excessive prices.

106. An excessive price has been defined by the Court of Justice as being "excessive in relation to the economic value of the service provided".[77] In addition the Court has made it clear that one of the ways this could be calculated is as follows:

"This excess could, *inter alia*, be determined objectively if it were possible for it to be calculated by making a comparison between the selling price of the product in question and its cost of production".[78]

107. It is necessary for the Commission to determine what the actual costs for the relevant product are. Appropriate cost allocation is therefore fundamental to determining whether a price is excessive. For example, where a company is engaged in a number of activities, it will be necessary to allocate relevant costs to the various activities, together with an appropriate contribution towards common costs. It may also be appropriate for the Commission to determine the proper cost allocation methodology where this is a subject of dispute.

108. The Court has also indicated that in determining what constitutes an excessive price, account may be taken of Community legislation setting out pricing principles for the particular sector.[79]

109. Further, comparison with other geographic areas can also be used as an indicator of an excessive price: the Court has held that if possible a comparison could be made between the prices charged by a dominant company, and those charged on markets which are open to competition.[80] Such a comparison could provide a basis for assessing whether or not the prices charged by the dominant company were fair.[81] In certain circumstances, where comparative data are not available, regulatory authorities have sought to determine what would have been the competitive price were a competitive market to exist.[82] In an

---

[76] The Commission Communication of 27 November 1996 on Assessment Criteria for National Schemes for the Costing and Financing of Universal Service and Guidelines for the Operation of such Schemes will be relevant for the determination of the extent to which the universal service obligation can be used to justify additional charges related to the sharing of the net cost in the provision of universal service (COM(96) 608). See also the reference to the universal service obligation in point 59.

[77] Case 26/75, *General Motors Continental v. Commission* [1975] ECR 1367, at paragraph 12.

[78] Case 27/76, *United Brands Company and United Brands Continental BV v. Commission* [1978] ECR 207.

[79] *Ahmed Saeed*, cited in footnote 19, at paragraph 43.

[80] Case 30–87, *Corinne Bodson v. Pompes funèbres des régions libérées* [1988] ECR 2479.
See also:
Joined cases 110/88, 241/88 and 242/88 *François Lucazeau and others v. Société des Auteurs, Compositeurs et Editeurs de Musique* (SACEM) and others [1989] ECR 2811, at paragraph 25: "When an undertaking holding a dominant position imposes scales of fees for its services which are appreciably higher than those charged in other Member States and where a comparison of the fee levels has been made on a consistent basis, that difference must be regarded as indicative of an abuse of a dominant position. In such a case it is for the undertaking in question to justify the difference by reference to objective dissimilarities between the situation in the Member State concerned and the situation prevailing in all the other Member States."

[81] See ONP rules and Commission Recommendation on Interconnection in a liberalised telecommunications market (OJ 1998 L73/42 (Text of Recommendation) and OJ 1998 C84/3 (Communication on Recommendation)).

[82] For example, in their calculation of interconnection tariffs.

appropriate case, such an analysis may be taken into account by the Commission in its determination of an excessive price.

Predatory pricing

110. Predatory pricing occurs, *inter alia*, where a dominant firm sells a good or service below cost for a sustained period of time, with the intention of deterring entry, or putting a rival out of business, enabling the dominant firm to further increase its market power and later its accumulated profits. Such unfairly low prices are in breach of Article 82(a). Such a problem could, for example, arise in the context of competition between different telecommunications infrastructure networks, where a dominant operator may tend to charge unfairly low prices for access in order to eliminate competition from other (emerging) infrastructure providers. In general a price is abusive if it is below the dominant company's average variable costs or if it is below average total costs and part of an anti-competitive plan.[83] In network industries a simple application of the above rule would not reflect the economic reality of network industries.

111. This rule was established in the *AKZO* case where the Court of Justice defined average variable costs as "those which vary depending on the quantities produced"[84] and explained the reasoning behind the rule as follows:

"A dominant undertaking has no interest in applying such prices except that of eliminating competitors so as to enable it subsequently to raise its prices by taking advantage of its monopolistic position, since each sale generates a loss, namely the total amount of the fixed costs (that is to say, those which remain constant regardless of the quantities produced) and, at least, part of the variable costs relating to the unit produced."

112. In order to trade a service or group of services profitably, an operator must adopt a pricing strategy whereby its total additional costs in providing that service or group of services are covered by the additional revenues earned as a result of the provision of that service or group of services. Where a dominant operator sets a price for a particular product or service which is below its average total costs of providing that service, the operator should justify this price in commercial terms: a dominant operator which would benefit from such a pricing policy only if one or more of its competitors was weakened would be committing an abuse.

113. As indicated by the Court of Justice in *AKZO*, the Commission must determine the price below which a company could only make a profit by weakening or eliminating one or more competitors. Cost structures in network industries tend to be quite different to most other industries since the former have much larger common and joint costs.

114. For example, in the case of the provision of telecommunications services, a price which equates to the variable cost of a service may be substantially lower than the price the operator needs in order to cover the cost of providing the service. To apply the *AKZO* test to prices which are to be applied over time by an operator, and which will form the basis of that operator's decisions to invest, the costs considered should include the total costs which are incremental to the provision of the service. In analysing the situation, consideration will have to be given to the appropriate time frame over which costs should be analysed. In most cases, there is reason to believe that neither the very short nor very long run are appropriate.

115. In these circumstances, the Commission will often need to examine the average incremental costs of providing a service, and may need to examine average incremental costs over a longer period than one year.

---

[83] *AKZO*, cited in footnote 63.
[84] *AKZO*, paragraph 71.

116. If a case arises, the ONP rules and Commission recommendations concerning accounting requirements and transparency will help to ensure the effective application of Article 82 in this context.

Price Squeeze

117. Where the operator is dominant in the product or services market, a price squeeze could constitute an abuse. A price squeeze could be demonstrated by showing that the dominant company's own downstream operations could not trade profitably on the basis of the upstream price charged to its competitors by the upstream operating arm of the dominant company. A loss-making downstream arm could be hidden if the dominant operator has allocated costs to its access operations which should properly be allocated to the downstream operations, or has otherwise improperly determined the transfer prices within the organisation. The Commission Recommendation on Accounting Separation in the context of Interconnection addresses this issue by recommending separate accounting for different business areas within a vertically integrated dominant operator. The Commission may, in an appropriate case, require the dominant company to produce audited separated accounts dealing with all necessary aspects of the dominant company's business. However, the existence of separated accounts does not guarantee that no abuse exists: the Commission will, where appropriate, examine the facts on a case-by-case basis.

118. In appropriate circumstances, a price squeeze could also be demonstrated by showing that the margin between the price charged to competitors on the downstream market (including the dominant company's own downstream operations, if any) for access and the price which the network operator charges in the downstream market is insufficient to allow a reasonably efficient service provider in the downstream market to obtain a normal profit (unless the dominant company can show that its downstream operation is exceptionally efficient).[85]

119. If either of these scenarios were to arise, competitors on the downstream market would be faced with a price squeeze which could force them out of the market.

Discrimination

120. A dominant access provider may not discriminate between the parties to different access agreements where such discrimination would restrict competition. Any differentiation based on the use which is to be made of the access rather than differences between the transactions for the access provider itself, if the discrimination is sufficiently likely to restrict or distort actual or potential competition, would be contrary to Article 82. This discrimination could take the form of imposing different conditions, including the charging of different prices, or otherwise differentiating between access agreements, except where such discrimination would be objectively justified, for example on the basis of cost or technical considerations or the fact that the users are operating at different levels. Such discrimination could be likely to restrict competition in the downstream market on which the company requesting access was seeking to operate, in that it might limit the possibility for that operator to enter the market or expand its operations on that market.[86]

---

[85] Commission Decision 88/518/EEC of 18 July 1988, *Napier Brown/British Sugar* (OJ 1988 L284/4): the margin between industrial and retail prices was reduced to the point where the wholesale purchaser with packaging operations as efficient as those of the wholesale supplier could not profitably serve the retail market. See also *National Carbonising Company*, cited in footnote 67.

[86] However, when infrastructure capacity is under-utilised, charging a different price for access depending on the demand in the different downstream markets may be justified to the extent that such differentiation permits a better development of certain markets, and where such differentiation does not restrict or distort competition. In such a case, the Commission will analyse the global effects of such price differentiation on all of the downstream markets.

121. Such discrimination could similarly have an effect on competition where the discrimination was between operators on closely related downstream markets. Where two distinct downstream product markets exist, but one product would be regarded as substitutable for another save for the fact that there was a price difference between the two products, discriminating in the price charged to the providers of these two products could decrease existing or potential competition. For example, although fixed and mobile voice telephony services at present probably constitute separate product markets, the markets are likely to converge. Charging higher interconnection prices to mobile operators as compared to fixed operators would tend to hamper this convergence, and would therefore have an effect on competition. Similar effects on competition are likely in other telecommunications markets.

Such discrimination would in any event be difficult to justify given the obligation to set cost-related prices.

122. With regard to price discrimination, Article 82(c) prohibits unfair discrimination by a dominant firm between customers of that firm[87] including discriminating between customers on the basis of whether or not they agree to deal exclusively with that dominant firm.

123. Article 7 of the Interconnection Directive provides that "different tariffs, terms and conditions for interconnection may be set for different categories of organisations which are authorised to provide networks and services, where such differences can be objectively justified on the basis of the type of interconnection provided and/or the relevant national licensing conditions ... " (provided that such differences do not result in distortions of competition).

124. A determination of whether such differences result in distortions of competition must be made in the particular case. It is important to remember that Articles 81 and 82 deal with competition and not regulatory matters. Article 82 cannot require a dominant company to treat different categories of customers differently, except where this is the result of market conditions and the principles of Article 82. On the contrary, Article 82 prohibits dominant companies from discriminating between similar transactions where such a discrimination would have an effect on competition.

125. Discrimination without objective justification as regards any aspects or conditions of an access agreement may constitute an abuse. Discrimination may relate to elements such as pricing, delays, technical access, routing,[88] numbering, restrictions on network use exceeding essential requirements and use of customer network data. However, the existence of discrimination can only be determined on a case-by-case basis. Discrimination is contrary to Article 82 whether or not it results from or is apparent from the terms of a particular access agreement.

126. There is, in this context, a general duty on the network operator to treat independent customers in the same way as its own subsidiary or downstream service arm. The nature of the customer and its demands may play a significant role in determining whether transactions are comparable. Different prices for customers at different levels (for example, wholesale and retail) do not necessarily constitute discrimination.

127. Discrimination issues may arise in respect of the technical configuration of the access, given its importance in the context of access.

The degree of technical sophistication of the access: restrictions on the type or "level" in the network hierarchy of exchange involved in the access or the technical capabilities of this exchange are of direct competitive significance. These could be the facilities available to support a connection or the type of interface and signalling system used to determine the type of service available to the party requesting access (for example, intelligent network facilities).

The number and/or location of connection points: the requirement to collect and distribute traffic for particular areas at the switch which directly serves that area rather

---

[87] Case C–310/93P, *BPB Industries and British Gypsum v. Commission* [1995] ECR I–865, at p. 904, applying to discrimination by BPB among customers in the related market for dry plaster.
[88] That is to say, to a preferred list of correspondent network operators.

than at a higher level of the network hierarchy may be important. The party requesting access incurs additional expense by either providing links at a greater distance from its own switching centre or being liable to pay higher conveyance charges.

Equal access: the possibility for customers of the party requesting access to obtain the services provided by the access provider using the same number of dialled digits as are used by the customers of the latter is a crucial feature of competitive telecommunications.

Objective justification

128. Justifications could include factors relating to the actual operation of the network owned by the access provider, or licensing restrictions consistent with, for example, the subject matter of intellectual property rights.

2.3. Abuses of joint dominant positions

129. In the case of joint dominance (see points 76 *et seq.*) behaviour by one of several jointly dominant companies may be abusive even if others are not behaving in the same way.

130. In addition to remedies under the competition rules, if no operator was willing to grant access, and if there was no technical or commercial justification for the refusal, one would expect that the NRA would resolve the problem by ordering one or more of the companies to offer access, under the terms of the relevant ONP Directive or under national law.

3. Access agreements (Article 81)

131. Restrictions of competition included in or resulting from access agreements may have two distinct effects: restriction of competition between the two parties to the access agreement, or restriction of competition from third parties, for example through exclusivity for one or both of the parties to the agreement. In addition, where one party is dominant, conditions of the access agreement may lead to a strengthening of that dominant position, or to an extension of that dominant position to a related market, or may constitute an unlawful exploitation of the dominant position through the imposition of unfair terms.

132. Access agreements where access is in principle unlimited are not likely to be restrictive of competition within the meaning of Article 81(1). Exclusivity obligations in contracts providing access to one company are likely to restrict competition because they limit access to infrastructure for other companies. Since most networks have more capacity than any single user is likely to need, this will normally be the case in the telecommunications sector.

133. Access agreements can have significant pro-competitive effects as they can improve access to the downstream market. Access agreements in the context of inter-connection are essential to inter-operability of services and infrastructure, thus increasing competition in the downstream market for services, which is likely to involve higher added value than local infrastructure.

134. There is, however, obvious potential for anti-competitive effects of certain access agreements or clauses therein. Access agreements may, for example:

(a) serve as a means of coordinating prices;
(b) serve as a means of market sharing;
(c) have exclusionary effects on third parties[89];

---

[89] Commission Decision 94/663/EC of 21 September 1994, *Night Services* (OJ 1994 L259/20); Commission Decision 94/894/EC, see footnote 49.

(d) lead to an exchange of commercially sensitive information between the parties.

135. The risk of price coordination is particularly acute in the telecommunications sector since interconnection charges often amount to 50% or more of the total cost of the services provided, and where interconnection with a dominant operator will usually be necessary. In these circumstances, the scope for price competition is limited and the risk (and the seriousness) of price coordination correspondingly greater.

136. Furthermore, interconnection agreements between network operators may under certain circumstances be an instrument of market sharing between the network operator providing access and the network operator seeking access, instead of the emergence of network competition between them.

137. In a liberalised telecommunications environment, the above types of restrictions of competition will be monitored by the national authorities and the Commission under the competition rules. The right of parties who suffer from any type of anti-competitive behaviour to complain to the Commission is unaffected by national regulation.

Clauses falling within Article 81(1)

138. The Commission has identified certain types of restriction which would potentially infringe Article 81(1) of the Treaty and therefore require individual exemption. These clauses will most commonly relate to the commercial framework of the access.

139. In the telecommunications sector, it is inherent in interconnection that parties will obtain certain customer and traffic information about their competitors. This information exchange could in certain cases influence the competitive behaviour of the undertakings concerned, and could easily be used by the parties for collusive practices, such as market sharing.[90] The Interconnection Directive requires that information received from an organisation seeking interconnection be used only for the purposes for which it was supplied. In order to comply with the competition rules and the Interconnection Directives, operators will have to introduce safeguards to ensure that confidential information is only disclosed to those parts of the companies involved in making the interconnection agreements, and to ensure that the information is not used for anti-competitive purposes. Provided that these safeguards are complete and function correctly, there should be no reason in principle why simple interconnection agreements should be caught by Article 85(1).

140. Exclusivity arrangements, for example where traffic would be conveyed exclusively through the telecommunications network of one or both parties rather than to the network of other parties with whom access agreements have been concluded will similarly require analysis under Article 81(3). If no justification is provided for such routing, such clauses will be prohibited. Such exclusivity clauses are not, however, an inherent part of interconnection agreements.

141. Access agreements that have been concluded with an anti-competitive object are extremely unlikely to fulfil the criteria for an individual exemption under Article 81(3).

142. Furthermore, access agreements may have an impact on the competitive structure of the market. Local access charges will often account for a considerable portion of the total cost of the services provided to end-users by the party requesting access, thus leaving limited scope for price competition. Because of the need to safeguard this limited degree of competition, the Commission will therefore pay particular attention to scrutinising access agreements in the context of their likely effects on the relevant markets in order to ensure that such agreements do not serve as a hidden and indirect means for fixing or

---

[90] Case T–34/92, *Fiatagri UK and New Holland Ford v. Commission* [1994] ECR II–905;
Case C–8/95 P, *New Holland Ford v. Commission*, judgment of 28 May 1988, not yet reported;
Case T–35/92, *John Deere v. Commission* [1994] ECR II–957;
Case C–7/95 P, *John Deere v. Commission*, judgment of 28 May 1988, not yet reported.
(Cases involving applications brought against Commission Decision 92/157/EEC of 17 February 1992, *UK Agricultural Tractor Registration Exchange*) (OJ 1992 L68/19).

coordinating end-prices for end-users, which constitutes one of the most serious infringements of Article 81 of the Treaty.[91] This would be of particular concern in oligopolistic markets.

143. In addition, clauses involving discrimination leading to the exclusion of third parties are similarly restrictive of competition. The most important is discrimination with regard to price, quality or other commercially significant aspects of the access to the detriment of the party requesting access, which will generally aim at unfairly favouring the operations of the access provider.

4. Effect on trade between Member States

144. The application of both Article 81 and Article 82 presupposes an effect on trade between Member States.

145. In order for an agreement to have an effect on trade between Member States, it must be possible for the Commission to "foresee with a sufficient degree of probability on the basis of a set of objective factors of law or of fact that the agreement in question may have an influence, direct or indirect, actual or potential, on the pattern of trade between Member States".[92]

It is not necessary for each of the restrictions of competition within the agreement to be capable of affecting trade,[93] provided the agreement as a whole does so.

146. As regards access agreements in the telecommunications sector, the Commission will consider not only the direct effect of restrictions of competition on inter-state trade in access markets, but also the effects on inter-state trade in downstream telecommunications services. The Commission will also consider the potential of these agreements to foreclose a given geographic market which could prevent undertakings already established in other Member States from competing in this geographic market.

147. Telecommunications access agreements will normally affect trade between Member States as services provided over a network are traded throughout the Community and access agreements may govern the ability of a service provider or an operator to provide any given service. Even where markets are mainly national, as is generally the case at present given the stage of development of liberalisation, abuses of dominance will normally speaking affect market structure, leading to repercussions on trade between Member States.

148. Cases in this area involving issues under Article 82 are likely to relate either to abusive clauses in access agreements, or a refusal to conclude an access agreement on appropriate terms or at all. As such, the criteria listed above for determining whether an access agreement is capable of affecting trade between Member States would be equally relevant here.

CONCLUSIONS

149. The Commission considers that competition rules and sector specific regulation form a coherent set of measures to ensure a liberalised and competitive market environment for telecommunications markets in the Community.

---

[91] Case 8/72, *Vereniging van Cementhandelaaren v. Commission* [1972] ECR 977;
  Case 123/85, *Bureau National Interprofessionnel du Cognac v. Clair* [1985] ECR 391.
[92] Case 56/65, *STM* [1966] ECR 235, p. 249.
[93] Case 193/83, *Windsurfing International v. Commission* [1986] ECR 611.

150. In taking action in this sector, the Commission will aim to avoid unnecessary duplication of procedures, in particular competition procedures and national/Community regulatory procedures as set out under the ONP framework.

151. Where competition rules are invoked, the Commission will consider which markets are relevant and will apply Articles 81 and 82 in accordance with the principles set out above.

REGULATION 141[1]

Exempting Transport from the Application of Regulation 17

The Council of the European Economic Community

Having regard to the Treaty establishing the European Economic Community, and in particular [Article 67][2] thereof;

Having regard to the first regulation made in implementation of Articles 81 and 82 of the Treaty (Regulation 17) of 6 February, 1962, as amended by Regulation 59 of 3 July 1962;

Having regard to the proposal from the Commission;

Having regard to the Opinion of the Economic and Social Committee;

Having regard to the Opinion of the Assembly;

Whereas, in pursuance of the common transport policy, account being taken of the distinctive features of the transport sector, it may prove necessary to lay down rules governing competition different from those laid down or to be laid down for other sectors of the economy, and whereas Regulation 17 should not therefore apply to transport;

Whereas, in the light of work in hand on the formulation of a common transport policy, it is possible, as regards transport by rail, road, and inland waterway, to envisage the introduction within a foreseeable period of rules of competition; whereas, on the other hand, as regards sea and air transport it is impossible to foresee whether and at what date the Council will adopt appropriate provisions; whereas accordingly a limit to the period during which Regulation 17 shall not apply can be set only for transport by rail, road and inland waterway;

Whereas the distinctive features of transport make it justifiable to exempt from the application of Regulation 17 only agreements, decisions and concerted practices directly relating to the provision of transport services:

Has Adopted This Regulation:

Article 1

Regulation 17 shall not apply to agreements, decisions or concerted practices in the transport sector which have as their object or effect the fixing of transport rates and conditions, the limitation or control of the supply of transport or the sharing of transport markets; nor shall it apply to the abuse of a dominant position, within the meaning of Article 82 of the Treaty, within the transport market.

---

[1] OJ 1962 2751; OJ 1959–62, 291.
[2] Repealed by the Treaty of Amsterdam.

Article 2

The Council, taking account of any measures that may be taken in pursuance of the common transport policy, shall adopt appropriate provisions in order to apply rules of competition to transport by rail, road and inland waterway. To this end, the Commission shall, before 30 June 1964, submit proposals to the Council.

Article 3

Article 1 of this regulation shall remain in force, as regards transport by rail, road and inland waterway, until 31 December 1965.

Article 4

This regulation shall enter into force on 13 March 1962. This provision shall not be invoked against undertakings or associations of undertakings which, before the day following the date of publication of this regulation in the *Official Journal of the European Communities*, shall have terminated any agreement, decision or concerted practice covered by Article 1.
This regulation shall be binding in its entirety and directly applicable in all Member States.

Done at Paris, 26 November 1962.

REGULATION 1017/68[1]

Applying Rules of Competition to Transport by Rail, Road and Inland Waterway

THE COUNCIL OF THE EUROPEAN COMMUNITIES

Having regard to the Treaty establishing the European Economic Community, and in particular Articles 71 and 83 thereof;

Having regard to the proposal from the Commission;

Having regard to the Opinion of the European Parliament;

Having regard to the Opinion of the Economic and Social Committee;

Whereas Council Regulation 141 exempting transport from the application of Regulation 17 provides that the said Regulation 17 shall not apply to agreements, decisions and concerted practices in the transport sector the effect of which is to fix transport rates and conditions, to limit or control the supply of transport or to share transport markets, nor to dominant positions, within the meaning of Article 86 of the Treaty, on the transport market;

Whereas, for transport by rail, road and inland waterway, Regulation 1002/67 provides that such exemption shall not extend beyond 30 June 1968;

Whereas the establishing of rules of competition for transport by rail, road and inland waterway is part of the common transport policy and of general economic policy;

Whereas, when rules of competition for these sectors are being settled, account must be taken of the distinctive features of transport;

Whereas, since the rules of competition for transport derogate from the general rules of competition, it must be made possible for undertakings to ascertain what rules apply in any particular case;

Whereas, with the introduction of a system of rules on competition for transport, it is desirable that such rules should apply equally to the joint financing or acquisition of transport equipment for the joint operation of services by certain groupings of undertakings, and also to certain operations in connection with transport by rail, road or inland waterway of providers of services ancillary to transport.

Whereas, in order to ensure that trade between Member States is not affected or competition within the common market distorted, it is necessary to prohibit in principle for the three modes of transport specified above all agreements between undertakings, decisions of associations of undertakings and concerted practices between undertakings and all instances of abuse of a dominant position within the common market which could have such effects;

Whereas certain types of agreement, decision and concerted practice in the transport sector the object and effect of which is merely to apply technical improvements or to achieve technical co-operation may be exempted from the prohibition on restrictive agreements since they contribute to improving productivity; whereas, in the light of

---

[1] JO 1968 L175/1.

experience following application of this regulation, the Council may, on a proposal from the Commission, amend the list of such types of agreement;

Whereas, in order that an improvement may be fostered in the sometimes too dispersed structure of the industry in the road and inland waterway sectors, there should also be exempted from the prohibition on restrictive agreements those agreements, decisions and concerted practices providing for the creation and operation of groupings of undertakings in these two transport sectors whose object is the carrying on of transport operations, including the joint financing or acquisition of transport equipment for the joint operation of services; whereas such overall exemption can be granted only on condition that the total carrying capacity of a grouping does not exceed a fixed maximum, and that the individual capacity of undertakings belonging to the grouping does not exceed certain limits so fixed as to ensure that no one undertaking can hold a dominant position within the grouping; whereas the Commission must, however, have power to intervene if, in specific cases, such agreements should have effects incompatible with the conditions under which a restrictive agreement may be recognised as lawful, and should constitute an abuse of the exemption; whereas, nevertheless, the fact that a grouping has a total carrying capacity greater than the fixed maximum, or cannot claim the overall exemption because of the individual capacity of the undertakings belonging to the grouping, does not in itself prevent such a grouping from constituting a lawful agreement, decision or concerted practice if it satisfies the conditions therefor laid down in this regulation;

Whereas, where an agreement, decision or concerted practice contributes towards improving the quality of transport services, or towards promoting greater continuity and stability in the satisfaction of transport needs on markets where supply and demand may be subject to considerable temporal fluctuation, or towards increasing the productivity of undertakings, or towards furthering technical or economic progress, it must be made possible for the prohibition to be declared not to apply, always provided, however, that the agreement, decision or concerted practice takes fair account of the interests of transport users, and neither imposes on the undertakings concerned any restriction not indispensable to the attainment of the above objectives nor makes it possible for such undertakings to eliminate competition in respect of a substantial part of the transport market concerned, having regard to competition from alternative modes of transport;

Whereas it is desirable until such time as the Council, acting in pursuance of the common transport policy, introduces appropriate measures to ensure a stable transport market, and subject to the condition that the Council shall have found that a state of crisis exists, to authorise, for the market in question, such agreements as are needed in order to reduce disturbance resulting from the structure of the transport market;

Whereas, in respect of transport by rail, road and inland waterway, it is desirable that Member States should neither enact nor maintain in force measures contrary to this regulation concerning public undertakings or undertakings to which they grant special or exclusive rights; whereas it is also desirable that undertakings entrusted with the operation of services of general economic importance should be subject to the provisions of this regulation in so far as the application thereof does not obstruct, in law or in fact, the accomplishment of the particular tasks assigned to them, always provided that the development of trade is not thereby affected to such an extent as would be contrary to the interests of the Community; whereas the Commission must have power to see that these principles are applied and to address the appropriate directives or decisions for this purpose to Member States;

Whereas the detailed rules for application of the basic principles of this regulation must be so drawn that they not only ensure effective supervision while simplifying administration as far as possible but also meet the needs of undertakings for certainty in the law;

Whereas it is for the undertakings themselves, in the first instance, to judge whether the predominant effects of their agreements, decisions or concerted practices are the restriction of competition or the economic benefits acceptable as justification for such restriction and to decide accordingly, on their own responsibility, as to the illegality or legality of such agreements, decisions of concerted practices;

Whereas, therefore, undertakings should be allowed to conclude or operate agreements without declaring them; whereas this exposes such agreements to the risk of being declared void with retroactive effect should they be examined following a complaint or on the Commission's own initiative, but does not prevent their being retroactively declared lawful in the event of such subsequent examination;

Whereas, however, undertakings may, in certain cases, desire the assistance of the competent authorities to ensure that their agreements, decisions or concerted practices are in conformity with the rules applicable; whereas for this purpose there should be made available to undertakings a procedure whereby they may submit applications to the Commission and a summary of each such application is published in the *Official Journal of the European Communities*, enabling any interested third parties to submit their comments on the agreement in question; whereas, in the absence of any complaint from Member States or interested third parties and unless the Commission notifies applicants within a fixed time limit, that there are serious doubts as to the legality of the agreement in question, that agrement should be deemed exempt from the prohibition for the time already elapsed and for a further period of three years;

Whereas, in view of the exceptional nature of agreements needed in order to reduce disturbances resulting from the structure of the transport market, once the Council has found that a state of crisis exists undertakings wishing to obtain authorisation for such an agreement should be required to notify it to the Commission; whereas authorisation by the Commission should have effect only from the date when it is decided to grant it; whereas the period of validity of such authorisation should not exceed three years from the finding of a state of crisis by the Council; whereas renewal of the decision should depend upon renewal of the finding of a state of crisis by the Council; whereas, in any event, the authorisation should cease to be valid not later than six months from the bringing into operation by the Council of appropriate measures to ensure the stability of the transport market to which the agreement relates;

Whereas, in order to secure uniform application within the common market of the rules of competition for transport, rules must be made under which the Commission, acting in close and constant liaison with the competent authorities of the Member States, may take the measures required for the application of such rules of competition;

Whereas, for this purpose the Commission must have the co-operation of the competent authorities of the Member States and be empowered throughout the common market to request such information and to carry out such investigations as are necessary to bring to light any agreement, decision or concerted practice prohibited under this regulation, or any abuse of a dominant position prohibited under this regulation.

Whereas, if on the application of the regulation to a specific case, a Member State is of the opinion that a question of principle concerning the common transport policy is involved, it should be possible for such questions of principle to be examined by the Council; whereas it should be possible for any general questions raised by the implementation of the competition policy in the transport sector to be referred to the Council; whereas a procedure must be provided for which ensures that any decision to apply the regulation in a specific case will be taken by the Commission only after the questions of principle have been examined by the Council, and in the light of the policy guidelines that emerge from that examination;

Whereas, in order to carry out its duty of ensuring that the provisions of this regulation are applied, the Commission must be empowered to address to undertakings or associations of undertakings recommendations and decisions for the purpose of bringing to an end infringements of the provisions of this regulation prohibiting certain agreements, decisions or practices;

Whereas compliance with the prohibitions laid down in this regulation and the fulfilment of obligations imposed on undertakings and associations of undertakings under this regulation must be enforceable by means of fines and periodic penalty payments;

Whereas undertakings concerned must be accorded the right to be heard by the Commission, third parties whose interests may be affected by a decision must be given the opportunity of submitting their comments beforehand, and it must be ensured that wide publicity is given to decisions taken;

Whereas, it is desirable to confer upon the Court of Justice, pursuant to Article 229, unlimited jurisdiction in respect of decisions under which the Commission imposes fines or periodic penalty payments;

Whereas it is expedient to postpone for six months, as regards agreements, decisions and concerted practices in existence at the date of publication of this regulation in the *Official Journal of the European Communities*, the entry into force of the prohibition laid down in the regulation, in order to make it easier for undertakings to adjust their operations so as to conform to its provisions;

Whereas, following discussions with the third countries signatories to the Revised Convention for the Navigation of the Rhine, and within an appropriate period of time from the conclusion of those discussions, this regulation as a whole should be amended as necessary in the light of the obligations arising out of the Revised Convention for the Navigation of the Rhine.

Whereas the regulation should be amended as necessary in the light of the experience gained over a three-year period; whereas it will in particular be desirable to consider whether, in the light of the development of the common transport policy over that period, the scope of the regulation should be extended to agreements, decisions and concerted practices, and to instances of abuse of a dominant position, not affecting trade between Member States;

HAS ADOPTED THIS REGULATION:

Article 1

Basic Provision

The provisions of this regulation shall, in the field of transport by rail, road and inland waterway, apply both to all agreements, decisions and concerted practices which have as their object or effect the fixing of transport rates and conditions, the limitation or control of the supply of transport, the sharing of transport markets, the application of technical improvements or technical co-operation, or the joint financing or acquisition of transport equipment or supplies where such operations are directly related to the provision of transport services and are necessary for the joint operation of services by a grouping within the meaning of Article 4 of road or inland waterway transport undertakings, and to the abuse of a dominant position on the transport market. These provisions shall apply also to operations of providers of services ancillary to transport which have any of the objects or effects listed above.

Article 2

Prohibition of Restrictive Practices

Subject to the provisions of Articles 3 to 6, the following shall be prohibited as incompatible with the common market, no prior decision to that effect being required: all agreements between undertakings, decisions by associations of undertakings and concerted practices liable to affect trade between Member States which have as their object or effect the prevention, restriction or distortion of competition within the common market, and in particular those which:

(a) directly or indirectly fix transport rate and conditions or any other trading conditions;
(b) limit or control the supply of transport, markets, technical development or investment;

(c) share transport markets;
(d) apply dissimilar conditions to equivalent transactions with other trading parties, thereby placing them at a competitive disadvantage;
(e) make the conclusion of contracts subject to acceptance by the other parties of additional obligations which, by their nature or according to commercial usage, have no connection with the provision of transport services.

Article 3

Exception for Technical Agreements

1. The prohibition laid down in Article 2 shall not apply to agreements, decisions or concerted practices the sole object and effect of which is to apply technical improvements or to achieve technical co-operation by means of:

(a) the standardisation of equipment, transport supplies, vehicles or fixed installations;
(b) the exchange or pooling, for the purpose of operating transport services, of staff, equipment, vehicles or fixed installations;
(c) the organisation and execution of successive, complementary, substitute or combined transport operations, and the fixing and application of inclusive rates and conditions for such operations, including special competitive rates;
(d) the use, for journeys by a single mode of transport, of the routes which are most rational from the operational point of view;
(e) the co-ordination of transport timetables for connecting routes;
(f) the grouping of single consignments;
(g) the establishment of uniform rules as to the structure of tariffs and their conditions of application, provided such rules do not lay down transport rates and conditions.

2. The Commission shall, where appropriate, submit proposals to the Council with a view to extending or reducing the list in paragraph (1).

Article 4

Exemption for Groups of Small and Medium-sized Undertakings

1. The agreements, decisions and concerted practices referred to in Article 2 shall be exempt from the prohibition in that article where their purpose is

— the constitution and operation of groupings of road or inland waterway transport undertakings with a view to carrying on transport activities;
— the joint financing or acquisition of transport equipment or supplies, where these operations are directly related to the provision of transport services and are necessary for the joint operations of the aforesaid groupings;

always provided that the total carrying capacity of any grouping does not exceed;

— 10,000 metric tons in the case of road transport,
— 500,000 metric tons in the case of transport by inland waterway.

The individual capacity of each undertaking belonging to a grouping shall not exceed 1,000 metric tons in the case of road transport or 50,000 metric tons in the case of transport by inland waterway.
2. If the implementation of any agreement, decision or concerted practice covered by paragraph 1 has, in a given case, effects which are incompatible with the requirements of

Article 5 and which constitute an abuse of the exemption from the provisions of Article 2, undertakings or associations of undertakings may be required to make such effects cease.

Article 5

Non-applicability of the Prohibition

The prohibition in Article 2 may be declared inapplicable with retroactive effect to:

— any agreement or category of agreement between undertakings;
— any decision or category of decision of an association of undertakings, or
— any concerted practice or category or concerted practice which contributes towards:
— improving the quality of transport services; or
— promoting greater continuity and stability in the satisfaction of transport needs on markets where supply and demand are subject to considerable temporal fluctuation; or
— increasing productivity of undertakings; or
— furthering technical or economic progress;

and at the same time takes fair account of the interests of transport users and neither:

(a) imposes on the transport undertakings concerned any restriction not essential to the attainment of the above objectives; nor
(b) makes it possible for such undertakings to eliminate competition in respect of a substantial part of the transport market concerned.

Article 6

Agreements Intended to Reduce Disturbances Resulting from the Structure of the Transport Market

1. Until such time as the Council, acting in pursuance of the common transport policy, introduces appropriate measures to ensure a stable transport market, the prohibition laid down in Article 2 may be declared inapplicable to any agreement, decision or concerted practice which tends to reduce disturbances on the market in question.

2. A decision not to apply the prohibition laid down in Article 2, made in accordance with the procedure laid down in Article 14, may not be taken until the Council, either acting by a qualified majority or, where any Member State considers that the conditions set out in Article 71(3) of the Treaty are satisfied, acting unanimously, has found, on the basis of a report by the Commission, that a state of crisis exists in all or part of a transport market.

3. Without prejudice to the provisions of paragraph (2), the prohibition in Article 2 may be declared inapplicable only where:

(a) the agreement, decision or concerted practice in question does not impose upon the undertakings concerned any restriction not indispensable to the reduction of disturbances; and
(b) does not make it possible for such undertakings to eliminate competition in respect of a substantial part of the transport market concerned.

661

Article 7

Invalidity of Agreements and Decisions

Any agreement or decision prohibited under the foregoing provisions shall be automatically void.

Article 8

Prohibition of Abuse of Dominant Positions

Any abuse by one or more undertakings of a dominant position within the common market or in a substantial part of it shall be prohibited as incompatible with the common market in so far as trade between Member States may be affected thereby.

Such abuse may, in particular, consist in:

(a) directly or indirectly imposing unfair transport rates or conditions;
(b) limiting the supply of transport, markets or technical development to the prejudice of consumers;
(c) applying dissimilar conditions to equivalent transactions with other trading parties, thereby placing them at a competitive disadvantage;
(d) making the conclusion of contracts subject to acceptance by the other parties of supplementary obligations which, by their nature or according to commercial usage, have no connection with the provision of transport services.

Article 9

Public Undertakings

1. In the case of public undertakings and undertakings to which Member States grant special or exclusive rights, Member States shall neither enact nor maintain in force any measure contrary to the provisions of the foregoing articles.

2. Undertakings entrusted with the operation of services of general economic importance shall be subject to the provisions of the foregoing articles, in so far as the application thereof does not obstruct, in law or in fact, the accomplishment of the particular tasks assigned to them. The development of trade must not be affected to such an extent as would be contrary to the interests of the Community.

3. The Commission shall see that the provisions of this article are applied and shall, where necessary, address appropriate directives or decisions to Member States.

Article 10

Procedures on Complaint or on the Commission's Own Initiative

Acting on receipt of a complaint or on its own initiative, the Commission shall initiate procedures to terminate any infringement of the provisions of Article 2 or of Article 8 or to enforce Article 4(2).

Complaints may be submitted by:

(a) Member States;
(b) natural or legal persons who claim a legitimate interest.

Article 11

Result of Procedures on Complaint or on the Commission's Own Initiative

1. Where the Commission finds that there has been an infringement of Article 2 or Article 8, it may by decision require the undertakings or associations of undertakings concerned to bring such infringement to an end.

Without prejudice to the other provisions of this regulation, the Commission may, before taking a decision under the preceding sub-paragraph, address to the undertakings or associations of undertakings concerned recommendations for termination of the infringement.

2. Paragraph (1) shall apply also to cases falling within Article 4(2).

3. If the Commission, acting on a complaint received, concludes that on the evidence before it there are no grounds for intervention under Article 2, Article 4(2) or Article 8 in respect of any agreement, decision or practice, it shall issue a decision rejecting the complaint as unfounded.

4. If the Commission, whether acting on a complaint received or on its own initiative, concludes that an agreement, decision or concerted practice satisfies the provisions both of Article 2 and of Article 5, it shall issue a decision applying Article 5. Such decision shall indicate that date from which it is to take effect. This date may be prior to that of the decision.

Article 12

Application of Article 5—Objections

1. Undertakings and associations of agreements which seek application of Article 5 in respect of agreements, decisions and concerted practices falling within the provisions of Article 2 to which they are parties may submit applications to the Commission.

2. If the Commission judges an application admissible and is in possession of all the available evidence, and no action under Article 10 has been taken against the agreement, decision or concerted practice in question, then it shall publish as soon as possible in the *Official Journal of the European Communities* a summary of the application and invite all interested third parties to submit their comments to the Commission within thirty days. Such publication shall have regard to the legitimate interest of undertakings in the protection of their business secrets.

3. Unless the Commission notifies applicants, within 90 days from the date of such publication in the *Official Journal of the European Communities*, that there are serious doubts as to the applicability of Article 5, the agreement, decision or concerted practice shall be deemed exempt, in so far as it conforms with the description given in the application, from the prohibition for the time already elapsed and for a maximum of three years from the date of publication in the *Official Journal of the European Communities*.

If the Commission finds, after expiry of the 90-day time limit, but before expiry of the three-year period, that the conditions for applying Article 5 are not satisfied, it shall issue a decision declaring that the prohibition in Article 2 is applicable. Such decision may be retroactive where the parties concerned have given inaccurate information or where they abuse the exemption from the provisions of Article 2.

4. If, within the 90-day time limit, the Commission notifies applicants as referred to in the first sub-paragraph of paragraph (3), it shall examine whether the provisions of Article 2 and of Article 5 are satisfied.

If it finds that the provisions of Article 2 and of Article 5 are satisfied it shall issue a decision applying Article 5. The decisions shall indicate the date from which it is to take effect. This date may be prior to that of the application.

Article 13

Duration and Revocation of Decisions Applying Article 5

1. Any decision applying Article 5 taken under Article 11(4) or under the second sub-paragraph of Article 12(4) shall indicate the period for which it is to be valid; normally such period shall not be less than six years. Conditions and obligations may be attached to the decision.

2. The decision may be renewed if the conditions for applying Article 5 continue to be satisfied.

3. The Commission may revoke or amend its decision or prohibit specified acts by the parties.

(a) where there has been a change in any of the facts which were basic to the making of the decision;
(b) where the parties commit a breach of any obligation attached to the decision;
(c) where the decision is based on incorrect information or was induced by deceit;
(d) where the parties abuse the exemption from the provisions of Article 2 granted to them by the decision.

In cases falling within (b), (c) or (d), the decision may be revoked with retroactive effect.

Article 14

Decisions Applying Article 6

1. Any agreement, decision or concerted practice covered by Article 2 in respect of which the parties seek application of Article 6 shall be notified to the Commission.

2. Any decision by the Commission to apply Article 6 shall have effect only from the date of its adoption. It shall state the period for which it is to be valid. Such period shall not exceed three years from the finding of a state of crisis by the Council provided for in Article 6(2).

3. Such decision may be renewed by the Commission if the Council again finds, acting under the procedure provided for in Article 6(2), that there is a state of crisis and if the other conditions laid down in Article 6 continue to be satisfied.

4. Conditions and obligations may be attached to this decision.

5. The decision of the Commission shall cease to have effect not later than six months from the coming into operation of the measures referred to in Article 6(1).

6. The provisions of Article 13(3) shall apply.

Article 15

Powers

Subject to review of its decision by the Court of Justice, the Commission shall have sole power:

— to impose obligations pursuant to Article 4(2);
— to issue decisions pursuant to Articles 5 and 6.

The authorities of the Member States shall retain the power to decide whether any case falls within the provisions of Article 2 or Article 8, until such time as the Commission has initiated a procedure with a view to formulating a decision in the case in question or has sent notification as provided for in the first sub-paragraph of Article 12(3).

Article 16

Liaison with the Authorities of the Member States

1. The Commission shall carry out the procedures provided for in this regulation in close and constant liaison with the competent authorities of the Member States; these authorities shall have the right to express their views on such procedures.

2. The Commission shall immediately forward to the competent authorities of the Member States copies of the complaints and applications, and of the most important document sent to it or which it sends out in the course of such procedure.

3. An Advisory Committee on Restrictive Practices and Monopolies in the Transport Industry shall be consulted prior to the taking of any decision following upon a procedure under Article 10 or of any decision under the second sub-paragraph of Article 12(3), or under the second sub-paragraph of paragraph (4) of the same Article, or under paragraph (2) or paragraph (3) of Article 14. The Advisory Committee shall also be consulted prior to adoption of the implementing provisions provided for in Article 29.

4. The Advisory Committee shall be composed of officials competent in the matter of restrictive practices and monopolies in transport. Each Member State shall appoint two officials to represent it, each of whom, if prevented from attending, may be replaced by some other official.

5. Consultation shall take place at a joint meeting convened by the Commission; such meeting shall be held not earlier than 14 days after dispatch of the notice convening it. This notice shall, in respect of each case to be examined, be accompanied by a summary of the case together with an indication of the most important documents, and a preliminary draft decision.

6. The Advisory Committee may deliver an opinion notwithstanding that some of its members or their alternates are not present. A report of the outcome of the consultative proceedings shall be annexed to the draft decision. It shall not be made public.

Article 17

Consideration by the Council of Questions of Principle Concerning the Common Transport Policy Raised in Connection with Specific Cases

1. The Commission shall not give a decision in respect of which consultation as laid down in Article 16 is compulsory until after the expiry of 20 days from the date on which the Advisory Committee has delivered its Opinion.

2. Before the expiry of the period specified in paragraph (1), any Member State may request that the Council be convened to examine with the Commission any question of principle concerning the common transport policy which such Member State considers to be involved in the particular case for decision.

The Council shall meet within 30 days from the request by the Member State concerned for the sole purpose of considering such questions of principle.

The Commission shall not give its decision until after the Council meeting.

3. Further, the Council may at any time, at the request of a Member State or of the Commission, consider general questions raised by the implementation of the competition policy in the transport sector.

4. In all cases where the Council is asked to meet to consider under paragraph (2) questions of principle or under paragraph (3) general questions, the Commission shall, for the purposes of this Regulation, take into account the policy guidelines which emerge from that meeting.

665

Article 18

Inquiries into Transport Sectors

1. If trends in transport, fluctuations in or inflexibility of transport rates, or other circumstances, suggest that competition in transport is being restricted or distorted within the common market in a specific geographical area, or over one or more transport links, or in respect of the carriage of passengers or goods belonging to one or more specific categories, the Commission may decide to conduct a general inquiry into the sector concerned, in the course of which it may request transport undertakings in that sector to supply the information and documentation necessary for giving effect to the principles formulated in Articles 2 to 8.

2. When making inquiries pursuant to paragraph (1), the Commission shall also request undertakings or groups of undertakings whose size suggests that they occupy a dominant position within the common market or a substantial part thereof to supply such particulars of the structure of the undertakings and of their behaviour as are requisite to an appraisal of their position in the light of the provisions of Article 8.

3. Article 16(2) to (6) and Articles 17, 19, 20 and 21 shall apply.

Article 19

Requests of Information

1. In carrying out the duties assigned to it by this regulation, the Commission may obtain all necessary information from the Governments and competent authorities of the Member States and from undertakings and associations of undertakings.

2. When sending a request for information to an undertaking or association of undertakings, the Commission shall at the same time forward a copy of the request of the competent authority of the Member State in whose territory the seat of the undertakings is situated.

3. In its request, the Commission shall state the legal basis and the purpose of the request, and also the penalties provided for in Article 22(1)(*b*) for supplying incorrect information.

4. The owners of the undertakings or their representatives and, in the case of legal persons, companies or firms, or of associations having no legal personality, the person authorised to represent them by law or by their constitution, shall be bound to supply the information requested.

5. Where an undertaking or association of undertakings does not supply the information requested within the time limit fixed by the Commission, or supplies incomplete information, the Commission shall by decision require the information to be supplied. The decision shall specify what information is required, fix an appropriate time limit within which it is to be supplied and indicate the penalties provided for in Article 22(1)(*b*) and Article 23(1)(*c*), and the right to have the decision reviewed by the Court of Justice.

6. The Commission shall at the same time forward a copy of its decision to the competent authority of the Member State in whose territory the seat of the undertaking or association of undertakings is situated.

Article 20

Investigations by the Authorities of the Member States

1. At the request of the Commission, the competent authorities of the Member States shall undertake the investigations which the Commission considers to be necessary under Article 21(1), or which it has ordered by decision pursuant to Article 21(3). The officials

of the competent authorities of the Member States responsible for conducting these investigations shall exercise their powers upon production of an authorisation in writing issued by the competent authority of the Member State in whose territory the investigation is to be made. Such authorisation shall specify the subject-matter and purpose of the investigation.

2. If so requested by the Commission or by the competent authority of the Member State in whose territory the investigation is to be made, the officials of the Commission may assist the officials of such authority in carrying out their duties.

Article 21

Investigating Powers of the Commission

1. In carrying out the duties assigned to it by this regulation, the Commission may undertake all necessary investigations into undertakings and associations of undertakings. To this end the officials authorised by the Commission are empowered:

(a) to examine the books and other business records;
(b) to take copies of or extracts from the books and business records;
(c) to ask for oral explanations on the spot;
(d) to enter any premises, land and vehicles of undertakings.

2. The officials of the Commission authorised for the purpose of these investigations shall exercise their powers upon production of an authorisation in writing specifying the subject-matter and purpose of the investigation and the penalties provided for in Article 22(1)(c) in cases where production of the required books or other business records is incomplete.

In good time before the investigation, the Commission shall inform the competent authority of the Member State in whose territory the same is to be made of the investigation and of the identity of the authorised officials.

3. Undertakings and associations of undertakings shall submit to investigations ordered by decision of the Commission. The decision shall specify the subject-matter and purpose of the investigation, appoint the date on which it is to begin and indicate the penalties provided for in Article 22(1)(c) and Article 23(1)(d) and the right to have the decision reviewed by the Court of Justice.

4. The Commission shall take decisions referred to in paragraph (3) after consultation with the competent authority of the Member State in whose territory the investigation is to be made.

5. Officials of the competent authority of the Member State in whose territory the investigation is to be made, may at the request of such authority or of the Commission, assist the officials of the Commission in carrying out their duties.

6. Where an undertaking opposes an investigation ordered pursuant to this article, the Member State concerned shall afford the necessary assistance to the officials authorised by the Commission to enable them to make their investigation. Member States shall, after consultation with the Commission, take the necessary measures to this end before 1 January 1970. [The Hellenic Republic shall, after consultation with the Commission, take the necessary measures to this end within a period of six months following accession.]

Amendment

In paragraph 6 the words in square brackets were added by the Act of Accession of the Hellenic Republic, Annex I(IV)(1).

Article 22

Fines

1. The Commission may by decision impose on undertakings or associations of undertakings fines of from 100 to 5,000 units of account where, intentionally or negligently:

(a) they supply incorrect or misleading information in an application pursuant to Article 12 or in a notification pursuant to Article 14; or

(b) they supply incorrect information in response to a request made pursuant to Article 18 or to Article 19(3) or (5), or do not supply information within the time limit fixed by a decision taken under Article 19(5); or

(c) they produce the required books or other business records in incomplete form during investigations under Article 20 or Article 21, or refuse to submit to an investigation ordered by decision issued in implementation of Article 21(3).

2. The Commission may by decision impose on undertakings or associations of undertakings fines of from 1,000 to 1,000,000 units of account, or a sum in excess thereof but not exceeding 10 per cent. of the turnover in the preceding business year of each of the undertakings participating in the infringement, where either intentionally or negligently:

(a) they infringe Article 2 or Article 8; or

(b) they commit a breach of any obligation imposed pursuant to Article 13(1) or Article 14(4).

In fixing the amount of the fine, regard shall be had both to the gravity and to the duration of the infringement.

3. Article 16(3) to (6) and Article 17 shall apply.

4. Decisions taken pursuant to paragraphs (1) and (2) shall not be of a criminal law nature.

Article 23

Periodic Penalty Payments

1. The Commission may by decision impose on undertakings or associations of undertakings periodic penalty payments of from 50 to 1,000 units of account per day, calculated from the date appointed by the decision, in order to compel them:

(a) to put an end to an infringement of Article 2 or Article 8 of this regulation the termination of which it has ordered pursuant to Article 11 or to comply with an obligation imposed pursuant to Article 4(2);

(b) to refrain from any act prohibited under Article 13(3);

(c) to supply complete and correct information which it has requested by decision taken pursuant to Article 19(5);

(d) to submit to an investigation which it has ordered by decision taken pursuant to Article 21(3).

2. Where the undertakings or associations of undertakings have satisfied the obligation which it was the purpose of periodic penalty payment to enforce, the Commission may fix the total amount of the periodic penalty payment at a lower figure than that which would arise under the original decision.

3. Article 6(3) to (6) and Article 17 shall apply.

Article 24

Review by the Court of Justice

The Court of Justice shall have unlimited jurisdiction within the meaning of Article 229 of the Treaty to review decisions whereby the Commission has fixed a fine or periodic penalty payment; it may cancel, reduce or increase the fine or periodic penalty payment imposed.

Article 25

Unit of Account

For the purpose of applying Articles 23 to 24 the unit of account shall be that adopted in drawing up the budget of the Community in accordance with Articles 277 and 279 of the Treaty.

Article 26

Hearing of the Parties and of Third Persons

1. Before taking decisions as provided for in Articles 11, 12(3), second sub-paragraph, and 12(4), 13(3), 14(2) and (3), 22 and 23, the Commission shall give the undertakings or associations of undertakings concerned the opportunity of being heard on the matters to which the Commission has taken objection.

2. If the Commission or the competent authorities of the Member States consider it necessary, they may also hear other natural or legal persons. Applications to be heard on the part of such persons where they show a sufficient interest shall be granted.

3. Where the Commission intends to give negative clearance pursuant to Article 5 or Article 6, it shall publish a summary of the relevant agreement, decision or concerted practice and invite all interested third parties to submit their observations within a time limit which it shall fix being not less than one month. Publication shall have regard to the legitimate interest of undertakings in the protection of their business secrets.

Article 27

Professional Secrecy

1. Information acquired as a result of the application of Articles 18, 19, 20 and 21 shall be used only for the purpose of the relevant request or investigation.

2. Without prejudice to the provisions of Articles 26 and 28, the Commission and the competent authorities of the Member States, their officials and other servants shall not disclose information acquired by them as a result of the application of this regulation and of the kind covered by the obligation of professional secrecy.

3. The provisions of paragraphs (1) and (2) shall not prevent publication of general information or surveys which do not contain information relating to particular undertakings or associations of undertakings.

Article 28

Publication of Decisions

1. The Commission shall publish the decisions which it takes pursuant to Articles 11, 12(3), second sub-paragraph, 12(4), 13(3) and 14(2) and (3).

2. The publication shall state the names of the parties and the main content of the decision; it shall have regard to the legitimate interest of undertakings in the protection of their business secrets.

Article 29

Implementing Provisions

The Commission shall have power to adopt implementing provisions concerning the form, content and other details of complaints pursuant to Article 10, applications pursuant to Article 12, notifications pursuant to Article 14(1) and the hearings provided for in Article 26(1) and (2).

Article 30

Entry into Force, Existing Agreements

1. This regulation shall enter into force on 1 July 1968.
2. Notwithstanding the provisions of paragraph 1, Article 8 shall enter into force on the day following the publication of this regulation in the *Official Journal of the European Communities*.
3. The prohibition in Article 2 shall apply form 1 January 1969, to all agreements, decision and concerted practices falling within Article 2 which were in existence at the date of entry into force of this regulation or which came into being between that date and the date of publication of this regulation in the *Official Journal of the European Communities*.

[The prohibition in Article 81(1) of the Treaty shall not apply to agreements, decisions and concerted practices which were in existence at the date of accession of Austria, Finland and Sweden and which, by reason of that accession, fall within the scope of Article 81(1) if, within six months from the date of accession, they are so amended that they comply with the conditions laid down in Articles 4 and 5 of this regulation. This subparagraph does not apply to agreements, decisions and concerted practices which at the date of accession already fall under Article 53(1) of the EEA Agreement.]

4. Paragraph (3) shall not be invoked against undertakings or associations of undertakings which, before the day following publication of this regulation in the *Official Journal of the European Communities*, shall have terminated any agreements, decisions or concerted practices to which they are party.

Amendment

Para. 3, second subparagraph was added by the Act of Accession of the Republic of Austria, the Republic of Finland and the Kingdom of Sweden, Annex 1(III)(B)2, as amended by Council Decision 95/1, Article 39.

Article 31

Review of the Regulation

1. Within six months of the conclusion of discussions with the third countries signatories of the Revised Convention for the Navigation of the Rhine; the Council, on a proposal from the Commission, shall make any amendments to this regulation which may prove necessary in the light of the obligations arising out of the Revised Convention for the Navigation of the Rhine.

2. The Commission shall submit to the Council, before 1 January 1971, a general report on the operation of this regulation and, before 1 July 1971, a proposal for a regulation to make the necessary amendments to this regulation.

This regulation shall be binding in its entirety and directly applicable in all Member States.

Done at Brussels, 19 July 1968.

APPENDIX 65

DIRECTIVE 91/440[1]

On The Development of the Community's Railways

THE COUNCIL OF THE EUROPEAN COMMUNITIES,

Having regard to the Treaty establishing the European Economic Community, and in particular Article 71 thereof,

Having regard to the proposal from the Commission,[2]

Having regard to the opinion of the European Parliament,[3]

Having regard to the opinion of the Economic and Social Committee,[4]

Whereas greater integration of the Community transport sector is an essential element of the internal market, and whereas the railways are a vital part of the Community transport sector;

Whereas the efficiency of the railway system should be improved, in order to integrate it into a competitive market, whilst taking account of the special features of the railways;

Whereas, in order to render railway transport efficient and competitive as compared with other modes of transport, Member States must guarantee that railway undertakings be accorded a status of independent operators behaving in a commercial manner and adapting to market needs;

Whereas the future development and efficient operation of the railway system may be made easier if a distinction is made between the provision of transport services and the operation of infrastructure; whereas given this situation, it is necessary for these two activities to be separately managed and have separate accounts;

Whereas, in order to boost competition in railway service management in terms of improved comfort and the services provided to users, it is appropriate for Member States to retain general responsibility for the development of the appropriate railway infrastructure;

Whereas, in the absence of common rules on allocation of infrastructure costs, Member States shall, after consulting the infrastructure management, lay down rules providing for the payment by railway undertakings and their groupings for the use of railway infrastructure; whereas such payments must comply with the principle of non-discrimination between railway undertakings;

Whereas Member States should ensure in particular that existing publicly owned or controlled railway transport undertakings are given a sound financial structure, whilst taking care that any financial rearrangement as may be necessary shall be made in accordance with the relevant rules laid down in the Treaty;

---

[1] OJ 1991 L237/25, of 29.7.1991.
[2] OJ 1990 L34/8 and OJ 1991 C87/7.
[3] OJ 1991 C19/254.
[4] OJ 1990 C225/27.

Whereas, in order to facilitate transport between Member States, railway undertakings should be free to form groupings with railway undertakings established in other Member States;

Whereas, such international groupings should be granted rights of access and transit in the Member States of establishment of their constituent undertakings, as well as transit rights in other Member States as required for the international service concerned;

Whereas, with a view to encouraging combined transport, it is appropriate that access to the railway infrastructure of the other Member States should be granted to railway undertakings engaged in the international combined transport of goods;

Whereas it is necessary to establish an advisory committee to monitor and assist the Commission with the implementation of this Directive;

Whereas, as a result, Council Directive 75/327/EEC of 20 May 1975 on the improvement of the situation of railway undertakings and the harmonization of rules governing financial relations between such undertakings and States[5] should be repealed,

HAS ADOPTED THIS DIRECTIVE:

SECTION I

Objective and scope

Article 1

The aim of this Directive is to facilitate the adoption of the Community railways to the needs of the Single Market and to increase their efficiency;

— by ensuring the management independence of railway undertakings;
— by separating the management of railway operation and infrastructure from the provision of railway transport services, separation of accounts being compulsory and organizational or institutional separation being optional,
— by improving the financial structure of undertakings,
— by ensuring access to the networks of member states for international groupings of railway undertakings and for railway undertakings engaged in the international combined transport of goods.

Article 2

1. This Directive shall apply to the management of railway infrastructure and to rail transport activities of the railway undertakings established or to be established in a Member State.

2. Member States may exclude from the scope of this Directive railway undertakings whose activity is limited to the provision of solely urban, suburban or regional services.

Article 3

For the purpose of this Directive:

— 'railway undertaking' shall mean any private or public undertaking whose main business is to provide rail transport services for goods and/or passengers with a requirement that the undertaking should ensure traction,

---

[5] OJ 1975 L152/3.

— 'infrastructure manager' shall mean any public body or undertaking responsible in particular for establishing and maintaining railway infrastructure, as well as for operating the control and safety systems,
— 'railway infrastructure' shall mean all the items listed in Annex I.A to Commission Regulation (EEC) No 2598/70 of 18 December 1970 specifying the items to be included under the various headings in the forms of accounts shown in Annex I to Regulation (EEC) No 1108/70,[6] with the exception of the final indent which, for the purposes of this Directive only, shall read as follows: 'Buildings used by the infrastructure department',
— 'international grouping' shall mean any association of at least two railway undertakings established in different Member States for the purpose of providing international transport services between Member States;
— 'urban and suburban services' shall mean transport services operated to meet the transport needs of an urban centre or conurbation, as well as the transport needs between such centre or conurbation and surrounding areas;
— 'regional services' shall mean transport services operated to meet the transport needs of a region.

SECTION II

Management independence of railway undertakings

Article 4

Member States shall take the measures necessary to ensure that as regards management, administration and internal control over administrative, economic and accounting matters railway undertakings have independent status in accordance with which they will hold, in particular, assets, budgets and accounts which are separate from those of the State.

Article 5

1. Member States shall take the measure necessary to enable railway undertakings to adjust their activities to the market and to manage those activities under the responsibility of their management bodies, in the interests of providing efficient and appropriate services at the lowest possible cost for the quality of service required.

Railway undertakings shall be managed according to the principles which apply to commercial companies; this shall also apply to their public services obligations imposed by the State and to public services contracts which they conclude with the competent authorities of the Member State.

2. Railway undertakings shall determine their business plans, including their investment and financing programme. Such plans shall be designed to achieve the undertakings' financial equilibrium and the other technical, commercial and financial management objectives; they shall also lay down the method of implementation.

3. In the context of the general policy guidelines determined by the State and taking into account national plans and contracts (which may be multiannual) including investment and financing plans, railway undertakings shall, in particular, be free to:

— establish with one or more other railway undertakings an international grouping;
— establish their internal organization, without prejudice to the provisions of Section III;

---

[6] OJ 1970 L278/1, Regulation amended by Regulation (EEC) No 2116/78 (OJ 1978 L246/7).

— control the supply and marketing of services and fix the pricing thereof, without prejudice to Council Regulation (EEC) No 1191/69 of 26 June 1969 on action by Member States concerning the obligation inherent in the concept of a public service in transport by rail, road and inland waterway,[7]
— take decisions on staff, assets and own procurement,
— expand their market share, develop new technologies and new services and adopt any innovative management techniques;
— establish new activities in fields associated with railway business.

SECTION III

Separation between infrastructure management and transport operations

Article 6

1. Member States shall take the measures necessary to ensure that the accounts for business relating to the provision of transport services and those for business relating to the management of railway infrastructure are kept separate. Aid paid to one of these two areas of activity may not be transferred to the other.

Accounts for the two areas of activity shall be kept in a way which reflects this prohibition.

2. Member States may also provide that this separation shall require the organization of distinct divisions within a single undertaking or that the infrastructure shall be managed by a separate entity.

Article 7

1. Member States shall take the necessary measures for the development of their national railway infrastructure taking into account, where necessary, the general needs of the Community.

They shall ensure that safety standards and rules are laid down and that their application is monitored.

2. Member States may assign to railway undertakings or any other manager the responsibility for managing the railway infrastructure and in particular for the investment, maintenance and funding required by the technical, commercial and financial aspects of that management.

3. Member States may also accord the infrastructure manager, having due regard to Articles 73, 87 and 88 of the Treaty, financing consistent with the tasks, size and financial requirements, in particular in order to cover new investments.

Article 8

The manager of the infrastructure shall charge a fee for the use of the railway infrastructure for which he is responsible, payable by railway undertakings and international groupings using that infrastructure. After consulting the manager, Member States shall lay down the rules for determining this fee.

The user fee, which shall be calculated in such a way as to avoid any discrimination between railway undertakings, may in particular take into account the mileage, the

---

[7] OJ 1969 156/1, p. 1; Regulation last amended by Regulation (EEC) No 1893/91 (OJ 1991 L169/1).

composition of the train and any specific requirements in terms of such factors as speed, axle load and the degree or period of utilization of the infrastructure.

SECTION IV

Improvement of the financial situation

Article 9

1. In conjunction with the existing publicly owned or controlled railway undertakings, Member States shall set up appropriate mechanisms to help reduce the indebtedness of such undertakings to a level which does not impede sound financial management and to improve their financial situation.

2. To that end, Member States may take the necessary measures requiring a separate debt amortization unit to be set up within the accounting departments of such undertakings.

The balance sheet of the unit may be charged, until they are extinguished, with all the loans raised by the undertaking both to finance investment and to cover excess operating expenditure resulting from the business of rail transport or from railway infrastructure management. Debts arising from subsidiaries' operations may not be taken into account.

3. Aid accorded by Member States to cancel the debts referred to in this Article shall be granted in accordance with Articles 73, 87 and 88 of the EEC Treaty.

SECTION V

Access to railway infrastructure

Article 10

1. International groupings shall be granted access and transit rights in the Member States of establishment of their constituent railway undertakings, as well as transit rights in other Member States, for international services between the Member States where the undertakings constituting the said groupings are established.

2. Railway undertakings within the scope of Article 2 shall be granted access on equitable conditions to the infrastructure in the other Member States for the purpose of operating international combined transport goods services.

3. Railway undertakings engaged in international combined transport of goods and international groupings shall conclude the necessary administrative, technical and financial agreements with the managers of the railway infrastructure used with a view to regulating traffic control and safety issues concerning the international transport services referred to in paragraphs 1 and 2. The conditions governing such agreements shall be non-discriminatory.

Section VI

Final provisions

Article 11

1. Member States may bring any question concerning the implementation of this Directive to the attention of the Commission. After consulting the committee provided for in paragraph 2 on these questions, the Commission shall take the appropriate decisions.

2. The Commission shall be assisted by an advisory committee composed of the representatives of the Member States and chaired by the representative of the Commission.

The representative of the Commission shall submit to the committee a draft of the measures to be taken. The committee shall deliver its opinion on the draft, within a time limit which the chairman may lay down according to the urgency of the matter, if necessary by taking a vote.

The opinion shall be recorded in the minutes; in addition, each Member State shall have the right to ask to have its position recorded in the minutes.

The Commission shall take the utmost account of the opinion delivered by the committee. It shall inform the committee of the manner in which its opinion has been taken into account.

Article 12

The provisions of this Directive shall be without prejudice to Council Directive 90/531/EEC of 17 September 1990 on the procurement procedure of entities operating in the water, energy, transport and telecommunications sectors.[8]

Article 13

Decision 75/327/EEC is hereby repealed as from 1 January 1993.

Reference to the repealed Decision shall be understood to refer to this Directive.

Article 14

Before 1 January 1995, the Commission shall submit to the Council a report on the implementation of this Directive accompanied, if necessary, by suitable proposals on continuing Community action to develop railways, in particular in the field of the international transport of goods.

Article 15

Member States shall, after consultation with the Commission, adopt the laws, regulations and administrative provisions necessary to comply with this Directive not later than 1 January 1993. They shall forthwith inform the Commission thereof.

When Member States adopt these provisions, they shall contain a reference to this Directive or be accompanied by such reference on the occasion of their official publication. The methods of making such a reference shall be laid down by the Member States.

---

[8] OJ 1990 L297/1.

Article 16

This Directive is addressed to the Member States.

Done at Brussels, 29 July 1991.

DIRECTIVE 95/19[1]

On the Allocation of Railway Infrastructure Capacity and the Charging of Infrastructure Fees

THE COUNCIL OF THE EUROPEAN UNION,

Having regard to the Treaty establishing the European Economic Community, and in particular Article 71 thereof,

Having regard to the proposal from the Commission,[2]

Having regard to the opinion of the Economic and Social Committee,[3]

Acting in accordance with the procedure laid down in Article 252 of the Treaty,[4]

Whereas greater integration of the Community transport sector is an essential element of the internal market and whereas the railways are a vital part of the Community transport sector;

Whereas the principle of the freedom to provide services needs to be applied in the railway sector, taking account of the specific characteristics of that sector;

Whereas Council Directive 91/440/EEC of 29 July 1991 on the development of the Community's railways[5] provides for certain access rights in international rail transport for railway undertakings and international groupings of railway undertakings;

Whereas it is important to ensure that, where railway undertakings and the international groupings which they constitute provide the services referred to in Article 10 of Directive 91/440/EEC, they benefit fully from the new access rights and whereas, to this end, it is appropriate to establish a system for the allocation of railway infrastructure and the charging of infrastructure fees which is non-discriminatory and uniform throughout the Community;

Whereas the scope of Directive 91/440/EEC should be maintained, including the exceptions laid down therein for regional, urban and suburban services, and whereas it should be specified that transport operations in the form of shuttle services through the Channel Tunnel are also excluded from the scope of that Directive;

Where, pursuant to the principle of subsidiarity, it is appropriate that the Community lay down the broad principles of such a system, leaving it to the Member States to put in place the detailed rules for the relevant practical implementation;

Whereas the Member States should ensure sufficient flexibility as regards the allocation of infrastructure capacity to allow efficient and optional use of the infrastructure;

---

[1] OJ 1995 L143/75, of 19.6.1995.

[2] OJ 1994 C24/2 and OJ 1994 C225/11.

[3] Opinion delivered on 14 September 1994 (OJ 1994 C393/56).

[4] Opinion of the European Parliament of 3 May 1994 (OJ 1994 C205/383), Council Common Position of 21 November 1994 (OJ 1994 C354/19) and Decision of the European Parliament of 14 March 1995 (OJ 1995 C89/31).

[5] OJ 1991 L237/25.

Whereas, however, it is necessary to grant certain priority rights with regard to the allocation of infrastructure capacity, notably for public services and services provided on a specific railway infrastructure;

Whereas it is also necessary to provide for the possibility of granting special rights in allocating infrastructure capacity if those rights are essential to ensure adequate transport services or to allow the financing of new infrastructure;

Whereas the accounts of the infrastructure manager should be in balance so that infrastructure expenditure can be covered;

Whereas, furthermore, it is necessary to define non-discriminatory rules as regards the charging of infrastructure fees in the same market;

Whereas efficient use of infrastructure capacity requires that fees be fixed according to a common set of general criteria;

Whereas, out of a general concern for transparency and non-discrimination, common rules should be adopted concerning the procedures for the allocation of infrastructure capacity and the charging of infrastructure fees;

Whereas, in the interests of traffic safety, railway undertakings must, in order to have access to a particular infrastructure, hold a certificate of safety based on certain common criteria and on national provisions, issued by the body competent for the infrastructure used; whereas they must also conclude with the infrastructure manager the requisite technical, administrative and financial agreements;

Whereas it is necessary to guarantee possibilities for making an appeal before an independent body against decisions taken by the authorities and bodies competent as regards the allocation of infrastructure capacity and the charging of infrastructure fees; whereas this possibility for making an appeal is required in particular to resolve any conflicts of interest in cases where an infrastructure manager is at the same time a transport services operator and is responsible for allocating train paths and/or collecting infrastructure fees,

HAS ADOPTED THIS DIRECTIVE:

SECTION I

Objective and scope

Article 1

1. The purpose of this Directive is to define the principles and procedures to be applied with regard to the allocation of railway infrastructure capacity and the charging of infrastructure fees for railway undertakings which are or will be established in the Community and the international groupings which they form, where such undertakings and groupings carry out services referred to in Article 10 of Directive 91/440/EEC under the conditions laid down in that Article.

2. Railway undertakings the activities of which are limited to the operation of urban, suburban and regional services shall be excluded from the scope of this Directive.

Railway undertakings and international groupings the business of which is limited to providing shuttle services for road vehicles through the Channel Tunnel are also excluded from the scope of this Directive.

3. Railway infrastructure capacity shall be granted in the form of the allocation of train paths in accordance with Community and national law.

Article 2

For the purpose of this Directive:

(a) "railway undertaking" means any public or private undertaking the main business of which is to provide rail transport services for goods and/or passengers, with a requirement that the undertaking must ensure traction;

(b) "international grouping" means any association of at least two railway undertakings established in different Member States for the purpose of providing international transport services between Member States;

(c) "infrastructure manager" means any public body or undertaking responsible in particular for establishing and maintaining railway infrastructure, as well as for operating the control and safety systems;

(d) "train path" means the infrastructure capacity needed to run a train between two places at a given time;

(e) "allocation" means the allocation of railway infrastructure capacity by an allocation body;

(f) "allocation body" means the authority and/or infrastructure manager designated by the Member States for the allocation of infrastructure capacity.

Section II

Allocation of railway infrastructure capacity

Article 3

Each Member State shall designate the allocation body in accordance with the requirements of this Directive. In particular, the allocation body, which shall be informed of all train paths available shall ensure that:

— railway infrastructure capacity is allocated on a fair and non-discriminatory basis and that,

— subject to Articles 4 and 5, the allocation procedure allows optimum effective use of the infrastructure.

Article 4

1. Member States may take the necessary measures to ensure that priority is given to the following rail services in the allocation of railway infrastructure capacity;

(a) services provided in the interest of the public, as defined in Council Regulation (EEC) No 1191/69 of 26 June 1969 on action by Member States concerning the obligations inherent in the concept of a public service in transport by rail, road and inland waterway[6];

(b) services wholly or partly operated on infrastructure constructed or developed for certain specific services (specialized high-speed or freight lines), without prejudice to Articles 81, 82 and 86 of the Treaty.

---

[6] OJ 1969 L156/1. Regulation as last amended by Regulation (EEC) No 1893/91 (OJ 1991 L109/1).

This provision shall apply without discrimination to all services within the scope of Article 1 having comparable characteristics and providing similar services.

2. With regard to services provided under paragraph 1(a), Member States may compensate the infrastructure manager for any financial losses incurred due to the imposition of a certain infrastructure capacity allocation in the interests of public service.

Article 5

Member States may grant special rights as regards infrastructure capacity allocation on a non-discriminatory basis to railway undertakings operating certain types of services or in certain areas if such rights are indispensable to ensure adequate public services or efficient use of infrastructure capacity or to allow the financing of new infrastructures, without prejudice to Articles 81, 82 and 86 of the Treaty.

SECTION III

Charging of infrastructure fees

Article 6

1. The accounts of an infrastructure manager shall, under normal business conditions over a reasonable time period, at least balance income from infrastructure fees plus State contributions on the one hand and infrastructure expenditure on the other.

2. The infrastructure manager may finance infrastructure development including provision or renewal of capital assets, and may make a return on capital employed.

Article 7

There shall be no discrimination in the charging for services of an equivalent nature in the same market.

after consulting the infrastructure manager, Member States shall lay down the rules for determining the infrastructure fees. These rules shall provide the infrastructure manager with the facility to market the available infrastructure capacity efficiently.

Article 8

1. The fees charged by the infrastructure manager shall be fixed according to the nature of the service, the time of the service, the market situation and the type and degree of wear and tear of the infrastructure.

2. As regards the procedures for the payment of fees, Member States may provide for the possibility that a global agreement be concluded with the infrastructure manager as regards public services, in accordance with Regulation (EEC) No 1191/69.

Article 9

1. The fees shall be paid to the infrastructure manager(s).

2. Member States may require the infrastructure manager to provide all the information on the fees necessary to satisfy them that they are charged on a non-discriminatory basis.

3. The infrastructure manager shall inform railway undertakings using its infrastructure to provide services referred to in Article 10 of Directive 91/440/EEC in good time of any major changes in the quality or capacity of the infrastructure concerned.

Section IV

General provisions

Article 10

1. Member States shall lay down the procedures for the allocation of railway infrastructure capacity referred to in Article 1(3). They shall publish their procedural rules and inform the Commission thereof.

2. An application for infrastructure capacity shall be submitted to the allocation body of the Member State on the territory of which the departure point of the service concerned is situated.

3. The allocation body to which an application has been submitted shall immediately inform the other allocation bodies concerned of this request. The latter shall take a decision as soon as possible but no later than one month after all relevant information has been submitted; each allocation body shall have the right to refuse an application. They shall immediately inform the allocation body to which the request has been submitted.

The allocation body to which an application has been submitted shall, together with the other allocation bodies concerned, take a decision on the application as soon as possible, but no later than two months after all relevant information has been submitted.

An application which has been refused on the grounds of insufficient capacity shall be reconsidered at the next time-table adjustment for the routes concerned if the applicant undertaking so requests. The dates for such adjustments and other administrative arrangements shall be available to interested parties.

The decision shall be communicated to the applicant undertaking. A refusal shall indicate the reason therefore.

4. An applicant undertaking may directly contact the other allocation bodies concerned with this request on condition that the allocation body to which the application has been submitted is informed.

5. The railway undertakings to which railway infrastructure capacity is allocated shall conclude the necessary administrative, technical and financial agreements with the infrastructure managers.

Article 11

1. The Member States shall provide that in addition a safety certificate in which the railway undertakings' safety requirements are set out be submitted in order to ensure safe service on the routes concerned.

2. In order to obtain the safety certificate, the railway undertaking must comply with the regulations under national law, compatible with Community law and applied in a non-discriminatory manner, laying down the technical and operational requirements specific to rail services and the safety requirements applying to staff, rolling stock and the undertaking's internal organization.

In particular, it must provide proof that the staff whom it employs to operate and accompany the trains providing services referred to in Article 10 of Directive 91/440/EEC has the necessary training to comply with the traffic rules applied by the infrastructure manager and to meet the safety requirements imposed on it in the interests of train movement.

The railway undertaking must also prove that the rolling stock comprising these trains has been approved by the public authority or by the infrastructure manager and checked in accordance with the operating rules applicable to the infrastructure used. The safety certificate shall be issued by the authority designated for the purpose by the Member State in which the infrastructure used is situated.

Article 12

Member States may provide for the possibility that applicants for infrastructure access are accompanied by a deposit or similar security.

If an applicant does not make use of an allocated train path, an amount may be deducted from the deposit which represents the cost incurred in processing the application and any subsequent loss of earnings due to the non-use of the infrastructure capacity concerned. In the other cases, the deposit/security shall be returned in its entirety.

SECTION V

Final provisions

Article 13

1. Member States shall take the measures necessary to ensure that decisions on the allocation of infrastructure capacity or the charging of fees shall be open to appeal before an independent body when so requested in writing by a railway undertaking. This body shall take its decision within two months of the submission of all relevant information.

2. Member States shall take the measures necessary to ensure that decisions taken in accordance with paragraph 1 are subject to judicial review.

Article 14

1. The Commission shall, two years after the application of this Directive, submit to the Council a report, accompanied — if necessary — by proposals regarding continued Community action, with particular regard to the possibility of enlarging the scope of the Directive.

2. Member States shall adopt the laws, regulations and administrative provisions necessary to comply with this Directive not later than two years following the date of the entry into force of this Directive. They shall forthwith inform the Commission thereof.

3. When Member States adopt the provisions referred to in paragraph 2, they shall contain a reference to this Directive or be accompanied by such reference at the time of their official publication. The methods of making such reference shall be laid down by the Member States.

Article 15

This Directive shall enter into force on the date of its publication in the *Official Journal of the European Communities*.

Article 16

This Directive is addressed to the Member States.

Done at Luxembourg, 19 June 1995.

684

REGULATION 4056/86[1]

Laying Down Detailed rules for the Application of Articles 81 and 82 of the Treaty to Maritime Transport

THE COUNCIL OF THE EUROPEAN COMMUNITIES

Having regard to the Treaty establishing the European Community, and in particular Articles 80(2) and 83 thereof,

Having regard to the proposal from the Commission,

Having regard to the opinion of the European Parliament,

Having regard to the opinion of the Economic and Social Committee,

Whereas the rules on competition form part of the Treaty's general provisions which also apply to maritime transport; whereas detailed rules for applying those provisions are set out in the Chapter of the Treaty dealing with the rules on competition or are to be determined by the procedures laid down therein;

Whereas according to Council Regulation No. 141, Council Regulation No. 17 does not apply to transport; whereas Council Regulation (EEC) No. 1017/68 applies to inland transport only; whereas, consequently, the Commission has no means at present of investigating directly cases of suspected infringement of Articles 81 and 82 in maritime transport; whereas, moreover, the Commission lacks such powers of its own to take decisions or impose penalties as are necessary for it to bring to an end infringements established by it;

Whereas this situation necessitates the adoption of a Regulation applying the rules of competition to maritime transport; whereas Council Regulation (EEC) No. 954/79 of 15 May 1979 concerning the ratification by Member States of, or their accession to, the United Nations Convention on a Code of Conduct for Liner Conference will result in the application of the Code of Conduct to a considerable number of conferences serving the Community; whereas the Regulation applying the rules of competition to maritime transport foreseen in the last recital of Regulation (EEC) No. 954/79 should take account of the adoption of the Code; whereas, as far as conferences subject to the Code of Conduct are concerned, the Regulation should supplement the Code or make it more precise;

Whereas it appears preferable to exclude tramp vessel services from the scope of this Regulation, rates for these services being freely negotiated on a case-by-case basis in accordance with supply and demand conditions;

Whereas this Regulation should take account of the necessity, on the one hand to provide for implementing rules that enable the Commission to ensure that competition is not unduly distorted within the common market, and on the other hand to avoid excessive regulation of the sector;

Whereas this Regulation should define the scope of the provisions of Articles 81 and 82 of the Treaty, taking into account the distinctive characteristics of maritime transport; whereas trade between Member States may be affected where restrictive practices or abuses concern international maritime transport, including intra-Community transport,

---

[1] OJ 1986 L378/4.

from or to Community ports; whereas such restrictive practices or abuses may influence competition, firstly, between ports in different Member States by altering their respective catchment areas, and secondly, between activities in those catchment areas, and disturb trade patterns within the common market;

Whereas certain types of technical agreement, decisions and concerted practices may be excluded from the prohibition on restrictive practices on the ground that they do not, as a general rule, restrict competition;

Whereas provision should be made for block exemption of liner conferences; whereas liner conferences have a stabilising effect, assuring shippers of reliable services; whereas they contribute generally to providing adequate efficient scheduled maritime transport services and give fair consideration to the interests of users; whereas such results cannot be obtained without the co-operation that shipping companies promote within conferences in relation to rates and, where appropriate, availability of capacity or allocation of cargo for shipment, and income; whereas in most cases conferences continue to be subject to effective competition from both non-conference scheduled services and, in certain circumstances, from tramp services and from other modes of transport; whereas the mobility of fleets, which is a characteristic feature of the structure of availability in the shipping field, subjects conferences to constant competition which they are unable as a rule to eliminate as far as a substantial proportion of the shipping services in question is concerned;

Whereas, however, in order to prevent conferences from engaging in practices which are incompatible with Article 81(3) of the Treaty, certain conditions and obligations should be attached to the exemption;

Whereas the aim of the conditions should be to prevent conferences from imposing restrictions on competition which are not indispensable to the attainment of the objectives on the basis of which exemption is granted; whereas to this end, conferences should not, in respect of a given route, apply rates and conditions of carriage which are differentiated solely by reference to the country of origin or destination of the goods carried and thus cause within the Community deflections of trade that are harmful to certain ports, shippers, carriers or providers of services ancillary to transport, whereas, furthermore, loyalty arrangements should be permitted only in accordance with rules which do not restrict unilaterally the freedom of users and consequently competition in the shipping industry, without prejudice, however, to the right of a conference to impose penalties on users who seek by improper means to evade the obligation of loyalty required in exchange for the rebates, reduced freight rates or commission granted to them by the conference; whereas users must be free to determine the undertakings to which they have recourse in respect of inland transport or quayside services not covered by the freight charge or by other charges agreed with the shipping line;

Whereas certain obligations should also be attached to the exemption; whereas in this respect users must at all times be in a position to acquaint themselves with the rates and conditions of carriage applied by members of the conference, since in the case of inland transports organised by shippers, the latter continue to be subject to Regulation (EEC) No. 1017/68; whereas provision should be made that awards given at arbitration and recommendations made by conciliators and accepted by the parties be notified forthwith to the Commission in order to enable it to verify that conferences are not thereby exempted from the conditions provided for in the Regulation and thus do not infringe the provisions of Articles 81 and 82;

Whereas consultations between users or associations of users and conferences are liable to secure a more efficient operation of maritime transport services which takes better account of users' requirements; whereas, consequently, certain restrictive practices which could ensue from such consultations should be exempted;

Whereas there can be no exemption if the conditions set out in Article 81(3) are not satisfied; whereas the Commission must therefore have power to take the appropriate measures where an agreement or concerted practice owing to special circumstances proves to have certain effects incompatible with Article 81(3); whereas, in view of the specific role fulfilled by the conferences in the sector of the liner services, the reaction of the

Commission should be progressive and proportionate; whereas the Commission should consequently have the power first to address recommendations, then to take decisions;

Whereas the automatic nullity provided for in Article 81(3) in respect of agreements or decisions which have not been granted exemption pursuant to Article 81(3) owing to their discriminatory or other features applies only to the elements of the agreement covered by the prohibition of Article 81(1) and applies to the agreement in its entirety only if those elements do not appear to be severable from the whole of the agreement; whereas the Commission should therefore, if it finds an infringement of the block exemption, either specify what elements of the agreement are, by the prohibition and consequently automatically void, or indicate the reasons why those elements are not severable from the rest of the agreement and why the agreement is therefore void in its entirety;

Whereas, in view of the characteristics of international maritime transport, account should be taken of the fact that the application of this Regulation to certain restrictive practices or abuses may result in conflicts with the laws and rules of certain third countries and prove harmful to important Community trading and shipping interests; whereas consultations and, where appropriate, negotiations authorised by the Council should be undertaken by the Commission with those countries in pursuance of the maritime transport policy of the Community;

Whereas this Regulation should make provision for the procedures, decision-making powers and penalties that are necessary to ensure compliance with the prohibitions laid down in Article 81(1) and Article 82, as well as the conditions governing the application of Article 81(3);

Whereas account should be taken in this respect of the procedural provisions of Regulation (EEC) No. 1017/68 applicable to inland transport operations which takes account of certain distinctive features of transport operations viewed as a whole;

Whereas, in particular, in view of the special characteristics of maritime transport, it is primarily the responsibility of undertakings to see to it that their agreements, decisions and concerted practices conform to the rules on competition, and consequently their notification to the Commission need not be made compulsory;

Whereas in certain circumstances undertakings may, however, wish to apply to the Commission for confirmation that their agreements, decisions and concerted practices are in conformity with the provisions in force; whereas a simplified procedure should be laid down for such cases,

HAS ADOPTED THIS REGULATION:

SECTION I

Article 1

Subject-matter and scope of the Regulation

1. This Regulation lays down detailed rules for the application of Articles 81 and 82 of the Treaty to maritime transport services.

2. It shall apply only to international maritime transport services from or to one or more Community ports, other than tramp vessel services.

3. For the purposes of this Regulation:

(a) "tramp vessel services" means the transport of goods in bulk or in break-bulk in a vessel chartered wholly or partly to one or more shippers on the basis of a voyage or time charter or any other form of contract for non-regularly scheduled or non-advertised sailings where the freight rates are freely negotiated case by case in accordance with the conditions of supply and demand;

687

(b) "liner conference" means a group of two or more vessel-operating carriers which provides international liner services for the carriage of cargo on a particular route or routes within specified geographical limits and which has an agreement or arrangement, whatever its nature, within the framework of which they operate under uniform or common freight rates and any other agreed conditions with respect to the provisions of liner services;

(c) "transport user" means an undertaking (*e.g.* shippers, consignees, forwarders, etc.) provided it has entered into, or demonstrates an intention to enter into, a contractual or other arrangement with a conference or shipping line for the shipment of goods, or any association of shippers.

Article 2

Technical agreements

1. The prohibition laid down in Article 81(1) of the Treaty shall not apply to agreements, decisions and concerted practices whose sole object and effect is to achieve technical improvements or co-operation by means of:

(a) the introduction or uniform application of standards or types in respect of vessels and other means of transport, equipment, supplies or fixed installations;

(b) the exchange or pooling for the purpose of operating transport services, of vessels, space on vessels or slots and other means of transport, staff, equipment or fixed installations;

(c) the organisation and execution of successive or supplementary maritime transport operations and the establishment or application of inclusive rates and conditions for such operations;

(d) the co-ordination of transport timetables for connecting routes;

(e) the consolidation of individual consignments;

(f) the establishment or application of uniform rules concerning the structure and the conditions governing the application of transport tariffs.

2. The Commission shall, if necessary, submit to the Council proposals for the amendment of the list contained in paragraph 1.

Article 3

Exemption for agreements between carriers concerning the operation of scheduled maritime transport services

Agreements, decisions and concerted practices of all or part of the members of one or more liner conferences are hereby exempted from the prohibition in Article 81(1) of the Treaty, subject to the condition imposed by Article 4 of this Regulation, when they have as their objective the fixing of rates and conditions of carriage, and, as the case may be, one or more of the following objectives:

(a) the co-ordination of shipping timetables, sailing dates or dates of calls;

(b) the determination of the frequency of sailings or calls;

(c) the co-ordination or allocation of sailings or calls among members of the conference;

(d) the regulation of the carrying capacity offered by each member;

(e) the allocation of cargo or revenue among members.

Article 4

Condition attaching to exemption

The exemption provided for in Articles 3 and 6 shall be granted subject to the condition that the agreement, decision or concerted practice shall not, within the common market, cause detriment to certain ports, transport users or carriers by applying for the carriage of the same goods and in the area covered by the agreement, decision or concerted practice, rates and conditions of carriage which differ according to the country of origin or destination or port of loading or discharge, unless such rates or conditions can be economically justified.

Any agreement or decision or, if it is severable, any part of such an agreement or decision not complying with the preceding paragraph shall automatically be void pursuant to Article 81(2) of the Treaty.

Article 5

Obligations attaching to exemption

The following obligations shall be attached to the exemption provided for in Article 3:

1. Consultations

There shall be consultations for the purpose of seeking solutions on general issues of principle between transport users on the one hand and conferences on the other concerning the rates, conditions and quality of scheduled maritime transport services.

These consultations shall take place whenever requested by any of the abovementioned parties.

2. Loyalty arrangements

The shipping lines' members of a conference shall be entitled to institute and maintain loyalty arrangements with transport users, the form and terms of which shall be matters for consultation between the conference and transport users' organisations. These loyalty arrangements shall provide safeguards making explicit the rights of transport users and conference members. These arrangements shall be based on the contract system or any other system which is also lawful.

Loyalty arrangements must comply with the following conditions:

(a) Each conference shall offer transport users a system of immediate rebates or the choice between such a system and a system of deferred rebates:
— under the system of immediate rebates each of the parties shall be entitled to terminate the loyalty arrangement at any time without penalty and subject to a period of notice of not more than six months; this period shall be reduced to three months when the conference rate is the subject of a dispute;
— under the system of deferred rebates neither the loyalty period on the basis of which the rebate is calculated nor the subsequent loyalty period required before payment of the rebate may exceed six months; this period shall be reduced to three months where the conference rate is the subject of a dispute.
(b) The conference shall, after consulting the transport users concerned, set out:
(i) a list of cargo and any portion of cargo agreed with transport users which is specifically excluded from the scope of the loyalty agreement; 100 per cent. loyalty arrangements may be offered but may not be unilaterally imposed;

(ii) a list of circumstances in which transport users are released from their obligation of loyalty; these shall include:

— circumstances in which consignments are dispatched from or to a port in the area covered by the conference but not advertised and where the request for a waiver can be justified, and

— those in which waiting time at a port exceeds a period to be determined for each port and for each commodity or class of commodities following consultation of the transport users directly concerned with the proper servicings of the port.

The conference must, however, be informed in advance by the transport user, within a specified period, of his intention to dispatch the consignment from a port not advertised by the conference or to make use of a non-conference vessel at a port served by the conference as soon as he has been able to establish from the published schedule of sailings that the maximum waiting period will be exceeded.

3. Services not covered by the freight charges

Transport users shall be entitled to approach the undertakings of their choice in respect of inland transport operations and quayside services not covered by the freight charge or charges on which the shipping line and the transport user have agreed.

4. Availability of tariffs

Tariffs, related to conditions, regulations and any amendments thereto shall be made available on request to transport users at reasonable cost, or they shall be available for examination at offices of shipping lines and their agents. They shall set out all the conditions concerning loading and discharge, the exact extent of the services covered by the freight charge in proportion to the sea transport and the land transport or by any other charge levied by the shipping line and customary practice in such matters.

5. Notification to the Commission of awards at arbitration and recommendations

Awards given at arbitration and recommendations made by conciliators that are accepted by the parties shall be notified forthwith to the Commission when they resolve disputes relating to the practices of conferences referred to in Article 4 and in points 2 and 3 above.

Article 6

Exemption for agreements between transport users and conferences concerning the use of scheduled maritime transport services

Agreements, decisions and concerted practices between transport users, on the one hand, and conferences, on the other hand, and agreements between transport users which may be necessary to that end, concerning the rates, conditions and quality of liner services, as long as they are provided for in Article 5(1) and (2) are hereby exempted from the prohibition laid down in Article 81(1) of the Treaty.

Article 7

Monitoring of exempted agreements

1. Breach of an obligation

Where the persons concerned are in breach of an obligation which, pursuant to Article 5, attaches to the exemption provided for in Article 3, the Commission may, in order to put an end to such breach and under the conditions laid down in Section II:

— address recommendations to the persons concerned;
— in the event of failure by such persons to observe those recommendations and depending upon the gravity of the breach concerned, adopt a decision that either prohibits them from carrying out or requires them to perform specific acts or, while withdrawing the benefit of the block exemption which they enjoyed, grants them an individual exemption according to Article 11(4) or withdraws the benefit of the block exemption which they enjoyed.

2. Effects incompatible with Article 81(3)

(a) Where, owing to special circumstances as described below, agreements, decisions and concerted practices which qualify for the exemption provided for in Articles 3 and 6 have nevertheless effects which are incompatible with the conditions laid down in Article 81(3) of the Treaty, the Commission, on receipt of a complaint or on its own initiative, under the conditions laid down in Section II, shall take the measures described in (c) below. The severity of these measures must be in proportion to the gravity of the situation.

(b) Special circumstances are, *inter alia*, created by:
   (i) acts of conferences or a change of market conditions in a given trade resulting in the absence or elimination of actual or potential competition such as restrictive practices whereby the trade is not available to competition; or
   (ii) acts of conference which may prevent technical or economic progress or user participation in the benefits;
   (iii) acts of third countries which:
      — prevent the operation of outsiders in a trade,
      — impose unfair tariffs on conference members,
      — impose arrangements which otherwise impede technical or economic progress (cargo-sharing, limitations on types of vessels).

(c) (i) If actual or potential competition is absent or may be eliminated as a result of action by a third country, the Commission shall enter into consultations with the competent authorities of the third country concerned, followed if necessary by negotiations under directives to be given by the Council, in order to remedy the situation. If the special circumstances result in the absence or elimination of actual or potential competition contrary to Article 81(3)(b) of the Treaty the Commission shall withdraw the benefit of the block exemption. At the same time it shall rule on whether and, if so, under what additional conditions and obligations an individual exemption should be granted to the relevant conference agreement with a view, *inter alia*, to obtaining access to the market for non-conference lines;
   (ii) If, as a result of special circumstances as set out in (b), there are effects other than those referred to in (i) hereof, the Commission shall take one or more of the measures described in paragraph 1.

Article 8

Effects incompatible with Article 82 of the Treaty

1. The abuse of a dominant position within the meaning of Article 82 of the Treaty shall be prohibited, no prior decision to that effect being required.

2. Where the Commission, either on its own initiative or at the request of a Member State or of natural or legal persons claiming a legitimate interest, finds that in any particular case the conduct of conferences benefiting from the exemption laid down in Article 3 nevertheless has effects which are incompatible with Article 82 of the Treaty, it may withdraw the benefit of the block exemption and take, pursuant to Article 10, all appropriate measures for the purpose of bringing to an end infringements of Article 82 of the Treaty.

3. Before taking a decision under paragraph 2, the Commission may address to the conference concerned recommendations for termination of the infringement.

Article 9

Conflicts of international law

1. Where the application of this Regulation to certain restrictive practices or clauses is liable to enter into conflict with the provisions laid down by law, regulation or administrative action of certain third countries which would compromise important Community trading and shipping interests, the Commission shall, at the earliest opportunity, undertake with the competent authorities of the third countries concerned, consultations aimed at reconciling as far as possible the abovementioned interest with the respect of Community law. The Commission shall inform the Advisory Committee referred to in Article 15 of the outcome of these consultations.

2. Where agreements with third countries need to be negotiated, the Commission shall make recommendations to the Council, which shall authorise the Commission to open the necessary negotiations.

The Commission shall conduct these negotiations in consultation with an Advisory Committee as referred to in Article 15 and within the framework of such directives as the Council may issue to it.

3. In exercising the powers conferred on it by this Article, the Council shall act in accordance with the decision-making procedure laid down in Article 80(2) of the Treaty.

SECTION II

RULES OF PROCEDURE

Article 10

Procedures on complaint or on the Commission's own initiative

Acting on receipt of a complaint or on its own initiative, the Commission shall initiate procedures to terminate any infringement of the provisions of Article 81(1) or 82 of the Treaty or to enforce Article 7 of this Regulation.

Complaints may be submitted by:

(a) Member States;
(b) natural or legal persons who claim a legitimate interest.

Article 11

Result of procedures on complaint or on the Commission's own initiative

1. Where the Commission finds that there has been an infringement of Article 81(1) or 82 of the Treaty, it may by decision require the undertakings or associations of undertakings concerned to bring such infringement to an end.

Without prejudice to the other provisions of this Regulation, the Commission may, before taking a decision under the preceding sub-paragraph, address to the undertakings or associations of undertakings concerned recommendations for termination of the infringement.

2. Paragraph 1 shall apply also to cases falling within Article 7 of this Regulation.

3. If the Commission, acting on a complaint received, concludes that on the evidence before it there are no grounds for intervention under Article 81(1) or 82 of the Treaty or Article 7 of this Regulation, in respect of any agreement, decision or practice, it shall issue a decision rejecting the complaint as unfounded.

4. If the Commission, whether acting on a complaint received or on its own initiative, concludes that an agreement, decision or concerted practice satisfies the provisions both of Article 81(1) and of Article 81(3) of the Treaty, it shall issue a decision applying Article 81(3). Such decision shall indicate the date from which it is to take effect. This date may be prior to that of the decision.

Article 12

Application of Article 81(3)—objections

1. Undertakings and associations of undertakings which seek application of Article 81(3) of the Treaty in respect of agreements, decisions and concerted practices falling within the provisions of Article 81(1) to which they are parties shall submit applications to the Commission.

2. If the Commission judges an application admissible and is in possession of all the available evidence, and no action under Article 10 has been taken against the agreement, decision or concerted practice in question, then it shall publish as soon as possible in the *Official Journal of the European Communities* a summary of the application and invite all interested parties and the Member States to submit their comments to the Commission within 30 days. Such publications shall have regard to the legitimate interest of undertakings in the protection of their business secrets.

3. Unless the Commission notifies applicants, within 90 days from the date of such publication in the *Official Journal of the European Communities*, that there are serious doubts as to the applicability of Article 81(3), the agreement, decision or concerted practice shall be deemed exempt, insofar as it conforms with the description given in the application, from the prohibition for the time already elapsed and for a maximum of six years from the date of publication in the *Official Journal of the European Communities*.

If the Commission finds, after expiry of the 90-day time limit, but before expiry of the six-year period, that the conditions for applying Article 81(3) are not satisfied, it shall issue a decision declaring that the prohibition in Article 81(1) is applicable. Such decision may be retroactive where the parties concerned have given inaccurate information or where they abuse the exemption from the provisions of Article 81(1).

4. The Commission may notify applicants as referred to in the first sub-paragraph of paragraph 3 and shall do so if requested by a Member State within 45 days of the

forwarding to the Member State of the application in accordance with Article 15(2). This request must be justified on the basis of considerations relating to the competition rules of the Treaty.

If it finds that the conditions of Article 81(1) and of Article 81(3) are satisfied, the Commission shall issue a decision applying Article 81(3). The decision shall indicate the date from which it is to take effect. This date may be prior to that of the application.

Article 13

Duration and revocation of decisions applying Article 81(3)

1. Any decision applying Article 81(3) taken under Article 11(4) or under the second subparagraph of Article 12(4) shall indicate the period for which it is to be valid; normally such period shall not be less than six years. Conditions and obligations may be attached to the decision.

2. The decision may be renewed if the conditions for applying Article 81(3) continue to be satisfied.

3. The Commission may revoke or amend its decision or prohibit specified acts by the parties:

(a) where there has been a change in any of the facts which were basic to the making of the decision;
(b) where the parties commit a breach of any obligation attached to the decision;
(c) where the decision is based on incorrect information or was induced by deceit, or
(d) where the parties abuse the exemption from the provisions of Article 81(1) granted to them by the decision.

In cases falling within (b), (c) or (d), the decision may be revoked with retroactive effect.

Article 14

Powers

Subject to review of its decision by the Court of Justice, the Commission shall have sole power:

— to impose obligations pursuant to Article 7;
— to issue decisions pursuant to Article 81(3).

The authorities of the Member States shall retain the power to decide whether any case falls within the provisions of Article 81(1) or Article 82, until such time as the Commission has initiated a procedure with a view to formulating a decision in the case in question or has sent notification as provided for in the first paragraph of Article 12(3).

Article 15

Liaison with the authorities of the Member States

1. The Commission shall carry out the procedures provided for in this Regulation in close and constant liaison with the competent authorities of the Member States; these authorities shall have the right to express their views on such procedures.

2. The Commission shall immediately forward to the competent authorities of the Member States copies of the complaints and applications, and of the most important documents sent to it or which it sends out in the course of such procedures.

3. An Advisory Committee on agreements and dominant positions in maritime transport shall be consulted prior to the taking of any decision following upon a procedure under Article 10 or of any decision issued under the second sub-paragraph of Article 12(3), or under the second sub-paragraph of paragraph 4 of the same Article. The Advisory Committee shall also be consulted prior to the adoption of the implementing provisions provided for in Article 26.

4. The Advisory Committee shall be composed of officials competent in the sphere of maritime transport and agreements and dominant positions. Each Member State shall nominate two officials to represent it, each of whom may be replaced, in the event of his being prevented from attending, by another official.

5. Consultation shall take place at a joint meeting convened by the Commission; such meeting shall be held not earlier than fourteen days after dispatch of the notice convening it. This notice shall, in respect of each case to be examined, be accompanied by a summary of the case together with an indication of the most important documents, and a preliminary draft decision.

6. The Advisory Committee may deliver an opinion notwithstanding that some of its members or their alternates are not present. A report of the outcome of the consultative proceedings shall be annexed to the draft decision. It shall not be made public.

Article 16

Requests for information

1. In carrying out the duties assigned to it by this Regulation, the Commission may obtain all necessary information from the Governments and competent authorities of the Member States and from undertakings and associations of undertakings.

2. When sending a request for information to an undertaking or association of undertakings, the Commission shall at the same time forward a copy of the request to the competent authority of the Member State in whose territory the seat of the undertaking or association of undertakings is situated.

3. In its request, the Commission shall state the legal basis and the purpose of the request, and also the penalties provided for in Article 19(1)(b) for supplying incorrect information.

4. The owners of the undertakings or their representatives and, in the case of legal persons, companies or firms, or of associations having no legal personality, the person authorised to represent them by law or by their constitution, shall be bound to supply the information requested.

5. Where an undertaking or association of undertakings does not supply the information requested within the time limit fixed by the Commission, or supplies incomplete information, the Commission shall by decision require the information to be supplied. The decision shall specify what information is required, fix an appropriate time limit within which it is to be supplied and indicate the penalties provided for in Article 19(1)(b) and Article 20(1)(c) and the right to have the decision reviewed by the Court of Justice.

6. The Commission shall at the same time forward a copy of its decision to the competent authority of the Member State in whose territory the seat of the undertaking or association of undertakings is situated.

Article 17

Investigations by the authorities of the Member States

1. At the request of the Commission, the competent authorities of the Member States shall undertake the investigations which the Commission considers to be necessary under Article 18(1), or which it has ordered by decision pursuant to Article 18(3). The officials

of the competent authorities of the Member States responsible for conducting these investigations shall exercise their powers upon production of an authorisation in writing issued by the competent authority of the Member State in whose territory the investigation is to be made. Such authorisation shall specify the subject matter and purpose of the investigation.

2. If so requested by the Commission or by the competent authority of the Member State in whose territory the investigation is to be made, Commission officials may assist the officials of such authority in carrying out their duties.

Article 18

Investigating powers of the Commission

1. In carrying out the duties assigned to it by this Regulation, the Commission may undertake all necessary investigations into undertakings and associations of undertakings.

To this end the officials authorised by the Commission are empowered:

(a) to examine the books and other business records;
(b) to take copies of or extracts from the books and business records;
(c) to ask for oral explanations on the spot;
(d) to enter any premises, land and vehicles of undertakings.

2. The officials of the Commission authorised for the purpose of these investigations shall exercise their powers upon production of an authorisation in writing specifying the subject matter and purpose of the investigation and the penalties provided for in Article 19(1)(c) in cases where production of the required books or other business records is incomplete. In good time before the investigation, the Commission shall inform the competent authority of the Member State in whose territory the same is to be made of the investigation and of the identity of the authorised officials.

3. Undertakings and associations of undertakings shall submit to investigations ordered by decisions of the Commission. The decision shall specify the subject matter and purpose of the investigation, appoint the date on which it is to begin and indicate the penalties provided for in Article 19(1)(c) and Article 20(1)(d) and the right to have the decision reviewed by the Court of Justice.

4. The Commission shall take decisions referred to in paragraph 3 after consultation with the competent authority of the Member State in whose territory the investigation is to be made.

5. Officials of the competent authority of the Member State in whose territory the investigation is to be made, may at the request of such authority or of the Commission, assist the officials of the Commission in carrying out their duties.

6. Where an undertaking opposes an investigation ordered pursuant to this Article, the Member State concerned shall afford the necessary assistance to the officials authorised by the Commission to enable them to make their investigation. To this end, Member States shall take the necessary measures, after consulting the Commission, before 1 January 1989.

Article 19

Fines

1. The Commission may by decision impose on undertakings or associations of undertakings fines of from 100 to 5,000 ECU where, intentionally or negligently:

(a) they supply incorrect or misleading information, either in a communication pursuant to Article 5(5) or in an application pursuant to Article 12; or

(b) they supply incorrect information in response to a request made pursuant to Article 16(3) or (5), or do not supply information within the time limit fixed by a decision taken under Article 16(5); or

(c) they produce the required books or other business records in incomplete form during investigations under Article 17 or Article 18, or refuse to submit to an investigation ordered by decision issued in implementation of Article 18(3).

2. The Commission may by decision impose on undertakings or associations of undertakings fines of from 1,000 to one million ECU, or a sum in excess thereof but not exceeding 10 per cent. of the turnover in the preceding business year of each of the undertakings participating in the infringement, where either intentionally or negligently:

(a) they infringe Article 81(1) or Article 82 of the Treaty, or do not comply with an obligation imposed under Article 7 of this Regulation;

(b) they commit a breach of any obligation imposed pursuant to Article 5 or to Article 13(1).

In fixing the amount of the fine, regard shall be had both to the gravity and to the duration of the infringement.

3. Article 15(3) and (4) shall apply.

4. Decisions taken pursuant to paragraphs 1 and 2 shall not be of criminal law nature.

The fines provided for in paragraph 2(a) shall not be imposed in respect of acts taking place after notification to the Commission and before its Decision in application of Article 81(3) of the Treaty, provided they fall within the limits of the activity described in the notification.

However, this provision shall not have effect where the Commission has informed the undertakings concerned that after preliminary examination it is of the opinion that Article 81(1) of the Treaty applies and that application of Article 81(3) is not justified.

Article 20

Periodic penalty payments

1. The Commission may by decision impose on undertakings or associations of undertakings periodic penalty payments of from 50 to 1,000 ECU per day, calculated from the date appointed by the decision, in order to compel them:

(a) to put an end to an infringement of Article 81(1) or Article 82 of the Treaty the termination of which it has ordered pursuant to Article 11, or to comply with an obligation imposed pursuant to Article 7;

(b) to refrain from any act prohibited under Article 13(3);

(c) to supply complete and correct information which it has requested by decision pursuant to Article 16(5);

(d) to submit to an investigation which it has ordered by decision taken pursuant to Article 18(3).

2. Where the undertakings or associations of undertakings have satisfied the obligation which it was the purpose of the periodic penalty payment to enforce, the Commission may fix the total amount of the periodic penalty payment at a lower figure than that which would arise under the original decision.

3. Article 15(3) and (4) shall apply.

Article 21

Review by the Court of Justice

The Court of Justice shall have unlimited jurisdiction within the meaning of Article 229 of the Treaty to review decisions whereby the Commission has fixed a fine or periodic penalty payment; it may cancel, reduce or increase the fine or periodic penalty payment imposed.

Article 22

Unit of account

For the purpose of applying Articles 19 to 21 the ECU shall be that adopted in drawing up the budget of the Community in accordance with Articles 277 and 279 of the Treaty.

Article 23

Hearing of the parties and of third persons

1. Before taking decisions as provided for in Articles 11, 12(3) second paragraph, and 12(4), 13(3), 19 and 20, the Commission shall give the undertakings or associations of undertakings concerned the opportunity of being heard on the matters to which the Commission has taken objection.

2. If the Commission or the competent authorities of the Member States consider it necessary, they may also hear other natural or legal persons. Applications to be heard on the part of such persons where they show a sufficient interest shall be granted.

3. Where the Commission intends to give negative clearance pursuant to Article 81(3) of the Treaty, it shall publish a summary of the relevant agreement, decision or concerted practice and invite all interested third parties to submit their observations within a time limit which it shall fix being not less than one month. Publication shall have regard to the legitimate interest of undertakings in the protection of their business secrets.

Article 24

Professional secrecy

1. Information acquired as a result of the application of Articles 17 and 18 shall be used only for the purposes of the relevant request or investigation.

2. Without prejudice to the provisions of Articles 23 and 25, the Commission and the competent authorities of the Member States, their officials and other servants shall not disclose information acquired by them as a result of the application of this Regulation and of the kind covered by the obligation of professional secrecy.

3. The provisions of paragraphs 1 and 2 shall not prevent publication of general information or surveys which do not contain information relating to particular undertakings or associations of undertakings.

Article 25

Publication of decisions

1. The Commission shall publish the decisions which it takes pursuant to Articles 11, 12(3), second paragraph, 12(4) and 13(3).

2. The publication shall state the names of the parties and the main content of the decision; it shall have regard to the legitimate interest of undertakings in the protection of their business secrets.

Article 26

Implementing provisions

The Commission shall have power to adopt implementing provisions concerning the scope of the obligation of communication pursuant to Article 5(5), the form, content and other details of complaints pursuant to Article 10, applications pursuant to Article 12 and the hearings provided for in Article 23(1) and (2).

[Article 26a

The prohibition in Article 81(1) of the Treaty shall not apply to agreements, decisions and concerted practices which were in existence at the date of accession of Austria, Finland and Sweden and which, by reason of that accession, fell within the scope of Article 81(1) if, within six months from the date of accession, they are so amended that they comply with the conditions laid down in Articles 3 to 6 of this Regulation. However, this Article shall not apply to agreements, decisions and concerted practices which at the date of accession already fall under Article 53(1) of the EEA Agreement.]

Amendment

Article 26a was added by the Act of Accession of the Republic of Austria, the Republic of Finland and the Kingdom of Sweden, Annex 1(III)(B)(3), as amended by Council Decision 95/1, Article 39.

Article 27

Entry into force

This Regulation shall enter into force on 1 July 1987. This Regulation shall be binding in its entirety and directly applicable in all Member States.

Done at Brussels, 22 December 1986.

APPENDIX 68

REGULATION 479/92[1]

On the Application of Article 81(3) of the Treaty to Certain Categories of Agreements, Decisions and Concerted Practices Between Liner Shipping Companies (Consortia)

THE COUNCIL OF THE EUROPEAN COMMUNITIES,

Having regard to the Treaty establishing the European Economic Community, and in particular Article 83 thereof,

Having regard to the proposal from the Commission[2],

Having regard to the opinion of the European Parliament[3],

Having regard to the opinion of the Economic and Social Committee[4],

Whereas Article 81(1) of the Treaty may in accordance with Article 81(3) thereof be declared inapplicable to categories of agreements, decisions and concerted practices which fulfil the conditions contained in Article 81(3);

Whereas, pursuant to Article 83 of the Treaty, the provisions for the application of Article 81(3) of the Treaty should be adopted by way of Regulation; whereas, according to Article 83(2)(b), such a Regulation must lay down detailed rules for the application of Article 81(3), taking into account the need to ensure effective supervision, on the one hand, and to simplify administration to the greatest possible extent on the other; whereas, according to Article 83(2)(d), such a Regulation is required to define the respective functions of the Commission and of the Court of Justice;

Whereas liner shipping is a capital intensive industry; whereas containerization has increased pressures for cooperation and rationalization; whereas the Community shipping industry needs to attain the necessary economies of scale in order to compete successfully on the world liner shipping market;

Whereas joint-service agreements between liner shipping companies with the aim of rationalizing their operations by means of technical, operational and/or commercial arrangements (described in shipping circles as consortia) can help to provide the necessary means for improving the productivity of liner shipping services and promoting technical and economic progress;

Having regard to the importance of maritime transport for the development of the Community's trade and the role which consortia agreements can fulfil in this respect, taking account of the special features of international liner shipping;

Whereas the legalization of these agreements is a measure which can make a positive contribution to improving the competitiveness of shipping in the Community;

Whereas users of the shipping services offered by consortia can obtain a share of the benefits resulting from the improvements in productivity and service, by means of, *inter*

---

[1] OJ 1992 L55/3, of 25.2.1992.

[2] OJ 1990 C167/9.

[3] OJ 1991 C305/39.

[4] OJ 1991 C69/16.

alia, regularity, cost reductions derived from higher levels of capacity utilization, and better service quality stemming from improved vessels and equipment;

Whereas the Commission should be enabled to declare by way of Regulation that the provisions of Article 81(1) of the Treaty do not apply to certain categories of consortia agreements, decisions and concerted practices, in order to make it easier for undertakings to cooperate in ways which are economically desirable and without adverse effect from the point of view of competition policy;

Whereas the Commission, in close and constant liaison with the competent authorities of the Member States, should be able to define precisely the scope of these exemptions and the conditions attached to them;

Whereas consortia in liner shipping are a specialized and complex type of joint venture; whereas there is a great variety of different consortia agreements operating in different circumstances; whereas the scope, parties, activities or terms of consortia are frequently altered; whereas the Commission should therefore be given the responsibility of defining from time to time the consortia to which a group exemption should apply;

Whereas, in order to ensure that all the conditions of Article 81(3) of the Treaty are met, conditions should be attached to group exemptions to ensure in particular that a fair share of the benefits will be passed on to shippers and that competition is not eliminated;

Whereas pursuant to Article 11(4) of Council Regulation (EEC) No 4056/86 of 22 December 1986 laying down detailed rules for the application of Articles 81 and 82 of the Treaty to maritime transport[5] the Commission may provide that a decision taken in accordance with Article 81(3) of the Treaty shall apply with retroactive effect; whereas it is desirable that the Commission be empowered to adopt, by Regulation, provisions to that effect;

Whereas notification of agreements, decisions and concerted practices falling within the scope of this Regulation must not be made compulsory, it being primarily the responsibility of undertakings to see to it that they conform to the rules on competition, and in particular to the conditions laid down by the subsequent Commission Regulation implementing this Regulation;

Whereas there can be no exemption if the conditions set out in Article 81(3) of the Treaty are not satisfied; whereas the Commission should therefore have power to take the appropriate measures where an agreement proves to have effects incompatible with Article 81(3) of the Treaty; whereas the Commission should be able first to address recommendations to the parties and then to take decisions,

HAS ADOPTED THIS REGULATION:

Article 1

1. Without prejudice to the application of Regulation (EEC) No 4056/86, the Commission may by regulation and in accordance with Article 81(3) of the Treaty, declare that Article 81(1) of the Treaty shall not apply to certain categories of agreements between undertakings, decisions of associations of undertakings and concerted practices that have as an object to promote or establish cooperation in the joint operation of maritime transport services between liner shipping companies, for the purpose of rationalizing their operations by means of technical, operational and/or commercial arrangements—with the exception of price fixing (consortia).

2. Such regulation adopted pursuant to paragraph 1 shall define the categories of agreements, decisions and concerted practices to which it applies and shall specify the conditions and obligations under which, pursuant to Article 81(3) of the Treaty, they shall be considered exempted from the application of Article 81(1) of the Treaty.

---

[5] OJ 1986 L378/4.

Article 2

1. The regulation adopted pursuant to Article 1 shall apply for a period of five years, calculated as from the date of its entry into force.

2. It may be repealed or amended where circumstances have changed with respect to any of the facts which were basic to its adoption.

Article 3

The regulation adopted pursuant to Article 1 may include a provision stating that it applies with retroactive effect to agreements, decisions and concerted practices which were in existence at the date of entry into force of such regulation, provided they comply with the conditions established in that regulation.

Article 4

Before adopting its regulation, the Commission shall publish a draft thereof to enable all the persons and organizations concerned to submit their comments within such reasonable time limit as the Commission shall fix, but in no case less than one month.

Article 5

1. Before publishing the draft regulation and before adopting the regulation, the Commission shall consult the Advisory Committee on Agreements and Dominant Positions in Maritime Transport established by Article 15(3) of Regulation (EEC) No 4056/86.

2. Paragraphs 5 and 6 of Article 15 of Regulation (EEC) No 4056/86 relating to consultation with the Advisory Committee, shall apply, it being understood that joint meetings with the Commission shall take place not earlier than one month after dispatch of the notice convening them.

Article 6

1. Where the persons concerned are in breach of a condition or obligation attaching to an exemption granted by the Regulation adopted pursuant to Article 1, the Commission may, in order to put an end to such a breach:

— address recommendations to the persons concerned, and
— in the event of failure by such persons to observe those recommendations, depending on the gravity of the breach concerned, adopt a decision that either prohibits them from carrying out, or requires them to perform specific acts or, while withdrawing the benefit of the group exemption which they enjoyed, grants them an individual exemption in accordance with Article 11 (4) of Regulation (EEC) No 4056/86, or withdraws the benefit of the group exemption which they enjoyed.

2. Where the Commission, either on its own initiative or at the request of a Member State or of natural or legal persons claiming a legitimate interest, finds that in a particular case an agreement, decision or concerted practice to which the group exemption granted by the Regulation adopted pursuant to Article 1 applies, nevertheless has effects which are incompatible with Article 81(3) of the Treaty or with the prohibition laid down in Article 82 of the Treaty, it may withdraw the benefit of the group exemption from those agreements, decisions or concerted practices and take all appropriate measures for the purpose of bringing these infringements to an end, pursuant to Article 13 of Regulation (EEC) No 4056/86.

3. Before taking a decision under paragraph 2, the Commission may address recommendations for termination of the infringement to the persons concerned.

Article 7

This Regulation shall enter into force on the day following its publication in the *Official Journal of the European Communities*.

This Regulation shall be binding in its entirety and directly applicable in all Member States.

Done at Brussels, 25 February 1992.

APPENDIX 69

REGULATION 823/2000[1]

On the Application of Article 81(3) of the Treaty to Certain Categories of Agreements, Decisions and Concerted Practices Between Liner Shipping Companies (Consortia)

(Text with EEA relevance)

THE COMMISSION OF THE EUROPEAN COMMUNITIES

Having regard to the Treaty establishing the European Community,

Having regard to Council Regulation (EEC) No 479/92 of 25 February 1992 on the application of Article 81(3) of the Treaty to certain categories of agreements, decisions and concerted practices between liner shipping companies (consortia),[2] as amended by the Act of Accession of Austria, Finland and Sweden, and in particular Article 1 thereof,

Having published a draft of this Regulation,[3]

Having consulted the Advisory Committee on Restrictive Practices and Dominant Positions in Maritime Transport,

Whereas:

(1) Regulation (EEC) No 479/92 empowers the Commission to apply Article 81(3) of the Treaty to certain categories of agreements, decisions and concerted practices between shipping companies (consortia) relating to the joint operation of liner transport services, which, through the cooperation they bring about between the shipping companies that are parties thereto, are liable to restrict competition within the common market and to affect trade between Member States and may therefore be caught by the prohibition contained in Article 81(1) of the Treaty.

(2) The Commission has made use of this power by adopting Commission Regulation (EC) No 870/95.[4] In the light of experience thus acquired so far, it is possible to define a category of consortia which are capable of falling within the scope Article 81(1) but which can normally be regarded as satisfying the conditions laid down in Article 81(3).

(3) The Commission has taken due account of the special features of maritime transport. Those features will also constitute a material factor in any Commission assessment of consortia not covered by this block exemption.

(4) Consortia, as defined in this Regulation, generally help to improve the productivity and quality of available liner shipping services by reason of the rationalisation they bring to the activities of member companies and through the economies of scale they allow in the operation of vessels and utilisation of port facilities. They also help to promote technical and economic progress by facilitating and encouraging greater utilisation of containers and more efficient use of vessel capacity.

---

[1] OJ 2000 L100/24, of 19.4.2000.
[2] OJ L 55, 29.2.1992, p. 3.
[3] OJ C 379, 31.12.1999, p. 13.
[4] OJ L 89, 21.4.1995, p. 7.

(5) Users of the shipping services provided by consortia generally obtain a fair share of the benefits resulting from the improvements in productivity and service quality which they bring about. Those benefits may also take the form of an improvement in the frequency of sailings and port calls, or an improvement in scheduling as well as better quality and personalised services through the use of more modern vessels and other equipment, including port facilities. Users can benefit effectively from consortia only if there is sufficient competition in the trades in which the consortia operate.

(6) Those agreements should therefore enjoy a block exemption, provided that they do not give the companies concerned the possibility of eliminating competition in a substantial part of the trades in question. In order to take account of the constant fluctuations in the maritime transport market and the frequent changes made by the parties to the terms of consortium agreements or to the activities covered by the agreements, one of the objects of this Regulation is to clarify the conditions to be met by consortia in order to benefit from the block exemption it grants.

(7) For the purpose of establishing and running a joint service, an essential feature inherent in consortia is the ability to make capacity adjustments. The non-utilisation of a certain percentage of vessel capacity within a consortium is not an essential feature of consortia.

(8) The block exemption granted by this Regulation should cover both consortia operating within a liner conference and consortia operating outside such conferences, except that it does not cover the joint fixing of freight rates.

(9) Rate-fixing activities come under Council Regulation (EEC) No 4056/86 of 22 December 1986 laying down detailed rules for the application of Articles 85 and 86 of the Treaty to maritime transport,[5] as amended by the Act of Accession of Austria, Finland and Sweden. Consortium members that wish to fix rates jointly and do not satisfy the criteria of Regulation (EFC) No 4056/86 must apply for individual exemption.

(10) The first of the conditions attaching to the block exemption should be that a fair share of the benefits resulting from the improved efficiency, as well as the other benefits offered by consortia, are passed on to transport users.

(11) This requirement of Article 81(3) should be regarded as being met when a consortium is in one or more of the three situations described below:

— there is effective price competition between the members of the conference within which the consortium operates as a result of independent rate action,
— there exists within the conference within which the consortium operates a sufficient degree of effective competition in terms of services provided between consortium members and other conference members that are not members of the consortium, as a result of the fact that the conference agreement expressly allows consortia to offer their own service arrangements, e.g. the provision by the consortium, alone of a "just-in-time delivery" service or an advanced "electronic data interchange" (EDI) service allowing users to be kept informed at all times of the whereabouts of their goods, or a significant increase in the frequency of sailings and calls in the service offered by a consortium compared with that offered by the conference,
— consortium members are subject to effective, actual or potential competition from non-consortium lines, whether or not a conference operates in the trade or trades in question.

(12) In order to satisfy this same requirement of Article 81(3), provision should be made for a further condition aimed at promoting individual competition as to quality of service between consortium members as well as between consortium members and other shipping companies operating in the trade or trades.

(13) It should be a condition that consortia and their members do not, in respect of a given route, apply rates and conditions of carriage which are differentiated solely by reference to the country of origin or destination of the goods carried and thus cause within

---

[5] OJ 1986 L378/4.

the Community deflections of trade that are harmful to certain ports, shippers, carriers or providers of services ancillary to transport, unless such rates or conditions can be economically justified.

(14) The aim of the conditions should also be to prevent consortia from imposing restrictions on competition which are not indispensable to the attainment of the objectives justifying the grant of the exemption. To this end, consortium agreements should contain a provision enabling each shipping line party to the agreement to withdraw from the consortium provided that it gives reasonable notice. However, provision should be made for a longer notice period in the case of highly integrated and/or high-investment consortia in order to take account of the higher investments undertaken to set them up and the more extensive reorganisation entailed in the event of a member's leaving. It should also be stipulated that, where a consortium operates with a joint marketing structure, each member should have the right to engage in independent marketing activities provided that it gives reasonable notice.

(15) Exemption must be limited to consortia which do not have the possibility of eliminating competition in a substantial part of the services in question.

(16) In order to determine for the purposes of exemption whether exemption competition exists on each market upon which the consortium operates, account should be taken not only of direct trade between the ports served by a consortium but also of any competition from other liner services sailing from ports which may be substituted for those served by the consortium and, where appropriate, of other modes of transport.

(17) The block exemption granted by this Regulation is therefore applicable only on condition that on each market upon which the consortium operates the market share held by a consortium does not exceed a given size.

(18) The market share held by a consortium within a conference should be smaller in view of the fact that the agreements is question are superimposed on an existing restrictive agreement.

(19) However, it is appropriate to offer consortia which exceed the limits laid down in this Regulation by a given percentage but which continue to be subject to effective competition in the trades in which they operate a simplified procedure so that they may benefit from the legal certainty afforded by block exemptions. Such a procedure should also enable the Commission to carry out effective monitoring and simplify the administrative control of agreements.

(20) However, consortia which exceed the limit should be able to obtain exemption by individual decision, provided that they satisfy the tests of Article 81(3), regard being had to the special features of maritime transport.

(21) This Regulation should apply only to agreements concluded between the members of a consortium. Therefore, the block exemption should not cover restrictive agreements concluded between, on the one hand, consortia or one or more of their members, and, on the other hand, other shipping companies. Nor should it apply to restrictive agreements between different consortia operating in the same trade or between the members of such consortia.

(22) Certain obligations should also be attached to the exemption. In this respect, transport users should at all times be in a position to acquaint themselves with the conditions for the provision of the maritime transport services jointly operated by the members of the consortium. Provision should be made for real and effective consultations between the consortia and transport users on the activities covered by the agreements. This Regulation also specifies what is meant by "real and effective consultations" and what main procedural stages are to be followed for such consultations. Provision should be made for such mandatory consultation, limited to the activities of consortia as such.

(23) Such consultations are likely to secure a more efficient operation of maritime transport services which takes account of users' requirements. Consequently, certain restrictive practices which could ensue from such consultations should be exempted.

(24) For the purposes of this Regulation, the concept of *force majeure* is that laid down by the Court of Justice of the European Communities in its established case-law.

(25) Provision should be made whereby awards given at arbitration and recommendations made by conciliators and accepted by the parties are to be notified to the Commission forthwith, in order to enable it to verify that consortia are not thereby exempted from the conditions and obligations provided for in the Regulation and thus do not infringe the provisions of Articles 81 and 82.

(26) It is necessary to specify, in accordance with Article 6 of Regulation (EEC) No 479/92, the cases in which the Commission may withdraw from companies the benefit of the block exemption.

(27) 11 consortia benefited from the block exemption contained in Regulation (EC) No 870/95 by application of the opposition procedure in that Regulation which enabled the Commission in particular to check that they were subject to effective competition. There is no indication that circumstances have since become such that those consortia are no longer subject to effective competition. Those consortia should therefore continue to be exempted on the terms laid down in this Regulation.

(28) No applications under Article 12 of Regulation (EEC) No 4056/86 should need to be made in respect of agreements automatically exempted by this Regulation. However, when real doubts exist, companies should be permitted to request the Commission to declare whether their agreements comply with this Regulation.

(29) This Regulation is without prejudice to the application of Article 82 of the Treaty.

(30) In view of the expiry of Regulation (EC) No 870/95, it is appropriate to adopt a new Regulation renewing the block exemption,

HAS ADOPTED THIS REGULATION:

CHAPTER 1

SCOPE AND DEFINITIONS

Article 1

Scope

This Regulation shall apply to consortia only in so far as they provide international liner transport services from or to one or more Community ports.

Article 2

Definitions

For the purposes of this Regulation:

1. "consortium" means an agreement between two or more vessel-operating carriers which provide international liner shipping services exclusively for the carriage of cargo, chiefly by container, relating to one or more trades, and the object of which is to bring about cooperation in the joint operation of a maritime transport service, and which improves the service that would be offered individually by each of its members in the absence of the consortium, in order to rationalise their operations by means of technical, operational and/or commercial arrangements, with the exception of price fixing;

2. "liner shipping" means the transport of goods on a regular basis on a particular route or routes between ports and in accordance with timetables and sailing dates advertised in

advance and available, even on an occasional basis, to any transport user against payment;

3. "service arrangement" means a contractual arrangement concluded between one or more transport users and an individual member of a consortium or a consortium itself under which, in return for an undertaking to commission the transportation of a certain quantity of goods over a given period of time, a user receives an individual undertaking from the consortium member or the consortium to provide an individualised service which is of a given quality and specially tailored to its needs;

4. "transport user" means any undertaking (such as shipper, consignee, forwarder) which has entered into, or demonstrated an intention to enter into, a contractual agreement with a consortium (or one of its members) for the shipment of goods, or any association of shippers;

5. "independent rate action" means the right of a maritime conference member to offer, on a case-by-case basis and in respect of goods, freight rates which differ from those laid down in the conference tariff, provided that notice is given to the other conference members.

CHAPTER II

EXEMPTIONS

Article 3

Exempted agreements

1. Pursuant to Article 81(3) of the Treaty and subject to the conditions and obligations laid down in this Regulation, it is hereby declared that Article 81(1) of the Treaty shall not apply to the activities listed in paragraph 2 of this Article when contained in consortium agreements as defined in Articles 1 and 2 of this Regulation.

2. The declaration of non-applicability shall apply only to the following activities:

(a) the joint operation of liner shipping transport services which comprise solely the following activities:
  (i) the coordination and/or joint fixing of sailing time-tables and the determination of ports of call;
  (ii) the exchange, sale or cross-chartering of space or slots on vessels;
  (iii) the pooling of vessels and/or port installations;
  (iv) the use of one or more joint operations offices;
  (v) the provision of containers, chassis and other equipment and/or the rental, leasing or purchase contracts for such equipment;
  (vi) the use of a computerised data exchange system and/or joint documentation system;
(b) temporary capacity adjustments;
(c) the joint operation or use of port terminals and related services (such as lighterage or stevedoring services);
(d) the participation in one or more of the following pools: cargo, revenue or net revenue;
(e) the joint exercise of voting rights held by the consortium in the conference within which its members operate, in so far as the vote being jointly exercised concerns the consortium's activities as such;
(f) a joint marketing structure and/or the issue of a joint bill of lading;

708

(g) any other activity ancillary to those referred to above in points (a) to (f) which is necessary for their implementation.

3. The following clauses shall in particular be considered ancillary activities within the meaning of paragraph 2(g):

(a) an obligation on members of the consortium to use on the trade or trades in question vessels allocated to the consortium and to refrain from chartering space on vessels belonging to third parties;
(b) an obligation on members of the consortium not to assign or charter space to other vessel-operating carriers on the trade or trades in question except with the prior consent of the other members of the consortium.

Article 4

Non-utilisation of capacity

The exemption provided for in Article 3 shall not apply to a consortium when the consortium includes arrangements concerning the non-utilisation of existing capacity whereby shipping line members of the consortium refrain from using a certain percentage of the capacity of vessels operated within the framework of the consortium.

CHAPTER III

CONDITIONS FOR EXEMPTION

Article 5

Basic condition for the grant of exemption

The exemption provided for in Article 3 shall apply only if one or more of the conditions set out below are met:

(a) there is effective price competition between the members of the conference within which the consortium operates, due to the fact that the members are expressly authorised by the conference agreement, whether by virtue of a statutory obligation or otherwise, to apply independent rate action to any freight rate provided for in the conference tariff; or
(b) there exists within the conference within which the consortium operates a sufficient degree of effective competition between the conference members in terms of the services provided, due to the fact that the conference agreement expressly allows the consortium to offer its own service arrangements, irrespective of form, concerning the frequency and quality of transport services provided as well as freedom at all times to adapt the services it offers in response to specific requests from transport users; or

(c)   whether or not a conference operates in the trade or trades in question, the consortium members are subject to effective competition, actual or potential, from shipping lines which are not members of that consortium.

Article 6

Conditions relating to market share

1. In order to qualify for the exemption provided for in Article 3, a consortium must possess on each market upon which it operates a market share of under 30% calculated by reference to the volume of goods carried (freight tonnes or 20-foot equivalent units) when it operates within a conference, and under 35% when it operates outside a conference.

2. The exemption provided for in Article 3 shall continue to apply if the market share referred to in paragraph 1 of this Article is exceeded during any period of two consecutive calendar years by not more than one tenth.

3. Where one of the limits specified in paragraphs 1 and 2 is exceeded, the exemption provided for in Article 3 shall continue to apply for a period of six months following the end of the calendar year during which it was exceeded. This period shall be extended to 12 months if the excess is due to the withdrawal from the market of a carrier which is not a member of the consortium.

Article 7

Opposition procedure

1. The exemption provided for in Articles 3 and 10 shall also apply to consortia whose market share on any market upon which it operates exceeds the limits laid down in Article 6 but does not, however, exceed 50% on any market, on condition that the agreements in question are notified to the Commission in accordance with the provisions of Commission Regulation (EC) No 2843/98,[6] and that the Commission does not oppose such exemption within a period of six months.

The period of six months shall run from the date on which notification takes effect in accordance with Article 4 of Regulation (EC) No 2843/98.

2. Paragraph 1 shall apply only if express reference is made to this Article in the notification or in a communication accompanying it.

3. The Commission may oppose the exemption.

It shall oppose the exemption if it receives a request to do so from a Member State within three months of the forwarding to the Member State of the notification referred to in paragraph 1. The request must be justified on the basis of considerations relating to the competition rules of the Treaty.

4. The Commission may withdraw its opposition to the exemption at any time. However, where the opposition was raised at the request of a Member State and the request is maintained, it may be withdrawn only after consultation of the Advisory Committee on Restrictive Practices and Dominant Positions in Maritime Transport.

5. If the opposition is withdrawn because the undertakings concerned have shown that the conditions of Article 81(3) are fulfilled, the exemption shall apply from the date of notification.

6. If the opposition is withdrawn because the undertakings concerned have amended the agreement so that the conditions of Article 81(3) are fulfilled, the exemption shall apply from the date on which the amendments take effect.

---

[6] OJ 1998 L354/22.

7. If the Commission opposes exemption and its opposition is not withdrawn, the effects of the notification shall be governed by the provisions of Section II of Regulation (EEC) No 4056/86.

Article 8

Other conditions

Eligibility for the exemptions provided for in Articles 3 and 10 shall be subject to the following conditions:

(a) the consortium must allow each of its members to offer, on the basis of an individual contract, its own service arrangements;

(b) the consortium agreement must give member companies the right to withdraw from the consortium without financial or other penalty such as, in particular, an obligation to cease all transport activity in the trade or trades in question, whether or not coupled with the condition that such activity may be resumed only after a certain period has elapsed. This right shall be subject to a maximum notice period of six months which may be given after an initial period of 18 months starting from the entry into force of the agreement.

However, in the case of a highly integrated consortium which has a net revenue pool and/or high level of investment due to the purchase or charter by its members of vessels specifically for the purpose of setting up the consortium, the maximum notice period shall be six months, which may be given after an initial period of 30 months starting from the entry into force of the agreement;

(c) where a consortium operates with a joint marketing structure, each member of the consortium must be free to engage in independent marketing without penalty subject to a maximum period of notice of six months;

(d) neither the consortium nor consortia members shall, within the common market, cause detriment to certain ports, users or carriers by applying to the carriage of the same goods and in the area covered by the agreement, rates and conditions of carriage which differ according to the country of origin or destination or port of loading or discharge, unless such rates or conditions can be economically justified.

CHAPTER IV

OBLIGATIONS

Article 9

Obligations attaching to exemption

1. The obligations provided for in paragraphs 2 to of this Article shall be attached to the exemptions provided for in Article 3 and Article 13(1).

2. There shall be real and effective consultations between users or their representative organisations, on the one hand, and the consortium, on the other hand, for the purpose of seeking solutions on all important matters, other than purely operational matters of minor

importance, concerning the conditions and quality of scheduled maritime transport services offered by the consortium or its members.

These consultations shall take place whenever requested by any of the abovementioned parties.

The consultations must take place, except in cases of *force majeure*, prior to the implementation of the measure forming the subject of the consultation. If, for reasons of *force majeure*, the members of the consortium are obliged to put a decision into effect before consultations have taken place, any consultations requested shall take place within 10 working days of the date of the request. Save in the case of such *force majeure*, to which reference shall be made in the notice announcing the measure, no public announcement of the measure shall be made before the consultations.

The consultations shall take place in accordance with the following procedural stages:

(a) prior to the consultation, details of the subject matter of the consultation shall be notified in writing by the consortium to the other party;

(b) an exchange of views shall take place between the parties either in writing or at meetings or both in the course of which the representatives of the consortium members and of the shippers taking part shall have authority to reach a common point of view and the parties shall use their best efforts to achieve that end;

(c) where no common point of view can be reached despite the efforts of both parties, the disagreement shall be acknowledged and publicly announced. It may be brought to the Commission's attention by either party;

(d) a reasonable period for the completion of consultations may be fixed, if possible, by common agreement between the two parties. That period shall be not less than one month, save in exceptional cases or by agreement between the parties.

3. The conditions concerning the maritime transport services provided by the consortium and its members, including those relating to the quality of such services and all relevant modifications, shall be made available on request to transport users at reasonable cost and shall be available for examination without cost at the offices of the consortium members, or the consortium itself, and their agents.

4. Arbitration awards and recommendations of conciliators, which have been accepted by the parties and which settle disputes concerning practices of consortia covered by this Regulation, shall be notified forthwith to the Commission by the consortium.

5. Any consortium claiming the benefit of this Regulation must be able, on being given a period of notice which the Commission shall determine on a case-by-case basis and which shall be not less than one month, to demonstrate at the Commission's request that the conditions and obligations imposed by Articles 5 to 8 and paragraphs 2 and 3 of this article are met and must submit to it the consortium agreement in question within this period.

Article 10

Exemption for agreements between transport users and consortia on the use of scheduled maritime transport services

Agreements, decisions and concerted practices between transport users or their representative organisations, on the one hand, and a consortium exempted under Article 3, on the other hand, concerning the conditions and quality of liner shipping services provided by the consortium and all general questions connected with such services in so far as they arise out of the consultations provided for in paragraph 2 of Article 9, are hereby exempted from the prohibition laid down in Article 81(1) of the Treaty.

CHAPTER V

MISCELLANEOUS PROVISIONS

Article 11

Professional secrecy

1. Information acquired as a result of the application of Article 7 and paragraph 5 of Article 9 shall be used only for the purposes of this Regulation.

2. The Commission and the authorities of the Member States, their officials and other servants shall not disclose information acquired by them as a result of the application of this Regulation which is of the kind covered by the obligation of professional secrecy.

3. The provisions of paragraphs 1 and 2 shall not prevent publication of general information or studies which do not contain information relating to particular undertakings or associations of undertakings.

Article 12

Withdrawal of block exemption

The Commission may withdraw the benefit of this Regulation, in accordance with Article 6 of Regulation (EEC) No 479/92, where it finds in a particular case that an agreement, decision or concerted practice exempted under Article 3 or Article 13(1) of this Regulation nevertheless has certain effects which are incompatible with the conditions laid down by Article 81(3) or are prohibited by Article 82 of the Treaty, in particular where:

(a) in a given trade, competition from outside the conference within which the con-sortium operates or from outside a particular consortium is not effective;

(b) a consortium fails repeatedly to comply with the obligations provided for in Article 9;

(c) the behaviour of a consortium produces effects that are incompatible with Article 82 of the Treaty;

(d) such effects result from an arbitration award.

Article 13

Transitional provisions

1. Article 81(1) of the Treaty shall not apply to agreements in force on 25 April 2000 which fulfil, on that date, the exemption requirements laid down by Regulation (EC) No 870/95 and to which the opposition procedure provided for by Article 7 of that Regulation was applied.

2. A notification made before the entry into force of this Regulation pursuant to Article 7 of Regulation (EC) No 870/95 and in respect of which the period of six months has not expired on 25 April 2000 shall be deemed to have been made pursuant to Article 7 of this Regulation.

Article 14

Entry into force

This Regulation shall enter into force on 26 April 2000.
It shall apply until 25 April 2005.

This Regulation shall be binding in its entirety and directly applicable in all Member States.

Done at Brussels, 19 April 2000.

REGULATION 3975/87[1]

Laying Down the Procedure for the Application of the Rules on Competition to Undertakings in the Air Transport Sector[2]

THE COUNCIL OF THE EUROPEAN COMMUNITIES

Having regard to the Treaty establishing the European Economic Community, and in particular Article 83 thereof,

Having regard to the proposal from the Commission,[3]

Having regard to the opinions of the European Parliament,[4]

Having regard to the opinion of the Economic and Social Committee,[5]

Whereas the rules on competition form part of the Treaty's general provisions which also apply to air transport; whereas the rules for applying these provisions are either specified in the Chapter on competition or fall to be determined by the procedures laid down therein;

Whereas, according to Council Regulation No. 141,[6] Council Regulation No. 17[7] does not apply to transport services; whereas Council Regulation (EEC) No. 1017/68[8] applies only to inland transport; whereas Council Regulation (EEC) No. 4056/86[9] applies only to maritime transport: whereas consequently the Commission has no means at present of investigating directly cases of suspected infringement of Articles 81 and 82 of the Treaty in air transport; whereas moreover the Commission lacks such powers of its own to take decisions or impose penalties as are necessary for it to bring to an end infringements established by it;

Whereas air transport is characterised by features which are specific to this sector; whereas, furthermore, international air transport is regulated by a network of bilateral agreements between States which define the conditions under which air carriers designated by the parties to the agreements may operate routes between their territories;

Whereas practices which affect competition relating to air transport between Member States may have a substantial effect on trade between Member States, whereas it is therefore desirable that rules should be laid down under which the Commission, acting in close and constant liaison with the competent authorities of the Member States, may take the requisite measures for the application of Articles 81 and 82 of the Treaty to international air transport between Community airports;

---

[1] OJ 1987 L374/1. Printed as amended by Council Reg. (EEC) No. 1284/91, OJ 1991 L122/2 and Council Reg. (EEC) No. 2410/92, OJ 1992 L240/18.

[2] As amended by Corrigendum (OJ 1988 L30/40).

[3] OJ 1984 C182/2.

[4] OJ 1982 C182/120 and OJ 1987 C345.

[5] OJ 1983 C77/20.

[6] OJ 1962 2751.

[7] OJ 1962 204.

[8] OJ 1968 L175/1.

[9] OJ 1986 L378/4.

Whereas such a regulation should provide for appropriate procedures, decision-making powers and penalties to ensure compliance with the prohibition laid down in Articles 81(1) and 82 of the Treaty; whereas account should be taken in this respect of the procedural provisions of Regulation (EEC) No. 1017/68 applicable to inland transport operations, which takes account of certain distinctive features of transport operations viewed as a whole;

Whereas undertakings concerned must be accorded the right to be heard by the Commission, third parties whose interests may be affected by a decision must be given the opportunity of submitting their comments beforehand and it must be ensured that wide publicity is given to decisions taken;

Whereas all decisions taken by the Commission under this Regulation are subject to review by the Court of Justice under the conditions specified in the Treaty; whereas it is moreover desirable, pursuant to Article 229 of the Treaty, to confer upon the Court of Justice unlimited jurisdiction in respect of decisions under which the Commission imposes fines or periodic penalty payments;

Whereas it is appropriate to except certain agreements, decisions and concerted practices from the prohibition laid down in Article 81(1) of the Treaty, insofar as their sole object and effect is to achieve technical improvements or cooperation;

Whereas, given the specific features of air transport, it will in the first instance be for undertakings themselves to see that their agreements, decisions and concerted practices conform to the competition rules, and notification to the Commission need not be compulsory;

Whereas undertakings may wish to apply to the Commission in certain cases for confirmation that their agreements, decisions and concerted practices conform to the law, and a simplified procedure should be laid down for such cases;

Whereas this Regulation does not prejudge the application of Article 86 of the Treaty,

HAS ADOPTED THIS REGULATION:

Article 1

Scope

1. This Regulation lays down detailed rules for the application of Articles 81 and 82 of the Treaty to air transport services.
2. This Regulation shall apply only to air transport between Community airports.

Amendment

Article 1 was amended by Council Regulation (EEC) No. 2410/92.

Article 2

Exceptions for certain technical agreements

1. The prohibition laid down in Article 81(1) of the Treaty shall not apply to the agreements, decisions and concerted practices listed in the Annex, in so far as their sole object and effect is to achieve technical improvements or co-operation. This list is not exhaustive.

2. If necessary, the Commission shall submit proposals to the Council for the amendment of the list in the Annex.

Article 3

Procedures on complaint or on the Commission's own initiative

1. Acting on receipt of a complaint or on its own initiative, the Commission shall initiate procedures to terminate any infringement of the provisions of Article 81(1) or 82 of the Treaty.
Complaints may be submitted by:

(a) Member States;
(b) natural or legal persons who claim a legitimate interest.

2. Upon application by the undertakings or associations of undertakings concerned, the Commission may certify that, on the basis of the facts in its possession, there are no grounds under Article 81(1) or Article 82 of the Treaty for action on its part in respect of an agreement, decision or concerted practice.

Article 4

Result of procedures on complaint or on the Commission's own initiative

1. Where the Commission finds that there has been an infringement of Articles 81(1) or 82 of the Treaty, it may by decision require the undertakings or associations of undertakings concerned to bring such an infringement to an end.
Without prejudice to the other provisions of this Regulation, the Commission may address recommendations for termination of the infringement to the undertakings or associations of undertakings concerned before taking a decision under the preceding subparagraph.
2. If the Commission, acting on a complaint received, concludes that, on the evidence before it, there are no grounds for intervention under Articles 81(1) or 82 of the Treaty in respect of any agreement, decision or concerted practice, it shall take a decision rejecting the complaint as unfounded.
3. If the Commission, whether acting on a complaint received or on its own initiative, concludes that an agreement, decision or concerted practice satisfies the provisions of both Article 81(1) and 81(3) of the Treaty, it shall take a decision applying paragraph 3 of the said Article. Such a decision shall indicate the date from which it is to take effect. This date may be prior to that of the decision.

[Article 4a

Interim measures against anti-competitive practices

1. Without prejudice to the application of Article 4(1), where the Commission has clear *prima facie* evidence that certain practices are contrary to Article 81 or 82 of the Treaty and have the object or effect of directly jeopardizing the existence of an air service, and where recourse to normal procedures may not be sufficient to protect the air service or the airline company concerned, it may by decision take interim measures to ensure that these practices are not implemented or cease to be implemented and give such instructions as are necessary to prevent the occurrence of these practices until a decision under Article 4(1) is taken.

2. A decision taken pursuant to paragraph 1 shall apply for a period not exceeding six months. Article 8(5) shall not apply.

The Commission may renew the initial decision, with or without modification, for a period not exceeding three months. In such case, Article 8(5) shall apply.]

Amendment

Article 4a was added by Council Regulation (EEC) No. 1284/91.

Article 5

Application of Article 81(3) of the Treaty

Objections

1. Undertakings and associations of undertakings which wish to seek application of Article 81(3) of the Treaty in respect of agreements, decisions and concerted practices falling within the provisions of paragraph 1 of the said Article to which they are parties shall submit applications to the Commission.

2. If the Commission judges an application admissible and is in possession of all the available evidence and no action under Article 3 has been taken against the agreement, decision or concerted practice in question, then it shall publish as soon as possible in the *Official Journal of the European Communities* a summary of the application and invite all interested third parties and the Member States to submit their comments to the Commission within 30 days. Such publications shall have regard to the legitimate interest of undertakings in the protection of their business secrets.

3. Unless the Commission notifies applicants, within 90 days of the date of such publication in the *Official Journal of the European Communities*, that there are serious doubts as to the applicability of Article 81(3) of the Treaty, the agreement, decision or concerted practice shall be deemed exempt, in so far as it conforms with the description given in the application, from the prohibition for the time already elapsed and for a maximum of six years from the date of publication in the *Official Journal of the European Communities*.

If the Commission finds, after expiry of the 90-day time limit, but before expiry of the six-year period, that the conditions for applying Article 81(3) of the Treaty are not satisfied, it shall issue a decision declaring that the prohibition in Article 81(1) applies. Such decision may be retroactive where the parties concerned have given inaccurate information or where they abuse an exemption from the provisions of Article 81(1) or have contravened Article 82.

4. The Commission may notify applicants as referred to in the first subparagraph 3; it shall do so if requested by a Member State within 45 days of the forwarding to the Member State of the application in accordance with Article 8(2). This request must be justified on the basis of considerations relating to the competition rules of the Treaty.

If it finds that the conditions of Article 81(1) and (3) of the Treaty are satisfied, the Commission shall issue a decision applying Article 81(3). The decision shall indicate the date from which it is to take effect. This date may be prior to that of the application.

Article 6

Duration and revocation of decisions applying Article 81(3)

1. Any decision applying Article 81(3) of the Treaty adopted under Articles 4 or 5 of this Regulation shall indicate the period for which it is to be valid; normally such period

shall not be less than six years. Conditions and obligations may be attached to the decision.

2. The decision may be renewed if the conditions for applying Article 81(3) of the Treaty continue to be satisfied.

3. The Commission may revoke or amend its decision or prohibit specific acts by the parties:

(a) where there has been a change in any of the facts which were basic to the making of the decision; or

(b) where the parties commit a breach of any obligation attached to the decision; or

(c) where the decision is based on incorrect information or was induced by deceit; or

(d) where the parties abuse the exemption from the provisions of Article 81(1) of the Treaty granted to them by the decision.

In cases falling under sub-paragraphs (b), (c) or (d), the decision may be revoked with retroactive effect.

Article 7

Powers

Subject to review of its decision by the Court of Justice, the Commission shall have sole power to issue decisions pursuant to Article 81(3) of the Treaty.

The authorities of the Member States shall retain the power to decide whether any case falls under the provisions of Article 81(1) or Article 82 of the Treaty, until such time as the Commission has initiated a procedure with a view to formulating a decision on the case in question or has sent notification as provided by the first subparagraph of Article 5(3) of this Regulation.

Article 8

Liaison with the authorities of the Member States

1. The Commission shall carry out the procedures provided for in this Regulation in close and constant liaison with the competent authorities of the Member States; these authorities shall have the right to express their views on such procedures.

2. The Commission shall immediately forward to the competent authorities of the Member States copies of the complaints and applications and of the most important documents sent to it or which it sends out in the course of such procedures.

3. An Advisory Committee on Agreements and Dominant Positions in Air Transport shall be consulted prior to the taking of any decision following upon a procedure under Article 3 or of any decision under the second subparagraph of Article 5(3), or under the second subparagraph of paragraph 4 of the same Article or under Article 6. The Advisory Committee shall also be consulted prior to adoption of the implementing provisions provided for in Article 19.

4. The Advisory Committee shall be composed of officials competent in the sphere of air transport and agreements and dominant positions. Each Member State shall nominate two officials to represent it, each of whom may be replaced, in the event of his being prevented from attending, by another official.

5. Consultation shall take place at a joint meeting convened by the Commission; such a meeting shall be held not earlier than 14 days after dispatch of the notice convening it.

In respect of each case to be examined, this notice shall be accompanied by a summary of the case, together with an indication of the most important documents, and a preliminary draft decision.

6. The advisory Committee may deliver an opinion notwithstanding that some of its members or their alternates are not present. A report of the outcome of the consultative proceedings shall be annexed to the draft decision. It shall not be made public.

Article 9

Requests for information

1. In carrying out the duties assigned to it by this Regulation, the Commission may obtain all necessary information from the governments and competent authorities of the Member States and from undertakings and associations of undertakings.

2. When sending a request for information to an undertaking or association of undertakings, the Commission shall forward a copy of the request at the same time to the competent authority of the Member State in whose territory the head office of the undertaking or association of undertakings is situated.

3. In its request, the Commission shall state the legal basis and purpose of the request and also the penalties for supplying incorrect information provided for in Article 12(1)(*b*).

4. The owners of the undertakings or their representatives and, in the case of legal persons or of companies, firms or associations having no legal personality, the person authorised to represent them by law or by their rules shall be bound to supply the information requested.

5. When an undertaking or association of undertakings does not supply the information requested within the time limit fixed by the Commission, or supplies incomplete information, the Commission shall by decision require the information to be supplied. The decision shall specify what information is required, fix an appropriate time limit within which it is to be supplied and indicate the penalties provided for in Article 12(1)(*b*) and Article 13(1)(*c*), as well as the right to have the decision reviewed by the Court of Justice.

6. At the same time the Commission shall send a copy of its decision to the competent authority of the Member State in whose territory the head office of the undertaking or association of undertakings is situated.

Article 10

Investigations by the authorities of the Member States

1. At the request of the Commission, the competent authorities of the Member States shall undertake the investigations which the Commission considers to be necessary under Article 11(1) or which it has ordered by decision adopted pursuant to Article 11(3). The officials of the competent authorities of the Member States responsible for conducting these investigations shall exercise their powers upon production of an authorisation in writing issued by the competent authority of the Member State in whose territory the investigation is to be made. Such an authorisation shall specify the subject matter and purpose of the investigation.

2. If so requested by the Commission or by the competent authority of the Member State in whose territory the investigation is to be made, Commission officials may assist the officials of the competent authority in carrying out their duties.

Article 11

Investigating powers of the Commission

1. In carrying out the duties assigned to it by this Regulation, the Commission may undertake all necessary investigations into undertakings and associations of undertakings. To this end the officials authorised by the Commission shall be empowered:

(a) to examine the books and other business records;
(b) to take copies of, or extracts from, the books and business records;
(c) to ask for oral explanations on the spot;
(d) to enter any premises, land and vehicles used by undertakings or associations of undertakings.

2. The authorised officials of the Commission shall exercise their powers upon production of an authorisation in writing specifying the subject matter and purpose of the investigation and the penalties provided for in Article 12(1)(c) in cases where production of the required books or other business records is incomplete. In good time, before the investigation, the Commission shall inform the competent authority of the Member State, in whose territory the same is to be made, of the investigation and the identity of the authorised officials.

3. Undertakings and associations of undertakings shall submit to investigations ordered by decision of the Commission. The decision shall specify the subject matter and purpose of the investigation, appoint the date on which it is to begin and indicate the penalties provided for in Article 12(1)(c) and 13(1)(d) and the right to have the decision reviewed by the Court of Justice.

4. The Commission shall take the decisions mentioned in paragraph 3 after consultation with the competent authority of the Member State in whose territory the investigation is to be made.

5. Officials of the competent authority of the Member State in whose territory the investigation is to be made may assist the Commission officials in carrying out their duties, at the request of such authority or of the Commission.

6. Where an undertaking opposes an investigation ordered pursuant to this Article, the Member State concerned shall afford the necessary assistance to the officials authorised by the Commission to enable them to make their investigation. To this end, Member States shall take the necessary measures after consultation of the Commission by 31 July 1989.

Article 12

Fines

1. The Commission may, by decision, impose fines on undertakings or associations of undertakings of from 100 to 5,000 ECU where, intentionally or negligently:

(a) they supply incorrect or misleading information in connection with an application pursuant to Article 3(2) or Article 5; or
(b) they supply incorrect information in response to a request made pursuant to Article 9(3) or (5), or do not supply information within the time limit fixed by a decision adopted under Article 9(5); or
(c) they produce the required books or other business records in incomplete form during investigations under Article 10 or Article 11, or refuse to submit to an investigation ordered by decision taken pursuant to Article 11(3).

2. The Commission may, by decision, impose fines on undertakings or associations of undertakings of from 1,000 to 1,000,000 ECUs, or a sum in excess thereof but not

exceeding 10 per cent. of the turnover in the preceding business year of the undertaking participating in the infringement, where either intentionally or negligently they:

(a) infringe Article 81(1) or Article 82 of the Treaty; or
(b) commit a breach of any obligation imposed pursuant to Article 6(1) of this Regulation.

In fixing the amount of the fine, regard shall be had both to the gravity and to the duration of the infringement.

3. Article 8 shall apply.

4. Decisions taken pursuant to paragraphs 1 and 2 shall not be of a penal nature.

5. The fines provided for in paragraph 2(a) shall not be imposed in respect of acts taking place after notification to the Commission and before its decision in application of Article 81(3) of the Treaty, provided they fall within the limits of the activity described in the notification.

However, this provision shall not have effect where the Commission has informed the undertakings or associations of undertakings concerned that, after preliminary examination, it is of the opinion that Article 81(1) of the Treaty applies and that application of Article 81(3) is not justified.

Article 13

Periodic penalty payments

By decision, the Commission may impose periodic penalty payments on undertakings or associations of undertakings of from 50 ECU to 1,000 ECU per day, calculated from the date appointed by the decision, in order to compel them:

(a) to put an end to an infringement of Article 81(1) or Article 82 of the Treaty, the termination of which has been ordered pursuant to Article 4 of this Regulation;
(b) to refrain from any act prohibited under Article 6(3);
(c) to supply complete and correct information which has been requested by decision taken pursuant to Article 9(5);
(d) to submit to an investigation which has been ordered by decision taken pursuant to Article 11(3).
[(e) to comply with any measure imposed by decision taken under Article 4a.]

2. Where the undertakings or associations of undertakings have satisfied the obligation which it was the purpose of the periodic penalty to enforce, the Commission may fix the total amount of the periodic penalty payment at a lower figure than that which would result from the original decision.

3. Article 8 shall apply.

Amendment

Article 13 was amended by Council Regulation (EEC) No. 1284/91.

Article 14

Review by the Court of Justice

The Court of Justice shall have unlimited jurisdiction within the meaning of Article 229 of the Treaty to review decisions whereby the Commission has fixed a fine or periodic penalty payment; it may cancel, reduce or increase the fine or periodic penalty payment imposed.

Article 15

Unit of account

For the purpose of applying Articles 12 to 14, the ECU shall be adopted in drawing up the budget of the Community in accordance with Articles 277 and 279 of the Treaty.

Article 16

Hearing of the parties and of third persons

1. Before refusing the certificate mentioned in Article 3(2), or taking decisions as provided for in Articles 4, [4a], 5(3) second sub-paragraph and 5(4), 6(3), 12 and 13, the Commission shall give the undertakings or associations of undertakings concerned the opportunity of being heard on the matters to which the Commission takes, or has taken, objection.

2. If the Commission or the competent authorities of the Member States consider it necessary, they may also hear other natural or legal persons. Applications by such persons to be heard shall be granted when they show a sufficient interest.

3. When the Commission intends to take a decision pursuant to Article 81(3) of the Treaty, it shall publish a summary of the relevant agreement, decision or concerted practice in the *Official Journal of the European Communities* and invite all interested third parties to submit their observations within a period, not being less than one month, which it shall fix. Publication shall have regard to the legitimate interest of undertakings in the protection of their business secrets.

Article 17

Professional secrecy

1. Information acquired as a result of the application of Articles 9 to 11 shall be used for the purpose of the relevant request or investigation.

2. Without prejudice to the provisions of Articles 16 and 18, the Commission and the competent authorities of the Member States, their officials and other servants shall not disclose information of a kind covered by the obligation of professional secrecy and which has been acquired by them as a result of the application of this Regulation.

3. The provisions of paragraphs 1 and 2 shall not prevent publication of general information or of surveys which do not contain information relating to particular undertakings or association of undertakings.

Article 18

Publication of decisions

1. The Commission shall publish the decision which it adopts pursuant to Articles 3(2), 4, 5(3) second sub-paragraph, 5(4) and 6(3).

2. The publication shall state the names of the parties and the main contents of the decision; it shall have regard to the legitimate interest of undertakings in the protection of their business secrets.

Article 19

Implementing provisions

The Commission shall have the power to adopt implementing provisions concerning the form, content and other details of complaints pursuant to Article 3, applications pursuant to Articles 3(2) and 5 and the hearings provided for in Article 16(1) and (2).

Article 20

Entry into force

This Regulation shall enter into force on January 1, 1988.

This Regulation shall be binding in its entirety and directly applicable in all Member States.

Done at Brussels, 14 December 1987.

ANNEX

LIST REFERRED TO IN ARTICLE 2

(a) The introduction or uniform application of mandatory or recommended technical standards for aircraft, aircraft parts, equipment and aircraft supplies, where such standards are set by an organisation normally accorded international recognition, or by an aircraft or equipment manufacturer;

(b) the introduction or uniform application of technical standards for fixed installations for aircraft, where such standards are set by an organisation normally accorded international recognition;

(c) the exchange, leasing, pooling, or maintenance of aircraft, aircraft parts, equipment or fixed installations for the purpose of operating air services and the joint purchase of aircraft parts, provided that such arrangements are made on a non-discriminatory basis;

(d) the introduction, operation and maintenance of technical communication networks, provided that such arrangements are made on a non-discriminatory basis;

(e) the exchange, pooling or training of personnel for technical or operational purposes;

(f) the organisation and execution of substitute transport operations for passengers, mail and baggage, in the event of breakdown/delay of aircraft, either under charter or by provision of substitute aircraft under contractual arrangements;

(g) the organisation and execution of successive or supplementary air transport operations, and the fixing and application of inclusive rates and conditions for such operations;

(h) the consolidation of individual consignments;

(i) the establishment or application of uniform rules concerning the structure and the conditions governing the application of transport tariffs, provided that such rules do not directly or indirectly fix transport fares and conditions;

(j) arrangements as to the sale, endorsement and acceptance of tickets between air carriers (interlining) as well as the refund, pro-rating and accounting schemes established for such purposes;

(k) the clearing and settling of accounts between air carriers by means of a clearing house, including such services as may be necessary or incidental thereto; the clearing and settling of accounts between air carriers and their appointed agents by means of a centralised and automated settlement plan or system, including such services as may be necessary or incidental thereto.

REGULATION 3976/87[1]

On the Application of Article 81(3) of the Treaty to Certain Categories of Agreements and Concerted Practices in the Air Transport Sector[2]

THE COUNCIL OF THE EUROPEAN COMMUNITIES

Having regard to the Treaty establishing the European Economic Community and in particular Article 83 thereof,

Having regard to the proposal from the Commission,[3]

Having regard to the opinions of the European Parliament,[4]

Having regard to the opinions of the Economic and Social Committee,[5]

Whereas Council Regulation (EEC) No. 3975/87[6] lays down the procedure for the application of the rules on competition to undertakings in the air transport sector; whereas Regulation No. 17 of the Council[7] lays down the procedure for the application of these rules to agreements, decisions and concerted practices other than those directly relating to the provision of air transport services;

Whereas Article 81(1) of the Treaty may be declared inapplicable to certain categories of agreements, decisions and concerted practices which fulfil the conditions contained in Article 81(3);

Whereas common provisions for the application of Article 81(3) should be adopted by way of Regulation pursuant to Article 83; whereas, according to Article 83(2)(*b*), such a Regulation must lay down detailed rules for the application of Article 81(3), taking into account the need to ensure effective supervision, on the one hand, and to simplify administration to the greatest possible extent, on the other; whereas, according to Article 83(2)(*d*), such a Regulation is required to define the respective functions of the Commission and of the Court of Justice;

Whereas the air transport sector has to date been governed by a network of international agreements, bilateral agreement between States and bilateral and multilateral agreements between air carriers; whereas the changes required to the international regulatory system to ensure increased competition should be effected gradually so as to provide time for the air-transport sector to adapt;

Whereas the Commission should be enabled for this reason to declare by way of Regulation that the provisions of Article 81(1) do not apply to certain categories of agreements between undertakings, decisions by associations of undertakings and concerted practices;

---

[1] OJ 1987 L374/9.

[2] As amended by Council Reg. (EEC) No. 2411/92, OJ 1992 L240/19.

[3] OJ 1984 C182/3.

[4] OJ 1985 C262/44, OJ 1987 C190/182 and OJ 1987 C345.

[5] OJ 1985 C303/31 and OJ 1986 C333/27.

[6] OJ 1987 L374/1.

[7] OJ 1962 204.

Whereas it should be laid down under what specific conditions and in what circumstances the Commission may exercise such powers in close and constant liaison with the competent authorities of the Member States;

Whereas it is desirable, in particular, that block exemptions be granted for certain categories of agreements, decisions and concerted practices: whereas these exemptions should be granted for a limited period during which air carriers can adapt to a more competitive environment; whereas the Commission, in close liaison with the Member States, should be able to define precisely the scope of these exemptions and the conditions attached to them;

Whereas there can be no exemption if the conditions set out in Article 81(3) are not satisfied; whereas the Commission should therefore have power to take the appropriate measures where an agreement proves to have effects incompatible with Article 81(3); whereas the Commission should consequently be able first to address recommendations to the parties and then to take decisions;

Whereas this Regulation does not prejudge the application of Article 86 of the Treaty;

Whereas the Heads of State and Government, at their meeting in June 1986, agreed that the internal market in air transport should be completed by 1992 in pursuance of Community action leading to the strengthening of its economic and social cohesion; whereas the provisions of this Regulation, together with those of Council Directive 87/601/EEC of 14 December 1987 on fares for scheduled air services between Member States[8] and those of Council Decision 87/602/EEC of 14 December 1987 on the sharing of passenger capacity between air carriers on scheduled air services between Member States and on access for air carriers to scheduled air service routes between Member States,[9] are a first step in this direction and the Council will therefore, in order to meet the objective set by the Heads of State and Government, adopt further measures of liberalisation at the end of a three year initial period,

HAS ADOPTED THIS REGULATION:

Article 1

This Regulation shall apply to air transport between Community airports.

Amendment

Article 1 was amended by Council Regulation (EEC) No. 2411/92.

Article 2

1. Without prejudice to the application of Regulation (EEC) No. 3975/87 and in accordance with Article 81(3) of the Treaty, the Commission may by regulation declare that Article 81(1) shall not apply to certain categories of agreements between undertakings, decisions of associations of undertakings and concerted practices.

[2. The Commission may, in particular, adopt such Regulations in respect of agreements, decisions or concerted practices which have as their object any of the following:

— joint planning and coordination of airline schedules,
— consultations on tariffs for the carriage of passengers and baggage and of freight on scheduled air services,

---

[8] OJ 1987 L374/12.
[9] OJ 1987 L374/19.

— joint operations on new less busy scheduled air services,
— slot allocation at airports and airport scheduling; the Commission shall take care to ensure consistency with the Code of Conduct adopted by the Council,
— common purchase, development and operation of computer reservation systems relating to timetabling, reservations and ticketing by air transport undertakings; the Commission shall take care to ensure consistency with the Code of Conduct adopted by the Council.]

3. Without prejudice to paragraph 2, such Commission regulations shall define the categories of agreements, decisions or concerted practices to which they apply and shall specify in particular:

(a) the restrictions or clauses which may, or may not, appear in the agreements, decisions and concerted practices;
(b) the clauses which must be contained in the agreements, decisions and concerted practices, or any other conditions which must be satisfied.

[Article 3

Any Regulation adopted pursuant to Article 2 shall be for a specified period.

It may be repealed or amended where circumstances have changed with respect to any of the factors which prompted its adoption; in such case, a period shall be fixed for amendment of the agreements and concerted practices to which the earlier Regulation applied before repeal or amendment.]

Amendment

Articles 2(2) and 3 were amended by Council Regulation (EEC) No. 2411/92.

Article 4

Regulations adopted pursuant to Article 2 shall include a provision that they apply with retroactive effect to agreements, decisions and concerted practices which were in existence at the date of the entry into force of such Regulations.

[Article 4a

A Regulation pursuant to Article 2 may stipulate that the prohibition contained in Article 81(1) of the Treaty shall not apply, for such period as fixed by that Regulation, to agreements, decisions and concerted practices already in existence at the date of accession to which Article 81(1) applies by virtue of the accession of Austria, Finland and Sweden, and which do not satisfy the conditions of Article 81(3). However, this Article shall not apply to agreements, decisions and concerted practices which at the date of accession already fell under Article 53(1) of the EEA Agreement.]

Amendment

Article 4a was added by the Act of Accession of the Republic of Austria, the Republic of Finland and the Kingdom of Sweden, Annex 1(III)(B)2, as amended by Council Decision 95/1, Article 39.

Article 5

Before adopting a regulation, the Commission shall publish a draft thereof and invite all persons and organisations concerned to submit their comments within such reasonable time limit, being not less than one month, as the Commission shall fix.

Article 6

The Commission shall consult the Advisory Committee on Agreements and Dominant Positions in Air Transport established by Article 8(3) of Regulation (EEC) No. 3975/87 before publishing a draft Regulation and before adopting a Regulation.

Article 7

1. Where the persons concerned are in breach of a condition or obligation which attaches to an exemption granted by a Regulation adopted pursuant to Article 2, the Commission may, in order to put an end of such a breach:

— address recommendations to the person concerned, and
— in the event of failure by such persons to observe those recommendations, and depending on the gravity of the breach concerned, adopt a decision that either prohibits them from carrying out, or requires them to perform, specific acts or, while withdrawing the benefit of the block exemption which they enjoyed, grants them an individual exemption in accordance with Article 4(2) of Regulation (EEC) No. 3975/87 or withdraws the benefit of the block exemption which they enjoyed.

2. Where the Commission, either on its own initiative or at the request of a Member State or of natural or legal persons claiming a legitimate interest, finds that in any particular case an agreement, decision or concerted practice to which a block exemption granted by a regulation adopted pursuant to Article 2(2) applies, nevertheless has effects which are incompatible with Article 81(3) or are prohibited by Article 82, it may withdraw the benefit of the block exemption from those agreements, decisions or concerted practices and take, pursuant to Article 13 of Regulation (EEC) No. 3975/87, all appropriate measures for the purpose of bringing these infringements to an end.

3. Before taking a decision under paragraph 2, the Commission may address recommendations for termination of the infringement to the persons concerned.

Article 8

[Article 8 was deleted by Council Regulation (EEC) No. 2411/92.]

Article 9

This Regulation shall enter into force on 1 January 1988.

This Regulation shall be binding in its entirety and directly applicable in all Member States.

Done at Brussels, 14 December 1987.

APPENDIX 72

REGULATION 1617/93[1]

On the Application of Article 81(3) of the Treaty to Certain Categories of
Agreements and Concerted Practices Concerning Joint Planning and
Coordination of Schedules, Joint Operations, Consultations on Passenger
[and Cargo] Tariffs on Scheduled Air Services and Slot Allocation at Airports

THE COMMISSION OF THE EUROPEAN COMMUNITIES,

Having regard to the Treaty establishing the European Economic Community,

Having regard to Council Regulation (EEC) No 3976/87 of 14 December 1987 on the application of Article 81(3) of the Treaty to certain categories of agreements and concerted practices in the air transport sector,[2] as last amended by Regulation (EEC) No 2411/92,[3] and in particular Article 2 thereof,

Having published a draft of this Regulation,[4]

Having consulted the Advisory Committee on Agreements and Dominant Positions in Air Transport,

Whereas:

(1) Regulation (EEC) No 3976/87 empowers the Commission to apply Article 81(3) of the Treaty by regulation to certain categories of agreements, decisions or concentrated practices relating directly or indirectly to the provision of air transport services.

(2) Agreements, decisions or concerted practices concerning joint planning and coordination of schedules, joint operations, consultations on tariffs and slot allocation at airports are liable to restrict competition and affect trade between Member States.

(3) Joint planning and coordination of the schedule of an air service can help to ensure the maintenance of services at less busy times of the day, during less busy periods or on less busy routes, and to develop onward connections, thus benefiting air transport users. However, any clauses concerning extra flights must not require the approval of the other parties or involve financial penalties. The arrangements must also allow parties to withdraw from them at reasonably short notice.

(4) Arrangements whereby a smaller airline receives marketing and financial support from another airline may help that smaller airline to operate air services on new or less busy routes. However, in order to avoid restrictions which are not indispensable to the attainment of that aim, the duration of such joint operations must be limited to the time necessary to gain sufficient commercial standing. The block exemption must not be

---

[1] OJ 1993 L 155/18, of 25.6.1993.
[2] OJ 1987 L 374/9.
[3] OJ 1992 L 240/19.
[4] OJ 1992 C253/5.

granted to joint operations where both parties could reasonably be expected to operate the air service independently. Those conditions are without prejudice to the possibility, in appropriate cases, of an application made under Article 5 of Council Regulation (EEC) No 3975/87,[5] as last amended by Regulation (EEC) No 2410/92,[6] with a view to obtaining an individual exemption where the conditions are not met or where the parties need to extend the duration of the joint operation. In particular where the parties wish to avail themselves, through a joint operation of the market access opportunities created by Council Regulation (EEC) No 2408/92[7] on routes which are neither new nor less busy, but which otherwise fulfil the conditions set forth herein, an individual exemption may be warranted.

(5) Consultations on passenger and cargo tariffs may contribute to the generalized acceptance of interlinable fares and rates to the benefit of air carriers as well as air transport users. However, consultations must not exceed the aim of facilitating interlining. Council Regulation (EEC) No 2409/92 of 23 July 1992 on fares and rates for air services,[8] is based on the principle of free pricing and therefore increases the possibility of price competition in air transport. Hence, competition may not be eliminated thereby. Consultations between air carriers on passenger and cargo tariffs may therefore be permitted for the time being, provided that they are limited to fares and rates which give rise to actual interlining, that the participation in such consultations is optional, that they do not lead to an agreement in respect of fares, rates or related conditions, that in the interests of transparency the Commission and the Member States concerned can send observers to them, and that air carriers participating in the consultation mechanism are obliged to interline with all other carriers concerned, at the tariffs applied by the carrying airline for the tariff category under discussion.

The Commission will reassess the effects of tariff consultations on price competition in the light of the operation of Regulation (EEC) No 2409/92 and in the light of the development of the Community air transport industry, and may make appropriate changes to the exemption in the course of its lifetime;

(6) Arrangements on slot allocation at airports and airport scheduling can improve the utilization of airport capacity and airspace, facilitate air-traffic control and help to spread the supply of air transport services from the airport. However, if competition is not to be eliminated, entry to congested airports must remain possible. In order to provide a satisfactory degree of security and transparency, such arrangements can only be accepted if all air carriers concerned can participate in the negotiations, and if the allocation is made on a non-discriminatory and transparent basis.

(7) In accordance with Article 4 of Regulation (EEC) No 3976/87, this Regulation should apply with retroactive effect to agreements, decisions and concerted practices in existence on the date of entry into force of this Regulation, provided that they meet the conditions for exemption set out in this Regulation.

(8) In conformity with Article 7 of Regulation (EEC) No 3976/87, this Regulation should also specify the circumstances in which the Commission may withdraw the block exemption in individual cases.

(9) No applications under Article 3 or 5 of Regulation (EEC) No 3975/87 need be made in respect of agreements automatically exempted by this Regulation. However, when real doubt exists, undertakings may request the Commission to declare whether their arrangements comply with this Regulation.

(10) This Regulation is without prejudice to the application of Article 86 of the Treaty,

---

[5] OJ 1987 L 374/1.
[6] OJ 1992 L 240/18.
[7] OJ 1992 L 240/8.
[8] OJ 1992 L 240/15.

HAS ADOPTED THIS REGULATION:

TITLE I

EXEMPTIONS

Article 1

Pursuant to Article 81(3) of the Treaty and subject to the provisions of this Regulation, it is hereby declared that Article 81(1) of the Treaty shall not apply to agreements between undertakings in the air transport sector, decisions by associations of such undertakings and concerted practices between such undertakings which have as their purpose one or more of the following:

— [...],
— [...],
— [the holding of consultations on tariffs for the carriage of passengers, with their baggage, on scheduled air services between Community airports,]
— slot-allocation and airport scheduling in so far as they concern air services between airports in the Community.

Amendment

The first and second indents were deleted by Reg. 1083/99; the third indent was replaced by Reg. 1523/96.

TITLE II

SPECIAL PROVISIONS

Article 2

[...]

Article 3

[...]

Special provisions for joint operations

Amendment

Articles 2 and 3 were deleted by Reg. 1083/99.

Article 4

[Special provisions for consultations on passenger and tariffs]

[1. The exemption concerning the holding of consultations on passenger tariffs shall apply only if the following conditions are met:]

[(a) the participants only discuss air fares and cargo rates to be paid by air transport users directly to a participating air carrier or to its authorized agents, for carriage as passengers or for the airport-to-airport transport of freight on a scheduled service, as well as the conditions relating to those fares and rates. The consultations shall not extend to the capacity for which such tariffs are to be available;]

(b) the consultations give rise to interlining, that is to say, air transport users must be able, in respect of the types of fares or rates and of the seasons which were the subject of the consultations:

(i) to combine on a single transportation document the service which was the subject of the consultations, with services on the same or on connecting routes operated by other air carriers, whereby the applicable fares, rates and conditions are set by the airline(s) effecting carriage; and

(ii) in so far as is permitted by the conditions governing the initial reservation, to change a reservation on a service which was the subject of the consultations onto a service on the same route operated by another air carrier at the fares, rates and conditions applied by that other carrier;

provided that an air carrier may refuse to allow such combinations and changes of reservation for objective and non-discriminatory reasons of a technical or commercial nature, in particular where the air carrier effecting carriage is concerned with the credi worthiness of the air carrier who would be collecting payment for this carriage; in such case the latter air carrier must be notified thereof in writing;

[(c) the passenger tariffs which are the subject of the consultations are applied by participating air carriers without discrimination on grounds of passengers nationality or place of residence or on ground of the origin of the freight within the Community;]

(d) participation in the consultations is voluntary and open to any air carrier who operates or intends to operate direct or indirect services on the route concerned;

[(e) the consultations are not binding on participants, that is to say, following the consultations the participants retain the right to act independently in respect of passenger tariffs;]

(f) the consultations do not entail agreement on agents' remuneration or other elements of the tariffs discussed;

(g) where filing of tariffs is required, each participant individually files each tariff which was not the subject of the consultations, with the competent authorities of the Member States concerned; in so doing it may act itself or through its filing agent or through its general sales agent.

2. (a) The Commission and the Member States concerned shall be entitled to send observers to tariff consultations. For this purpose, air carriers shall give the Member States concerned and the Commission the same notice as is given to participants, but not less than 10 days' notice, of the date, venue and subject matter of the consultations.

(b) Such notice shall be given:

(i) to the Member States concerned according to procedures to be established by the competent authorities of those Member States;

(ii) to the Commission according to procedures to be published in the *Official Journal of the European Communities*.

(c) A full report on these consultations shall be submitted to the Commission by or on behalf of the air carriers involved at the same time as it is submitted to participants, but not later than six weeks after those consultations were held.

Amendment

In para. 1, the introductory words and points (a), (c) and (e) were replaced by Commission Reg. 1523/96.

Article 5

Special provisions for slot allocation and airport scheduling

1. The exemption concerning slot allocation and airport scheduling shall apply only if the following conditions are met:

(a) the consultations on slot allocation and airport scheduling are open to all air carriers having expressed an interest in the slots which are the subject of the consultations;

(b) rules of priority are established and supplied without discrimination, that is to say that they neither directly nor indirectly relate to carrier identity or nationality or category of service, take into account constraints or air traffic distribution rules laid down by competent national or international authorities and give due consideration to the needs of the travelling publics and of the airport concerned. Subject to paragraph (d), such rules of priority may take account of rights acquired by air carriers through the use of particular slots in the previous corresponding season;

(c) the rules of priority, once established are made available on request to any interested party;

(d) new entrants as defined in Article 2(b) of Council Regulation (EEC) No 95/93[9] are allocated 50% of newly created or unused slots and slots which have been given up by a carrier during or by the end of the season or which otherwise become available, to the extent that those new entrants have outstanding slot requests;

(e) air carriers participating in the consultations have access, at the time of the consultations at the latest, to information relating to:
— historical slots by airline, chronologically, for all air carriers at the airport,
— requested slots (initial submissions) by air carriers and chronologically for all air carriers,
— allocated slots, and outstanding slot requests listed individually in chronological order, by air carriers, for air carriers,
— remaining slots available,
— full details on the criteria being used in the allocation.

If a request for slots is not accepted, the air carrier concerned shall be entitled to a statement of the reasons therefor.

2. (a) The Commission and the Member States concerned shall be entitled to send observers to consultations on slot allocation and airport scheduling held in the context of a multilateral meeting in advance of each season. For this purpose, air carriers shall give the Member States concerned and the Commission the same notice as is given to participants, but not less than 10 days' notice, of the date, venue and subject matter of the consultations.

   (b) Such notice shall be given:
      (i) to the Member States concerned according to procedures to be established by the competent authorities of those Member States;
      (ii) to the Commission according to procedures to be published in the *Official Journal of the European Communities*.

---

[9] OJ No L 14, 22.1.1993, p. 1.

TITLE III

FINAL PROVISIONS

Article 6

Withdrawal of the block exemption

The Commission may withdraw the benefit of the block exemption under this Regulation, pursuant to Article 7 of Regulation (EEC) No 3976/87 where it finds in a particular case that an agreement, decision or concerted practice exempted by this Regulation nevertheless has certain effects which are incompatible with the conditions laid down by Article 81(3) or are prohibited by Article 82 of the Treaty, and in particular where:

 (i) there is no effective price competition on any route or group of routes which was the subject of tariff consultations. In such cases the benefit of this Regulation shall be withdrawn in respect of the route or group of routes in question, and from the air carriers which participated in the tariff consultations concerning such routes;
 (ii) [. . .];
 (iii) the operation of Article 5 has not enabled new entrants to obtain such slots as may be required at a congested airport in order to establish schedules which enable those carriers to compete effectively with established carriers on any route to and from that airport, and where competition on those routes is thereby substantially impaired. In such cases the withdrawal of the benefit of this Regulation shall be in respect of the slot allocation at the airport in question.

Amendment

Article 6, point (ii) was deleted by Reg. 1083/99.

[Article 6a

The prohibition in Article 81(1) of the Treaty shall not apply to agreements, decisions and concerted practices which were in existence at the date of accession of Austria, Finland and Sweden and which, by reason of that accession, fell within the scope of Article 81(1) if, within six months from the date of accession, they are so amended that they comply with the conditions laid down in this Regulation. However, this Article shall not apply to agreements, decisions and concerted practices which at the date of accession already fell under Article 53(1) of the EEA Agreement.]

Amendment

Article 6a was added by the Act of Accession of the Republic of Austria, the Republic of Finland and the Kingdom of Sweden, Annex 1(III)(D)(10), as amended by Council Decision 95/1, Article 39.

Article 7

This Regulation shall enter into force on 1 July 1993.
It shall apply until 30 June [2001].

This Regulation shall apply with retroactive effect to agreements, decisions and concerted practices in existence when it enters into force, from the time when the conditions of application of this Regulation were fulfilled.

Amendment

Article 7 was amended by Reg. 1083/99

This Regulation shall be binding in its entirety and directly applicable in all Member States.

Done at Brussels, 25 June 1993.

CORRIGENDA

Corrigendum to Commission Regulation (EEC) No 1617/93 of 25 June 1993 on the application of Article 81(3) of the Treaty to certain categories of agreements and concerted practices concerning joint planning and coordination of schedules, joint operations, consultations on passenger and cargo tariffs on scheduled air services and slot allocation at airports

(Official Journal of the European Communities No L 155 of 26 June 1993)

Page 18, preamble, fourth recital, 20th line:
for: ' . . . , a joint operation, through of the market access . . . ',
read: ' . . . , through a joint operation, of the market access . . . '.
Page 19, preamble, sixth recital, sixth line:
for: ' . . . if competition is to be eliminated . . . ',
read: ' . . . if competition is not to be eliminated . . . '.
Page 20, Article 2(a)(ii), third line:
for: ' . . . for passengers of freight . . . ',
read: ' . . . for passengers or freight . . . '.
Page 20, Article 2(d), last line:
delete: 'notice'.
Page 22, Article 6(i), fourth line:
for: ' . . . in respect of the air carriers which participated . . . ',
read: ' . . . in respect of the route or group of routes in question, and from the air carriers which participated . . . '.

APPENDIX 73

REGULATION 2843/98[1]

On the Form, Content and other Details of Applications and Notifications Provided for in Council Regulations (EEC) No 1017/68, (EEC) No 4056/86 and (EEC) No 3975/87 Applying the Rules on Competition to the Transport Sector

(Text with EEA relevance)

THE COMMISSION OF THE EUROPEAN COMMUNITIES,

Having regard to the Treaty establishing the European Community,

Having regard to the Agreement on the European Economic Area,

Having regard to Council Regulation (EEC) No 1017/68 of 19 July 1968 applying rules of competition to transport by rail, road and inland waterway,[2] as last amended by the Act of Accession of Austria, Finland and Sweden, and in particular Article 29 thereof,

Having regard to Council Regulation (EEC) No 4056/86 of 22 December 1986 laying down detailed rules for the application of Articles 81 and 82 of the Treaty to maritime transport,[3] as last amended by the Act of Accession of Austria, Finland and Sweden, and in particular Article 26 thereof,

Having regard to Council Regulation (EEC) No 3975/87 of 14 December 1987 laying down the procedure for the application of the rules on competition to undertakings in the air transport sector,[4] as last amended by Regulation (EEC) No 2410/92,[5] and in particular Article 19 thereof,

Having consulted the Advisory Committee on Restrictive Practices and Monopolies in the transport industry, the Advisory Committee on Agreements and Dominant Positions in maritime transport, and the Advisory Committee on Agreements and Dominant Positions in air transport,

(1) Whereas experience in the application of Commission Regulation (EEC) No 1629/69 of 8 August 1969 on the form, content and other detail of complaints pursuant to Article 10, applications pursuant to Article 12 and notifications pursuant to Article 14(1) of Council Regulation (EEC) No 1017/68 of 19 July 1968,[6] as last amended by the Act of Accession of Austria, Finland and Sweden, and of Section I of Commission Regulation (EEC) No 4260/88 of 16 December 1988 on the communications, complaints and applications and the hearings provided for in Council Regulation (EEC) No 4056/86 laying down detailed rules for the application of Articles 85 and 86 of the Treaty to

---

[1] OJ 1998 L354/22, of 22.12.1998.
[2] OJ 1968 L175/1.
[3] OJ 1986 L378/4.
[4] OJ 1987 L374/1.
[5] OJ 1992 L240/18.
[6] OJ 1964 L204/1.

maritime transport,[7] as last amended by the Act of Accession of Austria, Finland and Sweden and also of Section I of Commission Regulation (EEC) No 4261/88 of 16 December 1988 on the complaints, applications and hearings provided for in Council Regulation (EEC) No 3975/87 laying down the procedure for the application of the rules on competition to undertakings in the air transport sector,[8] as last amended by the Act of Accession of Austria, Finland and Sweden, has shown the need to improve certain procedural aspects of those Regulations;

(2) Whereas it is appropriate, for the sake of clarity, to adopt a single Regulation on the procedures for applications and notifications in the transport sector; whereas, accordingly, Regulation (EEC) No 1629/69 and Regulations (EEC) No 4260/88 and (EEC) No 4261/88 should be replaced;

(3) Whereas the submission of applications under Article 12 of Regulation (EEC) No 1017/68 and notifications under Article 14(1) of that Regulation, and applications under Article 12 of Regulation (EEC) No 4056/86 and Articles 3(2) and 5 of Regulation (EEC) No 3975/87, may have important legal consequences for each undertaking which is a party to an agreement, a decision or a practice; whereas each party should therefore have the right to submit such applications or notifications to the Commission; whereas, furthermore, a party exercising the right should inform the other parties in order to enable them to protect their interests;

(4) Whereas it is for the applicants and the notifying parties to make full and honest disclosure to the Commission of the facts and circumstances which are relevant to reaching a decision on the agreements, decisions or practices concerned;

(5) Whereas, in order to simplify and expedite their examination, it is desirable to prescribe that a form be used for applications for negative clearance relating to Article 81(1) and for applications relating to Article 5 of Regulation (EEC) No 1017/68 and to Article 81(3); whereas the use of this form should also be possible in the case of applications for negative clearance relating to Article 82;

(6) Whereas, in order to simplify their handling, it is appropriate to introduce a single form for applications under Article 12 of Regulation (EEC) No 1017/68, under Article 12 of Regulation (EEC) No 4056/86 and under Articles 3(2) and 5 of Regulation (EEC) No 3975/87; whereas, in the case of notifications under Article 14(1) of Regulation (EEC) No 1017/68, it is appropriate to provide a separate form;

(7) Whereas the Commission, in appropriate cases, should continue to give the parties, if they so request, an opportunity before the application or the notification to discuss the intended agreement, decision or practice informally and in strict confidence; whereas, in addition, it should, after the application or notification, continue to maintain close contact with the parties to the extent necessary to discuss with them any practical or legal problems which it discovers on a first examination of the case and if possible to remove such problems by mutual agreement;

(8) Whereas the obligation of communication to the Commission, pursuant to point 5 of Article 5 of Regulation (EEC) No 4056/86, of awards at arbitration and recommendations by conciliators concerns the settlement of disputes relating to the practices of conferences referred to in Article 4 and in points 2 and 3 of Article 5 of that Regulation; whereas it seems appropriate to make the procedure for this notification as simple as possible; whereas it is appropriate, therefore, to provide for notifications to be made in writing, attaching the documents containing the text of the awards and recommendations concerned;

(9) Whereas the provisions of this Regulation should also cover cases in which complaints, applications and notifications are made under Articles 53 and 54 of the Agreement on the European Economic Area,

---

[7] OJ 1988 L376/1.
[8] OJ 1988 L376/10.

Has Adopted this Regulation

Article 1

Entitled persons

1. Any undertaking and any association of undertakings being a party to agreements or to concerted practices, or any association of undertakings adopting decisions, shall be permitted to submit applications or notifications to the Commission under any of the following provisions:

(a) Article 2 or Article 14(1) of Regulation (EEC) No 1017/68;
(b) Article 12 of Regulation (EEC) No 4056/86;
(c) Articles 3(2) and 5 of Regulation (EEC) No 3975/87.

2. Where the application or notification is submitted by some, but not all, of the parties referred to in paragraph 1, they shall give notice to the other parties.

3. Where the application or notification is signed by representatives of persons, undertakings or associations of undertakings, such representatives shall produce written proof that they are authorised to act.

4. Where a joint application or notification is made, a joint representative shall be appointed who is authorised to transmit and receive documents on behalf of all the applicants or notifying parties.

Article 2

Submission of applications and notifications

1. Applications under Article 3(2) of Regulation (EEC) No 3975/87 relating to Article 81(1) of the Treaty and applications under Article 12 of Regulation (EEC) No 1017/68, Article 12 of Regulation (EEC) No 4056/86 and Article 5 of Regulation (EEC) No 3975/87 shall be submitted in the manner prescribed by Form TR as shown in Annex I to this Regulation.

Form TR may also be used for applications under Article 3(2) of Regulation (EEC) No 3975/87 relating to Article 82 of the Treaty.

Notifications under Article 14(1) of Regulation (EEC) No 1017/68 shall be submitted on Form TR(B) shown in Annex II to this Regulation.

2. Joint applications and joint notifications shall be submitted on a single form.

3. One original and 17 copies of each application and notification, and three copies of the supporting documents, shall be submitted to the Commission at the address indicated on the forms.

4. The supporting documents shall be either originals or copies of the originals; in the latter case the applicant or notifying party shall certify that they are true and complete copies of the originals.

5. Applications and notifications shall be in one of the official languages of the Union. This language shall also be the language of the proceeding for the applicant or notifying party. Documents shall be submitted in their original language. Where the original language is not one of the official Union languages, a translation into the language of the proceeding shall be attached.

6. Where an application which purports to be submitted under Article 12 of Regulation (EEC) No 1017/68, Article 12 of Regulation (EEC) No 4056/86 or Articles 3(2) and 5 of Regulation (EEC) No 3975/87 is found to fall outside the scope of the Regulation or Regulations under which it has been submitted, the Commission shall without delay inform the applicant that it intends to examine the application under the provisions of such

739

other Regulation or Regulations as is or are applicable to the case; however, the date of submission of the application shall be the date resulting from Article 4. The Commission shall inform the applicant of its reasons and fix a period for the applicant to submit any comments in writing before it conducts its appraisal pursuant to that other Regulation or those other Regulations. The period fixed by the Commission shall be not less than two weeks; it may be extended.

Article 3

Content of applications and notifications

1. Applications and notifications shall contain the information, including the documents, required by the forms. The information shall be correct and complete.
2. The Commission may dispense with the obligation to provide any particular information, including documents, required by the forms where the Commission considers that such information is not necessary for the examination of the case.
3. The Commission shall, without delay, acknowledge in writing to the applicant or notifying party receipt of the application or notification, and of any reply to a letter sent by the Commission pursuant to Article 4(2).

Article 4

Effective date of submission of applications and notifications

1. Without prejudice to paragraphs 2 to 5, applications and notifications shall become effective on the date on which they are received by the Commission. Where, however, the application or notification is sent by registered post, it shall become effective on the date shown on the postmark of the place of posting.
2. Where the Commission finds that the information, including documents, contained in the application or notification is incomplete in any material respect, it shall, without delay, inform the applicant or notifying party in writing of this fact and shall fix an appropriate time limit for the supply of full information. In such cases, the application or notification shall become effective on the date on which the complete information is received by the Commission.
3. Material changes in the facts contained in the application or notification which the applicant or notifying party knows or ought to know shall be communicated to the Commission voluntarily and without delay.
4. Incorrect or misleading information shall be considered to be incomplete information.
5. Where, at the expiry of a period of one month following the date on which the application or notification has been received, the Commission has not provided the applicant or notifying party with the information referred to in paragraph 2, the application or notification shall be deemed to have become effective on the date of its receipt by the Commission.

Article 5

Notifications of awards given at arbitration and recommendations

1. Awards at arbitration and recommendations by conciliators accepted by the parties shall be notified to the Commission when they concern the settlement of disputes relating to the practices of conferences referred to in Article 4 and points 2 and 3 of Article 5 of Regulation (EEC) No 4056/86.

2. The obligation of notification applies to any party to the dispute resolved by the award or recommendation.

3. Notifications shall be submitted forthwith by registered letter with an acknowledgement of receipt or shall be delivered by hand against receipt. They shall be written in one of the official languages of the Union.

4. Supporting documents shall be either originals or copies. Copies shall be certified as true copies of the original. They shall be submitted in their original language. Where the original language is not one of the official languages of the Union, a translation in one of the official Union languages shall be attached.

5. When representatives of undertakings, of associations of undertakings, or of natural or legal persons sign such notifications, they shall produce written proof that they are authorised to act.

Article 6

Applications and notifications under Articles 53 and 54 of the EEA Agreement

Where applications and notifications as provided for in Articles 2(1) and 5(1) are made under Articles 53 or 54 of the Agreement on the European Economic Area, they may be made in one of the official Union languages or in one of the official languages of the EFTA States.

Article 7

Repeal

Regulations (EEC) No 1629/69, (EEC) No 4260/88 and (EEC) No 4261/88 are repealed.

Article 8

Entry into force

This Regulation shall enter into force on 1 February 1999.

This Regulation shall be binding in its entirety and directly applicable in all Member States.

Done at Brussels, 22 December 1998.

ANNEX I

FORM TR

Introduction

Form TR, as its Annex, is an integral part of Commission Regulation (EC) No 2843/98 of 22 December 1998 on the form, content and other details of applications and notifications provided for in Council Regulations (EEC) No 1017/68, (EEC) No 4056/86 and

(EEC) No 3975/87 applying the rules on competition to the transport sector (hereinafter referred to as "the Regulation"). It allows undertakings and associations of undertakings to make applications under Article 12 of Regulation (EEC) No 4056/86 and under Articles 3(2) and 5 of Regulation (EEC) No 3975/87.

Form TR is not a form to be filled in.

To facilitate the use of the Form TR the following pages set out:

— in which situations it is necessary to make an application (point A);
— to which authority (the Commission or the EFTA Surveillance Authority) the application should be made (point B);
— for which purposes the application can be used (point C);
— what information must be given in the application (points D, E, and F);
— who can make an application (point G);
— how to make an application (point H);
— how the business secrets of the undertakings can be protected (point I);
— the subsequent procedure after the application has been made (point J); and
— how certain technical terms used in the operational part of the Form TR should be interpreted (point K).

A. In which situations is it necessary to make an application?

I. Purpose of the competition of the EC Treaty and the EEA Agreement

1. Purpose of the EC competition rules

The purpose of the competition rules is to prevent the distortion of competition in the common market by restrictive practices or the abuse of dominant positions. They apply to any enterprise trading directly or indirectly in the common market, wherever established.

Article 81(1) of the EC Treaty (the text of Articles 81 and 82 is reproduced in Appendix I to this form) prohibits restrictive agreements, decisions or concerted practices (arrangements) which may affect trade between Member States, and Article 81(2) declares agreements and decisions containing such restrictions void (although the Court of Justice has held that if restrictive terms of agreements are severable, only those terms are void); Article 81(3), however, provides for exemption of arrangements with beneficial effects, if its conditions are met. Article 82 prohibits the abuse of a dominant position which may affect trade between Member States.

The original procedures for implementation Articles 81 and 82, which provide for "negative clearance" and exemption pursuant to Article 81(3), were laid down in Regulation No 17. However, Council Regulation No 14[9] rendered Regulation No 17 inapplicable in the transport sector. The procedures for implementing the EC competition rules in the transport sector have subsequently been laid down for transport by rail, road and inland waterway in Regulation (EEC) No 1017/68, for maritime transport by Regulation (EEC) No 4056/86 and for the air transport sector by Regulation (EEC) No 3975/87 (the references to these and other acts mentioned in this form or relevant to applications made on this form are listed in Appendix II to this form).

Regulations (EEC) No 4056/86 and (EEC) No 3975/87, like Regulation No 17, make reference to Articles 81 and 82 of the EC Treaty. By contrast, Regulation (EEC) No 1017/68 enacts substantive competition rules for the inland transport sector. Articles 2, 5, 7 and 8 of Regulation (EEC) No 1017/68 contain provisions which, with minor variations, mirror those respectively of Articles 81(1), (2) and (3) and 82 of the EC Treaty. Those

---

[9] Council Regulation No 141/62 of 26 November 1962 exempting transport from the application of Council Regulation No 17, (OJ 124, 28.11.1962, p. 2753); Regulation as last amended by Regulation No 1002/67/EEC, (OJ 306, 16.12.1967, p. 1).

provisions of Regulation (EEC) No 1017/68 are to be interpreted in the same way as Articles 81 and 82 of the Treaty.[10]

2. Purpose of the EEA competition rules

The competition rules of the Agreement on the European Economic Area (concluded between the Community, the Member States and the EFTA States[11] are based on the same principles as those contained in the Community competition rules and have the same purpose, i.e. to prevent the distortion of competition in the EEA by cartels or the abuse of dominant positions. They apply to any enterprise trading directly or indirectly in the EEA, wherever established.

Article 53(1) of the EEA Agreement (the text of Articles 53, 54 and 56 of the EEA Agreement is reproduced in Appendix I) prohibits restrictive agreements, decisions or concerted practices (arrangements) which may affect trade between the Community and one or more EFTA States (or between EFTA States), and Article 53(2) declares agreements or decisions containing such restrictions void; Article 53(3), however, provides for exemption of arrangements with beneficial effects, if its conditions are met. Article 54 prohibits the abuse of a dominant position which may affect trade between the Community and one or more EFTA States (or between EFTA States). The procedures for implementing the EEA competition rules in the transport sector are laid down for transport by rail, road and inland waterway in Regulation (EEC) No 1017/68, for maritime transport by Regulation (EEC) No 4056/86 and for the air transport sector by Regulation (EEC) No 3975/87, supplemented for EEA purposes, by Protocols 21, 22 and 23 to the EEA Agreement.

II. The scope of the competition rules of the EC Treaty and the EEA Agreement

The applicability of Articles 2, 5 and 8 of Regulation (EEC) No 1017/68, Articles 81 and 82 of the EC Treaty and Articles 53 and 54 of the EEA Agreement depends on the circumstances of each individual case. It presupposes that the arrangement or behaviour satisfies all the conditions set out in the relevant provisions. This question must consequently be examined before any application is made.

1. Negative clearance

In the transport sector, the negative clearance procedure has been provided for only in the air transport sector. Its purpose is to allow undertakings to ascertain whether the Commission considers that their arrangement or their behaviour is or is not prohibited by Article 81(1), or Article 82 of the EC Treaty or by Article 53(1) or Article 54 of the EEA Agreement. This procedure is governed by Article 3(2) of Regulation (EEC) No 3975/87. The negative clearance takes the form of a decision by which the Commission certifies that, on the basis of the facts in its possession, there are no grounds pursuant to Article 81(1) or Article 82 of the EC Treaty or under Article 53(1) or Article 54 of the EEA Agreement for action on its part in respect of the arrangement or behaviour.

There is, however, no point in making an application when the arrangements or the behaviour are manifestly not prohibited by the abovementioned provisions. Nor is the Commission obliged to give negative clearance. Article 3(2) of Regulation (EEC) No 3975/87 states that " ... the Commission may certify ... ". The Commission issues

---

[10] See Case T–224/94 *Deutsche Bahn v. Commission* [1997] ECR II–1689, at paragraph 77. The Court of First Instance held that Article 8 of the Regulation does not have a purpose which is substantially different from that of Article 82 of the Treaty.

[11] See list of Member States and EFTA States in Appendix III.

negative clearance decisions only where an important problem of interpretation has to be solved. In the other cases it reacts to the application by sending a comfort letter.

The Commission has published several notices relating the interpretation of Article 81(1) of the EC Treaty. They define certain categories of agreements which, by their nature or because of their minor importance, are not caught by the prohibition.[12]

2. Exemption

The procedure for exemption pursuant to Article 5 of Regulation (EEC) No 1017/68, Article 81(3) of the EC Treaty and Article 53(3) of the EEA Agreement allows companies to enter into arrangements which, in fact, offer economic advantages but which, without exemption, would be prohibited by Article 2 of Regulation (EEC) No 1017/68, Article 81(1) of the EC Treaty or by Article 53(1) of the EEA Agreement. This procedure is governed by Articles 12 and 13 of Regulation (EEC) No 1017/68, Articles 12 and 13 of Regulation (EEC) No 4056/86 and Articles 5 and 6 of Regulation (EEC) No 3975/87. The exemption takes the form of a decision by the Commission declaring Article 2 of Regulation (EEC) No 1017/68, Article 81(1) of the EC Treaty or Article 53(1) of the EEA Agreement to be inapplicable to the arrangements described in the decision. The Commission is required to specify the period of validity of any such decision, it can attach conditions and obligations and it can amend or revoke decisions or prohibit specified acts by the parties in certain circumstances, notably if the decisions were based on incorrect information or if there is any material change in the facts.

Regulations (EEC) No 1017/68, (EEC) No 4056/86 and (EEC) No 3975/87 provide for an objections procedure under which applications can be handled expeditiously. If an application is admissible pursuant to the relevant Regulation, if it is complete and if the arrangement which is the subject of the application has not given rise to a procedure as a result of a complaint or on the Commission's own initiative, the Commission publishes a summary of the request in the *Official Journal of the European Communities* and invites comments from interested third parties, from Member States and from EFTA States where requests relate to the EEA Agreement. Unless the Commission notifies the applicants within 90 days of the date of such publication that there are serious doubts as to the applicability of Article 5 of Regulation (EEC) No 1017/68, Article 81(3) of the EC Treaty or Article 53(3) of the EEA Agreement, the arrangement will be deemed exempt for the time already elapsed and for a maximum of three years from the date of publication, in the case of applications under Regulation (EEC) No 1017/68, and for a maximum of six years from the date of publication in the case of applications under Regulations (EEC) No 4056/86 and (EEC) No 3975/87.

The Commission has adopted a number of regulations granting exemptions to categories of agreements in the air transport sector and in the maritime sector.[13]

A decision granting exemption under Regulations (EEC) No 1017/68, (EEC) No 4056/86 or (EEC) No 3975/87 may have retroactive effect. Should the Commission find that notified arrangements are indeed prohibited and cannot be exempted and, therefore, take a decision condemning them, the participants are nevertheless protected, between the date of the application of the date of the decision, against fines for any infringement described in the application (Article 19(4) of Regulation (EEC) No 4056/86 and Article 12(5) of Regulation (EEC) No 3975/87). Regulation (EEC) No 1017/68 does not provide for such immunity from fines.

B. To which authority should an application be made?

The applications must be made to the authority which has competence for the matter. The Commission is responsible for the application of the competition rules of the EC

---

[12] See Appendix II.
[13] See Appendix II.

Treaty. However there is shared competence in relation to the application of the competition rules of the EEA Agreement.

The competence of the Commission and of the EFTA Surveillance Authority to apply the EEA competition rules follows from Article 56 of the EEA Agreement. Applications relating to agreements, decisions or concerted practices liable to affect trade between Member States should be addressed to the Commission unless their effects on trade between Member States or on competition within the Community are not appreciable within the meaning of the Commission notice of 1997 on agreements of minor importance.[14] Furthermore, all restrictive agreements, decisions or concerted practices affecting trade between one Member State and one or more EFTA States fall within the competence of the Commission, provided that the undertakings concerned achieve more than 67% of their combined EEA-wide turnover within the Community.[15] However, if the effects of such agreements, decisions or concerted practices on trade between Member States or on competition within the Community are not appreciable, the application should, where necessary, be addressed to the EFTA Surveillance Authority. All other agreements, decisions and concerted practices falling under Article 53 of the EEA Agreement should be notified to the EFTA Surveillance Authority (the address of which is given in Appendix III).

Applications for negative clearance regarding Article 54 of the EEA Agreement should be lodged with the Commission if the dominant position exists only in the Community, or with the EFTA Surveillance authority, if the dominant position exists only in the whole of the territory of the EFTA States, or a substantial part of it. Only where the dominant position exists within both territories should the rules outlined above with respect to Article 53 be applied.

The Commission will apply, as a basis for appraisal, the competition rules of the EC Treaty. Where the case falls under the EEA Agreement and is attributed to the Commission pursuant to Article 56 of that Agreement, it will simultaneously apply the EEA rules.

C. The purpose of this form

Form TR lists the questions that must be answered and the information and documents that must be provided when applying for the following:

— a negative clearance with regard to Article 81(1) of the EC Treaty and/or Article 53(1) of the EEA Agreement, pursuant to Article 3(2) of Regulation (EEC) No 3975/87, with respect to agreements between undertakings, decisions by associations of undertakings and concerted practices,
— an exemption pursuant to Article 5 of Regulation (EEC) No 1017/68, or Article 81(3) of the EC Treaty and/or Article 53(3) of the EEA Agreement with respect to agreements between undertakings, decisions by associations of undertakings and concerted practices.

Applications for exemption pursuant to Regulations (EEC) No 1017/68, (EEC) No 4056/86 and (EEC) No 3975/87 shall be submitted in the manner prescribed by form TR (see Article 2(1) of the Regulation).

This form can also be used by undertakings that wish to apply for a negative clearance from Article 82 of the EC Treaty or Article 53 of the EEA Agreement, pursuant to Article 3(2) of Regulation (EEC) No 3975/87. Applicants requesting negative clearance from Article 82 are not required to use form TR. They are none the less strongly recommended to give all the information requested below to ensure that their application gives a full statement of the facts (see Article 2(1)(a), second sentence of the Regulation).

---

[14] OJ 1997 C372/13.
[15] For a definition of "turnover" in this context, see Articles 2, 3 and 4 of Protocol 22 to the EEA Agreement reproduced in Appendix I.

The applications or notifications made on the form TR issued by the EFTA side are equally valid. However, if the agreements, decisions or practices concerned fall solely within Article 81 or 82 of the EC Treaty, i.e. have no EEA relevance whatsoever, it is advisable to use the present form established by the Commission.

D. Which chapters of the form should be completed?

Undertakings wishing to make an application must complete all three chapters of the operational part of this form. Notifications under Regulation No 17 of agreements concerning the creation of a cooperative joint venture of a structural character can benefit from an accelerated procedure. The accelerated procedure is not applied to applications under Regulations (EEC) No 1017/68, (EEC) No 4056/86 and (EEC) No 3975/87 because those Regulations provide for an objections procedure containing a specific timetable.

E. The need for complete information

The receipt by the Commission of a valid application has two main consequences. First, under Regulations (EEC) No 4056/86 and (EEC) No 3975/87, it affords immunity from fines from the date that the valid application is received by the Commission with regard to applications made in order to obtain exemption (see Article 19(4) of Regulation (EEC) No 4056/86 and Article 12(5) of Regulation (EEC) No 3975/87).

Second, until a valid application is received, the Commission is not "in possession of all the available evidence" which is necessary before it can publish a summary of the application under the opposition procedure in Article 12 of Regulation (EEC) No 1017/68, Article 12 of Regulation (EEC) No 4056/86 and Article 5 of Regulation (EEC) No 3975/87.

A valid application for this purpose means one that is not incomplete (see Article 3(1) of this Regulation). This is subject to two qualifications. First, if the information or documents required by this form are not reasonably available to you in part or in whole, the Commission will accept that an application is complete and thus valid notwithstanding the failure to provide such information, providing that you give reasons for the unavailability of the information, and provide your best estimates for missing data together with the sources for the estimates. Indications as to where any of the requested information or documents that are unavailable to you could be obtained by the Commission must also be provided. Secondly, the Commission only requires the submission of information relevant and necessary to its inquiry into the notified operation. In some cases not all the information required by this form will be necessary for this purpose.

The Commission may therefore dispense with the obligation to provide certain information required by this form (see Article 3(2) of the Regulation). This provision enables, where appropriate, each application to be tailored to each case so that only the information strictly necessary for the Commission's examination is provided. This avoids unnecessary administrative burdens being imposed on undertakings, in particular on small and medium-sized ones. Where the information or documents required by this form are not provided for this reason, the application should indicate the reasons why the information is considered to be unnecessary to the Commission's investigation.

Where the Commission finds that the information contained in the application is incomplete in a material respect, it will, within one month from receipt, inform the applicant or the notifying party in writing of this fact and the nature of the missing information. In such cases, the application shall become effective on the date on which the complete information is received by the Commission. If the Commission has not informed the applicant or the notifying party within the one month period that the application is incomplete in a material respect, the application will be deemed to be complete and valid (see Article 4 of the Regulation).

It is also important that undertakings inform the Commission of important changes in the factual situation including those of which they become aware after the application has been submitted. The Commission must, therefore, be informed immediately of any changes to an agreement, decision or practice which is the subject of an application (see Article 4(3) of the Regulation). Failure to inform the Commission of such relevant changes could result in any negative clearance decision being without effect or in the withdrawal of any exemption decision[16] adopted by the Commission on the basis of the application.

F. The need for accurate information

In addition to the requirement that the application be completed, it is important that you ensure that the information provided is accurate (see Article 3(1) of the Regulation). The Commission is empowered to impose, by decision, on undertakings or associations of undertakings, fines of up to EUR 5 000 where, intentionally or negligently, they supply incorrect or misleading information in an application (Article 22(1)(a) of Regulation (EEC) No 1017/68, Article 19(1)(a) of Regulation (EEC) No 4056/86 and Article 12 (1)(a) of Regulation (EEC) No 3975/87). Such information is, moreover, considered to be incomplete (see Article 4(4) of the Regulation).

G. Who can lodge an application?

Any of the undertakings party to an agreement, decision or practice of the kind described in Articles 81 or 82 of the EC Treaty and Articles 53 or 54 of the EEA Agreement may submit an application for negative clearance pursuant to Article 3(2) of Regulation (EEC) No 3975/87. Any of the undertakings party to an agreement, decision or practice of the kind described in Articles 2 and 5 of Regulation (EEC) No 1017/68, or Article 81 of the EC Treaty and Article 53 of the EEA Agreement, may submit an application requesting an exemption. An association of undertakings may submit an application in relation to decisions taken or practices pursued in the operation of the association.

In relation to agreements and concerted practices between undertakings it is common practice for all the parties involved to submit a joint application. Although the Commission strongly recommends this approach, because it is helpful to have the views of all the parties directly concerned at the same time, it is not obligatory. Any of the parties to an agreement may submit an application in their individual capacities, but in such circumstances the notifying party should inform all the other parties to the agreement, decision or practice of that fact (see Article 1(2) of the Regulation). They may also provide them with a copy of the completed form, where relevant, once confidential information and business secrets have been deleted (see below, operational part, question 1.2).

Where a joint application is submitted, it has also become common practice to appoint a joint representative to act on behalf of all the undertakings involved, both in making the application or notification, and in dealing with any subsequent contacts with the Commission (see Article 1(4) of the Regulation). Again, while this is helpful, it is not obligatory, and all the undertakings jointly submitting an application may sign it in their individual capacities.

H. How to submit an application

Applications may be submitted in any of the official languages of the European Union or of an EFTA State (see Articles 2(5) and 6 of the Regulation). In order to ensure rapid proceedings, it is, however, recommended to use, in case of an application to the EFTA Surveillance Authority one of the official languages of an EFTA State or the working

---

[16] See points (a) Article 13(3) of Regulation (EEC) No 1017/68, Article 13(3) of Regulation (EEC) No 4056/86 and Article 6(3) of Regulation (EEC) No 3975/87.

language of the EFTA Surveillance Authority, which is English, or, in case of an application to the Commission, one of the official languages of the Union or of the EFTA States or the working language of the EFTA Surveillance Authority. This language will thereafter be the language of the proceeding for the applicant.

Undertakings should provide the information requested by form TR, using its sections and paragraph numbers, signing a declaration as stated in Section 13, and annexing the required supporting documentation.

Supporting documents shall be submitted in their original language; where this is not an official language of the Union they must be translated into the language of the proceeding. The supporting documents may be originals or copies of the originals (see Article 2(4) of the Regulation).

All information requested in this form shall, unless otherwise stated, relate to the calendar year preceding that of the application. Where information is not reasonably available on this basis (for example if accounting periods are used that are not based on the calendar year, or the previous year's figures are not yet available), the most recently available information should be provided and reasons given why figures on the basis of the calendar year preceding that of the application cannot be provided.

Financial data may be provided in the currency in which the official audited accounts of the undertaking(s) concerned are prepared or in euros. In the latter case the exchange rate used for the conversion must be the average conversion rates prevailing for the years or other periods in question.

One original and 17 copies of each application, but only three copies of all supporting documents must be provided (see Article 2(3) of the Regulation).

The application is to be sent to:

European Commission
Directorate-General for Competition (DG IV),
The Registrar
Rue de la Loi/Wetstraat 200,
B–1049 Brussels,

or be delivered by hand during Commission working days and official working hours to the following address:

European Commission,
Directorate-General for Competition (DG IV),
The Registrar
Avenue de Cortenberg/Kortenberglaan 158,
B–1040 Brussels.

I. Confidentiality

Article 214 of the EC Treaty, Article 27 of Regulation (EEC) No 1017/68, Article 24 of Regulation (EEC) No 4056/86 and Article 17 of Regulation (EEC) No 3975/87, Article 9 of Protocol 23 to the EEA Agreement, Article 122 of the EEA Agreement and Article 27 of Chapter VI, Article 24 of Chapter IX and Article 17 of Chapter XI of Protocol 4 to the Agreement between the EFTA States on the establishment of a Surveillance Authority and of a Court of Justice require the Commission, the Member States, the EEA Surveillance Authority and EFTA States not to disclose information of the kind covered by the obligation of professional secrecy.

On the other hand, Regulations (EEC) No 1017/68, (EEC) No 4056/86 and (EEC) No 3975/87 require the Commission to publish a summary of an application for exemption. In this publication, the Commission " . . . shall have regard to the legitimate interest of undertakings in the protection of their business secrets" (Article 12(2) of Regulation (EEC) No 1017/68, Article 12(2) of Regulation (EEC) No 4056/86 and Article 5(2) of Regulation (EEC) No 3975/87).

Before publishing a summary of an application, the Commission will show the applicant(s) a copy of the proposed text.

In this connection, if an undertaking believes that its interests would be harmed if any of the information it is asked to supply were to be published or otherwise divulged to other undertakings, it should put all such information in one or more separate annexes with each page clearly marked "Business secrets". It should also give reasons why any information identified as confidential or secret should not be divulged or published.

J. Subsequent procedure

The application is registered in the Registry of the Directorate-General for Competition (DG IV). The date of receipt by the Commission (or the date of posting if sent by registered post) is the effective date of the submission (see Article 4(1) of the Regulation). However, special rules apply to incomplete applications (see under point E).

The Commission will acknowledge receipt of all applications in writing, indicating the case number attributed to the file. This number must be used in all future correspondence regarding the application. The receipt of acknowledgement does not prejudge the question whether the application is valid.

Further information may be sought from the parties or from third parties and suggestions may be made as to amendments to the arrangements that might make them acceptable.

An application for an exemption decision may be opposed by the Commission if it has serious doubts as to whether the arrangements should benefit from an exemption decision.

If, after having raised serious doubts under the opposition procedure, the Commission intends to issue an exemption decision, it is obliged to publish a summary and invite comments from third parties (Article 26(3) of Regulation (EEC) No 1017/68, Article 23(3) of Regulation (EEC) No 4056/86 and Article 16(3) of Regulation (EEC) No 3975/87). Subsequently, a preliminary draft decision has to be submitted to and discussed with the appropriate Advisory Committee composed of officials of the competent authorities of the Member States. Where the case falls under the EEA Agreement, representatives of the EFTA Surveillance Authority and the EFTA States will be invited to attend. Only then, and providing nothing has happened to change the Commission's intention, can it adopt a decision.

Sometimes files are closed without any formal decision being taken, for example, because it is found that the arrangements are already covered by a block exemption, or because they do not call for any action by the Commission, at least in circumstances at that time. In such cases comfort letters are sent. Although not a Commission decision, a comfort letter indicates how the Commission's Directorate-General for Competition (DG IV) views the case on the facts currently in their possession which means that the Commission could where necessary, for example, if it were to be asserted that a contract was void under Article 81(2) of the EC Treaty and/or Article 53(2) of the EEA Agreement, take an appropriate decision to clarify the legal situation.

K. Definitions used in the operational part of this form

Agreement: the word "agreement" is used to refer to all categories of arrangements, i.e. agreements between undertakings, decisions by associations of undertakings and concerted practices.

Year: all references to the word "year" in this form shall be read as meaning calendar year, unless otherwise stated.

Group: a group relationship exists for the purpose of this form where one undertaking:

— owns more than half the capital or business assets of another undertaking, or

— has the power to exercise more than half the voting rights in another undertaking, or
— has the power to appoint more than half the members of the supervisory board, board of directors or bodies legally representing the undertaking, or
— has the right to manage the affairs of another undertaking.

An undertaking which is jointly controlled by several other undertakings (joint venture) forms part of the group of each of these undertakings.

Notified agreement: a notified agreement is one that is the subject of an application using this form.

Relevant product market: question 5.1 of this form requires the undertaking or individual submitting the application to define the relevant product and/or service market(s) that are likely to be affected by the agreement in question. That definition(s) is then used as the basis for a number of other questions contained in this form. The definition(s) thus submitted by the applicants are referred to in this form as the relevant product market(s).

Relevant geographic market: question 5.2 of this form requires the undertaking or individual submitting the application to define the relevant geographic market(s) that are likely to be affected by the agreement in question. That definition(s) is then used as the basis for a number of other questions contained in this form. The definition(s) thus submitted by the applicants are referred to in this form as the relevant geographic market(s).

Relevant product and geographic market: by virtue of the combination of their replies to question 5 the parties provide their definition of the relevant market(s) affected by the notified agreement(s). That (those) definition(s) is (are) then used as the basis for a number of other questions contained in this form. The definition(s) thus submitted by the notifying parties is referred to in this form as the relevant geographic and product market(s).

Parties and applicant: the word "party" is used to refer to all the undertakings which are party to the agreement being notified. As an application may be submitted by only one of the undertakings which are party to an agreement, "applicant" is used to refer only to the undertaking or undertakings actually submitting the application.

FORM TR—OPERATIONAL PART

The first page of your application must contain the words "Application in accordance with form TR", and also one or more of the following indications as the case may be:

— "Application for exemption under Article 12 of Regulation (EEC) No 1017/68",
— "Application for exemption under Article 12 of Regulation (EEC) No 4056/86",
— "Application for negative clearance under Article 3(2) and/or exemption under Article 5 of Regulation (EEC) No 3975/87".

CHAPTER I

Sections Concerning the Parties, their Groups and the Agreement

Section 1

Identity of the undertakings or persons submitting the application

1.1. Please list the undertakings on behalf of which the application is being submitted and indicate their legal denomination or commercial name, shortened or commonly used as appropriate (if it differs from the legal denomination).

1.2. If the application is being submitted on behalf of only one or some of the undertakings party to the agreement being notified, please confirm that the remaining undertakings have been informed of that fact and indicate whether they have received a copy of the application, with relevant confidential information and business secrets deleted.[17] (In such circumstances a copy of the edited copy of the application which has been provided to such other undertakings should be annexed to this application).

1.3. If a joint application is being submitted, has a joint representative[18] been appointed?[19]

If yes, please give the details requested in 1.3.1. to 1.3.3.

If no, please give details of any representatives who have been authorised to act for each or either of the parties to the agreement indicating who they represent.

1.3.1. Name of representative.

1.3.2. Address of representative.

1.3.3. Telephone and fax number of representative.

1.4. In cases where one or more representatives have been appointed, an authority to act on behalf of the undertaking(s) submitting the application must accompany the application.

Section 2

Information on the parties to the agreement and the groups to which they belong

2.1. State the name and address of the parties to the agreement being notified, and the country of their incorporation.

2.2. State the nature of the business of each of the parties to the agreement being notified.

2.3. For each of the parties to the agreement, give the name of a person that can be contacted, together with his or her name, address, telephone number, fax number and position held in the undertaking.

2.4. Identify the corporate groups to which the parties to the agreement being notified belong. State the sectors in which these groups are active, and the worldwide turnover of each group.[20]

Section 3

Procedural matters

3.1. Please state whether you have made any formal submission to any other competition authorities in relation to the agreement in question. If yes, state which authorities, the individual or department in question, and the nature of the contact. In addition to this,

---

[17] The Commission is aware that in exceptional cases it may not be practicable to inform non-notifying parties to the notified agreement of the fact that it has been notified, or to provide them with a copy of the application. This may be the case, for example, where a standard agreement is being notified that is concluded with a large number of undertakings. Where this is the case you should state the reasons why it has not been practicable to follow the standard procedure set out in this question.

[18] For the purposes of this question a representative means an individual or undertaking formally appointed to make the application on behalf of the party or parties submitting the application. This should be distinguished from the situation where the application is signed by an officer of the company or companies in question. In the latter situation no representative is appointed.

[19] It is not mandatory to appoint representatives for the purpose of completing and/or submitting this application. This question only requires the identification of representatives where the applicants have chosen to appoint them.

[20] For the calculation of turnover in the banking and insurance sectors see Article 3 of Protocol 22 to the EEA Agreement.

mention any earlier proceedings or informal contacts, of which you are aware, with the Commission and/or the EFTA Surveillance Authority and any earlier proceedings with any national authorities or courts in the Community or in the territory of the EFTA States concerning these or any related agreements.

3.2. Please summarise any reasons for any claim that the case involves an issue of exceptional urgency.

3.3. State whether you intend to produce further supporting facts or arguments not yet available and, if so, on which points.[21]

Section 4

Full details of the arrangements

4.1. Please summarise the nature, content and objectives pursued by the agreement being notified.

4.2. Detail any provisions contained in the agreements which may restrict the parties in their freedom to take independent commercial decisions, for example regarding:

— buying or selling prices, discounts or other trading conditions,
— the quantities of services to be offered,
— technical development or investment,
— the choice of markets or sources of supply,
— purchases from or sales to third parties,
— whether to apply similar terms for the supply of equivalent services,
— whether to offer different services separately or together.

If you are claiming the benefit of an opposition procedure under a block exemption regulation, identify in this list the restrictions that exceed those automatically exempted by the relevant regulation.

4.3. State between which Member States of the Community and/or EFTA States[22] trade may be affected by the arrangements. Please give reasons for your reply to this question, giving data on trade flows where relevant. Furthermore please state whether trade between the Community or the EEA and any third countries is affected, again giving reasons for your reply.

CHAPTER II

Section Concerning the Relevant Market

Section 5

The relevant market

A relevant product market comprises all those products and/or services which are regarded as interchangeable or substitutable by the consumer, by reason of the products' characteristics, their prices and their intended use.[23]

---

[21] In so far as the notifying parties provide the information required by this form that was reasonably available to them at the time of notification, the fact that the parties intend to provide further supporting facts or documentation in due course does not prevent the notification being valid at the time of notification.

[22] See list in Appendix II.

[23] See Commission notice on the definition of relevant market for the purposes of Community competition law (OJ 1997 C372/5).

The following factors are normally considered to be relevant to the determination of the relevant product market and should be taken into account in this analysis[24]:

— the degree of similarity between the services in question,
— differences in price between two services,
— the cost of switching between two potentially competing services,
— established or entrenched consumer preferences for one type or category of service over another,
— industry-wide service classifications (e.g. classifications maintained by trade associations).

The relevant geographic market comprises the area in which the undertakings concerned are involved in the supply of products or services, in which the conditions of competition are sufficiently homogeneous and which can be distinguished from neighbouring areas because, in particular, conditions of competition are appreciably different in those areas.

Factors relevant to the assessment of the relevant geographic market include[25] the nature and characteristics of the services concerned, the existence of entry barriers or consumer preferences, and appreciable differences for the undertakings' market share or substantial price differences between neighbouring areas.

5.1. In the light of the above please explain the definition of the relevant product market or markets that in your opinion should form the basis of the Commission's analysis of the application.

In your answer, please give reasons for assumptions or findings, and explain how the factors outlined above have been taken into account. In particular, please state the specific products or services directly or indirectly affected by the agreement being notified and identify the categories of services viewed as substitutable in your market definition.

In the questions figuring below, this (or these) definition(s) will be referred to as "the relevant product market(s)".

5.2. Please explain the definition of the relevant geographic market or markets that in your opinion should form the basis of the Commission's analysis of the application.

In your answer, please give reasons for assumptions or findings, and explain how the factors outlined above have been taken into account. In particular, please identify the countries in which the parties are active in the relevant product market(s), and in the event that you consider the relevant geographic market to be wider than the individual Member States of the Community or the territory of the EFTA States on which the parties to the agreement are active, give the reasons for this.

In the questions below, this (or these) definitions will be referred to as "the relevant geographic market(s)".

Section 6

Group members operating on the same markets as the parties

6.1. For each of the parties to the agreement being notified, provide a list of all undertakings belonging to the same group which are:

6.1.1. active in the relevant product market(s);

---

[24] This is not however, exhaustive, and applicants may refer to other factors.
[25] This list is not, however, exhaustive, and applicants may refer to other factors.

6.1.2. active in markets neighbouring the relevant product market(s) (i.e. active in products and/or services that represent imperfect and partial substitutes for those included in your definition of the relevant product market(s)).

Such undertakings must be identified even if they sell the product or service in question in other geographic areas than those in which the parties to the notified agreement operate. Please list the name, country of incorporation, exact products or services provided and the geographic scope of operation of each group member.

Section 7

The position of the parties on the relevant product market(s)

Information requested in this section must be provided for the groups of the parties as a whole. It is not sufficient to provide such information only in relation to the individual undertakings directly concerned by the agreement.

7.1. In relation to each relevant product market(s) identified in your reply to question 5.1 please provide the following information:

7.1.1. the market shares of the parties on the relevant geographic market during the previous three years;

7.1.2. where different, the market shares of the parties in (a) the EEA as a whole, (b) the Community, (c) the territory of the EFTA States and (d) each EC Member State and EFTA State during the previous three years.[26] For this section, where market shares are less than 20%, please state simply which of the following bands are relevant: 0 to 5%, 5 to 10%, 10 to 15%, 15 to 20%.

For the purpose of answering these questions, market share may be calculated either on the basis of value or volume. Justification for the figures provided must be given. Thus, for each answer, total market value/volume must be stated, together with the sales/ turnover of each of the parties in question. The source or sources of the information should also be given (e.g. official statistics, estimates, etc.), and where possible, copies should be provided of documents from which information has been taken.

Section 8

The position of competitors and customers on the relevant product market(s)

Information requested in this section must be provided for the group of the parties as a whole and not in relation to the individual companies directly concerned by the agreement notified.

For the (all) relevant product and geographic market(s) in which the parties have a combined market share exceeding 15%, the following questions must be answered.

8.1. Please identify the five main competitors of the parties. Please identify the

---

[26] That is where the relevant geographic market has been defined as worldwide, these figures must be given regarding the EEA, the Community, the territory of the EFTA States, and each EC Member State. Where the relevant geographic market has been defined as the Community, these figures must be given for the EEA, the territory of the EFTA States, and each EC Member State. Where the market has been defined as national, these figures must be given for the EEA, the Community and the territory of the EFTA States.

company and give your best estimate as to their market share in the relevant geographic market(s). Please also provide address, telephone and fax number, and, where possible, the name of a contact person at each company identified.

8.2. Please identify the five main customers of each of the parties. State company name, address, telephone and fax numbers, together with the name of a contact person.

Section 9

Market entry and potential competition in product and geographic terms

For the (all) relevant product and geographic market(s) in which the parties have a combined market share exceeding 15%, the following questions must be answered.

9.1. Describe the various factors influencing entry in product terms into the relevant product market(s) that exist in the present case (i.e. what barriers exist to prevent undertakings that do not presently provide services within the relevant product market(s) entering this market(s)). In so doing take account of the following where appropriate:

— to what extent is entry to the markets influenced by the requirement of government authorisation or standard setting in any form? Are there any legal or regulatory controls on entry to these markets?
— to what extent is entry to the markets influenced by the need to have access to transport infrastructure?
— to what extent is entry to the markets influenced by the availability of rolling-stock vessels, aircraft, or other vehicles required for providing the services?
— to what extent is entry to the market influenced by the length of contracts between an undertaking and its suppliers and/or customers?
— describe the importance of research and development and in particular the importance of licensing patents, know-how and other rights in these markets.

9.2. Describe the various factors influencing entry in geographic terms into the relevant geographic market(s) that exist in the present case (i.e. what barriers exist to prevent undertakings already providing services within the relevant product market(s) but in areas outside the relevant geographic market(s) extending the scope of their activities into the relevant geographic market(s)?) Please give reasons for your answer, explaining, were relevant, the importance of the following factors:

— trade barriers imposed by law, such as tariffs, quotas etc.,
— local specification or technical requirements,
— procurement policies,
— the existence of adequate and available local distribution and retailing facilities,
— the need to have access to transport infrastructure,
— entrenched consumer preferences for local brands or products,
— language.

9.3. Have any new undertakings entered the relevant product market(s) in geographic areas where the parties are active during the last three years? Please provide this information with respect to both new entrants in product terms and new entrants in geographic terms. If such entry has occurred, please identify the undertaking(s) concerned (name, address, telephone and fax numbers, and, where possible, contact person), and provide your best estimate of their market share in the relevant product and geographic market(s).

Chapter III

Final Sections

Section 10

Reasons for the application for negative clearance

If you are applying for negative clearance state:

10.1. why, i.e. state which provision or effects of the agreement or behaviour might, in your view, raise questions of compatibility with the Community's and/or the EEA rules of competition. The object of this subheading is to give the Commission the clearest possible idea of the doubts you have about your agreement or behaviour that you wish to have resolved by a negative clearance.

Then, under the following three references, give a statement of the relevant facts and reasons as to why you consider Article 81(1) or 82 of the EC Treaty and/or Article 53(1) or 54 of the EEA Agreement to be inapplicable, i.e.:

10.2. why the agreements or behaviour do not have the object or effect of preventing, restricting or distorting competition within the common market or within the territory of the EFTA States to any appreciable extent, or why your undertaking does not have or its behaviour does not abuse a dominant position, and/or

10.3. why the agreements or behaviour do not have the objet or effect of preventing, restricting or distorting competition within the EEA to any appreciable extent, or why your undertaking does not have or its behaviour does not abuse a dominant position, and/or

10.4. why the agreements or behaviour are not such as may affect trade between Member States or between the Community and one or more EFTA States, or between EFTA States to any appreciable extent.

Section 11

Reasons for the application for exemption

If you are applying for an exemption under Article 5 of Regulation (EEC) No 1017/68, Article 81(3) of the EC Treaty and/or Article 53(3) of the EEA Agreement, explain how:

11.1. the agreement contributes to improving production or distribution, and/or promoting technical or economic progress. Explain in particular how the agreement contributes towards improving the quality of transport services, or promoting greater continuity and stability in the satisfaction of transport needs on markets where supply and demand are subject to considerable temporal fluctuation, or increasing the productivity of undertakings.

In particular, please explain the reasons why these benefits are expected to result from the collaboration; for example, do the parties to the agreement possess complementary technologies or distribution systems that will produce important synergies? (if so, please state which). Also please state whether any documents or studies were drawn up by the applicants when assessing the feasibility of the operations and the benefits likely to result therefrom, and whether any such documents or studies provided estimates of the savings or efficiencies likely to result. Please provide copies of any such documents or studies;

11.2. a proper share of the benefits arising from such improvement or progress accrues to consumers. Explain in particular how the agreement takes fair account of the interest of transport users;

11.3. all restrictive provisions of the agreement are indispensable to the attainment of the aims set out under 11.1 (if you are claiming the benefit of the opposition procedure, it is particularly important that you should identify and justify restrictions that exceed those automatically exempted by the relevant Regulations). In this respect please explain how the benefits resulting from the agreement identified in your reply to question 11.1 could not be achieved, or could not be achieved so quickly or efficiently or only at higher cost or with less certainty of success (i) without the conclusion of the agreement as a whole and (ii) without those particular clauses and provisions of the agreement identified in your reply to question 4.2;

11.4. the agreement does not eliminate competition in respect of a substantial part of the goods or services concerned.

Section 12

Supporting documentation

The completed application must be drawn up and submitted in one original. It shall contain the last versions of all agreements which are the subject of the application and be accompanied by the following:

(a) 17 copies of the application itself;
(b) three copies of the annual reports and accounts of all the parties to the notified agreement, decision or practice for the last three years;
(c) three copies of the most recent in-house or external long-term market studies or planning documents for the purpose of assessing or analysing the affected market(s) with respect to competitive conditions, competitors (actual and potential), and market conditions. Each document should indicate the name and position of the author,
(d) three copies of reports and analyses which have been prepared by or for any officer(s) or director(s) for the purposes of evaluating or analysing the notified agreement.

Section 13

Declaration

The application must conclude with the following declaration which is to be signed by or on behalf of all the applicants.

"The undersigned declare that the information given in this application is correct to the best of their knowledge and belief, that complete copies of all documents requested by form TR have been supplied to the extent that they are in the possession of the group of undertakings to which the applicant(s) belong(s) and are accessible to the latter, that all estimates are identified as such and are their best estimates of the underlying facts and that all the opinions expressed are sincere.

They are aware of the provisions of Article 22(1)(a) of Regulation (EEC) No 1017/68, Article 19(1)(a) of Regulation (EEC) No 4056/86 and Article 12(1)(a) of Regulation (EEC) No 3975/87.

Place and date:

Signatures:"

Please add the name(s) of the person(s) signing the application and their function(s). Applications which have not been signed are invalid.

TEXT OF ARTICLES 81 AND 82 OF THE EC TREATY, ARTICLES 53, 54 AND 56 OF THE EEA AGREEMENT, AND OF ARTICLES 2, 3 AND 4 OF PROTOCOL 22 TO THAT AGREEMENT

Article 81 of the EC Treaty

1. The following shall be prohibited as incompatible with the common market: all agreements between undertakings, decisions by associations of undertakings and concerted practices which may affect trade between Member States and which have as their object or effect the prevention, restriction or distortion of competition within the common market, and in particular those which:

(a) directly or indirectly fix purchase or selling prices or any other trading conditions;
(b) limit or control production, markets, technical development, or investment;
(c) share markets or sources of supply;
(d) apply dissimilar conditions to equivalent transactions with other trading parties, thereby placing them at a competitive disadvantage;
(e) make the conclusion of contracts subject to acceptance by the other parties of supplementary obligations which, by their nature or according to commercial usage, have no connection with the subject of such contracts.

2. Any agreements or decisions prohibited pursuant to this Article shall be automatically void.

3. The provisions of paragraph 1 may, however, be declared inapplicable in the case of:

— any agreement or category of agreements between undertakings,
— any decision or category of decisions by associations or undertakings,
— any concerted practice or category of concerted practices,

which contributes to improving the production or distribution of goods or to promoting technical or economic progress, while allowing consumers a fair share of the resulting benefit, and which does not:

(a) impose on the undertakings concerned restrictions which are not indispensable to the attainment of these objectives;
(b) afford such undertakings the possibility of eliminating competition in respect of a substantial part of the products in question.

Article 82 of the EC Treaty

Any abuse by one or more undertakings of a dominant position within the common market or in a substantial part of it shall be prohibited as incompatible with the common market in so far as it may affect trade between Member States.

Such abuse may, in particular, consist in:

(a) directly or indirectly imposing unfair purchase or selling prices or other unfair trading conditions;
(b) limiting production, markets or technical development to the prejudice of consumers;

(c)   applying dissimilar conditions to equivalent transactions with other trading parties, thereby placing them at a competitive disadvantage;
(d)   making the conclusion of contracts subject to acceptance by the other parties of supplementary obligations which, by their nature or according to commercial usage, have no connection with the subject of such contracts.

Article 53 of the EEA Agreement

1. The following shall be prohibited as incompatible with the functioning of this Agreement: all agreements between undertakings, decisions by associations of under-takings and concerted practices which may affect trade between Contracting Parties and which have as their object or effect the prevention, restriction or distortion of competition within the territory covered by this Agreement, and in particular those which:

(a)   directly or indirectly fix purchase or selling prices or any other trading conditions;
(b)   limit or control production, markets, technical development, or investment;
(c)   share markets or sources of supply;
(d)   apply dissimilar conditions to equivalent transactions with other trading parties, thereby placing them at a competitive disadvantage;
(e)   make the conclusion of contracts subject to acceptance by the other parties of supplementary obligations which, by their nature or according to commercial usage, have no connection with the subject of such contracts.

2. Any agreements or decisions prohibited pursuant to this Article shall be automat-ically void.
3. The provisions of paragraph 1 may, however, be declared inapplicable in the case of:

— any agreement or category of agreements between undertakings,
— any decision or category of decisions by associations of undertakings,
— any concerted practice or category of concerted practices,

which contributes to improving the production or distribution of goods or to promoting technical or economic progress, while allowing consumers a fair share of the resulting benefit, and which does not:

(a)   impose on the undertakings concerned restrictions which are not indispensable to the attainment of these objectives;
(b)   afford such undertakings the possibility of eliminating competition in respect of a substantial part of the products in question.

Article 54 of the EEA Agreement

Any abuse by one or more undertakings of a dominant position within the territory covered by this Agreement or in a substantial part of it shall be prohibited as incompatible with the functioning of this Agreement in so far as it may affect trade between Contracting Parties.
Such abuse may, in particular, consist in:

(a)   directly or indirectly imposing unfair purchase or selling prices or other unfair trading conditions;
(b)   limiting production, markets or technical development to the prejudice of consum-ers;
(c)   applying dissimilar conditions to equivalent transactions with other trading parties, thereby placing them at a competitive disadvantage;

(d) making the conclusion of contracts subject to acceptance by the other parties of supplementary obligations which, by their nature or according to commercial usage, have no connection with the subject of such contracts.

Article 56 of the EEA Agreement

1. Individual cases falling under Article 53 shall be decided on by the Surveillance Authorities in accordance with the following provisions:

(a) individual cases where only trade between EFTA States is affected shall be decided on by the EFTA Surveillance Authority;
(b) without prejudice to subparagraph (c), the EFTA Surveillance Authority decides, as provided for in the provisions set out in Article 58, Protocol 21 and the rules adopted for its implementation, Protocol 23 and Annex XIV, on cases where the turnover of the undertakings concerned in the territory of the EFTA States equals 33% or more of their turnover in the territory covered by this Agreement;
(c) the EC Commission decides on the other cases as well as on cases under (b) where trade between EC Member States is affected, taking into account the provisions set out in Article 58, Protocol 21, Protocol 23 and Annex XIV.

2. Individual cases falling under Article 54 shall be decided on by the Surveillance Authority in the territory of which a dominant position is found to exist. The rules set out in paragraph 1(b) and (c) shall apply only if dominance exists within the territories of both Surveillance Authorities.

3. Individual cases falling under subparagraph (c) of paragraph 1, whose effects on trade between EC Member States or on competition within the Community are not appreciable, shall be decided on by the EFTA Surveillance Authority.

4. The terms "undertaking" and "turnover" are, for the purpose of this Article, defined in Protocol 22.

Articles 2, 3 and 4 of Protocol 22 to the EEA Agreement

Article 2

"Turnover" within the meaning of Article 56 of the Agreement shall comprise the amounts derived by the undertaking concerned, in the territory covered by this Agreement, in the preceding financial year from the sale of products and the provision of services falling within the undertaking's ordinary scope of activities after deduction of sales rebates and of value-added tax and other taxes directly related to turnover.

Article 3

In place of turnover the following shall be used:

(a) for credit institutions and other financial institutions, their total assets multiplied by the ratio between loans and advances to credit institutions and customers in transactions with residents in the territory covered by this Agreement and the total sum of those loans and advances;
(b) for insurance undertakings, the value of gross premiums received from residents in the territory covered by this Agreement, which shall comprise all amounts received and receivable in respect of insurance contracts issued by or on behalf of the insurance undertakings, including also outgoing reinsurance premiums, and after deduction of taxes and parafiscal contributions or levies charged by reference to the amounts of individual premiums or the total value of premiums.

760

Article 4

1. In derogation from the definition of the turnover relevant for the application of Article 56 of the Agreement, as contained in Article 2 of this Protocol, the relevant turnover shall be constituted:

(a) as regards agreements, decisions of associations of undertakings and concerted practices related to distribution and supply arrangements between non-competing undertakings, of the amounts derived from the sale of goods or the provision of services which are the subject matter of the agreements, decisions or concerted practices, and from the other goods or services which are considered by users to be equivalent in view of their characteristics, price and intended use;

(b) as regards agreements, decisions of associations of undertakings and concerted practices related to arrangements on transfer of technology between non-competing undertakings, of the amounts derived from the sale of goods or the provision of services which result from the technology which is the subject matter of the agreements, decisions or concerted practices, and of the amounts derived from the sale of those goods or the provision of those services which that technology is designed to improve or replace.

2. However, where at the time of the coming into existence of arrangements as described in paragraph 1(a) and (b) turnover as regards the sale of products or the provision of services is not in evidence, the general provision as contained in Article 2 shall apply.

APPENDIX II

LIST OF RELEVANT ACTS

(as of 1 February 1999)

(If you think it possible that your arrangements do not need to be notified by virtue of any of these regulations or notices it may be worth your while to obtain a copy.)

Implementing regulations[27]

— Council Regulation (EEC) No 1017/68 of 19 July 1968 applying rules of competition to transport by rail, road and inland waterway (OJ L 175, 23.7.1968, p. 1), as last amended by the Act of Accession of Austria, Finland and Sweden,

— Council Regulation (EEC) No 4056/86 of 22 December 1986 laying down detailed rules for the application of Articles 81 and 82 of the Treaty to maritime transport (OJ L 378, 31.12.1986, p. 4), as last amended by the Act of Accession of Austria, Finland and Sweden,

— Council Regulation (EEC) No 3975/87 of 14 December 1987 laying down the procedure for the application of the rules on competition to undertakings in the air transport sector (OJ L 374, 31.12.1987, p. 1), as last amended by Regulation (EEC) No 2410/92 (OJ L 240, 24.8.1992, p. 18),

---

[27] As regards procedural rules applied by the EFTA Surveillance Authority, see Article 3 of Protocol 21 to the EEA Agreement and the relevant provisions in Protocol 4 to the Agreement between the EFTA States on the establishment of a Surveillance Authority and a Court of Justice.

— Commission Regulation (EC) No 2843/98 of 22 December 1998 on the form, content and other details of applications and notifications provided for in Council Regulation (EEC) No 1017/68, (EEC) No 4056/86 and (EEC) No 3975/87 applying the rules on competition to the transport sector.

Regulations granting block exemption

— Article 4 of Council Regulation (EEC) No 1017/68 of 19 July 1968 applying rules of competition to transport by rail, road and inland waterway, as last amended by the Act of Accession of Austria, Finland and Sweden (exemption for groups of small and medium-sized undertakings),
— Articles 3 and 6 of Council Regulation (EEC) No 4056/86 of 22 December 1986 laying down detailed rules for the application of Articles 81 and 82 of the Treaty to maritime transport, as last amended by the Act of Accession of Austria, Finland and Sweden (exemption for agreements between carriers concerning the operation of scheduled maritime transport services, and exemption for agreements between transport users and conferences concerning the use of scheduled maritime transport services),
— Commission Regulation (EC) No 870/95 of 20 April 1995 on the application of Article 81(3) of the Treaty to certain categories of agreements, decisions and concerted practices between liner shipping companies (consortia) pursuant to Council Regulation (EEC) No 479/92 (OJ L 89, 21.4.1992, p. 7). Article 7 of this Regulation provides for an opposition procedure,
— Commission Regulation (EEC) No 1617/93 of 25 June 1993 on the application of Article 81(3) of the Treaty to certain categories of agreements and concerted practices concerning joint planning and coordination of schedules, joint operations, consultations on passenger and cargo tariffs on scheduled air services and slot allocation at airports (OJ L 155, 26.6.1993, p. 18), as last amended by Regulation (EC) No 1523/96 (OJ L 190, 31.7.1996, p. 11). See also the notice concerning procedures for communications to the Commission pursuant to Articles 4 and 5 of Commission Regulation (EEC) No 1617/93 (OJ C 177, 29.6.1993, p. 6).

Notices of a general nature[28]

— Commission notice concerning agreements, decisions and concerted practices in the field of cooperation between enterprises (OJ C 75, 29.7.1968, p. 3, as corrected in OJ C 84, 28.8.1968, p. 17). This defines the sorts of cooperation on market studies, accounting, R&D, joint use of production, storage or transport, *ad hoc* consortia, selling or after-sales service, advertising or quality labelling that the Commission considers not to fall under the prohibition of Article 81(1),
— Commission notice concerning its assessment of certain subcontracting agreements in relation to Article 81(1) of the Treaty (OJ C 1, 3.1.1979, p. 2),
— Commission notice concerning the assessment of cooperative joint ventures pursuant to Article 81 of the EC Treaty (OJ C 43, 16.12.1993, p. 2). This notice sets out the principles on the assessment of joint ventures,
— Commission communication on clarification of the Commission recommendations on the application of the competition rules to new transport infrastructure projects (OJ C 298, 30.9.1997, p. 5),
— Commission notice on the non-imposition or reduction of fines in cartel cases (OJ C 207, 18.7.1996, p. 4),
— Commission notice on the internal rules of procedure for processing requests for access to the file in cases under Articles 81 and 82 of the EC Treaty, Articles 65 and

---

[28] See also the corresponding notices published by the EFTA Surveillance Authority.

66 of the ECSC Treaty and Council Regulation (EEC) No 4064/89 (OJ C 23, 23.1.1997, p. 3),
— notice on agreements of minor importance which do not fall under Article 81(1) of the Treaty establishing the European Community (OJ C 372, 9.12.1997, p. 13),
— Commission notice on the definition of the relevant market for the purposes of Community competition law (OJ C 372, 9.12.1997, p. 5).

A collection of these texts (as at 30 June 1994) was published by the Office for Official Publications of the European Communities (references Vol. I: ISBN 92–826–6759–6, catalogue No CM–29–93–A01–EN-C). These texts can also be found at DGIV homepage "DGIV—Competition on Europa":
http://europa.eu.int/comm/dg4home.htm
Pursuant to the Agreement, these texts will also cover the European Economic Area.

APPENDIX III

LIST OF MEMBER STATES AND EFTA STATES, ADDRESS OF THE COMMISSION AND OF THE EFTA SURVEILLANCE AUTHORITY, LIST OF COMMISSION INFORMATION OFFICES WITHIN THE COMMUNITY AND IN EFTA STATES AND ADDRESSES OF COMPETENT AUTHORITIES IN EFTA STATES

The Member States as at the date of this Annex are: Austria, Belgium, Denmark, Finland, France, Germany, Greece, Ireland, Italy, Luxembourg, the Netherlands, Portugal, Spain, Sweden and the United Kingdom.
The EFTA States which will be Contracting Parties to the EEA Agreement, as at the date of this Annex, are: Iceland, Liechtenstein and Norway.

The address of the Commission's Directorate-General for Competition is:

European Commission,
Directorate-General for Competition,
Rue de la Loi/Wetstraat 200,
B–1049 Brussels.
Tel. (32–2) 299 11 11
http://europa.eu.int/comm/dg04

The address of the EFTA Surveillance Authority's Competition Directorate is:

EFTA Surveillance Authority—ESA,
Competition and State Aid Directorate,
Rue de Trèves, 74,
B–1040 Brussels.
Tel. (32–2) 286 18 11
Fax (32–2) 286 18 00
http://www.efta.int

The addresses of the Commission's Information Offices in the Community are:

BELGIUM

Commission Européenne
Bureau en Belgique

763

Europese Commissie
Bureau in België
Rue Archiméde/Archimedesstraat 73
B–1040 Bruxelles/Brussels
Tel. (32–2) 295 38 44
Fax (32–2) 295 01 66
http://europa.eu.int/comm/represent/be

DENMARK

Europa-Kommissionen
Repræsentation i Danmark
Østergade 61 (Højbrohus)
Postboks 144
DK–1004 København K
Tel. (45) 33 14 41 40
Fax (45–33) 11 12 03
http://europa.eu.int/dk

FEDERAL REPUBLIC OF GERMANY

Europäische Kommission
Vertretung in der Bundesrepublik Deutschland
Zitelmannstraße 22
D–53113 Bonn
Tel. (49–228) 530 09–0
Fax (49–228) 530 09–50, 530 09–12

Europäische Kommission
Vertretung in der Bundesrepublik Deutschland
—Vertretung in Berlin
Kurfürstendamm 102
D–10711 Berlin 31
Tel. (49–30) 896 09 30
Fax (49–30) 892 20 59

Europäische Kommission
Vertretung in der Bundesrepublik Deutschland
—Vertretung in München
Erhardtstraße 27
D–80331 München
Tel. (49–89) 202 10 11
Fax (49–89) 202 10 15
http://www.eu-kommission.de

GREECE

Evropaiki Epitropi
Antiprosopia stin Ellada
2 Vassilissis Sofias
GR–10674 Athina
Tel. (30–1) 725 10 00
Fax (30–1) 724 46 20
http://www.forthnet.gr/ee

SPAIN

Comisión Europea

Representación en España
Paseo de la Castellana, 46
E–28046 Madrid
Tel. (34–1) 431 57 11
Fax (34–1) 432 17 64

Comisión Europea
Representación en Barcelona
Av. Diagonal, 407 bis, Planta 18
E–08008 Barcelona
Tel. (34–3) 415 81 77
Fax (34–3) 415 63 11
http://www.euroinfo.cce.es

FRANCE

Commission Européenne
Représentation en France
288, boulevard Saint-Germain
F–75007 Paris
Tel. (33–1) 40 63 38 00
Fax (33–1) 45 56 94 17/18/19

Commission Européenne
Représentation à Marseille
2, rue Henri Barbusse (CMCI)
F–13241 Marseille, Cedex 01
Tel. (33–4) 91 91 46 00
Fax (33–4) 91 90 98 07
http://europa.eu.int/france

IRELAND
European Commission
Representation in Ireland
18 Dawson Street
Dublin 2
Irelandlanda
Tel. (353–1) 662 51 13
Fax (353–1) 662 51 18

ITALY
Commissione Europea
Rappresentanza in Italia
Via Poli 29
I–00187 Roma
Tel. (39–6) 69 99 91
Fax (39–6) 679 16 58, 679 36 52

Commissione Europea
Ufficio di Milano
Corso Magenta 59
I–20123 Milano
Tel. (39–2) 467 51 41
Fax (39–2) 480 12 535

LUXEMBOURG

Commission Européenne
Représentation au Luxembourg
Bâtiment Jean-Monnet
Rue Alcide de Gasperi
L–2920 Luxembourg
Tel. (352) 43 01–34935
Fax (352) 43 01–34433

NETHERLANDS

Europese Commissie
Bureau in Nederland
Korte Vijverberg 5
NL–2513 AB Den Haag
Nederland
Tel. (31–70) 346 93 26
Fax (31–70) 364 66 19
http://www.dds.nl/plein/europa

AUSTRIA

Europäische Kommission
Vertretung in Österreich
Kärtner Ring 5–7
A–1010 Wien
Tel: (43–1) 516 18
Fax (43–1) 513 42 25
http://www.europa.or.at

PORTUGAL

Commissão Europeia
Gabinete em Portugal
Centro Europeu Jean Monnet
Largo Jean Monnet, 1–10°.
P–1250 Lisboa
Tel. (351–1) 350 98 00
Fax (351–1) 350 98 01/02/03
http://euroinfo.ce.pt

FINLAND

Euroopan komissio
Suomen edustusto
Europeiska kommissüonen
Representationen i Finland
31 Pohjoisesplanadi/Norra esplanaden 31
FIN–00100 Helsinki/Helsingfors
Tel. (358–9) 622 65 44
Fax (358–9) 65 67 28 (lehdistö ja tiedotus/press och information)

SWEDEN

Europeiska Kommissionen
Representation i Sverige
Nybrogatan 11, Box 7323
S–10390 Stockholm

Tel. (46–8) 562 444 11
Fax (46–8) 562 444 12
http://www.eukomm.se

UNITED KINGDOM

European Commission
Representation in the United Kingdom
Jean Monnet House
8 Storey's Gate
London SW1P 3AT
United Kingdom
Tel. (44–20) 7973 19 92
Fax (44–20) 7973 19 00, 7973 19 10

European Commission
Representation in Northern Ireland
9/15 Bedford Street (Windsor House)
Belfast BT2 7EG
United Kingdom
Tel. (44–1232) 24 07 08
Fax (44–1232) 24 82 41

European Commission
Representation in Wales
4 Cathedral Road
Cardiff CF1 9SG
United Kingdom
Tel. (44–1222) 37 16 31
Fax (44–1222) 39 54 89

European Commission
Representation in Scotland
9 Alva Street
Edinburgh EH2 4PH
United Kingdom
Tel. (44–131) 225 20 58
Fax (44–131) 226 41 05
http://www.cec.org.uk

The addresses of the Commission's Information Offices in the EFTA States are:

NORWAY

European Commission Delegation in Norway
Haakon VII's Gate 10 (9th floor)
N–0161 Oslo
Tel. (47–22) 83 35 83
Fax (47–22) 83 40 55

Forms for notifications and applications, as well as more detailed information on the EEA competition rules, can also be obtained from the following offices:

ICELAND

Samkeppnisstofnun (Icelandic Competition Authority)
Laugavegi 118
Pósthólf 5120

IS–125 Reykjavík
Iceland
Tel. (354–5) 527 422
Fax (354–5) 627 442

LIECHTENSTEIN

Amt Für Volkswirtschaft (Office of National Economy)
Gerberweg 5
FL–9490 Vaduz
Tel. (41–75) 236 68 73
Fax (41–75) 236 68 89

NORWAY

Norwegian Competition Authority
PO Box 8132 Dep.
0033 Oslo
Norway
Tel. (47–22) 40 09 00
Fax (47–22) 40 09 99

Annex II

FORM TR(B)[29]

This form and the supporting documents should be forwarded in one original and 17 copies together with proof in a single copy of the representative's authority to act.

If the space opposite each question is insufficient, please use extra pages, specifying to which item on the form they relate.

To the European Commission

Directorate-General for Competition
Rue de la Loi/Wetstraat 200
B–1049 Brussels.

Notification of an agreement, decision or concerted practice pursuant to Article 14(1) of Council Regulation (EEC) No 1017/68 with a view to obtaining a declaration of non-applicability of the prohibition in Article 2, available in states of crisis, pursuant to Article 6 of that Regulation.[30]

I. Information regarding parties

1. Name, forenames and address of person submitting the notification. If such person is acting as representative, state also the name and address of the undertaking or association of undertakings represented and the name, forenames and address of the proprietors or partners or, in the case of legal persons, of their legal representatives.

---

[29] Notifications made by using form TR(B) issued by the Commission and the equivalent form issued by the EFTA side are equally valid. Any reference to EFTA States shall be understood to mean those EFTA States which are Contracting Parties to the Agreement on the European Economic Area.

[30] See also this Regulation as adapted for EEA purposes (point 10 of Annex XIV to the Agreement on the European Economic Area, hereinafter referred to as "the EEA Agreement").

Proof of representative's authority to act must be supplied.

If the notification is submitted by a number of persons or on behalf of a number of undertakings, the information must be given in respect of each person or undertaking.

2. Name and address of the undertakings which are parties to the agreement, decision or concerted practice and name, forenames and address of the proprietors or partners, in the case of legal persons, of their legal representatives (unless this information has been given under I.1).

If the undertakings which are parties are not all associated in submitting the notification, state what steps have been taken to inform the other undertakings.

This information is not necessary in respect of standard contracts (see II.2(b)).

3. If a firm or joint agency has been formed in pursuance of the agreement, decision or concerted practice, state the name and address of such firm or agency and the names, forenames and addresses of its representatives.

4. If a firm or joint agency is responsible for operating the agreement, decision or concerted practice, state the name and address of such firm or agency and the names, forenames and addresses of its representatives.

Attach a copy of the statutes.

5. In the case of a decision of an association of undertakings, state the name and address of the association and the names, forenames and addresses of its representatives.

Attach a copy of the statutes.

6. If the undertakings are established or have their seat outside the EEA, state the name and address of a representative or branch established in the EEA.

II. Information regarding contents of agreement, decision or concerted practice

1. Does the agreement, decision or concerted practice concern transport:

— by rail,
— by road,
— by inland waterway,

or operations of providers of services ancillary to transport?

2. If the contents were reduced to writing, attach a copy of the full text unless (a) or (b) below provides otherwise.

(a) Is there only an outline agreement or outline decision?
    If so, attach also copy of the full text of the individual agreements and implementing provisions.
(b) Is there a standard contract, i.e. a contract which the undertaking submitting the notification regularly concludes with particular persons or groups of persons?
    If so, only the text of the standard contract need be attached.

3. If the contents were not, or were only partially, reduced to writing, state the contents in the space opposite.

4. In all cases give the following additional information:

(a) date of agreement, decision or concerted practice;
(b) date when it came into force and, where applicable, proposed period of validity;
(c) subject: exact description of the transport service or services involved, or of any other subject to which the agreement, decision or concerted practice relates;
(d) aims of the agreement, decision or concerted practice;
(e) terms of adherence, termination or withdrawal;
(f) sanctions which may be taken against participating undertakings (penalty clause, exclusion, etc.).

III. Means of achieving the aims of the agreement, decision or concerted practice

1. State whether and how far the agreement, decision or concerted practice relates to:

— adherence to certain rates and conditions of transport or other operating conditions,
— restriction or control of the supply of transport, technical development or investment,
— sharing of transport markets,
— restrictions on freedom to conclude transport contracts with third parties (exclusive contracts),
— application of different terms for supply of equivalent services.

2. Is the agreement, decision or concerted practice with transport services:

(a) within one Member State or EFTA State only?
(b) between Member States?
(c) between EFTA States?
(d) between the Community and one or more EFTA States?
(e) between a Member State or an EFTA State and third countries?
(f) between third countries in transit through one or more EC Member States and/or one or more EFTA States?

IV. Description of the conditions to be fulfilled by the agreement, decision or concerted practice so as to be exempt from the prohibition in Article 2

Describe to what extent:
1. the transport market is disturbed;
2. the agreement, decision or concerted practice is essential for reducing that disturbance;
3. the agreement, decision or concerted practice does not eliminate competition in respect of substantial parts of the transport market concerned.

V. State whether you intend to produce further supporting arguments and, if so, on which points

The undersigned declare that the information given above and in the Annexes attached hereto is correct. They are aware of the provisions of Article 22(1)(a) of Regulation (EEC) No 1017/68.

Place and date:

Signatures:

APPENDIX 74

REGULATION 26[1]

Applying Certain Rules of Competition to Production of and Trade in Agriculture Products

THE COUNCIL OF THE EUROPEAN ECONOMIC COMMUNITY

Having regard to the Treaty establishing the European Economic Community, and in particular Articles 36 and 37 thereof;

Having regard to the proposal from the commission;

Having regard to the Opinion of the European Parliament;

Whereas by virtue of Article 36 of the Treaty one of the matters to be decided under the common agricultural policy is whether the rules on competition laid down in the Treaty are to apply to production of and trade in agricultural products, and accordingly the provisions hereinafter contained will have to be supplemented in the light of developments in that policy;

Whereas the proposals submitted by the Commission for the formulation and implementation of the common agricultural policy show that certain rules on competition must forthwith be made applicable to production of and trade in agricultural products in order to eliminate practices contrary to the principles of the common market and prejudicial to attainment of the objectives set out in Article 33 of the Treaty and in order to provide a basis for the future establishment of a system of competition adapted to the development of the common agricultural policy;

Whereas special attention is warranted in the case of farmers' organisations which are particularly concerned with the joint production or marketing of agricultural products or the use of joint facilities, unless such joint action excludes competition or jeopardises attainment of the objectives of Articles 33 of the Treaty;

Whereas, in order both to avoid compromising the development of a common agricultural policy and to ensure certainty in the law and non-discriminatory treatment of the undertakings concerned, the Commission must have sole power, subject to review by the Court of Justice, to determine whether the conditions provided for in the two preceding recitals are fulfilled as regards the agreements, decisions and practices referred to in Article 81 of the Treaty;

Whereas, in order to enable the specific provisions of the Treaty regarding agriculture, and in particular those of Article 33 thereof, to be taken into consideration, the Commission must, in questions of dumping, assess all the causes of the practices complained of and in particular the price level at which products from other sources are imported into the market in question; whereas it must, in the light of its assessment, make recommendations and authorise protective measures as provided in Article [91(1)][2] of the Treaty;

---

[1] JO 1962, 993; O.J. 1959–62, 129.

[2] Art. 91(1) of the original EEC Treaty concerned control of dumping during the transitional period and was repealed by Art. 6(49) of the Treaty of Amsterdam.

Whereas, in order to implement, as part of the development of the common agricultural policy, the rules on aids for production of or trade in agricultural products, the Commission should be in a position to draw up a list of existing, new or proposed aids, to make appropriate observations to the Member States and to propose suitable measures to them;

HAS ADOPTED THIS REGULATION:

Article 1

From the entry into force of this regulation, Articles 81 to 86 of the Treaty and provisions made in implementation thereof shall, subject to Article 2 below, apply to all agreements, decisions and practices referred to in Articles 81(1) and 82 of the Treaty which relate to production of or trade in the products listed in Annex II to the Treaty;

Article 2

1. Article 81(1) of the Treaty shall not apply to such of the agreements, decisions and practices referred to in the preceding Article as form an integral part of a national market organisation or are necessary for attainment of the objectives set out in Article 33 of the Treaty. In particular, it shall not apply to agreements, decisions and practices of farmers, farmers' associations, or associations of such associations belonging to a single Member State which concern the production or sale of agricultural products or the use of joint facilities for the storage, treatment or processing of agricultural products, and under which there is no obligation to charge identical prices, unless the Commission finds that competition is thereby excluded or that the objectives of Article 33 of the Treaty are jeopardised.

2. After consulting the Member States and hearing the undertakings or associations of undertakings concerned and any other natural or legal person that it considers appropriate, the commission shall have sole power, subject to review by the Court of Justice, to determine, by decision which shall be published, which agreements, decisions and practices fulfil the conditions specified in paragraph (1).

3. The Commission shall undertake such determination either on its own initiative or at the request of a competent authority of a Member State or of an interested undertaking or association of undertakings.

4. The publication shall state the names of the parties and the main content of the decision; it shall have regard to the legitimate interest of undertakings in the protection of their business secrets.

Article 3

1. Without prejudice to Article 38 of the Treaty, Article [91(1)][3] thereof shall apply to trade in the products listed in Annex II to the Treaty.

2. With due regard for the provisions of the Treaty relating to agriculture, and in particular those of Article 33, the Commission shall assess all the causes of the practices complained of, in particular the price level at which products from other sources are imported into the market in question.

In the light of its assessment, it shall make recommendations, and authorise protective measures as provided in Article [91(1)][4] of the Treaty.

---

[3] See n. 2 *supra.*
[4] See n. 2 *supra.*

Article 4

The provisions of Article 88(1) and of the first sentence of Article 88(3) of the Treaty shall apply to aids granted for production of or trade in the products listed in Annex II to the Treaty.

Article 5

This regulation shall enter into force on the day following its publication in the *Official Journal of the European Communities*, with the exception of Articles 1 to 3, which shall enter into force on 1 July 1962.

This regulation shall be binding in its entirety and directly applicable in all Member States.

Done at Brussels, 4 April 1962.

COMMISSION COMMUNICATION TO THE MEMBER STATES[1]

Application of Articles 87 and 88 of the EEC Treaty and of Article 5 of Commission Directive 80/723/EEC to Public Undertakings in the Manufacturing Sector

I. INTRODUCTION

1. A reinforced application of policy towards State aids is necessary for the successful completion of the internal market. One of the areas identified as worthy of attention in this respect is public undertakings. There is need for both increased transparency and development of policy for public undertakings because they have not been sufficiently covered by State aid disciplines:

— in many cases only capital injections and not other forms of public funds have been fully included in aid disciplines for public undertakings,
— in addition, these disciplines in general only cover loss-making public undertakings,
— finally it also appears that there is a considerable volume of aid to public undertakings given other than through approved aid schemes (which are also available to private undertakings) which have not been notified under Article 88(3).

2. This communication is designed to remedy this situation. In the first place it explains the legal background of the Treaty and outlines the aid policy and case-law of the Council, Parliament, Commission and Court of Justice for public enterprises. This will, in particular, focus, on the one hand, on Directive 80/723/EEC on the transparency of the financial relationship between public undertakings and the State, and, on the other hand, it will develop the well established principle that where the State provides finances to a company in circumstances that would not be acceptable to an investor operating under normal market economy conditions, State aid is involved. The communication then explains how the Commission intends to increase transparency by applying this principle to all forms of public funds and to companies in all situations.

3. This communication does not deal with the question of the compatibility under one of the derogations provided for in the EC Treaty because no change is envisaged in this policy. Finally, this communication is limited to the manufacturing sector. This will not, however, preclude the Commission from using the approach described by this communication in individual cases or sectors outside manufacturing to the extent that the principles in this communication apply in these excluded sectors and where it feels that it is essential to determine if State aid is involved.

---

[1] OJ 1993 C307/3.

II. Public Undertakings and the Rules of Competition

4. Article 295 states: "This Treaty shall in no way prejudice the rules in Member States governing the system of property ownership". In other words the Treaty is neutral in the choice a Member State may make between public and private ownership and does not prejudice a Member State's right to run a mixed economy. However, these rights do not absolve public undertakings from the rules of competition because the institution of a system ensuring that competition in the common market is not distorted is one of the bases on which the Treaty is built (Article 3(1)(g)). The Treaty also provides the general rules for ensuring such a system (Articles 81 to 89). In addition the Treaty lays down that these general rules of competition shall apply to public undertakings (Article 86(1)). There is a specific derogation in Article 86(2) from the general rule of Article 86(1) in that the rules of competition apply to all public undertakings including those entrusted with the operation of services of general economic interest or having the character of a revenue-producing monopoly in so far as the application of such rules does not obstruct the performance in law or in fact of the particular tasks assigned to them. The development of trade must not be affected to such an extent as would be contrary to the interests of the Community. In the context of the State aid rules (Articles 87 to 89), this means that aid granted to public undertakings must, like any other State aid to private undertakings, be notified in advance to the Commission (Article 88(3)) to ascertain whether or not it falls within the scope of Article 87(1), i.e. aid that affects trade and competition between Member States. If it falls within Article 87(1), it is for the Commission to determine whether one of the general derogations provided for in the Treaty is applicable such that the aid becomes compatible with the common market. It is the Commission's role to ensure that there is no discrimination against either public or private undertakings when it applies the rules of competition.

5. It was to ensure this principle of non-discrimination, or neutrality of treatment, that the Commission adopted in 1980 a Directive on the transparency of financial relations between Member States and public undertakings.[2] The Commission was motivated by the fact that the complexity of the financial relations between national public authorities and public undertakings tended to hinder its duty of ensuring that aid incompatible with the common market was not granted. It further considered that the State aid rules could only be applied fairly to both public and private undertakings when the financial relations between public authorities and public undertakings were made transparent.

6. The Directive obliged Member States to ensure that the flow of all public funds to public undertakings and the uses to which these funds are put are made transparent (Article 1). Member States shall, when the Commission considers it necessary so to request, supply to it the information referred to in Article 1, together with any necessary background information, notably the objectives pursued (Article 5). Although the transparence in question applied to all public funds, the following were particularly mentioned as falling within its scope:

— the setting-off of operating losses,
— the provision of capital,
— non-refundable grants or loans on privileged terms,
— the granting of financial advantages by forgoing profits or the recovery of sums due,
— the forgoing of a normal return on public funds used,
— compensation for financial burdens imposed by the public authorities.

7. The Commission further considered that transparency of public funds must be achieved irrespective of the manner in which such provision of public funds is made.

---

[2] Directive 80/723/EEC (OJ 1980 L195/35), as amended by Directive 85/413/EEC (OJ 1985 L229/20), which included previously excluded sectors.

Thus, not only were the flows of funds directly from public authorities to public enter-prises deemed to fall within the scope of the Transparency Directive, but also the flows of funds indirectly from other public undertakings over which the public authority holds a dominant influence (Article 2).

8. The legality of the Transparency Directive was upheld by the Court of Justice in its judgment of 6 July 1982.[3]

8.1. On the argument that there was no necessity for the Directive and that it infringed the rule of proportionality, the Court held as follows (paragraph 18): "In view of the diverse forms of public undertakings in the various Member States and the ramifications of their activities, it is inevitable that their financial relations with public authorities should themselves be very diverse, often complex and therefore difficult to supervise, even with the assistance of the sources of published information to which the applicant governments have referred. In those circumstances there is an undeniable need for the Commission to seek additional information on those relations by establishing common criteria for all the Member States and for all the undertakings in question".

8.2. On the argument that the Directive in question infringed the principle of neutrality of Article 295 of the Treaty, the Court held that (paragraph 21), "it should be borne in mind that the principle of equality, to which the governments refer in connection with the relationship between public and private undertakings in general, presupposes that the two are in comparable situations. . . . private undertakings determine their industrial and com-mercial strategy by taking into account in particular requirements of profitability. Deci-sions of public undertakings, on the other hand, may be affected by factors of a different kind within the framework of the pursuit of objectives of public interest by public authorities which may exercise an influence over those decisions. The economic and financial consequences of the impact of such factors lead to the establishment between those undertakings and public authorities of financial relations of a special kind which differ from those existing between public authorities and private undertakings. As the Directive concerns precisely those special financial relations, the submission relating to discrimination cannot be accepted."

8.3. On the argument that the Directive's list of public funds to be made transparent (Article 3) was an attempt to define the notion of aid within the meaning of Articles 87 and 88, the Court stated as follows (paragraph 23): "In relation to the definition contained in Article 3 of the financial relations which are subject to the rules contained in the Directive, it is sufficient to state that it is not an attempt by the Commission to define the concept of aid which appears in Articles 87 and 88 of the Treaty, but only a statement of the financial transactions of which the Commission considers that it must be informed in order to check whether a Member State has granted aids to the undertakings in question, without complying with its obligation to notify the Commission under Article 88(3)".

8.4. On the argument that the public enterprises on which information was to be provided (Article 2) was an attempt to define the notion of public undertakings within the meaning of Article 86 of the Treaty, the Court stated that (paragraph 24), "it should be emphasized that the object of those provisions is not to define the concept as it appears in Article 86 of the Treaty, but to establish the necessary criteria to delimit the group of undertakings whose financial relations with the public authorities are to be subject to the duty laid down by the Directive to supply information". It continued in paragraph 25 as follows: "According to Article 2 of the Directive, the expression "public undertakings" means any undertaking over which the public authorities may exercise directly or indi-rectly a dominant influence. According to the second paragraph, such influence is to be presumed when the public authorities directly or indirectly hold the major part of the undertaking's subscribed capital, control the majority of the votes, or can appoint more than half of the members of its administrative, managerial or supervisory body". It continued in paragraph 26 as follows: "As the Court has already stated, the reason for the inclusion in the Treaty of the provisions of Article 90 [now 86] is precisely the influence

---

[3] Joined Cases 188 to 190/80, *France, Italy and the United Kingdom* v. *Commission* [1982] ECR 2545.

which the public authorities are able to exert over the commercial decisions of public undertakings. That influence may be exerted on the basis of financial participation or of rules governing the management of the undertaking. By choosing the same criteria to determine the financial relations on which it must be able to obtain information in order to perform its duty of surveillance under Article 86(3), the Commission has remained within the limits of the discretion conferred upon it by that provision".

9. The principles developed by the Court of Justice with respect to the Transparency Directive are now part of the established jurisprudence and of particular importance is the fact that the Court has confirmed that:

— making financial relations transparent and the provision, on request, of information under the Directive is necessary and respects the principle of proportionality,
— the Directive respects the principle of neutrality of treatment of public and private undertakings,
— for the purposes of monitoring compliance with Articles 87 and 88 the Commission has a legitimate interest to be informed of *all the types of flows of public funds* to public enterprises, and
— for the purposes of monitoring compliance with Articles 87 and 88 the Commission has a legitimate interest in the flows of public funds to public undertakings that come either *directly* from the public authorities or *indirectly* from other public undertakings.

III. Principles to be Used in Determining Whether Aid is Involved

10. Having established over which enterprises and over which funds the Commission has a legitimate interest for the purposes of Articles 86 and 87 it is necessary to examine the principles to be used in determining whether any aid is involved. Only if aid is involved is there any question of any prior notification. Where aid is involved it is necessary to then examine whether any of the derogations provided for in the Treaty are applicable.[4] This analysis of determining on the one hand whether aid is involved and on the other whether the aid is compatible under one of the derogations of the Treaty, must be kept as a two stage process if full transparency is to be assured.

11. When public undertakings, just like private ones, benefit from monies granted under transparent aid schemes approved by the Commission, then it is clear that aid is involved and under what conditions the Commission has authorized its approval. However, the situation with respect to the other forms of public funds listed in the Transparency Directive is not always so clear. In certain circumstances public enterprises can derive an advantage from the nature of their relationship with public authorities through the provision of public funds when this latter provides funds in circumstances that go beyond its simple role as proprietor. To ensure respect for the principle of neutrality the aid must be assessed as the difference between the terms on which the funds were made available by the State to the public enterprise, and the terms which a private investor would find acceptable in providing funds to a comparable private undertaking when the private investor is operating under normal market economy conditions (hereinafter "market economy investor principle"). As the Commission points out in its communication on "Industrial policy in an open and competitive environment" (COM(90) 556) "competition is becoming ever more global and more intense both on the world and on Community markets". This trend has many implications for European companies, for example with regards to R&D, investment strategies and their financing. Both public and private enterprises in similar sectors and in comparable economic and financial situations must be treated equally with respect to this financing. However if any public funds are provided

---

[4] See also points 32 and 33 below.

on terms more favourable (i.e. in economic terms more cheaply) than a private owner would provide them to a private undertaking in a comparable financial and competitive position, then the public undertaking is receiving an advantage not available to private undertakings from their proprietors. Unless the more favourable provision of public funds is treated as aid, and evaluated with respect to one of the derogations of the Treaty, then the principle of neutrality of treatment between public and private undertakings is infringed.

12. This principle of using an investor operating under normal market conditions as a benchmark to determine both whether aid is involved and if so to quantify it, has been adopted by the *Council* and the *Commission* in the steel and shipbuilding sectors, and has been endorsed by the *Parliament* in this context. In addition the Commission has adopted and applied this principle in numerous individual cases. The principle has also been accepted by the *Court* in every case submitted to it as a yardstick for the determination of whether aid was involved.

13. In 1981 the Council adopted the principle of the market economy investor principle on two occasions. Firstly it approved unanimously the Commission decision establishing Community rules for aids to the steel industry,[5] and secondly it approved, by a qualified majority, the Shipbuilding Code.[6] In both cases the Council stated that the concept of aid includes any aid elements contained in the financing measures taken by Member States in respect of the steel/shipbuilding undertakings which they *directly or indirectly control* and which do not count as the provision of equity capital *according to standard company practice in a market economy*. Thus not only did the Council approve or adopt the market economy principle, it went along the same lines as the Commission in the abovementioned Transparency Directive, which brought within its scope not only the direct provision of funds but also their indirect provision.

14. The Council has maintained this general principle, most recently in 1989 in the case of steel,[7] and in 1990 in the case of shipbuilding.[8] In fact in the 1989 steel aid code the Council agreed to prior notification of all provisions of capital or similar financing in order to allow the Commission to decide whether they constituted aid, i.e. could "be regarded as a genuine provision of risk capital *according to usual investment practice in a market economy*" (Article 1(2)). The Council also reaffirmed and approved unanimously this principle in Commission Decision 89/218/ECSC concerning new aid to Finsider/ILVA.[9]

15. The Parliament has been called upon to give its opinion on the market economy investor principle contained in the Shipbuilding Directives. For these Directives the Parliament agreed to the Commission drafts which included this principle.[10]

16. The Commission adopted the same market economy investor principle when it laid down its position in general on public holdings in company capital which still remains valid.[11] It stated "where it is apparent that a public authority which injects capital . . . in a company is not merely providing equity capital under normal market economy conditions, the case has to be assessed in the light of Article 87 of the EC Treaty" (paragraph 1). It considered in particular that State aid was involved "where the financial position of the company, and particularly the structure and volume of its debts, is such that a normal return (in dividends or capital gains) cannot be expected within a reasonable time from the capital invested".

17. The Commission has moreover applied this market economy investor principle in many individual cases to determine whether any aid was involved. The Commission

---

[5] Decision 81/2320/ECSC of 7 August 1981 (OJ 1981 L228/14). See, in particular, the second recital and Article 1.

[6] Council Directive 81/363/EEC of 28 April 1981 (OJ 1981 L137/39). See, in particular, the last recital and Article 1(e).

[7] Commission Decision 322/89/ECSC of 1 February 1989 (OJ 1989 L38/8).

[8] Council Directive 90/684/EEC of 21 December 1990, (OJ 1990 L380/27).

[9] OJ 1989 L86/76.

[10] See for example OJ 1987 C 28/23, and OJ 1987 C7/320.

[11] Communication to the Member States concerning public authorities holdings in company capital. (Bulletin EC 9–1984).

examined in each case the financial circumstances of the company which received the public funds to see if a market economy investor would have made the monies available on similar terms. In the *Leeuwarden* decision the Commission established that the capital injections constituted aid because "the overcapacity in the ... industry constituted handicaps indicating that the firm would *probably* have been unable to raise on the private capital market the funds essential to its survival. The situation on the market provides *no reasonable grounds* for hope that a firm urgently needing large-scale restructuring could generate sufficient cash flow to finance the replacement investment necessary ... ".[12] This policy has been applied consistently over a number of years. More recently in the *CdF/Orkem* decision,[13] the Commission established that the public authority "injected capital into an undertaking in conditions that are not those of a market economy". In fact, the company in question "had very little chance of obtaining sufficient capital from the private market to ensure its survival and long-term stability". In the *ENI-Lanerossi* decision,[14] the Commission stated that "finance was granted in circumstances that would not be acceptable to a private investor operating under normal market economy conditions, as in the present case the financial and economic position of these factories, particularly in view of the duration and volumes of their losses, was such that a normal return in dividends or capital gains could not be expected for the capital invested".[15] There have also been a number of cases where the Commission has clearly stated that capital injections by the State have not constituted aid because a reasonable return by way of dividends or capital growth could normally be expected.[16]

18. The Commission has also applied the market economy investor principle to many individual cases under the shipbuilding Directives and steel aid codes. In shipbuilding, for example in *Bremer Vulkan*,[17] the Commission considered that a bridging loan and the purchase of new shares constituted State aid because it did "not accept the argument put forward by the German Government that [it] ... only acted like a private investor who happened to be better at foreseeing future market developments than anyone else." In steel, for example, it took decisions in several individual cases where capital injections were considered as aid.[18]

19. It is noteworthy that in many of the above described cases the capital injected into the public undertaking came not directly from the State but indirectly from State holding companies or other public undertakings.

20. The Court has been called upon to examine a number of cases decided by the Commission in its application of the market economy investor principle set out in the 1984 guidelines. In each case submitted to it, the Court accepted the principle as an appropriate one to be used to determine whether or not aid was involved. It then examined whether the Commission decision sufficiently proved its application in the specific circumstances of the case in question. For example, in its judgment in Case 40/85[19] (*Boch*), the Court stated (paragraph 13):

---

[12] OJ 1982 L277/15.
[13] OJ 1990 C198/2.
[14] OJ 1989 L16/52.
[15] Decisions *Meura* (OJ 1984 L276/34), *Leeuwarden* (OJ 1982 L277/15), *Intermills I* (OJ 1982 L280/30), *Boch/Noviboch* (OJ 1985 L59/12), *Boussac* (OJ 1987 L352/42), *Alfa-Fiat* (OJ 1989 L394/9), *Pinault-Isoroy* (OJ 1988 L119/38), *Fabelta* (OJ 1984 L62/18), *Ideal Spun* (OJ 1984 L283/42), *Renault* (OJ 1988 L220/30), *Veneziana Vetro* (OJ 1989 L166/60), *Quimigal* (OJ 1990 C188/3) *and IOR/Finalp* (not yet published) where the same reasoning can be found.
[16] Decisions *CDF/Orkem*, in parts, (op. cit.), *Quimigal*, in parts, (op. cit.), *Intermills II* (Bulletin E.C. 4–1990, point 1.1.34) and *Ernaelsteen* (18th Competition Report, points 212 and 213).
[17] Not yet published.
[18] OJ 1983 L227/1. See also, in particular, cases relating to Arbed, Sidmar, ALZ, Hoogovens, Irish Steel, Sacilor/Usinor and British Steel where the same reasoning can be found. In all these steel cases the aid was held to be compatible. More recently, the Council unanimously approved this principle in the *Finsider/ILVA* case—see point 26 below.
[19] *Belgium* v. *Commission* [1986] ECR 2321.

"An appropriate way of establishing whether [the] measure is a State aid is to apply the criterion, which was mentioned in the Commission's decision and, moreover, was not contested by the Belgian Government, of determining to what extent the undertaking would be able to obtain the sums in question on the private capital markets. In the case of an undertaking whose capital is almost entirely held by the public authorities, the test is, in particular, whether in similar circumstances a private shareholder, having regard to the forseeability of obtaining a return and leaving aside all social, regional policy and sectoral considerations, would have subscribed the capital in question".

The Court has recently reaffirmed this principle in the *Boussac* judgment,[20] where it stated (paragraphs 39 and 40): "In order to determine if the measures constitute State aid, it is necessary to apply the criterion in the Commission's decision, which was not contested by the French Government, whether it would have been possible for the undertaking to obtain the funds on the private capital market", and "the financial situation of the company was such that it would not except an acceptable return on the investment within a reasonable time period and that Boussac would not have been able to find the necessary funds on the market" (unofficial translation).[21] The Court has recently further refined the market economy investor principle by making a distinction between a private investor whose time horizon is a short-term even speculative one, and that of a private holding group with a longer-term perspective (*Alfa/Fiat* and *Lanerossi*.[22] "It is necessary to make clear that the behaviour of a private investor with which the intervention of the public investor ... must be compared, whilst not necessarily that of an ordinary investor placing his capital with a more or less short-term view of its profitability, must at least be that of a private holding or group of enterprises which pursue a structural, global or sectoral policy and which are guided by a longer-term view of profitability". On the basis of the facts of the case "the Commission was able to correctly conclude that a private investor, even if taking decisions at the level of the whole group in a wider economic context, would not under normal market economy conditions, have been able to expect an acceptable rate of profitability (even in the long term) on the capital invested ... " (unofficial translation). "A private investor may well inject new capital to ensure the survival of a company experiencing temporary difficulties, but which after, if necessary, a restructuring will become profitable again. A mother company may also, during a limited time, carry the losses of a subsidiary in order to allow this latter to withdraw from the sector under the most favourable conditions. Such decisions can be motivated not only by the possibility to get a direct profit, but also by other concerns such as maintaining the image of the whole group or to redirect its activities. However, when the new injections of capital are divorced from all possibility of profitability, even in the long term, these injections must be considered as aid ... " (unofficial translation).

21. The fact that in many of the cases decided by the Court the injections came indirectly from State holding companies or from other public undertakings and not directly from the State, did not alter the aid character of the monies in question. The Court has always examined the economic reality of the situation to determine whether State resources were involved. In the *Steinicke and Weinlig* judgment,[23] the Court stated that " ... save for the reservation in Article [86(2)] of the Treaty, Article [87] covers all private and public undertakings and all their production" and that "in applying Article [87] regard must primarily be had to the effects of aid on the undertakings or producers favoured and not the status of the institutions entrusted with the distribution and administration of the aid". More recently in the *Crédit Agricole* judgment,[24] the Court confirmed this and added that " ... aid need not necessarily be financed from State resources to be classified as State aid ... there is no necessity to draw any distinction according to

---

[20] Case C–301/87 (not yet published).
[21] See also *Intermills* Case 323/82, *Leeuwarden* Joined Cases 296/318/82, *Meura* Case 234/84 where the same reasoning can be found.
[22] Cases C–305/89 and C–303/88 respectively (not yet published).
[23] Case 78/76.
[24] Case 290/83.

whether the aid is granted directly by the State or by public or private bodies established or appointed by it to administer aid".

IV. INCREASED TRANSPARENCY OF POLICY

22. To date most but by no means all of the cases which have come before the Council, the Commission and the Court where the market economy investor principle has been applied have concerned capital injections in loss-making or even near-bankrupt companies. One of the aims of this communication is to increase transparency by more systematically applying aid disciplines.

— to public undertakings in all situations, not just those making losses as is the case at present,
— to all the forms of public funds mentioned in the Transparency Directive (Article 3—see points 6 and 8.3 above), in particular, for loans, guarantees and the rate of return, not just for capital injections as is the case at present.

23. This increased transparency of policy is to be brought about by clearly applying the market economy investor principle to public undertakings in all situations and all public funds covered by the Transparency Directive. The market economy investor principle is used because:

— it is an appropriate yardstick both for measuring any financial advantage a public undertaking may enjoy over an equivalent private one and for ensuring neutrality of treatment between public and private undertakings,
— it has proved itself practical to the Commission in numerous cases,
— it has been confirmed by the Court (see particularly points 20 and 21 above), and
— it has been approved by the Council in the steel and shipbuilding sector.

Unless this clarification is implemented there is a danger not only of lack of transparency, but also of discrimination against private undertakings which do not have the same links with the public authorities nor the same access to public funds. The current communication is a logical development of existing policy rather than any radical new departure and is necessary to explain the application of the principle to a wider number of situations and a wider range of funds. In fact the Court, the Commission and the Council have already applied the principle of the market economy investor in a limited number of cases to the forms of public funds other than equity which are also the object of this communication— i.e. guarantees, loans, return on capital.[25]

24. *Guarantee.* In *IOR/Finalp* (op. cit.) the Commission considered that when a State holding company became the one and only owner of an ailing company (thereby exposing it to unlimited liability under Italian commercial law) this was equivalent to taking extra risk by giving in effect an open-ended *guarantee*. The Commission using its well established principle stated that a market economy investor would normally be reluctant to become the one and only shareholder of a company if as a consequence he must assume unlimited liability for it; he will make sure that this additional risk is outweighed by additional gains.

25. *Loan.* In *Boch* (op. cit.) the Court stated (paragraphs 12 and 13): "By virtue of Article [87(1)] . . . the provisions of the Treaty concerning State aid apply to aid granted by a Member State or through State resources in any form whatsoever. It follows . . . that

---

[25] It should be noted that this is not an exhaustive list of the different forms of financing which may entail aid. The Commission will act against the provision of any other advantages to public undertakings in a tangible or intangible form that may constitute aid.

no distinction can be drawn between aid granted in the form of *loans* and aid granted in the form of a subscription of capital of an undertaking ... An appropriate way of establishing whether such a measure is a State aid is to apply the criterion ... of determining to what extent the undertaking would be able to obtain the sums in question on the private capital markets."

26. *Return on capital.* When it opened the Article 88 procedure of the ECSC Treaty (letter to the Italian Government of 6 May 1988) in the *Finsider/ILVA* case, the Commission considered that the loans granted by State credit institutions were not granted to the undertaking in question under conditions acceptable to a private investor operating under normal market conditions, but were dependent on an *(implicit) guarantee* of the State and as such constituted State aid. In fact at a later date this implicit guarantee was made explicit when the debts were honoured. The opening of the procedure led to a decision with the unanimous approval of the Council[26] which imposed conditions on the enterprise in question to ensure that its *viability* would be re-established, and a *minimum return on capital* should be earned.

V. PRACTICALITY OF THE MARKET ECONOMY INVESTOR PRINCIPLE

27. The practical experience gained by the Commission from the application of State aid rules to public enterprises and the general support among the Community institutions for the basic themes of the market economy investor principle confirm the Commission's view that it is as such an appropriate yardstick to determine whether or not aid exists. However it is noted that the majority of cases to which the mechanism has been applied have been of a particular nature and the wider application of the mechanism may appear to cause certain difficulties. Some further explanations are therefore warranted. In addition, the fear has been expressed that the application of the market economy investor principle could lead to the Commission's judgment replacing the investor and his appreciation of investment projects. In the first place this criticism can be refuted by the fact that this principle has already shown itself to be both an appropriate and practical yardstick for determining which public funds constitute aid in numerous individual cases. Secondly it is not the aim of the Commission in the future, just as it has not been in the past, to replace the investor's judgment. Any requests for extra finance naturally calls for public undertakings and public authorities, just as it does for private undertakings and the private providers of finance, to analyse the risk and the likely outcome of the project.

In turn, the Commission realizes that this analysis of risk requires public undertakings, like private undertakings, to exercise entrepreneurial skills, which by the very nature of the problem implies a wide margin of judgment on the part of the investor. Within that wide margin the exercise of judgment by the investor cannot be regarded as involving State aid. It is in evaluation of the justification for the provision of funds that the Member State has to decide if a notification is necessary in conformity with its obligation under Article 88(3). In this context, it is useful to recall the arrangements of the 1984 communication on public authorities' holdings which stated that where there is a presumption that a financial flow from the State to a public holding constitutes aid, the Commission shall be informed in advance. On the basis of an examination of the information received it will decide within 15 working days whether the information should be regarded as notification for the purposes of Article 88(3) (point 4.4.2). Only where there are no objective grounds to reasonably expect that an investment will give an adequate rate of return that would be acceptable to a private investor in a comparable private undertaking operating under

---

[26] OJ 1989 L86/76. See also the Commission Communication to the Council of 25 October 1988—SEC(88) 1485 final and point 207 of the 14th Competition Report. In fact, the whole aim of the Steel Code for all Member States was to restore viability through a minimum return and self-financing according to market principles.

normal market conditions, is State aid involved even when this is financed wholly or partially by public funds. It is not the Commission's intention to analyse investment projects on an *ex-ante* basis (unless notification is received in advance in conformity with Article 88(3)).

28. There is no question of the Commission using the benefit of hindsight to state that the provision of public funds constituted State aid on the sole basis that the out-turn rate of return was not adequate. Only projects where the Commission considers that there were no objective or bona fide grounds to reasonably expect an adequate rate of return in a comparable private undertaking *at the moment the investment/financing* decision is made can be treated as State aid. It is only in such cases that funds are being provided more cheaply than would be available to a private undertaking, i.e. a subsidy is involved. It is obvious that, because of the inherent risks involved in any investment, not all projects will be successful and certain investments may produce a sub-normal rate of return or even be a complete failure. This is also the case for private investors whose investment can result in sub-normal rates of return or failures. Moreover such an approach makes no discrimination between projects which have short or long-term pay-back periods, as long as the risks are adequately and objectively assessed and discounted at the time the decision to invest is made, in the way that a private investor would.

29. This communication, by making clearer how the Commission applies the market economy investor principle and the criteria used to determine when aid is involved, will reduce uncertainty in this field. It is not the Commission's intention to apply the principles in this communication (in what is necessarily a complex field) in a dogmatic or doctrinaire fashion. It understands that a wide margin of judgment must come into entrepreneurial investment decisions. The principles have however to be applied when it is beyond reasonable doubt that there is no other plausible explanation for the provision of public funds other than considering them as State aid. This approach will also have to be applied to any cross-subsidization by a profitable part of a public group of undertakings of an unprofitable part. This happens in private undertakings when either the undertaking in question has a strategic plan with good hopes of long-term gain, or that the cross-subsidy has a net benefit to the group as a whole. In cases where there is cross-subsidization in public holding companies the Commission will take account of similar strategic goals. Such cross-subsidization will be considered as aid only where the Commission considers that there is no other reasonable explanation to explain the flow of funds other than that they constituted aid. For fiscal or other reasons certain enterprises, be they public or private, are often split into several legally distinct subsidiaries. However the Commission will not normally ask for information of the flow of funds between such legally distinct subsidiaries of companies for which one consolidated report is required.

30. The Commission is also aware of the differences in approach a market economy investor may have between his minority holding in a company on the one hand and full control of a large group on the other hand. The former relationship may often be characterized as more of a speculative or even short-term interest, whereas the latter usually implies a longer-term interest. Therefore where the public authority controls an individual public undertaking or group of undertakings it will normally be less motivated by purely short-term profit considerations than if it had merely a minority/non-controlling holding and its time horizon will accordingly be longer. The Commission will take account of the nature of the public authorities' holding in comparing their behaviour with the benchmark of the equivalent market economy investor. This remark is also valid for the evaluation of calls for extra funds to financially restructure a company as opposed to calls for funds required to finance specific projects.[27] In addition the Commission is also aware that a market economy investor's attitude is generally more favourably disposed towards calls for extra finance when the undertaking or group requiring the extra finance

---

[27] This may be particularly important for public undertakings that have been deliberately under-capitalized by the public authority owner for reasons extraneous to commercial justifications (e.g. public expenditure restrictions).

has a good record of providing adequate returns by way of dividends or capital accumulation on past investments. Where a company has underperformed in this respect in comparison with equivalent companies, this request for finance will normally be examined more sceptically by the private investor/owner called upon to provide the extra finance. Where this call for finance is necessary to protect the value of the whole investment the public authority like a private investor can be expected to take account of this wider context when examining whether the commitment of new funds is commercially justified. Finally where a decision is made to abandon a line of activity because of its lack of medium/long-term commercial viability, a public group, like a private group, can be expected to decide the timing and scale of its run down in the light of the impact on the overall credibility and structure of the group.

31. In evaluating any calls for extra finance a shareholder would typically have at his disposal the information necessary to judge whether he is justified in responding to these calls for additional finance. The extent and detail of the information provided by the undertaking requiring finance may vary according to the nature and volume of the funding required, to the relationship between the undertaking and the shareholder and even to the past performance of the undertaking in providing an adequate return.[28] A market economy investor would not usually provide any additional finance without the appropriate level of information. Similar considerations would normally apply to public undertakings seeking finance. This financial information in the form of the relevant documentation should be made available at the specific request of the Commission if it is considered that it would help in evaluating the investment proposals from the point of view of deciding whether or not their financing constitutes aid.[29] The Commission will not disclose information supplied to it as it is covered by the obligation of professional secrecy. Therefore investment projects will not be scrutinized by the Commission in advance except where aid is involved and prior notification in conformity with Article 88(3) is required. However where it has reasonable grounds to consider that aid may be granted in the provision of finance to public undertakings, the Commission, pursuant to its responsibilities under Articles 87 and 88, may ask for the information from Member States necessary to determine whether aid is involved in the specific case in question.

VI. COMPATIBILITY OF AID

32. Each Member State is free to choose the size and nature of its public sector and to vary it over time. The Commission recognizes that when the State decides to exercise its right to public ownership, commercial objectives are not always the essential motivation. Public enterprises are sometimes expected to fulfil non-commercial functions alongside or in addition to their basic commercial activities. For example, in some Member States public companies may be used as a locomotive for the economy, as part of efforts to counter recession, to restructure troubled industries or to act as catalysts for regional development. Public companies may be expected to locate in less developed regions where costs are higher or to maintain employment at levels beyond purely commercial levels. The Treaty enables the Commission to take account of such considerations where they are justified in the Community interest. In addition the provision of some services may entail a public service element, which may even be enforced by political or legal

---

[28] Minority shareholders who have no "inside" information on the running of the company may require a more formal justification for providing funds than a controlling owner who may in fact be involved at board level in formulating strategies and is already party to detailed information on the undertaking's financial situation.

[29] The provision of this information on request falls within the scope of the Commission's powers of investigation of aid under Articles 87 and 88 in combination with Article 10 of the EC Treaty and under Article 1(c) of the Transparency Directive which states that the use to which public funds are put should be made transparent.

constraints. These non-commercial objectives/functions (i.e. social goods) have a cost which ultimately has to be financed by the State (i.e. taxpayers) either in the form of new finance (e.g. capital injections) or a reduced rate of return on capital invested. This aiding of the provision of public services can in certain circumstances distort competition. Unless one of the derogations of the Treaty is applicable, public undertakings are not exempted from the rules of competition by the imposition of these non-commercial objectives.

33. If the Commission is to carry out its duties under the Treaty, it must have the information available to determine whether the financial flows to public undertakings constitute aid, to quantify such aid and then to determine if one of the derogations provided for in the Treaty is applicable. This communication limits itself to the objective of increasing transparency for the financial flows in question which is an essential first step. To decide, as a second step, whether any aid that is identified is compatible, is a question which is not dealt with because such a decision will be in accordance with the well known principles used by the Commission in the area to which no change is envisaged. (It should be stressed that the Commission is concerned with aid only when it has an impact on intra-Community trade and competition. Thus, if aid is granted for a non-commercial purpose to a public undertaking which has no impact on intra-Community trade and competition, Article 87(1) is not applicable). This obligation of submitting to Community control all aid having a Community dimension is the necessary counterpart to the right of Member States being able to export freely to other Member States and is the basis of a common market.

VII. DIFFERENT FORMS OF STATE INTERVENTION

34. In deciding whether any public funds to public undertakings constitute aid, the Commission must take into account the factors discussed below for each type of intervention covered by this communication—capital injections, guarantees, loans, return on investment.[30] These factors are given as a guide to Member States of the likely Commission attitude in individual cases. In applying this policy the Commission will bear in mind the practicability of the market economy investor principle described above. This communication takes over the definition of public funds and public undertakings used in the Transparency Directive. This is given as guidance for Member States as to the general attitude of the Commission. However, the Commission will obviously have to prove in individual cases of application of this policy that public undertakings within the meaning of Article 86 and State resources within the meaning of Article 87(1) are involved, just as it has in individual cases in the past. As far as any provision of information under the Transparency Directive is concerned, these definitions have been upheld by the Court for the purposes of the Directive and there is no further obligation on the Commission to justify them.

Capital injections

35. A capital injection is considered to be an aid when it is made in circumstances which would not be acceptable to an investor operating under normal market conditions. This is normally taken to mean a situation where the structure and future prospects for the company are such that a normal return (by way of dividend payments or capital appreciation) by reference to a comparable private enterprise cannot be expected within a reasonable time. Thus, the 1984 communication on capital injections remains valid.

A market economy investor would normally provide equity finance if the present value[31] of expected future cash flows from the intended project (accruing to the investor

---

[30] This list is not exhaustive—see footnote 25 above.
[31] Future cash flows discounted at the company's cost of capital (in-house discount rate).

by way of dividend payments and/or capital gains and adjusted for risk) exceed the new outlay. The context within which this will have to be interpreted was explained above in paragraphs 27 to 31.

36. In certain Member States investors are obliged by law to contribute additional equity to firms whose capital base has been eroded by continuous losses to below a predetermined level. Member States have claimed that these capital injections cannot be considered as aid as they are merely fulfilling a legal obligation. However, this "obligation" is more apparent than real. Commercial investors faced with such a situation must also consider all other options including the possibility of liquidating or otherwise running down their investment. If this liquidation or running down proves to be the more financially sound option taking into account the impact on the group and is not followed, then any subsequent capital injection or any other State intervention has to be considered as constituting aid.

37. When comparing the actions of the State and those of a market economy investor in particular when a company is not making a loss, the Commission will evaluate the financial position of the company at the time it is/was proposed to inject additional capital. On the basis of an evaluation of the following items the Commission will examine whether there is an element of aid contained in the amount of capital invested. This aid element consists in the *cost* of the investment less the *value* of the investment, appropriately discounted. It is stressed that the items listed below are indispensable to any analysis but not necessarily sufficient since account must also been taken of the principles set out in paragraphs 27 to 31 above and of the question whether the funds required are for investment projects or a financial restructuring.

37.1. *Profit and loss situation.* An analysis of the results of the company spread over several years. Relevant profitability ratios would be extracted and the underlying trends subject to evaluation.

37.2. *Financial indicators.* The debt/equity ratio (gearing of the company) would be compared with generally accepted norms, industry-sector averages and those of close competitors, etc. The calculation of various liquidity and solvency ratios would be undertaken to ascertain the financial standing of the company (this is particularly relevant in relation to the assessment of the loan-finance potential of a company operating under normal market conditions). The Commission is aware of the difficulties involved in making such comparisons between Member States due in particular to different accounting practices or standards. It will bear this in mind when choosing the appropriate reference points to be used as a comparison with the public undertakings receiving funds.

37.3. *Financial projections.* In cases where funding is sought to finance an investment programme then obviously this programme and the assumptions upon which it is based have to be studied in detail to see if the investment is justified.

37.4. *Market situation.* Market trends (past performance and most importantly future prospects) and the company's market share over a reasonable time period should be examined and future projections subjected to scrutiny.

Guarantees

38. The position currently adopted by the Commission in relation to loan guarantees has recently been communicated to Member States.[32] It regards all guarantees given by the State directly or by way of delegation through financial institutions as falling within the scope of Article 87(1) of the EC Treaty. It is only if guarantees are assessed at the granting stage that all the distortions or potential distortions of competition can be detected. The fact that a firm receives a guarantee even if it is never called in may enable it to continue trading, perhaps forcing competitors who do not enjoy such facilities to go out of business.

---

[32] Communication to all Member States dated 5 April 1989, as amended by letter of 12 October 1989.

The firm in question has therefore received support which has disadvantaged its competitors i.e. it has been aided and this has had an effect on competition. An assessment of the aid element of guarantees will involve an analysis of the borrower's financial situation (see point 37 above). The aid element of these guarantees would be the difference between the rate which the borrower would pay in a free market and that actually obtained with the benefit of the guarantee, net of any premium paid for the guarantee. Creditors can only safely claim against a government guarantee where this is made and given explicitly to either a public or a private undertaking. If this guarantee is deemed incompatible with the common market following evaluation with respect to the derogations under the Treaty, reimbursement of the value of any aid will be made by the undertaking to the Government even if this means a declaration of bankruptcy but creditors' claims will be honoured. These provisions apply equally to public and private undertakings and no additional special arrangements are necessary for public enterprises other than the remarks made below.

38.1. Public enterprises whose legal status does not allow bankruptcy are in effect in receipt of permanent aid on all borrowings equivalent to a guarantee when such status allows the enterprises in question to obtain credit on terms more favourable than would otherwise be available.

38.2. Where a public authority takes a hold in a public undertaking of a nature such that it is exposed to unlimited liability instead of the normal limited liability, the Commission will treat this as a guarantee on all the funds which are subject to unlimited liability.[33] It will then apply the above described principles to this guarantee.

Loans

39. When a lender operating under normal market economy conditions provides loan facilities for a client he is aware of the inherent risk involved in any such venture. The risk is of course that the client will be unable to repay the loan. The potential loss extends to the full amount advanced (the capital) and any interest due but unpaid at the time of default. The risk attached to any loan arrangement is usually reflected in two distinct parameters:

(a) the interest rate charged;
(b) the security sought to cover the loan.

40. Where the perceived risk attached to the loan is high then *ceteris paribus* both (a) and (b) above can be expected to reflect this fact. It is when this does not take place in practice that the Commission will consider that the firm in question has had an advantage conferred on it, i.e. has been aided. Similar considerations apply where the assets pledged by a fixed or floating charge on the company would be insufficient to repay the loan in full. The Commission will in future examine carefully the security used to cover loan finance. This evaluation process would be similar to that proposed for capital injections (see point 37 above).

41. The aid element amounts to the difference between the rate which the firm should pay (which itself is dependent on its financial position and the security which it can offer on foot of the loan) and that actually paid. (This one-stage analysis of the loan is based on the presumption that in the event of default the lender will exercise his legal right to recover any monies due to him). In the extreme case, i.e. where an unsecured loan is given to a company which under normal circumstances would be unable to obtain finance (for example because its prospects of repaying the loan are poor) then the loan effectively equates a grant payment and the Commission would evaluate it as such.

42. The situation would be viewed from the point of view of the lender at the moment the loan is approved. If he chooses to lend (or is directly or indirectly forced to do so as may be the case with State-controlled banks) on conditions which could not be considered

---

[33] See point 24 above.

as normal in banking terms, then there is an element of aid involved which has to be quantified. These provisions would of course also apply to private undertakings obtaining loans from public financial institutions.

Return on investments

43. The State, in common with any other market economy investor, should expect a normal return obtained by comparable private undertakings on its capital investments by way of dividends or capital appreciation.[34] The rate of return will be measured by the profit (after depreciation but before taxation and disposals) expressed as a percentage of assets employed. It is therefore a measure that is neutral with respect to the form of finance used in each undertaking (i.e. debt or equity) which for public undertakings may be decided for reasons extraneous to purely commercial considerations. If this normal return is neither forthcoming beyond the short term nor is likely to be forthcoming in the long term (with the uncertainty of this longer-term future gain not appropriately accounted for) and no remedial action has been taken by the public undertaking to rectify the situation, then it can be assumed that the entity is being indirectly aided as the State is foregoing the benefit which a market economy investor would expect from a similar investment. A normal rate of return will be defined with reference where possible being made to comparable private companies. The Commission is aware of the difficulties involved in making such comparisons between Member States—see particularly point 37. In addition the difference in capital markets, currency fluctuations and interest rates between Member States further complicate international comparisons of such ratios. Where accounting practices even within a single Member State make accurate asset valuation hazardous, thereby undermining rate of return calculations, the Commission will examine the possibility of using either adjusted valuations or other simpler criteria such as operating cash flow (after depreciation but before disposals) as a proxy of economic performance.

When faced with an inadequate rate of return a private undertaking would either take action to remedy the situation or be obliged to do so by its shareholders. This would normally involve the preparation of a detailed plan to increase overall profitability. If a public undertaking has an inadequate rate of return, the Commission could consider that this situation contains elements of aid, which should be analysed with respect to Article 87. In these circumstances, the public undertaking is effectively getting its capital cheaper than the market rate, i.e. equivalent to a subsidy.

44. Similarly, if the State foregoes dividend income from a public undertaking and the resultant retained profits do not earn a normal rate of return as defined above then the company in question is effectively being subsidized by the State. It may well be that the State sees it as preferable for reasons not connected with commercial considerations to forego dividends (or accept reduced dividend payments) rather than make regular capital injections into the company. The end result is the same and this regular "funding" has to be treated in the same way as new capital injections and evaluated in accordance with the principles set out above.

45. Duration

After an initial period of five years, the Commission will review the application of the policy described in this communication. On the basis of this review, and after consulting Member States, the Commission may propose any modifications which it considers appropriate.

---

[34] The foregoing of a normal return on public funds falls within the scope of the Transparency Directive.

APPENDIX 76

REGULATION 994/98[1]

On the Application of Articles 87 and 88 of the Treaty Establishing the
European Community to Certain Categories of Horizontal State Aid

THE COUNCIL OF THE EUROPEAN UNION,

Having regard to the Treaty establishing the European Community, and in particular
Article 89 thereof,
Having regard to the proposal from the Commission,[2]
After consulting the European Parliament,[3]
Having regard to the opinion of the Economic and Social Committee,[4]
(1) Whereas, pursuant to Article 89 of the Treaty, the Council may make any appropriate regulations for the application of Articles 87 and 88 and may, in particular,
determine the conditions in which Article 88(3) shall apply and the categories of aid
exempted from this procedure;
(2) Whereas, under the Treaty, the assessment of compatibility of aid with the common
market essentially rests with the Commission;
(3) Whereas the proper functioning of the internal market requires strict and efficient
application of the rules of competition with regard to State aids;
(4) Whereas the Commission has applied Articles 87 and 88 of the Treaty in numerous
decisions and has also stated its policy in a number of communications; whereas, in the
light of the Commission's considerable experience in applying Articles 87 and 88 of the
Treaty and the general texts issued by the Commission on the basis of those provisions,
it is appropriate, with a view to ensuring efficient supervision and simplifying administration, without weakening Commission monitoring, that the Commission should be enabled
to declare by means of regulations, in areas where the Commission has sufficient
experience to define general compatibility criteria, that certain categories of aid are
compatible with the common market pursuant to one or more of the provisions of Article
87(2) and (3) of the Treaty and are exempted from the procedure provided for in Article
88(3) thereof;
(5) Whereas group exemption regulations will increase transparency and legal certainty; whereas they can be directly applied by national courts, without prejudice to
Articles 10 and 234 of the Treaty;
(6) Whereas it is appropriate that the Commission, when it adopts regulations exempting categories of aid from the obligation to notify provided for in Article 88(3) of the
Treaty, specifies the purpose of the aid, the categories of beneficiaries and thresholds
limiting the exempted aid, the conditions governing the cumulation of aid and the
conditions of monitoring, in order to ensure the compatibility with the common market of
aid covered by this Regulation;

---

[1] OJ 1998 L142/1, of 7.5.1998.
[2] OJ 1997 C262/6.
[3] OJ 1998 C138.
[4] OJ 1998 C129/70.

(7) Whereas it is appropriate to enable the Commission, when it adopts regulations exempting certain categories of aid from the obligation to notify in Article 88(3) of the Treaty, to attach further detailed conditions in order to ensure the compatibility with the common market of aid covered by this Regulation;

(8) Whereas it may be useful to set thresholds of other appropriate conditions requiring the notification of awards of aid in order to allow the Commission to examine individually the effect of certain aid on competition and trade between Member States and its compatibility with the common market;

(9) Whereas the Commission, having regard to the development and the functioning of the common market, should be enabled to establish by means of a regulation that certain aid does not fulfil all the criteria of Article 87(1) of the Treaty and is therefore exempted from the notification procedure laid down in Article 88(3), provided that aid granted to the same undertaking over a given period of time does not exceed a certain fixed amount;

(10) Whereas in accordance with Article 88(1) of the Treaty the Commission is under an obligation, in cooperation with Member States, to keep under constant review all systems of existing aid; whereas for this purpose and in order to ensure the largest possible degree of transparency and adequate control it is desirable that the Commission ensures the establishment of a reliable system of recording and storing information about the application of the regulations it adopts, to which all Member States have access, and that it receives all necessary information from the Member States on the implementation of aid exempted from notification to fulfil this obligation, which may be examined and evaluated with the Member States within the Advisory Committee; whereas for this purpose it is also desirable that the Commission may require such information to be supplied as is necessary to ensure the efficiency of such review;

(11) Whereas the control of the granting of aid involves factual, legal and economic issues of a very complex nature and great variety in a constantly evolving environment; whereas the Commission should therefore regularly review the categories of aid which should be exempted from notification; whereas the Commission should be able to repeal or amend regulations it has adopted pursuant to this Regulation where circumstances have changed with respect to any important element which constituted grounds for their adoption or where the progressive development or the functioning of the common market so requires;

(12) Whereas the Commission, in close and constant liaison with the Member States, should be able to define precisely the scope of these regulations and the conditions attached to them; whereas, in order to provide for cooperation between the Commission and the competent authorities of the Member States, it is appropriate to set up an advisory committee on State aid to be consulted before the Commission adopts regulations pursuant to this Regulation,

HAS ADOPTED THIS REGULATION:

Article 1

Group exemptions

1. The Commission may, by means of regulations adopted in accordance with the procedures laid down in Article 8 of this Regulation and in accordance with Article 87 of the Treaty, declare that the following categories of aid should be compatible with the common market and shall not be subject to the notification requirements of Article 88(3) of the Treaty:

(a) aid in favour of:
    (i)   small and medium-sized enterprises;
    (ii) research and development;
    (iii) environmental protection:

(iv) employment and training;
(b) aid that complies with the map approved by the Commission for each Member State for the grant of regional aid.

2. The Regulations referred to in paragraph 1 shall specify for each category of aid:

(a) the purpose of the aid;
(b) the categories of beneficiaries;
(c) thresholds expressed either in terms of aid intensities in relation to a set of eligible costs or in terms of maximum aid amounts;
(d) the conditions governing the cumulation of aid;
(e) the conditions of monitoring as specified in Article 3.

3. In addition, the regulations referred to in paragraph 1 may, in particular:

(a) set thresholds or other conditions for the notification of awards of individual aid;
(b) exclude certain sectors from their scope;
(c) attach further conditions for the compatibility of aid exempted under such regulations.

Article 2

De minimis

1. The Commission may, by means of a Regulation adopted in accordance with the procedure laid down in Article 8 of this Regulation, decide that, having regard to the development and functioning of the common market, certain aids do not meet all the criteria of Article 87(1) and that they are therefore exempted from the notification procedure provided for in Article 88(3), provided that aid granted to the same undertaking over a given period of time does not exceed a certain fixed amount.
2. At the Commission's request, Member States shall, at any time, communicate to it any additional information relating to aid exempted under paragraph 1.

Article 3

Transparency and monitoring

1. When adopting regulations pursuant to Article 1, the Commission shall impose detailed rules upon Member States to ensure transparency and monitoring of the aid exempted from notification in accordance with those regulations. Such rules shall consist, in particular, of the requirements laid down in paragraphs 2, 3 and 4.
2. On implementation of aid systems or individual aids granted outside any system, which have been exempted pursuant to such regulations, Member States shall forward to the Commission, with a view to publication in the *Official Journal of the European Communities*, summaries of the information regarding such systems of aid or such individual aids as are not covered by exempted aid systems.
3. Member States shall record and compile all the information regarding the application of the group exemptions. If the Commission has information which leads it to doubt that an exemption regulation is being applied properly, the Member States shall forward to it any information it considers necessary to assess whether an aid complies with that regulation.
4. At least once a year, Member States shall supply the Commission with a report on the application of group exemptions, in accordance with the Commission's specific requirements, preferably in computerised form. The Commission shall make access to

791

those reports available to all the Member States. The Advisory Committee referred to in Article 7 shall examine and evaluate those reports once a year.

Article 4

Period of validity and amendment of regulations

1. Regulations adopted pursuant to Articles 1 and 2 shall apply for a specific period. Aid exempted by a regulation adopted pursuant to Articles 1 and 2 shall be exempted for the period of validity of that regulation and for the adjustment period provided for in paragraphs 2 and 3.

2. Regulations adopted pursuant to Articles 1 and 2 may be repeated or amended where circumstances have changed with respect to any important element that constituted grounds for their adoption or where the progressive development or the functioning of the common market so requires. In that case the new regulation shall set a period of adjustment of six months for the adjustment of aid covered by the previous regulation.

3. Regulations adopted pursuant to Articles 1 and 2 shall provide for a period as referred to in paragraph 2, should their application not be extended when they expire.

Article 5

Evaluation report

Every five years the Commission shall submit a report to the European Parliament and to the Council on the application of this Regulation. It shall submit a draft report for consideration by the Advisory Committee referred to in Article 7.

Article 6

Hearing of interested parties

Where the Commission intends to adopt a regulation, it shall publish a draft thereof to enable all interested persons and organisations to submit their comments to it within a reasonable time limit to be fixed by the Commission and which may not under any circumstances be less than one month.

Article 7

Advisory Committee

An advisory committee, hereinafter referred to as the Advisory Committee on State Aid, shall be set up. It shall be composed of representatives of the Member States and chaired by the representative of the Commission.

Article 8

Consultation of the Advisory Committee

1. The Commission shall consult the Advisory Committee on State Aid:

(a) before publishing any draft regulation;
(b) before adopting any regulation.

2. Consultation of the Committee shall take place at a meeting called by the Commission. The drafts and documents to be examined shall be annexed to the notification. The meeting shall take place no earlier than two months after notification has been sent.

This period may be reduced in the case of the consultations referred to in paragraph 1(b), when urgent or for simple extension of a regulation.

3. The representative of the Commission shall submit to the Committee a draft of the measures to be taken. The Committee shall deliver its opinion on the draft, within a time limit which the Chairman may lay down according to the urgency of the matter, if necessary by taking a vote.

APPENDIX 77

REGULATION 659/1999[1]

Laying Down Detailed Rules for the Application of Article 88 of the EC Treaty

THE COUNCIL OF THE EUROPEAN UNION,

Having regard to the Treaty establishing the European Community, and in particular Article 89 thereof,

Having regard to the proposal from the Commission,[2]

Having regard to the opinion of the European Parliament,[3]

Having regard to the opinion of the Economic and Social Committee,[4]

(1) Whereas, without prejudice to special procedural rules laid down in regulations for certain sectors, this Regulation should apply to aid in all sectors; whereas, for the purpose of applying Articles 73 and 87 of the Treaty, the Commission has specific competence under Article 88 thereof to decide on the compatibility of State aid with the common market when reviewing existing aid, when taking decisions on new or altered aid and when taking action regarding non-compliance with its decisions or with the requirement as to notification;

(2) Whereas the Commission, in accordance with the case-law of the Court of Justice of the European Communities, has developed and established a consistent practice for the application of Article 88 of the Treaty and has laid down certain procedural rules and principles in a number of communications; whereas it is appropriate, with a view to ensuring effective and efficient procedures pursuant to Article 88 of the Treaty, to codify and reinforce this practice by means of a regulation;

(3) Whereas a procedural regulation on the application of Article 88 of the Treaty will increase transparency and legal certainty;

(4) Whereas, in order to ensure legal certainty, it is appropriate to define the circumstances under which aid is to be considered as existing aid; whereas the completion and enhancement of the internal market is a gradual process, reflected in the permanent development of State aid policy; whereas, following these developments, certain measures, which at the moment they were put into effect did not constitute State aid, may since have become aid;

(5) Whereas, in accordance with Article 88(3) of the Treaty, any plans to grant new aid are to be notified to the Commission and should not be put into effect before the Commission has authorised it;

(6) Whereas, in accordance with Article 10 of the Treaty, Member States are under an obligation to cooperate with the Commission and to provide it with all information required to allow the Commission to carry out its duties under this Regulation;

(7) Whereas the period within which the Commission is to conclude the preliminary examination of notified aid should be set at two months from the receipt of a complete

---

[1] OJ 1999 L83/1, of 22.3.1999.

[2] OJ 1998 C116/13.

[3] Opinion delivered on 14 January 1999 (not yet published in the *Official Journal*).

[4] OJ 1998 C284/10.

notification or from the receipt of a duly reasoned statement of the Member State concerned that it considers the notification to be complete because the additional information requested by the Commission is not available or has already been provided; whereas, for reasons of legal certainty, that examination should be brought to an end by a decision;

(8) Whereas in all cases where, as a result of the preliminary examination, the Commission cannot find that the aid is compatible with the common market, the formal investigation procedure should be opened in order to enable the Commission to gather all the information it needs to assess the compatibility of the aid and to allow the interested parties to submit their comments; whereas the rights of the interested parties can best be safeguarded within the framework of the formal investigation procedure provided for under Article 88(2) of the Treaty;

(9) Whereas, after having considered the comments submitted by the interested parties, the Commission should conclude its examination by means of a final decision as soon as the doubts have been removed; whereas it is appropriate, should this examination not be concluded after a period of 18 months from the opening of the procedure, that the Member State concerned has the opportunity to request a decision, which the Commission should take within two months;

(10) Whereas, in order to ensure that the State aid rules are applied correctly and effectively, the Commission should have the opportunity of revoking a decision which was based on incorrect information;

(11) Whereas, in order to ensure compliance with Article 88 of the Treaty, and in particular with the notification obligation and the standstill clause in Article 88(3), the Commission should examine all cases of unlawful aid; whereas, in the interests of transparency and legal certainty, the procedures to be followed in such cases should be laid down; whereas when a Member State has not respected the notification obligation or the standstill clause, the Commission should not be bound by time limits;

(12) Whereas in cases of unlawful aid, the Commission should have the right to obtain all necessary information enabling it to take a decision and to restore immediately, where appropriate, undistorted competition; whereas it is therefore appropriate to enable the Commission to adopt interim measures addressed to the Member State concerned; whereas the interim measures may take the form of information injunctions, suspension injunctions and recovery injunctions; whereas the Commission should be enabled in the event of non-compliance with an information injunction, to decide on the basis of the information available and, in the event of non-compliance with suspension and recovery injunctions, to refer the matter to the Court of Justice direct, in accordance with the second subparagraph of Article 88(2) of the Treaty;

(13) Whereas in cases of unlawful aid which is not compatible with the common market, effective competition should be restored; whereas for this purpose it is necessary that the aid, including interest, be recovered without delay; whereas it is appropriate that recovery be effected in accordance with the procedures of national law; whereas the application of those procedures should not, by preventing the immediate and effective execution of the Commission decision, impede the restoration of effective competition; whereas to achieve this result, Member States should take all necessary measures ensuring the effectiveness of the Commission decision;

(14) Whereas for reasons of legal certainty it is appropriate to establish a period of limitation of 10 years with regard to unlawful aid, after the expiry of which no recovery can be ordered;

(15) Whereas misuse of aid may have effects on the functioning of the internal market which are similar to those of unlawful aid and should thus be treated according to similar procedures; whereas unlike unlawful aid, aid which has possibly been misused is aid which has been previously approved by the Commission; whereas therefore the Commission should not be allowed to use a recovery injunction with regard to misuse of aid;

(16) Whereas it is appropriate to define all the possibilities in which third parties have to defend their interests in State aid procedures;

795

(17) Whereas in accordance with Article 88(1) of the Treaty, the Commission is under an obligation, in cooperation with Member States, to keep under constant review all systems of existing aid; whereas in the interests of transparency and legal certainty, it is appropriate to specify the scope of cooperation under that Article;

(18) Whereas, in order to ensure compatibility of existing aid schemes with the common market and in accordance with Article 88(1) of the Treaty, the Commission should propose appropriate measures where an existing aid scheme is not, or is no longer, compatible with the common market and should initiate the procedure provided for in Article 88(2) of the Treaty if the Member State concerned declines to implement the proposed measures;

(19) Whereas, in order to allow the Commission to monitor effectively compliance with Commission decisions and to facilitate cooperation between the Commission and Member States for the purpose of the constant review of all existing aid schemes in the Member States in accordance with Article 88(1) of the Treaty, it is necessary to introduce a general reporting obligation with regard to all existing aid schemes;

(20) Whereas, where the Commission has serious doubts as to whether its decisions are being complied with, it should have at its disposal additional instruments allowing it to obtain the information necessary to verify that its decisions are being effectively complied with; whereas for this purpose on-site monitoring visits are an appropriate and useful instrument, in particular for cases where aid might have been misused; whereas therefore the Commission must be empowered to undertake on-site monitoring visits and must obtain the cooperation of the competent authorities of the Member States where an undertaking opposes such a visit;

(21) Whereas, in the interests of transparency and legal certainty, it is appropriate to give public information on Commission decisions while, at the same time, maintaining the principle that decisions in State aid cases are addressed to the Member State concerned; whereas it is therefore appropriate to publish all decisions which might affect the interests of interested parties either in full or in a summary form or to make copies of such decisions available to interested parties, where they have not been published or where they have not been published in full; whereas the Commission, when giving public information on its decisions, should respect the rules on professional secrecy, in accordance with Article 287 of the Treaty;

(22) Whereas the Commission, in close liaison with the Member States, should be able to adopt implementing provisions laying down detailed rules concerning the procedures under this Regulation; whereas, in order to provide for cooperation between the Commission and the competent authorities of the Member States, it is appropriate to create an Advisory Committee on State aid to be consulted before the Commission adopts provisions pursuant to this Regulation,

HAS ADOPTED THIS REGULATION:

CHAPTER I

GENERAL

Article 1

Definitions

For the purpose of this Regulation:

(a) "aid" shall mean any measure fulfilling all the criteria laid down in Article 87(1) of the Treaty;

(b) "existing aid" shall mean:
  (i) without prejudice to Articles 201 and 229 of the Act of Accession of Austria, Finland and Sweden, all aid which existed prior to the entry into force of the Treaty in the respective Member States, that is to say, aid schemes and individual aid which were put into effect before, and are still applicable after, the entry into force of the Treaty;
  (ii) authorised aid, that is to say, aid schemes and individual aid which have been authorised by the Commission or by the Council;
  (iii) aid which is deemed to have been authorised pursuant to Article 4(6) of this Regulation or prior to this Regulation but in accordance with this procedure;
  (iv) aid which is deemed to be existing aid pursuant to Article 15;
  (v) aid which is deemed to be an existing aid because it can be established that at the time it was put into effect it did not constitute an aid, and subsequently became an aid due to the evolution of the common market and without having been altered by the Member State. Where certain measures become aid following the liberalisation of an activity by Community law, such measures shall not be considered as existing aid after the date fixed for liberalisation;

(c) "new aid" shall mean all aid, that is to say, aid schemes and individual aid, which is not existing aid, including alterations to existing aid;

(d) "aid scheme" shall mean any act on the basis of which, without further implementing measures being required, individual aid awards may be made to undertakings defined within the act in a general and abstract manner and any act on the basis of which aid which is not linked to a specific project may be awarded to one or several undertakings for an indefinite period of time and/or for an indefinite amount;

(e) "individual aid" shall mean aid that is not awarded on the basis of an aid scheme and notifiable awards of aid on the basis of an aid scheme;

(f) "unlawful aid" shall mean new aid put into effect in contravention of Article 88(3) of the Treaty;

(g) "misuse of aid" shall mean aid used by the beneficiary in contravention of a decision taken pursuant to Article 4(3) or Article 7(3) or (4) of this Regulation;

(h) "interested party" shall mean any Member State and any person, undertaking or association of undertakings whose interests might be affected by the granting of aid, in particular the beneficiary of the aid, competing undertakings and trade associations.

CHAPTER II

PROCEDURE REGARDING NOTIFIED AID

Article 2

Notification of new aid

1. Save as otherwise provided in regulations made pursuant to Article 89 of the Treaty or to other relevant provisions thereof, any plans to grant new aid shall be notified to the Commission in sufficient time by the Member State concerned. The Commission shall inform the Member State concerned without delay of the receipt of a notification.

2. In a notification, the Member State concerned shall provide all necessary information in order to enable the Commission to take a decision pursuant to Articles 4 and 7 (hereinafter referred to as "complete notification").

Article 3

Standstill clause

Aid notifiable pursuant to Article 2(1) shall not be put into effect before the Commission has taken, or is deemed to have taken, a decision authorising such aid.

Article 4

Preliminary examination of the notification and decisions of the Commission

1. The Commission shall examine the notification as soon as it is received. Without prejudice to Article 8, the Commission shall take a decision pursuant to paragraphs 2, 3 or 4.

2. Where the Commission, after a preliminary examination, finds that the notified measure does not constitute aid, it shall record that finding by way of a decision.

3. Where the Commission, after a preliminary examination, finds that no doubts are raised as to the compatibility with the common market of a notified measure, in so far as it falls within the scope of Article 87(1) of the Treaty, it shall decide that the measure is compatible with the common market (hereinafter referred to as a "decision not to raise objections"). The decision shall specify which exception under the Treaty has been applied.

4. Where the Commission, after a preliminary examination, finds that doubts are raised as to the compatibility with the common market of a notified measure, it shall decide to initiate proceedings pursuant to Article 88(2) of the Treaty (hereinafter referred to as a "decision to initiate the formal investigation procedure").

5. The decisions referred to in paragraphs 2, 3 and 4 shall be taken within two months. That period shall begin on the day following the receipt of a complete notification. The notification will be considered as complete if, within two months from its receipt, or from the receipt of any additional information requested, the Commission does not request any further information. The period can be extended with the consent of both the Commission and the Member State concerned. Where appropriate, the Commission may fix shorter time limits.

6. Where the Commission has not taken a decision in accordance with paragraphs 2, 3 or 4 within the period laid down in paragraph 5, the aid shall be deemed to have been authorised by the Commission. The Member State concerned may thereupon implement the measures in question after giving the Commission prior notice thereof, unless the Commission takes a decision pursuant to this Article within a period of 15 working days following receipt of the notice.

Article 5

Request for information

1. Where the Commission considers that information provided by the Member State concerned with regard to a measure notified pursuant to Article 2 is incomplete, it shall request all necessary additional information. Where a Member State responds to such a request, the Commission shall inform the Member State of the receipt of the response.

2. Where the Member State concerned does not provide the information requested within the period prescribed by the Commission or provides incomplete information, the Commission shall send a reminder, allowing an appropriate additional period within which the information shall be provided.

3. The notification shall be deemed to be withdrawn if the requested information is not provided within the prescribed period, unless before the expiry of that period, either the period has been extended with the consent of both the Commission and the Member State concerned, or the Member State concerned, in a duly reasoned statement, informs the Commission that it considers the notification to be complete because the additional information requested is not available or has already been provided. In that case, the period referred to in Article 4(5) shall begin on the day following receipt of the statement. If the notification is deemed to be withdrawn, the Commission shall inform the Member State thereof.

Article 6

Formal investigation procedure

1. The decision to initiate the formal investigation procedure shall summarise the relevant issues of fact and law, shall include a preliminary assessment of the Commission as to the aid character of the proposed measure and shall set out the doubts as to its compatibility with the common market. The decision shall call upon the Member State concerned and upon other interested parties to submit comments within a prescribed period which shall normally not exceed one month. In duly justified cases, the Commission may extend the prescribed period.
2. The comments received shall be submitted to the Member State concerned. If an interested party so requests, on grounds of potential damage, its identity shall be withheld from the Member State concerned. The Member State concerned may reply to the comments submitted within a prescribed period which shall normally not exceed one month. In duly justified cases, the Commission may extend the prescribed period.

Article 7

Decisions of the Commission to close the formal investigation procedure

1. Without prejudice to Article 8, the formal investigation procedure shall be closed by means of a decision as provided for in paragraphs 2 to 5 of this Article.
2. Where the Commission finds that, where appropriate following modification by the Member State concerned, the notified measure does not constitute aid, it shall record that finding by way of a decision.
3. Where the Commission finds that, where appropriate following modification by the Member State concerned, the doubts as to the compatibility of the notified measure with the common market have been removed, it shall decide that the aid is compatible with the common market (hereinafter referred to as a "positive decision"). That decision shall specify which exception under the Treaty has been applied.
4. The Commission may attach to a positive decision conditions subject to which an aid may be considered compatible with the common market and may lay down obligations to enable compliance with the decision to be monitored (hereinafter referred to as a "conditional decision").
5. Where the Commission finds that the notified aid is not compatible with the common market, it shall decide that the aid shall not be put into effect (hereinafter referred to as a "negative decision").
6. Decisions taken pursuant to paragraphs 2, 3, 4 and 5 shall be taken as soon as the doubts referred to in Article 4(4) have been removed. The Commission shall as far as possible endeavour to adopt a decision within a period of 18 months from the opening of the procedure. This time limit may be extended by common agreement between the Commission and the Member State concerned.

7. Once the time limit referred to in paragraph 6 has expired, and should the Member State concerned so request, the Commission shall, within two months, take a decision on the basis of the information available to it. If appropriate, where the information provided is not sufficient to establish compatibility, the Commission shall take a negative decision.

Article 8

Withdrawal of notification

1. The Member State concerned may withdraw the notification within the meaning of Article 2 in due time before the Commission has taken a decision pursuant to Article 4 or 7.

2. In cases where the Commission initiated the formal investigation procedure, the Commission shall close that procedure.

Article 9

Revocation of a decision

The Commission may revoke a decision taken pursuant to Article 4(2) or (3), or Article 7(2), (3), (4), after having given the Member State concerned the opportunity to submit its comments, where the decision was based on incorrect information provided during the procedure which was a determining factor for the decision. Before revoking a decision and taking a new decision, the Commission shall open the formal investigation procedure pursuant to Article 4(4). Articles 6, 7 and 10, Article 11(1), Articles 13, 14 and 15 shall apply *mutatis mutandis*.

CHAPTER III

PROCEDURE REGARDING UNLAWFUL AID

Article 10

Examination, request for information and information injunction

1. Where the Commission has in its possession information from whatever source regarding alleged unlawful aid, it shall examine that information without delay.

2. If necessary, it shall request information from the Member State concerned. Article 2(2) and Article 5(1) and (2) shall apply *mutatis mutandis*.

3. Where, despite a reminder pursuant to Article 5(2), the Member State concerned does not provide the information requested within the period prescribed by the Commission, or where it provides incomplete information, the Commission shall by decision

require the information to be provided (hereinafter referred to as an "information injunc-tion"). The decision shall specify what information is required and prescribe an appro-priate period within which it is to be supplied.

Article 11

Injunction to suspend or provisionally recover aid

1. The Commission may, after giving the Member State concerned the opportunity to submit its comments, adopt a decision requiring the Member State to suspend any unlawful aid until the Commission has taken a decision on the compatibility of the aid with the common market (hereinafter referred to as a "suspension injunction").

2. The Commission may, after giving the Member State concerned the opportunity to submit its comments, adopt a decision requiring the Member State provisionally to recover any unlawful aid until the Commission has taken a decision on the compatibility of the aid with the common market (hereinafter referred to as a "recovery injunction"), if the following criteria are fulfilled:

— according to an established practice there are no doubts about the aid character of the measure concerned
   and
— there is an urgency to act
   and
— there is a serious risk of substantial and irreparable damage to a competitor.

Recovery shall be effected in accordance with the procedure set out in Article 14(2) and (3). After the aid has been effectively recovered, the Commission shall take a decision within the time limits applicable to notified aid.

The Commission may authorise the Member State to couple the refunding of the aid with the payment of rescue aid to the firm concerned.

The provisions of this paragraph shall be applicable only to unlawful aid implemented after the entry into force of this Regulation.

Article 12

Non-compliance with an injunction decision

If the Member State fails to comply with a suspension injunction or a recovery injunction, the Commission shall be entitled, while carrying out the examination on the substance of the matter on the basis of the information available, to refer the matter to the Court of Justice of the European Communities direct and apply for a declaration that the failure to comply constitutes an infringement of the Treaty.

Article 13

Decisions of the Commission

1. The examination of possible unlawful aid shall result in a decision pursuant to Article 4(2), (3) or (4). In the case of decisions to initiate the formal investigation procedure, proceedings shall be closed by means of a decision pursuant to Article 7. If a Member State fails to comply with an information injunction, that decision shall be taken on the basis of the information available.

2. In cases of possible unlawful aid and without prejudice to Article 11(2), the Commission shall not be bound by the time-limit set out in Articles 4(5), 7(6) and 7(7).

3. Article 9 shall apply *mutatis mutandis*.

Article 14

Recovery of aid

1. Where negative decisions are taken in cases of unlawful aid, the Commission shall decide that the Member State concerned shall take all necessary measures to recover the aid from the beneficiary (hereinafter referred to as a "recovery decision"). The Commission shall not require recovery of the aid if this would be contrary to a general principle of Community law.

2. The aid to be recovered pursuant to a recovery decision shall include interest at an appropriate rate fixed by the Commission. Interest shall be payable from the date on which the unlawful aid was at the disposal of the beneficiary until the date of its recovery.

3. Without prejudice to any order of the Court of Justice of the European Communities pursuant to Article 242 of the Treaty, recovery shall be effected without delay and in accordance with the procedures under the national law of the Member State concerned, provided that they allow the immediate and effective execution of the Commission's decision. To this effect and in the event of a procedure before national courts, the Member States concerned shall take all necessary steps which are available in their respective legal systems, including provisional measures, without prejudice to Community law.

Article 15

Limitation period

1. The powers of the Commission to recover aid shall be subject to a limitation period of ten years.

2. The limitation period shall begin on the day on which the unlawful aid is awarded to the beneficiary either as individual aid or as aid under an aid scheme. Any action taken by the Commission or by a Member State, acting at the request of the Commission, with regard to the unlawful aid shall interrupt the limitation period. Each interruption shall start time running afresh. The limitation period shall be suspended for as long as the decision of the Commission is the subject of proceedings pending before the Court of Justice of the European Communities.

3. Any aid with regard to which the limitation period has expired, shall be deemed to be existing aid.

CHAPTER IV

PROCEDURE REGARDING MISUSE OF AID

Article 16

Misuse of aid

Without prejudice to Article 23, the Commission may in cases of misuse of aid open the formal investigation procedure pursuant to Article 4(4). Articles 6, 7, 9 and 10, Article 11(1), Articles 12, 13, 14 and 15 shall apply *mutatis mutandis*.

Chapter V

Procedure Regarding Existing Aid Schemes

Article 17

Cooperation pursuant to Article 88(1) of the Treaty

1. The Commission shall obtain from the Member State concerned all necessary information for the review, in cooperation with the Member State, of existing aid schemes pursuant to Article 88(1) of the Treaty.

2. Where the Commission considers that an existing aid scheme is not, or is no longer, compatible with the common market, it shall inform the Member State concerned of its preliminary view and give the Member State concerned the opportunity to submit its comments within a period of one month. In duly justified cases, the Commission may extend this period.

Article 18

Proposal for appropriate measures

Where the Commission, in the light of the information submitted by the Member State pursuant to Article 17, concludes that the existing aid scheme is not, or is no longer, compatible with the common market, it shall issue a recommendation proposing appropriate measures to the Member State concerned. The recommendation may propose, in particular:

(a) substantive amendment of the aid scheme,
    or
(b) introduction of procedural requirements,
    or
(c) abolition of the aid scheme.

Article 19

Legal consequences of a proposal for appropriate measures

1. Where the Member State concerned accepts the proposed measures and informs the Commission thereof, the Commission shall record that finding and inform the Member State thereof. The Member State shall be bound by its acceptance to implement the appropriate measures.

2. Where the Member State concerned does not accept the proposed measures and the Commission, having taken into account the arguments of the Member State concerned, still considers that those measures are necessary, it shall initiate proceedings pursuant to Article 4(4). Articles 6, 7 and 9 shall apply *mutatis mutandis*.

CHAPTER VI

INTERESTED PARTIES

Article 20

Rights of interested parties

1. Any interested party may submit comments pursuant to Article 6 following a Commission decision to initiate the formal investigation procedure. Any interested party which has submitted such comments and any beneficiary of individual aid shall be sent a copy of the decision taken by the Commission pursuant to Article 7.

2. Any interested party may inform the Commission of any alleged unlawful aid and any alleged misuse of aid. Where the Commission considers that on the basis of the information in its possession there are insufficient grounds for taking a view on the case, it shall inform the interested party thereof. Where the Commission takes a decision on a case concerning the subject matter of the information supplied, it shall send a copy of that decision to the interested party.

3. At its request, any interested party shall obtain a copy of any decision pursuant to Articles 4 and 7, Article 10(3) and Article 11.

CHAPTER VII

MONITORING

Article 21

Annual reports

1. Member States shall submit to the Commission annual reports on all existing aid schemes with regard to which no specific reporting obligations have been imposed in a conditional decision pursuant to Article 7(4).

2. Where, despite a reminder, the Member State concerned fails to submit an annual report, the Commission may proceed in accordance with Article 18 with regard to the aid scheme concerned.

Article 22

On-site monitoring

1. Where the Commission has serious doubts as to whether decisions not to raise objections, positive decisions or conditional decisions with regard to individual aid are being complied with, the Member State concerned, after having been given the opportunity to submit its comments, shall allow the Commission to undertake on-site monitoring visits.

2. The officials authorised by the Commission shall be empowered, in order to verify compliance with the decision concerned:

(a) to enter any premises and land of the undertaking concerned;
(b) to ask for oral explanations on the spot;
(c) to examine books and other business records and take, or demand, copies.

The Commission may be assisted if necessary by independent experts.

3. The Commission shall inform the Member State concerned, in good time and in writing, of the on-site monitoring visit and of the identities of the authorised officials and experts. If the Member State has duly justified objections to the Commission's choice of experts, the experts shall be appointed in common agreement with the Member State. The officials of the Commission and the experts authorised to carry out the on-site monitoring shall produce an authorisation in writing specifying the subject-matter and purpose of the visit.

4. Officials authorised by the Member State in whose territory the monitoring visit is to be made may be present at the monitoring visit.

5. The Commission shall provide the Member State with a copy of any report produced as a result of the monitoring visit.

6. Where an undertaking opposes a monitoring visit ordered by a Commission decision pursuant to this Article, the Member State concerned shall afford the necessary assistance to the officials and experts authorised by the Commission to enable them to carry out the monitoring visit. To this end the Member States shall, after consulting the Commission, take the necessary measures within eighteen months after the entry into force of this Regulation.

Article 23

Non-compliance with decisions and judgments

1. Where the Member State concerned does not comply with conditional or negative decisions, in particular in cases referred to in Article 14, the Commission may refer the matter to the Court of Justice of the European Communities direct in accordance with Article 88(2) of the Treaty.

2. If the Commission considers that the Member State concerned has not complied with a judgment of the Court of Justice of the European Communities, the Commission may pursue the matter in accordance with Article 228 of the Treaty.

CHAPTER VIII

COMMON PROVISIONS

Article 24

Professional secrecy

The Commission and the Member States, their officials and other servants, including independent experts appointed by the Commission, shall not disclose information which they have acquired through the application of this Regulation and which is covered by the obligation of professional secrecy.

Article 25

Addressee of decisions

Decisions taken pursuant to Chapters II, III, IV, V and VII shall be addressed to the Member State concerned. The Commission shall notify them to the Member State concerned without delay and give the latter the opportunity to indicate to the Commission which information it considers to be covered by the obligation of professional secrecy.

Article 26

Publication of decisions

1. The Commission shall publish in the *Official Journal of the European Communities* a summary notice of the decisions which it takes pursuant to Article 4(2) and (3) and Article 18 in conjunction with Article 19(1). The summary notice shall state that a copy of the decision may be obtained in the authentic language version or versions.

2. The Commission shall publish in the *Official Journal of the European Communities* the decisions which it takes pursuant to Article 4(4) in their authentic language version. In the *Official Journal* published in languages other than the authentic language version, the authentic language version will be accompanied by a meaningful summary in the language of that *Official Journal.*

3. The Commission shall publish in the *Official Journal of the European Communities* the decisions which it takes pursuant to Article 7.

4. In cases where Article 4(6) or Article 8(2) applies, a short notice shall be published in the *Official Journal of the European Communities.*

5. The Council, acting unanimously, may decide to publish decisions pursuant to the third subparagraph of Article 88(2) of the Treaty in the *Official Journal of the European Communities.*

Article 27

Implementing provisions ·

The Commission, acting in accordance with the procedure laid down in Article 29, shall have the power to adopt implementing provisions concerning the form, content and other details of notifications, the form, content and other details of annual reports, details of time-limits and the calculation of time-limits, and the interest rate referred to in Article 14(2).

Article 28

Advisory Committee on State aid

An Advisory Committee on State aid (hereinafter referred to as the "Committee") shall be set up. It shall be composed of representatives of the Member States and chaired by the representative of the Commission.

Article 29

Consultation of the Committee

1. The Commission shall consult the Committee before adopting any implementing provision pursuant to Article 27.

2. Consultation of the Committee shall take place at a meeting called by the Commission. The drafts and documents to be examined shall be annexed to the notification. The meeting shall take place no earlier than two months after notification has been sent. This period may be reduced in the case of urgency.

3. The Commission representative shall submit to the Committee a draft of the measures to be taken. The Committee shall deliver an opinion on the draft, within a time-limit which the chairman may lay down according to the urgency of the matter, if necessary by taking a vote.

4. The opinion shall be recorded in the minutes; in addition, each Member State shall have the right to ask to have its position recorded in the minutes. The Committee may recommend the publication of this opinion in the *Official Journal of the European Communities*.

5. The Commission shall take the utmost account of the opinion delivered by the Committee. It shall inform the Committee on the manner in which its opinion has been taken into account.

Article 30

Entry into force

This Regulation shall enter into force on the twentieth day following that of its publication in the *Official Journal of the European Communities*.

This Regulation shall be binding in its entirety and directly applicable in all Member States.

Done at Brussels, 22 March 1999.

REGULATION 69/2001[1]

On the Application of Articles 87 and 88 of the EC Treaty to de minimis Aid

THE COMMISSION OF THE EUROPEAN COMMUNITIES,

Having regard to the Treaty establishing the European Community,

Having regard to Council Regulation (EC) No 994/98 of 7 May 1998 on the application of Articles 92 and 93 of the Treaty establishing the European Community to certain categories of horizontal State aid,[2] and in particular Article 2 thereof,

Having published a draft of this Regulation,[3]

Having consulted the Advisory Committee on State aid,

Whereas:

(1) Regulation (EC) No 994/98 empowers the Commission to set out in a regulation a threshold under which aid measures are deemed not to meet all the criteria of Article 87(1) of the Treaty and therefore do not fall under the notification procedure provided for in Article 88(3) of the Treaty.

(2) The Commission has applied Articles 87 and 88 of the Treaty and in particular clarified, in numerous decisions, the notion of aid within the meaning of Article 87(1) of the Treaty. The Commission has also stated its policy with regard to a *de minimis* ceiling, under which Article 87(1) can be considered not to apply, most recently in the notice on the *de minimis* rule for State aid.[4] In the light of this experience and with a view to increasing transparency and legal certainty, it is appropriate that the *de minimis* rule be laid down in a Regulation.

(3) In view of the special rules which apply in the sectors of agriculture, fisheries and aquaculture, and transport, and of the risk that even small amounts of aid could fulfil the criteria of Article 87(1) of the Treaty in those sectors, it is appropriate that this Regulation should not apply to those sectors.

(4) In the light of the World Trade Organisation (WTO) Agreement on Subsidies and Countervailing Measures,[5] this Regulation should not exempt export aid or aid favouring domestic over imported products. Aid towards the cost of participating in trade fairs, or of studies or consultancy services needed for the launch of a new or existing product on a new market does not normally constitute export aid.

(5) In light of the Commission's experience, it can be established that aid not exceeding a ceiling of EUR 100 000 over any period of three years does not affect trade between Member States and/or does not distort or threaten to distort competition and therefore does

---

[1] OJ 2001 L10/30, of 12.1.2001.
[2] OJ 1998 L142/1.
[3] OJ 2000 C89/6.
[4] OJ 1996 C68/9.
[5] OJ 1994 L336/156.

not fall under Article 87(1) of the Treaty. The relevant period of three years has a mobile character, so that for each new grant of *de minimis* aid, the total amount of *de minimis* aid granted during the previous three years needs to be determined. The *de minimis* aid should be considered to be granted at the moment the legal right to receive the aid is conferred to the beneficiary. The *de minimis* rule is without prejudice to the possibility that enterprises receive, also for the same project, State aid authorised by the Commission or covered by a group exemption Regulation.

(6) For the purpose of transparency, equal treatment and the correct application of the *de minimis* ceiling, it is appropriate that Member States should apply the same method of calculation. In order to facilitate this calculation and in accordance with the present practice of application of the *de minimis* rule, it is appropriate that aid amounts not taking the form of a cash grant should be converted into their gross grant equivalent. Calculation of the grant equivalent of aid payable in several instalments, and calculation of aid in the form of a soft loan, require the use of market interest rates prevailing at the time of grant. With a view to a uniform, transparent and simple application of the State aid rules, the market rates for the purposes of this Regulation should be deemed to be the reference rates, provided that, in the case of a soft loan, the loan is backed by normal security and does not involve abnormal risk. The reference rates should be those which are periodically fixed by the Commission on the basis of objective criteria and published in the *Official Journal of the European Communities* and on the Internet.

(7) The Commission has a duty to ensure that State aid rules are respected and in particular that aid granted under the *de minimis* rule adheres to the conditions thereof. In accordance with the cooperation principle laid down in Article 10 of the Treaty, Member States should facilitate the achievement of this task by establishing the necessary machinery in order to ensure that the total amount of aid, granted to the same beneficiary under the *de minimis* rule, does not exceed the ceiling of EUR 100 000 over a period of three years. To that end, it is appropriate that Member States when granting a *de minimis* aid, should inform the enterprise concerned of the *de minimis* character of the aid, receive full information about other *de minimis* aid received during the last three years and carefully check that the *de minimis* ceiling will not be exceeded by the new *de minimis* aid. Alternatively respect of the ceiling may also be ensured by means of a central register.

(8) Having regard to the Commission's experience and in particular the frequency with which it is generally necessary to revise State aid policy, it is appropriate to limit the period of application of this Regulation. Should this Regulation expire without being extended, Member States should have an adjustment period of six months with regard to *de minimis* aid schemes which were covered by this Regulation,

HAS ADOPTED THIS REGULATION:

Article 1

Scope

This Regulation applies to aid granted to enterprises in all sectors, with the exception of:

(a) the transport sector and the activities linked to the production, processing or marketing of products listed in Annex I to the Treaty;

(b) aid to export-related activities, namely aid directly linked to the quantities exported, to the establishment and operation of a distribution network or to other current expenditure linked to the export activity;

(c) aid contingent upon the use of domestic over imported goods.

809

Article 2

De minimis aid

1. Aid measures shall be deemed not to meet all the criteria of Article 87(1) of the Treaty and shall therefore not fall under the notification requirement of Article 88(3) of the Treaty, if they fulfil the conditions laid down in paragraphs 2 and 3.

2. The total *de minimis* aid granted to any one enterprise shall not exceed EUR 100 000 over any period of three years. This ceiling shall apply irrespective of the form of the aid or the objective pursued.

3. The ceiling in paragraph 2 shall be expressed as a cash grant. All figures used shall be gross, that is, before any deduction for direct taxation. Where aid is awarded in a form other than a grant, the aid amount shall be the gross grant equivalent of the aid.

Aid payable in several instalments shall be discounted to its value at the moment of its being granted. The interest rate to be used for discounting purposes and to calculate the aid amount in a soft loan shall be the reference rate applicable at the time of grant.

Article 3

Cumulation and monitoring

1. Where a Member State grants *de minimis* aid to an enterprise, it shall inform the enterprise about the *de minimis* character of the aid and obtain from the enterprise concerned full information about other *de minimis* aid received during the previous three years.

The Member State may only grant the new *de minimis* aid after having checked that this will not raise the total amount of *de minimis* aid received during the relevant period of three years to a level above the ceiling set out in Article 2(2).

2. Where a Member State has set up a central register of *de minimis* aid containing complete information on all *de minimis* aid granted by any authority within that Member State, the requirement in the first sub-paragraph of paragraph 1 no longer applies from the moment the register covers a period of three years.

3. Member States shall record and compile all the information regarding the application of this Regulation. Such records shall contain all information necessary to demonstrate that the conditions of this Regulation have been respected. Records regarding an individual *de minimis* aid shall be maintained for 10 years from the date on which it was granted and regarding a *de minimis* aid scheme, for 10 years from the date on which the last individual aid was granted under such scheme. On written request the Member State concerned shall provide the Commission, within a period of 20 working days, or such longer period as may be fixed in the request, with all the information that the Commission considers necessary for assessing whether the conditions of this Regulation have been complied with, in particular the total amount of *de minimis* aid received by any enterprise.

Article 4

Entry into force and period of validity

1. This Regulation shall enter into force on the 20th day following that of its publication in the *Official Journal of the European Communities*.

It shall remain in force until 31 December 2006.

2. At the end of the period of validity of this Regulation, *de minimis* aid schemes falling under this Regulation shall continue to benefit from it during an adjustment period of six months.

810

During the adjustment period, these schemes may continue to be applied under the conditions of this Regulation.

This Regulation shall be binding in its entirety and directly applicable in all Member States.

Done at Brussels, 12 January 2001.

REGULATION 68/2001[1]

On the Application of Articles 87 and 88 of the EC Treaty to Training Aid

THE COMMISSION OF THE EUROPEAN COMMUNITIES,

Having regard to the Treaty establishing the European Community,

Having regard to Council Regulation (EC) No 994/98 of 7 May 1998 on the application of Articles 92 and 93 of the Treaty establishing the European Community to certain categories of horizontal state aid,[2] and in particular point (a)(iv) of Article 1(1) thereof,

Having published a draft of this Regulation,[3]

Having consulted the Advisory Committee on State Aid,

Whereas:

(1) Regulation (EC) No 994/98 empowers the Commission to declare, in accordance with Article 87 of the Treaty, that under certain conditions training aid is compatible with the common market and not subject to the notification requirement of Article 88(3) of the Treaty.

(2) The Commission has applied Articles 87 and 88 of the Treaty to training aid in numerous decisions and has also stated its policy, most recently in the Community framework on training aid.[4] In the light of the Commission's considerable experience in applying those Articles to training aid, it is appropriate, with a view to ensuring efficient supervision and simplifying administration without weakening Commission monitoring, that the Commission should make use of the powers conferred by Regulation (EC) No 994/98.

(3) In order to establish a transparent and coherent policy for all sectors, it is appropriate that the scope of this Regulation be as broad as possible and include the agricultural sector, fisheries and aquaculture.

(4) This Regulation is without prejudice to the possibility for Member States to notify training aid. Such notifications will be assessed by the Commission in particular in the light of the criteria set out in this Regulation, or in accordance with the applicable Community guidelines and frameworks, if such guidelines and frameworks exist. This is currently the case for activities relating to the production, processing and marketing of products listed in Annex I to the Treaty and for the sector of maritime transport. The framework on training aid should be abolished from the date of entry into force of this Regulation, since its contents are replaced by this Regulation.

(5) For reasons of transparency, it should be recalled that in accordance with the second subparagraph of Article 51(1), of Council Regulation (EC) No 1257/1999 of 17 May 1999 on support for rural development from the European Agricultural Guidance and Guarantee

---

[1] OJ 2001 L10/20.
[2] OJ 1998 L142/1.
[3] OJ 2000 C89/8.
[4] OJ 1998 C343/10.

Fund (EAGGF) and amending and repealing certain Regulations,[5] Articles 87 to 89 of the Treaty do not apply to financial contributions provided by the Member States for measures subject to Community support for training according to Article 9 of the said Regulation.

(6) For reasons of transparency it should be underlined that this Regulation should only apply to training measures which constitute State aid within the meaning of Article 87(1) of the Treaty. Many training measures are not caught by that Article, but constitute general measures because they are open to all enterprises in all sectors without discrimination and without discretionary power for the authorities applying the measure, e.g. general tax incentive schemes, such as automatic tax credits, open to all firms investing in employee training. Other training measures do not fall within the scope of Article 87(1) of the Treaty because they directly benefit people everywhere and do not grant an advantage to certain enterprises or sectors. Examples are: schooling and initial training (such as apprenticeships and day-release schemes); the training or re-training of unemployed people, including traineeships in enterprises; measures directly targeted at workers or even at certain categories of workers, affording them the opportunity of receiving training unconnected with the firm or industry in which they work (for example the 'learning account'). On the other hand, it should be recalled that contributions from sectoral funds, if they are made compulsory by the State, are not considered as private resources, but constitute State resources within the meaning of Article 87(1) of the Treaty.

(7) This Regulation should exempt any aid that meets all the relevant requirements of this Regulation, and any aid scheme, provided that any aid that could be granted under such scheme meets all the relevant requirements of this Regulation. With a view to ensuring efficient supervision and simplifying administration without weakening Commission monitoring, aid schemes and individual grants, outside any aid scheme, should contain an express reference to this Regulation.

(8) In order to eliminate differences that might give rise to distortions of competition, in order to facilitate coordination between different Community and national initiatives concerning small and medium-sized enterprises, and for reasons of administrative clarity and legal certainty, the definition of 'small and medium-sized enterprises' used in this Regulation should be that laid down in Commission Recommendation 96/280/EC of 3 April 1996 concerning the definition of small and medium-sized enterprises.[6]

(9) In order to determine whether or not aid is compatible with the common market pursuant to this Regulation, it is necessary to take into consideration the aid intensity and thus the aid amount expressed as a grant equivalent. Calculation of the grant equivalent of aid payable in several instalments, and calculation of aid in the form of a soft loan, require the use of market interest rates prevailing at the time of grant. With a view to a uniform, transparent and simple application of the State aid rules, the market rates for the purposes of this Regulation should be deemed to be the reference rates, provided that, in the case of a soft loan, the loan is backed by normal security and does not involve abnormal risk. The reference rates should be those which are periodically fixed by the Commission on the basis of objective criteria and published in the *Official Journal of the European Communities* and on the Internet.

(10) Training usually has positive external effects for society as a whole since it increases the pool of skilled workers from which other firms may draw, improves the competitiveness of Community industry and plays an important role in employment strategy. In view of the fact that enterprises in the Community generally under-invest in the training of their workers, State aid might help to correct this market imperfection and therefore can be considered under certain conditions to be compatible with the common market and therefore exempted from prior notification.

---

[5] OJ 1999 L160/80.
[6] OJ 1996 L107/4.

(11) In order to ensure that State aid is limited to the minimum necessary to obtain the Community objective which market forces alone would not make possible, the permissible intensities of exempted aid should be modulated according to the type of training provided, the size of the enterprise and its geographical location.

(12) General training provides transferable qualifications and substantially improves the employability of the trained worker. Aid for this purpose has less distortive effects on competition, so that higher intensities of aid can be considered compatible with the common market and exempted from prior notification. Specific training, on the other hand, which mainly benefits the enterprise, involves a greater risk of distortion of competition so that the intensity of aid which can be considered compatible and exempted from prior notification should be much lower.

(13) In view of the handicaps with which SMEs are confronted and the higher relative costs that they have to bear when they invest in the training of their workers, the intensities of aid exempted by this Regulation should be increased for SMEs.

(14) In assisted areas under Article 87(3)(a) and (c) of the Treaty, training has a relatively greater external impact, since there is a substantial under-investment in training in those regions and a higher unemployment rate. Consequently, the intensities of aid exempted by this Regulation should be increased for those areas.

(15) The characteristics of training in the maritime transport sector justify a specific approach for that sector.

(16) It is appropriate that large amounts of aid remain subject to an individual assessment by the Commission before they are put into effect. Accordingly, aid amounts exceeding a fixed amount, which should be set at EUR 1 000 000, are excluded from the exemption provided for in this Regulation and remain subject to the requirements of Article 88(3) of the Treaty.

(17) This Regulation should not exempt aid cumulated with other State aid, including aid granted by national, regional and local authorities, or with Community assistance, in relation to the same eligible costs when such cumulation exceeds the thresholds fixed in this Regulation.

(18) In order to ensure transparency and effective monitoring in accordance with Article 3 of Regulation (EC) No 994/98, it is appropriate to establish a standard format in which Member States should provide the Commission with summary information whenever, in pursuance of this Regulation, an aid scheme is implemented or an individual aid outside such schemes is granted, with a view to publication in the *Official Journal of the European Communities*. For the same reasons, it is appropriate to establish rules concerning the records that Member States should keep regarding the aid exempted by this Regulation. For the purposes of the annual reports to be submitted to the Commission by Member States, it is appropriate for the Commission to establish its specific requirements, including, in view of the wide availability of the necessary technology, information in computerised form.

(19) Having regard to the Commission's experience and in particular the frequency with which it is generally necessary to revise State aid policy, it is appropriate to limit the period of application of this Regulation. Should this Regulation expire without being extended, aid schemes already exempted by this Regulation should continue to be exempted for six months,

HAS ADOPTED THIS REGULATION:

Article 1

Scope

This Regulation applies to aid in all sectors, including the activities relating to the production, processing and marketing of products listed in Annex 1 of the Treaty.

Article 2

Definitions

For the purpose of this Regulation:

(a) "aid" shall mean any measure fulfilling all the criteria laid down in Article 87(1) of the Treaty;

(b) "small and medium-sized enterprises" shall mean enterprises as defined in Annex I;

(c) "large enterprises" shall mean enterprises not coming under the definition of SME in Annex I;

(d) "specific training" shall mean training involving tuition directly and principally applicable to the employee's present or future position in the assisted firm and providing qualifications which are not or only to a limited extent transferable to other firms or fields of work;

(e) "general training" shall mean training involving tuition which is not applicable only or principally to the employee's present or future position in the assisted firm, but which provides qualifications that are largely transferable to other firms or fields of work and thereby substantially improve the employability of the employee. Training shall be considered "general" if, for example,

— it is jointly organised by different independent enterprises, or if employees of different enterprises may avail themselves of the training,

— it is recognised, certified or validated by public authorities or bodies or by other bodies or institutions on which a Member State or the Community has conferred the necessary powers;

(f) "aid intensity" shall mean the aid amount expressed as a percentage of the project's eligible costs. All figures used shall be taken before any deduction for direct taxation. Where aid is awarded in a form other than a grant, the aid amount shall be the grant equivalent of the aid. Aid payable in several instalments shall be discounted to its value at the time of granting. The interest rate to be used for discounting purposes and for calculating the aid amount in a soft loan shall be the reference rate applicable at the time of grant;

(g) "disadvantaged worker" shall mean:

— any young person under 25 who has not previously obtained his first regular paid employment,

— any person with serious disabilities which result from physical, mental or psychological impairments and yet capable of entering the labour market,

— any migrant worker who moves or has moved within the Community or becomes resident in the Community to take up work and who needs professional and/or language training,

— any person wishing to re-enter working life after a break of at least three years, and particularly any person who gave up work on account of the difficulty of reconciling his working life and family life, for the first six months after recruitment,

— any person older than 45 who has not attained an upper secondary educational qualification or its equivalent,

— any long-term unemployed person, i.e. any person who was without work for 12 consecutive months, for the first six months after recruitment.

Article 3

Conditions for exemption

1. Individual aid outside any scheme, fulfilling all the conditions of this Regulation, shall be compatible with the common market within the meaning of Article 87(3) of the

815

Treaty and shall be exempt from the notification requirement of Article 88(3) of the Treaty provided that it contains an express reference to this Regulation, by citing its title and publication reference in the *Official Journal of the European Communities*.

2. Aid schemes fulfilling all the conditions of this Regulation shall be compatible with the common market within the meaning of Article 87(3) of the Treaty and shall be exempt from the notification requirement of Article 88(3) of the Treaty provided that:

(a) any aid that could be awarded under such scheme fulfills all the conditions of this Regulation;
(b) the scheme contains an express reference to this Regulation, by citing its title and publication reference in the *Official Journal of the European Communities*.

3. Aid granted under the schemes referred to in paragraph 2 shall be compatible with the common market within the meaning of Article 87(3) of the Treaty and shall be exempt from the notification requirement of Article 88(3) of the Treaty provided that the aid granted directly fulfils all the conditions of this Regulation.

Article 4

Exempted training aid

1. Aid schemes and individual aid for training must fulfil the conditions laid down in paragraphs 2 to 7.

2. Where the aid is granted for specific training, its intensity shall not exceed 25% for large enterprises and 35% for small and medium-sized enterprises.

These intensities shall be increased by five percentage points for enterprises in areas which qualify for regional aid pursuant to Article 87(3)(c) of the Treaty and by 10 percentage points for enterprises in areas which qualify for regional aid pursuant to Article 87(3)(a) of the Treaty.

3. Where the aid is granted for general training, its intensity shall not exceed 50% for large enterprises and 70% for small and medium-sized enterprises.

These intensities shall be increased by five percentage points for enterprises in areas which qualify for regional aid pursuant to Article 87(3)(c) of the Treaty and by 10 percentage points for enterprises in areas which qualify for regional aid pursuant to Article 87(3)(a) of the Treaty.

4. The maximum intensities referred to in paragraphs 2 and 3 shall be increased by 10 percentage points if the training is given to disadvantaged workers.

5. In cases where the aid project involves both specific and general training components which cannot be separated for the calculation of the aid intensity, and in cases where the specific or general character of the training aid project cannot be established, the intensities applicable to specific training pursuant to paragraph 2 shall apply.

6. Where the aid is granted in the maritime transport sector, it may reach an intensity of 100%, whether the training project concerns specific or general training, provided that the following conditions are met:

(a) the trainee shall not be an active member of the crew but shall be supernumerary on board, and
(b) the training shall be carried out on board ships entered on Community registers.

7. The eligible costs of a training aid project shall be:

(a) trainers' personnel costs,
(b) trainers' and trainees' travel expenses,
(c) other current expenses such as materials and supplies,
(d) depreciation of tools and equipment, to the extent that they are used exclusively for the training project,

(e) cost of guidance and counselling services with regard to the training project,
(f) trainees' personnel costs up to the amount of the total of the other eligible costs referred to in (a) to (e). Only the hours during which the trainees actually participate in the training, after deduction of any productive hours or of their equivalent, may be taken into account.

The eligible costs shall be supported by documentary evidence, which shall be transparent and itemised.

Article 5

Large individual aid grants

The exemption shall not apply if the amount of aid granted to one enterprise for a single training project exceeds EUR 1 000 000.

Article 6

Cumulation

1. The aid ceilings fixed in Articles 4 and 5 shall apply regardless of whether the support for the project is financed entirely from State resources or is partly financed by the Community.
2. Aid exempted by this Regulation shall not be cumulated with any other State aid within the meaning of Article 87(1) of the Treaty, or with other Community funding, in relation to the same eligible costs, if such cumulation would result in an aid intensity exceeding that fixed by this Regulation.

Article 7

Transparency and monitoring

1. On implementation of an aid scheme, or grant of individual aid outside any scheme, exempted by this Regulation, Member States shall, within 20 working days, forward to the Commission, with a view to its publication in the *Official Journal of the European Communities*, a summary of the information regarding such aid scheme or individual aid according to the model laid down in Annex II.
2. Member States shall maintain detailed records regarding the aid schemes exempted by this Regulation, the individual aid granted under those schemes, and the individual aid exempted by this Regulation that is granted outside any existing aid scheme. Such records shall contain all information necessary to establish that the conditions for exemption, as laid down in this Regulation, are fulfilled. Member States shall keep a record regarding an individual aid for 10 years from the date on which it was granted, and regarding an aid scheme, for 10 years from the date on which the last individual aid was granted under such scheme. On written request, the Member State concerned shall provide the Commission, within a period of 20 working days or such longer period as may be fixed in the request, with all the information which the Commission considers necessary to assess whether the conditions of this Regulation have been complied with.
3. Member States shall compile a report on the application of this Regulation in respect of each whole or part calendar year during which this Regulation applies, in the form laid down in Annex III, also in computerised form. Member States shall provide the Commission with such report no later than three months after the expiry of the period to which the report relates.

Article 8

Entry into force and period of validity

1. This Regulation shall enter into force on the 20th day following its publication in the *Official Journal of the European Communities*.
It shall remain in force until 31 December 2006.
2. At the end of the period of validity of this Regulation, aid schemes exempted under this Regulation shall remain exempted during an adjustment period of six months.

This Regulation shall be binding in its entirety and directly applicable in all Member States.

Done at Brussels, 12 January 2001.

ANNEX I

Definition of small and medium-sized enterprises

(extract from Commission Recommendation 96/280/EC of 3 April 1996 Concerning the Definition of Small and Medium-sized enterprises (OJ 1996 L107/4))

'Article 1

1. Small and medium-sized enterprises, hereinafter referred to as "SMEs", are defined as enterprises which:

— have fewer than 250 employees, and
— have either,
    — an annual turnover not exceeding EUR 40 million, or
    — an annual balance-sheet total not exceeding EUR 27 million,
— conform to the criterion of independence as defined in paragraph 3.

2. Where it is necessary to distinguish between small and medium-sized enterprises, the "small enterprise" is defined as an enterprise which:

— has fewer than 50 employees and
— has either,
    — an annual turnover not exceeding EUR 7 million, or
    — an annual balance-sheet total not exceeding EUR 5 million,
— conforms to the criterion of independence as defined in paragraph 3.

3. Independent enterprises are those which are not owned as to 25% or more of the capital or the voting rights by one enterprise, or jointly by several enterprises, falling outside the definitions of an SME or a small enterprise, whichever may apply. This threshold may be exceeded in the following two cases:

— if the enterprise is held by public investment corporations, venture capital companies or institutional investors, provided no control is exercised either individually or jointly,

— if the capital is spread in such a way that it is not possible to determine by whom it is held and if the enterprise declares that it can legitimately presume that it is not owned as to 25% or more by one enterprise, or jointly by several enterprises, falling outside the definitions of an SME or a small enterprise, whichever may apply.

4. In calculating the thresholds referred to in paragraphs 1 and 2, it is therefore necessary to cumulate the relevant figures for the beneficiary enterprise and for all the enterprises that it directly or indirectly controls through possession of 25% or more of the capital or of the voting rights.

5. Where it is necessary to distinguish microenterprises from other SMEs, these are defined as enterprises having fewer than 10 employees.

6. Where, at the final balance-sheet date, an enterprise exceeds or falls below the employee thresholds or financial ceilings, this is to result in its acquiring or losing the status of "SME", "medium-sized enterprise", "small enterprise" or "microenterprise" only if the phenomenon is repeated over two consecutive financial years.

7. The number of persons employed corresponds to the number of annual working units (AWU), that is to say, the number of full-time workers employed during one year with part-time and seasonal workers being fractions of AWU. The reference year to be considered is that of the last approved accounting period.

8. The turnover and balance-sheet total thresholds are those of the last approved 12-month accounting period. In the case of newly established enterprises whose accounts have not yet been approved, the thresholds to apply shall be derived from a reliable estimate made in the course of the financial year.'

Annex II

Form of summary information to be provided whenever an aid scheme exempted by this Regulation is implemented and whenever an individual aid exempted by this Regulation is granted outside any aid scheme

Summary information on State aid granted in conformity with Commission Regulation (EC) No 68/2001	
Summary information to be filled in	*Explanatory remarks*
Member State	
Region	Indicate the name of the region if the aid is granted by a subcentral authority
Title of aid scheme or name of company receiving an individual aid	Indicate the name of the aid scheme or in the case of individual aid, the name of the beneficiary. In the latter case, no subsequent annual report is necessary!
Legal basis	Indicate the precise national legal reference for the aid scheme or for the individual aid
Annual expenditure planned under the scheme or overall amount of individual aid granted to the company	Amounts are to be given in euro or, if applicable, national currency.

Summary information to be filled in	*Explanatory remarks*
	In the case of an aid scheme:
	indicate the annual overall amount of the budget appropriation(s) or the estimated tax loss per year for all aid instruments contained in the scheme.
	In the case of an individual aid award:
	indicate the overall aid amount/tax loss. If appropriate, indicate also for how many years the aid will be paid in instalments or over how many years tax losses will be incurred.
	For guarantees in both cases, indicate the (maximum) amount of loans guaranteed
Maximum aid intensity	Indicate the maximum aid intensity or the maximum aid amount per eligible item
Date of implementation	Indicate the date from which aid may be granted under the scheme or when the individual aid is granted
Duration of scheme or individual aid award	Indicate the date (year and month) until which aid may be granted under the scheme or in the case of an individual aid and if appropriate the expected date (year and month) of the last instalment to be paid
Objective of aid	In the case of training aid, indicate whether the training is specific or general.
	In the case of general training, documentary evidence (e.g. description of the contents of the training) must be attached regarding the qualification of the training as general
Economic sector(s) concerned	Choose from the list, where relevant
☐ All sectors	
or	
☐ Agriculture	
☐ Fisheries and Aquaculture	
☐ Coalmining	
☐ All manufacturing	
or	
☐ Steel	
☐ Shipbuilding	
☐ Synthetic fibres	
☐ Motor vehicles	
☐ Other manufacturing	
☐ All services	
or	
☐ Maritime transport services	
☐ Other transport services	

Summary information to be filled in	Explanatory remarks
☐ Financial services ☐ Other services	
Remarks:	
Name and address of the granting authority	
Other information	

ANNEX III

Form of the periodic report to be provided to the Commission

Annual reporting format on aid schemes exempted under a group exemption regulation adopted pursuant to Article 1 of Council Regulation (EC) No 994/98

Member States are required to use the format below for their reporting obligations to the Commission under group exemption regulations adopted on the basis of Council Regulation (EC) No 994/98.

The reports should also be provided in computerised form.

Information required for all aid schemes exempted under group exemption regulations adopted pursuant to Article 1 of Council Regulation (EC) No 994/98

1. Title of aid scheme

2. Commission exemption regulation applicable

3. Expenditure

Separate figures have to be provided for each aid instrument within a scheme or individual aid (e.g. grant, soft loans, etc). The figures have to be expressed in euro or, if applicable, national currency. In the case of tax expenditure, annual tax losses have to be reported. If precise figures are not available, such losses may be estimated. These expenditure figures should be provided on the following basis:

for the year review indicate separately for each aid instrument within the scheme (e.g. grant, soft loan, guarantee, etc.):

3.1. amounts committed, (estimated) tax losses or other revenue forgone, data on guarantees, etc. for new assisted projects. In the case of guarantee schemes, the total amount of new guarantees handed out should be provided;

3.2. actual payments, (estimated) tax losses or other revenue forgone, data on guarantees, etc. for new and current projects. In the case of guarantee schemes, the

821

following should be provided: total amount of outstanding guarantees, premium income, recoveries, indemnities paid out, operating result of the scheme under the year under review;

3.3. number of new assisted projects;

3.4. estimated overall number of jobs created or maintained by new projects (if appropriate);

3.5. estimated overall amount of investment aided by new projects;

3.6. regional breakdown of amounts under point 3.1 either by regions defined at NUTS[7] level 2 or below or by Article 87(3)(a) regions, Article 87(3)(c) regions and non-assisted regions;

3.7. sectorial breakdown of amounts under point 3.1. by beneficiaries' sectors of activity (if more than one sector is covered, indicate the share of each):

— agriculture
— fisheries and/or aquaculture
— coalmining
— manufacturing
    of which:
    steel
    shipbuilding
    synthetic fibres
    motor vehicles
    other manufacturing (please specify)
— services
    of which:
    maritime transport services
    other transport services
    financial services
    other services (please specify)
— other sectors (please specify)

4. Other information and remarks

---

[7] NUTS is the nomenclature of territorial units for statistical purposes in the EC.

APPENDIX 80

REGULATION 70/2001[1]

On the Application of Articles 87 and 88 of the EC Treaty to State Aid to Small and Medium-sized Enterprises

THE COMMISSION OF THE EUROPEAN COMMUNITIES,

Having regard to the Treaty establishing the European Community,

Having regard to Council Regulation (EC) No 994/98 of 7 May 1998 on the application of Articles 92 and 93 of the Treaty establishing the European Community to certain categories of horizontal State aid,[2] and in particular points (a)(i) and (b) of Article 1(1) thereof,

Having published a draft of this Regulation,[3]

Having consulted the Advisory Committee on State Aid,

Whereas:

(1) Regulation (EC) No 994/98 empowers the Commission to declare, in accordance with Article 87 of the Treaty, that under certain conditions aid to small and medium-sized enterprises is compatible with the common market and not subject to the notification requirement of Article 88(3) of the Treaty.

(2) Regulation (EC) No 994/98 also empowers the Commission to declare, in accordance with Article 87 of the Treaty, that aid that complies with the map approved by the Commission for each Member State for the grant of regional aid is compatible with the common market and is not subject to the notification requirement of Article 88(3) of the Treaty.

(3) The Commission has applied Articles 87 and 88 of the Treaty to small and medium-sized enterprises in and outside assisted areas in numerous decisions and has also stated its policy, most recently in the Community guidelines on State aid for small and medium-sized enterprises[4] and in the guidelines on national regional aid.[5] In the light of the Commission's considerable experience in applying those Articles to small and medium-sized enterprises and in the light of the general texts relating to small and medium-sized enterprises and to regional aid issued by the Commission on the basis of those provisions, it is appropriate, with a view to ensuring efficient supervision and simplifying administration without weakening Commission monitoring, that the Commission should make use of the powers conferred by Regulation (EC) No 994/98.

(4) This Regulation is without prejudice to the possibility for Member States of notifying aid to small and medium-sized enterprises. Such notifications will be assessed by the Commission in particular in the light of the criteria set out in this Regulation. The guidelines on State aid for small and medium-sized enterprises should be abolished from

---

[1] OJ 2001 L10/33, of 12.1.2001.
[2] OJ 1998 L142/1.
[3] OJ 2000 C89/15.
[4] OJ 1996 C213/4.
[5] OJ 1998 C74/9.

the date of entry into force of this Regulation, since their contents are replaced by this Regulation.

(5) Small and medium-sized enterprises play a decisive role in job creation and, more generally, act as a factor of social stability and economic drive. However, their development may be limited by market imperfections. They often have difficulties in obtaining capital or credit, given the risk-shy nature of certain financial markets and the limited guarantees that they may be able to offer. Their limited resources may also restrict their access to information, notably regarding new technology and potential markets. Having regard to those considerations, the purpose of the aid exempted by this Regulation should be to facilitate the development of the economic activities of small and medium-sized enterprises, provided that such aid does not adversely affect trading conditions to an extent contrary to the common interest.

(6) This Regulation should exempt any aid that meets all the relevant requirements of this Regulation, and any aid scheme, provided that any aid that could be granted under such scheme meets all the relevant requirements of this Regulation. With a view to ensuring efficient supervision and simplifying administration without weakening Commission monitoring, aid schemes and individual grants outside any aid scheme should contain an express reference to this Regulation.

(7) This Regulation should apply without prejudice to special rules in regulations and directives concerning State aid in certain sectors, such as currently exist for shipbuilding, and should not apply to agriculture and fisheries and aquaculture.

(8) In order to eliminate differences that might give rise to distortions of competition, in order to facilitate coordination between different Community and national initiatives concerning small and medium-sized enterprises, and for reasons of administrative clarity and legal certainty, the definition of "small and medium-sized enterprises" used in this Regulation should be that laid down in Commission Recommendation 96/280/EC of 3 April 1996 concerning the definition of small and medium-sized enterprises.[6] That definition was also used in the Community guidelines on State aid for small and medium-sized enterprises.[7]

(9) In accordance with the established practice of the Commission, and with a view to better ensuring that aid is proportionate and limited to the amount necessary, thresholds should be expressed in terms of aid intensities in relation to a set of eligible costs, rather than in terms of maximum aid amounts.

(10) In order to determine whether or not aid is compatible with the common market pursuant to this Regulation, it is necessary to take into consideration the aid intensity and thus the aid amount expressed as a grant equivalent. The calculation of the grant equivalent of aid payable in several instalments and aid in the form of a soft loan requires the use of market interest rates prevailing at the time of grant. With a view to a uniform, transparent, and simple application of the State aid rules, the market rates for the purposes of this Regulation should be deemed to be the reference rates, provided that, in the case of a soft loan, the loan is backed by normal security and does not involve abnormal risk. The reference rates should be those which are periodically fixed by the Commission on the basis of objective criteria and published in the *Official Journal of the European Communities* and on the Internet.

(11) Having regard to the differences between small enterprises and medium sized enterprises, different ceilings of aid intensity should be set for small enterprises and for medium sized enterprises.

(12) The ceilings of aid intensity should be fixed, in the light of the Commission's experience, at a level that strikes the appropriate balance between minimising distortions of competition in the aided sector and the objective of facilitating the development of the economic activities of small and medium-sized enterprises.

(13) It is appropriate to establish further conditions that should be fulfilled by any aid scheme or individual aid exempted by this Regulation. Having regard to Article 87(3)(c)

---

[6] OJ 1996 L107/4.
[7] See footnote 4.

of the Treaty, such aid should not normally have the sole effect of continuously or periodically reducing the operating costs which the beneficiary would normally have to bear, and should be proportionate to the handicaps that have to be overcome in order to secure the socioeconomic benefits deemed to be in the Community interest. It is therefore appropriate to limit the scope of this Regulation to aid granted in relation to certain tangible and intangible investments, certain services supplied to beneficiaries and certain other activities. In the light of Community overcapacity in the transport sector, with the exception of railway rolling stock, eligible investment costs for enterprises having their main economic activity in the transport sector should not include transport means and equipment.

(14) The Regulation should exempt aid to small and medium-sized enterprises regardless of location. Investment and job creation can contribute to the economic development of less favoured regions in the Community. Small and medium-sized enterprises in those regions suffer from both the structural disadvantage of the location and the difficulties deriving from their size. It is therefore appropriate that small and medium-sized enterprises in assisted regions should benefit from higher ceilings.

(15) In order not to favour the capital factor of an investment over the labour factor, provision should be made for the possibility of measuring aid to investment on the basis of either the costs of the investment or the costs of new employment linked to the carrying-out of the investment project.

(16) In the light of the World Trade Organisation (WTO) Agreement on Subsidies and Countervailing Measures,[8] this Regulation should not exempt export aid or aid favouring domestic over imported products. Aid towards the costs of participation in trade fairs or of studies or consultancy services needed for the launch of a new or existing product on a new market does not normally constitute export aid.

(17) Having regard to the need to strike the appropriate balance between minimising distortions of competition in the aided sector and the objectives of this Regulation, it should not exempt individual aid grants which exceed a fixed maximum amount, whether or not made under an aid scheme exempted by this Regulation.

(18) In order to ensure that the aid is necessary and acts as an incentive to develop certain activities, this Regulation should not exempt aid for activities in which the beneficiary would already engage under market conditions alone.

(19) This Regulation should not exempt aid cumulated with other State aid, including aid granted by national, regional or local authorities, or with Community assistance, in relation to the same eligible costs, when such cumulation exceeds the thresholds fixed in this Regulation.

(20) In order to ensure transparency and effective monitoring, in accordance with Article 3 of Regulation (EC) No 994/98, it is appropriate to establish a standard format in which Member States should provide the Commission with summary information whenever, in pursuance of this Regulation, an aid scheme is implemented or an individual aid outside such schemes is granted, with a view to publication in the *Official Journal of the European Communities*. For the same reasons, it is appropriate to establish rules concerning the records that Member States should keep regarding the aid exempted by this Regulation. For the purposes of the annual report to be submitted to the Commission by Member States, it is appropriate for the Commission to establish its specific requirements, including, in view of the wide availability of the necessary technology, information in computerised form.

(21) Having regard to the Commission's experience in this area, and in particular the frequency with which it is generally necessary to revise State aid policy, it is appropriate to limit the period of application of this Regulation. Should this Regulation expire without being extended, aid schemes already exempted by this Regulation should continue to be exempted for six months,

---

[8] OJ 1994 L336/156.

HAS ADOPTED THIS REGULATION:

Article 1

Scope

1. Without prejudice to special Community Regulations or Directives under the EC Treaty governing the granting of State aid in specific sectors, whether more or less restrictive than this Regulation, this Regulation applies to aid granted to small and medium-sized enterprises in all sectors.

2. This Regulation shall not apply:

(a) to activities linked to the production, processing or marketing of products listed in Annex I to the Treaty;
(b) to aid to export-related activities, namely aid directly linked to the quantities exported, to the establishment and operation of a distribution network or to other current expenditure linked to the export activity;
(c) to aid contingent upon the use of domestic over imported goods.

Article 2

Definitions

For the purpose of this Regulation:

(a) "aid" shall mean any measure fulfilling all the criteria laid down in Article 87(1) of the Treaty;
(b) "small and medium-sized enterprises" shall mean enterprises as defined in Annex I;
(c) "investment in tangible assets" shall mean investment in fixed physical assets relating to the creation of a new establishment, the extension of an existing establishment, or the engagement in an activity involving a fundamental change in the product or production process of an existing establishment (in particular through rationalisation, diversification or modernisation). An investment in fixed assets undertaken in the form of the takeover of an establishment which has closed or which would have closed had it not been purchased shall also be regarded as tangible investment;
(d) "investment in intangible assets" shall mean investment in transfer of technology by the acquisition of patent rights, licences, know-how or unpatented technical knowledge;
(e) "gross aid intensity" shall mean the aid amount expressed as a percentage of the project's eligible costs. All figures used shall be taken before any deduction for direct taxation. Where aid is awarded in a form other than a grant, the aid amount shall be the grant equivalent of the aid. Aid payable in several instalments shall be discounted to its value at the moment of granting. The interest rate to be used for discounting purposes and for calculating the aid amount in a soft loan shall be the reference rate applicable at the time of grant;
(f) "net aid intensity" shall mean the aid amount net of tax expressed as a percentage of the project's eligible costs;
(g) "number of employees" shall mean the number of annual labour units (ALU), namely the number of persons employed full time in one year, part-time and seasonal work being ALU fractions.

Article 3

Conditions for exemption

1. Individual aid outside any scheme, fulfilling all the conditions of this Regulation, shall be compatible with the common market within the meaning of Article 87(3) of the Treaty and shall be exempt from the notification requirement of Article 88(3) of the Treaty provided that it contains an express reference to this Regulation, by citing its title and publication reference in the *Official Journal of the European Communities*.

2. Aid schemes fulfilling all the conditions of this Regulation shall be compatible with the common market within the meaning of Article 87(3) of the Treaty and shall be exempt from the notification requirement of Article 88(3) of the Treaty provided that:

(a) any aid that could be awarded under such scheme fulfils all the conditions of this Regulation;
(b) the scheme contains an express reference to this Regulation, by citing its title and publication reference in the *Official Journal of the European Communities*.

3. Aid granted under the schemes referred to in paragraph 2 shall be compatible with the common market within the meaning of Article 87(3) of the Treaty and shall be exempt from the notification requirement of Article 88(3) of the Treaty provided that the aid granted directly fulfils all the conditions of this Regulation.

Article 4

Investment

1. Aid for investment in tangible and intangible assets inside or outside the Community shall be compatible with the common market within the meaning of Article 87(3) of the Treaty and shall be exempt from the notification requirement of Article 88(3) of the Treaty if it fulfils the conditions of paragraphs 2 to 6.

2. The gross aid intensity shall not exceed:

(a) 15% in the case of small enterprises;
(b) 7,5% in the case of medium-sized enterprises.

3. Where the investment takes place in areas which qualify for regional aid, the aid intensity shall not exceed the ceiling of regional investment aid determined in the map approved by the Commission for each Member State by more than:

(a) 10 percentage points gross in areas covered by Article 87(3)(c), provided that the total net aid intensity does not exceed 30%; or
(b) 15 percentage points gross in areas covered by Article 87(3)(a), provided that the total net aid intensity does not exceed 75%.

The higher regional aid ceilings shall only apply if the aid is granted under the condition that the investment is maintained in the recipient region for at least five years and that the beneficiary's contribution to its financing is at least 25%.

4. The ceilings fixed in paragraphs 2 and 3 shall apply to intensity of the aid calculated either as a percentage of the investment's eligible costs or as a percentage of the wage costs of employment created by the carrying-out of an investment (aid to job creation) or a combination thereof, provided the aid does not exceed the most favourable amount resulting from the application of either calculation.

5. In cases where the aid is calculated on the basis of the investment's costs, the eligible costs of tangible investment shall be the costs relating to investment in land, buildings, machinery and equipment. In the transport sector, except for railway rolling stock,

transport means and transport equipment shall not be included in the eligible costs. The eligible costs of intangible investment shall be the costs of acquisition of the technology.

6. In cases where the aid is calculated on the basis of jobs created, the amount of the aid shall be expressed as a percentage of the wage costs over a period of two years relating to the employment created under the following conditions:

(a) job creation shall be linked to the carrying-out of a project of investment in tangible or intangible assets. Jobs shall be created within three years of the investment's completion;

(b) the investment project shall lead to a net increase in the number of employees in the establishment concerned, compared with the average over the previous twelve months; and

(c) the employment created shall be maintained during a minimum period of five years.

Article 5

Consultancy and other services and activities

Aid to small and medium-sized enterprises that fulfil the following conditions shall be compatible with the common market within the meaning of Article 87(3) of the Treaty and shall be exempt from the notification requirement of Article 88(3) of the Treaty:

(a) for services provided by outside consultants, the gross aid shall not exceed 50% of the costs of such services. The services concerned shall not be a continuous or periodic activity nor relate to the enterprise's usual operating expenditure, such as routine tax consultancy services, regular legal services, or advertising;

(b) for participation in fairs and exhibitions, the gross aid shall not exceed 50% of the additional costs incurred for renting, setting up and running the stand. This exemption shall only apply to the first participation of an enterprise in a particular fair or exhibition.

Article 6

Large individual aid grants

This Regulation shall not exempt an individual aid grant where one of the following thresholds is met:

(a) the total eligible costs of the whole project are at least EUR 25 000 000 and
    (i) in areas which do not qualify for regional aid, the gross aid intensity is at least 50% of the ceilings laid down in Article 4(2);
    (ii) in areas which qualify for regional aid, the net aid intensity is at least 50% of the net aid ceiling as determined in the regional aid map for the area concerned; or

(b) the total gross aid amount is at least EUR 15 000 000.

Article 7

Necessity for the aid

This Regulation shall only exempt aid if, before work on the aided project is started:

— either an application for aid has been submitted to the Member State by the beneficiary, or

— the Member State has adopted legal provisions establishing a legal right to aid according to objective criteria and without further exercise of discretion by the Member State.

Article 8

Cumulation

1. The aid ceilings fixed in Articles 4, 5 and 6 shall apply regardless of whether the support for the aided project is financed entirely from State resources or is partly financed by the Community.

2. Aid exempted by this Regulation shall not be cumulated with any other State aid within the meaning of Article 87(1) of the Treaty, or with other Community funding, in relation to the same eligible costs, if such cumulation would result in an aid intensity exceeding that fixed by this Regulation.

Article 9

Transparency and monitoring

1. On implementation of an aid scheme, or grant of individual aid outside any scheme, exempted by this Regulation, Member States shall, within 20 working days, forward to the Commission, with a view to its publication in the *Official Journal of the European Communities*, a summary of the information regarding such aid scheme or individual aid in the form laid down in Annex II.

2. Member States shall maintain detailed records regarding the aid schemes exempted by this Regulation, the individual aid granted under those schemes, and the individual aid exempted by this Regulation that is granted outside any existing aid scheme. Such records shall contain all information necessary to establish that the conditions for exemption, as laid down in this Regulation, are fulfilled, including information on the status of the company as an SME. Member States shall keep a record regarding an individual aid for 10 years from the date on which it was granted, and regarding an aid scheme, for 10 years from the date on which the last individual aid was granted under such scheme. On written request, the Member State concerned shall provide the Commission, within a period of 20 working days or such longer period as may be fixed in the request, with all the information which the Commission considers necessary to assess whether the conditions of this Regulation have been complied with.

3. Member States shall compile a report on the application of this Regulation in respect of each whole or part calendar year during which this Regulation applies, in the form laid down in Annex III, also in computerised form. Member States shall provide the Commission with such report no later than three months after the expiry of the period to which the report relates.

Article 10

Entry into force and period of validity

1. This Regulation shall enter into force on the 20th day following that of its publication in the *Official Journal of the European Communities*.

It shall remain in force until 31 December 2006.

2. At the end of the period of validity of this Regulation, aid schemes exempted under this Regulation shall remain exempted during an adjustment period of six months.

829

This Regulation shall be binding in its entirety and directly applicable in all Member States.

Done at Brussels, 12 January 2001.

ANNEX I

Definition of small and medium-sized enterprises

(extract from the Commission Recommendation 96/280/EC of 3 April 1996 concerning the definition of small and medium-sized enterprises (OJ 1996 L107/4))

"Article 1

1. Small and medium-sized enterprises, hereinafter referred to as 'SMEs', are defined as enterprises which:

— have fewer than 250 employees, and
— have either,
   — an annual turnover not exceeding EUR 40 million, or
   — an annual balance-sheet total not exceeding EUR 27 million,
— conform to the criterion of independence as defined in paragraph 3.

2. Where it is necessary to distinguish between small and medium-sized enterprises, the 'small enterprise' is defined as an enterprise which:

— has fewer than 50 employees and
— has either,
   — an annual turnover not exceeding EUR 7 million, or
   — an annual balance-sheet total not exceeding EUR 5 million,
— conforms to the criterion of independence as defined in paragraph 3.

3. Independent enterprises are those which are not owned as to 25% or more of the capital or the voting rights by one enterprise, or jointly by several enterprises, falling outside the definitions of an SME or a small enterprise, whichever may apply. This threshold may be exceeded in the following two cases:

— if the enterprise is held by public investment corporations, venture capital companies or institutional investors, provided no control is exercised either individually or jointly;
— if the capital is spread in such a way that it is not possible to determine by whom it is held and if the enterprise declares that it can legitimately presume that it is not owned as to 25% or more by one enterprise, or jointly by several enterprises, falling outside the definitions of an SME or a small enterprise, whichever may apply.

4. In calculating the thresholds referred to in paragraphs 1 and 2, it is therefore necessary to cumulate the relevant figures for the beneficiary enterprise and for all the enterprises that it directly or indirectly controls through possession of 25% or more of the capital or of the voting rights.

5. Where it is necessary to distinguish micro-enterprises from other SMEs, these are defined as enterprises having fewer than 10 employees.

6. Where, at the final balance sheet date, an enterprise exceeds or falls below the employee thresholds or financial ceilings, this is to result in its acquiring or losing the status of 'SME', 'medium-sized enterprise', 'small enterprise' or 'microenterprise' only if the phenomenon is repeated over two consecutive financial years.

7. The number of persons employed corresponds to the number of annual working units (AWU), that is to say, the number of full-time workers employed during one year with part-time and seasonal workers being fractions of AWU. The reference year to be considered is that of the last approved accounting period.

8. The turnover and balance sheet total thresholds are those of the last approved 12-month accounting period. In the case of newly-established enterprises whose accounts have not yet been approved, the thresholds to apply shall be derived from a reliable estimate made in the course of the financial year."

ANNEX II

Form of summary information to be provided whenever an aid scheme exempted by this Regulation is implemented and whenever an individual aid exempted by this Regulation is granted outside any aid scheme

Summary information on State aid granted in conformity with Commission Regulation (EC) No 70/2001

Summary information to be filled in	Explanatory remarks
Member state	
Region	Indicate the name of the region if the aid is granted by a subcentral authority
Title of aid scheme or name of company receiving an individual aid	Indicate the name of the aid scheme or in case of individual aid, the name of the beneficiary. In the latter case, no subsequent annual report is necessary!
Legal basis	Indicate the precise national legal reference for the aid scheme or for the individual aid
Annual expenditure planned under the scheme or overall amount of individual aid granted to the company	Amounts are to be given in euro or, if applicable, national currency. In case of an aid scheme: indicate the annual overally amount overrall amount of the budget appropriation(s) or the estimated tax loss per year for all aid instruments contained in the scheme.

Summary information to be filled in	*Explanatory remarks*
	In the case of an individual aid award:
	indicate the overall aid amount/tax loss. If appropriate, indicate also for how many years the aid will be paid in instalments or over how many years tax losses will be incurred.
	For guarantees in both cases, indicate the (maximum) amount of loans guaranteed
Maximum aid intensity	Indicate the maximum aid intensity or the maximum aid amount per eligible item
Date of implementation	Indicate the date from which aid may be granted under the scheme or when the individual aid is granted
Duration of scheme or individual aid award	Indicate the date (year and month) until which aid may be granted under the scheme or in the case of an individual aid and if appropriate the expected date (year and month) of the last instalment to be paid
Objective of aid	It is understood that the primary objective is aid to SME. This field gives the opportunity to indicate further (secondary) objectives pursued (e.g. small enterprises only or SME; investment aid/consultancy)
Economic Sector(s) concered	Choose from the list, where relevant

☐   All Sectors
    or
    ☐   Coalmining
    ☐   All manufacturing
      or
      ☐   Steel
      ☐   Shipbuilding
      ☐   Synthetic fibres
      ☐   Motor vehicles
      ☐   Other manufacturing
    ☐   All Services
      or
      ☐   Transport services
      ☐   Financial services
      ☐   Other services
 	
Remarks:	

Name and address of the granting authority	
Other information	

Form of periodic report to be provided to the Commission

Annual reporting format on aid schemes exempted under a group exemption regulation adopted pursuant to Article 1 of Council Regulation (EC) No 994/98

Member States are required to use the format below for their reporting obligations to the Commission under group exemption regulations adopted on the basis of Council Regulation (EC) No 994/98.

The reports should also be provided in computerised form.

Information required for all aid schemes exempted under group exemption regulations adopted pursuant to Article 1 of Council Regulation (EC) No 994/98

1. Title of aid scheme

2. Commission exemption regulation applicable

3. Expenditure

   Separate figures have to be provided for each aid instrument within a scheme or individual aid (e.g. grant, soft loans, etc.) The figures have to be expressed in euro or, if applicable, national currency. In the case of tax expenditure, annual tax losses have to be reported. If precise figures are not available, such losses may be estimated.

   These expenditure figures should be provided on the following basis.

   For the year under review indicate separately for each aid instrument within the scheme (e.g. grant, soft loan, guarantee, etc.):

   3.1. amounts committed, (estimated) tax losses or other revenue forgone, data on guarantees, etc. for new assisted projects. In the case of guarantee schemes, the total amount of new guarantees handed out should be provided;

   3.2. actual payments, (estimated) tax losses or other revenue forgone, data on guarantees, etc. for new and current projects. In the case of guarantee schemes, the following should be provided: total amount of outstanding guarantees, premium income, recoveries, indemnities paid out, operating result of the scheme under the year under review;

   3.3. number of new assisted projects;

   3.4. estimated overall number of jobs created or maintained by new projects (if appropriate);

   3.5. estimated overall amount of investment aid by new projects;

   3.6. Regional breakdown of amounts under point 3.1 either by regions defined at NUTS[9] level 2 or below or by Article 87(3)(a) regions, Article 87(3)(c) regions and non-assisted regions;

---

[9] NUTS is the nomenclature of territorial units for statistical purposes in the Community.

3.7. Sectorial breakdown of amounts under point 3.1. by beneficiaries' sectors of activity (if more than one sector is covered, indicate the share of each):

coalmining

manufacturing
of which:
    steel
    shipbuilding
    synthetic fibres
    motor vehicles
    other manufacturing (please specify)

services
of which:
    transport services
    financial services
    other services (please specify)

other sectors (please specify)

4. Other information and remarks.

APPENDIX 81

COMMISSION NOTICE[1]

On Co-operation Between National Courts and the Commission in the State Aid Field

The purpose of this Notice is to offer guidance on co-operation between national courts and the Commission in the State aid field. The Notice does not in any way limit the rights conferred on Member States, individuals or undertakings by Community law. It is without prejudice to any interpretation of Community law which may be given by the Court of Justice and the Court of First Instance of the European Communities. Finally, it does not seek to interfere in any way with the fulfilment by national courts of their duties.

I. Introduction

1. The elimination of internal frontiers between Member States enables undertakings in the Community to expand their activities throughout the internal market and consumers to benefit from increased competition. These advantages must not be jeopardized by distortions of competition caused by aid granted unjustifiably to undertakings. The completion of the internal market thus reaffirms the importance of enforcement of the Community's competition policy.

2. The Court of Justice has delivered a number of important judgments on the interpretation and application of Articles 87 and 88 of the EC Treaty. The Court of First Instance now has jurisdiction over actions by private parties against the Commission's State aid decisions and will thus also contribute to the development of case law in this field. The Commission is responsible for the day-to-day application of the competition rules under the supervision of the Court of First Instance and the Court of Justice. Public authorities and courts in the Member States, together with the Community's courts and the Commission each assume their own tasks and responsibilities for the enforcement of the EC Treaty's State aid rules, in accordance with the principles laid down by the case law of the Court of Justice.

3. The proper application of competition policy in the internal market may require effective co-operation between the Commission and national courts. This Notice explains how the Commission intends to assist national courts by instituting closer co-operation in the application of Articles 87 and 88 in individual cases. Concern is frequently expressed that the Commission's final decisions in State aid cases are reached some time after the distortions of competition have damaged the interests of third parties. While the Commission is not always in a position to act promptly to safeguard the interests of third parties

---

[1] OJ 1995 C312/18.

835

in State aid matters, national courts may be better placed to ensure that breaches of the last sentence of Article 88(3) are dealt with and remedied.

II. POWERS[2]

4. The Commission is the administrative authority responsible for the implementation and development of competition policy in the Community's public interest. National courts are responsible for the protection of rights and the enforcement of duties, usually at the behest of private parties. The Commission must examine all aid measures which fall under Article 87(1) in order to assess their compatibility with the common market. National courts must make sure that Member States comply with their procedural obligations.

5. The last sentence of Article 88(3) [*sic.*] has direct effect in the legal order of the Member States:

"The Commission shall be informed, in sufficient time to enable to submit its comments, of any plans to grant or alter aid. If it considers that any such plan is not compatible with the common market having regard to Article 87, it shall without delay initiate the procedure provided for in paragraph 2. The Member State concerned shall not put its proposed measures into effect until this procedure has resulted in a final decision."

---

[2] The Court of Justice has described the roles of the Commission and the national courts in the following way:

"9. As far as the role of the Commission is concerned, the Court pointed out in its Judgment in Case 78/96, *Steinlike and Weinlig v. Germany* [1977] ECR 595, at paragraph 9, that the intention of the Treaty, in providing through Article 88 for aid to be kept under constant review and supervised by the Commission, is that the finding that aid may be incompatible with the common market is to be arrived at, subject to review by the Court by means of an appropriate procedure which it is the Commission's responsibility to set in motion.

10. As far as the role of national courts is concerned, the Court held in the same judgment that proceedings may be commenced before national courts requiring those courts to interpret and apply the concept of aid contained in Article 87 in order to determine whether State aid introduced without observance of the preliminary examination procedure provided for in Article 88(3) ought to have been subject to this procedure.

11. The involvement of national courts is the result of the direct effect which the last sentence of Article 88(3) of the Treaty has been held to have. In this respect, the Court stated in its judgment in Case 120/73, *Lorenz v. Germany* [1973] ECR 1471 that the immediate enforceability of the prohibition on implementation referred to in that article extends to all aid which has been implemented without being notified and, in the event of notification, operates during the preliminary period, and if the Commission sets in motion the contentious procedure, until the final decision.

14. . . . The principal and exclusive role conferred on the Commission by Articles 87 and 88 of the Treaty, which is to hold aid to be incompatible with the common market where this is appropriate, is fundamentally different from the role of national courts in safeguarding rights which individuals enjoy as a result of the direct effect of the prohibition laid down in the last sentence of Article 88(3) of the Treaty. Whilst the Commission must examine the compatibility of the proposed aid with the common market, even where the Member State has acted in breach of the prohibition on giving effect to aid, national courts do no more than preserve, until the final decision of the Commission, the rights of individuals faced with a possible breach by State authorities of the prohibition laid down by the last sentence of Article 88(3)."

Case C–354/90, *Fédération nationale du commerce extérieur des produits alimentaires and Syndicat national des négociants et transformateurs de saumon v. France* [1991] ECR I–5505 paras. 9, 10, 11 and 14, at pp. 5527 and 5528.

6. The prohibition on implementation referred to in the last sentence of Article 88(3) extends to all aid which has been implemented without being notified[3] and, in the event of notification, operates during the preliminary period and, if the Commission sets in motion the contentious procedure, until the final decision.[4]

7. Of course a court will have to consider whether the "proposed measures" constitute State aid within the meaning of Article 87(1)[5] before reaching a decision under the last sentence of Article 88(3). The Commission's decisions and the Court's case law devote considerable attention to this important question. Accordingly, the notion of State aid must be interpreted widely to encompass not only subsidies, but also tax concessions and investments from public funds made in circumstances in which a private investor would have withheld support.[6] The aid must come from the "State", which includes all levels, manifestations and emanations of public authority.[7] The aid must favour certain undertakings or the production of certain goods: this serves to distinguish State aid to which Article 87(1) applies from general measures to which it does not.[8] For example, measures which have neither as their object nor as their effect the favouring of certain undertakings or the production of certain goods, or which apply to persons in accordance with objective criteria without regard to the location, sector or undertaking in which the beneficiary may be employed, are not considered to be State aid.

8. Only the Commission can decide that State aid is "compatible with the common market", *i.e.* authorised.

9. In applying Article 87(1), national courts may of course refer preliminary questions to the Court of Justice pursuant to Article 234 of the EC Treaty and indeed must do so in certain circumstances. They may also request assistance from the Commission by asking it for "legal or economic information" by analogy with the Court's Delimitis[9] judgment in respect of Article 81 of the EC Treaty.

10. The national court's role is to safeguard rights which individuals enjoy as a result of the direct effect of the prohibition laid down in the last sentence of Article 88(3). The court should use all appropriate devices and remedies and apply all relevant provisions of

---

[3] With the exception of "existing" aid. Such aid may be implemented until the Commission has decided that is it incompatible with the common market: see Case C–387/92, *Banco de Crédito Industrial*, now *Banco Exterior de Espana v. Ayuntamiento de Valencia* [1994] ECR I–877 and Case C–44/93, *Namur—Les Assurances du Crédit v. Office National du Ducroire and Belgium* [1994] ECR I–3829.

[4] Case C–354/90, cited at footnote 2, § 11 at p. 5527.

[5] See the Court of Justice's judgment in Case 78/76, *Steinlike and Weinlig v. Germany* [1977] ECR 595, § 14: " . . . a national court may have cause to interpret and apply the concept of aid contained in Article 87 in order to determine whether State aid introduced without observance of the preliminary examination procedure provided for in Article 88(3) ought to have been subject to this procedure."

[6] For a recent formulation, see Adv. Gen. Jacobs' Opinion in Joined Cases C–278/92, C–279/92 and C–280/92, *Spain v. Commission*, § 28: " . . . State aid is granted whenever a Member State makes available to an undertaking funds which in the normal course of events would not be provided by a private investor applying normal commercial criteria and disregarding other considerations of a social, political or philanthropic nature."

[7] The Court of Justice held in Case 290/83, *Commission v. France* [1985] ECR 439, that " . . . The prohibition contained in Article 87 covers all aid granted by a Member State or through State resources and there is no necessity to draw any distinction according to whether the aid is granted directly by the State or by public or private bodies established or appointed by it to administer the aid" (§ 4 at p. 449).

[8] A clear statement of this distinction is to be found in Adv. Gen. Darmon's Opinion in Joined Cases C–72 and C–73/91, *Sloman Neptun* [1993] ECR I–887.

[9] Case C–234/89, *Delimitis v. Henninger Bräu* [1991] ECR I–935; Commission notice on co-operation between national courts and the Commission in applying Articles [81] and [82] of the EC Treaty, OJ 1993 C39/6. See Adv. Gen. Lenz's Opinion in Case C–44/93, cited at footnote 3 (para. 106). See also Case C–2/88, *Imm. Zwartveld* [1990] ECR I–3365 and I–4405: "the Community institutions are under a duty of sincere co-operation with the judicial authorities of the Member States, which are responsible for ensuring that Community law is applied and respected in the national legal system" (§ 1 at p. I–3366 and para. 10 at pp. 4410 and 4411, respectively).

national law to implement the direct effect of this obligation placed by the Treaty on Member States.[10] A national court must, in a case within its jurisdiction, apply Community law in its entirety and protect rights which that law confers on individuals; it must therefore set aside any provision of national law which may conflict with it, whether prior or subsequent to the Community rule.[11] The judge may, as appropriate and in accordance with applicable rules of national law and the developing case law of the Court of Justice,[12] grant interim relief, for example by ordering the freezing or return of monies illegally paid, and award damages to parties whose interests are harmed.

11. The Court of Justice has held that the full effectiveness of Community rules would be impaired and the protection of the rights which they grant would be weakened if individuals were unable to obtain redress when their rights are infringed by a breach of Community law for which a Member State can be held responsible,[13] the principle whereby a State must be liable for loss and damage caused to individuals as a result of breaches of Community law for which the State can be held responsible is inherent in the system of the Treaty,[14] a national court which considers, in a case concerning Community law, that the sole obstacle precluding it from granting interim relief is a rule of national law, must set aside that rule.[15]

12. These principles apply in the event of a breach of the Community's competition rules. Individuals and undertakings must have access to all procedural rules and remedies provided for by national law on the same conditions as would apply if a comparable breach of national law were involved. This equality of treatment concerns not only the definitive finding of a breach of directly effective Community law, but extends also to all legal means capable of contributing to effective legal protection.

III. The Commission's Limited Powers

13. The application of Community competition law by the national courts has considerable advantages for individuals and undertakings. The Commission cannot award damages for loss suffered as a result of an infringement of Article 88(3). Such claims may be brought only before the national courts. National courts can usually adopt interim measures and order the termination of infringements quickly. Before national courts, it is possible to combine a claim under Community law with a claim under national law. This is not possible in a procedure before the Commission. In addition, courts may award costs

---

[10] As the Court of Justice held in Case C–354/90, cited at footnote 2, § 12 at p. 5528: " ... the validity of measures giving effect to aid is affected if national authorities act in breach of the last sentence of Article 88(3) of the Treaty. National courts must offer to individuals in a position to rely on such breach the certain prospect that all the necessary inferences will be drawn, in accordance with their national law, as regards the validity of measures giving effect to the aid, the recovery of financial support granted in disregard of that provision and possible interim measures."

[11] Case 106/77, *Amministrazione delle Finanze dello Stato v. Simmenthal* [1978] ECR 629, (§ 1 at p. 644). See also Case C–213/89, *The Queen v. Secretary of State for Transport, ex parte Factortame Ltd et al.* [1990] ECR I–2433, at p. 2475.

[12] Joined Cases C–6/90 and C–9/90, *Andrea Francovich et al. v. Italy* [1991] ECR I–5357. Other important cases are pending before the Court concerning the responsibilities of national courts in the application of Community law: Case C–48/93, *The Queen v. Secretary of State for Transport, ex parte Factortame Ltd and others*, OJ 1993 C94/13; Case C–46/93, *Brasserie du Pêcheur SA v. Germany*, OJ 1993 C92/4; Case C–312/93, *SCS Peterbroeck, Van Campenhout & Cie v. Belgian State*, OJ 1993 C189/9; Cases C–430 and C–431/93, *J. Van Schindel and J.N.C. Van Veen v. Stichting Pensioenfonds voor Fysiotherapeuten*, OJ 1993 C338/10.

[13] *Francovich*, cited at footnote 12, para. 33 at p. 5414.

[14] *Francovich*, cited at footnote 12, para. 35 at p. 5414.

[15] *The Queen v. Secretary of State for Transport, ex parte Factortame Ltd et al.*, cited at footnote 11.

to the successful applicant. This is never possible in the administrative procedure before the Commission.

IV. APPLICATION OF ARTICLE 88(3)

14. Member States are required to notify to the Commission all plans to grant aid or to alter aid plans already approved. This also applies to aid that may qualify for automatic approval under Article 87(2), because the Commission has to check that the requisite conditions are met. The only exception to the notification obligation is for aid classed as *de minimis* because it does not affect trade between Member States significantly and thus does not fall within Article 87(1).[16]

15. The Commission receives notification of general schemes or programmes of aid, as well as of plans to grant aid to individual firms. Once a scheme has been authorized by the Commission, individual awards of aid under the scheme do not normally have to be notified. However, under some of the aid codes or frameworks for particular industries or particular types of aid, individual notification is required of all awards of aid or of awards exceeding a certain amount. Individual notification may also be required in some cases by the terms of the Commission's authorization of a given scheme. Member States must notify aid which they wish to grant outside the framework of an authorized scheme. Notification is required in respect of planned measures, including plans to make financial transfers from public funds to public or private sector enterprises, which may involve aid within the meaning of Article 87(1).

16. The first question which national courts have to consider in an action under the last sentence of Article 88(3) is whether the measure constitutes new or existing State aid within the meaning aid of Article 87(1). The second question to be answered is whether the measure has been notified either individually or under a scheme and if so, whether the Commission has had sufficient time to come to a decision.[17]

17. With respect to aid schemes, a period of two months is considered by the Court of Justice to be "sufficient time", after which the Member State concerned may, after giving the Commission prior notice, implement the notified measure.[18] This period is reduced by the Commission voluntarily to 30 working days for individual cases and 20 working days under the "accelerated" procedure. The periods run from the time the Commission is satisfied that the information provided by the Member State is sufficient to enable it to reach a decision.[19]

18. If the Commission has decided to initiate the procedure provided for in Article 88(2) the period during which the implementation of an aid measure is prohibited runs until the Commission has reached a positive decision. For non-notified aid measures, no deadline exists for the Commission's decision-making process, although the Commission will act as speedily as possible. Aid may not be awarded before the Commission's final decision.

19. If the Commission has not ruled on an aid measure, national courts can always be guided, in interpreting Community law, by the case-law of the Court of First Instance and

---

[16] See point 3.2 of the Community guidelines on State aid for SMEs, OJ 1992 C213/2, and the letter to the Member States ref. IV/D/06878 of 23 March 1993, Competition Law in the European Communities, Volume II.

[17] Case 120/73, *Lorenz v. Germany* [1973] ECR 1471.

[18] Case 120/73, *Lorenz v. Germany*, cited at footnote 17, para. 4 at p. 1481; see also Case 84/42, *Germany v. Commission* [1984] ECR 1451, para. 11 at p. 1488.

[19] The Commission has issued a Guide to its procedures in State aid cases: see Competition Law in the European Communities, Volume II.

the Court of Justice, as well as by decisions issued by the Commission. The Commission has published a number of general notices which may be of assistance in this regard.[20]

20. National courts should thus be able to decide whether or not the measure at issue is illegal under Article 88(3). Where national courts have doubts, they may and in some cases must request a preliminary ruling from the Court of Justice in accordance with Article 234.

21. Where national courts give judgment finding that Article 88(3) has not been complied with, they must rule that the measure at issue infringes Community law and take the appropriate measures to safeguard the rights enjoyed by individuals and undertakings.

V. Effects of Commission Decisions

22. The Court of Justice has held[21] that a national court is bound by a Commission decision addressed to a Member State under Article 88(2) where the beneficiary of the aid in question seeks to question the validity of the decision of which it had been informed in writing by the Member State concerned and where it had failed to bring an action for annulment of the decision within the time limits prescribed by Article 230 of the EC Treaty.

VI. Co-operation Between National Courts and the Commission

23. The Commission realises that the principles set out above for the application of Articles 87 and 88 by national courts are complex and may sometimes be insufficiently developed to enable them to carry out their judicial duties properly. National courts may therefore ask the Commission for assistance.

24. Article 10 of the EC Treaty establishes the principle of loyal and constant co-operation between the Community institutions and the Member States with a view to attaining the objectives of the Treaty, including implementation of Article 3(h), which provides for the establishment of a system ensuring that competition in the internal market is not distorted. This principle involves obligations and duties of mutual assistance, both for the Member States and for the Community institutions. Under Article 10, the Commission has a duty of co-operation with the judicial authorities of the Member States which are responsible for ensuring that Community law is applied and respected in the national legal order.

25. The Commission considers that such co-operation is essential in order to guarantee the strict, effective and consistent application of Community competition law. In addition, participation by the national courts in the application of competition law in the field of State aid is necessary to give effect to Article 88(3). The Treaty obliges the Commission to follow the procedure laid down in Article 88(2) before it can order reimbursement of

---

[20] The Commission publishes and updates from time to time a compendium of State aid rules (Competition Law in the European Communities, Volume II).

[21] Case C–188/92, *TWD Textilwerke Deggendorf GmbH v. Germany* [1994] ECR I–833; see also Case 77/72, *Capolongo v. Maya* [1973] ECR 611.

aid which is incompatible with the common market.[22] The Court has ruled that Article 88(3) has direct effect and that the illegality of an aid measure, and the consequences that flow therefrom, can never be validated retroactively by a positive decision of the Commission on an aid measure. Application of the rules on notification in the field of State aid therefore constitutes an essential link in the chain of possible legal action by individuals and undertakings.

26. In the light of these considerations, the Commission intends to work towards closer co-operation with national courts in the following manner.

27. The Commission is committed to a policy of openness and transparency. The Commission conducts its policy so as to give the parties concerned useful information on the application of competition rules. To this end, it will continue to publish as much information as possible about State aid cases and policy. The case-law of the Court of Justice and Court of First Instance, general texts on State aid published by the Commission, decisions taken by the Commission, the Commission's annual reports on competition policy and the monthly Bulletin of the European Union may assist national courts in examining individual cases.

28. If these general pointers are insufficient, national courts may, within the limits of their national procedural law, ask the Commission, for information of a procedural nature to enable them to discover whether a certain case is pending before the Commission, whether a case has been the subject of a notification or whether the Commission has officially initiated a procedure or taken any other decision.

29. National courts may also consult the Commission where the application of Article 87(1) or Article 88(3) causes particular difficulties. As far as Article 87(1) is concerned, these difficulties may relate in particular to the characterisation of the measure as State aid, the possible distortion of competition to which it may give rise and the effect on trade between Member States. Courts may therefore consult the Commission on its customary practice in relation to these issues. They may obtain information from the Commission regarding factual data, statistics, market studies and economic analyses. Where possible, the Commission will communicate these data or will indicate the source from which they can be obtained.

30. In its answer, the Commission will not go into the substance of the individual case or the compatibility of the measure with the common market. The answer given by the Commission will not be binding on the requesting court. The Commission will make it clear that its view is not definitive and that the court's right to request a preliminary ruling from the Court of Justice pursuant to Article 234 is unaffected.

31. It is in the interests of the proper administration of justice that the Commission should answer requests for legal and factual information in the shortest possible time. Nevertheless, the Commission cannot accede to such requests unless several conditions are met. The requisite data must actually be at its disposal and the Commission may communicate only non-confidential information.

32. Article 287 of the EC Treaty requires the Commission not to disclose information of a confidential nature. In addition, the duty of loyal co-operation under Article 10 applies to the relationship between courts and the Commission, and does not concern the parties to the dispute pending before those courts. The Commission is obliged to respect legal neutrality and objectivity. Consequently, it will not accede to requests for information

---

[22] The Commission has informed the Member States that " . . . in appropriate cases it may—after giving the Member State concerned the opportunity to comment and to consider alternatively the granting of rescue aid, as defined by the Community guidelines—adopt a provisional decision ordering the Member State to recover any monies which have been disbursed in infringement of the procedural requirements. The aid would have to be recovered in accordance with the requirements of domestic law; the sum repayable would carry interest running from the time the aid was paid out." (Commission Communication to the Member States supplementing the Commission's letter No. SG(91) D/4577 of 4 March 1991 concerning the procedures for the notification of aid plans and procedures applicable when aid is provided in breach of the rules of Article 88(3) of the EEC Treaty), not yet published.

unless they come from a national court, either directly, or indirectly through parties which have been ordered by the court concerned to request certain information.

VII. Final Remarks

33. This Notice applies *mutatis mutandis* to relevant State aid rules, in so far as they have direct effect in the legal order of Member States, of:

— the Treaty establishing the European Coal and Steel Community and provisions adopted thereunder, and
— the Agreement on the European Economic Area.

34. This Notice is issued for guidance and does not in any way limit the rights conferred on Member States, individuals or undertakings by Community law.

35. This Notice is without prejudice to any interpretation of Community law which may be given by the Court of Justice and Court of First Instance of the European Communities.

36. A summary of the answers given by the Commission pursuant to this Notice will be published annually in the Report on Competition Policy.

Done at Brussels, 31 October 1995.